C000262955

The Way Of The Lover

MAY THIS BOOK BE A
BLESSING FOR YOUR LIFE,
AND BE AN INSPIRATION
AND BRING NEW TEACHINGS
TO ADD TO THE TREASURE
OF WHO YOU ARE.

With love,
Paule

The Way of the Lover

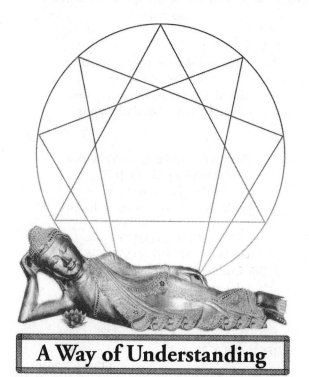

A Way of Understanding

The Fifth Way - Life at its Best

DR. PAULA BROMBERG

The Way of the Lover
Copyright © 2020 by Dr. Paula Bromberg
First Edition
All Rights Reserved
Limited Edition

No part of this book may be used or reproduced in any manner whatsoever without
written permission, except in the case of brief quotations embodied in critical articles
and reviews.

For reproduction rights, contact:
Dr. Paula Bromberg
E-mail: Goldoceandrive@gmail.com
Facebook:PaulaAmbikaBromberg

Publisher's Cataloging-in-Publication
Bromberg, Dr. Paula N.
The Way of the Lover
by Dr. Paula N. Bromberg. -- 1st Ed.
p. cm.
LCCN 2003112905
Hardcover ISBN 978-0-9715474-6-9
1. Self-actualization (Psychology) 2. Spiritual life.
3. Interpersonal relations. 4. New Age.
5. Self-help techniques. 6. Personal growth.

I. Title.
BF637.S4B76 2004   158.1
                           QBI03-700680
also available as an eBook

Printed in the United States of America

Book design: South Beach Grafix/Dr. Paula Bromberg

Acknowledgements

A Dedication of Gratitude and Praise

To my Teacher, who saw the angel in the marble—for her Love.

To my *Companions on the Way*, for their unceasing belief in me and their affirmation and direction so my dragons could turn into goddesses.

To those who joined hands in the climb up the mountain.

To the garden of the many who sat in a meeting of the heart; your rose fragrance flowered.

To Mama and Ammachi, for creating a safe space for me to challenge my personal windstorms...and discover the beauty of my carvings.

To my mother and the many godchildren with whom I practice Love.

To Sashie, my beloved, who stands at my side as the test and measure of All Love.

To Myself, for my persistence to chisel the angel out of the marble and set her free.

To the Universal Wisdom of Love, Truth, and Beauty, that accompanied me on the descent down the mountain.

To the Ocean, whose presence reflects the infinite grace that is my life.

About The Book Cover

The cover statue represents the awakened Buddha, reclining in a blissful state of peace. A Buddha is one who has awakened from the sleep of ignorance, expanding all senses and awareness. The root of suffering lies in our lack of understanding, and so the teaching is to change ignorance to wisdom through the love that is understanding. To know the nature of suffering is to also know the possibility of freedom from suffering. The way of understanding cultivates knowing within a framework of practicing mindfulness. It's to balance and harmonize everything that is arising now. The way of understanding which is centered in the heart of love, is concerned for the welfare of all beings. The state of buddhahood is the highest happiness, supreme compassion, powerful love, to which every living being can aspire. Over 25,000 years ago a person who it is said spent lifetimes looking for truth sat under a tree resolving to not get up until he was freed from all the delusions that were distractions, until he discovered his true nature. He understood that the jailkeeper, that the root was the ignorance of his true nature. This particular statue, the form of the awakened one, is in the home of Dr. Paula Bromberg.

The lotus, serenity and beauty, a simple water lily, symbolizes enlightenment, is grounded in earth, deeply rooted in mud, and blossoms in murky pools. The Buddha and the lotus are sacred symbols of our passage from darkness to light, from ignorance to wisdom, from bondage to liberation. They are reminders, expressions of the deep root of our timeless beauty. The lotus grows and floats in the water, still, water never touches it, its roots grounded in mud or suffering, its leaves pointing to the heavens. How to be in the world yet not of it, pristine, unaffected like the lotus. The paradox of the lotus serves as a metaphor for human wisdom. Unhindered, free of the mud and water that surrounds us we awaken to become unimpeded by our world of sorrow and change. The lotus is a symbol of the relationship between creation and spirituality as well as synonymous with love for its distinctive sensual aroma and physical structure.

The Enneagram, a compelling visual figure, a schematic diagram of perpetual motion demonstrates that life follows a circular movement. Seasons, sun, stars, planets, all of existence, like a wheel, is circular. This universal symbol of self-sustained transformation incorporates all wisdom of universal laws. It is both a model for what we do or study as well as a structure of intention. The inner triangle stands for the presence of higher elements, and the separate points represent the steps in the process of eternal return informing and giving meaning to the process. The Enneagram used as a way of understanding carries meaning, aliveness. It's a key that can be used as a model on any scale. The assertion, life is only real then, when I am, Gurdjieff's cosmic view, brings us to the ultimate inquiry, Who am I?

To offer life to symbols opens worlds of meaning since they have interpretive richness and flexibility. Through a sacred image we can connect directly with the source of that image. The reality behind the awakened Buddha, the lotus and the Enneagram, once combined with understanding, turn the world from chaos to cosmos. This, then, becomes the living Enneagram, the Buddha of our time, the lotus posture—now the circle is complete.

About the book

*T*he *Way of the Lover* is destined to become a classic work, bringing clear insightful new understanding into the lives of its readers. Beautifully written, this is the first time these numerous approaches to awakening have been brought together for our benefit. You now hold in your hands a map to find treasure and the keys; practical wisdom for true self-investigation. Look through the table of contents. This original work is based on ancient hidden sacred teachings and direct personal experience. Here are ways to use your life as the teaching. Included are 27 systems, tools to deepen self-understanding, never before printed in one book, that offer a direct way to know yourself. This book shows how to awaken to who you really are. A self-evaluation work-sheet is included that can be used repeatedly, as you study yourself and others.

The Way of the Lover arrives after more than five decades of study, practice and listening. This great feast of love inspires and uplifts. It is dedicated to the teaching, understanding and freedom of all people. It is entertaining as well as depthful, intended for those who love the creative process, have used psychotherapy and other methods as a means of self-knowledge, who recognize its limits and now want to awaken and satisfy the yearning for Truth, Love, and Beauty. That place beyond personality. No corner of the heart and mind can stay hidden and unexamined.

With great integrity Dr. Bromberg takes you directly to your heart. A book of truth and power that will make a difference.

Praise For
The Way Of The Lover

I treasure your masterpiece The Way of the Lover and love to read parts of it as soul food when I'm tired of answering thousands of letters. Thank you, thank you, thank you!!!

—Elisabeth Kübler-Ross, M.D.
author, psychiatrist, creator of the hospice movement, revolutionized the care of the terminally ill, a pioneer in near-death studies, inducted into the National Women's Hall of Fame

Paula Bromberg is a genuine big-hearted woman who has a rare and profound intelligence and a deep understanding of authentic compassion.

—Natalie Goldberg
renowned writing teacher, best-selling author of 15 books, painter, retreat leader, filmmaker, zen practitioner

The reminder of Paula's commitment to live her creative potential is what you receive in this book, the culmination of her life work. Paula is connected to the Source, empowering her to live her creative potential. May her journey lead her-lead her-lead her. Her book, The Way of the Lover, is a true teaching.

—Edith Wallace, M.D., Ph.D.
author, Jungian analyst who received her analytic training directly from Carl Jung M.D., prize winning painter, world-wide teacher

In my experience, Paula Bromberg is an extraordinarily knowledgeable Teacher who speaks with the authority of the heart and is gifted with the ability to articulate and clarify her deep understanding of the logos thus making it available to seekers and inquirers.

—José Stevens. Ph.D.
international lecturer, psychologist, corporate team builder, Shaman, author of 20 books

I have known Dr. Paula Bromberg for over 40 years. Thus I have been witness to a magnificent tapestry. Fierce warrior, yet gentle spirit. Seeker, teacher and disciple. The wide eyes and open heart of a child. She teaches us that everything is sacred yet nothing exists. Paula is both illumination and reflection. This book, The Way of the Lover, is a miracle.

—Rona Lieberman, M.D.
Physician practicing responsible medicine for over 35 years.

To aspire towards higher consciousness and spiritual growth defining and understanding one's authentic self is a major component of paramount importance. Dr. Bromberg's book The Way Of The Lover is an insightful and informative tool and as a co-companion can guide and support the enfoldment of this learning process, which is ongoing, joyous and eternal.
Namaste.

—Mara Howard
yoga and meditation teacher

Paula Bromberg is giftedly willing and able to look at love and all of its expressions with more clarity and honesty than most people would ever dare.

—David Deida
acclaimed author of 10 books, a founder of Integral Institute, teacher and researcher at University of California Medical School and École Polytechnique, Paris, France

I have learned much from Paula Bromberg's grasp of human types, as well as her moral sincerity.

—Kabir Helminski, Ph.D
Sufi teacher, psychologist, author and translator of Sufi literature, Shaikh of the Mevlevi order of Sufi which traces to Rumi, tours with the whirling dervishes of Turkey, director of the Threshold Society

Dr. Paula is a passionate soul whose vision penetrates the core mystery of what it means to be human.

—Rabbi Michael Ziegler
founder and leader of Song of Songs Minyan, guest faculty Naropa University, book reviewer

Some people write a book in a month and some in a year and others take their time, so the book grows as they do, until we have a living document of a life well-lived and well-considered. Such is this book by Dr. Paula Bromberg, The Way of the Lover, rich in her knowledge, abundant with her wisdom, and redolent with her deep understanding. Socrates said, "The unexamined life is not worth living." Paula's life has been overflowing with self-examination, and through the salient processes she offers, now a significant resource for those who wish to know themselves. Her brilliant opus is a work of art and courage.

—Aile Shebar
creative writing teacher, writing coach, editor and author

Paula Bromberg's The Way of the Lover in clear, simple terms brings tools for self-actualization and empowerment. Bromberg's book is poised to replace conventional psychotherapy and religion as the true journey, the way of choice.

—Larry Chang
author, director of Gnosophia Publishers

Paula Bromberg is a true intellect and a profound healer. Her teaching is magical and has helped me in my work with addicts using a spiritual approach. Deeply rooted in a massive knowledge of people and in life, her book The Way of the Lover is bold and beautiful.

—Kerry Riordan
addiction specialist counselor, New York, Puerto Rico

A gem filled with information and beautiful writing. The Way of the Lover is a book to read again and again.

—Fern Reiss
award winning author, syndicated columnist

I have known Paula Bromberg since elementary school days. Both of us traveled healing and spiritual paths. I established a Tibetan Medical Center and Paula became the on-call therapist for my clients in the New York and Massachusetts Centers. A brilliant team—Dr. Paula, Dr. Yeshi Dhonden and Dr. Marsha. Reading her book, The Way of the Lover is like sitting with a master: inspiring, uplifting, educational and enlightening. You must own this book, and carry it around, to actually use. The Way of the Lover fills an important need, finally a guide to understand who we are and how to love.

—Dr. Marsha Woolf
founder and director of New World Medical Center and Alternative Resources, director of Menla Tibetan Medical Institute, author, naturopath, worked for over 25 years with Dr. Yeshi Dhonden, personal senior physician to His Holiness the 14th Dalai Lama

The Way of the Lover encourages its reader to open their heart and let their energy flow sensing what life means. This book serves those who travel a spiritual road, who look for a healing breakthrough on their path to self-realization.

—Wulfing von Rohr
author, seminar leader, convention moderator and television journalist

A lifes work
A true understanding of the path
The recognition of the illusion
of our separateness
This is her guide book
and the tools that are needed
to plow the mind
into a vibrational frequency
of the real
Love upon love

—Charles Soloway, Udbodha
musical artist, created *Awakening*

Testimonial

The Work Works

Paula challenged me and gave me the courage to step into myself. Throughout the process I learned to truly be in the moment. The joy and freedom I feel is a gift I am grateful for everyday. She saved my life. She gave me my life.

I have worked with Paula for twelve years. Over those years, she challenged me and gave me the courage to be me. In the process I learned to love my nature and respect myself. With her guidance, I had the health, clarity, and energy to raise a beautiful family.

When I hear Paula's voice on the phone I know I am going to be ok. The work isn't always easy, but under her guidance, I have learned to love my nature. I crave her wisdom, clarity, and problem solving. She's both held my hand and kicked me in the butt. Because of Paula, I have been able to raise two beautiful children and keep a marriage strong. I'm also just more joyful, a gift I am grateful for everyday.

—Elizabeth Clair Flood
author, editor, photographer

Just sitting here at sunset, loving you. Hope you feel it. You've given me the greatest gift of my life, which is my life right now in this moment. I hold you in the same regard I hold my birth mother, in total gratitude for giving me an opportunity of a beautiful life.

I can never express my deep gratitude because not a day goes by that you don't wander (or firmly roll) into my thoughts. Thank you dear Paula for everything. My life is because of you. I love you now and always, and my children also know your presence because of the way I parent them. A deep exhale and deep bow to you, Paula my beloved mamaji.

—Amanda Botur
yoga teacher, leads yoga teacher trainings, masters in traditional chinese
medicine, classical homeopath, songwriter, musician—album *Confluence*

I have worked with other therapists in the past, but none of them enabled me to transcend my history and the pain entangled there in the way that Paula has.

Paula is exceedingly wise and compassionate. Her comprehension of an individual's particular nature, what I understand to be the truth of who a person is beyond her conditioning, is profound. With Paula's gentle yet powerful support I have come to recognize and embrace my true nature and this has given me much relief from suffering as well as enormous peace.

I consider Paula to be a teacher and mentor guiding me on an intimate journey of self-discovery. I am deeply grateful for her in my life.

—Cynthia S. DaCosta
psychotherapist, horse trainer, philanthropic foundation / grant-maker

Paula is my sage, a voice to my soul and heart. She has brought a voice to a perspective on myself that I wouldn't have otherwise. I am eternally grateful for her in my life.

Amanda, my wife, introduced me to Dr. Paula as we started working through our stories and problems as a married couple. She has been there through thick and thin, with guidance, compassion, and humor to our individual stories. She has come to our collective defenses and our indifference throughout our 18 years of marriage. Paula has added a strength and significance to bond our family journey.

—Freddie Botur
conservation pioneer and adviser, cowboy, cattle rancher, Cottonwood Ranch, climber and Alpinist, asset manager, entrepreneur

Paula Bromberg has given me one of the greatest gifts of my life— she gave me back myself. I began working with her over 20 years ago when I was emotionally lost, in unloving relationships, unhappy. Paula, through deep compassion, humor, and pushing me to do my work, helped me peel back the layers and patterns I'd hidden behind for decades. I began to re-discover my true self and, with that, true peace. I am now a joyful person, almost all the time, and even when facing several tragedies at once a few years ago, I knew I would be ok. And I was ok. Because Paula had given me the gift of myself. And isn't that really what we are all searching for? Isn't that where all our life's purposes and work and joy reside?

Paula is both a demanding teacher, always insisting I own every situation, every choice in my life. And never allowing me to blame another. She is also a deeply loving and hilariously funny teacher too. 21 years after meeting her, I still call her whenever there's turmoil in my life and her easy laugh and deep insight make me instantly feel better. Paula's work is so unusual in its depth, but also in its sensitivity. My emotional health doesn't look like my friend's health or my child's health. Paula leads us each to our own mountain top, and each peak is beautiful and each peak is different. She works with me, as me. And maybe most importantly of all, she never loses the connection between health and spirituality. She is grounded and present, but she always gently reminds me that I am part of something much larger than myself. That spiritual connection, coupled with a deep sense of knowing and loving who I am, has created a joy in my life, the depth of which still surprises me. It is resilient, it is generous and it is loving, because when we are connected to our true, healed selves and to the limitless love of the universe, life is beautiful.

Paula has made me rich because I have peace, I have compassion. And I have joy. I will always have profound gratitude and love for her and how she has enriched my life.

—Heather Pentland, L.Ac.
created New Leaf Healing Center, trained in China and New Mexico in
traditional chinese medicine, acupuncture and herbal medicine

Little did I know that when I contacted Dr. Paula Bromberg over 13 years ago how much of an impact on my life that initial call would have. I had sought counseling a few other times in my life so I was not a total stranger to entering therapy. In an hour over the phone, I could see my relationship issues and struggles more clearly. Working with her was different. She was not going to tell me what I thought I wanted or needed to hear. What ensued was a working journey into a better understanding of who I was and seeing why and how I reacted to situations that were presented in my life.

We used the Enneagram and other tools to help me explore and accept my true nature. I slowly began embracing that true nature. Stopped pushing against it and criticizing it. I shifted how I began to see and accept others, celebrating their differences, but keeping myself on course, my true way of being.

On I traveled staying in the relationship, keeping my professional practice going, navigating my father's death, my mother's illness, and her passing. That brought sibling challenges and how to negotiate what I needed. Each life event brought a chance to work on myself. I moved to another state, creating another phase of life. My beloved dog passed. There were professional challenges and opportunities to shift my business. As I grew and matured my marriage relationship changed and ended. As I enter this new phase of my life, I am forever in deep gratitude to Dr. Paula.

—Marybeth Minter, DVM
classical veterinary homeopath and nutritional counselor,
teacher and lecturer, Mariposa veterinary services

Always Beautiful

In memory of my Beloved Mother
Adele Rosalind Bromberg Hellman
January 18, 1915 – September 28, 2000

We Embrace in the Sh'ma

Thank You

Pain and happiness have the same shape in this world:
You may call the rose an open heart, or a broken heart.

Late In Winter
My Heart Is
Still A Rose In Bloom

The Way Of Love

The Message: Relationships challenge, Love awakens.

*L*ife repeats. When we learn to use our woundings for healing, as teachings, rather than let them use us, then we learn, transform and be in the Way of Love. That happens as we discover the sacredness of our essence, of our experiences and the remarkable beauty of our inner consciousness. Awakening is possible, as we embrace the transformative power of Love.

This book contains passages that appear to be memoir. Look further and you will find that I use my life as the teaching. Our life is the material, always available, the compost and fuel, once digested, for teaching ourselves and others. To learn through sitting at the feet of our own life, to drop the fascination and excitement with the story and understand its message and purpose—what a lifetime! My invitation is to no longer see where your story and teaching diverge, for your life to be an inspiration, a teaching, so that life and the teaching become one. As the *I* diminishes and your voice appears, may this book open a door to come home to who you truly are.

—*Dr. Paula Bromberg*

Contents

PART ONE
YOUR LIFE IS THE TEACHING

PART TWO
WHO AM I—TOOLS TO WAKE UP

PART ONE

Your Life Is The Teaching

Learn Through Sitting
At The Feet Of Your Own Life

And did you get
what you wanted from this life, even so?
I did.
And what did you want?
To call myself beloved,
to feel myself beloved on the earth.

—R. Carver

If the Beloved said,
pay homage to everything
that has helped you
enter my arms.

There would not be one experience of my life,
not one thought, not one feeling,
not any act,
I would not bow to.

—Rumi

PREFACE

With Certainty, Say Yes!

If understood, life is simply a jest;
If misunderstood, life becomes a pest.
Once overcome, life is ever at rest.
For pilgrims of the Path, life is a test.
When relinquished through love,
life is at its best.

—Meher Baba

WITH CERTAINTY,
SAY YES!

*T*hroughout the history of religion and philosophy there have been many paths towards truth and self-realization. All paths lead to five ways: the Way of the Fakir—awakening through the physical, the Way of the Monk—awakening through the emotions, the Way of the Yogi— awakening through the mind, and the Fourth Way—awakening through a balancing of the physical, mental and emotional. Each of these ways lead us into the realm of perfected beings, the inner circle of those who have attained.

I am proposing the Fifth Way, *The Way of the Lover,* A Way of Understanding—awakening in love; a transformative spirituality that speaks to our present time. The path leading towards this Way is a mindful path of the heart. *Sacred Psychology* is a tool along the Way honoring unconditional love as sacred, not only to be in love but to *become* love. Through our relationships, through learning to love, through mindful living, the practice of attention and studying the nature of mind we arrive into our potential, our possibility. Released love awakens us, committed intimate relationships challenge us.

In *Sacred Psychology* our woundings are used as a practice for self-purification. When we do not experience and understand our own creative process of self-healing we are not be able to mirror that to others.

7

Along the path our joy and sorrow are one, as we walk with one foot in heaven, one foot on the edge of the abyss. One foot steps out work, the other love. Our heart breaking open, we enter the Way of Love. The feminine, the mystical consciousness of regenerative birth that women have to teach is the bridge between psychology and spirituality. To cross that bridge is to move from the human heart to the divine heart.

To live our spiritual practice is a self-exploration. To look at family and its system, its collective history, transformational therapies and ancient sacred teachings, to look at our wounded relationship with love itself, and then to discover what constrains and what brings freedom. To find a spiritual path within everyday life is to live an inspired life. This means connecting our little stories to the big stories. To live our practice with presence is dying before we die, studying consciousness rather than pathology, and looking towards a psychology of the gods as we travel a journey towards unconditional love.

This book is an invitation, encouragement and inspiration to open to our heart, to polish the mind, to investigate through self-inquiry uplifting our personal experiences to universal truths: the ordinary to become extraordinary. This book is best read thoroughly, completely. It is a teaching as well as a pleasurable delight. I have read it many times and with each reading see in a new way.

—Dr. Paula Bromberg

INTRODUCTION

An Invitation: To remember

Pazienza! Patience! No man is born into
the world whose work is not born with him.

—*Michelangelo*

I was in the presence;

I was sent to earth;

My wings were taken;

My body entered matter;

My soul was caught by matter;

The earth sucked me down;

I came to rest.

I am inert;

Longing arises;

I gather my strength;

Will is born;

I receive and meditate; I adore;

I am in the presence.

—*Rodney Collin*

It does not matter what you have been or what you are

"What do you want?"

Say you are content with yourself.

Then you are dead.

You want nothing

and the journey is what you want

not what you were, or are,

but what you want now.

—*Maurice Nicoll*

AN INVITATION:
TO REMEMBER
YOURSELF

The Way of the Lover, A Way of Understanding, addresses what is eternal within, calling us to become and know who we are. To discover and know ourself, the secret is within, not lost, nonetheless forgotten.

> *Seeing a rose, Remember yourself.*
> *Hearing a song, Remember yourself.*
> *Watching yourself, Remember yourself.*

One approach towards self-knowledge is to perceive our life as pieces of a puzzle. One day one piece fits, the next day another, until eventually creating a recognizable harmonious pattern. We begin to see the configuration, although not necessarily while we are assembling it. As the pieces cohere we don't have the overall concept of our picture until the *Aha.* We might have that *Aha* at some point, yet still relate only to one aspect, not the totality. As a therapist-now-become teacher, I see that additionally we have moments of clarity and access to the greater picture. Those flashes of truth allow the brief intervals. Story drops away, we have glimpses, we wake from the dream, able now to remember and in time live into that consciousness called reality.

BRINGING AWARENESS
TO OUR LIFE

We each have our own story of the life we think that we are living. But underneath this story lies the deeper truth of who we are—our real nature—and a life that is fully present. —Llewellyn Vaughan-Lee

The topics I am writing about are themes in my life. I had a particular fantasy when I was young. I was intrigued by Lawrence Durrell's *Alexandria Quartet*, each book titled by the complexity of relationships that was his life: *Justine, Balthazar, Mountolive,* and *Clea*. Durrell investigated the numerous postures of love, moving between the personal and the political until all lines vanished. I imagined that I, too, would some day write about each person and the themes and unfolding that has been my life. Much of my inner work is rooted in themes that I hold as a meditation for long periods of time. The one that centered around relationships began when I was in my early teens. Themes often originate for me as questions: What is friendship? Who is family? What is my purpose? How to be intentional and say what I mean? How to have meaningful uplifted conversations. What is love? The ordinary experiences that we assume or take for granted became my yearly meditations. Listening to the questions leads us to discover who is the one doing the asking. From that place understanding arises. Our living questions form the love that is understanding; love is made of a substance called understanding, without it love has little meaning. The process that leads from illusion to realization, that wants to speak, to write, to serve awakening is who pays attention. Awakening, questioning the meaning of our living is key. We are the question. Who am I? What am I? Where am I? Experiencing brings us to live into the answer. Keeping our questions alive, not resolved with solutions and answers, living in the dialogue the inter-relationship with others, not escaping the questions—a risky endeavor in this material world where the concrete is idealized.

It is necessary to know how to sacrifice everything, including oneself. A price is to be paid for knowing and understanding. You yourself are this price. Question yourself always. Be Question. —G.I Gurdjieff

This is that book, my intention: awakening to becoming present to what is. A guidebook that looks deeply into our questions and directs us towards the conditions of higher states of consciousness. Navigating through this lifetime, placing ourself in the center of the now, to continuously begin again in the spirit and aliveness of the question, who am I? What do I want; along this journey into the unknown we learn to take responsibility for ourselves. And the more that we see, the more dearly we pay. Rumi enters the conversation and out of his love into his presence we feel the heart-center, the surrendered soul: *I would love to kiss you. 'The price of kissing is your life.' Now my life is running toward my life shouting, 'What a bargain. Let's buy it.'*

Jeanne de Salzmann wrote that *the first initiation into self-knowledge is to learn to see, but we will see that this is not easy. And it is not cheap. We must pay dearly. We must pay a lot, and pay immediately, pay in advance. Pay with ourself, by sincere, conscientious, disinterested efforts. The more we are prepared to pay without economizing, without cheating, without any falsification, the more we will receive.* Waking up comes from within, and so the second part of this book offers tools to lift the veil of what obscures our self-understanding. How to disengage from the adversities, the undesirable circumstances, from the unnecessary sufferings that hold us captive and obstruct us from opening to precious available higher energies.

See your success by what you had to give up in order to get it. —*the Dalai Lama*

The order of this book proceeds from a statement about the book cover, quotations of praise, followed by professional and literary acknowledgements. *Part One, Your life is the teaching,* begins with a *preface: With Certainty, say Yes!* explains the theme of the book. *The Introduction, an invitation: To Remember Yourself* extends the invitation to uplift our personal stories to universal truths, our small narratives to mythic tales, as we enter the way of love. The circumstances of our life are the invitation to connect and return to ourselves. This way of understanding for me has called forth significant teachers and teachings; here I speak to how they have impacted my journey.

In Chapter One, *Physician, Heal Thyself,* I explore a thread of my life which has been self-study and self-healing. Knowing ourself, genuine self-inquiry, finding meaning begins where we are. First to be one with ourself as we heal the illusion of separateness. Healing, a process of transformation that is powered by a persevering drive towards health to find our core wholeness, relinquishing our habitual self and diving deeper within to a self-awareness that liberates what lies fallow and unattended, therein lies the inner root that begs for tender understanding. Healing for me is a key aspect to my work and life. I can only bring a patient as far as I myself have gone; as I release more and go further inward, that energetic enables people who work with me to release and go forward. Otherwise something gets jammed; I jam them on my own unconsciousness when I haven't done a piece of work, whether physical, spiritual, or emotional.

Chapter Two, *Spiritual Conversation* is the very heart of relating, which is intimate conversation or *Sohbet.* This is spiritual dialogue as a practice. Mindful conversation trains us to listen, to pay attention and witness, to speak from the heart, it reflects inner wisdom, clarity and simplicity. Listening—attention to ourselves and others, being truthful—are present-moment expressions of how well we love and are loved. Here are two quite different conversations/interviews with Sufi teachers, one an instinctive-centered dervish from Baghdad in the Shattari Sufi order, the other a Shaikh of the Mevlevi order which traces its heritage to Mevlana Jelaluddin Rumi. Putting heart into our words, mutually agreeing to belong to the conversation, speaking through to the truth, a mindful conversation becomes a love offering. This sharing of our being creates an inward winding labyrinth while becoming reflecting mirrors as we mature our humanness.

Chapter Three, *The Path of the Heart,* trusting in the mystery of life, living into the questions, glimpses of other dimensions, this invisible fragrant celebration, beyond thought, a work of art, is our threshold to all relationships. This path is an umbrella for our spiritual work. The direction is inward, hidden away in the heart is where the treasure is found. The link, the unbroken chain for me was sound and words, the gorgeous music of holy chanting that penetrated me as a child. To enter the search, we walk through our life narrative until the fiction of our identity is released. To go beyond my story I traveled, gathered experiences; change scrambles our way of thinking: even so, what we come to know, this treasure is right here inside us, as close as our breath.

Chapter Four, *Let The Way Itself Arrive,* speaks to a daily life that becomes spiritualized: life itself as our meditation. The recovery of the sacred feminine, the mystical light of consciousness that has been a sleeping giant is now our greatest resource.

Chapter Five, *Mystery of the Feminine,* addresses my years in New York involved with feminism and spirituality. My first spiritual teacher was a woman, which was not what I consciously was looking for, but what was presented to me. My deepest connection to the feminist movement was the personal as the political, the relationships that were created and the visionary empowerment of becoming an agent of change. I worked as a therapist with trauma survivors. My interest was not in the politics of anger at the society for what had happened, rather it was in the nature, the energetics of each person and our relationship. To look at our responsibility to ourself and to others in a culture that doesn't value the years of practice it takes to unearth the parts of our psyche that obstructs our peace and loving kindness is the day labor. Psychological healing and spiritual maturation are interdependent. Recognizing what is particular to the feminine leads to an egalitarian reality where the consciousness of love is the love for life itself. This is the mystery of the feminine and seeing its impact on humanity we enter the Way of the Lover to honor all life as sacred.

While there are many paths to consciousness they all lead to five Ways. Chapter Six, *The Fifth Way,* A Way of Understanding, presents Sacred Psychology as the teaching and spiritual conversation as the tool to break the continuity of the narrative. Ordinary life provides the lessons, community becoming everyone. Chapter Seven, *Work is Love Made Visible* the practice of living mindfully, of studying ourself, a root for all paths, maximizes our possibilities. Self-study requires direct experience. The challenge of loving and being loved appeared in the form of a teacher. To step out of the constraints of this world I moved towards certain conditions that asked more of me. A reflection to break the trance, directed towards awakening. Being in the world but not of it I chose a teacher/teaching that became my guide. To know myself was to train myself to become accustomed to seeing in a higher way. The teacher, in the service of universal laws is our reflection, and was a mirror of my madness as well as my light, bringing me to see possibilities, to see *what is*. Chapter Eight, *The Circle of Angels*, a Metanoian Order, speaks to that invitation I accepted to live in a school of consciousness, to see every moment as the practice. A working environment with a teacher, Jean, serving as the instrument, a representative of my potential.

Chapter Nine, *The New Psychology* explores my vision of the bridge between psychology and spirituality. An invitation to move beyond the fiction of our biography, this science of the soul pays attention to those awakened beings who walk amongst us. Self-inquiry, to break the trance, less attention to pathology, a reverence towards ancient traditions, we become the miraculous. Chapter Ten, *The One Thing You Must Do*, expresses that yearning in the form of myth written as I approached my 50th birthday. The Beloved is found as we open to love, not through *shoulds* or *oughts*. Entering the magical kingdom where the simplicity of childlike essence is the divine play, then the openness and purity of a child brings forth this ultimate state of surprise and wonder. The pilgrimage through sacrifice to reconciliation; the teaching is to live generously, deeply ourselves and compassionately radiate a witnessing presence. Chapter Eleven, *The Way of the Lover*, sees healing as an experience of love and as a dying, discovering emptiness as the preparation to enter paradise on earth. Chapters One through Eleven point to our life as the material, always available, the compost and fuel, once digested, for teaching, to be lived as the overwhelming experience of Love, a continuous beginning. To learn through sitting at the feet of our own life, to drop the fascination and excitement with the story, and to understand that being present to our life creates our life.

Without presence there is no real life, only an imaginary life. Presence is divine. It is the divine spark that brings us to the great pearl, our highest self. —R. Burton

Part Two, *Who Am I—Tools to Wake Up, Wisdom Teachings* looks to *The Fifth Way* as a *Way of Understanding*. Understanding is the principal claim made upon us; it's the most powerful force we can create. Throughout this book are ways of understanding and Chapter Twelve is the courtroom of evidence—the how to live one day into the answer. This is the grist for the mill, the composting into awareness of our life's dramas. Tangible tools to assist our ascent up the mountain, to hold us steady, so as not to become fascinated by the view, and then to serve us in our descent down the mountain. Here is the linear—the proof and evidence of our humanity; that we are in a body, that we do have a personality, and how our human experiences have the potential for our transformation. These are the tools to point the direction to our specific work. The visible reality before we awaken to the invisible.

Chapter Thirteen, *Epilogue: Final Thoughts: Life At Its Best* addresses *The Way of the Lover* as a Way of Understanding. The voyage of the mud frog, the journey of the birds, as we locate what stops us from becoming, from awakening to the sacred while we proceed on the alchemical path of turning copper into gold. This is life at its best.

Open the Treasure Chest, names many of the books that have been my companions along the way; well crafted books of substance. *Books are the quietest and most constant of friends; they are the most accessible and wisest of counselors, and the most patient of teachers.* Yes, a carefully chosen book nurtures, draws me in, and I listen to each voice, drink deeply. Galway Kinnell says that *all beautifully written books have a certain quality in common, a tenderness toward existence.* Books speak to me, offer friendship and conversation, move me; I leave special hard cover books carefully placed around in my home sanctuary, and as I pass by I smile and feel happy—fruit blooming in my extravagant orchard.

Singing Creation Into Being, speaks to the music and musicians that fill the heart, uplift the soul and help create this beautiful world. Music, our true universal language: *The rhythm of the body, the melody of the mind, and the harmony of the soul create the symphony of life,* wrote B.K.S. Iyengar. *We have fallen into that place where everything is music,* says Rumi. *The strumming and the flute notes rise into the atmosphere, and even if the whole world's harp should burn up, there will still be hidden instruments playing.* Ours is to listen, to hear what the music is telling us, to rest in between the notes. Music fills my home, as I write, as I read, voices, instruments from across the sea, in every language from many continents. This music, breath generously carrying me into the moment where I visit myself and have great companionship. *Thank You* acknowledges my appreciation and gratitude to all who have ignited my fire and bless my life. *Further Deeper Work* offers possibilities to continue this work with me, to use the systems for self-study and inner investigation. *About the Author* gives a taste of a personal journey. *Book Order* provides options to purchase copies of *The Way of the Lover.*

The beginning of cultivating yourself is right in yourself; on a thousand mile journey, the first step is the most important. If you can do both of these well, the infinite sublime meanings of hundreds of thousands of teachings will be fulfilled. —Ying-An

FORMAL EDUCATION

I cannot imagine why one would dare to cross the shark-infested waters of the ego without a boatman. If you have not experienced an authentic teacher—or have had encounters with teachers who could not keep the boat afloat or tossed you overboard to fend for yourself—it is wholly understandable that you would be skeptical about finding a trustworthy teacher. But I remain convinced that true disciples in search of an authentic teacher will eventually find their way to the one they seek. —Mariana Caplan

*M*y earlier years in school were filled with the surprise of continuously discovering instructors who were apathetic and disinterested in teaching. That disappointment shifted when I attended the unique New School for Social Research in New York City. I recognized that the professors there were actually the artists, writers, philosophers and theorists who were creating and changing the world. They were human beings writing testimonies to their lives. I studied existential psychology with the American existential psychologist Rollo May, education with social critic and philosopher of education Paul Goodman and poetry with African-American poet laureate of New Jersey, Leroi Jones as well as poetry and literature with one of the leading figures of the Beat Generation, poet Allen Ginsberg. I was drawn to the presence of individuals who created a relationship with their students, teaching from an open dialogue, creatively cultivating intelligence, originality and initiative. I saw that it wasn't the ideas that were engaging me, it was the availability and exchange, the presence, energy, interest, cooperation and human interaction, the vitality and creativity that entered the classrooms, that created the background for teaching. True education has a spirit of inquiry that creates a new world.

We can only teach that which we are. —Jean Jaures

Studying literature, philosophy and psychology the overriding theme for me became the relationship, the connectedness, particularly the one between Jean Paul Sartre and Simone de Beauvoir. I wanted to know an intimate relationship without depending on society to lend it form or credence. To think independently and live a happy creative life takes real initiative. Our intelligence is awakened when we are in an honest dialogue looking at our inward psychological struggles as well as the points of view of moral and economic society. In this way we meet our life without fear or illusion. Living is a relationship, and the essential reason for friction and challenge is ourself, not how another acts but how we act or react. Once released from the beliefs, ideas and concepts that define relationships, we realize a mutual mature loving connection with all of life. All relationships serve as a mirror to see ourself in our distortions, in our truth. When we meet in love, knowing the reflection, when we embrace the relationship with tenderness, with attention, we enter heightened awareness to set a new paradigm, a discipline of the heart.

You must fall in love with the one inside your heart. Then you will see that it has always been there, but that you have wanted something else. To taste bliss, forget all other tastes and taste the wine served within. —Poonja

The Beloved And Universal Laws

You see, I want a lot. Perhaps I want everything. —Rainer Maria Rilke

The lack of available creative relationship role models prompted me to explore new ground. In my work as a therapist, teaching from a place of witnessing, attention empowers; bringing each moment alive, self-awareness is the key to healing. Often patients heal their relationship to their work and creativity and then look toward a similar integrity and aliveness in their primary relationship, recognizing how hindered they have been by the role models in their own family. I once told a patient, *If you came to learn good nutrition, I could send you to many people who understand and live in honest, clean relationship to their food. But to witness and spend time with two people in a healthy transformative committed relationship, that is rare.* There is a great lack in the modeling of the sacred marriage; finding a healthy, creative, autonomous couple to spend an evening with is no simple task. To begin to catch glimpses of open intimate relating between committed partnerships, to treasure the kindness that flows between couples imprints a delicious sensitivity, the possibility of honoring the sacred in marriage. A few hundred such partnerships could change the vibrational atmosphere and uplift this planet.

We walk through half our life as though in a fever dream barely touching the ground our eyes half open our heart half closed. Not knowing who we are or meaning half we say we watch the ghost of us drift from room to room through friends and lovers, never quite as real as advertised. Not saying half we mean we dream ourselves from birth to birth, seeking some true self. Until the fever breaks and the heart cannot abide a moment longer—and the rest of us awakens in the dream, summoned by the vastness to unrealized realms of being, born into a more authentic life not half caring for anything but love. —Stephen Levine

We have used and continue to use addiction in our effort to nurture ourselves. This is a country of intoxicants, co-dependents, alcoholics, workaholics, gamblers, sex, romance and love addicts and dysfunctional families. We use food, television and our electronic devises to distract and flatten our senses and to dull awareness. Rooted in insecurity, doubt and a need for recognition and acceptance our indulgence is in outside stimulus as entertainment. Thinking to be *happy* is a rosy fantasy, this being busy has moved us away from the still point of our interior journey. *The Way of the Lover* is directed to transcend the personality, not to develop it, to come to a quiet inner peaceful place so as to live in true spontaneity, in alignment with our deeper values, in integrity, connected and present. To break the narrow confines of our self-image, beyond the safety of our attachments and illusion and discover a sanctuary, that place of refuge where the enjoyment of our life becomes reality; says

Rumi: *Hey, that was joy that just stopped in for a visit! Glad it came by.* Life is the direct experience of what we contact, of living and being what we are in an awakened way—that's it!

All of our miseries stem from our inability to sit quietly in a room and do nothing. —*Blaise Pascal*

To learn to love another, one other human being, has been one of my most rigorous practice. It has been said that first you learn to love a plant, then an animal, only then are you ready and able to love another. This is a profound practice: learning to love. Rainer Maria Rilke speaks about this: *For one human being to love another: that is perhaps the most difficult of all our tasks, the ultimate, the last test and proof, the work for which all other work is but preparation.* Developing and strengthening our attention to create a new relationship to ourself to experience new levels of self-awareness as a way into mindfulness, our own being becomes the subject and object of our observation. And from that place of welcoming, of opening ourselves to ourselves, can we hope to meet, know, be intimate with and love another.

It is impossible to study a system of the universe without studying ourself. At the same time it is impossible to study ourselves without studying the universe. We are an image of the world, created by the same laws which create the whole of the world. By knowing and understanding ourself we will know and understand the whole world, all the laws that create and govern the world. And at the same time by studying the world and the laws that govern the world we will learn and understand the laws that govern us. In this connection some laws are understood and assimilated more easily by studying the objective world, while we can only understand other laws by studying ourself. The study of the world and the study of ourself must therefore run parallel, one helping the other. —*G.I.Gurdjieff*

Universal laws by which everything in the universe is governed beckon to give us understanding that awakens an intelligence deep inside, and with this influence we distinguish what is habit, what is conditioned and what is true and real. There is harmony in the universe by virtue of these laws; Chapter 12 in the second part of this book makes a study, an investigation into 21 universal laws. They are a bond between all experiences. There are laws that are beyond our subjective mind, understanding and living this knowing, gaining an impartial perception of *things as they are* creates harmonious balance. To live in this way our world expanded, we are more porous, penetrable, now with the possibility to become a lover of everything, to awaken to ourself, to go further....further.

The word Further is like a talisman, a power object. We must pull it out and gaze upon it after every battle, every time we think we must be done, that we must, at last, have arrived. As much as it may seem otherwise, there's always Further. Get up, dust off, and gird thy loins for the next fray. The day may come when there is no more Further and you will recognize that fact not with fanfare and ticker tape, not with radiant backlighting and choirs of angels, but with bemused and unenthusiastic observation that you are ...Done...Done means done. —Jed McKenna

SPIRITUAL TRAINING

The chances of someone awakening without a teacher are like the chances of getting pregnant without a partner. The spiritual teacher is the partner that is necessary for spiritual birth. Not too many immaculate conceptions happen. —Robert Ennis

My first spiritual teaching through Jean, a female Fourth Way teacher, was a path of affirmation, of great effort, a seeking and reaching to higher consciousness. I was asked to lean beyond my edge, my capacity, my fear—to lean slightly beyond my edge of comfort in every moment. My second teaching through Adnan, a male Sufi teacher, was more receptive, feminine, a surrender. To experience truth, or any real aspect of ourselves, look within, become the eyes, the ears, the heartbeat of the beloved. The more masculine path of taking action, of directionality, was traveled with a female teacher who sliced through obstacles like a warrior, while the gentle, graceful feminine path of flow was traveled with a male teacher who wrote songs, moving as dancing light in a garden of sound, clarifying for me that energy is about nature not gender.

Your body is the best home your mind will ever have. —*Matthew Sanford*

Initially, being with Adnan was an enigma. I couldn't understand his work through my intellect. Body-based practices to cultivate vital energy, to direct attention within, the integration of movement and stillness extending my energy. The days were spent doing trance-like, subtle, fluid movements followed by evenings of drumming, whirling, and belly-dancing. To let myself feel beautiful on the inside, not muscular strength but allowing the sensation of the body guide my movements, engaging aliveness, subtly easing into opened spaces. I trusted and gave myself permission to be in the experience. In the dance, in the drum, and especially in the music—the middle eastern splendorific pulse and beat, I became alive. This is a Sufi way of teaching. It is said that some are destined to know God, and some are destined to know God and His ways. I had mostly navigated in the world of thought. Adnan's work brought me tone and breath, to enter my body, a world of sensation; to move and dance with other goddesses, for my energy to then flow outward as receptivity.

Jean's teaching developed the craft of loving another human being, goals and projects, clarity and direction, challenging interpersonal relationships, large emotions, with life as theater. This theatre lets us glimpse the larger picture. A big plan is offered to us as a gift as we live our lives. When we defer to the flow that our life takes, we are in touch with the larger play: to be in the play of life, suspended between life and possibility.

How, indeed, could it be possible for man, who is limited on six sides—by east, west, south, north, deep, and sky—to understand a matter which is above the skies, which is beneath the deep, which stretches beyond the north and south, and which is present in every place, and fills all vacuity? —*St. Gregory the Wonderworker*

FIND THAT WHICH HOLDS US TO THE DIFFICULT

Even after all this time the sun never says to the earth 'you owe me'. Look what happens with a love like that, it lights the whole world. —*Hafiz*

The first month I met Jean I remember sitting in an Italian restaurant on 14th Street in New York City with her and three other students. She told us that we each have one particular quality that supports and inspires our spiritual work. I asked what she saw mine to be. She said, *Faith.* I realized that I had worn a gold medal of a blindfolded woman on the figurehead of a ship's prow. She was called *Blind Faith.* While I have had a guiding faith, at first it was blind. Until, eventually one day my faith developed sight, vision, wisdom. No longer blind faith, I threw the locket in the river, with connection to higher energy, with vision many things are possible.

Faith is a function of the heart. It must be reinforced by reason. The two are not antagonistic as some think. The more intense one's faith is, the more it whets one's reason. When faith becomes blind it dies. —*Mahatma Gandhi*

What I've had to develop alongside faith is trust, which is the groundedness I needed for balance. To me faith is having a hand extended upwards toward the unknown and trust is having a hand extended outward to another person. In faith and within trust life continues to reveal itself and flow without having a finished picture to make it be a certain way. This force of life arrives within our own experiences, our own knowing. All of our thoughts and expressions create currents of energy and activity. When thoughts are negative they create negativity around us, when thoughts are roses, they create a beautiful garden; what is within surrounds us. I once printed on a business card: *To heal the world is to heal ourselves.* The practice of healing ourself and thinking positive thoughts creates a wave of healing in the world. The atmosphere responds to our thoughts and actions. Following the Chernobyl nuclear accident in Russia, the air in Santa Fe, New Mexico was affected as was the air in upstate New York.

Thoughts have power; thoughts are energy. And you can make your world or break it by your own thinking. —*Susan L. Taylor*

Some of the universal laws behind energetic force are the physical laws of magnetic fields and attraction. Magnetic fields produce electric currents while a magnetic force attracts or repulses. We are cosmic magnets, our thoughts and feelings send out a magnetic field and universal energy for us to become a similar resonant energy, like the sun's rays hitting the earth, people in our life reflect and cast back as mirrors, one for the other sharing the energy we have generated. The interdependent web creates a substance that penetrates the moment and in itself is energy. Whatever is in our energy field and emotional life manifests in our environment to become apparent on a conscious and unconscious level. Our responsibility is to become a watchful guardian of everything within our arm span.

To think is to form patterns inside ourselves that are just as complex, fleeting, and rich in their diversity as reality itself. Thinking is no less than our mirror of the world. Science declares that we are physical machines that have somehow learned to think. Now it dawns that we are thoughts that have learned to create a physical machine. —Deepak Chopra

One corollary of the universal law of attraction and energy force is that we carry people only to the point where we are. Ram Dass said, *You can only be as high as your therapist.* In the early years of my work the first hour someone might say, *You seem so happy, how can you help me with my sadness,* in the second hour a different person might say, *you appear to be happy and that gives me confidence to look at my sadness,* in the third hour another person would say, *You seem so balanced, I don't know if I can work with you;* and in the fourth hour a new person would say, *if you don't tell me about your life how do I know if you live a balanced life.* It became clear that their projections were their obstruction as well as motivating force. In the later years and currently there is little to say about *me.* The reflection once claimed becomes a valuable and essential uncovering, the fiction that conceals truth. To look without buffers, to see the internal and external misconceptions; taking responsibility is preparation on a road to freedom, for the beloved and the lover to be experienced as one. My availability to serve people, leading them to reveal their unique spark, what obscures their divine voice; to become their naturalness, the romance begins. The telephone is the main instrument used to speak the unspeakable in this open experiment, journeying co-creation. Not to acquire more knowledge, instead to experience the truth of our life. Having this alchemical science of transformation available that I refer to throughout the book, everything is possible.

To meet a person at his center is to pass through a revolution in yourself. If you want to meet someone at his center, you will have to allow him to reach your center also. —Osho, Rajneesh

We magnetize the people who mirror the level and quality by which we live. As my practice has evolved, so has the relationship between me and the projection/reflection others bring. I don't doubt or question my work. I just do it. It's my service. I once asked (and that's the beginning work for all therapists), *Can I do it?* My ego was there. The less ego the more possibility for healing. Balanced, we balance the world. Transforming ourself gives light to the whole world. Once rooted/anchored into the present moment, the ability to recognize truth has a certainty and a promise, we are no longer an obstacle. This *yes* is the true discovery!

Relationship is life, and this relationship is a constant movement, a constant change. Only in relationship do you see the face of what is. Only in relationship can you know yourself, not in abstraction and certainly not in isolation. —Jiddu Krishnamurti

As We Are

There is no before, no after, only life itself. Freedom is not freedom from something, but freedom to be in the present, in a moment that never existed before. —Jeanne de Salzmann

This work incorporates the understanding that the past and the future are fused into the present. I move between the past, present, and future with patients—who they were in their family systems, to see and experience who they are now in the present moment, opening to who they are becoming. Our history, heritage, and traditions embraced, ultimately loved and forgiven, are here now to serve us. Forgiveness, not to justify the actions, rather to enable us to no longer be affected by them. What freedom to no longer be reactive from our past circumstances ! Whatever is arising, acknowledged and understood in the present, enables us to live daily life fully, from our core inner center.

Things are such, that someone lifting a cup, or watching the rain, petting a dog, or singing, just singing—could be doing as much for this universe as anyone. —*Rumi*

The path toward conscious love, which I call The Fifth Way, *The Way of the Lover,* A Way of Understanding, is the intention behind my life and work. Unconditional love is the sacred. We all yearn to give and receive love; when I'm at my best I'm putting love into my work and life. So the theme of *the Fifth Way,* conscious love, is visible and viable in all parts of life, whether I am an artist, scientist, musician, or painter. Rembrandt painted love, Mozart played love, Shakespeare wrote love. You could go to the nth degree and say, existence is love. It's everything and nothing. That's why it manifests in all shapes, colors, and forms.

Love is the only reality and it is not a mere sentiment. It is the ultimate truth that lies at the heart of creation. —*Rabindranath Tagore*

What has drawn me to particular teachers are their presence. If I were to say who was my teacher, I would say Love. The force that emanates is the teaching. When we experience the body of existence as Love, therapy becomes a way to live into our vulnerability. Each event not cleared is our obstruction that blocks us from receiving the love that is always available. Clearing our resistance, deepening attention, knowing our particular form we create a witness, someone home who becomes present and watchful to witness, observe ourselves, an essential first step towards awakening. Since we have the possibility to study ourselves, of recognizing how we show up in the world, noticing our mechanicalities frees us of illusion, confusion, self-preoccupation, subjectivity and opens worlds of understanding. Creating conditions to prepare our inner world to receive refined energy, to open to what is higher we sacrifice what keeps us agitated, our distractions.

Its like an exquisite spider web, this world, but I don't get trapped. I have ceased to tie the strings of one shoe to another in the morning, so now I don't trip over my wants. This leaves me nimble. Any mountain I can scamper up. A long rope shoved quickly into a sack can easily get tangled and not be of proper use when all of a sudden you need it. So I do everything, everything with care. It is like a miraculous weave of silk, the fabric of this tender-looking sphere where we are camping, but I don't get caught in any arms or lives, unless they are loving, loving me. —Rumi

Teachers work within the form of their constitutional type and transmit through their level of being, their presence. There are many styles which are the context and container for teachings. The Fourth Way Gurdjieff work uses the placement of attention, dances and movements as well as a typology called the Enneagram of body types as a map for understanding human nature. The Fifth *Way of the Lover*, works through the experience of the I am, through loving and relationships, cultivating presence from the totality of attention gained through intentional labor and directed effort. The Enneagram, which has been transmitted to us and preserved through oral tradition, classifies human nature objectively. It has not been until this century, that this system has become more than an oral tradition.

The understanding of human types is a necessary beginning in the development of consciousness because of the accumulation of artificial and illusory elements in the dreams we dream about ourselves. Not only are the elements that make up a person's essence complex, but they are usually obscured by the development of personality. It takes a very long time to separate those characteristics that are a part of personality from those that are a part of a person's essence. The essence of a person is that with which a person is born, what the person essentially is, and the personality is what the person learns. We are so conditioned to evaluate everything in terms of its relationship to the exterior, material world—the world that the greatest writers tell us is illusion, the shadows on the walls of Plato's cave, Maya—that we find it very hard to value consciousness itself as opposed to what it is we are conscious of. This, however, is the purpose of this system of classifying human types. We are the safe we are trying to crack, and we are trying to watch ourselves do it. The point is the watching. If we are watching then we exist. If we are not watching, then it doesn't matter whether we crack safes or what we do. —Susan Zannos

Reluctance to accept body type information is often a reflection of type, a lack of understanding or reaction of a younger soul person. We are at the mercy of our type until we consciously investigate, unravel, dismantle, and observe ourselves. What this book, *The Way of the Lover* and *The Fifth Way* communicate are ways to develop a witness, an observer, self-awareness, how to mindfully observe ourself, to escape, to be free; to awaken. The theory of body type is esoteric objective knowledge, new neither to this century nor to past history. It's depicted in the fairy tale *Snow White and the Seven Dwarfs*, where the dwarfs, tiny when compared to that of Snow White, suggest the magnificent potential within each of us and the tone of our personal work. We are directed by a definition of humanness while working within our particular framework. To find what is essential and true while knowing that we are exemplars of the whole universe, we look toward universal meaning.

In order to see types one must know one's own type and be able to 'depart' from it. What I speak of refers to the real type, that is to say, to essence. If

people were to live in essence, rather than in personality we would find each other easily. —*P.D. Ouspensky*

Born into a physical body, we awaken in the manner of the configuration of the container, of the seed of our birth. Roses are not going to become daffodils. There's a kernel that is our seed; we each have our own essence to mature. If one morning we were to wake up having the body of a dinosaur, and since self-image structures experience, it would pattern a new and different personality. Psychotherapy has been oriented towards strengthening the personality. Sacred Psychology, *The Way of the Lover* is directed towards finding the truth about ourself, about *what is*; ultimately diminishing personality, to find and mature our essence.

In the world to come, said Rabbi Zusya, I shall not be asked, Why were you not Moses? I shall be asked Why were you not Zusya? —*Martin Buber*

The acceptance of our type and the movement within that structure on its many levels becomes part of our mindfulness practice. The form is Apollonian, but the Dionysian aspect is the inner chaotic passion that moves through form to essence. Once we have allowed our nature to be what it is, for a rose to be a rose and not wish to be a daisy, accepting our limitations and our humanity we begin to allow the essence, which most often has been damaged in our personal life history, to mature until we awaken. This process occupies many lifetimes. Understanding type affords us the possibility to know others as they are to themselves, as well as identifying how we are, and from this kind place compassion grows.

It is possible to get out of a trap. However, in order to break out of a prison, one must first confess to being in a prison. The trap is man's emotional structure, his character structure. There is little use in devising systems of thought about the nature of the trap if the only thing to do is to know the trap and to find the exit. —*Wilhelm Reich*

MINDFULNESS REFLECTS OUR TRUE NATURE

The mind is a superb instrument if used rightly. Used wrongly, however, it becomes very destructive. It is not so much that you use your mind wrongly—you usually don't use it at all. It uses you. This is the disease. You believe that you are your mind. This is the delusion. The instrument has taken you over. —Eckhart Tolle

Disease is in the mind and the mind which encodes collective thought blinds us to the full spectrum of our existence. Our mind repeats little thoughts, images, and structures of what we imagine to be right or wrong—formitory thinking. We are part of a culture that says, It's wrong to be retarded, you belong in an institution. It's wrong to be old, you belong in a nursing home. It's right to be a woman and 5'6" and 120 pounds and it's wrong to be a woman and be 200 pounds. It's wrong to be a male under 5' tall, it's better to be a doctor than a truck driver, it's right to shake hands when you meet someone. This rule-bound aspect of the mind creates tremendous limitations and bigotry. It's right to be German but it's wrong to be a Jew in Germany. It's right to be white in America but it's wrong to be an Indian there. It's right to be heterosexual. It's wrong to be homosexual. It's better to be young than old, better to be white than black, better to have siblings than be an only child, better to have a college degree; the mind plays havoc with our imagination creating toxic unnecessary suffering and limitation, halting us from living in present moment awareness.

Man-made laws and rules, not universal or objective ones, create formitory thinking, fear and discrimination. On the psychological level the ego has a difficult time tolerating differences. It knows only itself. So the child becomes stuck and becomes a 40-year-old 3-year old, thinking that differences are bad and knowing only its own narcissistic needs, learning to love the similar and not tolerate differences. This thinking breeds fear and hate, promotes damage, hurt, and self-imposed, circular limitation, ultimately creating a pain-body, an inner negative energy-field, an invisible unconscious entity, the pain-body stores toxicity and restricts the experience of peace, calmness, equanimity and connection. The pain-body sets up circumstances that promote pain because happiness and enjoyment are indigestible to its existence. Wars, violent crime and unnecessary suffering emerges from this mind-set. Democrats belittle Republicans, many Americans demean Muslims, heterosexual men make fun of homosexual men, *ignorance*, says the Dalai Lama, *is the fundamental cause of the painful round and round of cyclic existence.* Yes, it's not the environment, but the mind itself that causes our mental suffering.

The mind, the mind, the mind—this is the beginning and end of it all. The quality of one's life depends on nothing but the mind. —the Buddha

The human mind has the immense potential for learning and processing information, for evolution. Wherever there is power and energy, there is also the possibility to distort. Because we have the capacity for consciousness, we also have the capability to create illusion. Wherever there is a possibility for growth there is also the possibility for destruction. We use our experiences or are used by them. This is also true of the mind. We can either use the mind to evolve or allow it to create chaos. The key to using the mind constructively is the practice of mindful living. Harnessing our mental chattering and distractions of the mind precedes connecting to higher, universal mind. We limit our access to universal mind, which is the positive, creative force of intellect through erecting obstacles and indulgent entertainment. Just as our emotions put up personal blocks, the mind puts up intellectual barriers, rigidly adhering to mechanical laws, missing what's behind the screen, which are universal, objective laws.

We have no reason to harbor any mistrust against our world, for it is not against us. If it has terrors, they are our terrors; if it has abysses, these abysses belong to us; if there are dangers, we must try to love them. And if only we arrange our life in accordance with the principle which tells us that we must always trust in the difficult, then what now appears to us as the most alien will become our most intimate and trusted experience. Only someone who is ready for everything, who doesn't exclude any experience, even the most incomprehensible, will live the relationship with another person as something alive and will himself sound the depths of his own being.
—*Rainer Maria Rilke*

In our original family system lies the message that some of our naturalness is ok while other aspects of our nature are not. We are educated towards imbalance and have created systems that continue that process. School teaches that if we excel in math then we should study math so as to maintain a high grade point average. Likewise, if we are not talented in languages, don't study French because it might lower our scholastic point average. We demonstrate athletic skills, therefore we are encouraged to pursue sports, not being athletically inclined, schools discontinue interesting us to participate in sporting events. The parts that are weak to begin with continue to atrophy and the parts that are skillful become more developed until we are quite out of balance, one-dimensional, with higher averages and lower lives. Lawyers relate to codes and not to persons, while doctors manipulate physiology yet lose touch with emotional and spiritual needs. We don't develop access to all the multifaceted aspects of ourselves.

Scientific studies have shown how little of the intellect we do use.

Sacrificing aspects of ourselves to develop one part, we burn out the percentage we are overusing. Large portions of our brain remain unused although fairly easily activated. The physiology of brain mapping suggests that most, if not all areas of the brain have a function. We meet a fraction, 5 to 10 % of our mental potential. And this beautiful brain composes concertos, arrives at brilliant thoughts, creates poetry and rhyme, expresses compassion, as well as remembers dates and experiences, and yet, rather than live in its expansiveness we live in squalor, a lower state of consciousness. Our birthright is a castle most splendid, yet we walk around asleep believing we are awake, barely entering the most wonderful parts of the castle where there is an ongoing garden of delight.

Mindfulness is the aware, balanced acceptance of present experiences. It is opening to or receiving the present moment, pleasant or unpleasant, just as it is, without either clinging to it or rejecting it. I have no desire to fix my mind so it will not feel saddened by loss. I want to feel deeply, and whenever I am brokenhearted I emerge more compassionate. I think I allow myself to be brokenhearted more easily, knowing I won't be irrevocably shattered.
—*Sylvia Boorstein*

Through mindfulness practice, bringing attention, cultivating cognitive traits that activate the brain and enhance the immune system we train our brain to be less reactive and more balanced. Mindfulness is the ability to pay attention to the present moment, to have self-observation and non-judgmental self-awareness, for us to be intimate with what's happening innerly. It impacts and changes our brain. It's like taking the brain to the gym. To be imbalanced and disharmonious our natural gifts move us towards our demise. To utilize our intelligence enriches ourselves and the world. The privilege of experiencing all of ourself as we go about the ordinary activities of life is to *be the lamp that lights the path and eliminates the darkness of ignorance.* Our mind can be our greatest friend. The whole range is available, within each of us, and that means to live total.

We must understand that, before acquiring new knowledge, we realize our limitations and the fact that our limitations are limitations of our being. Our knowledge remains on the same level. It grows in a certain direction, but this growth is very limited. What a restricted field we live in, deceiving ourselves, imagining things to be different from what they are. We think it is easy to change something, but only when we sincerely try can we realize how difficult, how almost impossible it is. The idea of change of being is the most important idea of all. Theories, systems, diagrams are a help; they help concentration and right thinking, but there is one real aim, and that is to change our being; if we want to change something in our own understanding of the world, we must change something in ourselves. —P.D. Ouspensky

THE LONGING THAT LIES HIDDEN IN THE HEART

What is the purpose and significance of life on earth and human life in particular? —G.I. Gurdjieff

The circumstances of our daily life are the invitation to bring our distracted scattered mind back home. It takes many years of traveling to know that we are sitting on the goal; there is no enlightenment outside of daily life. We search far away for what is as close as our heartbeat. Being truly present to what we do throughout our day, when we bring our mind to the here and now inviting ourselves to interface with the present moment, this is mindfulness. Mindfulness shines a light on whatever we pay attention to, and wherever I place my attention, there I am. Energy follows attention. Self-observation without judgment is considered to be the highest form of spiritual practice moving us away from our personal narrative and into life as it is, intentional, present, moment by moment, and when we are authentic we are a great benefit to all others.

A story about Nasrudin, the fool, has him looking for his key on a road under a street lamp. A dervish passed by and asked him more exactly where he lost it and the fool said, pointing elsewhere, *right where I was standing, but this is where the light is.* Our own key lies within, yet it is learning to make our inner understanding the source of all external actions before knowing what living mindfully is about. When the inside is harmonious the outside reflects accordingly. It's not just sitting and closing our eyes. Rather, it's finding the key, generating clarity, saying *yes* to the invitation, opening the door, stepping across the threshold: now enter and live on the burning *diamond-point of the present.*

Transform stamen on stamen fill your interior rose. —Rilke

*The art of medicine consists of amusing
the patient while nature cures the disease.*
　　　　　　　　　　—Voltaire

*If you see what needs to be repaired and how to repair
it, then you have found a piece of the world left for you
to complete. But if you only see what is wrong and how
ugly it is, then it is yourself that needs repair.*
　　　　　　　　—Menachem Mendel Schneerson

*I am the mirror as well as the face in it.
I am the song and the one who sings it.
I am illness and its cure
I am pain and what cures pain, both.
I am the sweet cold water and the jar that pours.*
　　　　　　　　　—Mevlana Jelaluddin Rumi

*I asked for wonder 'stead of comfort, And yes, You gave
me Wonder. —Abraham Joshua Heschel*

*Dear One: 'There is so much suffering and tragedy, so
much heartbreak and pain in this world —why haven't
you sent help?' and the Beloved answers, 'I did, I sent
beautiful help—I sent you." —source unknown*

CHAPTER ONE

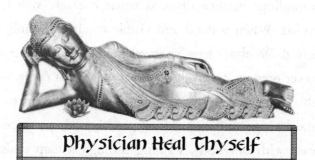

Physician Heal Thyself

PHYSICIAN
HEAL THYSELF

MEDICE, CURA TE IPSUM

*M*y first patient was myself. The piercing, my initiation at the age of two, was a wire from the ear of a stuffed bunny that penetrated my eye. Trauma, that great Teacher, carried me to my spiritual home. I traveled an inner journey of self-healing. My own daily life became the spiritual practice. To be available to another, I first must be available to myself. The only way to heal this world is to heal yourself. The first step begins at our own feet.

Our woundings become diseased when they are veiled, covered, left unattended. When washed and visible to air and sunlight, when opened we heal. We don't have to travel to distant countries when our own life is ever present. To break the dream is to first come face to face with ourself. We become alive at the core of our own heart. And this knowing and loving is curative. The wound is both entrance and exit: making peace with our body, walking through a map designed as a pilgrimage of descent brings us forward to a new beginning. Personal transformation, which is the healing, has been shown to invest us with the gift of a special knowledge earned through crossing that threshold, for the impossible to become routine. For it is not only to follow in the steps of those who have gone before us—it is to want for ourselves what they wanted. And each of us has our own particular song.

When you try to understand everything, you will not understand anything. The best way is to understand yourself, and then you will understand every-thing. —Shunru Suzuki

THE WOUNDED HEALER: PAIN MADE VISIBLE

Thirty-three years later, crossing 19th street in Manhattan the jutting outside mirror on a Ryder truck slammed into my head. A narrow thread between reality and an opening that brought me to a life teacher who made jokes about how I needed to have a truck hit me in the head before I could truly see. That is, before I could truly understand what vision and seeing were about I actually had to lose my vision in one eye. I had to live in a flattened dimension for 33 years before I could grasp the spiritual idea of seeing dimensionally. It was through love that I saw miracles become commonplace. I can now call impediments like my partial loss of vision, gifts. In my own experience these gifts, which other people might call hardships or obstacles have become ongoing miracles. The miracle of the truck moved me into my emotional self. When I came out of plastic surgery, because my nose had been moved to the wrong part of my face from the accident, the cast on my face let others see the black and blue skin under my eyes. I walked around like that in New York, where I had a psychology practice, good friends and was a supervisor at a clinic. I went into each familiar experience as if for the first time, because people would look at me and say, *Oh, my God, you must be in so much pain.* This response allowed me to breathe total. I was validated. What had been inside all of my life was finally out there to be seen. I felt alive and real, because inside and outside now matched. I had known I was in pain in my life. It was no big deal to me. But no one saw it, for I never let it show through.

Now, however, daily moments of acknowledgment came because of this black and blue face in cast and bandages. I even took pictures of it, the insurance company required them, and I sent photos to my mother. They were a second birth announcement. I was here now. This new visibility and validation led to my next experience, the task of traveling inward with a teacher. I understood how asleep I had been, to have run across a street and not see the Ryder truck, a huge yellow moving mass of steel. I realized that I was so ahead of myself and out of my body that eventually I would have been killed if I didn't stop, back up, go inside, and become quiet. My teacher offered me the opportunity to leave a life of acquisition. There was nowhere more to go in outward life. In its terms I was successful, competent, and financially secure. There was nowhere to travel, no further way to grow, except to back up and go inside. The bridge for this second journey in my life, was my pain made visible.

Lucky man. One accident like yours is worth ten thousand sittings in a monastery. —Soen Nakagwa Roshi

THE PERFECTION OF AN EMPTY POLISHED MIRROR

You can be helping many people, but if you are not helping yourself, you have missed the one person you were born to heal. —Alan Cohen

My own personal work of healing becomes a mirror reflection of my work with others. It is in the mirror that the key to our own identity lies. First, we look at what is here, to hold still and see what is reflected back. We open ourselves to project back what looks at us clearly and sharply without distortion. The mirror has no preferences. Look to imitate the perfect mirror, for when we become clear and empty like that mirror, this is the healing. When we leave, the mirror stands empty. It has no possessiveness, no sentimental memory, no likes or dislikes, no ways it wants us to be or not to be. It simply reflects back. When we stand before it, we are perfectly present and when we go we are totally gone. This represents the ultimate perfection of non-attachment.

The following notes were found among Rodney Collins' papers after his death and published in a book called *The Mirror of Light*:

We live our life in a mirror; everything is reversed. When we see a scene it is received in the brain reversed.

The same takes place in our thoughts; we think that cause is effect and effect, cause. For us, the physical is more real than the spiritual. We regard birth and death as antitheses and have altogether forgotten that to die is to be born.

The life we live, the world we live in, is a mirage. If we understand a mirage we understand a miracle. We should study more about the mirror. It is the key of the book that should soon be written.

The practice of paying attention, penetrating each moment, creates a deeper relationship with our inner world for us to see the visible manifestations of the invisible. Can we touch others through a glance, knowing who looks back at us. We polish our mind, we look into the mirror of the heart and our inner eye opens and sees light everywhere. Rumi says: *We are the mirror as well as the face in it.... You've no idea how hard I've looked for a gift to bring you. Nothing seemed right. What's the point of bringing gold to the gold mine, or water to the ocean? Everything I came up with was like taking spices to the Orient. So I brought you a mirror. Look at yourself and remember me.*

What is it we have to bring, to gift to others beyond our presence! We have been stuffed with things as a substitute for the lack of true gifting, and we continue accumulating, neglecting to grant ourself with the only gift that can deeply satisfy. We are the very thing we think we need. What a challenge to relinquish the materialism of this culture. To carefully consider what we bring, if not an undisturbed state. And to know when we receive less than that, or to ask less than that from ourselves we create suffering. Let us be careful to not fill our quiet space up with other stuff; our wholeness, our satisfaction rests on our insistence, on our looking deeply into the mirror of who am I? the most essential question we can ever ask of ourselves. This self-inquiry from the very mind that is asking is the reality that we are seeking. The practice of investigating, taming, asking for mental steadiness of our restless unrestrained mind slowly brings us to find peace within ourselves and the world. This discipline of the mind, quieting the inner disharmonies clears the dust from the mirror of our mind.

If you want to see yourself you will need a mirror. Only in the mirror will you see yourself, but then you will have to stand in front of the mirror. If your mind is a mirror, it can reflect the whole world. It cannot reflect you because you cannot stand before it. You are always behind, hidden behind the mirror. To keep the quality of mirroring continuously fresh is to remain young, is to remain pure, is to remain innocent. Reflect people, reflect the beauties of the world. —Bhagwan Shree Rajneesh, Osho

Healing the psychological is the first rung on the ladder and needs to be addressed before entering a spiritual realm. This accounts for the difficulty, the lack of intimacy skills that we encounter in the world; in marriage, friendship, government, in wherever people gather. Not addressing these early woundings, skipping the ground level of cellular pre-verbal essence childhood injuries leaves a hole in our capacity to love and receive love. To see who I am, to be a light to myself, to learn from the mirror, not about it, we need to know what to look at and have direct experiences of who is looking.

Look how a mirror will reflect with perfect equanimity all actions before it. There is no act in this world that will ever cause the mirror to look away. There is no act in this world that will ever make the mirror say 'no.' The mirror, like perfect love, will just keep giving of itself to all before it. How did the mirror ever get like that, so polite, so compassionate? It watched God. Yes, the mirror remembers the Beloved looking into itself as the Beloved shaped existence's heart and the mirror's soul. My eye has the nature of God, and looks upon all with perfect equanimity, as do my words dear. My poems will never tell you no, because the mirror is not like that, and if God ever hits you with a don't—He has His fingers crossed, He is just fibbing for your own good. —Hafiz

THERE WHERE I STAND: I AM

How does a word—uttered or read—open a channel between levels and bid us cross? When a word moves us, what in us moves and how can we be obedient? Listening, we go under the word's sign, pilgrims seeking the Way, uncertain, insecure, strangers in a foreign land. Could this be the raison d'etre of language, to transport thought beyond words, toward the wordless source of meaning—unless that wordlessness itself arouses, with a word? What leads from idle chatter to real meaning? It is important to heed the silent space between two words. —David Appelbaum

*L*anguage carries the power of the mirror. The moment a word is spoken we and the word disappear, the mirror is empty, clear once again. We live in a technological holographic world, a world of mirrors and virtual reality that capture images and reflect energy. We are the radio transmitters resonating, sometimes with a harmonious hum through the airwaves and at other moments forming interference patterns that vibrate dissonance. We receive and we transmit. When the mind is quiet we transmit clearly. Emptiness has no image. Words carry a relative sense for most people and enable us to make sense of another. When we see and know ourselves we go deeper in our understanding of others.

The power of the word when it is based on a special and mysterious energy initially gave rise to the word. One says something, and, depending on the energy behind it, the word or sentence arouses or fails to evoke a corresponding energy in the listener. The most important influence behind language is invisible, an invisible energy. From that point of view, a word or sentence, when spoken with attention, is charged with a special energy. Energy follows attention—where I put my attention there follows a flow of force—and where there's an inner presence accompanying what is expressed, power is added to whatever is spoken. —William Segal

According to the Hebraic tradition God spoke and the world was created. *In the beginning was the word,* as well as a void prior to the word, and so we pay attention, listen, to the word as well as to the silence, the pause between the words. Words and silence are regarded as the instruments of creation; to know them is to know reality itself. The meaning of words shift away from their original descriptions, just as we look different as we appear in the mirror of another's eye. Not to take words or images at face value; to perceive meaning we look further as we are drawn to live in the word. Our mind shows us an image of everything but ourself. How to see is to empty our mental processes, our thinking and be behind our mind. To go beyond the world of reflection, to inhabit the word, we receive glimpses of what is real and we are freed from our own limited perception, freed from living in a world of smoke and mirrors and empty words.

Spoken words are sounds occasioned by the vibration of thoughts; thoughts are vibrations sent forth by the ego or by the soul. Every word you utter should be potent with soul vibration. A man's words are lifeless if he fails to impregnate them with spiritual force. Talkativeness, exaggeration, or falsehood makes your words as ineffective as paper bullets shot from a toy gun. The speech and prayers of garrulous or inaccurate persons are unlikely to produce beneficial changes in the order of things. Man's words should represent not only truth but also his definite understanding and realization. Speech without soul force is like husks without corn. Words saturated with sincerity, conviction, faith, and intuition are like highly explosive vibration bombs, which, when set off, shatter rocks of difficulties and create the change desired. —Paramahansa Yogananda

The ancients saw words as living entities, carrying the power to speak the world into existence. The origin of our diversity of languages has been explained through the story of the tower of Babel which took place about 130 years after the flood. In the Bible version *the whole earth was of one language and the same words.* Heading west, the whole earth settled on *a plain in the land of Shinar,* which included Babylon located in Mesopotamia. The whole earth decided to build a city and a ziggurat, which were architecturally the Mesopotamian equivalent to the Egyptian pyramids. The purpose was to create a structure tall enough to reach heaven, to climb and learn all the secrets of the world. As the story goes, the qualities of pride and arrogance, the self-aggrandizement of people building an artificial mountain to acquire power created the scattering of men, women and children throughout the world, like seeds strewn across the whole earth destroying and scrambling their one original language. Eventually each tribe had to develop their own distinct language. There was no longer one speech or even a common border. In this action every newly developed culture and geographic location would hold their own piece of the puzzle. And so the tower of Babel has come to mean babble, the sound of people chattering that is incomprehensible or difficult to understand. This explanation of the origin of the world's many languages demonstrates how powerful language was regarded. The Talmud states that Babel is the root of all of our forgetting; the self-importance of the community building the tower which was to make a name for themselves, to sacrifice the individual for the sake of common good, led to a divine response which was to confuse language in the one creature that was endowed with speech. The workers had become incomprehensible to each other, as it was written in Genesis *their tongues became confused* and so the parable of Babel was a response that has tainted our ability to communicate with others. No longer one language, it is said that in spiritual terms Babel becomes an allegory for the discord between our inner and outer selves, as well as the impurity of our words with each other.

What the elements are to chemistry, what the sounds are to music, are words to language. However, words are not only the elements of a language but also the history of a people speaking it. They are the important milestones along the way leading to the majestic palace of human knowledge. We not only speak and think and even dream in words; language is a mirror in which the whole spiritual development of mankind reflects itself. Therefore in tracing words to their origin, we are tracing simultaneously civilization and culture and their real roots. —Ernest Klein

A writer and lover of dialogue I cherish words and their source; they are vessels carrying us along a voyage moving us into realms of meaning and purpose. Language informs and touches the heart through gestures, myths, allegory, parables, metaphors, through poetry and song; when it enters our heart the words turn into music, a language to refresh our spirit. Historically words were considered magical; I see that used with care and attention words become substance, create a powerful image, carry their own force. And we never quite know the day that we may have to eat our words, so let's keep them sweet and juicy.

In our Western tradition, a world made with words, they reveal or conceal, create atmosphere, describe the world, shape our attitude; spoken consciously they move the world. The early meaning, the etymology and philology of our language direct us towards those dimensions that bring the sacred to life. Words give meaning to sound, and throughout the world those sounds have been interpreted differently.

Words are the physicians of a mind diseased. —Aeschylus

We decode historical roots of words and discover, for example, that words like *medicine* and *meditation* have the same root; both are healing forces. Historically, the medicine man was also a spiritual being. In the same vein, Jesus' miracles with lepers and the blind were inspired through faith. *Health, healing, whole,* and *holy* all originate from similar roots. In current time, Ammachi, a Mahatma, a great soul, serves the sick without regard for her own immune system. Her *I* extinguished for *all,* she lives in ordinary activities, reflecting peace as her face of love. Her *I* becoming a swinging door which moves as she breathes. When we know ourselves as the timeless and spaceless possibility the *I* vanishes for us to become the heart of being, a understanding undisturbed, serene, witnessing presence.

A word is dead when it is said, some say. I say it just begins to live that day. —Emily Dickinson

THE SOURCE OF HEALTH

In the ultimate depth of being, we find ourselves no longer separate but, rather, part of the unity of the universe. That unity includes the sufferer and the suffering, and the healer and that which heals. Therefore, all acts of healing are ultimately our selves healing our Self. —Ram Dass

That the immune system restores itself from brokenness to wholeness is miraculous and mysterious. The physical body, a macrocosm of this universe, carries the inherent ability to repair itself. Energy flows out of openness and receptivity and when we learn to stay connected our energy circulates, builds; cells in our body continuously restore, reconstruct, rebuild, renew. We effect the health of our body with impressions, with the state of our presence, our ever-present thoughts and the quality of our attention. Discovering wholeness within our distress, that is our healing. When we know oneness it crushes the *me*, as I see that I am the one. As consciousness opens, the universe becomes our body, reflecting the macrocosm.

Shamanic cultures teach that a person is not fully healed until he/she takes on the mantle of the healer. A visit to a doctor for an hour, or a one-hour meditation practice, both prepare the ground. Their effectiveness depends on our ability to own the information we receive and bring it forward into a living, everyday practice. The term *incurable,* seen in a spiritual-meditative light suggests that our cure can be found by going in/within. Studies show that when a patient has an organ replaced but does not go to the source of what made that part of the body ill, the ailment reappears in a different part of the body. The body is essentially an electronic device and each cell is a tiny battery powering our electronics and energy system. Malfunctioning cells caused by deficiency and toxicity deplete and compromise us; we deserve to live with good health and increasing vitality.

Never go to a doctor whose office plants have died. —*Erma Bombeck*

The word *dis-ease,* or against ease, means disconnection; sickness is really a separation from the whole, lack of well-being, not in flow.

In ancient medicine it was not the business of the doctor to cure the disease, rather to restore alignment and create a harmonious balance. In fact, in the 3,000 year-old tradition of Chinese medicine, it had been the custom to pay a doctor only when one was well. When a patient remained ill the physician was not paid. There are no words in the ancient diagnostic systems for many of our modern illnesses, such as cancer or tuberculosis. The business of an allopathic doctor includes technology, diagnostics, repairing a mechanism, educating us to sustain our health. Combining the knowledge of the mechanics of the body teaching good nutrition, exercise, as well as addressing and recognizing the responsibility towards maintaining inner harmony and alignment heals the whole person. Western medicine has proposed that sickness, dis-ease, comes from an imbalance in the immune system. The Zohar, a 2,000 year old text, considered to be the soul of Kabbalah, teaches that the cure for disease is in the disease itself. Illness is an indication that something is out of balance, the orientation is to not fight the disease, but to bring us back to our natural equilibrium.

No mirror ever became iron again; no bread ever became wheat; no ripened grape ever became sour fruit. Mature yourself and be secure from a change for the worse. Become Light. —*Jalaluddin Rumi*

The work of a healer, whether as therapist, doctor, acupuncturist parent or friend is to be available to the whole which heals, to stay connected for energy to flow, enabling us to reconnect. What a beautiful world, to pay the physician to be available along the way, not after we become sick. A good season for the doctor would be when patients are well, instead of a wealth inspiring flu season. Hippocrates, the father of medicine, asked his medical students to swear to an oath of sanctification, a devotion which demanded their personal and professional lives be lived with integrity. He proclaimed: *The natural healing force within each one of us is the greatest force in getting well.* As early as Hippocrates, it was clear that when we don't experience and understand our own creative process of self-healing we will not be able to reflect it to others. Treating illness as a personal journey we emerge changed, embodying awareness.

Complete health and awakening are really the same. —*Tarthang Tulku*

Healing the world, an obligation of birthright in the Jewish tradition called *tikkun ha'olam* or the spiritual repair of creation, is knowing that we are this world, connected to everything in it, always affected. Each person is the whole world and all our actions are responsible for its reparation, a healing process, the liberation of light.

We are members of one great body, planted by nature in a mutual love, and fitted for a social life. We must consider that we were born for the good of the whole. —Seneca

METANOIA: CHANGE OF ATTITUDE

The miraculous is the entry into an action of a conscious force that knows why and how the action is performed. We cannot be without relation. Either we are related to something higher or we are taken by the lower. —*Jeanne de Salzmann*

Availability, opening to higher influences uplifts our life. And to live what we experience, to understand what happens to us is everything. We are fed through a current of energy and attuning to this force we strengthen and deepen our presence. To dedicate our work, ourselves, to become an instrument of service, mundane activities become our practice. Our everyday life supplies the material for our inner experience. Life can be a tale told from a place of hardship as easily as a place of joy. The choice is ours. To step out of our comfort zone we experience that the boundaries are what makes our world appear finite. True freedom is outside the limits the barriers and borders of the cages, it is present everywhere, it's a force that calls from deep within, a song of the soul dissolving the boundaries of our ordinary restricted self.

Beyond, to go beyond ourselves, is a life directed toward our highest possibilities. Further than the stories, the content that lives within us, the woundings, we access and experience what is higher as we open to a timeless spaceless field of consciousness. To dedicate our acts as Ghandi, Aug San Sui Kyi, Jeanne de Salzmann, Eve Ensler and Thich Nhat Hahn have is to risk everything, to inspire generosity in whatever we do, be it cooking, writing, raising children, peace making or mixing cement. All divine activities.

Every step of the practice path is an ordinary, everyday activity of human beings. The more we understand the causes of suffering, the greater our intention, the wiser and more compassionate our behavior, the clearer our minds, the deeper our understanding of suffering, the stronger our intention, over and over and on and on. If I want to be sure that I've made the point that acting wisely and compassionately is the inevitable, passionate imperative of the heart that comes from realizing the depth of suffering in the world, that we pay attention for goodness' sake, I say it this way: When we see clearly, we behave impeccably, out of love, on behalf of all beings.
—*Sylvia Boorstein*

An ancient story about three laborers illustrates this teaching. A wisdom teacher, sharp-witted and sensible, sees three workers hard at their job. He approaches, asking the first worker, *What are you doing?* Without looking up, in an annoyed impatient tone, the worker replies,

I'm laying brick. The teacher nods, walks on, asks the second workman, *What is it that you are doing?* The second man, tired and barely looking up, mutters, *I'm earning my living.* Hearing this the teacher goes on to the third workman, asking the same question. The man stops, looks up, walks over to the teacher and with an inspired smile and outstretched arms exclaims, *I'm building the most beautiful Temple in the world.* This account has been attributed to the building of the Taj Mahal, today one of the seven wonders of the world. This narration illustrates the value of attitude, how large, from what place of spirit and inspiration are we willing to see. People understand in proportion to their capacity. While all three workmen were performing the same task, only one ennobled it, celebrated his work within the perspective of his vision. It's the intention, the quality of attention that uplifts and brings meaning to our activities. Sufis call our real work self-remembrance, the only work worth doing is to remember ourself. The *Fifth Way* continues, asking us to open, to let bliss enter. The English poet and mystic William Blake lent eloquence to this idea when he wrote: *to see a world in a grain of sand and a heaven in a wildflower and hold infinity in the palm of your hand and eternity in an hour.* As we continue our inner work, the daily laying of brick, our ability to see levels and dimensions strengthens.

To penetrate into the essence of all being and significance and to release the fragrance of that inner attainment for the guidance and benefit of others— by expressing in the world of forms, truth, love, purity, and beauty—this is the sole game which has intrinsic and absolute worth. All other happenings, incidents and attainments in themselves can have no lasting importance.
—*Meher Baba*

Reb Nachman of Breslov, a Third century Hasidic master, taught that the sacred is in the ordinary, the remarkable within the common-place. His teaching stories point towards finding meaning in the midst of our life, to place our attention behind form. Learning how to see, we detect glimpses of the sacred in everything. Reb Nachman illustrated this in the story: As the wedding ceremony and reception was over a group gathered outside the Temple. First Speaker said: *Now that was a beautiful wedding, the food was out of this world. Not only did it look good, but it tasted better than any restaurant I recall eating at.* Second Speaker: *It was a great wedding. The music not only was terrific to listen to, it was as enjoyable to dance to.* Third Speaker: *I particularly had fun because I was introduced to more interesting people than I've met in years.* Reb Nachman, listening to the conversation said: *You were not really at a wedding.* A student of Reb Nachman then spoke: *How sacred and beautiful that those two people found each other, lover and beloved as one. A united spirit as great a miracle as any, bless these two beloveds.* Hearing this, at that moment, Reb Nachman said: *Now **you** were at a wedding.* The metaphor of marriage is the meaning of this world. To find the beloved of our soul, to witness and celebrate vows to each other beneath a bridal canopy is the rooting of the human in the realm of the sacred. To recognize and transmit the sacredness of the human heart, to hold connections to higher values and see what truly matters; this is the sacred marriage.

God creates new worlds constantly. In what way? By causing marriages to take place. —The Zohar.

It is taught that we are destined to marry our perfect soul partner from the time of creation, and the Talmud teaches that to find this partner is as great a miracle as that of the parting of the Red Sea, as that of the one day supply of oil miraculously lasting eight days, and as that of the burning bush remarkably not consumed by the flames. When we invite the sacred into our relationships, appreciating the sanctity of each moment as it appears, we introduce purpose, consequence, intention into our lives, now everything becomes greater than its appearance. Seeing a divine force brings this world to life. Love is the root and foundation on which our world is built, and marriage is seen as a microcosm of the soul's descent into this world.

From each person there emanates a light that reaches directly to heaven. And when two souls destined to be together find each other, their individual lights join as one, as a single shining beam issuing forth from their united spirit. —the Baal Shem Tov

Partners in this creation, our priorities when faithful to our inner self nourishes our soul. Our personality may be reactive, yet our essence is receptive. To look at our life as an intimate relationship with existence itself, spending the profits of our work as kindness and generosity in this world, the harvest we gather are the blessings that come from our service. To go beyond the personal, to go further than our limited conditioning and reactivity we shift our reality and unbind ourself from the sufferings that arise from subjective projections. This is a healing that takes place out of linear time, that releases us from endless repetitive patterns.

Come along! Today is a festival! Clap your hands and say,' this is a day of happiness!' Who in the world is like this bridal pair? The earth and the sky are full of sugar. Sugar cane is sprouting all around! We can hear the roar of the pearly ocean. The whole world is full of waves! The voices of Love are approaching from all sides. We are on our way to heaven. Once upon a time we played with angels. Let's all go back up there again. Heaven is our home! Yes, we are even higher up then heaven, higher than the angels! My dear, it's true that spiritual beauty is wonderful. But your loveliness in this world is even more so! —Rumi

At the age of seventeen I lived in a kibbutz in Israel. I knew that most of the people in my hometown, after finishing high school continued to remain in Providence, Rhode Island to work within their family business. Traveling to another country for me was expansive. In Israel I met a nineteen year old boy, born in a small village in Africa. He lived with the premonition that what had happened to the Jews in Germany would eventually happen to Jews in Africa; a slow but thorough extermination. Holding this thought form he dedicated his life to his dream of creating a safe place in Israel to relocate his small African Jewish population. Staying at his kibbutz I experienced how the universe responds to the quality of our dreams and actions. His simple example of service as a foundation of life, his determination as a practice, his efforts to actively impact and change his environment rather than passively tolerate it transformed his piece of the world. Yes, opening our arms to change without compromising our values, making an effort to dispel the darkness, the suffering of others, we take responsibility for our actions rather than accepting injustice and exploitation. Compassion is a priceless jewel. Meeting him I saw that one person changes history, that each of us has that possibility to affect lives, a capacity to think beyond our small town mind towards a greater dimension. I knew that once committed to a vision, I too could move worlds.

For hundreds of years—perhaps since the beginning of Creation—a piece of the world has been waiting for our soul to purify and repair it. And our soul, from the time it was first emanated and conceived, waited from above to descend to this world and carry out that mission. And our footsteps were guided to reach that place. And here you are there now.
—Menachem Mendel Schneerson

EXPANDED CONSCIOUSNESS

Your birthday is the date that existence decided that the world cannot exist without you. —the Rebbe

Within the code of my family system truisms were commonplace. Stock phrases filled our dining table: *be happy with what you have, a little extra money never hurts though; don't rock the boat, a clear sea is more trustworthy in a long swim, no one cares about you as much as your family, it's just as easy to love a rich man, just because you go to college, don't think you know more than we do, finish your food because people are starving in Europe, spirituality is not part of the Old Testament.* Creativity, self-discovery, inquiry, soul-searching were not high-priority in our family values. Questions were seen as pointless, they were *making a big deal over nothing. Stop analyzing everything* was my older sister's favorite remark to me. Conversations concerned what you did, entertainment and shopping were favorite activities. Life was presumed, outer appearances became the reality. A chill of silence that turned away from deeper emotions, that held disdain for processing, answers were solutions, while delight, wonder and surprise were effectively removed. And still, a voice that echoed timeless teachings penetrated me; my earth was tied to heaven. I read and wrote, words tucked away. I loved words, positioning and repositioning, jumbling the letters and sounds, maddening my mother and sister with the meaning and meaninglessness of phrases and noises. My performance pieces to them were a cacophony, a racket. What appeared as nonsensical to my family were my risk taking adventures to express myself openly, which startled and irritated, provoked and amused. I was motivated to infiltrate apathy, to pull me up from the ordinary conditions, to challenge others, to clarify what I experienced, to ask and ask and ask.

It is the infinite ocean of myself that the mind-creation called the world takes place. —*Ashtavakra Gita*

What is our true inheritance but this whole earth. Life is our relationship to ourself, to another, to society and to a global world. It lies in our question, who am I? A teacher of mine remarked: *without having a question we are only half alive.* And knowing how to ask a question, the quality of the question along with the willingness to live inside that question connects us historically to all traditions since the deepest questions are shared throughout humanity during all times. It is imperative to look multidimensionally, to enter the mystery of the unknown, to know that the voice resonating in my head is not all of who I am. The artist William Segal wrote: *what makes a person is their ability to question themselves. An authentic question, and, who am I is the most absorbing question that a human being can have. Everything is directed towards the question of who we really are.* Gurdjieff investigated the question: what is the purpose and significance of life on earth and human life in particular? all the while emphatic that we each verify for ourselves, learn to see, have a direct relational experience, face ourselves. Awakening to the meaning of our existence as well as the effort we demand of ourselves, the inner work to live what we learn, supplies the fuel, because all of the unanswerable questions are to be lived.

When indeed shall we learn that we are all related one to the other, that we are all members of one body? Until the spirit of love for our fellowmen, regardless of race, color or creed, shall fill the world, making real in our lives and our deeds the actuality of human brotherhood—until the great mass of the people shall be filled with the sense of responsibility for each other's welfare, social justice can never be attained. —*Helen Keller*

In therapy working on mother issues, regardless of our gender, includes unraveling who we are as mother as well as what universal mother means. This inquiry towards understanding, deceptively simple, births a new consciousness to step beyond our personality, to build something real for humanity. *The Way of the Lover* stretches/adds vision. Therefore, self-investigation, to unravel and release our own personal history, frees us to live and relate to what is truly around, not to remain imprisoned, imprinted, reactive from the past. The danger lies not in speaking, but in silencing ourselves and the world at large. Let's not be suffocated, muted, deadened, invisible before claiming our self, our voice. Thinking large opens doors, makes cracks in the walls, breaks form. The quality of self-attention in its process transforming, at its heart prepares our entry into the unknown, to make room for the experience of not knowing. The quality of our attention in itself is freeing.

When I chose to do my graduate work in philosophy, my mother was aghast. *What are you going to be when you grow up? A philosopher? You can't make money that way! Ah yes, a philosopher would be a high complement,* said I, *since that means a lover of wisdom.* I lived within a functional, practical family. Work was to make money. I knew I couldn't *make* money, I could work for work's sake to develop my possibilities in a world where most people work from ambition, obligation, compulsion or desperation. My pioneering spirit and willingness to step off the grid, to dedicate my life to unending work where everything becomes my practice, my opportunity, I saw as a force to assist my spiritual development. Work as a condition for living, as an integral act that connects us to ourself and this universe is a paying investment, not a wasteful expenditure. A mystic poet said: *Our work must be subjected to the scrutiny of our spiritual knowledge, which means to give up the rewards of compromise; choose a profession which endangers our moral and spiritual growth as little as possible.*

My own individuality, autonomy and dreams while not fostered in family or early school were confirmed by Jean, my Fourth Way teacher who pointed to a larger possibility: *If Christ could do it, you can do it too.* That had never been the code of anyone I had met. In fact, to say the word *Christ*, which I now see as consciousness itself, was alien to my family, they experienced it personally as a turning against family and Judaic tradition. They lived with fears and imposed limits, I chose to embrace the beauty of a consciousness not shrouded by the deadness of habit. Philosophical inquiry carries the wisdom that emphasizes the impulse to ask questions, the stretching of arms rather than folding them, determination to value the inquiring mind, to find meaning. Our mind can't capture the vastness of what is and yet the mind tries to reduce and limit with laws and form. Minds play games with reality wanting most of all to engage itself with the rising and falling of information, of minutae: the price of gasoline, the caloric content of a cookie, what flavors are best, which religion is better, what politician to listen to, how to play the stockmarket, where to buy real estate. Rather be concerned with: how to quiet the mind, to open and create relationship to higher energy, training the mind to pay attention to the sacredness of life; our underlying nature is so easily overwhelmed by the activity of the mind.

Bondage is of the mind; freedom too is of the mind. —*Ramakrishna*

I have come to understand that to live with indefatigable persistence and passion, bearing the indifference of others brings about inner freedom. Every once in a while I meet someone with an unquenchable flame, a Bonnie Whittingham, a Neith Nevelson, Maya Angelou, Leonard Cohen, Andrea Dworkin, Adrienne Rich, U.G. Krishnamurti, Kate Millet, Allen Ginsberg, Eve Ensler, Ram Dass, Jane Fonda; artists with daemonic mysterious energy refusing to bow to the banal; history remembers them as rebel, I, as lights unto themselves. Looking outward they looked inward, inviting us through their art, their music to do the same. Who am I? and Bonnie answered, *I am an English barmaid, a masked harlequin, a grain of sand, a great illumined planet.* To be guided by the lamp of our own light, illuminating itself; inner wealth and great generosity attended to will transform and bring change to this world. I remember standing in Israel with William Blake's lines running before me: *Arise and drink your bliss! For everything that lives is Holy.*

INTENTIONAL HEALING

What makes us human is our capacity of our questioning. Who am I is the most absorbing question that a human being can have. To know what we are here for, who we really are, our ability to question ourself is the quality that accompanies consciousness. The potentiality for the transformation of the human being is continuously present. —William Segal

William Segal, painter, writer, Gurdjieff student, relentless explorer of self-expression recounts that following a severe auto accident, lying broken, near death, he received a visit from friend and Zen teacher Soen Nakagwa. Seeing Bill, Soen grasped his hand and said: *Fine, fine, fine, lucky man, one accident like the one you had is worth ten thousand sittings in a monastery.* The broken places are cracks to let the light in. Shattered not only to be repaired but to embody a new vitality. Behind the idea that I am my body, that I am my thoughts a great discovery emerges. William Segal has said that the cultivation of the capacity for attention is possibly the most important thing a human being can do. *With attention a world uncovers itself.*

In Peter Brook's adaptation of Gurdjieff's autobiographical account of his youth and early travels, *Meetings With Remarkable Men,* Father Giovanni advises the young Gurdjieff: *Listen, you have now found the conditions in which the desire of your heart can become the reality of your being. Stay here, until you acquire a force in you that nothing can destroy.* And still the seeker is sent back into the world to test his understanding of the real meaning of inner struggle. Wholehearted attention, attending to what we are doing, whether it is listening to music, starting up the car, or feeding the dog, within the practice of applying ourself to each moment, to both that and to what's beyond the visible, we develop capacities that bridge the extraordinary.

Things are such, that someone lifting a cup, or watching the rain, petting a dog, or singing, just singing—could be doing as much for this universe as anyone. —Rumi

My beginnings incorporated a world of physicians and hospitals. An accident, an eye injury at the age of two, the subsequent thirteen years of medical intervention addressed the broken parts. I created a strategy for living. This shattering of the illusion of an ordinary life, for summer vacations hospital hallways became my playground. In an environment of specialization the human factor is overlooked. I was treated as an eye rather than as a child with an impairment who had feelings and thoughts, as well as physical needs; to the medical establishment I was an eye. The doctors and my family worked only on the injured eye, depersonalizing, fostering fragmentation. I had looked into a mirror to see a face cut open, a face stared back that had been hollowed out; for years I avoided catching myself in a mirror. Inward was more interesting, not an escape route but a circuitous redirection spiraling me away from a conventional suburban existence. I felt that, yes, they were repairing my eye, but another part of me felt hurt, affected, and it wasn't only my eye that felt injured. It was my being. I was wanting to be regarded as intact, unbroken, and until I enabled myself through age and maturity to go back and reclaim a self and a wholeness that happened to include an eye could I recover/integrate become a conscious physical/psychological and spiritual being. Health is a natural response to truth.

My experience with Balinese masks with actors, putting a plain, blank white mask on someone is a knockout exercise. The moment you take someone's face away in that way, it's the most electrifying impression: suddenly to find oneself knowing that that thing one lives with, and which knows is transmitting something all the time, is no longer there. It's the most extraordinary sense of liberation. It is one of those great exercises that whoever does for the first time counts as a great moment: to suddenly find oneself immediately for a certain time liberated from one's own subjectivity. And the awakening of a body awareness is immediately there with it, irresistibly; so that if you want to make an actor aware of his body, instead of explaining it to him and saying, 'You have a body and you need to be aware of it.' just put a bit of white paper on his face and say, 'Now look around.' He can't fail to be instantly aware of everything he normally forgets, because all the attention has been released from this great magnet on top. —Peter Brook

Our great challenges are from family of origin, outside influences and our automatic reactions. To find our driving force, look to where the greatest challenge appears. It either creates a seed of discontent, or it becomes a sanctuary for the heart. Often, when I was on exhibit in teaching hospital auditoriums and felt overwhelmed I experienced myself floating around the room. My strategy was to go out of body to maintain inner solitude. A profound healing came through one particular surgery in my adult years. I returned to the Massachusetts General Hospital where the earlier surgeries had incurred, mindful, not dissociative, neither compliant nor defiant, I reclaimed my history and the metal that had been left in my head was removed. My surrender to the healing process through years of self-investigation brought me to be present within the experience. This surgery was a life-changing experience. Existence offers opportunities, sometimes thinly disguised, either to redo a trauma in an intentional conscious way or to once again be traumatized. What a lucky lifetime, to find freedom within that which originally created confinement. I found a piece of self, a reconciliation and healing, an initiation, to meet and face myself; the universe moved. I was birthing myself, inside and connected, feeling my body integrated, instead of one part of my body having a disharmonious energy. This was a new beginning.

You learn to follow the inner self, the inner physician that tells you where to go. —Dr. O. Carl Simonton

When we set our conditioning and personal baggage aside to enter an inner space of stillness, then the one who is intended to be emerges, comes forth. I had artificial ideas and values implanted in me, as well as other people's needs and fears and I had to dislodge them. The original eye surgeries represented a conditioned definition, a concept about the acceptability of my body. Once exploring what vision, sight, wholeness really mean, understanding the esoteric intent to *let thine eye be single,* who I truly was stepped forth. Definitions of self, identifications, come and go, to discover ourself beyond name and form, as awareness itself, knowing this fullness redeems suffering. Availability, inviting the feminine, the receptive, surrendering, opening up to the surgeon and the power of nature during my later surgery, experience became the teaching. I made the conscious decision to say, *Okay, I'm going to receive these people so they can repair, move me towards my own restorative process.* What I was healing was receptivity itself; to open and receive with intention is a healing door to self-awareness. To randomly receive energy on other people's terms, their needs, values, fears, carries a toxicity that limits and cuts us off from our aliveness. This is what happened when I was a little girl. The medical procedures did not affirm my own strengths. The focus was cosmetic, on how it was going to look to other people, how the doctors were going to feel about their success, the techniques they had invented. The transformation in the later surgery came as I honored and owned my own heart and purpose, not for somebody else's interest and profit, but to bring new life to my own world; to a value system that mirrored what truly mattered in the understanding of heart. Rooted into life, taking in energies from higher sources, I came to know myself as a receptive vessel that when connected to my own life energy the wealth of the world was revealed.

Where silence and awareness meet, mingle and become one, there is receptivity. —Osho

T R U S T I N G   T H E   I N N E R   S E L F

Whatever you do, if you do it sincerely, will eventually become the bridge to your wholeness, a good ship that carries you through the darkness. —Carl Jung

Collaborative care, patient and doctor working together, affirms intuition, informs, directs. Naming the land we will travel, seeing where we have been, together looking at possibilities guides us to the heart of healing. Beyond a cure a dynamic relationship with a care-giver, with ourselves, not as a passive recipient, moves us towards well-being. From this blueprint we build an architecture of healing. Obstacles may appear on the landscape, with each expedition we set out on we become the Marco Polo of our world of possibilities. When I require medical treatment, I look for a person who dares walk fearlessly, respectfully, purposefully serving from their place of integrity—without intrusiveness or vanity—directing—with the means to both follow and lead me. Quite an assignment! Our woundedness, used for the purpose of self-purification will tap into hidden resources often quite close at hand. We hold the ingredients; meeting ourself we look for the landmarks, the routes, paying attention we become the author and creator of our own life. Mining the treasures as we embark on this healing journey, we are all prospectors.

During the physical curing process, the attention should not be on the disease, lest one's faith be dampened, but on the infinite powers of the mind. During mental overcoming of fear, anger, bad habits, and so on, one's concentration should be on the opposite quality; that is, the cure for fear is bravery; for anger, peace; for weakness, strength; for sickness, health. When a man has destroyed the mental bacteria of intolerance, rage, and fear, and has freed his soul from ignorance, he is unlikely to suffer from physical disease or mental lack. —Paramahansa Yogananda

Before surgery I spent time with Dr. Elisabeth Kübler-Ross re-experiencing the child that had disconnected, had become physically ungrounded. I recognized that to be imbalanced, to cut off from the root is to bypass the riches in this world of form. Discovering that balance between the form and formless, the home within and home without, eventually knowing they are one and the same; *gold coins may be raining down from heaven, but if one is not there to receive them, they are of no avail,* the observation states.

Mindful attention anchors us and is the foundation of all training and practice. The body has a beautiful wisdom. Body-work sessions brought me to gradually enter into and to inhabit my body. Connecting to this vibration, extending it to the atmosphere, being aware of ourself we develop sensitivity. Sensing and observation penetrate and transform; a connection with our body brings us a beautiful experience of energetic aliveness. Mindfulness shines its light to become one with itself. I have since learned that active attention comes directly from this body out into the world. Sensation of the body forms the basis for a connection to higher energy; to be as present as possible, always new.

I was preparing to enter surgery three decades past the original accident, with the intention of taking the metal out of my head, to contact the life force that had been sacrificed to survive trauma. Reclaiming what had been disowned behind the veil I discovered that my grandmother, my father and other invisible beings were available to me as guides. I learned to live in both worlds, tasting how the ordinary and extraordinary meet. During surgery my inner self offered no resistance. In surrender we are free. I went into the operating room having guided myself into my body. One child part wasn't certain for a moment, but another part, the adult, wanted to stay here in life. Allowing the past to fade, I arrived. To live into the moment, with understanding, we become finished with what has held onto us. The journey of acceptance in the light of awareness burns until nothing touches *us*, like the lotus blossom in the water, yet rooted in mud.

It is often said that our symptom or our pain is merely our visiting card towards the understanding of our true self. True healing is very much to do with becoming conscious. A real healer is able to add the necessary ingredient to a human being's life so that he or she is finally able to wake up to what is occurring in the present moment without being biased about what has happened in the past. —Reshad Feild

MINDFUL PRESENCE

Sacred Psychology, a way of leading by following, of healing through surrender, is illustrated in the following teaching story. A well-seasoned teacher/therapist named Sujin, living in the country, was outdoors, when a horse wandered into the backyard. The horse had no identifiable marking or tags, and Sujin had no idea to whom the horse belonged. In his desire to find the owner and return the horse, Sujin mounted and gently led her to the road. Holding the reins steady the horse felt reassured and began to slowly walk with rider on back. The horse sensed the direction ahead and Sujin rode, intervening only when the horse tried to stray off the road to eat grass or wander through tempting fields. Then they came to a path. The horse stopped at the path, so Sujin guided and then continued with her along the path until it opened to a farmhouse. A farmer walked out and said, *My goodness, how did you find my horse? Where was she? And how did you know where she came from and now lives?* Sujin replied, *I recognized a beautiful horse being lost, so I climbed on and we walked together. She led me as I reminded her to pay attention to what she instinctively knew. A few times I had to guide her back on the path, but she intuitively knew where she was going.* The journey of paying attention connects mind to body, horse and rider working together mindfully. To break through, to find what we are looking for is practical work. We pay attention, listen to the present moment. The mind like the horse tends to wander away, to get lost in distractions and wayward thoughts. To bring it back, to anchor it, to tame the wild horse mind, is to focus our attention and see things as they are rather than as we imagine or wishfully want them to be. Being here and not getting in the way are the quintessential elements, the beginning, the middle and the end. There are routes and landmarks, the key is to pay attention to our life, not the circumstances. A guide with presence awakens an intelligence that lies dormant, that is available and trained to discriminate. The peace that passes all understanding brings unwavering confidence. Our value as human beings resonates as we see our reactivity, our remembered sense of feeling lost. Life opposes quiet unfolding, distractions pull our attention, when we step forward into the unknown and remain present, then from this spaciousness we say *yes* to life. Mindfulness accepts what is, as it is. Witnessing without reaction we become a reliable instrument.

The horse and master reunited, body with mind and heart, this beautiful simple description of mindful presence, of healing, of the therapeutic process, of the teacher/student relationship, is our work. To use force creates resistance. The healing begins with the recognition that there is nowhere to go; there is nothing to do other than to be present to this moment. Being alert to what is creates clarity and removes clouds of static. Following our naturalness we grasp the essential destination. The work is to create a container, an environment, to receive what is already within, the gift of ourselves as we are. Not to erase ourselves in service to others, rather to co-create, self and others as partners in the process of repairing this world. Whether it's an animal, plant or human, animate or inanimate, a respect for all of life; healing sees everything as part of a greater whole. This broadening of our awareness are pores through which life breathes fresh air. Our very presence is the most powerful tool there is to enlist and offer others in their search. Jeanne de Salzmann, a masterful teacher called her quality of awareness *an attitude of vigilance, that she brought at all times and in all circumstances.* She lived her teaching, it was her way of being.

The most precious gift you can give is your true presence. What makes you alive? Mindfulness. Everything around you and in you can be the door to enter. Mindfulness is the energy that makes it possible for us to be aware of what is happening in the present moment. Whatever you do mindfully is a meditation. When you touch a flower, you can touch it with your fin-

gers, but better yet, you can touch it mindfully, with your full awareness.
—*Thich Nhat Hanh*

INITIATION: USING OUR WOUNDING

Our wound is the place where the Self finds entry into us. A window, we grow with the individuation urge, or it grows against us. The paradox is that the wound is also the treasure. The symptoms open you up, tear you open so that the things you need can flow in. The disease always carries its own cure and also the cure for your whole personality. –Kreinheder

Studies reveal that patients on hospital wards who ask questions are feisty and spunky and take responsibility for their own process tend to have a better prognosis and greater survival rate than patients who are passively compliant, accommodating, docile, cooperatively going along with a given treatment plan. Rebellion means you rebel as an individual, that will be true revolution—non-political; it is spiritual. I was headstrong, self-willed and rebellious, questioning, challenging every step of the way. And that was years before I read the statistics; challenging questions, intercepting my conditioning to give room as an active participant in the circumstances I found myself. *Blessed are you, who opens a gate in every moment, to enter in truth or tarry in hell,* wrote songwriter poet Leonard Cohen. To intercept what is experienced as shortsighted and inappropriate, to take responsibility for our life requires courage, takes risk and a willingness to dive further into the unknown.

The rebel is far closer to wisdom than the complacent child—as an ox is more powerful than a lamb. He only needs a wise person who can show him how to harness his strength and bring much good to the world.
—*Tzvi Freeman*

It's a given that the protocol for numerous medical procedures are debilitating and often eventually undermine a deeper process of healing. Weakening the immune system opens a door to pathogens and toxic invasion. To strengthen the immune system allowing symptoms to surface, gives the body an opportunity to cleanse despite recurring discomfort. Western medical practice in a one-two punch bombards the problem, the ailment, with little regard for the welfare and long range safety of the patient. The problem is extinguished, obliterated, and our body is left on the battlefield as a casualty of a war against it by a doctor's orders to destroy enemy foreign invasions. Oliver Wendell Holmes physician and Dean of Harvard Medical School at the annual meeting of the Massachusetts Medical Society commented about his medical community: *If we doctors threw all of our medicine, tossed the whole materia medica, sunk it to the bottom of the sea, it would be all the better for mankind and all the worse for the fishes.*

Our remedies are oftentimes more dangerous than the disease! Becoming inquiring participants in our own health care is a quality that advances a healthy sense of self. When we actively engage our physician and together manage our medical conditions statistics show that the success rate soars. *The next major advance in the health of the American people will be determined by what the individual is willing to do for himself,* was the headline in a investigative study that came from the Rockerfeller Foundation. Educating ourselves, preventing deficiencies and toxicity; and much of what we name biomarkers of aging are actually biomarkers of inactivity. Movement promotes the health of our cells. The cells in our body contribute to what we name as the mind, and what is happening in our mind affects our cells. Chronic stress inhibits immune response, releases tissue-damaging free radicals creating inflammation which damages tissues. Reducing stress in a lifestyle that thoughtfully combines food, exercise, relationships and work fortifies the immune system and empowers, affirms our own inner resources. Connections, to ourself as well as to others and to our whole life brings fresh air and balance to the physical and subtle levels of our being.

The greatest danger to your health is the doctor who practices Modern Medicine. —Robert Mendelsohn, M.D.

Stabilizing the physical self, bridging mind spirit and body, embarking on a quest for wholeness we move forward. The alchemy of change, transforming ourselves, refining and reshaping our reactions to life, uplifting the lead of our heart to gold, rests on our understanding. Only understanding and its application transmutes, transforms, metamorphosis us; changes our level of being. It's not about what we can do, this is about who we are in how we do what we do. It's about locating meaning, purpose, finding harmony within the dissonance of bodily betrayal. Reluctance to look deeply, to understand, to make fundamental changes that relinquish who we thought we were maintains imbalance. To depersonalize and split our selves off from our own experience brings us at risk to forces that can't locate our own path of healing.

We have a pharmacy inside us that is absolutely exquisite. It makes the right medicine, for the precise time, for the right target organ—with no side effects. The goal of health and healing is always the same—the revelation of wholeness that unites body, mind, and spirit as one. What lies behind the onset of disease: the body is sending a message that something lacking in the present—an imbalance existing somewhere—has given rise to highly visible, unarguable, physical symptoms. Life is like a tree and its root is consciousness. Therefore, once we tend the root, the tree as a whole will be healthy. Nature controls healing from this deeper level already, for every cell participates in the body's inner intelligence, responding to the patient's thoughts, emotions, desires, beliefs, and self-image. —Deepak Chopra

Studies confirm that the brain, organs and immune system work together to mobilize healing. Our mind as well as environmental circumstances and biology interact to create how we are. This journey of brokenness, an initiation when used to accelerate self-discovery, is a preparation for real change. Our wounds form scabs. The healing, a ladder descent down underneath, is for us to make this subterranean journey valuable, to allow the emergence of whatever arises out of the depths, infusing it to preserve the energy that was deposited and bring that forth with love. To not discount any part of our life, breaking patterns and habits we become new. As we travel across the waters of renewal our thoughts become our biology, looking for a partner in health, working together on a pilgrimage is empowering. I was clear not to exile myself from the medical world and looked to collaborate to participate in what Gurdjieff called *the experiment of life on earth*, to meet the challenge that was presented to me in the relative world. Could I turn an injury into a teaching, witness and redeem this life that I am custodian of; the care and understanding towards ourself is part of a hologram that holds the power of healing.

My body is either my master, a tyrant demanding satisfaction of its appetites, or my enemy, obliged to pay for all my thoughts and feelings. Yet my body could be the greatest support for experiencing my existence. It is on the level of the earth and draws its strength from it. I need stillness and great sensitivity to have a sensation of a presence in my body. —Jeanne de Salzman

THE ARROW OF

UNDERSTANDING

Talk to your cells. Praise your body. Tell your cells you believe in them and have confidence in them, and in their ability to do their work. The body is sensitive. It registers every thought and feeling. Be tender with it.
—Brendan O'Regan

*T*he legendary first doctor of medicine was Asclepius, his name meaning *the unceasingly gentle*. Masterful in the art and craft of medicine, the tale of Asclepius connects us to the origins of medical science and healing arts. Deified as the god of healing and medicine, he is traditionally depicted as the bearded man holding a staff with a revered single serpent coiled around it, symbolizing youthful renewal as the serpent casts off its skin. Temples were built in his honor. He put beds and created treatment areas in those temples which became what we know as our first hospitals. Leaning on a staff entwined with sacred serpents he was skillful in the vocation of medicine. Stories were passed along that he was able to bring the dead back to life. People came from throughout the Mediterranean countries to his temples to be cured. In the myths connected to him, the gods became angered as Asclepius was shifting the unique immortal characteristic of the gods to an ordinary place where mortals could have access to unique god-like qualities of eternal life. Provoked, Zeus killed Asclepius with a thunderbolt: both for accepting gold profits for services that used knowledge he had received from the master of the healing arts, Chiron, as well as going against the natural order of existence by resurrecting the dead to life. The legend is that following Asclepius' death Zeus and Apollo recognized the remark-able service Asclepius had offered to humanity, and his image was placed amongst the stars as the constellation the serpent holder to live eternally in the sky.

The temples and teachings of medical science continue. Historians speculate that a living Greek physician was the source of this legendary story. Asclepius is viewed as a founder of now so called alternative med-icine which in his times was considered traditional. His medical work was a process that encouraged natural healing mechanisms of the body, relying on active processes like touch, nutrition and the nature of our body to eventually heal itself. Asclepius is a fitting patron of a medical profession where skill and performance brought high esteem. His vision of body mind and spirit as a unity brings us to 21st century Western Functional Integrative Medicine, a holistic approach to health care emphasizing a nutritious diet, a toxin-free environment, daily exercise, adequate sleep, harmonious relationships, a low-stress life-style. He was an energetic wisdom messenger to be listened to, a guide for healing. Today, roots planted so many centuries ago continue to move in a direction that could improve our lives. As we make healthful choices that lower our levels of deficiency and toxicity and promote cellular health, the body can carry us in a progressive direction that is able to repair and regulate itself. The achievements of modern science wedded to the wisdom of past traditions as a collaboration have brought about wholesome living as well as a reverence for our modern landscape.

An intelligent person learns how by his own thought to derive benefit from his illness. It is far more important to know what person the disease has than what disease the person has. —Hippocrates

Modern medicine sits on the shoulders of shamans and practitioners who defined their practice at the height of ancient Greek and Egyptian medicine. Study the seers, the wise women, or witches, throughout the Middle Ages and Renaissance Period in Europe, Hippocrates, and the Yellow Emperor's Chinese classic of internal medicine. We hear the modern words of Hippocrates, *Let your food be your medicine and your medicine be your food* in 460BCE. 2500 years ago the Yellow Emperor's book taught that to live a quiet life and maintain pure energy and a peaceful spirit, disease won't enter the body. To remember the roots of our medical system, before it became a business brings us to its common sense wisdom.

A serious illness or an intense visionary episode has brought many healers to their spiritual awakening, and what followed often was to create a system out of their innate experiential learning. The knowledge that the body must be treated as a whole, not as a series of isolated broken parts, asks for us to become participants in our own ongoing healing, a mind-body-spirit approach. This is not a repair, it's a regeneration, a pilgrimage. Healing springs from what brings life to us, the emergence of wholeness from woundedness, the restoring and integration of self into a higher order.

Jung spoke of the archetype of the wounded healer. I believe that each wound that we suffer and eventually heal from is a soul-making experience with the potential to awaken our willingness to participate in the healing of the world. —Joan Borysenko

The word *patient* comes from a Latin root, *to suffer.* In the ancient traditions just having a body is to suffer. And yet, as well, is our possibility to overcome our suffering, not by ignoring it, but by also placing attention on the miraculous. Today we have the resources of practitioners who having lived through their own personal illness and studied the intelligence of their own process, have developed systems, techniques, methods and teachings from that personal source. Making a kind relationship to our symptoms we open our healing potential and become knowledgeable teachers for others. Through a heightened consciousness that often accompanies a healing crisis we can become an active player asserting independence and creativity which in turn enlivens the immune system and fortifies the psyche through granting it a vote of confidence.

We would rather be ruined than changed; We would rather die in our dread than climb the cross of the moment And let our illusions die. —W.H. Auden

When Australian actor, Frederick Alexander lost his voice on the stage in the 1890's he decided to investigate the process that made that happen. He founded a school of bodywork called the Alexander Technique based on a lingering ailment, chronic laryngitis, that had destroyed his acting career, while leading to a discovery which ultimately helped people around the world rid their bodies of tension and stress. Dr. Moishe Feldenkrais developed the Feldenkrais Method in response to his own injuries during the 1940's. Elsa Gindler, a German body worker, shaped the development of the gymnastic movement and somatic therapy, cured herself of tuberculosis by refining her awareness of her breathing as she taught herself to rest her diseased lung and breathe more fully with one healthy lung. Israeli healer Meir Schneider, born blind, underwent 5 operations and at the age of 17, through disciplined exercise, reversed his blindness, eventually creating a new system, a School for Self-Healing and the Miracle Eyesight Method; and the list continues. Matthew Sanford, paralyzed from the chest down in a car accident at age thirteen turned his unique experience through using yoga and his paralyses into a ground-breaking mind-body approach to living with a disability. Matthew has inspired and enhanced the lives of thousands through sharing the mind-body relationship. A paralyzed yoga teacher, he offers an unprecedented perspective, and is a pioneer in adaptive yoga. A keynote speaker at the Yoga Journal Conference, he teaches yoga practitioners and yoga teachers a revelation of wholeness, unifying the mind-body-spirit. The field of Adult Children of Alcoholics has burst forth with writers and psychologists coming from dysfunctional families who cured their own addictions and moved on to create clinics and institutes to treat others, including addiction disorders scholar, Dr. Claudia Black, author and addiction counselor John Bradshaw, Pia

Melody, founder of the Meadows treatment center for addictions, and author Dr. Susan Forward. Temple Grandin, diagnosed with autism as a child, with Asperger's Syndrome, now a professor and doctor of animal science and an autism self-advocate urges people to view the condition in a different light, without the focus on disability. Named a master intermediary between humans and our fellow animals, her insight into animal behavior from her unique position at the intersection of autism and science has changed the field of animal care. Recognized by Time Magazine as one of the 100 most influential people, her teaching is from her woundedness, her place of understanding.

The following comes from an interview with Jeanne Achterberg in *The Wounded Healer.*

> *Being disabled, or having had a serious disease, or being in recovery from an addiction, or even having a child with a significant handicap has been the wounding or the initiation for many in the health care field. For others of us, the wounding is our own private psychic pain; it is the richness and texture of our own lives, and the emotional ties we establish in our work. Getting wounded in this near-mortal sense can never occur simply by going to school and learning a trade. The tools and techniques that are taught in these professions serve as a shield to protect one from the wounding—from the arrow of understanding. In the interests of technology and dogma, the essence of what it means to be human was overlooked in medicine.*
>
> *There is an invisible bond of power between the wounded healer and the healee. The bond is the essence of the work of the healer. Some call this bond love. It comes forth from the desire to make and be made well or whole.*

Listening to our deeply rooted body, requires full attention. All things are circumstances to create awareness, to recharge ourself with energy to meet and undertake the huge task of healing. To awaken is to claim the events of our life, acknowledge and take responsibility, revise, refine and eventually rewrite them. We move from the periphery to the center, from the center to the periphery; the sum total of who we are is our presence as we create our personal mythology. In this body that houses our spirit we come to know and live our real self, which is free.

There is a saying in Tibetan, 'Tragedy should be utilized as a source of strength.' No matter what sort of difficulties, how painful experience is, if we lose our hope, that's our real disaster. —the Dalai Lama

PHYSICIAN AND PATIENT ARE ONE

The miracle of self-healing occurs when the inner patient yields to the inner physician. —Howard

*I*n early times the medicine man, physician, teacher, seer and sage were one, not separate. Healing is as natural as breathing, and breath is life. As fish live in the ocean, we live in this universe. To become harmonious, to be in relationship to the whole, a constant watchfulness, participation, relaxed and peaceful—a stillness comes out of understanding—all are results of true healing. Seeing what stands in our way, the barriers; eventually recognition deepens the witnessing; attention burns through the bridge that link heaven and earth. It's an in the moment let-go. The celebration is here in life. And the initiation into the core of our body-mind-spirit, this marriage of physician and patient, this inner sharing expresses the sacred as we break limited beliefs. At the heart of the universe we are one. The function of healing, that leads to wholeness is the expression of one face, the face worn by both the wounded and the healer.

Whatever limits the entrance of awareness limits healing. —*Stephen Levine.*

The healing energy is awareness in love, nourishment of a spiritual body. First, we heal what we imagine to be the separation between ourselves and the other, for the other is always our own true self. Once we experience our own illness, our own aging body, this direct experience, this taste of woundedness offers us the ingredients for love and compassion, the ultimate embodiment of emotional maturity. When the barriers that polarize dissolve, when we encompass rather than exclude or divide, bridges are built and crossed, a purposeful pattern co-creates a harmonious blend, a living blueprint for wholeness, a resource for healing. This is the soil in which we become agents of change. Our life as wounded healers is food to nurture and serve the world. The healer or practitioner once connected becomes an invaluable instrument, a link uniting inner world with outer, eventually distinctions disappear. We keep emptying the cup so that we don't make ourselves sick. It's the old Zen story about the teacher pouring until the student's cup spills over. There's no room left. The mind must be emptied of preconceptions for there to be space for something new to enter. Unhitched and present, now creative possibilities emerge, and here we enter into the experience to make our own discoveries. To live in the fullness of our being, regardless to the body-mind we arrive in; rigorous, using all of what is ours, the endurance of the human spirit creates the quality of our life.

To sit in the presence of suffering without trying to fix it; mind-body awareness helps us create compassionate boundaries. Learning to utilize the body as a means to deepen our presence is a profoundly simple insight. The body teaches the mind about presence, not vice versa. What we feel matters within the healing relationship. To learn to connect in both mind and body is mutually beneficial; it deepens our commitment to our own humanity. The frontiers of improving healthcare lies not in the promise of new and explosive technology. It lies within us. It lies in our ability to connect with both ourselves and each other. It lies within our humanity. —Matthew Sanford

To cultivate a relationship that holds the inner patient and the inner physician as one, we leave behind our ideas and opinions that have created that separation. The responsibility and balance to serve ourselves requires preparation. Becoming truly whole follows the recognition of a necessity for change. To make a bridge between this world and the invisible worlds we manage to know the world outside of us from within. To experience the stillness so our relationship with another force emerges we begin to know ourself and all the world as it is through that contact with Self.

Healing is far more than a return to a former condition. True healing means drawing the circle of our being larger and becoming more inclusive, more capable of loving. In this sense, healing is not for the sick alone, but for all humankind. In the end, healing must be a ceaseless process of relationship and rediscovery, moment by moment. The more we 'know' about healing, the more we are simultaneously carried toward something unknowable. For this reason all healing is in essence spiritual. —Richard Moss

CHAPTER TWO

Spiritual Conversation

Your own words are the bricks and mortar of the dreams you want to realize. Your words are the greatest power you have. The words you choose and use establish the life you experience. —Sonia Choquette

Those who do not have power over the story that dominates their lives, power to retell it, deconstruct it, joke about it, and change it as times change, truly are powerless, because they cannot think new thoughts. —Salman Rushdie

The self is revealed only in relationship. In observing the way I talk to my neighbor, I begin to awaken to the whole process of self-discovery. Listening is not merely hearing; listening is an art. It is part of self-knowing; and if one has really listened and gone into oneself profoundly, it is a purification. And what is purified receives a benediction. —J. Krishnamurti

This call to search, stronger in one than another, is to know who one is, what we are here for, what our destiny is, how to live more poetically. To include in our daily lives that element of light, a higher energy. The search begins with the realization that I don't know myself, Who am I becomes a burning question. It's the places in the interior of oneself. Eventually the teacher is in one's self. —William Segal

IN THE SUFI TRADITION

Come, Come, whoever you are,
Wanderer, worshipper, lover of leaving,
It doesn't matter.
Ours is not a caravan of despair.
Come, even if you have broken
your vows a thousand times.
Come, come yet again, come.

—*Inscription on Rumi's tombstone*

When a great Sufi master went on a pilgrimage to a holy place he was accompanied by a student who had traveled by his side for many years. The student had sacrificed worldly comforts, habits, and outer freedom to travel with his teacher. Each morning the Sufi teacher would ask the student to remind him what his name was. The day they were to arrive, the student overcome with emotion lamented: *I have been by your side for many years and still you ask my name.* The aged and wise Sufi replied: *Each day I learn your name, with a renewed heart. Words are veils over the truth, yet something new is born each time you remind me of your name.*

The longing of the student is a painful part of our journey, the invitation is to empty even from expectations. We sacrifice our wants, our sufferings for an appreciation to what we have received: the gift of life. The pain comes from the memory of when we were together, what the Sufis call *the sweetness that was before honey or bee.* This is the heartache that lives with every human being; the soul's pain of separation. The Sufi student was offered an experience of going beyond, beyond the search for intimacy with another, beyond hoping that some person might fulfill that need, beyond expectations and visibility. There are many levels to the story about recognition of the students name. Remembrance of the heart begins with a word, until all else is erased. The teacher's own name vanishes, as the distinction between *I* and *you* disappears. The student confronts the obstacles that appear in the mind, while the teacher, softening the heart, prepares the student for opening to a consciousness of the heart. This is the mystery, the connection between lover and beloved, the love that belongs to the soul. A surrender to an empty faceless no name, ultimate invisibility. Until that awakening the student lived within the limitations of self that created projection, seeing others through veils of illusion. Love is obscured when we close the door to our heart. To remember at every moment is to be awake. Rumi asks: *Do you love me or yourself more? There's nothing left of me. I'm like a ruby held up to the sunrise. Is it still a stone, or a world made up of redness? It has no resistance to sunlight. The ruby and the sunlight are one.*

Loving is the greatest freedom and fulfillment, so the wise, being wise, cash in on that. —*Rumi*

For the Sufi who lives in a universe created by love remembering is not something to do, it's a listening experience, an intimate conversation. To remember. That is the great gift. The voice of remembrance in the Sufi tradition recites dhikr—*La ilaha illa'llah, there is no god but God*—beautifies the heart, draws the mind deep into the heart sustaining the fire of longing as it burns away impurities, directing the attention. Dhikr, beyond language structure, is an internal rhythm which then becomes our own particular experience. The harmony we live in here on earth is orchestrated into other worlds, each time that we create a new beginning we change a way of seeing. It is said that the tongue mentions dhikr, the beautiful attributes of existence known as grace, yet it is the heart that understands. It is said that God does not fit into heavens or worlds, but fits into our hearts as a treasure of grace. The teaching serves, empties the vessel; the measure of our emptiness mirrors the quantity that can be taken in anew. We are travelers in this world and the pilgrimage is the mind itself. To bring the heart into the mind the mind becomes absorbed in beauty; this is awakened spiritual consciousness.

When does gold ore become gold? When it is put through a process of fire. So the human being becomes as pure as gold, it is the burning away of the dross. As a drop of water falling on the desert sand is sucked up immediately, so we become nothing and nowhere—we disappear. —Bhai Sahib

B E Y O N D   T H E   W O R L D   O F
A P P E A R A N C E

For Rumi the appearance of formal beauty comes as a natural response to being spoken to. The rose opens because it has heard something. The cypress grows strong and straight because a love-secret is being whispered. Elegance in language arrives in response. I have a friend who, when she wants to know who I am seeing, who I am in love with, asks. "Who are you talking to?" The exchange of deep friendship makes a fine entrance into love and trust, into the mysterious action that moves through the eyes, the voice, the heart. Love with no object, conversation with no subject, seeing with no image, light on light, pure possibility. —Coleman Barks

The Sufis say there are three ways of relating to the divine, of being with the mystery: there is prayer, higher than that is meditation, and the step up from that is conversation, *the mystical exchange they call sohbet: a human being is a conversation.* Coleman Barks, regarded as a foremost interpreter of Rumi, writes that *everything is conversation.* Mystical knowledge and devotional love are transmitted through sohbet circumventing the knots of the rational mind, connecting hearts. *Sohbet, spiritual dialogue, is a cleansing of the soul and a meeting of the hearts helping us reflect on the events of our everyday lives, guiding us in our search for unity,* writes Sherif Baba. A reflection in the moment, an investigation towards deeper understanding; the exchange to be lived within this way of love. A powerful practice, the lynch pin for our practices, used intelligently it brings meaning and understanding to all of our other activities. As a valuable process for sharing and connecting to our friends, our community, our circle of lovers, we train ourselves how to actively listen as well as how to speak from the heart, moving us to practice what we understand.

Our advantage as human beings lies in our power to speak, to articulate a nebulous world into meaningful words and phrases. God spoke and the world came into being. We speak and bring it into focus. Our words are the camera that determines reality: According to how we focus, so our world will be. With a small breath of air, we determine whether it is beauty that sprouts from the earth, or monsters growing as large as our imagination. True, there is a time for all things—even a time to speak in negative terms, to make clear that something is wrong and needs correcting. But there is a caveat to negative words. For if they do not reach their goal, their bitterness still remains. Speaking good words, kind words, words of wisdom, words of encouragement. Like gentle rain upon a dormant field. Eventually, they will coax the seeds beneath the soil to life. —*Tzvi Freeman*

Living within a universe of love, protecting the sensibility that reveals that aliveness is paramount. Intimate conversation dissolves the I thought, welcoming our vulnerability, our openness is an essential practice that places love at the center of this present moment. This is love transmitted through sohbet. In the Sufi tradition the purpose and meaning of creation is to discover the secret of love, and as students in the school of love we live to dissolve the illusion that imagines us to be separate from the object we love. Rumi calls: *Come, Come, whoever you are:* welcoming us, asking that we look with the eye of love at this world, with an inquiry of the heart. There is only one language, one religion, that of the heart which is recognized by all seekers of the Way. Quieting our identification with the demands of life awakens the spirit.

To be Sufi is to burn, to be so consumed by love that the distractions, the inessential concerns of life lose their pull. When Rumi asked the dervish Shams: *and where is the ladder on which I may climb to heaven?* Shams replied: *It's love. Learn to love. Earthly loves are mere shadow of divine love. Seek the love that cannot be caged. All that matters is love.* Not to focus on the form of religion and prayer, rather on the continuously moving conversation, the intimacy. The inner meaning is the companionship in which *friend and friendship become one sea-changing union,* a continuing conversation. The intimate conversation of self with deep self, with this book, *The Way of The Lover,* with all of our conversations to become open doors of possibilities is for us to know the truth within ourselves. When the *I* becomes a *we,* entering a maturity becoming love itself we transmit that particular fragrance through presence. Rumi wrote: *Yes, Love is my religion.* Rumi's Discourses, crafted to transmit sohbet within their teachings, transmit substance. Discussions on the nature of qualities, discourses to investigate what is a question, what is an answer, Rumi speaks: *O tongue, you are an endless treasure. O tongue, you are an endless disease. The world is like a mountain, and each action the shout that echoes back the speech of the speaker. Whatever you say, good or bad it echoes back to you. Don't say I sang nicely and mountain echoes an ugly voice. That is not possible.* Beyond all questions, beyond reason is the deep silence in which Rumi says *all lovers lose themselves.*

To see beneath the surface of things, beyond the world of appearances, to listen to the inside of the story we see signs without becoming caught in them. In love is there a lover and a beloved? There is only the beloved, because the lover disappears in love. Sufi, or Dervish, is universal in nature, as the inner esoteric dimension and reparation of the heart, what lies within the innermost sanctuary of the heart is expressed in the love of the lover for the beloved. Living in this world for it not to have sovereignty over us, the Sufi dies to the illusion of separation from the one reality. Now the call comes from inside the heart, and the Sufi dervish knows the source of the call and how to respond.

Every one of us is a vessel that contains a very great energy which goes unattended. There is something in us that is waiting to be called. And if we attend to it, if we acknowledge it, we will then be in touch with a force that can illuminate. It can transform and shape each one of us and can help to change the world. When one is still and one listens, then one begins to be in touch with this mysterious element which is within each of us. So here is the beginning. To do whatever one does with one's whole attention; the practice of attending wholeheartedly to the moment is most important.
—William Segal

Transmission through an oral tradition—teaching through a teacher, we use this world as a location to learn, grow to give service, rather than merely stage our own personal dramas. Learning to develop our ability for self-inquiry, to see through the pain to create an inner life is a craft and art that a teacher/therapist teach. Then life's trials and tribulations, challenges—a difficult phase in a relationship, an illness, friction on a job—become food for transformation, rather than a recipe for one more hard time.

Your task is not to seek for love, but merely to seek and find all the barriers within yourself that you have built against it. —Rumi

Playful Teachings:

A Conversation

There is a language older by far and deeper than words. It is the language of bodies, of bodies on bodies, wind on snow, rain on trees, wave on stone. It is the language of dreams, gesture, symbol, memory. We have forgotten the language. We do not even remember that it exists. —Derrick Jensen.

Nestled in the beautiful Manzano mountains in New Mexico is a Sufi retreat where Adnan, a Sufi teacher, and I had the following conversation. It is particularly representative of the simplicity, humor and style of his teaching.

> **PAULA:** *I wanted to ask you, Adnan, about your drum. In my own work, psychology, the first music or rhythm that a child hears happens before they are born. In the nine months before birth, while attached by a chord, they hear the mother's heart beat, like a drum beat, and that is their first contact with sound and music. And if you watch a mother with her very young when that child is upset, the mother will hold the child to her chest, where the sound of the heart beat will soothe the child. And even as we get older sometimes we put a clock in the room, and the ticking, again that beat, will soothe us. One can see all this from the viewpoint of psychology. In your work I feel that you use elemental rhythm or music as something to lift the spirit. I'd like to hear you explain the significance of this primary, originating beat for our spirit in the work.*

> **ADNAN:** *Well, before the baby is born he spends nine months within a birthing process—and if that baby didn't have any entertainment he'd be sick and bored because he's in the dark. Without sound for that time, there would be sickness and unhappiness, both at birth and throughout life. But because so much sound is happening in there, the baby is having a good time. He's getting high—like being in a nightclub. The baby is*

listening, and sometimes he moves and dances with the beat; that's when the mother gets kicked. The baby can get so enthused that it can even lose control and start jumping.

Within the adult body too there are all kinds of sounds happening, because there is blood flow and messages sent to the brain and to the heart. And with all of these functions you'd be amazed at the sounds that are created. Some are very fine, while some are powerful; and an orchestra is created with rhythm going boom boom boom di de boom boom di di di di boom di di di. This is going on in the body, while all of these kinds of sounds can be heard in the head.

Last year I had everyone do an exercise which involved listening to these sounds. The exercise ran for a long time, and following that everyone was in a trance for many hours. They were just there; not moving, not talking, or anything; because these sounds within your body are very powerful. So, actually, the baby is quite smart, he's in there enjoying all of these sounds each and every minute, and because that is happening he is in the moment. He is constantly living in the drum, which is all around him day and night—boom boom boom boom, all kinds of beats to hear. When he is finally born sometimes he will cry, because he's missing all of that entertainment from the nightclub show and wants to go back.

PAULA: *Having been in such a state of ease and lightness, a deep peace, encountering that again here in life is the mystery. Without sound there would be no silence. And only when we are present can we live in the fullness of the moment. There's a saying in the East that when a musician becomes perfect he throws away his instruments, and I was thinking about this and you, imagining that it would be very easy for you to not drum, and to inwardly hear your drum. Do you ever feel that you would no longer use your drum as an instrument for your work?*

ADNAN: *Exactly. When you develop very deeply into it, it becomes* *imprinted within you, and you constantly feel it—but in a different way. You function in the world, in whatever it is you need to be doing; but now any time that you are alone it's like turning the radio on—and you are in contact with it. It has a very vivid high level that is magnified, beyond the moment of when the drumming is actually happening. It actually becomes part of you, it exists all of the time and becomes part of the body. When you are playing and playing, then that sound becomes a part of you, and while it is there it is on a different vibration, and a different feeling takes place within you. This is one of the things that regulates life of the people, and this is actually one of the objectives of the drum; when people listen and hear the drum, that will regulate their function in life.*

As I have said before, rhythm exists for us before we are born, and then when we are born into this world we are in another state of rhythm. Everything in this world is rhythm, whatever we do—even our thoughts consist of rhythm. If our thoughts have the proper rhythm, they become positive. If our thoughts don't have the proper rhythm, they become negative. When we eat, when the food is in our mouth, you are playing the drum on the food with your teeth; and that, too, has a rhythm. For example, if you're eating and someone tries to get your attention, or if there's a tense situation happening, you lose the rhythm in your mouth and then you don't enjoy it. The entire digestive system is a rhythm. Any movement you do is rhythm.

In the Middle East, when people talk, and that's what they do all of their life—talk, talk, talk forever—they create all kinds of stories and situations. Even strangers who have never known each other, when they meet for the first time they will talk without feeling the time pass. There was once a story about an American who was in Saudi Arabia. He decided to go fishing with a fellow from Arabia. They would go to the sea at noontime and fish. The Arabian fellow, on his way to see the American and go to the sea, met his friend and started talking with him.

They decided to go somewhere and have tea and talk before he went to see the American fellow and do some fishing. They start talking for a long time until it's evening and gets dark. Then he tells his friend that now he has to go because he has promised his American friend to go fishing with him to the sea. In the meantime, the American was waiting and waiting and looking at his watch, and he felt nervous and tense. He couldn't call him because there was no telephone there. He decided not to go, since it was now getting dark. Then the fellow came, and the American was tense and nervous. Where have you been? I waited all day long, the sun went down, and you didn't come. He said, Oh, it's OK, I saw a friend and we sat talking, but now we'll go fishing at night. So when they talk, they talk; they don't stop...keep talking...and it puts them right in the moment.

PAULA: *Another level to that story is no appointments, no disappointments. Linear time being an illusion of the mind, it dissolves in present moment awareness. I often see people imagining that something stops them from having what they want in this life. And then pay great attention to what is missing, in anticipation of the imagined present moment. Waiting for the workshop to begin, they remain absent or uprooted in themselves. As if time were a true object, pulling at us so we are swept away banging against whatever debris comes floating by. Is that what's meant by Sufi time? A lot of people have a saying here. When they are asked, What time does the workshop start? I hear them say, Oh, it starts on Sufi time.*

ADNAN: *Sufi time means pure time: whatever is pure is the right thing; and purity could be anytime, anywhere. When it is pure, it means that you are in the right place.*

PAULA: *Yes. There is a saying that the person who has the pure heart of a child knows that everything is swimming in and arriving out of a sea of light. And I understand that this fresh unspoiled state can allow anything to arise without making it other, without doing something to it. Everything is in the*

*present moment, in this unborn mind state. This is the true
liberation; no motivation, no reward, no thought, no mind, no
past, no future, just immediacy. And now, for us too, we have
talked and talked, effortlessly, and it just happened!*

THE CONVERSATION OF
SILENCE

*Don't worry about the wine, the glass or the glass-blower. Immerse yourself in the
breath of the glass-blower. —Sufi teaching.*

Adnan, director of the Sufi Foundation, of the Shittari order, works
primarily through his predominant instinctive center. A master of
non-intrusiveness, he has a system of spiritual practices that are seated in
breath, movement, chant, prayer, fasting, belly dance and drum. Movement
is a training ground for sustained attention. There is a quality of energy
behind our thoughts and feelings and the practice of movements and
breath release identification with sensory traits associated with daily life.
Movements train us to keep our attention on the task at hand, and our
ability to direct our attention allows us to apply it to our inner work rather
than get lost in fascination to the activities and images of our circumstances.
When our force of attention is taken over by the events at hand we lose our
ability to be present.

Adnan, by not interfering in student's choice making, sets the stage for
a great range of possibilities in his work room. Oftentimes during hours of
silent meditation practice I chose to read the *Village Voice* or write notes in a
journal. He would open his eyes from a deep place and gaze at me, then
he would quietly roll his eyes back up, neither to judge nor criticize. In
those moments, the reflection was clear. Self awareness alone has the

power to activate and bring us to a higher understanding and level. I had room to explore my impulses, my resistance, an environment that mirrored back my actions, leaving me as my own gauge and measure. To change we have to go beyond our greatest obstacle called preferences, what we *like* or *don't like* about ourself. Freed from our selective self-images our attention gathers energy for experiences to become food for growth rather than opinions and judgements. Deconditioning ourselves, learning to go beyond our thoughts, to direct perceptions, to what is true, to what is new, awakens presence. True thinking is without conclusion. To see new is remarkable and requires not knowing. Recognizing our true nature, being undefended, present in our experiences encourages us on our search for truth. I came away from his work prepared, with a greater capacity to go inward, less distracted more connected to my breath and body.

Live in the present before it passes you by and becomes past. —Adnan Sarhan

This non-intrusiveness itself is an inner dialogue and exchange between teacher and student, a witnessing awareness, without judgment. A conversation dedicated to listen deeply to our inner voice, to the words of the heart carry an invitation: pay attention to the real needs of the moment. To take one thing and do it deeply, carefully, we are doing everything. I learned how to listen to myself, to slow down; true conversation depends on listening. To enter deeply into conversation as a path is to bring our psychology into the present moment with vulnerability, presence and a willingness to surrender to a creativity that reveals deep intimacy and true communion. Allowing the questions to percolate, to be together in the unfolding, the adventure of a new understanding is what children know organically. They live in endless inquisitiveness, engaging us again and again and again. And it is to ourselves that we turn for the answers, to have real exchange. Open, to look together, available to not knowing, open to inquire and to love the exchange, food for our sustenance, a collaboration, working together, co-operation, we join forces for new understandings.

Life is so short, we should all move more slowly. —*Thich Nhat Hahn*

The unfolding between two people can be an exquisite spiritual conversation. Dialogue like this in the Sufi tradition is named *sohbet.* It is said that while there is no word in the English language to translate this, one approximation would be *mystical conversation on mystical subjects.* To live the unknowable, to penetrate the inner unity and oneness of all things and beings is the mystery called mysticism; presence merging with presence, where the wave disappears and becomes the ocean. This experience, called spiritual conversation, is a sharing through the heart, like listening and absorbing the waves as they roll onto the beach. The conversation is harmonious, has risk, penetrates, is a love affair.

Rumi says: *Human beings are discourse. That flowing moves through you whether you say anything or not. Everything that happens is filled with pleasure and warmth because of the delight of the discourse that's always going on.* In the Tibetan Buddhist tradition, Milarepa, a student of Marpa, is portrayed with his hand held to his ear, deeply listening, named as the *Great liberation through hearing* in The Tibetan Book of the Dead, this path of listening is considered to be *like a golden mandala inlaid with precious stones. Listening to spiritual teachings eventually strikes a chord in us, memories of our true nature will start to trickle back, and a feeling of something familiar will slowly awaken. It's as if someone who loved and cared for us were whispering our real name in our ear, trying to bring us back to our knowledge of our lost identity.*

Sacred conversation, between beloved and lover, therapist and patient, teacher and student, between friend and companion, from self to self, soul to soul, is art, is creation, contains risk and all the ingredients for a harmonious union. This beautiful exchange, the distilled power of silence formed into words enables us to draw our mind deep into our heart.

Sohbet is so powerful that it can bring a much deeper realization in a short space of time than years of prayer or meditation. —Hilary Hart

LIVING PRESENCE: A CONVERSATION WITH KABIR HELMINSKI

Since in order to speak, one must first listen, learn to speak by listening. —*Rumi*

Kabir Edmund Helminski is recognized as a Shaikh of the Mevlevi Order of Sufis, which traces its inspiration to Mevlana Jalalu'ddin Rumi, appointed by the late Dr. Celebi head of the Mevlevi Order and twenty-first generation descendent of Mevlana Rumi. He is one of the major translators and interpreters of Sufi literature, a transpersonal psychologist and author of numerous books, amongst them: *Living Presence, The Knowing Heart,* and *The Rumi Collection.* Kabir was the co-founder and director of the Threshold Society, which embodies the roots of authentic Sufism, especially as reflected in the life and work of Rumi. Kabir is a wonderful storyteller and creatively brings the words and inspired life of Rumi to people throughout the world.

Life is a journey. The journey progresses from the heart of man to the heart of God. Life is an experience, a ceaseless inner unfolding through time. Our conversations reveal the meaning in our lives as well as who we are. To communicate accurately and to pass on tradition requires sincerity. Kabir Helminski speaks from the heart, neither inventing nor evading—simple sincerity invested with knowledge. A man of simplicity is one who directs his eyes to earth, his heart to heaven. It is a wise man who will give away his inner treasures; his understanding, kindness, passion and knowledge. As you read this conversation, you will catch glimpses of Kabir's love affair with Mevlana Jelalu'ddin Rumi; with his wife, Camille and his children; and with those true seekers on the way to love, compassion and service. You will witness the law of giving and receiving applied. Spiritual conversation grows out of human relating. The heart understands all truth; to communicate with the heart is to become more human. Our words are vessels which carry the energy of the Source.

Within the past three decades I have sat with great and ordinary beings engaged in conversation. Meeting Kabir Helminski, who honors the sacredness of *spiritual conversation,* created an opening to the following dialogue.

> PAULA: *It is my understanding that all life is energy. Sex is energy, and when valued properly and in balance, it is a tool for transformation. How does Sufism look at sexuality in relationships?*

> KABIR: *In Sufism in the Middle East, in most schools, the training of men takes place apart from the training of women. Often women will have their own circles and men will have their circles, or, if they're together, there is still a certain amount of separation in terms of practices. Zhikr is done apart; women will sit on one side and the men will sit on the other side. In the Sufi tradition, it has always been understood that in doing the*

spiritual work, you're awakening sexual energy. You awaken the energy of love. Their way of handling that from the beginning was simply to keep a separation in the outer world between the sexes. This has been typical of the Islamic world in general today. This was really arranged so that the energy awakened through spiritual exercises would not get confused with other kinds of attraction.

Marriage is held in very high esteem. Mohammed said marriage is half the faith. The basic premise of Islamic sexual morality is that of a committed relationship between two people. That relationship should be public. By public I mean there are no secret liaisons. Islam basically has a very positive attitude toward sexuality in the private realm and it is viewed to be completely consistent with a highly attained spiritual life. It is not something that needs to be sacrificed. However, any kind of casual sex is simply not part of the culture.

Now, in America, there is the very casual mixing of sexes in all kinds of activities. In spiritual circles in the West we even have a certain amount of hugging or physical contact between the sexes. The Sufi point of view encourages lifting that energy up—not to be afraid of it, not repress it. In a spiritual circle, people will find each other attractive. It is a natural result of awakening the energy. When love energy awakens, people simply become more beautiful. It doesn't have much to do with physical appearance.

PAULA: *Yes. The beauty of form is finite, the love energy, beauty, is endless. Since we are energy, and sexual energy moves with so rapid a vibration, how does Sufism—which works with energy—transform that?*

KABIR: *Sexuality is a fundamental energy of the universe. One transforms it through real spiritual love, through a love that is always becoming more comprehensive, and less exclusive. There are three levels of love. One level is eros which is the energy of life and desire. It is love of the lovable, or love of the attractive.*

Yet it tends to be somewhat self-oriented. Then there is philos, which is the love of sharing with others. Philos embraces more and is more comprehensive. Then there is agape, which is a love that ultimately embraces the whole universe, leading to something we might call making love with God. We are in a process of always making our love more comprehensive, but this does not negate either eros or philos. Eros can exist within the context of agape. In other words, one can have a love relationship with one person and still be in love with the universe. It is not an either/or situation. In spiritual groups, it is useful to be quite fastidious about these matters. Otherwise the waters get a little muddy.

PAULA: *Love without understanding, without knowledge and wisdom, can be fateful both to the lover and the beloved. This is why we are asked to love humbly, and study to know how to put our love into the service of the Divine. Love exists in the dimension of eternity, and in this state one can love anyone. How is it you chose to marry your wife, Camille? Beyond sentimentality and specialness, what makes your relationship to your wife work?*

KABIR: *We are attracted to certain people whose type is complimentary to our own essence type. In this matter we can really follow the heart. Yet a marriage from a Sufi point of view is most of all a marriage in and for the sake of God. Still, individual attraction and harmony has a place in that. However, marriage can deepen and yield much greater fruit if the love of God is at the heart of it.*

PAULA: *There is a saying that a loving marriage invites God into the relationship. I see this as adding a larger dimension, a divine force, to lift the daily concerns and serve as partner in the creation of the universe. In your marriage you both work together. Do you work together as student-teacher? How is that arranged in terms of the Work and the marriage and parenting?*

KABIR: *Camille is not my student; she is my wife. She also has a certain responsibility in our group work. We have recently been given a project by one of our teachers to do some translation work, and to do it together. This has channeled us into a kind of work where we have to develop real sensitivity and respect for the other's point of view on matters that are quite delicate, matters of expression. I think we both see that the translation on the whole is much better because both of us have given our best to it. We have to know when to back off from holding, being attached to a certain way of expression. It is probably a necessary stage in our education to merge into a single voice in this work.*

This brings up something that is a very fundamental issue that is not well understood in our culture—a fundamental moral issue in relationship to sexuality and partnership. Most of the abusive situations and, shall we say, ambiguous moral situations that spiritual teachers and human beings in general have gotten themselves into when it comes to sexuality arise out of a lack of equality between the two parties. To give a really obvious example, an adult having sex with a child is not a situation of equality, because how can a child understand the nature of the relationship? A relationship where one person exercises power over another is not a relationship of equality, nor is a relationship in which one person is extremely attached and the other indifferent to the relationship. One of the criteria for a healthy relationship, especially a healthy sexual relationship, is having as much equality in the relationship as possible. This means equality of love, equality of will, equality of maturity. Love is a surrender of two wills, not the annihilation of two individuals necessarily, but a surrender of two wills to a common purpose. If this surrender-in-equality is impossible, then you have all kinds of harmful situations arising, situations that involve manipulation, hypocrisy, and eventually harm to one or both parties.

This is why there seems to be a need for some kind of ethics related to a therapist or spiritual guide, a real fastidiousness in terms of the kinds of relationships that are appropriate.

PAULA: *Yes, spiritual teachers sometimes are of the illusion that they can live outside and above the ethical standards and morality that is applied to all others. To regard the teacher and the teaching with an eye of discernment, and to allow that process to continue moving inwardly takes responsible maturity. The integrity to help lift students to an independent level of awareness, while creating a relationship, as you so well say, of equality, is vital. Often we get a glimpse of the health of the teacher by seeing those around. I find that communities that are told to keep secrets, stifle their feelings, that profess their way is the only right way, are asked to violate their personal ethics, are not free to leave, are filled with people potentially deluding themselves. In this life our partner is a reflection of our own true self. And our teacher and community also mirror our consciousness and growth. A challenge on our journey is integrating what we know into how we live; the clue is in the gap between our spiritual practice and our level of personal development, our maturity. In light of this do you see your marriage as part of your work, as essential in your own journey?*

KABIR: *I have been married once and for 18 years by the grace of God. God willing, it will continue by the grace of God. My own spiritual development has taken place in this context. This is what my life has been. I see everything as part of my work, including marriage. Marriage is a relationship that matures, reflecting in many dimensions of one's life. The sexual dimension of it is one important part of it, but the totality of the relationship should keep on maturing. Marriage can keep on maturing. Our maturing together as a couple creates the context for a deeper and richer marriage.*

American culture is having a love affair with Rumi. Rumi has been taken up because so much of his poetry can be read as having a tinge of mystical eroticism. This is attracting many people. The ecstasy of love is very attractive in our culture today. This is particularly because we have for centuries viewed sexual love and spirituality as in some sense contrary to each other, or at best, marriage as a compromise we make in order to stay out of sin. Then we came into the 20th century, an era of relative sexual freedom and ending repression. Yet, on the whole, as a culture we still found ourselves suffering some unnameable guilt that we can't quite put our finger on. Then Rumi came along with this apparent depth of feeling—the ecstasy of love—and a seeming reconciliation of these two. Rumi is concerned with so much more than mystical eroticism that he is really not about that at all.

We are spiritually entering a more mature phase of our relationship with the ecstasy of love. It involves daily sacrifice, patience, acceptance, and discipline. Little by little, our culture may itself mature to the point where it can hear the more mature truth that Rumi offers. A mature spirituality is a spirituality that transcends individual desire and the body, and yet at the same time includes and respects our natural human self. In a certain sense we need to be born from the Mary of the body; we have to become the Jesus born from the Mary of this body and know that spiritual love. When we know it, we can then bring it back in, in a new way to everyday life, a more mature relationship.

Rumi's message is not a message of the wild man or wild woman living out unrestrained ecstasy. In fact, Rumi says the one without discipline or restraint not only burns himself, but sets the whole world in conflagration. In other words, there are some objective principles we can live by that involve self-discipline, sacrifice, and freedom from the demands of our physiology and our emotionality. When we have known it, we also find a new relationship to the body as the instrument of our essence. The greatest help will come to us from spiritual love, the depth of love. We cannot repress the ego or kill the ego—we can transform it with love.

PAULA: *I appreciate that you use the word love. It is devalued by a Western idea of sentimentality, associated with pop music,*

Valentine's Day greeting cards, and suicide. Rumi is known to the Sufi world as the Poet of Love. In the Mevlevi tradition, Rumi is the Religion of Love, love was his very being. Rumi's expression of love transcends all religious form. I'm drawn to that, his words uplift me, are a balm for my soul, a mirror of recognition, unveils my heart to the kingdom of love. When we maintain the beauty of this word love, and use it to elevate its use in this culture, rather than find a new concept or new word, love becomes an invitation to speak about the unspeakable. What does the word love mean to you?

KABIR: *Many of us have understood love as needing to attract something to us in order to possess it. We have thought of love as possession. We love something; we must possess it. The love that Rumi is talking about possesses us. Love is nonexistence. Love can only be found in nonexistence. When two lovers meet, they disappear in each other and God emerges from that disappearance. When a circle of lovers come together, a circle of spiritual lovers, they disappear in love without losing their individuality, but they lose their false selves. They lose those factors which have been keeping them in separation. They come into a kind of unity of will—whether it is a couple or a group—and bring the unique qualities of their own wills into harmony with the purpose of love. I remember walking into a little tailor shop in Istanbul, and his first words were, Find love in nonexistence.*

PAULA: *Yes, the beauty of love is the realization of oneness at the heart of creation. In your great love for Rumi, you have helped to make him accessible and among the most widely read poets of our time. As one of the major translators and interpreters of Rumi and Sufi literature, did you write Living Presence to say something of your own personal experience, or is this a statement that you feel is important for the world to hear?*

KABIR: *First of all, Living Presence is a book that lays a foundation for spiritual practice. The foundation is presence. Without presence, you're working or living in an imaginary way. Presence is a state of being which is on a higher energy level than our other functions, including thought, feeling, and action. It is the space around our thought, feeling, and action. It is the context in which these other functions take place. When presence is awakened in us, it gathers all of these different functions into a unified whole, so that we can become whole and not be fragmented and isolated.*

Presence is comprehensive awareness or consciousness that creates the space around the other functions. Presence is our birthright as human beings, although it exists in its fullness only very rarely in human beings because it has become a latent state rather than an actualized state. We have to activate what is latent in us.

Living Presence is a book about presence. Presence is the first requirement. There are other requirements. If I were to write a second book, it might be on the subject of what I call active submission. By that I mean developing our self-expression and creativity to the highest level possible for us, and at the same time surrendering that self-expression to a higher purpose. The higher purpose to which a Sufi surrenders is Allah, which is understood as the Reality of the universe, who is beneficent and merciful. Our surrender to that reality removes from us hesitation, doubt, resistance—the hesitation, doubt and resistance of the false self. When we can remove these, we will find life expressing itself perfectly, beautifully, lovingly through us.

PAULA: *This lies in certainty; not doubt, and the quality of presence establishes the quality of life. Whenever we feel the presence of life, of love, there is the Beloved. And everything has its own presence—the flower, the tree, the child; I might hold the flower but not its fragrance. Surrendering the illusion that we are separate opens the world of possibility. What a risk! To give up our false ideas and expectations. Children, sensitive to presence learn whatever is in the atmosphere through absorbing and* *imitating how we are. We build a presence through our inner work, can a child walk in a room and have a presence that is God-given; how do we create presence?*

KABIR: *It is a result of a certain kind of maturity. A child has many desirable qualities, but a child cannot have the kind of self-awareness that presence implies.*

PAULA: *To become again as a child, is to birth this child in us, to be like a child, childlike, comes from a place of maturity. In Living Presence, you speak to what it is that enables us to begin this inner investigation. I understand that through being a writer, it's a place of stillness. Hildegarde of Bingen, called creators of great art, those who emptied out, for the Divine to be present, feathers on the breath of God. Rather than becoming dulled by daily activities, to open the heart and remember our connection, in love, to all things, beings, and the Beloved, is that presence creative inspiration?*

KABIR: *Yes. This book was written because I see a clear need to marry the high truths of Sufism with something like a practical understanding of how we might develop some of these qualities. Presence could be developed entirely within the Islamic framework if one were able to follow it. One would realize that ablution and prayer five times a day, for instance, is the exercise of presence. Even in the outer religion, it has been taught very clearly by Mohammed that a moment of conscious presence is more valuable than 70 years of unmindful ritual worship. Nevertheless, this truth is widely ignored.*

PAULA: *It's what we bring to the practice: our desire, commitment, intention, reliability. To choose to sacrifice for freedom. It's who is doing the practice. Yet, not only the act of taking on practices and hours of meditation, but to live in that presence called Unity, Love. Yes, a moment of conscious presence is eternal, the statement that resonates for me is: a single conversation with a wise man is better than ten years of study.*

KABIR: *Right. In fact, in the Sufi point of view, the hours of meditation are not necessarily the most effective way to achieve this presence, because we're looking to develop a presence of life, not a presence of meditation. Sufism accepts and believes in the integration of an ordinary human life, sees raising a family or serving a guest or having a practical profession as being integral to one's spiritual life. Spirituality is not viewed as a specialization apart from life.*

Basically, Living Presence is what I would call the essential Islam. The qualities of the essential Islam are living in submission to the state of Divine Presence, presence not as a self-referential state, but as state of submission or surrender to Reality. The very presence that we experience in our being is the presence of God. The consciousness we are experiencing is God's consciousness exercising itself through us. We are God's servants awakening God's qualities in ourselves.

The knowledge and the practice in this book represent a kind of essential Islam or submission. Islam means submission. The Qur'an says there is and only has been one religion and that is the submission of the human being to Truth. Living Presence is a book that tries to relate these essential principles in a way that will be understood by our culture at this time. It adds a dimension in some ways to the more limited understanding of the individual practice of meditation which is so often viewed as solitary individual practice.

The viewpoint of Living Presence is the viewpoint of Unity and of our being merged with that Unity at the same time that we keep the pole of our individuality distinct. At the same time that we keep the pole of individuality distinct, we know that the other end of this pole is the whole. This is what the human being is, both individualized and integral to the One Being. We're not a piece of the One Being; we are integral in some way to that One Being. Living Presence presents a spiritual psychology of Oneness.

PAULA: *I recall that you once compared maturing a soul to culturing yogurt: It is not so difficult if you have the milk, the yogurt culture, the right environment, and the time necessary. Are you saying that we need community, living together, for this process of transformation and self-development?*

KABIR: *Yes. Sharing lives together, I would say. This doesn't imply you're all living in one location. We have such a need. In our culture we suffer greatly from our neurotic individualism, which sometimes includes an excessive need for privacy and an unrealistic sense of control over our individual lives. In Sufism it is viewed that the more we are alone, the more we live under the domination of the ego. The more we come together in loving brotherhood/sisterhood, the more this ego can be tamed by love. We say tamed by love—not destroyed, not obliterated, not sacrificed. When we have melted our false separation, what remains is a truer individuality. Our false separation is a product of our conditioning. Our false selves are actually in many ways more alike than our true selves. Our false selves are a product of social conditioning. What we really have to give up is not so much our real, essential individuality, but that part of ourselves which is more or less like other people but can't stand other people, becomes irritated with them, or resists real cooperation, real sharing.*

What we would see in a mature spiritual community would be a group of people with a high degree of personal autonomy at the same time that there is a very high degree of relatively selfless cooperation and creativity. We've had, for instance, an experience creating music together as a group, where beautiful things have emerged through the cooperation of individuals. It emerged as a whole in a very creative, spontaneous way.

PAULA: *You teach in a manner that doesn't make anyone in particular special, big or little, which creates a harmony and unity. You have the ability to create an environment so there's not a lot of personality in the room. Yet there is an order, someone who leads the way.*

KABIR: *I believe that one can escape the need to feel self-important and at the same time contact one's own heart, one's own inner truth, and be able to listen to it and not doubt it. This seems to be a gradual process, giving up the false self, the false personality, which is sometimes self-important and at other times self-blaming. Give up all of those voices and let the personality become something like a lens through which the essence is expressed. Part of my function is as a friend, a spiritual friend. What I have to share is my certainty concerning what dwells at the core of our human condition.*

PAULA: *Knowing that we are reflections, a mirror for others to see their pristine self as well as shadow, what is your relationship to being in the lineage of a wisdom teacher, a guide, a Shaikh, which in the Sufi tradition as I know it, is the one who is the servant of the student's yearning?*

KABIR: *One can be, in some ways, an example of something and still be a friend. In my function as a teacher or leader, I believe that a certain amount of respect is due to anyone who is serving us. The examples of this service in Islamic/Sufi tradition are not examples of people who have put themselves above others or have let others carry them. The real leader is ideally a servant. It is my job to help people trust their own hearts and know their own strength. I have seen in many spiritual groups, including some Sufi groups, a certain amount of damage done to people's authentic individuality. It was my experience at one stage that in the name of non-identification with the I, I lost my trust in myself. I have seen many people turn over their own inner authority and heart to another person without learning that they themselves must learn to listen to their own heart. I don't like the word empowerment very much, yet I believe that the spiritual process has to lead to both submission and a high level of self-expression. The self-expression has to come from the right place, not from the need for self-importance, or the need to dominate.*

PAULA: *Yes, self-importance is a great dis-service, the inauthenticity, ambition and lack of genuineness slowly erodes the possibility to connect hearts. To create a beautiful world, to be of service and make a difference requires a meeting of the hearts. Love brings us here, we live in a universe created by love. You live with that reminder reflected in the faces of your two children. Knowing what you know, having been touched by elders who have shared their teachings, how has this affected your being a father?*

KABIR: *Fatherhood itself has been my teacher. It has taught me lessons of love and patience and gentleness. It has also taught me lessons of setting boundaries and sacrifice. It is something I am always learning more about. It is a great teaching to be in a family because in a family it's much harder to live totally under the tyranny of your own ego—the need is there to always find just solutions to family problems. One is reminded to serve the needs of others who are not yet able to take care of themselves, and to make the kind of sacrifices for our children that our parents have made for us. It's a great teaching and maybe that's why Mohammed said, Marriage is half the faith. I enjoy working with other parents.*

Unfortunately, sometimes parents are too busy to have time to really give themselves to spiritual work. Thank God that many of the people we've worked with are couples and are people who have found the time. I am grateful for that.

People who are single are not less important or less spiritual. I'm sure whatever circumstance in which we find ourselves is appropriate for us to make the next step in our own spirituality. I have seen and experienced this spirituality and sacrifice in family life.

PAULA: *Yes, each life has its own unique way of expressing itself; this individuality is our birthright. What is it we need to understand so we can be responsible and proceed with our own inner work?*

KABIR: *Some of the so-called esoteric schools have been working with a model of creating conscious individuals as if this were a process of acquisition, as if the net result of the process is a more effective human being with unusual powers of consciousness and will. Yet many schools following this model end up in disillusionment and failure. The results of any school that does not have at its center the power of love, will eventually turn to ashes. Although it is important for us as individuals to become activated in our essence, the model of the Sufi brotherhood/sisterhood is not one of individual attainment, it is finding our most beautiful individual qualities in the context of a spiritual family. There was a group of Sufis living in Baghdad many centuries ago. Some of the local small minds of the time were jealous of these people, because they were attracting other students. These small minds accused this Sufi group of being nonbelievers and blasphemers. They were called before the judge of Baghdad and had a summary trial with a very quick conviction. The sentence was death. At their execution, there were three or four of them together. When the executioner brought one up first, the other three rushed forward saying, No, me first. They broke into a fight over who would be executed first. They were asked, Don't you value life? One said, Yes, we value a moment of life more than anything else. That is why I'm willing to die first, so that one of our brothers could have that extra moment of life. The Sultan was there. When he heard this he said, If these people are unbelievers, then there are no believers in my kingdom. Let them go. What's more I want you to grant them any wish they desire. What do you wish? Do you know what the Sufi said? I wish that you will forget about us.*

In our Sufi model we are working together as a team. Considering how to help our brothers and sisters come into their true individuality is even more of a concern than our attainment for ourselves. Our prayers are for our brothers and sisters. We don't pray for ourselves. I think this is a different model than what I've seen in many so-called esoteric schools.

PAULA: *The Sufi says you cannot search for God. He chooses you. To love God, we must first love people. The teacher is in service to the pupil. The awareness that while we stand in an intimate connection to presence, being present and creating sacredness comes naturally with a kinship, a connection, a love and regard for people.*

KABIR: *Yes. One of the lessons that we find, one of the things that needs to be learned, is for people to give up their own preoccupation with themselves. This includes the preoccupation with their spiritual attainment. It is one of the biggest.*

PAULA: *There are teachers in the Sufi and Fourth Way tradition who say to their students: I don't want to hear about your personal life, relationships, or work. I see our daily life as the fertile ground for our transformation and creativity. Do you encourage students to talk about their personal life and challenges?*

KABIR: *We exclude nothing from our spiritual conversation as a matter of principle. Yet at the same time, we do not wish to wallow in the issues of personality. We don't want to endlessly focus, for instance, on any particular problem. Perhaps you have seen certain schools where people have, not for years, but decades, brought attention to the problems of their own negativity without ever transforming it. We believe it can be transformed. We believe that love can transform it. The path of love is one of the quickest, most effective paths. We have to be open to people's authentic problems; this is the material of our life. It can't be denied. Yet we don't need to endlessly wallow—especially in personal problems—in the false suffering that people get into, the poor me's and if only's of life. A teacher has to know when it's appropriate to cut something off and when it's appropriate to draw someone out.*

PAULA: *Hafiz, the Persian poet, said I am happy even before I have a reason, and I now understand that awakening happens as we are in wonder, as the joy of life possesses us. Knowing that we are all one, caring for the One Body in which all of us dwell, is acting in accord with this awakened reality. In October you led a group of dervishes and musicians from Turkey around twenty different cities in the United States. Could you say something about this?*

KABIR: *I was asked by the head of the Mevlevi order in Turkey to facilitate a performance of the Mevlevi ceremony by the Konya dervishes and musicians. I agreed to do that and I found out that there was a great interest in this. We planned one or two dates that turned into a tour of fifteen cities during October and November. I felt it was important for our American culture to be exposed to this tradition, to its beauty, its music, its love. This is simply one way of getting some of these qualities out before the public. I honestly feel as if our Pir, Mevlana Jelalu'ddin Rumi, must have helped in this process in some way, because it really acquired its own momentum. I'm simply trying to be a servant of that momentum.*

PAULA: *It's with a big smile that I see that Rumi is currently one of the most widely read poets in the English language. In your Daylight book Rumi says: 'Everyone is so afraid of death, but the real Sufis just laugh: nothing tyrannizes their hearts. What strikes the oyster shell doesn't damage the pearl.' While we are always dying to what we have created, our life constantly brings opportunities to go deeper within our self. Since I teach hospice workers, and also work with life-and-death transitions, as a closure to this conversation I would like to know what the Sufi tradition would say to a mother whose child is dying of AIDS.*

KABIR: *Real grief has its place in human life—don't try to escape it. My attitude is not the attitude of escaping human suffering; it is not the premise on which my teaching is built. There is worth in the remembrance of God. This is a different perspective. There is acceptance. There is trust that we live in a beneficent universe, but we also feel grief, loss, suffering, value, and compassion. We do whatever we can to relieve others' suffering.*

PAULA: *Yes. Ancient wisdom has reminded us that what initially appears as a cup of sorrow ultimately becomes a goblet of immortal wine. Embracing everything, making loss meaningful and deepening our compassion, knowing how to sanctify life in the face of death we become human. To make darkness conscious, with light inside us, is to create the day and allow the night to fade away. The final question will always be: How well did you love? Not how much we do or give or have, but how much love has entered into the giving, having and doing.*

THIS IS FOR YOU: SOHBET

Spiritual conversation, or sohbet, is the heart of group practice. It is the connecting point of all the other activities: individual practice, group remembrance, music, study, social life, ethics. It is the primary relationship with the shaikh and the context in which people come to know one another. It is the activity that connects and makes sense of all others. Sohbet is not sermon or lecture, but discourse, storytelling, encounter and spiritual courtship. It is how God's lovers share and intensify their love. —Kabir Helminski

This sharing, this exchange, is friendship, is a companionship that matures and deepens us. It is conversation as a practice, educating and transmitting a state, discovering the ever-living possibility of actualizing the connection. The ingredients are presence, active/receptive listening, asking a real question, mindful inquiry, moving away from colloquialisms, pat expressions, generalizations, and, ultimately, sincerity. *Give each word light*, the Baal Shem Tov said, *for every letter contains worlds and souls and godliness.* The conversation with Adnan was at a Sufi camp in the mountains of New Mexico, in a morning meditation/exercise workroom where many other students were gathered and listening, whereas with Kabir the ground of the conversation was our dialogue, an interview.

Sohbet aims to train us to listen and speak from the heart, not only the intellect. The word *sohbet* comes from the root *hubb,* which means love or affection. And so we remember that conversation happens in a field of camaraderie. Mindful conversation is wholehearted. It happens out of love. And the reflection, as we deeply affect one another, is of harmony. Like constantly meeting a friend we recognize ancient travelers. Just being together in this way is transformative. This sharing of our being, this participation with understanding enlists true listening, which asks us to open and receive before we respond and is an essential part of the feminine. To enter into this inner conversation requires listeners with presence, whose personal needs vanish for the time. The energy creates a spiral, an inward winding labyrinth, a journey to the still center, and the potential within this spiral is simultaneous movement towards either direction. Putting heart into our words spiritual conversation becomes a love affair. Deep understanding arises and in this embrace words carry the life of the speaker. We become mirrors for others to reflect on our own divinity.

Written words cannot contain what I would tell you. Only conversation and presences. —*Rumi*

Parts of conversation with Dr. Paula Bromberg and Shaikh Kabir Helminsky were published in *Tantra, East/West* 1995.

CHAPTER THREE

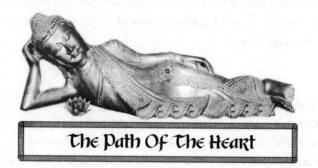

The Path Of The Heart

The path of love is like a bridge of hair across a chasm of fire.
—*anonymous early mystic*

*What makes a human being is the capacity of his/her questioning. Asking,
Who am I? is the most absorbing question that a human being can have. To
know what we are here for. Who are we?* —*William Segal*

*On this path we are seeking our own innermost essence, the pearl of great
price that lies hidden within the heart.* —*Llewellyn Vaughan-Lee*

*When you die you will not be called to account for the illegitimate things
you did do, but for all the legitimate pleasures you might have tasted and
did not.* —*Jerusalem Talmud*

*We must become ignorant of all we've been taught, and be, instead, bewil-
dered. Run from what's profitable and comfortable. If you drink those
liquors, you'll spill the spring water of your real life. Forget safety. Live where
you fear to live. Destroy your reputation. Be notorious. I have tried prudent
planning, long enough, from now on, I'll live mad.* —*Rumi*

I know a cure for sadness: let your hands touch something that makes your eyes smile. I bet there are a hundred objects close by that can do that. Look at beauty's gift to us—her power is so great she enlivens the earth, the sky, our soul. —Mirabai

To paint the portrait of a bird. First paint a cage with an open door. Then paint something pretty, something simple, something beautiful, something useful for the bird. Then place the canvas against a tree, in a garden, in a wood, or in a forest. Hide behind the tree, without speaking, without moving. Sometimes the bird comes quickly, but he may take long years before deciding. Don't get discouraged. Wait. Wait years if necessary. How fast or how slowly the bird comes has nothing to do with the success of the picture. When the bird comes, if he comes, observe the most profound silence 'til the bird enters the cage, and when he has entered gently close the door with a brush. Then erase all the bars one by one taking care not to touch any of the bird's feathers. Then paint the portrait of the tree choosing the most beautiful of its branches for the bird. Paint also the green foliage and the wind's freshness, the dust of the sun and the noise of the creatures in the grass in the summer heat. And then wait for the bird to decide to sing. If the bird doesn't sing it's a bad sign, a sign that the portrait is bad. But if he sings it's a good sign, a sign that you can sign. So, then, so very gently, you pull out one of the bird's feathers, and you write your name in a corner of the canvas. —Jacques Prevert

OPENING THE EYES OF THE HEART

*T*o live in the heart, the boundless universality of love, where still-ness resides, is to be intimate with the world. This is the soul of life, seeing with the eyes of love, for then what is concealed in the heart becomes grounded into everyday activity. To walk a path of the heart we cross the bridge of love. Love is the road that reveals life's teachings and is all inclusive. A well trodden path. And we are told to open com-pletely, to be in the aliveness, to go into the stillness that is the source of peace. Treating all relationships with care and tenderness, savoring each connection we are invited to look inside the treasure house, entering through the gate of the heart where the real jewels are stored. When we increase kindness, decrease harmfulness, wish to benefit others then our store house treasures profit, multiply, through gifting with heartfelt generosity. And the true measure of our life is in the daily moment-to-moment expressions of loving-kindness: life is the gymnasium of the spirit, and we are the instrument, the medium, the force that receives and anchors awareness. Through stillness we prepare for the energies, the vibrations, grounding to know the nature of mind: for in polishing the mind we step away from suffering and recognize the natural state of emptiness that opens into presence.

The capacity to love consciously, when developed, marks the highest achieve-ment in earthly life for a human being. —Fourth Way Tripod

Rumi says: *we are the mirror as well as the face in it.* What drives this great quest *is a special kind of love. Love so vast, love the sky cannot contain. How does all this fit inside my heart?* And we know, as it is told, that beyond all tradition and religion what we are really worshipping is each other—the shared essence visible in each human face. Rumi reminds us: *Stay together, friends. Don't scatter and sleep. Our friendship is made of being awake.* To know love, beyond the constraints of reason and rules, takes an awareness of what is happening in the body, the emotions, the mind as well as the world, and then to bring them together into this present moment. Living in this kind of awareness we become ourselves, and everything therefore is our practice. And the invitation is to change our awareness, shift our attention to enter vast spaciousness, to find wisdom in our most practical activities, to uplift the ordinary moments and for nothing to stand between us and other.

Loving is the greatest freedom and fulfillment, so the wise, being wise, cash in on that. —Rumi

To love is to be present, to bring our presence to wherever our attention is, whether it is ourself, another, or life itself. The core of love, understanding, is a consequence of looking deeply, paying attention. Love is a palpable force that holds great creative power. The primary obstacle to loving is our wandering mind and lack of harmony with ourself. Without self-harmony there won't be harmony with another. Rising above agitation, we become the messenger of love. We find our voice and expression in this physical world through acts of loving-kindness, named *gemilut chesed* in the Chassidic tradition; for both giver and receiver are lifted. Our distractions, our mind fullness; filled with thoughts and opinions and things and sufferings blocks heart energy. Present to our life we are also available to truth and wisdom. Practice, practice, practice. What passes though the heart flows into the world, and this is the force that effects change—of the planet—and of each one of us.

We ought to practice as if our hair is on fire. —*the Buddha*

Conscious beings—Krishna, Buddha, Meher Baba, Rabia, Aurobinda, Moses, Kali, Mirabai, Christ, Isis, Zulaikha, Kwan Yin, Ramakrishna, Sarada Devi, Kabir and the Baal Shem Tov—have all walked a path as servants of love bringing forth inspired teachings. Awakening and entering presence is the way of love, not dogma. Once the heart (Christ) has been taken out, and the religion (Christianity) is formed, the vitality dissipates. It closes the door of its own heart. The Christian who died on a cross centuries ago is said to have manifest great goodness in human form as well as expressing a language of teachings that continue to echo meaning: *Love your neighbor as yourself, what you would like people to do to you, do to them. You shall know the truth, and the truth shall make you free.* Concerned about humanity, suffering on its behalf, the recognition of the face of love inspired devotion; the organized religion seemingly forgetting about the surrender and transformation of the man called Jesus, both body and spirit broken and remade, that happened here on earth. Andrew Harvey commented: *This is the essential mystical process that Christ came to live out, embrace, and reveal to all of us, and it is because the churches have lost its secrets that they are mostly now so narrow and soulless, and largely impotent to birth the living Christ-consciousness.* Patron saint of the animals and ecology, Francis of Assisi had the passion, strength and penetrative vision to express: *This Church is rotten at its core. It is destroying the energy of Christ in the world, making it impossible for this glorious power to heal the world at the moment it needs it most.* More recently Pulitzer prize winning author, Annie Dillard, one of the most compelling writers of our time, said: *On the whole I do not find Christians, outside of the catacombs, sufficiently sensible of conditions. Does anyone have the foggiest idea what sort of power we so blithely invoke? Or, as I suspect, does no one believe a word of it? The churches are children playing on the floor with their chemistry sets, mixing up a batch of TNT to kill a Sunday morning. It is madness to wear ladies' straw hats and velvet hats to church, we should all be wearing crash helmets. Ushers should issue life preservers and signal flares, they should lash us to our pews. For the sleeping god may draw us out to where we can never return.* For love to be active, to be inspired, is to dedicate our actions to serve the welfare of more than ourselves.

My religion is very simple. My religion is kindness. —the Dalai Lama

There is a story that when the radiant Anandamayi Ma was visited by a group of middle agreed business men, investment bankers on a tour, as they tried to kneel at her feet she stopped them saying *I will prostrate myself at your feet. You are the true renunciates having given up peace of heart and the joy of serving the world as an instrument for the Divine.* Without real connection, lacking the experience of wonder and mystery, life become arid, moistureless. The ultimate revolution is that of the spirit. To run a business is easy, but to shift people's hearts and mind is the real work. We have named them teacher, guru, saint, tzadik, bodhisattva, sage, nabi, avatar, qutb, bhagavan, buddha. Now to capture our inheritance and awaken the energy and knowledge of our sacred identity. Rumi, witness of the heart, knew that the essential relationship on this earth is one of love saying: *I am neither Christian nor Jew, nor Gabr, nor Moslem. I am not of the East, nor of the West, nor of the land, nor of the sea. I am not of India, nor of China, nor of Bulgaria, nor of Saqsin, I am not of the kingdom of Iraquan, nor of the country of Khorasan. I am not of Adam, nor of Eve, nor of Eden and Rizwan. My place is the Placeless, my trace is the traceless; Tis neither body nor soul, for I belong to the soul of the Beloved. I am intoxicated with Love's cup. My religion is to live through love. If you have not been a lover, count not your life as lived; On the day of reckoning, it will not be counted. Everything has to do with loving and not loving.*

There's a story about a student who expressed her personal tragedies, hard times, to her spiritual teacher. Seeing that a smile never faded from her teacher's face the student paused in surprise to question *how can we smile at this brokenness. I feel crushed and defeated.* The teacher replied: *You are being shown the end of misery through the cracks that this misery is opening in your heart. Through them you can see the sun of the Self shining.* These words are attributed to Anandamayi Ma, the bliss permeated Mother who influenced the spirituality of thousands who came to see her throughout her life. This is to see behind the hardships, to learn to bring a flame into the darkness, to look into the mirror held up as a reminder of our essential divine nature. Rumi says: *Pain will be born from that look cast inside yourself and this pain will make you go behind the veil.* To be at peace with our pain and sorrow, to root and enter the darkness which is the source of light itself, each encounter, like Jonah in the belly of the whale, fully envelops us in the great mystery of the cloud of unknowing. Irina Tweedie speaking of her spiritual journey said: *The ego does not die with laughter and caresses; it must be chased with sorrow and drowned with tears.* Having met the demons, darkness embraced, opening to the full range and coming to peace with what is, pain is inevitable—suffering is optional.

Your pain is the breaking of the shell that encloses your suffering. And could you keep your heart in wonder at the daily miracles of your life, your pain would not seem less wondrous than your joy; And you would accept the seasons of your heart, even as you have always accepted the seasons that pass over your fields. And you would watch with serenity through the winters of your grief. Much of your pain is self-chosen. It is the bitter potion by which the physician within you heals your sick self. —Khalil Gibran

As long as we focus on appearance (dunya), we miss the essence, the source, the sustaining power behind beginnings and endings. The following story could be an ending story, but breaking form is a teaching itself; to begin at the end, since beginnings rely on endings. The story concerns a beloved teacher who had been lecturing to a class for weeks regarding the theme and question, *what is the essence of beauty, truth, and love?* Each morning he spoke about the essential nature of the heart, beauty and love. This particular morning, the window open, a clear summer day, the students sat waiting for the lecture to begin. A magnificent yellow and red bird, a warbler, with a brilliant plumage, settled on the window sill and began singing, chanting a lyrical melodious song. After it sang for a short while it flew off. When it was gone the teacher, and this story has been attributed to Krishnamurti, looked at the students and said, *The talk for this morning was presented by a yellow and red bird,* and Krishnamurti left the room. The experience of truth, beauty, and love had been revealed, recognized and experienced beyond intellect; this, then, becomes the path of the heart. The proof of the bird is the bird itself; if you want love, don't turn away from your heart. Love, truth, and beauty are not concepts but everyday realities to be lived. Dance, ecstasy, conversation, eating, walking, music, poetry, meditation and song are some of its practices.

More than all else do I cherish at heart that love that makes us to live a limitless life in this world. It is like the lotus, which lives in the water and blooms in the water: yet the water cannot touch its petals, they open beyond its reach. This ocean of the world is hard to cross: its waters are very deep.
—*Rabindranath Tagore*

It has been said that after God organized all six directions: above, below, east, west, south, and north, He then placed the source in the direction we would least likely look, naming it the secret direction. That direction is inward. Hidden away in the heart is where it is found, for the real work lies in the heart. Love seeks to reveal itself, since the meaning and purpose of life is to find the secret of love. *For all of the heavens and all earth cannot contain me, yet I can be contained within the heart of one faithful person. Who knows himself knows everything.* This, is where our treasure is found, for once we look through the eyes of love, we see all life as sacred. *The cause of creation is beauty and the first creation is love.* Love being the source, and beauty created to show love we see beauty through loving. When the heart is expanded to contain the universe everything is seen as the beautiful reflection of ourself.

When you begin to touch your heart or let your heart be touched, you begin to discover that it's bottomless, that it doesn't have any resolution, that this heart is huge, vast, and limitless. —Pema Chodron

This simple secret, that the journey, although essential and necessary still originates at self, unfolds for us to return and find the treasure where the journey began. We forget and become entangled and distracted by the illusions, the smoke and mirrors of life. Rumi tells us the way: *You wander from room to room, hunting for the diamond necklace, that is already around your neck!*

Our life is experienced remembering who we are.

Understanding is the essence of love. If you cannot understand, you cannot love. We must be there, attentive; we must observe, we must look deeply. And the fruit of this looking deeply is called understanding. Love is a true thing if it is made up of a substance called understanding. —Thich Nhat Hanh

THE HEART FINDS HOME

If going away is what it is to be a monk
then coming back
really
is what it is to be a Buddha
But surely you can only come back
if you've really gone away?
—Ko Un

I returned to retrieve the essence of a tradition that I had been born into and met the sweetness that stands at the center, at the heart that has been passed as a continuous chain from one generation to the next. Each custom brings new vision to the nature of reality. The tradition I had to confront was my own, its heart lost in the mechanical stories and events of staged holidays, prayers and practices emptied of presence, emotion, awe, devotion, newness, that forgot the *nefesh* and *ruach,* the *neshama,* levels of the soul; together all form a celestial light. How to recapture what Heschel called *a sense of radical amazement and wonder,* that feeling of wonderment that drives a child to *taste the thrill of discovery.* As adults we grow accustomed to the surprises, the miracles, taking for granted, we harden, restricting the opening that brings us into love. And arrive at a place of *boredom,* with the sweetness, the delight and enthusiasm emptied. We forget to love the questions themselves, to let them continuously unfold throughout our lives.

God revealed a sublime truth to the world when He sang, 'I am made whole by your life. Each soul, each soul completes me.' —Hafiz

Sitting one evening in a Sufi group watching Adnan moving as he recited the Koran, the practice of the Salat, his devotional prayer, both an invitation and obligation, his intimacy with Presence, I saw an image of my father rising in the morning and davvening, praying from his heart, his gestures of his traditional morning prayer. I remembered slipping down the stairs to peek into the dining room watching my father don tefillin, phylacteries, a small black cubic leather box with dark leather straps which he placed above his forehead, the strap going around his head and over his shoulders. The hand-tefillin he put on his upper arm and the strap was wrapped around his hand and fingers, to fulfill the instructions....*and you shall bind them as a sign upon your arm, and they shall be as frontlets between/above your eyes.* Two cube shaped black boxes that held scrolls with hand-scribed biblical quotations. The boxes were kept in a larger, protective box, placed in a dark burgundy velvet bag. Yarmulke or skull cap on his head, tallis or prayer shawl with tzitzit, tassels on each corner, around his shoulders, he stood the entire time he put them on, wrapping the straps from the forehead around his left arm spiraling down to his wrist and finally wrapping it around his palm, continuing to sway, move to and fro, as he removed them. My father, like Adnan, spoke sparingly, and yet both lived in a world of blessings, walking on a path of praise, of prayer. *Hineni muchan u'm'zuman, I am here, summoned, prepared, deliberate, ready.* I saw the value of using time with deliberateness. They both engaged in serving their world through prayer, through *tikkun ha' olam* and *salat*, repairing the world by fulfilling the commandments in Torah, in Koran, living *gemilut chesed*, with acts of loving-kindness. Entering a sacred space, *bismillah ir rahman ir raheem, in the name of God, boundlessly compassionate, boundlessly merciful.* One standing in the Presence davvening, a Yiddish term meaning *to pray*, the other stepping onto a prayer mat, with raised hands at the level of his ears, palms open upward, turning toward the qibla, the direction of prayer, both with beautiful gestures, both in a conversation with God. Ancient rituals, I was there witnessing two men in *shiviti*, in that sense of *I have set You always before me*, a reminder of sacred presence, one song, setting the stage for me to enter other realms, deepening, deepening.

All religions, all this singing, is one song. The differences are just illusion and vanity. The sun's light looks a little different on this wall than it does on that wall, and a lot different on this other one, but it's still one light. We have borrowed these clothes, these time and place personalities, from a light, and when we praise, we're pouring them back in. —Rumi

While I knew that Hebrew and Sufi traditions were radically different for most people, my heart joined the prayers, the harmony of sound, the devotional heart-surrender, the movement and reverence of these two men. Both, standing before what they knew as holy, saying, *here I am, Hineni, here I stand, in deep humility.* Words repeated inwardly in sacred languages of Arabic, of Hebrew, to enter a chamber of the heart and penetrate and direct the breath....*with all their heart, with all their soul, and with all their might.* Recognizing a light within both of these men, the ideals I cherished found a home. This was a living link to my father, standing rooted in prayer, an unbroken continuous breath proclaiming oneness, where the invisible and visible worlds meet. It was then that I could reclaim a tradition that I remembered and go to a Synagogue not bound by form or habit, instead, moved by the enormous spirit of my foremothers and forefathers. And from this, through the simple timeless music, the transcendent ancient Hebrew chants, I found my way to study, to absorb, to be ordained, a commitment to a practice. To anchor and root, song in my heart, lifting my voice with meaning and purpose, to a state of unwavering love, binding it to open a window that reveals light.

Know the true nature of your Beloved. In His loving eyes your every thought, word, and movement is always, always beautiful. —*Hafiz*

In the Bible Jacob falls asleep and has a vision, a dream. A two-way ladder standing on the ground with angels ascending and descending, its top reaching the heavens. Whatever goes up this ladder of prayer also comes down and vice-versa, connecting the mundane everyday experience with the sublime. The heavenly with the earthly. A glimpse connects the worlds, as they already exist, here and now, a sense of the sacred, we access awareness lifting ourselves, step-by-step to climb from earth to heaven, and from heaven to earth.

For those who have come to grow, the whole world is a garden. For those who wish to remain in the dream, the whole world is a stage. For those who have come to learn, the whole world is a university. For those who have come to know God, the whole world is a prayer mat. —*Bawa Muhaiyaddeen*

LIFE AS PRAYER

Words must open the mind and untie the heart. To those who remember, many of the words in our liturgy are still warm with the glow of our fathers' devotion. Such people we must inspire to recall. While those who have no such memory we must teach how to sense the spiritual life that pulsates through the throbbing words. We are the knot in which heaven and earth are interlaced. —*Abraham Joshua Heschel*

As a child, my father's daily rituals were foreign to me. As an adult experiencing my own connection to prayer, I recognized that his Torah was a human document he honored as a part of himself. Beauty lies intrinsically in all faiths and is echoed in prayer. For in prayer a deep silence occurs, a listening to—rather than a speaking to; our prayer is for our own prayerfulness—for it is for ourselves to change, not something outside. Within this turn from form to the mystery of the sacred, no particular sanctuary has to be erected. This prayer resonates in the heart sanctuary.

Only in embracing all can we become the arms of God. —*Rumi*

Following our life, allowing circumstance and our experiences to open us as we turn inward has been named *taking your life on the path.* Prayer polishes the heart. Listening from a still space, our life serves as an expression of love. When we meet our inner nature the work is not to do anything, it's to be who we really are, the core of our being. Life is a continuation, birth-death, no-birth no-death, what passes stays alive in our heart, we breath in the air and drink from the sea; they are all part of our body.

A certain holy man would tell people, *I never pray. I never need to pray because it is kind of foolish to ask God for what He knows already. God knows what I need so there's no need for me to ask for it.* The intention to live life mindfully, connected to the invisible, in the present, took me away from the form of the tradition and back again to the heart of it. The story about the holy man continues with his saying, *God knows when I need riches and God knows when I need poverty. Our life speaks prayer.* When prayer enters silence then each step, each breath connects to an invisible silence. The heart is the place of prayer—the inner quarters of the heart, both yours and mine, the place that is one and the same for both you and me. It is the way in which the devotion of our heart praises, so everything can be converted to praise and prayer. Depthful inner participation, what has been termed *kavanah*, focused awareness, directing our consciousness, prayers with wings, praying from the heart, our mind-set, intention, and alignment allows us to appreciate, brings us to experience how blessed this life is, expanding presence in this world, inspiring ourselves and others. Rebbe Nachman said: *Prayer is our main weapon—pray with all your might and with intense concentration to the point where your prayer will be like thunder. Prayer without kavanah is like a body without a soul.*

Inner devotion, surrendering to the unfolding, standing in the presence of the mystery of the universe; this is prayer. We make our heart and voice known. *For prayer,* said Heschel, *is our humble answer to the inconceivable surprise of living. To live our prayer is to add holiness to wherever we are—what attainment! It may be difficult to convey to others what we live. Our task is to echo and to reflect the light and spirit of prayer.*

Getting doors open one after another is the essence of prayer. Every door is a passage, another boundary we have to go beyond. We squeeze ourselves through, and then go farther. After all, the purpose of the Prayer is not to stand and bow all day long. The purpose is to possess continuously that fragrant state which appears to you in prayer. Asleep or awake, writing or reading, in every state never be empty of remembrance. Be rather one of those moving constantly within prayer. Remembering that you exist, and that your existence is an unbroken continuity with the existence of God.
—*Coleman Barks, Rumi*

TO BE IN THE MOMENT

Seek pearls from an oyster, skills from a craftsman. And if you find someone ripe in wisdom, don't go away empty-handed. Mastering a craft calls for practice; spiritual quickening needs intimate companionship with a true teacher. —*Rumi*

After leaving the Fourth Way School I recognized that I had become attached to the form and meaning of the School. I had substituted the idea that had been my life, what I experienced as my identity—and that had been my therapy practice, home and companions, I exchanged that with a new and different identity called Fourth Way School. The attachment shifted from the form of what had been my life, to the form of living in a spiritual school with students and a teacher and being on a journey towards consciousness. In the following years living in a Sufi community my identification again shifted, now to the formlessness of a Sufi path, that of traveling, fasting, chanting, drumming, belly dancing, living outdoors, and the circumstances of community life. Letting go of who we think we are may possibly be the greatest attachment, the one that is to ourselves. Since our very nature is freedom, allowing our images and concepts to dissolve, we chip away moving from one posture to another until we feel a harmonious balance. We are formless infinite beings, open emptiness. To know our self is to be in the moment, free of concepts, not identified with form. That dissolution happens with mindful practice, awakening to the truth of our essential nature. When the bondage of identification is broken, the burden removed, our true nature reveals itself. Once the ordinary concerns of life are put aside, with room for them within the context of a possibility to awaken as the primary essential value of our life, the determination to overcome the obstacles presented bring miraculous moments. Nothing achieved, letting go of identification, of conditioning which deceives and squanders our conscious energy through identification with mind structure, brings openness of consciousness. Ignorance is the root of all suffering, and our willingness to investigate our own unawareness, to bring about understanding changes the world. The suffering that blocks presence becomes the opening. What stands in the way is the way. Whatever you resist persists, to drop into the present moment is to become aware as presence, which carries love into this world.

Suppose a man in the course of a journey saw a great expanse of water, whose near shore was dangerous and fearful and whose further shore was safe and free from fear, but there was no ferryboat or bridge going to the far shore. And then the man collected grass, twigs, branches, and leaves and bound them together into a raft, and got safely to the far shore. Then, when he had got across and had arrived at the far shore, he might think thus: 'This raft has been very helpful to me. Suppose I were to hoist it on my head or load it on my shoulder, and then go wherever I want.' By doing so, would that man be doing what should be done with that raft? I have shown you how the Dhamma is similar to a raft, being for the purpose of crossing over, not for the purpose of grasping. —the Buddha

Traveling with a Sufi teacher an inner peace arrived in my heart, like a wealthy landowner giving away all of fields, anchored to find my own true place in this world, regardless to unsettled travel dates, unpredictable modes of transportation, not knowing ahead where I'd be staying from day to day. I learned to be available to the moment. I landed with my feet placed solidly in my heart, the whole earth in my arms. I might be in Madrid, Spain for two weeks involved with people there, and the following morning leave for Germany. I learned that relationships continue regardless to the proximity. I don't have to hold on physically for them to continue. They remain in my heart. Traveling for those years dedicated to a teaching created a greater mastery of life. Being open to the moment I was satisfied with life. This was a period of growth, a time of relinquishing control, understanding *Thy will be done,* participating in this magical creation rather than continuously trying to orchestrate the play. Conditions were created, the inner work evolved within those circumstances from the efforts to find a new dimension of meaning to my life. The practice of paying attention to the details of the moment, penetrating beneath the surface, to the invisible, we find what is essential.

We are starting out on a journey, didn't you know, a love journey. There's a boat waiting, but it's not so large, so we'll have to leave a lot behind, get used to traveling light. —Michael Green

And you, when will you begin that long journey into yourself? I waited centuries for this treasure to come into view. There's no turning aside now. I didn't buy this boat to hang around a harbor. —Rumi

BALANCE

Being a lover is close to being a worker. When the ruby becomes the sunrise, its transparency changes to a daily discipline. —Coleman Barks

I first met Adnan in New York City. I was brought to a bus stop in the middle of the night in a small rural town in Vermont, placed there to board a lone bus for anywhere, U.S.A. I got off in midtown Manhattan, with only the clothes on my back, $100, and a note from my teacher. I had been awakened in the night, given one hour to leave the Fourth Way School with whatever I could carry and handed a card with an angel on the front. Inside was a quote from St. Francis of Assisi: *Not enough, not enough, God cried. Man whines, I can't, I'll break. God replies, Then break.* There was a personal directive written from Jean, my Gurdjieff teacher: *go to the desert, extreme effort is necessary for real change, one more step towards true commitment to a better life. I love you with my whole being.—Jean.* I dropped into the immediate present. The willingness to lose everything, to meet myself, to be nothing and without owning much of anything was the invitation. My mind collapsed, the plug pulled, the future disappeared.

This existence of ours is as transient as autumn clouds. To watch the birth and death of beings is like looking at the movements of a dance. A lifetime is like a flash of lightening in the sky, rushing by, like a torrent down a steep mountain. —the Buddha

For the following years I continued to travel, read, speak to teachers and explore the possibilities of human consciousness. What I was looking for, a sense of stillness and aliveness was within myself, obscured by conditioning and identification. That recognition would only happen in time. A practical teaching to be lived that required a profound transformation; to realize myself as I was, through all of my experiences and to identify with none of them. Eventually the journey led me to the vast desert of New Mexico, to the expansive ocean in South Florida and inevitably to the spacious territory the desert of my mind, the unpolished tenderness of my heart.

The West has learned how to go to the moon but forgotten its own soul. This transition must begin with the understanding that every human being is a mystic in his or her own right. We are being called upon to act as enlightened revolutionaries, bodhisattvas of compassionate action to preserve the creation and to help usher in the next millennium. —*Mark Matousek*

Arriving in New York my first phone call landed me a weekly house-sit in Soho followed by a loft rehearsal space that had been used as a photography studio in Chinatown, I moved on to a 3 month house-sit living arrangement on the corner of Bleecker and Christopher Street in the heart of Greenwich Village. A chance encounter on Sixth Avenue in the Village with a former acquaintance, Peggy, led me to a job as a psychology consultant, traveling to different mental hospitals throughout New York. Life unfolded. As I relinquished the past and future each step was revealed. Working at Willowbrook State Hospital, one afternoon I read an ad in the *Village Voice,* a local newspaper, that carried an invitation to participate in an evening with a Sufi teacher, Adnan. It said that he had developed a technique of meditative drumming that blended material life and the spirit together and was a master of various traditions of scholarship, meditative sciences, physical exercise, mystical dance and music, leading people in timeless practices. I stepped across a threshold and entered a world filled with movement, chanting, meditation, fasting, belly dancing, whirling, drumming and traveling.

Before entering the Sufi teaching with Adnan I wrote a letter to Jean, my Fourth Way teacher, a grateful thank you with the intention of releasing our bond. Through a miraculous synchronistic series of events I was carrying the letter when I saw her and hand delivered it to her on a street corner in Greenwich Village, New York City. Sitting in a local Asian restaurant I wrote the letter to Jean, sealed it and walked to nearby Leroy Street where she sometimes visited a friend. As if orchestrated on some other level, within moments she arrived. I released our agreement with a glance and embrace. Miracles are commonplace as I continue to see that strong intention, certainty, deliberateness, availability to existence, courage and a willingness to surrender to the mystery penetrates form.

Lovers find secret places inside this violent world where they make transactions with beauty. Reason says, Nonsense. I have walked and measured the walls here. There are no places like that. Love says, There are. Reason sets up a market and begins doing business. Love has more hidden work. Lovers feel a truth inside themselves that rational people keep denying. —Rumi

EYE OF THE HEART

Love comes from you for no reason at all. It is your outpouring bliss, it is your sharing of your heart. It is the sharing of the song of your being. Love is the flower, compassion is the fragrance. —Osho

To the Sufi a breath that is not mindful, that does not say His name, is a treasure lost. Rumi's father, Bahayuddin taught him that love is the most effective and strongest force, the direct route; on the journey of self-discovery once we step aside to be pierced, emptied, burnt away, only love remains. This is the great work; to awaken, attuned to the inner and outer, freed from what imprisons, pure consciousness aware of itself. Clearing the mirror we purify our heart. No work for lightweights the heart must be broken open, torn apart, repeatedly opened, dying and blossoming, until the entire universe can be placed in the heart. True wealth is not blinded by opulence, the treasure lies in the heart, capable of reflecting divine attributes. This path of the heart leads to *The Way of the Lover.* Closing our eyes we open the eyes of the heart, the clarity of mind, to become the heartbeat of the beloved; for the world to no longer be a distraction, look within!

The true place of pilgrimage is the mind itself. —Shri Shankara

My lessons in letting go of what I assumed was security continued. I traveled to Sufi retreats in Puerto Rico, France, Spain, Germany, Hawaii, New Mexico and Colorado. One day I was brought to a beautiful first-class restaurant and was told by Adnan, *This is yours to live in while you are in Boulder, Colorado.* What a vision! Colorful cascading fountains spraying water, luxurious white and gold satin cushions, velvet brocaded couches, open clear light in the day, soft shades of comfort in evening, great spaciousness. The owners were on vacation and opened their space to this Sufi community and Adnan offered me this as my home sanctuary. A quiet place, a contemplative environment where I could create and luxuriate. Letting go of my loft in New York City, I released the form of what I had imagined as home and allowed this present moment to materialize a new and perfect home. Releasing, the cessation of resistance, opening to life energy arises and begins to flow. I wanted change and jumped into the fire, stepping out of a story through which I had interpreted reality. Learning to give away our stories, to author, edit, uplift and rewrite relocates us in this universe with a new vision.

But why think about that when all the golden land's ahead of you and all kinds of unforeseen events wait lurking to surprise you and make you glad you're alive to see? —Jack Kerouac

Meditation, wider horizons, drumming, whirling, belly-dancing, summer in New Mexico, living in the land of enchantment; I was under big sky and rolling mountains of Sufi Camp. Forty acres surrounded by 200 square miles of national forest, clear mountain air, 8000 feet elevation, distractions minimized, life was simplified. At the end of a four month retreat most of the students returned to the form of their daily life, while I, having given mine away before the retreat, remained in the desert of New Mexico. My belongings were sparse; a tent, hammock, tiny cook stove, wooden picnic table hammered together from nearby lumber and tree scraps, cotton bed sheets, sleeping bag, air mattress, some clothing, a few select books, a tiny silver bowl and a kerosene lantern, a simple used car. Four years later, after travels and Sufi practices I left the retreat center and drove to Santa Fe, New Mexico. During that drive my old used car broke down. It took four weeks for the necessary repair part to arrive; the signal was clear and loud—to remain in Santa Fe and reinvent a life. Within two weeks I moved in with a community of people, students at the Institute for Traditional Medicine and enrolled in a nine-month program to study medicine with Dr. Vasant Lad, an Ayurvedic teacher.

In this multifaceted, interruptive, too busy world, the conscious mind often closes down to the merely expedient. This is not true, however, of your invisible and uncharted creative vitality, which is reliably and sleeplessly a chamber of energy, and which, even when you are not aware of it, is full of restiveness and invention. —Mary Oliver

Shifting, balance reappears of its own accord. It happens, not from force, it comes from continuous movement. Balancing is not static, it's a dynamic process. I saw that my life had again moved out of balance. I had become attached to non-attachment—to change and travel, to not having a home and my own space, to few possessions. The *nots* were becoming bigger than the *haves*. I listened and put time and effort into reclaiming the possibility of a home with my own belongings. Paying attention with willingness, without expectation, to live honestly is a demanding commitment. The path of the heart becomes alive as we place awareness into practical action to mend the broken creation, to serve with our gifts. This transformation, one more shift, dropped me into being available to what was in the moment. Learning to be guided by circumstance obstacles become challenges as life maintains its energetic course. Opportunities are implicit each moment, to say *yes* to existence deepens openness, welcomes life.

In the driest, whitest stretch of pain's infinite desert, I lost my sanity and found this rose. —Rumi

SURRENDER: THERE IS A LARGER PLAN

The best rose bush, after all, is not that which has the fewest thorns, but that which bears the finest roses. —Henry Van Dyke

There is a teaching that when the weather is cold there are different ways to get warm. One is to wear suitable clothing, another is to light a fire. The first warms the individual, the second brings warmth impartially to all within range of the heat. With this understanding, thankful for what was provided, I made an agreement with Simon, a ten-year-old boy living in a community house who wanted to earn money to buy himself a computer. I would give him $45.00 a month as rent for his small room, he would save his money and move in to share a larger space in the same house with his mother. I became a work-study student of Ayurvedic medicine at the Institute for Traditional Medicine with an agreement to the school that I would create money for them to pay many tuitions, not just my own.

Dr. Vasant Lad, a medical doctor from India, the teacher of the program I was enrolled in, lived a connected personal life, a reflection of the depth of the ancient natural healing ways he practiced. Ayurveda, considered the mother of all medicine, means in Sanskrit *the science of life,* and has been practiced extensively in India for more than five thousand years. It is possibly the oldest authentically recorded healing science in existence today. The Institute was made up of five schools: Chinese Medicine and Acupuncture, Therapeutic Nutrition, Massage Therapy, Clinical Herbology, and Ayurvedic Medicine.

Ayurveda is not only a medical science, it is a science of life, it is the art of living life moment to moment, in harmony with the nature, so that Ayurveda will make the life whole. And such a person is holy. So Ayurveda truly brings that holiness in the life of the individual. —*Dr. Vasant Lad*

Ayurveda is a sympathetic model that encourages deepening knowledge of medicine as well as a personal application to one's own inner work. It explains that human beings, like the universe, are made up of each of the five elements—air, space, fire, water and earth, and a soul. Therefore, our bodies are a microcosm of the universe within itself. The principle behind Ayurveda is balance. Ayurveda is used both as a preventative health care modality, keeping our body balanced, and as a responsive health care system to bring our body back into balance.

As a psychologist I had trained to understand emotional life and behavior, now to examine and learn a model of the workings of the body, the nervous and energetic system, a wholistic approach. I had studied philosophy at the New School for many years and trained at several psychoanalytic institutes in New York, as well as interning at Bellevue Psychiatric Hospital. The integration of one's knowledge like that of linking heaven and earth has a powerful effect. Having fullness in our life, recognizing our true nature frees us to contact that inner spark that opens us to our possibilities. A beauty of the Ayurveda classes were Dr. Lad's particular way of teaching through sounds, vibrations, chants and mantras. Sound is considered one of the most important principles of existence, sound patterns engage the mind assisting it to focus. The creative force of the universe resides in all the letters of the alphabet. To hear Dr. Lad chant the names of the human systems in Sanskrit lifted the learning, brought poetry and music into a dialogue with science, a marriage of craft and art.

A poet is someone who can pour light into a spoon, then raise it to nourish your beautiful parched, holy mouth. —*Hafiz*

I began living in the group house, going to school. Patient, I knew direction would come, a directive that would enable me to pay tuition for my studies. That did happen, an opportunity to sponsor a seminar with Dr. Elisabeth Kübler-Ross at a large venue in a public space in Santa Fe which brought thousands of dollars to the Institute and led to my future journey with Elisabeth. I continued studying Ayurveda, selling hand and arm hanging puppets, Guatemalan fabrics of clothing and bags, Bolivian rugs, and Native American turquoise jewelry weekends at a local flea market to support myself. The smile I brought to the market opened doors, people were magnetically drawn to my table as I made contact with an essential part of my nature. Shifting what has been familiar and known and moving from the place where we have been we return to a new beginning. The aim is to maintain *beginner's mind,* that limitless rich original empty available mind. Only then are we invited into the realm of the creative moment where all situations hold a well of possibilities.

I created an intention to not work as a therapist, to step outside for a moment, to observe, to release the outer skin of personality. Before the Fourth Way School, if somebody had asked, *who are you?* I would have answered, *I'm a psychologist, a therapist with a private practice who worked at Bellevue Psychiatric Hospital.* I was my identity. Through dropping that identification, I realized that I was more than what I *did. Who* did it was significant. The shift removed any doubt that my identity did not lay outside of me, it also led me to understand that the teaching is *how* we show up, that I could *be* anything. I could and did sell Guatemalan fabric at a flea market, hawk puppets on a New York street corner, trade turquoise jewelry in Germany, roll and deliver newspapers in Santa Fe, New Mexico, sell Hawaiian shirts in Paris, work craft fairs and hot air balloon fiestas in Albuquerque, sell Bolivian rugs and bags of fruits and nuts at street fairs and still remain who I was, available to whatever needed to happen without making it my identity. The same people would come to the markets regularly to find me, bringing a running updated commentary on their life; who we are emerges regardless to the circumstance. This was living therapy, no fee for service, the focus— engagement in the conversation; true expression changes us, purposeful content, dialogue exchanged at a flea market, on a street corner, on an open field amongst vendors and hot air balloons, on a beach with many colored shirts. A conscious being can be a taxi driver or wait person in a restaurant. The authentic teacher might be the sweep cleaner in the lecture hall rather than the one offering the lecture. When the love in our heart and clarity of mind and spirit come through in the way we live our daily actions are ennobled and transformed. Our unfolding, like the mysterious force of a budding rose lies in *how* we are being, not *what* we are doing. It is through human love that we ascend to divine love. Living in awareness, our way makes us. This is the true surrender— *everything*—and out of that comes authentic presence.

Let us think of therapy as a conversational craft that we hone over a career with our client. The word 'craft' describes a skill set for producing useful things. Crafts are traditions passed down; we learn our craft from apprenticeship with masters. So if psychotherapy is a conversational craft, not merely a science or an art, what are the tools of the craft? They include words, gestures, statements, questions, listening, pausing, and the nonverbals that go with them. There's a knowledge base, too, for the craft of therapy, but here I'm focusing on the tools. Most therapists do not get better over time, though, because we plateau at a certain point and feel too confident and comfortable with our skills. —William Doherty

The joy of voluntary simplicity makes life the art form, and us the artists. It is important to know how to find truth in ordinary experiences. I spent a few mornings a week folding and delivering newspapers in Santa Fe. Everyday life, with her temptations and distractions is a great training ground. I saw the duality: in the business world people advance by compelling others to empower them, I was choosing to direct attention to present moment awareness, even while rolling newspapers; in our daily life we consecrate our activity. Paying attention—what joy to finally recognize everything as a spiritual act. Like the Zen cook in the kitchen, teaching as he stirs the pots of food, we rolled newspapers, our words, our conversations carried strength, rejuvenated. Over time I was asked to work with one or two of the friends of the paper deliverers, women who had walked away from conservative, traditional therapists. I agreed. Within a month they had referred another five or six people to me, and my practice was reinvented, restored. To love the world through our work is the wisdom. And so it has continued to evolve. And I continue to midwife the beautiful beings I encounter, as well as having profound teachings from the unfolding of their lives. *Everyone has in him/her something precious that is in no one else,* said Martin Buber. Being present to the polishing of each gemstone is a blessing.

Love and understanding never condemn but always seek to help and encourage. —Meher Baba

GOING BEYOND OUR STORY

Everything interpenetrates in the ecstatic core where heart-vision begins. The heart with its many regions moves more like interpenetrating spheres, concurrent universes, than a linear path. There is little one can 'say' about love. It has to be lived, and it's always in motion. —Coleman Barks

*O*nce the fiction of my public persona was released I was able to guide others beyond personality, out of their life narrative. The response became the work's verification. Truly, who am I? What matters? What do I want? began to emerge within our conversations. I used teaching stories, accounts about life that were pertinent and appropriate to the moment. This brought an honoring and dignifying of the personal stories of patients. We would unravel their narrative, look to hear in a new way, detached from old meanings. We brought attention and vision, air and energy, sincerity and understanding to breathe new life, able to witness and respond together at the deception and brutality, the dreams, visions and tender moments in their lives. To work in this way is to be attuned to the present, to be awake to who and what we are at any one moment. I finally understood that it's not the form of the therapy that matters, but the presence and the craft of the therapist. Conversation is a practice that when honed well is as much a skill and art as Tiger Woods golfing, or Martina Natrilova playing Tennis, Hemingway writing, as Dave Brubeck on piano, Pavarotti singing, Meryl Streep acting. Practice, practice, practice—to fine-tune our skill and art. This way of working has to do with making love; and by making love possible on earth everything and everyone becomes our lover. And so we strive to be lovers.

A married couple used to come see me once in a while. Among the many I knew who were wed, they appeared the most happy. One day I said to them, 'What marital advice could you offer to others that might help them achieve the grace you found?' And the young woman blushed and so did her husband; so I did not press them to answer. But I knew. Their secret was this: That once every day, for an hour, they treated each other as if they were gods and would, with all their heart, do anything, anything, their beloved desired. Sometimes that just meant holding hands and walking in a forest that renewed their souls. —Rumi

I had realized that a therapist could bring a patient only as far as they themselves have gone. I see the difference is not literal. It is in being. We can bring someone further once we come further, hearing stories never heard before, this is hearing in a new way. Bringing someone to the edge, to ignite their impulse to work, until eventually they eagerly enter, move to discover and own, stand firm and become in possession of their own practices. A lucky lifetime to embody service, opening the heart of compassion.

If you want to awaken all of humanity, then awaken all of yourself, if you want to eliminate the suffering in the world, then eliminate all that is dark and negative in yourself. Truly, the greatest gift you have to give is your own self-transformation. —Lao-Tzu

FORM UNRAVELS IN THE PRESENT MOMENT

*God gives us alarm clocks, then we fall asleep dreaming of alarm clocks.
—G.I. Gurdjieff*

Living in an intentional community, the friction used to prepare the way, to verify the reality of our perceptions, to know through observation, by direct experience, is essential. Attention, the under structure and fundamental principle of self-study opens a world of possibilities, the practice is, as always, to be present in each moment. And the daily practice moves from carefully serving a cup of tea, mindfully closing a door, not reacting when someone cuts you off as you drive, walking with attention placed into each step, listening deeply to music, really seeing the ocean, finding words that actually expresses what we mean, sitting down slowly and carefully, greeting others kindly and respectfully; attentive awareness as a teaching. I lived at a Gurdjieff school that used form to break attitude, create tension and lift energy. Discipline was a tool for transformation at the Fourth Way School. Years later I lived with a Sufi community that used formlessness to provide room for each student to find their way within the container of random looseness. A paradoxical mixture of contraction and expansion, of effort and effortlessness. A balance between perseverance and surrender are essential ingredients for this journeying process. Stepping away from duality I suspended judgment; neither was right, wrong or the better circumstance. To liberate our way of seeing, and enter this larger pasture of unknowing so that we see in a new way opens worlds of possibilities. And it is mindfulness, paying attention, self-awareness, that is the force needed to open the doors. The word attention, from the Latin attendere, to stretch, to reach towards, lets us know that if we want to pay attention, to reach towards, we make an effort towards relationship. Attention is an intimacy with myself. This reaching towards is a coming into relationship with myself. And it is built through effort and practice, maintained it becomes a force, an atmosphere, vibration; a beautiful presence.

Attention is the quintessential medium to reveal our dormant energies to ourself. Maintenance of a conscious energy is not easy. Open to the force of attention evokes a sense of wholeness and equilibrium. We can glimpse a possibility of a state of awareness immeasurably superior to that of our reactive mechanism. Cleared of all internal noise, conscious attention is an instrument which vibrates like a crystal at its own frequency. It is free to receive the signals broadcast at each moment from a creative universe in communication with all creation. To be at the service of conscious attention we prepare for its advent through active stillness. —William Segal

Rodney Collins in his *Theory of Conscious Harmony* claims that what we need to know is right in front of us, but we have to turn around and around or even go to another country to see it. When we don't resist, an unfamiliar environment scrambles our way of thinking, disarms set patterns, opens a window to fresh air. *To uproot—that is the only way to bring the future in. The past has to be destroyed, the old has to be destroyed to give birth to the new. The known has to be thrown; that is the only way to invite the unknown. I feel that one reason why it is important to travel is that one is able to go home and make a really new start. My experience is that it is almost impossible to begin anew simply by getting up and turning round in the same place. One has to step outside it for a moment, not only innerly, but also physically. Look at it and assess it from the outside. Then maybe one can return to it again and do what one has to do.* Years of mindful practice under our belt, our capacity to live with discomfort, to live close to the edge, to receive change in its newness and surprise expands, to look beyond the form, to see, to recognize the hidden treasure, buried, concealed for us to unearth; sometimes even stored in our cells, our atoms, our mind and heart. Many traditions speak of teachings hidden as treasures. Buddhism says that we awaken through understanding ourselves while bringing others to new understandings: from ignorance to wisdom. Our human life itself is the precious treasure, a jewel revealed, not to be treated lightly or thrown carelessly away. When the ground is well prepared, the soil turned, composted, then in its proper time, in our mysterious unfolding, we evolve.

Go forth, and teach the truth in the idiom of the people, for the happiness of many, out of compassion for the world. Strive on with diligence! —the Buddha

This was the teaching when I traveled with Sufi teacher Adnan and lived in Paris at the age of 35. A doorknob on a different part of the door, hearing a foreign language, showing my passport, food stores carrying one product, broken routines refreshed my way of seeing. The ability to look, think and respond to things in a new way resists conditioned automatic associations we have been trained to make. Unless awareness is touched our experiences can be lost to the wind. In Paris, my routine assumptions and concepts about living were challenged. It's in the simple daily ordinary moments that awareness develops. When I'd go into a bathroom, only a sink greeted me. There was no toilet, because in France that stands in another room. Disorientation fractures routine. While I was attending workshops at the Sorbonne and asked where the bathroom was, I went in to discover three men standing inside. I immediately walked out and asked someone again, until I recognized that the bathroom was co-ed. Each shift accelerated my process, pushed me to become mindful to what was in front of me; the process of awakening is being attentive to what is in front of us even if it's zebras in a French bathroom. Breaking form. In Spain, walking by soldiers, rifles cocked in their hands menacingly, I experienced the wounds of societal political change, the politics of fear and the grim reality of resignation and power. Fear manifests as we become slaves to culture. Having my passport taken from me in Paris cracked my image of myself as the invincible American, untouchable, able to roam freely in other countries. Beliefs are barriers, inquiry takes courage. To risk, to depart from the known, an imagined protected position in the world constitutes an illusionary identity for us to manage the precariousness of life. Each journey is unique, no two moments are alike. To proceed forward is to realize each thing in its own time. The ground is prepared by our attitude.

One thing that people can do wherever they are—and they can do it in a consistent, ongoing defined and focused way—is to take one step forward. Each person can move just a tiny bit, but still a tiny bit forward. The essence of all movement is that one does not remain in the same place.
—Rabbi Adin Steinsaltz

STREET SIGNS ALONG THE WAY: LOVE AS THE DIRECT ROUTE

Give me freedom to sing without an echo, give me freedom to fly without a shadow, and to love without leaving traces. —Irina Tweedie

The challenge and practice for us as custodians of this planet is to build a new world. We are placed here to learn how to love. Big thoughts, life is the teacher, our experiences serve us as we recognize the inherent beauty in life. Stepping forward into unchartered territory, to burn away, consumed in the smoke, dissolved, to be breathed in as fragrance for all who pass. An old Hasidic tale reminds us that in this world to see what needs to be repaired and how to repair it we find a piece of the world left for us to complete. But if you only see imperfection and how unpleasant it is, then it is ourself that needs repair.

Reason has no way to say its love. Only love opens that secret. If you want to be more alive, love is the truest health. —*Rumi*

Only the human heart can be broken and whole at once. Often we learn through a disorienting paradox. Although essentially *If we want truth as badly as a drowning person wants air, we will realize it in a split-second. For only a heart which has burned itself empty is capable of love.* This is what Irina Tweedie, wrote in her diary, her memoir, a classic work of a teacher of the 20th century. Irina was asked by her teacher to keep a complete diary of her spiritual training, predicting that it would one day become a book to benefit people around the world. *Daughter of Fire* was the record of her transformation, one of the most detailed accounts of a relationship between disciple and teacher that exists in

Western literature. The diary maps her process, perseverance, triumph, doubts and difficulties. *I expected wonderful teachings, but what the teacher did was to force me to face the darkness within myself, it almost killed me. It was written with the blood of my heart. A slow grinding down of the personality is a painful process.* This is knowing fire from having been consumed in it, living life by dying to it and being reborn. Letting ourself burn brings moments of great clarity; ignited, aglow, finally the space to be in communion with another. To surrender to that part in us that belongs to eternity, knowing that all things are rooted in the invisible world. The potential for transformation, towards conscious evolution, to become an instrument becomes our responsibility. This possibility sounds deep within us, to pay attention to something that penetrates, something greater than ourself. What makes us human is our capacity and willingness to question ourself. To ask of ourself an authentic question, from the heart, opening our heart to the question itself. Rilke, in his letters on love wrote: *to try to love the questions themselves like locked rooms and like books that are written in a very foreign tongue. Do not now seek the answers, which cannot be given you because you would not be able to live them. And the point is, to live everything. Live the questions now. Perhaps you will then gradually, without noticing it, live along some distant day into the answer. Resolve to be always beginning—to be a beginner.* For us to light the lamp, to see in the mirror of the heart, we have to burn away illusion. Fire is total. Rumi says, *Hey! Drink this fine fiery wine, these needles of fire, and fall so drunk that you will not wake on the day of resurrection.* To live with the heart broken open, a new tenderness appears.

I want a troublemaker for a lover, blood spiller, blood drinker, a heart of flame, who quarrels with the sky and fights with fate, who burns like fire on the rushing sea. —Rumi

There's a story about a teacher who hired a young student to come every day and remind him of death. He would visit daily to say, *remember that there is death.* After many years, the student was told he didn't need to come anymore, puzzled he asked, *coming here each day has been a great gift for me, because eventually reminding you of death began to point a reminder back to me of my own life and death. Why do you now stop this daily reflection?* The teacher responded, *because existence has now given me the gift of gray in my beard, and this gray hair reminds me that there is indeed an end to this body, impermanence, this life that has walked the earth in this body.*

The Baal Shem Tov taught that once you enter the heavenly court, because here on earth no one is able to judge your life, you are shown a person's life, their accomplishments, their shortcomings, their wise decisions and the poor choices, then you are asked: *what is it we should do with this person?* You offer the verdict, and it is accepted. Now you are told that this someone is you. Once entering heaven you don't remember. Those who judge favorably have a great advantage. Life is our place of practice; we are here to learn impermanence with soft, gentle, sweet, favorable and easy judgment.

A gem is not polished without rubbing, nor a person perfected without trials.
—*proverb*

DYING INTO LIFE

Teaching is a constant repetition. The pupil has to learn the lesson again and again in order to be able to master it, and the teacher must repeat the lesson, present it in a different light, sometimes in a different form, so that the pupil should understand and remember. —*Irina Tweedie*

*T*o trust in the mystery of life, each moment brings the possibility of awakening. What a beautiful lifetime, to have conscious love and a conscious death. Having that we master eternity. To avoid death is to avoid life, each moment we are dying something is leaving and something is entering. When we want incense to permeate the room we have to light it. Rumi says: *Light the incense! You have to burn to be fragrant. To scent the whole house you have to burn to the ground.* We become the sweet-scented burning aromatic incense. This coming and going, arriving and departing, all part of our voyage. To pay attention, we are told to remember two things every morning: the beloved and death; to look at our death is to have gratitude for life, to remember the beloved opens the inner eyes to see what is here as our birthright. Dying into life we come alive.

The struggle to leave the illusion of 'I' in which we live in order to come closer to a more real seeing, without this effort we remain separated with no measure to measure ourselves and live passively according to our likes and dislikes. Inner-development, work towards self-knowledge; for a true becoming we pay dearly. We pay with our ready-made theories, rooted convictions, prejudices, our conventions, our family life, what we think of ourselves— lies. We pay with sacrificing our lies, our life. —Jeanne de Salzmann

Our practice of awareness enables us to become deliberate with our ordinary experiences, the details of life, and then to elevate and refine them. In the Fourth Way School when my primary relationship was dissolved I experienced a small death. I was given exercises to work against my mechanicalness. For a period of time I was told not to use vehicles to carry myself about, and to not eat in restaurants. I had to find a new way to relate to people. I had been accustomed to moving about in cars, bikes, planes; I rarely walked locally other than to enter a moving vehicle: bus, subway, automobile, airport. My social life, for the large part had been driving to meet with friends, sitting in cafes and restaurants, dining out. Gurdjieff wrote on the wall of the Prieure, his school in 1923, *without struggle, no progress and no result. Every breaking of habit produces a change.* My exercises were an effort to barrage my personality. I felt I was dying, although I could see *I* wasn't dying. My Teacher offered: *Just because your brain can make up a 'reason' for something does not make it so.* Discipline, is from the Latin root, *to learn*; until we are connected to that which is the highest in ourself, our behavior transmits carelessness. The mind that wanders that is aimless and distracted does not penetrate to its fullest depths. Through discipline and perseverance we are able to arrive at a finer quality of attention, well developed, penetrating into the heart of things, this is the root and condition for love.

We had the experience but missed the meaning. What we have to do is build a bridge of remembrance, a way of recapitulation that can reengineer the same event again. This then is true mastery. The completion of understanding is to be able to recreate an insight at will. Progress takes place within the present moment as we integrate our experience in and out of time.
—*A.G.E. Blake*

Humility protects our awareness until we become effortless awareness. The years I traveled with Adnan, people would say, *Oh, you're a Sufi.* A Sufi is something to become, a *wayfayer,* or *traveler on a mystical path,* one who moves towards the truth through love and devotion. I said nothing. In humility, once aware, there are no claims, no labels, only beautiful beginnings. This attitude ties us to the sacred tradition of ancient wisdom. A fine line to walk. Nothing to do, only to become what you've always been, to be who you really are, able to say, *I am.*

We are both the Pilgrim and the Way. —*Irina Tweedie*

ONE INSTANT CAN ALTER ETERNITY

The Sufi opens his hands to the universe and gives away each instant, free. Unlike someone who begs on the street for money to survive, a dervish begs to give you his life. —Rumi

The beloved walks in the marketplace. Be mindful of who you are near, for you are always in the presence of the miraculous. Who might be rubbing shoulders with you in the supermarket? Behind appearances when we bring meaning even in the most simple contact we find a quality that transforms, brings aliveness. Gurdjieff himself used many disguises. He was the perfect flea market vendor, the trickster painting ordinary birds to sell as exotic feathered species, pushing his students out into the open market to work among everyday people, a clever master of his craft. This is a tradition that does not say go off to a mountain top, it says to be in the world with people, to see that as your work. Gurdjieff wrote that the greatest intentional suffering comes from *compelling ourselves to endure the displeasing manifestations of others towards ourselves.* And to be present to that. To enter into a covenant that asks for internal freedom while living mindfully in this world requires vigilance, a stable attention.

The Sufi says that we are here in this world to learn something. We attract our problems to ourself in order to learn something from them. One difference, if you like, between the individual who is on a spiritual journey as opposed to the person who is not, is the willingness to encounter a problem and ask: Why did I attract this? What does it have to teach me? To seek to discover the inner purpose of your problems, you are no longer the victim of misfortune. It's to go beneath the surface of your life and really learn something about yourself. If the Beloved is to live in your heart, you have to be burnt. You have to be the wood that is consumed in the fire of divine love. —Llewellyn Vaughan-Lee

In Paris I went to see the Mevlevi dervishes turning in their sacred dance ceremony, a turn towards the truth. Everyone attending becomes a participant offered the possibility of a glimpse into unseen worlds. For more than 700 years in a continuous unbroken line of transmission this spiritual journey expressed through the turn has taken place. Dressed in black cloaks, which represent a burial chamber and spiritual sleep, long white robes, symbols of the ego's shroud, their heads covered by tall camel hair wool hats designed to signify the tombstone of the ego, the dervishes enter a mystical journey, a stillpoint. The sound of the reed flute, the ney, penetrates the heart. It sounds a call to our relationship with everything; its frequency of finer vibrations and higher influences of an inner dimension are an enigmatic accompaniment to the turning Sufi dervish movements. The open-ended reed flute breathes life into all who hear the music of love. For Rumi the reed flute represented the soul torn from its home, our separation from the divine. *Now listen to the reed-flute tell its tale bringing forth its cry of separation: Ever since they wrenched me from the bed of reeds I have made this crying sound. ... What should we fear darlings? When were we ever less by dying? When I have relinquished every aspect of self, I shall become what the mind cannot conceive.*

This ceremony, called *Sema,* which literally means *hearing* is a cosmic dance of harmony and begins with a loud slap on the floor, a shock to awaken us from indifference, from the maya or illusion of this world. The semazens listening with the ear of the heart, rise and circle the floor three times. At the beginning of the Sema, holding their arms crosswise, the semazen visibly appear to represent the number one, testifying to the unity of existence. Revolving from right to left around the heart the semazens embracing humanity enter into the possibility of turning with love. At the end of the third turn, their black cloaks are removed, a liberation, a spiritual rebirth. Wearing white robes, which represent a new birth, one in truth, they ask permission to turn and slowly, arms outstretched, they turn. The ceremony has four sets; the turn at hearing the good news, of seeing the Beloved in all creation, the turn of knowing the truth within ourselves, and the turn back to the world, in service.

The whirling sacred dance was inspired by Rumi and organized by his son, Sultan Waled. Everything revolves, naturally. However, a dervish participates with conscious intention. In a circle of love, a whirling dance, a lamentation of the soul, dervishes turn toward their heart. In the turn, arms open, right arm directed to the sky ready to receive blessings, the left hand, upon which the eyes are focused, faced downward, positioned toward the earth, transmits the received energy, transformed through the heart to the world. Essentially it is a universal turn, a yearning for union, a final turn to Truth, and a return to the world remembering that light behind all of creation.

The Mevlevi turn, awakening the heart, is a meditation prayer that nourishes the soul. *The tale of love must be heard from love itself,* said Rumi. *For like a mirror it is both mute and expressive.* Turning, entering the gravity of the world to now become like a small universe. The earth and other planets turn on their axes. To allow gravity to take over, until we unravel the universal law of gravity under whose influence we are living. The semazen no longer experiences any distinction between who is turning and who is being turned. Eventually, so involved with the cosmic turning of the axis, a step away from mind, veils removed, worldly existence shattered; this is a true state of meditation. The left foot never leaving the ground symbolizes the way of the dervish both in this world and the next. The sacred ceremony, accompanied by turning music, in an otherwise silent room, ends with the semazens returning silently to their space of meditation, bowing, blessed, having cast off illusion, united in presence and oneness. The Sema has been remembered since Mevlana's marriage to eternity on December 17, 1273.

The one great turning, our souls are dancing with you, without feet, they dance. —Rumi

What has been named the remembrance of the innermost heart, a practice and ceremony to remind us of what is already known, the practices are devices, art forms to discover the secret of love through awakening or polishing the heart and mind.

I saw you whirling beneath the soft bright rose that hung from an invisible stem in the sky. I saw you dancing last night near the roof of this world. Hafiz feels your soul in mine calling for our Beloved. —Hafiz

Invited by Sufi Shaikh Muzaffer Effendi of the Halveti-Jerrahi order of dervishes to join a chanting ceremony of remembrance in New York City at St. John's Cathedral I was transported to a timeless experience. Participating in an energetic ritual of remembrance, chanting with men and women accompanied by rocking movements my body became one with the sounds. Closely connected, we stood shoulder-to-shoulder swaying in prayer, in this magnificent building which could have been anywhere. In that moment I knew the secret. In the realm of spirit, an instant can alter eternity. In one moment the gates open and we turn to enter.

A doorway to eternity flickered open, and in one pure outrageous act of faith, Rumi dove through. In an instant of mystical annihilation, fire met fire, ocean and Rumi fell into pure being. —Coleman Barks

THE FRAGRANCE OF LOVE:
THE LOVER OF LOVERS

Come, Come whoever you are. Wanderer, worshiper, lover of leaving; ours is not a caravan of despair. Come, even if you have broken your vows a thousand times. Come, yet again, come. —Inscribed on Rumi's shrine in Konya, Turkey

Faced with the mystery our inner experiences and glimpses of other dimensions may at times disturb customary ideas of love and reality. Vincent van Gogh painted trees that could reach stars and moon. He explained, *This is the longing of the earth, to transcend the stars.* He painted the longing, not the trees. Rabia, mystic lover and poet, married, went to her window each evening, lifting herself to sing and pray. Her husband, wildly jealous, thinking she was singing to another man did not understand that she was reciting her passionate poetry, her longing and devotional yearning to the beloved. Adoration and praise, surrounded by light, the songs themselves became inscribed on the walls of their room.

I pull a sun from my coin purse each day. And at night I let my pet the moon run freely into the sky meadow. If I whistled, she would turn her head and look at me. If I then waved my arms, she would come back wagging a marvelous tail of stars. —Hafiz

Mystical devotion has remained a thread in spiritual literature. It's prominent in the passionate Persian legend of Laila and Majnu. The story of Majnu, meaning *madman, absorption into a thought,* has become a symbol a testament to the living embodiment of love. Love-stricken, impelled by his undying adoration for a gypsy girl, Laila, the name meaning *sweetheart, a night of obscurity,* has represented romantic love carried to its ultimate level. Laila and Majnu have been a poetic teaching for Sufi poets memorialized in the late 1970's by Eric Clapton who was inspired by the legend and then recording one of rock musics most beautiful love songs, Layla. Woven into a narrative epic poem in the 11th or 12th century Laila and Majnu were moved by a love so compelling that even the repetition of each other's name carried them into ecstasy. Both from different tribes, they met at a young age and were immediately drawn to become each other's love song. The tribes in their effort to protect tribal lineage denied them contact. Through the years of separation Majnu's burning love intensified and he became fervently overcome with grief. Wandering, chanting poems of Laila's beauty and his devotion to her, Laila appeared in everything. Everyone in the Orient knew about Majnu's laments, songs, prayers and wailings of his love for Laila. All night, drunk with the wafting scent of love and melancholy, he would sing passionate songs to the stars, moon, and trees. One night, singing longingly by the palace: *Oh Laila, memories that burn, there sings no bird but calls your name to me. Each memory that has left its trace with me lingers for ever as if part of me.* The King summoned Majnu and bringing him to his court offered him a choice of any of the many beautiful women in his Kingdom, saying how common Laila was compared to these courtly well-bred women. Majnu faced each woman rejecting them one by one: *You are not Laila, you are not Laila, and you are not Laila.* He turned to his King and said, *You can never realize or see Laila's beauty until you love her. Only love reveals beauty. And my love for her, my eternal companion, has shown me her beauty.* Eventually within the parable, Majnun as a metaphor for the mystic, finds ultimate realization. *Love is not love that doesn't love the details of the beloved, the minute particulars,* says Rumi. *Zuleikha let everything be the name of Joseph. Anything she praises, it's Joseph's touch she means. Any complaint, it's his being away. Thirsty, his name is a sherbet. Cold, he's a fur. She loved him so much she concealed his name in many phrases, the inner meanings known only to her. When one is united to the core of another, to speak of that is to breathe the name "hu" empty of self and filled with love.* How do we understand this in a world where the cult of romance and sentiment flourish, considered an addiction and pleasure escape, an illusion that has brought both suffering and happiness.

It's this ecstatic state that is seen by the world as not being in the right mind. Sometimes we call it being in love. It's a feeling of being bewitched, cast under a spell; many are drawn treating this state of enchantment like an inconvenience, irritant, a nuisance, spellbound, hypnotized, some pull away, some sexualize or romanticize the intense emotional contact and charge, the darkness and overwhelmingness, the all consuming force feels crazy. Clapton penned his song: Layla *I'm begging darling please, before I finally go insane. Please don't say we'll never find a way and tell me all my love's in vain.* Our whole life becomes fixated and focused on one person. Some of us marry that person, but many don't dare because we can't continue to live in the urgency we experienced during the month or two that we were pierced and seared. To learn to be in the world opened, inspired, touched by something from another world, and then to elevate those feelings to what the Sufi calls a *splendor of awakening.* To be a knower, a mirror, elevated, inspired, to love another consciously with direction and purpose, is a practice that cultivates consciousness. In love we are drunk, with no need for liquor, entering an urgent wilderness without map or compass. This is one of the highest experiences, this love that Rumi speaks about; inspired, burned in the fire of love, we melt. Personal experiences uplifted, refined, transformed; expanded, this heart space willing to embrace all people, eventually there is no dissonance between the heart of the universe and the heart of humanity. Compassion, tonglen, expressed in so many ways; love songs to the world.

Where the divine and the human come together, this place where the two seas meet, where the dead fish become alive, is where spiritual teachings become a living substance that nourishes the wayfarer. We are the divine purpose made manifest. This is the hidden love story of the world, which the Sufis call the secret of the word 'Be!' —Llewellyn Vaughan-Lee

Gangaji writes about her correspondence with Papaji after their encounter, letters she states *that radiate the ecstatic bliss of their meeting.* She wrote: *By your glance, your touch, and your word you have caused the desert to bloom! A life wasted in personal suffering is revealed to exist only in thought. In raining your divine grace on that life, awe and gratitude bloom. What you have done cannot be spoken. The life that remains in your wake is the proof. This life belongs to you who is that one.*

The polished heart becomes an unceasing timeless state of self-remembrance. The theme of the dervish is to live in a state of remembrance to the beloved. To live in this state of a drunken lover's heart, unbounded, we become a threshold to all relationships, a door to the beloved. *Door* is the root of *darwish* or dervish, the one who turns. Love is the constant turn to knowing the divine, being pulled, a continuous inner dance, the *Way of the Lover,* an anchorless way of celebration. We are not in love, we become love, as a seed becomes a flower. A spiritual communion, finally to love another truly, considered to be the highest experience on earth. This path of love demands commitment, mindful devotion, presence. When we become like a flower in a garden all who pass receive our lingering scent.

Because I love
    There is an invisible way across the sky,
    Birds travel by that way, the sun and moon
    And all the stars travel that path by night.

Because I love
    There is a river flowing all night long.

Because I love
    All night the river flowers into my sleep,
    Ten thousand living things are sleeping in my arms,
    And sleeping wake, and flowing are at rest.
                                —Kathleen Raine

CHAPTER FOUR

Let The Way Itself Arrive

Enough talk of being on the path! Let the Way itself arrive. —*Rumi*

A long and difficult journey is before you. Remember where you are and why you are here. Do not protect yourselves and remember that no effort is made in vain. And now you can set out on the way. —*Gurdjieff*

Someday after we have mastered the winds, the waves, the tides, and gravity, we shall harness the energies of love. And then for the second time in the history of the world, we will have discovered fire. —*Teilhard de Chardin*

The best thermometer to the progress of a nation is its treatment of women. There is no chance for the welfare of the world unless the condition of women is improved. It is not possible for a bird to fly on only one wing. At the present time God should be worshiped as 'Mother,' the Infinite Energy. To all women every man, save her husband, should be as her son. To all men every woman, save his own wife, should be as his mother. We should not think that we are men and women, but only that we are human beings, born to cherish and help one another. —*Swami Vivekananda*

It is law that all things must be born in Woman, even things invented by men. —*Native American Indian saying*

Women are smarter than men. This is true, but it is also true that we now need the female power of the universe to bring us to the next step of our evolution. The male power was very important when we were still hunters and everything was about the survival of the fittest. Now it is about the survival of the wisest and about values like beauty, intuition, creativity, affection and awareness of our body and the universe. These are feminine values and they are not limited to women only, but women are more in tune with themselves and their bodies. For this simple reason that they have the ability to nurture an unborn child in their womb. —Deepak Chopra

The Mother's yoga comes down from transcendence into immanence, down from mystical illumination into heart-illumined action that is prepared to risk defeat. So the yoga of the Mother goes much deeper than the patriarchal ones, because instead of banning matter, it seeks to transfigure it from within. Instead of exiling death, it seeks to die again and again into a fuller and more passionate life. Instead of trying to escape time at any cost, it takes time and kisses it on the lips and accepts all of its conditions and suffering just as they are—in love, for love, as love; giving birth through suffering to a new reality. —Andrew Harvey

WOMEN AND SPIRITUALITY

The day the mountains move has come. I speak, no one believes me. For a time the mountains have been asleep. But long ago, they rose up in flames, they danced with fire. But even if you have forgotten—people! Remember! The sleeping women are now awake and moving. —Akiko Yosano

*I*n this age of spiritual transformation women have an important function, to disseminate the value of personal experience and reclaim the sacred feminine. Feminine consciousness is a creative force that carries wisdom, a spirituality lived in the body uniting spirit and matter. The sacred feminine is attuned to the oneness that is the interconnected wholeness of life. There is a story about a student who had traveled wide and far in search of enlightenment. He had recently returned from a monastery in Tibet and was visiting his mother. He said to her: *If only I could know God, I just want to be conscious and awakened.* She listened and said: *Did you have your breakfast? Yes,* he replied. She asked*: Were you present when you washed your dishes and did you carefully put them away? Yes,* he responded. And she wisely answered: *That's it.* These are the simple practicals that women have been actively engaged in for generations. What was once called *chop wood, carry water*, has been updated to *wash your dishes and put them away, cook dinner and feed the children.* This energy that brings us into awareness is the day labor, the pebble by pebble we build mountains, the daily moment-by-moment practice that is at the root of all true work.

Sometimes the most important thing in the whole day is the rest we take between two deep breaths. —Etty Hillesum

Embraced in the light of feminine energy, a mystical consciousness radiant and intuitive in truth unveils itself. Practicing the politics of an egalitarian not hierarchical world celebrates the ordinary and practical, cultivates an obedience to the moment, to what is given and received in the here and now. To find the divinity in life while holding the paradox of inhabiting as well as of leaving our body, our experiences in this world are essential. It is through this finite dimension that we open ourselves to the infinite bringing the sacred here to earth and into our ordinary life. Form and emptiness; bound as we are by body, by form, we are also rooted in the infinite. The secular and the sacred; looking for what is, was, and always will be.

The Mother is the ground, the energy and the always changing and flowering goal of evolution, the spider that spins the great cosmic web and lives in it, the web itself and the dark luminous womb a void out of which both spider and web are constantly being born. —Andrew Harvey

A well-known folk-tale attributed to Rabbi Simcha Bunam of Peschischa illustrates this delicate and fragile balance as follows: He would say: *I have two pockets, with a note in each pocket, I can reach into the one or the other, depending on the need. In one, there is a note that says: bishvilli nivra ha'olam, for my sake was the world created. In the second there is a note that says: saysanokhi afar va'efer, I am but dust and ashes.* Legendary, Simcha Bunam's practice and teaching were about how to appropriately use the pockets. When you feel alone, unique, notable and special read the note that celebrates your commonality with humanity, *anokhi afar va'efer, I am dust and ashes.* When you feel either self-important or worthless, pulled to surrender ego, a simple gratitude and appreciation for the everyday blessings, read the note that celebrates the uniqueness of your place in this world: *bishvili nivra ha'olam, for my sake was the world created.* The holy and the profane, nothing is left out. Life is patiently waiting for us to improve from our self-absorption, to empty our heart and remember that we are as dust and ashes, that we are created from the most elemental materials and will one day return to that. Even the mosquito was created before us, our body, our physical aspect, according to biblical sources, came about only after all other forms of life were created. And yet, to be created last makes everything else available, at our disposal.

At times we might even reach into both pockets. To know how to use the notes in their proper balance, their right time and place is essential, many make the error of using them with self-deception. To live well is to navigate between the seeming contradiction of everything and nothing. This mirrors the delicate balance of the masculine and feminine. To restore wholeness through equanimity, through presence of mind, we train ourself to open to both our feminine as well as our masculine. Uniting not polarizing, understanding energy so as to live from a place of real freedom; an engaged heart takes responsibility for the life of this world, sees our connection to all beings and things.

What can we learn from the cycle of the moon, how she ever waxes and wanes and waxes again? That a time of smallness is a time to become great; and a time of greatness is a time to become small. For in smallness lies the power to receive and in receiving lies the power to become great. And greatness endures only through its power to be small. —*the Rebbe, M.M. Schneerson*

There is a saying: *the person who removes a mountain begins by carrying away small stones.* It's our daily life that becomes spiritualized and women have long known this. Intuitively we understand that life itself is the meditation. Not to sit on a pillow with closed eyes when our children need dinner, linens require changing, plants are to be watered, or groceries need to be bought and put away. When women fill the yoga and meditation halls, shop for the food, cook the meals, care for the children, they become the heartbeat of community. Women's bodies are the organic connection to simple truths that are natures cycles as well as the elemental vibration of earth. Feminine wisdom has always known and seen the spiritual and material world together, have long understood that our responsibility is to be in service to the needs of the moment. In this lies the love and rebirth of spiritual awareness, the *Way of the Lover.*

This is what is needed now: to turn our mystical awareness into all corners of our lives so that everything is included. To allow the divine to flow into the world and awaken us all within the oneness and joy of that which is at once both infinite within the silence of our own hearts, and visible in the sparkling moments of light and love that are creation. —*Hilary Hart*

THE SACRED FEMININE

Women gives birth just as the earth gives birth to the plants. She gives nourishment, as the plants do, and the personification of the energy that gives birth to forms and nourishes forms is properly female. —*Joseph Campbell*

Mythology points, inspires, interprets, offers clues to our own inward mystery. The archetypes that provide information about life's experiences are a blueprint of the world explaining everyday natural phenomena. The stories based on legend and tradition have deep symbolic meaning, often the survival of a people and a culture rest on the creation of their mythology. The feminine commitment to life in all its forms draws us into a sensitivity towards ourself and all living things. The recovery of the sacred feminine brings a guardianship of the entire creation. Mother-goddess in ancient mythology was herself already earth and the universe, until male directed mythology recreated a new world, a motif of a universe made up of the body of the goddess with man as creator. This earth, the body of the goddess is sometimes plundered, sometimes sanctified, is reflected in how each particular culture regards women.

A woman's process takes on as many forms as there are women. But one thing is the same and that is love. The great Sufi master Bhai Sahib said that 'women need only a few spiritual practices. They are taken by the way of love' ... The mystery of feminine transformation is the mystery of creation, the Nothing that comes into being through love, the being that comes into the world through creative power, the world that appears with light and shadow. —Angela Fischer

Joseph Campbell, one of the world's greatest scholars of mythology, described the goddess as the form bearer, the Indian name for woman being, maya-shakti-devi; goddess-giver of life, mother of realization. The challenge lies in uniting the masculine and the feminine within ourselves, to relinquish thought forms that polarize women and men, to offer space for the light of awareness to shine through. Reclaiming the divine embodiment of universal mother, the feminine aspect, teaches us to be maternal, a nurturer to both ourself and to others. Shakti, feminine energy, radiant light, is the primordial cosmic energy the personification of female creative power.

Women have a particular knowledge about creation and the miracle of creation. This consciousness gives women a unique role to play within creation, It allows us natural access to the creative darkness through which all life emerges, We can access this darkness, and work within its silence to guide life from the emptiness. We live in two worlds, helping light enter existence, wherever it is needed, and we are attentive—with great care—to all that is born. —Angela Fischer

The feminine has an inherent access to the creative darkness from where birth emerges. Ancient wisdom teachings and feminine traditions connected to life asks women to ground into her body which is why violence against a woman's body interrupts the spiritual transformation of women, since earlier experiences of abuse tend to create disassociation from the body. Women, by nature do not typically set up meditations that invite sitting long hours on a cushion. Moving, stretching, yogic postures, singing, dancing, receiving energy through her body; we are a vessel, a container for creative forces to penetrate, connected with life through our longing for expression, transformed through love. To be in relationship with what is here and now, cherishing what we are offered—this gift called our life.

So fragile this petal the earth, as fragile as love. —*Mira*

The fertile earth represents life itself, is the agent for change, visible in this world and in our own life. The wisdom of the mother, embodiment of sacred feminine energy, spreads itself into all aspects of life, makes no division between the sacred and the profane. Women through the ages have been a doorway our connection to a direct unending relationship with life. As a representation of earth, as Gaia, as our mother and goddess we see that what comes to pass, how the earth is treated is how we treat ourselves. The ways of the feminine within us touch the extraordinary range of life from dark to light reflected in the many ways nature arrives, from ravaging hurricanes to pristine island beaches, from sudden tornadoes to beautiful mountain ranges. Sanctifying everything, from diaper changing to watching the ocean roll up along the shore, everything becomes sacred through the ways we love. This is the feminine energy, the radiance of light, creative, receptive; the locus of life is here, and we touch the earth and remember: who am I, sensing connection: to self, to life, knowing intuitively the mysteries of creation.

And the world needs this now, is waiting for this; the birthing of a feminine consciousness that embodies a sacredness in the unremarkable, the mundane, that glorifies with wisdom the presence of the beautiful right here in this world.

Concerning earth, the mother of all, shall I sing, from earth, eldest of the gods, that nourishes all things in the world; all things that fare on the sacred land, all things in the sea, all flying things that are fed out of her store. Through thee, revered goddess, are men happy in their children and fortunate in their harvest. Holy goddess, hail mother of the gods, thou wife of starry Ouranos, anon will I be mindful of thee. —Homeric hymn

The Way Of The Feminine:
Interdependence

Only a spiritual awakening among men will lead men to embrace women's equality. It takes a lot of dignity and inner motivation, to look at someone you have been able to control and treat them as an equal human being. —Naomi Wolfe

Myths have represented the qualities that pattern women's lives through the ages. Hestia, goddess of the hearth and home, oldest of the twelve great Olympians, tended the sacred fire in the hall of the palace, where light was eternal and every hearth on earth became her sacred altar. Her name means *essence, the true nature of things, the heart.* Offered one of the 12 thrones on Mt. Olympus, she gave her seat to Dionysus and presided instead over domestic life, making the hearth, the home, her throne. Hestia gained her self, her wholeness through relinquishing her seat on Olympus. Archetype of inner balance and harmony, she is an essential energy of benevolence, generosity and protection. Providing spaces she has symbolically given us gathering places, power places, dwelling places. For the feminine everything becomes our spiritual practice. Protectress of the home, keeper of the fires, Hestia offered refuge, created shelter, resting places for the body. Heart, hearth, both become the sanctuary at the center represented by the eternal flame symbolizing the midpoint within each one of us. Transformation originates at our core, moving outward. Women know this way, of honoring the sacred on earth in their daily life. The circle of creation, movement and growth reflect the beauty of nature that is the flow of life.

We come to know Hestia through the endless repetition of household chores. Hestia uplifted the mundane duties of household management to a stature, recognition and the value they merit. With Hestia animating the background of household duties, elevating an part of us that is fundamental to our well-being; the feminine finds quiet inner satisfaction in small chores and service. Hidden and consecrated in the details her image is architectural; she is the hearth itself, with the structure surrounding and protecting it. She found sacredness in the ordinary. This knowledge of Hestia as the ground of being creates a sense of inner space in the psychic domain, an awareness of elemental life. Historically, for cave-dwellers the single most important function was that of keeping the fire going, at its most basic level. This myth continued, women making a hearth and home for others. The home as a sacred space has empowered men throughout the centuries. In present times cultures have distanced themselves from these earlier teachings—household chores have been demeaned to lesser than, domestic services often looked down upon, to low pay or no pay jobs that might receive a tip, to expectations from husbands and children for free services from wife and mother. We have tipped the balance of humanity through forgetting what matters.

The way the world is now: the chaos, the violence, the emphasis on money instead of the human factor, the lack of love in many people's lives; it is very clear something needs to change and that can be done with female values: care and creativity, the importance of love, it is up to us women to lead the way in making changes for a better world; to be connected to heart energy.
—*Manon Tromp*

Each tradition has projected its image of the sacred feminine. Worshipped as Our Lady in the French Cathedrals Notre Dame, she is also Hildegarde of Bingen, Eleanor of Aquitaine, Sophia and Athena the goddesses of wisdom, Green Tara the Bodhisattva of compassion who steps from her lotus throne to help all sentient beings, White Buffalo Woman goddess of peace who brought the sacred buffalo calf pipe to the Native Americans, Shekinah tenderly called the Sabbath Queen and enjoyed as the visible majesty of radiant presence, Mary the divine mother, Rabia poet who set forth the doctrine of divine love, Lilith who according to Jewish folklore was the first independent woman, Ganga goddess of the Ganges river India's most sacred body of water descended to earth to raise and cleanse humanity and bring blessings, Kwan-Yin she who hears the cries of the world the goddess of compassion, Sarah the first matriarch and healer of souls, Miriam symbol of leadership and guardian of the promise, Kali Hindu goddess of liberation, Isis feminine archetype for creation, Gaia Greek goddess of mother earth, Ha Ha-i-wuhti Hopi divine mother, Venus Roman goddess of love and beauty. Where ever there is a celebration of love, beauty, compassion and mercy as well as responsibility toward our planet we see her divine presence.

The present moment is a powerful goddess. —*Johann von Goethe*

A DWELLING OF LIGHT

Deep inside the soul there exists the knowledge that in order to build a better world, what lies within the heart of the universe needs to express itself here in the relative world. This signpost points the way for all who long to return through the Mother into a world of pure light. The key is to be receptive, to open ourselves. The expression of love is the music of life, the rain that falls from the other world, here and now, if we will only listen, if we will only be receptive and awake. —Reshad Feild

In Jewish tradition the lighting of candles by the women of the household, mother or daughter, ushers in the Sabbath. The responsibility for the home rests with the women to bring light forward as consciousness. Symbolically the feminine brings the beauty of truth and the radiance of love's understanding into the home, revealing the grace of creation. Light, a metaphor for the divine presence in our world, the Shekhinah, is characterized as the feminine aspect of God which manifests in the material world. According to folk belief, Shekhinah, which means dwelling, is present, and in fact, wanders this world to radiate light upon the earth.

The soul of woman/man is the lamp of God. —Book of Proverbs

The following lines, from the Book of Proverbs, selected insights, beautiful poetry that extol the qualities of the ideal woman from a tradition where women the pillar of the household set the tone, create atmosphere of *a woman of valor*. The teaching, a parable, on one level speaking about the soul, explains that women lighting candles, blessing the home, illuminate the world, ultimately bringing peace to the universe.

> *A woman of valor, who can find?*
> *for her price is far above rubies.*
> *She looks well to the ways of her household,*

and does not eat the bread of idleness.
She opens her mouth with wisdom;
and the law of kindness is on her tongue.
Strength and dignity are her clothing;
Give her of the fruit of her hands;
and let her own works praise her in the gates.

Eshes Chayil, the woman of valor, is a completed woman. Her wealth lies in her appreciation, her gratitude and awareness of what is her life. A rich person is one who is satisfied with their portion. A woman of wealth knows what she has and is thankful. The ideal woman has the recognition of being blessed with abundance. The Jewish tradition teaches that women require very few practices, by nature she embodies love and a longing for oneness. This ode is a testimony to wholeness. Opening to creative power, feminine receptivity, is to remember and contact our essential vulnerable nature. The poem, *Eshes Chalil* is a parable, a song to wholeness, a look at what woman is, at what she can be, and the high esteem of her value. To make this world a dwelling place for the sacred, to bring light into the darkness, to offer spiritual guidance to the family of humanity; all are essential tasks of women.

In all cultural eras, the vocabulary of light has been used to express the deepest movements of our inner life. At one time or another, light has come to represent the forces of good, wisdom and enlightenment, spiritual abundance, and life itself. With the utterance and command, 'Let there be light!' the curtain was lifted on the pageant of existence...The elevation of the Feminine, for the Lamp as pure vessel is viewed as female—Shekhinah—in Kabbalistic sources. In relation to God, the whole created world is categorized as female, containers for sacred light. —Freema Gottlieb

History is a witness to women. She exists before recorded time, lives experientially, feels the pulse of life in the cells of her body, holds a key to completion. The past lives through the present moment. Discovering the inner meaning of the prophets within us, the hidden becomes available. Find the interface and awaken knowing the divine presence in our life.

Unless we awaken to the mystery of the sacred feminine, of the feminine as sacred, and allow it to glow into, irradiate, illumine, and penetrate every area of our activity and to create in them all harmony, justice, peace, love, ecstasy, and balance, we will die out and take nature, or a large part of it, with us. Unless we come to know what the sacred feminine really is—its subtlety and flexibility, but also its extraordinarily ruthless, radical power of dissolving all structures and dogmas, all prisons in which we have sought so passionately to imprison ourselves—we will be taken in by patriarchal projections of it. —Andrew Harvey

RECLAIMING TRUE POWER

A woman asking for equality in the church would be comparable to a black person's demanding equality of the Klu Klux Clan. All the so-called major religions from Buddhism and Hinduism to Islam, Judaism and Christianity as well as secular derivatives as Freudianism, Jungianism, Marxism and Maoism are mere sects, infrastructures of the edifice of patriarchy. Women have had the power of naming stolen from us. Our words have been reversed and twisted and shrunken. —Mary Daly

Within the history of world religion the popular image of God speaks through male figures. Religious political, and economic systems all patriarchal, image the feminine through a male lens. Thousands of years of male dominated society has created countless wars. Masculine power has lived in preparation to destroy, stockpiling weapons, funding war, actively killing. Without knowing how to transmute their life energy into creative loving visionary ways the masculine has externalized his vitality aggressively, competitively more from a fear of losing or gaining than from a love of service. The feminine has been more concerned with her own inner landscape than in conquering far away countries. Awareness of our interconnectedness, of the interdependent nature the sacred feminine holds is knowing that as we poison the air, pollute the waters, injure the animals, send armies to kill, we are toxifying, killing, murdering and undermining ourselves. The power of naming has been taken away from the feminine, until today language no longer sharpens thought, instead used carelessly words obscure meaning. The Way of the Lover recognizes our connection with the entire universe, walks along a path sensitively connected to language, to life force, to the presence in all beings and things animate and inanimate.

We're not going to solve our own problems or the problems of the world the old way. The masculine ways, the way of the warrior, of violence, don't work. This is a historic time for women, and for the feminine. Women who welcome and live their own power can help shift the consciousness of the world, to bring out a more positive side of the feminine, to bring out a new way of being into the world. Feminine spirit more than ever wants us to be truthful and honest about where its energy is, and to use it to heal. Feminine power is different from masculine power because you cannot see it so clearly. Hence the need to redefine what power is. Not as something that is seen, outgoing, but as something that is hidden. The one that is hidden can achieve a lot more than the one that is out there. Feminine power doesn't come out in showmanship, or doesn't overpower, it allows one to be oneself, it allows things to be as they are without aggressiveness or assertiveness. —Sobonfu Some´

Many contemporary male spiritual masters, teachers, and gurus have women guiding and inspiring their inner circle. Osho, spiritual leader for thousands throughout the world, relied upon a woman to run the commune, to be spokesperson for the ashram, stating: *this the first time in history a commune is run by women, they are the pillars of my temple.* The Eastern tradition has been steeped in a feminine, mystical, religious mode, often to the neglect of the material. The Western tradition has been scientific, materialistic and masculine. The *Book of Thomas,* speaks of integrating and unifying the masculine and feminine principles within our being, as a prerequisite to enter the *Kingdom*: to *make the two, one, to make the inner as the outer, and the above as the below.* And yet the discrepancy: the church has neglected to interrupt its injustices toward women. One of the best-kept secrets in the church is the enormous role that women have played in the early foundation of the church. Yet the sub-personal treatment of the man-woman relationship, the exaggerated male images of the priesthood, the sacraments, God, Christ, all are directives as to where we might lift and educate to shift the worlds consciousness providing the wisdom to change this imbalance.

Magu, Nanquan, and another monk were on a pilgrimage. Along the way they met a woman who had a teashop. The woman prepared a pot of tea and brought three cups. She said to them, 'Oh monks, let those of you with miraculous powers drink tea.' Silence follows. What to do, which monk will claim powers? The three looked at each other and the woman said, 'Watch this decrepit old woman show her own miraculous powers.' Then she picked up the cups, poured the tea, and went out. She knew that within the very ordinary lies the miraculous. She understood that waking up to the present is actually the miracle. Pour tea, it is miraculous! The entire universe is present in this act. This old woman knew that her powers were enough, just as they were, in that very moment. No leaning out for the next thing, the better thing, the more powerful thing, the more interesting thing. She didn't even stick around to see or to hear the results of her teaching. She knew what was miraculous, and she did it. It was enough. Just this. A cup of tea, Delicious!
—Mary Grace Orr

Constitutionally women feel the tides of the moon, are connected to nature through the rhythm of the body, whether giving birth to a child, an idea, or any creative possibility. Modern research has indicated that women have more sexual energy than men. Inherent sexual energy transformed into spiritual energy empowers women. When we convert energy we also revolutionize the world, this is an opening to recreate an earth rooted in spiritual energy. Feminism, spirituality and politics must be interwoven, elevated, before the real work of transformation heals the world. True power erupts as divine presence.

Women's power comes from being connected to the wholeness of life, to the great web of life and light that connects everything together. A sense of disconnection and isolation is damaging to feminine energy because isolation is counter to the nature of feminine spirit, which is about relationship and wholeness. It is the turning against its own nature that is the real source of vulnerability in feminine spirit. The only thing that can disempower feminine spirit is feminine power turning back on itself. Many prophesies in many indigenous traditions say that feminine spirit is resurging. It is a rising spirit. The most critical thing is to make it collective—feminine energy is an energy of connection. —Sobonfu Some'

Manifesting today as the light of feminine consciousness this force, a power I liken to a sleeping giant, rooted in ancient wisdom is filled with possibilities. To bring about this evolution is to alter our mind-set, free ourselves from an outmoded thinking that has diminished the feminine in these times. This now is our greatest resource—a mystical consciousness, transcendent and natural to the feminine. Having an innate quality that sees the connection between the physical and the spiritual, that discerns the spiritual in the midst of the physical finds meaning everywhere. The feminine nature; non-resistant, receptive, healing, rooted into the earth, has brought forth beautiful spiritual participants. Today there are a number of women seen as modern-day saint, teacher and Guru. Swami Chidvilasananda, also known as Gurumai, the woman who was Muktananda's translator, became his successor as a siddha master and guru. Ma Jaya, humanitarian and spiritual leader, Karunamayi revered as the embodiment of divine motherly love offers teachings, blessings, meditation and chants towards universal peace, Ammachi, the mother of compassion has been referred to as the hugging Ma. Her *darling chil-*

dren are told that she walks with and beside them, she speaks directly to each one as both the voice of our soul and as our own mother. The light that Mother Meera brings as she gives darshan, seeing and blessing, in silence; her force is claimed to charge, illuminate people. Gangaji, Buddhist teacher Pema Chodron, Mother Teresa, H.P. Blavatsky, Annie Besant, all inspire the experience of the feminine to those who have come to receive their blessings.

A human being is created to light up this world. —*Sefas Emes*

Brother David Steindl-Rast, a Benedictine monk, during an interview was asked to name the one thing that would change the world. He answered, *If women regain their power.* It is a great challenge to women, in this age of spiritual transformation, to claim, to remember, to reinvent, to design our spiritual heritage. Feminine wisdom allows for difference, yet embraces life as one. To know the sacred feminine is to understand mysticism. Buddha, Mirabai, Krishna, Rumi, Lao Tzu, Rabia, Paramahansa Yogananda, Rebbe Nachman of Breslov, Meister Eckhart, Hafiz, Simone Weil, Teresa of Avila, Rabia of Basra, Kabir, Tukaram, Francis of Assissi, the Baal Shem Tov, Hildegard of Bingen, St. Catherine of Siena, Sri Sri Ananda Mayi Ma; mystics who have embraced the feminine, all reflect a vision of the sacred. A deeper relationship with the inner world bringing power with wisdom joins the worlds.

As sugar is made into various figures of birds and beasts, so one sweet Divine Mother is worshipped in various times and ages under various names and forms, Different faiths are just different paths to reach the Supreme. —*Ramakrishna*

A HEART BURNED EMPTY

Friends, until you attain enlightenment you need a Teacher, so follow a supreme spiritual friend. —Atisha, Indian Master and Scholar

A teacher and student are mutually involved in a process of transformation. My teacher and I were in agreement that she would serve as an insistent and fearless force, the example of one who had been on a path before me. Her intention was to be a representative of my potential: an unwavering, objective mirror reflecting my manifestations and/or my perfection. A living embodiment is a gift, and to prepare the soil, to empty and to become available; for this I was challenged, inspired, directed, at a time in my life when there was yet to become any true possibility of refinement. This was a training and I was still foolish and course, the ground of my being not as yet prepared, wild and untamed, yet ready to embark on the voyage of unearthing, of following a call. Meeting a teacher and a teaching I jumped into the fire. A spark ignited and everything dropped away. This momentous design and devise, beautifully braided, perfection; for me to show up us as student, for her to be as teacher, an inner sharing reflecting myself and my separation from that self; for me to discover those obstacles, the boulders that stood in the doorway guarding essence. And so I proceeded to dismantle, to fight with the dragons guarding my heart. The soul's becoming is an extraordinary possibility and a preparation I embarked upon in those earlier years. Before practice what appeared was raw undisciplined eagerness. To bow to another, to find a personal integrity that allows the inner fire to be turned up; to take on the authority of a teacher says no to our own ego and yes to a love affair, to a surrender in remembrance of why we are here. Yes, it takes great time, patience, dedication and love to craft a human being.

A compassionate great ape, a prior incarnation of the Buddha, rescued a man who had fallen into a deep pit in the forest, carrying him to the top on his back. Exhausted, the ape said, 'I need to sleep so I'll have the strength to help you find the way out of the forest. You watch over me.' As he slept, the man, overcome by hunger, thought, 'I need to kill this ape and eat him.' He picked up a huge boulder and threw it—with all his might—on the sleeping ape. The ape awoke, startled. His eyes filled with tears. 'You poor man,' he said. 'Now you will never be happy.' —a Jataka Tale

I am reminded of my dedication and deep feeling for my teacher from a passage in *The Chasm Of Fire*, by Irina Tweedie, a Sufi teacher.

In one of the Upanishads there is a sentence which puts our quest for spirituality in a nutshell: 'If you want Truth as badly as a drowning man wants air, you will realize it in a split second.' But who wants Truth as badly as that? It is the task of the Teacher to set the heart aflame with an unquenchable fire of longing; it is his/her duty to keep it burning until it is reduced to ashes. For only a heart which has burned itself empty is capable of love.

The word *Upanishad* literally means sitting down near to learn inner or mystic teachings. The Upanishads, the inner mystical teachings, the final portion of the Vedas, are considered the most ancient and sacred scripture of India. This study leading towards self-knowledge removes the root cause of all unhappiness and unnecessary suffering which is ignorance, delusion about ourself. Self-knowledge is to withdraw the cause for unhappiness, the sorrows about life through recognition, clarity, attention, understanding while breaking the mistaken notion that we are separate from each other. Self-knowledge is the subject matter called Upanishad and it teaches that the guru or true teacher is none other than the conscious self; not *my self* but *the self*, housed in the body and mind of a teacher's compassionate embrace of humanity. The reflection; as distinctions collapse our hearts become so vast that we are able to hold great love under all circumstances.

Every incident, every circumstance, every word, every sound is nourishing, because the same love is in everything and in everyone.
—*Gurumayi Chidvilasananda*

Women, who inherently understand the position of creator as nurturer and carrier of the seed, rarely enter a spiritual path to assume a set philosophy. It was not practices, dogma, concepts, receiving a new name, or promises, that drew me to a teaching. A personal *daimon*, a silent voice, a guardian guided me to my own higher spirit that inner voice, my divine companion brought me to look at the question *how to awaken, how to love?* Meeting my teacher I looked at an aspect of the question, what is trust, how to open and live in the heart, and together we created a spiritual community, to live with students, mirrors to penetrate and energize the sacred wisdom of ordinary life, communicated through a way of life. To drop into recognition, to allow one Paula to die and another to be born, bringing challenges and heartbreak, my mind and heart were cracked open. When we allow our heart finally to break, when the longing for love overtakes us, when the heart is freed, as in the Sufi symbol of the heart with wings we are in the way of love.

Mevlana says:' Come, come whoever you are.' We can't take anything with us, because there has to be an empty space in our hearts. We need to die to the concepts and illusions that are held so tightly out of fear, the fear of facing ourselves in the mirror of life. This Way is not easy. And we have to give up something, which is ourselves. The door of the heart can only be opened from the inside. No one can open it for us. The doors open for us when we are empty, and in this emptiness we are free. It is not freedom from, but freedom within, life. Freedom is allowing the free flow of love to manifest in our lives and in all the kingdoms on earth. —Reshad Feild

TO BEAR WITNESS

If you look deeply into the palm of your hand, you will see your parents and all generations of your ancestors. All of them are alive in this moment. Each is present in your body. You are the continuation of each of these people. To be born means that something which did not exist comes into existence. But the day we are 'born' is not our beginning. It is a day of continuation. We celebrate our 'happy continuation day' and when we have the experience of non-birth and non-death we know ourselves beyond duality. Your hand proves that you have never been born and you will never die. The thread of life has never been interrupted from time without beginning until now. Previous generations, all the way back to single-celled beings, are present in your hand at this moment. You can observe and experience this. Your hand is always available as a subject for meditation. —Thich Nhat Hahn

This is the platform for humanity. Our link to memory connects us to our humanness. The power of memory opens us to wisdom, to teachings, builds bridges through history across into the future. Forgetfulness dehumanizes. *Liskor velolish koah: Remember and do not forget.* This statement, theme at Yad Vashem the memorial in Israel to those who died at the death camps is a call to remember, an encounter with this present moment. We are invited to be present to a reality which also exists on other levels. History wounds and elevates us. And we carry a responsibility, what is named memory; through awareness we become human. *Exile comes from forgetting. Memory is the source of redemption. Memory* says the Baal Shem Tov *is the gateway to redemption,* certainly it is key in our quest towards awakening.

Remembering is the source of redemption. Exile persists as long as one forgets. —Ba'al Shem Tov

Traditionally, included in a Passover ritual dinner, named *seder*, meaning order, Jews recite each year a line from the *Haggadah*, a telling of a narrative of the story of the Israelite exodus from Egypt: *In every single generation it is a sacred duty for each person to consider themselves as personally brought out of Egypt.* This unites and places us into the center of history, linking the past into the present moment. It is in the *here and now.* The questions themselves become testament and testimony to relive history, which miraculously unfolds without answers. Only in the silence do we know, until one day, satisfied with turning inward we ask ourselves to become present to this creation in its extraordinariness. Invited to personally know the events of our ancestors keeps history alive, for us to discover for ourselves the timelessness of memory, which is not bound by space or time. We remember and make history; as witness we stand outside the time-line of history. The history makers are those who have the capacity and courage to disclose the human process. This is transcending and transforming. The present moment contains the whole past, and in the present moment, the whole future as potential. The miracle is in our witnessing awareness; our quality of witnessing is the birth of consciousness.

We have a historical consciousness that transcends individual consciousness. Linked one to the other, tradition stresses the notion that each and every one of us stood at Sinai, that each and every one of us saw and heard, we are made to realize that we are older than we seem, that our memory does not begin with our own. The source of our strength is history, not geography. We want to live and uphold the sanctity of life, to create peace and bear witness that we are not each other's enemy, that every war is senseless, that the solution lies in compassion and that compassion is possible. We owe it to our past not to lose hope. To despair now after thousands of years would be a blasphemy—a profanation. What is essential in all things is peace which confers harmony on all beings and on our world. —Elie Wiesel

THIS WORLD OLAM HA-ZEH

*T*he sages have told us to remember six things daily: Going out from Egypt, Amalek, standing at Mount Sinai, how we tried God in the wilderness of the desert, Miriam and the Sabbath. They are the six remembrances recited daily after morning prayers. Zachor: to remember, is actually a commandment, a mitzvah, a worthy deed.

1. *To Remember the Exodus from the land of Egypt all the days of your life.* The Biblical word for Egypt is *mitzrayim,* meaning constraints, and on the holiday of Passover Jews celebrate *yetziat mitzrayim,* the perpetual exodus of the soul from all constraints. This eternal exodus has been at the core of a dynamic quest for meaning and purpose. The Talmudic dictum states: *In each generation, and every single day, an individual is obligated to see himself as though she/he departed from Egypt.* The immediacy and eternal relevance, experienced and actualized in the here and now to be lived every moment afresh; every day we are asked to create, live into a world where we work to transform oppression into liberation, to find freedom from ourself. To view ourselves as having personally experienced liberation from slavery, not only our ancestors, to bring ourselves to a new place, renewal. In the exodus story Egypt is that narrow place which is positioned between the mind and the heart. Once we are freed from our own inner narrowness the distortions of our self-interests, our personal *mitzrayim,* temptations to our personal integrity become less of a challenge. In each one of is an Egypt and a Pharaoh, and in every circumstance and moment there is an opportunity for another exodus. To remember the exodus is a call for compassion both towards ourselves as well as others; it is our personal story as we await and welcome both the stranger and the miracle-maker, the peacemaker and witness, proph-

et Elijah. The exodus, a focal point of Jewish history and tradition, is a continuing process towards liberation, not a one-time event, it is a present day hope and desire for freedom, liberation, redemption for all of humanity.

2. To Remember what the Amalekites did to you on the way, as you were leaving Egypt. How they attacked the weakest at your rear. Do not forget, erase their memory. Amalek in the spiritual sphere is the indifference, the dismissive *so what, it doesn't matter, whatever;* our apathy, cynicism and indifference. Everything matters; being dismissive of the ordinary creates disdain and sacrifices our reverence for life. To remember, *zachor*, is the antidote. It is our task to witness and to remember. To actively fulfill the directives, the suggestions that some call commandments, rather than only remember the atrocities, to speak out and actively pursue opportunities to obliterate Amalek: to call out, to recount with our mouth, to recall verbally and decry hatred and bigotry which are all aspects of Amalek—whenever and wherever they become manifest in our world.

The testimony of remembrance invites consciousness to pay attention through memory to presence in the history of humankind. The history of slavery of Blacks in America, the raping of women in Africa and all throughout the world, gender and sexual inequality, the oppression of children, are to name only a few. We are called upon to pay attention, to bring meaning to our life, to bring purpose to what was painful, to where there was/is injustice and suffering, uniting our innermost intentions with our outermost acts. The statement asks us to remember the action that Amalek took against us, eventually blotting out the remembrance of Amalek, of cruelty through actively pursuing opportunities to speak out, so that what we do and what we mean are aligned. The Amalekites were merciless, spreading cruelty, attacking the weakest in the wilderness. To remember tragedy and then to dedicate our lives to confronting injustice, pledging to work towards easing the oppression and suffering of the weak, making this a just and good world is to work with compassion for the betterment of humanity.

3. *Remember that you stood at Mt. Sinai and received the Law.* For one brief moment at Sinai we experienced the divine presence, to become, free of past and future we stood still, experiencing total presence and total being. The covenant that was received is ongoing. The ten declarations known as the ten commandments mark a spiritual dedication, where the sacred can be found everywhere. The divine presence is available in the present moment; our dedication is to uncover and to reveal this through study, service, keeping the newness and freshness of the marriage ceremony we experienced at Sinai between the *Life and Ground of Existence, the Beloved of the world,* and a people.

4. *Remember that you angered God in the wilderness by worshipping a golden calf.* Moses and those around him heard the ten commandments and Moses went up the mountain to bring down the stone tablets, saying he would return in 40 days. Waiting for Moses to return from Mt. Sinai the people becoming impatient, lost faith, decided to melt their gold and build a golden calf, an idol of worship. Impatience becomes a slave to time and distractions. A sign of how short our focus often is, leading to a lack of vision to our priorities, impatience is an obstacle that translates into having little presence. When Moses told the crowd to stop idolatry only a few had the mind-set, the clarity to get on track, so easily swayed by the mob we even fail to recognize that we all have the possibility to fall short, and then to remember that we can pick ourselves up and rise again. Having confidence, faith, trust, courage, is knowing how to let

go, to surrender. The teaching here is not about believing, it's about knowing, which is a form of trust; when faith is challenged dig deeper to find what is already known. Forgiveness follows as an essential part of this commandment. And the people were forgiven, and so the memory is to understand the steps that take us away from knowing as well as how to forgive ourselves and return again, to find our higher purpose.

5. *Remember that which the Lord your God did to Miriam on the way.* Miriam, born in Egypt at a time when the Jewish people were enslaved to hard labor, her name meaning sea of bitterness; sages tell that the spirit of prophecy came to her as she predicted that her mother would birth a son who would lead the Jewish people out of Egypt. Mid-wives, she and her mother were ordered to kill at birth any baby boy born to a Jewish mother. Risking their lives, disobeying the edict from Pharaoh; when Moses was born he was hidden in a basket, placed among the reeds at the river's bank. Found by Pharaoh's daughter who adopted baby Moses as her own; he lived to lead the Jewish people out of Egypt 80 years later. Miriam, sister to Moses and Aaron, together they became 3 devoted shepherd's accompanying their people throughout 40 years of desert wandering. The sages say that of the three gifts that sustained the Jewish people in the desert all were of great merit, called *zechus*, Miriam's well, a rolling rock that accompanied the Hebrews providing fresh water for the cattle, the sheep, the people and making the desert bloom green pastures was one of the three life-giving gifts. Miriam, inspired, led the women across the Red Sea singing with tambourine in hand. She has been revered and loved as a prophetess to become a popular figure in modern times.

Miriam, as it is told, spoke against her brother, publicly slandering him, challenging his marriage to an Ethiopian woman, she criticized his divorce from Tzipporah speaking derogatory words about Moses to her brother Aaron, following this she was stricken with leprosy and was quarantined outside the camp for 7 days. In order to impress the hardship that results from *lashon hora*, slanderous talk, we are told in Talmud: *Money can be reimbursed, but the hurt from words is irreparable.* and we are told to: *Remember what God did to Miriam on the way from Egypt.* What are we to remember here as a key to life? *Words are like arrows,* says the Psalmist, *and like smoldering coals. Like arrows,* explains the Midrash, *for a person stands in one place and his words wreak havoc on another person's life many miles away. And like a coal whose outer surface has been extinguished but whose interior remains aflame, so too do malevolent words continue to work their damage long after their external effect has evaporated.* Our words have the capacity to cause division and separation, and our purpose is to create unity and oneness. Words carry the power to sanctify and we have the ability to choose to elevate or to misuse the power of our speech. Words act upon the world, the words we choose determine how we experience our lives. *The mouth is the quill of the heart,* says Chovos HaLevavos. Our words define us. In the Jewish tradition *loshon hora*, the evil tongue, is a weapon of words, and is considered to keep the world in ruins. *Shmiras halashon,* carefully guarding the tongue, speaking mindfully, the antidote is the road to peace and unity, words of kindness, praise, encouragement, compassion and mercy, turning the speaker into an instrument for revealing the sacred in the other, in the world, is a source for a life of health, happiness and peace.

6. *Remember the Sabbath day and keep it holy.* Shabbos is considered to offer a taste of eternal life within time. On Shabbos there is only the present, simply being alive: a day devoted to being present. No tasks to finish, no plans to organize. The reminder has been: *more than we have*

kept the Sabbath, the Sabbath has kept us. To remember Shabbat means to remember the significance of Shabbat, both as a commemoration of creation and as a commemoration of freedom from slavery. *On this day we pay attention to the seed of eternity planted in the soul,* said Abraham Joshua Heschel. *To witness the perpetual marvel of the world's coming into being, to realize that the source of time is eternity, that the secret of being is the eternal within time. The act of bringing the world into existence is a continuous process.* Considered the Day of Being, this is a day we show up, devoted to being present. For a night and a day every week sacred time and space and the dream and promise of a perfect marriage: the Divine lover to the Shabbos queen: Lecha dodi: *Come my beloved to greet the bride, the Shabbat.* This renewal, a move inward, a day of becoming, for all—wealthy, poor, a time of equality, a beautiful taste of peace.

Within you there is a stillness and a sanctuary to which you can retreat at any time. —Hermann Hesse

HEAVEN ON EARTH

True remembrance means hearing, seeing and even knowing what is in any one moment of time, and yet not identifying with it in any way whatsoever. When we observe and remember at the same time, we are awake to the present moment. —Reshad Feild

There is a Hasidic teaching that states: there are three ascending levels of how one mourns: With tears —that is the lowest. With silence— That is higher. And with a song—That is the highest. According to tradition, when heaven arrives on earth the observance of all holidays will stop, except the one day that we laugh and rejoice singing the love that moves both heaven and earth.

A continuous chain is central to our outlook on tradition, therefore not as an inert inheritance, instead, it's a living organism. The notion of inspired persons who act as a link in the chain throughout the generations is a profound contribution, uncovering truths that are already there. A tradition cannot leave things in a state of unchanging status quo. —Adin Steinsaltz

The world is somewhat eased from its tragedy and suffering through being witnessed with aware compassionate recognition. To remember, we humanize the world, we create a more charitable, more welcoming world. The truth does not diminish, it elevates, brings people together; as we witness with compassionate love and understanding to save the future. We become the Moses, Hafiz, Mary, Lao Tzu, Rumi, Rebbe Nachman, Kwan Yin, Jesus, the Buddha of this time. In each one of us there is a promised land and every point in time is an opportunity for another exodus. We are the memory for the world and at the heart of memory is eternal consciousness. We are the living cemetery as well, standing on the backs of those who preceded us. Bearing witness we are evidence and affirmation. Now to know that there is no present moment without a conscious human being. Because we remember life continues. This is the secret of dedication. Once the matrix or pattern is recognized, we see ourself in the words of all sacred text. The essence of each image: angel, heaven, beloved, child, resonates once recognizing ourselves as personally going out from Egypt, standing now at Mt. Sinai, dancing with Adam, as gypsies of old lore. All ancient myths and teachings are present and current. They are so close, in fact, *they are in our mouth and in our heart.* To live in the present moment we cross a bridge between time and eternity. Our true heritage leads to the possibility of shifting consciousness, bringing emptiness into form, where the material and the spiritual world come together.

'In the Dalai Lama's words, 'Always remind. This is what I call the Jewish secret—to keep your tradition. In every important aspect of human life, there is something there to remind. We have to return, we have to return, we have to return, to take responsibility.' The Dalai Lama had grasped an essential Jewish secret of survival—memory. The Torah is full of exhortations to remember—to remember the Sabbath and keep it holy, to speak of the law constantly and teach it diligently to your children. The sacralization of memory has been an essential feature of Judaism throughout its history. We can see it today as Jews work hard to keep the memory of our Holocaust victims sacred. The Buddhist leader had now gained a more specific understanding of how Jews transformed the painful memory of exile into a source of strength and hope.... And now, next year in Lhasa.' —Rodger Kamenetz

To sit with the questions, to look at the world and be willing to stand as human representative, to re-present, to make present what has existed, beneath the mask of indifference and fear, to witness; *Liskor velo-lishkoah: remember and do not forget.* The Hebrew root *zakar*, suggests both remembrance and mindfulness. *Awake, awake, you sleepers from your sleep; examine your deeds, remember, those of you who forget the truth, look to your souls,* said *Rambam, Maimonides.*

Not to be overwhelmed by history, to be humanized by it. Here, in life, in our intentional participation, nothing is left out. The meaning of the phrases *tikkun ha-adam,* perfecting humanity, and *tikkun olam,* perfecting the world, are hidden meanings in my poem, *Zachor, To Remember.*

Zachor, To Remember

I Angel, Song of the Desert, moan of old terror.

Lone Angel, messenger taking form, to walk on earthly land.

I Caliph, Son of Sea, bring lumens to shore.

birth, mystery of creation, emerging from the ocean carrying emeralds in my mouth.

Heaven sounding new era bringing dawn to find home. Paradise—marked by light, its rays visions of sun flowering this earth.

Veiled, sorrow interrupts as sunset clouds my heart, hidden from the eyes, softly crying, yet tearless for all that's passed.

Mothers bear this pain. Daughters of Sin, dancing with Adam, O' so gently embrace here on Earthly shore, a ladder-climb down. A wingless place, desecrated until forgiveness becomes a petal blossoming in the sun's heart.

I, Singer of Song, plaintive wail send years of tumbling centuries old Ocean to trace my past.

I, Ocean of the rain, runner in the dawn, Gypsy of old lore, tell secrets in the wind.

Listen, all things pass. This to be learned, Love has memory. Don't be fooled—the price of admission is our recognition.

You, Beloved, remain. Buried in heartbreak.
One glance awakens this tender heart.

I, Lover of Light, wanderer with vision, looking inward remember the climb.
I am both Lover and Beloved with song I sing.
Of Rachel, Rebecca, Miriam, and Vashti,
of Sarah, Leah, Esther, Deborah, and Eve,
of Dinah, Delilah, Hagar, Ruth and Zipporah: I
Remember.
A woman bensching licht, head covered, weekly paradise, crown and memorial of creation, I Remember.

Once a slave in Egypt, we relive the miracle of liberation,
this exodus, ancestors on a trek to Mount Sinai
Today I am the one walking, witnessing, aching, awakened,
the Truth beyond all form.

We embrace in the cry of Sh'ma, memory is the heart of
our soul.
I stand in the center of history.
forefathers, I see our foremothers, eyes to earth, heart to
heaven, makes this world manifest.

Not separate, Lover and Beloved as one. Zechira,
remembrance. Zachor, I remember.

We Praise.
Soaring, liberation of the heart, freed to love. Out of great
Love, from this broken heart, Union. A universe revealed.

Come, come enter now: This emerald, this song, this
eternal dance, extended circle, is: *The Way of the Lover*.

—*Dr. Paula Bromberg*

CHAPTER FIVE

Mystery Of The Feminine

Life in its organic wholeness is absolutely a mystery. Such is the ultimate nature of things. My own vision is that the coming age will be the age of the woman. Man has tried for five thousand years and has failed. Now a chance has to be given to the woman. Now she should be given the reins of all the powers. She should be given an opportunity to bring her feminine energies to function, to work. Man has utterly failed. In three thousand years, five thousand wars—this is man's records. Man has simply butchered, killed, murdered; he has lived as if only for war. There are a few days in between two wars which we call days of peace. They are not days of peace; they are only days of preparation for the new war, they are preparation for the new war. Yes, a few years are needed to prepare, and again war, again we go on killing each other. It is enough! Man has been given enough chances. Now feminine energies have to be released: the energies of the Mother. —Osho

The whole human future depends on whether humankind can rediscover and restore the sacred feminine to the core of human awareness. An imbalance of the masculine has brought us to the moment when unless we recover the feminine powers of the psyche—of intuition, patience, reverence for nature, knowledge of the holy unity of things—and marry these powers with the masculine energies of will, reason, passion for order and control, life will end on the planet. This marriage of the masculine with the feminine has to take place in all of our hearts and minds, whether we are male or female. The health this brings is the goal of being human, the basis and energy of all true transformation. —Andrew Harvey

If there is to be a future, it will wear the crown of feminine design.
—*Aurobindo*

It is not surprising that the qualities that we have traditionally defined as feminine will be the qualities we need to develop and value in order to help the process of the evolution of our consciousness, the recognition of the divine wholeness of which we are a part. The ways of the feminine have traditionally honored all life as sacred, have emphasized receptive states of being rather than expressive states of doing, have reflected the inter-connectedness of life, and have not allowed the community to be forgotten in the pursuit of individual achievement. This is why it is important to look with new appreciation to a feminine understanding of spiritual transformation that has been, for so long, generally hidden from out collective consciousness. —*Hilary Hart*

Women are smarter than men. This is true, but it is also true that we now need the female power of the universe to bring us to the next step of our evolution. The male power was very important when we were still hunters and everything was about the survival of the fittest. Now it is about the survival of the wisest and about values like beauty, intuition, creativity, affection and the awareness of our body and the universe. These are female values and they are not limited to women only, but women are more in tune with themselves and their bodies, For the simple reason that they have the ability to nurture an unborn child in their womb. —*Deepak Chopra*

WOMEN AS HEALERS

Dedicate your practice in the Mother's name to the transformation of the earth into her living garden of love and justice and divine freedom. Imagine what such a world would be like—where the forests would be growing again and the vanishing of innumerable species halted and the whole of civic and political life dedicated not to the controlling of billions by fantasy and greed but to a liberation of soul force in every human being, until your whole being yearns for the establishment of the Mother's truth in all institutions, activities, relationships, and arenas. —Andrew Harvey

Healing is as natural an expression of love for women as breathing. The feminine moves into the mystery of love as it rises from a place of flowing harmonious wordless movement; from dancing, singing, gardens, ocean; receptive feminine qualities blossom: look to nature: the feminine surrounds us. The mystery of the feminine transcends the limits of time and space: love is her meditation, arising to live through the heart. Our Mother Earth is the transforming force of evolution, expressed within everyday life in our relationship to the physical world. In Egypt, the Goddess Nut, is the Mother Heaven who represents the heavenly sphere which arches over the earth with her protective body.

On the battlefield injured men often call out for their mother, that place of origin and refuge. The archetype, since all women are mothers, of a divinely created being is a counterweight to the limited popular image of a biological woman. How *mother* is known, her heritage and purpose, shifts to expand, becoming something more than biological mother. Giving birth is a woman's nature, yet society has regarded birthing as limited to the physical form of a child. All women are mothers and our lives are a testament. We birth ourselves as well as bringing into this world creative forms and ideas.

Ramakrishna compared Mother to *a spider who spins the entire creation out of herself and then goes and lives in every aspect of the web.* She lives in creation, rooted as radiant light Mother Earth. Represented in most every mythology of the world by our earth, Lao Tzu claimed that the nature of existence is more like the female, more feminine, is more balanced. And when we observe the earth, the lakes, rivers gliding, streams flowing, birds chirping, flowers as fragrance, we see the feminine everywhere. Jesus spoke to his disciples: *Look at the lilies in the field. How beautiful they are.* The mother is the earth, a womb for a new birth.

There is a web of connection, life, and light, a web of feminine energy that goes from the earth, to the moon, and to all other dimensions. The web is a form of consciousness, a consciousness of oneness, like a network linking all elements of life together. Women have a special access to this web because the web itself is a form of feminine energy. Connected to this web we will be able to live in a consciousness of oneness from which new solutions to our own evolutionary changes and the evolutionary challenges of the world will become available. —Sobonfu Some'

Regardless to how women have been offered expression they birthed through personal myth-making, story circles, piecing together afghans, quilts, clothing; spinning life and all of creation out of herself. Women can mother history, give birth to new values, be the mother for all humanity; her force and power is as visible as the earth giving birth to the plants. She gives birth to the human world. Her body is the universe, ocean, moon, and earth. The energy that gives rise to creation is the same energy needed for healing. Just as a mother is a link for the child, a healer is a connection between a person and the healing source. To recognize our human connection, our interconnectedness humanizes this world. Women intuitively know this.

The sacred is not in the sky, the place of transcendent, abstract principle, but rather is based on this earth, in the ordinary dwelling places of our lives, in our gardens and kitchens and bedrooms. —*Marilyn Sewell*

A female Canadian novelist once asked a male friend why men feel threatened by women, he answered: *They are afraid women will laugh at them.* She later asked a group of women why they feel threatened by men. They answered: *We are afraid of being killed.* A cavernous distance between pride and murder. A woman is statistically more likely to be killed by her husband or live-in boyfriend or former partner than by a stranger. The history of women is interspersed with stories of invasion and atrocities, as well as femicide, the killing of women and girls because of their gender. Amnesty International records cases of more than 300 million women having undergone genital mutilation, a dangerous procedure historically enacted to reduce woman's libido, deter promiscuity and maintain cleanliness, and still in the present generation there are over 2 million procedures being performed every day in reporting countries. In the Democratic Republic of the Congo 2.5 million girls are raped every year, with girls as young as five being brutally violated by gangs of soldiers. And these statistics have been on the rise each year. Rape has been used as a tool of war. Female trafficking and sexual harassment is the result of a systematic disregard for women's human rights. In the United States the trafficking of women and children on the back page of mainstream newspapers is a multi-billion dollar industry that violates the human rights of woman and girls. The Village Voice newspaper in New York City made over 2 million dollars a month, reported in 20012, on its BackPage, stating in 2013 it would be unwilling to stop its posting and lose this revenue. Countries still sanction breast ironing, a pounding of pubescent girls breasts to slow their development to limit the risk of sexual assault: to mutilate the body to protect girls from sexual harassment and rape so young girls can pursue education rather than being forced into an early marriage.

I don't believe that rape is inevitable or natural. If I did, I would have no reason to be here. If I did, my political practice would be different than it is. Have you ever wondered why we (women) are not just in armed combat against you? It's not because there's a shortage of kitchen knives in this country. It's because we believe in your humanity, against all evidence.
—*Andrea Dworkin*

History records foot-binding practices in China, where for 1,000 years women's feet were bound, reduced to stumps, as well as countless women who have been condemned and burned or stoned to death as witches from the 16th and 17th century and later. This continuum of terror named the global war against women includes incestuous and extrafamilial child sexual abuse, battery, sexual slavery, forced sterilization amongst a longer list of violations perpetuated against the faceless feminine. It is awareness and responsibility that has the power to bring us beyond, as we recognize our human connection and awaken from the mistaken notion that we are separate from each other.

We must recognize that the suffering of one person or one nation is the suffering of humanity. That the happiness of one person or nation is the happiness of humanity. —*the Dalai Lama*

Many religious themes as well as numerous fairy tales characterize women as stone-hearted, fiendish, evil, a cruel mother transformed into a wicked stepmother, a foolish damsel in distress, black-hearted seductress, a hateful witch laying in wait for children, weak and irksome; each of these characteristics, undermining and devaluing, reinforce and perpetuate the heartbreak that is ravaging the earth. Woman are depicted through the centuries as men perceived them. Veiled, women's potential, once sensed, has been covered and brought into line with imbalanced masculine power. All that is changing. This is a historic time, women will change the tone and texture, the consciousness of this world through making sacred their experience of birth, sex and death: keys to the miracle we call a mystery. It is now time to unveil, unbind, be taken off the stakes, to come into possession of self, rather than being owned and viewed as a property. Given men's last names, exchanged for goods or dowries, paid inferior wages, deleted from voting rights, dishonored in pornography, history reads unkindly. In the deepest sense of displaced ownership men have not owned the female inside themselves, personally dis-identified, they traditionally combined the institution of property-ownership with power over women.

When we try to pick out anything by itself we find it hitched to everything else in the universe. —John Muir

RECLAIMING THE FEMININE: WOMEN'S STRENGTH

Women, especially, seem to have difficulty finding and trusting that inner authority. I know very few women who trust their truth. I could count them on one hand. But I know hundreds of men who trust their truth because they're validated from the beginning by their culture, at their schools, in their professions. So women are going to have to find their authority, their courage. —Myosho Virginia Matthews

Historically, a special section was set aside in temples, dating as far back as the 13th century, that separated men and women, that created a space for men so as to not divert their mind from their prayer, to keep men from temptation. This continues today in Orthodox synagogues, as well as in Muslim countries, and various Indian cultures, sometimes erecting a curtain to avert eye contact. The Talmud states that the voice of a woman entices sexual arousal in men interfering with men's concentration for prayer. Women in the Jewish Orthodox tradition are asked not to sing, essentially, to not participate in the Temple service when men are in the room. The Talmud continues: when woman officiate at a religious service it detracts from the prayer mood because, *a woman's hair, voice and skin arouse sexual passion in men.* No thought to practice, evolve, educate or discipline the masculine, to create responsibility and elevate male sexual energy, rather the effort is to disenfranchise, to disown women from full participation. In a similar vein, the Vatican maintains its 2,000 year plus Catholic prohibition denying ordination for women to become priests or bishops. Canon law states: *Only a baptized man validly receives sacred ordination.* This is stated in fidelity to Christ's original intention, claiming that masculinity was integral to the personhood of Jesus. Tibetan Buddhism takes a small boy away from his mother eliminating a matrilineal tracing as he is trained to become the next Dalai Lama. The Tibetan word for woman literally means *lesser birth, inferior of birth.* Voices silenced that might have inspired, feminine energy undervalued; women's place in the evolution of consciousness has been overshadowed.

Women are by nature more independent than men, therefore down the ages men have tried to make her dependent in other ways—economically, socially. Naturally, she is more independent, and that hurts the man and his ego. So he has tried to make her dependent in some way; artificial dependence has been created for her. Economically she has been paralyzed, she has to depend on the man. This is a consolation for the man: if he depends on her, she also depends on him. It is a compensation and a consolation. Politically, socially, she has been thrown out of society; she has been forced to stay in the home so that man can feel, 'Not only I am dependent, she is dependent on me.' This is a psychological strategy of the male ego. Otherwise, if the woman is given total freedom—economic, social, political—man will look really poor compared to her. —Osho

Women's power, strong feminine energy has been minimized, our desire for intimacy treated as an irritation, women compensating have taken power not from true feminine strength which is intuitive and carries wisdom and light, instead, imitating masculine power, controlling through the intellect which has neutralized feminine differences. Departing from the ancient vision of divine mother, goddess of supreme wisdom, women in recent times have taken on patriarchal projections. What this betrayal has done to the psyche and the planet, this silencing of the sacred feminine, has been to disassociate ourselves from the mystical voice of nature while numbing our understanding of the natural interdependence of all things. Desensitizing intuition we have disconnected ourselves from the web of life. A collective global consciousness, a new spirituality of the earth, a gateway to the light, is to serve everything. Prophets and the teachers of this new century, connected to the wholeness of life must work together to work hand in hand to bring forth the world to come.

Life itself is the feminine, the ocean of energy that feeds and rejuvenates. The spirit of women is the uncompromising fullness of feminine energy, the radiance that embodies wild raw female life force, the goddess in her depth and wisdom. It is this goddess, queen mother of the universe, fountain of light who opens the door to radiant consciousness. The passage moves from a vision of the goddess towards the heart and light of the mother connecting to the wise grandmother who provides refuge, retreat and rest. The sacred feminine knows that all life is inherently sacred and one.

Your heart is full of fertile seeds, waiting to sprout. Just as a lotus flower springs from a mite to bloom splendidly, the interaction of the cosmic breath causes the flower of the spirit to bloom and bear fruit in this world.
—Motihei Ueshiba

To recover the feminine force, that source of all life, the vast energy that feeds and rejuvenates, restores, and renews will unite heaven to earth. To develop our feminine qualities, to assist the feminine spirit affirms life. Feminine power doesn't overpower, without the aggression and assertiveness of masculine power, without asserting ourselves it carries an invisibility yet creates a harmonious connection to the wholeness of life. This non-hierarchial matrilinear egalitarian connection to energy is a woman's way of living. As Choegyal Rinpoche said about life, *First you have an intellectual understanding, then you have a taste of it, then you become it.* When rightfully honored and allowed to show itself, the core of the feminine embodies radiance, is queen of heaven and earth.

To her who, purified, would break this vicious round and breathe once more the air of heaven—greeting! —Golden Tablet found in an Orphic tomb

SPIDER WEAVING COMMUNITIES

The power of the feminine is the power of being. It is power that just is, inherent in the substance of life, present in every moment all around us. We hold it in our bodies, But our culture is to do with competition and struggle for gain and so power is only understood and responded to in terms of what it could do to us. Harm, hinder, or help us subdue others. We need to see this terrible error! All life is under the tyranny engendered by this false perception!
—Jackie Crovetto

Women's wisdom, power and competence harshly portrayed as dark, sinister, scandalous and threatening has been a disservice to the consciousness of the planet. We read about Delilah, Pandora, Mara, Kali, Eve, Clytemnestra, Mata Hari, Jezebel, Baba Yaga, Persephone, the Succubus, Lilith, Medusa, Nemesis, Odyne, Cetus, Adicia, Hecate, Sabina Spielrein along with innumerable wicked witches, step-mothers and temptresses. Often women prominent in history, like Joan of Arc, had to dress like a man to gain a hearing. Feminine power is a silent energy of connection and will be the collective spirit that helps humanity take the next step out of separation to link this world throughout the planet, cosmos and other dimensions. Women do not flourish in a masculine hierarchical world. We live more as spider weaving communities, connected inside to inner authority. We have greater ease creating community. Women carry ancient feminine wisdom, are naturally relational, are the heart of life. Feminine wisdom is intuitive, radiant, devotional, mysterious, bridging a connection to the animals, to the body, to earth and to each other.

The dark feminine is a powerful archetype, a fierce ferocious mysteriousness that carries the creative force of life. We are invited to enter that darkness, a place where light can enter, where birth and transformation are fused from the mixture of light and dark. The Kali Durga, Medusa energy, are the vitality and dynamism that most often gets medicated, resisted, shamed away. Right here in life, to allow, acknowledge, include all our aspects we find the foundation of being. Where the light enters the darkness is the force that powers, the vision, the energy that transforms.

The black Madonna has the capacity to see in the night, then to gestate and be fecund. The womb of the Divine Mother, the mysterious darkness of the

Tao, gives birth to divine light. The black Madonna is the dark matrix of this endless divine birth. The way of the feminine invites us to enter that darkness, to break gently apart in that womb, to be remade as a divine child who is happy to re-enter the dark again and again, aware that this darkness is the source itself of light, this 'divine ignorance' a constant fountain of gnosis. The Mother wants us to get to her by whatever way we choose, and each of us has a path to her. But we have to take that path with intense fervor and passion. The way of the Mother stands always open, but to walk to the end we will need every kind of courage and stamina and discrimination.
—Andrew Harvey

The sacred feminine, radiance of the heart, magnetism and light, center of who we are, lives and bears all circumstances, strengthened by each heartbreak, delighted to cherish all life celebrations. In many ancient traditions the heart sustains and nurtures not only the human body but also the entire universes in which the mind lives. *The Way of the Lover* is the way of birthing creation, of waking the inner eye, divinizing heart and mind, body and soul together. What freedom to move beyond the limitation of holding dependent our children and partner, to come to know universal mother and woman's wisdom. Holding all life as sacred, knowing the unity behind all variety, an end to exclusivity with the understanding that the rhythm of universal laws illuminate the natural flow and processes of life.

Dissolving roles and postures: mother, wife, sister, aunt, god-mother, child; stripped away, who am I? From this place the constructed walls of conditioning and habits taken down, we become who we really are in its fullest sense. Bringing our roles into the light of consciousness, placing our attention on how we limit awareness, the labels that block the door of understanding obstructs pure experience. This is the importance of women's participation: life reflects our relationships. Our way is engagement. Involvement, the organic experience of connected-ness with all growth, with the world, with nature. Every life we touch is carried in heart-wisdom to be placed into service to help mend this broken creation. The feminine extends out to embrace the well-being of community. Knowing the inherent sacredness of everything in life we birth a conscious world.

When Buddha was asked if the community of spiritual friends, good companionship is at least half of the holy life, Buddha said, *No, community is the whole of the spiritual path.* A feminine attitude, a mystical approach, is crucial for both men and women. A path of the heart means an attitude of nurturing protective receptiveness. What is distinctly feminine is the tenderness and embrace that sees everything as sacred. It's how the Gopis saw Krishna in all things, the world becoming a dance of light, how Zuleikha let everything be the name of Joseph, how Ma Ammachi, holy woman, enfolds each of us, opening, softening with each breath. To the sacred feminine, to the divine mother, all of creation is her and is precious. This vision is essential to stop us from destroying her body/nature, her children/each other. To know that our male and female nature come from the same source, and to be whole creates an inner meeting of both.

The virtues of the Direct Path—tenderness, supple sensitivity, peaceful-ness, generosity, charity towards all embodied creatures, a steady passion to serve all beings—are primarily those of the Mother aspect of the Godhead. For earth to transform into heaven cannot be realized without conscious, loving, patient, and continual cooperation with the force of the Mother.
—Andrew Harvey

BIRTHING OURSELVES

The light that shines above the heavens and above this world, the light that shines in the highest world, beyond which there are no others—that is the light that shines in human hearts. Truly, this universe has come forth from Reality. It lives and has its being in Reality. Assuredly, all is Reality.
—*Upanishads*

*A*love which is guarding the solitude of the other originates to protect our own solitude, honoring, paying attention, nurturing so that our own creative process will emerge. Each family has its personal myth, in mine we were told that we were uncreative. There was little reverence for culture or original visioning in our home. I had to put the badge of my family on the table to rebirth myself into a creative woman, to awaken inspiration, to initiate my intention toward what mattered. Daring to be attentive, to listen and ask real questions, willing to risk; all this has brought me to a teaching and a writing life. To say what I see, to write what I know. *If you want to work at your art, work at your life,* said Anton Chekhov, and both, for me, have been dedicated to truth-telling. In a personal letter Rene Daumal wrote: *Yes, Genevieve, work for others is first of all an effort for oneself.*

I have discovered that one of the most challenging illusions to dispel is the misperception, the well-known myth that we help others. We educate, teach, demystify ignorance, and then it's up to the other to initiate, to practice. By being diligent to my own inner world, there is the offering; if we want to develop our inner practice, we decide when and whether to proceed. We bring maps, tools and our life as the example; our presence. Contacting our creative impulses, gifting the world through expression we become the guardian of a sacred trust. With courage we take the journey, to bear witness, to risk and reveal the truth of our lives. No moment is insignificant or meaningless, they are each a bridge leading to our awakening while rousing the world. Monk and spiritual leader Thich Nhat Hahn following a brain aneurysm at age 88 years old continues to teach in silence, through his awakened awareness, as a presence; reminding those around him as he mindfully drinks a cup of tea, chews his food, living what he has practiced throughout his lifetime. At age 80 he was asked if he planned to retire. He remarked that *teaching is not only by talking but also by living your own life. Your life is the teaching, is the message. I'll continue to teach, if not by Dharma talks, then in my way of sitting, eating, smiling, interaction with the sangha. You don't need to talk in order to teach. You need to live your life mindfully and deeply.*

The world has a beginning that is the mother of the world. Once you've found the mother, thereby you know the child. Once you know the child, you return to keep the mother, not perishing through the body. —*Tao Te Ching*

Women throughout the ages have been creative; from telling family stories, which is beautiful, to sitting in circles where with skilled hands we designed fabrics and fashioned crafts which have been beautiful. The immature notions of romantic love, the control and attachment to the lives of sons, daughters and husbands has not always been so beautiful. Women's emotional landscape when reduced to sentiment erodes family systems and love-life. Now, it's to be creative with our own lives, giving birth to ourselves. Meeting ourselves authentically, placing our attention, which is energy, we become a vessel. The possibility to be attentive to ourselves offers moments of inner silence that become the teaching. To bring experience to our actions, to embody what we teach while being open to others and attentive to what appears we see the sacred as always present. Birthing the feminine brings a receptivity and awareness to our own interconnectedness. Developing a quality of attention, an alert stillness, helps us to become a stable presence. Caretakers for that space which is at the core of our own connection we birth the hidden into light. To be spirited, alive, is an encounter with the power of the Mother which is inherent in the substance of life itself. Present within ourself we change the world.

O Wisdom Goddess! Your essence alone is present within every life, every event. Your living power flows freely as this universe. You are expressed fully, even by the smallest movement. Wherever I go, and wherever I look, I perceive only you, my blissful Mother, radiating as pure cosmic play, Earth, water, fire, air, space, and consciousness, are simply your projected forms. There is nothing else. —Ramprasad

CHANGING REALITIES

What is the source of our first suffering? It lies in the fact that we hesitated to speak. It was born in the moment when we accumulated silent things within us. —Gaston Bachelard

We were ten empowered women, we met for meaningful conversation. Kate Millet having written *Sexual Politics,* which was named by Doubleday Publishers as one of the ten most important books of the past century, Phyllis Birkby, an architect who founded the Women's School of Architecture in New York, Alma Routsong, a.k.a. Isabel Miller, who wrote the novel *Patience and Sarah* which was staged on Broadway and recreated again as an opera at Lincoln Center, Barbara Love and Sydney Abbott who together wrote *Sappho was a Right On Woman,* Bonnie Whittingham, a fine arts painter whose work was exhibited and maintained in permanent museum collections, Myra Carter, award-winning equity actress on stage a favorite of playwright Edward Albee and cast in many of his productions, Linda Clark who lived in a Sri Chinmoy meditation community in Connecticut, and myself, a psychologist and teacher who spent years educating parents, working with children, in a therapeutic dialogue; it was an unusual empowered effective cross section.

We are women. We are a subject people who have inherited an alien culture.
—Kate Millett

We met once a week and told our stories: about our mothers, fathers, sexual abuse, schooling, surgeries, dreams, joys, disappointments, accomplishments and survival. Experiences that had not yet been verbalized, hidden, now acknowledged, recognized and named. And then it was time to give back what we received. Each of us went out to form a new group. From the original ten we each created a ten-member consciousness-raising group to become one hundred women. When we gathered in my Chelsea loft in one large circle it was remarkable to see our growth. The seed for consciousness-raising groups in New York City had been planted and the result became a powerful instrument for women to listen to other women, instead of sitting home isolated. We spoke to break the silence. We heard private thoughts lifted to universal ideas. Small intimate accounts now connected to a big universal story. And to learn to listen, to open, to become alert and actively receptive is the starting point and the healing. We were remaking, reshaping ourselves, testifying, witnessing, embracing the nightmares, shattering illusions to find the treasure that can never be destroyed. We held conferences in public school and university auditoriums on topics that the media, the public had ignored: prostitution, spousal battery, pornography, unequal hiring practices and wages, abortion, same-sex relationships, incest, child-abuse, woman-hating, trafficking, menopause, pedophilia, rape, and we accomplished the primary step towards change: breaking the deep silence. We were joined, supported and encouraged in our speak-outs and conferences by writer Andrea Dworkin, lawyer Bella Abzug, author Ti-Grace Atkinson, writer Grace Paley, writer John Stoltenberg, Poet Robin Morgan, journalist Susan Brownmiler, author Shulamith Firestone, writer Susan Griffin, professor of psychology Phyllis Chesler, lawyer Florynce Kennedy, Author Rita Mae Brown; courageous feminist spokespeople in our nearby community.

Power, however it is evolved, whatever its origins, will not be given up without a struggle. —Shulamith Firestone

We trained ourselves to think large, expanding a vision that could penetrate and break personal and social boundaries. No longer silently imprisoned in our house or body where fathers seduce/rage at us, brothers distract and compete, husbands violate the sanctity of the marriage or boyfriends date-rape photograph and intimidate. *Around the world,* says Amnesty International, *at least one in every three women has been beaten and sexually abused in her lifetime.* Violence in the home and the community devastate the lives of millions of women. Gender-based violence kills or disables more women between the ages of fifteen and fifty-four than cancer or heart attacks, and its toll on women's health far surpasses that of traffic accidents and war fatalities combined. Every 10 seconds a woman is beaten, a child is abused and a woman is raped. 86% of emergency room treatments are women seeking hospital treatment for an injury by an intimate assailant. The majority of female molestation and homicides are not from a dangerous stranger, are from a boyfriend, husband, in community, priest, family member, someone known to her. Women live in a foreign culture, we need to educate and create a safe atmosphere to heal our wounds, to design a culture based on the fostering of individuality and the uniqueness that incorporates women's values. To have a society where women have the power to name, with sexual equality to males, where there is ultimately not the predominance of *I* or *mine*, is to unite our hearts and to realize oneness.

Men who want to support women in our struggle for freedom and justice should understand that it is not terrifically important to us that they learn to cry; it is important to us that they stop the crimes of violence against us and against each other. —Andrea Dworkin

UNVEILING THE HEART

The entire universe is condensed in the body, and the entire body in the heart. Thus the heart is the nucleus of the whole universe. —Sri Ramana Maharshi

Through weaving the personal into the universal, our stories are interconnected. We proceed from the stories of our lives, to the kingdom of myth and fable, to magic and mystery, until finally there becomes more than the narrative. Bridging worlds, we join ancestors, wise ones, for these now become our teachings. Our initiation is in the heart, the spiritual center of the soul. Because the heart understands all languages, when we live in the heart its voice penetrates all barriers and differences. Within the inner heart we come to know the unity of life.

What is this precious love and laughter budding in our hearts? It is the glorious sound of a soul waking up! —Hafiz

A teaching story speaks about Hannah who traveled a great distance to visit the Rebbe for a Shabbos weekend. She had never been a particularly happy or appreciative person, often lonely, selfish and sad, yet she had always wanted to meet the great Rebbe. When she arrived Friday morning she went directly to see the Rebbe. Now the hallmark of the Rebbe's leadership was his special gift of seeing into the future.

He looked at Hannah and told her not to stay for Shabbos. Hannah was shocked, taken off guard. The Rebbe, which means teacher, looked at Hannah with sad eyes saying: I *see death surrounding you—it appears that you are destined to die this Shabbos. Best that you go to a nearby small village and die there.* Hannah's heart was broken. Can you imagine how she felt? Told she had one day to live by a great seer of the future. She slowly walked out of town. She walked many miles and eventually on the road encountered a wagon loaded with people going to join the great Rebbe for the Shabbos celebration. They were singing and having a great time. *You're going the wrong way,* they called out, *come with us for Shabbos celebration. I cannot, I have been told that I am going to die and to find a small village. Nonsense,* said the group. *If you get sick and need help be with us, don't worry about anything.* So Hannah joined the happy singing group, climbing into the wagon. Soon they stopped at a tavern and one of the group said *Friend, since you are going to die soon spend some money on buying us a drink to keep warm.* And she did. Each time someone lifted their cup to drink they turned to their benefactor, Hannah, and toasted *L'Chaim, May you live a long healthy life.* Blessing after blessing. Soon Hannah forgot to be sad, put aside what the Rebbe predicted, released her worries and concerns and began enjoying herself. Rounds of blessings poured over her. Much later that afternoon they all arrived at the Rebbe's house. When Hannah walked in the Rebbe looked and exclaimed: *what a miracle, the angel of death is gone. What a Rebbe can't do, a joyful singing community of companions can do for another. The power of L'Chaim, of blessings. So you see while a Rebbe may have merit and good things can be done in my name, when a circle of friends gather as a collective to offer blessings, this has the force, the leverage, the influence. May all be blessed to have a generous community of beloveds who praise us in the heavenly realms.* We learn when our lesson is presented in a different light, sometimes in a different form. The Rebbe pushed Hannah to face a darkness within herself, simply done, her mind, initially confused, was finally switched off. Existence expresses itself through relationships. Welcoming others as ourselves heals what isolates us in our illusion of separateness. Hannah was brought to experience interdependence. That comradeship was food for her heart, and her heart needed nourishment to become healthy.

Hafiz knows the torments and the agonies that every mind on the way to annihilation in the sun must endure. So at night in my prayers I often stop and ask a thousand angels to join in and applaud, and applaud anything, anything in this world that can bring your heart comfort. —Hafiz

Sobonfu Somé, whose name means *keeper of the rituals*, leading authority on African women's spirituality, explains that in her small village everyone works together. An American company failing to succeed at setting up a predominantly male run business in the village organized a gathering, a dialogue with the village population to learn what stood in the way of their project succeeding, what had contributed to its failure. An elder spoke out: *What do you expect when you cut our tongue out from our mouth? What do you expect when you cut our heart out from our chest? You cannot isolate a part of the community and still get things done. You have disconnected us from our tongue and our heart. Women must be part of what happens.* Respect and commitment to everyone in the community, where both men and women are welcomed into any domain, restores and revitalizes energy. Through shared interests we strengthen community. May we all together complete the journey.

It is possible that the next Buddha will not take the form of an individual. The next Buddha may take the form of a community—a community practicing understanding and loving kindness, a community practicing mindful living. This may be the most important thing we can do for the survival of the earth. —Thich Nhat Hahn

David Steindl-Rast, Benedictine monk and author when asked to identify the one thing that would change the world, replied, *If women regain their power.* We have neglected to feed the heart, to be imprinted from what is beautiful, we shifted our attention from heart to head, abdicated our natural power and blinded our hearts. Women charged with a feminist battle cry for liberation, to emancipate, brought a masculine sounding voice out into this world. Liberating our energy preceded reclaiming the emotional and spiritual life that was sacrificed. We relinquished the sacredness of our home and sexuality during those years of imitating male ambition and promiscuity, under the guise of freedom and liberation. We sacrificed our radiant heart, the source of female energy. Small mind and personal feelings reduced our ability to connect to love, diminished love to sentimental experiences sung to the top ten on a hit parade. Recognizing the wounding, forfeiting our deeper nature we lost access to our connection to the love that comes from within. Instead we got a mirror ruthlessly held up to the mask. This world is saturated with divinity. The awareness of our interconnectedness is our natural resource. Women, the heartbeat of this earth, bring a natural connection to sacred energy.

Women know intuitively the mysteries of creation, of how form is birthed from formlessness and flows back into the eternal. Women have the potential to live this wisdom consciously, for their own sake and the sake of the whole. In doing so, they can help awaken a sacredness here, reveal the presence of a divine here in this world. It is time to come down from the mountains to bring the beautiful clarity, the vastness of the sky, deep into the valleys where life is waiting. The clear and icy wind of the mountaintops is still with us. But if it descends, the earth will warm this wind, and the wind will refresh the land. —*Angela Fischer*

Claiming power in powerless situations includes a dialogue as well as developing an inner core of confidence and well-being. We know the rhythms of nature through our bodies, from the heart of the earth we have learned how life comes and goes. Our knowing is buried deep within the whole process of creation. Intuitively we know, and we have the possibility of offering that to the world, of enlivening this world with a new consciousness, that of inclusion and wholeness. This link has been interrupted with the disenfranchisement of women and now the flow of energy throughout this planet is congested. We are informed of suffering and violence through newspapers, magazines, TV images and the internet. Whatever affects the world affects us all. Feminine power is a collective memory of a nature that cultivates life, and having been cut off from our nature with centuries of violence that is what must be retrieved, renewed, reconnected and recharged. Can we turn towards this new state of inter-blending where both the masculine and the feminine live in equanimity? Birthing this vision will transform the evolution of human consciousness. What is needed is an empowerment that liberates and uplifts the heart, connecting us to universal mind which is the beloved. Universal mind removes the blinders of personal sentiment bridging our alliance with all humanity.

The Divine has no body now on earth but yours, no hands but yours, no feet but yours, yours are the eyes through which to look out seeing the divine's compassion to the world; yours are the feet with which the divine is to go about doing good, yours are the hands with which the divine is to bless all beings now. —*Teresa of Avila*

MYSTERY OF THE SACRED FEMININE

The bad news is that you are falling through the air, there is nothing to hang onto and you have no parachute. The good news is that there is no ground.
—*Chogyam Trungpa Rinpoche*

*T*he sacred feminine, mirroring the rhythm of the universe, unlocks secrets of universal laws. Through opening to a feminine understanding of receptivity, intuition and wonder as well as to the wild, charging, lawless, turbulent Kali energy we enter a woman's way of wisdom. Living into our wholeness daring to step into the unknowable, to claim our power, our naturalness the passion that is the force to move us is essential to birth the illumined heart called feminine consciousness. The initiation and transformation will come through the poetry and song of our life. Love, not reason, becomes the evidence and women know this, through experiencing we absorb life. The dancer becomes the dance. Taking risks: pick a practice that penetrates us, a practice to live intentionally, mindfully, to live within the wholeness, the mystical in ourselves. The mystics, both male and female, embrace the feminine spirit. This journey of risk asks us to open and meet ourselves in the fire of love. The radiance of the feminine, unresisted, brings the masculine to his knees, finally stopping the mind. The intellect becomes empty. This inner power of the feminine lies in the heart of mystical imagination, and is expressed through embracing the oneness within our differences. Ramakrishna tells a story of the Mother cooking the whole fish of awareness in the many ways that suited the tastes of her children. Some prefer it sweet, some spicy, others without condiments and raw, a few like it with ginger sauce, possibly a little salsa, others with curry. Yet everyone is eating the same fish. The feminine has room for differences, all the children are eating the same fish, just with different tastes. This is the vision of the banquet at the feast of life, expansive and spacious, embracing all.

To dare to look, to find that center that remains still and from that place to watch the constant movement of life, to what is here, what lives on earth, to our humanity, is the important missing part in psychology, and the link that creates the crossover or bridge to the new *Sacred Psychology*. For there to be transformation we begin with ourselves. The enlivened core of the mystical feminine is delight, celebration, song, laughter, dancing pure energy, surrender; like the ocean; immense, ever changing, beautiful, anarchic, fierce, full of life, the source of life. An ocean that is already full with sea life, and still we are invited to enter. The history of psychology in the last century has been nearly devoid of this, has excluded the mystical, the spiritual element from its daily practice. When we use everything that inspires us, see life as art, sing our own inner song, dance the dance of life, this quality of participation leads to the storehouse of the treasure.

I am happy even before I have a reason. I am full of Light even before the sky can greet the sun or the moon. Dear companions, we have been in love with God for so very, very long. What can Hafiz now do but Forever Dance!
—*Hafiz*

To become co-creators, partners entering the mysterious, anointing the miraculous, this life as poetry and music is the mystical journey. So within reach, as close as our breath. Attachment to our suffering, not seeing that the other side of pain is pleasure, makes us heavy; we walk with one foot in pain, one foot in pleasure, one foot in hell, one foot on earth. Life may be serious and still not heavy. Here is a vision where our feet step out heaven, to leap free of ourself, both feet land in absolute love. A heart that breaks, rather than defends becomes strengthened. To yield, to be a simple open presence, love is always ready to respond, then we become tender. Joy and sorrow become one, we can have pain without unnecessary personal suffering. Freedom is knowing when this is not my pain, my suffering, my thought; once developing compassion, we see this as the pain, the thought, a collective consciousness shared by all who walk through life, deepening our connection to all people. Life happens through us—we are a door, a vehicle.

The great Persian poet Hafiz, in a generous compassionate statement, spoke what I consider the essence of *The Fifth Way, The Way of the Lover*: *Dear, they have dropped the knife. They have dropped the cruel knife most so often use upon their tender self and others...I have found the power to say no to any actions that might harm myself or another.* Not to go towards heartache, nor to move away. The treasure lies in being still and present. Once one with love we will radiate true peace.

For only in praising is my heart still mine. —Rainer Maria Rilke

The Feminine Force Of Life

Every human being with whom we seek relatedness is a koan, that is to say, an impossibility. —Bernard Phillips.

Koans are riddles to be approached not from the conceptual mind, instead, from a wider intuitive knowing. A feminine way of knowing, freed from the linear, constructs how to bring the sacred to the here and now. Ripening, our creative energies emerge. Love blooms from a mysterious unknown place deep within, opening to find the treasure is finding our heart where the treasure has been hidden. Art lives in the heart where invisible forces inform. The ways of women embrace life. We are the mystery of beautiful scents, of lavender and rose. We hear the song of the wind and birds, the dance of the trees and seasons, the laughter of the children and the out-breath of those who are terminal. Feminine power is like a storm moving across the ocean, where the wind knows the rhythm and makes its course and still remains in unity with all of life, aware of its preciousness. This radiance of light, life-sustaining, reflects the fullness, the community of this world. All is miraculous to the feminine: the taste of an apple, the color of the sky, the sound of the birds wings flapping. The universe is the mother, as is the moon and ocean and earth. All is here in life to celebrate, to enjoy.

Our male patriarchal culture has defined women and distorted, concealed, oppressed our nature. The feminine is about absorbency and nurturance, receptivity, radiance, creativity, fierceness, melting and softness; the heart of a lamb as well as a lion. Birthing this spirit will bring civilization to a renaissance. The feminine lives in the language of garden, storm and ocean, volcanoes and hurricanes, sweet chocolate and prima ballerina, a world filled with beauty and energy, we are that energy that creates the waves, flowers and rejuvenates; the feminine is a force of life. Since we have no direct memory of a woman-centered language we will have to invent ourselves, renew our scarred self-image, contact our inner power and affirm our lives.

The feminine is the force of life. There is never a shortage of feminine energy, only a resistance to receiving, trusting, and embracing it. —David Deida

I lived with a creative and productive artist, each day began in front of an easel, painting. I marveled at the possibility of having a work that was self-contained, inspired, creative, inner-directed, personal, self-reflective. Giving birth to this book is a woman's way of healing; to work with what we have been given. The truth of creation is to create ourselves, making room inside for something new, a seed to grow; birth and rebirth. This is a woman's essence. Between birth and death is all of life. A woman's body is designed to give up, to die and to give birth to the new. Psychologically, this effects all of humanity. The masculine, learning the difference between action and activity, experiences the need to be released from constraints, likes challenge. Men, identified with thought, relax into strengthened intelligence. When the masculine, directive and forceful, embraces the death of ego, life will begin. The sacred feminine, with her mystical vision knows achievements can be continuously experienced, standing in front of the ocean, looking at a sunset, dancing, hiking in the forest, writing a poem, painting a canvas; out of this inspiration emerges creativity, sustains life.

The people I love the best jump into work head first without dallying in the shallows and swim off with sure strokes almost out of sight...I love people who harness themselves, an ox to a heavy cart, who pull like water buffalo, with massive patience, who strain in the mud and the muck to move things forward, who do what has to be done, again and again. I want to be with people who submerge in the task, who go into the fields to harvest and work in a row and pass the bags along...The work of the world is common as mud...The thing worth doing well done has a shape that satisfies, clean and evident. The pitcher cries for water to carry and a person for work that is real. —Marge Piercy

Conscious Love

There is no necessary relation between love and children; but there is a necessary relation between love and creation. The aim of conscious love is to bring about rebirth. —A.R. Orage

Love is the reason for creation. We are in this world because of love. There is male energy—Shiva, the masculine principle; penetrating, all-pervading, challenged, present. There is female energy—Shakti, the feminine principle; receptive, radiant, beautiful, praiseworthy, oceanic. The feminine seeks fullness and love. An open heart in surrender recognizes the limitlessness of love. The masculine, wanting to be released from constraints and to experience freedom lives at the edge challenged by purpose and mission. Understanding, honoring and celebrating the diversity, both are responsible to gift, serve, embrace the world, to risk everything. To live in this way is to have a feminine reverence for life and a masculine consciousness aligned to a life with purpose birthing her or his own true self. This prepares the ground to live as the ultimate freedom in the vertical dimension of love where everything is possible. *The Way of the Lover* addresses woundedness, speaks to the leader in each of us, not the imitator. When that wound is acknowledged, made visible, it becomes a reliable source of spiritual power.

Be like a lion outside but like a flower within. Let us strive to reach a state in which we are able to see all beings on earth as part of our own Self.
—Amma, the Mother of bliss

CHAPTER SIX

The Fifth Way

Man remains a mystery transmitted, is taught by someone who has tasted, experienced himself. He has a nostalgia for Being, a longing for duration, for permanence, for absoluteness—a longing to be. Yet everything that constitutes his life is temporary, ephemeral, limited. He aspires to another order, another life, a world that is beyond him. He senses that he is meant to participate in it. He searches for an idea, an inspiration, that could move him in this direction, It arises as a question: Who am I—who am I in this world? If this question becomes sufficiently alive, it could direct the course of his life. He cannot answer. He has nothing with which to answer—no knowledge of himself to face this question, no knowledge of his own. But he feels he must welcome it. He asks himself what he is. This is the first step on the way. He wants to open his eyes. He wants to wake up, to awaken. —Jeanne de Salzmann

To know how to be mercilessly sincere with ourselves, then to ask ourselves 'what am I', not expecting a comforting reply, nor to ask 'what does that mean' since that shows that we haven't asked much of ourselves. People pay so little attention to themselves in the sense of self-knowledge. With dull complacency they shut their eyes to what they really are and spend their lives in the pleasant conviction that they represent something valuable. Who is this 'I'? Who is 'myself'? Socrates words 'know thyself' remain for all those who seek true knowledge and being. —G.I. Gurdjieff

Wherever you are and in whatever circumstance, try always to be a lover and a passionate lover. Once you have possessed love, you will remain a lover, forever. To be born in love is to serve all beings and all creation. Real lovers serve ardently, hopefully, and in an ecstasy of awe. Look for the happiness of the servant of love—all the joys of the world are nothing to that. —Rumi

A man meets his life most poignantly in moments of painful contraction and expansion. At those moments he senses the difference between being present and being taken. If he keeps himself open to the question, he will move in what he believes is a fruitful direction. At that moment a door opens. He may or may not go further; the chances are that the pull of gravity will close the door. He will be shut away from his ever-present possibility. Back to the office and workplace, to vacations, to family, to having a good/bad time, getting and spending. The door may never open again—or will it?
—William Segal

Right questions, right problems are those that refer to being and change of being, how to find the weak sides of our being and how to fight against them. We must understand that, before acquiring new knowledge, we must realize our limitations and the fact that our limitations are really limitations of our being. Our knowledge remains on the same level. It grows in a certain direction, but this growth is very limited. We must see what a restricted field we live in, always deceiving ourselves, always imagining things to be different from what they are. We think it is very easy to change something, but it is only when we sincerely try that we realize how difficult, how almost impossible it is. The idea of change of being is the most important idea of all. Theories, systems, diagrams are only a help; they help concentration and right thinking, but there can be only one real aim, and that is to change our being, for if we want to change something in our own understanding of the world, we must change something in ourselves. —P.D. Ouspensky

LIFE IS REAL ONLY
WHEN I AM

*A*remarkable man, G.I. Gurdjieff made the ordinary extraordinary. He has been described as magician, scoundrel, philosopher, master, sly man, spiritual teacher, rascal, prophet, hypnotist, fate-changer, iron-like, mystic, clairvoyant, the devil, remarkable, resourceful, gentle, an impressive figure. One can imagine the stories and sagas that accompany each attribute. Pay attention to the wit and teaching flavor of the following tales. After a gentleman joined Gurdjieff and students for lunch one of the students commented on the *nice* man who had joined them. Gurdjieff responded: *Nice man, because everyone at the table was asleep. If you press on one of his corns, then you see what kind of man he really is.* Another time, in a conversation in which a student asked for a task to begin work on himself, Gurdjieff's reply was: *You want to be a successful and useful man. Since you ask I will tell. When you go to the lavatory, always remember pull plug.*

On a visit to the Ouspensky estate at Mendham, New Jersey, Franklin Farms, Gurdjieff entered the stately hall and seeing the well-dressed people, the ones that were considered important in Ouspensy's community, sitting there around the banquet table Gurdjieff requested to see the people who were behind the scenes, the day laborers, the ones creating the food: *Who is in the kitchen? Bring out the people who are in the kitchen doing the work.* Gurdjieff's presence here on earth was to awaken humanity. The priceless gifts he left as a teaching were what he named *the work, self-remembering, the Enneagram, the Fourth Way, the movements,* and *the search.* The work worthy of human effort is to

234

remember yourself. All and everything becomes the work when we do it with attention, are creative, see it as a challenge, are playful using it as opportunity; then it becomes the only work there is. The search itself is transforming, not as a search for transformation but in paying attention to the journey and our encounter with ourself as the teaching.

The sole means now for the saving of the beings of the planet Earth would be to implant again into their presences a new organ... of such properties that every one of these unfortunates during the process of existence should constantly sense and be cognisant of the inevitability of his own death as well as the death of everyone upon whom his eyes or attention rests. Only such a sensation and such a cognizance can now destroy the egoism completely crystallized in them.
—*G.I. Gurdjieff*

One of the most enigmatic teachers of this time, Gurdjieff devoted his life to developing a system, a methodology for the possible evolution of consciousness to liberate humanity from the state of walking sleep in which he claimed that most of us live. Part of a group called *Seekers of the Truth,* his quest was to find the hidden knowledge, the sacred teachings that could awaken humanity. For this purpose he traveled throughout the world, to spiritual communities, monasteries, Sufi orders and ruins of ancient civilizations. He established the *Institute for the Harmonious Development of Man* at the Chateau du Prieure in Fontainebleau-Avon, France, a training establishment to restore the energy that Western civilization was being crushed under, the activity Gurdjieff called *modern life.* His design was to heal humanity through a total reform of the self. This was a teaching that was not to become a religion or a philosophy, it was intended as a practical teaching to be lived, a teaching that questioned the entire outlook of the life of man on this earth. His intention was to make esoteric knowledge usable and sensible, experiential, for everyday living, setting forth a heroic task. To awaken higher intelligence, to come to our fullest potential, full consciousness, he presented a world view of a universe that has purpose and stated that with extraordinary efforts we will awaken to serve that purpose.

To be in a room with others where keeping a question alive is more important than thinking one has the answer. —G.I. Gurdjieff

Waking up is a daily process, first we learn what it is to pay attention, which is alert stillness, to be present, all the while recognizing the forces that have kept us asleep. *Awakening begins,* said Gurdjieff *when a person realizes that they are going nowhere and they do not know where to go.* Creating individual conditions for each student, teaching through presence, he knew how to open the door to the hidden. Gurdjieff had a relationship with his own inner world that was so strong that it emanated, reached out and touched others.

One's own presence is the ultimate mysticism. —Robert Burton

Prior to his death in 1949 Gurdjieff entrusted the rights to his writings, music and dance exercises called *the movements* to his pupil Jeanne de Salzmann. *Live to be over 100,* he instructed De Salzmann, aware of the monumental responsibility he was asking: that of bringing his work to the world. *I charge you with doing everything possible—even impossible, in order that what I brought will have an action. Publish the writings as and when you are sure that the time has come.* De Salzmann's first meeting with Gurdjieff made a profound impact on her and she wrote about it: *The presence of Gurdjieff, and especially his penetrating look, made an extraordinary impression. You felt that you were truly seen, exposed by a vision that left nothing in shadow, and at the same time you were not judged or condemned. A relationship was immediately established which removed all fear and at the same time brought you face to face with your own reality.*

Using the next 40 years to establish his teachings, Mme. de Salzmann created Gurdjieff centers in New York, Paris, London and Venezuela, had his books published, produced films of the movements including the Peter Brook movie *Meetings with Remarkable Men*. She guided, led, brought life to the teachings, her reflections, questions and devotion to truth offered the possibility to breathe life into a dynamic journey of self-knowing for numerous people throughout the world. She died at the age of 101 in 1990, a radiant light of the feminine, paying attention to the extraordinary teachings that she transmitted. Not designating teachers, she wrote: *this is a way of understanding, not of faith or obedience to a charismatic leader; the teaching is the guide, and only he who questions more deeply can be responsible to serve.* Jeanne de Salzmann realized within herself the essence of the teaching, and like Gurdjieff was the source that reflected it, teaching through her presence. She was a voice that embodied higher influences and that infused a sacred work. For forty years she continuously wrote, and at ninety-one she commented *I am writing a book on how to be in life.* Reflecting on the reality of being, her writings provided a forty year account of her life's work, written thoughts that she often brought to her meetings. The book, based on her notebooks, *The Reality of Being*, edited and prepared after her death and later published in 2010 is an expression of one who knows. She said: *I am writing a book on how to be in life, on the path to take in order to live on two levels. It will show how to find a balance, to go from one to the other, or rather to find the way in between. We have to see beyond and through our ordinary thinking in order to open to another mind. Otherwise, we remain at the threshold in front of the door, and the door does not open.*

Gurdjieff and Mme. de Salzmann prepared the way towards greater awareness and a deeper relationship with the inner world. They both demanded sincerity from themselves as well as from others. Socrates words *know thyself* were the root and essential core that produced their dictum *verify everything*, understanding that our state of being is key to self-knowledge and change. *Who am I? Life is real only when I am*, resounds and resounds; for both Gurdjieff and De Salzmann life was lived as the real.

I cannot develop you; I can create conditions in which you can develop yourself. —G.I. Gurdjieff

Help us always and everywhere to be able to remember ourselves at all times in order that we may avoid involuntary actions. —the last words pronounced over Gurdjieff's coffin

To Become A Real Person

This moment is a meditation. Just as, on the other hand, one can be sitting in a monastery in a formal position, and there will be no meditation. —William Segal

The influence of Gurdjieff currently continues. The Enneagram was unknown in the West until he introduced it as a way to pictorially symbolize many of the objective laws of cosmology intrinsic to his system. A universal symbol, *all knowledge can be included in the Enneagram and with the help of the Enneagram it can be interpreted*, taught Gurdjieff. As a template it can be used and translated in different ways, essentially what we bring to it determines our understanding of it. The Enneagram which has since become popularized are teachings about the personality, the conditioned self and the spiritual; the what that is beyond our conditioned self. As a map, grounded in both our true nature, our essence and our individual consciousness, it offers a profound possibility for inquiry into the process and patterns of awakening.

The Enneagram symbol introduced by Gurdjieff near the turn of the century has captivated minds for generations. It is a masterpiece of symbolic art. He integrates all that we can gain from looking within with all that we can gain from seeing far into the world 'out there.' Without the knowing of oneself in the moment, one's understanding is incomplete and misleading. Gurdjieff pictured two intelligent strangers meeting in the wilderness and squatting down to draw Enneagram symbols in the sand to compare their understanding. These diagrams will soon be erased, just as in the sand-painting traditions. The Enneagram is to be used to enable us to communicate in understanding. It is in the flow of meaning between people—or dia-logue—that the Enneagram comes to life. The Enneagram is not just a model for what we do or study, but an intent. It is a stubborn human cry of desire for meaning. —A.G.E. Blake

Verify everything, Gurdjieff's consistent statement asks us to believe nothing that we are not able to verify ourself since understanding grows through self-observation, through our own experience. The probability of being seduced by our own ego stands in the way of our experiencing the true teacher, which is life. Foremost then is learning how to learn, how not to be guarded and tricky and mechanical towards the moment-by-moment offerings that life brings.

If life is the teacher, then there are a lot of bad students. —Georg Feuerstein.

In a recent book *Search for Truth*, Hugh Brockwill Ripman, First Secretary to the British Embassy in Washington, describes the impact his initial meeting with Gurdjieff created for him: *Then Gurdjieff came in—and instead of there being seventy-one people in the room, there was one man and seventy two-dimensional figures. This was a man whom one could never forget.* William Segal, artist, publisher, student of Gurdjieff, in an interview at age 96 remarked: *Gurdjieff was too big to teach you directly. You had to watch him. So I watched. I saw in the way he walked, the way he handled people, the way he helped them. He kept his cool, as it were. The mystery we must all take into consideration lies in the moment that trans-forms everything. If we're able to evoke this silence, it would be the clear sign of the presence of a master—not a master in the formal sense, but in our ability to change things around us, to do without doing. The great masters are able both to evoke this mysterious opening to the new energy and sustain it. Gurdjieff could do it. There would be silence in those moments with him where we would possess a much greater attention. The Japanese express this as satori. The call coming from a true master is so strong that it reverberates over the ages, and is able to attract people after the master himself is gone. The teaching is fortified, not by the will of the master, but by the energy with which he imbues everything he says and touches. The aim of the master is to link heaven and earth.*

To truly live the teachings without clinging to them, to awaken to the truth of the human condition, for our life to be a work of love, this then is the practice—to become a real person. To live established in a practice, placing our attention in front of us, in the immediate present, on each moment, brings us to a clarity of the heart. There are no useless moments, presence is our anchor. The cosmos is regulated by universal laws and since the universe is also within us, through cultivating spaciousness or awareness we allow for our humanity to come forth. This recognition, once we put our personal commentary aside, opens us to the dynamic nature of our own being. The real work, to create a human being of ourself happens deep down inside. The true nature of our mind is as a natural clarity of awareness, becoming aware of our awareness, of placing attention without tension, we become easy effortless watchfulness.

Nothing stays still or remains the same. Nothing lasts forever or ends com-pletely. All that lives evolves or declines in an endless movement of energy. The laws underlying this universal process were known to ancient science, which assigned man his proper place in the cosmic order. —*Jeanne de Salzmann*

Many students who have left Fourth Way Schools have stated that: *One of the greatest things that happened to me after finding the School was leaving it.* The very decision to leave is a valuable aspect, an initiation itself. An esoteric school is not based on authority nor on the demand of a teacher for recognition and obedience. The only authority to recognize is that of truth itself, intuitively perceived and then subjected to the mental analysis and interpretation of each individual. Gurdjieff knew this and set up circumstances that would foster his students to not become followers, to move on rather than hold on. He liberated the power and force of individuality. The teaching in its deepest meaning is to awaken the power of conscience in a human being, not morality in the social sense of convention. There are fundamental laws of conscience which are the same in each culture throughout the world. It is a universal view of an organic conscious universe that has purpose. It is only when we realize that life is taking us nowhere that it begins to have meaning.

The question for a human being that's the most absorbing one is, who are we? Napoleon said something very interesting when Goethe walked into the room, Ah, voila un homme! He didn't say he was a strong person, a beautiful person, a rich person or a talented person. He said Voila un homme! This is the specificity again; when you see someone like Gurdjieff, or Madame de Salzmann you say, This is a person! This is a quality that accompanies consciousness, this is the fruit that I hope will arise from Gurdjieff's original appearance in the West. —*William Segal*

PRACTICAL TIPS FOR INNER FREEDOM

*I*nscribed in a special script above the walls of the Study House at the Prieure were the following aphorisms:

1. Remember yourself always and everywhere.
2. Remember you come here having already understood the necessity of struggling with yourself—only with yourself. Therefore thank everyone who gives you the opportunity.
3. Here we can only direct and create conditions, but not help.
4. Like what *it* does not like.
5. The highest that a man can attain is to be able to do.
6. Know that this House can be useful only to those who have recognized their nothingness and who believe in the possibility of changing.
7. The chief means of happiness in this life is the ability to consider externally always, internally never.
8. I love him who loves work.
9. Only conscious suffering has any sense.
10. Practice love first on animals, they are more sensitive.
11. By teaching others you will learn yourself.
12. Remember that here work is not for work's sake but is only a means.
13. Blessed is he who has a soul, blessed is he who has none, but woe and grief to him who has it in embryo.
14. Rest comes not from quantity but from the quality of sleep.
15. Sleep little without regret.
16. The energy spent on active inner work is then and there trans-

formed into a fresh supply, but that spent on passive work is lost forever.

17. One of the best means for arousing the wish to work on yourself is to realize that you may die at any moment. But first you must learn how to keep it in mind.

18. Conscious love evokes the same in response. Emotional love evokes the opposite. Physical love depends on type and polarity.

19. Conscious faith is freedom. Emotional faith is slavery. Mechanical faith is foolishness.

20. Hope, when bold, is strength. Hope, with doubt, is cowardice. Hope, with fear, is weakness.

21. Man is given a definite number of experiences - economizing them, he prolongs his life.

22. Here there are neither Russians nor English, Jews nor Christians, but only those who pursue one aim—to be able to be.

23. Take the understanding of the East and the knowledge of the West—and then seek.

—G.I. Gurdjieff

Conversations were filled with teachings and Gurdjieff's words informed and spoke to fundamental and essential questions:

What do I teach? I teach people how to listen to themselves- ...I cannot develop you; I can create conditions in which you can develop yourself, be continuously reminded of the sense and aim of your existence by an unavoidable friction between your conscience and the automatic manifes-

tations of your nature.....To go for the pocketbook nerve or the sex nerve is to take a short cut to a person's psychology. Man never on any account wants to pay for anything; and above all he does not want to pay for what is most important for him. You now know that everything must be paid for and that it must be paid for in proportion to what is received. But usually a man thinks to the contrary. For trifles, for things that are perfectly useless to him, he will pay anything. But for something important, never. This must come to him of itself. Nothing shows up people so much as their attitude toward money..... Cannot be understanding between rich and poor, because rich and poor, both, only understand money. One does not understand life without money and hate people who have money. This woman now hate self because guilty about being rich. Poor man hate self—or sometimes just life—because feel guilty about not having money or feel cheated by world. With such unreal, false attitude, impossible any serious thing like my work. Even when people give money still almost always impossible for them to learn anything. Already, they think of reward. Now I owe them something because they give me money. When think of reward in this way, impossible learn anything from me.....I teach, that when it rains, the pavements get wet.....In order to free ourself from hypnotic sleep it is necessary, above all, to know it and see it. This is an effort involving conscious and lucid presence of the whole being: thought, feeling, perception, sensation of self, all simultaneously.....The first task, the first exercise, due to the constant lying to oneself, and our own inability to be sincere, is to learn to be sincere and honest in relation to ourself, otherwise everything is only lies, imagination and fantasy. People who *have an inner searching, have a general unified rhythm, an economy of movement and tone of voice. There are not unnecessary words or movements. Everything is connected. Conscious attention prepares for real thought. Do not believe what I tell you, but experience it for yourselves.....*A story Gurdjieff related one evening: *A certain people eating snake wished to take vows and become a monk, agreed to stop killing and attacking. One year later the monk passed by and saw the snake covered in wounds. The snake said he had kept his promise, the vows and now people would throw stones at him. 'I see,' said the monk, yes, you were told not to attack, but you were not forbidden to hiss!' Learn to play the role suited to each situation, objectively and clearly, while being free inside and open to the other people.....The fundamental striving of every man should be to create for himself an inner freedom towards life and to prepare for himself a happy old age. A considerable percentage of the people we meet on the street are empty inside, that is, they are actually already dead. Lucky we don't see and know it, if we knew how many of these dead people govern our live, we should go mad with horror......We attain knowledge with the help of those who possess it. One learns from one who knows.*

William Segal commenting on Gurdjieff wrote: *What makes a man is his ability to question himself. And when someone at Mr. Gurdjieff's table really did that in front of him, you would see him smile with a special kindness emanating from him, because an authentic question had arisen. This is what sustained him the most.*

Gurdjieff's influence in mainstream thought carries across multiple disciplines. *Self-observation,* the *observer,* as well as our western use of bowls, bells, sound and movement have been penetrated by his teachings. Masters of wisdom possess the power to record teachings using sacred artifacts which resonate as others come in contact with those artifacts. A pioneer, whose ideas echo through today's wisdom teachings; *raising a new awareness of what it is to breathe, move, think and pay attention, to experience something of the zen-like quality of ordinary life two inches off the ground, bringing into question the most ordinary and everyday things we take for granted, based on the living action of deep enquiry,* wrote Anthony Blake. Pay attention, listen, work together, know differences, build substance; such simple yet deep and meaningful reliable ways to promote presence. To inhabit life we must be clothed by our life, has been the force, the reminder, the invitation into a world that continues through our self-awareness, love and understanding.

Gurdjieff died in Paris in 1949. Words pronounced over his coffin were: *Help us always and everywhere to be able to remember ourselves at all times in order that we may avoid involuntary actions.*

THE FIVE WAYS

It's up to us to see what comes out of this deeper relationship with our inner world. The rigor of the Work is to be continuously listening, listening to another vibration while going about one's everyday activities. It's the capacity to encompass the inner world. All the practices eventually lead one to the brink where you leap over the precipice and you make your own discovery. Eventually the teacher is in one's self. —William Segal

While there are many paths to consciousness, they all lead to one of the five Ways: the Way of the Fakir, the Way of the Monk, the Way of the Yogi, the Way of the Sly Man or The Fourth Way, and The Way of the Lover or The Fifth Way. Each Way offers the possibility of consciousness through complete awakening. The fakir focuses on awakening the instinctive center through developing mastery over the physical body. Using discipline he/she achieves control over the instinctive senses. Lying on nails, walking on fire, standing motionless in one position for days, all this is in the effort to develop will in the physical body. The monk attains mastery of emotions through prayer, devotion, sacrifice, religious feelings, faith, through rising above life's desires. Along this Way of faith and concentration of feeling the monk subjects all other emotions to one emotion, faith, to develop will in the emotional body. The yogi brings mental attention to an intellectual path of knowledge to gain control over the mind. Along this Way of knowledge the yogi develops the mind and will in the intellectual body. Each of these three Ways requires withdrawal from the world, from day-to-day life. It has been generally accepted that to be on one of these paths entails a renunciation of the world and a commitment to a regulated type of living. The Fourth Way, that of the Sly Man, rooted in the Gurdjieff tradition, is a system to develop all the bodies or centers simultaneously and has claimed to be more efficient and accelerated. *The sly man knows the secret,* said Gurdjieff, *and with its help outstrips the fakir, the monk, and the yogi.* The work on this Way includes balancing the instincts and senses, mastering emotions and developing the intellect. Effort is made in all three centers; body, feeling and mind. Essentially, Gurdjieff's work was, and remains, in the tradition of a Fourth Way School.

The real work is to create integral human beings, to create wakefulness. The real work will simply disappear from the world's eyes. I am creating a mystery school—such schools existed when Zarathustra was alive, they existed in Egypt, India, Tibet. Pythagoras noted the fact of mystery schools. Jesus was trained by the Essenes, a very secret mystery school. All that is beautiful and all that is great in human history has happened only through a few people who put their energies together for the inner exploration. It is the greatest adventure there is, and the greatest dance too. —*Osho*

What becomes problematic is that history has shown Fourth Way Schools and teachers to involute, to separate from society, to withdraw from the world, to create separation, and that becomes antithetical to awakening. Their belief system has been that their ideas can't be communicated outside the conditions and activities of a Gurdjieff school. Fourth Way schools remain contained, sequestered, having little broad impact on today's spiritual communities. Even the books are now relatively unpopular and difficult to find. Students often remain cloistered, unapproachable, giving little back to the world, draped in the illusion of their uniqueness and self-importance, fostering separation; missing the essence of spiritual work, which speaks to connection, to breaking the dream of separation, to create a flow of love, compassion and generosity.

The Fifth Way, The Way of the Lover, is a way of understanding, and understanding is rooted from within, grows out of us, comes through our opened heart, is based on our state of presence, liberating and transforming life. To learn the art of love, to become a lover, to show up as presence, training and practice is essential. We show up in the world according to our level of understanding. The Fifth Way, awakening to our own presence, is a training, a loving teaching and the foundation of my work. —*Dr. Paula Bromberg*

The Fifth Way, The Way of the Lover, dissolves separation. Our relationship to everything is always taking place. To be a friend to our inner life while in relationship to our everyday activity leads us to realize that contact with the sacred can happen in any setting or activity. Our daily personal encounters are both mundane and mystical. Relationships become the food and sustenance, the meditation and the practice. Without a distinction between above and below, seeing everything that appears in our life as sacred is to be here in our fullness, in our celebration of this life. If the essence of life is the expression of beauty then we all become artists.

Doing selfless and loving actions brings you to the door that leads to the realm of the Self. It is through such actions that you gain entry into that world. We are not isolated islands. We are joined to one another like the links of a chain. —Amma

THE FIFTH WAY
THE WAY OF THE LOVER

Our loving is the way Existence's secret gets told! —Rumi

The Fifth Way, The Way of the Lover, my design and creation, explored and expressed throughout this book, standing on the shoulders of the first four Ways, is a Way of understanding, is about our relationships, is a path of love leading through mindful self-awareness to awakening. Walking along the path of the heart, *Sacred Psychology* is the teaching, the entrance way to union with the creative feminine that awakens us to our sweetest dance, to universal playfulness. It incorporates the mystical consciousness of the sacred feminine, the unknowable. Life must be directly experienced, digested, to be understood. Spiritual conversation, a psychological tool, assists in removing the burden of the personal story to break the continuity of the narrative, of past and future, for us to awaken to live a conscious life. Stories released we become storyless. Along *the Fifth Way*, ordinary life provides the lessons within the adventure of living. Our daily conditions are a reflection, teachings on how to love, how to live in a way where there is no inward violence, a way that has inner stability, that is not touched by outward circumstances. Community becomes everyone, no longer is exclusivity a value, all beings are aspects of our own true self. Embodying esoteric traditions and the extracted essence of many teachings and paths, *The Way of the Lover* blesses human transformation to reveal truth in a practical manner. This teaching elevates the essential, not deadening into a formal structure, a reminder that we come alive through our presence.

The present moment is the point of escape from the three dimensional prison of space and time. —*Rodney Collin*

The Fifth Way is kind, offering tools, many included in this book, to serve our journey along our path. Ramakrishna said he walked in this world as if with a broken arm walking amongst a crowd. Maps and tools assist the challenge to not react, to remain balanced, regardless. Its the intelligence behind the attention that brings substance. The impulse to work, while maintaining our individuality is what is fostered, treated with great care and tenderness. To dismantle our story, to choose tools that sharpen our eyes and ears, that open clarity and objectivity to the mind, frees energy *to be in the world and not of it.* Part 1 of this book teaches us to use our own biography, unraveled and digested, to sit at the feet of our own life, to become conscious of our stories and how they have shaped and molded us, as well as to know who we are beneath our stories. And then to see the visible manifestations of the invisible, to bring that presence into the world of form, the world of here and now. Part 2 sets forth the systems, provides maps and guidelines, upholding them as objective, neutral tools to arrive at essence, to mature essence, to awaken.

Hafiz describes and invites us along the journey: *What is this precious love and laughter, budding in our hearts? It is the glorious sound of a soul waking up! The subject tonight is Love and for tomorrow night as well. As a matter of fact, I know of no better topic for us to discuss until we all die! Come this way.*

SCHOOLS FOR SELF-INQUIRY

Wanting to reform the world without discovering one's true self is like trying to cover the world with leather to avoid the pain of walking on stones and thorns. It is much simpler to wear shoes. —Ramana Maharshi

Life is a school and we are both the students as well as its teachers. Traces of schools on earth with higher influence pass through our magnetic center. Most people do not recognize the esoteric teaching that is inherent within the conditions of life. Ordinary life has conditions, and these conditions our ourself. Through understanding choices are born and the circumstances to develop are everywhere when our intention is to awaken to ourself, when we are the witness to our thoughts. *I cannot know anything if I don't know the knower itself, if I don't know the one who seeks to know,* becomes the inquiry. Self-investigation is discovering who is in our heart, a reality that is neither inside nor outside of the body. To understand our true nature and the timelessness of being penetrates the suffering. Focused attention, an ancient technique, is to concentrate inwardly until the inner self is located in the heart, where the deeper truth of who we are becomes our true and natural state.

Our minds should be like mirrors, not cameras. —Amma

Intentional communities and conscious schools are environments that present specific conditions for learning. History can be looked at as a play of school influence. It has been a theory that conscious beings at one time or other have been connected to an esoteric school of regeneration. Jesus Christ's formation was drawn from the School of the Essenes. Rodney Collin, in *The Theory of Celestial Influence,* describes with great detail the history of mystery schools:

Conscious Schools constitute the real life on earth. Between 20,000 and

10,000 years ago, schools for the attainment of consciousness seemed to have been established upon Earth. Probably schools always exist, in some form or another. All true civilizing effects are indirectly produced by conscious people. But they in turn depend on the existence of schools to create conscious beings. The destruction of the old personality and the imparting of conscious souls constitute the whole work of schools. All human history is history of schools and school influence, its growth, its transfer elsewhere, this is human history, there isn't anything else.

The Fifth Way invites us to use this planet as the environment, the conditions for our development, to educate ourselves to be ourselves, to not be enslaved by our thoughts. The ancient dictum, *Know Thyself*, echoed through the centuries validates this inner pilgrimage. Our self-study is learning to see in order to know how to love. The fruit of our labor is Love. Our own awakening is the greatest service we can offer to this planet. To find peace inside shines a light of peace into this world. To look deeply into ourselves, to live deeply within each moment is the practice for loving. This is to listen, to look and to speak deeply, peacefully, with the whole of our being. Mindful attention, simply looking at what is, softening our heart, being receptive; mindful attention directs awareness. To unlock the secrets of what we can become we practice seeing into the true nature of everything, so then each moment becomes the miracle.

The Fifth Way has to do with making love, making love possible on this earth. This is being present, understanding with a mind of love. There is a saying that every time a bird drinks water it lifts its head in gratefulness to the heavens. To be present with the bird's chanting song in our heart, we have all and everything. Knowing that life happens through us, to take responsibility for ourselves in appreciation for this precious human birth, contacting that force within, connecting to higher energy, finding balance, is to know and act from that place that is *the love that moves the earth and the stars.* Kabir the 15th century Indian poet-saint remarked that rather than dye his clothes saffron he wished to dye his heart with divine love. We are one heart, and our practices remind us of our connection as we awaken in love. *The Fifth Way* enables us to participate in a journey to bring creation to its fullest for all beings. Expanding our heart from the personal to the universal, that enormous spaciousness of our true being, is a road sign of *The Fifth Way.*

A hundred times a day I remind myself that my inner and outer life depends on the labors of other men, living and dead, and that I must exert myself in order to give in the measure as I have received and am still receiving. —*Albert Einstein.*

A STUDY OF OUR POSSIBILITIES

Ego, or separate personal identity, is at the root of all suffering in life. Therefore, it is to be destroyed by any means possible. This is Liberation or Enlightenment or Self-realization. —*Ramana Maharshi*

The word, psychology, is a combination of two terms, *psyche,* which is soul or spirit, and *ology,* meaning study. This study of the soul has a long history and tradition. For thousands of years, psychology has been an exploration of the human spirit, soul and mind. Our word therapy derives from the Greek therapeia, which means healing. In the Greek myth Psyche, the beautiful goddess of love, was told by Eros/Cupid not to look into his face and was tricked by her jealous sisters to break her agreement. Eros/Cupid left and Psyche had to overcome great obstacles to learn how to love. Psyche is seen as the human soul purified through strife in the quest for joy and the happiness of love. Her/our suffering is not from an illness, it's part of the quest of our journey towards union with love. Understanding the root of psychology changes the stigmatizing, the labeling that is taught in universities and hospitals, the branding that happens in clinics and offices under the guise of mental health. Modern psychology and psychoanalysis have lost touch with their origins, which included philosophy, yoga, Sufism, conscious breathing, as well as other ancient systems and wisdom traditions. Based in the study of our possibilities and consciousness, Sacred Psychology, continues where Western psychology leaves off. Not to follow guidelines that label *good mental health*, we are here to serve as facilitator, educator, conversationalist, guide; to create an environment, a container, to live as presence, paying attention, with compassion and availability.

Certainly it seems more and more clear that what we call 'normal' in psychology is really a psychopathology of the average. —Abraham Maslow

Historically, there is a large difference between the century or so tradition of psychoanalysis, and the ancient Eastern psychologies which claim a tradition and history of at least several thousand years. For over five thousand years some form of psychological healing has been practiced in India. Sacred Psychology, the teaching of *The Way of the Lover*, returns to its roots, the wisdom of psychology, addressing the full possibility of a human being, not only adjustment and comfort, rather, a freedom from illusion with the possibility of total awakening. Escaping from our small ego to look toward an understanding of how we show up in this world, of the spaciousness of big mind, the pure boundless awareness that is the ground of our being, frees us. No longer looking to pathology there is a neutrality and objectivity in our recognition. Within the frame work of systems lies the greater intention for mindfulness, for self-remembering, for developing greater consciousness, for waking up.

Psychology addresses the content of our consciousness, it helps us understand the forces that inform our egoic, or personality, structure. It looks at the stories, relationships, patterns, and perceptions that make up the life, that run our life. Spirituality addresses the context of consciousness. It helps us access and experience the field of consciousness from which all manifestations arise, helping us to access something that is larger than our own story—to open to the perennial truths that mystics from all traditions have known.
—*Mariana Caplan*

Trying to work on ourselves without a map to navigate our exploration, without reliable strategies, devices and tools is limiting. The new psychology brings maps and tools, has a blueprint to carry us along to awaken to our true nature. A map for our consciousness assists us to see through the poses and gyrations of the mind and our diversity, to recognize and to orient ourselves.

A comprehensive psychology must work toward increasing wholeness and psychospiritual integration rather than simply trying to 'fix' people so they comply with a socially agreed upon norm for mental health that is profoundly limited in its conception of what is possible for a human being.
—*Mariana Caplan*

Our resistance to the now, to fully dropping into each moment, stands in our way, furthering our sleep. Emily Dickinson wrote about this trance that envelops us: *There is a pain so utter it swallows being up, then covers the abyss with trance, so memory can step around, across, upon it.*

Concrete tools to address our wounding, opening and gaining access to our inner resources, to hold to the difficult, finally to have permanent access to ourself, finding that source inside, the depth of connection between all existence transforms the trance into the gold of our true nature. What is possible for a human being changes the focus from adjusting and fixing people to guiding us to open, to understand, to awaken to our true nature and become one with that, to live within a context of a life that is of service. To have a deep loving connection challenges and inspires us. To integrate our story with self dissolves the fiction of who we think we are, to learn and use the tools with awareness: this, then, is the Fifth Way.

If you want to be free, get to know your real self. It has no form, no appearance, no root, no basis, no abode; it is lively buoyant and responsive.
—*Zen teaching*

AWAKENING IN LOVE

You will see that in life you receive exactly what you give. Your life is the mirror of what you are. It is in your image. ...The first requirement, the first condition, the first test for one who wishes to work on himself is to see things in himself which he has never seen before, see them actually, and in order to see, he must learn to see; this is the first initiation of man into self-knowledge. You will see that it is not easy. And it is not cheap. You must pay dearly. You must pay, pay a lot, and pay immediately, pay in advance. Pay with yourself. By sincere, conscientious, disinterested efforts. The more you are prepared to pay without economizing, without cheating, without any falsification, the more you will receive. —*Jeanne de Salzmann*

This dance of relationship shakes us to our roots. The journey of discovery admidst turbulent waters of intimacy, of perceived threats from childhoods that created defensive postures, makes partnering powerful journeying. A relationship is a luxury, not a necessity, and for this practice we need tools, vigilance, attention, imagination, constant self-examination, and an appreciation for the miraculous. *The Fifth Way* incorporates, makes available, tools (refer to chapter 12) to study ourself to keep the beauty in our chosen partnership, to learn the simple joy of being. Our responsiveness to life need not be dependent on whether current circumstances are fortunate or unfortunate. From our aliveness we respond to the world as our expression of open awareness. Transformation becomes a possibility without getting lost in the forest of blame, envy, resentment, fear and pride, which breeds separation. To remain in the open field with big sky and bountiful earth, in the words of Hafiz: *Dear ones, Let's anoint this earth with dance!*

Along this path of the heart we hear Rumi's words: *My religion is to live through love. If you have not been a lover, count not your life as lived.* We are called upon in our private and public lives to offer our loving relationships, to radiate light. To cherish our deep friendships, to look at how we show up for the children, our intimacy towards ourselves: described by a teacher of these times: *this engaged love gives us the strength of the mother who lifts a car off of her child.* The possibility of creating sacred partnerships that will transform all that surrounds us, enfolds the world, the essence of the sacred feminine, the interdependence of all things is a force that embraces everything, has room for differences, infuses energy into life. With great respect to the rhythm of this planet, to be in the body, in life, the betrayal of the feminine permeates most cultures, is sounding an alarm. This path of the heart speaks to maintaining a polarity that heightens intensity, engaging in intimate conversations, in seeing the other as sacred.

How did the rose ever open its heart and give to the world all of its beauty? It felt the encouragement of light against its being, otherwise we all remain too frightened. —Hafiz

The new psychology incorporates tantric sexuality, making love in a playful and responsible manner, speaks to connecting with our natural sexual energies. The joyful dance between Shiva and Shakti—pure consciousness and pure energy—allows us to dance, sing and weep for joy in the sacred marriage of lover and beloved. And yet so often we forget the simplicity and ordinariness that becomes the ground for daily living. What has initially drawn two people together is most often what creates their dissolution or divorce. The quality that creates attraction becomes the same characteristic that is magnified and objected to, until two people, now discontent, want only distance. We might *fall in love* with privacy and quietness, yet 5 years later want out because the initial attractive quality called privacy and quietness, now irritates. What was once a passionate pull, over time, grows into dissatisfaction with a raw edge. A close friend of Frieda and D.H. Lawrence described their marriage: *what in the first days must have been the passionate attention of love had now become the attack and the defense between enemies.*

So long as we remember our purpose in this triangle of love, its third dimension, so long as we invite the beloved into our relationships will we live to see the fruit from our labor. Our partnerships flower when we love consciously. Without the sacred our partnership burns up. This discipline of the heart, called spiritual communion, is one of the highest experiences known to us. Hafiz describes and names it: *The Gift.*

Our union is like this: You feel cold I reach for a blanket to cover our shivering feet. A hunger comes into your body I run to my garden and start digging potatoes. You ask for a few words of comfort and guidance, I quickly kneel at your side offering you this whole book, as a gift. You ache with loneliness one night so much you weep. And I say, here's a rope, tie it around me. Hafiz will be your companion, for life.

There is a teaching story that the Buddha, reached into a pond and pulled a lotus flower out of the mud. Holding it silently before him, its roots dripping of water and mud, he smiled. This soft smile, often depicted on statues and paintings is said to be the measure of illumination, a smile from a light soul and an enlightened mind. The smile, on Buddha's lips, on our childhood photos and perpetually on the face of the dolphin demonstrates the wordless metaphorical smile within us. Women intrinsically know this kingdom of innocence and when history listens and takes itself with less heaviness we enter paradise to find the peace that lies within the smile, a sign of realization. Within our divine child essence we let all things be as we live into our authentic nature. What a beautiful and simple teaching is *The Way of the Lover*, to soar on the wings of Love.

There is a beautiful creature living in a hole you have dug. So at night I set fruit and grains and little pots of wine and milk beside your soft earthen mounds, and I often sing. But still, my dear, you do not come out. I have fallen in love with someone who hides inside you. We should talk about this problem—otherwise, I will never leave you alone. ....And love says. 'I will take care of you,' to everything that is near. —Hafiz

Our ordinary life, everything we enjoy, comes along with us on this journey. Realization is fed at the root of daily life. This is not a dreary path, it invokes laughter, passion, enthusiasm, excitement and playfulness as well as the willingness to experience the suffering and needs of the world. There's a story about an aging, health-challenged woman who approached a great teacher exclaiming that she had never meditated, chanted or prayed, she found those activities to be grim and distant. But now she felt an urgency to open her heart to something meaningful to what is at the very core of her life. The teacher smiled and said *who or what do you love most?* Quite easily she replied; *my dog, my plants and the ocean. So simple,* the teacher said, *go home and adore your dog, plants, and the ocean as if, for they are the divine holy blessing on all the earth.* For it is Love that connects us to meaning and purpose. To love purely, anything, anyone, is the miracle.

Those tender words we said to one another, are stored in the secret heart of heaven. One day, like the rain, they will fall and spread and our love will grow green over the world. —Rumi

AUTOBIOGRAPHY IN FIVE CHAPTERS

1. *I walk down the street.*
   There is a deep hole in the sidewalk
   I fall in.
   I am lost...........I am hopeless.
   It isn't my responsibility.
   It takes forever to find a way out.

2. *I walk down the same street,*
   There is a deep hole in the sidewalk.
   I pretend I don't see it.
   I fall in again.
   I can't believe I'm in the same place.
   But it isn't my responsibility.
   It still takes a long time to get out.

3. *I walk down the same street.*
   There is a deep hole in the sidewalk.
   I see it there.
   I still fall in...........It's a habit.
   My eyes are open
   I know where I am
   It is my responsibility.
   I get out immediately.

4. *I walk down the same street.*
   There is a deep hole in the sidewalk
   I walk around it.

5. *I walk down another street.*

—Anonymous

CHAPTER SEVEN

Work Is Love Made Visible

Wherever your work be—in the kitchen, the cowshed, or the toilet—let that be your Temple. —*Mata Amritanandamayi*

No conscious work is ever wasted. The only real satisfaction in life is to work not from compulsion but consciously. The work is to remember oneself. The only work worth doing is to remember oneself. —*G.I. Gurdjieff*

We are called to witness the existence of the finite and the presence of the infinite. Both call, both are here. They only lack a witness to their presence. Witnessing/watching is the quintessential human task. —*William Segal*

When you work you are a flute through whose heart the whispering of the hours turns to music.

And to love life through labor is to be intimate with life's inmost secret. All work is empty save when there is love?

It is to weave the cloth with threads drawn from your heart, even as if your beloved were to wear that cloth. It is to charge all things you fashion with a breath of your own spirit.

Work is love made visible. —*Kahlil Gibran*

Then I asked: Does a firm persuasion that a thing is so, make it so? He replied: All poets believe that it does, and in ages of imagination this firm persuasion removed mountains; but many are not capable of a firm persuasion of anything. —*William Blake*

I dream'd in a dream I saw a city invincible to the attacks of the whole of the rest of the earth,

I dream'd that was the new city of Friends,

Nothing was greater there than the quality of robust love, it led the rest

It was seen every hour in the actions of the men of that city,

And in all their looks and words. —Walt Whitman

To Be of Use

The people I love the best jump into work head first without dallying in the shallows and swim off with sure strokes almost out of sight. They seem to become natives of that element, the black sleek heads of seals bouncing like half-submerged balls.

I love people who harness themselves, an ox to a heavy cart, who pull like water buffalo, with massive patience, who strain in the mud and the muck to move things forward, who do what has to be done, again and again.

I want to be with people who submerge in the task, who go into the fields to harvest and work in a row and pass the bags along, who are not parlor generals and field deserters but move in a common rhythm when the food must come in or the fire be put out.

The work of the world is common as mud. Botched, it smears the hands, crumbles to dust. But the thing worth doing well done has a shape that satisfies, clean and evident. Greek amphoras for wine or oil, Hopi vases that held corn, are put in museums but you know they were made to be used. The pitcher cries for water to carry and a person for a work that is real. —Marge Piercy

LOVE MADE VISIBLE

When you are in love, everything you touch is a blessing. Love and work are our two feet, as we walk along the path of the heart. To forget one is to be out of balance, disharmonious, to embrace both opens us to a great secret of life called the true art of living. Work is a way to distribute the gifts of our love. And in life it can look like writing a book, making breakfast, emptying the garbage, choreographing a dance, smiling with a child, painting a wall, washing dishes. The slight shift of emphasis from what we are doing to how we are doing it—to the love, the embodied compassion with which we are doing it—creates the presence and radiance of the act. Our acts are eternal gestures of love for all who choose to partake, and each opportunity is an inquiry. Life is a school, and the real work is happening deep down inside. What comes out is the true treasure, a perfect cup of tea served to a friend. Perform each task as if your life depends on it. It does!

The Fourth Way teaching was for me a death and a rebirth. The school opened me to an ongoing investigation of values, conscience, standards; not ones I had been taught as a child: about love, relationships, right living, what an aim is, to be loved for who I am, how to live. The school burned values inside of me. What I had relied on was shattered, the many life-illusions I carried were broken. Throughout a long dark night I was protected and guided. While I was learning, I was also unlearning. To learn as a blank slate there is no contradiction, it's following sequence without the intrusion of fixed concepts and opinions. I had been taught to move in the world with locked muscles, so I had to grasp two things at once, how to unlock and how to retrain muscles to move without restriction. Adjusting to a new reality, freeing up distortions lib-

264

erates energy. To move beyond the influences that have been imprinted our reactions have to slow down, for particular qualities to find a place to see unself-consciously. Rumi's son, Sultan Walad, described this becoming: *The human being has to be born twice, once from his or her mother, and then out of his or her body and of its own existence.* Withdrawing from the fictional realm of life we go back into the world to live naturally. Wherever we are and within each moment, becomes the practice.

I can thoroughly study the system of ideas, but if I do not realize my mechanicalness and my powerlessness, this will not lead me very far. Conditions can change and I can lose all possibility. The thinking must not remain lazy. I have to understand the necessity of introducing the principles of work into my personal life. I cannot accept that one part of myself is mechanical and at the same time hope that another part is going to be conscious. I need to live the teaching with all of myself. —Jeanne de Salzmann

The Fifth Way, The Way of the Lover, speaks to placing attention, to finding a language that matches our experience as we step out of a narrow well and onto dry land. Burning our house, taking down the walls that keep us from the treasure; within this act of liberation we become a furnace room igniting, creating fire within, living like a flame. Then to sit quietly and witness, how many lifetimes does it take to see that nothing is worth clinging to, not our thoughts, not our things; only after we pay homage to what has brought us this far, sanctifying our history, our birthright and inheritance, our heritage and lineage; shattering the cage we heal ourselves in the fire of understanding. And in this way of understanding we penetrate into the heart of things, awaken to the beauty that grows from within and is the creation of love, for us to now have the possibility of a conscious life.

The distinction between understanding and opinion has to be made clear, as well as various illusions of self-importance have to be broken. The key of this way is 'understanding', and every effort made with understanding of its reason and possible effect was worth ten times as much as the same effort made without understanding. With understanding, time and persistence, many things become possible. —Rodney Collin

My teacher, Jean, offered the possibility of not only being in the play but of writing the play. Life for her was theatre. Her presence carried focused attention, an awareness of being here, heart vision, energy that touched the longing inside love. In her wisdom she lent vision to see what had been invisible. When I first met Jean my dearest friendship was with Bonnie, an artist who experienced occasional breakdowns and hospitalizations. Jean arrived at my loft accompanied by Bonnie, who had taken on a word exercise, a Gurdjieffian tool. One of the beginning steps of the Gurdjieff work is to not use certain words like *I*. Since we are not a unified *I*, do not have a permanent *I*, we remind ourselves that we are fragmented through not saying *I*. We pay attention to our mechanicalness, creating an observer, a witness, within ourselves. Constrained by the opinions of others, we have many sub personalities or *I*'s, and these exercises are ways to verify how easily we are pulled away from our core. Learning to detach, observe, create a witness that acknowledges ourself is a starting point for inner work. The next step is to struggle against our negativity. So they came to my loft and were replacing *I* with *it*. Bonnie would say, *It would like a glass of water*, and I thought, *Oh, wow, she's falling apart again. Another hospitalization.* My mind went wild. Jean sensed this and she said, *Oh, Bonnie, Paula thinks you're having a breakdown. Don't do the word exercise.* When Bonnie was in a breakdown she couldn't slow down or stop. Her ability and willingness to stop on that occasion led me to see that Jean was mindfully creating a process of self-awareness. Jean's determination to know, her authenticity and persistence reflected back a mirror that revealed my own yearning to love and know truth. Her energy generated and increased my love, I became more alive. I was drawn to the possibility that I could learn to love consciously, to become a lover. I felt verified in turning to the work. I have always been moved by people who through their presence communicate and bring forth the beauty in others. Love with knowledge makes us conscious lovers, at that moment I understood my life's work.

Surely love is a big part of the truth we are here to live. —*Coleman Barks*

CHOOSING A TEACHER

The teacher is the one who points the way to wisdom. —*Krishnamurti*

More and more, as I spent time with Jean, I understood that she saw me. That recognition, to be seen, a connecting point, penetrated my heart. I tested her over and over again. I was in therapy and even took her to my analyst-therapist, Gabrielle. Watching the two of them together, I experienced the qualitative difference. In that room stories dropped away and I entered another reality. I was connecting to my nature, a knowing beyond words, stepping out of time. This invitation was a reminder of what mattered, about the generosity of a life of meaning and purpose, of truth and responsibility. I had asked for truth, and now to have a glimpse. A fire was lit. Gradually, I realized that Jean was not like any human being I had ever met. She was mindful, intentional, pointing the way, guiding me to know what was needed; constantly I verified her to be a remarkable woman. A teacher opens a window for the inner knowledge to pour down, to open conscious mind. Jean's presence allowed synchronistic events to unfold, even the environment testified to her force. We would have inexplicable miraculous experiences. Often as we walked down the street our energy would be so high that street lights would blow out overhead. One early evening as Jean and I were riding the subway to Lincoln Center to meet 7 students every couple of stops a student from our school would enter our car on the train and join us. Until all 9 of us arrived at the final stop. We didn't talk about these moments, Jean was training us to live in the miraculous, to not diminish ordinary experiences with our fascination.

If you meet a person of developed being, of real presence, you feel something in their presence, it makes you quiet, you become yourself, if only for a moment, in their presence. That's what we need: real people. —*Jacob Needleman*

Nonetheless, while living out these extraordinary qualities she often remained insignificant, sort of hidden. She would take on mundane tasks, like painting the hallways in the building where I lived and worked, which were massive, shabby, and neglectfully in need of repair. She bought paint brushes and began to work. When my patients came up the stairs to enter my loft-office, they would pass by her. I was uptight, trained to believe that therapy should maintain strong external boundaries, that a therapist does not intrude on the patient's life in the world. Jean would say hello, observe and after the session go out with me for coffee, to tell me a story about this person that she had met for a moment on the staircase while painting the walls in the hallway. Until one day she transformed the whole building into a golden castle. This is one of the ways in which she taught. She was never afraid of hard work.

We are here on this planet to learn about love, to come into the knowledge of love. And we are here to manifest this love in our daily lives. —*Reshad Feild*

Eventually I left the life I had created to go for the bigger life. I had lived in a small arena until meeting Jean who viewed daily life as the universal game called Life and Love and Truth. Jean told me that she had known that one day a one-eyed messenger who would be her right arm would arrive. I was, for her, that person. We started having meetings. The first people who came had varying connections to one another. Jean took that to mean we were destined to work together in a boundless spiritual dimension. People came out of the woodwork of our lives to become a part of what we named the *Circle of Angels*. Sons and daughters, husbands and wives, brothers and sisters, past lovers and friends, drawn to become part of *The Circle*, a Fourth Way School of Consciousness. The pursuit was a relentless unsentimental odyssey of polishing the heart, of daily practice, unglamorous and maddening.

I was given the task of finding a house where we could live and continue our work together. I rented a car and Jean told me to leave New York with another student, Alexandra, and drive to Cape Cod to find a house for the school. She gave the same assignment, without my knowing it, to a student, Elaine, who I had often struggled with; now one of us was to find the *right* environment. This was typical of the way in which Jean worked, intentional friction to create heat, challenges that bring us into contact with ordinary life, that break habits and have the possibility of carrying higher energy. The necessity of working with others, to break our conditioning and move beyond personal preferences touches our knowing of truth which is always at our level of being. Recognizing our limitations and strengths are paramount to walking a true path. I became aware that I was finding a house as my personal work as well as offering community service. Eventually the decision as to which one of us had found the most fitting, suitable living space was made by Jean. Elaine chose a classic weathered Cape Cod house that belonged to Norman Mailer. Located at the East End of town its natural cedar shingles had oxidized to a silver gray, so it had character, albeit lowered ceilings, tight nooks and crannies which made it comfortable for a family or couple, but not spacious for a working community. We didn't move into his house and years later, Mailer saying he didn't want his home to be lost to history dedicated it to a charitable foundation to support the Norman Mailer Writer's Colony in Provincetown, Massachusetts.

I found a dream house and recognized it as that when it appeared. It was a split-level mansion dropping from back to front down into the beach sand, water as far as the eye could see, three levels, panoramic windows, and a top floor built as a widow's whale watch. The front of the house had a protruding open air porch with a blue grey slatted deck and huge bay windows which faced over the water of old Cape Cod. The house sat in the more secluded West End of town. A private beach in front was spacious with clean well-packed sand. The owner, Harris, a medical doctor, had never rented his house until now, deciding he wanted to take a year off to live in Boston. What was remarkable is that although a young man in his fifties, during our first year living in his home he died. Late one evening the police arrived with the news of his death. Harris released the house and we had our space for our experiment, Jean and the nineteen of us continued to live there as community, an intentional Fourth Way School.

Insist on constant verification of the teaching, take nothing on faith, Understanding cannot be handed over from teacher to student like a sackful of grain. Real understanding is the child of knowledge and being. A teacher's greatest gift may be to be a living embodiment of the great mystery and beauty of existence. —David Appelbaum

Exercises: Seeing What Is

To go up alone into the mountains and come back as an ambassador to the world, has been the method of humanity's best friends. —Evelyn Underhill

In the house we explored many disciplines and forms of group work—from dynamic meditation and levitation movement to encounter exercises and psychodrama. Each student worked individually with aloneness and silence through daily meditation practice, a 54-hour isolation octave, and time spent privately in a dune shack which we had access to from winter through spring. We surpassed what we set out to do in our sanctuary by the sea.

I submitted to break down what was mechanical and programmed, to notice my associative thinking, to essentialize everything. By agreeing to live in conditions that are temporarily removed from life demands is a reprieve from being taken over by the activities in life that diminish focus and fragment attention. Living together creating exercises, cultivating awareness set the stage to do the impossible. We are accustomed to doing what is possible, while remaining in our comfort zone. Transformation implies doing the unthinkable, to live where we fear to live. Direct inner experience brings us to clarify, to verify, to discoveries; ultimately to live into the questions. To midwife our spiritual rebirth we cultivate mindful awareness and anchor clear vision.

This work has service at its apex not its foundation. At its foundation it has understanding what our situation really is. Right sensitivity towards life, towards living things, is one of the first and most valuable forms of sensitivity to acquire. —John G. Bennett

The following is an example of exercises that were offered to me by the teacher as first-line work, which is work on ourself. Second-line work is work for others, and third-line work is work for the school or community.

Paula: Possibilities for 1st Line Work (3-week Program)

1. *Upon arising—20 minute "sitting" exercise (prop your back up—watch your mind).*
2. *Shower **only** 2 mornings per week.*
3. *No verbal speech before noon or between 7-8 p.m.*
4. *3 hours minimum per day 3rd line work.*
5. *No 2nd line work—**Help** no one!*
6. *Repeat mantra "No resistance" 3 or 7 minutes 7 times a day on the hour.*
7. *Continue food exercises—any type—form.*
8. *Walk alone in nature (not town) at least 30 minutes a day.*
9. *Lying—dying exercise 30 minutes in evening.*
10. *30 minutes "Jack of Spades" daily.*
11. *30 minutes silent-sitting— "Listen" to music.*
12. *Observe—don't think!!! in all the above.*

If and when you can within the above:

a. *Don't answer phone until someone asks for you.*
b. *Paint a serious canvas—express something for the world of your present understanding. Plan it.*
c. *Stay out of cars.*
d. *Quiet down and observe—Be still.*
e. *Don't resist—Bring everything home.*
f. *Don't bother with externals—observe internals.*
g. *Watch your machine's "wants."*
h. *Take on responsibility of one plant and one animal.*
i. *Play piano 15 minutes daily.*
j. *Learn sign language.*
k. *Learn Spanish.*

*Please set up a strict 3-week program for yourself and observe, **only** observe your thoughts and emotions and movements. No judgment of your machine—or excuses—or reasons—or connections—just **observe**.*

I love you, JR

What had been known to me as *Paula* was breaking, chipped away through the practices that Jean offered. For example, I agreed to take on an exercise to go out for one hour a day, whereas I had always been out and about in the streets, often without limit or aim, as distraction. My customary lifestyle had routinely been to come and go throughout a day, hours filled with idle wandering, activity, often fun, but at the expense of the enormous ground of stillness that is the simplicity of *being*. This simple exercise of mindful restraint harnessed my energy, an opportunity to learn to focus inward, to rein in my spiritedness and power; to know *how* I am is to taste a quality different from the habitual conditioned ways of behavior, and this done in quiet attentiveness, undistracted, not on the surface, creates a foundation for inner work. To develop and strengthen attention opens a new relationship, one that cultivates self-awareness. Within the activity of life the illusions of who we imagine ourselves to be are strengthened. A wandering body supports a drifting agitated mind, conditioned habitual attitudes set up barriers to awakening. There are moments in life that bring us to the door of the unknown, dangers and illness and death, job and financial loss, accidents and divorce. One of the functions of our practice teaches us to remain present in the face of uncertainty. Discipline and discrimination, the force of attention, like love, must enhance personal dignity.

A similar exercise had me limit all outdoor activity to a radius of 6 blocks, for two hours a day. Whatever was needed had to be located within those six blocks. The practices were grounded in the daily routines of life. Paying close attention creates aliveness. A new kind of energy becomes available, to live in an electric field, beyond mind or concepts, shocks us to light up, to enter a new world. Dispersed and scattered we lack presence. This exploration, creating a magnetic force, began with the practice of witnessing, an investigation of energy, of developing an observer for there to be someone home. One essential truth to life is that we make payment for what we receive. Every hair is counted as we work to find the quality, the state that opens us to understanding and meaning and possibility.

Without preparing ourselves through preliminary practices, the only answer to the question, 'Who am I?' is 'The same old fool.' —*Swami Sivananda*

TRUE HUMILITY IS FREEDOM FROM FEAR

Awake, arise, having approached the Great Teacher, learn the road is diffi-cult, the crossing is as the sharp edge of a razor. —*Katha Upanishad III*

The exercises were intended to increase substance and presence; to face our fears, to find the meaning behind our efforts. Simple chal-lenges; self-observation has to be approached as a new relationship to ourself, and so we were offered practices, not techniques. Practices help us arrive into the present moment, they build invisible muscle, maturity, teach us to understand the unfolding of process. And there might come a day when what we call our practice becomes our life.

I want to teach students to develop a curiosity, not a blunt acceptance, a thirst for understanding, connecting links; creating wrinkles in the gray matter of our brains feeds a penchant to see below the surface. Surfaces do not make the cut...Most of all pay attention. Deep attention. Developing a practice helps, creating space, a connection to the heart, a grounding in the wisdom of impermanence, egolessness, a coming back to zero. Otherwise the world's troubles are hard to bear. We become numb, callous, or continually angry. —*Natalie Goldberg*

I was ready to journey into the exploration of blindness that continued to catch my attention. Visually impaired, losing my vision had been an unresolved question, and to unravel this, for myself, for all beings that foray into darkness: the power of the practices lie in the freedom of release from everything that might catch us, that might hold us hostage; to not be blackmailable, not be reactive, is social freedom. We were given an exercise in which one student was blindfolded for 24 hours, while another student would assist us during that time. To come together with what Jeanne de Salzmann names as *conscious exchange* is imperative. To learn to ask a real question, to listen deeply, to take the other seriously, to hold ourself responsible, to not pretend, to remain open; this is what to ask of ourself.

I accompanied a student named Deborah, spending 24 hours with her blindfolded, observing people's responses to what appeared to be her blindness. I watched her being tentative as she made her way, sometimes people would stare, more often they carefully offered her the space to easily walk past. I paid attention, trying to know blindness from the outside in. The next morning I was offered the exercise unassisted. Once the blindfold was in place I heard Jean calling me from downstairs. I remember thinking, *She must be nuts to think I'm going to go down those windy long stairs blind-folded.* Yet, I did, and was amazed.

When I walked in I was so impressed with myself that I could barely believe that she then said, *Go get me a cup of coffee.* I thought, *What do you mean? I just walked down these stairs blind. Now I have to go get coffee?* But I did, even though my inner voice was saying, *Blind people don't do this.* I made her coffee and brought it to her, not knowing who else was in the room. Then she said, *Go pick out some music and put it on.* I walked to where I sensed the music was shelved and easily slid a disc onto the player. Each task was the way Jean taught. As soon as you could do one thing, she asked you to do the next. There was no praise. The work was constantly stretching my limits. Inside that exercise I was breaking down a formative apparatus which believed that blind people don't function and that I couldn't function if I were blind. The work prepared me for future events in my life. Ultimately, our spiritual work is to prepare us for a conscious death through meeting our fears.

Years later, when I was not able to wear my eye glasses following eye surgery, with bandages over my eyes, I did not miss a beat. This was now a dance. I walked around the hotel, I did my laundry one evening in the laundry room. I couldn't see a foot in front of me, yet I spent the days enjoying the simplicity: walking around the hotel grounds, going into town, going to a restaurant. Knowing I might have to fly home from Boston to Santa Fe without my vision, I knew I could go to an airport and be wheeled onto a plane. Others could take care of me if I needed to be guided somewhere. I wouldn't be crippled by my body. What I learned at the School is totally usable. I know I don't have to become a vegetable if life renders me blind or paralyzed. There is a spirit inside which doesn't have to be frayed or afraid. The exercises, practices, were tremendously useful. When I stagger I can also see the miracle in life and begin to understand Walt Whitman's great and humble lines of gratitude and appreciation: *Old poor and paralyzed on bended knee I thank Thee.*

Perhaps all the dragons in our lives are princesses, who are only waiting to see us act, just once, with beauty and courage. Perhaps everything terrible is, in its deepest sense, something helpless that needs our love. —Rainer Maria Rilke

SELF-STUDY AND PRECISION

The word 'further' is like a talisman, a power object. We must pull it out and gaze upon it after every battle, every time we think we must be done,

that we must, at last, have arrived. As much as it may seem otherwise, there's always 'further'. Get up, dust off, and gird thy loins for the next fray. The day may come when there is no more 'further' and you will recognize that fact with the bemused and unenthusiastic observation that you are...'done'.
—Jed McKenna

How to walk through our day, step-by-step-by-step, becomes the *how* of walking towards consciousness. The practice of living in mindfulness, of not being habitual in daily life, will break our machinery, the mental rigidities of our attitudes. We called ourselves a Metanoian Order because *metanoia* means change of mind, change of attitude. It's our attitude that creates limitations. What kind of attitude does the star have towards the sky, the branch towards the tree, the wave for the ocean? These are our human mental prejudices and my yearning was to allow life to be, without my mental imposition. To go beyond limits and definitions we first study ourselves. *Know thyself. The unexamined life is not worth living,* said Socrates. Years later Gurdjieff remarked: *Know thyself always and everywhere.* Our first task is to know, to understand how this machine is put together, what this instrument is for, otherwise, how can we distinguish how to use it and how to be available to this life that we have been gifted? This is the root and foundation of all psychological and spiritual paths. Who am I? What is my life purpose? What is my true self? *Who am I standing in the midst of this thought traffic?* asked Rumi. How can I liberate myself from these persistent thoughts, the habitual tendencies that stand in the way of awareness and certainty? The task continues, to look inward, to know our essential nature, to allow the light of our presence to shine, to live truthfully in accordance to our nature, our natural self.

A practical aim: To help people to learn how to 'work on themselves' in their search for the imperishable. If you are the person I hope for, you are in search of a satisfying answer to the question: 'What is the sense and purpose of my life and how am I to achieve it? We are needed to maintain the balance of energies in the Solar System and to help its spiritual evolution. We exist to serve Nature rather than to make use of Her. If we serve consciously the purpose of our existence we become 'real' beings. —J.G. Bennett

The systems in the second part of this book are tools to see ourself as well as to recognize and study, know others, tools to defuse our projections and distortions, maps to bring clarity to our explorations. The understanding of type and energy through ancient personality theory accelerates our inner work, deepens our psychological development and creates a bridge to our spiritual unfoldment. By knowing energy we maximize our possibilities. This information assists in our daily life so we can move mindfully through the world in accurate relationships to others, not projecting, to use our personality to embark on a larger journey, that of conscious awareness. Seeing life just as it is, this is the true awakening. Intentional exercises offer a direct perception as we awaken from the trance, having a greater range of choices in our climb up and down the ladder to discover unwavering freedom.

Why cannot all men develop and become different beings? The answer is very simple. Because they do not want it. Because they do not know about it and will not understand that without a long preparation what it means, even if they are told. The chief idea is that in order to become a different man we must want it very much and for a very long time. A passing desire or a vague desire based on dissatisfaction with external conditions will not create a sufficient impulse. The evolution of man depends on his understanding of what he may get and what he must give for it. If man does not want it, or if he does not want it strongly enough, and does not make necessary efforts, he will never develop. So there is no injustice in this. Why should man have what he does not want? If man were forced to become a different being when he is satisfied with what he is then this would be injustice. —P.D. Ouspensky

Recognize Everything: Present Moment Practices

By the power and truth of this practice may all beings have happiness, and the causes of happiness; May all be free from sorrow, and the cause of sorrow, may all never be separated from the sacred happiness which is sorrowless: And may all live in equanimity, without too much attachment and too much aversion, and live believing in the equality of all that lives. —Tibetan prayer

To serve another, we first work on ourself. Exercises and practices built around self-study move us out of a narrow subjective world towards objective awareness while forming a base of self-understanding. Observing both ourself and the external world at the same time begins to break the habit of being fascinated and hypnotized by an object of our attention. We have to be able to see ourselves as well as to understand since most of how we picture ourselves to be is imaginary. Our growth and development is directly proportional to our understanding; self-study, self-observation is without pre-conceived ideas. The process of familiarizing ourself with how we are needs a quality of attention that enables us to recognize ourself. *For consciousness, attention is necessary. Attention is as oil in the lamp. Consciousness is the light,* said Robert de Ropp in a conversation with Madame Ouspensky. The direction of our attention, the creation of a witness, someone who is present to register, who is open and available; practices used well hold us to the truth of the moment.

The words 'believe' and 'worship' are unfamiliar to true practitioners because we do not 'believe' we understand, and we do not 'worship' we practice what we understand. —Nyogen Senzaki

Our education and conditioning have trained us to disconnect from our essence, that seed inside that is ourself. Inner development requires direct experience as our guide. To see and confront the contradictions of our temperament requires study until we learn to differentiate between essence and personality. We begin slowly, simply, observing as we are, in the situation of the moment. Know that our effort easily gets rooted in a laziness to not do the harder work of inner evolution: accommodating others avoids the more difficult work required to take responsibility for our own happiness. When we are natural, open and alert to a sense of direction, soft yet not drifting, wide and present, we flower.

Do not give rise to good and bad thoughts. When a thought arises—be aware of it—awareness dissolves the thought. When this method is applied over a long period of time—all thoughts are forgotten and oneness is attained.
—*Bai Zhang*

Using a group to generate energy we began as The Circle of Angels with First Line work which emphasizes personal work for and on ourself. We proceeded next to Second Line Work which is with and for others. Third Line Work serves the work itself and is for the school or for the community and engages a larger scale, that of true service. Wisdom and awareness integrated into action, refined into our own lives minimizes unnecessary suffering optimizing the possibilities for awakening and healing this planet. During the years I lived at the school exercises were changed often so as not to become habitual or too comfortable. For example, from October 13, 1979, to May 13, 1980, the following exercises were for all students:

1. *Commitment to an agreed-upon sexual straitjacket for study of that center.*
2. *Silence at evening meals and from noon to 6 p.m. on Sunday.*

3. 24-hour liquid fast from Saturday midnight to Sunday midnight each week.
4. Shower schedule and procedure—never on Sunday or between midnight and 5 a.m.
5. Sleep 6 to 7 hours, except on Sunday.
6. Doors open from 7 a.m. to 11 p.m. except Sunday.
7. Daily 30 - minute group silent meditation at 7 p.m. except Thursdays and Saturdays. On Saturday, meditation will be replaced with a King of Hearts Ceremony.
8. No cigarettes in community room.
9. No drugs - and alcohol only during meshing hours.
10. No cars to be used on Sunday except for an emergency.
11. No third line tasks or projects on Sunday except essentials.
12. Work against unnecessary talk. Be more, say less.
13. Work with first I's.
14. Each student is responsible for a personal weekly food discipline.
15. Daily looking and listening exercise.
16. Day's replay—in reverse—before sleep.
17. Morning prayer of gratitude.
18. Slow motion exercise each evening before retiring.
19. Learn to rest without unconsciousness.
20. Each student is responsible for their own animals.
21. Each student is responsible for their own medical bills or insurance.
22. Dress-in-your-best for dinner on Tuesday, Friday and Saturday.
23. Concentrate on precision.
24. Each student is daily responsible for the information on the bulletin board and in the mailbox.
25. Once a week lying and dying exercise.
26. Word and posture exercises.
27. No one to touch thermostat except JG/JR, unless an emergency.

28. Each student is to give and receive a total body massage to and from every student before May 13. Completion to be indicated on checklist.

Each student is to set up a checklist/chart (to be kept by their bed for me to see) indicating all your exercises and tasks, and whether or not they have been completed. This is an imperative octave. We are connected and affected by each other. Students are responsible for photographing those who have forgotten or are unwilling to comply with each detail of this seven-month octave. If photographed, and they still persist in resistance, you are responsible for informing JR or JG. (All of this is subject to change at any moment.)

Each student also had a separate personal list of exercises, based on our type, personal psychology, level of being, and what Jean observed as our particular work. Preparation and practices that inform, that impart authentic insights bring understanding. To live into the questions, why we are here and who and what we are, to reflectively experience what is around us, to make a shift in our being are what exercises and practices are capable of creating. The journey, to find what we already have is to pierce the hundred thousand veils of illusion. Most people presume to know. To be free of delusions, of pretense, of false selfhood is a process that recognizes this state of disguise, the imprisonment that catches us as we dream that we are awake. And in our sleep everything *just* happens. As the English nursery rhyme goes: *Row, row, row your boat, gently down the stream, merrily, merrily, merrily, merrily; life is but a dream.* Without sleep, there would be no awakening; and in life we are here to awaken, to awaken from the dream.

If we are going to build real being we need real experience. Admittedly, we can have it by remembering ourselves while watching television, but as long as we are going to make the effort to be present, why settle for being present to something that is at best neutral to our aim? Why not try to be present to something that will further our evolution, something that will promote the growth of our being, something we will wish to make a permanent part of ourself? After all, awakening means immortality, and the simple pastimes which seem harmless to us now could be something we will have to live with through eternity. —Girard Haven

OPENING PANDORA'S BOX

We have been given a mind, we have to know it. We have been given higher mind, we have to earn it, to find it. We have been given receptivity, we have to develop it. —William Segal

Individuals engaged in inner work activate and influence our climb, our ascent up the mountain, reminding us of what is possible. We speak not of our exercises and practices, but through them. Indiscriminate numbers do not necessarily strengthen. Understanding, knowing what is, to penetrate and be one with our purpose and maturity is a path towards overcoming our illusion of separateness. A mutual primary interest—to wake up—to live in a more conscious way, to stretch further, further than we even imagine possible, we step off the grid of the ordinary life. Common purpose, working together; sincerity, perseverance, honesty, and particularly the willingness to not be distracted by life's entertainment or our self-importance assist us to recognize and serve that which is larger than ourselves. When awareness fades we think we want something: ambition, fame, success, amusement, amassing money, all surface posed as distractions. Recognizing awareness as embracing the actual moment, being undistracted, practicing; eventually this pebble by pebble training builds mountains, this slow droplet of water eventually fills the bucket.

To be true to ourself we sacrifice the irrelevant. Life is a tragedy without

the work, because there is no life without it. There are few people interested in hearing about the opportunity to develop a mature soul, they think they already have one; being present is the only way one can help. Eventually, one teaches by becoming the words one speaks. We advance in relation to our ability to eliminate illusions. William Shakespeare said, 'And this above all, to thine own self be true.' How can so vital a statement be absent from one's life? —R.E Burton

A movement towards the unknown; risky to drop our limiting beliefs, to shift from our small personal story and cramped view of this world to come into an alignment with the unbounded inexhaustible limitless world that Always Is. This becomes true conversation, that place that Rumi described as *a step up from prayer and meditation.* The answers disappear. Finding people who are willing to have their rest, relaxation, their sleep disturbed are a great find. This dialogue, wordless and at other times with words, removes the fiction of our identity—to be together with another presence the world becomes clear. Who we are when met and seen, witnessed in a timeless presence of another generates energy. Gurdjieff's vision states that *we exist on earth to serve a very great purpose,* he is compelling us to wake up, to alleviate unnecessary suffering. And still, our journey is very much solitary, like the writer, the long distance runner, the mountain climber and painter. Truth, always here, imperceptible to those who are not really interested, is here to pass along, to teach others what we know; to climb the mountain requires great powers of observation needed for the long descent back to that place where we will abide.

The mountain is the connection between Earth and Sky. Its highest summit touches the sphere of eternity, and its base branches out in manifold foothills into the world of mortals. It is the path by which humanity can raise itself to the divine and the divine reveal itself to humanity.... If I couldn't scale the mountains, (after being told no more climbing due to my tuberculosis),

I would sing of them from below. Then I began to think seriously with the heaviness and awkwardness with which one jostles one's thought processes, when one has conquered one's body by conquering rock and ice. I will not speak about the mountain but through the mountain. With this mountain as language, I would speak of another mountain which is the path uniting the earth and heaven, I will speak of it, not in order to resign myself but to exhort myself. —Rene Daumal

Through my years with the school I was presented with exercises, both as a resident and subsequently as a non-resident student. I took on many practices studying myself, training myself to non-reactivity to break conditioning and preferences. To not react, to act from a place of connection we become creative rather than automatic. To be *compos mentis*, clear minded, is to notice, be watchful, observant, in a state of attention, and I see practices and exercises as a movement to see ourselves and to be seen. The following were given to me by JR (Jean) when we lived in Vermont:

Individual First line Tasks—Seven Months
(Please try to help each other remember and photograph.)

Paula
1. *Do not drive any school vehicle (red or blue VW-truck, red van, Sirocco station wagon) unless asked by JR.*
2. *Celibacy.*
3. *No special dishes or foods (plates, bowls, glasses).*
4. *Live in room at top of stairwell.*
5. *Acquire your personal needs from Country Store—Do not go shopping!!!*
6. *Weigh in each Saturday noon on doctor's scale.*
7. *Present me with a monthly list of "every" phone call.*
8. *Do not acquire a separate mailbox.*
9. *Buy no clothes. Borrow or trade or make do.*
10. *Pay $44 to third line fund for excess baggage transport.*

11. Wear a dress to Saturday meal.

*12. Do **not** answer phone unless no one else is around.*

Amongst many other activities we printed a journal several times a year, mailed out to the particular people we felt to be our personal connections. The April, 1979 issue of the journal, *Steppes*, asked the question, *To find something that does not change, that is to find oneself, how to discover that?*

I wrote:

Teach yourself to see what you imagine as the impossible, and then you will find what is possible. It is said that a conscious being only has to look at an old person once to understand aging and dying, a child to understand innocence, a flower to unravel the universe. We exist from day to day, but without any remembrance of who we are. Caught in a circle, we find no way out. Each act becomes a repetition, creating pleasure or displeasure with no chance for real change. Our effort here is to change the lower into the higher, a transformation that makes each moment coincide with what is true, and that lets us find what is truly remarkable, to live in the miraculous. Here, through self-remembering, the miracle begins—directing, leading the way, ultimately eliminating the smaller self, leaving only remembering until there is nothing.

For me now, each moment has led to this one. The single most consistent thread in the tapestry has been light, even though there have been times of darkness. And now, in this moment, the search is over. No more to seek, now only this honest battle, my own civil war. The moment-by-moment task is to kill off those parts which have enabled illusion to flourish. The responsibility is to become my own witness. Self-luminous. To go across. To live in the state of grace I have touched upon with a gratefulness for each breath, whereby all the accumulated treasures of my past, through love, can be given away. I have received a conscious teaching and the universe awaits. —Dr. Paula Bromberg

Once we recognize that the universe also sits quietly within ourselves, compassion for the world blossoms. Through the years I have seen that traveling this path of love gives rise to an invisible energy. Seeing from a love space, having a smile in the heart is a key that unlocks universes. A genuine smile brings inspiration and freshness. Beyond our everyday issues are the world's issues. One and the same. To live poetically, mythically, heroically, to surrender all that we imagine ourselves to be, is to give up this something that we think we are. Once our heart is broken open this initiation lights the fire of purpose.

Only from the heart can you reach the sky. The rose of glory grows from the heart. When the agony of love has broken open your life, roses and lilacs take over the garden of your soul. Open your hidden eyes and come, return to the root of the root of your own self. —Rumi

Preparation: Then Patience

Our efforts to work in life are, first of all, to discover how far we are from our highest possibilities. —Jeanne de Salzmann

To discover ourselves as the teaching we are available to transmit our experiences through seeing the miraculous. It's recorded that saint Teresa of Avila would say to her nuns: *You are not ready for the task. Go back in the kitchen and peel potatoes.* To surrender to what life brings, to what is asked of us; in this education of the heart we are preparing the ground, creating inner space, opening to something higher through sacrificing what stands in our way. Within each of us there is a theatre piece that we live out for our own conscious awakening. Jean said to me, *Yours will be a wild play, having lived so passionate a life. The surrender will be an expression, reflection of the vitality you've lived.* Our practice is to create a witness, an observer, someone home taking up primary residence in self rather than in the position, the role we are doing. Then when the time comes to go through the knot, the black hole, we maintain balance so as not to fall off the razor's edge into madness. We enlist perseverance based on exercise and the willingness to stop fooling ourselves, for our conditioned responses to drop away. Being alert and present in our life follows training ourselves to pay attention. There is a transformative power in developing attention, in self-remembering. The latter movement towards awakening is a grace note, while along the way our mindful effort, attention, dedication, perseverance, integrity and energy are the day labor.

I am dead because I have no desire, I have no desire because I think I possess, I think I possess because I do not try to give; Trying to give, we see that we have nothing, Seeing that we have nothing, we try to give ourselves, Trying to give ourselves, we see that we 'are' nothing, Seeing that we are nothing, we desire to become, Desiring to become, we live. —Rene Daumal

This brings to mind the myth of Pandora's Box, a classic tale of women's curiosity. Pandora, considered to be the Greek version of the biblical Eve, speaks to the myth of woman having navigated a searching questioning quality of curiosity that carries shattering consequences. Eve, warned to not eat from the tree of knowledge of good and evil, Pandora, cautioned not to look inside a box, both were tempted to step into the darkness where it is still possible to create light and compassion. Both women, longing to know, to look, to taste, took risks. We live in a world where dreams and fears are unopened, the lid tightly shut, where most resist not going deeper, further. Opening Pandora's box releases the judgment of the tree of good and evil through bringing light into the dark, for us to decide whether to wound or to console. No longer is there a duality of good and evil. Sitting with whatever arises we learn to own, take responsibility, to uplift and transform all aspects. Fear becomes awe, heartbreak becomes yearning, greed becomes heartfelt passion, anger transforms to courage. To awaken in the dream begins the process of awakening from the dream.

When you reach the top, keep climbing. —Zen proverb

WORK IS LOVE MADE VISIBLE

Conscious work is the effort to sense, remember and observe oneself.
—C.S. Nott

I learn while I work. Living from the center of life demands clear intention. Creating a channel between giver and receiver sets into place a mutuality that extends beyond the moment of need, a gratifying bond that becomes compassionate teaching. Working with others has taught me the endless possibilities of reciprocal relationships. Listening inward, becoming aware of another, bringing loving attention to the other we begin to see the world as it is...through the heart. To be of service, having been provided with our life, to work harnessing the energies of love and compassion creates a new world, allows us to see the wonder and purpose, the transformed world of all that we are, now alchemically turned to gold. It has been taught that the only work worth doing is to remember ourself; that only one thing is real work and that is remembering the forgotten, but not the lost; easing suffering. Whether we remember or not it is here to be discovered, called self-awareness, attentiveness, reminders to find out who I am.

At the still point of the turning world. Neither flesh nor fleshless; Neither from nor towards; at the still point, there the dance is, but neither arrest nor movement. And do not call it fixity. Where past and future are gathered.

Neither movement from nor towards, Neither ascent nor decline. Except for the point, the still point, There would be no dance, and there is only the dance. —*T.S. Eliot*

My teacher used the friction of working with the intensity that I brought as a student for her own awakening. Jean often said that I was a hardworking challenging student and therefore a gift for her. I tested, pushed, loved, was committed to the whole journey. In the beginning I provoked, prodded, questioned, as well as jumped passionately into a commitment to serve and to live with Jean and any student who made the intention to work. Initially Jean made herself accessible. To establish a way of living that reflects our highest truth brings about a naturalness to live in the heart. Jean had little fear. I remember her saying: *If you break your fear, you will be able to teach others who live with fear. Because I don't know fear. I was afraid only once.* That episode occurred when a shark was after her in the water. The resistance entices the fear—watching it, learning, unraveling these obstructions we gain understanding—and that liberates us from our reactions.

She made herself available for what we needed, not concerned that she would run out of resources, energy or time. Many people feel the needs of others as boundless, endless and exhausting and are put at ease only when limits are set. So often I have observed amongst therapists and teachers that what they name as boundaries rules and limitations are really auxiliaries of their own personal fear. My experience has allowed me the confidence to know that when someone asks for five sessions a week, I see them five times a week, trusting that this will eventually pass and something deep will become satisfied, to ultimately shift. Likewise, if they need call, e-mail, or text me many times a day, they can, and I maintain trust in the process. This way of teaching, serving the moment, without withholding or adhering to rules or fear of consequence, trusting the innate core and health of people has consistently proven to guide, restore, to heal and deepen an opening: the value is in the heart... to continue opening. This manner of teaching speaks to the autonomy, the wholeness, the integrity and strength of each person. We have a tender place where satisfaction can be touched, once addressed. I have had remarkable successful verification of this experience. A true teaching.

The shop-foreman, irritation showing plainly on his face, strode over to Jules, a non-conformist free spirit. 'Listen,' he growled, 'do me and everyone else in the shop a big favor and quit whistling while you are here at this job.' 'Hey,' retorted Sam, 'who is working at a job? Whatsoever I have done in my life, it has never been a job. I have been simply whistling. To say that I work at a job? This is the way I am. It is not a business; it is simply the way I am. It is happening, I cannot do otherwise.' —Osho

When I worked with autistic children, I directly entered their world, imitating and whirling with them. I listened to children who had never spoken, finally speak. Such results confirmed my instinct to follow the child rather than follow the rules and guidelines. Our minds are afraid to tap into universal energy, we construct little worlds and boundaries and then declare that to be the way. To continue to live in the present moment is to be courageously willing to try new ways, not having to follow precedent, staying connected to the heart—to make love visible. In my work that is what I try to do.

All work is empty save when there is love; And when you work with love you bind yourself to yourself, and to one another. —Kahlil Gibran

HOMAGE TO A TEACHER:
OPENING THE INNER SELF

Old, torn and patched is an honest place to begin without silly illusions and some healthy experience. —JR

You told me to sleep five hours a day.
You told me to feed the wolf to save the lamb.
You told me every hair is counted.
You told me that lies are the greatest sin,
that the mind is the devil, that gold alchemy
can be achieved, that you would sacrifice every
student for one to be enlightened.
And now you have brain cancer.

You told me you loved me,
that I was your one eye messenger,
to love my precious self,
that consciousness is possible,
that I am worth something;
and now your brain tumor is malignant.

Do Teachers die?
I imagined your death to be before me
so I could be led,
be guided through the tunnel into your arms.
I would call your name: Jean, my Teacher
my one forever Teacher birthing me into myself.
My whole past and history begins with your name.

You told me to give up my attachments—no ketchup,
no moving vehicles, no stores or shopping, no restaurants.
To sit while I ate, to sleep alone,
to go to a strange town—to go to the desert alone:
and I did.
I listened and learned a self built on love and wisdom.

If you die a space will open for me.
For life.
When a Teacher dies the earth moves.

You told me the first come last the last come first.
You went before me and I will remember.
I remember Dover Fox-Croft, Maine.
You on a hill.
I remember baptism in a stream.
You lifting airplanes.
I remember you dancing naked in Central Park,
peeing anywhere anytime,
our swimming across Cape Cod bay.
I remember finding eternity holding on to a bed post,
living in a dune shack, surviving a car crash,
hearing Bonnie die, surviving your fist in my jaw.

My life began again there out in the woods:
baptism in a stream, tossing away blind faith,
living the Christ drama,
being Paul the Apostle, becoming living history.

And now I have myself to face,
and your love, the test and measure of my life.

—*Dr. Paula Bromberg*

CHAPTER EIGHT

The Circle Of Angels

Reason took us as far as the door; but it was presence that let us in. —*Sanai*

Believe in the impossible, for then you will find it possible. —*P. D. Ouspensky*

I complained to the universe when my foundation was shaking, only to discover that it was the universe shaking it. —*Charles Weston*

Want nothing with all your heart. Stop the stream. When the world dissolves. Everything becomes clear. —*Dhammapada*

> *The angels were looking Jacob over*
> *and deciding which*
> *one was to wrestle with him*
> *all the night long,*
> *and towards dawn to wound him in the thigh*
> *so that he limped forever after.*
> *An angel is a messenger of God, is God,*
> *and whoever touches God bears the wound*
> *and can be recognized by it, forever.*
> *How many of God's people bear the wound?*
> —*Ladder of Angels*

THE CIRCLE OF ANGELS

*T*he whole universe unfolds in a circle—the sun, moon, planets—bringing here to earth the angels of light, purity, messengers, wounded innocence in communion with all of existence.

Through the years Jean has loved me with nudges, blows, and directives—some subtle and some explicit. The following are few of her love-teachings:

- *Listen to your innocence, not your mind.*

- *The peace that passeth all understanding is devoid of personality.*

- *Be more, say less.*

- *Love makes one sensitive and your thickness brings blood.*

- *Love, being what it is—tough, eternal, and drastically necessary—I leave it to you to inform me, who loves you, just what you wish to take, give and/or share—just how we may proceed in this grand and pathetic love affair.*

- *No pain, no growth. Look at your proper and improper behavior according to natural laws—those of Love. If you do not see your errors and practice ridding yourself of such habits, naught can be understood or changed ... and your life will be forever incomplete, with only death holding the keys.*

- *Love is a difficult game. Have fun and be serious.*

- *The emphasis is on Spring, re-birth, resurrection, fertility, beginning anew, transcendence over suffering, consciousness over unconsciousness, life over death—a re-dedication to all that is life and love.*

- *Old, torn and patched is a wonderful place to begin—without silly illusions and with some healthy experience.*

- *The only reason you view me as a 'powerful' person is because I love you.*

- *The real issue is your grotesque condition; don't throw a bone to the wrong side in your civil war towards clarity and sanity.*

- *We must all treat love with care, sensitivity and precision ... and it must not be denied. It takes years and scars and scores of intentional careful discipline.*

- *This is a School, not just an AA support group. Your tiny or massive ego is supposed to be hurt for Christ's sake! We have work to do. I do not intend to spend years tip-toeing around your madness. We're either going for it or we should throw in the rag.*

- *May this find you ready and willing to begin the process of integration. Try to remember and create situations that keep your heart free. Learn to breathe before reacting.*

- *Extreme effort is necessary in order for any real change to occur. If you will not make it by living in our communities, then you must be asked to do so by making extra effort in the community at large.*

- *Just because your brain can make up a reason for something does not make it so.*

- *Gossip is a part of unconsciousness and will continue until the species is complete. Don't fight it except in yourself. Why are you so surprised by human nature, when theoretically you have made a life study of it; is it because you've never studied yourself? It is one of God's great truths that unconscious people are like pigs—why do you complain? It's like complaining of rain on Tuesday, or that cars can have flat tires!*

- *Your main problem is you still see your problems as outside yourself—(maybe not in mental reflection but in momentary action)—as all unconscious people, you blame the world around you for the viciousness while patting your own sweet vulnerable self on the back. We all must stop this way of thinking and being by observing honestly and verifying that we are what we are witnessing—the mind projects.*

- *Stop complaining—God says it's all right for things to be as they are—it can rain on Monday, people die, suffering exists,—and, there is the Master Game for those who want out of it—The others prefer the story in it—hush up and watch!!!*

Thank you, Paula I love you—& wait Eternally—For we know, don't we! My love, JR

CEREMONY AS CELEBRATION

A ceremony is a book in which a great deal is written. Anyone who understands can read it. One rite often contains more than a hundred books.
—G. I. Gurdjieff

The wonder of living with a teacher and a teaching is particularly visible during times of ceremony. At those moments the direction is clear, the giving of our life to higher purpose, a journey of imperishable being. On the occasion of my thirty-fifth birthday Jean created a ceremony at the school. With each of the 7 gifts she offered me she said the following:

*In honor of your valiant Rebirthing Process I present to you **seven** symbols for Self-Remembering:*

A. Three symbols to represent the highest aims of the lower self:

1. A soft, pink King of Hearts = Compassion.

2. *A gold, fertile egg = Female Receptive Principle—Temporal—
   Mother Earth—Form.*

3. *A gold, erect penis = Male Penetrating Principle—Spiritual
   Father : idea of Consciousness—Formlessness.*

   a. *Gold = The highest, purest valuation/understanding.*

   b. *Sexuality = The most potent, refined energy from the lower
      Self...the seat/seed of our beginning...The foundation/base-
      ment/acceptance upon which we must stand to begin the
      Spiritual Stretch. To "be"/crystallize these internal phenom-
      ena allow the building of bridges/ladders/extensions toward
      final completion...spiritual existence... closure of the circle...
      merging of Heaven and Earth (Male/Female) all dualities.*

B. *And three symbols to represent the attainment of higher worlds/
   levels/bodies:*

   4. *The exotic, unusual flowering conscious effusion and penetra
      with its perfume/power... its fragility and receptive acceptance
      upon the coarse Earth, merging the male/female principles.*

   5. *The Angel of Light...conscious innocence/essence bear-
      ing the gift of pure, clear, unobstructed, imperson-
      al, objective vision..."and a child shall lead them"
      " as an angel with authority"—essence with Truth.*

   6. *Collaged symbols of attainment...objective gods/Laws/
      Relationships in form of service. c. One to represent Air-con-
      taining the minuscule molecules of my expanded/contracted/
      exploded/ego self, now merged and dancing with-in-on the
      Air...the breath of life...mine in yours...yours in mine...One.*

   7. *The breath of my kiss upon your third eye (consciousness,
      compassion, vision).*

STATEMENT

*T*he following was written January, 1979, by Jean, and included in a workbook that was given to each student:

General Statement (from the teacher)

Since our first crystallization/inception in New York City in October, through our most recent crystallization in Maine in August, and subsequent life on Cape Cod, we have perused and pursued a myriad of forms. Essentially, in psychological realms at least, we may appear Gurdjieffian. Esoterically, we may at most appear Sufistic. In fact, we are many and all forms available through us at any given moment...stuck in none, averse to none, fearless through death.

An Esoteric School is not a democracy. The blind student acquires sight slowly until he "sees" the Teacher and the Teaching consistently, and wants only what the Teacher and the Teaching wants...Conscious Beings.

The aim of this School is to provide a contained, refined energy, a positive working environment, vigilant surveillance, and reliable Love so that the student may attain to crystallized God-Consciousness. It is to reliably manifest the one value system in accordance with universal laws, thereby transcending them... allowing one to exist freely in a spontaneous innocence, harmony and balance with oneself and all that is.

This (Friend, Lover, Teacher, Entity) serves as the force, the insistence, the fearlessness and the example of one who has trod the path before you. This (Friend, Lover, Teacher, Entity) serves as a representative of your potential, as an unwavering, objective mirror reflecting your manifestations and/or your perfect seed. This Presence is present to you whether or not you are present to her presence. She-It sees through and around your uncon-

scious manifestations to the Love-Core...and reminds you...and reminds you...and reminds you. This (Friend, Lover, Teacher, Entity) functions as fuel to fire your dormant conscience, breathes Life into your near-dead truth cells which have been blocked by cancerous lies. This (Friend, Lover, Teacher, Entity) is relentless and will go on through eternity awaiting you, shocking you at every instance to wakefulness. She-It has vowed to train negativity out of the minds in her presence, and to bust every lie wide open.

This (Friend, Lover, Teacher, Entity) acts out many roles but is not the roles she acts out...through a female Martial energy-form. Her Work, Love, Lives, Bodies, and Breath are all the same...energy designed to unburden you and our World, however grandly or minutely. This (Friend, Lover, Teacher, Entity) is to be used, and used and used again...but abuse is blasphemous. She-It cares not for being "liked," "disliked," or "understood"... and approaches you with Love in its highest form, to unshackle that Love of your own, that you might fly freely and breathe life into others.

YOU GET WHAT YOU NEED

People rarely see the beauty and the greatness around them. They live their lives in half sleep. Paying attention we go deeper, attention, well developed equips us with the capacity to be open to what would ordinarily escape us. The ability 'to see' is rarely deep enough. With sustained attention, we grasp relationships which usually are overlooked. To nurture an attention which penetrates into the heart of things whole new worlds reveal themselves. To give meaning to the humblest encounter, no subject is too small, to insignificant, to receive attention and care. —William Segal

Jean's acceleration intensified while the school was in Doverfoxcroft, Maine. Jean's brother, Billy, owned land and we camped on it for several months, living in tents and working together as a school of consciousness. We came to Maine as a group directly from New York. Most of the students had a contemporary essence and were accustomed to city life, therefore some of the challenges, resistance, frustration, obstacles, as well as the learning, centered on the organic Maine country lifestyle. This was definitely not an easy vacation in the woods. The instinctive friction was relentless; whenever we are hard-pressed our least developed places rise to the surface. The friction to transform suffering increases the level of available attention. The poet Rilke praised the tenderness and value of this essential suffering : *How dear you are to me, you nights of sorrow, Why do I not kneel more to receive you, and give myself more loosely unto you? We, wasters of sorrow. How we gaze beyond them into some drab duration to see if they might not end there.*

Our attitudes are acquired, are personal, limiting and arbitrary. Studying what creates our attitudes loosens them, expands our possibilities; meaning comes from our way of seeing, not from the circumstance. How we see life changes the way life appears. Through the process of self-observation and self-study, watching ourselves behave mechanically we familiarize ourselves. Practicing to let what we see penetrate through the exterior we go further. Intention subdues the mechanicalness that reacts automatically, impacted by the conditions of life we are held captive to our thoughts and actions. With understanding our positions and reactions dissolve, turn into playful gestures usable for whatever aim we are trying to further. Seeing everything as a play with ourself as an actor, circumstances lose their power and we are less bothered by what happens. Training ourselves in this way we become more available to life as it is. To live in this way self-study is necessary which begins with a decision, and a teaching. Real change happens from the inside. The conditions of our daily routine, the practical day labor prepares us to become available to forces that pave the way to higher states.

Since we cannot change reality, let us change the eyes which see reality.
—*Nikos Kazantzakis*

We had regular meetings, were offered individual tasks, exercises to gather information, to bring to light and verify as well as experience and study ourselves. Practicing new ways of being with others we worked together to build a chapel and meditation space. Living as students doing practical exercises of self observation to generate energy and develop awareness, collaborating in the effort to gain awareness we were paving the way for a richer relationship with ourself and others, for greater awareness, for being a presence which then becomes meditation-in-action. Elaine, a hardworking, ascetic student, was sawing wood for the chapel. She looked up and said: *Oh, God, I need more friction. I need friction.* Within moments she sawed her finger off. She was taken to a hospital and Jean asked me to go there with her that afternoon. Jean stood over Elaine's bed and told Elaine, *If you ask for something you will get it. Ask only for what you really want.* When you've taken on a teaching and live in agreement as travelers within a community everything becomes accelerated and intentional. Pooling our consciousness together we affect each other as our energy circulates. Consciousness moves and so we cannot be too flip because we will get what we need, which is not always what we want, and we *will* get what we ask for.

Look at you, you madman, Screaming you are thirsty. And are dying in a desert. When all around you there is nothing but water! —*Kabir.*

As Jean and I were waiting for Elaine to come out of surgery, we saw a patient covered with a sheet being wheeled down the corridor. Jean turned to me. *If she's dead, don't miss a beat.* Friction used well is transformed, not identified with; the school was intended to produce consciousness. Un-transformed moments are missed opportunities. The teaching for me has been to learn to live as function, without the embellishments of drama, sentiment, and high emotion. Many moments call for action free of the storms of emotional madness, in mental preparedness and alertness.

Evaluate how you spend each moment: with presence or negligence.
—*Shah Naqshband*

WITNESSING IS PURE CONSCIOUSNESS

If you have the choice between enlightenment and a million dollars, take the million dollars! Because if you get the million dollars, there will be somebody there to enjoy the million dollars; but if you get enlightenment there's no one there to enjoy the enlightenment. —*Ramesh Balsekar*

A demonstration of a martial or warrior body type, Jean's acceleration released and burned up excess parts of her life. Acceleration means speeding up, living in another time, space and dimension, living in higher parts, manifesting in a way to eliminate the daily stress of mental activity, worry and fear. Jean was a visual electric energy field, her dynamic rocking tempo created an energy which became a stable presence, like a second body; she called her movement *the rock of ages*. The high vibrational frequency created a rhythm that moved her force of life to an expressed energy field that grounded her attention. The unfolding through her body acted as a spiral penetrating through the spheres, quickening her flow of movement. We are made up of a multitude of bodies, including water, air, earth, fire and ether. The etheric or vital body enters the fifth dimension carrying the force of electro-magnetic waves. The entire universe is filled with substance and since we are transmitting stations able to transform matter everything in motion is transformed to a finer or to a more dense matter, dependent on its ascending or descending direction. Creating heat to saturate her body with lighter, refined hydrogen Jean brought all matter to a higher level. She grounded through the accumulated substance of her inner work practices, drawing upon the state that was produced, like a lamp that is wired and on, she was a dynamo collecting impulse energy from the atmosphere. The sound of our force resonates to ionize our body. Outer work spends energy. Inner work accumulates energy. The universe operates through dynamic exchange. The higher our vibration the more quickly energy is refueled.

In the Movements the important thing is not the positions, but the impulse, the energy from one position to another. And nobody can teach you that. You have to watch yourself. —*Jeanne de Salzmann*

During Jean's acceleration, I was asked to watch over her body as well as the body of Jo Grady, who was in the tent with Jean. I was carefully poised to maintain attention. The students sat outside the blue 2 pole domed 8x8 Eureka camping tent, in a half circle configuration looking into the tent where we three sat cross-legged. Jean and Jo sitting on a rectangular blue goose down sleeping bag had no clothes on and Jean's body appeared to be on fire. She was astrally projecting at this point. My task, as it was given to me, was to prevent Jo from leaving her body. Jo was to watch Jean and I was to watch Jo; I also was watching both Jean and Jo and trying to create tension in my own body so as not to become overwhelmed by the gravitational force, the curvature of space-time waves that were pulling/pushing me to collapse. I was focused, vigilant, an axis of balance, centered to serve. This process went on well through the night.

During this time, Jean gave me an assignment, to choose someone for a particular task, with my own life depending on it. So my choice became urgently consequential. I didn't pick someone from my likes or dislikes, but out of function. The task itself was simple: to fill a bucket of water; I asked Kathleen. I remember choosing her because I knew she was efficient, precise, taking her responsibilities seriously, someone who followed through with whatever she was asked. For the first time I chose with conscious intention, with reference not to my own preferences, instead, to objective law—who properly suited the function for the job.

The true purpose is to see things as they are, to observe things as they are, and to let everything go as it goes. —Shunryu Suzuki

Jean's change of consciousness affected her form. She was lifting from someone who was conscious for herself to a new level, burning off elements; her radiations gave off a vibration like electrical currents which had an electromagnetic force. The movement was perpetual; she was breaking down impressions, refined to the grade of psychic hydrogen of a higher order pulled by invisible strings. This was her epiphany, a quickening, and we were immersed. The energy was high, and Jean was unraveling her life in front of us. We played different parts in it, as she was releasing, as she was moving between worlds. There were no apparent life rules. It was beyond imagination: her unfastening of bodily control, the intensity, the disregard for convention, all appeared as energy taking over the entire world. Jean chose people to ring the space, to walk around the outside of the tent. We were monitoring to keep negative forces from entering the area during her acceleration. Darkness is no longer visible in the atmosphere of light, similarly, unconsciousness dissolves and is disabled in the presence of luminous consciousness. When the mind is still, time vanishes. We entered a timeless world of weeks or months in the tent and on the mountaintop. At one point we became parts of a Biblical drama. I remember being Paul, Elaine becoming Peter, Bonnie as Barabas, and Jean being John. We went down to a deep stream on this land and were baptized.

Truth is a bird in flight, not a bird in a cage. Transformation, relaxing into what is, brings a higher state of being. Around consciousness, miracles, the workings of divine laws, happen simply and naturally. The real miracle is a change of heart, new understanding, releasing of habits. Great things are not what is demanded. *The previous generations did all that for us.* We have now to do the small things—while living in a more challenging time.

The Teacher is the one who instruments your illumination, who helps clear the way. While one lusts for food or sex and is beset by such thoughts, nothing is possible. So the Teacher challenges the student, sometimes quite harshly, until we are willing to give up those attachments. A Teacher carries the responsibility of refining the capacities of the student so that we can begin to realize our true nature. —William Segal

During another acceleration encountering an inward dimension, within and without dissolved and I was initiated into being both the universe and nothing. This happened in the house on Cape Cod bay. I was in the same room with Jean, both of us reclining on separate twin beds. She was in higher frequency and I felt my body starting literally to burn. To be close to the fire, to melt, absorb and receive ignited a spark that penetrated to a deeper core. I experienced my mind withdraw, become empty and I transcended the body. In the realm of pure being, that formless realm, there is stillness and great aliveness. These spontaneous moments, unfathomable, yet real, bring the teaching into our life to continue even beyond the teachers form. The determination to remain connected to a higher energy, once contacting the inner teacher, brings up a well of energy that is a preparation for this encounter. Learning with devotion brings about a finer quality of attention. The presence of the teacher and the teaching has always been our own true self. This discovery of limitless openness, in a realm beyond imagination, was consuming. On the particular occasion, two other students, Lori and Deborah were appointed to watch over/protect Jean's and my body. Deborah had to continuously put cold water on my body, and I to hold on to the metal headboard of the bed to stay grounded in the flesh. Jean explained that I was going into the electronic world, of pure electricity, the world of the speed of light, the world of the sun. Like sunlight which interpenetrates everything, conscious food from light has continued to nourish me throughout these many years. Being shown a higher plan fed my desire to live into that possibility. When the acceleration slowed down, much of my gum tissue was burned away. This required first-time periodontal work.

Thus if the Tibetan Book of the Dead may be taken as probable, most unprepared men would never experience the life of the spirit, or the electronic world at all, even though by the arrangement of the universe, each man is entitled to do so. It is his deathright, which he sells for the mess of potage of material attachments. Passage from the physical world into the molecular world may be compared with the explosion of a bomb, the constituents of which in one moment change from a few cubic inches of gelatine into thousands of cubic feet of gas. But passage from the physical world into the electronic world would be literally akin to the detonation of an atom bomb, the expansion being so great that vortex was created right through the earth's atmosphere and out into solar space. But what man's consciousness is strong enough to become attached to the explosion of an atomic bomb and retain its awareness? When irritation or flattery or a sudden shout may instantly deprive men of all sense of their own individual presence and existence, what possibility is there of them retaining such a sense through the unimaginable shock of death? —Rodney Collin

On one hand experiencing what is immortal and indestructible, and on the other hand living in a body that is effected daily on a cellular level requires tenderness, patience and deep surrender. I have since understood that accessing the molecular world is the world of the speed of scents, sounds and atmosphere, the cellular world is the world of the speed of the lives of cellular bodies and the mineral world is the slow dense world of rocks, stones, minerals and the core of the earth. The training and preparation to enter the infinite forms, to break free of ordinary perceptions, to penetrate consciously into the unknown and beyond; these small tastes of worlds began what for me has been years of building bridges, of dissolving selves, of paying attention, and of practices. And still there are miles to go, continuously starting new again entering the spiraling labyrinth of understanding.

To Wake Up

There are no answers to be found, only the questions that define our limitations. Understand the question, and you destroy the limitation. It is through courageous thought and clear-seeing that delusion is destroyed. —Jed McKenna

Jean used me, and I her in our mutual quest for Self. There were moments when I was swept into a pool of energy, experiences on the cellular level, times surrendered to an unfathomable realm of peace. It was as if the sides of the stage, which are the boundaries of life, dropped away. Jean's body during acceleration would become red, sizzling, heat waves radiating from her body with such intensity that one could barely enter the room. Students walking in were jolted, before long they would leave the space. It was like walking into a drug den, yet there were no drugs. Being present created a visible change in being. Accepting what was offered, *Yes,* to what is, nonresistance, is the key.

We see and touch the world around us, but we do not realize that it is not this world but the higher worlds that are substantially real, and we cannot understand this until we have begun to experience it for ourselves. To do this we have to learn how to exist differently, how to exist in more than one world at a time. —*J.G. Bennett*

On one such occasion Jean told me to give water to the cat. I remember trying to figure out how to put water in a bowl, normally a simple task, but not so easy when walking a tightrope. My awareness was spread out along an interval between thoughts. Everything except the present moment vanished. How does a transparent liquid fill a bowl with water, to be carried and placed on a floor that is superimposed on a background? Space became vastness. Our state of mind is reflected as we walk on this earth, connecting our body and soul with the here and now. I learned to let go of fascination to use each precious moment, remaining present to each function. Years later, having sat with those who have realized their true nature, I know that to open, to awaken to who we are beyond name and form, moving away from the present moment to an imaginary future and being caught in the narrative of the past stands in the way of our presence. Life is right now and we obstruct our opening. Absorbed with the objects of our thoughts life becomes filtered through the thoughts in our head that buffer the world, interfering with our being present to the world as it is. Being here-now is our natural state, our true nature. To become what we know: to know freedom is to be free, to know love is to be love. To experience love as compassion, finally the noises stop. A life of learning is to come to know ourself through cultivating understanding. True wisdom is a liberation from concepts and a willingness to live at the abyss of emptiness, which is infinite openness or oneness, without losing sanity. And when we know ourself in this way we will know the needs of the moment. For this is the love that anchors knowledge. And love needs us to manifest.

At some point in your growth it starts to become quieter inside. This happens quite naturally as you take a deeper seat within yourself. You then come to realize though you have always been in there, you have been completely overwhelmed by the constant barrage of thoughts, emotions, and sensory inputs that draw on your consciousness. As you see this, it begins to dawn on you that you might actually be able to go beyond all these disturbances.
—*Michael Singer*

Jean had the discipline to give up fascination with the process, to use her acceleration to embody the teachings. To cleanse our personality through intention, discipline and action, to make it a carrier of information, we serve an authentic teaching. We live in a play produced not by the President of the United States but by the conscious beings who are available to guide us. At the Circle of Angels the students and Jean worked many months to harness energy, to get energy tight, anchored, until something would hit, with transforming impact on at least one of us. An accelerated environment can produce a conscious being. Jean would say, *If I were told that I could make one student conscious by having you jump off a roof, I would have you all jump.* She would also say, *I don't want a bunch of disciples. I want a friend. So hurry up.*

To Live What We Know

*E*veryday life is the practice. Everything that touches our life has levels of meaning, learn how to be a student of life. The more attuned we are to living in the sweetness of blessings, to look with the eyes of love, the closer to entering a heightened appreciation for life. Everyday challenges create the setting. Once we live in the open space of awareness to our true nature we become transmitters of love. To seek the reality that gives meaning to each experience, to be in contact with *what is* we draw upon our internal energy source. Being present to understanding becomes our foundation. Having experiences does not necessarily mean we learn anything. Knowledge is ultimately the knowledge of ourself. Discovering the still point of the turning world removes us from the treadmill of action and unnecessary suffering. To withdraw from the action allows us to find what is real. The steadiness of our mind permits a deepening of attention, now we can be present to our own life. Peace, the wheel revolves, and we move inward. Controlling and directing lower emotions supports inner health. We receive according to our capacity, and then knowledge becomes wisdom. As we transform ourselves, living what we know, we build a bridge of love.

Silence is the fence around wisdom. —*Hebrew proverb, Pirkei Avot*

A tortoise and two geese sharing a small pond for many years became close friends. A drought slowly drying up the pond made it apparent that the geese would soon have to fly away to find a new home. The two geese bid farewell to the tortoise. The tortoise hearing this news feared that he would eventually die of loneliness and so pleaded to the two geese to let him join them. Since the tortoise couldn't fly the geese said, *No*. Begging to join them the geese figured out that only if the tortoise agreed not to open his mouth, not to speak a word, could he come. Agreeing to be silent rather than die alone in the dry pond, allowed the geese to show tortoise a strong stick and then had tortoise grasp it tightly in his mouth and with each goose holding an end and tortoise clamping his mouth on the stick they could fly to their new pond. As they flew over several villages many people looked up and pointing heckled at how very silly the tortoise looked. People jeered and laughed at the foolishness of a tortoise flying mid-air. The tortoise growing more and more prideful and indignant at the stares and ridicule from the villagers finally couldn't tolerate the insulting teasing anymore and opening his mouth to explain fell to the ground and was smashed to pieces.

Who undertakes the task of self knowledge and further self development, must put it first in their life which is not so long that we can afford to squander our time on trifles. —*G.I. Gurdjieff*

Yearning, longing and striving are the deepest and surest guides when tempered by teaching and direction. As form dissolves and veils are lifted invisible worlds appear. During this acceleration period, moving beyond the relative world, beyond mind, in a flash, a moment, I was living in another dimension—a fourth state. My hand was taken and I was flown around the world, shown many things, and then gently brought down to hear my inner voice say, *Okay, now live this.* The following years what I experienced was incorporated into the everyday material of my life, and it continues and continues. What I tasted and knew in the fifth dimension reinvests itself into this present time reality. The experience of consciousness initiated me to know that it is possible, and, in fact, necessary, to live a mindful life. As veils parted I had tastes, sightings; indestructible reality penetrated my being, opened me to the higher, and that remains with me, the responsibility for my life, the experience that is beyond all form. The inner eye opens revealing the mystery, to be lived, still distant and beyond, further, further, and further still.

Our practices ground and balance us inside as we open to higher worlds. Writing, having a teacher—*a servant of the student's yearning,* formal study of sacred text, mindful conversation, my beloved, these have been my daily practices. There is a story about a student who questioned his teacher: *What shall I do now that I have learned all there was to be learnt?* The teacher replied: *Practice what you have learned, for theory without practice is like a body without spirit.* My experiences were glimpses, before full practice. I was given clear visions of what life is, to allow them to unfold within me, my practice, my work. Since I was out of time, what I saw was to return to time, here in this world, a timeless beginner. I envisioned a world lived without negativity, free of personal whims, beyond personality. When worldly connection to time ceases, seeking stops and we arrive. Returning to form, entering back into my body, my preferences reclaimed me, my likes and dislikes, my wants and aversions. I snapped back into my personality out of an expanded state, this time, though, I brought with me a true inner observer, and a deepened sense of being. All else pales before the experience of enlivened awareness.

Sail forth! Steer for the deep waters only! Reckless, O soul, exploring. I with thee, and thou with me. For we are bound where mariner has not yet dared to go. And we will risk the ship, ourselves and all. O my brave soul! O farther, farther sail! O daring joy, but safe! Are they not all the seas of God? O farther, farther, farther sail! —Walt Whitman

YOU ARE NOT THE PERSON
YOU TAKE YOURSELF TO BE

When your real, effortless, joyful nature is realized, it will not be inconsistent with the ordinary activities of life. —Ramana Maharshi

Self-knowledge as awareness is the beginning of wisdom. There is no distance in love, dropping the illusion of separation there are no walls. *Life is Real Only Then, When "I Am"*, Gurdjieff's book is titled. The focus is on what happens within the human being, within the heart, where the little *I am* and the big *I am* become one. The outer is always changing, is fleeting. To move inward is to find what never changes, who is always present, permanent. Invited into the banquet of love, seeing through the cracks in our heart, love is our state of being, an expression of our matured essence. We move from needing to giving, from wanting to sharing. Our illusions have created the unnecessary suffering, the wounds that carry us across the threshold of change, sometimes on our knees, broken. The baggage that we have carried throughout our years have brought us to the door, have been the reason for the search. *Why struggle to open a door between us*, asked Rumi, *when the whole wall is an illusion*. Sri Nisargadatta Maharaj speaking to a seeker stated: *all that a teacher can tell you is: My dear, you are quite mistaken about yourself. You are not the person you take yourself to be.* We journey around the world and still return to the entry point, the search begins and ends with our self. In the process of placing ourself in the fire, miracles and heartbreaks melt form, leaving spacious consciousness to shine through. Recognizing our true nature as totally open, flawless, clear, limitless, and perfected is the freedom. To serve the world from this openness honors the highest within ourself. Speaking about the passion to serve, Vivekananda said: *By thinking intensely of the good of others, by devoting yourself to their service, you will purify your heart by that work and through it you will arrive at the vision of Self which penetrates all living things.* Serving the world we help to mend this broken creation. The privilege to be of service manifests in many forms, essentially its primary ingredient is presence, we each have our function, our purpose and responsibility: all of our thoughts and actions impact the whole galaxy.

This self of which you speak, whether it is the great self or the small self, is only a concept that does not correspond to any reality. —the *Buddha*

The invitation presented itself to me in the form of my Gurdjieff teacher. When I first met Jean, I lived in New York City, in Chelsea, in a loft with twenty foot ceilings and walls and walls of books. She said to me that my first task was to create a home so that if my teacher were to walk in, only the things that were now *me* would be visible. She sat on the oversized leather couch in the office section of the loft while I tried to complete that task, to discard excess stuff; her presence lent a powerful focus. One challenging part, though, came in dealing with a wall of books on Existentialism. I had many books by Jean Paul Sartre, Simone de Beauvoir, Friedrich Nietzsche, Albert Camus, and a number of other philosophers and had carried them through different moves for years. I placed them in a carton to sell at Barnes and Noble book store. I recognized that they weren't who I was anymore. Before I left New York I removed everything that was no longer me in the present, and I continue to try to update the hard drive, to live with that intention.

Enlightenment is an accident, but spiritual practice makes you accident-prone. —*Jack Kornfield*

I've kept the gifts, the pearls from my teachers as a compass, a direction to live into for meeting the needs of the moment. Having experienced a source of higher energy, now to step out of the way, to enter a silent place, where quiet is said to be *unceasing eloquence*. In Sanskrit, sound is considered to be the distilled power of silence. And so practices of music, chanting, mantra, bhajans become the poetry of the heart.

When the heart has found quietness, wisdom has also found peace. —*Gita*

I continue to scan my home and remove unnecessary belongings. Memorabilia and old stored collections often perpetuate sentiment, an emotional quality of attachment that diminishes spiritual capacity. It's often acted out with hits of the pop music charts which have lyric titles like: *Nobody knows you when you're down, Bad blood, Bitch better have my money, He left me and now I'm going to die, Jealous lover, Break up with him, The other woman, Breaking up is hard to do* or *I'll never love again.* Most of our holidays have been reduced to sentiment. Statistics reflect that Christmas, the number one holiday that people celebrate in America, has the highest suicide and homicide rate, the most document-ed sexual abuse time, the largest admissions into psychiatric hospitals over all other periods of the year. I see that as a by-product of sentimen-tal thinking which says: *I wish I were with my family, our holidays were so wonderful,* or, *if only I had a good family to go home to like everybody else.* Each of those statements may be far from the reality of truth yet they tend to create feelings of hurt, rejection, self-victimization, disappoint-ment, jealousy, anger, sadness and self-pity which often lead to drinking, drugs, marital fights, suicide, homicide. Caught in a spiritually impov-erished world happiness is taught to be an acquisition and a commodity. *Money buys happiness,* say the magazines and television. Spiritual matu-rity addresses what is hidden, what we turn away from: aging, loss, dis-appointment, illness, death; impermanence. A mature vision, one that embraces the darkness will carry us along a journey into truth, honoring the sacred texts and practices that are our heritage.

The cause of misery is not in life without; it is within you as the ego. Be as you really are. It is not a matter of becoming but of Being. Remain aware of yourself and all else will be known. —Ramana Maharshi

THE HEART KNOWS

At the end of the talk someone from the audience asked the Dalai Lama, 'Why didn't you fight back against the Chinese?' The Dalai Lama looked down, swung his feet just a bit, then looked back up at us and said, with a gentle smile, 'Well, war is obsolete, you know.' Then, after a few moments, his face grave, he said 'Of course, the mind can rationalize fighting back.... but the heart, the heart would never understand. Then you would be divided in yourself, the heart and the mind. And the war would be inside you.'
—reported from a 2012 talk in the USA.

While living at the School I was not primed to live in the woods. Having a contemporary, not organic essence, living outdoors was for me an uncharacteristic foreign experience. I kept a bucket in my tent. To go to the bathroom in the woods felt lame. I remember walking down the hill to empty my bag of shit. Like a child I was swinging my garbage bag and singing, *It's Howdy Doody time*. Jean was living in a trailer, grieving from an emotional loss. She said the center of her heart had fractured and she was preparing to leave her body. Just then she happened to look out the window, and seeing me in my determination, my purest child essence, captured her attention, reawakened her focus. She realized that what she had to live for were her students. She made a choice at that moment to not let go of her body, to align with her life purpose. She said to me, *the work is to let your heart break*. I began to understand that my work, too, would be to live in the heart, pierced, penetrated to let love be revealed, to let my heart shatter, uncompromised, cracking until one day breaking open. It has been taught that there is nothing more whole than a broken heart, the heart must break to become large, and then the whole universe fits inside. And now it has happened. I have become that broken-hearted authority living at the center of love itself, having finally dared to turn to love. For it's in an open heart that the mystery appears, when the *beloved is born in the heart, the entire creation participates in this birth.* To pay attention to the present as the focal point of our life, it is all here and available for us to be in this everyday life. And the work is to be rooted, anchored within, to build love with a sense of aliveness that is right here originating from consciousness itself.

In her biographical movie, the Jungian analyst Marie-Louise von Franz states, *The alchemists said that the gold is found in the shit. After reaching illumination, one returns to the common life. There is no contrast between consciousness and the shitty life. If we see the hand of God in the shit, then we don't suffocate in the shit.* Beyond our aversions, beyond our pain, facing our darkest concerns we look to practices that hold us to the difficult, that create a container strong enough for us to weather these challenges. To look into our woundedness not for relief, instead to meet in recognition; we gain patience towards the scars by looking towards a peaceful recognition of *what is.* Ramakrishna, self-realized, was able to bless even the pain of his throat cancer. To see the sacred, to feel presence when the mind stops making sense, the heart knows beyond all reason. When we allow our heart finally to break, when the longing to love overtakes us, when the heart is freed as in the Sufi symbol of the heart with wings, we are finally in the Way of Love, a continual celebration of each ordinary moment.

Reason is powerless in the expression of love. Love alone is capable of revealing the truth of love and of being a lover. Mount the stallion of love and do not fear the path—Love's stallion knows the way exactly. With one leap, Love's horse will carry you home however black with obstacles the way may be. There is no salvation for love but to fall in love. Only lovers can escape out of these worlds. The whole world could be choked with thorns, A lover's heart will stay a rose garden. Only from the heart can you reach the sky. The rose of glory grows from the heart, when the agony of love has broken up your life, roses and lilacs take over the garden of your soul. —*Rumi*

BEYOND PERSONALITY

Don't just do something. Stand there. —*the Buddha*

By worldly standards I had a lot. My psychotherapy practice was successful, I was speaking on panels for television and radio shows, enrolled in a Ph.D. program, had a familiar group of acquaintances, a primary love relationship, good health and lots of outside adventures. Life was filled with distractions, innerly though I felt like an outsider. The treasure inside was far away, covered over by longing, excessive energy and agitation. The narratives were absorbing. I had been on a searching quest, a mariner of sorts, devoted to finding treasure. Sophisticated journeyer, I had already traipsed continents, now holding my inner world together through its sweeps and movements of energy. When I met my teacher I knew that I had come into contact with somebody who was much more than I. Knowing that there was nowhere else to go with the things I already had, that there was nothing more to *do*. I realized somebody was offering me the possibility to *be* more, not to *have* or *do* more.

All of your life you have been taught to do, to strive. You have been sold a self-improvement plan. You have been conditioned to believe that you are the body and the mind. All of this is a reflection of ignorance. It has been the blind leading the blind. —*Adyashanti*

In Jean I found a conscience and a bridge to teachings that brought meaning, that became a center for my being, a link to internalize the teaching for myself. I have the capacity now to live the teaching. I remember her saying *There is no Jean.* There is a universal law that the lower can not see the higher, accounting for why there are such diverse stories from students about their teacher. I remember days when Jean would be elusive and silent and meditative; I would find her in her room, but she'd be who knows where. You couldn't put a finger on her. In the beginning she was more approachable. She was accessible and saw me and met my needs, both as teacher and friend, meeting me on a personal level. I see now that I don't have to be at the school to live the teaching, the teaching is me.

Jean was a lover, she didn't love out of self-interest. She loved. Whatever exercises she gave to me were really for me. She was a hard task-master, sometimes it was challenging to feel myself being loved, yet I felt it, even when she was pushing and I was questioning/resisting. Entering that love, anchored into each encounter as a meeting with the beloved I perceived and understood her conscious light through the light in my heart. Trungpa Rinpoche said *Even your struggle with the guru is devotion. Your resistance and your anger can be a sign of your devotion.* Surrender is bowing before the unknown, simply in that everything is a blessing and to pay attention knowing there is a greater force; being relieved of this *personality*, the identity that is projected onto us; to finally be nothing as well as to be of service.

Transformation happens to us and for us, depending on the degree of work we do. People often talk about working on themselves without knowing what this means. You cannot transform personality with personality. When you work on yourself what is working on what? If you try to destroy the ego with the ego, you create a thousand-headed serpent. So what can you do? It is said that love can turn even copper into gold. Love will melt the personality, because love redeems all into itself. We have to allow ourselves to be loved, which is to be transformed in the fire of love. —Reshad Feild

There were so many teachings, practices, and unravelings. How can it be that we live within these bodies, personalities, with our names for years, and yet don't really know what they are made of and how we function. The invisible has to be brought to light; recognizing ourselves is a real beginning. I had shied away from my middle name for many years until one day a whisper in my ear told me its inner significance. Paula Nada—nothing. In Hebrew, *ayin*, The Ba'al Shem Tov teaches that the Hebrew word *ayin* means nothing, the divine nothing from which all reality, something, is continuously recreated. The implied negation transferred into a positive assertion, diminishing we become truly eternal. In the Buddhist tradition, *sunyata*, nothing, impermanence, nothing lasts, nothing remains the same. What a surprise! Continually diminishing myself, the impossibility of not teaching, not practicing; and there is always more. This life force sensing the depth of possibility available, continues....it's ongoing. Beginning, always beginning.

If a teacher does not tend to his or her human experience as well as to her awareness the teacher's students will pay the price, and he or she will also suffer the karmic consequences of premature assumptions of spiritual enlightenment or awakening. Like Claudio Naranjo, who came to understand that his great illumination had been sacrificed in order to integrate that which was still 'dark,' or unconscious, within him, we must be willing to suffer our own darkness if we truly aspire to know the deeper spiritual potentialities that exist within us. —Mariana Caplan

Jean's limitation and demise was in not seeing each student as her own true self. There remained a slight separation. Just enough for the mirror to lack total emptiness. We recognize ourselves as we look into the mirror. We vanish in an empty pure reflection. The teacher is a door. For me it was to cross that threshold and open that door to consciousness. I had to let go of life attachments; the possessive inclination to having a lover rather than being a lover as well as the attachment to personal comfort. And once let go, everything is given back—now in freedom.

Believe in a love that is being stored up for you like an inheritance, and have faith that in this love there is a strength and a blessing so large that you can travel as far as you wish without having to step outside it. —Rilke

A Heart Alive, By The Sound Of It's Own Weeping

The hardest thing for a person is to endure the manifestations of others.
—G. I. Gurdjieff

I remember one time at the school, in inner turmoil, feeling lost and broken, my partner was holding me while I cried. Jean opened the door and bellowed: *Don't you hold her when she's in that condition!* I came to understand that I wanted somebody to take away my fear and pain, to make me feel good, to protect me from heartbreak. To push myself further would be to walk through the fear to the other side, to courage, conviction, strength, a heart expanded and awakened. Jean called to me to enter into the nameless and affirm my inner truth, to trust my own possibilities. That's the response of a good lover. Most people aren't that kind of lover, wanting to hold us when we feel bad, to comfort so as to make us feel good while obstructing our deeper experience; and that is our own responsibility to our tender relationship with our precious inner world. Remaining with our feelings, not escaping from them tears down walls, opens doors, breaks the dream, pulls us out of the dream, asks open-ended questions. Henry David Thoreau wrote: *that only that day dawns to which we are awake.* We are on a journey that has no map or edges, how to be vigilant, connecting to higher energy, dropping into the interior of ourselves? *You shall not look through my eyes, nor take things from me, you shall listen to all sides and filter them from your self, one world is aware and by far the largest to me, and that is myself, not I, not any one else can travel that road for you, you must travel it for yourself, it is not far, it is within reach, now I will you to be a bold swimmer, to jump off in the midst of the sea, rise again, nod to me, shout, and laughingly dash with your hair,* wrote Walt Whitman. My persistence and dedication to know love, became unwavering.

We're all afloat in a boundless sea, and the way we cope is by massing together in groups and pretending in unison that the situation is other than it is. We reinforce the illusion for each other. That's what a society really is, a little band of humanity huddled together against the specter of a pitch black sea. Everyone is treading water to keep their heads above the surface even though they have no reason to believe that the life they're preserving is better than the alternative they're avoiding. It's just that one is known and one is not. Fear of the unknown is what keeps everyone busily treading water. —Jed McKenna

I was told to not physically leave the school for two years. This created tremendous friction, because I strongly wanted to make a trip to New York City. It sounds so simple: I was attached to my desires, my wants; relief and distraction pulled at me to go away, to distance myself from the very core that I needed to drop into. I felt like I was dying; Jean's refusal to let me travel left me feeling broken and twisted mentally and physically. By harnessing my center of gravity—moving center—and not letting me indulge it, Jean led one part of me to die, which allowed other parts to surface and bloom, bringing me into a new balance. Withdrawing energy from the world and rerouting energy to myself allowed me to practice dying to the external world and to be born into myself.

Philosopher Jean-Paul Sartre said: Freedom is what you do with what's been done to you. In other words: freedom consists in finding the point of power, which is always in the present moment. It also means: how you respond to what happens is more important that what happens. —Eckhart Tolle

FINDING THE INNER SANCTUARY

It is no use saying, "We are doing our best." You have got to succeed in doing what is necessary. —Winston Churchill

The exercises were a challenge. In one particular practice we were confined to a bed to experience *not doing*. For several days Jean assigned one student to take charge of our physical needs. To relinquish control and surrender was a powerful exercise, what would be discovered was quite unknown. Paying attention, seeing our work; self-study is doing what is asked and then to look inside to understand the value and what it means to follow a task, to be intentional. The inner journey includes a destruction of life-illusions which can be experienced as a death. To make our personality passive in relationship to essence; personality provides the information for us to study including the obstacles that stand in our way, our temptation and illusions. Knowledge about ourself through observing and gathering information without making change is pure collecting information. Direct, neutral, dispassionate collection of data. And, then, to investigate. And which *self* of ourself are we to know? The elusive multi-selves that appear and disappear, that rise and fall, that pull and tug, that amuse and confuse. Through all the mirages and mirrors there is a root, one true self that is me.

This above all: to thine own self be true, and it must follow, as the night the day, thou canst not then be false to any man. —William Shakespeare

Over time we create an observer, a witness, someone home who watches, experiences ourselves even in the midst of activities and major circumstances. How sophisticated this is! It becomes a practice and it is essentially the beginning of our inner work. Adding the component of intention, taking responsibility, not necessarily to achieve or to become something, for this inner work is free of ambition, instead it's to lift awareness, to deepen, to have states of consciousness and know who I am. That burning question—who is this that I am? To come to know the mystery of the darkness, the unity of opposites, what is beyond all concepts, what is ultimately created in the cold hard earth of winter to later awaken in spring. This happens with a willingness to enter again that dark womb of the Mother, just as the mystics chose to enter and bless the darkness in the mountain caves of India. The difficulty of our inner spiritual journey has been pointed out in the gospels which say: *it is easier for a camel to pass through the eye of a needle than for a rich man to enter a kingdom.* The wealth comes from having learned to rest in the darkness, to allow the light in the heart to teach us the peace and wisdom of dying before we die. To reach a depth of silence, to awaken to ourself as we are and enter into that experience, is to be.

Perhaps the whole root of our trouble, the human trouble, is that we will sacrifice all the beauty of our lives, will imprison ourselves in totems, taboos, crosses, blood sacrifices, steeples, mosques, races, armies, flags, nations, in order to deny the fact of death, which is the only fact we have. —*James Baldwin*

My desire to love deepened my faith. At the school the yearning that kept the fire burning, that held me standing steady when my knees were shaky, was to love my god-son, Mitchell, and a friend, Harriet. Through the years I have moved beyond the sentimentality and the preferences to embrace who is in my arm-span, and that one becomes the smile, the commitment and agreement to work and study, to gift and protect the integrity that I know that I am. Who shows up, who is available becomes the guest. Who sits with me in visibility are my *sangha*, the Sanskrit word for *inseparable;* the community looking to serve from their place of kindness and compassion. Liberation does not arrive from preferences, ignorance is the suffering, as we enter into understanding the truth of what has always been. My connection to my teacher has remained an enduring bond, a rope to heaven that has passed into the hands of other teachers since then, and is now held securely within my own hands with arms outstretched and opened wide.

The divine has no body now on earth but yours, no hands but yours, no feet but yours, yours are the eyes through which to look out the divine's compassion to the world; yours are the feet with which the divine is to go about doing good; yours are the hands with which the divine is to bless all beings now. —*Teresa of Avila*

Another exercise brought me into a room for 36 hours deprived of most stimuli. The shades were drawn, I had no books, or paper or pen, only bread and cheese and water and Kleenex. I thought I would be agitated, yet contrary to my expectations something very wonderful and quiet emerged that I had not allowed myself to find, a place beyond suffering, an inner sanctuary where quiet bliss reigned. When the veil lifted during that episode I experienced being held in the arms of silence; a taste of meditation, of stillness. I entered the tenderness of the silence beyond the mind, and emerged opened with love.

Love creates the unity of heaven and earth. Love tears apart heaven and earth. Is love sympathy. Is love gentleness. Is love possessiveness. Is love sexuality. Is love friendship. Who knows? Maybe the rock knows, Sitting diligently on earth, Not flinching from cold snowstorms or baking heat. O rock, How much I love you: You are the only lovable one. Would you let me grow a little flower of love on you? —*Chogyam Trungpa*

The exercises continued to stretch my edges. In one, we exchanged a massage with each student, both of us nude, then wrote about our experiences and read them to the group. Confronting my own illusions, meeting resistance, learning to be home connected to my body, quieting mental chatter, were intense teachings. Encountering my dark side, facing and recognizing and ultimately embracing my demons has been a powerful and uplifting experience equipping me with insight into myself throughout the years. The once self-conscious exercise of nude massage and public description shifted into a practice of my own in Santa Fe, New Mexico. I would spend an hour in the afternoon at a hot tub oasis high in the mountains with five or ten other women in full sunlight, honoring the beauty of individual bodies, pushing beyond normal comfort while upholding my limitations, being fully within community, this time in the name of wholeness and health and celebration. Once finding a safe place within, and sanctifying the right to enjoy, this freedom traveled from the mountains of New Mexico to a beautiful public nude beach in South Florida, where men and women appreciate the beach and ocean in a clothing optional space. Discovering the root of our being, staying connected to that, this energy that is always available directs us to live harmoniously, connected, no longer imprisoned in ours and others thought forms. Dissolving our unnatural self-consciousness and our inner demons allows us to then follow the natural spontaneous curve of our life.

Remember that you are an actor in a play and the playwright chooses the manner of it...your business is to act the character that is given you and act it well; the choice of the cast is another's. —*Epictetus*

THE ROAD TO HEAVEN

Life is a bridge, cross over it, don't build a house on it. —*proverb*

A thin line separates madness from consciousness. On one side is fascination, on the other awakening. When I worked at

Bellevue Psychiatric Hospital with schizophrenic children I had a deep connection and ability to enter their unrestrained whirling stream. I was unafraid of the world of madness. *The sharp edge of a razor is difficult to pass over, thus the wise say the path to salvation is hard,* reads the epigraph. It's a narrow, difficult path, a hard journey to freedom. My ability to walk that line and face my own dark terrors, to walk with one foot in heaven and one foot in hell has brought me into the here and now. Not to step over the line into fascination, to remain mindful, placing attention, contacting what is, this knowing, in the face of the unknown, is the source of our creativity. An inner life that is quiet, unflappable and alive, as things appear and disappear to remain serene, penetrable, open, steady. Our greatest attachment is to our unnecessary suffering, to the fascination side of the line called madness. It is the last thing we drop. This compulsion, attraction, preoccupation that draws, lures us, I understand now that what we call our suffering is often an illusion, our mind-set directed from circumstances. The things that Jean provoked us to let go of looked to be our faith and suffering, but were not real. We aren't really asked to let go of any thing, we are asked to set our sail in new directions, to reboot our inner hard drive, to put our baggage in the baggage car, to shift our stance; as we deepen our understanding and revise our attitude life takes on a new appearance. The work is beautiful, bringing us to the true stuff of life, its actual substance. When we work, the teaching works.

The one who is rich is able to appreciate what she has, to realize and live into the truth that what we need is nowhere else. —*Joshua Boettiger*

We named the school, The Circle of Angels—a Metanoian Order. Metanoia, change of attitude, a transformational change of heart, is to build a recognition of the essential impermanence of all forms until surrender becomes a way of living. This awareness towards the ever present challenges that are part of living continue to burst the dream bubbles until the teaching drops, roots, settles deep inside ourself. To go beyond a set attitude opens a door to the vastness and mystery, while keeping us honest. Our vulnerability is to look at the fleeting nature of life and the challenges and opportunities that come and go. Being present to the moment with open-heart, open-hands, to ordinary daily moments, is the road to heaven, the miraculous, for us to live as we are, the surprise and prize of presence.

We created our friction our challenges with purpose, to experience intentional suffering for something higher. The exercises in the school were designed with this in mind. Most people would say that to intentionally make ourself suffer is senseless since life itself brings hardship. And yet our environment acts upon us, to look and to study ourself, to experience ourself in the midst of life's activities we disarm our personality and prepare a way to live in choiceless awareness of what is appropriate to each circumstance. Everything depends on our quality of attention which is restorative. This inquiry of self-investigation has enabled me to live life with more clarity and love. Pain and suffering are not parallel, refusing our pain creates our suffering. If we want pearls we have to dive deep, where there is always danger.

I wanted to have a clear mind instead of a mind filled with chatter. To find clarity I subjected my mind to the insanity that was there already. The work I did allowed my distorted thinking to become visible. Now, when distortions arise, I can recognize them, smile, and lose interest in engaging and entertaining them.

Attention or awareness is the secret of life and the heart of practice. Every moment in life is absolute itself. That's all there is. There is nothing other than this present moment; there is no past, there is no future; there is nothing but this. So when we don't pay attention to each little this, we miss the whole thing. And the contents of this can be anything. This can be straightening out our sitting mats. Chopping an onion, visiting one we don't want to visit. It doesn't matter what the contents of the moment are; each moment is absolute. That's all there is, and all there ever will be. If we could totally pay attention, we would never be upset. If we're upset, it's axiomatic that we're not paying attention. —Charlotte Joko Beck

The Mask Becomes The Face: the Fall Of A Teacher

My only vow is to remain here in the land of utmost suffering through count-less lifetimes in order to benefit all living beings. —the Avatamsaka Sutra

Jean's life was unremarkable, a warrior, she had built a house, was close to nature and had an organic essence. Hers was a journey of remarkable effort. I had not known her when she was a student at The Fellowship of Friends, her Fourth Way School. She spoke about break-ing, climbing exhausted up a hill to come home at night to the exercises of the school. Her life included working in a prison as assistant to the warden, a high school counselor and business teacher, sorting fish at a fish packing plant, numerous relationships, and heavy alcohol consump-tion. I may never know what broke her or of her dismantling, her earlier spiritual quest, her crazy-wisdom teachings or what led to her faltering, to make choices that ultimately attracted those students with vitality and juice and enough self to make the difficult and necessary choice to leave, some broken into exhaustion. I know only that she lived her remaining years with a desperate and limited partner who possessively encroached on her teaching and apparently was the shadow side of a being who had displayed great light.

When you awake, you have to awaken again. You try to understand this adversary. Make an effort, not struggle. —*Lord Pentland*

A conscious partnership has an inclusive deepening love for humanity. It is a being together while turning together towards others. The light of the conscious relationship increases as all others are embraced. The holy marriage is designed to expand and deepen our spirit. Jean and Jo, as a partnership turned away and blocked kindness. Others perished as they became bitter company. Lacking all encompassing benevolence we saw the wounds that had not healed. Unconditional love, the acceptance of everything is the sacred partnership, and Jean with Jo missed the mark.

You yourself are your own barrier—rise from within it. —*Hafiz*

Jean died a painful and difficult death from cancer. We must each answer to our own wisdom, and Jean still had impediments that created her own version of hell, especially for one so close to awakening, yet also blinded on so holy a path of love. In her insistence on uncompromised unconventional teaching ways, when the goal is the absolute then obstacles create dangers. Jean may have sacrificed her humanness in her presumption of God-Consciousness. The expression of compassion for all humanity which is the essence of a spiritual life is far greater than taking up residence, refuge in spiritual attainment.

The Great Master attended a class disguised as a Lowly Student. The Inept Teacher held up the Great Book and spoke words that were loathsome to the Great Master's ears. Unable to endure the Inept Teacher's false interpretation of the Great Book any longer, the Great Master picked up his chair and beat the Inept Teacher to death. Instantly, the Lowly Students burst into Full Enlightenment. —*the Zen Teachings of Master Addlebrain*

Initially, I tested Jean to see if she would fall. In the beginning she made herself available to me, rarely letting her mechanical self get in the way. I could wake her at any hour of the night and she would get up and work with me, or with any student. It was amazing to see the design of the school unfold. There was no school, then suddenly we would call meetings and create form. Together we developed a workbook which differentiated the body types. In the beginning she had endless energy, like a battery charger, at the end she dried up and ate her own tail.

Consciousness is a delicate journey. My understanding is to walk with great care, dissolving into love. Knowing there is no separation the lover and the beloved become one. I imagine that Jean's eventual demise lay in choosing a partner who was an imprecise mirror to her consciousness and then faltering in her final attachment. At those heights the fall is a long and hard one. Her freedom would have been to express a love that unlocked the heart of all the world, and to dissolve every trace of separateness; instead, Jean opened and cultivated a wound of separation.

The truth of awakening lies in knowing that we are part of each other, there is no separation. To walk the path of unity, with generosity and compassion for all; to embrace the world is the vision. This, then, as Rumi describes, is the step Jean missed:

The whole world could be choked with thorns:
A lover's heart will stay a rose garden.
The wheel of heaven could wind to a halt:
The world of lovers will go on turning.
Even if every being grew sad, a lover's soul
Will stay fresh, vibrant, light.

Embrace the world. Say, *I am you.*

I have since come to understand that the journey begins with the ascent up the mountain until we arrive at a view that is astounding. The climb down, however, is where we bring with us everything we know in love and service. This climb down takes dedication and precision. Jean never quite made it down. She experienced some great views and she brought some of us up. When she accelerated I had no fear, while most of the other students were afraid to let themselves go. I eventually learned to access energy through my own day labor, to find what is real in me, to open to a higher energy and great patience in order to maintain clarity and understanding for both the climb and the descent. There is a beautiful Hadith (saying): *I was a hidden treasure, and I wished to be known, so I created man in order that I may be known.* What a wealthy bounty we have available. To be present here in this ocean of bliss is the treasure, and I thank myself, eternally, for joining hands with Jean, and her for leading me up the mountain.

In every action that we do,
In everything we do,
We should treat each other
with the soft hand.
Not the callused hand of the woodcutter,
But the soft hand of the flower
Anpu, the inner flower of the heart. —Rumi

DEAR COMPANIONS, WE ARE ALL LOVERS

May every action I do be worship. May each word I utter be a mantra and each time I lie down May it be a prostration. —Amma

Over the years something in me refined itself. I don't need to be pushed so grossly. I remember the last time I was at the Circle of

Angels, and we were singing with a student named Deanna, a woman with untamed vanity. Her eyes were closed while she was singing, and Jean leaned over and cracked her across the face. I figured that this was because Deanna wasn't really singing with anybody else, but was on her own little toot. Deanna opened her eyes and continued singing. When it was over Jean said, *That's what happens when a student has been with me this long. She's sophisticated enough not to ask why, but to just keep going on.* At that moment I realized that I no longer needed a gross teaching at that unrefined level. I knew then that I had internalized the true teaching and my work was to live it with the inner conviction and strength that had finally awakened within me. For me, what had been the form of my school dissolved. I understood that there comes a time to leave the small teacher and the small teaching that served as an experiment and exercise, and to bring all that we know into the world as our community. To live without separation.

A billion stars go spinning through the night, blazing high above your head. But in you is the presence that will be, when all the stars are dead.
—*Rainer Maria Rilke*

To carry that true love and knowledge into this world is the completion of such teaching, and much more difficult than remaining sequestered in a school, guarding what is perceived as true and ultimately turning consciousness back into Dunya (the world of appearance). It is said that a conscious teaching is the *noblest dimension of humanity.* It is the highest offering to the human race and has been the inspiration and fuel for *The Way of the Lover.* To help build this beautiful new world, cooperation and inclusion are essential, a kindness to all humanity. *The function of a Teacher is to bring each person to their own beginning and then to release them. The responsibility of this work is the reciprocal maintenance of the planet on a global level.*

To have tasted this freedom, to have had doors and windows opened—is to understand how even walls disappear. Custodians of this planet, we are interconnected, we stand out here in the world—inside our heart—and begin to love now.

Without love, life is impossible. We have to learn the art of loving. This world very much needs love. I am more and more convinced that the next Buddha may not be just one person, but a community, a community of love. We need to support each other to build a community where love is something tangible. This may be the most important thing we can do for the survival of the Earth. We have everything except love. We have to renew our way of loving. We have to really learn to love. The well-being of the world depends on us on the way we live our daily lives, on the way we take care of the world, and on the way we love. —*Thich Nhat Hahn*

Like all things, relationships are impermanent. The point is not to make the relationship last forever, because it can't. Serve the intention of the relationship: wake up to the mystery of being. We are what we experience. Presence is knowing directly in the moment, that we are what we experience. The path does not rest on fiction, beliefs or peak experiences. It consists of taking apart, brick by brick, the wall that prevents us from knowing what we are. To dismantle that wall is the work of a lifetime. It requires an outlook to show us a way, a practice to develop the abilities we need, and a way of living that brings the practice into life. The practice is attention: Cultivating attention and using it to dismantle the sense of separation. The way of living is presence: we live in attention, aware and awake in the mystery of being. —Ken McLeod

All of us look out at the same world. And we all see a different version of it, depending on what's already in our minds. Practice is to notice how the dust of our mind obscures the clear reflection of the world, how our values and preferences determine our interpretations. These 'dusty' tendencies are delusions. Experiences enter the mind as distortions of mind itself. True intimacy occurs when we directly experience reality for ourselves. Each one must find intimacy directly, not through thinking mind, but from immediate direct experience. —Katherine Thanas

CHAPTER NINE

The New Psychology

What we need is a completely new psychology, one which has as its end not a decent sanity but a transfiguration of the being. What is possible is liberation, and any psychology which does not have as its end the complete liberation of human beings from the bounds of illusion is of limited value. —*Andrew Harvey*

Who am I?" Behind the misleading screen of all our other questions it is the question of each one of us in our human existence. It is humanity's first and last question. —*Michel de Salzmann*

Unless we understand the whole psychological structure of society of which we are a part, which we have put together through the centuries, and are entirely free from that structure, there can be no total psychological revolution—and a revolution of that kind is absolutely essential. —*Jiddu Krishnamurti*

The family is the basic group most of us have established in us, and it is a barrier to being on a level with each other. The family is the small, cramped group which most of us never get beyond. It is based on emotion and power. —*Anthony Blake*

Ego doesn't need to be killed because it was never really alive. You don't have to destroy your false self because it's not real, which is really the whole point. It's just a character we play, and what needs to be killed is that part of us that identifies with the character. Once that's done—REALLY done, and it can take years—then you can wear the costume and play the character as it suits you to do so, now IN the character but not OF the character. —*Jed McKenna*

All circumstances must change in time; and if one can pass through them equally, without being borne too much up or too much down, one becomes ready for other change. It is not the happy or tragic role that makes the difference between actors, but the way the role is played. Some parts of life are very hard. At the same time one can no longer wish it to be otherwise; for perhaps it is better to be called upon to pay up to the limit of one's capacity for a while, so that one's debt to life is reduced, and one may be that much nearer to becoming free. Though we do not know how it works, I am very sure that this paying off of accumulated debts is essential before really new things can enter one's life, from a different level. —Rodney Collin

At the most basic level, spiritual maturity has to do with the realization that you are not in control. Being willing to lose everything is a blessed surrender. The invitation to accept the diamond of life is not an invitation to safety and comfort. It is an invitation to live life fully and completely, which is never safe and is often uncomfortable. —Gangaji

SOCRATES: I want to hear from him what is the nature of his art, and what it is which he professes and teaches; he may, as you suggest, defer the exhibition to some other time. CALLICLES: There is nothing like asking him, Socrates; and indeed to answer questions is a part of his exhibition, for he was saying only just now, that any one in my house might put any questions to him, and that he would answer. SOCRATES: How fortunate! Will you ask him, Chaerephon? CHAEREPHON: What shall I ask him? SOCRATES: Ask him who he is. —Plato

A NEW PSYCHOLOGY OF HUMAN POSSIBILITIES

What has been offered to us is a seed which holds the unfolding of our possibilities; what we transmit is our being, a presence that flows through us: we are tools for the spirit. To awaken to our true nature, to unfold and know who and how we are, to live consciously and intentionally is our possibility. Discovering who we are intended to be and to live spiritually mature in all circumstances is the inherent principle of *The Fifth Way, The Way of the Lover*—new, ongoing, transcendent, each moment a first time. To awaken and live the life of our spirit is both challenging and a necessity. The new psychology seeks liberation from illusion, a willingness to pursue the dream, to take risks, to give birth to ourself so that we penetrate conditioned patterns to transform our being as a whole. In a poignant tale, Martin Buber's parable, *The Query of Queries,* that question of inner authenticity is asked: Before his death, Rabbi Zusya said, *In the coming world, they will not ask me: Why were you not a teacher like Moses? Why were you not devout like Elijah? They will ask me: Why were you not Zusya?* There is no answer to this. Four questions to myself are: do I deceive ourself, am I imitating another, am I being myself. Who am I? Our life constantly brings opportunities to go deeper within ourselves, where the door to the real opens and our treasure, no one else's, pours forth.

Once, after a hard day's forage two bears sat together in silence on a beautiful vista watching the sun go down and feeling deeply grateful for life. Though, after a while a thought-provoking conversation began which turned to the topic of fame. The one bear said, 'Did you hear about Rustam? He has become famous and travels from city to city in a golden cage; he performs to hundreds of people who laugh and applaud his carnival stunts.' The other bear thought for a few seconds then started weeping. —Hafiz

Sacred Psychology is a bridge between psychology and spirituality. To move beyond the fiction of our biography and learn to live a mature spirituality includes self-investigation, a look at the psychology of our family, our historical development and its process—our spiritual life then penetrates our conditioned personality releasing whatever has blocked our energy. Self-knowledge is the threshold, the invitation to unfold and reveal, to know ourselves. Our freedom from illusion begins with the examined life, with the acknowledgment of how and where we covered over our essential nature, our true self. Nothing to hide in the maya of darkness. To integrate our biography into awareness and to allow it to dissolve is like moving from the book store fiction section to the non-fiction section, that place beyond personality. Initially projected images, then an empty screen until that too disappears, taking with it our desires, affairs, stories, ambitions and greed. Screen disappears and what's left is the light. This is the psychological base of my work. We enter a period of mourning for the person we were created to be but gave up to survive a frozen family structure. We mourn for the sacrifice of possibility, of who we might have become. Even when we are removed from our family system, we carry a role, that of a bad, good or rebellious child, daddy's princess, the under-or-over-achiever, a surrogate father if our father ran off or died while we were young, the caretaker, or whatever strategy we had adapted to keep our family system intact. When we live current, turned toward the inside, to the practice of presence, of making conscious efforts, we become free to change the direction of our life.

We are all born in a post-hypnotic trance induced in early infancy. —Ronald Laing

PSYCHOLOGY:

SCIENCE OF THE SOUL

We are transformers of subtle energies producing a refined alchemical substance, called soul, which travels with us and spreads out into the world. The soul is made up of the stuff that comes through sacrifice and surrender. The soul, a knowing substance, its true heritage is freedom. The untransformed mind cannot understand the nature of the soul, the essential self.
—*Reshad Feild*

As children we are born with an undeveloped spiritual life. Dr. Elisabeth Kübler-Ross has said that we are equipped with four quadrants at birth: the spiritual, physical, intellectual, and emotional. The intellectual and physical quadrants become developed overshadowing the other two parts, unless a child is ill or faces death at a very young age. In those life threatening scenarios the spiritual quadrant then becomes greater and more developed. The cultural message given children is to close off their spiritual aspect, even though a spiritual sense is innate and directly experienced by children right from birth. Our educational system offers little support or encouragement despite the fact that to develop any of our quadrants they each need to be specifically addressed; our spiritual aspects need to be spoken to for there to be growth. *Sacred Psychology, The Way of the Lover,* speaks to, embraces the spiritual quadrant; it is no longer regarded to be a vague, esoteric concept.

We are born into the world of nature; our second birth is into the world of spirit. —*Bhagavad Gita*

Originally psychology meant *science of the soul*. Psyche in Greek mythology is the personification of the soul. *Psyche* in Greek means soul, breath or butterfly, and the word *therapy* is derived from the Greek *to serve, to heal.* Psychology has moved far from her origins and true meaning. In classical mythology, Psyche was a personification of the soul in the form of a beautiful girl who was loved by Eros/Cupid; her suffering transformed her in her preparation for eternal happiness. Suffering has no intrinsic value, it is like a heat, it fuses things. Suffering is a raw material and when transformed into presence strengthens the aspects of yourself you want to encourage. When we have released old patterns and are ready to fuse, to integrate our many parts, then the irritations and difficulties that arise, rather than being swept away by them can be used to elevate, to change, to strengthen our capacity to be loving and compassionate. Psyche was made immortal and was represented in ancient Greek art as a goddess with butterfly wings. The derivation of the word is the soul or spirit approached with love. In Roman mythology Psyche was the lover of Cupid. Their story, that of soul and love portrays Psyche as the beautiful butterfly winged goddess. The illustration of the immortality of the soul is strikingly portrayed as a butterfly bursting on wings from its caterpillar existence flying into air and light. Dr. Elisabeth Kübler-Ross discovered from her lifetime of working with terminal patients that when children face death they paint and draw butterflies. Death is simply a shedding of the physical body like the butterfly shedding its cocoon. The butterfly, its wings strengthened by its struggle to exit the cocoon, gracefully emerges from its chrysalis and takes flight. The new psychology, that of our possibilities and of our development, looks to what we may become, from the point of view of our possible evolution, our unfolding.

In fact, the obsession with therapy can fix you in biography when the whole point of the journey is to integrate biography with the Self, the relative with the Absolute. Without an integration of these two dimensions, without an awareness of transcendence, no therapy can help us to freedom.
—Mark Matousek

The new psychology unites higher consciousness, mystical awareness and a commitment to life in all its forms. Becoming aware that we
are buddhas, are Moses and Miriam, gods and goddesses, opens a link to
higher levels of consciousness. To bring this realization into the world,
to others, to nature, allows for a greater sense of unity. The distillation
of our essence creates a fragrance, invisible yet permeating all planes and
dimensions to carry us into the unknown. Forms dissolve to the mystery.
Soul is the inner eternal light, beyond the limits of time; it's through
witnessing that we first become aware that we are eternal beings, that we
have a soul. The soul created pure is neither spirit nor body, it's an ocean
without shore. This knowing substance called soul manifests through us
as we are creating it. Possibly the most profound undertaking we commit
to in our lifetime comes about, is formed through the impressions we
take in, the efforts we make and the illusions we release.

Soul bridges the divine and the worldly, the body its repository. A
link between realms our soul evolves, a mirror polished reflecting clear
light. *How are souls to be made,* asked the poet John Keats, *How, but by
the medium of a world like this. A world of pains and struggles is necessary
to school an Intelligence and make it a soul.* Wrestling, engaging with life
deepens the soul's response to this world. The poet Yeats called this
world *the vale of soul making,* this invisible part that effects everything
we do. Gold, metaphor for the soul, is precious and enduring, is alloyed
with other metals, combining with metals makes gold stronger, workable
and useful; the soul created pure, also needs to be mixed with the material world in order to evolve.

*Unless western psychology starts seeking and searching for the soul it will
remain a very ordinary thing with much jargon. It has created a great system
but the essential core is missing. 'Psyche' is a beautiful word, the most signif-*

icant word in any language, because it indicates something in you which is beyond you. You are not the body, not the mind either: you are the witness of it all. Unless one starts growing more and more in witnessing one will not know that one is a soul. —Osho

The Fifth Way, The Way of the Lover, strengthens witnessing awareness, fortifies an inner life, anchors soul's growth. Soul, transcendent by nature, experiences fullness, takes on a body, for the sacred marriage between soul and body. This is what Rumi called *the marriage feast, the place where soul and body celebrate their eternal wedding in time.* The body is symbolically referred to as the chalice or sacred vessel out of which the soul drinks enabling a divine human life to flower in the heart of ordinary life. To stand aside and watch the play is to experience what is eternal and exists beyond ourselves; when love appears all else disappears. As the quality of witnessing develops, identification loosens; a new consciousness reflects the birth of soul. In the experience of eternity the opportunity to penetrate light and come to the center, which is beyond light and dark, emerges. As witness we have the possibility for the awareness that beyond body and mind there is soul that is untouched by death, and our possibility to know the mystery of soul.

When experience is viewed in a certain way, it presents nothing but doorways into the domain of the soul, and they are all found in the present moment. You give care and attention to your life as it unfolds in actuality. Thoreau called it the greatest practice in life: 'To affect the quality of the day, that is the highest of arts.' —Jon Kabat-Zinn

There's a story that Adam was created soulless and as the soul was invited into the body it said *I'm no fool to want to be trapped in there.* So angels entered the body with harps and played beautiful music to lure his soul into his body. In the Jewish tradition four Hebrew words for soul: *nefesh,* self, *ruah,* spirit, *neshamah,* the essence of a person, breath, or life-force, and *yechidah,* the highest and innermost called the higher self are looked to as a key to the spiritual nature of the universe as well as the essence of each person. And the Kabbalists, the Jewish mystical teaching regard the soul as divine presence, with sparks of light throughout the world that are linked to each unique soul. The fabric of who we are, the soul, encompasses the spiritual, directly reflecting our connection—the ideas and meaning behind the words that arise from our very core, unbounded spaciousness, infinite silence.

When you are left behind, when you cannot walk anymore, travel anymore, your soul continues the journey. —*Rumi*

Often in Sufi literature the soul is a bird imprisoned in the body longing to fly home, or a fish in the ocean thrown onto dry land, or a reed cut and separated from the reed bed, longing to go back, expressing itself in its reed flute song or the glory of the body as a robe for the soul. Rumi uses the elements of nature that come alive in spring as the outward signs of the soul's inner awakening. In Rumi's poetry, love is the infinite soul of the universe, embracing all of humanity. Through the Koranic lens, original sin was that Adam forgot, and the cure for forgetfulness *dhikr, remembrance,* frees spiritual energy, awakens the soul. Initially it's a repetition of the tongue, then remembrance of the heart, as the heart deepens *dhikr* becomes remembrance of the soul. Hafiz asks: *The dust of my body veils the face of my soul. How can I fly if I am imprisoned in the body?* The soul's becoming, despite constraints placed upon it through physical embodiment shines through our awareness and increases in substance until it no longer needs a body to make its qualities manifest. Through our soul development we know value, see our true nature, find the inner meaning of our experience.

A soul—our own I, our individuality—must be earned before it can be bestowed. It is up to us to build our cathedral, to become a worthy vessel, before the spark can become a living fire, transforming every cell of the body into an instrument for the individual expression of the divine here on earth.
—Rainer Maria Rilke

SOUL-MAKING:
REPAIRING THE WORLD

The soul that moves in the world of the senses and yet keeps the senses in harmony finds rest in quietness. —Bhagavad Gita

The *Way of the Lover* brings psychology to its original meaning, a science of the soul, concerned with awakened human beings incorporating the psychology of Buddha, Moses, Rumi, Hafiz, the Baal Shem Tov, Ramana Maharshi and other awakened beings into our books, conversations and personal relationships; paying attention to those beings who reflect light—the Dalai Lama, Ram Dass, Ammachi, Pico Iyar, Reb Zalman Schachter-Shalomi, Eckhart Tolle, Mirabai, Anandamayi Ma, Mother Meera, Thich Nhat Hahn; those who live an awakened life. This is finding our spiritual home through looking into the eyes of those who have first discovered theirs. This is a psychology about being healthy, natural, mature, peaceful, loving and compassionate as we learn to embody our larger nature in this world, feeling the meaning of our life as it connects with the boundless universal life that flows through us as awareness and presence.

The human self is not a point, or an essence, but a unique contingency called to give expression to the glory of the body being raised from the inertness of matter and to the exhilaration of the soul's response to this mutual contact.
—Adin Steinsaltz

The teaching in *the Fifth Way, The Way of the Lover,* asks us to quiet the personality, contact essence and to liberate it from personality. We are born with essence, personality is imprinted and is learned through imitation. Essence stops developing around the age of five, until we return to retrieve and mature it. (See Chapter 12, System 9.) Developing and maturing essence is the day labor of the new psychology. Freeing ourselves and transcending the constraints of our material existence to discover a life of harmony between body and soul we become a force that could transform the world. So to reintroduce soul to psychology is to bring back the original meaning of the word and its related myths. The definition of psychology, as P. D. Ouspensky stated, maintains its original integrity: *Psychology is the study of the principles, laws and facts of man's possible evolution.* And his teacher, Gurdjieff, inscribed on the wall of his school: *Blessed is he who has a soul, blessed also is he who has none, but woe and grief to him who has it in embryo.*

The sacred cosmic substance required for the coating of the highest being-body, which they call soul, is a luxury. No one has yet been born with a fully developed soul. Man is born without a soul, but it is possible to make one. Our aim is to develop our soul, to fulfill our higher destiny. —*G.I. Gurdjieff*

Since we have the possibility of awakening into full consciousness, let's talk about this when someone enters therapy. Is that ever put out as an option behind office doors? Here in *Sacred Psychology* we learn to have an inner compass that senses life's internal tempo, able to pace our outer movements by our inner rhythms. *The Fifth Way, The Way of the Lover* is the study of our mind, self-inquiry, a willingness to experience, describe and know how we are, to dismantle and detach, create an observer, to break the trance while studying awakened beings who have walked before us. The journey, the series of odysseys on which we move along continues until we discover the deeper light and sweetness that is embedded within the dark, until we awaken to live within humanity as one person with one heart. The new psychology turns away from dysfunction, labels and disease and moves towards joyful wisdom teachings. Humor creates a space for the observer to enter. This is not about being funny, but about seeing funny, using humor to gain perspective. Joy is the spiritual dimension of happiness, not dependent on circumstance, an inner state, to look within and find what is most often looked for outside. And humor is the entrance way. It liberates playfulness, punctuates reason, enlivens deadness, explodes the ego, as we live within the smile. *The Way of the Lover* embraces the task of repairing the world, raising the level of the universe, to discover our particular spark in this sacred world. To spiritualize our life, to self-actualize, is to find a deep calm that accompanies seasoned wisdom and brings love and harmony. Thus we become inspired agents for future generations.

Soul is a joy when kindness comes, a weeping at injury, a growing consciousness. Pain will be born from that look cast inside yourself and this pain will make you go behind the veil. —Rumi

BEGINNER'S MIND

In the beginner's mind there are many possibilities, but in the expert's there are few. —Shunryu Suzuki

Bringing spirit into matter everyday moments reveal their sacredness. This is beginner's mind where the impossible is defeated to become an ordinary daily experience. The everyday practice of washing dishes, cooking dinner, driving to work, paying a bill, brushing our teeth, answering the phone, smiling, making love, writing a book, contain the material for our spiritual growth. The mystical is not some aspect far removed from our life, but rests within moment-to-moment everyday reality. When our attention has quality and presence we become meditation in action. Freed from a reactive mind, quiet, sitting in the open space away from monkey mind brings truth into our daily life. I don't need to go away to a retreat to be spiritual, rather to bring my attention into each event, to move myself into the eternal present. I use the word *practice* intentionally since it's not *only* washing the dishes, paying a bill, cooking a meal, it's who is at home, an interior witness, present and mindful throughout the activities of our day. There is someone observing me, who is my self washing the dishes. Releasing story and history, eventually there will no longer be the introjected critical parent saying, *You'll never do the dishes right.* The old chatter ceases, the dishes can be washed as a present moment meditation. Self-observation is the first step towards self-remembering. Life is the arena, the stage where real internal work is done. This ordinary routine world is where the true miraculous nature of creation is located. Each moment is unique; and so to retain a child's wonder and surprise through seeing and celebrating the simple delights of each thing for its own sake, this, then would be our refusal to be worn down from the outrages, the suffering, bringing heart to a broken world, becoming one more compassionate energy to help to heal and awaken this world.

It is said that meditation on love even for a moment far exceeds the merits accumulated through making infinite offering to infinite Buddhas.
—*the Dalai Lama*

There's a story about a farmer who lived a simple, peaceful life. One day his horse got loose and ran off. His neighbors came by to say, *Oh, we're so sorry. What a terrible thing. Your one horse got loose and ran away.* The farmer said, *Well, I don't know if it's so terrible. It's just something that happened. Maybe it's a blessing, maybe a curse. Only existence knows. Let's see what wants to happen.* Two days later his horse came running back with seven wild horses and a beautiful stallion and they all entered into his covered paddock. The neighbors heard this and returned to say, *Oh, what a wonderful thing. Your horse came back with eight more horses.* And the farmer said, *Well, I don't know if it's a good thing or a difficult thing. It's just something that happened. Maybe it's a blessing, maybe a curse, only existence knows. Let's see what wants to happen.* The next day his son, who had always wanted to ride a stallion, went out, rode the stallion, fell off and broke his leg. Then the neighbors returned to say, *What a terrible thing. Your son broke his leg.* And the farmer said, *I don't know if it's a dreadful thing or a wonderful thing. It's something that just happened. Maybe it's a blessing, maybe a curse, only existence knows. Let's see what wants to happen.* Two days later soldiers came marching through the town gathering all eligible young men to go off and fight a war for the country. Knocking on the farmer's door and seeing the son with his leg shattered in two places, they told him they could not take him with them. The neighbors came back and said, *What a wonderful thing that your son has a broken leg. He doesn't have to go off to war, but will remain to help you work the land.* The farmer again said, *I don't know if it's an awful thing or an excellent thing. Maybe it's a blessing, maybe a curse, only existence will reveal this. Let's see what wants to happen.*

Freedom is this surrender to the unfolding so that we are adaptable like water to live our life empty of concepts regarding circumstances, regarding our self. The farmer was continuously reborn in each moment, his mind available—not occupied, open to higher forces. The simple choice, to use the events of our lives or they use us, not judging our experiences, instead, being present to them; a way of understanding follows.

Life is not a concept, to plan ahead or to think about, it's here to live into the immediate present. By remaining available and going deep into what is, with awareness, we develop true presence. Each moment brings food to nourish everything we are. Life provides the necessary material to study ourself, to learn to live higher values until we are brought step by step into the present moment, the Way of Love.

It is not the strongest of the species that survives, nor the most intelligent that survives. It is the most adaptable to change. —Charles Darwin

Ego And Spaciousness: Against A Wide Sky

Ego has always been a paradox—it is the point from which you see, but it also makes you blind. —Bill Russell

The ego with its inflated sense of self and personality wrapped around it does not like differences. Our ego structure, a rational representative of the outside world develops a protective shell that establishes the self as something bound and separate keeping us imprisoned in a narrow conceptual world. Explained as a fabricated or constructed self, our ego identity is built to think of ourself as *somebody*, as a definite identity rather than as the openness that is awareness. We are born without self-consciousness, remembering impressions we form an identity composed of beliefs and the memory of our childhood that become our identity. The conditioned self-structure established early in childhood limits as well as disconnects us from our own being as well as from our connectedness to all sentient beings. The ego is the primary obstruction to spiritual realization and limits the open unboundedness of soul presence. Rather than a source of strength, it's weakness in disguise, since it's entering our inner core, that place of our true inheritance that contains the authentic heroic. Discover the open space of our being, then egoity, the constrictions that limit, the narrowness that bring suffering, will release, will be defeated. This constriction is the source of anxiety, depression, dread and the countless sufferings that shut down the spaciousness that is expansive consciousness. Unbounded, vast, formless, ungraspable, impartial, free of preference, discriminating, and stable—the ever-present ground which is always what it is, is open free and spacious. Rilke names it as the essential ingredient for loving relationships: *Once the realization is accepted that even between the closest human beings infinite distance continues to exist, a wonderful living side by side can grow up, if they succeed in loving the distance between them which makes it possible for each to see the other whole and against a wide sky.*

The ego sees itself as separate from the rest of the universe. While a strong ego offers competence in worldly functioning, it interferes with the connection to our true nature and supports the community impulse to imprint according to the needs of the family. Strengthened by others opinions, creating confusion about who we really are, the ego supports separation as we identify it as ourself. This obstruction to spiritual development loosens as we come to understand that we are not that separate identity. Our personal essence is our natural identity, therefore, as ego dissolves, we appear. Developing an ego and personality is necessary, in fact it is an important device for observing habits, mannerisms, and attitudes, yet most of us become attached and identified and have difficulty moving forward from this stage of illusion. The ego depends on outward external focus and becomes its own projection of reality.

Ego serves a useful developmental purpose as a kind of business manager or agent that learns and masters the ways of the world. The tragedy of the ego, however is that we start to believe that this manager— this frontal self that interfaces with the world—is who we are. This is like the manager of a business pretending to be the owner. This pretense creates confusion about who we really are. If we want to move beyond self-involvement we must work on overcoming our identification with whatever we imagine ourselves to be—any image of ourselves as something solid, separate, or defined. The less involved we are with images of who we are, the more we will be able to recognize our deep bond with all sentient beings. —John Welwood

We make contact with our essence through psychological work, self-inquiry, cutting through aspects of personality, loosening defenses, the conditioned personality structures that cover our deeper parts. Children conditioned into a restrictive personality weaken their essence losing the aliveness known as spontaneous joy. The magic and wonder diminish as preferences form into concepts of like and don't like, good and bad, shoulds and should nots. Family constellations set a tone, imprinting preferences and directing impulses. Watching and listening to our children allowing their unfolding to be in its purest form, essence will thrive along with personality.

The Hindu, Sufi and alchemical systems of thought are far more profound in their understanding of psychology and full possibility of the human being than the writings of Freud and Winnicott. Both Freud and Jung fell short of the kind of all-embracing mystical psychology that I see the future giving birth to. —Andrew Harvey

When a family is predominantly intellectual and one child is by nature emotional, the emotional child sacrifices their feelings to fit into the family system. The loss of responsive spontaneity in children creates false personality, eventually relinquishes essence connection. When an essential quality is overlooked or ridiculed, we grow up losing contact with it. Every time we cry or feel sad, if criticized or ridiculed, we feel as if we are not ok, when actually what appeared was our natural behavior. In Sacred Psychology space is opened to recover the buried, secretive, shamed, lost parts; learning to embrace contradiction and dissimilarity without judgment and recognizing that differences have vitality shifts us towards becoming truly who we are. Discovering our self we release attachment to the story. The narrative will disappear once we are free to experience who's behind the story. Soul work is steady day labor, planting, cultivating, refining until we become clear light, a sun to the earth. When heart and soul meet our small identities fade as *I* exists in relation to *thou*. Rumi speaks to this: *Do not think that the drop only becomes the ocean. The ocean too becomes the drop.*

Go on a journey from self to Self, my friend. Such a journey transforms the earth into a mine of gold. If you desire the Self, get out of the self. Leave the shallow stream behind and flow into the river deep and wide. Don't be an ox pulling the wheel of the plow, turn with the wheel above you. —Rumi

TO LIBERATE
THE TRAPPED GOLD

What seems at first a cup of sorrow is found in the end immortal wine.
—*Gita*

Life continues in cycles, an important step on the journey is to name, to acknowledge events in our life. My family had given me the message to not tell anyone about my eye accident. In order to participate in the family's system, I concealed parts of my life. They felt ashamed, guilty, angry and responsible that a two year old had an accident. The mother experienced having an injured child as a reflection of her incompetence; her distortion of reasoning: she imagined that a physical handicap, what she experienced as a flawed child, is caused by inadequate mothering. The father was irritated by yet another disruption in his desire for a peaceful household. Their feelings, based on their history and personal needs led them to shroud the event in secrecy. The humorless, self-absorbed elder sister, instinctive centered, with limited ability to process and extrapolate, who saw life through ready made phrases, angry and resentful that attention was taken away from her, no longer in the limelight, became cruel, punishing, resentful and envious. To sidestep naming the elder sister's lightweight intellectual limits, focus was placed on her attractive physical looks; the avoidance to acknowledge perpetuates the suffering. As if some characteristics are to be ashamed of, and thereby are unnamed elephants in the closet. Known, ignored, compensated for, pretended to be otherwise, until an innocence arrives and exclaims: *the emperor has no clothes on,* and the child gets shushed or whisked away to wonder what was wrong in naming the obvious. Frightened, anxious, distracted people, my families shame became their secret; that kind of shame runs like a red thread through all dysfunctional families, whether it's about alcoholism *(Don't tell anybody your father drinks),* incest *(this is our family secret),* cultural and personal dissatisfaction *(having less, wanting more),* a relative's unwanted pregnancy *(send her away so neighbors can't see),* adultery *(the illusion of happiness hangs as a cloud of doubt),* or parents who survived a concentration camp *(silent guilt and shame for surviving, festering anger at the enemy).* Secrecy, dissatisfaction, fear, denial, addictions, rage, power and control are the great sins and disease of family systems, adding to life's suffering. Bringing light into the darkness, examining and owning our history, not judging it as either good or bad, as in the farmer's story—simply saying to ourselves, *maybe a blessing, maybe a curse, only existence knows, let's see what wants to happen,* is the freedom. The wounds remain, addressed they lose their steam, no longer holding power over our lives they hold the possibility to look at, digest and transform our family story, to not endlessly pass it and its dysfunction on. This diminishes the suffering, and strengthens our ability to step into a joyful world that includes both pain and happiness, bringing kindness into our lives.

Count your salted wounds then name them like the stars of a bright constellation. Count your scars and bruises then give them the wings of forgiveness to fly. —*Malak El Halabi*

Year's later, following my mother's death, I made a choice to not allow my sister's endless dissatisfaction, now named money, drown the family in a long court battle. A decision in our family of origin can disrupt the seed of discontent that lies fallow in the heart of family. To stand against our personal family betrayal and feel the immensity of the measureless greed that touches the world—in the environment, the animal kingdom, children's lives, brings about an explosion of protection. The courage to stand in compassion and forgiveness against generations of hypocrisy will open the possibility of a conscious communal planet. For those who dare to challenge, that act will eventually secure and protect the beauty that is at the heart of all people. Courageous, to forego safety and comfort, to no longer be part of the web of communal deceit we join the family of humanity sometimes relinquishing the smaller pod people so tightly cloister themselves around. Jung wrote: *One does not become enlightened by imagining figures of light, but by making the darkness conscious.* Facing the wound is the substance that deepens our understanding and pushes us forward. All parts of our life need to be looked at, *to liberate the trapped gold.*

The modern nuclear family has become a pressure cooker in which the parents' problems with love and intimacy are passed on directly to their children. How each of us expresses and receives love in relationships—and fears doing

so—was established long ago, in our very first intimate relationships—with our mothers and fathers. Our parents have a tremendous influence over us, not just because our well-being depended so totally on them, but because they were the first people we loved deeply. Unfortunately, our first loves usually leave us with wounds that we carry with us for the rest of our lives.
—John Welwood

To disengage from preserving the fiction of our identity, we need to understand what has actually bruised us. Released to bring our secrets forward into light, we leave no corner or facet of our life or mind unexamined. For every part of life to be sacred, every detail has to be owned. As Andrew Harvey said in an interview: *No aspect of grief, lust, rage, jealousy, envy or violence can be glossed over. For each of the so-called dark emotions has secrets to yield and trapped gold to liberate.* The past and the future are transformed through the present moment; for everything is sacred, here and now. To insulate and limit our inward look interferes with our ability to establish a trust inside that strengthens our core to open to the world as it is. The ego, not tolerating differences and variation tries to establish rules to protect the illusion of being in control. All other solutions, short of facing everything, allowing truth to penetrate our wounding, stops short of our opening to the heart of compassion, for that to bring change.

Our lives are essentially meaningless if we do not claim our birthright to become who we truly are and to live in accordance with that truth.
—Mariana Caplan

To turn away from grief is to turn away from life. —Roshi Joan Halifax

The invitation the universe handed me to live with my mother the final chapter of her life brought me to deepen what I had practiced and prepared for most of my adult life. A quiet intimate sharing with the spark that created my own life. In ancient traditions it is written: *If you were to carry your parents on your back, you could hardly repay them for giving you life.* What a gorgeous and satisfying time in my life, to know my mother as she prepared to leave her body. Yes, the true spiritual community has one heartbeat.

Bless and accept fully everything that is most painful and dark in you. For all of life to be divinized, all of life has to be owned. Dark emotions have secrets to yield and trapped gold to liberate. Final wisdom can only flower from transformation of everything in the psyche, the bringing up into the light of spiritual consciousness and the releasing there of everything hidden in the dark depths. —Andrew Harvey

BREAKING OUR PATTERNS

For memory is a blessing : it creates bonds rather than destroys them. Bonds between present and past, between individuals and groups. It is because I remember our common beginning that I move closer to my fellow human beings. It is because I refuse to forget that their future is as important as my own. Opening the doors of memory arouses our curiosity. All questions are important; there is nothing worse than indifference. Why so much indifference to suffering, to the anguish of others? Forgetfulness leads to indifference; indifference to complicity and thus to dishonor. —Elie Wiesel

We form our identity based on memory, the reflection we have seen in our families eyes, on learned behavior and imprinting. Separated from our essential nature we lose spontaneous expression to live instead in a distorted reality of projection. Our childhood produces family systems made up of various roles based on an image of ourselves. Most families fail to see that the symptoms are the salvation. The rebellious child is functionally the same as the good child, the motivating force for both is their expression of discomfort. There is a time when we discover that most of our personality patterns are based on survival tactics that, at one time necessary, have truly outlived usefulness; what once protected, now incarcerates. Initially we need to appreciate and bring awareness to the cleverness of our strategies, those inner resources that promoted survival. The importance of reclaiming with compassion our disowned aspects is crucial to achieve wholeness. Each part needs to be affirmed before it can be transformed.

It may be considered indiscreet to open the doors of someone else's house and rummage around in other people's family histories. Since so many of us still have the tendency to idealize our parents, my undertaking may be regarded as improper. And yet it is something that I think must be done, for the amazing knowledge that comes to light from behind those previously locked doors contributes substantially toward helping people rescue themselves from their dangerous sleep and all its grave consequences. —Alice Miller

The shared collective denial, not being available to who each family member is, creates a hole in the spirit of the family, blocking deepening intimacy. Silencing parts of ourselves creates a barrier in our relationship to everyone. So many in this world live in mistaken identities, fighting to maintain the facade of untruth. Once we no longer identify with the belief systems, dynamics, and who our family thought we were; in seeing the masks, we are given the opportunity to break the trance. We may disenfranchise ourselves from members of our nuclear family, yet the larger context of community, those near and dear, those with familiar values, those willing to risk and love as we are bring us to the open hearted inclusion of the life of wholeness, that of being true to our highest ideals. When forgetfulness takes hold we forget the why of why we are here. To hold to the difficult, as we raise our consciousness, we raise the consciousness of those around us, as well as mending this broken creation.

It is the idea of private property that has created the family. The family conditions the child to a certain religious ideology, political dogma, is the root cause of all our neurosis. And the child is so innocent and so accepting, so vulnerable that he can be exploited. He is so helpless and utterly dependent that he has to agree with the family, with whatever nonsense the family wants him to agree. Once the child becomes burdened with beliefs his enquiry is crippled, paralyzed, his wings are cut. Each child comes with a tremendous intelligence but to live with an intelligent child is troublesome. He doubts, is skeptical, enquires, is disobedient, is rebellious—and family wants someone obedient, who imitates. From the very beginning the seed of intelligence is almost completely burned. —Osho

ALL OF EXISTENCE IS ENERGY

Looking deeply at any one thing, we see the whole cosmos. The one is made of the many. —Thich Nhat Hahn

Existence is energy. All life, body, soul, mind and matter, everything we are is energy. To understand energy is invaluable information. We only use a minimal amount of our vitality, yet the substantial leaks of energy throughout our day from unproductive and negative thoughts, unnecessary emotions, aimless chatter and mental rummaging depletes and exhausts us. When we feel spent or tired at the end of the day most often it's from misuse of energy. The first steps are to find where we are leaking energy. To become aware of the movement of energy in ourselves takes practice, requires a specific quality of attention and observation. To understand our life force and how to store energy and tap into reservoirs of the endless energy that exists is an essential step on a path of awakening. (Part Two in this book addresses this). How we live directly affects our energy.

We are like a chalice holding the spirit of life. What we can give is dependent upon our degree of emptiness. If we can be like the chalice, empty and giving all the time, then we can have the capacity for Spirit to enter through us and into whatever we do, or whomever we meet. Being has to do with capacity, and it comes about through consciously giving ourselves totally to whatever we do in the present moment. —Reshad Feild

Vitality spent on conscious work is transformed, creates new fire, is a good investment, while energy used mechanically is depleted, wasted, lost forever. This is revealed in a study of alchemy; learning to hold reserves of energy they become available for the work of transformation. We lift ourselves to a higher plane through economizing our energy and freeing ourselves from tensions. Learning to catch and manage negative energy—not by repressing, since expression not repression is health—by transforming it, a tremendous amount of power will be released or stored and saved rather than discharged. Through our relationship to the higher force that lives deep within ourself we become our own battery charge renewed through the source of life. Opening we receive the finer elements and vibrations that come to us, enabling us to balance, to center in stillness, to become a presence. Presence is our essence; living alert, abundantly alive, in awareness we know things as they are. This is a major principle in *The Fifth Way, The Way of the Lover.* Why not learn how to become our own battery source! (further elaborated in Chapter 12)

Gathering information serves us as we absorb, digest, assimilate what we observe, which is what is meant by understanding. When we come out of little mind, and move into big, universal mind, we gain rather than lose energy, seeing things anew without labeling them, not systematizing experiences and ideas into good or bad, right or wrong, wonderful and terrible. We abuse our vital force through our formitory apparatus—thinking in terms of black or white, as did the farmer's neighbors in the story. A clear open state brings a substantial boost to our immune system. Reinventing ourselves, cultivating a sense of wonder and surprise, fresh and new, is like standing in front of the ocean and breathing it into our being rather than limiting it with cliches. *What a pretty ocean, a dangerous, scary ocean, a deep blue ocean;* rather to be available to know it as it is. Reaction, objection, retaliation, resistance, repression, rejection, defenses, demands, fighting, excess, turning outward, wanting more, the automatic personal wilfulness, the habitual patterns of conditioning squander our energy. Conserving, holding, experiencing, understanding, knowing, integrating, moving into inspired creativity to become an instrument is our initiation into self-knowledge. To use this theory properly is to experience the difference between rowing across a lake with arms and hands or using two well-made oars.

There are parts of man's inner structure that are perfectly adapted to receive forces of a finer nature than those energies which ordinarily fuel our thoughts, feelings, and perceptions. Most of the time these are covered up by the passage of coarser energies which the organism elaborates in the routine of daily activities...The role of a conscious human being is to provide the phenomenal earth world with energies which otherwise would not be effectively transmitted to the creations and unities which make up our world. Attention is the quintessential medium to reveal the dormant energies in ourselves....Philosophers and scientists are coming to agree that not only do we need a deep alteration in the present state of mankind, but that a radical shift depends solely upon our relationship to consciousness—the invisible, fundamental energy behind phenomenal existence. —William Segal

TO BEAR WITNESS

The you I love is everywhere. —Rumi

At the school I discovered myself held captive within a small relationship story. My energy was disrupted, drained through focusing on one specific love object. My thoughts, attention, and concerns were aimed and directed towards one particular personal relationship.

My teacher at the time, Jean, who often overstated what she saw as needing to be corrected, dissolved the partnership. Jean rarely underplayed. She walked into the room and declared, *God giveth and God taketh away.* Arrangements were made for us to live separately with little access to each other, I would remain at the school house in Massachusetts and my lover was moved to the farm house in Vermont and immediately created a new romantic partnership with a very close friend of mine. I dropped into a painful emotional state. Grief met expands on a spiritual path. The substance of a spiritual life develops from rooting yourself in such strength of silence and purity of love that you open completely to pain, yours and others, to assist the healing. To allow the pain body to vibrate like a bell, letting the sound penetrate, struck not fixing or finding a solution, opens a space for deepening. We are here to heal, which includes ourselves, this planet and our illusions of separateness. During that time I knew little, I understood less; pierced, blinded and lost, grief became my partner. Deep into this painful darkness I noticed that when I would go to bed at night a beautiful rose had been placed on my pillow. In the morning I would wake to see a candle lit by my bedside. I recognized the abundance of gifts that surrounded me. These gifts were from other students who, sensing the darkness in my heartbreak would leave gestures to signal that I was cared for and seen. I recognized that they were all lovers and that I could receive tenderness from everyone, not just from the one person on whom I had focused my identification. Love itself was my teacher, found at the bottom of the well, under the darkness and beneath the water, and I had to choose what to birth; pain, dying to myself was the calling card, love, the beloved as in all creation the reminding awakener. To enter into the darkness and become that, to taste our responsibility in the world's madness is to see into and withstand the darkness knowing very well that we are participants in a cosmic play where we will one day emerge whole and compassionate. We are also the murderer, the rapist, those who threw children into the ovens, the homeless, the dark Kali. A descent into the darkness, a dangerous holy path, can release us from duality; everything is eaten up as we go down into this mysterious heartbreak that defies all thought. And so we bow to even that, freed from complaint and judgment, undefeated in our heart we root and open to bear witness to the world's grief. Tenderized, unafraid, having faced our nightmares we can look with a compassionate gaze at this world. Our level of descent mirrors precisely our level of ascent.

With this understanding my energy shifted. It was as if the telescope of life, which apparently I sometimes looked through backwards was turned around. Now, I could focus and see at great distances. The lens became clear and expanded. I was able to see panoramas rather than one oversized item. My vitality deepened and I could feel a reserve building. With this seed planted, many have entered my life. When a person lives in the present moment, nothing is held back. Therefore, energy is free to circulate; how beautiful is this dance of transformation!

Pain will be born from that look cast inside yourself and this pain will make you go behind the veil. Desperation, let me always know how to welcome you, and put in your hands the torch to burn down the house. —*Rumi*

TRUST WHAT IS

Accept what is, as it is, here and now, without judgment. —*Swami Prajnanpad*

Trust is at the very core of love. The poet Goethe said: *As soon as you trust yourself, you will know how to live.* To develop trust within this unpredictable world, practice. To be vulnerable in our experiences of living is what brings us to the aliveness that connects us with ourselves, with others and with life itself. Not trusting we close down, step away from experiences; won't go into the ocean, avoid airplanes, refrain from intimacy. We live in experiences, and when our mind is chattering we miss that we are in the midst of a moment. Our lack of trust, and unwillingness to surrender to the what is in each moment keeps us from the aliveness that is our possibility. Voluntary attention, which is something to be practiced leads us to being present in our experiences until trust takes over. Trust happens to you. To trust who you are. We live in a visible world of facts, information, reason and logic and when combined with ideas and principles they become partners in our process of building trust. To discriminate based on the information we are taught impedes what would develop through our own seeing, learning, and ultimately understanding through awareness. Verify everything for yourself. Wisdom-in-action is discrimination through awareness. To live while we are alive, to trust ourself, to enter experiences knowing and ultimately through understanding, is love energy penetrating and transforming our life. Within ourselves is a tremendous force and power of inner independence and that eases that state of dependence on external authority and creates integrity, a time tested source for developing trust.

In some moments of grace trust is revealed, relax into that trust and let it be done. What is left is clarity itself. —Gangaji

We are conditioned to believe that our success lies in mastering what is out there. I don't master the sea by learning to swim; instead I learn to become familiar with the ways of the sea as I learn to swim in the ocean. The ocean remains the ocean. I change. Knowing that brings me to trust in my own ability, therein lies liberation. And when the self stretches into the Self, beyond our accumulated identities, we trust, regardless to what life brings that we will find the resources to be guided. Trust may not cure, stop things from happening or limit suffering, but it does allow us to find the strength to open to existence and the resources to be available to the needs of the moment. It may not save a job, but it gives us the courage to find a different vocation, the strength to sit with a friend who is dying, the determination to turn within and take responsibility for what we see. Trust does not give us the words to say to our broken hearted friend, yet, nevertheless, it creates an opening for us to be patient and listen. Once the resistance to each moment is dropped, love arrives/arises. We are loving *what is.*

Risk! Risk anything! Care no more for the opinion of others, for those voices. Do the hardest thing on earth for you. Act for yourself. Face the truth.
—*Katherine Mansfield*

My experience at the school which dis-identified me as the lover of one person reflects my creation, the dis-identified self as model. We are all lovers. I sit as a lover-therapist, as teacher, witness, open to a living relationship, together to go to that place beyond personality, deprogrammed, unconditioned, such love is the guiding principle of this work. This path is a Way of Love and we need to cultivate the possibility of being each other's lover, not just being a lover to the one person with whom we partner. To bring dinner to a home bound neighbor, patience to others on the road while driving, forgiveness to ourself, kindness to a friend; these are the seeds of conscious or unconditional love. Ordinarily, psychology has dealt with emotion by encouraging people to experience and release the love, hate, jealousy and possessiveness that blocks or drives us. *The Way of the Lover* goes beyond that, encouraging elevated states of being, a psychology of the gods modeled on awakening. There are no longer casual shifts of feelings when you are in an objective non-possessional state. To experience peace is to be in a state of joy. We don't have to shift up and down at the mercy of inconsistent moods, we can live reliably in a higher state.

The 19th century Indian Swami Ramakrishna was approached by one of his students, who said, 'Sir, if one gave up the I, nothing whatsoever would remain.' 'I am not asking you to give up all of the I,' Swami Ramakrishna responded. 'You should give up only the unripe I. The Unripe I makes one feel : I am the doer. These are my wife and children. I am a teacher. Renounce this unripe I and keep the ripe I which will make you feel that you are the servant of Existence, a devotee, and that Existence is the doer and you are the instrument.'—Mariana Caplan

Being watchful of energy, we learn to play the instrument called self. Like a maestro informed by each instrument as to what melodies are produced, we also listen to our own voice, paying mindful careful attention. Self-regulating—to wake up in a low energy state suggests quiet reflection, a high energy state lends to doing. We become a soul doctor, knowing when and what to read, eat, exercise, whether to stay home or to go out, who to call or not call, when to answer the phone and when to wait for a message, how to say yes and no; understanding the nuances of the instrument called self. This leads to living in a state of being. Rather than only to explore the world, particularly to explore and pay kind attention to our own nature, and then to live with simplicity from our own true center.

Most people lack the tools to develop trustworthiness and are mechanically unreliable forgetting an aim and promise, allowing disappointments to compromise and constrict, the separation that brings us to construct a personality that is not a true reflection of who we are. To develop a trustworthy voice of the heart happens through a process of watching ourselves, seeing clearly amid suffering and challenges, choosing the life we are given. Expanded this becomes an emotional and intellectual life of trust within a universal perspective, the *what is*, not to remain limited to a personal realm, enabling us to evolve in a natural, full, safe and confident way, to drink the sweetness of this birth. Love is the golden ring and trust is the horse we ride on the carousel.

A night full of talking that hurts, my worst held-back secrets: Everything has to do with loving and not loving. —Rumi

TOOLS TO WAKE-UP

'Who are you?' said the Caterpillar. This was not an encouraging opening for a conversation. Alice replied, rather shyly, 'I—I hardly know, Sir, just at present—at least I know who I was when I got up this morning, but I think I must have changed several times since then.' —Lewis Carroll

Psychologists work to resolve conflicts on a psychological level. *The Fifth Way, The Way of the Lover,* seeing this limitation, the inadequacy of Western Psychology, instead looks to imperishable truths, to who we are. Nothing left unexamined, self-inquiry, the exploration of spiritual transformation opens a portal to freedom. Without understanding universal laws and the nature of consciousness, psychology as it appears today helps to maintain the story, keeping us imprisoned in a finite mirror. Our disconnection from our essence is the essential conflict. Resolving early psychological discord and emotional traumas is not a full healing. The new psychology speaks to reconnecting and maturing essence. We all know and feel loss, only when essence is acknowledged and experienced will we experience wholeness. Psychology as it is, tries to strengthen the personality to make us feel better. *The Way of the Lover, a Way of Understanding,* is about finding the truth of who we are within an awareness of transcendence. The teaching is for us to be connected to the highest in our self, to nurture an attention so that we awaken to see the beauty in the particular and the ordinary for it to become the food of impressions that nurtures our being. The unconditioned, beyond our identifications, through self-awareness; living as our meditation, we come to live in our eternal smile.

The Way of the Lover makes conscious information available to objectively explain our nature and type. The systems in this book are reliable and assist in quieting personality as well as identifying tools to mature essence. Once explained, they are easy to use, revealing how to see ourselves objectivity, clearly. They do not focus on systems of pathology or dysfunction. With this help most everyone can move from unhealthy states to average and healthy ones, and to higher states freed from the clutter of personal distortion. Our body, personality type, our nature influences our viewpoint of life. We are at the mercy of type and so to study objective systems we identify our issues and how to work with them; the information now becomes usable as a jumping-off base towards higher consciousness.

Man's noblest quality is the will to discover an imperishable Reality beyond the changes and chances of this mortal world. This quality is what I mean by 'spiritual.' Man's spirit is his will. Since will is commitment to action, it follows that a spiritual psychology must be a practical psychology, One can go further and say that it must be a 'do-it-yourself psychology,' by which I mean that we must find and live by our will and not look to anyone else to do the work for us. This is where a spiritual psychology differs from most clinical psychology. The practical aim in view is to help people to learn how to 'work on themselves' in their search for the imperishable Real. —*J.G. Bennett*

The short history of modern psychology, barely one hundred years old, like Western Medicine, has not fully integrated the wisdom of the ancients. Using the systems as a map and guide we are offered real tools that reveal the framework and patterns that have taken us away from our essence and essential nature. This opens the possibility of exploring the deep-rooted question about the meaning and purpose of life along with giving us the skills needed to communicate in our relationships, to understand behavior freeing us from comparative thinking and judgment. To design and chart our exit, to integrate our biography is freedom from its constraints. Self-study softens our heart toward ourself through offering meaning to our historical and present life. Engaging mindful conversation, honoring differences through understanding has the power to bring peace; the systems in the second part of this book serve consciousness. Understanding self and others develops through knowing and reading energy, the fundamental teaching in Chapter 12 is the entry into the profound, the wonder in what's unremarkable.

The miraculous is the entry into an action of a conscious force that knows why and how the action is performed. —Jeanne de Salzmann

LIVING INTO OUR POTENTIAL

Not what we say about our blessings, but how we use them, is the true measure of our thanksgiving. —W.T. Purkiser

I see myself as a stimulus-response machine. A well-tuned-sensing instrument of consciousness. A lover. Ultimately we become our own gauge. What happens in an hour in a session is the laboratory and the proof of the lab experiment appears as we go out to live what we have explored. The work of therapy goes on in the moments outside the office; the teaching emerges from our time together, to be practiced and lived beyond it. To deepen kindness and compassion, to acknowledge yet limit suffering—ours and others, is a deep spiritual path.

Good therapy, like all work of transformation is a relentless mirror held up to the mask, the illusion, asking for wholeness, perseverance, stamina and the courage for us to become who we are, to live into our possibilities. Inner work rests on strong intention, to study and explore new territory to develop the highest potential within ourselves. The strength we bring supports the destruction of what is not healthy, and when we face and investigate, expand health, we diminish the dis-ease, the part that is not at ease with transformation. To acknowledge, encounter, go into, bless and accept what has been painful and dark, to live with the truth and the love it requires is liberation, freedom from the smoke and mirrors of our imprisonment—to find that place beyond personality.

Love awakens us. Relationships challenge us. Relationships are the strength and impulse of life, and show up as our connection to every-thing: to our self, our partner, friends, house, computer, money, plants, car, food, community, sleep, work and animals, to existence itself. Life cannot be without relationship. I use my relationship to the client, the student, the guest, the sangha, and theirs to me, a solid and distinct reflection of our work, a mirror that reflects back. Together we resonate awareness, understanding and harmony. Training ourselves every day to see each thing in a higher way, to become mindful, to bring our atten-tion to the here and now; the circumstances of our life are the invitation. A person in a loving state has a sacred relationship to everything that he or she touches, demonstrating that the way to heal this world is to heal ourself. This is not surprising, once we realize that love is the source and energy behind and within all of life.

Unless we establish right relationship, all our lives will be constant battle, individually as well as collectively. If we can deeply understand the relation-

ship between oneself and another then perhaps we shall understand and solve the problems of our relationship with society, for society is but an extension of ourselves. —J. Krishnamurti

HEAR, AND YOU SHALL LOVE

A person who practices the mysteries of love will be in contact not with a reflection, but with truth itself. To know this blessing of human nature, one can find no better helper than love. —Socrates

We are the bridge between heaven and earth. *Practice what you know*, has been a practical Sufi comment, *for knowledge without practice is a body without life.* Meher Baba observed that he had come here not to teach, but to awaken. Not speaking the final 44 years of his life, out of that silence his being continuously expressed love. Love blossoms when we diminish the personal. Our practice extends through awakening the heart, the pure energy we call love. The essential message of our time has been a directive in the Jewish tradition, the Ve'ahavta: *Hear, And you shall love. And these words which I command you, teach them, recite them..... you shall love.* A challenge, a commandment; and now the day labor, how to love? *with all your heart and with all your soul and with all your might.* To embrace, cherish, to love: our obligation, an impossibly possible task. And then to teach this with *our heart and soul* is to teach through example, to recite these words as our mantra, to chant, to sing these words till they fill the world. This is the practice. How to live within obedience to this inner voice? The password and key is in its first word: *Hear*, listen, pay attention, be attentive. Hearing equals presence: in order to really listen requires our presence. To hear the pure voice of love, to come alive, to awaken to love as the soul of the universe is opening to a great love, to our true nature, embracing a world of love. Rumi spoke to this when he said: *Wherever you are and whatever you do, be in love. It is love that holds everything together, and it is the everything also. Love rests on no foundation. It is an endless ocean, with no beginning or end.*

The one I love is everywhere. —*Rumi*

Approaching the door of the heart, opening to love we enter a state of heightened awareness. Love is pure energy and certain artists have created this state through their work—Nijinsky's leaps, Rembrandt's paintings, Vivaldi's music, Walt Whitman's poetry, Hafiz, Rumi, Shakespeare, their words beyond this world of appearances as we know it carry the ingredients to bring us into the present moment. The conscious artist is rare, and we know who they are, their works remain alive and when we read their books, listen to their music, look at their art we are carried on the inhalation and exhalation of their inspired breath. A conscious breath has endurance. When we are conscious whatever we do is an expression of love.

To love is first of all to accept yourself as you actually are. 'Knowing thyself' is the first practice of love. May I learn to look at myself with the eyes of understanding and love. May he learn to look at himself with the eyes of understanding and love. May she learn to look at herself with the eyes of understanding and love. May they learn to look at themselves with the eyes of understanding and love. —*Thich Nhat Hahn*

THE JOURNEY OF ORDINARY MOMENTS

There are relationships which must be a very great, almost unbearable happiness, but they can occur only between very rich matures and between those who, each for themselves are richly ordered and composed; they can unite only two wide, deep individual worlds. Young people, it is obvious, cannot achieve such a relationship, but they can, if they understand their life properly, grow up slowly to such happiness and prepare themselves for it. They must not forget, when they love, that they are beginners, bunglers of life, apprentices in love, must learn love, and that, like all learning, wants peace, patience, and composure. —Rainer Maria Rilke

We use the challenge of relationships. They are a source of our development. Everything is linked to everything else, and our relationship to it, our connection to its wholeness becomes who we are. We resemble what we love. Our partners bring forward our flaws and our willingness to recognize and accept responsibility produces the personal integrity that is the bedrock for deep creative intimacy. The friction, opposition, obstacles, personal impact and compelling connection in a relationship creates energy that awakens us to love. The practice of a marriage or living with another, of writing a book, teaching yoga, creating a dance performance, a business partnership, caring for a pet, close friendships, of being a parent, a god-parent, of cleaning our home, caring for children, all are the food and sustenance, the challenges and practice that fuel the adventure called conscious love. When we pay attention that becomes the meditation. This meeting, new each time, is to take notice, to be mindful, *to resolve to be a beginner*, each moment is our practice, that's what relating is: we are as mirrors reflecting and the state of our being brings love into a larger dimension that is unlimited and enduring. Our relationship with our inner world, our discovery of the teacher within through our practices, through a personal encounter; for us to become as present as we can, to awaken to ourself and go deeper into the question of who we are becomes the recognition of why we are here, along our journey of ordinary moments.

Spirit entering into form, breaks off from itself, breaks itself into pieces, is broken. Wherever we see spirit, there is something broken. Here the heart is broken, here the spirit enters. The prayers of a broken heart call the spirit in, inevitably heal, are therefore whole. When great hearts break, we take the pieces into ourselves. Then everything is singing. —Deena Metzger

The legendary devotional partnership of Govinda and Gayatri recalls his simple request of her when asked if there was anything he wanted her to do solely for him. He asked that each time she served him a meal that she place a small bowl of water and a needle next to his food. During the 60 years of their life together he sat at the dining table with a small bowl of water and a needle next to his plate and while she never saw Govinda use either, the request remained his personal wish. Towards his final days he asked Gayatri if there was anything that would settle her mind, was there an unanswered question that had passed between them. She replied, *just one thing. Many, many years ago you requested a small bowl of water and a needle beside your plate. Although I never saw you use either of them, what was their purpose?* Govinda's face lit up and the smile that was often there grew larger as he replied: *I have felt such love and appreciation for every meal that you have cooked. Your attention and devotion while cooking, the love you serve with, I imagined that if in a moment of carelessness, if I was not mindful for a second and would drop even one grain of rice onto the table, in appreciation I wanted to be able to pick it up with the needle and wash it in the water, so that I could eat it, to not waste even a morsel of the love that you tended to so diligently.*

The sincerity behind our daily practice infuses our relationships. Whatever holds us steady, and we might use a range of reminders from music to photos, statues, candles, chanting, books, anything that inspires us, sometimes even a small bowl of water and a needle. Training ourselves each day, until we become accustomed to seeing things in a higher way, named memory of the heart, infusing our life with that fragrance brings energy and beauty to our every day. This discipline of the heart brings us to love consciously, illuminating the heart to unveil the oneness that opens us to all dimensions. As a magnet, blessings are drawn towards us, surrounding us, once we dedicate our practice to opening our heart.

Love is the true means by which the world is enjoyed: our love to others and others' love to us. We ought therefore above all things to get acquainted with the nature of love. For love is the root and foundation of nature: love is the soul of life and crown of rewards. Never was anything in this world loved too much, but many things have been loved in a false way: and all in too short a measure. —Traherne

In earlier centuries it was common for people to go off to a mountain and initiate the ascetic practices of a Buddha or Ramana, leaving to go on a pilgrimage, removing ourself from this world on a journey towards enlightenment. Today our practice is in the challenge of ordinary moments, to awaken, the invitation is now, we need only to recognize the reminders. Our times suggest we live here in the mundane world. We are asked to teach and to engage in this world with one of the most difficult of tasks, which is to live through the manifestations of other human beings and to keep our heart open. To be in a world where most people are strongly attached to their suffering, to their dissatisfactions, makes it a challenge to go to the cleaners and pick up our shirt, to allow a workman to bring his negativity into our home, drive a car amongst others' aggression and impatience, be married and live with someone who comes home complaining, and yet continue to maintain a joyful loving state. People hold on to their unnecessary suffering, often it's the last attachment to slip away. It's in how we love that offers the opening. In a relationship of integrity we ask the most of ourselves and of each other. It's who we are, not what we do that creates the miraculous.

Says Rilke: To take love seriously and to bear and to learn it like a task; people have misunderstood the place of love in life, they have made it into play and pleasure because they thought that play and pleasure were more blissful than work; but there is nothing happier than work, and love, just because it is the extreme happiness can be nothing else but work. So whoever loves must try to act as if he had a great work: he must be so much alone and go into himself and collect himself and hold fast to himself; he must work; he must become something! The more one is, the richer is all that one experiences. And whoever wants to have a deep love in his life must collect and save for it and gather honey.

This companionship and the practices that we enter into that help us claim them are here to remind us that we are the guardians of this world and these relationships are our responsibility. Love feeds us, and we become co-creators, dedicated instruments infused with the realization that everything is our partner in this walk through life. That's quite a practice, the reminder of the sacredness of everything that enters our life. What fun, to be tender and caring; washing the dishes is as much a mindful activity as driving the car as painting on a canvas as being in the office as feeding the dog. And it all leads to how we are with our self, a child, friend, the neighbor, a person on the street, a parent, a book, our car; the presence we bring touches the present moment, transmits energy making the ordinary extraordinary.

Every person needs to know that she is called to serve based on the model of perception and feeling which is unique to her, based on the core root of her soul. In that root, which contains infinite worlds, she will find the treasure of her life. A person needs to say: 'Bi-shvili nivrah ha-olam, the world was created for me.' —Abraham Isaac Kook

The New Psychology, which is the Path of the Heart and *The Way of the Lover*, lays out a basis for spirituality. Are we opening or closing? Do we fill our time with trivialities, distractions and non-essentials or are we leaving wide empty spaces for existence to play through us as presence? Do we rest in stillness regardless to the circumstances that appear? As we allow ourself our own humanness, who we are comes forth, emerges to be grist for the mill expressed through the daily events of life. If the aim and intention is to learn a skill, yet we find ourself distracted, our reactions habits and outside influences hinder us from maintaining attention and completing our aim. Through resolving to harness and build energy the challenge becomes noticing what's happening within ourself and creating our own self-healing in the process. To trust that our small experiment will lead into a greater experience is the surrender. It's going back and forth in this way from the little experiments on ourself to the greater experience of life that verifies our trust in our heart connection showing us that we're not isolated and that everything we do feeds a greater plan.

The end of therapy is to rescue our divinity from its unconscious state.
—Andrew Harvey

OUR LIFE THEME

If your mind becomes firm like a rock and no longer shakes in a world where everything is shaking, your mind will be your greatest friend and suffering will not come your way. —Theragatha

We each have a theme that binds us to our personal exploration. Discover, then uplift the theme that is woven throughout your life. Mine has been both faith and endurance. To bring blind faith to conscious faith, to continue beyond to a strength of character; an integrity while knowing suffering, yet still continuing; so that what is submerged must emerge. This is a liberation of our psychology, using what appears in our life. *How can we fulfill the meaning of our existence on earth?* asked *Martin Buber,* and most traditions offer that to be devoted to this creation, love towards each other is the crowning jewel of the heart. *For there is no rung of being* answers Buber, *on which we cannot find holiness everywhere and at all times.* As witness to the silence that is beyond words, how to find the statement, the voice that speaks to who I am.

To this thought I hold unswerving, to wisdom's final fruit profoundly true: of freedom and of life one only is deserving, who ever day doth master them anew. —Goethe

A story about conscious faith, one of the themes that is prominent in my life, is the ancient tale of Sarai and Abel, both very much in love, who venture out to holiday in a small boat. As they cross the lake, rowing in their modest craft, the day is quite beautiful. Sudden and abruptly the seas become rough, shaking the vessel as a storm approaches. The sky turns dark and cloudy with fog rolling in, the high winds forbidding and Sarai becomes afraid and alarmed. The boat is small and the storm is impending. She looks at Abel who sits quietly peaceful, still smiling, and she says, *Are you crazy? Look at this storm. The clouds are dark and menacing. Why aren't you upset? We could drown.* He continues to calmly row. So she exclaims, *This may be our last moment, only a miracle can save us. Are you immovable? Why aren't you afraid?* Abel stands up in the boat, takes his sword out of its sheath, and holds it to her neck, asking, *Do I frighten you?* She nervously laughs, quite puzzled, and says, *Why would I be afraid? You may be holding a sword, yet in this moment I know you love me.* He puts the sword back and sits down. As he looks up at the sky he says, *I know Existence loves me and holds its sword to my throat, and I also know that the storm is in the hands of existence, even so, I trust that I will find how to best use this moment.* Understanding comes from inner stillness, from being present. Deep trust is an expression of love, and means that while in the midst of circumstances we remain calm in our heart. Compassion, understanding, true presence are the greatest gifts we can bring to the love and life we have. Our life is the art form. Maintaining tranquility in the midst of challenges and throughout our ordinary day is the consequence of a life of practice. To be with life and just be in it as it is, seeing reality as it is means that the personal considerations about our life diminishes. To discover the still point on which the universe turns, in that space it is said that there is *no yesterday, no tomorrow and no today.*

It isn't the things that happen to us that cause us to suffer, it's how we relate to the things that happen to us that causes us to suffer. —*Pema Chodron*

This is blind faith untethered. The blindfold off, we discover trust deep within, welling up in agreement with universal laws to bring us to a doubtless certainty that happens spontaneously; then all barriers dissolve. Regardless to the storms that appear, to how rocky our days seem to be, there is something greater that embraces us, so in each moment while our presence may or may not change the circumstances, our receptivity to what is births consciousness. Relationships are here to connect us to our aliveness to something higher; when we experience separation rather than openness woundedness emerges. When smaller emotions lose sight of the big picture during a storm, leading into doubt, our ability to step back, to witness in awareness, the ability to observe ourself brings wisdom and compassion, lets us ride challenges, flow with the currents. That quality of understanding is capable of transforming our life. We burn steadily and everything becomes our liberation.

Faith is a function of the heart. It must be reinforced by reason. The two are not antagonistic as some think. The more intense one's faith is, the more it whets one's reason. When faith becomes blind it dies. —Mahatma Gandhi

Endurance, the other prominent theme in my life has drawn me to learn and understand endurance more deeply through a classic folktale about Bontscha Schweig, Bontscha the silent, by Isaac Peretz. It has been said that acts of kindness are their own reward and misdeeds carry their own justice. Bontscha was a simple being who lived unnoticed in this world, he lived *as a grain of sand until the wind at last lifted him up and carried him across to the other shore.* An uncomplaining man, he endured life's humiliations, never protesting or asking for more. This passive meekness is not the humility or courage of Abel who met the changing circumstances of life with an equitable spirit. There is a fine line to balance between the acceptance of what befalls us, perseverance, certainty, determination and endurance. His life and death went unnoticed in this world. Dying, Bontscha, who having endured life's humiliations entered Paradise. His arrival was a considerable event. Trumpets sounded, important angels came to meet with him as he was given a golden crown and honorary staff. Bontscha initially thought there was an error, a mistaken identity until he stood before a tribunal and listened to the prosecuting as well as the defending angel address a long list of mistreatment and hardship that had been his life. Bontscha recognized his life of humiliations. The defending angel overwhelmed the trial portraying a man who had never blamed or protested or asked for retribution towards his parents or community. Bontscha's silence and lack of complaints in the face of constant hardship, his resignation and fortitude stopped the prosecuting angel's objections. The tribunal judge addressed Bontscha:

You never understood that you need not have been silent, that you could have cried out and that your outcries would have brought down the world itself and ended it. You never understood your sleeping strength. Here, in Paradise, you will be rewarded, ask for anything you want. And Bontscha, smiled and asked for a simple breakfast for each morning, a fresh roll with a little butter. Both judge and angels silently were in awe for having created this level of meekness and poverty of spirit. The forbearance, resignation, determination of Bontscha is not the courage of Abel. A nineteenth century Hasidic teacher said: *the cry unuttered is the loudest.* The wounded sensibility of Bontscha, the silent, when dignified reaches out to the indifference of those communities who betray through justification. How to invent hope in a world that closes its eyes? Contact with higher energy, brings meaning when we allow it to penetrate, for suffering to then dissolve. Our thoughts and actions are not only ours, they are for and affect this entire creation. To look seriously at the Bontscha and the Abel's a quality of unease might rise as we enter the risky world of relationship, and discover our humanity; claiming threads that brought us to this moment reveals a rich tapestry. The greatness of spirit that brings us to pay attention, to understand and to stand up and be present, to live responsibly what we know is spiritual maturity.

Seek the wise and realize, the path is difficult to walk upon, as sharp as the razor's edge. —Katha Upanishad

To discover and cast a light on a theme that permeates our life and then to elevate it brings us to make sense and understand the significance of our life. Understanding grows as we see the clues, find a sense of direction, discover truths in our life, information and signs, and then create the meaning and purpose for the transformation of our whole being. We are capable of greatness, follow the threads of our life, observing how we arrived at this moment; awakening to the meaning of our existence is a work of great love. The rewards are countless.

The soul's extravagance is endless: spring after spring....we are your gardens dying, blossoming. To die into life is to become life. The wind stops skirting you and enters. All the roses, suddenly, are blooming in your skull. —Rumi

FAITH IS THE PILGRIMAGE, TRUST IS THE DESTINY

It is said that Trust means faith has arrived at the goal.
Faith is fulfilled. One has come to know,
Then trust arises. Only those who have faith reach trust.
Faith is the pilgrimage and trust is the destiny.
Begin in faith, end in trust. —Osho

My pilgrimage of faith combined with enduring trust carried me through my mother's death. Death, the wake-up call, taught me to trust existence. Standing with her as she took her final breath informed me, pointed to my own mortality, brought serenity in the face of death. At that moment all separation ceased and my mother was born into my heart. I would never be alone again. Our mutual acceptance brought me to trust in the exquisite beauty of living. I understood for the first time that trust was not outside. Trust is confidence and self-reliance, the guardian and custodian of what truly matters. Can I truly trust myself is the real question. Through facing death are we then able to love. The silence that appeared to me in the face of my mother's death brought me to the ocean. And there I spent the morning (mourning). My mother stopped breathing, like the wave that vanishes; still the ocean remained. She became invisible, leaving her body, parting from the shore our separation vanished forever. Trust revealed herself to me that day. The outer mother became the inner, she who I had taken care of in her final years offered this great experience of understanding. Now I am able to hold love for my beloved partner. The knowledge that one of us may die first, deepens the love and beauty in the relationship. Every human relationship is a metaphor to awaken to the divinity within, with a heart that understands, ears that listen, and eyes that see. This willingness to vulnerability, this fullness in life, brings about inner peace.

What is our particular strength emerges to be called upon as a resource. When we are able to remember that what we are grieving today in sadness and pain was yesterday the source of our joy, we learn to walk with one foot in sorrow, one foot in joy, making grief usable. We learn to move with one foot in heaven, one foot in hell until we ascend to a clarity of crystallized, reliable, consistent consciousness.

When we see eternity in things that pass away and infinity in finite things, then we have pure knowledge. —Bhagavad Gita

THE LOVE THAT MOVES BOTH HEAVEN AND EARTH

When consciousness has been cleansed of psychological images there is a flowering of the purified heart. Then love blossoms of its own accord as easily and effortlessly as the act of breathing in and out. The person whose innermost nature has undergone such a radical change starts loving because he cannot help loving. Such a person is indeed the very embodiment of love.
—*J. Krishnamurti*

The New Psychology is a testament to living in freedom with wisdom and few constraints, placing less attention on pathology, instead looking towards ancient traditions that carry the mystery of gods and goddesses who have blossomed into their own true nature. The value of preserving the great treasures of traditions is not only about keeping those ancient cultures alive, it also is about our further understanding of the inner life, the inner resources of a people. The stories, myths, scrolls and books, the rituals and folklore, important in literature and the arts, are ways to remember as well as to understand the world and what it means to be human. It might be the most significant way that the human race creates meaning. In the light of keeping the fires of civilization burning we have been offered depthful tools to look at traditions and ourselves. When we learn to view our own life and its stories through new lenses the personal drops away, and we have the space to offer an inward bow to everything that has brought us to this point, as we step out into greater expansiveness, stretching and uplifting the meaning and purpose of our lives.

If you look deeply into the palm of your hand, you will see your parents and all generations of your ancestors, all of them are alive in this moment. Each is present in your body. You are the continuation of these people.
—*Thich Nhat Hahn*

According to Kabbalistic wisdom-teachings, all stories and text can be read, approached, studied and understood from four perspectives, from four levels of meaning, four dimensions, teaching us to see in a new way. The four dimensions gave rise from the acronym *pardes* which in Hebrew means an orchard or garden. Derived from the ancient Persian word that also gives us paradise in English, and has come to refer to those who stroll in the orchard as the ones who undertake and enter into mystical reflection. There is *peshat*, where we look for the obvious, the simple, surface, straight, literal direct or contextual meaning which includes the historical and factual. *Peshat* is considered closer to the overt concerns of the text. *Remez* hints at something deeper, a philosophical or moralizing allegory, a symbolic meaning moving beyond the literal sense. *Derash,* synonymous with the term *midrash* is the next level and is slightly deeper than the first level. From the *derash* viewpoint through inquiry, interpreting, examining, investigating, looking to the comparative midrashic meaning, the contextual and non-contextual, the moral and philosophic we expand meaning. *Derash* regards the story and its interpretation to derive deeper meaning, sometimes to reveal an ethical lesson, a metaphorical meaning. *Sod* operates on the secret hidden mystical esoteric meaning as given through inspiration or revelation which speaks to the mysteries of the upper and lower worlds. The *sod* dimension of the text implies that there us a deeper layer of meaning projected onto the more intrinsic understanding and the *sod* interpretation may have less to say, on the face of it with the texts manifest content.

In order to see, we must first learn to see; this is the first initiation into self-knowledge. First of all, we have to know what we must look at. When we know, we must make efforts, keep our attention, look constantly with persistence. Only through maintaining our attention and not forgetting to look, one day, perhaps, we will be able to see. If we see one time we can see a second time, and if that continues we will no longer be able not to see. This is the state to be looked for; it is the aim of our observation; it is from there that the true wish will be born, the irresistible wish to become: from cold we shall become warm, vibrant; we shall be touched by our reality.
—*Jeanne de Salzmann*

Pardes represents an ideal place, one that has been portrayed in a well-known account of mystical experience depicted in Jewish sources. There is a story in the Talmud that serves as a warning to the uninitiated against entering the deepest levels of *pardes*. The story recounts how four scholars, all respected sages, Rabbi Akiva, Ben Zoma, Ben Azzai and

Elisha ben Avuya entered *pardes*, meaning that together they delved into the most hidden secrets. As a result, Ben Azzai lost his life, Ben Zoma lost his mind, and Elisha ben Avuya lost, betrayed his faith and went astray. Of the four scholars only Rabbi Akiva. who entered in peace, left in peace, emerged unscathed. This cautionary tale is a teaching to exercise caution and relentless self-honesty to both teachers and students. Students and self-appointed teachers are warned to cultivate awareness and compassion, to take time before leaping into hidden mysteries. The inclination to aggrandize ourselves and our own accomplishments, to live in self-importance or inferiority, worthy and unworthiness, is, indeed, often presumptuous. Without true experience and self-inquiry how can we make distinctions, see fraud, or fool ourselves that we know the difference between psychological self-development and spiritual life, between diversion and distraction, or discrimination and clarity? When our mind is not at peace, when we are not balanced and well-prepared we become lost in distortions, inaccurate presumptions, self-delusion and spiritual materialism; this journey of spiritual evolution has many levels.

This is not a journey for those who expect love and bliss; rather, it is for the hardy who have been tried in fire and have come to rest in the tough, immovable trust in 'that' which lies beyond the known, beyond the self, beyond union, and even beyond love and trust itself. —Bernadette Peters

The study of myth and the study of self assist one another. While each symbol teaches us about ourself, in order to understand something we see its connection to a bigger whole. Stories have the possibility to throw open a door to hidden mysteries, to illuminate truth, to hold our attention and awaken us to new energy. And when doors open that have been closed or locked we expand, become more alive. Through mythic story we are reminded of vast worlds, locating meaning and insights to awaken curiosity, to question and hold dear that union with our concealed self. In the new psychology we move beyond the personal through looking at stories, and our own stories mythically, through the lens of the four worlds, multi-dimensionally, adding a richness to our life stories that carries us from the personal to the universal.

The juncture in history and the zeitgeist we live in is something we choose, setting the scene for the spiritual fodder we need to grow and achieve deeper elevation of our souls. —Raquel Cepeda

This following story speaks to the heart of humanity: it is said by the Buddhas that if you were to gather all the pleasures and happiness of the world and put them together, it would not approach one tiny fraction of the bliss that you would experience upon realizing your own true nature. This teaching-story expresses that the possibility of our greatness was designed in the effort God made when he asked an angel to come to earth to look for the most exceptional quality of human experience, the one quality that has allowed this creation to continue. The story continues with the angel arriving here on earth to see a man disoriented standing in the middle of a public road. Suddenly a truck traveling with great speed appeared. At that moment a stranger raced from the curb side pushing the elderly fellow out of the way and was hit by the truck and killed. The angel took a drop of the good samaritan's blood and brought it to God saying: *This is indeed the most exceptional human quality, the willingness to sacrifice a life for another.* God, in agreement to the nobility of that thought and effort nonetheless told the angel: *that's not the most exceptional quality and so to return again to earth to find what is the most excellent human quality, the one that allows creation to continue.*

The angel returned to earth and came upon a mother giving birth.

In labor, enduring great pain for many hours she was lying in a pool of sweat. Finally, after a long struggle an infant emerged. Seeing the baby the mother's tired face transformed to radiate light and love. The angel gathered a drop of the mother's sweat, returned to God saying: *The most profound and excellent characteristic of the human experience is the courage to move through pain to bring life into this world.* Again, God, in agreement to the worthiness, the courage, still prodded the angel to return to earth to find the one quality in the human experience that is the *most* excellent. Once again the angel returned to earth to find the most excellent human quality, the one that allows creation to continue.

The angel returned to earth a third time, carefully watching to find an experience that would enable him to better understand humanity. What caught the angels attention was a man running through a wooded area in distress and in a furious rage. Quickly reviewing the life of the man the angel discovered that this man had recently been released from prison, having served 7 years for a crime another man committed and was festering with hate, bitterness and revenge. Carefully following the released prisoner the angel felt the spite and venom in the ex-convict as he stormed through the woods in hot pursuit of the man who he had served time for, the one who had left him to sit in prison, hoping now to inflict punishment, to pay off the old debt. The angel watched him come upon a cabin where the offending man lived. A light was on in the living room, and peering through the window the revengeful bitter ex-con could see the man who he had served prison time for, could see him inside looking peaceful, joyful, smiling. Inside the cabin the man and his wife were holding newly born infants. Their faces filled with light and happiness, since they had recently returned from the hospital with their twin son and daughter. There was no mistaking the bliss and light and beauty in the cabin living room. The angry vengeful ex-convict seeing the beauty fell to his knees while slowly his heart broke into pieces. Weeping he got up, speechless he moved to one side, mindful awareness brought him into the present moment, forgiveness opened his heart and he slowly, quietly walked away.

The angel gathered one tear and returned to God. *This is the most exceptional of all human qualities—mindful awareness, it allows forgiveness to rise. Mindful presence opens the heart and brings the ability to transcend anger, bitterness and revenge. Authentic transformation in the service of love.* Mindful awareness, an open heart, brings the realization that the well-being of others is our own well-being, it's when we are truly here, mind and body together. Real forgiveness has no judgment, so that true luminosity shines through. God praised the angel. *Yes, mindful presence opens the heart, brings the ability to forgive, to look truth in the face; to become mindful, kind, present, open hearted—this is the human trait that distinguishes human possibilities and is the reason creation continues. Without paying attention, mindful awareness which opens us to truth in forgiveness, standing on compassion and loving kindness, creation might disappear.*

To live with our human potential, to serve life, this most sacred of gifts, through our actions giving ourselves with totality we become the miraculous. When the heart blossoms we become the expression of love. Truth/mindful presence/ awareness/forgiveness/compassion/loving kindness all unite as one; they live together as a transformation of energy that lifts us above the darkness of sleep. Awareness knows only the present. It is at this place that we become one with humanity. This is where we sanctify life. In mindfulness we are truly here, the stories disappear, the heart opens and we become the blessing and have the power to alter the destiny of this universe.

Those who enter the gates of heaven are not beings who have no passions or who have curbed their passions, but those who have cultivated an understanding of them. —William Blake

CHAPTER TEN

The One Thing You Must Do

The One Thing You Must Do

There is one thing in this world that must never be forgotten. If you were to forget all else, but did not forget this, then you would have everything. But if you performed everything else, yet forgot that one thing, then you would have done nothing whatsoever.

It's as if a King had sent you to some country for a specific task, and you accomplish a hundred other tasks, but not the particular task, then, you did nothing at all. Everyone comes into this world for a particular task, that is your purpose. If you do not perform it, then you will have done nothing, to say that you have done other work is nothing. You were not created for those other tasks.

It's as if you were to come by a priceless golden sword, such as is found only in the treasures of Kings and treat it as a butcher's knife for slicing rotten meat saying 'I am not letting this sword stand idle, look, I am putting it to so many useful purposes.'

You are more precious than heaven and earth. You do not know your own worth. If we keep our life for ourself, doing just what we like and are good at, then we only love the treasures we have been granted. Of all, learning what is truly important touches us most closely, know your own Self, and knowledge about the root of the matter: life's purpose. Remember the deep root of your being, or you will be wasting valuable keenness and forgetting your dignity and purpose. —Mevlana Jalaluddin Rumi

We forget our purpose. All else is distraction, our pre-occupation with the trivialities, the nonessential. We are not here to become something. Remember the root of our being, life is for awakening, where the human and the divine meet, this burning of the heart that calls the beloved silently into the night. Forgetfulness of our true nature creates separation. To remember; our witnessing is a compass that brings attention to the moment. Awakening to our true nature we open to the love that always is: greater awareness, a deeper relationship to the inner world, awakened presence. We pause to claim our history, our connections that link the past and future into a freedom called this present moment, which carry us into a timelessness called eternity. No longer a trace of *me*, I am. The following tale is my memory/memoir of entering the deep root of being, along *The Way of the Lover*.

—*Dr. Paula Bromberg*

THE SOUND
THE COLOR OF LOVE

*A*s stories go, this King had lived a great life; wise, understanding and kind. But during that time a corner of his noble heart had remained locked up, despite the immense respect and reverence his subjects and family had paid to him. There was always a silence in one part of his heart. A silence that contained every sound ever heard. Like the white which held every color in his Kingdom.

This King of Kings, as he was known throughout the lands, addressed in this equally fine way, had a great chamber, in which he would ruminate when he wasn't serving his Kingdom. All near to him understood that late evenings when most would sleep he then retired to his chamber in a remote part of the castle, disappearing until dawn.

Only one daughter—his third by his seventh wife had the privilege to meet and greet with him when he would emerge from this seemingly private time. Daughter of daughters, as she was known, had never married although she was a magnificent sight to behold. Her hair shone like the stars had arrived and created a night cap reaching to her slender shoulders. Her skin—pale—cast a silver glow and her eyes burned like black embers, almost unbearable to gaze into.

Everyone knew that the King of Kings had a special place for his daughter of daughters, and it was never questioned that the key to his heart lay in the mystery of her soul.

Every year—on the 29th of April the King of Kings held a ceremony whereby the entire Kingdom was invited to a festivity that lasted through the night and into early morning. All calendars began and ended on that one designated day. So it was to everyone's surprise when a proclamation on March 31st stated that this year would not follow past protocol. The King of Kings was preparing for a long journey that would take him outside his own borders for the first time.

The entire Kingdom rocked as word quickly spread. No personage had ever gone beyond the borders of this holy land and return to tell of it. A great gloom descended upon the entire land and speculation was that the Kingdom could/would never survive this. Everyone felt that this would be the demise of the 50 years of joy and prosperity that had been showered upon this exemplary Kingdom.

As the dawn of April 1st arrived all eyes looked toward the many turreted castle. People began slowly gathering, until by sunrise all of the Kingdom had arrived to hear the edict officially announced. The enormous seriousness of the expedition became visible when the King of Kings himself stepped out this April 1st morning and stood side by side with his daughter of daughters, this third child of his seventh wife.

A great hush fell upon the Kingdom. An expectant silence so total that even the wind engaged in quieting the trees. The animals hushed their animal noises. The seas stopped moving, clouds disappeared to show an empty sky, birds held their wings and breath. Rocks sat motion-less. It was as if all eternity had waited for this moment.

The King of Kings ceremoniously took the silver hued hand of his priceless jewel the daughter of daughters as she stood most regally by his side.

No one of us has ever ventured out beyond the borders of this country and come back to tell it. I have lived in this Kingdom a very long life watching time pass. Great beauty has dwelt in my heart, but a corner of it has remained locked by a dark secret.

When I was three years old my childhood years of play and fancy were robbed from me. An angel took one tear from my childhood and stated a sacred prophesy. I was barely able to comprehend the magnitude of it at the time of its occurrence. Forty-seven years would first pass: time nearly beyond the age people lived, and during which I could only hold the awe and mystery of this beautiful angel in silence.

I had been sitting alone in the garden when she appeared. Wings luminescent, face brilliant like the sun. A dream to awaken me from my childhood fancy.

I never was the same again. Childhood vanished and I became a serious adult. Slowly growing into the King of Kings that you have known. Except that each night while my Kingdom slept I have secluded away into my great chamber room and devoted time to this question revealed to me as a small child. The angel who took my tear offered me the gift of eternity and said that on my 50th birthday I would have to choose between eternal life in this Kingdom or be banished forever. If I chose eternal life I would remain alive to watch my people, my friends, all of nature, the birds, clouds, trees, rivers die and dry up. If I didn't want to grieve over the loss of all that I have loved I would have to walk out of my Kingdom forevermore.

But on my 35th Birthday a miracle occurred. My seventh wife gave birth to my third daughter. Looking at this child I saw a divine spark and remembered that early visit at age three. For my daughter of daughters grew to have the same pale skin the same luminescent face as the angel who stole the tear from my childhood.

The years passed and I grew to cherish my angel daughter, help-

ing her to stay in form as the continuous light of this Kingdom. On the night before my 50th birthday, the night I was to make this decision, I went to my chamber. I heard a light tapping on my window, it was my daughter of daughters. To my astonishment two silver wings appeared on her shoulders. When I opened the forever shut window she floated in and hovering to my left, she landed on her small feet and stood by my side. "Oh King of Kings" she said: and she had never called me this before; only "Father" had ever come from her precious lips: "I have known about your prophecy from the day I was born. I have carried this, your mysterious secret, deep in my soul, and I took form to stand by your side as a reminder of that angel in all of us, of the seed that yearns.

I am what is within you, and all that has been in your Kingdom. But this morning at dawn you must make your decision. An initiation into eternity, or the unknown. If you leave this Kingdom I will vanish having used up my purpose in life. If you remain to watch everything you've known wither you will face what no one has ever known; life without death." With this she disappeared as if she had never been there.

And so I have come to you my devoted people to ask your mercy, to beg your loving kindness and forgiveness. For I have to depart. The decision made, I must leave, even though inside my heart I have touched eternity. I have been and am the King of Kings —with or without my Kingdom. And, I have birthed and loved this daughter of daughters whether she remains in form or not. I have taught all who lived by me to live naturally, I love you all who have touched my life, and so now...

And as he spoke a small child stepped forward and walked towards the King.

Life and death are one and the same, said the child. *We are always beginning just as the seasons change, and your people have been blessed to live in this Kingdom of joy and prosperity for these 50 years. I am a child of your land and I need to grow, wisely led. This country needs your guidance to allow the fruit to ripen on the vine, the rivers stay clean and clear, the seas remain free from foe, love abloom in our hearts—to keep fear from growing in our bellies.*

I am a child of your people. Yet I speak with age and wisdom. Like you did when your tear was plucked at three by the angel. No one could hear you then, yet I know you hear me now. Weeping, I appeal: Remain with us.

The King became very silent. A silence that contained every sound ever heard. After looking far out into the distance he brought his gaze back to the child.

For you I will stay. Here, in silence. In deep golden silence I will rule. I will rule for eternity in silence.

And the King of Kings sacrificed his tongue as he had sacrificed the tear that had been taken at three. And he ruled as the most royal leader that had ever lived. And he lives, alive in fullness, still in that far away Kingdom where people know joy and prosperity. There every sound is the great silence, like every color is white.

CHAPTER ELEVEN

The Way of the Lover

What can we gain by sailing to the moon if we are not able to cross the abyss that separates us from ourselves? This is the most important of all voyages of discovery, and without it, all the rest are not only useless, but disastrous.
—*Thomas Merton*

We can let the circumstances of our lives harden us so that we become increasingly resentful and afraid, or we can let them soften us, and make us kinder. We always have the choice. Awareness of death is the very bedrock of the entire path. Until you have developed this awareness, all other practices are obstructed. —*the Dalai Lama*

Within each individual human being, there is this spark of the divine. But we have been trained to ignore it. We don't know how to be in touch with it except in special moments. What makes life more meaningful. This is what we are really here for. We do know that we're bound to experience periods of suffering, of stress, of joy and of happiness. So, when I say to make life more meaningful, it becomes a serious question. I believe that life becomes more meaningful when one is present to this moment. All of life is a challenge which has to be met and one can't meet it without being in the marketplace. With intention, one leads a more harmonious existence. With intention, one remembers that there's more to life, more in life than the mechanical associative actions and thoughts to which we're subject for most of the time. One pauses and in this stop, there's a great in-gathering which can help to change life. To be open to the atmosphere and to receive impressions of a very fine order, there is the marketplace full of harmony and color and light and activity, very important in developing one's inner life. Life is joyous.
—*William Segal*

If you want to work on your art, work on your life. —Chekhov

Perhaps the deepest reason we are afraid of death is because we do not know who we are. It is on a fragile and transient support that we rely for our security. So when they are all taken away, will we have any idea of who we really are? Without our familiar props, we are faced with just ourselves, a person we do not know, an unnerving stranger with whom we have been living all the time but we never really wanted to meet. Isn't that why we have tried to fill every moment of time with noise and activity, however boring or trivial, to ensure that we are never left in silence with this stranger on our own? And doesn't this point to something fundamentally tragic about our way of life? Hypnotized by the thrill of building, we have raised the houses of our lives on sand. This world can seem marvelously convincing until death collapses the illusion and evicts us from our hiding place. —Sogyal Rinpoche

It is our responsibility to learn how to love. By learning what love is, and its purpose, we will break through the world of illusions into the real world and we will come upon the great secret. —Reshad Feild

Each of us has a divine name. Mindfulness is the key to unlocking its secret. The term in the Talmud for mindfulness is kavanat lev, 'the directing of the heart.' Real mindfulness comes about not by an act of violence against our consciousness, not by force, not by trying to control our consciousness, but rather, by a kind of directed compassion, a softening of our awareness, a loving embrace of our lives, a soft letting be. —Alan Lew

Lucky Life

Dear waves, what will you do for me this year? Will you drown out my scream? Will you let me rise through the fog? Will you fill me with that old salt feeling? Will you let me take my long steps in the cold sand? Will you let me lie on the white bedspread and study the black clouds with the blue holes in them? Will you let me see the rusty trees and the old monoplanes one more year? Will you let me draw my sacred figures and move the kites and birds around with my dark mind?

Lucky life is like this. Lucky there is an ocean to come to. Lucky you can judge yourself in this water. Lucky you can be purified over and over again. Lucky there is the same cleanliness for everyone. Lucky life is like that. Lucky life. Oh lucky life. Oh lucky lucky life. Lucky life. —Gerald Stern

Long past the time he could walk from his home to shul on Shabbos, I was riding with Reb Zalman to a Lubavitcher shtiebl (prayer space) in Boulder, Colorado. The shrill pinging of a Tibetan bell that was hanging from Reb Zalman's rearview mirror continually interrupted our time together. Every pothole elicited the ringing of the bell, and while I did my best to ignore it, the tinny clanging finally got the better of me.

What's with bell? I asked.

It is my blessing bell. Everytime it rings I say Baruch HaShem, thanks God. This way if, God forbid, I should get into a fatal accident, the bell would ring and the last words I would utter would be Baruch HaShem.
—*Rami Shapiro*

TO DIE BEFORE WE DIE

I remember singing a song at night in bed:

Each night before I go to sleep I ask the Lord my soul to keep, and if I die before I wake, a prayer for mother and dad. May I grow up some day to be, a sweet and loving child for Thee, and if I die before I wake, a prayer for mother and dad.

Now, years later this child's bedtime prayer holds the key to that innocent surrender; says the mystic poet: *a child presses on to lose his own life upon the summits, in that simplicity which does not know itself.* I remember working in the children's ward of a New York hospital seeing children admitted bearing burns and cuts from their parents, and yet still eager to be reunited with that same parent. Says the poet: *To find the heart of the child behind the door of scars. That golden room where all things blaze.*

I see that my next teacher will be death. That nightly passage, dropping off to sleep, my introductory initiation. Disappearing to reappear into the surprise of awakening each morning. The greatest mystery of life is not life itself, it's death. This daily experience with impermanence, emphasized by loss, brought me to know what truly does endure. Early experiences taught me to live gently, that the physical is impermanent, to be shaken out of the dream is to look for what really matters. Life and death cannot be separated, they are aspects of each other. *There is no one exempt. Before death we are all equal.* When we ask *for whom the bell tolls,* we are forgetting the endless extravagance of life—the continual renewal of seasons, from summer to winter to spring.

From childhood I knew that the true spiritual path is revealed through loss, not acquisition or gain. Self-inquiry is to find what remains free of death. How to have a relationship to what is never born, never dies, unborn, imminent until it is realized and silent. And therein lie the innumerable deaths in life that accompany us on our journey. I understood loss at a young age. Through sorrow and eventually self-recognition came a teaching that all things remain alive and present, the reality of life and death continuously meet in the heart.

Any death diminishes me, because I am involved with humanity; and therefore never send to know for whom the bell tolls—it tolls for thee.
—John Donne

Death is a great teacher, asking us to pay attention, to trust existence, it brings a vulnerability to knowing what is important, to live fully, to have no regrets. And in recognizing limitation, mortality, our life gains preciousness, like a rare diamond or gold its scarcity teaches us to place a high price on that jewel. We cannot buy more time. Death awareness is a great teacher because it represents the definition, the shape and context, an unavoidable mirror in life. How ironic that what holds the key to personal responsibility to this planet, future generations, the environment, the meaning of life, our spiritual dimension, the state of medicine and health care is so often underplayed and dismissed. Listen to those who have faced life threatening illness or near-death accidents. The intensity of those wake-up calls often generates renewed appreciation, births understanding, brings unfamiliar aliveness from clearing away the unnecessary, the distractions and pettiness that keep us too busy to notice deaths hand in our daily life. It's fear that closes us, not our truthful recognition and willingness to see what's there in front of our eyes. We turn away from the illusion we perpetuate when hiding the most simple facts of life, hidden in our language when we say we lost our husband, hidden from children when we won't take them to a funeral, and we hide it from ourself when we consider death a depressing morbid avoidable topic. We prefer to keep it out of sight; denial often based on a terror of death. *Men come and they go and they trot and they dance, and never a word about death. All well and good. Yet when death does come—to them, their wives, their children, their friends—catching them unawares and unprepared, then what storms of passion overwhelm them, what cries, what fury, what despair! To begin depriving death of its greatest advantage over us, let us adopt a way clean contrary to that common one; let us deprive death of its strangeness, let us frequent it. Let us get used to it, let us have nothing more often in mind than death,* said Michel de Montaigne. *We do not know where death awaits us: so let us wait for it everywhere. To practice death is to practice freedom. A man who has learned how to die has unlearned how to be a slave.*

Death does not squander our years, we do. To enunciate the transience of their meditation, yogis have sat by burning funeral pyres and in graveyards as one of their practices. Reminders, all here to promote our great appreciation of what we do have. Reminders of our impermanence, practices loosening the bindings that restrain us, preparations for us to live deliberately, to live well. To embrace death is to embrace life. And the great ones have always known this. Mozart wrote: *I have formed a close relationship to this best and truest friend of mankind that death's image is no longer terrifying to me, but is indeed very soothing and consoling. I have learned that death is the key which unlocks the door to our true happiness.*

Deathlessness is hidden at the center of the house. You have to be killed in every room of the house before you can get to the room where death-lessness is. The mercy is that after the first couple of killings, you know that you are being killed into life, and participate in the killing willingly.
—Andrew Harvey

In ancient Rome the Latin words *Momento Mori: Remember you must die* were spoken to Roman generals as they paraded through the streets during their triumphant victory march. Standing behind each general the attendant's task was to repeat the words *Momento mori. respice post te! Hominem te memento. Remember you will die. Look behind you! Remember you are but a man!* Reminding the general that, though his glory, his greatness was at this peak today, tomorrow he could fall or be brought down.

If we are all dying how can we actually hate another person. If we are all going in the same cart to execution, to see every other being as bound for death is to experience real compassion. —Sir Thomas Moore

There is a beautiful story about Plato. Dying, he called his students, told them to come close, saying: *I have one teaching of wisdom. All of my learning I give to you in a simple statement: Practice to die.* In the same manner, Gurdjieff stated: *As we are without inner evolution, death is the end for us. But immortality is a possibility. The Way of the Lover, The Fifth Way, Sacred Psychology* extends an invitation to come along the journey of inner evolution, to die before we die, while still in form, to die into life; the more we die the more we are alive, appearing within the in and out of each breath. We are born with each inhalation of our breath and we are released—die—as we breathe out. We enter and exit this life on the breath, and in between those two breaths is a world connected to all beings. Awakened breathers could clothe this atmosphere into a blossoming garden.

How did the rose ever open its heart and give to this world all its beauty? It felt the encouragement of light against its being. —Hafiz

WISDOM TEACHINGS

The realization that every act, every word, every thought of ours not only influences our environment but for some mysterious reason forms an integral and important part of the Universe, fits into it as if by necessity so to say, in the very moment we do, or say, or think it —is an overwhelming and even shattering experience. The tremendous responsibility of it is terrifying. If all of us only knew that the smallest act of ours, or a tiny thought, has such far-reaching effects as to set in motion forces which perhaps could shatter a galaxy....If we know it deeply and absolutely, if this realization becomes engraved permanently on our hearts, on our minds, how careful we would act and speak and think. How precious life would become in its integral oneness. And this, I think, is a far as the human mind and heart can go.
—*Irina Tweedie*

*H*emingway wrote that every true story ends in death. How then to open our heart, embrace our beloved, knowing that one us will most likely live beyond the other's death? What brings meaning, the rich fullness to life is, even though; to awaken and become human, to treasure the sweetness while it is, to defy and break all illusion, what enduring hearts we have! To stand before death, as I was in my mother's presence at her last breath, and still continue to love. True love asks for nothing in return. Not for my mother to take another breath, not for existence to keep her here, it is utter surrender with great compassion for ourselves. *How could the lover ever die?* asks Rumi. *When we are dead, seek not our tomb in the earth. But find it in the hearts of man.* This is the sacred, the lover never dies. The eternity of life is found at the door of death, to burn away, to let go of our attachments, to become vigilant, life-affirming; to live well we approach the center of deathlessness. *Only that day dawns to which we are awake,* said Thoreau who went to the woods asking of himself to now live deliberately.

No thought exists in me which death has not carved with his chisel.
—*Michelangelo*

After winning the Nobel prize, Isaac Bashevis Singer was questioned why he writes in Yiddish, a dying language. *Yes, you are right, Yiddish is a dying language. But in Jewish history, the distance between dying and dead is very great.* To place attention to what is, the movement of the mind becomes self-directed. When out attention is freed from its attachments, no longer held captive by our associative thinking, our experiences carry the possibility of unifying our thoughts and bring us to a deeper understanding. This changes the state of our consciousness. The past is welcomed into this present moment for us to appreciate the richness of what is still here, now. Death teaches us to live. The courage to face our mortality is a doorway to compassion. We are all terminal. There is no us or them, we are all them, all of them are really us.

When we remember who we are, we will see where we are. We will see that we are in the rose garden and that we are its guardians. We have been given the extraordinary dignity of being the interpreters, adorers and guardians of that place. When we remember, we will wake up to our transcendent responsibility to save the planet. —*Andrew Harvey*

Becoming interior beings we hear a sacred voice deep inside. The soil for our growth in this world stands at the entrance into the wilderness of temptation. Leaving everything behind, to experience who we are, truth is discovered rising from the deepest source of our being. Now to sit with this. The continual rise and fall, like our breath, we flow between worlds, to appear and disappear, to relax into our inner home, to feel at home; uprooted, yet planted, allowing nature to take her course.

The esoteric aspect of this work is to be able to die consciously each and every moment, and this serves the world in a particular way. As we die to our illusions a little more each day, a certain kind of energy is made available for the conscious evolution of mankind. Can you accept the fact that you don't know who you are? To question, 'Who am I?' for through this ultimate question, and the yearning to know the answer, the substance of the soul comes into being. Something comes about through the sacrifice of our self-concepts and our concepts of all things of this world, which are the illusions of the world, the shadow world of the real world. What starts to come about is the substance of the soul coming into being. —Reshad Feild

Numerous cultures include a folklore legend of a mythical Phoenix bird. The beautiful scarlet and golden plumed Phoenix, a source of inspiration, peace and regeneration, has radiant bold feathers and a melodious cry. Each morning it bathes and sings with a voice said to be so entrancing that all of creation stops and listens. The Phoenix resides in the tree of knowledge that is heavy with the seeds of all of the plant life in the world, having lived to see the world destroyed three various times. Not harming anything the bird lives on dewdrops, its power of healing and regeneration contain the entire universe, risking everything, its death is beyond time and change, agent of love dissolving into the very essence of life itself, like a chrysalis turned into a butterfly the Phoenix unites death with life.

The Phoenix knows the exact day of his death. In this manner death becomes key to liberation in life. Every thousand years, as the end of its life approaches, the Phoenix builds itself a pyre nest of incense, aromatic branches and spices, sets the fire and burns in the flames. Both nest and bird are consumed and reduced to ashes. As the bird leaves the tree seeds fly in all directions. A new Phoenix arises from the midst of the ashes and flames. Birth and death in fire make the Phoenix a sacred fire bird, a sacrificing figure of renewal courageously setting itself ablaze to live eternally through birth, death and renewal. The spirit never dies, what was is continuously becoming new, a further passage.

Death is a vast mystery., but there are two things we can say about it: It is absolutely certain that we will die, and it is uncertain when or how we will die. The only surety we have, then, is this uncertainty about the hour of our death, which we seize on as an excuse to postpone facing death directly. We are like children who cover their eyes in a game of hide-and-seek and think that no one can see us. —Sogyal Rinpoche

Every continent has its Phoenix myth. In the Jewish tradition, it is named Micham and called the guardian of the terrestrial sphere. On its right wing are the words, *neither the earth produces me, nor the heavens, but only wings of fire*. In certain other cultures it is spoken of as the bird of paradise, the swan of song, the Chinese Feng, Japanese Ho-oo. This King of the Birds sustained on the dew neither kills or crushes anything it touches. The Phoenix, mirror of the universe, is birthed at the same moment that all the stars return to their starting position beginning a new orbit in an eternal cycle. Attar, a 12th century Sufi poet wrote an allegorical poem, *Conference of the Birds*; naming the Phoenix, Simurgh. The Simurg's beak, flute-like, is long and pierced with 44 holes each giving out a different tone. When the bird takes flight the wind creates its beautiful music that floats around the world. Living 1,000 years, knowing the moment of its death, the celestial music at the moment of death expresses its sound of recognition.

A spiritual allegory, *Conference of the Birds* is a journey to find the Simurg, a teaching about the rigors and trials of our spiritual quest. Andrew Harvey, scholar, mystic and poet says he reads it every three years because: *it is a divine mirror that reflects back to us transformed what we have come to understand.* The birds who journeyed to the court of the Simurg eventually arrived worn, their bodies reduced to ashes, yet the light of the Simurg brought life to their souls saying: *Once love penetrates the heart you become brave as a lion even when feeble as an ant. How can one who takes a leap into the ocean of adventure accept any drink but the blood of your heart?* The risk and the sacrifice becomes our life! The whole personality, the false self, is claimed and the mirror blazes light as the Phoenix rises. The riddle of I and Thou is revealed when the Simurg spoke: *The sum of my majesty is a mirror, Whoever beholds himself in this mirror sees there his soul and body.* There in the Simurg's radiant face the birds see themselves as the Simurg of the world with awe. They gazed, and dared, finally knowing, understanding, who is in the mirror.

The secret of death is in the heart of life. For life and death are one, even as the river and the sea are one. —*Kahlil Gibran*

THE PSYCHOLOGY
OF THE GODS

Man is that being who invented the gas chambers of Auschwitz; however, he is also that being who entered those chambers upright, with the Shema Yisrael on his lips. We who lived in concentration camps can remember the men and women who walked through the huts comforting others, giving away their last piece of bread. They may have been few in numbers, but they offer sufficient proof that everything can be taken away from a man but one thing: The last of the human freedoms—to choose one's attitude in any given set of circumstances, to choose one's own way. Even in the most severe suffering a human being can find meaning and thus hope. Those who have a why to live can bear with almost any how. A person is then not the son of his past but the father/daughter of his/her future. Everything can be taken from a person but the last of the human freedoms—to choose one's attitude in any given set of circumstances, to choose one's own way. —*Victor Frankl*

*T*he new psychology recognizes unconditional love, not pathology, as the model for a natural life. During the process of inner work, we chip away and refine, coming closer to who we really are. Open, deconstructing the false self, we live what we know. In our culture we say that someone is going to a *shrink* when they are in therapy. Therapy is not only shrinking, it's stretching ourselves to increase, to become spacious, extending into a heart constantly widened, expanding. People bring issues exploring how to live with clarity, honesty, mindfully. Learning to empower ourselves, we use our life's experiences and eventually teach others what we have unraveled. *The Way of the Lover* is a teacher training, not patient perpetuation, to impart what we have discovered. It supports authenticity and aliveness. *Sacred Psychology* develops gardeners and midwives—that's the true nature of teaching—to plant seeds of truth for nature to birth us into our aliveness.

It is not the end of the physical body that should worry us. Rather, our concern must be to live while we're alive—to release our inner selves from the spiritual death that comes with living behind a facade designed to conform to external definitions of who and what we are...... If we were to protect all ravines against all storms and avalanches we would never be able to admire the beauty of their scarred surfaces. —Dr. Elisabeth Kübler-Ross

Teaching in this way cracks open the heart, until one day breaking, released from the barrier of ego that binds. Sacrificing our wounds to ennoble our journey, this is the psychology of the gods. We open, we become through understanding our wounding. We look to Jacob, Jesus, Joseph, Jeanne D'Arc, Mansur, Rumi, Mirabai, Akiva and the esoteric symbol of their wounds. Jacob wrestling with the angels, wounded to forever walk haltingly, to limp. A ladder ascended into heaven and descended to earth. Joseph thrown into a pit by his brothers, envious that he might receive a greater proportion of the family inheritance.

Moses, leaving Egypt, running for his life from Pharaoh who wanted him murdered, Jeanne D'Arc, burned, yet holding to the truth of her faith, Rumi cast into love's furnace, teaching: *if you have not been a lover, count not your life as lived. Die with love and remain alive, blessed is the one who burns away like this,* Sufi Mansur, publicly executed, entered the truth lived at the bottom of his heart, cut into pieces, arms, legs, tongue, finally his head; laughing *because you are killing somebody else, this poor body has done nothing, this body is not Mansur,* open as he forgave his tormentors, recognizing them, too, as ways that existence appears to test love, and Akiva, tortured, executed, joyful of heart, steadfast in his faith as he was mercilessly murdered, died saying: *I rejoice at the opportunity now given me to love my God with all my life.* It is the Akiva's, the Joseph's, the Mansur's of the world that hold spiritual integrity, the connection to their essence, mind and body silent, not pulled to be lost in the persuasion and glitter of this world. Holding a vision, Joseph held on to the promise. To bring something good and life affirming out of the wounding, for that becomes our instrument of survival for future generations. We can become heroic, faced with challenges, trials, yet remain inspired to continuously undergo a transformation of consciousness. A hero offers life to something greater, to a new way of being. Life evokes our character. To bring meaning to this world, to be used as an instrument, shaped by our life, is the heroic way. It's Hamlet asking: *are you up to your destiny?* It's accepting the trials, ordeals and joys along the way. In healing we become strong in the broken places.

Ring the bells that still can ring, forget your perfect offering, there is a crack, there is a crack in everything, that's how the light get's in, that's how the light gets in. —Leonard Cohen

To become rooted in the ground of self we are freed to offer our practice of loving kindness, calming the water within as well as on the other side of the world. Says Rumi: *The moment you accept what troubles you've been given, the door will open.* To be awake to the moment of the ordinary we need to lean into the difficult, touching the soft spot in our core, the one that teaches us that we are all vulnerable and available to connect to limitless generosity and compassion. Embracing all, our awakening gives us the vision to make real change. To die to everything we imagine ourselves to be, the concepts and illusions, and then to even let go of the empty space we took refuge in, is the surrender. The preparation, the study and intention, the clues point the direction, yet only from within can the door open, previously barricaded by our preconcepts and fears which eventually are left outside, left behind. To deeply penetrate, realize our true nature, to come into a full and mature awakening, to have died before we die; absent we increase in presence.

Spiritual traditions recognize that awakening is the beginning rather than the end of an open-ended process of spiritual transformation. It is one thing to thoroughly wake up to one's true nature as the formless ground of being or no-self; it is another to actualize or embody this awareness in one's daily life in the body and in relationship and to transpose these changes to collective, societal structures. —Prendergast and Bradford

Since breath is life, and our out breath fills the atmosphere, one conscious breath changes the atmosphere of the world. Our breathing is a stable solid ground to take refuge in, we are responsible for the air we breathe, we all share the same air. Accountability opens true compassion; to see every one facing the same precariousness, this focus on impermanence now lends to living fully. Spiritual maturity is surrendering resistance, nothing to give up, since nothing is owned. We don't give up our house when we go out, it just drops from our consciousness. We are in this world as guardians, the interpreters, heirs of this world and all of its inhabitants are our family.

A human being is part of a whole, called by us the 'Universe,' a part limited in time and space. He experiences himself, his thoughts and feelings, as something separated from the rest—a kind of optical delusion of his consciousness. This delusion is a kind of prison for us, restricting us to our personal desires and to affection for a few persons nearest us. Our task must be to free ourselves from this prison by widening our circle of compassion to embrace all living creatures and the whole of nature in its beauty. —*Albert Einstein*

An esoteric teacher, in his later years, when asked about his life, told what he had held secret and was willing to reveal as his most important teaching: *I don't mind what happens.* This becomes visible on the beautiful faces of Buddha, Ramana, Meher Baba, Ammachi; peaceful deathlessness, the smile that penetrates, the eyes of fearlessness: awakened in love. To renew ourselves; one essential step is to empower our stories, to rewrite our history—not the way family or society told it, but to find the essence of our experience and rewrite it that way. Otherwise, we walk around with introjected inner voices; critical, judgmental, self-righteous, often negative. Even when a parental voice says, *You are such a good child,* that still may not have been our experience. To release those voices, remembering how we felt before we first heard, thought, spoke those words. To no longer defend ourselves against what was our initial wounding. Once surviving the first time, to look again, sliding free, less impacted from the original suffering. The going back is to unravel our own truth, finding the kernel—the original seed. When we recognize that the voice inside that pretends to be us is not who we are, the one who is aware of that voice who brings attention from a still place within, awakening to that, a glimpse into what is unchanging, a link between us and our true name, brings a new level of realization.

Thoughts change but not you. Hold to the self even during mental activity.

Happiness is inherent in everyone and is not due to external causes. When your real, effortless, joyful nature is realized, it will not be inconsistent with the ordinary activities of life. —Ramana Maharshi

Traveling the unprotected journey, study those who have gone the entire route. Be nourished, remembering who has walked this path before. Life is here to use, as we connect to the stories of awakened beings. The bodhisattva voluntarily joins life to participate with compassion in the sorrows of others. Unconditional love is the awakening of the heart from self-interest to an unwavering commitment to love humanity. Living with our heart open to others here in the midst of life is to experience the vastness of who we are.

I am now 74 years old. And yet I feel that I am an infant. I feel clearly that in spite of all the changes I am a child. My guru tells me that child which is you even now is your real self. I used to sit for hours with nothing but the "I am" in my mind. Soon peace and joy and a deep all embracing love became my normal state. In it, all disappeared: my self, my guru, the life I lived, the world around me. Only peace remained and unfathomable silence. —Nisargadatta

UNCONDITIONAL LOVE

The childish work for their own benefit. The Buddhas work for the benefit of others. Just look at the difference between them! —Shantideva

Unconditional love speaks directly to the heart. To love for its own sake, to savor and protect each encounter for its connection to what is higher touches the heart of unconditional friendship for ourselves. The mindful practice of Tonglen, the path of compassion, asks us to look at ourselves and life with a gentle brave forgiving heart. To practice compassion we first need compassion for ourselves. We develop the ability to breathe in the suffering that is in this world as we breathe out peaceful well-being. Through giving and receiving, becoming agents of healing, hearing the cries of the world, taking in the sorrow we breath it out with a desire for peace. To dissolve the barriers in our heart we enter a land that looks to meet suffering as we breath out well-being. This is a practice as well as a way of life.

The birth of a man is the birth of his sorrow. The longer he lives, the more stupid he becomes, because his anxiety to avoid unavoidable death becomes more and more acute. What bitterness! He lives for what is always out of reach! His thirst for survival in the future makes him incapable of living in the present. —*Chuang Tzu*

During one of Elisabeth Kübler-Ross' Life, Death and Transition, week-long seminars, there was a man who had served in Vietnam, who had molested his girlfriend's child. I watched my inner response, listening to Richard I felt closed and judgmental. I saw him as violent and injurious to a child. As the days progressed, however, Elisabeth Kübler-Ross was embracing, compassionate towards him, creating a safe environment in the room and throughout the retreat for him to express his personal wounding, as well as for us to hear and touch our humanity. His father had beaten and molested him; as the days unfolded, his heart touched, he felt and expressed shame, remorse and grief for his actions that had harmed another child. My heart opened to see his humanity as not separate from mine or anyone else's. At the end of the workshop we made a circle around this wounded soldier, sang the national anthem, opening our arms. He cried as Elisabeth said, *Welcome home.* I was deeply moved as this battered child who had returned from an ugly war, had a brutal past as both victim and perpetrator rewrote his history now moving us to reshape our own responses. Unconditional love or total acceptance and love towards others, the ability to see through the acts that people perform to feel and to see their divinity enables us to contact our humanity, to humanize this world, to dissolve judgment until all that's left is life's essential sacredness. As that young man was able to feel and express his pain and innermost longings, we opened. Both parties were healed. Unconditional love inspires reciprocal healing and redeems the suffering; witnessed, we awaken into the present moment, freed from the self-imposed limitations of the past.

With each experience we grow and become more aware of the inner beauty that lies within us. Ultimately we are truly our own leader. We lead the connection and flow of life that is our inheritance. —Rabbi Yossi

This story stands as an illustration: the meeting of personal wounds with the world's sufferings. It speaks to, in its communal way, the inter-penetration of death and life. There is only the present moment. To awaken and live, to die before we die, we must dive deep to make real change. But how to do this inner work, and break our fixations, the patterns? A transformative path does not trivialize awakening by suggest-ing that by wanting it to be so, consciousness, knowledge and living in peace and balance will be accessible and available. Glimpses and tastes of stillness and peace often fleeting become more than glimpses, become a real possibility. This book is my offering, it holds secrets of the mystery, our soul beauty, so that we might give ourselves to the love that already owns our breath and life.

The earth and the sand are burning. Put your face on the burning sand and on the earth of the road, since all those who are wounded by love must have the imprint on their face, and the scar must be seen. Let the scar of the heart be seen, for by their scars are known the persons who are in the way of love. —Wisdom sayings, Hadith

SELF-INQUIRY: PARADISE HERE AND NOW

Creative vision only belongs to one who dares to look into the depths of himself as far as the void. We are the calm center of the whirlwind of life. Then everything is done without attachment, as though we have nothing to do, living wherever it is necessary. Things arise by themselves brought by the current of life. If I understand the totality of life in a connected world, I will see that in order to transform things outside of me, I have to transform myself, voluntarily assuming the role given to me within this life, I understand my part in the struggle within the totality of existence.
—*Jeanne de Salzmann*

The Fifth Way, *The Way of the Lover,* calls us to turn inward to find the truth that is our very being and bring it forward into the world. Spiritual work is not about arriving, journeying itself is the way. This knowing, a living realization, self-inquiry, to discover ourself arises naturally in the soft light of compassion. For this precarious journey, an awakening of consciousness, there are tools to discover what enslaves us to the narrow places in our lives. Our greatest gifts are obscured by our obstructions and that makes us see the world not as *it* is, but as *we* are.

Blessed are you, who opens a gate in every moment, to enter in truth or tarry in hell, sang Leonard Cohen, because life will certainly throw a veil over our path, and still we have the possibility to choose intention, integrity, to proceed with clarity and discernment. Part Two, Chapter 12, completes the invitation of Part One, and offers tools, maps to study, ways to break out of our limited awareness, to become visible and see, to infuse the planet with our awareness. To navigate our life here on earth, to become mindful of what is distorted, from a place of childishness toward a responsible maturity; having a toolbox with conscious teachings guides us within the spirit of the adage: *Give a person a fish and you feed him for a day: teach him to fish and you feed him for a lifetime.*

The Five Precepts: Do no harm to anyone, Take nothing that is not freely given, Speak truthfully and helpfully, Use your sexual energy wisely, And keep your mind clear. —the Buddha

The place where you are standing is holy, it's our forgetting that creates exile; memory and awareness are our source for redemption. The birth of consciousness comes when inner space creates a ledge for witnessing. I become aware of my thoughts, feelings, and actions, without judgment. In fact, I enjoy myself, whatever the circumstance. Deep humor transforms the world. Longchempa, a Buddhist teacher said: *When you actually see what's going on, you nearly die of laughter.* Ramana spoke: *On the day of liberation, you will laugh, but what is on the day of laughter is also now.* The Dalai Lama's signature mischievous grin greets his life with the good humor that finds voice in frequent peals of deep reverberating laughter. For tragedy not to overwhelm us *we chuckle from inside as we see the facade of samsara and nirvana; the view will constantly keep us amused, with a little inner smile bubbling away all the time,* commented Tibetan Khyentse. The awakened smile of love and compassion enjoys this world. And what goes on is all usable, my life becomes mine to use rather than a power that will go on using me. To know ourself, to live in the wisdom of the heart, without separation, this is true freedom. Now we become the endless love story, having discovered, *The Way of the Lover*—paradise.

Dying, Laughing

A lover was telling his beloved how much he loved her,
how self-sacrificing he had been, getting up at dawn
every morning, fasting, all for her.

There was a fire in him.
He didn't know where it came from,
but it made him weep and melt like a candle.

You've done well, she said, but listen to me.
All this is the decor of love, the branches and leaves
and blossoms. You must live at the root to be a true lover.

Where is that! Tell me!

You've done the outward acts, but you haven't died.

You must die.

When he heard that, he lay back on the ground laughing,
and died. He opened like a rose that drops to the ground
and died laughing.

That laughter was his freedom, and his gift to the eternal.
—Rumi

PART TWO

Who Am I: Tools To Wake Up

The unexamined life is not worth living. —Socrates

Man remains a mystery to himself. He has a nostalgia for Being, to be. He searches for an idea, an inspiration, that could move him in this direction. It arises as a question, Who am I—who am I in this world? If this question becomes sufficiently alive, it could direct the course of his life. He cannot answer. He has nothing with which to answer—no knowledge of himself to face this question, no knowledge of his own. To welcome this question, to ask himself what he is. This is the first step on the way. He wants to open his eyes He wants to wake up, to awaken. —Jeanne de Salzmann

I tell you, whosoever you be that wish to explore the depths of nature, if what you seek is not found inside yourself you will never find it outside. Know thyself, for in thee is hidden the treasure of treasures. —Isis

My child, it's your business to understand. Now be completely present, give me your whole attention, with all the understanding that you are capable of, with all the subtlety you can muster. For the teaching requires a divine concentration of consciousness if it's to be understood. —the Asclepius

The object of your study is, first of all, yourself. Your love for the other, your ability to love another person, depends on your ability to understand/love yourself. —the Buddha

At the moment of his awakening at the foot of the bodhi tree, the Buddha declared, 'How strange—all beings possess the capacity to be awakened, to understand, to love, to be free—yet they allow themselves to be carried away on the ocean of suffering.' He saw that, day and night, we're seeking what is already there within us. We can call it buddhanature, awakened nature, the true freedom that is the foundation for all peace and happiness. The capacity to be enlightened isn't something that someone else can offer to you. A teacher can only help you to remove the non-enlightened elements in you so that enlightenment can be revealed. If you have confidence that beauty, goodness, and the true teacher are in you, and if you take refuge in them, you will practice in a way that reveals these qualities more clearly each day. —Thich Nhat Hahn

Wisdom Teachings

*B*e *a lamp unto yourself*—Buddha's final words to his student, Ananda. As Buddha lay dying: *You are the lamp that lights the path,* and Part Two of **The Way of the Lover** provides tools to penetrate to the very core of that light. Know yourself : from that place you know the universe and its laws. The teachings, from conscious sources, direct us to use our ordinary life—to come to *real* life; to consciously live in awareness, with open-heart. To turn more actively to the unexplored domain of our inner world is the challenge. To access the inner compass, to reach that invisible center of the labyrinth, tools are essential. Each of us travels a distinct path, and the initiation, the unfolding, the sacrifice and cost, this challenging upheaval becomes the transformation of our own being. The tools are tested, our comfort disturbed, our habits disarranged. They can be verified: for knowledge without understanding creates intolerance. Knowledge with understanding lifts our level of being. Listen to the systems, listen without knowing or deciding, then we are available to understand, free to respond creatively, to the challenges, the joys that arrive moment to moment.

This is the Way: To awaken in the present moment, to pay attention, remembering to use this time to repair the past, prepare the future, and to know our very nature and purpose of life. Here are practical teachings that offer awakening and transformation. The results of our efforts reflect proportionally to our understanding. It is an esoteric principle that whatever is taught has to be adapted to the level of understanding of each particular person. Only when we see a connection to a larger whole, when the recognition starts to come from an entirely different level, do we understand. This crack between worlds, the opening for real change, awakens authority in our heart.

Shifting from one dimension of awareness to another, *The Way of the Lover* is a Way of Understanding, a direct relationship between knowledge and being. What distinguishes the *Fifth Way* from most approaches is that the teaching is lived in the present moment; to wake up and see that the real work is not out there, it's inside ourself. The relationship between knowledge and being, the integration of knowledge and experience results in understanding. Real knowledge, not so easily accessible, is what this book offers. How to recognize, understand our behavior, who we are and why we manifest in these ways, why our relationships to ourself and others are the way they are; how to *see and know thyself.* The extent to which we can see ourselves is the measure of our being. And it follows that we understand others only so much as we understand ourself and only on the level of our own being. People's reluctance to see the truth about themselves keeps this Way for the few.

For travelers on a path of love having tools, road maps, reminders, prepares us for the immediacy, the moment of knowing. The strategies become alive used well towards the discovery of our true nature, tools to unearth a treasure deposited deeply within. These powerful instruments of inquiry and investigation, living oral tradition teachings, cover both psychological and spiritual terrain. Psychological dynamics wreak havoc on so many spiritual communities. Years of meditation and insight, and still students and teachers repeating unhealthy personality patterns. This is visible in spiritual communities, as well as at retreats and new age classes. What a contradiction! The sacred needs psychology as much as psychology needs the sacred.

Perfect Understanding is a great mantra, is the highest mantra, is the unequalled mantra, the destroyer of all suffering, the incorruptible truth.
—Heart Sutra

SPIRITUAL MATURITY

I recommend never adopting the attitude toward one's spiritual teacher of seeing his or her every action as divine or noble. When a teacher is engaging in unsuitable or wrong behavior, it is appropriate for the student to criticize that behavior. —the Dalai Lama

Moral and ethical negligence, the indiscretion of standards and values supports the need for tangible tools to be brought into spiritual communities. Spirituality cannot be on one level and behavior on a different level. Conduct and integrity, uprightness and sincerity; how we are to money, sexuality, time commitments, how we treat our belongings, the way we show up, our relationships to family, friends and acquaintances, our attitude to the elderly and the environment; all a direct reflection and connection to our being. There is an ethical complement to the work we do on ourself, we are all responsible to live what we know. Self-observation is a key; to witness our life is to come into real life aligned with higher consciousness.

There is no reality in the absence of observation. —Quantum Mechanics

Within a meditative community, in the presence of a self-realized master, a Mahatma, a Guru, a spiritual teacher, we have moments even days of bliss and recognition to who we really are. Then, once again immersed in daily life, our habits and routines cloud awareness until variations of distractions, anxiety, stress, fear or worry arise. To become present, within the heart, once we step out of the way of ourself, veils are lifted. Said the poet, Attar: *The true lover finds the light only if, like the candle, he is his own fuel, consuming himself.*

The Way of the Lover directly addresses the habits of the conditioned personality. Living in reactivity, tension, stress, defenses, living with blind spots and self-deception points to the difficulty of integrating spiritual consciousness into the daily fabric of life. Even with years of spiritual practice our self-interest and self-deprecation will mask ego defenses; the distorted projections and habitual emotional reactions become obstacles to an authentic wholesome relationship to self. Years of meditation for someone who has low self-esteem creates a confusion of spiritual laws. Self-negation gets mixed up with selflessness, self-importance becomes confused with surrender, feeling comfortable and blaming replaces a willingness to live into the discomfort of the unknown, apology is substituted for forgiveness, emotion often reduced to sentimentality. Natural feelings are dismissed for misunderstood impersonal laws. The discrepancy between personal development and spiritual practice often occupies a large space.

Choose your thoughts carefully. Keep what brings you peace, release what brings you suffering, and know that happiness is just a thought away.
—*Nishan Panwar*

The spiritual world speaks to emptiness, the impersonal, transformation, universal truth, transcendence through surrender, silence. The psychological world looks to developing individual personal truth, individuation, pathology, neurosis, personal meaning, treatment and cure. *The Way of the Lover* integrates both worlds and is about self-development and awakening, the study of our possible evolution and transformation. Most peoples lives need to be emptied of their fullness—stories, details about numerous dramas and circumstance, things that have happened. The lives of those on a spiritual path, conversely, could use emptying and fullness; eliminating distractions while deepening quiet time, a grounded sense of self-confidence, a willingness to drop into a quiet inner space and allow our creativity to emerge, as well as to step into life and teach what is known. The world must not be ignored in pursuit of consciousness. The Dalai Lama has acknowledged this error in his judgment in his *not joining international communities for protection,* and separating his inner search from making commitments to the world. There is no separation. To remember our soul, our global responsibility, our life in the body as well as in spirit. This is the *Fifth Way;* love as a daily practice and meditation in this world, to cultivate a compassionate heart of unity and love.

Your acts of kindness are iridescent wings of divine love, which linger and continue to uplift others long after your sharing. —Rumi

The bridge between psychology and spirituality is the distinction between the temporary and the eternal. The difficulty maintaining balance, perseverance, rests here. For a spiritual door to open we need time devoted to a peaceful space without distractions, the ability to easily financially support a life free of debt, to live within a mended past. A harmonious inner life requires a harmonious outer life. This means not getting lost in life's temptation to work more, distract more, travel more. The Fifth Way proposes to live as if on vacation 365 days a year. To be where one would want to visit. To spend time alone, silently enjoying what we have acquired. Stillness of the mind draws us beyond the mind, into our center, for us to balance reason, emotions, imagination, body and spirit. The tools are offered to support this quality of growth as our daily way to live.

When the heart has found quietness, wisdom has also found peace. —the Gita

Maturity brings a steady reliable inner state. Life's playground filled with toys for pleasure are fun, having the awareness of its fleeting brief nature is essential. Impermanence is our ally, reminding us to anchor ourselves in the awareness of life and death as we engage with the full sadness of loss and the striking generosity of life. The tools offered in this chapter are presented in the light of remaining in this world, teaching how to shift the flow of attention from the cravings and appetite for the world, back again to the self; from outer adventures to inner journeying. Not repression, suppression, not denouncing or leaving the world, instead; through noticing what captures our attention and directing it to the present moment, presence. Paying attention, having awareness is to become conscious of ourselves and our relation to the surrounding universe. This chapter is dedicated to offering tools that will make this possible. Observing the world within and without, balanced each clarifies the other. To understand, to pay attention to what we see by being sensitive to the world, to know, pay attention to how we feel, to walk towards excellence; this is harmonizing our life. We use our body and the world, or they use us. Ultimately, what directs us is passionate sincerity; the heart aflame with longing for freedom. The ability to hear the call, deep down knowing, longing, some call it a *spiritual need*, Rumi said: *open your hidden eyes and return to the root of the root of your own self*. Realize that there is no break, no time off, finally we are burning in the fire of awakening.

Understanding grows out of experience, meeting the universe from the inside it wells up within, grows out of us and is ultimately liberating. First listen, then open, now understand, finally transform. True wisdom, being a light unto yourself, is in the present moment, this is the witness, the lotus of one thousand petals suddenly opening, time to wake up!

As your love grows, as your love petals open and your heart becomes a lotus, something tremendously beautiful starts descending on you—that is wisdom. And wisdom follows understanding and brings freedom. —Osho

I had to seek the Physician because of the pain this world caused me. I could not believe what happened when I got there— I found my Teacher. Before I left, he said, "Up for a little homework, yet?" "Okay," I replied, "Well then, try thanking all the people who have caused you pain, they helped you come to me. —Kabir

Any relationship you are in that is not with someone who is committed with you to serve the depths of your being is a wasted moment, because you are less than you could be. —Anonymous

It seems impossible to love people who hurt and disappoint us. Yet there are no other kinds of people. —Frank Andrews

No one can have understanding. Understanding arises, but no one can have it or cause it to arise. To understand is to see things clearly and from all sides. Understanding means to be close to, to be with. Understanding and love always go together! Love requires understanding, a true and profound appreciation of the object of affection. Understanding isn't about understanding something. It isn't about what we know or even how we know. It's about who we are and how we navigate this human journey. Compassion arises as a natural consequence. Understanding amounts to this: the whole world, as it appears in consciousness and time, is nothing other than perfection of understanding constantly expressed in the simple actions of our daily living.

The perfection of understanding is recognizing that nothing is as we think it is; that there is no separation, no tragedy; that nothing is fixed or solid; that there is only love and endless hopelessness beyond and within what happens and doesn't happen. Understanding and love are possible. —Norman Fischer

Understanding is the substance out of which we fabricate compassion. —Thich Nhat Hahn

CHAPTER TWELVE

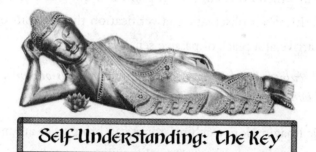

Self-Understanding: The Key

SELF-UNDERSTANDING: THE KEY

*I*n this invitation to awaken, tools of knowledge used to deepen self-understanding become part of our spiritual landscape. The key lies in *understanding*. We understand information and people only to the degree that we understand ourself. Systems are the bridge between psychology and spirituality. They offer us the possibility to become our own teacher, to carry timeless practical tools wherever we go. What power in the face of the mystery! To go beyond the personality brings us to the threshold of the spiritual. These teachings empower us to move beyond what we have come to know of as ourself, as well as to grasp the reality in which others live, their point of view. The starting point is always uncritical self-observation, a verification through our own experience, to arrive at a place of passive self-awareness.

We are all sculptors and painters, and our material is our own flesh and blood and bones. —Henry David Thoreau

Mythic imagination, teaching stories can bring us to an understanding of our place in the natural world, offering timeless wisdom and power. Our primal ancestors told stories about the animals and the great mysteries. The art, paintings on cave walls and oral literature, handiwork of the ancients, of the spirit that offered clues to our potential, reveal the mysteries of life, of what lies behind the visible world calling us to a deeper awareness of the very act of living itself.

One of the problems today is that we are not well acquainted with the literature of the spirit. We're interested in the news of the day and the problems of the hour. As we turn to the inner life, if we don't know where it is or what it is, of the magnificent heritage we have in our traditions—Plato, Confucius, the Buddha, Goethe, and others who speak of the eternal values that have to do with the centering of our lives—we've lost perspective. What we have in common is revealed in myths, clues to the spiritual potentialities of the human life, the experience of being alive so that our life experiences on the purely physical plane will have resonances within our own innermost being and reality, so that we actually feel the rapture of being alive. That's what these clues help us find within ourselves. —*Joseph Campbell*

OUR TRUE NATURE

*I*n days of old there was a particular rabbit residing in an uncrowded, unspoiled town. The clear open sky, conducive to a spirit of freedom characterized a way of life that treated the natural environment with respect. Rabbit, his heart a precious orchard, for years had yearned for a learning community of mindful loving friends. Creating a school of consciousness he wrote a friendly invitation to all the forest mountain and sea creatures to come and fill their spirit, to spend time and offer attention to practicing at this new academy. The animals enrolled, eager to study, enthusiastic to be part of a learning community. The first course was swimming. The duck, horse, dog, frog, donkey and beaver all had a natural aptitude and performed quite well. The pig, though, was not very good in this class and the animals criticized the pig saying he was lazy and not trying. The next day there were jumping classes and again the duck, horse, dog, frog, donkey and beaver performed well, in fact the frog won the jumping match. But, again, the pig could barely compete and felt humiliated. Everyone made fun of pig until finally he felt enough of a failure to decide to quit the school. But the rabbit teacher had prepared for student frustration and called in the old soul owl counselor. The owl gathered the class in the barnyard meeting area and wisely explained that *we all have natural skills and talents and* *through observation, exercises, experience and living we learn what our true nature is. We have much to gain by studying ourselves rather than living in comparison and judgment. Real learning,* he said, *is ultimately knowing about yourself. Working with others is essential. As keepers of the earth, we are responsible for this planet; the welfare of our forest, mountains and lakes depends upon kindness, cooperation and day-to-day responsibility, to the land, the trees, the water and to each other. Let us realize our inter-connectedness and continue this experiment; with awareness, understanding and love everything becomes simple and most things become possible.*

Some will be good at swimming, others at running, or climbing, some as guide and companion; best is to preserve our uniqueness as we learn who we are. Each creature is a different facet of the diamond, yet there is a secret connection between all things and to live in harmony is to understand cooperation, community, and service; all steps on our exploration. In this way we protect what's at the heart of ourselves, each creature and the planet. Treasure what you've been given as a gift. If you try to learn without knowing yourself you will just read into everything whatever you want. Life is a school. Now, understanding this, you will be ready to enjoy learning the secrets in our community school. Soon pig began to oink, dog barked, duck quacked, the beaver smacked his tail and they felt ready to embark on their own inner journey, the recognition that we all have the possibility of joy in our experience of life.

Find the work of your life, and the worker too, for both exist as one—this is you. Discover vocation, creation, and joy will come like clairvoyance, where blindness is gone before. —*Rumi*

EXPLANATION OF SYSTEMS

We awaken through our own relentless efforts. We awaken by becoming aware of our current situation and learning which tools to use. We awaken

through our friendships and work with other people who have the same aim together with the assistance of someone who has awakened already.
—*Labbate & Herold*

The 27 systems in Chapter 12, some of which existed before recorded history, are for the recognition of who we are, why we are here, and how to wake up. They are esoteric teachings of self-transformation, the creation of presence, comprised of practice as well as theory; the why of why we came here. Knowing changes behavior. Psychology as the knowledge of the soul offers us a glimpse into the unknown. Knowledge anchors love, not information; to actually know ourself.

Self-realization is the realization of our true nature, without doubt or misconception, our real nature is distinguishing the eternal from the transient, and not swerving from our natural state. —Ramana

The Way of the Lover combines ancient tradition and present-day practices with a commitment to a maturity of life that offers a deepening appreciation of who we are. Ultimately we see beyond temperament, as we dissolve habits, vanity, comparative thinking and self-importance; all typical stumbling blocks to growth. With the use of these tools we recognize others as energy and see ourselves free from distortion and fantasy, without judgment or illusion. In this way the purpose of existence is to live it; to be present and available to serve life.

The most standard error is to compare systems, they are aspects. It would be like comparing a section of an orange to a section of an apple, or the color orange to the color green. One could—but first understand orange. Real knowledge, which is beyond all comparison, comes when there is a yearning for truth with a willingness to sacrifice self-deception and illusion. Recognizing our type allows for a particular work on ourself—to see the forest as well as each tree. Recognition and acknowledgement is to consciousness and awakening as diagnosis and treatment plan is to recovery in Western medicine. Typing ourself is no different than taking a blood test to discover we have diabetes, or a slow metabolism, and then to work creatively with a plan to maintain a healthy lifestyle according to our particular needs.

The tools provide information that reveal fundamental truths. They are best used not to justify our type; the systems are offered for self-understanding and transformation and are at their optimum when looked at from a spiritual context. Characterological insight brings about a quality of detachment from our automatic psyche. In order to see traits we must first know our own character, and then to be able to depart from it.

Enquiring minds that long for the truth of the heart, and penetrate to the essence of things, phenomena and into ourselves; no matter what path followed we must inevitably arrive back at ourself and begin with the question and solution of who we are and what is our place in the world around ourself. —G.I Gurdjieff

BLUEPRINTS OF AWAKENING

I see the potential for a new world being born in front of me and all around me, and I feel the only way to bring that potential into being is to know myself. —14th Dalai Lama

The systems exist to show us how we keep the light hidden, that we are already boxed; they are not intended to limit. Value-free, they are maps with information, penetrating spiritual teachings for these modern times, specific methodology for the development of consciousness. To see our limitations parts the veil: a screen that is the difference between prison and freedom. Each of us has a basic blueprint that we work with in life, yet to know who we are, to awaken to the real self is only experienced after the personality, or ego, is recognized and dislodged. Moving from system to system, we assemble a picture, a neutral photomontage. No longer any need to shift the image, when we see ourself through another's reflection, often judgment colors the image, now, impartial, we are free to recognize, acknowledge, take in, affirm; this is an essential step on the journey. Eric Weihenmayer, blind mountaineer, after climbing the seven greatest summits, understood that critical to his success was the fact that he assembled his expedition teams based on tools that taught personality traits, not only on climbing skills. *My method for assembling my climbing teams was based on personality traits, not just on performance expertise. The only way to cross a glacier is on a rope to which your entire team is tied. You either all plunge together or succeed together.*

Once choosing awakening as our purpose we become instruments of conscious influence. How to use this ordinary life, with it's daily happenings, its uncertainty, negativity, suffering, pleasures, to come into a real life. To learn to live mindfully, to use the tools to develop self-knowledge and being which lead to understanding and objective conscience; to enter the journey into love is why we are here. The tools open a door to the higher world. *The Fifth Way, The Way of The Lover*, offers wisdom and a direct path to emerge from daily living into the light of full consciousness. The systems bring about a new level for us, to love in a way that otherwise might be inconceivable. These rich, priceless guidelines allow us the wisdom to go forward. Who we thought we were; the concepts, labels, judgments, reactions and opinions dissolve, until *who* I thought I was starts to disappear.

You've no idea how hard our work is to polish the mirror. With one mirror I see my face. With a combination of mirrors I see what's around me. The reflection lights the way. The systems as tools are mirrors; to see and reflect. These blueprints for awakening are an alchemical process of changing brass to silver to gold. A silversmith uses fire and heat to separate pure silver from impurities. *The Way of the Lover* turns on the heat offering tools for life's challenges to help us distinguish between the valuable and the peripheral. Each moment inspires us to practice the art of a spiritual silversmith/goldsmith creating purity of mind and heart, allowing the heat of life experience to draw the best from within; ultimately pure gold.

You do not realize enough that your attention is your only chance. Without it you can do nothing. —*Jeanne de Salzmann*

A self-evaluation worksheet precedes the systems; to gather, record and refer to, for our own self-study. To come to the systems with self-observation and neutrality quickens the process of self-recognition. To pay attention, discover, see, identify and become aware is the beginning of freedom from our habit-energy, our patterns, and a real move towards unconditioned consciousness. The study of the liberation of attention, an essential discipline, using every circumstance of life as a means to feel the whole truth about ourselves, to participate and learn to rely on our own impressions; settling our mind prepares the ground for our inner evolution. The limits of our self-understanding are the limits of our life. Through this journey of self-exploration the tools offer insight into both ourself and others. Continue to return to the self-evaluation worksheet on the following two pages as you read through the chapter. They are a remarkable comprehensive resource.

It seems to me that before we set out on a journey to find reality, to find God, before we can act, before we can have any relationship with another; it is essential that we begin to understand ourselves first. —*Krishnamurti*

444

SELF-EVALUATION WORKSHEETS

BE PRESENT AND MINDFUL

Active	Passive	Neutral
a_____	a_____	a_____
b_____	b_____	b_____
c_____	c_____	c_____

1st_____
2nd_____
3rd_____

SYSTEM ONE

ENNEAGRAM OF PERSONALITY TYPE
A MANDALA FOR ALL
TIME

The Enneagram reveals the patterns by which we organize and give meaning to all of our experiences. If we could see the core pattern around which we organize and interpret all of our experiences, the framework on which we hang the events of our lives, we could make much quicker progress in our spiritual and psychological growth. This core patterning is our personality type. —Riso and Hudson

The Enneagram is an ancient geometric figure, a symbol of self-sustained transformation, a new age mandala rooted in time-honored traditions. The Enneagram as a diagram reveals the fundamental nature and process of any phenomenon in the universe; in itself it's a complete cosmos, therefore every process may be represented in its totality. A map embedded in the mystical wings of all sacred traditions, the figure is used to identify nine distinctive character types, personality styles, and strategies of human nature. An ancient philosopher remarked that *when the world was imagined it was geometrized*; lines, curves and angles are a necessary pre-requisite before anything can be built. Everything we know has been represented by a geometric design or symbol.

Earliest simple geometric designs have been the circle and equilateral triangle. The figure of the Enneagram, a spacial structure is a pattern of sustained motion embodying universal laws containing the elements of the circle, triangle, and hexad; it is a nine-pointed star in a circular setting. The three primary parts of the symbol represent three universal laws that govern all of existence. The circle is the most common and universal sign found in all cultures; symbol of the sun, moon and world, it has no beginning or end, no divisions, making it the symbol of completeness, eternity, and the soul, the cyclical nature of change and its movement through time. The Sanskrit word for circle is mandala, representing wholeness, seen as a model for the organizational structure of life itself; a cosmic diagram that reminds us of our relation to the infinite, the world that extends both beyond and within our bodies and minds. The lines contain the direction that self-study takes to actuate growth around the outer circle. The equilateral triangle inscribed in its circle at the numbers 9,3,6, is an emblem of the universal threefoldness that permeates all existence. Buckminster Fuller named the triangle *the most important building block of the universe.* The completely closed symmetrical figure is frequently used in construction dating back to the great pyramids in Egypt because of its strength and stability. Pointing upward's it's called the symbol of manifestation on the material plane, imaging humanity looking towards the heavens.

In order to understand the Enneagram it must be thought of in motion, as moving. A motionless Enneagram is a dead symbol, the living symbol is in motion. The knowledge of the Enneagram has for a very long time been preserved in secret, and if it now is, so to speak, made available to us all it is only in an incomplete and theoretical form without instruction from a person who knows. —G.I. Gurdjieff

The irregular hexagon, named a hexad, tracing the numbers 1,4,2,8,5,7, opening wide downward was described by Gurdjieff as: the line in the course of the forces—which is interrupted constantly and whose ends combine again. It suggests movement rather than stability, symbolizing the law of seven, that nothing remains at rest—all things move in the direction of integration or disintegration. The circle is the wholeness that is able to contain and reconcile these two diverse elements. These three elements together—the triangle, hexad and circle—make up the Enneagram, expressing the wholeness of all things in the circle, and how they are made up of the interaction of three forces in the triangle and how everything moves over time as in the hexad.

The original cosmic figure of the Enneagram was a dynamic process-oriented model used to understand universal activities at work. The nine points following around the circle represent the steps of the undertaking. The circle is unbroken and the process repeats itself. Point 3 and 6 introduce outside influences into the practices, named *shock points* to shock the process onward to subsequent steps. The primary difference between how the Enneagram is currently used as a template for personality types and the totality of the Enneagram as a structure is the difference between a process and a system. This system represents nine different categories of character type patterns; how to maintain this as a dynamic process still moving around the circle will reflect the consciousness that is using this tool. All symbols have levels of meaning, the exoteric, the outer or surface is based on the literal everyday logical explanation, using reason to explain, and the esoteric, inner, the contemplative mystical understanding asks for transformation of consciousness.

Exoteric knowledge without esoteric knowledge is a great mischief.
—*R.A. Gohar Shahi*

Be who you truly are all else will take care of itself. —Serge Benyahon

The system of personality types of the Enneagram, popularized in recent years has made the figure of the Enneagram an accessible tool.

Current teachings present the Enneagram as a psychological typology that structures our behavior, offering a map of our character and the diverse possibilities toward change. There is a movement within each type towards integration or disintegration. The study of our type and our ability to not be mechanical in the movement of the chart is of great assistance for self-understanding, growth, empathy, harmony and balance. One type is not better or worse than another, each type represents its own impression and perception of the world. The recognition that different types have their own internal logic and integrity, offers different and correctly perceived parts or versions of reality to be revealed in this study. Learning to use this system we understand differences and are offered direction to loosen the compulsive hold that mechanical reactivity has over us, but first, through self-observation is to reveal and verify our own particular personality type. Identifying our type offers a guidebook to our behavior that stems from the restriction of our world view, routines, compulsions, ways we limit and bring suffering to ourselves, a way to look at our habit-energy, our hypnotic trance. The type structures are based upon Vedic cosmology, Egyptian astrology and terminology stemming from ancient esoteric traditions.

With a graph like the nine-pointed star, everything depends upon a correct placement of the types on the diagram, because they relate to one another in such specific ways. Once personality is formed, attention becomes immersed in the preoccupations that characterize our type. We lose the essential childlike ability to respond to the world as it really is and begin to become selectively sensitive to the information that supports our type's worldview. We see what we need to see in order to survive and become oblivious to the rest. —Helen Palmer

Essentially, each of us expresses ourself at one particular point which sets a tone, a strategy for our life. This is the way we see and pay attention. We all have access to a wing on both sides, a Two has a 1 and 3 wing, a Three has a 2 and 4 wing, a Five has a 4 and 6 wing and so on. (Refer to Chart 1, page 453). There is a small percentage of each type in all of us and to use the Enneagram well is to see the connections, interplay, and how we inherit the types that preceded ours. Unless there is a conscious integration of the motion of the whole Enneagram we live an isolated static fragment, missing the experience of living the fullness that is part of a totality. We move from a previous type and then fall asleep to what once was. To know the original intention of the octave and continue the journey is living the esoteric Enneagram as it was intended in its earliest development to be used as a living process. This is collective humanity, overcoming the illusion of separateness within wholeness. The separateness paves the way for us to proceed and have learning experiences that then can be recognized and remembered. To find our specific type in the most accurate way is through intuition, self-observation, considering how we were in childhood, recounting our negative manifestations, learning about each point and studying for verification from a true teacher.

This construction (the Enneagram) shows the inner laws of one octave and it points out a method of cognizing the essential nature of a thing examined in itself. —P.D.Ouspensky

HISTORY

The knowledge of the Enneagram has for a very long time been preserved in secret and if it now is, so to speak, made available at all, it is only in an incomplete and theoretical form of which nobody could make any practical use without instruction from a person who knows. —P.D. Ouspensky

No one has been able to track the exact origins of the system, although the symbol called Enneagram was brought to the west about 90 years ago by the Armenian teacher, G.I. Gurdjieff. He viewed the figure of the Enneagram as a cosmological model, teaching that it demonstrates the laws of our cosmos, having learned about it at Sufi mystery schools located in remote mountain regions originating with the Sarmaun Brotherhood 2500 years ago in Central Asia. The Sarmauni were custodians of the secrets of transformation and reciprocal maintenance embodied in symbols and sacred dances (Refer to Universal Laws, System 27). An oral, mystical tradition, the symbol itself, the circle with the inner triangle and hexad, also dates back at least 2500 years.

The study of type has centuries of history. Gurdjieff taught the idea of chief feature, which is the basic characteristic of our personality, one we are generally oblivious to and our primary obstacle to awakening. (Developed in System 1 & System 18). The possibility of converting our primary attitude relieves us of our mechanicalness. He pointed out our blemishes, our false personality, in a notable effort to shock and push recognition. Looking at negative aspects of personality forces comprehension and accelerates the process, since our primary illusion is self-deception. Self-observation with the assistance of these tools, puts us in a position to see through our clouds of distortion. Understanding the Enneagram we see the basic projections that people make and we have a tool that will shine a light on how to free ourselves. The figure of the Enneagram itself has no values. Gurdjieff's position was, to truly understand it is to imagine it in constant motion.

The Enneagram is the fundamental hieroglyph of a universal language which has as many different meanings as there are levels of men.
—G.I. Gurdjieff

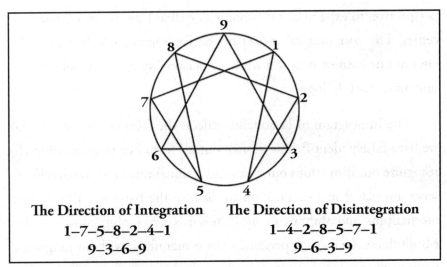

Chart 1: Integration, Disintegration

A COSMIC SYMBOL

To understand the Enneagram's history it is necessary to distinguish between the Enneagram symbol and the nine personality types. The core truth that the Enneagram conveys to us is that we are much more than our personality. The Enneagram also helps us by giving us a direction in which to work, but only as long as we remember that it is not telling us who we are, but how we have limited who we are. Remember the Enneagram does not put us in a box, it shows us the box we are already in—and the way out.
—Riso and Hudson

The Enneagram of Personality, a vehicle for self-inquiry, is a valuable tool along the path of Sacred Psychology, and is a noteworthy means to create and develop an observer. A cosmic symbol employed effectively points to something universal in our nature. In order to understand something we look to see its connection with the larger whole. A symbol clarifies something unknown, inner participation from the observer to recognize and unravel the mystery opens us to a new perspective, to expand our viewpoint as well as lead us toward our own center. The cosmological model of the Enneagram which depicts the laws of our cosmos is now a study of personality types, popularized in humanistic psychology.

The Enneagram of Personality reflects the faces of ego, to see who we have falsely identified as, to free ourself from our programming. To recognize our distortions our flaws and rationalizations through self-observation places us in a position to dissolve the barriers called defense mechanisms and shift us to move towards developing consciousness. Mindfulness, seeing our personality as it manifests, without judgment, without distraction, permits something deeper to surface, called *waking up*. To come into unity and release unnecessary suffering is the power of this and all the systems listed in this book, *The Way of the Lover*. Knowing that the personality is false, we need assistance to subdue it. Most essential is to see, make conscious, our flaws. The transmission of this system, best done in the oral tradition, studied in written form, deepens its use as a sensible tool for self-knowledge. When we believe our physical, mental, and emotional body to be who we are, we limit our possibilities. The strategies we devise become a barrier obscuring our true nature. Once we acknowledge who we thought we were is not a unique manifestation, rather it is a regulated predictable habit, we can have space to access compassion and forgiveness towards ourself and others.

The essential features of the Enneagram are really universal. I have found them in science, business, myth, and movies. They are locked up in the ancient liturgies. Please remember, however, that the Enneagram is not just a model for what we do or study, but an intent. It is a stubborn human cry of desire for meaning. —A.G.E. Blake

Applying the Enneagram to *personality fixations* was developed by Oscar Ichazo in the 1960's as a means of mapping the human psyche and its character fixations. Ichazo added the arrows and the movements of change, the subtypes, using them as a psychological model and study of personality types. Claudio Naranjo, inspired by its theoretical picture and techniques codified it into a system, connecting it to a psychological typology, adding the arrows indicating stress and security for each type. He correlated it to Christianity's seven deadly sins as well as relating it to the Diagnostic and Statistical Manual of Mental Disorders. Helen Palmer, another pioneer, took the teaching and integrated it to parallel her interest in the field of intuition. She brought the Enneagram mainstream promoting studies as well as interviewing panels of men and women each demonstrating their type. Don Riso and Russ Hudson further developed a systematic description noting developmental levels from unhealthy to average to healthy ranges in each type. In the late 1980's the Enneagram of personality reached the market place. The CIA uses it to train its agents, Christian monasteries teach it for enhanced harmony in community, human resource people use it as a hiring tool.

The Enneagram gives you the structure of who you are not: with this insight it is immediately possible to realize who you really are. —Eli Jaxon-Bear

THE ENNEAGRAM IN MOTION

The Enneagram is not something that you can understand passively. You have to struggle with it, as Jacob struggled with the angel. —Anthony Blake

In the Enneagram of Personality there are three fixations in the emotional body, three in the physical body and three in the mental body. Each have patterns that we think are our identity. When we see the repetition that directs our life we have a choice to make a shift. Each of the types is connected on a line to two other types. Following the lines in a positive direction, the heart space, allows for integration, this is the relief route. Following the lines in a negative direction creates disintegration, this is the stress route. Each point has a wing on each side. Using the movement of the Enneagram in a fluid manner allows for balance, harmony and an easing out of personality. There will be one place that we each fixate, where our attention habitually goes, and to find that we need to be starkly honest with ourself. The Enneagram brought to life is always in movement, an energy transformer. Only that which moves and changes expresses life. (Refer to Chart 1, page 453).

The Enneagram provides profound insight into human nature. It explains some of the major difference between people by pointing out the broad range of goals, values, desires, and interests which motivate human behavior. Each of the nine types is an entire 'culture,' with its own language, fears, goals, beliefs, passions and challenges. Each type has a unique power, or 'gift,' which he needs to share with the world in order to grow spiritually.
—*Miriam Adahan*

All of the strategies are present as flavors, yet we express ourselves through one predominant point of view. Doubting, or seeing ourselves everywhere, are also descriptions of type. A willingness to learn what drives our behavior, to relinquish our primary coping tactic, brings forth our true nature. Recognizing and knowing our true nature is essential to moving easily in the world, is critical for living in a natural joyful manner. To identify our point offers us a glimpse of the hypnotic trance that envelops us as we relate to an idea of the world rather than the world itself.

The Enneagram portrays nine distinct views, nine different perspectives, nine particular strategies. They are all, ultimately, distractions from our essential self. The following descriptions break the nine points into three main categories.

2-3-4 Emotional body: The image points. The relating group moves towards people to gauge feelings The core issue for the image points are finding ways to be loved. These are the feeling or heart types, involved with subjects regarding personal value, emotional needs and self-image.

5-6-7 Mental body: The fear points. They move away from people. These points have retreated from their feelings and body to use their mind as a protection in what they consider to be a threatening uncertain world. Their energy moves inward. For the thinking head types, knowledge is a defense against fear. Anxiety about doing, all three: Five, Six, Seven, have issues involving security, worry, internal dialogue and thinking.

8-9-1 Physical body: The anger points. They move against people. The body centered instinctive gut types, the core issue centers around the difference between being true to themselves and being controlled: which are all issues of power. All three deal with aggression, repression and new experiences, they first connect to physical and bodily sensations before connecting to feelings or the intellect, and share issues concerning relating. Anger originates in the physical body. Attention is placed around taking a position. Ones want the right position, Eights have a strong position, while Nines avoid taking a personal position.

In each of the three groups, one point under-expresses their chief quality, one point over-expresses it, and one point avoids and disconnects from their chief fixation. The Two over-expresses feelings, the Three is out of touch with feelings, suppressing them to be more effective. The Four internalizes, thinks about their feelings and under-expresses them. Point Five over-expresses thinking and has the fear interiorized. The Six, the central fear point, is out of touch with thinking. The Seven under-expresses, has an undeveloped thinking style, their thoughts jump. Point Eight over expresses anger. The Nine, although the central anger point, avoids and disconnects from anger. Point One has internalized their anger and under-expresses it, to live with a relentless internal voice. The anger of the One and Nine is often repressed until they no longer have connection to it, inhibiting natural self-expression.

The ability to parent well depends on accurate observation. The Enneagram helps parents 'see' children more in alignment with how the children experience themselves. —Elizabeth Wagele

The Enneagram, a tool for understanding, is a pattern of perpetual motion, a living moving symbol containing the oneness that is. Symbols are the tools to bring about transformation, they offer a vision to life, once we recognize what they hold. To realize processes in a new way, our own growth and its movement, not as a closed circle but in its openness, is a great gift of the Enneagram. Meaning opens up to us in relationship to the level of consciousness that we access. A symbol, once experienced and understood, made one's own, deepens, to teach us about ourselves. The Enneagram does not put us in a box, it shows us the boxes that we are already in—and the way out. It points to the veiling, our patterns, shows us the structure of our mind, clearing the way for us to realize our true nature.

To get along in this world each of us, of necessity acquires a veil of personality. This lets us interact with our world while protecting the privacy of the inner self. As our life unfolds, we forget our true selves and turn an increasing deaf ear. How can we distinguish between these acquired personality traits and the essential self hidden underneath? A feature of the Enneagram is that the center type of each triad, located at three core points on the enclosed triangle, actually appears to repress it's triad's own dominant faculty. Rather than being the prime example of their triad's predominate faculty, the respective core types might not outwardly show that trait at all. Our individual personality types are not a static collection of habits and traits. —Rabbi Howard Addison

Moving around the Enneagram is an interplay and evolving process, opportunities for self-discovery. The direction of integration and disintegration create a moving interaction among the types. We move towards a specific type when under strife or pressure and toward another specific type when we feel comfortable and cushioned. Each point is an aspect and continuation on a journey of discovery with the possibility to be used to awaken to the nature of reality. Used properly and with patience, it complements all other systems in this chapter. The descriptions give us in beautiful detail, a guide. These are the characteristics that mask essence. Understanding the Enneagram we see the basic projections that people make. Our willingness to relinquish personal identity opens the door to discover our true self. Wrestling with the Enneagram orients us to better know ourself. On one hand we all contain a small percentage of each type and could learn to knowingly work to remain in the positive part of each point, on the other hand, once authentically seated in our natural birth type, looking around the Enneagram we see the next step in our development. The Enneagram represents a journey to our own center and back out into the world. The following table lists the types, their primary theme, distortion, avoidance, healing and awakening.

Through our senses the world appears. Through our reactions we create delusions. Without reactions the world becomes clear. —the *Buddha*

TYPE	THEME	DISTORTION	AVOIDANCE	HEALING	AWAKENING
One perfectionist	critic idealist	resentment self-righteous	anger impropriety mistakes	serenity acceptance	clarity right action integrity
Two caregiver	helping	pride advice-giving manipulation hurt feelings	personal needs	self-nurture love humility	understanding
Three doer	achievement net-worker	self-deception self-image	failure	authenticity honesty veracity	inter-connected
Four temperamental	specialnesss self absorbed intensity	moody nostalgia envy dissatisfaction drama	ordinariness shame	equanimity balance forgiveness	self-remember
Five observer	withdrawal witholding	avarice greed isolation	involvement emptiness looking foolish	wisdom detachment	true non-attach- ment
Six questioner	security skeptic	doubt fear defensiveness	deviance spontaneity	faith courage	conscious trust
Seven optimist enthusiast	adventure planning	gluttony happiness	pain boredom self-restraint suffering commitment	gratitude joy moderation sobriety	attentive
Eight boss	justice self-reliance	lust arrogance punitiveness	weakness vulnerability	truth innocence self-surrender	dedication through service
Nine accomodator mediator	peaceful indecision accomodate work-money	neglectful forgetfulness sloth non-esssential task anxiety secret life	conflict discomfort	awareness deliberate aliveness presence right action	mindfulness mindful aware- ness intentional

Chart 2: The Enneagram of Personality Types

Template For Self-Realization

Awareness is our sword, and the Enneagram shows us the precise structure of the knot of ego that needs to be cut. In this way enlightenment or self-realization is possible. —Eli Jaxon-Bear

Having fallen asleep to our true nature, our essence so overpowered by our personality and entrenched in our psychology, loses contact with a direct experience of ourself. Bringing awareness to our personality we experience and contact our essence directly. This model of consciousness is an invitation to investigate, to discover what we have falsely identified with as ourself. These personality tendencies are great teachers, carrying awareness to lift us into higher states. To set the personality aside we must first know it. To look at and attend to our wounding is the beginning of our healing. Studying and understanding our personality and circumstances does not change either the story or our life or the context and particulars. To dig deeper, into the stronghold of where ego resides, to loosen the egoic identity, to recognize and see through it is the freedom. This is a tool to penetrate our identification with the ego, to end the cycle of ignorance and unnecessary suffering.

To see clearly is to get our personality out of the way. Otherwise we are seeing through a distorted lens—that of our personal preferences rather than seeing things as they are. For most, the recognition of the negative side of our personality is more immediate, when looked at this way we are less apt to fool ourselves and more willing to attend to serious work on ourselves. This viewpoint accents the self-deception that is the characteristic trait of humanity, caused by wishful thinking, impeding and interfering with self-development. To begin the journey first apply the Enneagram to yourself, know your own type and projections before you begin to apply it to others. In this manner we will be guided to use it to expand awareness rather than as a projection instrument which limits and distorts.

The recognition that we are a type, and how that affects our point of view is often quite surprising, along with the realization that this personality type limits us, narrows our point of view, controls much of our life. With self-observation we develop a witness, someone home, nonjudgmental awareness. A tool like the Enneagram is a guide to serve as a reminder, to enliven presence, to deepen attention. Freed of the shackles of identified personality awareness grows and expands.

This simple and elegant Enneagram provides a rare tool for seeing the etiology of neurosis, psychosis, or, in another language, sleep, how we go from a state of openness and awakening as children to a state of dullness and atrophy as adults. The essential self's identification with the sleep of the machine; although the Being or essence does not sleep, it agrees to permit itself to be hypnotized , or becomes seduced by the attraction of something about the life. There is no magic in the system itself. Like any genuine teaching it works for you only if you do the work. Choice of one system over another is usually just a question of preference based on immediate working application. What is esoteric about this teaching is the appropriate use of the knowledge. This you must learn from a practitioner who knows. One who knows the use of such a system for the separation of machine from essence is free to modify and adapt that system. —E.J. Gold

Each point has distinct patterns. Point One, easily dissatisfied, knowing something must be changed, collects information, to awaken through *clarity* and *right action.* Developing the ability to pay attention to the present moment without judgment, remembering the integrity of the perfection they know, brings the One to awakening. Point Two, listening, informing and interpreting what has been gathered, opens to enter their own inner world, becomes the experience, is penetrated, awakening as *understanding*. The treasures are buried deep inside, that's where understanding lives, at the root where it grows out of you. Listening, opening; truth has such love that once understood—there is the awakening!

At point Three an outside force effects a course of change. The rough draft, the layout and blueprint have arrived and point Three is ready to go to production. Soliciting for the team, the enthusiasm creates connections that strengthen the task. All life is interconnected, realize the deep connection with everyone, the recognition that generating energy through cooperative work, living a bond of community, being truthful in honoring the *interconnectedness* of all beings, awakens the Three. Point Four is the crisis point, from this space, on the right side of the Enneagram, having journeyed from point One, Two and Three, the difficulties, now known, loom large. The information is available, yet seeing how difficult real change is, the awareness of personal inability, limitation and inadequacy appears. Point Four becomes a place of true practice, day labor. Breaking through the resistance of self-involvement and preoccupation with their personal feelings, developing *self-remembering* is the awakening. Rebuilding their point of view towards themselves and others, remembering to remain out of imagination and be attentive, being present is independent to what's happening outside; minimizing distractions; wandering energy divides the mind, being still we empty into the present moment.

Point Five sees the direction, is no longer immersed in their emotional life, has clear vision and reorders, organizes, detaches and unifies what has been learned. Within the silence the Five, finding a spirit of real happiness, through that door arrives at non-attachment. Remaining with a sense of emptiness energizes and advances their journey into awakening. The Five can easily renounce the world, here, though, non-attachment is not withdrawal. Rather, it follows inner joy, otherwise it would be repression. Having made the most difficult crossover of the whole Enneagram map, the jump from the large gap of Four to Five, a quality of frustration permeates; now the goal up the left side of the diagram appears; still a long trek. The difficulty of the jump and the residue from Four lingers, yet observing, while holding to the difficult, keeps the heart and head open. Awakening for the Five arrives through *true non-attachment*.

Point Six, the second shock point, looks outside for assistance. This urging, or push, from an outside force is an important part of proceeding onward. Without it everything might stop and back up. The willingness to remain undistracted from the details, act decisively and learn to recognize projections, even to refrain from making them, absorbs the outside influence. Consciousness is our real nature, it is the truth of who we are, everything else comes and goes. When the Six arrives at this place, knowing what is unlimited, permanent, this recognition, as *conscious trust*, becomes the awakening. Point Seven, coming towards the end of the journey, needs to be attentive, to prepare the ground, to settle down and focus, knowing that the search is for something one already has, a necessary journey, now requiring bringing back wandering attention. Love is attentive, it fosters growth to both the inner and outer world. To be attentive when there is outside stimulus is involuntary. To bring and sustain attention comes from ourself, is to act from the will and develops through concentration and meditation. The power of attention penetrates, breaks fascination, masters time, brings us into presence. As concentration deepens, in the stillness of an attentive mind, wisdom emerges. It's the wisdom of emptiness, strengthening attention quiets and turns the extraneous away; what becomes interesting is the practice of attention itself. Withdrawing attention from distractions and adventures, to focus careful attention on what actually is, requires the engagement of the whole person. Emily Dickenson knew this well, she was attentive, saw with sensitivity and precision describing her experience: *To live is so startling, there's little time for anything else.* Point Seven gathering one-pointed attention, scattered energies coming together to converge around a single point, infusing it into the present moment, becomes unified, bursts into flames. Close attention opens the heart, creates the power to cut through surface appearance. Seven awakens through *attention*.

Point Eight, able to focus, embodies the work. *Dedication through service* to others, learning from what has preceded throughout the journey along the Enneagram structure is possible. Awakening comes to an Eight, surrendered to consciousness, dropping defenses and agendas, with both hands open, not closed in a warrior pose, a 100% person. The greatest warrior is the one who leaves no trace of themselves because there isn't ego involved in what they do; they are choosing effectiveness and preserving life over fame and glory. Awakening for the Eight is in serving something greater than themself. The greatest battle is against their own ego, mechanical nature and habits. To serve humanity compassionately, surrendering self-interest, is the awakening for Point Eight. Point Nine, the third and final shock point, the transition place, enters a new process. To know the Nine is to understand the dynamics of the Enneagram. Everything that has happened before and all that will continue, begins here. A choice appears; to compromise, resist, to accept what is or to move on to a new and higher level. The Nine, in discovering the difference between peace and laziness, is the beginning and end point. This is a laziness of the psyche and of the spirit, manifesting as forgetfulness, missed opportunities to recognize, to create change. In Tarot, hermit #9, being of introspection and withdrawal, is the fool #0, demonstrating a world of infinite possibilities, in disguise. The light, hidden inside the darkness is found in a solitary passage. The hermit, illuminating what is already known, stands as a hidden symbol. The fool, having forgotten the meaning to what he does, daydreamer, doesn't see the cliff in front of him, yet his actions still maintain power. The fool, on the way to a new beginning, needs to stop forgetting and start self-remembering, and live in mindful awareness, so he won't fall like a fool. Intentional and effective, the transition to begin again, to resolve to live as a beginner, decided from a place of love, is the wake up call. Living intentionally brings a state of aliveness, of presence, to the Nine. *Mindful awareness,* paying attention to what is both within and without, taking charge of their life, forging ahead, becoming visible the Nine anchors in their gentle manner those who appreciate their kind ways. To agree to a decision, the committing of oneself with the ability to intentionally carry through requires persistence and holding consciousness, inner detachment, for it to remain a sacred act. To live intentionally, to live with risk, to enter/go wholeheartedly into risk, decisiveness is necessary; from that place of intention the Nine will be birthed into peaceful stillness, awakened *as is.*

The wisdom of the Enneagram is revealed in its extraordinary accuracy in describing human nature, thus forcing each individual who studies it seriously to know him-or herself. Through self-knowledge each person is then able to relate freely with self, others, the universe, and God. It is an evolving knowledge that begins with an awakening—to the truth of human nature and to the true potential human beings possess and to the ways people get caught in an ever-narrowing labyrinth that compresses and distorts their true selves. This awakening process is the invitation to embark on the journey of genuine personal growth. —K. Hurley and T. Dobson

The Enneagram, brought to life, maintaining its movement, as an energy transformer, is a remarkable tool, a wisdom mirror, to be used in the service of self-inquiry. Promoting self-knowledge it complements all the other systems in this chapter. Each personality type revealed in detail is a guide. Detailing the motivations, thought patterns and position of different types, we come up with portraits of ourselves as well as others. These are characteristics that mask essence. Our willingness to relinquish personal identity opens the door to discover the true self. Following are the nine types, descriptions of the variations of the illusion that we are separate and limited.

When your real effortless, joyful nature is realized, it will be consistent with the ordinary activities of life. —Ramana Maharshi

TYPE ONE

PERFECTIONIST, REFORMER, GOOD PERSON, JUDGE, PREACHER, CRUSADER, IDEALIST, EGO-RESENTMENT

I am righteous.

I may have faults, but being wrong ain't one of them.—Jimmy Hoffa

Righteous indignation is the substitute for the anger that I feel toward the world and myself for not being perfect. Excessive control of my behavior, I live in a world of principles, not feelings, controlling my anger through internalized rules. Often I overlook people's feelings as I pay attention to doing what is right. Right is right; I could be the moral conscience of this world. I see what is right, I want to tell everybody what to do, yet feel too perfect to express my anger. When I suppress it, the shadow side of perfection is rage. I want to be right to avoid being criticized, if I'm perfect, there is little possibility of being wrong. At times I make the issue more important than the relationship, like scolding people for making a mess, my priorities get scrambled.

Avoiding anger, yet propelled by anger, I am a Honda automobile driving around town with my brakes on. Scanning for how the world is and should be, measuring myself and the world around me by standards that I value takes sustained effort as well as inner criticalness. My secret resentment focuses on why other people don't have principles and standards. My natural energy is constrained, over-controlled, obsessive and held down with rigidity because I am afraid of doing the wrong thing. Called anal-retentive, rarely will my anger leak out, I prefer to be sensible, oftentimes enjoying a good debate all the while trying to live up to my point of view. Keeping my environment in order, sometimes seen as compulsive behavior, comes from wanting things to be clean and in their proper place. I sometimes monitor my diet in an orderly methodical style, self-control is natural although I secretly have indiscretions like eating a good piece of chocolate and pound cake with a cup of coffee, smoking marijuana, or behind closed doors looking at porn on-line. Striving for improvement, correcting others, being pedantic, irritated, moralizing and sometimes intolerant, I can be condemning, demanding and even cruel. An inner voice on my shoulder often talks to me, even corrects my errors. My irritation and frustration lie in the thought that others do not care to be as diligent, and the world has low standards.

If you look for perfection, you'll never be content. —Leo Tolstoy

There is a possibility to shift to the dark side, especially when I drink and am at a party. For men the good boy/philanderer or Jekyll-Hyde personality is a One phenomenon. This is the priest who gets drunk, assaults a child and forgets, Bob Dole advertising for viagra, the Amish woman dressing in Victorias Secret lingerie to have kinky sex. For women, the madonna/whore syndrome engages once we let go. Fun, which has been on reserve until now, unburdens my behavior, so my usual compulsion to be correct and blameless gets set aside.

How many crimes are permitted just because their authors could not endure being wrong. A man without ethics is a wild beast loosed upon this world.
—*Albert Camus*

Precise in my work, I could be a good dentist, book designer, accountant, excellent house cleaner, a precise vascular or brain surgeon. The obsessive-compulsive type, my talking mode is to preach, teach (uninvited), sermonize. When my irritation comes through I make sharp-tongued remarks, sounding scolding. *You should* is often the energetic atmosphere that permeates a long-winded conversation. This appears as a constructive desire to make others better, yet behind it is a disapproving manipulation to correct another's behavior and suit my needs. Often the model child, I push myself, become nitpicking and crabby without realizing it. My stance is to be morally correct, to reform. My internal battle to keep the anger down is rarely visible. The phrase tight ass must have been invented after meeting me; in the psych books they call it anal retentive. Less than perfection is unacceptable, I often lose the beauty of the process. My strength is in my sense of responsibility, order, reliability, self-discipline and productivity, and I will persist with diligence. Supportive of other people's rights, popular opinion does not sway my viewpoint. My weakness is that I can be dogmatic, lack spontaneity, judgmental, critical, resentful and controlling. The primary relationship I invest in is to an impersonal principle.

My finances tend to be overseen in a thrifty manner, material things are important. Working independently, I can be a good business person. Making lists helps my pursuit to set things right. America started as a One culture. Puritanical and connected to principles, I often have an intellectual and moral superiority. Internally I can live as if there is an angel on one shoulder and the devil on the other. Cleanliness is high on my list of obsessions. Not neatness or order, I mean rubbing, scrubbing, really removing dirt. I don't tidy the house, I keep it clean. Even the garden stays trim and manicured, no lush overgrowth for me. Time management is used wisely or I feel on edge, many days have full schedules, I get a lot done, which may include a morning of straightening up and taking a walk as two of the activities that make me feel that the day is not wasted. Point One Martha Stewart when facing jail time for lying to investigators about her sale of stocks invoked the name of Nelson Mandela by saying: *many, many good people have gone to prison.*

How dreadful it is when the right judge judges wrong. —Sophocles

The Enneagram point One, the first stage, is not only a beginning but an aspect of a movement that has already started, representing the foundation for new beginnings expressed through dissatisfaction and a desire for change. I see my discontent and realize that if I am not true to myself I will be unhappy. The Enneagram circle implies an ongoing process which will eventually find completion. I prepare by bringing order into my life for a 9-step process around the Enneagram. A successful journey begins with learning how to carry out, accomplish and complete each task. This reality-based, well-behaved, civilized type, the beginner, knows the importance of getting things right. Reality is matched up with a set of ideal standards, what *should* be, and those ideals might be spiritual, moral, social or objective. Reliability reflects my fussy ways, working independently I want to execute each task perfectly. Here, I look at issues, often disguised, I gather and collect information, often concealed, and have direct experiences. Point One is about clarity, integrity, right action and is the beginning of self-remembering and self-observation, and to increase self-acceptance and decrease self-judgment, impatience, self-criticism and resentment. Right action is the practice of non-violence toward ourselves and others. Seeing every thought as an action, then right thinking is an action to heal this shattered world; it is an action toward forgiveness and self-nurturance.

I have learned through bitter experience the one supreme lesson: to conserve my anger, and as heat conserved is transmuted into energy, even so our anger controlled can be transmuted into a power which can move the world.
—*Mohandas K. Gandhi*

TRANSFORMATION: HEALING

Learn what is true in order to do what is right, is the summing up of the whole duty of mankind. —*Thomas Henry Huxley*

Once free of the fixation, One's have deep integrity, focused concentration, are conscientious and live by flexible values and principles. As the excessive concern for form and detail and a life lived aimed at being right loosens, life in fullness blooms. Arriving at an objective accurate evaluation from a dispassionate place, this becomes a life of heroic integrity. Finding the inherent perfection that already exists in the unfolding of life is a healthy posture. Responsible and ethical, once learning to live in their own energy they live as a moral conscience free of judgment and inner voices. Knowing through the body, intuitively, that perfection is in each moments unfolding and reward comes not for the self but for the excellence of a priceless creation. Learning to embrace a less-than-perfect world, taking in daily pleasures, moving towards balance are keys. Awakened as clarity, inhabiting awareness, frees the One from unnecessary suffering. Right action, to do everything mindfully, experienced by the One as integrity, brings about the idealism that One's yearn for, a harmonious world. Relaxed into effortlessness, dropped into the center, life is enjoyable. The bell of mindfulness allows the One to touch the deep presence inside themselves. Rooted inside, the One can leave the surface uncontrolled. The transformational shift is from anger to serenity and in lifting the idea of perfection to mean wholeness, which is perfection in the present moment. To move from critical faultfinding and intolerance towards what is not *right*, to seeing that what is, has an inherent rightness, a wholeness, just because it is. Serenity becomes ease with all feelings. In the absence of good or bad, right or wrong, resentment and judging subside. There is balance, wisdom and self-acceptance of all their parts, with an allowance for all others. Finally releasing the knowing mind, the One is free to discover what is beyond the mind; what is limitless. They become a reflection of the Serenity prayer: wisdom, discernment and peace.

If the Angel decides to come it will be because you have convinced her, not by tears, but by your humble resolve to be always beginning, to be a beginner.
—*Ranier Maria Rilke*

Some known Ones include: *George Washington, Jane Fonda, Ralph Nader, Mahatma Gandhi, Margaret Thatcher, Raoul Wallenberg, Taylor Swift, Britney Spears, Prince Charles, Dr. Jack Kevorkian, Jennifer Garner, Mary Baker Eddy, Fred Astaire, Arthur Ashe, William F. Buckley, Gwyneth Paltrow, Kenneth Starr, Anita Bryant, Emma Thompson, Maggie Smith,*

Billy Graham, Bob Dole, Martin Luther King, H. Ross Perot, Jennifer Aniston, Anderson Cooper, Colin Powell, Tony Randall, Emily Post, Abigail Van Buren, Martha Stewart, Ida Rolf, Eliot Spitzer, Jodie Foster, Ayn Rand, Irina Tweedie, Julie Andrews, Dr. Laura Schlesinger, George Bernard Shaw, John Stuart Mill, Barry Goldwater, Peter Jennings, Nelson Mandela, The Amish, Mary Poppins, Phylis Schafly, Joan Baez, Gene Siskal, Tom Brokaw, Jiddu Krishnamurti, Grant Wood's painting *American Gothic, Victorianism, England, Amsterdam, Switzerland, Sweden* are One cultures. The industrious *ant* and *bee.* Integrates/heals at 7, disintegrates at 4.

TYPE TWO

CAREGIVER, HELPER, MOTHER GODDESS, LOVING PERSON, RESCUER, EGO-FLATTERY

I am helpful

It is through selfless sharing that the flower of life becomes beautiful and fragrant. —Amma

I am the feeling type, mostly focused on other peoples feelings and needs. I move through life in relationship to others, they are part of my thoughts and heart. The most interpersonally oriented of all the personality types, life is seen in relational terms. Sometimes I confuse who I am with the role I am playing, of how I actually feel, getting lost in how I feel in the image of who I seem to be, aware of others needs; it may take a while before returning to my own self. This relocating in another pushes me to lose my own self and then I start to compensate by reminding myself that I'm really helping someone and this is what is important, my service to others. *You owe me* becomes a quiet inner theme. My preference is to be the giver, not the receiver, to be the lover not the beloved. As a point in the relating group, I move towards people in an effort to be loved, needed and indispensable. This selling out for love, stems from my lack of self-worth. I truly believe I can not be loved for myself. My ongoing need for recognition, approval and affirmation does not abate, as I continue to adapt to other's needs in the effort to gain love. Giving help and advice whether others want it or not, I need to learn to give only what is needed, this, then, moves me to develop a sense of a separate integrated self. Often my emotional dependency is experienced as intrusive. My world revolves around relationships. I am dedicated, generous and supportive, often at the expense of my own rhythm and personal needs.

If you want to be loved, be lovable. —Ovid

My attention migrates to another person. How I am to others, who I am needed to be, is essential. I take pride in being the best giver, and helping to potentiate people, especially those well-known, to fulfillment, it's actually my driving force and is connected to my self-image as helper, advice giver. My antenna is tuned to what is needed and wanted. I move forward towards others, sending attention over to others, positioning myself, a slight alteration and adaptation, using flattery and manipulation I easily get lost in others needs, forgetting my own. Sometimes I satisfy needs I have ignored in myself and relocated in others. It's so easy for me to take another out to a restaurant or make a meal at home for them, I create a beautiful evening, but to take myself out to eat becomes less clear, in fact, I may forget to eat or just snack on fast food. The idea that I have to give to get pushes me to meet my needs through giving what is needed with the secret wish that I will receive that back. Once feeling love, I remain in a relationship, often giving up the experience of finding myself. I have many acquaintances, all very different types. Easily merging, I take on the attitude and agenda of others, even reflecting the atmosphere of a group. I am energized when there is a pull of the heart connection, feel inspired, sometimes empowered through the person I am drawn towards.

To love one that is great is almost to be great oneself. —S. Churchod

My talking style is advice-giving, helping. Comfortable to be around, easy to talk to, I listen with understanding and sensitivity, often hearing particularly personal and private information. My door opens easily to offer advice. I either find myself in this position, or will put myself there, even when not asked. Easily showing emotions, you might not notice that most of my feelings relate to the moods and preferences of others, often I am out of touch with my own feelings. Hurt feelings easily surface; the connection to my true feelings have been sacrificed in my many adaptations as I alter to other's moods and preferences.

Repressing, therefore neglecting my own needs, giving so much over to another and overextending myself, I easily become sick. In service to another, my needs are met, particularly when it is someone who has power. Of course, having buried my own needs and desires I am barely able to recognize what I personally need. By helping you I am carried along on your trip. Positioned around someone empowered and I am highly psychic, I easily sense the mood and tone of another. Empathetic connections, effortlessly establishing rapport, being attuned to others, actually being on their wavelength, supports my belief that I am loved for how well I take care of you.

The burning conviction that we have a holy duty towards others is often a way of attaching our drowning selves to a passing raft. —Eric Hoffer

There can be a waiting for someone to want me, a phone call, a door knock. I sometimes have a weight problem since this is one way to give to myself. Putting others in the spotlight, I ignore my own abilities. To have my own needs addressed feels selfish, embarrassing and shameful. Keeping my needs in check I am drawn to children and those who require protection, this satisfies my love need, perpetuates my persona as the giver rather than the receiver and supports my self-image of being lovable and happy. I hope for gratitude and recognition for making things nice for others. Only when I am in a healthy place can there be genuine giving.

What I want is intimacy—for someone to get to their deepest place, and ironically, it is also what I most defend against. I like to affect others, to be of service, to be challenged by difficult odds, often choosing people who are not easily accessible. The other is the referent point. Feelings that are inspired by those who matter are in the forefront. I don't have needs, but knowing yours I can align with them. Often displaying entitlement, rarely do others know its root. Giving so much of myself away, I legitimately feel deserving of the extra privileges that I take. Pushing in front of others, taking an extra dessert, having someone pay for me, walking away with an unpaid item, taking an extra turn or going out of turn; having given excessively this is my moment of pay back.

My home is accessible when you arrive. Instantly you will feel at ease. Often I arrange things for your comfort, so my surroundings will look beautiful to you. The healthier I become, the more I give *what* people need; the less healthy, I tend to give and give *anything,* more is better. Only when I am connected to my own needs can I be altruistic, giving without conditions and from a selfless place.

For it is in giving that we receive—Francis of Assisi

Where I am is in the dance between the relationship. I give myself away, without the other demanding it. False generosity, the attempt to be loved for how well I take care of you, originates from a lack of self-worth. Creating dependency, forcing closeness, I enjoy feeling valued. Seeking praise, recognition and appreciation, there is great disappointment when my help is not acknowledged and appreciated. Pride in being the best giver pushes me to demand attention, so as to relieve the hurtful feelings that are close to the surface. In negativity, I might get physically sick and be a drain on your time and attention, suffering and feeling self-pity to receive the benefits that my illness brings, proving that no one caretakes as well as I do. It's difficult to feel satisfied until I can look in the mirror and love *that* reflection, believing I am worthwhile, valuable, precious, whether appreciated or not.

No matter what happens in life, be good to people. Being good to people is a wonderful legacy. —Taylor Swift

Continuing along the movement of the Enneagram, the second point on the circumference of the Enneagram, Two, continues the work necessary for transformation. I am involved with interpreting how I am, informing myself in preparation for change, seeing the consequences. There is a vision of the direction towards the goal, yet I need more understanding. As the second type I see the possibilities for a beautiful world and plan to create it for myself and others. I have to take care not to react too easily and be pulled by my need for recognition, wanting not to be overlooked by the people around me.

Your task is not to seek for love, but merely to seek and find all the barriers within yourself that you have built against it. —Rumi

TRANSFORMATION: HEALING

You can't take care of anyone else until you know how to take care of yourself.

The deep work for a Two is developing self-esteem, listening to their own needs, sinking into their own rhythm, letting go of the identification as the giver. Finding the real self in the midst of many selves brings integration. Placing attention on how they feel inside, to develop a stable self that will not shift to meet others needs deepens the experience of self for the Two. Spending quality time alone, focusing on their own needs and creative desires, seeing what part of self they are denying, assists them in becoming reflective, self-aware and whole. Contacting the source of love from within as a reliable constant, knowing how to recognize and nurture their own needs, boundaries are created that maintain their connectedness back to self. Distinguishing their needs from the needs of others, strengthens their core. Balanced, able to be intimate, humility arises calming the need to call attention to themselves or to receive praise. The ease of loving is supported by a happy internal image and fulfillment through loving another. The ability to nurture themselves, to recognize love, ends the need to get love from the outside, now they are free to truly enjoy others good fortune. Envisioning and planning for a beautiful world for all people is a real possibility for the Two.

You can't pour from an empty cup. Take care of yourself first.

Once allowing people their pain and struggle liberates the burden of having to help heal all others; releasing any idea of *helping* others, giving itself is the experience. Reclaiming freedom from the tyranny of a world that only approves if fulfilling others needs, releases an endless promise. Developing a separate self, paying attention to their own needs, not over-emoting or over-feeling, watching for emotions that convey unmet needs the open-hearted generosity that is the essence of a balanced Two emerges. Valuing and showing up for themselves, knowing their own truth, not having expectations, cultivating a receptivity that focuses on self allows the kindness that is at the heart of the Two to come forth. Knowing themself not through the eyes of another, through the connection that returns the attention back to self deepens autonomy. Love in this manner is a being with others, not to eliminate their pain or *fix* them, it's to be available and present to wherever they are.

Awakening as understanding; listening to their own voice welling up from within; resting in their own being arrives from silently moving inward. Two, as a heart type, once penetrated, entered deeply, becomes understanding. The transformational shift is from pride to humility, from being a dependent person to the freedom of knowing their own desire and following it, rather than giving over to others wishes. Finding value in themselves outside of the context of a relationship, releasing the need for recognition, for being appreciated, easing up the inflated prideful idea of being the best giver, finding love inside themselves, the Two is free, kind, compassionate, and caring. Unconditionally loving, the Two now expects nothing in return. Finding their own power, the evolved Two is capable of true service, offering exactly what is needed, the Two then lives in a place of compassion and humility, encouraging others independence and autonomy. Truth understood liberates. When evolved, this is the most genuinely loving and altruistic of all the types; open-hearted, they open our heart.

Help thy brother's boat across, and lo! thine own has reached the shore.
—*Hindu Proverb*

Some known Twos include: *Mata Amritananda Ma (known as Ammachi), Rosa Parks, Eleanor Roosevelt, Rob Kardashian, John Travolta, Kelly Clarkson, George Clooney, Amy Schumer, Kim Kardashian, Florence Nightingale, Elvis Presley, Ken Burns, Doris Day, Monica Lewinsky, Selena Gomez, Tammy Faye Baker, Barbara Bush, John Legend, Katy Perry, Virginia Satir, Karen Horney, Jimmy Kimmel, Leo Buscaglia, Richard Simmons, Elizabeth Taylor, Ben Affleck, Jerry Lewis, Carol Channing, Archbishop Desmond Tutu, Blake Shelton, Dolly Parton, Princess Diana, Bali* and *Thailand.* Integrates/heals at 4, disintegrates at 8.

TYPE THREE

PERFORMER, MOTIVATOR, FRAUD, NET-WORKER, ACHIEVER, EFFECTIVE PERSON, MASTER OF APPEARANCES, WINNER, DOER, EGO-VANITY

I am successful

Losers visualize the penalties of failure. Winners visualize the rewards of success. —Dr. Rob Gilbert

I pay attention to affecting others favorably, playing to an audience creating images that work best. Identifying with the character I sell, I market my appearance and the mask becomes the face. A fast tempo, I sparkle without much access to deep feelings. My performance is my identity. I am a production machine and see myself winning, even if this is not the outside reality. There is non-stop activity at a fast tempo because I am enthusiastic and immersed in doing things out in the world. Conversations are often about how well I am doing, self-promoting my productivity, abilities, personal achievements, as well as explaining my efficiency and organizational skills. I am persistent, survival oriented and yet I have a nagging fear of being disabled or not having enough money. Happiness is equated with material security and I easily blame anyone or circumstances if my finances are jeopardized.

The fear of boredom is at the expense of creating an interior world. My relationship to feelings has to be built very slowly, since feelings are not efficient. Multi-tasks are easy: loading the dishwasher, listening to a tape, talking on the phone and making dinner can all be done in the same moment. In the car, listening to messages on my cell phone I have lunch on my lap. Sitting at a lecture, I make good use of time and stay occupied planning my next day. Focused on the mechanics of the performance I enjoy evaluations, job tasks, and action. I am not particularly empathetic, friendships sometimes become expendable as I drive myself to accomplish, to meet my expectations. My sense of self is connected to outside recognition, real evidence that I am performing well. I will not tolerate the discomfort of blame or self-reproach. The reactions of those who notice are extracted, whether it is my children, parents, institutions, the media. The ability to rely on inner assessment rarely exists. I feel comfortable at work, where productivity and performance are required. I am popular, a team-builder, motivator, an energetic manager and self-assured. I expect to be loved for what I do, not for who I am, for the package that covers me as a commodity. What you see is what you get, there is little depth beneath the surface.

For me life is continuously being hungry. The meaning of life is not simply to exist, to survive, but to move ahead, to go up, to achieve, to conquer.
—Arnold Schwarzenegger

My talking style is propaganda, enthusiastically promoting myself, convincing you that what I do is who I am. Driving and agitated, often exhausted from overload, what's called type A behavior, the core hysteric type, my tone may be assertive and impatient. While there appears to be an absence of hysteria, my hyperactivity may lead to burnout, to physical exhaustion. Cheerfully marketing and inflating myself, you can expect the correct feelings to be displayed when you see me in a social circumstance. But first you will listen to what I do; moments into meeting someone I trot out my work badge and anyone else's in my family that might have impressive credentials. You'll hear about my son's accomplishments, my daughter's column in the paper, my granddaughter's piano recital, my doctor's latest opinion of my health, my grandson's dance performance, my friend's promotion. And if I don't see you I'll e-mail you the articles, regularly.

The toughest thing about success is that you've got to keep on being a success.
—*Irving Berlin*

I have many of the right products to show off; add up this list to get a high score: the right amount of children, a good car brand, a nice address, a well-behaved husband or wife, achievements and a full schedule. I play by the rules, with one aim: to win. Rarely will I march to the tune of a different drummer, and this helps in my achieving. I stay focused on the star and am driven to perform well. Very easy to spot, because I will throw my achievements on you. I am less apt to engage in growth work and spiritual meetings, since I am rarely introspective. Rather to go to theater, movies, shopping, errands, organizing events, traveling to other countries, museum shows, sometimes lectures and classes that I can boast having attended. Stress is high. Full appointment books with little time for relaxation, I usually feel the pressure of time. I can manage eating breakfast in the car while driving to work, reading e-mail while on my phone, ironing or shaving while listening to a self-improvement tape, grabbing a snack in between appointments, running to the gym, going over my notes while making lunch for the kids, meeting a friend for a walk. Practical, everything is an opportunity for shortcuts, organizing and keeping active. Production, getting something accomplished keeps the experience of feeling my fragile self far away, while serving to keep relationships distant. Personal relationships are not efficient, they waste time and threaten performance. Friendships are maintained by scheduled meetings, fitting into an appointment list.

Feelings are like speed bumps—they just slow me down. —*anonymous*

My emotional range is small, yet I am unaware of having so limited a repertoire. Life for me is think, do, think, do, think, do. I equate feelings with doing and energy, not suffering over the fact that I have no real connection to my inner life. There is a real willingness to work, I will not be a *nobody*. Often I do not give full attention or quality time to my children or partner. I will support the families activities, but not just hang out and do nothing with people, that would be an enigma; what others call quality time is not on my list. Love is productive and fun, scheduling activities to do together as a team. Little attention to process, anything can be sacrificed for the goal. Covering up information, from my age to my weight, hiding my self, avoiding looking inward, I project and see others as deceitful, eventually disbelieving what people tell me. Life becomes high maintenance; only when I resolve my need to impress others, confront my fear of worthlessness, of not being valuable if I am not doing things, will I awaken my heart to see myself. Playwright Luigi Pirandello made a classic Three statement: *Pretending is a virtue. If you can't pretend, you can't be king.*

America is a Three culture, mass marketing; everything mainstream. Appearance, image, productivity, performance, ambition, achievement, recognition, greed, success are the primary values that motivate this country. Pocketbooks and clothes with the name label on the outside; Louis Vuitton bags, Gucci collection, Yves Saint Laurent, Giorgio Armani, Prada, Oscar de la Renta, Versace, Calvin Klein, Ralph Lauren, these are the names I esteem. Whoever came up with the idea of putting the brand name label on the outside to market status, success and position had to be a Three. Power yoga, EST, lifestyle as if rich and famous, there is a need to be number one, the star. Self-deception is big, because there is no connection to the inside and the image gets shifted based on what others need me to look like. Without my accomplishments I feel worthless and without value. My day-timer is filled to the brim. A self-important imposter, I am often driven to impress. Packaging myself and projecting a role limits the ability to enter a spiritual realm and makes taking a quiet vacation a large project. Without the busy schedule life is threatening. I am talkative and charming, have many acquaintances, although personally I get embarrassed when others are rude or lazy, since being thought well of matters. My dodging intimacy is a tactic to keep outsiders from suspecting the inner emptiness I avoid. Propaganda covers the hollow impatience I experience. Any childhood traumas become forgotten to maintain the image of success. Those experiences seem so meaningless; you will rarely find me in therapy—generally life is going well and there's little time left over to sit and discuss issues unless there are clear goals and objectives. Therapy is short term, not too interesting to get bogged down in emotions, I fix things and move it up and onward. Being in emotional pain equates to being a loser. Dynamic energy, youthfulness, garnering attention; the opposite are laziness and failure.

I could lie and pretend that I hunt and camp, but that wouldn't be me. Clothes? Shopping? That's stuff I like. —Ryan Seacrest

As a Three culture we like a smooth slick even a billionaire President. We did not know that Roosevelt was in a wheelchair. We want to look first-rate and feel good. The deceit is in fashioning the image; aging and deformities are hard to tolerate. Ken and Barbie are a natural posture for my Enneagram type. We are the big cosmetic users, liking to have a sexually attractive appearance, although frigidity has its high population among Threes. Botox, cosmetic surgery, all assist to create and maintain a youthful appearance. Energetic, I exhaust myself with drive, enthusiasm and a large range of interests. Turning on the adrenalin can be at a demanding physical price. I look for results and measure myself by the requirements and reflection of the outside world. Even emotions can be called upon, the world points to the needed emotion and I often call that up; easier than spending time and effort digging deep to access it, and less trouble.

I'll quit tanning when the satchel handle grows out of my back. If I feel any sort of emotional upheaval, I just go for a jog and I feel better. —Kelly Ripa

I can do everything, while sacrificing depth. The win is in the speed, wanting to be liked, praised, applauded, I sell everything, including myself; in America we admire that and don't see gloss as superficial. Braggarts, wanting admiration, competing, everything becomes an opportunity to promote and come out ahead. We go to other countries and say, *do you like America?* without knowing anything about that country; we don't know their language or history or culture. We want to be admired by other countries without learning about them. Within this mask of *vanity of vanities*, appearance holds court.

I might hang artwork and artifacts in my home or office that have little personal connection to my life, sometimes consulting a decorator and telling them the image I want to convey. At times lacking integrity, I think my role, what I represent, is who I am. Even if you don't buy the whole image I can alter myself to continue getting your positive feedback. In a marriage I am not necessarily looking for deep intimate love. My energy is used up on external activities and nothing is left to know what I feel inside. I rarely integrate anything, I learn it, Xerox it, then e-mail it to someone. In one class I learn, then I turn around and teach the subject. My kindness is usually a mask and an act. The desire is to be loved for what I do. A great motivator, I like doing volunteer work and encouraging others to be the best they can be and develop their potential. Poised under pressure, I have a sense of humor about myself and enjoy retaining a youthful appearance.

I wish I had a twin, so I could know what I'd look like without plastic surgery. —*Joan Rivers*

At the third point on the Enneagram, the first shock point, an outside force is needed to spark and direct movement towards the goal. Like an alarm clock each of the 3 shocks are a reminder of the energy necessary to fuel the change process. Point Three marks the beginning of new energy coming in from an external mechanical shock. This is the moment in the wheel of change where some form of outside energetic stimulus is essential to sustain the process, so I won't get stuck. This point is about surrendering myself to a support structure that includes others. Work on myself starts to bear upon my inner life. I take the order of the One and the feeling vision of beauty of the Two and turn to the outside world to receive help to make change. Point Three is a mediator between the beginning of the Enneagram and its middle part. New ideas and impulses enter to freshen and refuel the journey, for at this point observation and understanding have been presented, yet I don't quite know how to proceed. The outside world brings in support for me to move in the direction of change. Here the details of life meet the aesthetics, successfully collaborating. Now, the impressive production happens once I enlist others in a team effort. I know what the world likes and I go after it. The infusion of energy at point Three, where the triangle intersects, supplies the process with enough force to continue the journey of discovery.

If I blunder, everyone can see it; not so, if I lie. —Goethe

TRANSFORMATION: HEALING

Foolishness is caused less by a lack of information than by a lack of self-awareness and self-honesty.

For a Three to work on themselves they need to ask, *what have I not examined? Am I willing to experience failure, to go to the root, to experience inefficiency*, what they consider to be *failure*. As the unconscious need for image loosens, the deception subsides. The transformational shift is from deceit to truthfulness, from efficiency to a hope and trust based on understanding that the world continues without their intervention. Meditation, sitting and doing nothing, dropping below the surface of activity, entering into a silent peaceful world creates this shift. *Meditation,* said a Tibetan, is *not a magic pill, it is like a waterfall falling for years on the rocks before they are worn away.* Knowing change this way not as achievement but as a calm alert relaxation can bring a state of mind to be carried throughout the day that invites in presence. When the Three allows life to work through them rather than making it happen, they become in tune with their true self. This is life's networker and once connected to themselves life flows through them with beautiful ease. Developing a sense of what is right and wrong, being honest and truthful, showing themselves to their community just the way they really are in the present (not acting), a healthy Three helps others attain the outstanding qualities they embody.

A creative person is motivated by the desire to achieve, not by the desire to beat others. —Ayn Rand

As a Three is working on themselves they begin to discover what has real depth, finding what is true they have the ability to manifest authentically. The turning point is when they admit to being tired of their lack of integrity and deceit. Noticing where they are lying to themselves brings their attention to an inner world so they begin to develop true substance. The growth continues with the shift from high energy doing to connecting to a broader repertoire of feelings. Highly motivational to others, once authentic they become admirable, effective, candid, forthright, truthful and are able to make a real contribution to people. Overcoming a sense of separateness, connections to others from a place of love allows the Three freedom from attachments to activities and to live from their depth of sincerity. In our country the Three has no real incentive to self-develop, to stop selling themselves, the great temptation of appearance since the world remains impressed and rewards/awards the product. This is the practice for the Three, to pursue the ambitions of the world and to live with love as the friend, within the experience that all life is interconnected. Cooperation in the path of service melts separation, is a communion between hearts. Through these connections, harmony is created. The Three awakens honoring the interconnectedness of all beings. Within this oneness the Three touches life and is touched, recognized, realizing their deep connection with all beings.

People need some kind of external activity, because they are inactive within.
—Schopenhauer

Some known Threes include: *Tony Robbins, O. J. Simpson, Paula Abdul, Barbie and Ken, John F. Kennedy, Pat Boone, Kelly Ripa, Doris Day, Arnold Schwarzenegger, Sarah Palin, Debbie Reynolds, Kris Kardashian, Kristin Chenoweth, Farrah Fawcett, Pamela Anderson, Christie Brinkley, Joseph Biden, Jennifer Lopez, Joan Rivers, Dick Clark, Ryan Seacrest, Kathie Lee Gifford, Shirley Temple, Werner Erhard, Michael Jordin, U.S.A., Miss America, Hong Kong,* the *peacock.* Integrates/heals at 6 disintegrates at 9.

TYPE FOUR

TRAGIC ROMANTIC, INDIVIDUALIST,

ARTIST, UNAVAILABLE BELOVED,

MOODY NOSTALGIC, TEMPERAMENTAL,

EGO-MELANCHOLY

I am unique

It's terribly amusing how many different climates of feeling one can go through in a day. —Anne Morrow Lindbergh

I feel alive from big emotions, dramas and moods and live in an ever changing emotional atmosphere. Today is a rehearsal for a time when those things I have longed for will appear—in the future. Self-absorbed, I listen to others only if the topic interests me. A job, home, loved one, new place to live; my attention is usually elsewhere, on what is missing. What is already present in my life becomes mundane and overlooked. Living an ordinary life, to which I am generally an outsider, seems flat and a concession for the richness I experience through my moods and melodrama. I hold on to my hope of finding the love of my life, my real self, the depth I want, the feeling of connection, the promise of love. Sensitive and temperamental I easily feel misunderstood and take care to not feel shamed, which sometimes wears me out. Miniscule annoyances become major irritants, especially when they are from an intimate relationship. My feelings are important to me, yet I find myself imagining closeness to someone, and then find it difficult to have current experiences that match my imagination. I review, remember and remind my family and friends about the past nostalgically. Memories don't make demands and aren't routine like a relationship, and the reminders help to keep stories alive and me separate from who I am beneath those experiences. Contact for me is about the possibility of connection. Tuning in to what it is I feel, the experience itself can elude me.

Happiness is beneficial for the body, but it is grief that develops the powers of the mind. —*Marcel Proust*

I have eliminated a number of possible feelings from my repertoire for the many times I want to remember, mull over select occasions that were meaningful, and then be able to run them in my mind my own way. I have learned how to manipulate my moods and temperament, I fix the environment and create a self that will match whatever it is I want to play out; this helps keep old thoughts and stories alive and me safely out of the world. This requires a bit of effort and energy since I have to push away everyone and everything that doesn't support my idea of myself. Not certain which set of feelings, what persona is me, I create a fantasy idealized self-image in my imagination. This holds the shame and the uncertainty at bay, the image of being defective, as well as allowing me to maintain a steady identity separate from the ever-shifting pattern of emotional reactions I could feel. At times I create an exotic off-beat persona to cover the uncertainty; this works since I reject certain feelings as ones that don't work for me, now I don't allow myself to experience particular moods.

The dream was always running ahead of me. To catch up, to live for a moment in unison with it, that was the miracle. —Anais Nin

Feeling out of place, I need proof in different forms that someone cares about me, comparing, longing and waiting, self-absorbed, disenchanted, never having enough. It could be a gift, or a phone call or complement, so long as it connects me, is a meeting-of-hearts, then I temporarily see the glass half-full. I catch myself exaggerating my value in someone's life. Reminding another about the meaningfulness of our relationship helps to reassure me that someone cares about me.

One may have a blazing hearth in one's soul, and yet no one ever comes to sit by it. —Vincent van Gogh

I live in the future waiting for life to begin, it's not time for the beautiful house or the longed for partner, or to get married and have children. Focused on what's missing or unavailable I use my emotional intensity and artistry to romanticize other times and places. A special beach I walked on as a child, an earlier boyfriend, an old school romance that might have been the love of my life, I cherish some of those beautiful moments, paradise lost, and pull them out as a reference point for the present. Judy Garland's *Somewhere Over The Rainbow* and Carol King's *So Far Away* are great Four songs. Ordinary people and the humdrum world are boring. Feeling more deeply than most others I dream up my life, refashioning and designing it, putting my own stamp on how it could be.

The world will be saved by beauty. —Fyodor Dostoyevsky

Mediocrity is everywhere, in people, in stores, restaurants, movies, conversations. I have a heart for beauty and being in tasteless places that lack character and feeling is disheartening. An uninspired middle-of-the-road relationship or plastic polyester clothing are dissatisfying. I am moody, self-absorbed, melancholic, sensitive; living with me has its difficulties and challenges. The attraction to deep emotion pulls me, regardless to my feeling joy or pain. I am drawn to find depth of meaning, craving intense emotions, romance, beauty and nostalgia. My most consistent feeling is one of longing. I look to be understood, and am willing to be courageously self-revealing. Wanting to make everything significant, I give meaning to whatever emotional pain I feel. Seeking something that will complete me, I spend years in therapy, am in and out of numerous relationships, and most often have a romance addiction— being in love with love.

Do not fear death so much, but rather the inadequate life. —Bertolt Brecht

On one hand I value my sensitivity and depth, yet inside I feel a hopelessness about ever really being content. Underneath the veneer of specialness I feel flawed and defective and know the shame that surfaces. Others happiness and good relationships are a reminder of my lack of lightheartedness. Moved by the passion of envy, I compare myself to others, and then become dissatisfied with my own life. Something is missing, others have it, and I envy them. Feeling the shame of being disharmonious, damaged, wounded, I push love away, sometimes becoming alternately clinging and self-absorbed. This frustration keeps me in turmoil and supports my demanding disposition, as I claim victimization.

Dying is an art, like everything else. I do it exceptionally well. —Sylvia Plath

Daily life just seems to be a rehearsal for that loving partnership I long for, while I wish the companion I have were someone or somewhere else. A Four commentary is: *I feel so bad since you've gone, it's almost like having you here.* Self-frustration and self-victimization are the backdrop for the appearance of a neediness that sits at the pit of my stomach. On the one hand I like to be admired, on the other hand I also feel drawn to pull out the beauty and specialness in others. Exaggerating dependency through clinging either to suffering or to a person or situation that I experience as a separation marks me as emotional. I need connection and yet my attitude of standoffishness to the outer world complicates the ease that might supply me with this contact need. Elitist and separate, pursuing the unreachable, longing for the past or future opens the door to melancholy and isolation. Having failed to meet the model image of self that I have imagined, the unattainable remains a goal. I may feel socially insecure while appearing special and that intensifies my isolation and feelings of being misunderstood. Sometimes it becomes a strain to be interested and listen and learn about others, to focus on anything that is not directly relevant to my own personal concerns. Unrequited love is the painstaking lament. The feeling of loss, whether it is true or not, constantly reappears; each friendship becomes a possibility of being left. Push-pull is characteristic, rejecting what I have and longing for what is missing. Living on the emotional edge enlivens me. At times I choose to compete with those who are the most close to me, pushing up the ante if I feel driven, whether it's to have more lovers than my partner or friend, to know more high powered people, or a larger wardrobe of clothing, or pursuing the unnameable darkness that others avoid.

What a wonderful life I've had. I only wish I'd realized it sooner. —Colette

I am a difficult child to raise, live in all emotional states of amplified feelings, and am up and down, loving theatrics. Posing, acting and pretending, I shift moods throughout the day, even entering dark tragic dramas. Taking everything personally, feeling special and therefore separate has overtaken my time and energy. Turning away from what might be easily available, I perpetuate feeling victimized, paying, instead, attention to what has been unavailable. My emotional drama fills my inner world and drains attention from my having an easy relaxed day.

I can stand almost anything except a succession of ordinary days. —Goethe

My talking style has a distinct emotional quality. A solemn thoughtful tone tinged with dissatisfaction and melancholy appears as an expression of sorrow, disappointment, grief or regret towards something. People are attracted to my sensitive and expressive aesthetic, yet once my lover you are on the roller coaster of exaggerated emotions. I actually believe that I have deeper feelings than most others, both due to my strong sensing the emotional atmosphere wherever I go and supported by making often insignificant daily things a disaster of Hurricane Katrina proportion. I prefer the intensity of feelings, the simplicity of an ordinary feeling seems so trivial compared to the passion, sadness, angst and nostalgia that can transport me. Billie Holiday, Judy Garland, Edith Piaf, Janis Joplin, Maria Callas, Prince, Lenny Kravitz, Martha Graham and Leonard Cohen, all Fours, soulfully expressed the hopelessness, betrayal, aspirations and tragedy in their great style as musical divas.

I greet you from the other side of sorrow and despair/ With a love so vast and shattered it will reach you everywhere. —Leonard Cohen

Finding true love evokes pain, since the focus is on the absent lover. Love received may get invalidated, which continues the cycle of frustration and supports my viewpoint of being misunderstood. Close relationships with a pet or child, places where I am in charge and in imagination, are more common as partnerships. I live on the edge of depression. When I move towards people, intimacy threatens, as then I remember loss and feel insecure in vulnerability. Spiteful, I find myself comparing others lives, unable to drop into my own without comparing. The ideal is not in the present moment. Endlessly needing to be reassured and cared for I act it out through the need for financial protection. Somebody who claims to love me, footing the bill, loaning me money, setting up a trust fund, covering my rent; I feel deserving of these emotional tokens. Creating my own financial success compensates for my underlying feeling of being defective, although there never is quite enough to fill the deep sense of lack which includes feeling displaced. I give to get, sometimes in a seductive way, but, ultimately end up enslaved by the frustration, pain and melodrama that my need for love activates. I have strong emotions and a wide range, including sadness and feeling flawed, so hate erupts which produces guilt and regret. My own emotional drama fills my life and often there is little energy left for the rest of what is out there. Early family connections are anchored in feeling different and the loss of parental love, real or imagined, especially from my father, persists through adulthood. Abandonment becomes a theme.

We are all sentenced to solitary confinement inside our own skins-for-life.
—*Tennessee Williams*

Hiding within artful self-presentation I make the effort to dress and look casual and natural. When I think I am being subtle expressing my specialness, it is still stated quite directly. Loving to look casually elegant, natural, a scarf turned the right way, sporty relaxed pants appear original and creative, most important is that they fit the mood.

Understated, clothing may have a smooth rich feel, yet informal and carefree is the style of the day. I can be found dancing, modeling, writing poetry, giving public readings, the special guest speaker, invited to perform prayer services and meditations, any project that offers exhibitionist rewards. I like the ritual and beauty of ceremony, live in my emotional imagination, creating an atmosphere in my home, sometimes with flowers, art work, photos, candles, incense or music. Going through phases of hyperactivity, I travel and have lots of experiences out in the world, or I alternately move inward and stay home, sad and nostalgic.

I have sometimes been wildly, despairingly, acutely miserable, racked with sorrow, but through it all I still know quite certainly that just to be alive is a grand thing. —Dame Agatha Christie

The nine-pointed star diagram called Enneagram as a template for sequencing methods of change and development places type Four as making the shift in the movement and geometry of the Enneagram structure itself. The bottom right hand side on the structure has the only chasm—between 4 and 5, making this the most difficult maneuver, from the right to the left side of the Enneagram figure. It's as if this chasm can never be crossed and, so, point Four has been called the crisis point. The Four fails to meet the idealized image suggested in point One, Two and Three, instead living in frustration, separateness, chronic dissatisfaction, while craving protection. Looking back at the other types, there is a yearning to move forward. This is a place of struggle and tension. The Three set up a structure of support, moving to the fourth type sets in motion the possibility for inquiry and experimentation that brings about change. The fourth point is a place of true practice, often filled with failure and broken promises. As a place of discovery and creation, possibilities appear. Experiencing the tension, the Four, emotionally unstable, balances through remaining current, less preoccupied with self, grounded and present.

We look before and after, and pine for what is not; Our sincerest laughter With some pain is fraught; Our sweetest songs are those that tell of saddest thought. —*Percy Shelley*

TRANSFORMATION: HEALING

This is the material plane and every outward thing we do is inner work. This is the material plane and it could use a good sanding. —*Rumi*

When they can see the extraordinary in the ordinary there is a real shift. Offering recognition and value to what already exists in their life balances the tremendous self-doubt that cripples the Four. Satisfaction with their own world, being a good sport—cooperating with others as another part of a team, not a special part, not the star, without recognition, shifts the self-absorption and indulgence that has a stronghold on the unhappiness and suffering a Four experiences. Giving without the thought of getting, awareness of another's needs, free of any need of appreciation, opens a door to growth and transformation. Healthy Fours can reveal shameful aspects in their pursuit to understand, integrate and heal their chronic dissatisfaction. An evolved Four has developed inner composure and emotional presence—a consistent nature even under stress—has creative depth and the capacity for self-awareness. Once they stop trying so hard to be free or to be themselves, and release the narrative of their suffering, who they really are can emerge. Protecting their self-image has tied them up to avoid things, people, experiences; the idea of being different and needing special treatment and props to create the illusion takes a toll and prevents the spaciousness of spontaneous living. The movement from what is missing to noticing what is presently available allows them to enter a realm of peace that is presence itself. When developed, Fours have the ability to transform all experiences into authentic creative beauty.

Happiness always sneaks in through a door you didn't know you left open.
—*John Barrymore*

The transformational shift is from envy to equanimity. Open to knowing and feeling satisfied, the experience of already having everything one needs quiets the envy and makes room for the ordinary. No longer missing anything, waiting to be noticed or to receive attention quiets down into present moment acceptance of others; relationships become ordinary day-to-day, not idealized or imaginary. No longer immersed in their own story, their self-absorption, self-indulgence and dramas, open to flow and experience the ordinary, life *is*. Relinquishing the need for only intensity to have value, from taking it all personally, one feeling at a time allows for a balanced emotional life. Their creativity is inside, and when used constructively they are an inspiration and encouragement. Once free they can teach others how to give meaning to life.

How strange when an illusion dies. It's as though you've lost a child.
—*Judy Garland*

The shift from being self-involved to self-remembering brings the Four to penetrate the present moment, and this is the ticket to freedom, their awakening. Bringing themselves into the present moment, rather than escaping into idealized fantasy, appreciating what they have now, not what is lacking, moves them out of their habit of unnecessary suffering to feel the tensions so they can be transformed and now live in balanced equanimity. Avoiding *if only*, rather to find meaning, understanding here in this world and its universal implications, then taking meaningful action breaks the trance. Staying present to the world and to self, grounded in the moment, no longer will life be taken so personally. Standing aside, seeing relationships outside themselves; not being the center, not being separate, births consciousness. Remembering oneself consciously brings immediate contact with *what is*, self-remembering, balanced, the person has disappeared, this is presence.

So much of the world is plunged in darkness and chaos. So ring the bells that can still ring Forget your perfect offering There is a crack in everything That's how the light gets in. —Leonard Cohen

Some known Fours include: *Judy Garland, Lady Gaga, Amy Winehouse, Tennessee Williams, Marlon Brando, Madonna, Beyonce, Amal Clooney, Barbra Streisand, Rihanna, Shakespeare, Soren Kierkegaard, Ingrid Bergman, Robert Downey Jr., Whitney Houston, Angelina Jolie, Prince, Charlie Chaplin, Anne Sexton, Frida Kahlo, Cher, Karina Smirnoff, Lenny Kravitz, Diane Arbus, Leonard Cohen, Judy Collins, Michael Jackson, Violette Le Duc, Percy Shelley, Andrew Harvey, Isadora Duncan, Rudolf Nureyev, Johnny Depp, Anais Nin, Martha Graham, Christina Aguilera, Winona Ryder, D.H. Lawrence, Kate Winslet, Marguerite Duras, Maria Callas, Sylvia Plath, Kurt Cobain, Mevlana Jelaluddin Rumi, Don Riso, Isabelle Allende, Madame Bovary by Flaubert, Marcel Proust, Edith Piaf, Sarah Bernhardt, Janis Joplin, Charles Baudelaire, Gangaji, Billie Holiday, Santa Fe-the city different, Japan, France,* the *dove.* Integrates/heals at 1 disintegrates at 2.

TYPE FIVE

OBSERVER, THINKER, MYSTIC PHILOSOPHER,
RECLUSE, INVESTIGATOR, EGO-STINGINESS

I know.

People say life is the thing, but I prefer reading. —*Logan Pearsall Smith*

*T*he most internal, emotionally detached and constricted of all the types, I substitute thinking for doing, working things out in my mind, experiencing the preparation as the doing. The computer world and analytical thinking are my ideal domain since my need is to know why things are the way they are, to search and to learn. I give of myself sparingly, likewise holding on to those minimal things that do matter to me. I am insatiable as I gather, collect and study, there is never enough knowledge or any limits to improving my skills. Rarely a risk taker; the data is seldom all in, so I only occasionally make that final commitment. I am emotionally stingy, like a vacuum cleaner I keep taking in and taking in, facts, information, giving little back out.

I don't enjoy hugging or excessive social physical contact, those are energy drains. I stay away from most engagement in the outside world, except in the library, a business meeting or meditation hall. Privacy is a great place, no interruptions through another's expectations; this is my time to reflect, to come to my own opinions. My viewpoint was well expressed by Herman Hesse in Siddhartha, who became Buddha : *I can think, I can wait, I can fast.* Creating small secret places to hide, self-discipline develops my skills of concentration and studying for extended periods of time. I retreat when I get depleted from being in the world. My talking style creates distance rather than intimacy and sounds like a commentary or, if I get started, a sermon or dissertation. Once I feel the limit of words I shift into my secondary mode of communicating: silence. Meher Baba, a Five mystic was silent for the last forty-four years of his life stating that: *Things that are real are given and received in silence.*

I fell in love with the darkroom, and that was part of being a photographer at the time. The darkroom was unbelievably sexy. I would spend all night in the darkroom. —Annie Leibovitz

In my own home I need guaranteed private space. Deprived of quality time in the house, I become irritated and move to Eight, forbidding anyone to come into my room, I close the door and lock it, this is my no trespassing zone. As long as I have some small place to retreat to I maintain undisturbed, a tent set up in the yard, an attic or garage, a little office big enough for one at the back of the house: a getaway. I will defend my right to protect my space, my privacy, my freedom from disturbance, otherwise I feel invaded. I need little, but my own space is where I recharge. An uncontrolled living area where people come in and out of my space, where I can't maintain privacy; for me that level of intrusiveness is too much of a challenge. Zen meditation centers are one of my favorite places, although not a great choice for growth, since my ability to detach and minimize is already mechanically present. Sometimes I would like to cancel the outside world from all consideration, that would be a peaceful life, since it is not so easy for me to protect myself from what is out there, even my sun sensitive complexion reflects this.

I never found the companion that was so companionable as solitude. —Henry David Thoreau

Preferring manageable and managed space I work as an endodontist peering into the small cavity of a root canal, making homeopathic remedies, a truck driver on long hauls, drawing lines on an architectural plan, a writer, constructing computer programs or living a limited lifestyle like a hermit. Meditation, physical lone running or long distance bike riding, lack of availability, lack of involvement, the monastic life; I just will not react. I often feel drained, depleted, from the exhausting experience of holding back. Giving up easily, resignation closes down the future. I seal off and the visibility of my thoughts and feelings become elusive and invisible. I might agree just to eliminate conversation and confrontation, eventually I'm even concealed from myself, hidden away, resigned and isolated.

The stoical scheme of supplying our wants by lopping off our desires is like cutting off our feet when we want shoes. —Jonathan Swift

My avoidance of life and relationships does not convey my sensitive inner world, where I am inwardly gentle, soft and tender. Personal freedom is essential. I have a rich interior world and am an acute observer which makes for a good writer and thinker, as well as my having an inner life that pulls away interest from the external world. Often too overwhelmed to play the success oriented economic game, I sit on the sidelines, avoiding vocations that involve high-powered selling, advertising, marketing, disclosure, direct confrontation, abrasive people or power struggles. Instead, I prefer jobs that protect my mild solitary nature. I am the most antisocial of all types on the Enneagram, and guard against being intruded, inundated by others needs and energy. Teaching, forest ranger, research, writing, meditation guide, scientist, all fitting jobs and lifestyles.

Hell is other people. I had found my religion: nothing seemed more important to me than a book. I saw the library as a temple. —Jean-Paul Sartre

We can hoard or be miserly with money and energy. Many of the other types will threaten suicide for drama and histrionics, I am the type that will quietly do it. I am not so accessible, often will not answer the telephone, even though I am standing next to it when it is ringing. I enjoy the mind and inventing, gathering data and doing projects that are of particular interest to me. Fives as actors are prominent. There is a love of knowing, which is the trap. I take careful time in gathering information and like to pass along this knowledge. I hold on too long, hold back, hold in, yet easily will give up. Fixating on what is within my own focus of attention I close down to the unfolding of possibilities.

Less is more. —*Robert Browning*

Under stress I move to Seven and may look happy, charming and relating, yet putting myself out there, any impulsive activity feels like a demand and is consuming. My intimate partner becomes an emotional lifeline. Being emotionally distanced I need a person who puts energy into the relationship. Once I have extended periods of time alone I can show up and be loving, although I still withdraw when I experience boundary invasion. Thinking gets substituted for feelings creating confusion for my partner; when asked for energy and enthusiasm, instead, you get dissection and analysis. I can speak up more easily in the protection of my own home and from the vantage point of the predictability of one partner; I imagine my study and evaluation to be my feelings. Nonverbal communication, most often my decisions are made in private and the other is not privy to the process and may even be misled by the blank screen you see during our meetings. Easily overwhelmed and drained by the needs of my partner, I try to divert the attention when it's aimed at my feelings. Sharing a project together, be it planning a wedding, our children, or house hunting; intimacy is voiced through agreed commitments. In relationships I am patient, steadfast, restrained. I create and maintain a separate secretive world that I engage in, a way to experience my own sphere of nonintrusion. When intruded upon I become caustic and skeptical, hoping to push people away with my abrasive viewpoint. I appear emotionally distant, with a cool demeanor, because I am fearful of getting involved in my own and others feelings. Hiking, gardening, cross country skiing, running, silently sharing, is my strong and important bond. Exploring the environment deepens my confidence and allows me to engage in the reality of a world safely.

One reason I like boats so much, is that you have to pare everything down to the bare necessities, and there you are, the captain of a little boat, without a shelter, without a past, without future hopes. —*Peter Matthiessen*

When I withdraw, I recharge, I need a lot of breathing room and rarely intrude on anyone, just wishing for the same in return. Living is replaced with my pursuit of creative ideas. I am full of information as well as quite independent, well able to take care of myself. An array of complex mental configuration sometimes leads me to make remarkable insight and inventions, although sometimes at the expense of practical day to day interactions. Personal relationships suffer the most. I tend to deal with topics systematically and extensively. Examining my thoughts, reviewing my day, liking to investigate and categorize, there is a reserve even in my subtle British-type humor. I am interesting to talk to, my conversations are easy and informative, my emotional needs are small, although you might not be too successful at picking my brain for additional information. I could enjoy sporting a beard, wearing neutral colors, not being flashy, living a minimalist lifestyle. At times I disassociate, cut myself off from what I feel, am emotionally unavailable: I could sit through a party or a dinner with people and say nothing, talk to no one, and the next day report that I had a good time. My position on the few things that matter to me is clearly stated, I want the world to pass by and leave my select things intact.

Sometimes I think, sometimes I am. —*Paul Valery*

I live in between the devil and the deep blue sea, otherwise referred to as between a rock and a hard place. The outer world is uncomfortable and draining and when I go inside to hide and avoid it, eventually I contact a gaping hole. When I retreat inside I am judged as cold and aloof. I do not like open-ended meetings, often withdrawing out of habit. Avoiding most people, their expectations overwhelm me, muddies my own clarity of mind, and often leaves me feeling invaded. My energy goes towards analytical thinking and endless extrapolations, not to help or serve the world, but to sit like the owl and watch. I might position myself in the back of a room, taking everything in, giving nothing in return. My ability to have non-verbal communication is highly developed. I spend hours happily at my computer doing research, inventing, surfing for information, investigating. I am more at home in my head than in my heart or body.

Why one has to have a body, I don't know. A necessary appendage to the head, I suppose. —*Paul Bowles*

While I know a lot, I do not easily take action since that involves feelings and entanglements. Setting boundaries for personal time is helpful, too much contact, being in people's company I lose myself. Alone is a quality experienced even when people are around. The ability to be solitary holds a large range. The companionship is with my own world. There is emotional relief in the detail since I can get smaller and smaller and more hidden. A Five commentary is the story of Immanuel

Kant. He left a note on the door of his lecture hall: *Cannot come today, have not finished thinking yet.* German-American Maria Ludwig Michael Mies, a pioneering master of modern architecture designed in a style described as extreme clarity and simplicity. A Five, his aphorisms, *Less is more* and *God is in the details* are great Five commentaries. He aptly called his buildings *skin and bones.* A minimalist, true to his type he found the world interesting as he so carefully planned, focusing on the projects that drew him into his resourcefulness and creativity.

At the fifth point on the 9 pointed star diagram the bottom left side of the Enneagram, the goal is clearly in sight. This transition from the Four on the right, to the left side of the figure, is the largest and most dramatic shift spatially possible. This is a point of maximum tension and of the greatest hazard, having taken the largest spacial step. I have direction, see where I have to go, yet feel impatient that the distance exists. I look ahead to point 7 and 8, no longer gazing behind, like 4 looked to 1 and 2. But my mind gets caught and my life can become projecting and thinking rather than insightful doing. The fifth point shifts from looking for an answer, feeling not yet capable to act. Knowing does not make something happen. Obstacles appear, this is the point where ambition wanes. A stuck quality brings old habits back, and I retreat, looking restrained and restricted.

Those who know their minds do not necessarily know their hearts.
—*La Rochefoucauld*

TRANSFORMATION: HEALING

That's been one of my mantras—focus and simplicity. Simple can be harder than complex: you have to work hard to get your thinking clean to make it simple. But it's worth it in the end because once you get there, you can move mountains. —*Steve Jobs*

*I*n the highest awareness the Five is a visionary, insightful and attentive. The mystic philosopher, non-attached, able to see without imposing their personality, they pioneer new areas of knowledge. Keeping an open mind, risking, being seen, acknowledging personal needs, links them to humanity. Once evolved the Five allows life and others to matter to them. To go out into the world with confidence and make use of the knowledge they have gathered, to share their wisdom by simplifying their ideas and to experience themselves as a meaningful part of the world often results in masterfully successful discoveries. The transformational shift is from the appetite for gathering and hoarding information and the greed for privacy, to dispassionate calm non-attachment, not being identified with any one point of view. To loosen the attachment to detachment, the defensive posture of separating emotions from mind, from being penetrated by people, outside events and feelings, then awareness, along with satisfaction from experiencing *enough*, true non-attachment grows. The movement is from intellectualization to understanding, from imposing and projecting to seeing with clarity. To become touched by life, to have direct experience, direct understanding, an open mind, unselfconscious, they thrive. The transformation is from contemplation to action, from eccentric intellectual to innovative brilliance. Five's awaken through digested self-observation, true non-attachment. They obstruct their awakening by clinging, holding on to concepts, by moving away from involvement. Non-attachment, a real let go, is participation with the way things are, no resistance. Life is a coming and a going, like the breath. This is the awakened life of non-attachment, open and spacious. Non-attachment displays an absence of a sense of emptiness and meaninglessness, demonstrating patience even under trying conditions, a freedom from irritation, with a good-humored attitude. What a joyful awakening!

As thoughts arrive, destroying them utterly without any residue, in the very peace of their origin is non-attachment. Just as the pearl-diver ties a stone to his waist, sinks to the bottom of the sea and there takes the pearls, so each of us should be endowed with non-attachment, dive within oneself and obtain the Self-Pearl. —Ramana Maharshi

Growthful work is to attach to feelings, thoughts, experiences; to make contact. Training themselves to have real skills repairs their deep sense of insecurity, offering confidence to step into the world and participate rather than to live privately in their world of ideas and distortions. Involvement in life and connection with people, presence rather than solitary isolation, allows for the opening. As the greed for time, energy and personal space relaxes, a spiritual realm opens that now understands that everything we need to know is always available. Moving towards being involved, learning how to self-renew, making contact, opening feelings, finding a spirit of true happiness, connecting with others, remaining present through the shifts and moods of others; these are ways in which the Five develops, opens and offers their gifts to the world.

We are what we think, all that we are arises with our thoughts, with our thoughts we make our world. —the Buddha

Some known Fives include: *Franz Kafka, Emily Dickinson, Jonas Salk, Joan Didion, Gautama the Buddha, Martin Heidegger, Clint Eastwood, Ingmar Bergman, Bobby Fischer, Oliver Sacks, Rene Descartes, Ebenezer Scrooge, Ted Kaczynsky, Mark Twain, J. D. Salinger, Karl Marx, Jean-Paul Sartre, Albert Camus, Marlene Dietrich, Henry David Thoreau, Claudio Naranjo, Robert Pattinson, Kristen Stewart, Glenn Close, Georgia O'Keefe, Eckhart Tolle, Rainer Maria Rilke, Albert Camus, Kabir Helminski, Samuel Beckett, Russ Hudson, Alan Greenspan, Jane Goodall,*

Kurt Vonnegut, Howard Hughes, Bill Gates, Bob Dylan, St. Francis, May Sarton, Ken Wilbur, Jacqueline Onassis Kennedy, Robert Browning, Mitch Chefitz, Jose Stevens, Simone Weil, R.Crumb, Charles Darwin, Greta Garbo, Annie Leibowitz, Immanuel Kant, Ken Wilbur, Friedrich Nietzsche, Ludwig Wittgenstein, Dustin Hoffman, Raymond Carver, Philip Glass, Laurie Anderson, Osama bin Laden, Dirk Bogarde, William S. Burroughs, Meryl Streep, Steve Jobs, Claudio Naranjo, A.H. Almaas, Albert Einstein, Stephen Hawking, J.Paul Getty, Ramana Maharshi, the *owl, Great Britain, Old China*. Integrates/heals at 8, disintegrates at 7.

TYPE SIX

QUESTIONER, DEVIL'S ADVOCATE, DOUBTER, LOYALIST, CHESS PLAYER, PARANOID PERSONALITY, EGO-COWARDICE

I am doing my duty.

It is clear the future holds opportunities—it also holds pitfalls. The trick will be to seize the opportunities, avoid the pitfalls, and get back home by 6:00. —*Woody Allen*

I am questioning, suspicious, doubting, sarcastic, anxiously hesitant, hard-working, inflexible and hyper-vigilant. This is the world of the psychic and the lawyer, the taxi driver, the politician, comedian, police officer, sky diver and the chess player. In the quest for certainty I am looking for predictability. I like to know where the danger is and then play out all possible scenarios. Once I slip into doubt I question each action outside of myself, eventually leading me to uncertainty. A smile on my face may misrepresent what's underneath. I want logical reasonable answers and clear-cut guidelines to what is expected. I use my mind for protection against how I imagine the world to be threatening. The core fear point, although I am also dissociated from the emotion of fear, living in or between one of two worlds: phobic or counter phobic. Phobic means I lay low, am vigilant or compliant, hesitant, at times melodramatic, dogmatic, victim, scanning in anticipation of danger—counter phobic means I manifest as provocative and outspoken, restless, catching trouble before it catches me. Addicted to insecurity, contentious, I might take action impulsively sometimes making poor decisions. The paranoia of impending possible danger is handled with challenging bravado. Not only do I avoid fear, it is absent from view, rarely displayed. Disconnected from my emotions because I live mostly in my head leads me to hesitate and distrust. Easily reactive until I ground myself inside to address my insecurities, the ambiguities of my personality shift; at times you might see fear or courageousness, a loner or me mingling in a group, trust or paranoid distrust, strength or weakness, me acting defensively or me acting on the offense; full range contradictions. I am like a time-bomb of anxiety, hyper-vigilant, alerted for the next impending doom. Once danger strikes, I will step forward to meet it.

Suspicion always haunts the guilty mind. —*Shakespeare*

My speaking posture is to set limits, to make life more ordered, reasonable, and certain. Often avoiding eye contact, at times a helmet like hair style, looking somewhat like the original musical crew of the Beetles. Careful not to miscalculate or get it wrong, I want to stay out of the firing line and not become anyone's target practice. This is my idea of communicating, being within the margin to stay clear of other's eruptions. I live in a world I perceive as intimidating; even reassurance is food for mistrust. Comfort is to know how things will play out. Argumentative, contrary, stubborn, defensive, skeptical and cynical, often we are militarists. Duty and loyalty to an outside authority eases the inner doubt and paralysis that occurs from my near constant lack of certainty. Germany as a Six country displays how deeply the fear and paranoia lie. They are obsessed with law and authority, either against or for it.

A thief believes everybody steals. —E.W. Howe

In the search for security and certainty, I fight with authority. I am the person who worries and takes care of others with loyalty and duty to create my own safety. I am the type that argues to deny the Enneagram, and all systems that I see as boxing or limiting. A disbeliever, I am not convinced that I am a Six or that I have fear. Sometimes I adopt dog behavior, but rather than barking to back you off, I bluff and strong arm others. Authority holds a charge for me, I might aggress on those subordinate to me, although I submit to those above. Anxiety is a frozen fear, an imagined danger and my inhibited response feeds the uneasiness. It is unsafe to feel that my impulses are not reliable, yet the consequences bring me to distrust my spontaneity. I become hyper-vigilant, watching for hints and indications before taking action. Lack of certainty, fear of change and even fear of loving keeps me careful and double checking. Problem seeking, I reason my way trying to build a safe place in this world often avoiding my own inner world which is charged with worry and thinking.

I don't like being afraid. It scares me. —Margaret Houlihan

In relation to other people, power is a preoccupation. Entering a room my attention goes to who is in authority. This is a habit, projection and reaction. Vocations with clear guidelines, known boundaries, I like to know what to expect, predictability keeps my anxiety at ease. We often become police officers, and as lawyers we check out all possible scenarios before going to trial. Often, for safety, I choose a strong partner, although this ups my competitive edge. The key issue to the friction in partnerships eludes me. It just fits better to help others satisfy their aims. Over-protectiveness is a cover for my need to control, I rarely share my inner doubts and shifts of thought, expecting failure, I get it, since others are unaware of my distrust and doubt. Success feels too exposed, and the pleasure from achieving gets worn away by constantly looking for the problem areas. I am hard working, well-informed, prudent and constant.

Nothing will ever be attempted, if all possible objections must be first overcome. —*Samuel Johnson*

Being rewarded for hard work, receiving acknowledgment, achieving success, accomplishment, fame and recognition can bring on paranoia and heighten doubt. Referred to as *the trooper, the hero,* and *the co-fighter,* I move away from leadership when it is handed to me. In one of my two postures: phobic, I step back from fear and when counter-phobic I enter high-risk experiences to face fear until it dissipates. Drawn to the edge I find comfort in challenging situations learning how to make the fear go away. The opposite of fear is courage, and grounding myself in a trust of my own resourcefulness, my inner guidance to rely on myself, a relaxed peacefulness arrives. Sometimes drawn to activities with an adrenalin high, I sky-dive, join rodeos, become a stunt-person, Green Beret, rock climb; all ways to briefly contact real fear, leading towards courage, as opposed to living with persistent imagined fear.

I'm not afraid to die. I just don't want to be there when it happens. —*Woody Allen*

I make a good trouble-shooter, since I am naturally prudent, apprehensive, skeptical, cautious, loyal, motivated through finding my own actual belief, stepping up to the plate once the consequences hit the fan. Doubt brings me to procrastinate, to not take action, there's invariably that *yes, but,* going on in my head, and when I'm complimented or praised I look for the inner intentions, as well as to duck for cover following my suspicious inclinations. I am the over-rehearsed problem seeker, scanning for obstacles, looking for clues, falling back on logic and reason. This protects my fear, anxiety and paranoia. Doubting most things I invariably will be uncertain that I am a Six on the Enneagram. Another dilemma, since I ride between self-invalidation and grandness; I will choose the most appealing type in this system to say *that's me* and demonstrate certainty. More often, though, I will doubt the system in an effort not to be pegged and to maintain what I see as my unique point of view.

I don't know if you've noticed, but our two-party system is a bowl of shit looking at itself in the mirror. —Lewis Black

Betrayal and bad faith are my secret frame of mind. While defending the underdog, I am steaming to knock the topdog off their perch. Sometimes referred to as the *devil's advocate,* I scan to find redemptive qualities in the underdog at times aligning with a person or cause that's irreconcilable. Usually not flashy we are the glue that holds small businesses, corporations, taxi fleets, academia, and the justice system together; we are the salt of the earth people. I look to find the security that will ease my tension and anxiety through my loyal performance of duty and once I commit to a task I follow it through with a sense of responsibility that is dedicated even through difficulties and conflicts. In my mind I divide the world into the good and the bad guys. I can follow rules and standards that aren't mine when accepting responsibility to be an integral part of an organization, even going down with the ship. We are the people who endlessly persist on the job, getting up and going to work every day. Liking the stability and security of the known, I will not risk; I don't want unpredictable or unwelcome consequences. Friendships, people who I am at ease with, who listen to my doubts and offer reassurance and consistency, when I trust that they like me this is where I finally let my guard down. The questioning eases, the analysis weakens, arguments and scanning quiets, and I am warm and caring.

A pessimist is one who feels bad when he feels good for fear he'll feel worse when he feels better. —*anonymous*

My doubting mind in a partnership craves reassurance and encouragement. I avoid making essential decisions, equally resisting others who try to make them for me; rather to pick the brain of someone who serves as a sounding board, someone who's had experiences in areas that I might want, then I create an alliance with that person. Attracted to beauty and strength, I look for assurance, safe bets; I want a relationship that will support, not reject or harm me. I need a reality check, when I am not prepared since what is unknown has me feeling unprotected and uncomfortable, trusting my gut and heart is not a natural direction for me, my head and talking excessively take over. Romance is not a big item in my world, the doubts wander into my mind, although they don't necessarily push me out of the partnership. Adversity awakens my vitality, faced without opposition I slow down, procrastinate, delay decisions. Knowing that I am accepted, liked, the paranoia lightens and fades; with certainty I become a team player rather than a disruptive partner. My awareness of the negative implications, my doubts in the relationship are always there, although, ironically they sustain me to stay in the partnership by reducing the fear. It is less intimidating when I know what the issues are, the hazards won't come up and grab me; the proverb: *forewarned is to be forearmed* must have referred to me. Knowledge of imminent danger prepares me to overcome it, I like to know the trouble spots. This is the tool that enables me to open in love, the shelter of doubt. Following this I am quite manageable, loyal, protective, imaginative and committed.

Pessimist—One who, when he has the choice of two evils, chooses both.
—Oscar Wilde

Enneagram point Six is the second shock point, a place where an external pressure offers an intake of energy. Energy coming from outside can be used to break old habits and upgrade the system to a higher level. This final point of the energy triangle needs a spark, momentum, inner strength, a faith in something to undertake the change that is about to happen. Point Six enters as belief, moves to faith and ultimately becomes trust. The surrender needed at this point asks for questions to drop away. Standing at the edge, ready to take the jump into the unknown, this is the letting go point. The right side of the Enneagram is based on preparation, recognition and understanding; much is hidden. The transformational left side knows what needs to happen and experiences a change in the fundamental nature of their whole life. Point Six has been called the hardest to understand, their contradictions and unpredictability are both external and internal, aimed at others as well as at themself.

I've developed a new philosophy—I only dread one day at a time.
—Charles M. Schulz

TRANSFORMATION: HEALING

*W*hen they do not feel threatened and trust is established, they are loyal, practical, self-reliant, responsible and fair, often supporting those with less power. The transformational shift is from fear, doubt, dogma—to courage, faith and trust. Questioning as an objective reality check is an excellent way out of the fear. To remain clear even when facing fear, to allow the fear to be an energy rather than an obstacle, this is the trust that is the courage that transforms. Faith brings a possibility to move into taking action even within the worry. Once acknowledging the stronghold fear has and recognizing the energy of distress; turning to trust, intuition, faith and courage is a way to create a solid presence. An integrated Six resolves their anxiety, connects and works with others as an equal and is no longer reactive. Trusting themselves they are now able to trust others. The ability to live in the apprehension, the tension, the insecurity and to still find the courage to take action is enlivening. To turn away from doubt, trusting intuition and clear-sighted faith is an evolved place for the Six to live.

The only security is courage. —*La Rochefoucauld*

Healthy Sixes are courageous in protecting the underdog, and hold a space in the world as a reliable mainstay. Developing intuition, deepening certainty, moving from blind faith to conscious faith, all of these bring awareness into a daily life that now becomes positive and hopeful. Allowing courage to commingle with fear, the Six is able to move forward with self-reliance and steadfastness. No longer emotionally guarded they are able to be carefree and trusting of others. Transformed, they appear solid and manifest a faith based on certainty rather than blind beliefs. An insightful Six comment is: *Courage is not the absence of fear, but rather the judgment that something else is more important than fear.*

Life shrinks or expands in proportion to one's courage. —Anais Nin

Awakened through their courage to enter into the heart of love: *conscious trust.* All distinctions vanish, and they see things as they are; otherwise they confuse reality with appearance. To overcome the mind which has always been the great obstacle, doubts vanish, the courage to trust captures the light. The Six, arriving at an inner place of stillness, feels grounded and supported, certain about what is, allowing life to unfold. Rooted and connected, inviting seeds of certainty, the ground of being supports their solidity of consciousness, their discovered true nature. Peace and harmony are restored as essence emerges and matures.

A reasonable probability is the only certainty. —Edgar Watson Howe

Some known Sixes include: *Sherlock Holmes, Adolf Hitler, Sigmund Freud, Woody Allen, J. Edgar Hoover, Warren Beatty, Mel Gibson, Spike Lee, Ellen DeGeneres, David Letterman, Rosie O'Donnell, Kanye West, Nick Nolte, Robert Redford, Janet Reno, Michael Moore, Jim Jones, Oliver North, Jay Leno, Elton John, Charlie Sheen, Dick Cavett, William Buckley, Ricky Gervais, Evel Kneivel, Diane Keaton, Malcolm X, Johnny Carson, Jim Jones, George W. Bush, John McCain, Simon Cowell, Jack Lemmon, David Koresh, Charles Manson, Louis Black, Helen Palmer, David Daniels, Gloria Steinem, Sylvester Stallone, Rush Limbaugh, Whoopie Goldberg, Humphrey Bogart, Billy Crystal, Richard Nixon, Robert F. Kennedy, Hamlet, Germany,* the *wolf.* Integrates/heals at 9 disintegrates at 3.

TYPE SEVEN

ADVENTURER, HEDONIST, WORLD TRAVELER,

CHARMER, ENTHUSIAST, GENERALIST,

OPTIMIST, EGO-PLANNING

I am happy.

You could make yourself so happy, that by looking at you other people become happy. —*Yogi Bhajan*

I am the upbeat excessive extrovert, ruled by fear, fun-loving, light-hearted, sometimes irresponsible. In my move away from painful and limiting experiences, I keep options open. I do not like to be pinned down or restrained and feel frustrated when the momentum slows down. Fears are avoided by focusing on the positive, I turn away from my pain as well as that in others; until I make commitments it's difficult to hit a moving target. Buoyant, stimulating and charming, I am not so interested in what meaning or emotions may be connected to experiences. Driven by the need to avoid unhappiness, I am a glutton for more and more fun, sometimes excessive. Good with children, because we are children, I play and am light-hearted at any age. When I know life will be hard, I make light of everything and have more fun escaping my fear by focusing on the positive and looking at all of my choices to stay on the bright side of life. Untroubled, free and easy, devil-may-care, upbeat; I don't want to be brought down. I smile easily, it is permanently there on my face. I could read a dictionary or a phone book and smile. No guilt. I will always up the fun, overdoing.

The world is so full of a number of things, I'm sure we should all be as happy as kings. —*A Child's Garden of Verses*

I try to figure out how to maximize the pleasure and minimize the pain. Once it becomes humdrum and hard daily work, I disengage. Overextending myself, light-hearted in anticipation, looking forward to new plans and opportunities is a high. *Think good thoughts* is my mantra. When something is hard, I imagine a brighter future. Exciting to be with, I see the bright side and am an optimist who brings fresh experiences and endless possibilities to the lives of those around. Eating life without digesting it, the practice of step-by-step eludes me. Rarely setting limits on myself, I put another in the position to frustrate or restrain me, and then get annoyed. I am busy and fast-paced, moving quickly to avoid boredom or pain, liking to live in the fast lane. Learning to take care of my own needs, I find innumerable transitional objects as distractions, filling my life with an array of experiences, learning the hard way to discriminate. Highly productive, easily dissatisfied, self-absorbed, I am good at pumping up energy and drawing attention to myself. Financially exploitative, my big ideas and promises sometimes turn sour and friends are left owed money. I fall in and out of addictions, being pleasure-oriented and an impulsive sensualist, I have to be careful to remember to discipline myself with physical exercise and moderation.

You only live once—but if you work it right, once is enough. —*Joe E. Lewis*

My talking posture is stories, I turn adventures into entertaining tales to sparkle and make people happy. Life is an exciting activity, rarely is there a problem, and if so it surely is not mine, nor will I take yours on. Emotions are self-serving. Does this make me feel good? Life is a delightful playground, each event is here for my pleasure. I appear spontaneous, going with the flow, yet a closer look shows me planning experiences, maneuvering and trying to direct the river. Looking at his life Ram Dass, Enneagram point Seven, remarked that: *I am embarrassed* to admit what drew me to psychology. I didn't want to go to medical school. I was getting good grades in psychology and I was charismatic and people in the psychology department liked me. It was as low a level as that. We miss out on the quality of satisfaction that comes from working hard at something that strengthens character. Entitlement is my own feeling of superiority. I am of the opinion that my way is not only the right way, it is also slightly above all others. I will not be brought down.

I have a lightness of being—I take things in a very happy, amused way. —Julia Roberts

If my situation or relationship does not work out I have at least two or three others up my sleeve. A skillful explainer, I slip out of a relationship or adventure and there is another one waiting in the wings. This is the expression of being on top of it, there is always somewhere to go. I make certain that I won't give up the superior position and be caught. My relationship remains uncommitted. This serves to keep my heart from breaking and manages to keep emotional pain right where I want it, at a distance. Mae West expressed this Seven sentiment when she stated: *When choosing between two evils, I always like to take the one I've never tried before.* Rarely do I let the options close down, otherwise fear emerges. Manic-depressive cycles can overtake me. I do not age well, since choices begin to become limited. To hold myself to one venue creates a dilemma, since I quickly see the other options and opportunities that I have to say no to, so for balance I create short term plans. In my weakness for pleasure, missing out looms large. What didn't I choose and what's out there that I didn't pick; that keeps me busy scheming. My insatiability aims towards variety and surprise. Traveling always holds the promise, *it* might appear in the next destination, and certainly there will be a new experience. I cloak any remote possibility of frustration and dissatisfaction under the disguise of enthusiasm.

Variety is the mother of enjoyment. —*Benjamin Disraelli*

An indulgent trickster, confident escapist swindler, I am a schemer offering dreams as reality. Seeking surprise and variety, my enthusiasm protects me from frustration, dissatisfaction and unpleasant painful experiences. I am the fix-it personality; when put in a position of listening to others, and I rarely volunteer an ear, I pull a solution quickly at hand, or at least a good reason to keep my listening time short. My tolerance for negative or painful emotions is low, mostly I see them as a limitation and waste of time. With a cavalier, devil-may-care imagination, life is the playground buffet and enjoyment is my required ticket. Diplomatic and charming, I seduce with generosity and helpfulness, buying appreciation and good feelings towards me, while under cover I might be exploiting you. People feel good around me, charged up by my lighthearted, lively merrymaking. Persuasive and having lots of new ideas, I engage you into my long range projects, even though there is a thin line between potential, possibilities and realized achievements.

The devil's name is dullness. —*Robert E. Lee*

In the avoidance of pain, I have a hard time seeing the value of holding steady. My mind jumps, I have surface experiences and enjoy interesting distractions. I am fun loving, good-natured, charming, restless, spontaneous, opinionated, self-centered, imaginative and defensive. Too much of a good thing and you probably have a Seven. Not noticing that activity is an escape, or a diversion from my feelings, I continuously am drawn away from intimacy and home base, rationalizing most situations away, mostly envisioning a positive outcome. I find a way to make light of the heavy, since I am resourceful at avoiding what I find boring. Rarely do I get into guilt, I am attracted to depth in other people, yet stay shallow in my own private world. My greed is for a variety of experiences, not wanting to miss anything. My other mantra is: *nothing succeeds like excess, the more the better.*

I have a story, easily rationalizing with my magical thinking statement: *just go with the flow, so let it go,* rarely taking in anything that might cause duress. Having fun, I make a joke and keep my inner world smooth, just to keep moving. I am the playboy/girl of the Enneagram, life is here to enjoy—without obligations, wrongdoing, blame, should, guilt, duties, and rather than fighting or opposing I prefer to be a diplomatic charmer. Sevens and Threes stay on the surface. We know how to cut corners and make our money work. Great at creating businesses, not so great at the follow through which requires routine daily management. I lose interest as the project comes to its completion. I feel trapped, unless I can open it up again and be playful. We are the big deceivers, the con men, if I am not tricking you then I am surely tricking myself. Originally the attention is strong and focused, whether on a person or project, I begin full and powerful. Planning is a mental preoccupation and its activity keeps my anxiety quite minimized. At certain times I get mixed up between my potential and the actual realizations.

The wandering mind is always rushing about in empty effort among the deceptive delights of the world. —*Bernard of Clarvaux*

Even when problems arise, I rarely address them—you won't find me sitting in the therapists office. If the going gets tough I can make believe everything is fine. When I get involved with a spiritual community it's often to gather more experiences, I don't want to miss out. The idea can easily replace the actual activity. A day might include yoga, spa, flea market to buy fruit, meeting with investors to show drawings of my building project, rushing to an office for a conference call to present bankers with a new idea, hiking, going to a movie or rehearsal, and then finding an interesting party to hang out and maybe meet a date for the evening. That, to me, is a growthful, intimate day. *Don't Fence Me In* is a good Seven song. It's easier for me to be enlightened in theory, since I appear to be awakened, and the world enjoys my magical charm. Photographer Edward Steichen caught the quality of the Seven when he said: *My only advise is this, we don't know where we are going, but we shall give life all the gas we've got.*

On the Enneagram, point Seven attracts new experiences along with a map and definition of how to create completion. This is the third and last section of the Enneagram, that of future thinkers and planners, where life will become better and better. Point Seven is about experiencing loss and liberation and within this is the foundation and dawning of happiness. It is not enough to have experiences, since it is in the surrender; the letting go of them is where true freedom is found. This is the world of possibilities and the kindness that is generated is one we then offer to all humanity.

Happiness is not a destination. It is a method of life. —Burton Hills

TRANSFORMATION: HEALING

Follow your bliss. People say that we're seeking a meaning for life. No. What we are seeking is an experience of being alive, so that we actually feel the rapture of being alive. —Joseph Campbell

To feel the Seven needs to stop, limit experiences and options, and go within to find the bliss inside, rather than running after it outside. The willingness and ability to shift inward, to leave the thrills of the outside world even though there's still fun and interest, then an inner spaciousness opens up for them to deepen and to live from that place. An evolved Seven can allow a routine of consistent relationships, go deeply, having quality rather than quantity, postpone pleasure, slow the daily pace, now having a greater range of emotional life which means including pain. Do they want fun or freedom? Are they willing to give up mind racing plans and ideas? To acknowledge and look at the fear, is the first step. The transformational shift is from gluttony of experiences to sobriety and focus/self-restraint, from pleasure and avoidance of pain to authentic and depthful work, from restlessness and superficiality to grounding and healing, to become discriminating so depth and quality instead of quantity become the flavor of new experiences and quiets agitation to bring about a soothing calmness. Carefully completing tasks, developing self-control and self-restraint, a genuine follow through, paying attention to the details; all open a door to wisdom and depth for the Seven. Slowing down and honoring a commitment to one job, partner, home, to being attentive allows for self-development. Taking life seriously, living focused in the present rather than in the plans, increases self-understanding and develops purpose. Happiness will find you once facing the pain that self-honesty brings. Personal depth increases, once learning how to face painful issues—happiness is hidden deep inside. An evolved Seven will focus on a place of true inner bliss offering their life as a reminder that the true spirit of joy is in the service to the universe, to humanity. These are the people, when transformed, remind us that life is a gift to be lived, as simple events appear in this bountiful playground called life.

To be able to be unhurried when hurried; to be able not to slack off when relaxed; to be able not to be frightened and at a loss for what to do, when frightened and at a loss; this is the learning that returns us to our natural state and transforms our lives. —Liu Wenmin

The Seven awakens from a heightened sense of awareness, named attention. Resisting the wandering fluttering of attention, the roaming mind, dropping into focused attention, what Zen practitioners call beginners mind, the Seven becomes still and finds satisfaction. This is empty mind, free of the habits of the expert, who clearly sees things as they are. Looking with full attention, each moment is a first time. *In the beginner's mind there are many possibilities, but in the expert's there are few,* said Shunryu Suzuki. Often the Seven begins with a practice offering compassionate attention to others and experiences, having been so habituated to a noisy mind. Unconditioned attention is unconditional love, is showing up, to be present to each moment, to exist, and not one thought has to go into that. To live from the silent witness, attention is clear. The intellect is a tool; when the Seven understands that thinking that there is somewhere to go other than the present, and that there is something to do other than to be present to their own life; that quality of attention is the awakening. When the ongoing projects, planning and chatter stop, for the Seven to return to the wonder and joy that originally filled them as a child, they live out of truth and now present that beauty to the world.

The essence of boredom is to be found in the obsessive search for novelty. Satisfaction lies in mindful repetition, the discovery of endless richness in subtle variations on familiar themes. —George Leonard

Some known Sevens include: *Ram Dass, Miley Cyrus, Timothy Leary, Jim Carrey, Steve Allen, Julia Roberts, Tom Cruise, Amy Schumer, Andy Sanberg, Tina Fey, Jerry Seinfeld, Robert Bly, Goldie Hawn, Lama Surya Das, Chris Griscom, Katie Couric, Tom Wolfe, Larry King, Lucille Ball, Victor Borge, Sid Caeser, Louise Hay, Bobby McFerrin, Jack Nicholson, Carol Burnett, Little Richard, Eddie Murphy, Martin Short, Jerry Rubin,*

Chevy Chase, Rod Stewart, Jerry Garcia, Cary Grant, Peter Pan, Walt Disney, David Niven, Groucho Marx, Robert Benigni, Eddie Murphy, Regis Philbin, George Plimpton, Magic Johnson, Jack Benny, Richard Branson, Reshad Feild, Joseph Campbell, Bernie Siegel, Dr. A.J. Farschian, Don King, Osho Bhagwan Rajneesh, Prince Harry of Wales, Danny Kaye, Robin Williams, Barack Obama, Brazil, Sedona. Integrates/heals at 5 disintegrates at 1.

TYPE EIGHT

BOSS, CONFRONTER, POWERFUL PERSON,

MAFIA GOD-FATHER, FIGHTER, BULLY,

CHALLENGER, PROTECTOR, EGO-REVENGE

I am strong

Life is like a dogsled team, if you ain't the lead dog, the scenery never changes.
—*Lewis Grizzard*

Confident and strong-willed, I strengthen and empower others. I am supportive to friends, enjoy a challenge and a good time. Intensity, stimulation, taking control, the desire to be right overpowers me. In a relationship I am forceful, strong-willed, overly attentive, protective, straightforward, loyal, possessive and consuming, focused on maximizing my power, rarely paying attention to my softer feelings. Filling a room with a confident presence, I have selective memory, using denial as my priority defense. Insight is low, as is my ability and regard for introspection.

Pay attention to your enemies, for they are the first to discover your mistakes.
—*Antisthenes*

Similar to the Three I am under-represented in growth classes, mainly due to my lack of interest as well as not liking to sit with others who teach. I am the boss, uncompromising in my position. Before trusting, I accuse, belittle your credentials, assassinate your character, until you are unseated or prove yourself a worthy adversary. The tough fighter who holds my ground, I am eager to win and also want you to be a worthy opponent who believes in your own position. Once you are my ally, you are in, forever protected. Betrayal is dramatized, once loyalty is established I still take precautions that you won't let me down. The focus is clearly that others do not have power or control over me. Independent, I fear being disempowered, and avoid vulnerability. I have inflexible determination, meeting life head on.

What I wanted to be when I grew up was—in charge.
—*Brigadier General Wilma Vaught*

Sometimes I am drawn to be bad, or against, using foul language, feeling no shame or desire to back off. Inside is a little girl or boy, yet I rarely show it. Often my real needs are not met, simply because I don't know them. I appreciate family life and can be surprisingly attentive in my home to all household members. Allowing comfort and support is difficult. Anger is easy to access, it often covers my softness. I like to even the score, and mete out justice with revenge. Once I catch you doing something wrong I hold you accountable and tell you, all in the name of justice. Moderation is low on my list. I am larger than life, big energy, no middle of the road lukewarm backing off for me. Living intensely, with enthusiasm; action suits me better than thinking things through. I can handle whatever comes my way, enjoying feeling and looking competent and being in the dominant position, seeing myself as street-wise. Blaming lays the groundwork for the need to punish, prevail over others, and in my personal view this is considered retribution. I reprimand and feel justified to enforce my authority.

The art of living is more like wrestling than dancing. Stand firm and be ready for an unforeseen attack. —Marcus Aurelius

While my partner feels protected and taken care of, I am also regarded as overbearing, possessive and demanding. As long as you don't withhold or hide information; like a bull I see a red flag and imagine betrayal, escalating a small matter into a major event. Life with me is no easy journey. I look to take charge of your life sometimes even more than dealing with my own. You will be protected, but unless I feel secure my blunt emotional stance will ebb and flow sometimes like a hurricane season. I excuse my behavior because if I were consulted for everything then I would make good decisions for our life. Just remember to keep me informed. Overdoing, it helps to have someone oversee and modify my words and actions. I don't realize how my anger and energy affects others. Often a loner as well as a good friend, don't forget to keep me in the loop.

Never go to bed mad—stay up and fight! —Anonymous Eight

I am generous with my thoughts and time. Independence is prime, I am supportive and determined, but don't try to control me. I become punitive when I feel I am being taken advantage of, compromise is not in my vocabulary. You get what you see, no big hidden story here. Contact for me can be many things; a fight or disagreement, sex, a motorcycle ride or other action adventure, conversation or bullying. Self-expression is important, I see myself as a free agent and turn to myself when the going gets tough. I know what I want and often act oblivious to any one else having thoughts. Energy gets stirred up and I am most comfortable with that; overwhelming the home front, action might disrupt the status quo, rarely is there boredom living around me. I make the home rules and am the first to break them.

Never settle with words what you can accomplish with a flame-thrower.
—*Bruce Feirstein*

My talking style is laying a trip. I like telling others where and how they are off-track, although I am strongly resistant to having any flaws pointed out or being considered wrong. Blunt, sarcastic and hostile, sometimes humiliating and frustrating others becomes part of my repertoire. The rhinoceros, thick-skinned and charging is an Eight type animal. My denial is my way of self-forgetting. It is useful to set up ground rules with me, this helps generate trust. Once trust is established I am reliably loyal and will use my confidence to influence, contribute, and build up others. In stress, I move to Five and withdraw. This extreme contraction unnerves me. I may become secretive and reclusive, isolate myself, retreating from the world, sometimes turning the aggression towards myself. On the other hand, when I move to Two, which is healing, I become tender, enabling or engulfing, opening myself to others, rather than governing them, unguarded, touched, I see the needs and the beauty of love rather than the beauty of power. Enneagram point Eight Tallulah Bankhead said: *I'd rather be strongly wrong than weakly right,* and point Eight Frank Sinatra sang an Eight theme song, *My Way.* Fritz Perls, in his effort to prevail over all circumstances, fatally ill was told to use a bedpan, and still, somehow, managed to crawl out of bed. His last words on his way to the bathroom were: *No one tells me what to do.*

It's hard to be humble, when you're as great as I am. —*Muhammad Ali*

Resourceful, self reliant, high energy; spiritual leaders and wisdom teachers making a real impact on the world are most often Eights. Inspiring, magnanimous, passion-driven, strong minded; people easily turn to me for leadership. We are a tremendous force for change and good. The toughness, as I ward off tender feelings, distancing myself from softer feelings, creates a brusque quality that is not the image of femininity. Society does not support the strength of Eight women. Decisiveness, self confidence, letting others know where I stand, fearlessness and leadership are considered masculine traits. Abusing my body, believing that the neediness and dependency I felt as a child was a natural experience for children—I have looked at that as something that was wrong with me and I hesitate to open myself to those qualities that now keep me apart and separate and lacking feminine softness. Since I do not fit the picture of the feminine type, out in the world I try to appear polished.

There's no defense like a good offense. —anonymous Eight

Right is whatever benefits the stronger person said point Eight Machiavelli, a fifteenth century philosopher; and that is a clear expression of how I think. I am generally unaware that the world is not operating along the thought form *might makes right.* Most of my interactions feel like an imminent challenge. Pleasure often comes from the struggle topped only by victory. Full steam ahead, I enjoy the intensity that keeps the flatness of daily life at bay. I would not want to live a lackluster, drab, wishy-washy, unexciting life and actually like being an expressive type. Intensity is the constant overstimulation to avoid feeling flat and bored from simple day-to-day living in moderation. My aliveness is experienced through over-stimulation as well as avoiding inwardness, which also reinforces my insensitivity. This shows particularly when I'm blunt, sarcastic, putting others down, intimidating, sometimes feeling pleasure as others feel frustrated or humiliated. When I lose control of the people who have been following my lead and protecting my interests, although it is hard for me to look at this part of my behavior, I strong-arm and punish, being in the driver's seat, ruling the roost; sometimes I play for high stakes. Aggression comes from my need to hold on to power. Retaliatory, justice means vengeance; getting even means I punish the offender. Revolutionaries, we love to take on the big systems.

The Eighth point on the Enneagram symbol completes the cycle around the circle. I now become the leader willing to stand my ground. A new cycle is close, only a short step away. Competent, strong, self-confident and able to act with assurance, I am the all-or-nothing boss and leader. Immersed in my pursuit for truth, the destination becomes passionately lived. This is the single-focused position, devoted, fully engaged in serving the task at hand. Having circled the device called the Enneagram the eighth point ends the existing cycle. The challenge at this point on the circle is to incorporate sensitivity and empathy for other types, and to go beyond my own type.

Bitterness is like cancer. It eats upon the host. But anger is like fire. It burns it all clean. —*Maya Angelou*

TRANSFORMATION: HEALING

He who conquers others is strong: He who conquers himself is mighty. —*Tao Te Ching*

Evolved Eights have empathy, moral courage and are willing to be tender and view vulnerability as strength. They genuinely protect and serve others out of generosity, compassion, and regard for the greater good. It takes courage on their part to be willing to not be right, regardless to whether they are, simply because it does not matter. Justice can be a veil that covers truth. The transformational shift is from lust

to innocence, turning away from excessiveness, intensity and demandingness, and turning towards satisfaction with everything just the way
it is. Sexual pleasure now includes a relationship where the Eight is
vulnerable, shows their weakness and receives love. Unguarded they
manifest an innocence of perception that allows vulnerability and kindness, gentleness and generosity. The healing lies in moderating strong
opinions and passionate lust, making time to go inward, connecting
their hearts to others. In this manner they open and expand from the
small personal playing field of blunt truth, to a universal language that
speaks to all people.

It is your work in life that is the ultimate seduction. —*Pablo Picasso*

An insensitive type on the Enneagram, once the disdain for others
weakness is released, as well as the perpetual blaming of people and
the world for everything they don't agree with, allowing vulnerability,
concern for the welfare of others, humility and love to emerge, this is
the real hero, which is true power. The second shift is from vindication,
or getting even, to true justice or truth, which is an acceptance that
the universe itself takes care of righting things. They like honesty and
have the strength to enforce what is fair and just. Moving from a small
personal sense of truth that has been used to bully and dominate and
coming to live in the truth of life, the Eight softens in the variation of
the landscape, surrendering control. This will appear as they back off
from dominating center stage and now demonstrate public tenderness.
Eights become heroes, heroines, and respected teachers, who offer great
opportunities for others to connect to their own personal self. They nurture with the same energy and passion that was used to attack, finding
kindness that now needs no recognition. Overcoming willfulness, they
develop true will. This is a powerful type, when evolved and connected

to their essential nature they embody the heroic.

We either make ourselves miserable, or we make ourselves strong. The amount of work is the same. —Carlos Casteneda

Awakening through dedication in service, the Eight gives up their willfulness, expresses vulnerability, relinquishing their *it's me against the world attitude.* Laying down the sword, and placing their attention inward, being in charge of their impulsivity, opening their heart, compassion shines through the largeness of their generous spirit. Their awakening as dedication through service to others allows them to become vessels for a higher purpose, once connected to their hearts, willing to take a stand for something beyond themselves. A relationship to the world of dedicated love, of love-in-action, impacts the universe through a large vision, in service. The Eight lived as a barrier to their own awakening, once dissolving separation through an inner experience of unity they can establish justice for all, to cherish life through dedication in service. Stepping out of their defensive structure, their fear of being controlled or harmed, surrendered to their vulnerability, to something greater than themselves; understanding that self-realization is the ultimate goal of all action. To serve as a compassionate guide to humankind, to become a vessel for a higher purpose, available to the world, the Eight awakens. This is the bodhisattva, who serves the welfare of all, regardless.

I want to be thoroughly used up when I die, for the harder I work the more I live. Life is a splendid torch which I have got hold of for a moment, and I want to make it burn as brightly as possible before I hand it off to future generations. —George Bernard Shaw

Some known Eights include: *G.I. Gurdjieff, Pablo Picasso, Al Pacino, Fritz Perls, Anthony Quinn, Zorba the Greek, Nikos Kaztanzakis, Ernest*

Hemingway, Roseanne, Ann Richards, George Forman, Jerry Lee Lewis, Mae West, Henry Miller, Norman Mailer, Bette Davis, Gertrude Stein, Frank Sinatra, Robert DeNiro, Nora Ephron, Leona Helmsley, Angela Davis, Charles Bronson, Da Free John, Mike Tyson, H.W.L. Poonja, Mohammed Ali, Hillary Clinton, Don Rickles, Eli Jaxon-Bear, Tallulah Bankhead, Billie Jean King, Madame Helena Blavatsky, Fidel Castro, Evil Knievel, Leah Remini, Gloria Allred, Humphrey Bogart, Johnny Cash, Kirk Douglas, Eldridge Cleaver, Paula Deen, Sadam Hussein, F. Lee Bailey, Moshe Feldenkrais, Chogyam Trungpa, Oskar Schindler, Arnold Schwarzenegger, Sean Penn, Ma Jaya Sati Bhagavati, Nelson Mandela, Apache warrior Geronimo, Archie Bunker, Ike Turner, Jimmy Hoffa, Golda Meir, Katherine Hepburn, Humphrey Bogart, Oprah Winfrey, Bea Arthur, Melissa Etheridge, Marge Schott, Bella Abzug, Henry Miller, Janis Joplin, Ethel Merman, James Brown, Swami Muktananda, Dr. Elisabeth Kübler-Ross, Susan Sarandon, Richard Burton, the *mafia godfather, Mexico, Israel, Palestine.* Integrates/heals at 2 disintegrates at 5.

TYPE NINE

MEDIATOR, PEACEFUL PERSON, CHAMELEON,

MR.–MS. NICE GUY, NOBODY SPECIAL,

FENCE-SITTER, INDOLENT, ACCOMODATOR,

EGO-INDOLENCE

I am pleasant.

I have so much to do that I'm going to bed. —Savoyard *Proverb*

I am the go with the flow type, focused on keeping peace of mind at any price. It may appear surprising that I am the core anger point, you will rarely see me angry. Nice, easy-going, unassuming, comfortable to be with, I appear to fit in with the group. I cover up and control my anger with extreme gentleness. My primary defense strategy is to blend with and accommodate my environment. When asked to do things I almost always say *yes* but can't do all of them, my passive-aggressiveness takes over and projects are left unfinished. Mostly I say no through silence or stubborn slowing down, or circling around an idea; but watch out because snide nastiness might jump out at you if I am pushed too far. I am the sell out person, often out of touch with my higher values, eager to maintain my inner balance regardless of the bombs bursting in air. Needing to avoid, I roll with the punches, and glaze over. I even avoid my own focus and point of view. Falling asleep to my own needs, my energy is often not felt so you might not notice or remember me. My thoughts are simple. I am unassuming. What you see is what you get, there is no underneath complexity.

I'm a really nice guy when you meet me. I like to just chill out with friends and not get in people's faces. —KSI Olatunji

In childhood I disassociated from commotion for self-protection and was low maintenance. Now, in the present moment, I still ask for little, and hope you will ask very little in return. Most things are not worth arguing about, therefore I am able to maintain the illusion of peace. Generally unaware of myself, instead concentrating on many others, I am supportive to those in my world. To stay this way I resist everything that offers awareness of my inner rage, anxiety, frustration and disappointment. I admit, though, that sometimes anxiety creeps in. My response time lags and I am as far from authentic inner peace as is possible. Real peace expresses itself in vitality, aliveness, enthusiasm, exquisite self-awareness; not numbness, detachment, resignation, withdrawal, daydreaming, passivity, disengagement, or loss of vitality.

The lust for comfort, that stealthy thing that enters the house as a guest, and then becomes a host, and then a master. —*Kahlil Gibran*

If you look around my home or office you will probably spot the almost finished obsessive-compulsive piles. Things are saved, garage is full, the attic serves to store items that one day may be needed. Habits and routines help me to stay comfortable, fall asleep and stay asleep. The trance deepens as I eat the same cereal every morning for 15 years. Comfortable means falling asleep on a pile of fireworks. To keep all conflict away, I do not take a point of view. To make a decision takes tremendous effort. I keep myself away from real goals, being ambivalent about them, replacing important agendas with incidental tasks. What kind of work do I want to do? How can I make money? These are two often repeated Nine questions, and often the answers spin and whirl and create anxiety for myself and for others. Working hard, but off track— the Three is right on track, the Nine is way off track. I live between the Three—the performer/image, and the Six—the doubter /in lack of certainty. I live in the quest of right action.

I always procrastinate when I get around to it. —*Nine theme*

Even under pressure from friends and family to *make something of myself,* I still find it difficult to take initiative and become self-reli-ant. One inconsequential moment can cause that major eruption, not towards the person who created the error, that would be too threat-ening. Often accidents appear, it's safer to hurt myself than face the anger directly with the person violating me. I might bump my knee, break a glass, cut myself opening the mail that my partner wouldn't open. Injuries are a safe way to express anger, self-inflicted hurts are the step before taking the gun into the school yard and letting loose. I find myself running a conversation in my head about what I would say to someone and answering the other side, and on and on. I will stew and project and then act fine. The internal questioning continues, eventually creating a holding pattern.

The fine art of executive decision consists in not deciding questions that are not now pertinent, in not deciding prematurely, in not making decisions that cannot be made effective, and in not making decisions that others should make. —Chester I. Barnard

Decisions happen by default. Distractions create a large portion of the day, options are so plentiful it becomes hard to follow the thread of the essential. I finally just get caught in other peoples emotions and agendas throughout the day. Blending, scanning for points of agreement, concealing discomfort; what you don't feel around me is a true presence. Often I engage in time consuming interests like reading, gardening, cooking, E-mail, following a favorite TV show, small errands for others, yoga, sitting around; all to keep the primary agenda from getting accomplished. Spaced out for myself, I see what others are doing, but fog in to my own plan. Indolence and laziness are not my fear of hard work, they are my detached avoidance to create meaning to my life. Lazy for me is accepting what comes my way, settling, entrenched, resigned to not make waves. My strategy is similar to that of an ostrich, not wanting to see, maybe it's not there—not the outer world, not my inner world, not even an intellectual world. I just simplify my thinking into a concrete literal zone; all of this supports the purpose of dulling out. This avoidance keeps me from the intimate realm in relationships. People feel my lack of charge or life-force. Passive, I often appear content and satisified, until I become irritable, especially if I feel pushed out of compliance and my appearance of tranquility.

I have left orders to be awakened at any time in case of a national emergency—even if I'm in a cabinet meeting. —Ronald Reagan

I might have energy in a group, but sitting alone, away from team energy, I pass out, or repeat a familiar routine rather than initiate a new process. Easily merging with another and their agenda, time gets filled with interesting chores, yet the essential aim is put aside. Focusing on irrelevant details I under-perform, minimizing the importance of a task at hand. Looking involved, it still may not be my own aim. Apparently I need assistance, because doubts arise as soon as I am involved in my own projects. It is a tremendous risk to stand alone and have a life with my priorities. Now the belief becomes: *no one will care about my interests and I will forever be left alone.* Adapting to everyone's needs, diplomatic, compliant to other's demands, taking care of everyone before myself; rather than deal with the pain and anger about that, I live in self-forgetfulness. To identify a Nine, look for what's missing—the absence of something—whether it's a position or a definite proclaimed stance —that would make my presence known. The more I erase, eliminate myself from my own life, the greater is the sensation that nothing really matters.

I can't figure out why to pay attention to myself. —9 comment

Accommodating, the saying *peace at any price* must have been said by a Nine. It's easier to go along with and accommodate people than to oppose them. I prefer that nothing interferes with my calm and ignore things that carry the potential to disrupt comfort and tranquility. People take my easy going nature for granted, not knowing how hard I try to go along with others wishes, or seeing my resignation they disregard the high price I pay for comfort. Often I ask questions about how you are doing, and keep myself distant. The question is: *whose agenda am I following, my own or someone else's?* Merging, I don't distinguish whose wishes I have incorporated. I basically play dead to remain alive. Initiating an action, changing a habit; I prefer to maintain a holding pattern, to postpone, repeat, generally unsure as to what's really that important. Self-observation diminishes, I forget myself and become filled with other peoples agenda, other peoples stories and lives. The strategy for a Nine is *not wanting to see,* and to live in this context I have to simplify as well as limit any personal psychological insight, and remain concrete and literal. Few can imagine my loss of inwardness, since I appear so available for others, so content and peaceful, and neither are they participating in my hours of numbness and narcotizing. Having fallen asleep to my own yearnings, passion and desires, I have just forgotten.

Spending time with a Nine is calming and reassuring, we make less than few demands, allow others to take the lead, are overly adaptable and unassuming. On the other hand, the forgetfulness, the self-neglect, lack of assertion and spacey passive-aggressiveness follows a withdrawn pattern. We are hidden, secretive, anxious, spaced-out, unexpressed and don't see ourselves as making an impact on the world. Nor are we driven to be stage center famous. We seek more self-protection than is realistic, are easy-going, good natured, yet impersonal. Knowing what I don't want, yet ambivalent about my position for my personal life, for my work and whether it's important to create change in the present moment, I need to recognize my own value. I like the predictable because it serves to offer me inner space free from anxiety and pressure, further away from any surge of energy that might imbalance or awaken me out of my comfort and sleep. When I feel pushed my loud stubborn silence is deafening. This is my way of expressing anger: nothing—no comment, no action, no words, no withdrawal. Hopefully you will feel foolish, frustrated, insulted, ignored, offended, and I will say: *but, I haven't done anything, I haven't said anything, what's the offense?*

There is a wide range of meandering in conversation, the talking posture being a saga. Long round about explanations keep me comfortably distanced from peoples insistence and aggression. Group memberships are made up of Nines, we can't leave, have difficulty discriminating, are resigned creatures of habit, so we stay in the Chamber of Commerce, the Toastmasters, the job and school committees, and the Ashram. I can be angry and driven when I go out for a cause. Vicariously living through others, I take on the groups qualities. My conservative inclination protects me from experiencing unexpected open mysteries of life. What is missing is the observer, that inner witnessing critical for deep spiritual transformation. My top feeling is sadness, under that, fear, and under that is rage, mixed in with anxiety if I allow it to surface; to experience all of them is freeing. It is the willingness to be uncomfortable and face emotions that releases my years of sleep-walking.

I bear the wounds of all the battles I avoided. —*Fernando Pessoa*

In a friendship or partnership I appear agreeable, yet one can never be sure if this is what I really want to do. I defer, and say *I don't care what store, movie, restaurant we go to.* I have spent years looking at choices and positions trying to discover priorities and be available to myself. This point possibly takes the longest on the journey of awakening, yet once on course I am steadfast. Most people cannot believe that I really don't know my position, since I appear productive, yet inside there is still that question, what do I want? The learning doesn't come through my mind, because doubt or opposition stop the change. I learn through outside support to enter into experiences, rather than drifting and going with the flow, or going inside to find my passion and be devoted to that. Looking within there is a scarcity of my own inner experiences, instead, I first find everyone else's agendas, then I find tremendous anger. I have deadened myself to my own inner voice and imagination. Having over-adapted, under-performed, over-controlled and denied myself, now winter has ended, and the bear is ready to leave the den hideout. What a roar, for how many years have I neglected myself, been lethargic and distracted! Kindness towards myself, looking inward, space opens and my determination releases my habitual move towards ease and comfort.

Don't just fit in; make it a point to brighten your corner. Decide to resolve your challenges. —Israelmore Ayivor

The final type and the third shock point of the Enneagram is the transition, the return point. Nine is at the apex of the triangle, a reminder that all endings also represent beginnings. Knowing that a line of time is a curve that *the path up and down is one and the same, identical the beginning and the end.* Life, not in a state of rest, always moving, helps me visualize the Enneagram as a moving rotational spiral. It is important in understanding this point to fully grasp the dynamic of the whole Enneagram. This is birth at nine months, either to move onward or to remain stagnant. This is our legacy and inheritance; what preceded is brought to me, and effects and imprints my present day life. We are not responsible for the past, but we are responsible to restore and renew what can be changed. It is the connection between what appears transitory and what appears eternal. As a transition point to a new process the option to uplift, to begin again in a new and creative way is always waiting. The door to a new possibility of consciousness opens.

Point Nine stands at the threshold. Laziness, resistance and lack of motivation are in the balance, carrying weight in the decision between starting anew or remaining passive and idle. On the held back side, my avoidance to psychological exploration, my impoverished inwardness keep me holding tightly to stability. Resistant to sacrificing the seemingly harmonious known for what could bring conflict and an interruption to tranquility, I hesitate, resist change, refuse to see. Will I enter the sacred journey, the labyrinth which expands the vision of what is possible, stretching, taking courageous challenges and step into a new cycle to go forward? The path around the Enneagram has me shift direction and awareness, discovering and integrating within this powerful design. It is a metaphor for the journey of life; transformation, with the goal of being where you are meant to be.

The end of all our exploring will be to arrive where we started and know the place for the first time. —T.S. Eliot

Transformation: Healing

Setting our intentions outside of time, beyond mind, beyond the world of comparison, we begin on what is called the way. Intention is the bridge between the two worlds, illusion and the real world. —Reshad Feild

This is the Enneagram point that needs support, not opposition. The Nine must find family and friends that unconditionally support as well as prod, yet not oppose them. Only from a position of self-acceptance and self-love can the Nine evolve. Then it no longer matters if others agree or oppose. Right action emerges from an awareness of what is meaningful in life and the inner connection to an integrity that stands behind and for one's truth. To have a deep-seated sense of their own identity is essential for a Nine. They can easily be like every other type on the Enneagram, except the Nine. *Don't rock the boat,* the refusal to see and to resist change is sustained by a joylessness, a sadness, an emotional context that avoids deep probing. The transformational shift, rocking the boat, moves from indolence and resignation towards intentional action, love and aliveness. Once finding their own position, the Nine becomes a leader of great stance; not for self-importance or image or to promote themselves.

A ship is safe in harbor, but that's not what ships are for. —*William G. T. Shedd*

Over-adapting to the world, living vicariously, supports their need to space out, often acted out with drinking, smoking dope, fading out watching TV or exercising, having a secret life, overeating, until lapsing into forgetfulness. The Nine makes molehills out of mountains, abandoning themselves to avoid conflict. Shifting out of addictive behavior, focused and on track, the Nine needs to participate and engage their energy through addressing issues. They must be willing to allow themselves to be affected, rather than left undisturbed, turning on their stalled motor and joining the human race, rather than blaming the world for trying to prod them alive. For the Nine to no longer fall asleep to their own yearning, to find their own dreams, rather than living vicariously through others joyful moments, to connect first to their own high priorities is their direction of growth and self-development. Standing for what is true, intentional action, speaking up and out for what is noble and dignified, taking a risk, not silently allowing others to engage while they remain on the sidelines, feeling their own conviction enlivens and integrates them. The healing comes with the acknowledgement that they matter, that their presence and participation can change the world.

Most people think of peace as a state of Nothing Bad Happening, or Nothing Much Happening. Yet if peace is to overtake us and make us the gift of serenity and well-being, it will have to be the state of Something Good Happening. —*E. B. White*

The absence of passion and fire, ignited and substituted and confused with excessive eating, drinking and drug taking can be shifted to become that which constitutes true aliveness. This is the person who through years of adaptation to the world and yielding to the demands of others covers their pain of lack of recognition by self-forgetting. The Nine misunderstands their transitional passage for a resting place. This shift and switching station serves as a lifting off point to a whole new level or octave of consciousness. Not a time to rest, instead this becomes the moment to look at ourself and life with a new level of consciousness that arrives through the long journey from point One to point Eight. This is the elephant and dolphin, peaceful and easy-going. Finally learning the difference between laziness and peace, to live with risk, the Nine moves on to a higher level.

Forgetfulness is the darkness, mindfulness is the light. —*Thich Nhat Hanh*

Anger as body energy can be engaged and used to accomplish growthful goals. Moving anger from the gut upward will activate them. Peaceful, not compromised, they now have the opportunity to become deliberate and independent. At one with yourself and the world dignity is effortless. The Nine is the one type that thrives and activates with positive regard and constant love. They need to know that even if they oppose they will still be accepted. For the Nine to awaken they first must embrace life in its fullness, and really inhabit themselves, only then can they be the true bearer of peace, harmony and unity for the world.

The art of leisure lies, to me, in the power of absorbing without effort the spirit of one's surroundings; to look, without speculation, at the sky and sea;

to become part of a green plain; to rejoice, with a tranquil mind, in the feast of colour in a bed of flowers. —*Dion Calthrop*

To bring forth the enlivened vitality needed to penetrate, the dullness of a Nine becomes a real presence. The quality of awareness brought to each moment connects the Nine to a stream of aliveness. This experience of their true nature and the ability to continue in this manner quiets the inner restlessness. To be attentive while in motion, to bring the attention back to self rather then let it wander, to remain intentional, attentive while inactive as well as active, shifts the numbness, activates the aliveness. Otherwise, they are able to move along, accomplish a lot, function well in routines without ever showing up and being present. Intentional right action, taking charge of their life, forging ahead, allowing visibility by stating through action: I am here, the Nine anchors peacefully, gently, those who appreciate their kind nature.

To understand Presence, one must make the effort to be Present. —*Robert Earl Burton*

The Sioux Indian phrase: *with all beings and all things we shall be as relatives,* captures the Nine's essence that experiences the knowing that all things are of the same nature. To look at the tree is to see the sun and the clouds, is to see that nothing exists separately. This quality of oneness, the nature of the Nine, when awakened, restores wholeness and connects the Nine to the nature of awakening that is within them. Realizing one's true nature liberates. The intention towards awakening for the Nine is the way to awakening. All that stands in the way for the Nine is their forgetfulness. Opening to the deepest meaning in their life, holding sustained intention, remembering that impulse to create the intention; trained intentions transmit into every action. Mindfulness, mindful awareness releases the numbness, overcomes the isolation; the bell of mindfulness allows the Nine to touch the deep presence inside themselves. For the Nine to keep their intention each step of the way, regardless of discomfort, to break the trance, is to open and look into the face of the mystery and remember to be happy and to love.

Those who are awake live in a state of constant amazement. This most subtle awakening comes about through moment-to-moment intention.
—the Buddha

Self-realization is only the realization of one's true nature. The seeker of liberation realizes, without doubts or misconceptions, his real nature by distinguishing the eternal from the transient, and never swerves from his natural state. —Ramana Maharshi

Some known Nines include: *Julia Child, Tom Hanks, Alfred Hitchcock, Ed McMann, Al Gore, Bruce Kaitlyn Jenner, John Kerry, Brad Pitt, Gerald Ford, Albert Einstein, Tony Bennett, Karl Malden, The Dalai Lama, Walter Matthau, Buckminster Fuller, Carl Jung, Carl Rogers, Thich Nhat Hanh, Dean Martin, George Burns, Art Carney, Hubert Humphrey, Dwight D. Eisenhower, Milton Erickson, Ramana Maharishi, Ezra Pound, Mel Torme, Carl Rogers, Gracie Allen, Walter Cronkite, Connie Chung, Johnny Mathis, Tipper Gore, Andy Williams, Martin Sheen, Eva Marie Saint, Nat King Cole, Warren Christopher, Perry Como, Dean Martin, Renee Zelleweger, Dan Quayle, Ronald Reagan, Edith Bunker, Mr. Magoo, Abraham Lincoln, Austria, India, Russia.* Integrates/heals at 3 disintegrates at 6.

Sy s t e m   Tw o

ROLE

Se r v e r ,   Ar t i s a n ,   Wa r r i o r ,
Sc h o l a r ,   Sa g e ,   Pr i e s t ,   Ki n g

Everything announces your own true nature. Everything speaks to you and reflects back to you what you are, the Essence itself. Whether you call it life, Buddha nature, spirit or God—everything reflects that back to you when you can see it. —Adyashanti

All people have one primary and one secondary of seven essence energies, personality types or Roles. We are born with this way of being in the world. Each of the seven Roles sees and experiences the world through the lens of their particular Role. Our Role is our nature and remains constant in all lifetimes, is developed and deepened throughout each lifetime, and is a comfort not a confinement, since it remains enduring and dependable. This is how we are and have been, our underlying personality archetype. The more we understand our Role, the more self-acceptance and greater range to see others in their Role. Studying and understanding each Role creates variety in our life. Knowing only yellow, one day learning about green, then blue, now red, brings richness and contrast to the world we live in. The secondary Role, since we all have a primary and secondary Role, flavours, colors, and sets a tone. What follows is a study of the design of the seven primary Roles.

We have to dare to be ourselves, however frightening or strange that self may prove to be. —May Sarton

ROLE	THEME	ENERGY	FLAVOR	POSITIVE	NEGATIVE
1. Server	service	ordinal	inspiration	nurturance	bondage
2. Artisan	creation	ordinal	expressive	imaginative	self-deceptive
3. Warrior	persuasion	ordinal	action	focused	aggressive
4. Scholar	knowledge inquiry	neutral	assimilative	comprehensive	hypothesizing
5. Sage	expression	exalted	expressive	entertaining	loud
6. Priest	compassion	exalted	inspiration	uplifting	proselytizing
7. King	mastery	exalted	action	commanding	tyrannical

Chart 3: Roles

THE SEVEN ROLES AS UNIVERSAL ARCHETYPES

The Role we are, the template for how we see the world, regardless to our experiences, determines the predominant way that we show up in the choices we make. They are a description of human behavior that bring insightful teachings to those who are walking a path of self-discovery and self-knowledge. The Roles are universal archetypes. This system has no hierarchy, it is describing, offering a key and map; to know our human nature. Each Role has a positive and a negative expression. In the negative, we are in false personality and distortion, the positive is true personality. The positive has a significant connection to the negative, for example, the Scholar gathers knowledge in the positive, but distorts the information to make up a theory in the negative. The Artisan is creative in the positive, yet in the negative convincingly creates a reality that is wishful thinking or a personal invented fantasy. The Role is the vehicle we have for us to express who we are. It is our style and determines how we do what we choose, not necessarily what we choose, it is not a vocation, it is a style, a manner of being that we embody.

I'm not playing a role. I'm being myself, whatever the hell that is.
—*Bea Arthur*

The Roles have particular ways of perceiving, comprehending the world, and are divided into three types of energy; ordinal, exalted, and neutral. The ordinal Roles: Server, Artisan, Warrior, enter the world in a narrow, focused, relating one-to-one way, taking care of what is practical and immediate. Less comfortable with large groups, their energy is primarily affected and ordered by what's directly in their life, their personal relationships. The exalted Roles: Priest, Sage, King, energetically appear wide and full and tend to have a stronger affect on others. They like to deal with groups, are less likely to work for someone, and tend to work for big causes like teaching, healing, preaching, influencing many. These are the big picture people, offering leadership and standing out. The one neutral Role is the Scholar. They interact with all types assisting the Roles to understand each other and are able to offer uncommitted neutral information. Vocations are not necessarily predicted by a person's Role, a Warrior may be an musician, police officer or painter, a King may be a performer, politician, or business person, while a Server can be a world leader or a veterinarian.

All the world's a stage, And all the men and women merely players; They have their exits and their entrances. —*William Shakespeare*

The Roles have four different properties or flavors; expressive, inspiration, action and assimilation. The expressive Roles—Artisan and Sage—live their lives through expression, not through doing. They set a tone, mood, and atmosphere, setting the stage for bringing beauty and drama into people's lives. The inspirational Roles—Servers and Priests—experience their essence inspired through life, as they nurture and motivate, encourage and look after. Concerned with serving and supporting people and the environment, other's well-being is their focus. The action Roles—Warrior and King—are energetic, productive, effective, accomplishing and manifesting on the physical plane. Getting things done is a comfortable place for them to live; these are spirited enterprising people. The neutral or assimilative Role is the Scholar who experiences life absorbing, inquiring, retaining, gathering and digesting information.

A lamp cannot play the role of the Sun and the Sun cannot play the role of a lamp. —Amit Kalantri

Ordinal Roles are needed in greater proportion on the planet and therefore noticeably outnumber exalted Roles. The earth's population is mostly comprised of ordinal energy; Server, Artisan, Warrior; practical and more pulled back. Servers make up 28% of the world population, Warriors 25%, Artisans 24%, Scholars 12%, Sages 7%, Priests 3%, Kings 1%.

The essence of each Role carries a vibrational frequency, this vibrational rate accounts for the differences between each Role. *Frequency is the specific rate of vibration that characterizes your essence, and manifests through the body as well as personality.* Like the natural color of water taking on the hues of sun, sky and earth, like the color white before passing through a prism and refracting into seven frequencies, each Role appears to be separate, yet are actually fragments of a whole. This is true in the Enneagram of Personality, the Enneagram of Body Type, and the Role (refer to System One, Two and Five).

Life is for a specific mission. Find your role and fulfill it. —Lailah Gifty Akita

Relationships are easier when the numbers add under 11, like a Server 1 and a King 7 = 8. Numbers over 11 add intensity, like two

Kings 7 + 7. Lower numbers tend to manifest their role earlier than higher numbers. The high frequency Roles—Priests and Artisans, are more fluid and are visionaries, like Don Quixote, wishful, yet impractical, less comfortable in their body they have easier access to out-of-body experiences. Mid-range frequency are the Servers and Sages. Low-frequency solid Roles—Kings, Warriors and Scholars—live more grounded, in a one-day-at-a time mode. One's range can vary, as well as shift throughout this life.

Try to hear the frequency or vibration of each Role, see each one as true essence, the better we know our Role, just as a seasoned actor/actress offers a grander portrayal when studying their Role to understand the character being played, the more meaningful memorable and masterful their performance becomes. This truly engages the dictum: *know thyself.*

What can we gain by sailing to the moon if we are not able to cross the abyss that separates us from ourselves? —*Thomas Merton*

SERVER

POSITIVE: SERVICE

NEGATIVE: BONDAGE

Whoever is spared personal pain must feel himself called to help in diminishing the pain of others. We must all carry our share of the misery which lies upon the world. —*Albert Schweitzer*

The essence of my Server role is service, an ordinal role, assisting, nurturing, supporting and providing for others, putting their needs before my own, at times I don't notice that this is my modus operandi. I show my love by what I do for you. Most often I care for one person at a time and am a mid-frequency stable inspirational role. Hands-on, my tireless support makes me innately a servant of humanity. My contribution may be approached modestly although often covertly manipulative. I inspire others as well as being inspired through service. To attend to you I stay in control and have everything in order. I am the one running the show; a waiter, an emergency room doctor or fitness trainer, generally positioned in the background. Orchestrating your lifestyle by choosing your diet, setting up an exercise regime, preparing the food as well as cleaning up, cutting and creating your hairstyle, listening to your personal problems, I will massage you, even pick up after you. I am the support, aiming for your best interest, enjoying to be steering each situation. Ordinal, serving one person at a time, paying attention to your needs and interests, I prefer to work behind the scenes.

My religion is very simple. My religion is kindness. —*the Dalai Lama*

Young soul service reflects *my* personal interests and wants, while as an older soul I now serve according to *your* want and interests. Love and devotion are displayed by what I do for you. Other-directed in care-taking, serving deepens my spiritual growth through stepping aside and putting your needs foremost. This inspires me as well as opens me to develop humility and devotion. I like controlling situations that I provide services for, organizing how others needs are taken care of and even though I may be well intentioned, as a care-giver I slide from being sweet and warm to being distant, downtrodden and self-involved. My manner is usually low-key, an ordinary person who is sometimes undervalued and overlooked.

When my energy is in a negative direction I feel self-sacrificing, often enslaved to a person, job, project, or possession. Feeling victimized I slide to martyrdom. Once bondage sets in, my freedom controlled, I feel tied down, frustrated and have difficulty expressing my concerns eventually becoming underhanded. Resentful, exhausted, imagining that I have been condemned to a life of hard work, bitter and a victim, neglecting my own needs, feeling exploited, taken for granted, unappreciated, mistreated, undervalued, disappointed, I dull down. Feeling like I have no choice other than frustration, certainly little time to focus on my own needs. As bondage sets in, and it almost always does, for me to stay away from that disintegration and not become entrapped by whatever I add into my life I need deeper inquiry; to know what is true service and what really matters, to see when I am over-extended, to be watchful and know what leads me to step into bondage and how to honestly embody true service. Choosing to look inward, listening to a larger viewpoint, I find a deeper source. In this positive direction I am careful not to over-extend and self-deny, I maintain a caring self. At my best you will feel inspired to be in my presence.

I feel my family's needs are a priority. I'm not comfortable with the idea of serving the many and ignoring my family. —Susan Sarandon

It's a challenge to have direct communication. I wish people could mind-read—because once I am overworked, frustrated and feeling enslaved, although dropping hints I still prefer not to receive the spotlight of attention or confrontation, I just hope to keep things stabilized. Preferably not to shake my world, I'm even careful to not ask questions that could lead to problems. My way of letting others know my plight is quite round about protecting the stability of my day-to-day world. At times it would be best if I was stopped from ruining the fun of an adventure, like making the kids stop eating birthday cake cause they might get a stomach ache or interfering when they try to pop the balloons cause they might get scared of the loud noise.

Following orders indiscriminately I might get into unsavory situations; like serving a money making boss, a corrupt politician, a tricky husband or wife, or an unsavory guru. When living mindfully, intentionally I am uplifted through devotion, I become steadfast and loyal. My love is expressed through what I do, it might be making dinner or the bed, moving chairs in an auditorium, cleaning someone's kitchen at a potluck invitation, going to war for my country, or taking care of gorillas in Africa.

It is better to lead from behind and to put others in front, especially when you celebrate victory when nice things occur. You take the front line when there is danger. Then people will appreciate your leadership. —Nelson Mandela

Accommodating, I will volunteer for the unpopular job, pick up your sister at the airport, come to your house to feed your dog while you are on vacation, get up to make coffee when eating dinner at a friends house, be the family member that provides for the aging parent, putting clothes back on the hangar for others who forgot while I'm shopping, tidying up bathrooms, give up my seat on the subway, saying hello and being nice to strangers, bending over to pick up the thing you dropped. Often considered an invaluable staff worker, I slot into the mainstay of the companies and organizations that I work for, regardless if I am the secretary, the nurse, the librarian, the social worker, or the accountant. I work longer hours, clear up the paper work, do the practical jobs that are needed. Unassuming, I am not looking to be front and center, to push my way up the corporate ladder, rather I like to improve the place where I work. Actually, I become so needed and functional for the others that I am not the first to get laid off, nor am I the first to get promoted due to my usefulness. At my best I am angelic, the unsung hero that is brought into sainthood.

It is not the magnitude of our actions but the amount of love that is put into them that matters. —Mother Teresa

I can be spotted locally as the waiter, hairstylist, beautician, social worker, psychotherapist, butler, massage therapist, nurse, mechanic, accountant, personal trainer, midwife in the boy scout troops, and other volunteer and community organizations; most behind the scenes service occupations that still have direct one-to-one contact with people. I like helping out, putting people at ease, and am ultimately the support that enables all other roles to function and continue. In a love relationship I am devoted, attentive, willing to do more than my share of household jobs. Ordinal and hardworking, the most numerous of all the roles, I like to volunteer for charity groups, the simple practical jobs that are the substance of organizations suit me well. Knowing myself to be an inspiration to others, as well as inspired by the work I do, liking to serve the well-being of all, in clear moments I see my role as my personal path to spiritual growth and in many faith-based devotional communities this role is regarded as the path of growth.

The meek shall inherit the earth. —Beatitudes, Sermon on the Mount

Known Servers include: *Albert Schweitzer, Mother Teresa, The Dalai Lama, Meher Baba, Thich Nhat Hahn, Florence Nightingale, Jimmy Carter, Nelson Mandela, Mia Farrow, Jane Goodall, Susan Sarandon, Dian Fossey, Jonas Salk, Prince Charles, John Kerry, Eleanor Roosevelt, Elisabeth11, Rosa Parks, Desmond Tutu, Linda McCartney, Diana Princess of Wales, Anna Freud, Cinderella, John of God, Harriet Tubman, Alice B. Toklas* and *Mata Amritananda Mayi Ma* (known as *Ammachi*).

ARTISAN

POSITIVE: CREATION

NEGATIVE: ARTIFICE,

SELF-DECEPTION

The ultimate work of art is ourselves, our personality. We are endowed with the faculty of being able to become what we want to become; life is a great loss if we don't avail ourselves of this potential. —Vilayat Khan

I am the ordinal expressive role inventive and creative in my approach to life. The world and my body is my canvas and I decorate, shape, re-invent, imagine, refashion in whatever medium I engage; whether it's the business, fine arts, science, crafts, or simple day-to-day living, I am constantly re-inventing things around me. The job of the Artisan is to design and create new forms that will bring about change on this planet. Finding a venue of expression, my creativity is rarely surpassed; it flows like an open channel—new, fresh, fun, innovative, entertaining with visions that cross cultural roadways accessing universal understanding.

Looking to do things in a new way, a tattoo, piercing, colorful clothing, offbeat or innovative style in my home, even how I wrap and present a gift; all in a fresh perspective. I might decorate my body with piercings, tattoos, unique haircuts and colorings, wear a beaded glove on only one hand, have a unique mustache, draw designs on my bedroom wall, paint each fingernail a different color, wear an unusual hat, personally design my office space with inventive colors and designs putting up statues, collages and other symbols; I have my own particular style, which very often is geared to making a statement. Ungrounded, fluid, you can find us in many fields: as actors, inventors, computer designers, hairstylists, film makers, fashion models, florists, clothes designers, tailors, chefs, repairman, auto mechanics, plumbers, manufacturers of things to sell, engineers, people who can fix, create or invent anything. We are creating forms, the structure behind imagination, seeking originality, giving shape to the universe.

If you can dream it, you can do it. Always remember that this whole thing was started with a dream and a mouse. —Walt Disney

Creating reality according to my personal vision, self-deception, artifice leading to delusion is how I disintegrate when I become negative. The illusion of who I am is often far-fetched from the truth and my clever mind generates distortion. Wishful delusional thinking convincingly replaces accuracy and self-understanding. My world may barely have any slight resemblance to reality. To connect me to a truthful reality is to break through the constructed invention of my belief system, since I tend to see life through a mask with rose-tinted glasses, firmly convinced that this is how I am and this is who you are—sometimes quite far off from honesty or accuracy. I will re-invent myself according to what suits me at the present moment, as well as to convince myself, I *pull the wool over my own eyes.* My understanding of a situation may have no bearing on facts and so I either fall into depression, act impulsively, become irresponsible and confused, all in the effort to beat the ordinary routine day-to-day boredom.

Happiness lies in the joy of achievement, in the thrill of creative effort. —Vincent Van Gogh

It takes tremendous effort on my part to see when I am deceiving myself and others and find myself living in a wishful thinking mode, rather than in the present moment. Inventing my own reality when

I lose interest or feel constrained by the present one, I creatively fool myself as well as others. I often make people think and see me as the image and fantasy that I make up and elaborate. A challenging type for therapists, I require constant tapping back onto the truthful road, since I so easily veer into believing my own inventive stories about myself, life and others. Steer me back on course by keeping me grounded in the world; once I fragment, become scattered moody or depressed I can be the most crazed, not right in the head, of all the roles. Deluded and distracted, I take the easy lazy way and sacrifice originality for copy and imitation. I will imagine myself to be a film-maker but ignore the hard work and discipline that goes into writing and filming. I day-dream my life into a series of all the things I could do, meanwhile getting further away from its possibility by time, age, lack of muscle tone; a kind of propensity to pretending which some call lying. This false sense of self or false identity gets enabled by hanging out with more productive artisans. Differentiating between my inner world and the truth becomes divided by a thinning line. On the other hand success can also drive me to delusion, poor choice making, an early death; ie. Artisans Kurt Cobain, Michael Jackson, River Phoenix, Elvis Presley, Andy Warhol, Vincent Van Gogh, Amy Winehouse, Whitney Houston, Jerry Garcia, Marilyn Monroe.

The finest day I ever had was when tomorrow never came. There are a lot of things I wish I would have done, instead of just sitting around and complaining about having a boring life. So I really need life to shake it up. I started being really proud of the fact that I was gay, even though I wasn't.
—*Kurt Cobain*

Don't box me in or rigidify a schedule for me, routine and rules hem me in, fluidity allows my intuitive and sensitive imagination to flourish. In the positive direction I am naturally creative, imaginative, stylish.

The world is my blank canvas to fill in creating, imagining, visioning, being original and inventive. Something as simple as dinner at my house might become a memorable event for you as I design the presentation embellished with candles, music—a creation to fill your senses. In the negative direction my smoke and mirror relationships become filled with drama, imitation takes over originality, projects are unfinished, I get moody, chaotic and self-destructive. Woman Artisans are generally quite feminine, and male Artisans appear to be less macho tough often re-inventing themselves with long hair, short hair, a mustache, side-burns, unique footwear, a shaved head, tattoos, earrings and piercings.

When I was a child my mother said to me, 'If you become a soldier, you'll be a general. If you become a monk, you'll be the pope.' Instead I became a painter and wound up as Picasso. —Pablo Picasso

Staying healthy is generally a reflection of the ease and flow of my creativity. I do have to be careful though, since I can manifest-create tumors and growths and odd symptoms with ease, and also I can make them disappear as well. Light and flowing, self-indulgent and change-able, sensitive and spontaneous, sometimes a bit eccentric, I love to find the new, the imaginative, and am often ahead of the times with my inno-vations. Experiencing life as my canvas, I can make this a beautiful or ugly world. My originality, my ideas and creative energetics express and reflect how I process and tune in to life. The atmosphere will become charged by my mood, as I spontaneously move things around excited by my visions and charged by my quick thoughts. I set a tone and change the tenor of a room with my aura. A connoisseur of the new, day to day jobs tire me. Expression-oriented, I experiment with fashion and imagination, ways that make me appear distinctive. People might sense an erratic scatteredness, sometimes considered bohemian, avant-garde, or nutty, this becomes a useful tenure for fermenting creative ventures.

Spending time with other Artisans keeps me connected, and sometimes I vacation in artsy Artisan communities like Cape Cod, Santa Fe, Sedona, Key West, Asheville, Byron Bay Australia, New Hope, San Francisco, Bali, Miami Beach, Boulder, Maui, Pune or Kerala India, Paris, Barcelona, Berlin, Venice, Santa Cruz, Taos, many island communities, places Artisans gravitate to where I feel support, connections and understanding.

When the artist is alive in any person, whatever his kind of work may be, he becomes an inventive, searching, daring, self-expressive creature. He becomes interesting to other people. He disturbs, upsets, enlightens, and opens ways for a better understanding. Where those who are not artists are trying to close the book, he opens it and shows there are still more pages possible.
—*Robert Henri*

Known Artisans include: *Michelangelo, Cher, Halle Berry, Jamie Fox, Frank Lloyd Wright, Mozart, Vincent Van Gogh, Victoria Beckham, Paul Gauguin, Edgar Degas, Auguste Renoir, Walt Whitman, Brittany Spears, Kelly Clarkson, David Beckham, Boy George, Albert Einstein, David Bowie, River Phoenix, Hugh Grant, Dr. Christian Barnard, Paris Hilton, Andy Warhol, Jerry Garcia, Beyonce, Jennifer Lopez, Angelina Jolie, Lady GaGa, Katie Perry, David Bowie, Yoko Ono, Usher, Calvin Klein, Prince, Brad Pitt, Whitney Houston, Bjork, Paula Abdul, Kristen Stewart, Robert Pattinson, Johnny Depp, Janet Jackson, Salvador Dali, Bjork, Elizabeth Taylor, Shirley MacLaine, George Lucas, Steven Spielberg, Billy Joel, Elton John, Lewis Carroll, Elvis Presley, Grace Kelly, John Lennon, Bob Marley, Coco Chanel, Tom Cruise, Twiggy, Amy Winehouse, Justin Timberlake, Gary Larson, Kurt Cobain, Tiger Woods, Charlize Theron, Prince, Justin Bieber, Liberace, Walt Disney, Woody Allen, Leonardo DaVinci, Marilyn Monroe, Michael Jackson.*

WARRIOR

POSITIVE: PERSUASION

NEGATIVE: COERCION

From this arises the question whether it is better to be loved rather than feared, or feared rather than loved. It might perhaps be answered that we should wish to be both: but since love and fear can hardly exist together, if we must choose between them, it is far safer to be feared than loved.
—*Niccolo Machiavelli*

I am the practical, principled, ordinal action role, setting an aim, and slowly, steadily going towards its completion. A solid physical role, I am determined, focused, productive, resourceful, goal oriented, expressing myself through action, organization, strategy and resourcefulness. The structures and order that hold society together, the systems— schools, banks, health care, welfare—are set up by me. Then, I enforce the rules to protect bureaucratic organizations, watching out that people don't abuse those systems. You are less apt to find my type taking advantage of the welfare system that I have carefully put together; I would see that as giving others power over me, creating my indebtedness. It's a jungle out there and although I am street savvy, my preference is hard work, even through to exhaustion, so that I know whatever I get is because my day labor earned it. Challenges summon me to focus and organize, in fact sometimes a personal battle is a great test for me to rise to the occasion, moving me to take practical step-by-step action. I know I am a survivor and I pride myself on the hardships I can go through, often looking at them as tests to my resilience and backbone.

Never, ever give up. —*Diana Nyad*

Grounded, I tether those around, keeping them in line and on course. Disorganization and disorder push me to impose my chain of command. Strength and perseverance are assets I fall back upon to get a job well done. There are times when I rely on no one and still the projects get completed; once I set a goal and devise a straight forward strategy I know what to do and what comes next. Enjoying a challenge, not shirking hard work, I straighten up the mess that others cause; I roll up my sleeves, set a target and proceed. I tend to see and feel things in a black and white formatory manner, people are either with me or not with me, and if you are with me I certainly will be supportive.

Social protocol works for me, when I invite you to a holiday dinner, answer the invitation, because to offend me with your poor manners you'll be placed on the outsider or as some call it *the shit list*, and it's quite difficult to redeem yourself once you've crossed me.

If people bring so much courage to this world the world has to kill them to break them, so of course it kills them. The world breaks every one and afterward many are strong at the broken places. But those it will not break it kills. It kills the very good and the very gentle and the brave impartially. If you are none of these you can be sure it will kill you too but there will be no special hurry....There is no rule on how to write. Sometimes it's like drilling rock and then blasting it out with charges. —Ernest Hemingway

Notice that my firm grounded eyes look straight at you. Oriented towards protection, similar to a mother bear or a guard dog my direct confrontational stance looks right into the camera, here I am, a Warrior! Posturing, sometimes I will strut like a military commander, hand on hip, whatever it takes to show you who is in charge. I have a strong body, high threshold of pain, and am full into living on this physical plane. I like food, sex, sports, cars, and using my body for labor. You won't see a luke-warm response from me, provoked, I bluntly speak out. Good at business and politics I appear competent and self-assured, able to close a deal with my persuasive logical approach. You will get a pumped up armed forces when I am in office because I believe in that protection, a strong defense, and if that fails I will set out to conquer—countries, people, principles that oppose mine.

Everyone has a plan 'till they get punched in the mouth. I don't try to intimidate anybody before a fight. That's nonsense. I intimidate people by hitting them. —*Mike Tyson*

Goal-oriented, strong-willed, a practical persuader, deliberate, I like excitement, intensity and working for whatever I want to achieve. I enjoy a challenge, especially when I am the winner, in fact, rather than lose I may become a bully. History books and movies speak about the gladiators who have fought to their death. Fighting for whatever I believe in, I might go to war, protect my family, work as a fireman, a professional boxer, prison guard, an athlete, run a shelter for battered women or children, bouncer at the door of a local bar, head a corporation, become a cop or a national guardsman. I certainly enjoy wearing a uniform so people can see what position or function I serve: whether it is a fireman, judo, karate, soccer, or marine garb, as well as wearing a suit if I go to a business meeting: this way you *get* my position of authority and activity. You can find us on the football field, movie screen or bull riding at the rodeo, fighting in gangs, in the Mafia, joining the police force, on the courtroom floor, working at the F.B.I. or C.I.A., truck drivers, country western singers, lawyers, pirates on ships, prostitutes on the street, emergency room physicians, managing a big corporate organization, security guard, politicians in Washington, any military branch, most sports as well as construction sites.

My heart has been stolen too—but I've gone and got it back every single time. I keep waiting to meet a man who has more balls than I do. —*Salma Hayek*

Maternal and paternal, honest, willing to earn what's needed, I make a good workhorse parent even though I was a difficult child to manage. Throughout my childhood I was described as a cross between Dennis the Menace, Superman, the Bash Street Kids, Minnie the Minx and Wonder Woman. Scraped knees and broken bones don't deter me as I compete, ride dirt bikes, skate board, inline skate along steep hills, jump off curbs, fall out of jungle gyms, play soccer, football; danger and courage are in my bloodstream.

Blind faith in your leaders, or in anything, will get you killed.
—*Bruce Springsteen*

Life is an adventure. I am persuasive, practical and determined, will work hard, don't back off from violent outbursts, expressing myself through action. A single-minded go-getter, things get done when I am involved. I like results. Life is an undertaking and I stay productive, conquering each thing that I take on. Blunt and forthright, sometimes abrasive and crude, live with me and over time my soft sweet side will become visible. Some see me as a grizzly bear, others say I'm a harmless teddy bear. In the positive direction I encourage and champion, promote and strengthen, firing others up I renew their spirit rousing them to action.

Sometimes if you want to see a change for the better, you have to take things into your own hands. I tried being reasonable, I didn't like it. I have a very strict gun control policy: if there's a gun around I want to be in control of it. —Clint Eastwood.

You'll often find me forcefully behind the wheel of a big black SUV, watch out, because I commandeer that, owning the road, sometimes risk-taking as I drive by cutting you off, plowing ahead at lights. Off the road I can be a protective no-nonsense parent, a good team player,

I can strategize and with the right team or tools will get the job done. Throughout the centuries I show up as gladiator, Viking, Greek and Roman hero, mercenary soldier, cowboy, outlaw, long-distance trucker, auctioneer, airline pilot, rock star, football hero, tennis champ. Rarely big on long flowery explanations, I prefer plain-spoken, unadorned, frank descriptions; not too much to read between the lines, I say what you hear and true or not I probably believe it. Processing thoughts wears thin with me, and slow inner therapeutic approaches don't call to my nature. Coaching, a quick one-day work-shop, martial arts, techniques that offer solutions and practical approaches; once engaged I can stay with practices and enjoy the focus of hard work along with the accomplishment of results.

There is nothing to writing. All you do is sit down at a typewriter and bleed.
—*Ernest Hemingway*

Countries have a Role, and certainly Germany, The United States, and Japan have impacted and at times dominated the world with Warrior influence. My ability to deal with, to mobilize and set into action in the positive direction makes a real impact in business, the community, and on the world. But in the negative direction I also impact lives: I am the school bully, the gang leader in the prisons, intimidating, dominating, cruel. Entering enemy territory during war, unrestrained, out-of-control, we plunder, rape, destroy; the disastrous bloodbaths you read about are Warrior dominated. I am the marine sergeant that makes the private crawl through the woods until he drops from exhaustion sometimes even dies due to my insensitivity. The prison guard who turns the hot water on the prisoner until his skin peels: *Toughen up,* I am saying innerly. On the other hand, people will feel confident and reassured around me when I show up firm and reassuring, determined;

my voice in itself, resonant and strong will take command, and they know that as a workhorse I will skillfully fight to protect what I see as needed and fair, and that I will defend at whatever the cost.

When I don't get my way, feeling frustrated, I stand my ground, willing to fight it out. The biblical *an eye for an eye* is my style along with an inflexible stance bringing me to feeling impenetrable. When I slide to the negative I go into a strong-armed coercion and become intimidating, bullying, dismissive, gutsy, emotionally withheld, argumentative, ruthless, single-minded and narrow-minded, a rabble rouser, looking for danger often intimidating others and making trouble. Not beating around the bush, subtlety to me is new age airy fairy stuff. The comment: *To a real warrior power perceived may be power achieved,* satisfies me. Using strong-arm techniques, insisting or laying down the law are a couple of tactics I use to keep others in line. Protecting the environment, my family, my company, I'll employ whatever strategy suits me best. I loved the adventures of Robin Hood, Billy the Kid, Wonder Woman, Xena the Warrior Princess, Tarzan, Indiana Jones, Spiderman, Captain America, Thor, Iron Man, The Black Widow—now those are great Warriors!

It is fatal to enter any war without the will to win it. —Douglas Mac Arthur

Known Warriors include: *G. I. Gurdjieff, Fidel Castro, Diana Nyad, Billie Jean King, Manuel Noriega, Baby Doc Duvalier, Judi Dench, Ernest Hemingway, Hillary Clinton, Theodore Roosevelt, John Wayne, Gertrude Stein, Golda Meier, Frank Sinatra, Rosie O'Donnell, Salma Hayek, Pink Hart, Clint Eastwood, Venus and Serena Williams, Sylvester Stallone, Mike Tyson, Yogi Bhajan, Mitt Romney, Mohammed Ali, Martina Navratilova, Mark Wahlberg, Sean Penn, Joan Rivers, Bruce Springsteen, Davy Crockett, Madonna, Lauren Bacall, Sun Bear, Barbara Bush, Tina Turner, Mary Lou*

Retton, Mae West, Frida Kahlo, Geronimo, Condoleeeza Rice, Charlton Heston, Norman Mailer, Bette Davis, John Grisham, Demi Moore, Dick Cheney, John McCain, Charles Bronson, H.W.L. Poonja, George W. Bush, Joe Biden, Colin Powell, Madeleine Albright, Janis Joplin, Jimi Hendrix, Melissa Etheridge, Arnold Schwarzenegger, Teresa Giudice, Mark Wahlberg, Calamity Jane, Dwight Eisenhower, Winston Churchill.

SCHOLAR

POSITIVE: KNOWLEDGE

NEGATIVE: THEORY

And let a scholar all earth's volumes carry, he will be but a walking dictionary; a mere articulate clock. —George Chapman

As the only neutral role I easily interact and help facilitate communication between all other roles. They come to me for data and a practical viewpoint. I take note of what's going on. Not strongly opinionated, I see many sides to a situation. Gathering information is fun, I am a born observer. To know me is like having a card catalogue on hand, since I have facts and lists on many topics. Studying people and watching situations, my position is to hold information, what has been called the library of the universe—the Akashic Records—so nothing will ever be forgotten. I act as a conduit, gathering facts and passing them along, experiencing knowledge, not only possessing it. The transcriber, the historical pen person of humanity, my function is to accumulate and hold information, as well as to make it available when asked.

Doing what little one can to increase the general stock of knowledge is as respectable an object of life as one can in any likelihood pursue. —Charles Darwin

It's an adventure to play a sport, I care less for the action or winning than participating for the curiosity to find out about the sport whether it be tennis or tai chi. I'm not driven to competitively excel. A solid role, I am grounded but have to be careful not to store unnecessary information in my body. This can lead to tightness and physical unease, unless over time I learn how to let go of experiences that no longer need to be accessed. You will find me often in academia as a teacher, university professor or life-long student, a doctor, scientist, veterinarian, a museum curator, writer, yoga instructor, librarian. Sometimes I look at life as a classroom, an experiment, distancing myself from being immersed in life. I also am good as a detective, historian, publishing books, a research specialist, I sit at meetings taking extensive notes, and like getting on a game show that shows off my encyclopedic knowledge. Not highly sociable, I enjoy staying home with a good book or rummaging through magazines or researching on my computer. My preference is to study the world, not to change it; I would rather think and study, observe and record, than go out and do big actions.

There is much pleasure to be gained from useless knowledge. —*Bertrand Russell*

As the neutral position I am colored and activated by the essence or energy of the type I associate with. Alone I appear bland, even my clothing is conservative and muted, although around certain roles, especially a King, I brighten and move forward. Left to my own I would dress in a manner that blends rather than stands out, and that works for the times I want to look around and not be the focal point, like at a social get-together. At a party I often like to hang out on the sidelines, near a wall watching, observing. If you want to engage me in a conversation ask me what I am currently reading, rather than start with a personal question, my comfortable information is about whatever my work or research project is; self-disclosure is something I warm up to, but not right out of the starting gate. Gathering knowledge, I make lists, organize and easily handle the details. In my house there are areas with piles of magazines, articles cut out, files, pamphlets, books, a container of pencils and pens. Find me a good map, I can get lost studying it.

I am an old scholar, better-looking now than when I was young. That's what sitting on your ass does to your face. —Leonard Cohen

Much of the data I accumulate is not timely, since I excel at looking at data after the fact. Best as a historian, I seek out and track material storing it for future reference. I am thorough with detail work and actually enjoy going over material that others might find tedious or boring. Methodical, I pursue something I am interested finding out about, and then have lists, catalogs, reminder notes, scraps of paper, pamphlets, the topics ranging A to Z. My curiosity takes me on adventures, to the northern California coast to learn about Sequoia Redwood trees, to the Galapagos to study island turtles, trekking across a mountain to know the history of its stone formation, to conferences where I find other scholars, traveling to South Florida to investigate the real estate market boom, walking the island barriers with a metal detector, sitting at my computer looking up my family genealogy, an electronics fair in a nearby city to see the new products. I know a Scholar who got arrested and went to jail to investigate prison conditions. Places that have access to lots of information like libraries or bookstores and museums are fun, since I can study a leaf of a flower or insect as easily as figuring out where a place is on a map or how a boat capsized on a rock on an obscure island in Maine.

There must be no barriers to freedom of inquiry. There is no place for dogma in science. The scientist is free, and must be free to ask any ques-

tion, to doubt any assertion, to seek for any evidence, to correct any errors.
—*Julius Robert Oppenheimer*

At my highest I have wisdom, am an authority, a master specialist, while at my lower range I quickly tell people what I know, I am excessively concerned with minor details and rules, a nitpicker, I may give an appearance of learning, yet am hypothesizing and theorizing with random bits of information, easily fooling myself and others. I cover up what I don't know and then appear knowing, but actually I am creating some made-up abstract confused rendition of a theory. I like to theorize when I am too lazy to research and test what I find or just don't truly understand, then I become opinionated, narrow-minded, pedantic, a quibbler and in that arena I am slow to take action. Information is useful only to the degree that it's absorbed, assimilated by one's being and understood. If facts and data are known but not understood, then I am unknowingly lying, since I can't convey a truth I don't understand. The intellect is the primary place of lying. When I develop my inner work I become less popular and I talk less about what I don't know, then my lying diminishes. In the positive direction, knowledge is about the experience of knowing and moving beyond the beliefs and theories that distort my perception of truth.

My mind seems to have become a kind of machine for grinding general laws out of larger collection of facts. If a person asked my advice before undertaking a long voyage, my answer would depend upon his possessing a decided taste for some branch of knowledge, which could by this means be advanced.
—*Charles Darwin*

As the integration Role, a knowledge person, history has shown Scholars to have been influential and essential in almost every arena. The compiler of the first dictionary—Dr. Samuel Johnson, chronicler of mythological stories—Joseph Campbell, Galileo—the father of science, Charles Darwin—who laid the foundation of modern evolutionary studies, Socrates—a founder of Western philosophy, Sigmund Freud—the father of psychoanalyses, Stephen Hawking—theoretical physicist regarded as the wisest person of this age; yes, the Scholar is on the cutting edge of all branches of learning. We care about knowledge, which is the positive direction of my Role, then I become unassuming and diligent going beyond cerebral book information. I have the patience to delve into activities that might find me trudging up a mountain to find a particular species of butterfly, or research tribal customs in Borneo, or investigate animal behavior in Alaska, or sit at the computer researching articles on vitamins after being diagnosed with a digestive disorder, before organizing my nutritional needs. Understanding is a substance arrived at through a practice of looking deeply into the heart of the matter, through penetrating into the essence of things; real change comes through understanding.

To talk in public, to think in solitude, to read and to hear, to inquire and answer inquiries, is the business of the scholar. —Samuel Johnson

Known Scholars include: *P.D. Ouspensky, Rodney Collins, Carlos Casteneda, Galileo, Margaret Mead, Marco Polo, Anderson Cooper, Ken Wilber, Prince William, Sigmund Freud, Eckhart Tolle, Susan Boyle, Ben Affleck, Isaac Newton, Immanuel Kant, Marcel Proust, Christopher Columbus, Dr. Samuel Johnson, Alan Greenspan, Hannah Arendt, Supreme Court Justice Souter, Margaret Thatcher, Mr. Rodgers, Plato, Socrates, Alfred Kinsey, Ken Burns, Marie Curie, Arthur Miller, Nicolas Tesla, Jane Goodall, Steve Jobs, Helen Palmer, Jose Stevens, Aristotle, P. M. Roget, Bobby Fischer, Al Gore, Larry Chang, Rene Descartes, Gloria Steinem, Sherlock Holmes, Iris Murdoch, Joseph Campbell, Bill Moyers,*

Charles Darwin, Heraclitus, Bertrand Russell, Margaret Atwood, Dan Rather, Ludwig Wittgenstein, Dr. Strangelove, Osho Rajneesh, Julius Robert Oppenheimer, James Joyce, Noam Chomsky, Elie Wiesel, Stephen Hawking.

S A G E

POSITIVE: EXPRESSION, DISSEMINATION

NEGATIVE: VERBOSITY

The story is not told to lift you up, to make you feel better, or to entertain you, although all those things can be true. The story is meant to take the spirit into a descent to find something that is lost or missing and to bring it back to consciousness again. Stories are medicine. —*Clarissa Pinkola Estes*

I am the overgrown kid who says: *I like to play so don't give me too much responsibility.* I am inquisitive and dramatic as well as informative, quite perceptive and will offer you an upbeat humorous side of life. Entertaining, keeping it light; I'd love to teach the world how to handle life cheerfully. Most things can be fun, regardless to its seriousness. I can turn almost anything into a joke or really funny story. The exalted expressive role, friendly, optimistic, a twinkle in my eyes, I gather information, passing it on to as many people as possible, often in the form of stories, witticism, one-liners, through performance. The world is my audience, and I certainly come alive in the lime light. Although this is the Role most people are drawn to, many Sages rarely dig down deep inside to find their authenticity or real self, instead we take the popular route of getting laughs, winning popularity votes for the pleasure people receive being in our company. I like throwing parties, getting people together; you will notice me because I am creative at attention getting, whether I put on a costume or just raise my voice. A jokester, witty and friendly, I play to the audience and will tell you stories, making anything fun to learn. When you see a group and hear one voice louder than the others, expect a Sage. Standing out in the crowd, my voice is just a notch bigger. I enjoy being center stage, youthful looking, charismatic, lifting everyone's spirits. Theatre is my forte, playing to the audience energizes and enlivens me.

There's no business like show business. —Irving Berlin

Once wound up my conversation is non-stop, people say I have *the gift of gab*. In this negative direction silence unnerves me and is not as entertaining as comic relief. I'd rather sit with friends and have fun, readily reporting on any topic, embellishing to keep you smiling than be in the discomfort of silence. What you learn from my story is less important to me than that you pay attention to me while I cheer you up. In this negative posture I talk too much sometimes only for the sound of my voice or for the sake of talking, am intrusive, attention grabbing, I exaggerate and stretch the truth, occasionally at another's expense. Once on a downhill roll, I gossip, am deceptive and tasteless, loud and verbose, chatty, commanding attention without engaging in true communication. Indulging myself in soap opera dramas I get pulled into other peoples stories and sometimes jump into my own histrionics. During those moments I lose connection and interest in anyone else's needs. Sometimes I will go on and on, talking till the cows jump over the moon. Some people say I was born talking, in fact I wake up and start right from the first get go. Loving to sit around and hear the news on everyone's life, later to spice it up and spread it, keeping others up to date with what's happening. Center stage, I rarely refuse the opportunity to add a word, or story. I easily shirk the daily humdrum routines for the fun of a party. Generally a poor listener; you have probably fallen into the Sage con man who swindles and wheels and deals, clever and sharp-witted, often called the *spin-doctors* thinking that charming someone's money out of them is ok since I have also entertained, showed you a good time, lightened you up with an enjoyable performance.

Gentlemen, you have just been listening to that Chinese sage, On Too Long. —*Will Rogers*

In the arts I am less likely to be concerned with technique, more focused on expression. My paintings are more symbolic less involved with technical elements like perspective and proportion. My music playing is geared to having and giving a good time not mastering complex sonatas and overtures. I offer a voice to the pulse of the times and can be found reporting, newscasting, somewhere in the entertainment field. Whether I am singing, writing or acting, I tend to maintain a sense of humor and energy towards what I do. Life, to me, is a theatrical production and I have to be careful not to perform my life rather than authentically dropping into it. My enthusiasm is catching. The clown Punchinello, a trickster or fool, one of the characters in the Renaissance of the Italian theatrical tradition, the Commedia dell' Art, had my Sage ability to draw attention while he entertained.

Laughter without a twinge of philosophy is but a sneeze of humor. Genuine humor is replete with wisdom. —*Mark Twain*

I am a great salesperson, funny comedian, fiery preacher, loud auctioneer, a colorful actor, skillful courtroom lawyer, a lively TV announcer, author, interesting speaker, and easily found in the middle of a coffee klatch. I am good with children, in fact I am like a child much of the time. My clothing includes colorful often theatrical items, a scarf with a splash of sparkle, costume-like garments, Hawaiian shirts, red Reebok high-top sneakers, a T-shirt that says something you will notice, an outfit that is connected to the event I am attending, a necklace that has a hanging symbol to tell you what I'm into or to announce something, verging on the eccentric—you will notice me! Dressing for effect, not always for style, when I dress up I still find room for a flashy watch, tie, cape, scarf, purse or hat for that special Sage flavor, calling attention to me. Throwing larger than life parties, clever with words and bending the truth, I stretch, exaggerate and embellish a one-minute story into a long evening. With a deep resonant voice, I get loud and out of hand. Unscrupulous huckster, trickster, spin doctor, insensitive; watch out, I can con you into buying the Brooklyn Bridge. Words, words, words, I can make them shake and shine. I feel naturally exuberant, generally positive, smiling, with twinkling eyes, hoping to stay young at heart forever.

We have all, at one time or another, been performers, and many of us still are—politicians, playboys, cardinals and kings. —Sir Laurence Olivier

Sage as a noun means learned person, wise one. This deeper side in its positive direction holds a mirror up to the world, disseminating, informing with insightful observations, witty comments letting the world see with new eyes, pointing towards societies flaws and hypocrisy. Writing, teaching classes, lecturing, courtroom influencing, light-hearted we make a mark on our culture. The task for me is to express myself genuinely not just through my performance. Once authentic and inner directed I use my natural gifts to elevate the arts as well as good causes that uplift and expose the travesty of justice. Noted Holocaust survivor Elie Wiesel, called *a messenger to mankind,* awarded the Nobel Peace Prize, writing numerous books, stories about his life, truth-teller Sage, informing and disseminating has made a profound impact through his expressive wise visibility.

Storytelling is at the heart of life. As a child I was never bored because I could always get on with my story. I still love to walk by the water or in the woods listening to the story that never ends. Always my imagination is creating a form that gives shape to otherwise sporadic events in everyday life. Gradually I am recognizing the meaning of my existence through my own myth. —Marion Woodman

I am the troubadour, the bard, minstrel, the one with a silver tongue, the raconteur, Scheherazade. The mythical story of Scheherazade, the Tales of a 1001 Arabian Nights speaks to how Scheherazade, the narrator of the tales educates the king and saves her life with her nightly storytelling of magic, riches and myth. The background story has the Persian king discover his wife's infidelity and then has her executed along with a declaration that for this betrayal he will marry a virgin and each day behead yesterday's wife. Three thousand women had already been beheaded when Scheherazade, the daughter of the high official who was responsible for finding the women, volunteered herself to marry the king. Scheherazade, a Sage, was well read and had great wit and wisdom, and against her father's protestations chose to become the next bride. Reluctantly her father, the official vizier, agreed.

Throughout their wedding night she slowly narrated, unfolded a mythic story that had no end, instead, it was a ..more to follow... saga. The newly married king, drawn into the tale, listened with great interest, curious and eager to hear the narrative and its ending, thereby postponing her execution. The following evening as she concludes the narrative Scheherazade begins another stirring, gripping story. As morning dawns another night passes in which the Sultan abstained from his killing, choosing to wait one more day and night for a further tale before he executes Scheherazade; and so another day arrives in which the county lives in peace. Now, as the king desires to hear the end of each tale he postpones executing her until the succeeding night, keeping Scheherazade alive as he anticipates each evening of storytelling. 1001 nights and three sons later the king, through hearing these beautiful teaching tales becomes educated in morality and kindness with a deepened understanding of love, patience and his connection to Scheherazade. Continuing for 1001 nights, we have the magical tales of Aladdin and the Wonderful Lamp, The 7 Voyages of Sinbad the Sailor, Ali Baba and the 40 Thieves, adventures of love, magic, destiny, of genies, of gossiping barbers and scheming matchmakers, fables, folk stories. This is Sage storytelling at its highest most powerful art of expression.

God made man because he loves stories. —*Elie Wiesel*

The Sage gives voice to the thoughts of the culture. Indries Shah, a Sage exemplar and mystic who died in 1996 made use of traditional teaching stories and parables that contained multiple layers of meaning designed to trigger insight and self-reflection within the reader. He was careful not to make his teaching community his social or family life and not to indulge his *sageness* in *exciting* psychic experiences. In the Sage tradition he transmitted esoteric teachings through simple and entertaining stories. Teaching stories meant to be studied carefully for reflection on their inner meanings, the inspiring tales that have a collective as well as personal meaning presented a distillation of spiritual wisdom. In his introduction to the collection of Mulla Nasrudin rascal Sage stories, Indries Shah relates that Nasrudin, when a boy, had the strange power of keeping his schoolfellow's attention with his stories. Their academic work suffered. The teacher, unable to prevent Nasrudin's magnetism was himself a Sage. He put a spell on the young man saying: *From now, however wise you become, people will always laugh at you, from now, whenever one Nasrudin tale is told, people will feel compelled to tell them until at least seven have been recited.*

Learning how to learn involves examining assumptions and Shah's Nasrudin stories are wonderful examples of serving this function. Indries Shah, an evolved Sage, explained that awakening to reality requires complete mutuality: *if you seek a teacher, try to become a real student. Awakening must come little by little; otherwise it will overwhelm. A spiritual teacher must be a person who can be totally balanced.* This speaks to our work of developing and maturing our essence and nature; often people gauge health by someone that they feel comfortable with rather than recognizing what is their nature and then what has been the intentional labor of deepening and maturing our original essence and nature. Often we think that someone with a *nice* nature is more evolved than a person with a cynical nature. When, in fact both might be mechanical lacking any true inner development. Said Shah: *This is a civilization that has the knowledge, yet is not using it.* This is reflected in our world where there is starvation, homelessness, war, in a world where we have the knowledge and production to create change, yet, as Shah says, *as a civilization we aren't using the knowledge that we have access to;* perceptive, truthful, concerned words of a wise Sage.

Stories move in circles. They don't move in straight lines. So it helps if you listen in circles. There are stories inside stories and stories between stories, and finding your way through them is as easy and as hard as finding your way home. And part of the finding is the getting lost. And when you're lost, you start to look around and to listen. —Fischer, Greenberg, Newman

Learning that what we tell about ourselves *is* story and ultimately leads to the discovery that what is true about every story is not the account but the connection to the larger story, the one that opens us to wisdom. We listen to more than the story as we penetrate the veil of illusion that has obscured our life to a small singular dimension. Stories are a way of experiencing the world and open us up to the mystery that informs all things. The bard, the troubadour, the Sage, the raconteur, the story keepers instruct, entertain and invite us into the center of a larger story.

All sorrows can be borne if you put them into a story or tell a story about them. —Isak Dinesen

Known Sages include: *Indries Shah, Robin Williams, Elie Wiesel, Will Rogers, Bill Clinton, Salvador Dali, Groucho Marx, Geraldo Rivera, Bette Midler, Stephen King, Bella Abzug, Lenny Bruce, Bill Cosby, Tina Fey, Regis Philbun, Sammy Davis Jr., Milton Berle, John Stewart, Jay Leno, Jack Black, Peter Sellers, Clarissa Pinkola Estes, Roseanne Barr, Richard Pryor, Ethel Merman, Muhammad Ali, Fran Drescher, Drew Barrymore, Jerry Springer, Oscar Wilde, Bill Murray, David Letterman, James Brown, Elton John, Johnny Carson, Jim Carrey, Dolly Parton, Michael Moore, Sir Laurence Olivier, Jack Nicholson, Osho Rajneesh, Mark Twain, Chris Rock, Red Skelton, Harpo Marx, Conan O'Brien, Whoopi Goldberg, Chevy Chase, Sacha Baron Cohen, Borat Sagdiyev, Richard Burton, Deena Metzger, Howard Stern, Charlie Chaplin, Shirley MacLaine, George Lopez, Lily Tomlin, Scheherazade, Sandra Bernhard, Luciano Pavarotti, Tom Lehrer, Lewis Black, Carmen Miranda, Stephen Colbert, Ellen DeGeneres, Dennis Rodman, Zalman Schacter-Shalomi, Rami Shapiro, Mitch Chefitz, Danny DeVito, Shakespeare, Truman Capote, Eddie Murphy, Sarah Silverman, Miley Cyrus, Mae West, Dr. Ruth Westheimer, Billy Crystal, Steve Martin, Rodney Dangerfield, Lucille Ball.*

PRIEST

POSITIVE: COMPASSION

NEGATIVE: ZEAL

All that we have hoped for is coming into view at this auspicious moment of our evolution. We are awakening to a new era of human potential and experience. We must open the Windows to the Sky so that we can access the hologram of our Soul. If we could see past our emotions, our beliefs, our fears, we would realize that every dilemma has its purpose as an experience of consciousness. —Chris Griscom

A high-frequency role, like a violin, when tuned well I am an inspirational visionary. Learning to properly tune a violin, no simple feat, requires study and attuning the ear to differentiate pitch. Tuned well I am fluid and others are deeply moved by my beautiful, almost divinely inspired presence. I am less attached to the physical world than other roles, often ungrounded, energetic, high spirited, encouraging people to improve their life. In this realm I experience compassion and inspire healing. A cardinal exalted inspiration role, I push others towards spiritual advancement, I serve the higher good through being a source of inspiration, a spark that encourages people to change. Sometimes impulsive, my intensity fires a visionary mission that aims to stir emotions so others will stretch and feel moved and animated. I like rituals and symbols and often use them as well as visualizations in my healing practice, although when I am too extreme I proselytize, becoming impractical and overly-enthusiastic.

Our aspirations are our possibilities. —Samuel Johnson

I have a striking look, a pulpit appearance, often attractive looking with a stylized manner of speaking, along with a mysterious or penetrating bright look in my eyes. Inspired, I enjoy having a mission. Personal relationships are hard for me to develop, instead I get involved with causes, politics, single-minded gung-ho issues, places where my vision will reach the greatest number. Instigating global or mass healing, I look to serve the highest good. I am the exalted server, facilitating spiritual growth, reminding you that there is more than a physical plane, there is a consciousness that includes all realms. Having a sense of mission, my energy is optimistic, goading people to look and change their ways. Enthusiastic, my mission takes me from communicating about politics, to making people aware of planetary needs, all working for what I see as the higher good. Sometimes I'll advocate for something before much of the data is in, a bit over enthusiastic, a tad irrational, still, I feel concerned and want to encourage people in their healing and learning. Referred to as the heart of the body, the shepherd of humanity, I have been known to see the world as my congregation.

Change will not come if we wait for some other person or some other time. We are the ones we've been waiting for. We are the change we seek. Focusing your life solely on making a buck shows a certain poverty of ambition. It asks too little of yourself. Because it's only when you hitch your wagon to something larger than yourself that you realize your true potential.
—*Barack Obama*

In the negative direction, my driven sense of purpose and cause creates a fanatic with insensitive pacing. Evangelistic, crusading bigot, flaky, sermonizing, zealous fanatic, arrogant and impractical, often not concerned with the accuracy of information, sometimes needlessly leading many into battle. For me a congregation could be ten people at a Thanksgiving dinner, a board meeting, or a group of musicians gathered at a friends house, and, once turned on, whether people want to hear or not, if I feel a sense of purpose, you will get a teaching. Self-motivated, it doesn't take a lot to get me going. Sometimes, though, I just like pushing people, encouraging them in areas that I think they need. Placing too much stock on faith I get carried away and force my beliefs on those around. I can inspire people to be excited about their life or to be enthusiastic about marching to war. Disclaiming disbelievers, I lose my balance getting lost in indignation and self-righteousness, imagining my belief as the right and only way.

You must be the change you want to see in the world. —Mahatma Gandhi

40 Billion a year spent on beauty products. Stop fixing your bodies and start fixing the world. —Eve Ensler

Rarely are people neutral about me: disliked or loved, my charismatic visibility and often my title: counselor, shaikh, rabbi, shaman, healer, priest, mullah, president, preacher, doctor, makes me a target of love or ire. I really like making a difference, my faith carries me a long way. In the positive direction I am compassionate towards humanity and want to uplift, to have an influential positive impact on the world. Drawn to movements and causes: environmental groups like Green Peace, civil rights, third world countries, AIDS and Cancer projects, are comfortable places for me to promote my dream. Swaying an audience or congregation, many listen and support my vision of the world as I see it.

Man is something that shall be overcome. Man is a rope over an abyss. What is great in man is that he is a bridge and not an end. —Zarathustra, Nietzsche

Many are emotionally moved and uplifted by me. My leadership charisma, my charm strongly impacts people, and in the world you see me as class president or reverend, a basketball player inspiring my team towards a win, a playwright activist creating theatre that speaks to informing and rousing the world to end violence against women and girls, a musician writing and singing music that inspires change, president of the United States or prime minister of England. I tend to be delicate, extending myself by getting involved with many tasks while forgetting to be attentive to my own physical needs. Grounding myself in my body can be challenging, I sometimes neglect day-to-day physical well being, instead, involved in causes of service. In the positive realm, knowing that we are all divine beings, my effort is to direct, shape, uplift the current of life and that of the planet. Encouraging people to fulfill their dreams I inspire them to go beyond their fears, to have optimism. My natural ability to make connections with people, to transmit the light of my spark creates memorable associations and stirring moments. This is not an easy role to live in, yet, when balanced, I am a beautiful humanitarian with the desire and ability to heal the planet.

There is no hidden poet in me, just a little piece of God that might grow into poetry. And a camp needs a poet, one who experiences life there as a bard and is able to sing about it. At night, as I lay in the camp on my plank bed, surrounded by women and girls gently snoring, dreaming aloud, quietly sobbing. Women and girls who often told me during the day: We don't want to think, feel, otherwise we are sure to go out of our minds. I was sometimes filled with an infinite tenderness. And I prayed: Let me be the thinking heart of these barracks. And that is what I want to be again. The thinking heart of a whole concentration camp. —Etty Hillesum

Known Priests include: *Princess Diana, Barack Obama, Billy Graham, Malcolm X, Chris Griscom, Gangaji, Tony Blair, Marianne Williamson, Thomas Merton, Thomas Aquinas, Etty Hillesum, Moamar Khadafy, Rasaputin, Martin Luther, Lynn Andrews, St. Francis of Assisi, Allen Ginsberg, Martin Luther King Jr, Adolph Hitler, Stevie Wonder, Jesse Jackson, Bob Dylan, Kabir Helminski, Marianne Williamson, Natalie Goldberg, Leo Tolstoy, Louise Hay, Jim Bakker, Coretta Scott King, Sigmund Freud, Joan Baez, Joel Ostein, Friedrich Nietzsche, D.H. Lawrence, Cesar Chavez, Rosa Parks, Reverend SunMyung Moon, Bono, John Lennon,*

Leonard Cohen, Eve Ensler, Charles Manson, Idi Amin, Bob Marley, Anne Frank, George Harrison, Ayatollah Khomeini, Milarepa, Jesse Jackson, Napoleon, Siddhartha Guatama, Katherine Mansfield, Zarathustra, Ernsto Che Guevara, Eartha Kitt, Timothy Leary, Moses, Henry David Thoreau, Byron Katie, Rudolf Steiner, Edgar Cayce, H.P. Blavatsky, Ayn Rand, St. Joan of Arc.

KING

POSITIVE: MASTERY

NEGATIVE: TYRANNY

If there is no wind, row. —*Latin Proverb*

Your crown is already paid for. Just put it on your head. —*James Baldwin*

I aspire to master whatever I undertake, whether it's buying a car or house, making a birthday party celebration, choosing a gift, or setting up a business plan. Wanting to become expert in a situation, I feel responsible for the outcome. Privately, self-mastery impels me, publicly, I strive for excellence, especially when I am visibly in the center of an activity. I delegate and oversee. Informed, I am able to get the results I want, even if it means reading through numerous booklets and brochures, investigating online, interviewing people before buying a product. I consider the welfare of many, when I am assigning tasks, advising, I am relentlessly checking up, maintaining self-direction, seeing just what needs to be accomplished. Preferably I am self-employed or at the top position, head of a corporation, foreman in a factory, chairman of a board, owner of a sports team, managing my own business, teaching a class, holding court; in each position I am imprinting style and a sense of vision. In the work that I choose I am an authority, this, though, is not true for all interests I might have, so I have to be diligent not to overextend, to know my limitations, and to assign tasks, to delegate assignments to people who are willing to serve me, and when they do I pay, rewarding them well, sometimes with money and other times with gifts and direct help with their life.

I believe in benevolent dictatorship, provided I am the dictator.
—*Richard Branson*

It's better to be a pirate than to join the navy. —*Steve Jobs*

An active exalted role I have an overview that sees the forest and the trees. I view the whole picture before noticing the details. In my deepest part I experience myself as the ultimate authority, the King. Seeing myself as unrestricted, feeling like a crowned head of state; others may view me as an entitled person who doesn't follow rules, for me, to experience people as my subjects, to live in a world where only 1% of those around are Kings, to regard the world as my domain requires some trimming of the arrogance factor. I learn that by being diplomatic when I feel authoritative. Liking to initiate the course of events, not afraid of hard work, I pay attention to my surroundings both immediate and in the larger context. Remember, throughout history Kings had the *divine right* to rule, which asserted that the King is subject to no earthly rule, as God's vice regent upon the earth and therefore subject to no inferior power; we are considered as the head and arms of the body of man. This symbolism remains in the coronations of the British monarchs, in which they are anointed with Holy oils, ordaining them to monarchy, traced to the genealogy to King David of the old testament. The British Royal Families motto remains as: *God and my birthright—I rule with God's blessings.* For those of us in the King role, whether we are aware on a conscious level or not, we experience ourselves as sovereign, with others as our subjects.

People accuse me of being arrogant all the time. I'm not arrogant, I'm focused. —Russell Crowe

I often magnetize people as well as the accoutrements that are exactly needed. This could be a place to live, job, investment opportunity, party invitation, pair of shoes, the perfect scarf, a teacher at a timely moment or a special doctor. Thriving on overseeing and directing activities, I excel in self-direction. Working in someone else's organization is OK if I am in charge of the aspect that I work with: leader of the team, head of the department, superintendent of the school system, police captain, manager of the hotel, mayor of the town, leader of the union, president of the bank, CEO of the radio station, my own TV show, and then I direct, having great vision for success. I am not satisfied until I have mastered the project I am engaged in, and can be objective in evaluating what is necessary to complete the task. In my field I am an authority, and a good delegator. Not so great at compromise. People feel right as well as motivated and confident when a King is at the helm. And I reward them well, loyalty to me means you are awarded gifts; good expense accounts, fringe benefits called perks. I may not be forceful or strong arm, and I might look relaxed, but you will sense and follow my power and inner authority. Once I am publicly humiliated, contradicted, offended you are on my list, regarded as rebellious even thought of as trying to take over when you come up with ideas that are new and oppose mine. When I have not been taken seriously I feel a certain indignity, insult and surprise, this especially happens in childhood, and with family, when not trusted or not placing confidence in my decisions, especially towards a girl King. School was rough, I really didn't feel like a typical child and found the rules didn't make sense, so I was often not cooperative, not obedient, in trouble, although I actually took life more seriously than the other kids.

No matter what the outcome is, we have to keep our eyes on the bigger picture. —*Michelle Obama*

The King role has the most impact on imprinting those around us, an influence lasting for generations. This comes from my drive to master and perfect, as well as my willingness to be involved in others lives, helping to order and orchestrate the details of their lives. Feeling responsibility for family and others in my empire, I remain loyal to serving those who I take into my kingdom. For me it is no light matter to make a friend, since that act brings the person into my domain, and now under my protection. Of course, the down side is, if betrayed, you are banished from my kingdom—off with your head. Quite a large life to live internally with such big responses.

Love him or hate him, Trump is a man who is certain about what he wants and sets out to get it, no holds barred. —*Donald Trump (describing himself)*

Good speaking tone we are quite facile at oration. Often I set an example through living so large a style. My presence rarely goes unnoticed, some people feel intimidated by my directness and confidence, although I am generally not intending to intimidate. I serve many different types of people, watching responsibly for their welfare and the outcome of their adventures. A Server focuses on one person, I tend to many at one time. Personal relationships are more about projects than friendship. Private, I may look intimate but not really, you might think you are my friend, but I see you as an acquaintance. I rarely just *hang out* as part of a group. People are drawn to me, yet I don't feel that I am their *friend*. I know that I don't *hang out*. Although I might go to a gathering, it has to have a function, like celebrating someone's birthday or a meditation, and then I go to check in with the community. I am careful who I include in my community, since I feel responsible for their welfare once I make that commitment. And the range is large—from ex-convicts to street/homeless people to the well-to-do entertainers and famous aristocrats; I am comfortable with them all.

There's going to be very painful moments in your life that will change your entire world in a matter of minutes. These moments will change 'you.' Let them make you stronger, smarter, and kinder. But don't you go and become someone that you're not. Cry. Scream if you have to, Then you straighten out that crown and keep it moving. —anonymous

Moving toward the negative direction of tyranny I become overbearing, impatient feeling a real need to be in control, in charge, bullying my children, or business associates. When I feel betrayed or deceived, disobeyed, or belittled, then this disloyalty feels like treason. Watch out because I don't forget and the banishment you experience is a real happening. You are removed from being around me. I may not always get the full impact of how people are effected by my behavior. Hard on myself translates to being hard on many in my kingdom. When tyrannical my perspective says: there are only 2 possibilities: my right way or the other, the wrong way. The way out of my disdain for weakness is through compassion for those who don't have the strength to manifest as fearlessly. If you imagine a life in the jungle you can get why the lion is called the King of the beasts!

I would really, really, really like to be a legend like Madonna. Madonna knows what to do next, and when she's performing the audience is just in awe of her. —Britney Spears

I have the same goal I've had ever since I was a little girl. I want to rule the world. Better to live one year as a tiger, than a hundred years as a sheep. I won't be happy till I'm as famous as God. —Madonna

Regardless to what work I am engaged in, I become informed and gather information to know the lay of the land. Driven to be a cut above, to master what projects I take on, I expect the same from others. I like to do what I say, my honor and character matter. I might re-invent the rules when I see more direct and easier ways to do things; in my mind I am the ruler and some rules are outdated and archaic and need to be replaced and who but a King should be laying down the rules! I don't like to labor over decisions, generally the ones I make are good and will work out, and I will stand by what I decide. Drawing up a game plan I am a good strategist, designing with the big picture in view as well as the particulars, and I love the projects: whether they be publishing a book, planning a wedding, orchestrating a class reunion, buying a car, helping a friend find a nursing home for her mother, running a political campaign, rearranging a house, setting up a new health care system for the country. I watch how all the parts interplay and what the choices are, and I pay attention as the project is unfolding. This is not an easy role, often I feel people's energy pulling towards me, sensing my need and ability for self-rule. This can also bring trouble; since I see the world as my kingdom and in this modern world there are very few literal thrones to be filled. Others sometimes feel frustration at my entitlement and privilege-taking, and, yet I am driven to motivate others to want the kind of excellence that I like for my own personal tasks.

Life is too short to be living someone else's dream. Someone once asked me, 'What's your best pickup line?' I said, 'My best pickup line is, Hi, my name is Hugh Hefner.' —Hugh Hefner

Head-strong, I prefer to maintain composure and be directive. An exalted action role, I do things in a big way, whether it is amassing a fortune or losing a bundle. I can be a condo president or the informed bartender, the President's wife, military officer, guru, a movie director or actress, heading up a charity, driving my own private limousine, a therapist or writer, the one in the audience or the person running the class. When I am a Psychologist that allows me to oversee the lives of those who sign on to work with me. I see the whole picture and slowly the person's life unfolds in a new and uplifted way as they capture their power and deepen their understanding. I believe that whatever my work is it adds to making this a better world and from this position, even when I work at home, in my own castle, behind the scene, I am self-empowered. For me, though, it's difficult to ask for personal help, I almost have to become disabled before I'm able to receive assistance. My high energy and empowerment doesn't offer too much of a peek into the personal suffering I have; insomnia ranks high since sleep is no easy matter for the King.

I don't say it in a cocky way, but I take pride in being one of the best at what I do. People respect me as a marketer, brand builder. I want to have a cultural impact. I want to be an inspiration, to show people what can be done. —Sean Combs-P. Diddy

Friendships are few, although acquaintances are many. You might think I have lots of friends —that's because the word is casually used by people, and yet rarely do I consider anyone my *friend*. Conscious of my dignity, when belittled or not taken seriously or not consulted, I withdraw. Male Kings like Richard Branson creating his own airline, John F. Kennedy, President of the United States, Ted Turner creating CNN, Robert Mondavi putting California wine on the map, Hugh Hefner's Playboy domain, Donald Trumps real estate empire and President of the United States, we imprint the field we are in with our vision. It is doubly difficult to be a female King, the world is less apt to support the empowerment of a woman and more easily takes offense at my demanding, self-assured authority. This was apparent with Leona Helmsley and Martha Stewart, both publicly visible Kings, zealously prosecuted less for the magnitude of their crimes than to set an example, convicted more for their temperament than their transgressions. Both judged more harshly than a man in the King role, held to different standards. Men are not attacked as severely for being strong or dominant. Their personalities were their undoing, both having a persona that made it difficult to feel bad for them. Each carried themselves with an hauteur that asked: do you know who I am? Helmsley, one of the richest women in the U.S., referred to as the Queen of Helmsley, has been quoted as saying: *Only little people pay taxes. We don't pay taxes. Only the little people pay taxes.* (Whereas Trump, a male King, not paying taxes, is often smiled at by business men who proclaim him to be a very clever business man.) Both women were sentenced and served prison time, undone by public opinion, portrayed as entitled and condescending. The public spoke of them both using similar language. *They had a chance to be liked if they would have been humble and carry a low profile.* Not exactly a simple prescription for a King!

I had the notion that we could make great wines equal to the greatest wines in the world, and everybody said it was impossible. Whether I played marbles, whether I played football or anything else, I always wanted to excel.
—*Robert Mondavi*

Rarely ordinary, a commanding presence, easily found holding court, delivering commands quite naturally; some of us make so much money we could form our own country. Extravagant and generous, demanding yet responsible to the business I create, I hold court even when I am alone at home. Huge oversized desk—sometimes made of granite or mahogany, an oversized desk chair; a throne to sit on in our castle. Royal colors like purples and gold, fabrics like silks either on clothing or bedding, I certainly have expensive taste. At a conference I inadvertently get the best chair, at a restaurant I also am handed the prime table, sometimes I look for that King spot, the throne to sit on when I attend a function, other times it just is offered to me.

Deals are my art form. Other people paint beautifully on canvas or write wonderful poetry. I like making deals, preferably big deals. I like thinking big, if you're going to be thinking anything, you might as well think big.
—*Donald Trump*

Most of us are either the youngest or the oldest in a family and dominate how the family works, also maintaining a responsibility for the welfare of each member. This same approach continues in business and in community, although when I am an old soul King around younger souls there is the greatest possibility that they won't get my empowerment and will demean my expertise. Easier for younger soul Kings who manifest in the business world where empire building and acquiring wealth is respectable and respected. I like running hotels—they become my kingdom, as well as holding political office or controlling a newspaper or engaging in the power of technology. As a visionary I like entering realms that are the cutting edge, the forefront: I think large, see ahead, don't mind risk, have fun setting up new systems and, in fact, enjoy the challenge. I do poorly in working conditions where inefficiency, laziness, cutting corners or carelessness are permitted or encouraged, even if it's to save a dollar; especially uncomfortable if I am not at the helm or when my opinion is not respected. I prefer motivating through excellence and quality, although bullying can also be a powerful motivator. I get away with more than most, I think it's because I feel entitled and ask or move into the spaces that I want. A distinctive partner, if allowed to be in charge. My impact is so far-reaching and so pervasive that there really does not need to be so many of us around. My imprinting carries through generations. Since there are not a lot of us around, only 1-2% of the population; much of what I figure out is intuitively sensing where energy needs to be balanced. Socially a loner, no one really appears as an equal, even so, my acquaintances get the benefits of my lavishness with the added risk of being cast away, banished from the kingdom.

You set goals beyond your reach so you always have something to live for. I didn't care what, how much adversity life threw at me. I intended to get to the top. —Ted Turner

A visionary, I see possibilities, the big picture, the unfolding that may appear along people's journey. Those who know me are loyal, especially since I encourage or impose loyalty, experiencing me as a good advisor, clever investor, creating businesses and projects, as well as a willingness to include and supervise, be interested in their undertakings. In the negative direction, I am overly demanding on both myself and others by having too exacting standards. I can be relentless, intolerant, over-bearing and tyrannical. Composed and matter-of-fact in my evaluation of a situation, sometimes I straddle between unmerciful kindness and heartless intolerance. My energy can get lost in care-taking one person, whether it is an ordinal partner or demanding parent. It's as if a King set up their kingdom for one solitary gardener and allowed his/her energy and time to be isolated and immersed in that one attendant. This can lead to a quality of dissatisfied unrealized potential. I like to be catered to, yet to erect a kingdom for one solitary mate and contract my energy to fill their need may be a choice for certain lifetimes. Since easily misunderstood my attention needs to be placed on where I best serve, what brings me sovereignty, self-determination and cultivates benevolence.

All of life is a foreign country.....My witness is the empty sky....Accept loss forever. —*Jack Kerouac*

I am at home directing others. Even as a child I had expensive taste, cheaply constructed hand-me-downs have always been unacceptable. What was difficult was being misunderstood by others. I am so unlike most all children that a lot of the time I felt like a loner. Although Kings are rare, oftentimes there are several in one family. I make an effort to imprint a sense of competency in those whose lives I touch. As I grow older in years and interact with children I see that they become strongly effected by my lavish gifts, my wisdom; I am a strong role model. Older soul Kings are generous, private loners, compassionate and benevolent, younger soul Kings, more driven, are ambitious to acquire money, prestige, and fame. Regardless to what soul age, I often feel like this throne is a hot seat, could be that since I am self-assured and informed, in the process of reaching this point, people easily take, and really enjoy taking, a pot shot at me. Generally I am thinking about how to skillfully handle myself and life, all in the most masterful way.

Think like a queen/king. A queen/king is not afraid to fail. Failure is another stepping stone to greatness. Do one thing you think you cannot do. Fail at it. Try again. Do it better the second time. The only people who never tumble are those who never mount the high wire. Cheers to a new year and for another chance for us to get it right. —*Oprah Winfrey*

Known Kings include: *John F. Kennedy, Jacqueline Kennedy Onassis, Madonna, Steve Jobs, Sean Connery, Elvis Presley, James Cameron, Donald Trump, Adele, Mussolini, Mitt Romney, Richard Branson, Martha Stewart, Sean Combs-P. Diddy, Ted Turner, Cate Blanchett, Leona*

Helmsley, Jack Kerouac, Christopher Plummer, Benazir Bhutto, Mario Cuomo, Fidel Castro, John Muir, Barbra Streisand, Hugh Hefner, Aristotle Onassis, Robert Mondavi, Britney Spears, Michelle Obama, Jeff Bezos, Katherine Hepburn, Orson Wells, Alice Miller, Otto Preminger, Rupert Murdoch, Oprah Winfrey, Queen Latifah, Arianna Huffington, J. Paul Getty, Maya Angelou, Franklin Roosevelt, Barbara Walters, Hugh Hefner, Madeleine Albright, Indira Gandhi, Deepak Chopra, William Randolph Hearst, Helena Rubenstein, Susan B. Anthony, King David, Claus von Bulow, Gordon Ramsey, Charles de Gaulle, Zeus, Russell Crowe, Simon Cowell, Sarah Palin, Neem Karoli Baba, Katherine the Great, Lorenzo de Medici, Stalin, Lenin, Hitler, Alexander the Great, Thomas Jefferson, Queen Elizabeth I, Jesus, the Queen of Hearts, C. Everett Koop, Dwight Eisenhower, Maria Callas, Buddha.

S Y S T E M   T H R E E

S O U L   A G E

I N F A N T   S O U L ,   B A B Y   S O U L , Y O U N G   S O U L ,   M A T U R E   S O U L ,   O L D S O U L ,   T R A N S C E N D E N T A L   S O U L , I N F I N I T E   S O U L — A V A T A R

The body is the grail cup out of which the soul drinks the wine of divine ecstasy and can embrace all the terms of a living and dying creation and so becomes boundless and infinite. —Andrew Harvey

Soul is what is eternal within, transcendental to time. The word *soul* and the word *psychology* come from the same root; *psyche*. Soul, an ethereal substance particular to each unique being incorporates the inner essence of a person. Without the soul our body becomes like a light bulb lacking a source of electricity, a computer with no software or system to turn it on; it imbues being, spirit and significance into our life. Soul Age refers to how we have grown from our experiences on this planet, as well as to how many lifetimes we have lived. *The Fifth Way, The Way of the Lover*, is devoted to the well-being and development of the soul. Life, the systems and the tools in *The Way of the Lover* all serve to grow awareness, witnessing; growing a soul, that which is beyond birth and death. Our body, an instrument of the soul, may or may not be healthy. As a dense form of spirit we caretake our body, regardless to its distress—whether the cause is genetic, over-indulgent lifestyle, environmental hazards or karma; still, behind the body and each mani-festation is the energy of the soul. Soul Age development while invisible to the eye, as a spark of light, our breath, is our eternal link with truth. It is a defining quality of human consciousness. As we progress through levels, paying off karma, advancing, growing through our experience, our soul—beyond birth and death, unlimited consciousness, the beginningless, the endless, is immortal. Cumulative intensity of specific life experiences and the reflection and understanding of it may lead to Soul Age advancement as well as life maturity.

Let loving lead your soul, make it a place to retire to, a kind of monastery cave, a retreat for the deepest core of being. Then build a road from there to God. Let every action be in harmony with your soul and its soul-place, but don't parade these doings down the street on the end of a stick! Keep quiet and secret with soul-work. Don't worry so much about your body. God sewed that robe. Leave it as it is. —Attar

When the violinist breaks a hand is the solution to repair the violin? When the tennis player injures a leg, does it change the ability to play by getting a new tennis racket? The instruments obey the player, and what comes out is relevant to the state and condition of the musician or athlete. And so in psychology we don't seek to repair the personality, we study creating a witness, someone home called Self. You are not the body, you are not the mind, you are not the emotions; you are the watcher standing by the side of the mountain. Witnessing is the function of the soul. To realize that you are not the tennis racket, not the violin, you are not the mountain, nor the cars that drive along on the road by the side of the mountain; nobody. You are the watcher, the *I am*. Through witnessing we become aware that we have a soul.

The soul is the intelligence that praises this world's beauty—its roses, its wine, its beautiful women and men, its poems and its prayers. The soul is a grateful guest of the earth. The spirit is a guest of the soul, who is constantly trying to leave. —Robert Bly

Through witnessing we connect to a spark that is a fragment of the whole. The age of our soul is not in direct correlation to our life years, it's in relationship to our lives, our experiences and our comprehension of both. Soul Age is connected to our level of perception and understanding. It is our perspective from this life plane. Through awareness and deep understanding obstacles vanish and we awaken. Soul Age refers to how a person has grown from their experience on the planet, not just to how many lifetimes he or she has lived. At some point we experience it all, moving continually along to different levels of understanding and responsibility. It is said that the soul is a knowing substance, and needs the body. Experience, knowing, and awakening, are keys to Soul Age. Buddha looked at an old person once and understood death, he saw a child and subsequently understood birth. Just how many experiences have we had and do we need to have before we understand, before our self-awareness, before we know! This is the key to assessing Soul Age.

About soul: We are born with a certain property and, thanks to this property, in the course of our life 'something' does form itself in us: this, for me, is beyond all doubt. We are born with a certain property, and, thanks to this property, in the course of our life experiencings elaborate in us a certain substance, and from this substance there is gradually formed in us 'something or other' which can acquire a life almost independent of the physical body. Although this 'something' is formed from the same substance as the physical body, it has a much finer materiality and, it must be assumed, a much greater sensitivity towards all kinds of perceptions. —G. I. Gurdjieff

Since the soul is eternal, our ability to know the soul develops as our ability to witness evolves. Our life experiences, our living in physical form bring us to have experiences, and our learning and self-awareness which is at our level of consciousness affects how our personality appears. The key lies in the development of our awareness. I am not only the body, mind, or my emotions. As the quality of witnessing grows, as awareness deepens, a new birth of consciousness—the birth of the soul, that which is beyond birth and death, transcendental to time. And you are the witness to it all. By witnessing, we become aware of having a soul. The world hangs on the thread of consciousness, Gurdjieff names this in his teaching: *Life Is Real Only Then When I am*. He stated that the first exercise for awakening is that of *I Am*.

The Baal Shem Tov taught that a soul may descend from its place high in the heavens down into this world for 70-80 years, just to do a favor for another. —Rabbi Tzvi Freeman

To turn more actively to the unplumbed places inside ourselves, not to necessarily become a healthy person, but for the soul, for the mystery of what we don't know we contact that which lies at the core of our being. The words of Rumi are filled with accounts of soul: A beautiful image appears in his lines:

> *Out beyond ideas of wrongdoing and rightdoing, is a field. I'll meet you there. When the soul lies down in that grass, the world is too full to talk about. Ideas, language, even the phrase, each other doesn't make any sense.*

Hafiz says:

> *What is this precious love and laughter*
> *Budding in our hearts?*
> *It is the glorious sound*
> *of a soul waking up!*

And so soul, beyond birth and death, is what this study is about. Soul, a timeless substance grows from our experience. There are seven Soul Ages and seven soul levels. Each age has a positive and a negative viewpoint, and a focus; except transcendental, infinite and avatar. I have included life year examples to offer conceptual and visual clarity to this study of Soul Age.

Every moment and every event of our life on earth plants something in our soul. —*Thomas Merton*

The following parallel between human development each lifetime and the development of the soul over many lifetimes are used as illustrations to bring clarity to the teaching; their blossoming and maturing assists our consciousness and lifts our planet's vibration. The relationship connections are quite apparent, in other words knowing that infants, appropriately so, see life in relationship to their survival. Babies look for structure, youngsters learn about the world as it appears outside of themselves, and adolescents create peer one-to-one relationships as they tentatively experience their world. As we move away from adolescence towards old soul time, we begin to see the world at large from a broader perspective. To be aware of the differences in each Soul Age and level opens the door to true understanding, which accelerates our development. Soul Age tells us the type of lessons that are dominant at particular stages. Our life years, our age, is a superficial detail of who we are; our true Soul Age is more meaningful, more impactful, more significant—it is the perspective of our inner self. The older the soul, the more desire and capacity to be truthful, although at all ages there are those who delude themselves. Our Soul Age is where we are on a spiral that has no beginning or end and describes our primary perspective and lessons with regard to the physical plane.

The soul is placed in a body like a rough diamond, and must be polished, or the luster of it will never appear. —*Daniel Defoe*

Souls exist in light form and each soul projects a specific color of the spectrum. The color scale of the soul's aura portrays the gradations of hues and colors that mark the evolution of the soul. Off-white and gray with tints of pink mark the infant soul. Orange-red are the core colors for the baby soul. Light orange-yellow, moving into yellow are the colors for the young soul. Various hues of green are the mark for the mature soul. The old soul is portrayed with hues of blue moving from light blue and teal and turqouise to deeper blue, violet. The transcendental and infinite souls are seen with an aura of purple.

Perhaps a stable order can only be established on earth if man always remains acutely conscious that his condition is that of a traveler. It is precisely the soul that is the traveler; it is of the soul and of the soul alone that we can say with supreme truth that being necessarily means being on the way: en route. —*Gabriel Marcel*

INFANT SOUL

TODDLER

BIRTH TO 3 YEARS

Simple, Open, Animalistic, Terrified, Survial-Oriented

Positive: simple, innocent, openness, environmental awareness
Negative: frightened, myopic, helpless, avoidant, aggressive, ruthless
Focus: being alive, survival choices

Such as are your habitual thoughts, such also will be the character of your mind; for the soul becomes dyed with the color of its thoughts. —*Marcus Aurelius*

Primitive and tribal cultures are predominately made up of Infant Souls. Primarily involved with survival needs, environmental awareness, not knowing right from wrong, they are naive, fearful, impulsive, have a basic curiosity about this physical plane and see themselves as the center of the universe. Initially, we all enter the planet manifesting at an Infant Soul age. We are toddlers focused on strong instinctive needs and attractions, enjoying the touch and taste of dirt, clay, water, as well as a fascination with small bugs, butterflies and lizards. Infant Souls are instinctive centered with an organic essence; there is an ease and comfort to being without clothing, sleeping outdoors, fishing, hunting, as well as eating plants and other naturally grown foods. Little pretense and no real strong agenda, they act from habit or impulse. We remember our Infant Soul self when our survival is threatened.

To put it simply, the lizard brain is purely concerned with survival.
—*Stephen Richards*

New to the world, barely socialized, Infant Souls don't easily fit in with mainstream society, have a near impossible time knowing the difference between right and wrong, and are routinely being told to grow up. Being newly incarnate they often have a mystical air. Infant Souls have to be educated about right and wrong regardless to their intelligence or I.Q. Ethical understanding and morality does not bleed through this beginning incarnation. Self-involved, they often live in a state of incompetence and terror, their small daily circumstances are about all they can deal with. Little understanding of life, their impulsive issues keep them from expanding beyond their immediate world, what is known and familiar is where they tend to remain. Novices at physical existence, making headway in simple natural environments, they are not skillful in contemporary modern settings. Short attention span and hesitant to experiment, there is still a freshness about them. Infant Souls are intolerant of those who lead complicated lives and lack survival skills. Justice and morality, appropriateness and ethics are unclear concepts, murder is an easy instinctive fear-based response, it's their survival strategy. Mental hospitals, psychiatric locked wards and prisons are oftentimes where Infant Souls are placed.

I'm not very wise to many things. I'm not of this generation. —*Charles Manson*

Infant Souls do not like to be public, the few we hear about have been serial murderers, like Richard Ramirez a California serial killer, and Joel Steinberg who murdered his adopted daughter. Jeffrey Daimer was an example of an Infant Soul serial killer born into a time when other soul ages could not comprehend that he was not crazy and was, in fact, acting in accordance to his natural instincts, appropriate to his soul age. Infant Soul cannibalism is frightening to all other soul ages and eventually he was murdered in prison, the baby and young soul population found him too threatening and quite bizarre to their baby and young soul reality. What we see as uncivilized, is an Infant Soul acting on impulse minus social understanding, and with no regard to consequences, without conscience, unable to sense right from wrong without guided instruction.

In the beginning, soul is inexperienced and often overwhelmed by the challenge of learning to operate a physical body. The initial focus is naturally going to be primarily on the physical plane and social plane as soul learns to imitate in order to survive. —*Kit Cain*

Without a tradition of history and old-fashioned values to rely upon, the theme is *why not!* They might barbecue their brother or throw him out of a window, to stop his crying. Antisocial and immoral acts arise from their lack of socialization and what follows is no real sense of wrongdoing. They are wide eyed, innocent, one with nature, yet lacking life time experiences. Often they cluster around the equator. Survival is of essential importance since the Infant Soul carries many fears. Places like Ethiopia, the Amazon basin, Iraq, Iran, rural Guatemala, the Gaza,

New Guinea, Sri Lanka, Borneo, and the Sudan have populations that include simple, earthy Infant Souls that appear to be quite out of step with their current society. Threats to them are often simplistic survival issues—earthquakes, tsunamis, plagues, inadequate shelter, typhoons, Ebola, poisonous foods, war, aggressive animals; life lived close to the bone. With these unavoidable dangers, the Infant Soul lifetime might be brief.

The law of evolution is that the strongest survive. Yes, and the strongest in the existence of any social species, are those who are most social, in human terms, most ethical..There is no strength to be gained from hurting one another. Only weakness. —Ursula K. Le Guin

We have currently shifted to a mature soul era, making Infant Soul birth rare. It would be difficult for that child to fit into this society and a challenge to our community's ability to tolerate an Infant Souls way of being. The current century demands more socializing, less opportunity to hunt, fewer places to live intuitively close to nature. At this time Infant Soul's are rarely born in most of the Western world.

Not choice but habit rules the unreflecting herd. —William Wordsworth

Known Infant souls include: *Jeffrey Daimer, Richard Ramirez, Joel Steinberg, Fred West, Charles Manson.*

BABY SOUL

CHILD: PRE-SCHOOL THRU ELEMENTARY

3 TO 12 YEARS

Structure, Conformity, Rigid, Dogmatic, Rule-Oriented

Positive: structure, organizing society, social awareness

Negative: rigid, dogmatic, strong belief systems, lack of originality
Focus: belonging to a culture, moral code and ethical choices

Most of the things we do, we do for no better reason than that our fathers have done them or our neighbors do them, and the same is true of a larger part than what we suspect of what we think. —*Oliver Wendell Holmes, Jr.*

Once survival skills are mastered, the Baby Soul stage is concerned with civilizing instincts and accepting cultural imprinting through controlling primitive urges. Slowly the Baby Soul develops a sense of self along with pride in being molded and socialized. It is that aspect of ourself that was taught acceptable eating habits, proper toilet training, managing emotions, watching our language and obeying restrictions. Elementary childhood children are comforted when given ordered clear consistent rules. Parents, the school system, the police, religious leaders all work to create human beings out of what they perceive as rude, coarse, unmannered, savage, newcomers that were once infant souls. Essentially Baby Souls develop and maintain the authority standards and the beliefs and form of civilization.

Any fool can make a rule, and any fool will mind it. —*Henry David Thoreau*

This is a stage when puritanical and conventional pride aims to structure the culture. With the memory remnants of having sat in a mud hut for tribal meetings, this soul age sits in churches and organizations like Rotary Club, Parent Teacher Association, National Rifle Association, evangelical activists, Ku Klux Klan meetings; groups that aim to set what they deem as correct methods and guidelines. Laws to maintain marriage standards, anti-abortion, defined social behavior and dress code at family gatherings, as well as the structure of the Mafia, are manifestations of this soul age. Tattling is a common way to attract adult attention. Winning, leading, being first or in charge as the boss are important; losing creates unhappiness for the Baby Soul. Essentially, structure helps support comfort in the world, as Baby Souls over apply rules that become set in their minds. Life at this stage is about security and safety, what's deemed right is right, there's no room for the grey and possibilities, or living in the question. In this context discipline and authority are used as a way to educate and improve themselves. Medical doctors, religious leaders, military leaders, even a prison system can become the recognized, looked-up-to authority.

It's the rule, and that's what will do. I'm a pillar of this community, and I love my country, and I will protect the country, my community and my family at all costs. —Baby Soul comment.

A week after the December 2012 school shooting in Newton, Connecticut Wayne La Pierre, Vice President of the National Rifle Association gave a defiant address advocating placing armed officers in schools. LaPierre speaking to a Baby Soul mentality claimed that Americans are buying firearms and ammunition because *there is no greater freedom than the right to survive and protect our families with all the rifles, shotguns, and handguns we want. The only thing that stops a bad gun with a gun is a good guy with a gun. I call on Congress today to act immediately to appropriate whatever it is necessary to put armed officers in every single school in this nation.* The Alternative Right, commonly known as the Alt-Right, is a set of far-right ideologies, groups and individuals geared towards what they call the preservation of *Western civilization*, adhering to *scientific racism;* there has been a fascist overtone to their comments. This is a soul age that takes strong positions and is put on edge, unnerved when feeling threatened by what they deem as lawlessness.

Government comes from a Baby Soul desire for order. Things are polarized. Often a collective experience like the army, jail, hospitals and bureaucracies are formed from a Baby Soul mentality. There is good and bad, right and wrong. There is a gun in one hand, and life is about law and breaking the law. You join us or we kill you. If you argue, confusion and anger become part of the solution, rather than the raising of a question. Evangelical, with concepts of evil and salvation, they work to influence government with strong standards regarding obedience, anti-abortion, firm laws and a tough stance on criminals and lawbreakers. Litigation, fundamentalist religions, religiously devout, ultraconservative; if the rule book doesn't speak to a circumstance their self-importance kicks in to make them still believe they are right. Baby Souls need a framework and direction and will impose the rules that they are comfortable living under onto the public at large. If they feel homosexuality is against the Scripture, that nude beaches are objectionable, that abortion is offensive, that marijuana and euthanasia are appalling, then laws need to be passed to ban these things for all people at all times in the effort to save the world from *eternal damnation*. Behavior that does not conform to their standards and rules is sinful.

Evolution is a bankrupt speculative philosophy. Only a spiritually bankrupt society could ever believe it. Only atheists could accept this Satanic theory. If I do not return to the pulpit this weekend, millions of people will go to hell. —Jimmy Swaggart

Structure, law and order and rules offer a quality of protection that becomes a welcome relief. Baby Souls are critical of those who don't follow the program. Once in a position of power the violence of beatings and other abuse become justified to enforce the credo of: *follow the rules*. Problems have solutions, not psychological reasons, since this is not a self-reflective time. There is almost no awareness or understanding of motives, their own or others, there is only good or bad, right or wrong. Therefore the medical model of surgery and medication, of going to war, water boarding as punishment for opposition, obeying the school principal, are the one correct way to live. There are no insights, life is approached in a black and white routine. Literal; therapy or looking to understand deeper meaning is not a natural part of any equation. The preferred mode is to be directed from the outside, with clear guidelines. The medical establishment is a good example. Go to the doctor, get a prescription, take the medicine, go to surgery, cut out/solve the problem.

Guns are neat little things, aren't they? They can kill extraordinary people with very little effort. —John W. Hinckley Jr.

These are the so-called good citizens, not questioning authority, and sometimes becoming the authority. They make popular politicians and propose clear direct policies, in fact they can't imagine any other way but their own policy. Much of the Middle East, Latin countries like Argentina, Brazil, and Central and South America, Haiti, Iran, Iraq, Bangladesh and the Caribbean Islands have large Baby Soul populations. This creates civil wars, killing for undisputable beliefs, imposing punishment. Totalitarian regimes, one-party absolute and dictatorial, requiring complete subservience to the state, are the product of Baby Souls.

What we call morals is simply blind obedience to words of command. —Havelock Ellis

Known Baby Souls include: *Ayatollah Khomeini, John Ashcroft, Jesse Helms, Hitler, Mohammar Kaddafy, Idi Amin, Pat Boone, Richard Nixon, Papa Doc Duvalier, John W. Hinckley Jr., Jimmy Swaggart, Joseph McCarthy, Pat Robertson, Senator Ted Cruz, Rick Santorum, Jerry Falwell, Oral Roberts, Charlton Heston.*

YOUNG SOUL

JUVENILE TO ADOLESCENT
TO YOUTHFUL TEENAGE
TO EARLY ADULTHOOD
13 TO 28 YEARS

Productive, Materialistic, Competitive, Success-Oriented

Positive: prosperous, effective, productive, industrious, independence, personal achievement

Negative: self-centered, materialistic, lacking insight, formatory, ego-driven

Focus: being a free agent, choices about mastering achievement

Get going. Move forward. Aim high. Plan a takeoff. Don't just sit on the runway and hope someone will come along and push the airplane. It simply won't happen. Change your attitude and gain some altitude. Believe me, you'll love it up here. —Donald Trump

The characteristics of the Young Soul age are geared towards lessons about worldly success. Moving away from baby soul experiences concerning survival on the physical plane the Young Soul learns to negotiate in the world. Adolescents move away from being constantly monitored by their parents and create peer groups, becoming the authority the infant and baby souls look up to, asserting independence. All three soul ages, infant, baby and young, focus on the external world until shifting to a mature soul age when the direction changes to looking towards an inner world. Why? is rarely asked; this is a soul age that has little insight or interest into other people's behavior. When issues arise there are momentary excursions for help and direction, which quickly pass as a solution appears. The earlier soul ages are not directed to patiently examine their life. Young Souls are identified with the body. This is a very physical stage. There is almost no awareness about being more than a body, consciousness does not survive the physical form, death is avoided and denied, so extreme measures are taken to maintain a high level of bodily energy regardless to inner needs. Young adults, not aware of future consequences, push the physical, eat randomly and indiscriminately and the Young Soul age reflects this kind of brash, cocky attitude. Extreme measures are taken to keep the body looking toned and fit, all to project a self-confident youthful image and appearance. People reach their competitive Young Soul mind-set sometime in mid-school years. Energetic, enjoying action films, the United States entertains the world until competitiveness sets in—then they plunder to dominate, destroying each other and the planet.

I wish I had a twin, so I could know what I'd look like without plastic surgery. —*Joan Rivers*

There is a high motivation towards wealth, success and power, not based on any particular personal interest; the aim is to amass money, to look good, to be prosperous, all for self-advancement and personal achievement. There is no interest in using money for service or to make others lives better. Their basic motivation is materialism. Young souls tend to be critical of those who are not successful in the world. Achievement is foremost, fame and fortune, this is success! Exceptionally adept at building civilizations, experiencing themselves as separate, they see each idea as their own. Wanting to impact the outer world to prove independence and learn the world game, they enjoy mastering the game of life. Personal interest does not weigh much in the equation, one's work is based on function, convenience, monetary possibilities, image and competition. Stepping into the business one's parent set up, studying at a fashionable Ivy League college, higher education and graduate-level degrees, the majority of people organizing this country are Young Soul: productive, competitive and ambitious, wanting power and prestige in their lives as well as globally. More ego-driven than other soul ages, there is a lot of amped-up energy to keep busy, to prove themselves, to assert their opinions in the world. We are all imprinted by the values of the Young Soul community; it seeps into our education, corporations, politics, medical establishment, legal system, advertisements, sports, movies, television and magazines. Young Soul governments are always watching to one-up other countries, whether it is in the arms race or in developing a rich economy.

My sons are all adults and they've made decisions about their careers and they've chosen not to serve in the military and active duty and I respect their decision in that regard. One of the ways my sons are showing support for our nation is helping me get elected because they think I'd be a good president.
—*Mitt Romney*

Young Souls have moved from having experienced infant and baby soul stages of survival, fear, structure and order; now the energy shifts to amassing power in the world. This, then becomes a competitive, wealth gathering, finding prominence, stage. Things are bought not because they necessarily like them, instead, they are based on what projects an image of success. The house, body, job, bank account, wife/husband, parties, car and jewelry are acquired in a style that will best express prominence, achievement and status. What you have is who you are, the younger the body looks the more successful one appears. Youth, wealth and fashion are pursued regardless to the long term health of the body, in the competitive hope of projecting an image of rich and famous. A strong identification with looks; cosmetic surgeons are the solution to the bodies aging process. A makeover to look younger, to have the face that is remembered in the mind's eye—not the one in the mirror. Gray hair carefully covered, wrinkles and lines create the urge to tighten the skin, veneers on the teeth, dental and breast implants; looking younger helps them to feel younger and allows the Younger Soul to tackle the world with greater tenacity. Creative innovation is absent, instead, copying what has been popular and mass marketing, the clone becomes the production. Imitation everything, so long as it sells, whether it's a TV show, a smart looking electronic device, clothing, or jewelry that looks like the real thing; the Young Soul mentality is to crank out copies and then, once the money making dries up, to move on, cleverly lifting and replicating the next popular item.

If the social order judges success by material gain, the most successful will be the most corruptible and selfish. —Khemetic saying

Cosmetic surgery, ambition, having and doing a lot, pursuing plastic lives, best describes this soul age. Fingernails covered with long shiny press-ons, wearing cologne or perfume, going to the mall regularly to shop, on-line purchases, tweeting opinions and preferences, rarely identifying their true age; they have a strong avoidance to aging as well as fear of dying. This fear helps motivate the drive to make a symbolic immortal impact on the world. In fact, the death word is often dropped and replaced by the word *lost, gone* or *passed away.* This masks the Young Soul fear of death, which is the distinctive, the most noticeable of all other soul ages.

I long for the day that 'Roe V. Wade' is sent to the ash heap of history. Do I believe in evolution? I embrace the view that God created the heavens and the earth, the seas and all that's in them. —Mike Pence

The Young Soul will go along with change if it is in their favor. The idea of not dying your hair, not being thin, not being an investor, not having a 401K, not having health and life insurance; not being seen as a winner, makes one a loser. This is a fun time, with interest in running things, looking good, eating in the right restaurants, living with the attractive and affluent people and getting elected to high positions. They like living in large cities like Los Angeles, Washington D.C., Dallas, Boston, Miami, New York and Chicago. The previous infant soul age was more about rural locations. This is the America that is based on the corporate world of 9 to 5, the Madison Avenue Corporate America, working sometimes very long days to have more, these are the movers and shakers. Materialism at its peak cultivates the workaholic Young Soul who is pressed to build an empire based on the goal of making money, of parking a polished new BMW or Tesla in their driveway for the neighbors to see, of the driving ambition that fuels the chasing after success and winning toys, of membership in Trump's Mar-a-Lago and sporting the newest digital products along with named brand sporting equipment. The doctrine of *I win* has created the extravagant challenger, contender competitions that exist in our business world, in our adversarial legal system, in the building of big cars and high-rise condominiums that blot out light and our natural environment, in the corruption of the banks and the housing industries. These are the people who have excess money while others live in poverty, of the Ponzi scheme strategy where there is a winner and many losers.

How you play the game is for college ball. When you're playing for money, winning is the only thing that matters. Win anyway you can as long as you can get away with it. If I was playing third base and my mother rounded third base with the winning run, I'd trip her up. Nice guys finish last. As long as I've got a chance to beat you I'm going to take it. —Leo Durocher

Imperialistic, all people, all countries should subscribe to their way; particularly because they won't listen to any other way and don't like to be told what to do. They see the world as their club, differences are difficult to tolerate, so join and conform or they will make jokes about you, or wipe you out. This is the community that cannot accept same-sex adoption and will vote against same-sex marriage. Organizations, fraternity and sorority houses, competitive sports like football regardless to the consequence of concussions and gross injuries, conventions and seminars, the stock market, the Chamber of Commerce, all are backed by the Young Soul collective mentality that believes strength of achievement comes from large numbers. Countries like Australia, Canada, parts of Europe, Mexico, Hong Kong, Taiwan, Japan, South Korea, Vietnam, as well as progressive Arab states like Oman and Saudia Arabia, and large areas of the United States like Silicon Valley, and Los Angeles all have large Young Soul populations.

I have five draft deferments because I had other priorities in the sixties than military service. My current health: except for the occasional heart attack, I never felt better. —Dick Cheney

There is no real psychological study, regard for motives, interest or depth in connection to one's personal inner life. *Don't analyze everything* is the comment to older souls for placing interest and attention on understanding. Younger souls don't understand older souls, and have no concern or issue for that to be different. Thinking they know it all, resistant Young Souls do not make innovative perceptive students. Good grades are more meaningful than what is learned and diplomas and certificates are pridefully framed and hung on the wall as achievement. Psychology and Psychiatry are valued for prescribing medication and maintaining a normal anxiety-less life. Labeling the problem—

depression, hyperactivity disorder, erectile dysfunction, postpartum depression, attention-deficit disorder—always the solution remains the same. Drugstore pharmacology. In fact, one goes to therapy to receive a label and get the prescription. Inserting metal into bone to replace hips and knees without any regard for alternative choices or after effect and repercussion; this is the quick fix-me conclusion community. There is no true interest in self-understanding, fixing the issue, solving the problem; designing and shaping civilization is the thrust and personal issues are viewed as an interference, to be cleared up and straightened out. The following comments by Clarence Thomas who sits on the Supreme Court and popular Tom Cruise reflect the thinking of this soul age:

I was smart enough to use pot without getting caught, and now I am on the Supreme Court. If you were stupid enough to get caught, that's your problem. Your appeal is denied. This 40 year sentence just might teach you a lesson. —Clarence Thomas

Nothing ends nicely, that's why it ends. My job is as brutal, as hard as fighting in Afghanistan. —Tom Cruise

Young Soul values as reflected in parenting promote children for what they can do and is interesting as a way to chat with family and acquaintances. Baby carriages and strollers that make you want to look in, fancy infant clothing, music classes and recital performances for the younger child; appearance offers status to the parent and grand-parents. This is not a soul age that engages children to express feelings or bonds from a place of intimacy and understanding. Friends are someone to do things with, as entertainment; to go places with, to small talk with on the phone, to share business thoughts or to play cards. One mark of a Young Soul person is the lack of capacity for self-awareness, instead, there are simplistic solutions for resolving situations. Cargo gets dumped as toxic waste, with little regard for the environment. They act out, often with aggression. This is the world of sports, lawyers, insurance and medical fraud, government and nationalistic wars. Conquer is a big motivation and shows up in the business, sports and imperialistic world view. Television is filled with Young Soul soap operas, sports competition, and other unimaginative uninspired shows. Religion is geared to the familiar, to what has been known and has worked in the family. Insurance and law suits are based on getting what is imagined to be deserved, manipulating major settlements and investing large amounts of time and energy in feeling cheated, blaming, pointing fingers, looking for the win even at the detriment of others.

I knew I was a winner back in the late sixties. I knew I was destined for great things. People will say that that kind of thinking is totally immodest. I agree. Modesty is not a word that applies to me in any way—I hope it never will. —Arnold Schwarzenegger

In the political arena, issues are framed by us versus them, a black and white approach, avoiding complexities and perspectives. The Young Soul is dedicated to ambition and winning at any price. The power of war is energizing, might make the economy rise, and the drive to forcefully get the upper hand is the success. Waging war is primarily a Young Soul happening; they love to make their mark on the world. The human consequence is rarely in the equation, since country is more of an amorphous concept than the vision of individual humanity.

It's possible to think that we are mentally healthy because we share our mistaken values and understandings with those around us. Collectively, our ill minds create a society that is itself ill and we consider ourselves healthy because we see our values reflected in our fellow wordlings. —Bodhipaksa

Known Young Souls include: *Clint Eastwood, George Bush Jr., Tom Cruise, Arnold Schwarzenegger, Mitt Romney, Osama Bin Laden, Clarence Thomas, Jim Bakker, Alan Greenspan, Nancy Reagan, Billy Graham, Mohammed Ali, Dick Clark, Liberace, Carly Fiorina, Dr. Ben Carson, Mike Pence, Paul Ryan, Sean Hannity, Rush Limaugh, Mitch McConnell, Ted Cruz, Marco Rubio, Dick Cheney, Imelda Marcus, Donald Trump.*

MATURE SOUL

ADULT

29 TO 49 YEARS

Intensity, Social Interaction, Inner Exploration, Issues,

Relationship-Oriented

Positive: exploring personal relatedness, interest in a spiritual path, concern for the environment, tolerance of differences, looking at boundary issues, interdependence, empathy, intimacy
Negative: identified, emotional turmoil and melodrama, subjective projections, suffering, rebelliousness, addictions, confused
Focus: co-existence with others, relationship choice

It's time for human beings to grow up emotionally, Only through emotions can you encounter the force field of your own soul. —Doc Childre

*B*etween ages 28 and 30, called the first Saturn Return, marks the end of youth and the beginning of the productive adult years. The planet Saturn takes 29.5 years to make its orbit around the sun. When Saturn moves back to the place it was the moment you were first born, you are metaphorically reborn, but only after certain lessons. Saturn occupies a space in everyone's chart that is considered the astrological thumbprint of the soul and indicates the lessons you came here to learn. The Saturn Return identifies the time when an individual comes to terms with adulthood and leaves behind many of the vestiges of childhood and early adulthood. This life passage is equated with *growing up*. The first Saturn Return is a time of serious self examination; many consider the first return to be one of the most difficult times of their life, as well as the most rewarding. To meet this event with responsibility we step forward onto a path with a clarity that supports our lifestyle. This is a time to be building a platform to stand on in life. On the other hand setting an imprint of confusion and roadblocks imprints difficulty throughout the following 29 years. Saturn rules structures, and at age 29 people look at the structures in their life: job, career, relationships, education, household. These are forms in the material world which define and describe who and how we are and are up for review and change at this time. Since ancient history Saturn has been identified with father time even though, like the moon, Saturn is feminine and we are all his/her children; our mortal bodies devoured while our immortal souls liberated as we understand who and what we are—life in the kingdom of time. Saturn is the archetypal symbol for a way of being, a process that brings an opportunity to stand in our life and face what is, to see the landmarks and take direction.

Saturn's beat and pressure are needed in order that we can develop what Buddhists call the diamond soul. —A. Whitaker

During Saturn Return practical experiences match the truth in the saying: *Endings are beginnings.* This event brings the opportunity to turn inward, reflecting on our personal destiny. Awareness of age and time, a Saturn issue, pushes us to move forward or holds us to feeling blocked. When the action we take mirrors the measure of understanding and maturity that has deepened over time we harvest the bounty and enter adulthood. Stepping forward into our life, risk-taking; holding to the difficult creates a new beginning. When lessons are not understood and the clutter that impedes progress is not swept away, the second Saturn Return at age 58 to 60 presents a second major opportunity to accept responsibility for the life that is our own. Reviewing and taking responsibility for our circumstances—how has our body held up, does our work sing to us, is this the partner I cherish; this is the moment the blame train stops and we can get off, or at least deposit everything in the baggage car as well as rewrite our script, minus the illusions of unresolved issues. Or, we become excessive, disagreeable, bitter, in poor health, disillusioned, disappointed; the structures we have created are challenged and we experience a quality of satisfaction or one of regret. We see what has been sown. The door opens and elderhood arrives: the age of wisdom. A new moment to create ourselves. At the time of our third Saturn Return, age 86 to 89, there have been three full passages of Saturn through our birth chart, three full opportunities and we have completed three full phases of our life; each cycle turning up the heat and pressure and bringing opportunities to grow, learn, produce, and to mentor others.

It has often been said that under strong Saturn transits one can choose between exhaustion and depression—some choice! It implies that because Saturn is often about doing real work in the mundane world that exhaustion is the better choice—hinting that 'its better to wear out than rust out' as Mark Twain once said. —Elizabeth Spring

The shift to a Mature Soul age, a reflection of the first Saturn Return, is marked by discomfort from an earlier soul age emphasis on an external life; now the stirring of an inner life is calling attention. Young souls, little energy spent on personal life, had time to focus on the outside, amassing wealth and prestige. No longer satisfied by the drive to acquire, the challenge changes. Mature Souls, more interested in personal questions and feelings, start to gravitate to other Mature Souls and create communities to live close by or together. Learning takes on a personal tone, grades and diplomas are no longer priority, the meaning of life, regard for the planet and other people, being informed, all matter more than receiving the status that motivated the younger soul person. There is a move towards lesser paid smaller jobs, away from large bureaucratic organizations, much to the surprise and disapproval of the younger soul. Downsizing salary and gaining less prestige baffles the younger soul. The adolescent and young adult are now becoming adult with deeper questions, *who am I?* replaces, *whoever has the most toys when he dies wins.* Day to day living carries a tone of intensity; feelings surface, relationships carry pain and bring suffering. Stress plays havoc on the brain and body, creating physical and mental illness. Therapy becomes a model of healing for many of the high maintenance Mature Souls often times fascinated with their own dramas they magnetize acquaintances, family members and therapists who indulge the stories.

Saturn brings to mind the two ancient Greek maxims inscribed at the Temple Delphi: 'Know Thyself' and 'Nothing in Excess.' One might think that by understanding and trying to live by these wise sayings one could avoid the great troubles in life. Perhaps they help; but still we seem to suffer. Our understanding of these words change as we age, but life often plays some nasty tricks on us in the meantime. Perhaps this is why we have Saturn transits—it's a chance to get it right this time. Saturn is the archetypal symbol for a way of being, or a 'process' that slows us down and makes us take a cold hard look at reality. —Elizabeth Spring

This stage marks the entry into a spiritual life. The challenge to stop building personality, instead to pay attention to essence, rocks the emotional world. Mature souls become judgmental towards those who do not care to take life as they do. Connections with others, an emotion-based life-style, focus on the environment, on what health foods they eat and a real concern for politics are markers for Mature Souls. Their desire to impact the world lies in finding a meaning for life. The lessons are now about relationships, emotions and an inner world. A child's viewpoint matures to become that of an adult. Mature Soul consciousness arrives and brings up-and-down emotional turmoil, full-of-drama experiences. Mature Souls shifting into the soul age of 29-plus years evaluate their life, their goals, take workshops and classes to learn about themselves, enter therapy looking to find a meaning to life. Earlier soul ages studied to achieve more money and status; this soul age is clearly concerned with personal fulfillment.

If conversation was the lyrics, laughter was the music, making time spent together a melody that could be replayed over and over without getting stale.
—*Nicolas Sparks*

Relationships and emotional life are significant. Personal life has a quality of melodrama. Moving through the infant, baby and young soul stages into the Mature Soul age begins to create unease. The wealth, prestige and power that once engaged one's interest in the external world shifts to an inner direction of questioning and noticing the emptiness of a life without meaningful relationships. Things now begin to personally matter. *I want a house that I design and care about, not just a house like everyone else.* Feelings begin to hold interest, even noticing that other people have feelings becomes a possibility. Living harmoniously follows the awareness that coarse rough energy effects them. Vacations become places to retreat to, sanctuaries, spas and centers with like minded people; to be away from the competitive world and share concerns with like minded people is important. This is the soul age that inspires the world, forming environmental groups, social reforms, peace movements, all within the desire to create a better planet for the world.

Why aren't people in recovery good dancers? They lose interest after 12-steps.
—*Recovery program joke*

Often the Mature Soul is identified with dramas involving addictions and will create community around meetings, 12-step programs, Course in Miracle classes, men's drumming and Warrior Way circles and support groups. Health food stores, vegetarian, vegan and raw food life style, Waldorf and other school communities that promote a particular lifestyle, protesting the wearing of fur and leather to protect animals; all are Mature Soul causes. Concern for animals becomes an issue, pet cemeteries, swimming with the dolphins and whales, protecting certain species from extinction, not killing animals and wearing their fur; this follows the awareness that other sentient beings have rights, and wanting to work to protect those rights. The large emotional content of experiences are created by the Mature Soul in order to open themselves emotionally. The questions arise: Who am I ? Why am I here? What is my life purpose? How can I find my soul mate? What is my sexuality? Does my gender match my birth body? How can I heal the planet and find peace on earth? Many times the questions are unanswerable, and need to be lived into until shifting into the old soul age. Those questions sometimes open a door for the Mature Soul to turn to using drugs and alcohol. Anxiety, fear, worry, suicide, and much of the acting out and early departures that we read about in the news are products of the intensification of feelings; earlier soul ages had little if any interest in their inner life and so the questions and lifestyle of the Mature Soul are looked at as disturbed instead of understood as searching for meaning and creativity.

Robin Williams, Michael Jackson, Amy Winehouse, River Phoenix, Truman Capote, J.D. Salinger, Janis Joplin, Philip Seymour Hoffman, Marilyn Monroe, Judy Garland, Mature Souls who struggled with life, eventually succumbing to their early departure. It's inordinately difficult to be recognized and *famous* in a world of younger souls who regard soul searching and emotional force as unbalanced and troubled; young souls see a departure from the established traditional life that they esteem; money, status, family, fame, unequal distribution of wealth, as puzzling.

Since I was 16 I've felt like a black cloud hangs over me. Since then, I have taken pills for depression. —Amy Winehouse

Mature Souls initiate change. They recruit for the rights of any minority that they see needs a voice: civil rights, immigrants' rights, gay rights, animal rights, transgender rights, marijuana rights, earth rights, equality for women, native american injustices, sex trafficking, voter rights. Relationships play a large part in the life, there is a flavor of family to the relationships, with a lot of role playing imprinted from the original family. They often endure difficult family connections and trying problematic partners, perhaps believing that through their sense of duty and struggle the difficult lessons to be handled dealing with family and unlikely partners, that they will come out on top. Green Peace expresses the relationship to the environment, group therapy expresses the interest in other people's dramas, as well as the ability to connect, relate, and see the mirror of self in others lives. Elizabeth Taylor and Richard Burton, both examples of Mature Souls, acted this out on stage in the Mature Soul play: *Who's Afraid of Virginia Woolf.*

I'm sick of not having the courage to be an absolute nothing. The worst thing that being an artist could do to you would be that it would make you slightly unhappy constantly. —J.D. Salinger

In the business world the individual matters. These are the companies that institute health care for same-sex partners, paid time for maternity leave, exercise programs for staff, policies that care for the worker. Tolerant of differences, this is the *la dolce vita* swinging excessive time of self-gratification and dissipation, doing whatever is wanted. Seeing the beauty in the world, they want to enjoy life, rather than place disproportionate time and energy into a career, job, and achievement. You might notice a well-known doctor or lawyer give up his prominence and financial gain to pursue an interest in writing, or build an environmentally sound house while going deeper into a relationship commitment to a partner to explore living a more meaningful lifestyle. There is great angst and suffering, making this not always a fun cycle. Upsets and issues concern family of origin, drugs and alcohol, divorce and legal wrangling, financial injustice and inequality, emotional boundaries, ecology and environment, treatment of animals and political protests. They feel misunderstood and rebellious. This is the time for sensationalism and melodramas, involving suicide, date rape, group sex, mental illness, sex change, divorce, eating disorders, incest, drug abuse, wasting and painful terminal disease, as well as gathering strong collective support. The largest population in therapy, Mature Souls sit on both sides; they are the therapists as well as the clients. Emotional upheaval keeps the waters churning, any drug that might take the edge off, anesthetizing the pain, calming the uneasiness, is often considered, tried, and sometimes offers a respite.

It is no measure of health to be well-adjusted to a profoundly sick society.
—*Krishnamurti*

Vacations and second homes are less for status and become retreats and places of nurturance. Religion and politics have moral values, Unity

Church and Renewal Judaism, places where all are welcome and music and meditation become part of the service. There is an attraction to traditions like Jewish Renewal, Yoga, Quaker, Unitarian, Buddhism, and a dissatisfaction with the rigid dogma of right extremists. Group gatherings include support circles, networks for personal growth, interpersonal therapy, sitting in a sangha group, stress reduction meetings, friends of the earth, non-violent communication process, anger management classes, to name a few. Countries like New Zealand, Russia, England, Denmark, Belgium, Finland, Holland, Greece, Norway, Italy, Sweden, and the United States, have large pockets of Mature Souls because they gravitate to places that explore sociological issues; places where fundamental human rights are publicly addressed.

You can't wring your hands and roll up your sleeves at the same time.
—Pat Schroeder

Mature Souls are at the vanguard for developing technology, stem cell research, the arts, and for contributing to the welfare of the poor. They write about mature themes in their music as expressed by Paul McCartney, Janis Joplin, Adele, Leonard Cohen, Madonna, and Bruce Springstein. In the political arena, these are not the people who wage war, the hesitance to fight and kill is based on a vision that we are all related. In the 60's the flower children, communes, anti-nuclear energy, Ralph Nader, Green Peace caring for the environment, Peta protecting the animals, the Sierra Club, habitat for humanity building homes for everyone; all Mature Soul movements that contribute to changing conditions. The Bernie Sanders popularity addressed inequalities and fueled a grass-roots movement that spoke to Mature Soul ideals. These are the people who care about the planet and truly want to make it a long lasting better place for all to inhabit.

A man has many skins in himself, covering the depths of his heart. Man knows so many things; he does not know himself. Why, thirty or forty skins or hides, just like an ox's or a bear's, so thick and hard, cover the soul. Go into your own ground and learn to know yourself there. —*Meister Eckhart*

Known Mature Souls include: *Marilyn Monroe, Judy Garland, Jean Genet, Al Gore Jr., Colin Powell, Truman Capote, Barack Obama, Janis Joplin, Robin Williams, Boy George, Marlon Brando, Sean Penn, Russell Crowe, Richard Burton, Elizabeth Taylor, Ralph Nader, Barbara Walters, Paul Gauguin, J.D.Salinger, Jack Nicholson, Billy Crystal, Mario Cuomo, Lily Tomlin, Woody Allen, Robert Downey Jr., Roseanne Barr, Mel Brooks, Jimmy Carter, Bette Midler, Ernest Hemingway, Sigmund Freud, James Dean, Jimmy Hendrix, Robert DeNiro, Robin Morgan, Vincent Van Gogh, Paul Gauguin, Jim Morrison, Rodney Dangerfield, Shirley MacLaine, Jon Stewart, Princess Diana, Barbra Streisand, Kitty Dukakis, Betty Ford, Steven Spielberg, Paul McCartney, Bruce Springstein, Madonna, Abbie Hoffman, Patty Hearst, Gloria Steinem, Amy Winehouse, Yoko Ono, Adele, Kevin Costner, Willlie Nelson, Shirley MacLaine, Michael Jackson, Winnie Mandela, Pee Wee Herman, Alice Walker, Jane Goodall, Warren Beatty, Ruth Westheimer, River Phoenix, Philip Seymour Hoffman.*

OLD SOUL

ELDER

50 YEARS AND ONWARD

Spiritually Aware, Perceptive, Teaching, Self-Deprecation,

Philosophically-Oriented

Positive: inclusiveness, detached, sees the world in a large context, views relationships three-dimensionally, respects all points of view, sees

aspect of self in everyone, individualistic, easygoing, autonomy, wise counsel, spiritual awareness
Negative: lacking direction, unmotivated, unpleasant personality, self-deprecation
Focus: Being part of all-that-is, choices about the nature of oneness

If a man does not keep pace with his companions, perhaps it is because he hears the beat of a different drummer. —Henry David Thoreau

The second Saturn Return, age 56 to 59 will be experienced based on the decisions one has made at the first Saturn Return, age 28 to 30. For those who made choices that supported a purpose in alignment with their essence, this is a time of payment; inner peace, satisfaction and achievement, rewards from the past 30 years. The second Saturn Return reveals what our life has become, what is too late to alter, and what can be harvested. The price for avoiding one's life direction at the first Saturn Return, at age 30, can be redeemed at this time. Energetically the resilience of the body, less able to tolerate life's battering and self-abuse, as well as the personal benefit from good choices, reduces the current margin for error.

This is your life. You are responsible for it. You will not live forever; stress is an ignorant state. It believes that everything is an emergency. —Natalie Goldberg

My actions are my only true belongings. —Thich Nhat Hahn

Old Soul age is a time to release the relationships and attitudes that no longer reflect the present. Decisions are made about what needs to be reorganized and altered to continue developing while making room for the new. The three major cycles of Saturn are 28-30, an energetic becoming stage, 56-60 an awareness stage, 85-89, the synthesis stage. Throughout our life these processes are happening, at these three times they intensify. Each Saturn Return opens the opportunity to find a wisdom that will carry us to the next stage of life, along with the skills necessary to meet the challenges that arrive during our lifetime.

On one side, a heart so tender it can weep in a moment from sadness and all the suffering in the world, and on the other side—there's wild humor and an eye that can seemingly (with just a tiny flex of inner will) behold great splendor. That is where I camp these days, between those poles. I plow a field there. Songs rise. —Daniel Ladinsky

An Old Soul is not consistently acting out of Old Soul awareness until about age 49 and even then it may only be in some areas of life while not in others. Old Souls will drop most of the rigid, rule-oriented baby soul discipline, young soul materialism, competitive ambition, and mature soul intense emotionality once those qualities have been uplifted and integrated into the personality; then one can access them when necessary. The second Saturn Return, a time of major assessment, offers the opportunity to refine, refocus, review, revise, renew and regroup. Old Soul responsibility for what has been created is a reality check. It is accountability to your soul. Experience provides a wide range for the wisdom and understanding that the Old Soul has gathered.

Wake up first. Wake up, and then you can double back and perhaps be of some use to others if you still have the urge. Wake up first, with pure and unapologetic selfishness, or you're just another shipwreck victim floundering in the ocean and all the compassion in the world is of absolutely no use to the other victims floundering around you. —Jeb McKenna

At an early age this child is walking to the tune of a different drum beat, not necessarily the one the crowd hears. The work interest now shifts to support spiritual and emotional development, rather than financial gain. Competent, they choose work that is undemanding and agreeable, not looking for fame or great wealth, time is a high value.

Old Souls teach just through being who they are. Not too involved in the game of life, accomplishment and amassing wealth; they seem to be peacefully on vacation. You see detachment with a measure of saying: *don't worry, be happy.* Spiritual values becomes part of life. There is a lightness of being now that the mature soul conflicts, tensions and searching have loosened; moving into a freedom to enjoy their life, that of being part of *what is* as it arrives. Harmlessly eccentric; nude beaches and off-beat humor seem an odd fit to meditation and a sacred home life. Having sat with numerous spiritual teachers the Old Soul creates their own practice, one that is harmoniously in alignment with their created life, each day is the lived spirituality. This might include Tibetan singing bowls and bells, Hebrew chants, Vedic music, walking mindfully, Buddha statues, sitting quietly on a beach, photos of holy people adorning their home, belly dancing, practices that allow an inner smile to keep the heart alight. Energy is directed from ambition to spiritual development. Less effort is made to accomplish, for these are not the doers and shakers of the world. Not climbing corporate ladders, these are the teachers, not always acknowledged as such, their form is not easily recognized by mainstream society.

Work and interests are growthful and in the realm of study, teaching and creativity. Daily life is about creating beauty and while living within a predominately younger soul age world that shouts competitiveness, image and emotional turmoil, the Older Soul remains on the edge or outside of that, less caught by external values. Being in the world and yet not of it is the delicate dance. Teaching their spiritual understanding, going after the route of least resistance, not much dogma, personal practices take precedence over organized formal tradition; passing undetected in public they are free to pursue their truth. Visibility and recognition becomes less important than authenticity and harmony.

Elders serve as conduits between the divine realm and the mundane world, making the abstract truth of spirituality accessible to the community by embodying them in their everyday behavior. —*Zalman Schachter-Shalomi*

Less attached to personal relationships with blood family members; spiritual connections, people with similar lifestyle orientation predominates, karmic agreements that have been groomed and formed become companionship. Relationships are not for business purposes and financial advancement, they exist for being together. Political campaigns or social clubs have little pull, government, corporate and business hierarchical structures lack the quality of integrity and competence to resonate with Old Souls. Ethics and decency are just there and don't have to be taught and trained by society; rules no longer need to be imposed from the outside. Aging becomes a sign of wisdom rather than a fear that is covered in secrecy, operations, and illusion.

A child-like person is not someone whose development has been arrested; on the contrary, it is someone who has given himself a chance of continuing to develop long after most adults have muffled themselves in the cocoon of middle-aged habit and convention. —*Aldous Huxley*

Time is spent having a massage, meditation, listening to beautiful music, quietly at home, gardening, a continued consciousness around healthy food, often a vegan/vegetarian lifestyle, hiking, going to the beach, swimming in the ocean, time spent quietly alone, bike riding, pot luck dinners, reading books by awakened beings, assorted projects, going to a good movie, being creative, alternative medicine like homeopathy, ayurveda, salt rooms and acupuncture; essentially a wholistic lifestyle. They like it here, are easygoing, and can do whatever they want, yet are not so motivated. Old Souls will go along with change if it starts inside.

Not too often found in religious structures, they know we are all one, all inter-connected. Very little political drive, with more attention paid to unconventionally doing what they want, in fact, they rarely do things they don't like. Self-employment is high on the list, since the freedom to come and go, to live mindfully, is a higher priority than a steady income. The inclination is not to make a business out of life, rather to continue to do what is creative and ordinary, not getting tied to appointments, creating the opportunity to stay home. *Don't work for a living, create for a life* is the Old Soul motto. What has value is the connection to inner spirit and the willingness to live from that place. You will rarely see an Old Soul working long at a job they don't like.

Just as we manage the external world, it is equally important to learn how to manage our internal world. —Amma

Friends and acquaintances become global, no longer local. Switzerland, Northern California, Iceland, Australia, sections of the United States like parts of New Mexico, Sedona, the Florida Keys, New York City, Boulder, Colorado, sections of India and Bali, parts of Hawaii; these places have pockets where Old Soul's can expand beyond the immediate family and into the universe as a whole. Having more resources available the connections to people from many parts of the world develop easily into kindred on-the-same-wavelength intimates. Traveling becomes part of the search for truth, looking for what is out there, until embarking on the inner journey, may fill earlier years. The family idea is expanded to include many, most often people from all parts of the world. Relationships are about seeing aspects of ourself, there are no real others, everyone is a particular expression of ourself, interconnected; secrets and judgments vanish, everyone is everywhere and everything. Rules loosen, acceptance looms large. Male and female differentiation becomes hazy, sexuality between equals, whether male or female, is the norm. Gender is less defined by society in terms of interests, colors and costumes, living arrangements, and energy. There are few geographic or time constraints. Momentary feelings of unworthiness emerge, knowing we are not part of the mainstream, feeling little ambition and desire to get ahead, being judged and misunderstood, humility can turn against the self. Early efforts to work in corporate jobs rarely were satisfying, the willingness to trust the process and remain confident in the vision brings the satisfaction.

Step away from mass movements and quietly go to work on your own self-awareness. If you want to awaken all of humanity, then awaken all of yourself. If you want to eliminate the suffering in the world, then eliminate all that is negative in yourself. Truly, the greatest gift you have to give is that of your own self-transformation. —Hua Hu Ching

Younger souls are in too much of a rush to stop and truly listen to Old Soul pearls of wisdom that have been cultured. And the Old Soul, now aware of the shortened life-span of things and investments and material objects, of impermanence, has little energy for contributing to the society. Seeing death as the end of life is like seeing the horizon as the end of the ocean. Tired and driven as they may be, there is a relaxation and mellowness, with little emphasis on changing the world. This is a time to loosen life entanglements—those with friends, family, and possessions, while strengthening one's life purpose, deepening understanding, wisdom and spiritual chords. Time to slip off the incarnation wheel, smiling at the games people play; rarely worked up about causes, it's all illusion, this is marching to the tune of one's own drum.

If you meet a person of developed being, of real presence, you feel something in their presence, it makes you quiet, you become yourself, if only for a moment, in their presence. That's what we need: real people. —Jacob Needleman

Self-esteem, forgiveness and unconditional love are the prominent lessons for the Old Soul. Psychological distress was more of a hardship in earlier soul ages. How to live in accord with our vision, so that the inside and outside match. How to have a personal and career life that suits our life purpose. Finding balance living in a society that doesn't value how we are, the Old Soul sees what a tiny part they truly play in the large scheme of the universe. The challenge lies in there being very few living examples; present-day society does not support this vision. The practice is to be mindful, to be aware with each thing that you are doing: when you walk to know you are walking, when you talk to know you are talking. Self-forgiveness and self-acceptance are paramount; how to truly enjoy life without the world valuing you. To see all people as aspects of ourself—poor, rich, victim, perpetrator—to prefer alternative medicine while your insurance or medicare only covers conventional treatment—to avoid self-pity, judgment and self-deprecation—to feel little pull to emotional intensity, thereby sidestepping the land mines of peoples dramas—and through this, to master unconditional love for oneself and others! This is the script for the Old Soul. The focus is off what others think, external appearances become background, reputation is no longer an issue, schooling and learning are less about grades than wanting to know. The medical establishment comes off the pedestal, in fact, is only used under extreme circumstances, and then still includes alternative and holistic.

Suffering just means you're having a bad dream. Happiness means you're having a good dream. Enlightenment means getting out of the dream altogether. —Jed McKenna

Walking to the tune of their own drumbeat, this is not mainstream society. Often abrasive and irritating, the challenge of having chosen intense lessons, the Older Soul person, depthful, outspoken and perceptive, is not always an externally peaceful person to be around. The interest in doing and running, sexual conquests and complex relationships diminish, a partnership is the desire for a soul mate, a beloved. Off-beat, a sense of the ridiculous, humor is a great healing agent for the Old Soul. Jokes, even bawdy off-color stories to bring laughter, sometimes part of a teaching, are way more entertaining than the heavy dramas younger souls engage in for their entertainment. Humor is a large part of the Older Soul life, capturing essence, pointing out the great cosmic joke, living in the smile. Much of the *heaviness* of the physical plane is transcended for periods of time with playfulness in the awareness of Self and spaciousness. Diversity now becomes cherished; with younger soul age differences were friction and hard to tolerate. Old Souls, the most accepting, are often criticized by those who are more rigid and quite intolerant.

We must become ignorant of all we've been taught, and, be, instead, bewildered. Run from what's profitable and comfortable. If you drink those liquors, you'll spill the spring water of your real life. Forget safety,! Live where you fear to live! Destroy your reputation! Be notorious! I have tried prudent planning long enough, from now on, I'll live mad. No more words. Hear only the voice within. This dance to the joy of existence. —Rumi

An interest in spirituality or health food is not necessarily an indication of an Old Soul. Being on a spiritual path as a daily practice, continuous self-examination and a commitment to higher values as well as a mature understanding of love are revealing evidence of an Old Soul. Further, rather than acquiring more as the initiation—*steer for the deep waters only* said Old Soul Walt Whitman. Rarely interested in making a mark or succeeding or learning the life game; *it doesn't matter* may be a misunderstood mantra, since inner excellence is a driving force. Teaching is a daily event, the Old Soul demonstrates by example; their life is the lesson. This soul age is cycling off and its work is to learn self-acceptance, forgiveness, unconditional love and to teach at least one other person everything they know.

I believe in the absolute oneness of humanity. We have but one soul. The truly noble know all men as one, and return with gladness good for evil done. —Mahatma Gandhi

The third Saturn Return age 85-89 is the synthesis stage. A time of reflection and recognition. This is spiritual elderhood, the twilight of our life. How we have lived, whatever we have done, everything counts. Old Soul Zalman Schachter-Shalomi who died a month before his 90th birthday spoke often of the privilege of having this lifetime, he said: *Living at the intersection between time and eternity in this way the elder asks,'what is the meaning of my life? What have I contributed to the world to make a difference?'* Zalman made a significant difference, fearless, he was a living flame of wisdom with large vision. His life was a representation of, in the language of William Wordsworth: *A presence that disturbs with the joy of elevated thoughts; a sense sublime of something far more deeply interfused, whose dwelling is the light of setting suns, and the round ocean and the living air, and the blue sky, and in the mind of man.*

Ring the bells that still can ring. Forget your perfect offering. There is a crack in everything, That's how the light gets in... If you don't become the ocean, you'll be seasick every day. —Leonard Cohen

Living mindfully and wisely sharpens our awareness for us to harvest our experiences to hold a wider vision. *If we wish to die well we must learn to live well,* said the Dalai Lama. Accepting the pain of living, remembering those who have died, understanding life's losses, allowing the heart to break, learning to pass through the pain of life without resistance, called suffering; for those who are gifted the longevity of a third

Saturn Return, these are the Old Soul teachings. Making life matter is a beautiful lifestyle.

My work is a daily reminder that we are not our bodies or our brains, but our souls. That's the part of us that is eternal. Our souls keep returning, as though we were in a large school, until we are able to understand and to graduate. —Brian Weiss

Known Old Souls include: *Walt Whitman, Carl Jung, G. I. Gurdjieff, Abraham Lincoln, Carlos Castaneda, Joan Baez, Jerry Garcia, Bob Marley, Paul Winter, Kitaro, Henry David Thoreau, Mark Twain, Ram Dass, Judy Collins, Rabbi David Ingber, Mitchell Chefitz, Rami Shapiro, Roshi Joan Halifax, Marc and Shoni Lebowitz, Leonard Cohen, James Taylor, Bobby McFerrin, Chris Griscom, John Lennon, Albert Einstein, Eckhart Tolle, Mathew Fox, Stevie Wonder, Jed McKenna, Natalie Goldberg, Elisabeth Kübler-Ross, David Deida, Maya Angelou, Sogyal Rinpoche, Jack Kornfield, Helen Palmer, Lama Surya Das, John Welwood, Mariana Caplan, Kabir Helminski, Reshad Feild, Yongey Mingur Rinpoche, Mahatma Gandhi, William Segal, Jeanne de Salzmann, Andrew Harvey, Stephen Hawking, Coleman Barks, Gangaji, Eli Jaxson Bear, Zalman Schachter-Shalomi, Alice Walker, Ram Dass, Stephen Levine, Michael Green, Daniel Ladinsky, Thomas Merton.*

TRANSCENDENTAL SOUL

GREAT WISDOM, A CATALYST

FOR SOCIAL TRANSFORMATION,

BODHISATTVA

Though the eye is small, the soul which sees through it is greater and vaster than all things it perceives. In fact, it is so great that it includes all objects, however large or numerous, within itself. For it is not so much that you are within the cosmos as that the cosmos is within you. —Meher Baba

After completing all old soul lives, and cycling off, we may choose to return to the physical plane to prepare the way for the infinite soul. Knowing harmony, not as sentiment, the Transcendental Soul has great wisdom and lives as a representative of something much greater than the one body they appear in, while assisting in social or spiritual transformation. Referred to as a volunteer soul, having completed karma and able to cycle off, they live here in a positive force field, no longer limited to a personality or the illusions that exist on this physical plane.

Join me in the pure atmosphere of gratitude. —Hafiz

Let my soul smile through my heart and my heart smile through my eyes, that I may scatter rich smiles into sad hearts. —Paramanhansa Yogananda

Transcendental Souls perceive others as self, directly experiencing what people are feeling. Transcendental Soul, Meher Baba said: *I have come not to teach but to awaken.* The world recognizes a Transcendental Soul; they have access to great wisdom and freedom, no longer relating from their personal agenda. Transcending the personality they are no longer attached to form. Many people are dedicated to assist in the care of this physical form that so easily wears out. A balanced being, they easily access higher centers and expansive states of consciousness.

The Transcendental Soul is focused on the connectivity of the universe. Having an indelible influence on their communities, sometimes to receive global recognition; always their teachings are recognized.

Where can the soul go? Where is it not already? —*Swami Vivekananda*

There are times when the Transcendental Soul might misperceive that their teaching is all and everything; it is a focus on one perspective. Perceived as *leading the way;* often a foundation, religion or institution is created to continue in the flavor of their style. A Transcendental Soul is the incarnation of a representative of a reunited entity, living from the perspective of *all that is,* helping others to awaken.

She caught me off guard when my soul said to me, "Have we met?" So surprised I was to hear her speak like that I chuckled. She began to sing a tale: "There was once a hard working man who used to worry so much because he could not feed and clothe his children and wife the way he wanted. There was a beautiful little chapel in the village where the man lived and one day while he was praying, meditating, an angel appeared. The angel said, "Follow me." And he did out into an ancient forest. "Now dig here," the angel said. And the man felt strength in his limbs he had not known since youth and with just his bare hands he dug deep and found a lost treasure, and his relationship with the world changed." Finding our soul's beauty does that—gives us tremendous freedom from worry. "Dig here," the angel said—"in your soul, in your soul." —*St. John of the Cross*

Known Transcendental Souls are: *Paramahansa Yogananda, Zoroaster, Mahatma Gandhi, Socrates, Mata Amritananda Mayi Ma (known as Ammachi), Mevlana Jalaluddin Rumi, Hafiz, Sai Baba, Mohammed, Al-Hillaj Mansoor, Nanak, Baal Shem Tov, Swami Vivekananda, Ramakrishna, Maimonides, Babaji, Kabir, St. Francis of Assisi, Meher Baba.*

INFINITE SOUL — AVATAR

A CATALYST FOR THE

SPIRITUAL TRANSFORMATION

OF HUMANITY

I say to thee weapons reach not the Life, flame burns it not, waters cannot o'er whelm, not dry winds wither it. Impenetrable, unentered, unassailed, unharmed, untouched, immortal, all-arriving, stable, sure, invisible, ineffable, by word and thought uncompassed. Ever all itself, thus is the Soul declared! —the Bhagavad-Gita

The Infinite Soul is the intensity high frequency vibration of the Tao, the ultimate principle that binds existence together, expressing the spiritual heart. Tao means the harmony of the whole, the ground of all being; all planes have a direct connection. The Tao, already complete is in equilibrium, while the universe, incomplete, expanding, continues in motion. When the totality is there, no self is left—no yours or mine— and when the self is there, there is no longer totality. The whole universe is consciously held in the one body of the Infinite Soul.

The world is continuous flux and is impermanent. —the Buddha

The Infinite Soul creates a body using a 7th level old soul and the energy of the transcendental soul, remaining only briefly on the planet. They live in oneness with everything, a messenger of the Tao, permeating the universe with love. *The life of Lord Krishna has been misunderstood by many Western commentators. Scriptural allegory is baffling to literal minds,* said transcendental soul Yogananda Paramahansa. The birth of an Infinite Soul is predicted long before its arrival. There is an energy and a presence that impacts the world, even before the exalted presence appears. This energy has been compared to an impending supernova.

The Infinite Soul rarely comes directly to the physical plane, and then only to assist in social or spiritual transformation, living in oneness with everything.

Each moment fills my chalice with presence; this is my wine, I drink from the present moment. —*Bahauddin*

An Infinite Soul incarnates in order to catalyze massive spiritual change in a civilization, generally during a shift from one soul age to another. Jesus incarnated when Western civilization was shifting from predominantly baby soul to primarily young. We are currently in a similar transition, from young to mature. Always an Avatar, the reverberation of this being lasts thousands of years. Jesus was a 7th level old soul king, living briefly as an Infinite Soul; some say 30 days, others say 3 years. Siddhartha Gautama, a 7th level old soul priest, gave his body over to the Buddha form of an Infinite Soul. Once the Infinite Soul takes over a physical body, the body literally begins to burn out.

If they say to you 'From where have you originated?' say to them, 'We have come from the light, where the light originated through itself.' —*Jesus the Christ*

The Infinite Soul is a manifestation of part of the highest levels of the spirit of energy. The Infinite Soul is thought to have incarnated among mankind four times, as Sri Krishna, Lao Tzu, Buddha and Christ. These four are denoted as Avatars of the Infinite Soul. An Avatar is an embodiment, a bodily manifestation located in the spiritual realm, descending to this physical realm. The qualities of transcendental and Infinite Soul are not materially different, they are amplified. It's been about 2,000 years, therefore the next possible appearance of an Infinite Soul is calculated to be between the year 2020 and 2054. Avataric periods bring to everyone more energy and awareness. The Infinite Soul supports the planets move to the next soul age. Life's circumstances become the liberation. The Infinite Soul is the ultimate unflowering of consciousness, the one-thousand petaled lotus flowering. Impelled towards expression, the Infinite Soul is an explanation of how the truth moves, of the deep love for *what is*. It has been predicted that the new Avatar will be named Maitreya which means *loving-kindness,* bringing peace to this earth. Maitreya, a transcendent bodhisattva is the universal Budda of a future time, born to teach enlightenment in the next age. Ushering in an era of peace and prosperity, the name Maitreya means loving kindness, the *Benevolent One;* she is the embodiment of all-encompassing love.

An infinite soul incarnates in order to catalyze massive spiritual change in a civilization, generally during a shift from one average soul age to another. An incarnation of a transcendental soul usually precedes it in order to catalyze massive social change. —Shepherd Hoodwin

When humanity slides into decay, an Infinite Soul arrives in form to jump-start mankind. Now, 2,000 years later we are ready. Always teaching oneness and love, highly visible, no one mistakes their presence. The earth may have up to five Infinite Souls walking the planet during the next fifty years. Some may refer to them as trouble makers or rabble rousers, some see them as an anointed saviors, prophets of humanity. The planets next transition from young soul to the group consciousness of mature soul will be assisted by the Infinite Soul manifesting in an incarnated form of one or more individuals.

That in whom resides all beings and who resides in all beings, who is the giver of grace to all, the Supreme Soul of the universe, the limitless being—I am that. —Amritbindu Upanishad

Known Infinite Souls—Avatars are: *Buddha, Krishna, Lao Tzu, Moses, Chuang Tzu, Zarathustra, Jesus Christ, Maitreya.*

SYSTEM FOUR

SOUL LEVEL

FIRST LEVEL: SIMPLE ACTION

SECOND LEVEL: UNCERTAINTY

THIRD LEVEL: REASONING INTELLECT

FOURTH LEVEL: MOMENTUM INTENSITY

FIFTH LEVEL: ECCENTRIC EXPLORER

SIXTH LEVEL: COMPELLED KARMIC TEACHER

SEVENTH LEVEL: HARMONIOUS INTEGRATION

The soul of man functions through its instrument or vessel, which is the body. Higher forces unite souls in their work of repairing the world, of raising the level of the universe. As the souls return and strive to correct the world they reach their highest peak. —Adin Steinsaltz

Within each soul age there are seven distinct learning steps or levels. Each soul age has many lifetimes, and we spend numerous lives at each level to become acquainted with our life lessons. There are seven soul age levels for an infant soul, seven levels for a young soul, and this continues throughout all ages through seventh level old soul. There are 35 learning steps or levels total and each single step takes at least one life time to complete. Like fudge ripple ice cream, the vanilla soul age is expressed through the flavor of the fudge or level. There is a definite characteristic as well as a particular way each level influences our life. Every level makes specific demands regarding the type of experience we will have before moving on to the next stage. The first levels are here to experience life and the lessons that we either use or that use us, in the last levels we demonstrate and express in action what we have experienced. And in the middle stage we are integrating and synthesizing these happenings. Eventually we are teaching what we have learned along our journey of Soul Levels.

Something of our soul goes forth into the world, embodied in air. The invisible, inwardly experiencing soul thus announces its presence through the body. —Lory Widmer Hess

ETCHING A SOUL

Soul Levels don't move from positive to negative aspects, having experiences and understanding them lays the ground for Soul Level development. Ultimately, we connect to what appears, all experiences having value to the Soul Level; how to use them is the learning. The aim is to bring meaning to our experience at each level, since every stage is a necessary step along the way. Attitude shapes growth, life presents situations; how they are received, understood, and lived through etches our soul. And when a soul volunteers for this great passage, this adventure of reincarnation as human beings to evolve as souls, that in itself is heroic. We've signed on to this evolutionary journey which has these 35 sequential steps, and we use a human form as the instrument from beginning to end.

Let our fragile spirit have eternal life. The soul lives, the body wears out like a cloak. —Rumi

Each level effects a lifetime's behavior. Higher intensity living generates an increase in level, while lower intensity allows for more time to move along the way. The reflection, the lack of resistance, ultimately the deep understanding creates the shift. Being stuck, distractions and dramas that are not digested, non-movement, being thrown off course and gathering non-essential experiences also prolongs the journey. Every soul age level is a distinct phase in a process of forming a particular soul age's perspective. The true nature of life is veiled on each level and circumstances appear differently depending on the perspective of each person. The younger soul ages and earlier levels see aspects and particulars, older soul ages and later levels see less detail and more panorama. Each stage along the way brings value; the illusions, called maya, become more subtle for older soul ages and levels. The physical world and the Soul Levels are based on the fundamental law of maya or *that which is not,* our illusions. The illusionary false veil loses its density, becomes thinner and lighter after many lifetimes as truth is uncovered.

You don't have a soul. You are a soul. You have a body. —*C.S. Lewis*

SEVEN SOUL LEVELS

The first three levels are ordinal, focused on down to earth smaller issues, living and being immersed in life. The next three levels are oriented to the abstract, considering the world in general, questioning to understand the world at large. An increase in the range of awareness, self-examination and self-consciousness develops within each progressive level. Invisible to the eye, a new layer of soul development which are layers of energy is added to essence from the cumulative intensity of priceless occurrences. Meaningful experiences differ between individuals. Understanding happens in a moment, Freud called it the *aha* experience. Resistance, rigidity, fear, distractions, slow down the process. Many life experiences happen, not necessarily leading to soul advancement. As the soul is aging, during the last 3 levels, growth happens more from joyful lessons than from suffering, and with greater resources and deepened understanding recovery time definitely shortens. Levels shift from cumulative intensity of experiences. People who are careful and slow, who keep themselves away from experiences, from looking to understand, will take additional time to generate a level increase. The amount of resistance there is to overcome also slows level shifts. Many life events do not lead to soul age advancement; ultimately not everything we do directly leads to what we choose. For example, if we want to have a partner, not everything that we create is valuable to that pursuit. The integration and understanding of cumulative intensity of experience advances Soul Level. Essentially it's the situation and the understanding that matter. Many experiences are of no real value. The older the soul the less time spent recovering from negative situations.

I first believed without any hesitation in the existence of the soul, and then I wondered about the secret of its nature. I persevered and strove in search of the soul, and found at last that I myself was the cover over my own soul. I realized that that in me which believed and that in me that wondered, that which was found at last, was no other than my soul. I thanked the darkness that brought me to the light, and I valued this veil that prepared for me the vision in which I saw myself reflected, the vision produced in the mirror of my soul. —Hazrat Inayat Khan

The following is an ocean analogy of the Soul Levels:

First Level: Simple Action. I put my toes in the water. The ocean is cold, and not too enticing. This is actively entering the purpose of the soul age, an inauguration, a glimpse, a taste and introduction. I move tentatively to find what this ocean is about. I am not ready to get wet, jump waves or swim.

Second Level: Uncertanity. I go into the water up to my waist. Now I am half in and half out. This is stabilizing my new perceptions. Still uncertain whether to go in further; I am wading in and out. The sand has ridges and is unstable. I am not quite sure of my footing. I walk along the sand exploring my balance and the arrangement and shape of edges as water touches beach.

Third Level: Reasoning Intellect. I enter the water, assessing how it is. Water is cold, I am beginning to get used to it. Off by myself, fully immersed, hidden by the water, I am motivated to actively explore the sea. Taking quiet time to just be in the ocean, figuring how long to stay in, I determine the value of my time in the ocean until eventually I step out.

Fourth Level: Momentum Intensity. I re-emerge, fully wet within this soul level perspective. Exciting! Wow! Now I begin to swim around and exercise in the water, interacting with others, doing laps, this is a workout. Energizing, yet exhausting. Comfortable, confident, relaxing into it, the sea holds plenty of possibilities and I keep busy. This is a basic stereotypical water person, looks the part and appears to let the ocean be ocean, in all of its shifts and changes from wild waves, rip tides, currents and mild calm no surf days. This is thrilling and exhilarating, *I'm in.*

Fifth Level: Eccentric Explorer. I splash around and play, finding other people to swim with and have fun. I am celebrating and sharing this new level. Exploring the ocean, wearing snorkel, face mask and fins, some think I look strange, others see me as cute. I enjoy pushing boundaries, finding my ocean limits. Experimenting, how to hold my breath under water, handstands without nose plugs, putting seaweed on my head; interesting adventures. Burning off karma as I live into this fifth level of consciousness. Looking around I see how much more the ocean holds; sea life, the colors magnified by the sky. This begins my awareness that there are other worlds that impact the ocean.

Sixth Level: Compelled Karmic Teacher. Others splash me, it's like a pay back, and I am busy dodging the waves, the splashes, trying to move harmoniously in the ocean, all the while trying to teach those around how to stay afloat and not drown. So much to do! This ocean has sharks, Portuguese men-of-war with long tentacles, jellyfish that sting as well as sleek torpedo-shaped barracuda with razor-sharp teeth. Predatory fish that inhabit open waters, waiting in bay areas in the shadows, all making floating or hanging out rare moments. Driven to teach others how to enjoy the sea, regardless; I know the inherent joys in the beautiful ocean and am driven to share that with those who enter. Developing presence, I become a reflection for others. Lending some of my water gear to friends, they have the time to float around, and the good luck to get clear weather. My luck seems to come and go, not so simple to trust an ocean that has churned up unexpectedly so often, as well as dodging boaters who seem to be aiming at me when I try to take a momentary break for fun. What an intense demanding experience this beautiful blue sea, as I move around in the water having many moments of harmonious associations. Enough ocean. I get out and lie on the beach letting the sounds of the waves penetrate me, the pure oxygen oxygenates throughout my body, smelling the clean air, I smile. A lucky lifetime. I know this and feel privileged. Everything is a teaching, and to be with me is to receive the distillation of my ocean life.

Seventh Level: Harmonious Interation. Enough of this intensity! Floating around in the deep blue-green waters, relaxed, delighted, enjoying the ease of being held by the ocean. Having a mastery of ocean, it arises through me, what unfolds is the teaching moving deep within me. A hint of sea breeze blows gently, the surf glides up onto the sand. Peaceful, this is comfort. I head back and return to shore finding someone on the beach who wants to learn about the ocean. Sitting on a beach blanket I impart understanding, teachings, experience and knowledge about the wonders of the sea that have brought me to this level. I am a role model as I master living harmoniously.

God revealed a sublime truth to the world when He sang, 'I am made whole by your life. Each soul, each soul completes me.' —Hafiz

Issues and events come and go, yet each Soul Level has a different perception of similar circumstances. Point of view shifts and deepens, as we move along, changing level of understanding and responsibility. Each level may take 200-350 years or one to five lifetimes to complete. Moving quickly one might go through a level in one lifetime, or moving slowly an individual could take ten lifetimes to master one level. The type of lessons that one creates and the willingness to learn, speeds or slows the process. The soul is eternal and so we have time to learn, to grow in consciousness through experiencing in physical form, to know ourself making choices; the primary choice that of being here.

Soul is our appetite, driving us to eat from the banquet of life. People filled with the hunger of soul take food from every dish before them, whether it be sweet or bitter. —Matthew Fox

FIRST LEVEL: SIMPLE ACTION

Why should I apologize because God throws in crystal chandeliers, mahogany floors, and the best construction in the world. —Jim Bakker

The First Level soul age is a beginning introduction, like nursery school, when everything is carefully tried, as in testing a situation. This level, whether infant, baby, young, mature or old is a sampling, taste, exploration of the new soul age and is not rushed. Simple, First Level is about entering the purpose of the soul age. Looking at and experimenting with new perceptions, accompanied by a sense of tentative uneasiness; sometimes it feels like not fitting in. At those moments there is a retreat to the last soul age remembered. Here one has a sample of things to come, a glimpse of life as it will unfold.

Activity centers around reactivity and busyness, more than creativity. Life is happening outside, so they try to manipulate the circumstances. Without an inner life we rarely question as we live in a superficial perspective of our own actions. Single-mindedness, a stuck quality, often unsophisticated in understanding the times; there is not much motivation to step out and know life. First Level souls live much of the time from the place of their previous level of understanding, as well as investigating what this level is about. First Level mature souls live from the perspective of a seventh level young soul. First Level old souls will appear old part of the time and then might appear young. First Level infant souls are connected to the universal Tao, the everything and nothing of *what is*, the infinite and eternal, that which is inexpressible. The new level is a taste of things to come.

One morning I woke up and found my favorite pigeon, Julius had died. I was devastated and was gonna use his crate as my stickball bat to honor him. I left the crate on my stoop and went in to get something and I returned to see the sanitation person put the crate into a crusher. I rushed him and caught him flush on the temple with a titanic left hand and he was out cold convulsing on the floor like an infantile retard. —Mike Tyson

Examples are: *Mike Tyson, Jim Bakker;* first level baby. *Tammy Bakker,* first level young. *Yoko Ono, Andrew Weil;* first level old soul.

SECOND LEVEL: UNCERTANITY

Vertigo is the conflict between the fear of falling and the desire to fall. Doubt, it seems to me, is the central condition of a human being in the twentieth century. —Salman Rushdie

This level brings the conflict of wanting to become more involved, and yet still sliding back to the remembered comfort of carefully trying things out. What appears is a push-pull person displaying contradiction; torn between whether to proceed forward or to revert to the comfort and reassurance of what had been previously known. Half in, half out, unsure about advancing, backing up, the footing is unsteady. There is uncertainty about the new perceptions, while hanging on to the initial learnings that came through first level. A stuck quality from experiencing inconsistency, until moving ahead to new information.

I think if you're going to put an artist's eye to it, you're going to put a critical eye to it. I've always been interested in the gray area that exists between the black and white, or the red and blue, and that's where complexity lies. —Robert Redford

Second Level is a transition stage, not quite certain whether to push outward or to go inward. The predicament of life situations that are contradictory sets up a demanding, sometimes wearisome lifetime. There are many relapses back to the experimenting first level until extracting those habits and hankerings that belonged to the earlier perceptions that held disappointment and thwarted movement.

And I don't believe that I have to stay on one side of the fence or the other. I don't believe that there is any good career move or bad career move. I believe there are only the things that make me happy. —Whoopie Goldberg

What is resisted, persists. Situations that reassure are held onto, comparisons are the framework for decisions, until eventually the structure is broken to discover the new. Unsure, apprehensive, internal warfare, feeling the dilemma as frustration, wanting to experiment makes moving on less than routine. The dilema of hesitation creates anxiety and instablity, and colors many of the Second Level experiences.

The message is: slow down and think about what you're doing before you do it. Weigh the pros and cons, what's best for you. Of course you can get paranoid analyzing each situation you're faced with. Sometimes you've got to go with your own instinct. —River Phoenix

Examples are: *Princess Diana, Salman Rushdie;* second level mature. *River Phoenix, James Taylor, John Lennon, Alice Walker, Whoopie Goldberg, Robert Redford, Jesse Jackson;* second level old souls.

THIRD LEVEL:
REASONING INTELLECT

That's the whole trouble. You can't ever find a place that's nice and peaceful, because there isn't any. You may think there is, but once you get there, when you're not looking, somebody'll sneak up and write fuck you right under your nose. —J.D. Salinger

*A*t the Third Level the shift is internalized. The perceptions are not integrated enough to comfortably display outside in the world, therefore the quiet inward process brings about restraint, seclusion and introversion. The inside and the outside do not match and so the person generally removes himself from the world. Fame and prominence create pressure, discomfort and tension. What's needed is time alone, privacy, seclusion, quiet moments at home. This is an understated time, addressing internally issues that appear, and when pushed into the public eye there is unease and a lack of confidence to sustain the outward persona.

I wish people were all trees and I think I could enjoy them then. —Georgia O'Keefe

There is a neutral and intellectual quality to the Third soul age Level. Discriminating about lifestyle, enterprising and energetic, the care taken to funnel energy brings them to feel that being curious might make their projects scattered to remain incomplete. Introspective, inward, unyielding and internalized, often a loner, there is a real possibility to know the subject matter that engages them, once making peace with themselves. A bit stiff, taking quiet time to be alone; life becomes more gratifying. Self-acceptance, allowing themselves to be the way they are, paves the way to internalize new understandings. Often self-conscious, apprehensive, and lacking confidence, they may appear pensive and absorbed.

I want to be alone. If only those who dream of Hollywood knew how difficult it all is. Being a movie star means being looked at from every possible direction. You are never left at peace, you're just fair game. —Greta Garbo

Dropping into the fullness of the soul age at the Third Level, their experiences are not integrated, therefore they are not balanced and have difficulty functioning confidently at the Third Level out in the world. During this long process of evaluating and developing conviction, poise and self-assurance, what manifests is reclusivity and their need for space and privacy.

I feel more comfortable with gorillas than people. I can anticipate what a gorilla's going to do, and they're purely motivated. The man who kills the animals today is the man who kills the people who get in his way tomorrow.
—Dian Fossey

Examples are: *Howard Hughes, George W. Bush, Greta Garbo;* third level young. *J.D. Salinger, Ralph Nader, Georgia O'Keefe;* third level mature. *Dian Fosse,* third level old soul.

FOURTH LEVEL:
MOMENTUM INTENSITY

A little more moderation would be good. Of course, my life hasn't exactly been one of moderation. —Donald Trump

At this heavily karmic formation level, life is intense, emotions run the gamut, and they are easily submerged with problems. The balance point, mid-way between first and seventh levels, is a grounding point. High visibility, for this extroverted level. What has been learned is brought out into the world. A karma gathering stage, there is an edge of intensity to the Fourth Level, which may also bring about emotional breakdowns. The difficulty, by not developing an observer, a witness, they identify with their issues, losing perspective. Sometimes a personality disintegration leads to medication or hospitalization. Easily losing themselves in the identification of whatever they are involved with in life, there is little separation between self, life, problems and emotions. All seems to blend together into one big disturbance.

Behind every beautiful thing there's some kind of pain. Gotta head full of ideas that are driving me insane. No one is free, even the birds are chained to the sky. —Bob Dylan

Fourth Level people show up, are visible, out there, achieving, participating and busy. This is a time to be out in the world, involved and *doing* life. Friendly, busy, engaged, noticeable, even front-and-center, the high amount of doing and interacting minus a witnessing self, forms karma, creates intensity, allows little respite. Extending, reaching out to others, life is busy and engaging until the solution become the problem. Subjective responses, engaged feelings create fiery times. Strengthening one's position, new viewpoints are trotted out into the world, often expressed, definitely experienced in relationship to others. This adventuresome time can be exhausting; intense emotions without discrimination is wearisome.

It is extraordinary how the house and the simplest possessions of someone who has been left become so quickly sordid. Even the stain on the coffee cup seems not coffee but the physical manifestation of one's inner stain, the fatal bid that from the beginning had marked me for ultimate aloneness. —Jane Fonda

Examples are: *Donald Trump, Fidel Castro, Ronald Reagan;* fourth level young. *Jane Fonda, Stephen Colbert, Bob Dylan;* fourth level mature. *Bonnie Whittingham, Ken Wilbur, Mark Twain;* fourth level old soul.

FIFTH LEVEL: ECCENTRIC EXPLORER

When I was growing up I always had the feeling I was dropped from somewhere else, that's how I was treated at school. —Bjork

Notably distinguished by their eccentricities, this soul level is the easiest to spot. On one hand there is the known feeling of not fitting in, on the other hand their unconventional curious behavior offers an immense opportunity to push the parameters and explore unusual urges. This level is the step towards integrating earlier levels. Feeling unstable, there continues to be unorthodox exploring, venturing out, breaking with tradition, searching, manifesting and expanding in new directions. Gathering earlier experiences until they fit, at the Fifth Level they notice what else is possible. Preparation time is for what is sensed to be forthcoming in the near future. Offbeat, and a bit quirky, makes stability a bit shaky.

I was thrown out of college for cheating on the metaphysics final. I looked within the soul of the boy next to me. —Woody Allen

People are sometimes drawn to the unorthodox, whimsical, often playful Fifth Level person, as well as at times being put off by what looks bizarre. This level is about expansion and having adventures in the soul age exploration. You might find a surgeon, a medical doctor recognizing the brutality of surgical procedures and pioneering non-invasive techniques; actually writing their own rules as to how to live and work in this world. Broadening their horizons, looking to find the limits of thought, they discover unusual creative possibilities within each particular field. An artist pushing boundaries, finding where the limits will go, sometimes re-inventing relationships, coming up with their own dress code, altering rules, walking the edge of what's acceptable, exploring sexuality. This fringe of society person can be viewed as innovative, novel, unorthodox, an individualist, or an odd peculiar misfit. Unconventional, they live on the edge of what is considered normal or dangerous. Sometimes overextended, an experiment without exercising judgment becomes an impulse for drama and useless adventure.

If I died tomorrow I would be a happy girl. —Amy Winehouse

People think they know me, but they don't. I am one of the loneliest people on this planet. —Michael Jackson

It is not uncommon for people to feel protective and enchanted by these soul age individuals, even to become drawn in to their lively fantasy world. Often they dress a bit out of the ordinary, as well as having bizarre habits. It could be painting soup cans, napping in an oxygen chamber or clothing a monkey named Bubbles. The Fifth level instability rests on the reality that having climbed this high, the glimpse, seeing what may be ahead; old realities could topple. Experimenting and exploring limits becomes a great adventure. Possibilities show up as endless.

I've always wondered what it would be like if somebody from outer space landed with three heads. Then all of a sudden everybody else wouldn't look so bad, huh? Well, ok you're a little different from me but, hey, ya got one head. —Cyndi Lauper

Examples are: *Jerry Lee Lewis,* fifth level baby. *Weird Al Yankovitch, Mr. T., Liberace;* fifth level young. *PeeWee Herman, Frank Zappa, Andy Warhol, Cyndi Lauper, Divine, Janis Joplin, Boy George, Woody Allen;* fifth level mature. *Dr. Jay Victor Scherer, Michael Jackson, Fran Leibowitz, Szuzsanna Budapest;* fifth level old. *Salvatore Dali, Robin Williams, Gary Larson, Madonna, Amy Winehouse, Bjork, Adele, Liberace, Mick Jagger,*

John Waters, Dr. Allmorad Farshchian, Abbie Hoffman; fifth level soul age.

SIXTH LEVEL:
COMPELLED KARMIC TEACHER

Should you shield the canyons from the windstorms you would never see the true beauty of their carvings. The most beautiful people we have known are those who have known defeat, known suffering, known struggle, known loss, and have found their way out of the depths. These persons have an appreciation, a sensitivity and an understanding of life that fills them with compassion, gentleness, and a deep loving concern. Beautiful people do not just happen. —Elisabeth Kübler-Ross

The Sixth Level soul age is the most challenging, intense and demanding. Infant baby and young Sixth Level souls are gathering karma, while mature and old soul Sixth Levels are managing, sorting out and taking charge of their actions. For the Sixth Level mature and old soul there is completion, a handling of the accumulated karma of all the levels, plus teaching as a preparation for what follows. Much of what has previously been avoided is now up to be dealt with, handled, and there seems to be few breaks in between. At this point the experiences of the previous five levels come together. The energy imbalance that was created in the past seeks resolve, often through an intense, growthful experience. Karma is a compelling influence.

Growth, in some curious way, I suspect, depends on being always in motion just a little bit, one way or another. I don't think life is absurd. I think we are all here for a huge purpose. I think we shrink from the immensity of the purpose we are here for. —Norman Mailer

You are the purpose of life on earth. How to proceed? Firstly with love and

lastly with love, but in the space in between, work on yourselves. Don't expect anyone to do it for you. —Reshad Feild

This is a full demanding time, packed with *hard-luck* and obligations from the past, as well as in the present. Payback time, this is when an *eye for an eye,* a *tooth for a tooth,* may look like bad luck, but bearing with it, handling all old debts, juggling responsibilities, teaching by how we approach circumstances, may not seem like fun, but if the effort is made to pay attention to ourselves, much gets accomplished. Driven to be done with this world, fast-paced, piecing together and taking care of responsibilities and obligations that have added up through lifetimes, this is an engrossing soul level. What's often considered *hard-luck,* presents opportunities for completion and resolving obligations and makes for a busy, demanding, difficult, challenging lifetime. It's like pay-back, and a lot of time is spent dodging the bullets, as well as teaching others through experiencing the vicissitudes, changes of circumstances that life presents.

This is your life. You are responsible for it. You will not live forever. Don't wait. Be willing to split open. —Natalie Goldberg

Inwardly there is hope and a need for a harmonious environment, for relationships that are in accordance with the sensitivity and higher aspects of a life that the Sixth Level person innerly feels. The heightened self-awareness and quality of oneness towards others drives the mature and old Sixth Level person to look for conditions that are harmonious. Other soul levels are less able to step up to the plate and be as available, making personal connections challenging. The Sixth level person sees the limitations, struggles with trust issues and is driven to teach within an accelerated framework. To overcome this constant dilemma the Sixth Level soul person needs to stay focused on their intention, aim and purpose, remember to take care of their own personal needs while maintaining clarity and focus. In preparation for the next level, teaching what is known becomes a way of life.

Look down at me and you see a fool. Look up at me and you see a god; look straight at me and you see yourself. —Charles Manson

Your career, interests and relationships are important, but they are only important insofar as they lead you towards a deeper understanding of yourself. Otherwise, they are irrelevant. —A.H. Almaas

Examples are: *Ayatollah Khomeini, Dick Cheney;* Sixth Level baby. *Charles Manson,* Sixth Level infant. *Adolph Hitler, John Hinckley;* sixth level young. *Jesse Jackson, Elizabeth Taylor, Norman Mailer, Winnie Mandela;* Sixth Level mature. *Werner Erhard, Chris Griscom, Natalie Goldberg, David Deida, David Zeller, Shlomo Carlebach, Kabir Helminski, Mimi Feigelson, Bernie Siegel, A.H. Almaas, Roshi Joan Halifax, Jean Houston, Eli Jaxson-Bear, Rami Shapiro, Mitchell Chefitz, Gershon Winkler, Dr. Elisabeth Kübler-Ross, Dr. Paula Bromberg, Mary Oliver, Andrew Harvey, Arthur Green, Matthew Fox, Alice Miller, Stephen Levine, Jose Stevens, Reshad Feild, Mother Theresa;* Sixth Level old soul age.

SEVENTH LEVEL:
HARMONIOUS INTEGRATION

Everything we do, everything we are, rests on our personal power. If we have enough of it, one word is enough to change the course of our lives. If we don't, the most magnificent piece of wisdom can be revealed to us and that revelation won't make a damn bit of difference. Do you know that at this moment you are surrounded by eternity? And do you know that you can extend yourself forever in any direction? Do you know that one moment can be eternity? If you had enough personal power, my words alone would serve as a means to round up the totality of yourself and get to the crucial part of it out of the boundaries in which it is contained. —Don Juan Matus

Seventh Level is a well earned time of rest, recovery, relaxation and composure. Following the activity and demands of the sixth level, arriving at a zone of reassurance, there are few challenges, attention is focused on completing unfinished business with themselves more than with others. Because this is a resolution and moving on level there is an emphasis on reviewing, and what better way than to teach what we have accumulated in the six previous levels. Instilling the lessons, we sum up the soul age.

There are very few things that surprise me. —Judi Dench

You can't stop the waves but you can learn how to surf. —Swami Muktananda

There is noticeable unfolding, an ease and flow to sharing, plus teaching in a more reserved and private manner. They may be born to wealth, have comfort in their knowledge; this is an enjoyable time. Few obstructions, this is a *let's see what wants to happen time*. Relaxing from the intensity of sixth level, the reflection now mirrors the soul age. Seventh Level young soul, teaching for all younger soul ages, they could be a business counselor or advising stock investors and teaching companies how to set up credit card processing to become financially successful. The Seventh Level young soul will be guiding others on how to create a successful life of wealth and financial prosperity. A Seventh Level mature soul, teaching all that was learned until that point, might be a drug or divorce counselor, assisting emotional balance to those whose emotional life is off-kilter.

When we have done all the work we were sent to do, we are allowed to

shed our body, which imprisons our soul, like a cocoon encloses a butterfly.
—*Elisabeth Kübler-Ross*

A Seventh Level old soul teaches what has been integrated through all lifetimes, guiding often just one other, passing along how they are and what they know. Engaged, the Seventh Level old soul person either wants to master and pass on insight, what has been gained, to others, or gathers and mixes prior experiences, hanging out, not very outwardly directed. Since this is a preparation for the next cycle for the old soul there are one-to-one teachings that look like a mentorship or apprenticing or a disciple, in preparation to cycle off.

I did not come to collect students, but to train teachers. Your strength is how calmly, quietly and peacefully you face life. —*Yogi Bhajan*

Worldwide about one percent are Seventh Level old; this appears more as a teaching lifetime than a learning lifetime. A requirement for cycling off from the physical plane is successfully imparting knowledge and understanding to another person. This was apparent in Carlos Casteneda, disciple apprentice to Don Juan Matus for three decades. Lessons now are internal, therefore the Seventh Level person appears less a part of the world than any other level. Not fitting into the system, or really caring to fit; this is truly the outsider.

I have been training myself since I was young for the moment I would die. I'd ride the subway to Brooklyn, to the Yeshiva, and imagine that I was ready to depart from life and be gone by the next station. Then I would repeat the Shema by myself several times so I would be saying the ancient prayers with my last breath. Zalman Schachter-Shalomi left his body a month before his 90th birthday and was said to be a friend, teacher, purveyor of joy, a spiritual visionary, Reb Zalman, *with a heart as big as the world* created Jewish Renewal, ordained over 150 Rabbi's to impart new teachings and song for future generations.

Forgiveness is not an occasional act. It is a permanent attitude.
—*Martin Luther King*

The Seventh Level person must find a form to teach what has been learned. It might be taking care of a parent or protecting the environment; ultimately it is teaching those on the level they live what has been their unique understanding. Often carrying a wisdom that draws people to them, although it is difficult to understand a soul age older than one's own, Seventh Level always has a larger perspective than the ones preceding it. The focus is more on completing and deepening self-awareness not on completing unfinished affairs with others. Instilling lessons within ourselves, and connecting to one other person; this is a time to synopsize succinctly what has preceded. The older the soul age level the greater the ability to allow others to be, along with the urge to owe little, have fewer obligations. Since the Seventh Level is mostly about inner karma, much learning has happened along with a maturity of experience, bringing one to an end of a level.

We are not going to change the whole world, but we can change ourselves and feel free as birds. We can be serene even in the midst of calamities and, by our serenity, make others more tranquil. Serenity is contagious. If we smile at someone, he or she will smile back. And a smile costs nothing. We should plague everyone with joy, If we are to die in a minute, why not die happily, laughing? —*Swami Satchidananda*

Examples are: *Mohammar Khadafy, Sarah Palin, Richard Nixon;* Seventh Level baby. *Ruth Westheimer, Judi Dench, Ayn Rand, Ringo Starr, Rachel Maddow, Shirley MacLaine;* Seventh Level mature, *Swami Muktananda, Swami Satchidananda, Ram Dass, Martin Luther King, Yogi Bhajan, Zalman Schachter-Shalomi, Don Juan Matus;* Seventh Level old.

SYSTEM FIVE

ENNEAGRAM OF BODY TYPES

LUNAR, VENUSIAN, MERCURY, SATURN, MARS, JOVIAL, SOLAR, NEPTUNE, URANUS, PLUTO, CHIRON

Because you think you are the body, for a long time you have been bound. Know you are pure awareness. With this knowledge as your sword, cut through your chains and be happy! —Ashtavakra Gita

This system of typology, placed on the Enneagram, an ancient symbol of transformation, a symbolic device reminiscent of the Mandala, was brought to the West by G. I. Gurdjieff. The Enneagram is a cosmic map that embodies the universal ideas that Gurdjieff called the *Law of Three* and the *Law of Seven* (refer to Universal Laws, System 27). It is a triangle inscribed in a circle that is divided into nine equal segments by points connected in a precise way. A universal model of processes, the law of 7 united with the law of 3; its roots are in the mystical wings of all sacred traditions. The Enneagram is a model that can be applied to any process happening in the universe, mirroring its concealed structure. The Enneagram embodies the progress, explaining what we inscribe into the system, yet it is in the observing intelligence, the act of self-observation that brings about the understanding which precedes our transformation. In the system of body and personality types available for this study, the teaching perspective is that both the mechanical body and the personality stand in the way between ordinary life and the planes of spiritual life.

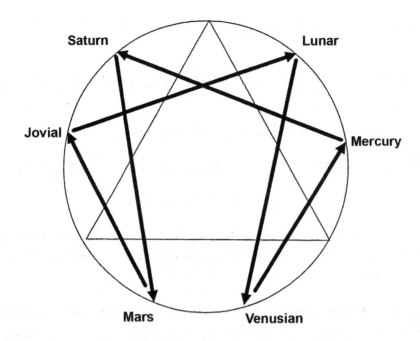

Chart 4: The Circulation of Types on the Enneagram of Body Types

The Enneagram is a subtle and interwoven teaching. It is a challenge to keep in mind its multidimensional perspectives. The Enneagram describes a pattern and a process, something invariant and something that changes in steps. Think of the pattern as the basic plot of a drama and the process as the action that unfolds it. Or, as the "idea" of a piece of art, which has to be realized through a line of work. In the Enneagram, the plot or the idea is not a thing but a "relationship", and it appears in the form of the triangular figure. The process, the action, or the work appears in the sequence of steps around the circle. —A.G.E. Blake

The Enneagram of Body Type describes eleven types that travel around the Enneagram design. Body Types are easily observable and therefore accessible to study. The continuous and orderly circulation of type is: Lunar, Venusian, Mercury, Saturn, Mars, Jovial. An additional five types: Solar, Neptune, Uranus, Pluto and Chiron join any of the Body Types in a random manner. The additional five types point the physical way to something metaphysically higher. The long cycles existing between the three outer planets means essentially that Neptune, Uranus and Pluto do not directly deal with individuals, they deal with collective, planetary and cosmic factors—with humanity, the earth, the solar system and the galaxy as wholes. The Body Types connected to the outer planets express themselves more through the eyes and vibrational atmosphere of individuals than through physical characteristics. The direction of the movement of the first six types plus Solar, charted on the Enneagram contain an integration and balance for each type. What appears as we look to our next type is a correction as well as the available strengths to assist growth. The Body Type we start out with moves gradually throughout our lifetime towards the characteristics of the next Body Type. Our physical and psychological traits stem from the influences of the celestial bodies on our physical body.

GLANDULAR CONTRIBUTIONS TO OUR LIVES

This system links the cosmos of a person to the cosmos of the solar system, establishing a link between the endocrine glands of the body and the celestial bodies of the solar system.

Each endocrine gland or its associated nerve-plexus is sensitive to the magnetism of a particular planet. This particular magnetism will naturally be strongest when the planet is in the zenith and shining vertically through the minimum thickness of the atmosphere, exactly as the sun's light and warmth are strongest at midday. The height of a given planet in the sky will thus be an exact measure of the degree of stimulation imparted to the corresponding gland at a given moment. —Rodney Collin

The eleven Body Types correspond to the Sun, Moon, Venus,

Mercury, Saturn, Mars, Jupiter, Neptune, Uranus, Pluto and Chiron. Each Body Type has a planetary influence and a ruling gland. If all the glands were perfectly balanced, the astrological influence would be harmonious. When we choose to be under the direction of a particular glandular influence, when one gland is actively predominant, the increased activity of that gland gives us the physical and psychological characteristics corresponding to that gland. The glands in the order of their distance from the heart obey the same laws as the planets in the order of their distance from the sun. Similarly designed, each responds to the other. Each gland is a sensitive instrument tuned to the frequency of a corresponding planet, transforming human energy, obeying its guidance. This implies that our body appears, like the Milky Way, to be a spiral with the sun and its source being the heart, releasing through the thymus, the pancreas, the thyroid, and continuing. On a cosmic scale we are receptors for the influences broadcasting through our body.

Glands are organs consisting of specialized tissues which produce and/or secrete materials essential to body harmony. The energy-form of each type is controlled by a particular endocrine gland. These ductless glands regulate many of our physiological processes: growth, metabolism, reproduction, the body's electrical balance, its temperature and the rate it burns energy; essentially the glands act like guardians, the survival of our species depends on their functioning. It may take a malfunction or the exhaustion of a gland before real appreciation of glandular contributions in our physical and psychic lives appears. Individual survival depends on the endocrine system making accurate readings of stimuli and situations and its continuing to respond with appropriate adjustments. The glands are the intercommunicating instruments, the transformers, or transmitters between the spiritual, divine, cosmic self and the more gross, earthly and physical self bringing about within us a divine alchemy. Our personal magnetism is the result of the proper functioning of our glands.

The heart is the sun of the body, and the bloodstream, like the sun's radiation in the solar system, extends to its every part. No corner of the body is too remote to be warmed and vitalized by it. It suffuses the endocrine organs, as the Sun's light and heat shines upon all the planets, supplying them with life and uniting them into a single whole. The order in which the glands pour their influence into the blood-stream follows a definite sequence, similar to that in which the planets sound their characteristic notes in the stream of time. —Rodney Collin

The Body Type as a tool is a road map, the circumstances and challenges of living continue and here is a street guide. Loving begins with self-acceptance, as we are, as others are, and the question of living mindfully eases when we have a map that offers true insight. The wisdom of *know thyself* as a directive echoed in the Socratic statement *the unexamined life is not worth living* supports the system of Body Types as a valuable tool of study. In the dog world we can clearly observe the difference between body types; ie: a Poodle and a German Shepherd, each breed has recognizeable characteristics and nature. In the animal world the Siamese cat and the Calico cat are strikingly different. Lunars do not look like Martials, a Solar appearance is markedly different from a Jovial, a Saturn's body is easily distinguished from a Mercury body. Looking at physical characteristics of each type will reveal, sometimes by the process of elimination, our Body Type. A close examination of the body and its structure, regardless to the efforts made to alter it, discloses important information. The information about how the glands affect development and behavior offers insight into why the different types look and behave as they do. The distinction between the different types of human beings becomes apparent once we have the tools, the maps; this information is available to study throughout this book.

Astrologers speak of three kinds of planets. The personal or inner planets, the Sun, Moon, Mercury, Venus and Mars; the transpersonal planets, Jupiter and Saturn; and the outer planets, Uranus, Neptune and Pluto. The Sun represents who we feel we really are, the Moon represents our most basic needs, and security issues, the place in consciousness where emotions are manifested, as well as the physical body. Mercury is the process of communication, the inner light of the mind, and the self that is not bound by definitions but rather flits from one idea about itself to another. Basically Venus and Mars like to have sex, eat good food and play out the polarity of maleness and femaleness. The transpersonal planets, Jupiter and Saturn represent forces that don't seem to be so internal, but rather function as a part of society. Jupiter represents good fortune (as if from the outside), and the aspects of a person that are magnanimous, excessive, and full of hot air. Saturn represents concrete structures, the boundaries and structures of mind, body and interaction with and within which we must live. Without Saturn functioning normally, which includes tending to our process of becoming mature and creating structures to live within, we have a hard time staying sane or stable.

The outer modern planets, represent humanity's delves into deep space of consciousness in the form of psychoanalyses, spirituality, invention, industry and mysticism—not to mention mass insanity, holocausts, world wars and genocide. Uranus is the planet of revolution, innovation, and the divine electricity of the mind. Neptune represents the presence of the numinous, the supernatural, the unspeakable, the invisible and the mysterious. Pluto, takes what seems to be negative force and possibilities and with awareness transforms them. The further away the planets are, the more difficult their energy is to grasp or comprehend. Enter Chiron, functioning as an inner planet, and an outer planet, a bridge between the outer planets and the transpersonal planets. We know Chiron is active when we strive to make difficulty meaningful, when we seek healing rather than escape, and when we strive for awareness when in the past we desired to go to sleep. —Eric Francis

OUR BODY TYPE AS A COSMOS

The esoteric information called Body Typing offers the possibility of working through the 48 universal or phenomenal laws to higher levels of consciousness that surpass the Body Types. All Body Types have the possibility to awaken into a conscious life. Each Body Type has the potential to be a complete cosmos. About 45% of our traits come from our primary Body Type, 25% from the type before, 25% from the following type, about 5% from all other types. The other possible and common composition is: 70% our primary type, 20% second type and 10% a third type. We have access to each type, although primarily we are a combination of two or three types. The part that our family of origin preferred becomes strengthened, while the characteristics they rejected influences us to deny, dilute, and believe those aspects of ourself to be less than acceptable. The positive and negative characteristics are similar to electrical currents and color our attitude as to whether we see the glass as half full or half empty. The positive types are more like the day; brighter, lighter, emphasizing the outer, overlooking flaws. The negative types are more like the night; darker, shadowy, emphasizing the inner, observing what needs correcting. Each Body Type is either active—having a tendency *to do*, they muscle up with exercise, are often naturally thin; or passive—having a *to be* quality, not strengthening with exercise and have a tendency to be round bodied.

Weakness and predominant traits of one Body Type are strengths for the next type circulating on the Enneagram. The progression of types originates with Lunar and moves to Venusian, Mercury, Saturn, Mars, Jovial and then returns to Lunar, always in that order. The other types exist separately and are found in any combination along with the basic

TYPE	THEME	ENERGY	GENDER	CHARGE	GLAND
Lunar	coldness willful aloof timidity	passive	feminine	negative	pancreas
Venusian	non-existence earth mother sensual slothful	passive	feminine	positive	parathyroids
Mercury	high-spirited live-wire trickster talkative	active	masculine	negative	thyroid
Saturn	self-control domination predictable quiet	active	masculine	positive	anterior pituitary
Mars	combative direct single-focused forceful	active	masculine	negative	adrenals
Jovial	vanity grandiosity periodicity maternal	passive	feminine	positive	posterior pituitary
Solar	child-like energetic naiveté	active	androgynous	positive	thymus
Neptune	mysterious aesthetic psychic	passive	feminine	positive	pineal
Uranus	extreme individualist inventive the rebel	active	androgynous	negative	gonads
Pluto	penetrating eccentric cruel	passive	masculine	negative	hypothalamus
Chiron	integration maverick wounded healer	active	androgynous	positive	pineal hypothalamus

Chart 5: Eleven Body Types

types. The following step for each resolves the weakness of the present type and introduces new friction. The aloof, coldness of Lunar goes towards the sensuous warmth of Venusian. The slothful non-existent Venusian moves towards the live-wire Mercury. The talkative Mercury circulates towards Saturn self-control, the quiet Saturn goes towards the direction of the feisty Martial, the forceful Martial moves towards the ease of the Jovial, and the vain Jovial goes towards the timidity of Lunar. As one leaves Jupiter and ascends to Lunar, the same circular movement on the Enneagram continues, each cycle at a new, higher level. (Refer to Chart 4 and 5)

We can look to the ancient gods of Greece for another example of the historical existence of types. Seven of these gods became associated with the seven heavenly bodies visible from the Earth with the naked eye, and their qualities have been bound together ever since. These connections have lasted through more than two thousand years and occupy a place now in the names we use for the planets an the days of the week. Each day has its god, and we have no difficulty in considering the whole week as a complete and self-contained system. —*Joel Friedlander*

The 7-day week and the stories of the Greek and Roman gods are some of the expressive history of this system. Each day of the week has been named for a heavenly body and a human Body Type. The energy of each celestial body is linked to mythological symbols. For example, Mars, the red planet, is named after the Roman god of war and people with a Martial Body Type tend to be aggressive. The ancients were convinced that there were just seven planets including the Sun and Moon; Mercury, Venus, Mars, Jupiter and Saturn. Each of the seven were believed to have a special influence over their designated day of the week: Sunday-Sun-Solar, ruled by Phoebus. Monday-Moon-Lunar, ruled by Selene. Tuesday-Mars-Martial, under Ares. Wednesday-Mercury-Mercurial, the day of Hermes. Thursday-Jupiter-Jovial, and the god is Zeus. Friday-Venus-Venusian, ruled by Aphrodite. Saturday-Saturn-Saturnine, of the Greek Kronos. The alchemists of the Middle Ages noted that there were seven planets and seven metals that coordinate with the planets. The seven metals presented by the alchemists matched with the planets: gold (Sun), silver (Moon), copper (Venus) iron (Mars), tin (Jupiter), lead (Saturn), and quicksilver (Mercury).

We should spend out lives upgrading energies, This is the hidden meaning behind alchemy. 'To be born again.' —*Margaret Anderson*

Each of the planets has rulership over one or two of the twelve zodiac signs exerting its most powerful energy over the Body Type it rules as well as being mirrors of basic organizing principles in the universe. Planets exert their influence directly through gravitational power. The esoteric tradition of the Emerald Tablets, *as above, so below*, is verified in the corresponding celestial body that influences each type. The basic patterns of the universe repeat themselves and the stars in the sky become linked to life here on earth.

PLANETARY INFLUENCES

The planets exert a very great influence on the life of the earth, and on all existing and living organisms—a far greater influence than our science imagines. —*G.I. Gurdjieff*

Originally, astrology's primary function was that of a calendar. Early astrologers, based on observations of qualities and energies of both the planets and the zodiac signs began to match them. Some of the combinations have remained unchanged since the earliest days of astrology, while other pairings were made after the discovery of Uranus in 1781, Neptune in 1846 and Pluto in 1930. The discovery of Chiron in 1977 and the demotion of Pluto to dwarf planet continues to create new associations. That a planet rules a particular sign means that the ruling planet and all its energies are in charge and influence the expression of the individual. The listing of planets that rule sun zodiac signs are: the Sun rules Leo, the Moon rules Cancer, Mercury rules Gemini and Virgo, Venus rules Taurus and Libra, Mars rules Aries and Scorpio, Jupiter rules Sagittarius, Saturn rules Capricorn, Uranus rules Pisces, Pluto rules Scorpio.

All great events in the life of the human masses are caused by planetary influences. Human society is a highly sensitive mass for the reception of planetary influences; and any accidental small tension in planetary spheres can be reflected for years in an increased animation in one or another sphere of human activity. —P.D. Ouspensky

This ancient system of the Enneagram of Body Type offers greater insight towards seeing ourself and others more distinctly, which minimizes subjective opinions, expectations and other personal distortions. A compass of impartiality, this tool offers a way to study and discover mysteries of human psychology. The understanding of energy through Body Type information accelerates our inner work, deepens our psychological development and creates a bridge to spiritual development. By knowing the energy and nature of the types, we learn to draw on and borrow the assets, resources and attributes of other constitutional types. This information assists us in our daily life to move through the world in more accurate relationships with others, projecting far less, offering a tool to use our personality as a point to embark on a larger journey into the awakened world of conscious awareness. All of the tools expose the mechanicalness of our habits and once we see, acknowledge and stop taking ourselves personally we become free to unlock a door to our true nature. A Body Type is a form in which to create a soul.

Each body type is potentially a complete cosmos and contains all seven types within it. According to the school of Pythagoras a cosmos is a self-evolving or self-transcending whole. Logically, according to this definition a human being would be the only being found on this planet that can be rightfully called a cosmos as it is the only instrument capable of transcending itself and creating an astral body, that is a soul. —Robert Burton

L U N A R

Positive: receptive, calm, sensitive, patient, determined, persevering, methodical, reflective, gentle, introspective, imaginative, careful attention to detail
Negative: willful, moody, obstinate, depressive, unapproachable, cold-hearted, withdrawn, unforgiving, stubborn, rigid, internal rage, uncommunicative, sarcastic humor, unresponsive, remote, cynical, obstinate, eccentric, secretive
Maximum attraction: Saturn
Ruling astrological sign: Cancer
Ruling gland: pancreas
Mid-most Point: femininity
Type: passive/negative, feminine

The moon, the moon, so silver and cold. Her fickle temper has oft been told, now shade—now bright and sunny. But of all the Lunar things that change, the one that shows most fickle and strange, and takes the most eccentric range, is the moon—so called—of honey! —Thomas Hood

The Lunar body type is a receiver for a celestial body, the moon, which is under 96 laws. The earth is under 48 laws, the planets under 24 and the sun is under 12. This is important to know in understanding the moody, heavy, cold, stubborn, obstinate, detached, introspective nature of the Lunar type. The moon, closest planetary body to the earth, has the strongest influence, pulling on the water element. The water of the moon quenches the fire, thereby making Lunar slow to react as well as subject to display cool emotions.

She is the most powerful in operation of all the other planets on Elementary bodies by reason of her proximity to us and her swiftness, by which she transfers the light and influence of all Superiors to us, by configuration with them. —Ramesey. This passage, written by the 17th century astrologer conveys something of the great importance attached to the interpretation of the moon.

PHASES OF THE MOON

The Romans called her Diana and Selene, the Greeks, Artemis and Hecate, goddess of the night. The Moon is the goddess with three forms: Selene in the sky, Artemis on earth, and Hecate in the lower world; the world cloaked in darkness. These forms are reflected in the moon's phases. As the new moon she is the maiden goddess Artemis, always new and virginal, reborn and ready for the hunt. As the waxing moon, increasing in fullness she is the fertile mother goddess, pregnant with life. And as she wanes to darkness, she is the wise crone or witch Hecate, knowledgeable in the magical arts, with the power to heal or transform. Driving her silver chariot she carries the moon across the sky, shooting arrows of silver moonlight to the earth below. She is the lady of wild things and the goddess of the hunt. Through Diana, Artemis, Hecate, Selene, the many faces of women and of the changing moon are displayed.

I have a little secret I'd like to impart. The man in the moon is a lady, she winks at the stars from her bed of green cheese. She sends the big dipper a kiss. So don't ever offend her, remember her gender. The man in the moon is a miss. —Lyrics by Blake McGrath

Our moon's revolutions equal its rotation and therefore shows only one side of itself to us on earth, just like the Lunar type, both sides are secretive and private. Always half-hidden, maintaining mystery, the moon influences ocean tides and the body. The moon has been viewed as feminine, and woman's bodies respond to Lunar cycles, mirroring woman's menstrual cycles. Women's characteristics are as changeable as the three faces of the moon, waxing (maiden, youth and vitality) full (mother, nurturer and protector) and waning (crone, age and wisdom). The Lunar type is the mid-most point of femininity. The Lunar, willful, eccentric and aloof, a passive and negative type, appears indifferent, impervious and unapproachable. Often lovers of solitude, aloof, they prefer quiet company and simple friendship. They are the singular type whose governing body is considered to be a satellite, an object that orbit's another object; the moon is earth's satellite.

The moon is the swiftest moving body. It travels through the zodiac every 28 days. As Lady of the Night the Moon is feminine and can represent the mother. At a universal level it is a powerful symbol of womankind and feminine energy, and it rules motherhood, babies, childhood, and fertility. The Moon's 28-day cycle taps us into the menstrual cycle. —Martin Gansten

LUNAR TYPES

Ruled by the pancreas, which is important in the digestion of food and connected to the lymphatic system, Lunar types are subject to poor digestion. An abundance of lymph is said to be responsible for the Lunar's luminous appearance. Tall, or short and rounded, they have an awkward unfinished look. The Lunar body is immature with longer arms and legs than torso, graceful and fluid. Often hunched over in an effort to not be noticed, once pushed the Lunar resists, when urged they decline, when dominated, they rebel. Pale-skin, round moon-shaped faces, gray, pale or light blue eyes, often deeply set and protected the pupils having a luminescent appearance, the upper lid is barely visible.

Small ears set close to the head, their nose is long and prominent or low, flat and formless. Lunar types have a weak chin, some have no appreciable jaw development, the frontal chin and jaw outline continue the circle of the facial shape, sometimes there is instead a narrow jaw and often a meek, mild high key voice. Either you will see a tiny slit mouth or a large, loose-lipped mouth that is not defined. The face has a sad, dreamy and somewhat woe-begone expression. When youthful, the body is slender, although with age they may put on watery weight. Reticent, reserved, shy, they often live and work alone, enjoying their solitude and moods. Liking sunlight less than most other types, reticent and introspective they sometimes have a flare for bizarre humor. This type can be hauntingly beautiful one day and quite plain the next.

Do not swear by the moon, for she changes constantly. Then your love would also change. —William Shakespeare

The pancreas, the ruling gland, is located in the abdomen. Its secretions, insulin and glucagon, create the proper environment for the digestion of complex foods, as well as regulating blood sugar levels. The pancreas has a lot to teach in regard to its judicious storage and dispensation of psychic energy, which flows naturally along the channels of our thoughts and experiences. The impressions we ingest must be broken down, similar to food, to then be digested. Since Lunar and the pancreas are closely connected to the lymphatic system, the abundance of lymph is responsible for the round watery translucent appearance. Lymph, colorless in hue turns opalescent from fat absorbed after a meal, representing the moist aspect of the Lunar nature, subject to the pull of the moon. This tends to quench the fire, making Lunar slow to respond, cool in emotions, their pale skin, low digestive fire, often constipated, they display *steel icy blue* eye energy.

The Moon is the queen of mesmerism and mystification. Enticing us with her delicate aura, intriguing us with her inconstant appearance, the Moon is a wanton creature; sometimes appearing low on the horizon, illuminating the night in her full orb, sometimes appearing briefly, dressed in her flimsiest crescent. It is now established that the Moon affects us; a cosmic trigger for many natural rhythms and breeding cycles. —Deborah Houlding

GODDESS OF THE MOON

Diana, Roman goddess of hunting, virginity and the moon, is a perfect example of a Lunar woman. Named Artemis in the Greek myth, goddess of the hunt, she fiercely defended her right to eternal virginity. Furious when a mortal saw her bathing naked in the woods, Artemis transformed him into a stag. She carried a silver bow and arrows, giving a painless death to anyone she chose to kill. The goddess Diana was a huntress, as well as nurturer of children and feminine values, a protector of the weak and vulnerable. Goddess of the moon, the heavenly light that illuminates the darkness, she is portrayed as a torchbearer whose torch or candle lit the way. Regal and dignified, she held the reins of her life, and drove her own chariot through unchartered territory. Diana ruled the wilderness, the untamed frontiers of nature. This independent, yet compassionate goddess was available to others, yet challenged by her relationships with men. Her brother Apollo tricked her into a hunting competition, whereby, as Artemis, she unintentionally beheaded her lover Orion and then proceeded to make him a star in the sky since he could no longer be the star that brightened her time on earth.

We are all like the bright moon, we still have our darker side. —Kahlil Gibran

The passive power of a Lunar is like a person holding onto a tight rope, steady and immovable, a tough obstacle to be reckoned with since there is an immediate *no*, and a stubborn refusal to change to *yes*. They resist new ideas, often feeling empowered by their refusal which feels to them like independence. The only passive and negative type, as well as the only type whose governing celestial body is thought to be a satellite, coming from Jovial moving to Venusian they may have a residual interest in people or when a Lunar Venusian type they then carry the softness of the Venusian ease. Often nocturnal, they prefer a dimly-lit home and solitude over time spent out socializing. The fear of exposure, of visibility, constrains and constricts them. Unmovable, misunderstood, cautious, tender, self-reliant, afraid to be unmasked, hiding their feelings, willful, their aloofness exaggerates their mysteriousness.

The moon is a white strange world, great, white, soft-seeming globe in the night sky, and what she actually communicates to me across space I shall never fully know. But the moon that pulls the tides, and the moon that controls the menstrual periods of women, and the moon that touches the lunatics, she is not the mere dead lump of the astronomist. When we describe the moon as dead, we are describing the deadness in ourselves. When we find space so hideously void, we are describing our own unbearable emptiness. —D.H. Lawrence

Don't worry if you make waves simply by being yourself; the moon does it all the time. —Scott Stabile

Some known Lunar types are: *Emily Dickinson, Woody Allen, Gwyneth Paltrow, Meryl Streep, David Letterman, Glenn Close, Ranier Maria Rilke, Paris Hilton, Meg Ryan, Andy Warhol, Gary Larson, Charles Addams, Truman Capote, Tom Wolfe, St. Theresa, Stephen Hawking, Steven Wright, Anne Heche, Kate Bosworth, Taylor Swift, Miley Cyrus;* lunar venusian mercury, *Lady Gaga, Prince William, Ellen DeGeneres, Nicole Kidman;* jovial lunar venusian, *Mr. Magoo.*

V E N U S I A N

Positive: easy-going, loyal, healing, nurturing, kind, supportive, devotee, good health, loves pleasure, easily satisfied, sympathetic, accepting, voluptuous

Negative: non-existence, careless, slothful, low self-esteem, easily victimized, vegetative/comatose in front of a TV, lack of focus, lazy, poor teeth, vague, impractical

Maximum attraction: martial

Ruling astrological sign: Taurus and Libra

Ruling gland: parathyroid

Type: passive/positive, feminine

I will sing to Aphrodite/Venus, bestower of love, gold-crowned and beautiful. Hail, sweetly-winning, coy-eyed goddess! She gives kindly gifts to men, smiles are ever on her lovely face, and lovely is the brightness that plays over it. —Homeric Hymn

G O D D E S S   O F   L O V E

The art world has flourished with paintings of beautiful shapely sensual Venusian bodies. Soft velvety skin, lovely and smooth to the touch, of average height, Venus, the goddess of love and fertility appreciates pleasure and beauty. This cellular bulk body type is evenly proportioned, often over-weight. Aphrodite was the goddess of love and beauty. In Rome she was named Venus, the mother of Cupid. She rose out of the ocean and was so lovely to behold that the wind almost lost his breath. All the gods rejoiced in her beauty and made her one of them. Venus/Aphrodite, goddess of love and fertility, beauty and regeneration, who calms the seas and pacifies nature; her qualities balance and harmonize human instincts and emotions. The myths around the goddess represent her as having power over the sexual and carnal urges of the energy of love and able to imprison others in their animalistic instincts, or to transform them into heroes, rewarding them. In her myths she rules over the heart of all humans and, according to her will, she either saves people from their trials and ordeals, or recklessly pushes them into adventurous love affairs that usually end up disastrously, such as those of Helen of Troy, Medea and Phaedra, as well as those we read about in Hollywood headlines; ie. Venusians Marilyn Monroe, Anna Nicole Smith, Mariah Carey, Justin Bieber, Brad Pitt. Venus, considered a feminine planet, in the past century, a best-selling non-fiction book equated the feminine with the planet: Men are from Mars, Women are from Venus, wrote John Gray.

When you are the flower I am the shadow cast by the flower. When I am the fire you are the mirror reflecting the fire. And when Venus has entered the disc of the Sun then you are that Venus and I am the Sun. —Harry Crosby

Aphrodite/Venus carries the most essential of all the gifts; divine love. Without pure love's impulse other gifts remain untapped. They need the vibrant, pulsating impulse of divine love to stay nourished and sustained. The essence of love carries the lover and the beloved, creating wholeness, making the world a livelier and more beautiful place. While all the other gods and goddesses had lengthy lists of divine duties to perform, the goddess Venus/Aphrodite was assigned only one: to bring love into the world.

The pattern of Venus around the Earth portrays a 5-petalled rose when viewed from the geometric position. Every 8 years, when the Earth and Venus 'kiss' to form another petal, Venus presents the same face to the Earth. Astronomer Johannes Kepler understood such patterns as a mathematician aware of the mystical qualities of the universe. The patterns of Venus are extremely beautiful—the heart and the rose. They reveal the essence of Venus in her role of celestial guardian of love and beauty to those of us here on earth. —Nick Kollerstrom

Loyal and reliable, the healing professions attract the caring Venusian, whether male or female. This is a passive, feminine, positive, receptive body type, malleable and earthbound. A living sponge, absorbing, sensual, animal, positioned to life in the flesh, having an aura of naturalness about things, Venusians have an appreciation of pleasure and beauty. Form-aware, often catering to the gaze of others, their contours represent physicality. The Venusian is ruled by the parathyroids, the glands which complement the thyroid by stabilizing the metabolism and producing a calm, adaptable, flexible effect. These four small glands that sit on the corners of the thyroid gland produce parathormone, which serves to monitor calcium levels in the blood.

Venus rules beauty and its physical attributes are good looks, prettiness, dimples, softness, roundness, and a tendency to put on weight. It also rules beautifying, such as make-up, perfume, jewelry, and all adornments.
—Joanna Watters

THE VENUSIAN TYPE

The slow quality of the body type correlates to the fact that Venus rotates once every 243 days, one of the slowest planets. Remember that the earth rotates once in less than 24 hours. Never more than 47 degrees from the sun, Venus reflects 57% of the sun's light, rather than retaining it for its own nurturance, this is representative of the Venusian quality of non-existence. Venus, the second closest planet to the sun, is perfectly round and white, with a pearly soft appearance, having the most circular orbit of all the planets. Venus, closest known planet to earth, second planet in distance from the sun, brightest object in the sky, is the planet most similar to the earth. She appears to welcome both the dawn and the dusk. The Chinese call this slowest rotating and hottest of all recognized planets, *beautiful white one*. Temperatures climb to 900 degrees F (482C), owing to the dense, heat-trapping atmosphere.

A transit of Venus over the sun being, beyond comparison, the most curious and uncommon appearance the heavens afford; the near approach so rare a phenomenon. —*John Winthrop*

Venus, the warm planet, is surrounded by an atmosphere of clouds of carbon dioxide gas, and the Venusian type is hazy and indistinct often difficult to bring into focus. Slow, sometimes emanating a humid air of sensuality, their open generosity often too indiscriminate, easily losing themselves in others, living through and letting the lives of others take over. Preferring to wear loose comfortable clothing, their full-bodied contour has few edges. The limbs are smooth and graceful, with little muscular or boney prominence. Often addicted to sugar, rarely bald, the hair tends towards a brown earthy color. Easy to talk to, they're happy to listen and inviting to confide in, accepting and friendly. An excessive need for contact; generating energy themselves is difficult, therefore, leaning against, hand holding, massaging, hugging; all physical contact speeds up their slow metabolism. Touching—food, material, people, pets, children; all stimulate their senses. Sensuality keeps them uplifted. Almost irresistible to hug, soft and easy-going, their physical warmth expresses a benevolent spirit. Venusians are an agreeable type, comfortable to be around, enjoying shared pleasure. Venusians ask us to indulge our senses and revel in the beauty of our world. It's a sensual world, not necessarily sexual; and relating to others, good food and drink, appreciation for luxury possessions, a sense of the aesthetic, all pleases the Venusian interests. Often edema, the buildup of fluid between the tissue cells, creates discomfort and swelling in their legs, as well as unhealthy soft gums and teeth. The Venusian can also grow quite large, sometimes pear-shaped with thick ankles. The habitual expression is either vacant, tender, or enticing and inviting.

Known as the morning or evening star, Venus is visible just before sunrise or after sunset. In Greek mythology Venus is Aphrodite, the goddess of love, from whose name comes the word 'aphrodisiac', that which induces desire. From Venus' name comes the word 'venereal,' which literally means 'of lust'. Venus is feminine and rules our world of love and all desires. Through it we experience joy, rapture, lust, and the nature of our sexuality. Venusian types are generally wonderful lovers, but they are also lovers of beauty, art, music, and food. Venus rules sensuality and earthly pleasures as discovered through the senses of touch, taste, smell, sight, and sound. In this sense it is the opposite principle of Mercury, as our physical appetites are a response to need and want rather than being part of an analytical process. In fact, our most powerful desires drive out judgment—we all know that trying to reason with anyone 'in love' is useless. —Martin Gansten

Venusians, sometimes considered non-existent, live life indirectly, often through others, having little desire to make the necessary efforts required towards consciousness. There are piles of things—papers, clothing, projects unfinished, scattered around, as they happily vegetate, blending in with whatever is around. Absorbent, difficult to say *no* when pressured, later having resentment build, Venusians make a bigger deal out of experiences, fueling their quality of non-existence. Sexual energy easily dissipates, although the earthy, gracefully rounded soft body, bulky or voluptuous, pulls others easily towards them. This is Earth Mother, generous and reliable, comforting and healing, approachable and friendly.

Some known Venusian types are: *Marilyn Monroe, Charlize Theron, Elvis Presley, James Dean, John Travolta, Britney Spears, Jessica Simpson, Jean Harlow, Marlon Brando, Mariah Carey, Mama Cass;* Venusian Mercury, *Elizabeth Taylor, Kim Kadashian, Anna Nicole Smith, Scarlett Johansson, Justin Bieber;* jovial lunar venusian, *Venus di Milo.*

MERCURY

Positive: entertaining, perceptive, energetic, rich melodious voice, witty, cheerful, clever, clean appearance, lively
Negative: manipulative, nervous, opinionated, low pain threshold, restless, impulsive, controlling, tricky, scattered, finicky
Maximum attraction: Jovial
Ruling astrological sign: Gemini and Virgo
Ruling gland: thyroid
Type: active/negative, masculine

Mercury is the closest planet to the sun and moves with the greatest speed. Because of its proximity to the sun and earth, the influence of Mercury is somewhat more visible than that of the slower moving planets. This is particularly true when the planet is retrograde, visibly influencing communication and mechanical devices. —Skyscript

MERCURIAL ENERGY

*M*ercury is the smallest planet in the solar system, the one closest to the sun. Called the baby planet, the orbit of Mercury travels around the sun with more speed than any other planet, 315 times compared to the earth's 76 times in the same period of about 70 years. Its visibility is approximately 85 hours a year. A Mercury year, 88 earth days, is half as long as a Mercury day, because it rotates one-and-a-half times during each of its orbits around the sun. There is no day and night for the planet Mercury, only light and heat on one side and cold and darkness on the other side of the rapidly moving little planet. If orbits were racetracks, speedy Mercury would leave the other planets behind. It zips along at about one and a half times the speed of the earth. It is one of the five planets known to the ancients who referred to them as *wandering stars.*

An active, masculine, negative type, Mercury influences the thyroid gland which regulates combustion in the organism. This, then, affects the speed of the whole mechanism. The thyroid and the hormones it produces strongly effect our metabolism. A strong thyroid creates sharp, quick excitability and nervous energy in a person, a healthful functioning thyroid keeps the body warm, controls the body's burning of caloric content to keep our weight balanced. A deficient thyroid causes the body to store fat deposits rather than converting the caloric intake into energy.

At the physical level, our bodies are like a miniature replica of the solar system. Our hearts perform the function of the sun—the center of its system. Other organs within our body are also used by our souls to find a means of expression. The planets exert vibrations upon our bodies that influence our personalities and soul patterns. At the soul level, the solar system is our larger body, and our bodies act as a miniature solar system. We are connected to the planets, the stars, spiritual realms and entities. On the spirit level, we are one with the whole. —Kevin Williams

The person with a Mercury body type energy is agile, speedy, a live wire, high-spirited, with a sunny disposition, compact, neat and trim like a sports car. They lighten and brighten, bringing curiosity and a child-like quality; this is the witty chatter box. An overactive mind, speedy thoughts and quick mental perception, a mercurial nature brings to mind motion. The planet Mercury implores us to express ourselves, and when it goes retrograde giving the appearance of traveling backward, communication becomes challenged. Mercury, the cosmic trickster, when retrograde sends communications, travel, appointments and mail into a muddle, as well as bringing personal misunderstandings, flawed or delayed negotiations, glitches and breakdowns that arise because a crucial piece of information or component has gone astray. Mercury is about mental clarity and the power of the mind over critical faculties, dimmed and less acute during a retrograde period. Moving forward, sometimes we do need to move backward to rethink actions and fix what might be broken. This, then, is an opportunity to review past ideas, to revise, re-evaluate and reconsider in preparation for when Mercury goes direct. A planet is described retrograde when it appears to be moving backwards through the zodiac. According to modern science, this traditional concept appears in the illusory planetary motion created by the orbital rotation of the earth with relation to other planets in our solar system. Planets are never actually retrograde or stationary, they just seem that way due to a cosmic shadow-play.

The purpose of Mercury retrograde is to review and revise our life and our connection with reality. The timing of this universe is geared toward the Sun as it moves through the zodiac. Mercury has an orbit that at times gets ahead of the Sun allowing us to look into the future toward new and innovative ideas. However, we cannot continue in that vein until we come back to the present designated by the Sun and put our new ideas into manifestation. During the time that Mercury jumps ahead, we ultimately have to bring the ideas back into the present to test and evaluate to see how they fit into our life. —Karyl Jackson

MERCURY: MESSENGER OF THE GODS

The body type ruled by Mercury enters the active sphere, involved with doing, compelled to move, easily apt to notice what's missing, eager to point out defects, often quite sharp-witted, savvy, outmaneuvering, perceptive and sly. Playful, they look more *girlish* and *boyish* than manly or womanly. Insecure, they like an appreciative audience, so as to be admired and convinced of their worth. Easily influencing people with their schemes, charm and convincing tone; what's necessary to complete an aim will be presented persuasively. The excessive electric energy might create a nervous tic and while those around won't be bored, it sometimes gets tiring. Needing a lot of reassuring, cheerful on the outside, referred to as the sunshine person, similar to the little planet—one side in active sunlight—they sparkle, as well as having a dark side that is not so visible. The lighthearted exterior masks an inside lack of confidence and inner insecurities regarding their self-worth. Ruling the animal spirit they are the author of subtlety, tricks, devices, and perjury.

When one is in love, one always begins by deceiving one's self, and one always ends by deceiving others. That is what the world calls a romance.
—*Oscar Wilde*

In Greek mythology Hermes was the messenger of the gods. The most elusive and deceptive of the gods, the swift, wing-footed messenger, Hermes, his Roman counterpart; Mercury inherited his attributes. He was the wittiest of the gods. Mercury was the Roman god of commerce and rhetoric, a messenger between humans and gods, as well as god of thieves and those who lived by their wit, a patron of literature and music. He was the Greek god wearing a golden hat with wings, curly hair, winged sandals, a cape under which he could hide his magic tricks, carrying either a phallus or the magic wand of one who communicates with the dead. Snakes entwined on his staff protected the messenger. In ancient times information from one ruler to another or between armies were carried by messengers who displayed a special staff as a sign of their position, so they would not be harmed, and this was called a caduceus; Hermes/Mercury carried such a staff. In a flash he would move from place to place, even escorting the souls of the dead to the underworld river Styx that separated the world of the living from the world of the dead. Precocious as a child, even for a god, his mischievous nature helped create abundant stories about his ways. This was the guide for travelers, the musician with the beautiful lyre, the merriest messenger god. When the planets were given names related to the gods, in the days of Greek astronomy, the fastest planet was named for the winged one.

Mercury as our mental power planet gives us the gift to 'write the script' by which we make choices of all levels of life experience. Mercury in astrology is not explained simply through the story of a little Greek upstart who thought he could beat all-comers at the game of cunning, but is our access to more profound arcane levels of wisdom, and evolution. It is embedded in the archetypal images of Hermes, the healer Asklepios, in the legends of Hermes Trisnagistos, and in those of Thoth. A key to many of these allegories is that all these archetypes are of both godly and mortal parentage. All of them aspired to a greater position in the ethnogeny yet maintained their human creation. —Linda Reid

Type cast in movie or theatre roles, Mercury is usually a quick talker, crook, thief, schemer or charmer. Childish, maintaining a youthful look at any age, impulsive, ready to take action, they are restless, having a wandering attention span. The overactive quick racing mind, observant and perceptive, flits and matches the changing moods. Small in stature, lean and short, agile without being muscular, slightly curly hair that tends to be thin, fine, brown, black or mousy in color, they have an oval to round head with small alert twinkling sparkling dark eyes. A petite and fine nose, with small, clearly defined nostrils, thin lips, small evenly set teeth, a clean appearance, agile, a non-muscular type, wiry, well coordinated and flexible, you might notice a Mercury fidgeting as they sit or move around. The Mercury body is energetic but not geared for physical activity so much as for mental activity—the creation and conveyance of ideas and words. Impatient with those not as quick and clever, and that includes most others. The voice is of medium timbre and has a warm full rich quality, resonant, like a radio announcer or singer.

Whatever deceives men seems to produce a magical enchantment. —*Plato*

A bundle of energy, the lively entertaining Mercury is flirtatious in a mischievous way, their arms active, hands often gesturing. All motions are completed with ease as quick as the twinkling of an eye. Regardless to the amount of movement, Mercuries have a natural neatness, their clothing appearing freshly ironed. Bright young clean appearance, good grooming is a noticeable characteristic. Sensitive to the environment, they have a low pain threshold and a tendency to hypochondria. The high metabolic rate creates sleep disturbance leading to insomnia. Light sleepers, inquisitive, sometimes unaware of there own needs, imagining illness they investigate special diets and miracle cures.

THE SUNNY TRICKSTER

In the greater arcana of the tarot, Mercury is always associated with the first trump, the Magus or Juggler—names which sum up the extremes of the planet, sage and trickster. —*David McCann*

Mercury children are precocious, mischievous with a sunny disposition. Like the planet they are bright and swift, sparkling with warmth and humor, as well as having a hidden dark side. Shoplifting candy bars or a toy, grows into taking pens from the office, silverware from a restaurant, looking for creative tax loopholes, investment schemes, or collecting rents on unrentable apartments, a card shark or juggler, cunning until overcoming their self-interest and tempering themselves with Saturn restraint. It's the childish side that stretches principles, with an agility that is quicker than the eye when they swipe something. Teasing and joking, that disposition continues throughout their years of aging. Mercurial thoughts produce fine, thin, pointy, quick and mobile shapes. The Mercury type avoids entanglements. Like the planet, they have aimless movements and are the most sharp-witted of all the body types. Whirling, indirect, youthful, agile in perception, they live well by their smarts. Great salesmen, animated and persuasive, good at all communication careers, center stage, they glitter and dress to flash and charm. The Mercury Body Type, as archetype, once studied is fairly easy to spot; they enjoy being visible.

Your physical body provides a means of communication, allows you to experience higher levels of consciousness and to attain mastery over the physical realm. The fifth energy center, the throat chakra which is communication is connected to the thyroid. —Laura Hyde

Some known Mercury types are: *Sammy Davis Jr., Billy Crystal, Chris Rock, Paula Abdul, Howie Mandel, Mario Lopez, Joan Rivers, Jennifer Lopez, Bill Maher;* mercury saturn, *Jon Stewart, Richard Nixon, Fran Drescher, Jimmy Kimmel;* mercury venusian, *Steve-O, Nick Lachey, Joey Fatone, Cantinflas, Kelly Ripa, Jillian Michaels, Tina Fey, Eddie Murphy, Seth Myers, Andy Samberg, David Spade, Marcel Marceau, Margot Fonteyn, Arsenio Hall, Kathy Griffin;* mercury saturn mars, *Jennifer Lawrence.*

SATURN

Positive: balance, moderation, fair, discreet, predictable, ascetic, practical, self-control, judicious, prudent, disciplined, frugal, wise, responsible
Negative: domineering, indecisive, joyless, dogmatic, inflexible, despondent, secretive, fearful, melancholic, inhibited, stingy, loveless, bureaucratic, dense, cold, depressed, unsympathetic
Maximum attraction: Lunar
Ruling astrological sign: Capricorn
Ruling gland: anterior pituitary
Mid-most point: masculinity
Type: positive/active

Saturn rules old age. Those who have learned the lessons of Saturn; persever-
ance, confrontations of limitations, tyrannies, and inner darkness; who learn
to accept the world around them with tolerance of others and self-acceptance,
age with dignity and acquire wisdom. —Hamilton, Woolfolk, Guttman, Parker

SATURNINE MODERATION

*S*aturn as a body type is somewhat stiff; the formality of their movements gives rise to people advising them to loosen up. Moderation is their mantra. Preferring predictability, life is serious and every day should be accounted for; in their quest for orderly thinking and discipline there is little room for a foolish spontaneous moment. The Saturn type is the mid-most point of masculinity. Saturn, maker of order, does not inspire others to impulsively run up and hug them. Carrying themselves with the simple dignity of great yogis, they have a beautiful erect posture. Their air is firm and pensive, subdued, the vibration slow and deep, ponderous, touching off seriousness in others, not lightheartedness. Sincerity and contemplativeness along with an expression of concerned concentration and self-denial, Saturn has a restrained stance towards life. Their need for constancy, regularity and assuredness overrides any drive for variety. This is the person who counts on the *sure thing*, sticking with what's known, not the one ordering the unfamiliar unusual special of the evening from a exotic restaurant.

Saturn is known as Father Time, and is concerned with old age, boundaries,
limitations, and death. Saturn is associated with fear and despondency, with
dreary virtues of caution, self-control and thrift. —Joanna Waters

A year on the planet Saturn would be about 25,000 days. Careful consideration, long deliberation precedes action, sometimes a Saturn type makes decisions that eventually become irrelevant to the new moment. Saturn is an active, positive body type with breadth, overview and wisdom, ruling the anterior pituitary gland, regarded as the gland of intelligence. It is through pituitary responsiveness or lack of it, that the intelligence of the psychic self may or may not manifest in an individual's behavior. When the anterior pituitary functions are subnormal a person of very low intelligence is created, conversely, when the anterior pituitary is hyperactive in its functions, a genius, or someone extremely sensitive to stimuli may develop. The anterior pituitary exerts considerable influence on the size of the body, promoting masculine traits; its exaggerated secretion creates long bones, particularly large hands, feet and chin. The anterior pituitary gland is considered the master gland due to its function of promoting and releasing the hormones that stimulate the other endocrine glands to produce and release their hormones. This mirrors the characteristics of domination that Saturn types carry and use to monitor others. Saturns can direct others effectively, just as the dominant gland directs the activities of the other endocrine glands.

Saturn is the membrane which separates the personal unconscious from the collective unconscious. —Liz Greene

The most distant planet known to the ancients, Saturn has a bland atmosphere, and a prominent system of rings. When compared with its colorful neighbor, Jupiter, it looks lackluster and dreary. Yet, best known for its rings, it is considered the grandest of the planets, a total of 62 individual moons have been identified. Fifty-three have been named, many after actual Titans of Greek mythology, who were a sister and brothers of Cronus, the Greek Saturn. Cronus was the leader and youngest of the first generation of Titans, divine descendants of Gaia, the earth, and Uranus, the sky. Seven magnificently complex cosmic jewelry rings decorate Saturn, filling more space than any other planet.

The second largest planet in the solar system, its mass is 95 times that of earth, with enough space to contain close to 800 planets the size of earth. It is the only planet of the solar system that has been found to be less dense than water.

FATHER TIME

The Body Type of the leader, Saturn is a god of greatest adoration to the Greeks. His beauty rests in the eternal, his habits were precise and his countenance sharp, attentive and devotional to duty. This Body Type controls the pituitary gland which governs skeletal growth. Essence's desired use for height is secondary to the tendency of this type to endure great deprivation and exhibit a willingness to maintain personal discipline. —S.J. Cocconi

Saturn, called Cronus by the Greeks, was the god of agriculture, the protector and sower of seeds, ruler of the universe during the Golden Age. Cronus, lord of the universe, sat on the highest mountain and ruled over heaven and earth with a firm hand. The other gods obeyed his will and early man worshipped him. But Mother Earth was angry with him for his dominating ways and it was prophesied that one day Cronus would lose his power to one of his children who would overthrow his supremacy. To prevent this from happening, each time his wife gave birth Cronus would swallow the newborn. Zeus, the sixth child was hidden away, and Cronus was duped into swallowing a stone wrapped in baby clothing. Zeus grew up and eventually returned to trick Cronus into eating poison, and throwing up the stone and the five children. His six children, now grown gods, all turned against him; Cronus surrendered his powers and fled. In Roman mythology Cronus became Saturn and in Rome established the Golden Age, a time of peace, harmony and equality, which continued throughout his reign. In memory of the Saturn peaceful era the feast of Saturnalia was held at winter solstice, a time of gift giving and kindness. Christians adopted the feast and renamed it Christmas.

This body type, referred to as father and teacher, is often found counseling or in courtrooms sitting as a judge. Restrained, impartial, patient, solemn, introspective, a strong regard for equality and justice are some of the Saturnine characteristics. Not known for their charm or wit, tall and well proportioned, they are the classic male and female American model. Long-boned, a chiseled or angular face, the neck lean and long, large hands and feet, long fingers, high notable cheekbones, a pronounced forehead, a prominent nose, the tallest of all types, Saturns are called the *bone people*. They have an upright stature with straight shoulders and strong muscles. They have great self-confidence in their sound judgment and perseverance, determined to see their objectives realized. Carefully deliberating, they are effective in determining a definitive course of action.

Saturn is the slowest moving of the traditional planets, completing its cycle around the sun every 29-30 years. It is also dim and unimpressive to view. Both its lackluster appearance and its sluggish motion have contributed to astrological signification over old age and poor vitality, as well as careful, determined and slow but disciplined approach, There is no heat and fire in the characteristics of Saturn, no burning passion or inflamed desire, its movement is deliberate, steady and predictable. —Deborah Houlding

Statuesque, with good posture, graceful bearing, a long narrow and medium head and face, they have thick hair, thoughtful sad eyes, sunken cheeks, a long straight thin nose and a tall lean neck. The skin of the nose is pulled tight, clearly revealing the bones at the bridge. Hairlines around the lips are common, teeth are large and frequently in poor condition; chipped, yellow, or misshapen. Facial angles and bony protrusions are well-defined, sometimes beautifully chiseled. Jaw line, neck cords and the Adam's apple may be visible in both male and female. The forehead is high and narrow. They have clean, sharp tapered shapes and lines, forms that tend towards squares, rectangles, and angles. The skin is dry and flaky, with deep lines adding to the overall appearance of respectable age. The hair is stiff, brittle, dry and prone to premature graying, hair luster goes early. The body is narrow throughout, with protruding shoulder blades, ribs and knees. Various joints and knobs of the structure are large, including hands and feet. Shoulders are narrow, held high and stiff. Long, bony hands with noticeable knuckles and finger joints. An inclination to dress tailored, conservative and simple, they wear beige, dark blue, blacks, browns, and other subdued colors of clothing; gray surrounds them, like the joy that's been drained. Saturn types wear a tasteful suit, or work clothes, sensible shoes, generally moving away from anything ostentatious.

The discipline that ballet requires is obsessive. And only the ones who dedicate their whole lives are able to make it. Your toenails fall off and you peel them away and then you are asked to dance again and keep smiling. I wanted to become a professional ballet dancer. — Penelope Cruz

Each day and every project fits neatly into a structure, life is controlled, arranged in detail, and begins in the morning with the plan to wake up. Great powers of endurance, this is the father, filled with restrictions, self-control, domination, and self-denial; he kows what is best for you, in fact, Uncle Sam knows what's best for the country. The need for constancy keeps Saturn regimented with the same meals, the same restaurants, all guarantees of how it will turn out. The less evolved Saturn type creates a negative, misanthropic, dejected, melancholic, inflexible, unsympathetic tone, with a stooped posture, as if beaten down by the woes of the world, like Scrooge in *A Christmas Carol*. This is the taskmaster, asking us to get to work and work hard, manage our limitations, restrictions are the province of this body type, as is any form of discipline or delay; perseverance gets well applauded. It takes Saturn nearly 30 years to complete one orbit, which offers a valuable clue to their relationship to their life situation. In its mythological representation, Saturn refers to the cosmic power that brings cycles to their conclusion. Saturn symbolizes time; its glyph is the sickle of Cronos, the god of time. Saturn is the archetypal symbol for a way of being, or a process that slows us down to look at reality. In ancient times it was seen as *the old malefic*, or moments of misfortune, and its passage in an astrological chart was viewed carefully. Saturn has also represented reward for hard work and effort, once one is willing to wait; the Saturn return in a chart marks a time when one has an opportunity for revision, reshaping, and life-changing rewards.

In traditional texts Saturn is known as the Greater Malefic because it is placed furthest from the creative warmth of the Sun and the fertile moisture of the Earth and Moon. Its qualities are therefore defined as 'cold and dry', conditions that are antipathetic to growth and healthy development. Standing on the perimeter of our personal cosmos it is also considered dark, incapable of receiving or generating much luminosity. The absence of light further defines it as heavy, inclined to fall or weigh down—gravity and grave are two words that respond directly to its essentially serious, ponderous and somber nature. —Deborah Houlding

U.S.A.: SATURN COUNTRY

This is a Saturn country and time; important things are measured. Bank accounts, IQ, College degrees, school report cards, the weather and the wind chill factor, hurricanes, population, good movie ratings, 4-star hotels, restaurants, we rank our athletes, the sexual quotient of women

1-10, the best places to live; everything is well assessed, properly judged and placed, and Saturn rules again. Like the planet, the Saturn body type appears aloof and distant, moving slowly, looking out with a level gaze. Their prominent bone structure and height makes them photogenic as the ideal type of beauty, often chosen as fashion models.

Indecision can block action, since all the figures and information have to be detailed, gone over, measured, compared, numbers calculated, leaving little room for intuition or emotional decisions. Sometimes Saturns are introverted, enjoying spending time with another Saturn and make a striking visually balancing couple. Often loners, unless finding another willing to have high standards, be instructed or keep a progress report. Serious, yet having a gentle demeanor, they think and move slowly. This is not the party person, life is more serious and frivolity has little room, time is spent preparing and studying to be efficient. Their slow response time is deceiving, because once figuring something out they then become more efficient than others. Careful planners, determined, their course of action includes smug self-confidence. This is the person who will decide where to put your coat, when to turn the light on, very often assuming the other's incompetency.

Predictability is the Saturn dream, and the road of reason is taken, often with sacrifice, to arrive at a chosen destination. Easily we can recall images of the priests and teachers who kept a somber eye on our impulses, while we made fun of their stiffness and dogma. Fun for them is in the accomplishment. Steady progress, for this serious approach to life in its predictability, brings pleasure. Sports that include endurance, physical stamina, activities that require discipline are fun for them. This is the old child, able to stand alone under pressure, once they determine their strategy of action. Rational and democratic, they tend to provide balance to situations.

Medieval and Renaissance scholars associate Saturn with melancholy, serenity and wisdom. Astrological Saturn is associated with the letter of the law. Cronus, from the Greek word meaning time represents limitations. He is the symbol of Father Time, for he brought all things to an end that have a beginning. Saturn's domain is patience, stability, maturity and realism. Saturn effects us by delaying rewards until they are earned.
—*Hamilton, Woolfolk, Guttman, Parker*

Some known Saturn types are: *Abraham Lincoln, Jesus Christ, Al Gore, Osama bin Laden, Adrien Brody, Cher, Scrooge, Ichabod Crane, J.Krishnamurti, Jeff Goldblum, C.G. Jung, Barack Obama, Henry Fonda, Daniel Day-Lewis, John Kerry, Cat Deeley, Duchess Kate, Naomi Campbell, Lupita Nyong'o, Nicholas Cage, Rumer Willis, Greta Garbo, James Stewart, Penelope Cruz, Angelina Jolie, Uncle Sam U.S.A. symbol, Amal Alamuddin, Jennifer Lopez, Nelson Mandela, Melania Trump.*

MARTIAL

Positive: direct, protective, persistent, vigorous, straight forward, loyal, self-reliant, independent, defender of the weak, decisive, forthright, energetic, purposeful, resourceful, heroic, dedicated, fearless, determined, courageous, perseverant, strong leader in a crisis
Negative: rude, destructive, blunt, rageful, over-reactive, quarrelsome, unpredictable, bully, ruthless, rash, aggressive, combative, intrusive, war-like, angry, lacking forethought, tunnel-vision, impulsive, boisterous, violent, menacing
Maximum attraction: Venusian
Ruling astrological sign: Aries and Scorpio and Pluto
Ruling gland: adrenal
Type: active/negative, masculine

To fight and conquer in all our battles is not supreme excellence; supreme excellence consists in breaking the enemy's resistance without fighting.
—*Sun Tzu*

MARS: GOD OF WAR

The Martial, a fiery warrior, ready for action, blunt and forthright, is an active, negative, masculine body type with chief qualities of aggression and destructiveness. Mars, in Roman mythology the god of war, third smallest planet in the solar system, first planet beyond the orbit of the earth, is called the red planet because of its red surface area. Named after the ancient Roman god of war, as befitting the red planet's bloody color; the Romans copied the ancient Greeks who had named Mars after their god of war, Ares.

Mars, composed of craggy rocks, along with its two planets, Phobos and Deimos, named fear and panic, is commonly referred to as the angry planet. The adrenal glands influenced by Mars produce adrenaline and noradrenaline, hormones which elicit rage and fear, responding with *fight or flight* activity. On the planet Mars, cyclones run wild, clouds and volcanoes erupt and landslides thunder through the mountains. The most impressive storms in the solar system blow upon Mars, sending raging clouds of dust over the planet, darkening it for months. And in life circumstances the Martial type lives within the intensity of those commotions and fires that fills their life, moving towards challenges carrying a high level of energy, pushing aside obstacles, going towards the action as their adrenaline rush keeps pumping out hormones that propel the Martial type forward.

Psychologically, Mars is the assertive and self-determining factor that allows us to survive and express our humaneness openly and fearlessly. It is a

very clear energy—purposeful, not complicated by emotion and mindset.
—Linda Reid

The combative and passionate energy of Mars connects to the body through the adrenals, the glands of self-preservation. The adrenals, a pair of glands one on top of each kidney manifest the energies associated with self-assertiveness and self-expression. The functions of the adrenal cortex, the outer portion of the glands, control the development of the human brain. The hormones of the center layer of the adrenal cortex are responsible for the body's reaction to stressors such as trauma, infections and exercise. The adrenal medulla, the inner portion of the adrenals are a collection of nerve cells belonging to the sympathetic arm of the autonomic nervous system regarded as the mirror of our emotions. All sympathetic stimulation, whether an experience of love, joy, fear, ecstasy, pain, or anger, will trigger the release of the hormones from the adrenal medulla, also the gland of energy mobilization. Adrenalin stimulates the release of liver glycogen to the cells and causes the heart to beat faster and stronger increasing the rate of breathing and speed of blood reaching vital areas. Adrenalin in the bloodstream reaches the heart, sending it to the brain.

In astrology Mars represents the compelling force of action and initiative. In personal horoscopes the position of this planet indicates an area where we are challenged to defend or assert our will. The redness on the surface of the planet Mars are from the surface of the planet being covered by heavy deposits of iron, the metal it has been said to rule. The color reflects the characteristics of the planet, denoting heat, energy and danger. Like fire its quality is hot and dry; burning, activating, inflaming passions and arousing emotions. The Mars influence is capable of mass destruction when allowed to rage out of control or remain untempered by the softer qualities of a more beneficial planet such as its female partner, Venus. —Deborah Houlding

Adrenaline prepares the body and its systems for immediate action. The adrenal glands produce the adrenal steroids long known to affect strong emotional and instinctive reactions like rage, intense fear, sexual response and violent behavior in both humans and animals. The purpose which underlies adrenal mobilization is defined by the interplay between head and heart. Because of their influence on the chemistry of the blood, the functions of the adrenal glands are associated with the electrical conductivity and electromagnetic properties of the body. We exist in an ocean of electromagnetic waves and so it follows that the adrenal glands have much to do with the quality of our psychic attunement to our environment. Exhausting the capabilities of the adrenals to meet the demand for hormones happens when excessive fear and explosive anger run through the body, what follows feels like fatigue or depression. When we balance our emotional life we minimize adrenal depletion and receive the benefits of the influences inherent in the electromagnetic aspects of our environment. Just as emotions trigger the release of adrenal hormones which mobilize or propel our physical being into action, so, too, our emotions propel our psychic being in accordance with our desires and aspirations. Integrating our experiences with our values our life moves towards a harmonious balance. Understanding how negative emotions of fear and anger can be uplifted and transformed to build energy assists us in avoiding burnout; all creative work requires vitality.

Mars symbolizes everything to do with how we go into battle and handle the cut and thrust of life. The nature of Mars is assertive, or aggressive and confrontational. It speaks of our sense of drive and urgency. As the god of war it rules strife, combat, conquerors, and weapons. Venus may speak of our sexuality in terms of enjoyment but Mars is the sex drive and the phallus. Where Venus is soft and slow, Mars is sharp and quick, and its nature is to attack, pierce, penetrate, cut, or wound. It rules knives and all who work with them, everything from the surgeon and his precise scalpel to the butcher and the hacksaw. —Martin Gansten

MARTIAL: ACTION AND ENERGY

A Martial, athletic, robust and strongly built is of average short to medium height, with a tight, sinewy, dense and tough, compact muscular body. The Martial body is built for action and endurance. Shoulders back, they walk with a determined march-like stride. Red or dark hair that flairs out from the head, freckles, when light-skinned, a mottled look, ruddy complexion, rough and thick skin with pits, gashes, scars and moles being the common marks of Mars, dark eyes that look directly at you, a short thick neck sitting on rounded or square powerful shoulders, a well-developed barrel chest, and short bandy muscular legs that maintain a firm and ready stance, strong arms; this is a decidedly athletic type. A high threshold for pain, this is raw power primed to jump into action. There might be visible scars since they are prone to injury, happening when they have exerted more force than a situation warranted. Their habitual posture is challenging or defensive, solidly grounded, with an aura of taut intense raw power, geared to spring into victory. Unpredictable, a determined look, a loyal and protective nature, they walk around with vigor and a cadence of resolve as if always poised to defend themselves. Enjoying action, thriving on exercise and hard work, they may be ruthless or courageous, have uncontrolled rash impulses or be heroic with no apparent regard for danger. Forthright and candid, rarely diplomatic, blurting out what's on their mind, their nature magnifies rather than inspires resolve or diminishing problems. The Martial body is built for endurance, thrives on exercise and hard work, withstanding a lot of pain and abuse. A harsh voice, barking impatiently when under pressure, a zest for life, Martials want to satisfy urges *right now.*

When you are angry, the chemicals of anger are synthesized and flow throughout the body, bonding to and influencing millions of cells. Soon the liver is angry; the white cells are angry. If this is unhealthy anger—repressed or inappropriately expressed (as opposed to a positive cathartic release of pent-up feeling)—then the white blood cells and liver may become belligerent, refusing to perform their tasks. On the other hand, if you feel happy and secure, all of the cells feel happy. —Kenneth S. Cohen

Typically they work as a police officer, stunt-person, attorney, physical educator, construction worker, an ideal soldier or law enforcement officer, lifeguard, rock star, drummer, drug rehabilitation coach, butcher or race car driver. Visible in the boxing rings, the military, street and bar brawls, rushing into a fiery building, in contact sports; rarely found sitting behind a desk or standing in a laboratory. They are spunky, forthright, lustful, protective, steadfast, fierce, self-reliant and sturdy. Energy and power are at the maximum in this type. Intensity and urgency are the pace, setting goals, living as if life is a military academy and each disciplined achievement pins a medal on a Martial chest. Girls are tomboys during childhood, and continue to compete and gain control, stepping forth to be the only woman in a position of power, whether to head a real estate company, TV station, school administration, rock band, dance troupe or condominium board. The Martial child is Dennis the Menace, sometimes shocking people, taking charge, behaving exuberantly, making their presence known. Bumped skinned knees, broken bones, falling out of trees are everyday happenings for this roughneck child. Self-reliant, rebellious, impatient, excitement and conquest fuel them. Jokes and humor for a Martial generally includes sex and violence.

The core meaning of Mars is energy, pure and simple, without conscience, value judgement, attachment, thought, principles, emotions or concern for civility; just a clear and constant source of action and vitality. It is through Mars that the 'Divine Self' expresses its will and capacity to survive on earth. It is the tool by which the Divine seeds humanity, so it is with little

surprise that the various cults of Mars, in different forms, always include a phallus. Psychologically, Mars is the assertive and self-determining factor that allows us to survive and express our humaneness openly and fearlessly. It is a very clear energy—purposeful, not complicated by emotion and mindset. At best, it allows us to be assertive without aggression, to be forthright without being offensive, and to relate to others by being able to express our point of view without clouding the right of another to express theirs. It is willpower and self-determination, the desire to experience life and initiate activity.
—*Linda Reid*

Truthful, they sacrifice subtle suggestions for quick right to the point blunt statements and expect receiving the same in return. The Martial action role has little patience for dragging their feet or wasting time with indecision. *Do it now*, is the motto, *and don't quit till finished.* Theirs is a narrow single focus, sometimes unstoppable, yet the job does get done. If a Martial doll was built it would be wound up to walk straight into a wall. Forging ahead, straight-line oriented, tunnel vision, walking into; breaking down a wall is not seen as an obstacle, it's the persistence and direction in sight. Whatever's in the way easily gets broken, destroyed. Martial energy can be constructive or destructive. The god of war in ancient times, Mars, could be brutally violent. While this energy still emanates from the planet, it can also be harnessed for good. In conversations they enjoy finding the opening to prove you wrong and are energized by any argument. Fight or flight as the mantra, once criticized, insulted, they take flight or are right in your face. Sitting on the sidelines is not in this script; Martials speak to the power and confident expression of the individual, encouraging others to be their best, or better. Relationships are not calm and easy. The ancient Romans, the Vikings, Germans, Turks and the Irish are all Martial races. The Pit Bull Terrier as well as the freshwater fish called Piranhas, known for their sharp teeth and called the *wolves of the water* are both Martial.

Mars expressed as rage or anger is inappropriate, regardless of the primitive, brutal force embedded in its meaning. Mars as the killer is not clear archetypal imagery because anger implies emotion and Mars is not about emotion but pure action and energy. Emotions blur the edges. The 'core' energy of Mars is embedded in the 'seed' of life. Therefore, it has sexual overtones. Mars, not expressed, but constantly 'nice', seemly and decorous, suppress their natural instincts. Eventually the repressed and enraged energy of Mars bursts forth in bouts of anger, violence and aggression. Rage is the dysfunctional expression of a suppressed Mars. Mars ought to be expressed directly, spontaneously, immediately at the start of things, whatever the situation. Clarity of source is essential to expressing Mars in an assertive, non-aggressive way.
—Linda Reid

Sexually more active than any of the body types, uplifting sexual tension is rarely a choice. Instead, out in the world testing sexual limits, rules and safety are thrown to the wind. Punishing, challenging and driving their body, the Martial can be found entering a rodeo while wearing an ankle brace, rock climbing after turning a wrist, playing football with a cracked shoulder, skydiving, training horses, precariously working on an oil rig, and regardless to their injuries still setting records. This is all for a big adrenal rush, dedicated for the win, with a robust constitution, they are urgently charging ahead. These are the doers in life, the mountain movers, not the couch potatoes sitting around watching TV. Appearing ready-to-spring, easily capable of socially unacceptable behavior, they are often unconscious of their effect; life is to satisfy their impulses, now.

Holding on to anger is like grasping a hot coal with the intent of throwing it at someone else; you are the one who gets burned. —the Buddha

Some known Martial types are: *G.I. Gurdjieff, George W. Bush Jr., Janet Reno, Sylvester Stallone, James Cagney, Katherine Hepburn, Kelly Osbourne, Simon Cowell, Dave Navarro, Sean Penn, Ross Perot, Tina Turner, Mel Gibson, Harrison Ford, Arnold Schwarzenegger, Janis Joplin,*

John Kennedy, Pablo Picasso, Denzel Washington, Chuck Norris, Kirk Douglas, Michelle Obama, Quentin Tarantino, Pink, Melissa McCarthy, Vincent Van Gogh, Madonna, Hillary Clinton, Niecy Nash, Robert Redford, Sissy Spacek, Paul Newman, Mitt Romney, Mark Wahlberg, John Mellencamp, Clint Eastwood, Muhammad Ali, Mike Tyson, Richard Burton, Nick Nolte, Ludwig van Beethovan, Popeye, Jean Claude Van Damme, Robert DeNiro, Bruce Willis, Dolph Lundgren, Thor, Chris Hemsworth, Teresa Giudice, Dennis Quaid, Liev Schreiber, Justin Theroux, Chelsea Handler.

JOVIAL

Positive: creative, generous, good tempered, magnanimous, maternal, just, cheerful, ambitious, benevolent, cultured, epicurean, easygoing, enthusiastic, optimistic

Negative: vain, grandiose, deceitful, conceited, bombastic, overconfident, arrogant, wasteful, pompous, indiscriminate, self-indulgence, dilettante, flamboyant, boastful, periodicity, extravagant

Maximum attraction: Mercury

Ruling astrological sign: Sagittarius

Ruling gland: posterior pituitary

Type: positive/passive, feminine

The majestic ruler of the skies sits in regal splendor presiding over the heavens. Golden planet Jupiter is Deva Guru, preceptor to the gods. Jupiter is the planet of expansion, his indisputable status is evidenced by the breadth of his gaze in the expanse of his gestures. —Chakrapani Ullal

THE LORD OF PLENTY

A Jovial is a passive, positive, feminine, maternal type with a chief quality of vanity. Known as Zeus, in Greek mythology he dethroned his father, Saturn, and sat on the highest throne with a bucketful of thunderbolts to subdue the gods when they quarrelled. Zeus was stronger than all the other gods and in Roman mythology became Jupiter, king of the gods. The planet that influences the Jovial body type, Jupiter, is considered by scientists to be the most evolved of the planets, the only known planet to produce its own heat and light, continuing on its evolutionary step to becoming a sun or star. Jupiter has 67 observed satellites or moons orbiting the giant planet; the irregular satellites are cloistered in *families* with similar orbits and colors. In life the Jovial type energetically supports many who then serve as satellites.

Jupiter is the only planet that gives off its own source of energy, two times more heat than it receives from the sun. Jupiter, the largest of all the planets, is so enormous that all of the other planets in the solar system could fit inside. Brighter in our skies than most any planet, even while being so remote, visually startling, the largest and most colorful planet in the solar system, producing the most powerful magnetic field of all the planets. Jupiter forms a kind of miniature solar system. Known as the Lord of Plenty, rotund and warm, giving and cheerful, a prodigal type, sometimes wastefully extravagant. The short axial rotation period and high speed produces enormous centrifugal force in the equatorial zone of Jupiter, which makes it bulge in the middle. This is reflected in the Jovial body type, carrying their weight most often as a bulge around the waist.

The planet of liberation and freedom of expression, Jupiter seeks expansion, though sometimes through exaggeration and over-inflation. Hope and optimism spring from this planet; although tolerant and broad-minded, its natives suffer when being too generous with assets they don't possess or committing themselves to schemes that surpass realistic expectations.
—Martin Gansten

The Jovial type can be grandiose and flamboyant and is remarkably able to appear simultaneously lordly and grand, friendly, pompous and evasive. The preference is to wearing bright colors, rich fabrics, flowing, loose, robe-like garments. Women tend to pile their hair dome-like on their head. They like sandals and non-restrictive footwear due to their tendency to overheat. Partial to rich foods and good wine, there is a tendency to be overfed, overindulged, and self-indulgent; their homes reflect their many interests as well as their tendency to over acquire. Complementary type is the quick, charming, child-like Mercury. Both are fun, witty, enjoying to be in the spotlight; together they thrive. Vanity is the strong Achilles heel, since flattery about most anything will pump up and engage the Jovial. Flourishing when admired, maintaining the genial image of getting along with everyone, loyalty means that you will never criticize them, which protects their fragile self-esteem. Disappointed, they exile you forever from their good graces.

Thin people are beautiful, but fat people are adorable. —*Jackie Gleason*

Fancying to live the big life, Jovial becomes patron of the arts, restaurateurs, more generous than they want, ultimately surrounded by belongings that feed their excess, their acquired appetite for momentos and driven knack for self-indulgence. Artistic with a creative flair, they are found in restaurants as chefs or bakers, as diplomats, bartenders, priests, university department heads in classics, music, philosophy, spending their earned money extravagantly. Maternal in outlook, whether female or male, the Jovial type enjoys being in the kitchen and other essential home-making tasks. As the planet Jupiter attracts satellites, so does the body type; the tendency to nurture, feed and help others keeps them engaged in people's lives, sometimes risky, when they relegate you to remain as a satellite to their celestial body. Similar to the planet

Jupiter, warm-blooded, they produce their own heat well, and may wear short sleeves and open shoes minus socks even as other types bundle up. Their habitual expression is smiling and benevolent, dignified or dramatic. An optimistic disposition, the voice is resonant, cheerful, confident and compelling.

Jupiter rules the grand scheme of things. As the king of the gods, Jupiter's main characteristic is largeness and its nature is to enlarge and expand. Jupiterian types are often physically large, larger than life, characterized by a horror of being restricted in any way. They will always push the boundaries, physically or mentally, and are at their happiest when roaming, exploring, and learning. —Joanna Watters

J O V I A L   R H Y T H M

Periodicity, the on-again, off-again gusto that brings enthusiasm to new projects and leaves them mid-way, is a prominent Jovial characteristic. That quality of starting with enthusiasm and then losing interest, the momentum fading, is a reflection of Jupiter's sporadic emanations. Launching new endeavours and following varied pursuits, the range spans a large expanse. Cooking, arts and crafts, organizing a book club, finding a new diet plan, looking after the neighbors animals, learning a new language, buying new costly products to then be put aside, the interests and cravings come and go. Loving to start projects, an activity that had held full interest, quite suddenly takes a back seat or just disappears from the screen. This is a creative fun-loving type, haphazardly returning to postponed ideas after a long interval. While success, accomplishments and prosperity are all within Jovial's realm, their legacy can, at times, deteriorate into laziness and sloth, gaining weight as they step away from revolving interests and activities. Routine living is seen as drab, yet their succession of shifts and changes may keep the Jovial from accomplishing anything meaningful. Fading interest doesn't allow for follow through and deepening, and once the enthusiasm wanes projects are set aside. Up and down the mountains and valleys of excitement, then fading away, entertaining, gathering people they are influential and public-hearted.

Every 12 years Jupiter returns to the same position in the sky; every 370 days it disappears in the fire of the sun in the evening to the west, 30 days later it reappears in the morning to the east.(observation in the 4th century B.C.) —Suixing Jing

Often identified by their bulbous or cherry nose, sometimes slightly turned up, they are of medium height, solid build, overweight, big waist, full-bodied, the nose turns up at the end showing the nostrils which are flared, referred to as a pug, pig, or Howdy Doody puppet nose, also called a clown's tip. Jovials have a large frame, stomach paunch, a big waist on top of thin legs, often appearing overstuffed, resembling a football blocker. The appearance of both male and female is tank-like. Jovials having thin legs for their bulk, appear out of proportion, some-one once said: *like a ball balanced on matchsticks.* Even when the body is overweight, the excessive ample, beefy flesh is solid and firm rather than sloppy, watery or spongy. Large round heads, brown hair, often the men bald early on the top of their head. Abundant body hair is a trait of Jovial men. There's a quality of roundness displayed in the face, cheeks and shoulders. The bones and muscles are heavy-duty, but the body does not emphasize muscularity as does the Martial, rather, it presents an imposing, regal bearing. The neck is short and thick. The trunk and limbs are heavy. Their back, chest, shoulders and upper arms are broad and thick, predominating over the hips and legs. The gait is stately and dignified, a frame built to carry heavy weight. The body, whether overweight or not, is carried with a stately grandeur. Whales are considered a Jovial body type, as well as Santa Claus who embodies the Jovial type of big-bellied generous souls.

Jupiter is the largest of the planets, aptly reflecting its principle of drawing in towards a sense of fullness and offering a grander more expansive vision of reality. It expresses the qualities of abundance, freedom, growth and fertility; broadening our horizons and bringing relief from the restraints that cause us to view the world in narrow, constricting terms. Its sense of liberation allows us to move, explore, think and act with greater acknowledgement of the power of our own self-will. Its nature is to enlarge, inflate and augment; its extremes are connected to exaggeration, over-indulgence, wastefulness, superficial promotion and false promises that distort reality beyond recognition. —Deborah Houlding

Jovial is ruled by the posterior pituitary gland which influences distinctive maternal qualities such as the production of milk, bladder and uterus functions; considered the gland of maternal traits. One of the two hormones released by the gland, oxytocin, is also released in nursing mothers and is considered the maternal hormone that is associated with childbearing. Quite fitting, since the maternal characteristics of Jovial, that of nurturing, protecting and feeding others are prominent whether male or female, or even actually having biological children. The pituitary gland represents the lower end of the sympathetic system through which the psychic self directly controls and coordinates the entire glandular system. The posterior pituitary gland, or back portion, is an outgrowth of the base of the brain. The activities of the pituitary gland influence every aspect of life's expressions in the human body. The hormone released into the body helps to keep the body's internal environment in balance. This equilibrium, called homeostasis, assists to insure human survival, and serves as a channel through which the psychic self maintains the best possible harmony within the body.

I'm a big woman. I need big hair. —Aretha Franklin

Maternal, cheerful, ample and improvident, often flamboyant, squandering and extravagant; even promises go unheeded. Planning grandiose ideas for others might happen while ignoring what they need to do for themselves. The collector, storing things from numerous adventures; clutter signals to them how varied and pleasurable their life has been. Jovial homes reflect their beautiful taste and many acquisitions. The diplomatic world has seen its Jovials, good at statesmanship, enjoying the social interactions, the required banquets, the indulgence and admiration that comes with the traveling position. Often found in the art world, either as patron, art historian, curator, fund-raiser for the symphony, opera affectianados; the love of the arts are a strong connection to the harmony for humanity that the Jovial envisions.

Jupiter, a giant self-illuminating planet, the center of a mini-solar system of its own, is the principle of expansion, a kind of cosmic Santa Claus, the teacher or the con man, the priest or used car salesman, the gambler or crusader. In Greek mythology Jupiter was always seeking a further adventure symbolized by his pursuit of ever new objects of desire, and governs luck and well-being, providing opportunities for expansion and success. —Robert Couteau

Some known Jovial types are: *Orson Welles, Oprah Winfrey, Johann Sebastian Bach, Walt Whitman, Dame Judi Dench, Charles Dickens, Helen Thomas, Kate Winslet, Emma Thompson, James Beard, Mama Cass Elliot, Jackie Gleason, Benjamin Franklin, James Cagney, Sylvia Boorstein, Peter Ouspensky, Thomas Edison, Wolfgang Puck, Benny Hill, Penny Marshall, Elton John, Aretha Franklin, Roseanne, Ethel Merman, Queen Latifah, Mario Batali, Mariah Carey, Tracy Morgan, Melissa McCarthy;* mars jovial, *Martha Stewart, Jack Nicholson, Winston Churchill, Shelley Winters,*

Rembrandt van Rijn, Julia Child, Meryl Streep, Falstaff, Socrates, Friar
Tuck, Burl Ives. Santa Claus is a perfect Jovial figure, as well as the figures
painted by Rubens, Michaelangelo and Rodin.

S O L A R

Positive: child-like, energetic, creative, optimistic, exuberant, sunny,
refined, artistic, graceful, enthusiastic, radiant, imaginative
Negative: naive, indiscriminate, over-sensitive, gullible, vain, manip-
ulative, frail, restless, intolerant, greedy, self-destructive, childish
Maximum attraction: none
Ruling star: Sun
Ruling gland: thymus
Type: active/positive, neutral/androgynous

*The Sun, by whose energy the planets revolve and the world of Nature lives,
appears to us as a great radiant ball which we calculate to be a million
times larger than the Earth. The Sun transmits life and form to Earth by
means of light and magnetism. All things, all influences, all life, matter
and form may be regarded as emanating from the Sun in the fullness and
totality of time.* —Rodney Collin

S O L A R   E L E C T R I F I E S

*T*he Solar type combines randomly with all other body types on the
Enneagram. An active positive type, when any body type mixes with
a Solar the faster vibration of Solar energy intensifies and is enlivening.
A Jovial Solar would be a more electrified Jovial with a naive generosity,
sometimes falling prey to financial schemes, and on the other hand the
Jovial influences the Solar to shift the straight lines into curves and bulg-
es. A Venusian Solar energizes the Venusian while quieting the electricity
of the Solar. A Saturn Solar speeds up and moves to a higher level of

activity as Solar counteracts the Saturn's sedentary ways lightening up their serious nature. Solar Martial helps ease up the warrior, although the extra shot of energy might endanger their health by creating burn-out. Solar Lunar mixes the passive negative Lunar with positive active Solar to create someone who looks porcelain yet might drive a tractor trailer. This combining element continues throughout the Enneagram. Blending with the Solar influence imparts a delicate and more intense energy accompanied by a more refined appearance to the characteristics of any type it combines with, like a supercharger handily fitted on to any other body type.

In natal astrology the Sun represents the heart of one's being, the true spirit, individuality and creative self-expression. It is a symbol of glory and indicates where we can tap in to the strength of our will to overcome instinctive fears, rise above habitual patterns of behavior, and find a majestic quality within ourselves. —Skyscript

The Solar body type is influenced from a different order of existence and does not have a fixed placement unlike the six earlier named types around the Enneagram. The celestial body that influences the Solar is the sun, which is a star, not a planet. This type is also of a different order of creation influenced by increased emanations of the sun and the sunspot cycles. The sun, the star at the center of the solar system, makes life possible on our planet by providing light and heat. Sunlight, the main source of energy to the surface of the earth supports almost all life on earth via photosynthesis and drives earth's climate and weather. The sun is a magnetically active star, sunlight being the main source of energy to the surface of the earth. Solar activity played a large role in the formation and evolution of the solar system and strongly affects the structure of Earth's outer atmosphere.

In Greek mythology Apollo was the god of sunlight and music, who, in a chariot drawn by white swans, wearing a shining crown, using 1,000 silver arrows, slew the dragon that guarded the sacred Delphi, thereby winning claim to the shrine. Named Helios in Roman mythology, he was the radiant god of the sun, driving his golden chariot across the sky from east to west each day bringing light to the earth. Traveling the journey of the sun to begin in the east and end in the west, at which point Hellos completed his daily rounds and floated back to his eastern palace in a golden bowl.

Once a year the Sun 'travels' around the zodiac, so our birthday is our Solar Return, the day that the Sun returns to the same sign and degree as on the day we were born, hence, 'Many Happy Returns of the Day'. The Sun is traditionally known as the 'Lord of the Day' and, along with the Moon, is one of the 'lights'—the Sun being the light of the day, the Moon being the light of the night. —Joanna Watters

SOLAR ENERGIZES

The ruling gland for the Solar body type, the sun is considered to control the thymus, located in the upper chest and under the breastbone, governing the immune system and growth, especially noticeable in children. The thymus gland is most prominent during early life, after puberty it begins to undergo an involution and progressively decreases in size throughout adult life. It produces hormone-like substances that affect the immune system's development and functioning. Physiologically the thymus has two major functions, growth promotion and immunological competence. During childhood, the thymus coordinates the physical body in relationship to what is in the environment. In the Solar body type thymosins, the hormone produced by the thymus, continues producing the hormone which is responsible for a child's delicate skin and fine hair. This allows the Solar type to retain childlike physical delicacy and a quality of naivete. The place and function of the thymus indicate it as being the regulator of the undifferentiated life impulse derived from the sun.

I've always taken 'The Wizard of Oz' very seriously, you know. I believe in the idea of the rainbow. And I've spent my entire life trying to get over it.
—*Judy Garland*

The Sun: Pure Energy

The sun, sitting at the center of our solar system, generating extreme energy, has conditions well beyond our imagination and is considered to influence the center of our personality. The one element in nature that consistently has the most impact is the energetic force, the sun. Felt, regardless to whether blocked by clouds or other planets, the world is continuously reinvented due to the sun. Never going retrograde, all other planets reflect the light of the sun. We have connected the light and heat generated by the sun with its evolution and see in the sun the embodiment of our own highest functions, that of love, thought and awareness. The significance of the relationship between our perceptions, stress, and the preparedness of the body to defend itself against invasion is remarkable. Studies have proven that our thoughts, our feelings, our spirit have tremendous influence over the internal reactions of our body's defense capability.

As Lord of the Day the Sun is masculine and can represent the father. At a universal level the Sun is associated with royalty, majesty, stateliness, dignity, and authority. Strong Solar types exude seemingly boundless energy and vitality and share many of the positive characteristics—generosity, courage, confidence, clarity of vision, loyalty, strength of character and glowing health. An afflicted Sun has the reverse of the previous qualities, such as arrogance, attention-seeking, insecurity, lack of confidence, and a shaky sense of identity. Poor health and a lack of vitality can also be manifestations of an afflicted Sun. As the source of being and illumination the Sun represents your day world, consciousness, and psychological purpose; the Sun symbolizes your essential self and who you are struggling to become. If you were to repress your own Sun sign attributes you would cease to shine, living only in other people's light—self-conscious, lifeless or depressed. In claiming your own light you can embrace a healthy self-love and experience a sense of feeling integrated and centered. This is reflected in the Sun's glyph, the dot making the centre of the circle, symbolizing the point of consciousness from which all life will emerge. —Joanna Watters

The Solar is recognized by their pale skin, broad forehead, wide-set eyes, thin waist and electrical vibration. The classic type is thin, and waif-like, gracefully proportioned, with a light, supple, child-like body, a slender waist and scant body hair. A distinctly androgynous appearance, they have transparent milk and roses skin, which appears almost see-through if not luminescent, almost translucent, with delicate features and bone structure. Silky and shiny hair, the overall impression is ethereal, otherworldly. Quite often their eyes are further apart and slightly larger than in other types. Their other-worldly beauty may appear too refined for this coarse planet. Their habitual posture or expression is wide-eyed and innocent inspiring people to want to take care of them. No one type is a maximum attraction. They retain a Peter Pan-like immaturity and vibrate at a high frequency. More pure energy than any of the types, seeming not of this earth, shape-shifter, they come to this planet with a mechanical spiritual understanding. Quick in movement, energy enlivens their body as they electrically prance around leaving animated energetic traces in the atmosphere. Child-like, fantasy-filled, sometimes costumed and absorbed in self-image and the world of make-believe, yet graceful and supple, there is a tendency to be too trusting and become prey to victimization. A sunny disposition, light and sparkly, with fragile health, lacking sophistication regarding human limitations, they often burn up due to the high-frequency vibration energetic world in which they live. They do not fare well exposed to the sun for long periods.

Let us dream of tomorrow where we can truly love from the soul, and know love is the ultimate truth at the heart of all creation. Why can't you share your bed? The most loving thing to do is to share your bed with someone. It's very charming. It's very sweet. It's what the whole world should do.
—*Michael Jackson.*

The Solar experience is one of not quite belonging here on this planet, of not having strong attractions or an affinity to other types. This is a mechanical example of the next higher world, a world of suns. Most people have strong pulls and interest in others, the Solar lacking this, along with a naiveté about what is tricky or corrupt, may choose acquaintances unwisely. Living in a fairy tale world of endless possibilities their enthusiasm and immaturity often interferes with knowing when to rest, when to eat. Like the sun, Solars are almost pure energy. Working and playing hard they are able to move from one project to the next. Having refined sensibilities and preference for fantasy, the arts become a favorite field of work. The fantasy is usually the reality, and they show up as charming, endearing and romantic. Their weak constitution, loneliness and poor habits sometimes create short lives. Not quite suited to living on this planet, their beauty appears to be not of the earth, and gives the impression of delicate fine porcelain.

In universal terms it is a small, insignificant star, fairly average in the great scheme of things. Move in closer and it is a roaring, explosive mass of volatile radioactivity— a glowing white-hot ball of nuclear reaction, many millions of degrees Celsius and continually blasting out huge flares of electrically charges particles. This is the 'solar wind', it flows through the solar system and interacts with all the planets. The Sun is the very essence of creative energy and it is the central heart of our solar system. Its gravitational attraction keeps the planets in their courses; its creative energy provides nearly all their heat and light, and its wind bathes them in a solar atmosphere that circulates around the planetary system just like the blood that pulsates though our veins. —Deborah Houlding

Solars are of medium height, gracefully proportioned, with a broad full forehead. Large wide-set almond-shaped spread out eyes slanting upwards in the feline manner, brown or blue, and look out with an honest and sweet expression, rapidly changing from playful to tearful. At other times the eyes have a self-contented haughty gaze, yet sparkle with vitality and magnetism. Solar features are refined, with a finely shaped straight nose and mouth, everything well formed, ears and chin, well-countoured head and neck, graceful legs, feet carrying a high instep. The face is broad, particularly in the region of the eyes and cheekbones. There is a musical voice that has a distinctive vibrating quality distinguishing Solar energy graceful, they display an elegant impression. Strain or shock is hard on their body since they have a small heart and fragile blood vessels, which can interrupt their life at an early age.

Dressing in bright warm colors, often costume-like clothing, fun is to have companions to charm. They are like a sunny day, playful and carefree, hopeful and singing, like Annie: *the sun comes out tomorrow.* Gold is the metal, Ruby the gem. Most always in motion, they dance, whether walking or talking they radiate. That energy heightens whoever is around a Solar type. Delicate, like children, they easily forget to take proper care of their physical needs. Skipping meals, walking in the rain without protection, under dressed in the winter, their body is susceptible like a child's. Often found in the arts a Solar may be a ballet dancer, poet, cabaret singer, fashion model, belly dancer or actor. Creative and sensitive they charge the atmosphere. When performing, we like to watch; their charisma draws us to notice, at times be captivated, as they glow and stand out.

Come with me, where dreams are born, and time is never planned. Just think of happy things, and your heart will fly on wings, forever, in Never Never Land. —Peter Pan

Some known Solar types are: *Michael Jackson*; solar mercury, *Judy Garland*; solar jovial, *Liza Minelli, David Bowie, Prince, Madonna, Peter Pan, Snow White, Mozart, Percy Shelley, John Keats, Nicole Kidman*; solar lunar, *Madonna*; martial solar, *Mozart, Drew Barrymore, Marilyn Monroe*; solar venusian, *Anna Nicole Smith, Rudolph Nureyev, Iman, Elizabeth Taylor, Rainer Maria Rilke, Scarlett Johansson, Eddie Redmayne, Goldie Hawn.*

NEPTUNE

Positive: psychic, imaginative, mood-shifts, aesthetic, sensitive, subtle, restless, mystical, selfless, devotional, non-possessive, universal

Negative: diffuse and at times subjectively unclear or confused, impractical, unrealistic, self-deceptive, addictive, indiscriminate, glamour, decadence, sensationalism, unstable, fear, bondage, sadism, fanaticism

Maximum attraction: none

Ruling gland: pineal

Ruling astrological sign: Pisces and Jupiter

Type: passive/positive, feminine

The tidal wave starts as a minor oceanic event and swells to a magnitude that can erase cities from the earth. Nothing personal, says the wave, it's immutably decreed. And so it is. —Jed McKenna

PINEAL GLAND: SEAT OF THE SOUL

*T*his body type, has a random order of placement on the Enneagram, combining with any other type. When Neptune is prominent it is expressed through their eyes and into the vibrational atmosphere. The gland connected to Neptune is the pineal gland, buried in the brain, behind the hypothalamus and producing melatonin. Scientific research is currently being performed to study this small pine-cone-shaped gland centered directly behind the eyes at the center of the head. The pineal gland buried deep in the brain has been seen as an organ of perception and two thousand years ago was referred to as the seat of the soul. Philosopher Rene Descartes said: *it's the seat of the rational soul, the gland of knowing.* This organ of perception, the pineal, represents a portal through which the psychic self exerts very definite influences on the physical self. A regulator of regulators, it governs many activities of the hypothalamus-pituitary, thyroid, gonads, pancreas, adrenal cortex, thymus. Pineal activities are responsive to environmental lighting; the visual experience of light itself has great effect on our glandular system. The pineal reacts to the amount of light our eyes take in. The pineal gland is an important organ linking the environment with and through the endocrine system via the eyes and other organs of perception. The pineal gland may be the link between the larger universe and human, the smaller universe; the *eye* through which we harmonize both the inner and outer worlds. The pineal gland is considered to be a third eye, a new organ, a possibility to develop higher psychic functions.

We see Neptune as the as-yet unseen, probable new planet, the way Columbus saw America from the coast of Spain. Its movements have been felt, trembling along the far-reaching line of our analysis with a certainty hardly inferior to that of ocular demonstration. —*Sir William Herschel*

Neptune is the eighth planet from the sun in our solar system. An outer planet, its orbit lying outside the range of human vision, its slow orbit around the zodiac ensures that its effect is generational in nature. It takes Neptune 165 years to complete its travel through the zodiac, spending about 14 years in each sign. Since Neptune was discovered in 1846 it has not yet completed a single revolution around the sun. Therefore, the planet tends to have an influence on an entire generation rather than on one individual. More than two billion miles from the sun, it cannot be seen without a telescope.

Neptune, the planet of idealism, mystery and imagination, is also the planet of illusion, self-delusion and dissolution. It is a subtle yet powerful disintegrator, source of hallucinations and the deceptive forces of the subconscious mind. Its principle is to dissolve barriers, being capable of raising us up to mystical experiences, or pulling us down into chaos and confusion.
—*Martin Gansten*

THE EARTH-SHAKER: GOD OF THE SEA

In Greek mythology Poseidon was lord of the sea. Neptune's glyph is the trident of Poseidon. Much about this planet is fluid, Neptune rules the oceans of the earth, changeable and illusory in nature, abstract thought and the mysterious are all governed by Neptune. Administering all the lakes and rivers, Neptune is associated with Pisces, the most watery of the signs. Pisces, the water sign, considered mystically inclined, represents the return to the great ocean from which life evolved, and where all boundaries are dissolved. Pisces, ruled by Neptune, lord of illusion and imagination, and Jupiter, lord of inspiration and drama, both appear different to others than to themselves and is why Pisceans tend to lack clarity on how they appear to others. Neptune, in Roman mythology was a moody and violent god. He carried a three-pronged spear or trident so forceful that when he struck the ground with his trident the earth trembled and split open, and when he struck the sea frothing waves rose mountain high, wrecking ships and drowning those who lived near the shore. Tranquil, he would put his hand out to still the sea, raising new land from the water. A restless god, he enjoyed racing the waves with his team of snow-white horses. His fierce blue eyes pierced the haze and his sea-blue hair streamed out behind him. The trident of the Roman sea god shows Neptune as a vast, deep, mysterious and unknown force.

Neptune, symbolizing the vast ocean, fills the larger part of the earth's surface; the one ocean out of which all land masses have arisen and into which flow the refuse of the myriad of life activities that developed on the continent. Neptune presents to the land-bound or ego-bound consciousness a transcendent kind of vision. Because the Neptune cycle takes about 164 years to be completed, Neptune opposes the place it occupied in the zodiac at birth at about age 81 or 82.

The world of photographs and movies was born in Neptune's era. The first still photograph was taken in 1872 and the first 'illusion toys' were invented in the early 1830's—devices that gave the appearance of moving pictures. The world of illusion is Neptunian and, maybe for this reason, its nature is elusive and difficult to define. Neptune's discovery also coincided with advancement in the world of pharmaceuticals, ether being first used in surgery; in many of these ways, Neptune has come to speak of escapism in all its guises. Whether it's the glamour of the movies or the hazy world of drugs and drink, the Neptunian world is cut off from reality or anesthetized from pain. To seek existence in such a world is illusory, The movie finishes, the drugs wear off, the hangover brings sickness, and suffering is even more acute. Thus, the two sides of Neptune are rapture or despair, delirious happiness versus pain and confusion. Life is either full of meaning and euphoric or it's pointless. In Greek mythology Neptune is Poseidon, god of the sea, as illustrated in Neptune's glyph of the trident. Thus Neptune rules the ocean

and all that is related to it, such as sailing, boats, fishing and marine life. In the 'Neptunian world' we can be 'all at sea' with no land in sight— drifting and floundering—and typical Neptune types know no boundaries.
—Joanna Watters

A Neptune person has open psychic abilities, functioning on a higher plane than most. This body type can access and harmonize the inner and outer worlds. Neptune rules dreams, imagination and intuition, as well as pointing to an avoidance towards any reality that appears as personally unpleasant. This might be a rejection of the mystical, a blockage of intuitive faculties, ultimately creating low vitality; at times taking the path of least resistance supports their escapist tendencies. Neptune is a symbol of a higher type of person, one in whom a new function operates. Having other worldly appearance, their intense and wild eyes are particularly memorable. Called the earth-shaker, their nature is both violent as well as serene.

Neptune is amorphous, attuned to the finest nuances of beauty, feeling and mind, blissful, compassionate, dreamy, ethereal; highly emotional imitative, and impressionable through extra-sensory channels. Neptune the planet in its influence resembles an ocean in its boundlessness, fluctuation and emotional pulls and its function as a repository for the undifferentiated, anonymous and unknown that becomes a mysterious source of individualized life under certain conditions, only to serve later as an unforgiving void into which what once appeared vital dissipates and dissolves, and thus is an agent of death through release from the confines of matter. —Philip Graves

We rarely see this body type with its mysterious, elusive, magnetic aura. They are beguiling and enigmatic, yet, also at times, appearing listless and sad. With an other-worldly expression, their heavy-lidded eyes shift from sadness to angelic sparkling warmth. Hypnotic eyes, sharp almost cruel features, sometimes bald at the temples, Neptune people are challenged to differentiate between the subtle and the mirage of sensory information. Evoking visions that are expressed idealistically or through escapism, this type tends to be soft and non-muscular, sometimes having a watery natured obesity. Large facial features, sometimes ill-defined, lips too big, poorly outlined, their voice is sweet and tired. Things seem to fall apart about them and their aura is both soothing and draining. Neptune types are compassionate and illusionary, often found as an actor, writer, or oceanographer. Evolved Neptune types are quite angelic. Neptune offers us de-conditioning and liberation from the past on one hand, and a dreamlike, glamorous escape on the other.

From beneath his slouched hat Ahab dropped a tear into the sea; nor did all the Pacific contain such wealth as that one wee drop. —Herman Melville, Moby Dick.

Known Neptune types are: *Mr. Spock* on Star Trek, *James Dean;* Neptune Martial, *Anna Pavlova, Marilyn Monroe;* Venus Solar Neptune, *Jared Leto, Billie Holiday, Edgar Cayce, Oscar Wilde, Bing Crosby, George Harrison, Angelina Jolie;* Solar Neptune.

URANUS

Positive: creative, inventive, ambitious, versatile, unique, inspired, individualist, original, independent, ingenious, self-reliant, innovative
Negative: rebellious, uncooperative, aberrant, eccentric, perverse, extremist, odd-ball professional, bizarre, nervous energy, erratic, impulsive, peculiar, enervating, fanatical when restricted
Maximum attraction: none
Ruling glands: gonads
Ruling astrological sign: Aquarius and Saturn
Type: active/negative, androgynous
Great primeval god of the sky, Uranus, born of Gaia, the earth, covered the world in the form of a vast bronze dome and ruled over everything.
—*Mythology*

The Great Awakener

*T*his body type combines with any other type at random. Expressed predominately through the eyes and vibrational atmosphere rather than through physical characteristics, a decidedly electrical feeling pervades the aura of an Uranian individual. Uranians possess a highly-charged mental atmosphere and sometimes less electrically charged types feel uneasy around the abrupt spasmodic odd-ball energetics. Uranus was discovered in 1781 and carries the character of that century of invention and revolution. Uranus is the seventh smallest planet, the seventh planet from the sun and takes 84 years to complete its orbit. Uranus's rotation is most unusual, having been tipped to its side in the early years of the solar system, rolling on its side like a ball. Blue-green in color, caused by the methane in its atmosphere which absorbs red light, it has 17 satellites, all named for characters in Shakespearean plays.

Uranus signifies the urge to stand apart from the collective and offers independence through invention, and individualism through the capacity to deviate from the expected. Its energy is lively startling and dramatic—often associated with breaking down or breaking out. —Skyscript

This is the first planet discovered in modern times. Uranus is the great awakener, ruling over change and the future, symbolizing the urge to go beyond. As a body type they are inventive, powerful, mentally impacting the making of sudden changes, destroying the old to bring about the new. Uranus also symbolizes directionless rebellion. The planet of technology and invention, Uranus represents the technocrat and technology for its own sake, as well as inspiring a step into the unknown. Representing revolutionary forces that shatter Saturn's barriers, challenging the authority of Saturn, Uranus is the first planet discovered beyond the orbit of Saturn. Uranus offers that we can be more, that a next step in human evolution is possible, stepping into the unchartered and unfamiliar. Saturn's orbit marks the outer reach of the solar winds, the sun's electro-magnetic current, which provide a strong clue to the symbology of Uranus. Over a century ago it was stated that Uranus and Neptune are in but not of the solar system, subjected to the pull of the galactic center.

A New World

Uranus sees no need for status quo, preferring instead to break with tradition and develop an avant garde approach. While the building blocks, science and electricity, are reliably maintained, this planet focuses its gaze on a new world order. To that end, rebellion, revolution, dictators, autonomous state and free will all fall under the aegis of this planet. This is the planet which coaxes erratic and bizarre behavior and excessively complicated underhanded schemes. A bohemian, utopian society is Uranus' tendency, as are humanitarian ideals, freedom and creativity. Originality, inventions, computers, cutting-edge technologies and future events are ruled by this planet. Having a sudden, sometimes violent and often unexpected manner, Uranus rules earthquakes and other natural disasters.

Uranus symbolizes the rebel and says that rules are there to be broken or challenged. Uranus throws caution to the wind. Its nature is innovative, explosive, and unexpected, scorning authority and convention. Uranus rules accidents, shocks, and all that's unpredictable. In mythology it is the sky god and it rules all that 'comes out of the blue'. In the natural world Uranus rules earthquakes and electrical storms. The typical Uranian type is primarily different. He or she may be fascinating, brilliant, eccentric, chaotic, unstable, a wild child, or a genius, but is always unconventional or original.
—*Joanna Watters*

In Greek mythology, Uranus, also called Father Sky, was the god of the sky, ruler of the heavens, first son and husband of Gaia, Mother Earth. Their children loved this mother of all living things, yet feared their father. The first twelve children were beautiful, but the next six, Uranus saw as ugly and so flung them into a pit under the earth. Mother Earth loving all her children, wanting to protect them, feeling great loss, asked them to depose their father. Only Cronus, the youngest, dared take on the challenge, overpowering and castrating Uranus with a sickle. Losing his powers, Uranus, the sky god separated from Gaia, the Earth, and Cronus took over, becoming king of the gods.

Uranus is one of the most chaotic and disruptive systems in the solar system. The new discoveries demonstrate that Uranus has a youthful and dynamic system of rings and moons. —Mark Showalter

The Uranus body type is unusually tall, with an egg-shaped head and large forehead. They have cool, light, sparkling blue eyes set far apart with a peculiarly electric, composed, intelligent, deliberate, impersonal gaze. Often blonde-haired, considered to be an inspired individualist, they can be extreme and unique in their brilliance. Speech is fast, full of multi-syllable words, talking with peculiar observations and comments. Vocal tone is sometimes unpleasant, there may be a computer-type quality to the voice. The body temperature is cool and clothing tends to be mismatched, wearing bright-colored outfits, randomly put together.

I don't have a bank account because I don't know my mother's maiden name. —Paula Poundstone

The sex organs, men's testes and women's ovaries, are associated with Uranus. The gonads are the ruling glands. The word gonad means *seed* and *to become*. The gonads provide the *seeds of becoming* for the species. The gonads are associated with the concept of generation or becoming, equally applicable on the physical and psychic planes of existence, the psychic seeds of becoming manifest as our yearning and dreams. The gonads secrete male and female sex hormones which influence the central nervous system. Producing steroids, the female gonads, the ovaries, produce estrogen, the male gonads or testes produce androgens. The hormones that control these organs for the male determine the quality of his secondary sex characteristics; the deepness of voice, quantity of body hair and shape of body. Similarly, women's ovaries influence the feminine development necessary for changes in a woman's body that influence the proportions of a female body.

Uranus evokes originality, which when positively expressed manifests as inventiveness; when negatively expressed, as deviance. Uranus confers contempt for conventional conceptions of morality, distaste at being controlled by arbitrary forms of outside authority. It is aloof, cool, critical, crushingly assertive, impersonal, prophetic, and sarcastic without provocation. It also signifies bereavements, blind impulses, catastrophes, sudden events, sorrows, and uncertain fortunes. —Philip Graves

The Uranus type, creative, individualistic, non-conforming, is innovative often reaching for prominence in their field of choice. In many instances it is theatre. Astrologers, antiquarians, inventors, phrenologists, and people pursuing uncommon forms of work are often Neptunian. Recognizable by their unusual body presentation, sometimes albino, bald as male, they are quite versatile and strong-willed. Large, light, brilliant keen eyes and irregular features are some of their physical characteristics. Generally the response to a Uranus type is strong and extreme—they are extremists and produce similarly notable reactions—they are loved or loathed.

We are all a little weird and life's a little weird, and when we find someone whose weirdness is compatible with ours, we join up with them and fall in mutual weirdness and call it love. —Otto Preminger

Known Uranus types are: *Otto Preminger;* Jupiter Uranus, *Steve Jobs, Yul Brynner;* Mars Uranus, *Alfred Hitchcock;* Lunar Uranus, *Paula Poundstone, Verne Troyer;* Mercury Uranus, *Quasimodo-the hunchback of Notre Dame, Gabourey Sidibe, Pan.*

PLUTO

Positive: penetrating, analytical, powerful, resourceful, investigative, intellectually bright, confident, managerial, exacting, cerebral, determined, passionate, resolution
Negative: shrewd, calculating, manipulative, murderous, cynical, sardonic, cruel, domineering, sly, contriving, far-sighted, intolerant, aloof, scheming, harnessed aggression, forcefulness, demanding, unscrupulous terrorists, coercive
Maximum attraction: none
Ruling gland: hypothalamus
Ruling astrological sign: Scorpio and Mars
Type: passive/negative, masculine

He knows himself, and all that's in him, who knows adversity. To scale great heights, we must come out of lowermost depths. The way to heaven is through hell. We need fiery baptisms in the fiercest flames of our own bosoms. We must feel our hearts hot—hissing in us. And ere their fire is revealed, it must burn its way out of us; though it consume us and itself.
—*Herman Melville*

GROWTH OR DESTRUCTION

*T*he planet Pluto's eccentric orbit maps out a strange and unusual winding path. All other outer planets are gaseous giants, Pluto's composition is a mixture of rock and ice. Pluto is a misfit, the most distant planet in the solar system, the smallest in diameter, considered to be a dwarf planet, the furthest from the sun. Considered the black sheep of the planet family, or its favorite child, the debate over Pluto's planetary status continues. Discovered in 1930, during the time when nuclear power was developed, just as the great depression, fascism, the atomic bomb and LSD were having their impact. Pluto takes 247.9 earth years to complete a single circuit of the sun. Since its discovery Pluto has yet to complete one revolution of its orbit, and so, essentially, we need to gather more information in order to understand the variations of the planet as well as the physical body type. Pluto signifies the huge power that could release untold energy, even annihilate and destroy all and everything. The outermost planet in our solar system, farthest from the sun, Pluto's energy may be subtle, yet it's possibilities hold potentially great power.

Pluto has always been a problem because it's less massive than the moon and it's only about one 500th as massive as the Earth. So is it just a rock or is it a real planet? —Donald Schneider

Pluto is one of the only known planets not visited by a spacecraft, remaining somewhat of a mystery. The Hubble Space Telescope can resolve only the largest features on its surface. It is the only known planet to rotate simultaneously with the orbit of its satellite. Images have shown it to be unusually complex, with more large-scale contrast than any planet, except earth. In 2006, Pluto lost its status as a planet, failing to dominate its orbit around the sun in the same way as the other planets. It is now referred to as a dwarf planet; Pluto was automatically disqualified because its highly elliptical orbit overlaps with that of Neptune.

Pluto is so unlike any planet we have ever visited. It's this strange little duck, sitting out there, this mixture of rock and ice but with an atmosphere. There is so much to learn about this planet. —Bill Gibson

Pluto is the great reducer, stripping away all that is unessential, leaving what is. Destroying glamour, Pluto is a brooding force presenting the possibility of rebirth, producing the conditions that lead to reintegration around a new way of being, representing a stage of questioning everything. The Pluto body type has a penetrating and deliberate manner. Their psychic atmosphere is unusually intense. They are emotionally detached, ardent and ruminating, intellectually brilliant, resourceful, oftentimes manipulative and domineering. They are analytic and cerebral, creating an atmosphere of mystery and elusive dark power, all held in reserve. Strategists, they are secretive, exuding a tone of brooding intensity. Excelling in positions of danger, authority and specialization, they easily know how to remove anything that interferes with their scheme. Pluto asks us to go deep, to contact and transform whatever obstructs our power, to revitalize what is hidden, inviting us into new relationships that stretch us to evolve. In the Plutonian intensity we are brought into an atmosphere to root out new parts of ourself through encountering our limitations. When we resist, Pluto is known to force a crisis or shock that may impact our growth or lead to our destruction.

On the outer reaches of the solar system, Pluto represents the principle of regeneration and transformation through elimination and renewal. Discovered in the period that saw the development of atomic power, the Great Depression and the birth of dreadful dictatorships, Jeff Mayo called it the symbol of the great heights or fearful depths to which man can rise or fall. —Skyscript

In Greek mythology this is Hades, the underworld kingdom inhabited by the souls of the dead. Hades, lord of the dead, a somber god of few words lived in a dark palace. Called the *god of the invisibles*, mortals feared him, didn't dare mention his name in hopes of not attracting his attention, believing that he might therefore not send for them. Also called *the Rich One*, all the treasures in the underworld belonged to him as he was lord over all the mineral wealth below the ground. He was also called *the Hospitable One*, for in his desolate, joyless underground realm he always had room for another dead soul. Astrologically where we find Pluto in our chart is where we find change, regardless to our acceptance or willingness to embrace it. Hades, invisible and remote without representative attributes in myth, his name was seldom spoken, as well are there no Greek/Roman art pieces easily available to identify as a portrait of him; it was considered bad luck to even mention his name. Eventually, all mortals arrived in Hades.

In Greek mythology Pluto is Hades, god of the underworld, and the era of Pluto, including both Nazism and the use of nuclear bombs, certainly presents an unparalleled vision of hell. At its worst, Pluto symbolizes the abuse of power, hellish experiences, and the threat of death, either physically or to a sense of self. In mythology we learn that Hades donned the helmet of invisibility when leaving the underworld. Thus Pluto also speaks of that which is invisible or absent. —Joanna Watters

Precious metals and crops were believed to come from Pluto's underground realm. The planet Pluto was named after the Roman god of the under-world who had a helmet of invisibility made for him by Cyclops, one-eyed giants who were trapped in Tartarus along with Pluto. Pluto used the helmet to make himself invisible to everyone. The energy of the planet Pluto is cold and exact. Nothing can exist there that is not exactly in place. The energy of Pluto is death and transformation and represents subconscious forces, ruling all that is *below the surface*. Plutonian energy used in a search for truth and deeper meaning is transformative, whether it be birth or death. Scorpio is ruled by Pluto, the scorpion, representing sex, death and rebirth; it will sting itself to death rather than yield to a predator. The Scorpion ambushes their prey, lying in wait as they sense its approach. Like Pluto who suddenly opened up the earth to abduct Persephone, Scorpio was behind the scene for the right moment to make one powerful move. Even when appearing self-controlled there is a seething intensity of emotional energy under the placid exterior. They are like a volcano, not far under the surface of a calm sea, bursting into eruption at any moment.

This small but mighty planet rules over the Underworld. He is Osiris who rises up daily from the dead in order to bestow new life. His is not the easiest path to follow. When his energy is abused, he is devastating in his ruthlessness. When his law is obeyed and his energy is well used, he is the giver of incredible creative potency. Pluto always demands death as he is the door to the process of transformation and transmutation. Talk about paying ones karmic dues! Pluto is so far away that he is more of a force that is related to a subconscious process undertaken in order to grow. Such a force can be positive—there are definite aspects of ourselves that need to be destroyed from time to time —this periodic cleansing and divesting of form is central to the Pluto process. —Alan Oken

The influencing gland is the hypothalamus, which is in the brain, between the midbrain and the cerebrum, just below the thalamus. The hypothalamus is part of the floor of the third chamber of the brain and serves as a bridge linking the activities of the central nervous system with those of the glandular system and the activities of the psychic self. Thus, the hypothalamus responds to a blend of impulses representing the best possible balance between the urges of the inner and the outer selves. In so responding, the hypothalamus releases neurohumors which direct the activities of the pituitary gland. The hypothalamus is the agent for the autonomic nervous system, relaying impulses along the chain of neurons in the spinal cord and moves them to muscles and glands all over the body. Through these impulses it directly or indirectly manages many of our organs, our heartbeat, respiration, the opening and closing of blood vessels and the tightening of the stomach and intestines. Pluto also governs the reproductive system. The hypothalamus directly controls the digestion of food and governs our experience of hunger and thirst. The hypothalamus produces a class of morphine-like chemicals, endorphins, serving as neurotransmitters or chemical messengers in the central nervous system which stimulate the activity of neurons and are associated with experiences of exaltation, ecstasy and higher states of consciousness, as well as affecting our experience of pain. The hypothalamus is a bridge between the body and the psyche, plays a role in body harmony as well as in our experience of self, and serves as an instrument of an intelligence we experience as exaltation and oneness.

R E N E W A L   A N D   R E B I R T H

Pluto is powerful and penetrating on an unconscious and psychological level. It gradually permeates the subconscious with its drive, leaving the unconscious unaware until suddenly and explosively it emerges in an instinctive response that brings sweeping and often devastating change in the psyche and way of living. It can thus be a force for great personal good or ill. It evokes the principles of resurrection and determination, which when positively expressed bring resolution; when negatively expressed, coercion. —Philip Graves

For all that Pluto (re)creates, it loves to destroy. This planet rules destruction, death, obsession, kidnapping, beheading, coercion, viruses and waste. Pluto also governs crime and the underworld, along with many forms of subversive activity, like terrorism and dictatorships. Pluto is about all that is secret and undercover, what is hidden from view. Pluto's energy is focused on the masses and what the collective will do, asking people to look inward, to the subconscious. Pluto is the button pusher, ignoring what is fearful, going for intensity. Pluto represents chaos, dictators, totalitarianism and holocausts, the drive towards absolute power and control over others.

It used to be said that Pluto is a misfit. But now we know Earth is the misfit. This is the most populous class of planet in our solar system and we have never sent a mission to this class. —Alan Stern

The Pluto body type combining with any other body type at random is negative, masculine, passive. Plutonians have an inverted V-shaped head, dramatically overhanging brows that shadow deep-set prominent dark and penetrating eyes that have a steely intensity that appears to look through you and into your soul. Deliberate in their manner, at times they display a hypnotic beauty. The nose is eagle-like, quite pronounced. Average stature, they are thickset, swarthy, strong, having an abundance of hair, although little body hair. Illnesses include ailments resulting from mineral deposition caused by acidosis, arthritis, and arteriosclerosis. Intellectually astute, they are above average intelligence, yet emotionally detached. A severe and otherworldly appearance, they are often intolerant of what does not work in their intellectual scheme, and are known as the intensifier. They often work as a detective, mortician, narcotics agent, professional chess player, FBI or CIA agent, archaeologists, those working underground: coal miner, subway work person, excavator, *sandhogs* who dig water tunnels under the streets, an exterminator, nuclear power worker, investigator.

All men live enveloped in the whale-lines. All are born with halters round their neck; but it is only when caught in the swift, sudden turn of death, that mortals realize the silent, subtle, ever-present perils of life. —Herman Melville

Pluto is the ultimate test, once transformed, uplifted out of its darkness, demanding, abandoning the thought of holding power and authority over others, or any desire to be a radiant sun to a group of dark planets, they become the strongest most resilient type. This is the test of the true initiator; to become a spiritual friend, no longer a teacher or leader. Elevated, Pluto asks that we transcend and forget what we've been taught so as to remember what we know. A new sense of identity, through mind change is the conclusion of the Pluto cycle. The large cycle of Pluto could, over time, impact our lives through collective factors. The planets in the cosmos exert a unique influence on us, and the world we live in, much the same way as the Moon affects the tides. Scientists have redefined Pluto as the ninth member of the solar system and the first ever spacecraft arrived at the planet in 2015. Pictures of the dwarf planet's icy surface and observations of Pluto's moon Charon are revolutionizing our understanding of solar system objects that are far from the sun. The mirror of this is displayed in the intensity of the current era.

To begin depriving death of it's greatest advantage over us, let us adopt a way clean contrary to that common one; let us deprive death of it's strangeness, let us frequent it, let us get used to it; let us have nothing more often in mind than death. We do not know where death awaits us: so let us wait for it everywhere. To practice death is to practice freedom. A man who has learned how to die has unlearned how to be a slave. — *Michel de Montaigne*

Known Pluto types are: *Adolf Hitler;* Mars Pluto, *Rasputin;* Saturn Pluto, *Osama Bin Laden, Marlon Brando, Kojac, Batman, Sinead O'Connor, Donald Trump, Saddam Hussein, Bhagwan Rajneesh.*

C H I R O N

Positive: healing, hero, wholemaking, maverick, quest, guide, key, doorway, loophole, qualifier, teacher, guru, mentor, foster parent, turning point, now, catalyst, bridge, passageway, stepping-stone, holistic, mediator, essence, charitable
Negative: a wound that will not heal
Maximum attraction: none
Ruling gland: pineal, hypothalmus
Ruling astrological sign: Sagittarius, (Chiron is also a ruler for Libra and Virgo)
Type: androgynous

We heal others by virtue of our own wounds. —*Rollo May*

M A V E R I C K

A Native American prophecy states that when the planet of *healing* is discovered in the sky, the ancient sacred warrior teachings will return to the Earth. Chiron, discovered and named in 1977 reawakened teachings that were rooted in antiquity. Its origins pre-date recorded Western history showing up in the mythologies, philosophies, religions, arts and customs worldwide. The Hermetic teachings derived from the ancient Egyptian mystery traditions identifies the universal law: *as above, so below, as below, so above.* This ancient key, over 10,000 years ago, engraved in the Emerald Tablet reveals that the microcosm of mankind and the earth are a reflection of the heavens. The tablet said: *What is above is like what is below. What is below is like what is above. That which is above is the same as that which is below.* The recognition and naming of Chiron has been reflected here on Earth, having innumerable implications for our modern times.

Just weeks after its discovery by scientists in 1977, a new planet found its way into astrology. It was named Chiron, after the famous surgeon and healer of Greek mythology. It's themes have had an undeniable effect on astrology, providing us with the most spiritually-oriented planetary influence since Neptune, and guiding astrology to the level of a holistic healing art. Around the time of Chiron's discovery something else happened that provided the first clues to the meaning of Chiron: the emergence of holistic consciousness in popular culture. We take for granted that you can stroll into a health food store and buy kava kava, ginseng or colloidal silver, or receive Reiki for your migraine. Back then, people were, after years of philosophical discussion of 'holism' among intellects and occultists, beginning to dig deeper into the mind-body-spirit connection. —Eric Francis

A heavenly body in the outer solar system, Chiron is the first major planetary discovery following the naming of Pluto in 1930. In its orbit Chiron encircles both Saturn and Uranus, considered to be a bridge between the structure of Saturn and the chaos of Uranus, co-rulers of Aquarius. Considered an unstable path, it has been traveling along it for only a couple of thousand years. Chiron's symbol resembles an old-fashioned key. Orbiting the sun every 51 years it is regarded as a key to the outer planets as well as to those spheres of life shown by its role in classical mythology.

Chiron's translation from Greek is 'one who has hands'. Massage therapy, acupuncture and other hands-on-arts began to surface around the time Chiron entered astrology. The first clue to Chiron's theme actually came from an astronomer, Dr. Marsden, who termed it a 'maverick' because it did not fit any typical scientific definitions. It broke all the rules. People with strong Chiron placements are almost always mavericks, too. The second keyword was 'bridge'. Chiron serves as a connecting point between different worlds. Chironic people often strive to ground new ideas into existing forms, and bring structure to innovative ideas. —Eric Francis

THE GENTLE CENTAUR

Chiron's discovery signals evolutionary change or revolutionary destruction. It was the first known member of a new class of objects now named centaurs and is classified as both a comet and a minor planet. Centaurs were a race of beings, half-horse and half-human—head, arms and chest of a man, along with the body and legs of a horse. Lawless, uncontrollable, unfriendly creatures they symbolized the dark unruly forces of nature and were depicted as drunken revellers, given to rape and pillage, with the exception being the most famous centaur, Chiron. Centaurs, notorious for indulgent drinking, uncultured, violent when intoxicated. Chiron, by contrast, was intelligent, kind, civilized and known for his knowledge and skill with medicine. Chiron was considered the most gentle soul in Greek mythology.

Without meaningful rites, we sustain the most grievous wounds to the soul— life without depth. Rites of passage are essential—for all passages imply something ending, a death of sorts, and something beginning, hopefully a rebirth. Initiation implies entry into something new and mysterious. Given the fact that the rites of passage have largely disappeared from our culture. What is not available through our culture, we are now obliged to find ourselves. Since Chiron's discovery, the call to unlock the sacred warrior teachings and the quest for wholeness have bestowed empowerment and healing upon those who choose to walk between the two worlds of spirit and instinct in a sacred and earth-honoring manner. —Larry Williamson

His centaur-like form was a birth-defect. Son of the god Cronus/ Saturn, a Titan, Cronus had disguised himself in the form of a horse in order to seduce and ultimately rape the beautiful nymph Philyra, who, to escape his unwelcome advances had turned herself into a mare. Cronus returned to his god form and Philyra seeing her newborn son, half horse, half man was appalled and rejected him. The first wounding tragedy for Chiron was to be born through a violent rape as a centaur and to be abandoned by both parents. Immortal, the infant lived to grow up alone, later to be adopted and foster parented by the sun god Apollo who taught him music, medicine, poetry and healing. Apollo, god of music, poetry, prophecy, healing and mysteries taught Chiron all that he knew, enabling him to rise above his beast nature. Chiron became known to the Olympian community as a wise and honorable being, unlike other centaurs, becoming a teacher to the great heroes of the Hellenic world. And we see the reflection here on earth at this time, in the struggle to rise above our reactive animal nature and to evolve into self-awareness, higher consciousness, to manifest kindness and compassion.

Until you make the unconscious conscious, it will direct your life. —Carl Jung

THE WOUNDED HEALER

The second wounding came from his friend and mentor Hercules who carelessly and accidently shot him in the knee with a poison arrow. Arrows coated with the blood of the monster Hydra were known to create agonizing incurable wounds. The pain led to a healing pilgrimage. Under the guidance of Apollo, the god of light, Chiron journeyed through the darkness to find the gift in the wound. Being immortal Chiron would eternally live with the incurable malady. To be relieved of the unrelenting torment of the wound inflicted by Hercules, Chiron sacrificed his own immortality to the Titan Prometheus, changing places with Prometheus, allowing the world the use of fire, and saving Prometheus from being chained to a rock, from being doomed for eternity in punishment for stealing the fire of the gods and giving it to humankind. Prometheus would only be released if an immortal sacrificed his status as an immortal. And so Prometheus was freed from his unending struggles. This turnabout marks a transition from one realm to another, from the above to the below, from the known to the unknown. Chiron's incurable wound offered him intimate knowledge of suffering, and he tapped the wisdom within to ease the pain of others. No longer disconnected and separate from the deepest most fundamental aspects of himself, like most people who identify with the surface as opposed to the deeper mind, which makes the unexplored inner symbolic aspects of consciousness appear forbidding. We all have a moment where a continued struggle against the inevitable is futile and damaging, adding to pain and suffering; a let go. Chiron, the master of the healing arts willingly sacrificed his own immortality, and Zeus honored him by placing him forever in the sky as the constellation Centaurus or Sagittarius. Chiron's discovery moved humanity to want an existence that is healed and whole. Astrologically Chiron's placement in a chart demonstrates a deep early wound that cannot heal until it is embraced, exposed to the light, the energy released.

In the current models of medicine and psychiatry, we view the patient as an entirely passive entity in the healing process. In holistic healing, astrology and many other more balanced models of growth and wellness, a person is far from passive but rather the central figure in the healing journey, with a greater element of control over his or her destiny, In this way, the healing crisis is a call to growth, personal empowerment, and most of all consciousness. Chiron, as a healer is a bridge between humanity and the outer forces.
—*Eric Francis*

The heroic stance and the way of descent are also themes of the Chiron myth for this time. Chiron was compassionate and kind, devoted to teaching. Among the gods of the Greek myths he alone is portrayed as being without a tragic character flaw, while all others had obstructions such as vanity and vengefulness, were unfaithful, deceptive; all common properties of Greek deities and mirrored here in humanity. Chiron's flaw was how he was born, used by him as an opportunity to learn compassion and create distance and detachment, to study and teach. Chiron's lessons are mirrored in the mythology of its namesake, the centaur. Here couched in the myth lies the issue of whether humanity is half-animal, half-human, and which impulse rules. The integration of the physical, emotional, mental, social, spiritual is the heart of Chiron.

In mythology Chiron was a great healer and teacher. The word 'chirurgerie' means surgery, and Chiron was the teacher of Aesclepius, the Greek god of medicine (incidentally, early forms of chiropractic were called 'Aesclepian manipulation.') Consider that before Chiron, there was no planetary energy that specifically represented healing. Now we have Chiron, and by using its natal placement and transits, we work on a level where astrology is raised to the level of a holistic art and a spiritual science. —Eric Francis

In his search for a cure for his own wound, Chiron was a discoverer of medicine. A painful defect that was unhealable, while he was unable to find his own cure he became wise in the use of healing herbs and compassionate to the suffering of others. Chiron is the wounded healer for those who, rather than giving in to despair amid their own suffering, overcome their personal issues and receive teachings and lessons as a source of wisdom and healing powers for others. Chiron's teachings focused on guiding the heroes to realize their own true nature. Astrologically Chiron represents mastery over the inner darkness. Incurably wounded he tapped a well of wisdom within the recesses of his inner being. Representing our deepest trauma in a natal chart Chiron symbolizes the wounding we sustain in life. Represented as half human/ half animal it asks us to overcome our animal nature and serve the higher form of life, service, to release suffering and move forward in life, moving into our higher self. When our consciousness resists, life becomes disharmonious. Our wounds live as our teachers. In our wounding lies a key to our healing, for our transformation. Chiron represents the pain of embodiment; to learn freedom within the confines of flesh and blood, to learn peace as we move through the denseness of matter, of form and life. As an archetype, Chiron expresses how to link the mundane with the profound and create a bridge for others: between the realm of earth and spirit.

The Centaur planet Chiron is an astrological force for healing, transformation, service, spiritual growth and the lifelong process of becoming aware. In a word it could be summed up as 'holistic,' which means making whole. Most people who have heard of Chiron associate it with the words 'wounded healer,' but this would be like summing up the life of Albert Einstein as the 'confused physicist.' Include the theme of Maverick, because Chiron was different and stood out as a unique scientific discovery. —Eric Francis

HEALING AS WHOLENESS

Astrologers view the planetoid orbiting the outer realms of our solar system named Chiron as heralding the possibility of deeper self-knowledge, and through this, a way of addressing the suffering of our modern times. The template that unfolds for our recent planetary discoveries speaks to the evolution of consciousness. In this century astronomers uncovered a new class of similar objects found beyond Neptune, beyond Pluto. Healing in its larger context concerns wholeness, which is our source, where we come from, where we are at every moment. This is to make peace rather than war with this universe, we are born into it and will disappear into it. Losing resistance we are protected and begin the healing. Chiron, as a representative, as healer, became a force of love, the agent for wholeness. Healing as the journey of our consciousness towards greater wholeness and harmony is mapped out by Chiron: the wounding, itself the teacher and teaching. It is healing to be available to others to live through a pain we have lived through. The centaur Chiron, the figure of philosopher and teacher within Greek mythology demonstrates the conflict between the spirit and the carnal instinct of human nature, that humanity is at least half animal in nature. The glyph represents an arrow slung in a bow, aiming at the stars. The Centaur planet Chiron is an astrological force for healing, transformation, service. When the Chiron return arrives in our personal life, it can be an evolutionary leap, a time to move ahead and actualize our purpose on earth. For many, the leap is too far and, therefore, not made.

The wounded healer refers psychologically to the capacity to be at home in the darkness of suffering and there to find germs of light and recovery with which, as though by enchantment, to bring forth Aeschlepius, the sunlike healer. —Kerenyi

You might find Chiron working as a spiritual teacher, a light healer, preacher, astronaut, giving satsang, or teaching martial arts like t'ai chi, aikido, tae kwon do, or the way of the sword. In recent times the legalization of medical marijuana in many states offers a possibility to ease physical pain that is not connected to the medical model, and instead refers back to ancient shamanic traditions that relax the body out of pain and discomfort and into more meditative places without visits to doctors for prescription drugs. We can recall the biblical imagery of Jacob wrestling with the angel, initiated through his wounding, becoming Israel, literally meaning *he who wrestles, struggles with God.* And it is within our wrestling, our struggles for truth that we can recognize our wholeness, the part that has never been wounded, that is invulnerable and transcendent to the wound; this is health, our wholeness. True health is harmonious and happens somewhere inside, in our consciousness which knows no birth, no death. It is eternal.

The archetype of the wounded healer reveals to us that it is only by being willing to face, consciously experience and go through our wound do we receive its blessing. To go through our wound is to embrace, assent, and say 'yes' to the mysteriously painful new place in ourselves where the wound is leading us. Going through our wound, we can allow ourselves to be re-created by the wound. Our wound is not a static entity, but rather a continually unfolding dynamic process that manifests, reveals and incarnates itself through us, which is to say that our wound is teaching us something about ourselves. —Paul Levy

OUR GLOBAL VISION

When a new astronomical object is discovered looking at its mythology is a way to gather insight into its meaning as well as its significance for this time. Chiron is a major key to understanding, not only our solar system, but healing and mentorship. Often the teacher, guide, adviser, counselor, mentor, is overlooked, forgotten. To remember in whose footsteps we have walked is to remain connected to tradition, history and community. The folklore holds the meaning behind all things. Our reality is formed not by the events we see, but by the stories we tell about them. And the memory and ability to remember, to reinvent, to bring new meaning and renew ourselves makes us human. Myths live in the collective unconscious, to be reflected consciously or unconsciously. Myths are our own stories.

Ken Wilbur's first book A Spectrum of Consciousness, appeared in 1977, the year of Chiron's discovery, and is credited with officially ushering in the transpersonal psychology revolution. Wilbur associates Chiron's 'centuric consciousness' with a search for meaning, self-actualization, freedom, integration, and autonomy. A number of writers have intuitively called Chiron the planet of the New or Aquarian age. We are participating in

the construction of a new world view, a new consciousness, a global vision.
—Candy Hillenbrand

Chiron's effect on our life has to do with where we need to seek meaning, and where we are likely to find meaning in our lives. Chiron calls the root cause, the wound. Medicine and psychology have a pattern of naming the symptoms the disease, and works to eradicate and fix the wound. Chiron is directing the healing journey to discover, to not resist the wounding, to journey through the dark, to bring light into all of life. The psychospiritual significance of the Chiron myth continues to evolve. Its direction is to accept, without reservation the issues and scars that we find within our life. The Chironic or psychic wound is today addressed in the shamanic experience of self-discovery, leading to awakening.

The doctor is effective only when he himself is affected. Only the wounded physician heals. When the doctor wears his personality like a coat of armor, he has no effect. —Carl Jung

Known Chiron types are: many young children having notable qualities and energy that reflect Chiron wisdom, Parkland High School, Florida, *Emma Gonzalez & David Hogg, Christopher Reeve, Chris Griscom, Stephen Hawking, Malala Yousafzai,* The two dozen planets identified as belonging to the Centaur class that have been discovered since include: *Pholus,*1992; *Nessus,* 1993.

System Six

GUIDE TO HAPPINESS:

Points Or Needs

Acceptance, Adventure, Expansion, Exchange, Expression, Communion, Freedom, Security, Power

I believe that the very purpose of our life is to seek happiness. That is clear. Whether one believes in religion or not, whether one believes in this religion or that religion, we are all seeking something better in life, so, I think, the very motion of our life is towards happiness. —*the Dalai Lama*

ACCEPTANCE: Positive: friendly **Negative:** ingratiating

ADVENTURE: Positive: exploration **Negative:** drama

EXPANSION: Positive: abundance **Negative:** indiscriminate greed

EXCHANGE: Positive: creative dialogue **Negative:** chatter

EXPRESSION: Positive: artistic self-expression **Negative:** exaggerated

COMMUNION: Positive: true community **Negative:** constant socializing

FREEDOM: Positive: present moment **Negative:** irresponsible aimlessness

SECURITY: Positive: trust **Negative:** fear

POWER: Positive: authority **Negative:** authoritarian

Finding Our 3 Active, 3 Passive, 3 Neutral Needs

Happiness is the meaning and the purpose of life, the whole aim, and end of human existence. —Aristotle

We are responsible for our daily happiness. This system describes nine universal points or needs, in no particular order or hierarchy. Unconscious motivators, our needs carry a huge impact on our daily life, when addressed and met they provide a surprising sense of inner peace. Each of us has three active, three passive and three neutral needs. These are chosen at a young age and remain constant throughout our lifetime. To identify our three active or primary needs offers us the possibility to create and change the tone of each day. The extent that our three primary needs are satisfied daily, we feel happy. The longer that our active points are missing, not engaged in daily life, the greater is our frustration and dissatisfaction. In fact, an unmet need creates discontent and emptiness, a feeling of not being nourished. On the other hand when our primary points are satisfied our life feels full, of higher quality, and we are focused and nourished. Our needs animate us to seek out our lessons, the teachings that engage and propel us along on our journey, they also distract and keep us a participant in the aimless searching of repeat activities and reruns which offer repetitive sensations of compulsive pleasure.

When a person can't find a deep sense of meaning, they distract themselves with pleasure. —Victor Frankl

This remarkable system teaches us what we need to address in order to be satisfied and happy each day. A great tool to observe how and where we are held hostage to our urges and habits. The realization of our needs is the responsibility of the person with the need, a reflection of our inner world, not the *job* of a partner or friend or parent. Needs are either expressed negatively, indiscriminately, or with intention and discrimination. We each have three primary needs within the nine possibilities, and so the teaching is to know our three key needs, to understand them and their different expressions and to learn how to meet them. Ultimately, we learn to create environments and relationships that support our essential points. All nine basic human points are experienced from birth throughout life. They are fundamental needs held as a piece of common human experience. Three of the nine basic points become highlighted, they resonate the loudest for each of us, as they become priority. To figure out for ourselves which are of greatest importance and then to meet them; we live balanced. To enjoy the play of learning skills that are a support for self-understanding makes it possible to live satisfied in the world. Growth comes from being unconditionally accepting of ourself. Another opportunity to realize the truth of who we are. This tool works!

Earth provides enough to satisfy every person's needs, but not every person's greed. —Mahatma Gandhi

Relationships maintain an ease when both people have similar points. Contradictory and opposing points stretch, sometimes strain a friendship. There is stress and friction and sometimes a karmic relationship as well as difficulty in understanding/grasping the other when our three primary active needs are not similar. Each point incorporates positive and negative aspects. When our three passive points are initiated or activated by someone else we respond and enjoy. The three neutral points are least important, we feel little pull towards them.

Happiness is not something that happens. It is not the result of good fortune or random chance. It is not something that money can buy or power

command. It does not depend on outside events, but, rather on how we interpret them. Happiness, in fact, is a condition that must be prepared for, cultivated, and defended privately by each person. People who learn to defend inner experience will be able to determine the quality of their lives, which is as close as any of us can come to being happy. It is by being involved with every detail of out lives, whether good or bad, that we find happiness.
—*Mihaly Csikszentmihalyi*

THREE PRIMARY NEEDS

It is essential to pay attention to primary needs in our relationships. They are as important over time in sustaining fulfilling partnerships as is good sex, money and open conversations. Met needs inspire intimacy. Understanding our needs as well as the different needs of a partner, child, or friend, keeps relationships vital. From early childhood, our needs are apparent and should be supported, not shamed or compared. The child with an Adventure point will investigate and explore, the child with a Security point will stay by your side. Our needs remain with us throughout life, they mature and evolve as we mature and evolve. The youthful expression of Security for a young person is a stuffed animal, for an adult it could be a 9-5 job. The lowest level of expression for an Adventure point is commotion and drama, addictions, and travel, an evolved Adventure point explores inner travel, the mind, investigates teachings, ultimately wakes up. There's a great adventure!

The more our needs are not met, the higher will be the pressure, stress, agitation, unhappiness, tension, physical illness, and even acting out in ways of addiction, destructive behavior and inability to sustain an intimate partnership. There are moments, though, when the friction of not having our needs met creates lessons that we can use that push our personal growth. Yet, still, these unconscious influences command a huge impact in our lives. Family life reflects how well the parents are meeting their own needs, as well as how successful they are at addressing their children's points. When children have an Expression point and you force them to dress a certain way or choose the decor of their room, their retaliation might be to crayon on their wall or somehow lose the sweater that you picked out; better to compliment their efforts to dress, and let them name their own color schemes, ultimately, that will bring peace and harmony to the home.

Know Yourself

The needs that are satisfied through our own energy, and do not rely on others, offer us direct access to a happy time. Those are: Adventure, Expansion, Power, Expression. Exchange, Security, Freedom, Acceptance and Communion, are impacted by outside constraints and unpredictability, therefore making them more difficult to satisfy on a daily basis. Finding creative ways to meet our points enhances our life. Essentially we choose specific needs to better facilitate our life task. Soul age and our inner work are revealed as we manifest a higher level of our needs.

Become aware of what is going on—in our bodies, our feelings, our minds, and in the world. When we settle into the present moment, we can see beauties and wonders right before our eyes—a newborn baby, the sun rising in the sky. We can be very happy being aware of what is in front of us.
—*Thich Nhat Hanh*

Needs also shift from negative to positive, as we work on ourself. The negative expression of Exchange is gossip, the positive expression is free-flowing deep creative conversation. The dialogue can be with another, with an author through their written word; A writer often meets their exchange point alone, through writing and editing and being connected to their own written words. But essentially the drive to have a direct conversation, based in earnest consideration and mindful thought can not be duplicated and is difficult to find. The imbalance of being with people who chat mindlessly is debilitating; young soul environments make for a difficult challenging place to meet this point.

Using the telephone: Words can travel thousands of miles. May my words create mutual understanding and love. May they be as beautiful as gems, as lovely as flowers. —Thich Nhat Hahn

People express their needs according to their level of being. One person with a Communion point may have a group of friends they meet with regularly to gamble and get drunk, or to travel with on a subway or bus, another may meet at a nearby house to do yoga practice, or sing together in a chorale, or sit quietly reading or using a computer in a library room amongst others. One person with a Security point may walk around with a license to carry a loaded gun, another takes out a life insurance policy or maintains a 401K plan. As we learn more about our needs and what satisfies them we heighten our awareness and become connected to living our life in a more joyful way.

Happiness is not something you postpone for the future, it is something to design for the present. —Jim Rohn

Ultimately needs that go unmet, our unrequited needs, rear their heads and make themselves known. They are like a well, a hunger that can't be filled and when not satisfied bring about unsettled, uncertainty, foggy feelings of sadness and self-doubt. Divorce, getting called to school because your child acts out, physical symptoms, dramas, depression, anger, frustration, are just a few of the symptoms of unfulfilled needs. Through knowing our points we can intentionally arrange our time to have our needs fulfilled. Once we name our active points, and know another's points, we can directly see if we are compatible. People with no points in common will come up with distinct communication barriers, whereas having similar points can quickly open intimacy. Ultimately it is the responsibility of the individual to meet our own needs, which are a reflection of our inner world. To be fully alive and happy, joy follows. In the words of Meher Baba: *Don't worry, be happy.*

Following is a more detailed exploration of the nine points on the Guide To Happiness. Look to find your 3 active, 3 passive and 3 neutral points.

If you want happiness for an hour, take a nap. If you want happiness for a day, go fishing. If you want happiness for a month, get married. If you want happiness for a year, inherit a fortune. If you want happiness for a lifetime, help someone else. If you want eternal happiness, know yourself.
—Chinese saying

ACCEPTANCE

Positive: agape, open, agreeable, compassionate, devoted, friendly, goodwill.
Negative: non-confrontation, manipulative, ingratiation, cunning, sneaky, indirect, inertia, resignation, pleasing others.

SELF-ACCEPTANCE: THE KEY

Our entire life, with our fine moral code and our precious freedom, consists ultimately in accepting ourselves as we are. —Jean Anouilh

*B*eing well-received, greeted with a friendly hello, included and liked, are comfortable, uplifting, important experiences for me. I have ease being accepting and friendly, especially when it might make someone feel better, I feel constrained in a social situation when I am told to be guarded or neutral. Recognition that carries approval matters; I am relaxed knowing that people feel carefree and happy in my presence. Agreement, the willingness to receive and comply, feels respectful to me, and I try to keep social situations harmonious and trouble-free.

We cannot change anything unless we accept it. Condemnation does not liberate, it oppresses. —Carl Jung

At my best, I carry an energy that allows others to experience Acceptance, particularly through my reassuring encouragement. Having an Acceptance point I often stretch to maintain an openness and ease in relationships, since arguing and friction is uncomfortable. I clearly prefer agreeable interchanges and watch out for stepping on others toes. One way to meet my needs is to offer me the space to be my friendly self. Rather than thwarting and pushing me, it is more useful to think of ways to be supportive and complimentary. It is in my nature to thrive with nurturance and to be in a friendly welcoming environment. I am generally a forgiving person, comfortable to be around, and usually have a significant partner. The quality of safety from bonding with a life partner is important to me and serves as a safety net.

We walk through so many myths of each other and ourselves: we are so thankful when someone sees us for who we are and accepts us. —Natalie Goldberg

Acceptance of self and others is the basic learning before we leave this planet. The truth of reflecting this back to others lies in the willingness to dive deeper into the pool of self-exploration and self-acceptance, since lying and dishonesty robs others of an accurate mirror. Misrepresentation is based on lack of self-acceptance and fear of not being accepted, and undermines the integrity and dignity of the moment. Accepting what is further beyond compromise or submission is an acknowledgement and a great devotion.

Everything in life that we really accept undergoes a change. So suffering must become love. That is the mystery. —Katherine Mansfield

Everything is usable, non-resistance is a great step in overcoming anything. While all of the points are a door to happiness, Acceptance is the key. Self-acceptance begins our ability to learn to love. Agape and compassion, towards myself and others while recognizing and allowing what is, opens me to the joy of life. Tolerance, love, compassion, agape, understanding, are life lessons before we leave this planet and Acceptance is the seed for these deep teachings.

Every morning a new arrival. A joy, a depression, a meanness. Welcome and entertain them all! —Rumi

In the negative direction I am superficial, ingratiating, manipulative, tricky, and concerned, even worried about being *nice* and *liked*. Flattery, a superficial smile, unreal phony laughter, and lying are some of my skillful cunning ways of dealing with unpleasant situations as well as getting my needs met. I lie, manipulate and ingratiate to protect myself from what I imagine as not being acceptable, as well as to dodge the pain of being hurt or rejected. In the positive, to accept all, is the highest peak—all the sweetness of life and all the bitterness, to accept what appears as well as disappears; this is blissful happiness.

Accept—then act. Whatever the present moment contains, accept it as if you had chosen it. Always work with it, not against it. Make it your friend and ally—not your enemy. This will miraculously transform your life. —Eckhart Tolle

People with an Acceptance point: *Bill Cosby, Ellen Degeneres, Paula Abdul, Kelly Ripa, Sofia Vergara, Tony Bennett, Selena Gomez.*

ADVENTURE

Positive: being in the moment, open, vulnerable, inner discovery, new learnings, free-flowing, presence.
Negative: aimless, drama, risk-taking, busy, adrenaline rush addictions, distractions, forced, ungrounded, hedonist, gadabout, glamour, crisis.

EXPLORATION AND DISCOVERY

Life is either a daring adventure or nothing at all. —Helen Keller

I enjoy new experiences, challenges, traveling, and will create explorations even in small daily moments. Curious and inquisitive, searching and investigating unusual approaches to everyday things and places feeds my spirit. If I were to visit a new town and learn they have three waterfalls I'd have a good time going to all three, seeing the view from each perspective. Different angles are new Adventures.

Life is a blank canvas and you need to throw all the paint on it you can.
—Danny Kaye

I have fun trying out a new innovative restaurant, an imaginative theme movie theatre, traveling to places I have never seen, I like the exploration. I am independent, enterprising, checking out interesting unfamiliar ways, while speculating where the next stimulating venture will appear. A wilderness trip, watching the Amazing Race TV reality show or Indiana Jones movies, investing in Bitcoin, overland bike trek, having a romantic affair, starting a new business, Club Med, gambling, unprotected sex, swimming with the dolphins, a fire walk, traveling, all allow me to loosen the constraints of my persona of everyday reality. Sometimes looking for an Adventure can rule me, yet I feel purposeful along the journey of discovery. Approaching new experiences, *stepping to a different beat* keeps me playful and young.

There is something about jumping a horse over a fence, something that makes you feel good. Perhaps it's the risk, the gamble. In any event it's a thing I need. —William Faulkner

I am energized out in the world when I become risk taking, trying things; every day encounters could lead me into the unknown. The Adventure of discovery, inquiry, directs me to gather knowledge. Looking to something fresh and exciting my independence and confidence is promoted and I become self-reliant as I fulfill my need for Adventure. The adrenaline rush and stimulation keep me focused, although I have to be careful not to fall into dramas. A flair for theatrics/commotion, its stimulation and excitement brings forth the crisis Adventure, a destructive space I have known well.

If you don't take risks you'll have a wasted soul. —Drew Barrymore

Sometimes an emotional adventure will pull me, like when I am enamored, infatuated or stimulated by someone. Enthusiastic about beginning a project, I can turn that into a treasure hunt, searching and looking for the parts to make the whole thing work. At other times I am attracted and drawn to the thrill and fascination of things like parasailing, mountain climbing or deep sea diving. Participating when there is uncertainty, that keeps that sense of Adventure resonating in me. When the Adventure is not what I expected or wanted, I still learn, possibly choosing not to do that again.

The very basic core of a man's living spirit is his passion for adventure. The joy of life comes from our encounters with new experiences, and hence there is no greater joy than to have an endlessly changing horizon, for each day to have a new and different sun. —John Krakaver

In the positive direction I come away with a feeling of excitement, turned on, enlivened. Experimenting, pushing myself into direct experiences, curious, I am willing to peer underneath and in between the crevices to see new worlds and strange places. Inquisitive, at my best there is no end to the adventures and so much can be revealed.

There is nowhere to go but everywhere, so just keep on rolling under the stars. —Jack Kerouac

The positive and uplifting of my point is to find the Adventure close to where I already am; that brings new meaning to everything. No longer drawn to find the craters in the moon I look to the ridges and terrains in myself until coming to the center of my own life, discovering who it is that's having the Adventure. In the negative direction I get intoxicated, even hung over. Keeping busy looking for external stimulation, the idea of an inner Adventure, of *doing nothing* and naming this a new experience is a remote concept, not one that I easily understand.

The growth of the human mind is still high adventure, in many ways the highest adventure on earth. —Norman Cousins

I exhaust myself trying unfamiliar things and jeopardize running risks that are a long shot, proving to be unwise, reckless or dare devilish. Sometimes I am rash and hasty creating uncertain situations, although people tend to enjoy my company because things happen and there's usually fun. I also see that it's negative when I am irresponsible, cutting off relationships because I want to go into an offbeat Adventure, pulling me away from intimacy. My Adventure point is a place where I can be arrogant, showing self-importance with a disregard for others. I want to be with new people trying out different things, drawn at times to the glamour, sometimes neglecting the established relations that already exist.

No, no! The adventures first, explanations take such a dreadful time.
—Lewis Carroll

I like novelty, traveling, meeting new people, doing things that involve challenge or a gamble. I am pushed to stay awake and present as the Adventure takes me out of the safe mundane everyday routines. Essentially, the goal is to enjoy life. The appeal of Adventure can be in many domains: starting a business, attending a spiritual retreat, booking a first class airline flight, an unexpected hotel upgrade and its unknown amenities, foraging through a flea market, gambling, even having an affair, or finding a different health store or new clothing store. Ultimately, I enjoy experiences of unpredictability and varied change in routine. The rush of discovery is the excitement, although I see that in the endless repetition I become trapped in the maze of echoing redundancy. Life can be tedious and boring when I don't have something I am planning or creating. Sometimes people mix-up an Adventure point with a freedom point; stimulation is not necessarily important to a freedom need, we externally look similar, yet, internally we are quite different. When my Adventure need is held back for too long I can slide into a lethargy or an apathetic state, stuck, not quite knowing what's missing but feeling no real enthusiasm for the day.

Never forget that life can only be nobly inspired and rightly lived if you take it bravely and gallantly, as a splendid adventure in which you are setting out into an unknown country, to meet many a joy, to find many a comrade, to win and lose many a battle. —Annie Besant

People with an Adventure point: *Bill Clinton, Ernest Hemingway, Spider-Man, Angelina Jolie, Richard Branson, Brad Pitt, Jack Kerouac, Paris Hilton, William Faulkner, Cameron Diaz, George Clooney, Pink Hart, Lady Gaga, Prince Harry, Justin Bieber, Christopher Columbus, Amelia Earhart.*

We live in a wonderful world that is full of beauty, charm and adventure. There is no end to the adventures we can have if only we seek them with our eyes open. —*Jawaharlal Nehru*

EXPANSION

Positive: evolution, transformation, prosperity, abundance.
Negative: grows/expands to anything indiscriminately, fragmentation, complexity, confusion, stretched out, greed, hoarding, arrogant false pride.

INVESTMENTS: PRODUCTIVE VERSUS INDISCRIMINATE

The need of expansion is as genuine an instinct in man as the need in a plant for the light, or the need in man himself for going upright. The love of liberty is simply the instinct in man for expansion. —*Mathew Arnold.*

I enjoy developing new ideas, growing businesses and having more from what already exists. Often when there are one or two ventures succeeding I thrive on creating additional businesses with the perspective of increasing and improving what was originally there. Prosperity and juggling many projects work well together. I see the possibilities and enjoy taking on work projects that successfully double what I have. The fun is in the limitlessness, adding more and watching my world expand. I am either creating new things or continuing to build and re-invent the things that are already in my life. This ranges from my stamp and book collection, to real estate, to being overweight, to hoarding, to growing a family and money. There are times that, rather than revel in what exists, I lose my aim and come up with ideas that dilute the strength of the original undertaking and then I get set off creating excess without a true need or purpose.

I like thinking big. If you're going to be thinking anything, you might as well think big. Go beyond the limits of what classifies the average person and be exceptional. —Donald Trump

Essentially, Expansion is empire building, annexation, wanting to make *it* bigger. This might be in business, developing chain stores, or incorporating and opening branches throughout the country, in real estate buying properties and buildings, investing in stocks and cryptocurrency like Bitcoin or in collecting gold. It might be in a group, increasing membership or starting other groups with the same name or theme. In music it is in mass production, in the art world it's building a large collection. Soul age often directs what is amassed and how the wealth is used. I could build a vast real estate empire and donate money to third world countries to fight poverty and develop new medicines; the advancement and direction becomes far-reaching. Making a difference in the world, advancing the causes of people; when I am in a growthful direction these are desires that motivate me. I think big and don't like containment or feeling boxed in without room to expand. Essentially I am entrepreneurial and uneasy with status quo. I am more at ease with the future. Married, I find adding onto my family is as fulfilling as the challenge of developing and branching out my business. Having one child quickly gives me the idea to make a larger family.

I consider my contributions of more than 1.3 billion dollars to various causes over the years to be one of my proudest accomplishment and the best investment I've ever made. Those dollars have improved lives, saved species, fought disease, educated children, inspired change, challenged ideas and opened minds; at the time of my death virtually all of my wealth will have gone to charity. —Ted Turner

Without discernment I expand, gaining weight, spreading cancer throughout my body, unselectively hoard things that I have received, overextend myself to friends and acquaintances, buy more things I don't need; I just burn out. Once spiralling in a negative zone, greed and false pride pull me towards patronizing and feeling superior as I indiscriminately sprawl, accumulate and develop. My indulgence is fueled by the energy I receive developing new projects. Complexity is the step before confusion, I envision a wider scope, see the bigger picture, yet have to show care to pursue true prosperity with discrimination. In that negative mode I become greedy and vain, feeling superior and cocky, sometimes hoarding and arbitrary about what's expanded and careless about how it develops. In the positive direction I want to impact the world, to expand awareness and make a difference. Amassing a business empire I often become a philanthropist, supporting causes, investing, creating endowments and foundations. The world takes notice of the men and women who engage their Expansion point to both benefit as well as fill up, add on to the world. I am either creating new things or continuing to build and re-invent the things that are already in my life. This fluctuates between my clothing and shoe assortment to my friends and businesses.

The first 'dream of success' is part of our youth. To start over after failing the initial dream is a part of our maturing process. —Kathleen de Azevedo

The uplifting evolution of this need is to feel the expansiveness of the earth, sky, and ocean, experiencing the space around, expanding my energy field and aura, reaching out to extend my circle of relationships. To evolve in a productive manner dedictated to learning and understanding more, bulding foundations to assist humanity, is a beautiful way to live. To maintain balance and still satisfy this need, I keep in mind the difference between making a living and making a life.

Should you find yourself in a chronically leaking boat, energy devoted to changing vessels is likely to be more productive than energy devoted to patching leaks. —Warren Buffett

People with an Expansion point: *Donald Trump, Sam Walton, Rupert Murdoch, Ted Turner, Richard Branson, Martha Stewart, Steve Jobs, George Soros, Mark Zuckerberg, Michael Bloomberg, Angelina Jolie, Warren Buffet, Nadya Suleman, Paul Allen, Hugh Hefner, Colonel Sanders, Joel Ostein, Bill Gates, Melinda Gates.*

EXCHANGE

Positive: disseminating, building, relationships are for creative dialogue, informed and concerned, conversation.
Negative: gossip, slander, unrelated verbosity, chatter.

RECIPROCITY

Words can help us move or keep us paralyzed. Our choices of language and verbal tone have a great deal to do with how we live our lives and whom we end up speaking with and hearing. We can deflect words by trivialization and ritualized respect; or we can let them enter our souls and mix with the juices of our minds. —Adrienne Rich

I have a stimulating and satisfying time with free-flowing, deep, creative conversations. Social functions, lectures and outings are best when there is learning, teaching and interesting information passed back and forth. It is disconcerting to be with people who speak in a manner that is close ended, reporting about their day with little self-reflection or give-and-take. Companionship is satisfying when something I value is exchanged. This might be a new understanding, an idea, a teaching story, jokes, knowledge, or even sexual energy. Workshops and seminars are fun when there is an engaging lively format. Being around people who fill the space with chatter takes away energy, is depleting. I prefer socializing when there is something I want to Exchange, otherwise the contact feels somewhat irritating, less than satisfying and frivolous.

There is nothing so good to the heart as well agreed conversation, when you know that your companion will answer to your thought as the anvil meets the hammer, ringing sound to merry stroke; better than wine, better than sleep, like love itself—for love is agreement of thought. —Richard Jeffries

Some of our early American thinkers elevated the art of conversation, regarding it as a skill and craft. Ralph Waldo Emerson called *great conversation as an absolute running of two souls into one,* and Henry David Thoreau once remarked that *the greatest compliment ever paid me was when someone asked what I thought, and attended to my answer. Commonly, if anything is wanted of me, it's to only know how many aces I make of land, since I am a surveyor, or trivial news. They never want my meat, they prefer the shell.* Reciprocity, valuable meaningful exchange is the key. Understanding evolves from this position; and understanding transforms life, is the definition of love.

Conversation. What is it? A mystery! It's the art of never seeming bored, of touching everything with interest, of pleasing with trifles, of being fascinating with nothing at all. How do we define this lively darting about with words, of hitting them back and forth, this sort of brief smile of ideas which should be conversation? —Guy de Maupassant

Reciprocity, connections that maintain integrity, quality time with others is meaningful to me and the open flow of interchange that deepens understanding satisfies my Exchange point. I am engaged when others share neutral information as long as the openness allows for mutual sharing. As a resource I am valuable, able to easily share knowledge.

True conversation is an interpenetration of worlds, a genuine intercourse of souls, which doesn't have to be self-consciously profound but does have to touch matters of concern to the soul. —Thomas Moore

I slide to the negative part of Exchange when I gossip, make small talk, pass rumors, share unnecessary details, chat mindlessly, report or listen to reports about someone's day, ask frivolous questions, tell reductive stories, brag about myself and my children, offer unasked for advice, become a talebearer; often entertaining but rarely uplifting. When people don't have an Exchange point, I sometimes slide and amuse myself by telling jokes, or with idle banter, casual chatter, inappropriate comments or chit chat. Gossip is my downfall, when the other does not have Exchange I lose myself sharing stories about those not present, and the negativity of that bantering depletes and creates cellular unhealth in my physical being. I might find myself eating mindlessly in a social situation to counteract the mindlessness of the conversations, and then leave quite dissatisfied.

T R U E   C O N V E R S A T I O N

Ultimately the bond of all companionship, whether in marriage or in friendship, is conversation. —*Oscar Wilde*

During a conversation I find it unsettling and disconcerting when someone holds back information, withdraws, or blocks the flow by being superficial or shifts the topic without any exploration or meaningful dialogue. I process my experiences and readily communicate them to deepen intimacy. Finding myself without people to have a significant, relevant conversation, I satisfy this point studying the thoughts of spiritual teachers, writing, creating projects that include research, study, exchanging e-mail, going on Facebook, sometimes even a well documented reality TV show meets this need. Socializing for the intention to learn is happiness.

The fact is, people seldom truly speak with or listen to one another; more often than they care to admit, they deliver soliloquies, with each individual using another's remark merely as a launching pad for his or her own performance. —*Tuan Yi-Fu*

Exchange is a predominant theme and way of teaching in many sacred traditions; called Sohbet or spiritual conversation in the Sufi tradition. Dardedel, in Persian, means a heart-to-heart talk, it's sharing the most private, sincere and important things uniting our soul with another. Also named Satsang, a Sanskrit word that means gathering together for truth, in the company of the truth, Satsang, ranges from sitting in an ashram to a gathering of various people in a friendly home. The intention, to share heart connection can range from words to meditation to kirtan/chanting, regardless, the Exchange is intentional, uplifting, depthful and satisfying to those with this point. This is how I share and intensify my most important relationships.

A good conversation is better than a good bed. —*Ethiopian Saying*

True dialogue, which requires active receptive listening, also requires understanding, self-expression, and awakened observation of oneself and life. To speak truth from the heart, in sincerity, can be a developed practice for those on the Way of Love. *The Fifth Way* speaks to those with an Exchange point. This book resonates to those who appreciate learning, change, and greater understanding; offering real tools to deepen awareness.

The best conversation is rare. Society seems to have agreed to treat fictions as realities, and realities as fictions; and the simple lover of truth, especially if on very high grounds, as a religious or intellectual seeker, finds himself a stranger and alien. —*Ralph Waldo Emerson*

People with an Exchange point: *Whoopi Goldberg, Eckhart Tolle, Kabir Helminski, Larry King, Adyashanti, Jane Fonda, Thomas Moore, Barbara Walters, Daniel Ladinsky, Thich Nhat Hahn, Oscar Wilde, José Stevens, Eve Ensler, Maya Angelou, Elie Weisel, Reshad Feild, Oprah Winfrey, Andrew Harvey, Fran Lebowitz, Zalman Schachter-Shalomi,*

Arthur Greene, Eli Jaxon-Bear, Helen Palmer, Deva Premal, Natalie Goldberg. Leonard Cohen, Michelle Obama, Meryl Streep, Barack Obama, Gangaji, Stephen Colbert.

EXPRESSION

Positive: creative, definitive, imaginative, artistic self expression, promote understanding through revealing myself.
Negative: exaggerated, artificial, superficial, flaky, destructive acts, childish insistence, intrusiveness on others space, use of shock value.

PERSONAL CREATIVITY

To know what you prefer instead of saying Amen to what the world tells you you ought to prefer, is to have kept your soul alive. —*Robert Lewis Stevenson*

Expression is an aesthetic. The pleasure of what I see as beautiful energetically engages me, expressing creativity in the selection of the watch I wear, the earrings, the color scarf, the jacket I put on in the morning; all of these choices for me is artistry. Who I am comes forth in small choices. Preferences are more than thoughts, for me they are connected to moods and meaning. I love the hand-picked perfect ring, scarf, frame, candle, incense, bicycle, card, computer, car, cell phone; not just the one that works or is handy. Most all of my possessions have personal meaning. Articles of clothing are worn to convey a feeling. They are not arbitrarily bought. Jewelry and all accouterments are thought about and chosen for a significant reason and are inventive artistic creations.

Style is knowing who you are, what you want to say, and not giving a damn. —*Gore Vidal*

Belongings take on a particular meaning each having their own story. Colors, shape, design, who gave it to me, the memory of an object, its symbol and use, are variations that endear me as well as having significance. I have personal relationships to those objects that are in my life. A beautiful pen that writes a certain shade of blue, an oddly shaped soap, earrings that hang just so, high-topped sneakers, the car that I drive, the special name on my license plate, the scarf that best expresses the mood of the day, my brightly colored collection of Hawaiian shirts, an artistically designed handbag made of bottle caps, the exact shape and size wallet that fits my specifications, the image that's displayed on my iphone as well as the personal ring tones for different friends, the material and shape and color of my hat, a gift that fits the person it's going to, luggage that is unique, all become my personal friends. I receive satisfaction from my belongings and wear and carry them with that in mind. Tattoos, body piercing, a computer with a personality, colored cell phone that takes photos or a tiny credit card camera that fits into a neat leather case; I basically want my belongings to have a characteristic personality. I think about what I buy and use, how it fits into my life and what I need to satisfy me at this time in my life. I won't buy a practical Toyoto or Honda to drive around in if I feel a need for a sporty Jaguar or vintage Volvo. The kind of leather interior and wood on the dash and wheel can influence me as much as the horsepower and gas mileage in making a choice.

Become aware of what is in you. Announce it, pronounce it, produce it and give birth to it. —Meister Eckhart

People with an expression point may have a costume quality, particularly when in the public eye. Creatively expressing myself through any medium, whether clothing, speech, dance, food, home decor, music, satisfies this need. I like when people notice my Expression point and compliment it favorably. Parents best give space and room for this child to choose their own clothing as well as letting them participate in decorating their own room, or there will be frequent outbursts and discontented rumblings. Temper tantrums and complaining, even lying can be a negative form of Expression. Children with Expression might choose to wear their special cowboy boots day after day to school and to interfere because you feel embarrassed, or it doesn't seem practical wearing leather boots on a sunny day, can escalate into an out and out war. Giving room to your child who has an Expression point so they can experiment and be creative; letting them design their bedroom, pick the paint color, make gifts of candles, scarves, cards, cupcakes, for friends parties, participate in picking the fabrics and colors of their clothing; all can offer a sense of well-being to your child as well as bring peace to the home front.

Life lived as art finds its own way, makes its own friends and its own music, sees with its own eyes. Joy is in risking, in making new. —Marilyn Ferguson

There is great pleasure and satisfaction in a creative endeavor like writing or singing that offers room to convey who I am. Cooking a meal will have my characteristic signature, whether its sprinkling coconut, cinnamon, or drizzling chocolate on top, cutting vegetables in a stylish manner, serving the food in dishes that make a statement, just as what I wear to a dance or evening out will include something that expresses my mood and personality for the occasion. I like to make a statement, even if it's only a silent one to myself, through what belongs to me. Accessories actually express who I am, my inner self. Theatre with flashy performances often have designers and performers who love the process of sharing their dancing and singing as a creative presentation.

All the arts we practice are apprenticeship. The big art is our life. —Richards

My pleasure and ease to communicate meaning through Expression stirs the emotions of those around. My willingness to represent personal feelings and moods through a stylized statement promotes understanding, as I reveal myself while encouraging others to disclose themselves, to have their own creative expression.

It's my body and if I want to do it like Michael Jackson I will. My nose bothered me for a long time. Now it's smaller and I'm happy. If I wanna put my tits on my back, they're mine. —Cher

People with an Expression point: *Cher, Elton John, Georgia O'Keeffe, Lady Gaga, Miley Cyrus, Rihanna, Gwen Stefani, David Bowie, Christian Dior, Pablo Picasso, Britney Spears, Cindy Crawford, Rita Ora, Jennifer Hudson, Sarah Jessica Parker, Justin Bieber, Lance Bass, Blac Chyna, Dr. Edith Wallace, Drew Barrymore, Boy George, Bjork, Tom Wolfe, Paris Hilton, Avril Lavigne, Pink, Madonna, Michael Jackson, Marilyn Manson, Angelina Jolie, Diane Arbus,* graffiti artists.

There is a center in us which, if we could but open to it, would give us direction, strength, wisdom and the capacity to live our creative potential. Connection with this source gives our lives presence and vitality. Our creativity depends on it. —Dr. Edith Wallace

COMMUNION

Positive: sharing, unity, true community, interbeing, mutuality, intimacy, interdependent.
Negative: indiscriminate contact, disconnected chatter, overwhelming neediness, lacking boundaries, constant socializing.

COMFORTABLE CONNECTIONS

A healthy social life is found when in the mirror of each soul the whole community finds its reflection, and when in the whole community the virtue of each one is living. —*Rudolf Steiner*

*L*iving in community or having people nearby to share time and space with has a naturalness, I keep my own rhythm, and knowing that people are nearby is relaxing. There is an easy manner to having guests, pot-luck dinners or organizational meetings at my house; it's all an extension of community. I also have fun going out to small group gatherings at the end of the day, slipping into an informal environment, having people available. I like the familiar feeling of fellowship. The day unfolds and I am comfortable with the awareness that we will all meet later for dinner, or a walk, a movie, or gather at a meditation. I tend to be tribal and family oriented, enjoying celebrating occasions with my friends. Most any reason to have a get-together, a gathering, sharing; community events feel like a good opportunity to come together in one place. The occasion is less important than the social gathering. I like living in an neighborhood knowing others are available within close range. My preferred working conditions are when I feel the proximity of other workers in the building who might walk over for a momentary smile or hello.

All things and beings in the universe are connected with each other—visibly or invisibly and through vibrations a communication is established between them on all the planes of existence. —Hazrat Khan

Sometimes I'll sit at Starbucks or Barnes and Noble Cafe with my laptop computer, ipad or cell phone, while others around me are reading magazines, newspapers or drinking coffee. I have lived communally with friends, sharing meals and open spaces, once even in an ashram environment. People drop by my home, which I keep user-friendly, easily accessible. When I go to the gym I enjoy working out while others are in the room. Meeting to watch a favorite TV show or video with companions, setting up a group to watch the Emmy's or Academy awards, these are clues to my having a Communion point. Partnering with someone who isolates me eventually leads to unhappiness; instead availability to people and working in a way that offers contact with others meets my need.

Without community there is no liberation; but community must not mean a shedding of our differences nor the pathetic pretense that these differences do not exist. —Andre Lorde

I like my alone space as well, yet knowing that others will share their time and life with me promotes additional richness and pleasure. Having an ease to sharing, interaction, cooperation, joint participation, collaboration, connectedness, the day is harmonious. Sharing meals, whether I visit or have people drop by, I am an informal host, putting others at ease unless I overwhelm them with my urge to please. Pot-luck dinners, getting together to walk, bike-ride, cook together, even chatting on the phone fills my enjoyment for contact. Memberships or belonging to a community center a local synagogue or church, I like the affiliation and having a brotherhood/sisterhood that offers a continuity to feel part of, with a group of people that I get to be with over time.

More than anything else we need communion with everyone. Struggles for power has nothing to do with communion. Communion extends beyond borders. It is with one's enemies also. —John Cage

COMMUNITY

I openly share my space and generate a quality of community. Seen as a community builder and a good host, I bond and experience connectedness. Yoga, water aerobic classes, conferences; whatever draws me I either register for events or drop by and informally participate. Cities like New York, and Boston resonate for me. Sitting in a subway car, riding a bus, eating in restaurants; New Yorkers, once they step out are rarely alone. Outdoor cafes, flea markets, a cafeteria, green market, a beach; I sense the life force around me. The subway, train, airplane, airport and bus are great examples of being connected with strangers all going somewhere, sitting close by, and sometimes even looking at each other; all ways to satisfy my Communion point. Lifted to a higher place this is one family and one world and at my best I feel a closeness when I experience connectedness with my brothers and sisters on this planet, cancelling out any illusion of separateness.

Weave real connections, create real nodes, build real houses. Live a life you can endure, make love that is loving. Keep tangling and interweaving and taking more in, a thicket and bramble wilderness to the outside but to us interconnected with the rabbit runs and burrows and lairs. —Marge Piercy

Many spiritual traditions have created environments, ashrams, communes, sangha, communities, centers all over the world to create what Rajneesh called an energy field, a *Buddhafield*; an unworldly world that offers conditions for spiritual growth, where one is not distracted by the world, to no longer be lost in the apparent. Teilhard de Chardin coined the word *Noosphere*; an atmosphere, a climate with a world of subtle vibrations, thoughts, feelings that surround us allowing us to deepen our vulnerability, to drop defenses, withdraw arguments; a place attuned to a teaching that offers an energetic field, a space that fosters openness and receptivity. *Sangha*, a Sanskrit word translated as commune or community of kindred spirits refers to the friends and community often considered to be the body of a spiritual teacher or Guru. Gathered around the presence of a Buddha a sangha brings together people who have mutual interests and live harmoniously. Meeting with a sangha to practice mindfulness we see that our happiness is not separate from the happiness of others. Thich Nhat Hahn, a Vietnamese spiritual teacher has said that the coming Buddha of the future is the community, not the individual person. This quality of connectedness, which first originates from an authentic self-connection, then expands outward, honors our differences and has a reverence for all of life.

The task before us now, if we would not perish, is to build the Earth. This is a passionate concern for our common destiny. The only truly natural and real human unity is the spirit of the Earth, the irresistible pressure to invite humankind in a common passion. The Age of Nations is past. The Earth in its evolutionary unfolding is growing a new organ of consciousness called the Noosphere, a planetary thinking network an interlinked system of consciousness and information, a global net of self-awareness, instantaneous feedback and planetary communication. It is not our heads or our bodies which we must bring together, but our hearts—humanity is building its composite brain beneath our eyes. This convergence, through a global information network is not a convergence of merely mind and bodies, but of heart.
—Teilhard de Chardin

INTENTIONAL COMMUNITIES

Spiritual communities have flourished, and are representative of the

Communion point in their approach to communal lifestyle, usually with large open spaces to encourage meals, meditation, meetings and easily available personal contact with those living in the community. Thich Nhat Hahn created a contemplative community, Plum Village Monastery, a retreat center near Bordeaux, France, in the Dordogne region in the Southwest of France, the Dalai Lama lives at Dharamsala, a village in the mountains north of New Delhi India, establishing a government-in-exile, with monasteries, temples and Tibetan teachings, Gurdjieff pioneered teachings, setting up the Prieure, The Institute—a School for the Harmonious Development of Man at Fontainebleau, France. Parahamansa Yogananda created the Self-Realization Center in Encinitas, California, Ammachi has her main Ashram in Kerala, India, Chogyam Trungpa founded Naropa Institute in Boulder, Colorado, and established Shambala Meditation Centers and the Karme Choling retreat center in Barnet, Vermont. Bhagwan Shree Rajneesh, Osho having hundreds of meditation centres throughout the world, masterful at setting up community, his main commune considered to be a meditation resort, offers a place where people can have a direct personal experience of a new way of living, is in Pune, India. Yogi Bhajan, established an ashram and Sikh Temple while living at Hacienda de Guru Ram Das in Espanola, New Mexico, Mother Meera holding the light, offering silent darshan in Thalheim, a quiet German village, Michael Singer created the Temple of the Universe on 600 acres outside of Gainesville, Florida, Gangaji located her center in Ashland, Oregon. Adyashanti, based in California invites people to his meditation retreats, Adnan Sarhan has a Sufi retreat Center in Torreon, New Mexio, Ma Jaya founding Kashi Ashram, a healing center in Sebastien, Florida, Ram Dass sitting in Maui, Hawaii offers Sunday meditations. Intentional communities, kindling light. Sacred spots that radiate kindness, generosity, clean food, and a holisitic healthy lifestyle. Jesus is reported to have said; *wherever four of my disciples are gathered together, I will be there.* This presence of teachers, teaching places, communities, carries the force to shift the world, and the Communion point is in the forefront once it uplifts to its positive direction to bring about this possibility.

The need for group work and group cooperation is vital at this time in history. Now is the time to work together, to fulfill our obligation to life. We become human as we cross the threshold to be responsible at last, responding to the call that, if we could but listen and hear, is in every moment. Spiritual community is totally involved with the pain and suffering of the world, and yet not identified with it. We ask how this suffering can be alleviated. This is work for a spiritual community. Let us be considerate and truly learn about brotherhood/sisterhood; living this way we will be free. —Reshad Feild

The history of communes speak to the Communion point. Steven Gaskin in 1970 created the Farm in Tennessee, an intentional community, a non violent eco-friendly cooperative community that ushered in the new age. At one point 1500 people lived together with a commitment to simple living. Kat Kinkade, inspired by B.F. Skinner's *Walden Two*, established Twin Oaks, in 1967 an eco-village tucked away on 465 acres of farmland in rural Virginia. The desire to be a model social system was propelled by a strong Communion point, and both communities still thrive. Israel currently has societies dedicated to mutual aid called Kibbutzim, which are the largest commutarian movement in the world. Kibbutz members work and live cooperatively, mostly in rural communities. An allusion is often made to the Snow Leopard or snow lion who lives alone and is more from past times. Tibetan folklore says that only the snow lion can go into the icy wilderness forest alone. All others need community.

GATHERINGS

Only in relationship can you know yourself, not in abstraction and certainly not in isolation. —*Krishnamurti*

Jimmy Carter past president of the United States advanced peace and human rights through the model of the homeless and volunteers working side by side, promoting housing and other benefits for those who could not afford basic comforts of living. Our times speak to meetings and gatherings like twelve-step programs, religious rituals such as Easter or Passover dinners, joyfully sitting in a Sukkah together, examples of collective joint ventures, shared ceremonial meals, holidays where families and friends meet throughout the year. Gatherings and most social events generate energy for those with a Communion point. The quality of that energy and where we choose to find it is our personal choice; ranging from a writing group, a meditation circle, a racetrack, a comedy club, Shabbat dinner, studying in a library with others around, working on the computer in a public place like Einsteins or Starbucks, sitting at a public beach, a business or board meeting, sitting with people and getting drunk or smoking pot, a silent retreat, a shooting range, a gang; the level of the individual and their aim, values and intention sets the course for how that decision is made. When we select with fore-thought, arranging our time with an understanding of what we are truly seeking, then our needs are met without reducing ourselves to attending events out of loneliness, instead our outings become uplifting produc-tive occasions that might shift the tone of this earth.

Community. Somewhere, a circle of hands will open to receive us, eyes will light up as we enter, voices will celebrate with us. A circle of friends. —*Starhawk*

People with a Communion point: *Jimmy Carter, Ram Dass, Steven Gaskin, Starhawk, Rudolf Steiner, Thich Nhat Hahn, Willie Robertson, Ammachi, Martin Luther King Jr., Oprah Winfrey, Drew Barrymore, Ashton Kutcher, Kim Kardashian, Blake Shelton, Ellen DeGenerous, Kat Kincade* and many people living in ashrams, monasteries and convents, repeat criminals in jail, and, often, street people.

The universe is a vast interconnected network. All our thoughts and actions reverberate throughout it. —*Mata Amritanandamayi*

FREEDOM

Positive: independent, in the present moment, spontaneous, vitally aware of the rhythms of life, aware of unlimited possibilities, understands impermanence.
Negative: unreliable, unaccountable, irresponsible, aimless, unfocused.

No Appointments

No Disappointments

True freedom is always spiritual. It has something to do with your innermost being, which cannot be chained, handcuffed, or put into a jail. —*Osho*

The experience of having no appointments, being spontaneous, and in the moment, the future fairly wide-open, brings delight. Little structure is required for a fun occasion. This type of mobility feels like an open field of opportunity. Fitting in to a scheduled vacation would take away some of my fun. Many of us are self-employed. Traveling without a schedule or reservation is simple and enjoyable. Often I prefer to drive rather than to be confined to the structure of an airline schedule. Not to be confused with an adventure point, I am not necessarily looking for an adventure, or distraction or entertainment, rather to hold an empty space for the pleasure of the empty space; to have an unlimited quality of choices. No appointments, no disappointments is my Freedom point motto.

Caged birds accept each other but flight is what they long for.
—*Tennessee Williams*

A plan or reservation can feel like a nail in a coffin, fenced-in; it's an interruption of the ease and pleasure of a day. Society is gauged to take this point lightly and create a world of schedules and deadlines defending their position of structure with the rationale that things would not work and people need plans. Times when there are several choices and I feel pushed to land on one are somewhat challenging, unless I have certainty in which direction I want my day or evening to go. When people say *I want to see you,* or, *when can we get together,* there's a squeezed sensation of obligation and limit. My preference would be that meetings happen either spontaneously or the plan is made quite close to the meeting time.

The only time I've made plans the cosmic sledgehammer has intervened and something else has happened. You just have to wait and see what comes your way, so that's what I do. —*Peter Capaldi*

WANDERING SPIRIT

I'm a person that doesn't have that many goals or plans. I feel like I'm the wind and I blow through life; it's whatever comes to me. I very much respect nature. Whatever happens to me, I'm happy and I embrace it. —*Bai Ling*

I am best in relationships that have good flexibility, with people who don't try to entrap me or throw guilt trips, allowing me the room to make independent decisions. I am productive creating my own work rules with unrestricted time frames, leaving space for spontaneity and openness. Unconventional, free-lancing or self-employed; in a job with rules imposed I begin to feel bound and obstructed. Often people minimize my wandering spirit, not understanding how plans limit my Freedom point, instead justifying their need to block in a time slot, a plan. Even a restaurant reservation made two days ahead, or the information that someone will be a house guest in two weeks diminishes my breathing space.

Our plans never turn out as tasty as reality. —*Ram Dass*

Understanding the open spaciousness of this need for people who don't have Freedom as an essential point becomes a stretch. This country is organized for those with a security point, the pleasures of a Freedom Point person are truly an enigma to those who do not carry this point, the difference creates a gap of understanding. Designated parking places brings comfort to those who do not have a Freedom point; open parking becomes an anarchistic thought form for community and condominium living. To my Freedom point, to drive home and park my car in whatever spot appears makes the most sense. Often viewed as *too loose* or told *you can't live in the world without a schedule* or reminded that *everyone makes plans* or *if you don't make a plan to see me I'll be too busy to see you*; yet these rationalizations discount what brings happiness to this point. Asking to meet me at 6pm seems to be a benign request, yet the thought form, a containment, a reference point in the day, fences in the unblocked unrestricted *let's see what wants to happen* day. Once the idea is formed that we will be meeting later in the day, that plan interrupts my thought form of an easy happy-go-lucky wandering, roaming day.

I never make plans, I never set goals, I don't like to futurize, I barely know what I will do tomorrow, and because there is a working plan here I've never futurized because life always surprises me with things even better.
—*Kate del Castillo*

Certainly I can make and keep schedules and appointments, knowing that this world caters to routines and time structures; but what happiness in the open field of not knowing, the unfolding of letting the moment be my guide! Yes, I can meet schedules people make, even though it puts a slight squash on my fun. Avoiding confinement is a difficult dance. I am easily drawn into another's time frame, since I rarely have a firm schedule, so a telephone call asking me to be somewhere might pull me off my loose open day. Unguarded, my easy range gets roped in, since living casually as I choose in this world always has some restriction. A knock at the door, interruptions, invitations, movie times, classes I want to take; all moments that point a finger to come here, schedule this.

A good traveler has no fixed plans, and is not intent on arriving. —*Lao Tzu*

AIMLESS OR MINDFUL

We cannot lead a choiceless life. Every day, every moment, every second, there is a choice. If it were not so, we would not be individuals. —*Ernest Holmes*

When I slide to the negative of my Freedom point I cancel appointments at whim, or just don't show up under the guise of *being in the moment.* Those around are then stuck paying for my illusion of Freedom. Losing focus, aimlessness overtakes me. Not taking responsibility for a plan I agreed to, or an agreement I made, I explain that I am *being in the flow.* Relationships often suffer from the gratification of this need. In the effort to satisfy my Freedom point I mistake true freedom with irresponsibility and promises that override commitment as I pretend to be a free flowing open person and don't see the consequences of my behavior on other people's lives. I easily step on toes when I arrive late, don't show up, act surprised when someone holds me to an arrangement I might have casually made; I become highly unreliable although I imagine myself to be the more evolved casual easy going one. I avoid commitments and sometimes distance myself, even sabotage closeness when I feel someone is trying to bind my spirit. Resentment surfaces when I feel controlled by another's need for scheduling and plans, or judged for wanting to have a choice as I navigate around others belief systems. For me the enjoyment and the experience of my Freedom point is to not have restrictions, constraints, to feel mobile, not controlled by culture or other's insistence on rules, plans and time schedules.

The best laid plans of mice and men often go awry, and leave us naught but grief and pain, for promised joy. —*Robert Burns*

Maturity brings a quality of responsibility so that my word and my plans become reliable. In the positive direction I am exceedingly responsible honoring the commitments I do make. I am reliably independent, a free thinker, willing to dream my own dream and follow it, regardless of the price, sacrifice or judgment of others. A plan becomes solid and clear and I am quite mature in my agreements and commitments. There is a subtle distinction between plans and planning. Dwight D. Eisenhower understood this when he stated *In preparing for battle I have always found that plans are useless, but planning is indispensable.* I love to think through a plan and to create order, and live with an intention, and then, to live in the free-fall. A developed Freedom point person holds to their promises, regardless. The way I achieve this is through being careful and mindful when I agree to a date, rather than a casual intention, knowing that it is made as an interruption to my Freedom point, I become careful before saying yes. I just don't like having rules or restrictions imposed; breathing room, leeway to maneuver, having a range of choices I maintain balance and openness. Discrimination, discernment, mindful breathing, are valuable tools in the art of living in the moment.

I try to avoid plans and that way I can more easily deal with anything new that comes up. —Linus Torvalos

There seems to be a law that governs all our actions so I never make plans. —Greta Garbo

LIFESTYLE

I'm poor but happy a man of the Way all my needs are satisfied by chance last night the west wind downed an old tree at daybreak firewood covered the ground gauze silk clouds adorned red scarps dew drop pearls bejeweled green cliffs what's present has always decided my living why should I burden myself with plans. —the Zen works of Stonehouse

Most people, having learned the concept of a Freedom point, imagine they have it. But only 5% of the population has it as their top three needs. The Adventure point focuses on stimulation; a Freedom point is about being unrestricted, having the power of self-determination. Generally Freedom point people work for themselves. One woman, having no home, car, bank account, credit card, or cell phone, travels by bus and offers astrology readings, asking for a donation, and stays at different friends homes or at a known bookstore in Chicago. She happily lives her free-flowing life. Freedom point people are often subjected to criticism and judgment, referred to as ADD, irresponsible, learning disordered, hyperactive, neurotic, yet, may be healthy and balanced, just different in our personal needs.

She asked why people are sad. That's simple, said the old man. They are the prisoners of their personal history. Everyone believes that the main aim in life is to follow a plan. They never ask if that plan is theirs or if it was created by another person. They accumulate experiences, memories, things, other people's ideas, and it is more than they can possibly cope with. And that is why they forget their dreams. —Paulo Coelho

True Freedom is outside of time, and to avoid a world that continuously challenges this point through organizing and justifying imposed order and restrictions is a daily dance for all of us with this need.

You cannot parcel out freedom in pieces because freedom is all or nothing. —Tertullian

People with a Freedom point: *Baba-Ji, Krishnamurti, Howie Mandel, Abbie Hoffman, Robin Williams, Tom Green, Greta Garbo, Janis Joplin, John Lennon, Yoko Ono, Paul McCartney, Owen Wilson, Britney Spears, Ozzy Osbourne, Ram Dass, Bhavani, Marlon Brando, Neem Keroli Baba.*

For to be free is not merely to cast off one's chains, but to live in a way that reflects and enhances the freedom of others. —Nelson Mandela

SECURITY

Positive: trust, secure that the universe is ordered and taking care of you, responsible to commitments, reliable to the order of planned events, stable, self-confident, comfortable, security and trust that is grounded in experience and knowledge and tradition.
Negative: fear, controlled and controlling, lacks spontaneity and passion, unwilling to let go of form or try new things, limited, conventional, phobic, narrow-minded, blind trust, false hope and illusion, irrational caution, clinging to tradition, beliefs and opinions.

PLANNING AHEAD

I never attempt to make money on the stock market. I buy on the assumption that they could close the market the next day and not reopen it for five years. Our favorite holding period is forever. —Warren Buffett

*E*njoyment comes from knowing the boundaries of a plan. Before moving to a new town, I like to have a job as well as a place to stay, confident that, for me, this is the right way to relocate. Renting a house offers comfort before purchasing it, so I can gradually ease into the change, or at least to check out the area for reassurance. I like plans and don't hesitate to make appointments, dates and reservations ahead of time. Scheduling in a vacation two months to one year ahead adds to my pleasure, then I will also have the added benefit of looking forward to the trip. Planning ahead, the enjoyment that follows is in the thought about the vacation or the dinner date that's up coming. I can think about what I want to do, read books on places I might visit, and imagine what I might order in the restaurant I'll be going to, or what I'll wear at the theatre I have tickets for on the following month. Organizing for upcoming occasions satisfies my Security need and gives me confidence as I arrange for my needs and pleasure.

There cannot be a crisis next week. My schedule is already full. —Henry A. Kissinger

Many of us are people with schedules, routines and 9-to-5 jobs. The form of the plan, like the booked airline ticket with the set date, plus the structure of having to return to work after my vacation, offers a sense of relief and the space to have a good time. Time shares are a good investment, the dependability of knowing when my trip away from home will happen each year, what clothing to pack and knowing what to expect, allows me to more fully enjoy the experience. Thinking ahead about my meals, figuring out dinner in advance, often before breakfast is eaten; sometimes my meals are worked out for the entire week.

A schedule defends from chaos and whim. It is a net for catching days. It is a scaffolding on which a worker can stand and labor with both hands at sections of time. —Annie Dillard

We are rarely caught in the moment with nothing doing, with an empty date book or alone, just hanging out for a couple of unstructured days. My plans usually have plans following the plans. Work ends at five p.m., meet one friend for dinner at six, then meet three friends to go bowling at eight, have to go home at ten, in order to get up and be at work by nine a.m. the next morning. This amazes a freedom point person, who enjoys living within the possibility of—what if at dinner I meet someone exciting at the next table who invites me to a party? The Security point person prefers to have an orderly, safe and predictable sequence to their day and evening. Wanting to make things certain and foreseeable, worked out according to my ideas; no surprises when I arrive is comforting. The corporate and bureaucratic world relies on the scheduling that appeals and is familiar to a Security point person. Having a permanent income and health insurance through work overrides the time sacrifice.

Always plan ahead. It wasn't raining when Noah built the ark. —Richard C. Cushing

I don't object to my partner checking in with me regularly, telling me their plans and offering information. I like knowing that both myself and my loved ones are safe. What might create Security for one person, varies from person to person. To some it may mean knowing that their investments are sound, to another it means that their home has good protective devices and their partner won't have an affair, or having a secure job with numerous benefits and a sizeable bank account along with good life insurance; but definitely order and a blueprint leaves me room to have a better time.

Plan your progress carefully; hour-by-hour, day-by-day, month-by-month. Organized activity and maintained enthusiasm are the wellsprings of your power. —Paul J. Meyer

When in the negative part of the Security point, I plan the future from a place of fear and insecurity, not trusting myself. I become attached to the details believing that the play is real, blocking spontaneity, trying to know the outcome before confirming the date. Following through with a plan regardless to its use or value sometimes misses the mark when opportunity arises. I organize an outing and might miss a delightful sunny day at the beach because I arranged to go to the mall with a friend, this, though, doesn't make me feel bad because the knowledge that my day is organized overrides the temptation to shift for external weather conditions. I tell myself there will be other beach days, and enjoy following through with the plan.

I do better with routines and predictability. I don't react well when there's a sudden change in the schedule. —Gretchen Rubin

This is a popular point, about 35% of the population have the need for Security. They satisfy this need by having a *safety net*, are concerned about resources, money, personal safety, home security, car/home/health/life insurance, a will, cemetery plot, secured summer or winter plans with dates and reservations, airline tickets and hotel accommodations booked well in advance, jobs that come with benefits—like insurance and a 401K, long term investments. Buying stocks or gold, keeping papers tucked away in a bank deposit box or safe, balancing my checkbook; knowing what's available keeps me feeling anchored. Having a Security point creates an interest in wanting more guidelines, additional information, more facts, more direction, more clarity, more rules, and more predictability. It is comfortable knowing how much money I have, to keep the bills paid, when traveling to be clear about the weather report and what to expect. Without these things in order life is stressful and feelings of unhappiness arise. I stay at my job since it is familiar and known, as well as its promise of a good medical insurance plan, a steady paycheck, benefits, as do most people with a Security point, and those of us that don't like our job still maintain enough hours to keep up our medical coverage, blocking out and strategizing how many years it will take to ensure protection. Old age is considered, and plans are made in advance to take care of needs that might result from aging. A life insurance policy and long term health care insurance protection offers confidence that life will turn out manageable.

If you want total security, go to prison. There you're fed, clothed, given medical care and so on. The only thing lacking is freedom. —*Dwight D. Eisenhower*

SELF-CONFIDENCE

Many memorable proverbs and slogans are based on this point: *Better safe than sorry. An ounce of prevention is worth a pound of cure. Safety brings first aid to the uninjured. Safety is a cheap and effective insurance policy. Better a thousand times careful than once dead.*

I like to know the details before I move forward, planning the event, researching, gathering the facts are part of my caretaking. Knowing the whereabouts of the people I care about, their schedules and plans speaks to my security point. I have been referred to as a status quo person, *the state of things as it was before*, liking to keep things the way they currently are, in fact, I could hold on to a stale marriage or partnership for years, and have been known to maintain my living quarters and a job for long years even after realizing that I'm done with them. Rocking the boat is not a favorite activity; essentially I don't want to jeopardize those things that are already in place. Change is not high on my list of favorite things. I seem to need reassurance before trying something new. The configuration of my other points tempers this point: for example, having an Adventure need eases up my rigidity, and once plans are in place I roam around looking for surprises within the boundaries of a plan.

Security is like virginity: you're either a virgin or you're not. You either have security or you don't. —Lennart Meri

To feel safe from terrorism, politicians convince people to give up daily freedom, and that raises the fear and threat level, which raises the Security needs higher, which creates an unwillingness to invest and spend money, making more economic issues and raising fear levels which irritates Security needs. *The only real prison is fear, and the only real freedom is freedom from fear,* said Burmese Nobel peace prize laureate Ang San Suu Kyi. Trust, which contains certainty and reliability, offering confidence, is the positive move of a Security point. Taking care not to immerse oneself in fear, which accompanies misgivings, suspicion, worry and concern maintains the balance and offers satisfaction for a person with a Security point.

There is only one security, and when you've lost that security, you've lost everything you've got. And that is the security of confidence in yourself; to be, to create, to make any position you want to make for yourself. And when you lose that confidence, you've lost the only security you can have. Self-confidence is self-determinism. One's belief in one's ability to determine his own course. As long as one has that, he's got the universe in his pocket. And

when he hasn't got that, not all the pearls in China nor all the grain and corn in Iowa can give him security, because that's the only security there is.
—L. Ron Hubbard

People with a Security point are: *George W. Bush Jr., Nancy Reagan, P.D Ouspensky, Warren Buffett, Henry A. Kissinger, Martha Stewart, David Hasselhoff, John Travolta, Gretchen Rubin, Anderson Cooper, Jennifer Hudson, David Letterman, many in the Corporate business world.*

POWER

Positive: authority, masterful, empowerment, leadership, self-discipline.
Negative: authoritarian, dictator, oppressor, tyranny, viciousness, abuse, inappropriate control, manipulation of others.

TAKING CHARGE

Power is of two kinds. One is obtained by the fear of punishment and the other by acts of love. Power based on love is a thousand times more effective and permanent than the one derived from fear of punishment.
—*Mahatma Gandhi*

The Power point is about capability, potency, flair, leadership, might, brute force, formidableness and control. I influence people and situations, because I want to, self-assured I step forward convincingly taking control; being in charge. Moving with confidence, assertively taking over a situation that is not going well is an instinctive and predictable experience. I feel more comfortable with authority than most. I like to run the show, to take responsibility and to be the leader. I feel accomplished and this is felt by others and gives them added trust in my authority.

My relationship to power is that I'm all for it. People need someone to watch over them. Ninety-five percent of the people in the world need to be told what to do and how to behave. —*Arnold Schwarzenegger*

I learn to organize myself, so that I have Power over my space. Coordinating many parts I bring things together so every part works efficiently. I am responsible and can make things happen, eventually most people see me as effective and allow me to take a commanding posture. Finding myself in a position of influence, as long as my personal agenda doesn't take over, my diplomacy and good leadership helps empower others. Sometimes I am satisfied just to be around someone who is powerful, and still I exude confidence.

True power is the falling away of individual identity. —*Sri Saradamani Devi*

In the positive direction there is a genuine willingness to accept responsibility, to take charge and become a leader. I step forward and use the opportunity to teach, lead and guide others. In the negative direction there is terrorism and oppression, which has been demonstrated in organizations that work with power like the CIA, the IRA, the IRS, the Mafia the KGB, Al-Queda, and ISIS militants. In a negative downward spiral I become destructive and obsessed with control, have explosive outbursts, am manipulative, get the upper hand through force, and will crush any opposition even if it means oppressing myself and others. Once blinded by my personal agenda, carried away, I become disempowered.

Power never takes a back step—only in the face of more power. —*Malcolm X*

Theodore Roosevelt understood when he spoke the words: *Speak softly and carry a big stick; you will go far.* The language of a person with a Power point reveals entitled grandiosity, an attitude of privilege. In the words of Castro: *I am Fidel Castro and have come to liberate Cuba. The universities are available only to those who share my revolutionary beliefs. I never saw a contradiction between the ideas that sustain me and the ideas of that symbol, of that extraordinary figure, Jesus Christ.* The license and permission to make such powerful statements emanates from a self-assured belief that encourages people like Castro to come across as effective to some while outrageous to others. Clearly when the Power point is engaged we are not luke-warm people; we step up to the plate and speak with force and conviction.

Let not thy will roar, when thy power can but whisper. —Dr. *Thomas Fuller*

I have a commanding presence, and am regarded as sturdy and effective. Persuasive and influential, I enjoy exerting superiority and displaying actions that make me feel and appear powerful and able to *call the shots.* This need has a strong positive as well as negative force and moves from authority to authoritarianism. I encourage and empower others, or oppress, enslave and terrorize them. This point has pushed women like Mary Kay Ash to rise to great financial success. Asked about her power she stated, *You can have anything in this world you want, if you want it badly enough and you're willing to pay the price.* Nerves of steel, world class cut throat card shark poker champ Annie Duke, and savvy business veteran comedian diva Joan Rivers have both cashed in on having Power points as has Tony Robbins who fathered the life coaching industry and is considered one of the top business leaders in the world. Tony states: *One reason so few people achieve what they truly want is that they never direct their focus; they never concentrate their power.* Using her Power point to crush opposition is the popular story of cosmetic business pioneer Elizabeth Arden and her comment to her husband. *Dear, never forget one little point. It's my business. You just work here. There's only one other Elizabeth like me and that's the Queen.* Calling the shots, Arden's name became a force in the world of fashion.

Heart empowerment of each individual—mentally, emotionally and physically—accelerates human evolution. Uncovering this hidden power is a personal process of understanding how it works and understanding yourself.
—Sara Paddison

People with a Power point: *Fidel Castro, George Bush, Jr., Mary Kay Ash, Chairman Mao, Mikhail Gorbachev, Piers Morgan, Charlton Heston, Elizabeth Arden, Tony Robbins, Annie Duke, Bette Davis, Dick Cheney, Ferdinand Marcos, Joan Rivers, Malcolm X, Niccolo Machiavelli, Hitler, Donald Trump, Vladimir Putin, Nelson Mandela, Hillary Clinton.*

Ultimately, the only power to which man should aspire is that which he exercises over himself. —Elie Weisel

SYSTEM SEVEN

RHYTHMS OF TIME

LINEAR, EXISTENTIAL, CIRCULAR

Time isn't precious at all, because it is an illusion. What you perceive as precious is not time but the one point that is out of time: the Now. That is precious indeed. The more you are focused on time—past and future—the more you miss the Now, the most precious thing there is. —Eckhart Tolle

THE DIMENSIONS OF TIME

Time is the fourth dimension. The first dimension is form, physical space—a line. A surface is of two dimensions, neither being able to exist by themselves. The third dimension is space: length, breadth, height; the infinite sphere; and there is no time in three dimensional space. Every cosmos is three-dimensional for itself. Life is the fourth dimension, a circle, the completion of one possibility. When this comes to an end, it meets its own beginning. Understanding the nature and mystery of time, which as we feel it is the fourth dimension, has concerned scientists, astronomers, theologians, philosophers and economists for decades; we are placed within a time-bound reality and have the ability to contemplate its limits plus experience timelessness. The economic measurement of time, *time is money*, impacts our social system and personal life.

Dost thou love life? Then do not squander time, for that's the stuff life is made of. —Benjamin Franklin

Nothing is more precious than being in the present moment. Fully alive. Fully aware. —Thich Nhat Hahn

The fifth dimension is eternity, life eternally repeating, a repetition of the fourth dimension. Time is a measure of motion, which is how we are able to speak of parallel universes and spirals. The more we know, the more time we have. The less we know, the less time we have. Six dimensions mean the realization of all possibilities. As we go into higher dimensions, who we are extends in time: like Buddha and Christ, the influence spreads. Starting life in a different way is the sixth dimension, time is no longer on a straight line it is now also lived on the vertical.

Time is an invisible web on which everything may be embroidered. We kill time; time buries us. —*Joaquim Machado de Assis*

Essence is always in the present moment, the physical body is history anticipating the future; therefore we are able to position ourselves in all three modes: past, present and future. Without time there would be no physical plane and, accordingly, without the physical plane there would be no time. As a necessary element to our physical plane experience, while time in itself does not exist, like divine-love, it flows always independently by itself and blends proportionately with all the phenomena present. Existence is existence in time, and time is breath. The difference between telling time and knowing time lies in understanding that time is in us and we are in time.

From early morning to late at night, from preschool to retirement, we rush through our lives in order to scrimp on time. But what if time did not control us? What if we felt that our time and our lives were our own? Buddhist wisdom tells us that there is a level of consciousness or awakefulness within us that exists and operates independently of time, transcending birth and death. —*Lama Surya Das*

Time is something we measure based on its passing, although its nature and origin have remained baffling, a mystery. In measuring time we learn that in a single second 2.4 million red blood cells are produced in our bone marrow, that in one second 4 billion impulses are exchanged between the cortical hemisphere in our brain. This quantity that we name *a second*, that we measure moments and events by, appears to be both an inexhaustible well, as well as limitable. The brain has its own internal clock and neurochemically we can speed up or slow down to experience *time* passing at different rates. In certain experiences, though physical and mental things happen, the self is absorbed and energy is not structured onto cause and effect relations. In other experiences, a time duration, how long things last, particularly when feelings are engaged, we are in linear time. Strong feelings of time passing, feeling that the present time is separate from the future, is intensified by procrastination. Time is more flexible than Western culture teaches.

All cosmic phenomena have a sense of objectivity. Only time alone has no sense of objectivity. —*G.I Gurdjieff*

TIME AND OUR MIND

Time is the infinite, absolute, potential of all existence. —*C.S. Nott*

To truly know time we have to be living in the fourth dimension; to be on time brings us out of time. Time does not exist, when you are. The mind, not the physical world, creates time divisions, sets up the notion of past, present and future, measures what is truly measureless. When the mind stops, psychological time stops. Cultivating an understanding of the nature of our mind, coming to know and taste the mind's true emptiness we also understand the nature of time. Time disappears when the mind is quiet.

The present moment contains past and future. The secret of transformation is in the way we handle this very moment. —*Thich Nhat Hahn*

Time, the potential of all existence, has at its center the vast dimension of space about which Rumi says: *Come out of the circle of time and into the circle of love.* Awakening, another universe emerges. The Eastern theory of Time sees an alternately expanding and contracting universe, not always linear, as in the Western viewpoint which proceeds from past to present to future. When we change our perspective on time we break through the temporal structure of seeking happiness ahead, of trying to get satisfaction from objects, events or relationships outside ourselves. Looking forward to things, trying to get there, stops the experience of being here. To be in timelessness is to be here in peace and presence, no longer to attain; anxiety, pressure, worry, concern and stress disappear.

Have you also learned that secret from the river; that there is no such thing as time? That the river is everywhere at the same time, at the source and at the mouth, at the waterfall, at the ferry, at the current, in the ocean and in the mountains, everywhere and that the present only exists for it, not the shadow of the past nor the shadow of the future. —Herman Hesse

Small children have no feeling of time passing. They are full into feeling. Sadness once felt, eliminates the repressed experience of *missing*, which is associated as time passing. A sense of time passing is often repressed energy that arises from resistance. To be in the present moment is to allow the here and now feelings to surface, to avoid the present is to plan the future and reminisce about the past. Energy is changed into an experience of time passing from past, present and future. What is not bound by a time-space universe allows terms like past and present to lose their meaning. Impermanence makes all things possible, and eases all suffering.

It is not impermanence that makes us suffer. What makes us suffer is wanting things to be permanent when they are not. —Thich Nhat Hahn

We must make every effort to break our usual ideas of time. Sometimes this is the chief illusion of all, and becoming free of it our chief preparation. Try to think of different speeds of time, of time passing faster and faster, or slower and slower, of time going backwards, of parallel times, of times coexisting or standing still, of all these different motions of time going on simultaneously in different parts of the universe. Think out the effect on our perception of different motions of time, how they would effect our values, ideas of cause and effect, and so on, It may sound theoretical. After some time it ceases to be theoretical and can become very emotional. One's attitude to many things may begin to change from it. —Rodney Collin

THREE RHYTHMS OF TIME

Time and space are interrelated phenomena. To see all time as one is to know eternity in our consciousness, a sense of endlessness. *Time is a companion that goes with us on a journey,* said Captain Jean-Luc Picard in the film Star Trek, continuing with, *It reminds us to cherish each moment, because it will never come again. What we leave behind is not as important as how we have lived.* The word *Time*, in Sanskrit is the same word as *death*. To live in time means to live in death. Once time disappears, death disappears. This is the timeless eternal world entered when the clock of the mind stops. Beyond thought, time does not exist. What does exist is a cadence, a tempo, a pulse rhythm. We easily know the rhythm through the pacing of our breath. It began when we listened to the rhythm of our mother's heartbeat, the only life and time that we knew. All events have rhythm. People essentially set up their lives to live in one of three Rhythms Of Time; Linear, Existential, or Circular.

To be free of time is not to carry psychological damage over, which is time. The very ending of it is the ending of time. Time is a theory which everybody adopts for psychological purposes. Time is the common factor and the psychological enemy of man. When man becomes aware of the movement of his own thoughts he will discover that this division is an illusion. Then only is there pure observation which is insight with out any shadow of the past or of time. It is the mind, it is thought that creates time. Thought is time, and whatever thought projects must be of time; therefore, thought cannot possibly go beyond itself. To discover what is beyond time, thought must come to an end. Thought ends only when we understand the whole process of thinking, and to understand thinking there must be self-knowledge. —*Jiddu Krishnamurti*

LINEAR

If you don't feel comfortable owning something for ten years, then don't own it for ten minutes. —*Warren Buffet*

L inear people make plans and time travels a familiar path. There is a uniformity to Linear time. Life is understood in the sequential consecutive framework of a, b, c, d, e, f, g. There is order and arrangement. The Christmas hangings are stored for the following year, the baby clothing is put away for the next pregnancy, the job is maintained so as to receive a 30-year retirement, money is stored in an IRA, a time share is purchased for the vacation and then handed down to the children, membership is bought in the Temple for the following year's High Holiday Services, parents and children are called on Sunday, theatre tickets are chosen and bought as a pre-arranged packet for the upcoming season, a summer week is decided and the rental is made during the winter time to secure the spot, three mornings a week is a plan to go to the gym and exercise, it's fun to visit the local organic market each weekend; life has a practical ordered familiar sequence. Life is understood as a succession of events that have a direct impact, fairly proportionately, developed and followed through with few variables.

Time is the coin of your life. It is the only coin you have, and only you can determine how it will be spent. Be careful lest you let other people spend it for you. —*Carl Sandburg*

Time for the Linear person has a story line, like a chain with links, there is an orderly sequence, and the understanding of time has a methodical well-arranged succession. The regular steady pulse, the uniformity of a time-bound reality, where events occur in an irreversible order is standard for Linear time people. Units of time are agreed upon to quantify the duration of events and the intervals between them. Regularly recurring events serve as familiar markers. A day is the duration of time it takes for the earth to rotate all the way around, a year is the time it takes the earth to orbit the sun. The recognition for those with Linear time supports stability and has a safety net, not too many surprises here. The routine rhythm of time creates containment. These are the people in our culture who assume that time is measured and quantitative, it is an objective measurable flow of *befores* and *afters* interspersed with the transient *now*.

He who every morning plans the transactions of the day and follows out that plan carries a thread that will guide him through the labyrinth of the most busy life. If the disposal of time is surrendered merely to the chance of incident, chaos will soon reign. —*Victor Hugo*

Linear time, characterized in the Western world by Newton three-hundred-plus years ago displays time as an absolute physical reality and claims that the passage of time is independent of consciousness. In a Linear perspective time flows like a conveyor belt that moves horizontally from past to present to future at the same unchangeable speed for all people. Our feelings about it adapt to the reality.

Someone's sitting in the shade today because someone planted a tree a long time ago. —*Warren Buffet*

EXISTENTIAL

The moment has no time. —*Leonardo da Vinci*

$\mathcal{E}$xistential people live in the moment with little regard for other peoples moment. They set up their life with few commitments, preferring to live into life as it happens. The order to their life is random and connected to the personal *I*; essentially based on whim, feelings, mood, and a concept of freedom. Often there is a good deal of spontaneity, energy and adventure. Life unfolds and has an edge of excitement, although there can also be a dodging quality to the desire to be free of commitments. Cancelling or changing plans at the last minute, arriving late, not finding a parking place due to poor planning, missing appointments; you will hear phrases like: *it just wasn't meant—the parking angels are busy, it's not in flow, this isn't in the moment, whatever,* and, *there will always be another time.* This is a popular rhythm for people with adventure or freedom points, for mature soul and the self-employed. The desire to keep an openness for free play and not be task oriented often gets confused with what we know of as a child's awareness of subjective time.

To realize the unimportance of time is the gate of wisdom. —*Bertrand Russell*

The Existential person experiences a void, empty space, understanding that everything is always new. Time is experienced with its curves and masses and they see themselves as creating reality. Focused less on an orderly sequence, chance plays a large part in the long term management of life. Hoping to not need medical assistance, not choosing to work in an undesirable job just to maintain benefits, there can be a scrambling to figure out how to live in mainstream society. Attention is given to what's personally interesting, free time is considered important. Socializing and availability, taking a break from routine, are equal priorities to saving money or making a will. The Existential rhythm of time person has an aversion to the linear approach, which is viewed as limiting choices and problem solving for solutions. This is the type who might take a week to go somewhere and many week-ends to do *something*. Life is not linear, a job might get left for another job, even willing to give up saved benefits to make-up for the repetitiveness of the last job. New careers are chosen, divorces happen due to lack of satisfaction, moves across country are possibilities and life continues on a time line with broken chain links.

This year I want to stick a net into time and say 'now,' as men plant flags on the ice and snow and say 'here'. —*Annie Dillard*

The Existential time person makes room for paradox and is responding to those who not only live on clock time, but talk as though they are clocks. These are the people who try to learn the meaning of authentic existential time. Objectivity is one dimension of time, another dimension is subjectivity. Martin Heidegger perceived that we are temporal beings who exist as time, within time. Time in the *authentic mode* is experiential time, a process of living within a pure present. This is living simultaneously the three temporal moments of past, present and future. In this linked relationship of time spaces, the past is construed not as simply the *past*, nor is the future simply not yet, both come together and are integrated in the time present.

Time is a created thing. To say 'I don't have time,' is like saying, 'I don't want to.' —*Lao Tzu*

The Existential rhythm of time person may have difficulty maintaining a tempo that assumes responsibility for time measured. Within the maturing of essence, one learns to become steady; dependability is a mark of one's trustworthiness, reliability and intention are a reflection of one's consciousness, one's level of being. The courage to be as oneself is the orientation for Existential time. Outside things are not seen as dependable, therefore they are not used as guideposts or anchors over one's behavior. Time here is used to become oneself.

Do not be afraid of the past. If people tell you that it is irrevocable, do not believe them. The past, the present and the future are but one moment. Time and space, succession and extension, are merely accidental conditions of thought. —Oscar Wilde

CIRCULAR

Time exists no more for me. Every moment is the same, all differences have disappeared. My mind is being used, but my consciousness is centered in absolute beauty and silence. —Osho

Circular people create a bridge between responsibility to themselves and their responsibility to the world. Each day is an open flow. This is a highly mature position and not typical in this world. Plans are made when they appear, in alignment to true values. Availability is the key. Willingness to make commitments aligns with the integrity to maintain the plan, without the need to have rigid routines or schedules. Essentially appointments are made to keep connections and be in the world, not out of need or duty, and there is a mature responsibility to each commitment once it is negotiated. Future thoughts are based on intention, work flows throughout the day and evening, with a willingness to be interrupted. Lunch does not need to be at noon, as time begins to have a bendable movement, met with maturity. This is the rhythm of the circle, and existence moves circularly. Stars, seasons, suns, planets: enfolding and unfolding.

The one who forces time is forced back by time, but the one who yields to time finds time standing at one's side. —Babylonian Talmud

Time Is Breath

While the universe is being created every moment, once birthed into time, everything is subjected to the laws of evolution. The Circular person understands the interrelationship between past, present and future, and is willing to drop into the present moment, to become immersed into the now. What is time? Time is breath. *All transformation takes place in the present moment.* The secret of time, understood by the Circular person, has been stated by Reshad Feild, *Make the mind your friend and time will be on your side at last.* He illustrates this with the image of a train coming from the past, already set in motion at the time of our birth. Out there is another train, the driver waiting for the signal. When we agree to our commitment and send the signal to the driver it sets the motion. This train comes through a world of possibility, filled with helpers, waiting for the first train to get close. They pass in the present moment, the driver of the train coming in, and the one going out, both wave to the station-master at the same time. *We make time by agreement. God makes the seasons, but we make time.*

Let a person fix their mind on the reality and, having done this, they will transcend time. —Mahabhatata

To the Circular person all time is significant. *No better love than love with no object, no more satisfying work than work with no purpose,* said Rumi. A distinction between wasted time or no time holds no real meaning. Pleasure perseveres in the present; having to do something elsewhere does not have to interrupt the enjoyment, all minutes are used. Rushing, hurrying, wasting time, impatience, dawdling, catching up, later, anticipation, routine, urgency, enough time, how long, no time, waiting; all learned concepts that we are taught, short-circuiting intimacy to get something done so as to move to the next thing. It is all qualitative time. The rhythm of time for the Circular person does not have a tempo or cadence that is fast or slow, instead, time becomes a personal expression of one's own tempo. For the child, who lives out of clock time, in a timeless state, time has no duration, life is infinite, only inconvenienced by sleep. The required sleep duration, beyond all control or comprehension, has a finality, and is based on nature's day-night cycle.

There is no past, present or future. Using tenses to divide time is like making chalk marks on water. —Nadine Gordimer

Time, for the Circular person, does not have a logical nature. The plan is there, things happen, and we fit in with ease. The only thing we can do is to change our attitude, preparation implies time, since truth is time-free, we can be led, life flows on its own. Answerability, accountability, are the maturity of this type. An inner integrity creates the freedom from structures, so the circle can end where it began.

The long road turns to joy: Take my hand. We will walk. We will only walk. We will enjoy our walk without thinking of arriving anywhere. When you touch one moment with deep awareness, you touch all moments. If you live one moment deeply, that moment contains all the past and all the future in it. The one contains the all. Touching the present moment does not mean getting rid of the past or the future. As you touch the present moment, you realize that the present is made of the past and is creating the future. Touching the present, you touch the past and the future at the same time. You touch globally the infinity of time, the ultimate dimension of reality. When you drink a cup of tea very deeply, you touch the present moment and you touch the whole of time. —Thich Nhat Hanh

S Y S T E M   E I G H T

F O U R   M I N D S

C O N C R E T E - S E Q U E N T I A L ,
A B S T R A C T - R A N D O M ,
C O N C R E T E - R A N D O M ,
A B S T R A C T - S E Q U E N T I A L

Our life is shaped by our mind. The mind is everything. What we think, we become. Suffering follows negative thoughts as the wheels of a cart follow the oxen that draw it. Joy follows pure thoughts, like a shadow that never leaves. There is nothing so disobedient as an undisciplined mind, and there is nothing so obedient as a disciplined mind. The mind, the mind, the mind—this is the beginning and end of it all. The quality of one's life depends on nothing but the mind. —the Buddha

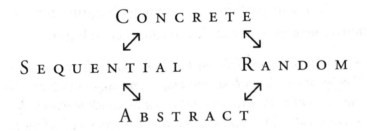

To know and understand how your Mind fires, and the manner in which it operates, actually puts you in charge of yourself. Using the Mind, not letting it continuously wander, understanding and maintaining control, is an expression of self-remembering. Our Mind is limited by our self-consciousness, so to become self-aware is to expand the Mind. One step towards this is knowing how your personal Mind takes in information. Everyone has a two-mode way of thinking. The Mind cannot be concrete-abstract and it cannot be sequential-random, all the other combinations are possible. You either have a concrete-sequential or a concrete-random Mind; or on the other axis you have an abstract-sequential or an abstract-random Mind. Two of the four different approaches are seated in a concrete type, which has to do with objects and things, two are seated in an abstract type, which has to do with thoughts and ideas. Two of the approaches are a sequential type which has to do with ordering and organizing, and two are a random type, which is arbitrary, in-the-moment and subject to shift and change. Each of us has one predominant mind-set in the four quadrants which remains the same during our lifetime.

If the practitioner knows his own mind clearly he will obtain results with little effort. But if he does not know anything about his own mind, all of his effort will be wasted. When we understand how our mind works, our practice becomes easy. —Zen master Thuong Chieu

THE MIND

We use the Mind when we are self-reflective and insightful, creating ideas, thoughts, memories, to build, analyze, compare, reason, collect information, process, structure, imagine, judge, choose, synthesize, know and understand. Connected to time, the Mind is aware of past and future and creates history, records, plans for the future, dreams, sets goals, envisions, has intelligence, comprehension and wisdom. The mind is a conjurer, it appears to magically summon and create happiness, sadness, good and bad, beauty, success and failure, it intensifies pain and pleasure. When we come upon challenges in life, we look at the circumstance or people as the problem, when in reality the problem we experience is located in the mind. A problem is something created by the mind. To create a witness, an observer, and to not be driven by the mind, is to live in truth, and greatly diminishes our suffering.

The single most vital step on your journey toward enlightenment is this: learn to disidentify from your mind. Every time you create a gap in the stream of mind, the light of your consciousness grows stronger. Your mind is an instrument, a tool. It is there to be used for a specific task, and when that task is completed, you lay it down. As it is, I would say about 80 to 90 percent of most people's thinking is not only repetitive and useless, but because of its dysfunctional and often negative nature, much of it is harmful. Observe your mind and you will find this to be true. It causes a serious leakage of vital energy. —Eckhart Tolle

For most people the mind wanders, is filled with distractions. This reality brought Swami Sivananda to observe: *Thought binds a man. Whoever controls his thoughts, is a veritable God on this earth.* Self-observation confirms that, unchecked, the mind drifts, gets sidetracked; it is to our advantage that thinking can reflect upon itself and correct itself, yet cannot escape itself. The mind's ability to know itself is the ingredient to create an observer; it lets us know when our mind wanders and becomes distracted. The ability to watch our reactions, to reflect and apply the teachings we receive back to our own life, requires a trained mind. The focus shifts from taming the mind to training the mind. Following and training the mind, we learn to recognize and release fascination, negative, self-centered and possessive thoughts.

In the Buddhist tradition we talk of taming the mind. By working with various forms of unmindfulness we begin to become thorough and precise, and our discipline becomes good. Then we speak in terms of training the mind. That is the next step. The mind is, when tamed, then it can be trained. Having domesticated our mind we can use it further. —Chogyam Trungpa

Training Our Mind

Buddha placed mindfulness at the heart of all training. Gurdjieff positioned self-remembering as the primary key to awakening. So many on a spiritual path confuse their desire to quiet or drop the Mind, falsely thinking that meditation is about stopping thoughts. Without studying, knowing and training the Mind, to live at the mercy of passing thoughts and moods brings many to over indulge, drink, take medication and other endless external methods and distractions in the quest to quiet their Mind. Unable to remain relaxed, open, to look at our own Mind admidst challenges; not holding attention during the difficult brings us to make Mind be a mysterious enemy.

If you want to know your own mind there is only one way: to observe and recognize everything about it. This must be done at all times, during your day-to-day life no less than during your hour of meditation.
—*Thich Nhat Hahn*

The Mind creates time, when the Mind is suspended, stops, time is suspended, stops. The clock continues to move, like in Einstein's theory of relativity, time becomes a flexible phenomenon. When thoughts stop, there is no time left. Yet, who is watching, remains. Once the Mind engages, then we are able to study this instrument, and be at home as the driver, the one who knows and is behind the wheel, called Mind. Time is an extension of mental events. Certain activities are easy and natural, while some are difficult, according to the kind of Mind we have. Knowing that we are separate, a witness to the Mind, we can choose to study the mechanism of Mind activity, this instrument, essential tool along the journey. The Mind has provided us with great benefits, we have used it to evolve into this century. Technology, scientific discoveries, the ease of our lifestyle, all have developed through the use of the

Mind. It has also exhausted us with our excessive identifications and overuse. To watch it, allow it to rest, is to be in charge of handling it as an instrument under our control. A reliable car is important to get us somewhere. But we are not the car, it is only an instrument, a tool in the hands of the driver. Good use of this tool, the Mind, helps create a witness, to have a watchful consciousness, to become aware, to go beyond the Mind.

Keep your mind quiet, steady and firm. One who cannot restrain his tongue cannot restrain his mind; one who cannot restrain his mind cannot restrain his action; one who cannot restrain his actions cannot restrain himself; and one who cannot restrain himself cannot attain his Infinite Self. —Meher Baba

The Mind is a beautiful instrument when used intelligently. Learning when to drop it, how and when to empty it, how to purify and live within its silence is using the Mind well, allowing it to serve. The Mind can either be a barrier or a bridge. Mindfulness, witnessing the Mind, allows understanding to arise. To study, rather than identify with the Mind is to ultimately see that only the watcher is constant. The Mind moves and changes, the watcher who studies the activities of the Mind is steady, is not the Mind.

We all agree that training the body through exercise and diet and relaxation is a good idea, but why don't we think of training our mind. Once we see how our mind works we see how our life works, too. That changes us. —Sakyong Mipham Rinpoche

CONCRETE-ABSTRACT

There are two perceptual qualities, ways in which we see the world: concrete or abstract. Concrete deals with the obvious and registers information directly through the 6 senses: smell, touch, taste, sight, hearing and knowing. To a concrete Mind things are what they are, not perceived as hidden or in relationship to one another; information is what it is. Abstract registers information intuitively, through the imagination and its subtle implications. Here, information is not what it seems to be. The Mind visualizes and believes what cannot be seen. The Mind looks beyond what is presented, has flexibility, leaving space for interpretation and discussion.

What is called 'mind' is a wondrous power residing in the self. It causes all thoughts to arise. Apart from thoughts, there is no such thing as the mind. Therefore, thought is the nature of the mind. The thought "I" is the first thought of the mind; and that is egoity. That which rises as "I" in this body is the mind. Of all the thoughts that arise in the mind, the "I" thought is the first. It is only after the rise of this that the other thoughts arise.
—*Ramana Maharshi*

SEQUENTIAL - RANDOM

The two ordering abilities of the Mind are sequential or random. **Sequential** organizes information in a step-by-step, logical, uniform, linear train of thought. It has a plan and follows it. A Random Mind organizes information by chunks, in no particular direction. The arrangement of thinking is casual, sometimes arbitrary. Steps might be skipped, impulses followed, ideas, projects and thoughts might start in the middle or at the end, sometimes working backwards, plans dropped to be in the moment; still, the intended result arrives.

Stand firm in the seat of the witness and release the hold that the habitual mind has on you. —*Michael Singer*

STUDYING MIND

Once we study and understand the Mind, through the use of any of the tools in chapter twelve, we train it to serve us. A simple Zen saying reminds us to: *Be the master of the mind, rather than mastered by the mind.* Not to reject the Mind, to use it to learn, to keep moving on and learning something else, something new. We learn a function on the computer or our cell phone and then we are free to use the equipment creatively. This system, Four Minds, identifies differences in learning and the manner people comprehend and organize their perceptions of themselves and the world. Understanding how we naturally take in and process information, knowing what our learning style is, are valuable clues and keys to growth. Learning how to learn, how to keep learning, how to be life-long learners can be accessed through understanding this system.

It is wrong to think that misfortunes come from the east or from the west; they originate within one's own mind. Therefore, it is foolish to guard against misfortunes from the external world and leave the inner mind uncontrolled. —the Buddha

The Mind functions through currents and waves, to understand the mechanism, to use it well, to become disidentified with it, is to awaken. When the small Mind is liberated from all limitations, it disappears, like a drop of water that enters the ocean. Find which of the following 4 possible two-mode ways your Mind works.

This mind, perfectly and fully realized, moves with a clear, tranquil spiritual awareness. It encompasses heaven, covers the earth, penetrates form, and rides with forbidding abruptness. It is a radiant light shining from the crown of your head, illuminating wherever you are; it is an awesome wind, rising up at each step you take, enveloping all things. If you are able to make this mind your own, then even though you do not seek excellence yourself, excellence comes to you of its own accord. Without seeking emancipation, you are not hindered by a single thought. —Daito

CONCRETE-SEQUENTIAL

The discovery that the mind can regulate its thoughts, fostering some, and dismissing others is one of the most important stages in the art of self-culture. It is astonishing how little this art is practiced. —John Cowper Powys

A Concrete-Sequential mind is especially useful for balancing a checkbook or following a direction manual. Putting things in order, following a recipe, teaching others by breaking things down, to have a basic foundation for the subject matter; these are some of the strengths of a Concrete-Sequential mind. Programming a cell phone, buying a piece of electronic equipment and figuring out how to install it, putting together a bookcase that arrived in a box with many pieces, organizing your taxes; with this mind-set all of these become manageable ordinary experiences. Collectors of data, statistics, liking to keep records, this type of mind is good at research that involves specific and logical organization. An eye for detail, they focus their attention on material reality and physical objects. They can study anatomy, learn yoga postures, accurately balance a checkbook, follow directions, make spreadsheets and double check the monthly bills. They like to identify the issues, gather facts, maintain files and focus on keeping track, as they look at material that concretizes, that offer sound solutions.

First comes thought; then organization of that thought, into ideas and plans; then transformation of those plans into reality. Anything that the mind of man can conceive and believe, it can achieve. —Napoleon Hill

Linear reasoning, immediately looking for a solution or resolution, this mind lands quickly and is most comfortable grounded and having an answer without wrestling with the question. Good organizers, excess easily gets carted away, quickly able to decide what stays and what goes, this mind is the daily backbone of a company. Told what to do, this mind receives and accepts. Competent secretaries, a natural editor, grounded accountants, precise yoga instructors or physical trainers, they are particular, liking hands-on projects, clear-cut, literal and practical. They like a structured environment and predictability, they do not like to be wrong or sit still for long periods of time. Experiences are approached in a sequential manner, communication leaves no ledge to dig into the unconscious. This is a person who rarely internally processes their experiences. Thinking is logical, grounded, sensible and solution oriented.

When fate hands you a lemon, make lemonade. —Dale Carnegie

Having a vision, seeing and valuing what is not concrete, soaring into unknown worlds, living in the paradox, are all difficult for the Concrete-Sequential mind. Having to work in groups when the discussion is disorganized, being faced with questions that have no clear-cut right or wrong answers, dealing with opposing views, processing and understanding thoughts and feelings, all stretch their natural inclination. Preferring hands-on projects with a product based effort, seeing the visible outcome, knowing what is expected, as well as the time frame; they are logical, instinctive and deliberate. Making choices, open ended assignments and *what if* questions are a challenge, as is coming face to face with opposing views or jumping into a new approach for a familiar solution. Creativity is not about originality, but function. What is developed may be more effective than the original. These are the solid, practical, reliable *A goes to B goes to C and then D* thinkers, step by step, based in reality, systematic, liking to know the facts, and the accepted way of doing things, maintaining routine and order.

Logic is an organized way of going wrong with confidence. —Robert Heinlein

Educational school teachers who are Concrete-Sequential develop projects for their students, relying on worksheets to reinforce content, stress practical lessons, work under strict time limitations, process information methodically; they are oriented to testing and to results. Direct, hands-on activities, step-by-step instructions, workbooks with detailed information, exact directions, diagrams, flowcharts, computer assisted instruction, documentation; ideas are best applied in pragmatics. Their preferred working and teaching environment is ordered, evidence-based, quiet and stable; they are competent when faced with predictable situations.

The question is not whether to adjust or to rebel against reality but, rather, how to discriminate between those realities that must be recognized as unalterable and those that we should continue to try to change however unyielding they may appear. —Helen Merrell Lynd

Examples of Concrete-Sequential mind: *Napoleon Hill, Dale Carnegie,* hopefully your tax accountant.

ABSTRACT-RANDOM

Like the imaginary lines created between countries, we create separation in our minds. All our distinctions are like lines on water. The mystery of intelligent love brings us together regardless of the lines we imagine. —Eli Jaxson-Bear

An Abstract-Random mind works well with theorizing and Zen koans. Listening, they easily follow the mind, pulling out pieces of thought, creating a story with or without an ending, while staying open to the inherent flow. Looking at the whole situation, a big picture view of the challenges and choices available, they quiet the *drunken monkey with, don't know mind.* This is the person who does not think in a manner that appears logical, and would explain how A goes to H without touching BCDEFG. It could be because heaven begins with an H and follows G for goodness, and today has been a heavenly day. This is the intuitive, orderless imaginative thought, based more on theories, principles and flow, than on specific concrete facts.

Realize that the world is in you and not vice versa. If this blows the circuits of your rational mind, Congratulations. If we spend our time trying to figure out what causes what in this crazy world, we can end up going crazy. The so called rational mind tends to make everything seem very complicated, In reality, things may be much simpler than we think. —Isaac Shamaya

The mystic, poet, sometimes homeless wanderer, big mind in a larger field to roam, not always easy to follow, unless they tame this wild horse of a mind. Schools and the bureaucratic world disregard the fertile soil of creativity of this mind, turned off by its random jumps. Not successful at test taking or memorizing and grabbing information, they feel the frustration of trying to follow linear directions and listening to what seems like endless details. Harnessing this free flowing, rolling stone gypsy mind is no easy job. The joy comes in sudden inspiration and connections that resonate as energy pulses while recognition drops the pieces into a harmonious musical composition. The mind is a device, falling in tune with it, letting the paradox disappear, the incomprehensible, as it happens, vanishes. This way of thinking will remain a mystery; when you try to think reasonably, logically, you will miss it. To know this mind is to enter the mysterious without any reasoning. The Universities often turn away this philosophic mind, just based on examination scores, yet once a form is found, society runs to buy the books and fill the lecture halls to hear their big thoughts and striking ideas.

To speak of waves apart from water or water apart from waves is a delusion. Water and waves are one. Big mind and small mind are one. When you understand your mind in this way, you have some security in your feeling. As your mind does not expect anything from outside, it is always filled. A mind with waves in it is not a disturbed mind, but actually an amplified one. Whatever you experience is an expression of big mind. The activity of big mind is to amplify itself through various experiences. In one sense our experiences coming one by one are always fresh and new, but in another sense they are nothing but a continuous or repeated unfolding of the one big mind. —Shunryu Suzuki

The downfall lies in their difficulty doing the day to day functions: like balancing a check-book, reading an instruction manual, communicating details to an insurance adjuster, filing taxes, preparing for and taking an exam; in other words cooperating in a linear world. Trying to learn the form in a Taoist Tai Chi session, or follow the teacher in an aerobics class is a great challenge; it's hard to internalize and incorporate outside instructions that have sequential movements. Philosophizing, seeing the forest as well as certain trees of choice, they are often the large minds of the world. Information is perceived and used through absorption. Pushed when there are time constraints, they are sensitive to feelings, both their own and others. Routines and orderliness are less than popular, rather, discussion and dialogue are the preferred learning and teaching atmosphere.

Perceive freshly as you enter the world of continual emergence; that rock-bottomed essence of your mind. Is always still, but ever emerging; Always there, as if waiting to be noticed. —Ji Aoi Issi

Abstract-Random people focus on relationships and their emotions, are extra sensitive to feelings—their own as well as others. Assignments with room for interpretation, working best in a noncompetitive atmosphere, collaborative work with a personal touch keeps them balanced and flourishing. They respond to visual methods of instruction, group discussion, and time for reflection. Building rapport is part of the learning experience. They like to evaluate, to process personal experiences. Self-paced learning, such as computer-assisted instruction is difficult. Picking up e-mail in the middle of a project, reading: *said the caterpillar to the butterfly: You'll never get me up in one of those things*, brings a welcome smile. This, makes sense in a nonsensical world of order.

Peace is your natural state. It is the mind that obstructs the natural state.
—*Ramana Maharshi*

Educational school teachers who are Abstract-Random are more at ease setting up a personalized class which emphasizes high morale, humor, journaling and self-expression, rather than focus on grades or achievement charts. Discussions, sharing ideas, video clips, video conferencing, case studies, guest speakers, having a personal focus; learning within these modes is easy and natural. Using a thematic approach to address content, the primary teaching tools are media, writing practice, dialogue and discussion. The technique of theme to direct the mental attitude towards one object focuses the mind to penetrate in depth. In this way the mind has less risk of wandering off, attention is engaged, idle associations have less room to occupy the mind. Thinking processes are based in feelings, connecting with others is easy, since attention is focused on emotional attachments, relationships and memories. Their world is ordered in a non-linear, multi-dimensional way and events are experienced in a holistic style. Perceptive, critical, wanting to be liked, artistically imaginative; information is organized through reflection. This imaginative mind-set has difficulty following an ordered routine, working with unfriendly competitive people, having to give facts and details. People with this mind-set learn best in a beautiful and personalized environment, good relationships, a lot of flexibility in hours and scheduling, are best when treated with emotional sensitivity. Adaptable, easily able to go with the flow, resilient, they handle change well, thinking outside of the box.

The mind within the senses does not dwell; it has no place in outer things, like form, and in between, the mind does not abide: not out, not in, not elsewhere can the mind be found. —Shantideva

Examples of Abstract-Random mind are: *Rumi, Andrew Harvey Hafiz.*

CONCRETE-RANDOM

Does the wind move or does grass move? asks the pupil. Your mind moves, answers the Zen master. —Martha Heyneman

A Concrete-Random mind will often have an idea and not know how to materialize that thought; like adding a room onto their house. The concept is definitive, how to go about and do the task is vague. On one hand they want to have something concrete manifest, on the other hand they are stymied as to what is needed to make that happen. They miss seeing the order that is necessary to produce the thought. The skipping around, not knowing how to pace and prioritize and the avoidance of limiting their options to get into a routine, restricts their creative pleasure.

Killing the mind does not mean quietism, it means undivided concentration. Place the mind on one point, and everything can be done. —Lu Dong Bin

They are good at multi-tasking, at diversity. Having a solid practical idea, they follow that idea in a random manner. Deciding to invest in real estate they might look at places when the opportunity arises, like visiting a friend who recently bought a house, or looking through a classified paper on a trip, but as to actually figure out the financial arrangements and hire a realtor and make the decisive decision, this would be a much longer journey. The particulars and details are obvious and acceptable. The reasoning is well-defined, yet the disorganization and irregular intervals of the project often keep the results from manifesting.

The mind is the flow of information as it moves among the cells, organs and systems of the body. The mind, as we experience it, is immaterial, yet it has a physical substrate that is both the body and the brain. —Candace Pert

Lots of substantial ideas, they research and find sensible material to back those projects, the execution and fulfillment of the plans become protracted, snail-like, caused by the multitude of credible ideas; they have difficulty finding a good sequence to manifest a project. Keeping detailed records and formal reports is a stretch, and so many plans go by the wayside. Trying to buy a used car, they drive around looking at used car lots; eventually when the plan works out and the concrete original thought lands, they feel satisfied. They like not having a routine, knowing there are many choices and not being required to do things the same way each time.

The snake which cannot cast its skin has to die. As well the minds which are prevented from changing their opinions; they cease to be mind. —Friedrich Nietzsche

Once in the flow of allowing the sensible to hit ground, this mind-set of Concrete-Random can be creative, their unmethodical arrangement, not following the thread in the ball of yarn, often leads to finding the knitting needles and hopefully landing in the center. This trial and error approach thrives on brainstorming and has an original and unique approach to problem solving. A risk-taker they are self-directed. Trouble arises when they feel time limitations, when projects need to be completed and expectations are placed on them to come up with one definitive answer, or when they experience being corrected, or having to maintain detailed records, or are in a position to surrender without explanation to another's ideas. Those are challenging and sometimes stressful situations for the Concrete-Random person.

The reasonable mind keeps a balance when the logical mind has lost it.
—*Lin Yutang*

Educational school teachers who are Concrete-Random employ a problem-solving approach to curriculum; using games, independent study, computer activities, multimedia, discovery and experiments. Learning best in a trial-and-error approach, they have breakthroughs with intuitive insight. Focusing attention on applications, methods and process, a good working and learning environment is stimulus rich. They are often competitive, once free to use their wits. The Concrete-Random student needs to challenge and probe, to ask why, to be challenged to think. Naturally curious, risk-takers, learning happens through hands-on experimenting, investigating, finding their own original, new and unique way of doing things. This is not the type who follows someone else's routine plan, they are independent, pushing themselves to come up with originality, their natural curiosity inspires others to take action. Viewing the world in a concrete way, they are still intuitive. Ordering happens in three-dimensional patterns, events manifest in a linear sequence allowing the space to be affected by outside variables. This is not your read the instructions and directions person; sidestepping some of the details, this is an experimenter who prefers to find their own way and style of doing things. Thinking processes for the Concrete-Random mind-set are instinctive, intuitive and impulsive; these are the implementors of change.

Example of Concrete-Random mind: *George W. Bush, Donald Trump.*

ABSTRACT-SEQUENTIAL

Education is not the learning of facts, but the training of the mind to think. Logic will take you from A to B. Imagination will take you everywhere.
—*Albert Einstein*

An Abstract-Sequential mind will create theory, be imaginative and inventive and able to bring their ideas into ordered form. Significant scientific concepts have come into being from this research type of mind. Albert Einstein was able to bring his theory of relativity into form and manifest his work, because his mind, once it wandered out into large pastures could then be reigned in to process and work out his vision. Many stories about Einstein's personal life exemplify the quirks of this mind type. One evening, he was sitting for hours at a neighbors house, eventually the neighbor said, *I am tired and waiting for you to go home so I can go to bed*, Einstein replied, *Oh, I thought I was home. I was waiting for you to leave.*

A great memory does not make a mind, any more than a dictionary is a piece of literature. —*John Henry Newman*

The idiosyncratic manner of landing on a plan or project might seem difficult to follow, yet the results show up clean and clear. Assumptions and explanations are further investigated, ideas and possibilities are put forth and brought to the drawing board, research and gathered facts prove or disprove theories. Satisfaction is reached once the starting point is grounded. The world of abstract ideas and its organization both make sense; they like to know what's needed for a project to happen and are willing to reason logically, taking time and care. Often metaphysical visionaries, sometimes impractical, gathering, experimenting, inquiring helps them to figure out what needs to be done. Using well-researched information, following traditional procedures, they gather and analyze facts to refute or prove ideas, having the patience to work out a project before coming up with a protocol.

The fact that it's in the nature of minds for storms to arise and pass away is not a problem. It helps in keeping the spirits up to remember that the weather is going to change. Our difficult mind states become a problem only if we believe they are going to go on forever. —Sylvia Boorstein

Many grant writers and Nobel Prize winners have an Abstract-Sequential mind. Loving ideas, they see how things fit together. This self-directed mind is respected for its intellectual prowess. Grant writing requires both the visionary and the pedestrian to make something materialize. Comfortable in the world of abstract ideas, less comfortable expressing their emotions. Too much regulation or having to work with people who oppose their views is challenging. Much of the learning comes from watching rather than doing. This mind-set works well, doing research, following traditional procedures, working well alone, having logical explanations. Reading, they prefer information that is presented logically. They avoid appearing ridiculous or uninformed. Diplomatic, often monopolizing conversations, they like having a forum for intellectual debate. Conversely, expressing emotions, taking risks, writing creatively and having too many specific rules are difficult for the Abstract-Sequential person. Big visions, a finger pointing to the moon, this way of thinking knows the finger is not the moon, and has tools to diagram the blueprint, then sets up a program to land on the moon.

The mind fits into the world and shapes it as a river fits and shapes its own banks. —Annie Dillard

Educational school teachers who are Abstract-Sequential heavily rely on lecture format, guided individual study, outlines, well-organized material, syllabi with an emphasis on reading assignments. Asking for documented evidence, an intellectual debate must have solid content, precise information, logical reasoning. This is not the type that shines in creative writing or open ended issues, or uncertainty and large unguided groups. They like written, verbal, visual instruction and the time to think about their responses. Grades bear more weight, intellectual recognition is important. Formal testing is a solid method to evaluate work. Not comfortable taking risks, facing the unpredictable, their creative strength lies in theories, internet searches, synthesizing. Arranging ideas is two-dimensional, beginning with a common core and then branching into parts in a tree-like manner is a common style for the Abstract-Sequential mind. Attention is focused on knowledge, concepts and ideas. This is the book lover working in a quiet ordered environment whose thinking processes are intellectual, analytical, correlative, fluid and quick.

Although I cannot move and I have to speak through a computer, in my mind I am free. Quiet people have the loudest minds. —Stephen Hawking

Example of Abstract-Sequential mind are: *Albert Einstein, Annie Dillard, Stephen Hawking.*

S Y S T E M   N I N E

E S S E N C E   N A T U R E
T H R E E   E S S E N C E   S T Y L E S :
C O N T E M P O R A R Y ,   O R G A N I C ,   C L A S S I C A L

The universe is the periodical manifestation of this unknown absolute essence. —H.P. Blavatsky

O U R   T R U E   N A T U R E

Our Essence is the natural and true part of us, our original face, our essential nature. Essence is what we carry into this lifetime. Essence is quite simple, quite naive, and anticipates kindness from life. It is trusting and due to it's chemical composition cannot be taught to love everyone. You, on the other hand can be taught to love. This essential self, the fundamental ground of our being, awakens us to the beauty all around; allows us to experience the world with the innocence of a child, experiencing its mystery. At birth we have an essential nature, with its preferences, urges and tendencies. Small children respond to the world in ways that show who they are, and only as they socialize do they begin to modify, to fit in and imitate what appears acceptable. Most of us have an Essence that stopped maturing by the age of five or six. Falling asleep to our true nature sabotages authenticity, creates suffering for both ourself and those who are in relationship with us.

According to Gurdjieff, 'as a rule a man's essence is either primitive, savage and childish, or else simply stupid.' The essences of many are actually dead, though they continue to live seemingly normal lives. The development of essence to maturity, when it will embody everything that is true and real in a person's being, depends on work on oneself, and work on oneself depends on a balance between a relatively healthy essence and a personality that is not crushingly heavy—as in the case of the 'rich man' who cannot get into heaven. Both are necessary for self-development, for without the acquisition of personality there will be no wish to attain higher states of consciousness, no dissatisfaction with everyday existence; and without essence there will be no basis of development. —Kathleen Riordan Speeth

At the moment of birth, Essence is saturated by the configuration in the sky, how the planets and stars are arranged. Children essentially grow up acting their natural self until socialization sets in, and then personality forms. The naturalness gets slightly adjusted, temperament restrained, then diminished, even revised, so as to be accepted, liked or to fit in. This all happens through observation, imitation and instruction. The outcome of the years of social dependence that span our childhood are fairly firmly set; ideas, habits, opinions, tastes, concepts, prejudice reflect the status, values and flavor of the family and culture, even though they are not necessarily an inner reflection of the child.

The object of Essence in coming down to earth and seeking a body is to enable it to reach full development. We are told that Essence can only grow to a certain limited extent under ordinary circumstances and that it requires a special food to develop any further. We may be sure that this special food will involve the death of something else. In this case it involves the death of personality. A person who lives and dies when Personality is active and Essence is passive is incomplete, unfinished. In a general sense he is called man asleep. We live and die a seed-asleep, in a world of people asleep. And we do not guess that this is the actual case, although we may have heard this. —Maurice Nicoll

Essence is surrounded by personality, one of our tasks is to loosen that grip, to nourish our Essence so that it continues to evolve in its understanding. To shift our conditioned response opens a space for Essence to pop forward. Our mind does not influence and is not able to observe our Essence. The spontaneity that we knew as children, the wonder and disregard of judgment or repercussion, free of interruption, fully engaged in the immediacy of the moment becomes matured or paralyzed. To see that the personality is not really who we are, to be shaken loose from that misconception, Essence, without the mental image of ourself, lives as life unfolds naturally, everything happening at the right moment, a sense of self growing. Not always sweet and agreeable, all real change of being is a change in Essence.

Every human being is born with an essential nature. This essence is not a 'table rasa' a blank or amorphous mass, although it has blank areas in which the influences of life experience make their imprints. It is a real individual identity with its own tendencies and predispositions, already collected by the configuration of stars and planets at the moment of its birth, and it will grow, if not stifled, into self-conscious adulthood. In this process every one of us falls into the stupor that is ordinary waking state and forgets his origin and destiny. —Kathleen Riordan Speeth

Essence is a gift from nature, personality is a gift from society. Psychology has been geared to study and work with training and taming the personality. *The Way of the Lover* is a teaching that identifies, nourishes, awakens and matures Essence. Eventually we will know to ask and answer, *which one is operating, Essence or personality?* When we shake someone's hand, when we say *how are you*, is that coming from our Essence or our personality. Both express themselves. When it comes from personality, it continues to strengthen personality, when it comes from Essence, Essence grows. When personality is strongly developed it suffocates Essence. Most people relate to the outer garment, and we impersonate what appears from the confined *me.* The false self is who you think yourself to be. The true self is a limitless expanse of conscious intelligence.

One of the chief purposes of a person is to develop from a substance called 'essence', a special kind of reason—objective reason—which will establish him as a permanent brain-cell of all life. Essence is truth about oneself in contrast to social and expected opinions of oneself. Essence is truth irrespective of time, place, and the feelings of anyone. It is truth before God. Personality is truth before men—before the world, conditioned by 'what will people think?' —C.S. Nott

TRUE AND FALSE PERSONALITY

Essence is everything we are born with: type, heredity, nature, character, and is a process, not a fixed identity. There is true personality as well as false personality. The stronger the true personality, the more assistance it can offer to grow Essence. Existence offers us Essence, society gives us false personality which develops while we learn through imitation. False personality expresses itself through our attitudes, postures, thoughts and feelings. True personality, on the other hand develops as a result of working on ourself in light of an authentic teaching, it is geared towards finding our purpose, breaking down untruths, becoming an intentional protection for Essence. False personality is developed in the world, acquired, and at the expense of Essence, although it does shield Essence. False personality, accidental and influenced by outside—events, upbringing, opinions, circumstances, developed through imitation and influences can be altered just like clothing. False personality reacts to the constantly changing outer environment with predictable and conditioned reactions, it restrains, stifles and strangles and is a barricade to Essence. True personality, like the oyster to the pearl, holds, supports and feeds Essence, co-creating for it to emerge, grow, be directed and matured; to be present.

False personality is a compilation of unconscious acts acquired from others, but essence is intrinsic to one, is one's own. Essence in its undeveloped state is severely limited because it cannot divide its attention. True personality is designed to develop essence. —Robert Earl Burton

Our individuality grows as we develop our Essence. But it does not have the strength to evolve and flourish by itself much further than the age of three to seven. To continue the process something has to form that protects and surrounds Essence while offering it room to breathe, and that becomes our true personality. False personality, best kept modestly developed, provides the information and friction that is the basis of work on oneself, it is also one of the chief obstacles to awakening.

Only a conscious man can distinguish between essence and personality. All the ordinary roles we play are personality. Under the shock of grief, the stern business man or the statesman may become human and tender. Some grown-up men, when they have had a good deal to drink, or are under the influence of some young woman, will behave like little boys—which essentially they are. Our task is to die to this personality, which is a false thing, not our own; it may be necessary to melt it down in the fires of great suffering, but when this is done correctly, in its place will grow individuality; a man will become an individual, possessing real will and an 'I'. He will be himself.
—*G.I. Gurdjieff*

Essence does have its limitations, some of which are its subjectivity and its fascination with what it is looking at, and its mechanical negativity. Having a combination of character traits that make up true personality, we have our choice to be in the positive or negative aspect of those traits. Our identification with our personality, as well as the fear patterns that drive us into its negative parts, create false personality. True personality cannot exist apart from its foundation, the Essence self. Wisdom teachers have known throughout the ages that they can communicate with most anyone by appealing directly to that person's Essence, even when the person is not in contact or is unfamiliar with their own Essence. Humor, one of the greatest most powerful tools for awakening, speaks directly to Essence, in its playful emotional disengagement, its enjoyment of incongruity; comedy is used to see funny, to gain wisdom and perspective. Humor and spiritual life require an underlying self and simultaneous regard for others and offers another perspective on the world. It is a gauge for spiritual growth and nurtures Essence. Lack of humor implies a dullness of the soul.

Duality is obviously designed into our machines. We have two eyes, two ear, two arms, two hands, two legs, two feet and two different nostrils. If one studies physiognomy, one can see two different people in one machine because the left side of the body, essence, is different from the right side. A person's right eye harbors personality, the left eye is where his essence resides.
—Robert Earl Burton

The Fifth Way provides tools, which, when used well, creates true personality, feeding Essence to grow and to mature, ultimately to come forth as our individuality. True personality deflects mechanicality and promotes presence, it nourishes what is true. Children up to age 7 and remote secluded tribal community people have an Essence that predominates their personality. This delicate balance of true personality, protecting our pearl or seed, not too much so that it withers, yet enough so that it flourishes, allows Essence of individuality to mature and emerge.

Watch the child involved in an activity. Whatever the child is doing, there is the child. —M.M. Schneerson

MATURING OUR ESSENCE

Real development is in Essence. We still remain constitutional types from birth, yet no longer imprisoned to be used by our mechanicalness. When we resist expressing our true self we are blocked from serving our purpose. We are much more than our personality. Once connected to Essence, true personality becomes transparent and flexible. Essence steps forward, distractions and preoccupations fall away for the world to be experienced from a place of wonder. One of the most simple statements about Essence was spoken by the Hasidic master Moshe Leib of Sassov. *Three Things I learned from a Child. 1. Everyday, children are busy; they are never unoccupied. 2. When they need something, they cry. 3. When that need is met, they are joyful and leave their sadness behind.* To reclaim, recapture and recover our beautiful natural spirit is the beginning. Maturity is a true rebirth, it requires inner integrity, responsibility—freed of blaming, neither society, parents, nor others; we are the creators of our own inner life. Diminishing ego, personality, born and in the present; available to our heart and wisdom we mature our Essence.

Essence is I — it is our heredity, type, character, nature. When a man is born, three separate machines are born with him which continue to form till his death. These machines have nothing in common with one another: they are our body, our essence and our personality. The development of each one separately, depends on the data a man possesses and the data which surround him. For the body these are heredity, geographical conditions, food and movement. Personality is formed exclusively through what a man hears and through reading. Essence is purely emotional. It consists of what is received from heredity before the formation of personality, and later, only those sensations and feelings among which a man lives. What comes after merely depends on the transition. In our essence we have almost nothing, because from the time we were babies we have absorbed almost nothing. Except that, by accident, sometimes something may enter. —G.I. Gurdjieff

Creating a life in the world, one of some success and popularity, hopefully a feeling of *is this enough* takes over. From that place, Essence, the genuine part, progresses, replacing the feeling of emptiness with a feeling of meaning. As adults it is only through weakening false personality that we develop and mature our Essence. This sacrifice of personality is a visible reversal. After receiving the education that life offers, and the better the student—meaning our ability to shine in life, gather money, prestige, experiences—then, feeling a quality of discomfort, brings us to several roads. It is this dissatisfaction that either leads us to develop false personality constraining us to live under more laws—or, we seek something deeper—an inner life. This means that no matter what college we attended, what newspapers we have read, how involved we are in politics and saving the environment; essentially, what we have gathered goes towards developing false personality, not towards creating an authentic self. Until eventually it's not that we are not accepted as we are, it's now that we don't accept ourselves as we are. Or—we step onto a road that is a path of dismantling what we've acquired, that is not about image and persona and acquiring more; we perceive that we could live in a manner that is not a compromise to what is innately our own.

In most of us personality is active and essence passive: personality determines our values and beliefs, profession, religious convictions, and philosophy of living. Personality, not essence, is responsible for the vast quantities of books and articles that fill the libraries of the world, for few indeed speak from or to essence; personality creates most visual art; it speaks in the highest sentiments of statesmen. Personality even projects a God and prays to that projection. Essence is what is one's own. Personality is what is not one's own, what may be changed by changing conditions, or artificially removed with hypnosis, drugs or special exercises. —Kathleen Riordan Speeth

Life itself is this large field to explore, to investigate and learn about ourselves. When you let the false personality or dinosaur scales fall off, you get the energy for the journey. And there are many who have gone before and led the way, there is a trail. So many paths, each leading to five different Ways, this book being about the Fifth Way. Our enthusiasm, enjoyment and valuing the Way is what changes our Essence and being. When we have an authentic desire to "*do*" something, we find the ability to follow that one vision and then that following becomes energizing, effortless. When we have an inauthentic urge to "*do*" something, to recognize our insincerity and allow it to fall away, that awareness brings us into the process of taking responsibility for the maturing of our Essence.

Essence is a bridge to higher centers. If essence is aware both of itself and of the object viewed, higher centers are functioning, otherwise essence has no value, it basically ornaments the earth. We need essence in order to experience higher centers. It takes a number of years, in reality lifetimes, to transform essence into higher centers. Many people use their entire lives to strengthen their features rather than their essence. —Robert Earl Burton

False personality is essentially a mask. It is the lifetime accumulation of mental and emotional patterns that constitute the personal, the person we believe ourself to be, and then we present that image to the world. Just imagine, most everything we know in the world is created by people's false personality, which is not their truth. It is through inner work and inner development that we grow our Essence; not to acquire more, instead to discover and remember our true nature. This is achieved through observing and reconstructing what has been lost, discriminating between personality and Essence, and then seeing what needs to be shifted. And so the work is to study and know our true self. Creating the change comes from continuing to do whatever we did—and now to do it differently, from the inside, without identifying, without being resentful. Life has the food and sustenance to develop false personality. Life does not have the food or sustenance to develop Essence. A strong false personality, a rugged, solid influence gathering around Essence makes it difficult to penetrate, to reach what we are. Essence aware of itself is presence.

Rilke said, 'Never imagine wisdom to be more than the understanding of a child.' Unless one is like a child—in a state of essence—one will not experience one's self. —Robert Earl Burton

The center of gravity of Essence is the emotional center, the center of gravity of the personality is the intellectual center. The center of gravity of the body is the moving center. Personality comes from earth and is under 48 laws. Essence comes from all planets of the solar system and is under 24 laws. Therefore, Essence is on a higher level than personality; and to mature our Essence we need food that comes from a higher source than life. To turn to authentic teachings and teachers and receive energy through mindfulness and meditation becomes a way to feed our Essence. Now, inwardly we are alive. This voyage, from personality to Essence—once we remember and recognize ourself—through effort—is a vertical one. Yet so much time and energy is used in linear, horizontal thinking, moving along on the surface of things. Once we stop and become still, another world opens. Think of Jacob and the ladder. For our Essence descended to earth and we want to take hold of the ladder and climb back up. Personality never descended, it grew here, so there is no need for a climb. Essence, unlike the body and the personality, is deathless; any change in Essence is outside of time.

When we speak of inner development and inner change, we speak of the growth of essence. The question now is not to acquire anything new but to recover and reconstruct what has been lost. This is the purpose of development. When you have learnt to distinguish personality from essence and to separate them you will understand what has to be changed. At present you have only one aim—to study. Essence is truth about oneself, in contrast to social and expected image of oneself. Truth irrespective of time, place, and the feelings of anyone. Personality is truth before men. —C.S. Nott

THREE ESSENCE STYLES

Essence maintains a presence within the physical realm by focusing a part of itself into creating a shell, a body. This is the part of you that is visible, recognized as being alive, the physical representation of you. Essence sees no difference between the physical self and the auric self. Just as there are parts to the physical body, there are different aspects to Essence. To see and understand Essence assists us to know ourself. Our interests, strengths and weaknesses are influenced, sometimes determined by qualities of our Essence; our type, center of gravity, obstacles, and alchemy, to name a few. There are numerous attributes to Essence and as we study other systems in this book we further learn how they can be addressed. This system addresses and describes Essence Style, one form and mode of Essence. In the investigation of Essence nature we begin through learning which Essence style we carry.

Style is joyful if you allow yourself to have joy. —Stacy London

We are born with one of three Essence Styles. Connecting to our particular Style assists us to remember, in this process of waking up in the dream of time, our eternal identity. In claiming a form that has arrived from no form, we receive another means to live in this world connected to our divine identity.

The belief that I am a body casts a veil over my reality. I cling to the form and always take the object as real, hypnotized by the attraction toward matter. In my effort to be present, I always want to have a sensation of a form, a new form, but nonetheless a form. My ordinary functioning and the way I sense my body prevent me from becoming conscious of what I am in my true nature. A knowledge beyond my usual imagination, a new knowledge, will be revealed only when the notion I have of myself is no longer rooted in my body. —Jeanne de Salzmann

CONTEMPORARY

When you look at a city it's like reading the hopes, aspirations and pride of everyone who built it. —Hugh Newell Jacobsen

*A*Contemporary Essence person vibrates to living in the city and enjoys being current with the pulse of the times. They remain informed, reading the newspaper, watching television, listening to the news, opening their mail, paying attention to the tone of life. Movies, shopping, driving into town, knowing what is in their neighborhood, are all common experiences, and the Contemporary Essence person is comfortable in this modern-day milieu.

I have never felt salvation in nature. I love cities above all. —Michelangelo

The city's got the right name-New York. Nothing ever gets old around here, a popular comment that expresses this present-day essence style and its attitude. They are of this time and keep the culture alive by going to restaurants, movies, updating their wardrobe, noting the real estate market, being on-line, current with the award shows, fielding e-mail, checking in with Facebook, tweeting, watching a favorite TV show, reading the newspaper headlines, being of the here-and-now knowledgeable. They upgrade with a new electronic goody every once in a while, be it a digital camera, cell phone, i-pad, lap-top computer, high-tech gadget or acoustic headphones. There is an interest in the newest movie released, noticing up-to-date fashion, being familiar with the diet of the day as well as the health releases of the times, who is the known lecturer in town in their field of interest, knowing which TV shows are popular, the entertainers that hold current value, trying the talked about restaurant. When traveling they buy the local paper and sample the culture and city in the locale where they are staying. Visiting a flea market, using a credit card that accumulates airline miles, going to a book fair, green market, concert, being familiar with the reality shows, all of this feels right and adds vitality to the Contemporary Essence person. This is a present-time type, of this century, and up-to-date.

The chief function of the city is to convert power into form, energy into culture, dead matter into the living symbols of art, biological reproduction into social creativity. —Lewis Mumford

I have an affection for a great city. I feel safe in the neighborhood of man, and enjoy the sweet security of the streets. —Henry Wadsworth Longfellow

Example of Contemporary Essence style person: *Madonna, Kim Kardashian, Jennifer Lopez, Lady Gaga, Ryan Seacrest, Kathy Griffin, Cardi B, Sofia Vergara, Channing Tatum, Prince Harry, Beyonce.*

All great art is born of the metropolis. —Ezra Pound

ORGANIC

Everything that slows us down and forces patience, everything that sets us back into the slow circles of nature, is a help. Gardening is an instrument of grace. —May Sarton

The Organic Essence person vibrates to nature and the country. This person has ease and comfort in the woods, on an island, outside in the natural environment and feels little pull to stay on top of current events, watch the TV news with regularity, go to big department stores or read a daily newspaper. Going to a mall would not be a relaxing time or of much interest, except as a novelty. Nurturing for this style type is a simple day in nature, gardening, hiking, sitting by the ocean, horseback riding, reading in the yard, puttering around the house by an open door or window, an unpretentious modest afternoon feels eventful. The kitchen might have special herbs, and eating in is more of a treat than eating out, unless a restaurant is a once a month event. The comfort and relaxing zone here is in the smell of nature, canning fruits and vegetables, yard work, plants, flowers in the house, long walks, animals and living where nature is easily accessible.

What is this life if, full of care, we have no time to stand and stare? No time to stand beneath the boughs, and stare as long as sheep and sows: No time to see, when woods we pass, where squirrels hide their nuts in grass: No time to see, in broad daylight, streams full of stars, like skies at night: No time to turn at Beauty's glance, and watch her feet, how they can dance: No time to wait till her mouth can enrich that smile her eye began? A poor life this if, full of care, we have no time to stand and stare. —*W.H. Davies*

Intrinsically, the gradual natural development of a day feeds this type. The physical world, the countryside, the environment unaffected by human activity, all support this type to live close to their own nature. To be deeply ourself demands we meet and become the person we are. Communion with nature, sometimes contradicting the rational mind, heals the Organic Essence type through a personal connection to the elemental world. Animals, cats, dogs, horses bring easy comfort, swimming with dolphins or whales in their own environment would be a wonderful vacation. Fishing, mountain climbing and biking, wandering through the woods, a pond, a cabin; natural pleasures through the seasons gratify and make a rich satisfying life.

Those who contemplate the beauty of the earth find reserves of strength that will endure as long as life lasts. —*Rachel Carson*

Too much city stimulation would cause an overload. This person might have a garden regardless of where they live. Even hanging pots on a window sill or balcony will create a satisfying connection and carry nurturance and energy. Sustained by blending their life with Earth Mother and relations in the animal, plant and mineral kingdoms, the Organic person is connected to the elements. Energy is refreshed by the powers of the forces: earth, air, fire and water. A tree is a pipeline or conductor bringing energy from the earth to the sky. For those with this essence nature, to be open to the lessons that creation has to teach; the earth is a magical place and a source of constant marvels. The natural world makes living worthwhile.

I said to the grasshopper bounding along the road—how excellent you are at what you do! —Mary Oliver

Mostly, I spend my time being a mother to my two children, working in my organic garden, raising masses of sweet peas, being passionately involved in conservation, recycling and solar energy. —Blythe Danner

Example of Organic Essence style person: *Mary Oliver, Thoreau, Ellen DeGeneres, JK Rowling, Adele, Willie Nelson, Britney Spears, Harrison Ford, Matt Damon, Blythe Danner, Chis Hemsworth, George Clooney, Rihana, Scott Eastwood, Joaquin Phoenix, Carrie Underwood, Blake Shelton.*

Rivers and rocks and trees have always been talking to us, but we've forgotten how to listen. —Michael Roads

CLASSICAL

All the world's a stage, And all the men and women merely players. They have their exits and their entrances. And one man in his time plays many parts. His acts being seven ages. —Shakespeare

A person with a Classical Essence style is drawn to a different time. Their home, even their office, displays art and collectibles from a historic or renaissance period. Their clothing is often of that older period. It's as if they are living and working in a Shakespearean Globe theatre set. They have a higher frequency as if not really here in this century, on this planet. Walking into their home conveys a theatre quality; now, instead of plants, animals wandering around, newspapers, magazines and a TV set, you will find tapestry, antique collectibles, art items of another era, costumes, classical music, all an ageless aura of times past.

There is no present or future, only the past, happening over and over and over again, now. —*Eugene O'Neill*

A stylistic refinement, music tastes are traditional or formal, not only genres of pop or rock; now to incorporate 17th, 18th and 19th century music composed in Europe. Often the home looks like a Renaissance fair, a Baroque museum, or else sparse and without visible popular consumer items. This essence type is fed by their music and home environment, going to concerts and museums, an old park with classical sculpture, reading about ancient cultures and ways. Bells, lutes, the sounds of ocarinas; shopping for something that was carried on the back of an explorer from the wilds of the far off Indies rather than looking to find something in a sterile mall atmosphere under fluorescent lighting. Bright modern looking shiny colors like bright reds and pastels are ignored for earth tones, browns, mauve, greens, golds, rusts and variations there-of, the color palate is drawn to what looks antique as opposed to newly acquired. Medieval, Renaissance and Baroque flavor, hats from a milliner, gold carved frames, drugstore reminiscent of an apothecary; this current century is not quite comfortable. Pageantry, color and a vital spirit, *where love hath a holiday humour*, is the heart of the Classical Essence style. Listening to the harpsichord, hammered dulcimer, wooden flute, harp, jukebox tunes; music reflecting the mood of earlier times.

Golden lads and girls all must as chimney-sweepers come to dust. —*Shakespeare*

Often a fifth level soul, there is an aura of difference, of not quite fitting, of stepping out of another time zone or planet. These are the crafts people with memory of apprenticeships at guilds, carrying the spirit of rich age-old customs, English spring-time markets, learning a trade to be proud of and practicing it carefully, sometimes only for their own enjoyment. One medical practitioner with a Classical Essence style keeps an old fashioned Wurlitzer jukebox in the authentic design of classical yesteryear in his office and wears a bow-tie at work. With back-illuminated color drums and bubble tubes generating illumination effects, music fills his office transporting a feel of stepping into another period.

I decorated my house like a medieval gothic castle—European-style. Chandeliers and red velvet curtains. My bedroom is pink and black. My bathroom is totally Hello Kitty, I have a massive pink couch and a big antique gold cross. —Avril Lavigne

Different times have personalities similar to people. The person with a Classical essence carries the energy of an older age, and exudes that in their temperament, manner and sophistication. The literature, art and culture of the ancient world, the high period of an art form, temper the style of this person. The energy from old traditional modes, of lasting value and quality, carry venerable meaning. Particular times speak to each of us. To honor our essence, regardless to its nature, keeps us aligned, balanced, refreshed, nurtured and on course, allowing a deepening, a maturing of that which is our natural essence nature.

Sure, I could have done it different. Put my clown in a closet and dressed up in straight clothing. I could of compromised my essence and swallowed my soul. —Wavy Gravy

Example of Classical Essence style person: *Viola Da Gamba, Michael Jackson, Wolfgang Amadeus Mozart, Ludwig van Beethoven. Avril Lavigne, Dr. Alimorad Farshchian, Virginia Henley.*

SYSTEM TEN

ENERGY FORCE
ACTIVE, PASSIVE, NEUTRAL
THE LAW OF THREE

Threeness is one of the master ideas of human culture. It is integrally linked with a vision of creativity, of making the new from the old. It draws upon our intuitions of a spiritual order intervening in the workings of the world—without violating any of the restrictions under which we exist, such as cause and effect. When we speak of it as a law, we can become too fixed. It is an open-minded principle, capable of endless interpretations. Gurdjieff's formulations of the law of three are masterly works of art in their own right. We should remember his injunction that to understand is to think, feel, and sense together: to have the law of three working in us. We understand the law by making it happen in ourselves. It is this that enables us to link with the phenomena of the physical world and begin to see how real change is possible. —A.G.E Blake

LIFE IS ENERGY

*E*ach of us has a predominant Energetic posture or Force. Energy is expressed through us in one of three ways. Ultimately it is useful to have access to all three. These qualities of interacting with life are: Active, Passive, and Neutral. Right use of energy is the science of alchemy. All of existence is energy: mind, body and consciousness. To understand the nature of our energy, the possibilities available, and to use them well, we attain maximum realization of our resources. Every whole phenomenon is composed of three separate sources, named Active, Passive and Neutral. This law applies to everything in the universe and humanity, as well as all structures and processes. It is important to know and to think of the three forces as essential to transforming our own energy. The process of transformation requires the three actions of affirmation, denial and reconciliation. There is at any one time three Forces acting.

Wisdom has to do with our relationship to the whole, to the cosmos, to nature. Wisdom is finding the balance between active and passive, energy and rest, cosmos and psyche. —Matthew Fox

The first Energy Force is Active or positive, second is Passive or negative, and third is Neutral or reconciling. Simply put, the Active Force is the Force that is acting, the Passive Force is what is acted upon, and the Neutralizing Force is what allows the other two Forces to interact. All three are equally Active, showing up with their expression only in relation to one another. Since our natural inclination is to one primary posture, it takes study and practice to access and shift our Energy Force, according to circumstances. Once we learn to do this, our range of relating and living becomes larger, more developed.

To challenge ourselves to mature and to have choices in our interactions we create conditions that will train and teach us to move in modes that might not be our most natural response. We could make an intention to take on a leadership role (Active). We might listen and repeat a story as close to the details as the original (Passive). We could moderate a discussion in which we have strong opinions with the aim to remain disengaged and neutral towards both sides (Neutral). To come out of our natural posture requires concentrated intentional energy, as well as perseverance. We can tell how developed a person is by their mastery of all three energy manifestations, along with their ease of switching from Active to Passive to Neutral.

The energy used in conscious work is converted for future use; that used unconsciously is lost forever. You cannot think about storing energy before you learn to stop leaks. We spend our energy in the wrong way, on identification and negative emotions. Inner considering, lying, idle talk, expressing of negative emotions, these are open taps from which our energy runs out. Stop these leaks and then it is possible to store energy. —P.D. Ouspensky

This is a tool of empowerment, through becoming aware of our options and then choosing with intention, instead of living in patterns or reactive responses, we discover neglected parts of ourself which enables us to have the ability to develop a wider range in life. Often conditioned to see in duality, which generally blocks resolution, using this tool of Energy Force, we open to third possibility, or Third Force. Dualistic thinking engenders conflict. It's me or them, my country or the other country, right or wrong, good or bad, win or lose. Becoming Third Force sensitive, opens a new point of view, organizes thought, assists in creative, self-aware choice making. Learning to access all Three Energy Forces breaks our automatic response patterns and allows us to make determinations based on present realities not on past conditioning or habit.

THREE ENERGY FORCES

According to many ancient systems of philosophy, all phenomena that exist arise from the interaction of three forces. One is described as of an active or creative nature; the second as passive or material; and the third as mediating or formative. The characteristics of the three forces depend, not upon the phenomena through which they manifest, but upon their relation to each other. —Rodney Collin

The most fundamental law of nature, the Law of Three, Energy Forces, is the mainstay of all creative processes, its influence manifests practically everywhere. Nothing in this universe can be created without the combined action of the Three Forces described by it: Active, Passive and Neutral. The three main constituents of atoms—protons, electrons and neutrons—the three-pin-plug, two opposing teams and a Neutral referee, the three primary colors of the spectrum of light, two chemical compounds and an intermediary catalyst—all of these trinities exist and interact as a direct result of the Three fundamental Forces described by the first law of nature. Whenever and wherever something is created, these Three Forces will inevitably be there.

Threeness is implicit in nearly all our human relationships. Our linkages with other people in relation to our various purposes show what is at stake. To associate three with change is the first part of the law of three. Change can happen only when three independent forces come together. If there are only two forces, they either affirm or deny each other, and the situation is static. If there is to be a real change, there needs to be something independent of yes and no, plus and minus. When a third force enters, the other two forces are no longer locked into each other in the same way as before. There is an extra degree of freedom and a higher level of awareness. —A.G.E. Blake

Matter differs by its density. Active Force, called life, has the highest density of vibrations and the lowest density of matter, Passive Force, called matter, has the lowest density of vibration and highest density of matter, and Neutralizing Force, form, is intermediate between life and matter in density of both matter and energy. We can study these three processes on many scales and levels; essentially it assists our self-understanding. There are six possible sequences or orders to how they exist. These are, active/passive/neutral, passive/neutral/active, neutral/active/passive, active/neutral/passive, neutral/passive/active and passive/active/neutral.

An illustration of each sequence, translated: life as Active, matter as Passive and form as Neutral, is:

active/passive/neutral: life acting on matter, produces a form: A potter making a cup; the potter is active, takes the clay, which is passive, and shapes it into a cup, which is neutral.

neutral/active/passive: form, applied to life, results in matter: A creative idea is forced into a structure which kills the idea.

passive/neutral/active: matter, aided by form, is restored to life. A broken bone aligned with a splint grows back and becomes functional.

active/neutral/passive: life, acting on form, produces matter. Smashing the cup, destroying form, thereby bringing it into matter.

passive/active/neutral: matter, acted on by life, becomes a form. We cook carrots, then chew them, and we have the pulverized, disintegrated carrots.

neutral/passive/active: right form applied to matter brings it to life. Rumi used words to inform people, and this continues through time into the present day, Rumi's words have become fashionable, sought after and found in popular bookstores and mass marketed on greetings cards.

THIRD FORCE

There can be no new thing without the third force—the law as above, so below, we have within us the sun, the moon, and the planets, all on a small scale. —Gurdjieff

The same object can have separate forces acting through it in different processes. The Three Forces always are about the particular relation between things. This system of Energy Force teaches balance, perspective, and a way to understand all processes and developments. As we allow opinions and beliefs to drop away our energy is freed up. To observe the three invisible energetic Forces one starts with self, knowing that what we see is also resonating throughout the entire organic world. All events that happen in the universe are resolvable into Three Forces, arising from the meeting of the Three Forces at some point in time and space.

Nothing happens unless there are three forces. If we have any two rules, then they cannot operate on each other without a third. —A.G.E. Blake

The art of using this tool comes from training yourself to see three aspects of a process, until you automatically look for Third Force, rather than thinking in terms of black and white. Each are appropriate at different times, ideally you could switch to any of the three, according to the circumstances. However, each person has a strong leaning toward one Energy Force over the other two and will tend to take that position most often. First, find your natural energy, this is your position of strength.

In order to accomplish what we wish three forces are necessary, of which our own desire or interest is only one. If we accomplished something, it is because three forces were present. We may sometimes understand that something was only achieved through another's help, or through a chance encounter that made everything fall into place. By making use of the idea of three forces, one comes to understand that what seems to be chance may not be, and that our own efforts, though necessary and important, will not of themselves produce a result. —Girard Haven

ACTIVE

Thought is the blossom; language the bud; action the fruit behind it.
—*Ralph Waldo Emerson*

An Active person takes a leadership position in a group and, in general, effects others. An Active Force is most often projecting energy. We, as an Active, make a suggestion about what activity to do, choose, often start conversation subject matter and switch the topic to follow our interest. Active Force acts on the environment as well as people and is the energetic stimulation, impression and impact that initiates; the cause to make something happen. Entering a room, we decide who we want to stand or sit near, easily start a conversation, as well as ending the contact by moving away at our own choosing. Similarly, on a telephone, we are the person who starts talking, initiates the dialogue, sets and directs the tone. Bike or horseback riding, we easily lead the pack, driving, we are a Force to contend with, often choosing to go first, pulling out ahead of the line, sometimes cutting off other cars to speed ahead. We have strong debating skills, will change the rules in the middle of a game, or enter a card game or theatre while it is already in progress, interrupt a conversation having questions before the other people are finished, choose the line to wait in at the check-out counter, and certainly speak out when the person at the head of the line forgets to move quickly enough to my liking, this repeats itself when I am at the ticket counter at the movie theatre box and become impatient. Active energy people view the world as something we can affect. The Active Force is what one wants; the Active role is energy and provides motive Force.

The study of the three forces begins with the study of them in oneself. Active or 1st force can be taken as what one wants. Passive or 2nd force can be taken as what resists or prevents what one wants. It is impossible to see 3rd force until one sees 1st and 2nd force. —*Maurice Nicoll*

Active Force corresponds with the Chinese *yang*, the focused energy of a laser beam, the fiery essence of the mid-day sun, and the Western idea of male energy. It is assertive, decisive, firm, insistent, determined, action-oriented, potent, clear, effective, effecting, focused, specific, initiating and risk-taking, exerting force toward another person, usually doing something to create an effect on others. Yang represents everything about the world that is illuminated, evident, controlling, hot, hard, the sun and heat, extroversion. Difficulty receiving input, and rarely able to take the observer's position of clarity and witnessing, this posture easily shifts, encourages, opens conversations and circumstances, suggesting the restaurant or time to eat and meet, and even when quiet is influencing the gathering. Too much Active energy in a room and we might find ourselves agitated and restless, like drinking a cup of expresso coffee right before going to bed.

Action is the real measure of intelligence. Don't wait. The time will never be just right. —*Napolean Hill*

The Active Force is a derivative of the dynamic condition, it is the realizer. An exercise to develop Active Force in a passive or neutral person is to offer to be in charge of a project, team effort or another person, without following a previous plan. It's the ability to carve out a new routine, to step forward and come up with a fresh way of doing things that brings the Active energy forward. The Active team members need to be, or choose to remain, passive or neutral or they will take over the leadership. The project should be one that requires an Active plan, not one that engages consulting others or books. For an Active to understand passive, they might receive instructions for a project, then follow precisely the way it was given. Active is a persevering, forceful, enterprising posture—pursuing at whim, operative and easily engaged.

I never worry about action, but only inaction. —Winston Churchill

Never mistake motion for action. —Ernest Hemingway

PASSIVE

In the solitude of your mind are the answers to all your questions about life. You must take the time to ask and listen. —Bawa Mahaiyaddeen

A Passive energy person absorbs. They have no true protection and take in what is happening around them. Strongly affected by their environment, they gravitate to an active type and are absorbent, receptive and observant. Socially, conversations are followed and rarely switched or directed. It is more comfortable to participate in a planned event than to be the organizer. Passive offers feedback and is responsive and suggestible. This Force can be devouring and engulfing, since, like a sponge or blotter the compliant energy retains and is consuming. The Passive tone corresponds with the Chinese *yin*, receptive, unfocused, unassertive, dark, mysterious, hidden, yielding, drawing, cool, introverted, feminine. Earth is the ultimate yin object. Yin, meaning shady, corresponds to midnight and dormancy, north and winter. A Passive energy receives and absorbs another's input. They are not eager to have a direct effect on others, incorporating everything that is around, unable to step back from the action and watch unaffectedly. Passive is contained, accommodating and giving of feedback; it is essentially what is considered to be matter and characterized by inertia.

The passive or 2nd force or force of resistance exists in everything. That is, to what we want there is inevitably a force of resistance. If people realize this they will not blame so much as they do, nor will they feel that their difficulties are unique. In making an aim, 2nd force must be calculated, otherwise the aim will be impractical. If you make an aim, you must count the cost of keeping it. When you do so, you will probably make your aim more practical, and not so difficult. Everything that prevents you from keeping your aim is 2nd force, provided you wish to keep your aim. —Maurice Nicoll

The Passive Force is what resists one's efforts. Trying not to express resentment, feeling annoyed by a friends forceful greeting, or disliking the chosen music being played at the pool, emotions try to stay hidden, although energetics may be felt. Entering a restaurant, this type holds back, follows the person with them (if an active) or allows the waiter to choose the seating. Phone conversations have a hesitation, allowing the other person to begin, regardless to who made the call. When in a partnership with an active force, the Passive type asks: *What do you want for dinner, when do you want to eat, would you like to go to a movie?* A lot of easy compliance, as well as wanting to be guided and given structure and decisions. There is a frequent waiting mode to this energy type, seeming non-participatory to the active, and definitely nonresistant a majority of the time. Action is expressed through letting others make decisions. Passive energy people view the world as something that presses on them and over which they are relatively powerless.

A Passive child can learn to take an active role by being given leadership in an area known and comfortable. An exercise to develop Passive Force in a active or neutral person might be to listen to a report or story and then retell it to someone exactly as you heard it. The nonresistant, compliant containment of Passive energy sets the stage at an early age to good learning, which is a successful childhood mode of imitation, a solid

Passive style of learning. An illustration of a Passive position, showing all three elements visibly is in the leavening of dough: the ingredients are flour which is Passive and the raw material to be transformed, yeast which is an active agent of transformation, water which is neutralizing providing a medium for the flour and yeast to meet and the reaction take place.

Contemporary thought realizes the existence of two forces for the production of a phenomenon: force and resistance, positive and negative magnetism, positive and negative electricity, male and female cells. To work on ourself and change certain characteristics, to attain a higher level of being, our desire is the active force, while the inertia of all our habitual psychological life which shows opposition to our initiative will be the passive or negative force. —P.D. Ouspensky

The Passive Force is a derivative of the static condition. It contains all the possibilities for creating the phenomenon. A Passive energy type from a young age creates the defensive structure of resistance, which is an unproductive style of creating real change. Outwardly, going along with an activity, yet inwardly in resistance and feeling negative; this state strongly affects everyone around, as well as their own experience. Passive, absorbing everything, physically present, this energy withdraws through daydreaming, blanking out and being in imagination. As a defense this feels safe and protective, yet is inefficient, disconnected and filled with distraction. The avoidance and fear of having direct impact on others, the inability to step back from action and watch unaffected creates a need for this defensive posture. Learning a simple triad of *participate/redirect/leave*, which presents three viable responses to an interaction opens the door to options that use all three energetic Forces. Shifting and using one of the other two available energies offers a practical response and conscious choice-making. When we have true insight, beyond thinking of ourselves as the *doer* and see our place in this huge cosmos, knowing Passive Force we become closer to liberating ourself.

The world is ruled by letting things take their course. —*Lao-Tzu*

NEUTRAL

The great self reflects things, but does not change them. —*Chang Chung-yuan*

Allowing things to happen: the sky is not doing anything at all, just remaining there. Just be and remain under the sky—vulnerable, open,—and then the sky will penetrate you. —*Osho*

A Neutral energy is neither affected nor influenced by what is going on around them. They are excellent energy in a room with many children, since they easily Neutralize confusion or fragmented energy. They neither act, receive nor respond. Rarely initiating events, socially caught up by others conversations, they do not easily disengage or change a topic. The Neutralizing Force, while it equalizes and offsets, can also obstruct and thwart, as it cancels out undoing the effect of other Forces. The person with a Neutral energy sits and observes—they are the perpetual witness. They have difficulty in receiving input. Neutral neither acts nor receives, it observes, unaffected and uninfluenced by other Forces and events and is considered to add to the category of information.

Every situation in the world is like a problem in mathematics—has a positive, a negative, a neutralizing force (active, passive, neutralizing). The neutralizing force is the form-giving force. —*Margaret Anderson*

To ignore, do nothing, to be indifferent; essentially Neutral force is noninterventional, nonpartisan, it observes. At times the slow, gradual response, like glass sitting on the bottom of the ocean, still creates an affect; over the years a broken soda bottle becomes a beautifully worn piece of beach glass. Doing nothing sometimes is ineffective, yet, not responding, leaving someone alone, sometimes creates real change. A Neutral posture is not giving any response at all—as if a situation or conversation never happened. The caricature of the ostrich planting his head under the sand until the event passes, watching the Emperor parade nude, saying nothing, as if he were well-dressed, are instances of Neutral Force. Sometimes an equalizer, this style creates balance, equilibrium and is a stabilizer. This happens by counterbalancing the two other Forces, when the opposing Forces balance each other out stability is attained. This generally results in a situation where there will be no resultant change, where balance is maintained and brings about a state of calmness and composure. This posture, formless and free from the impress of what will be received from the outside, does not intrude. It is like making perfume, initially taking care to start with a Neutral nonodorous liquid substance.

With ordinary man life is the neutralizing force, but when we have a real aim, the aim becomes the neutralizing or reconciling force. —Orage

Neutral energy is the basis of all meditative states and a source of deep peace. Seng-Ts'an, the third great patriarch of Zen stated: *The perfect way is only difficult for those who pick and choose; do not like, do not dislike: all will then be clear.* Nothing needs to be done. Sit in front of the ocean. Sometimes a pelican sits on top of the water, sometimes a fish jumps, someone is swimming—you do nothing. It is the ocean's business. You sit. This is not effort, but effortlessness. Relaxing in doing nothing, resting in one's own being, indifference, unconcern. The Neutralizing connecting Force ensures the maintenance of equilibrium in all of the universe. It is always from the Neutralizing Force that a new triad springs, it is the Force that allows the other two Forces to interact. It is impossible to see Third Force, Neutral, until you can see first Force, active, and second force, passive. If you want nothing, there is no second Force, in so far as your desire is concerned. Active Force is what one wants, passive is what resists. The Three Forces always act, not just when we think we can see them. When we have an inner struggle between yes or no something may come along acting as Third Force or Neutral, with the result that at this time, something happens.

Without neutralizing force, active and passive forces stand in useless opposition and nothing new can emerge, but when this third force is present, active and passive forces can join and produce results. Man in his present state of consciousness is blind to third force: it requires a higher level of awareness than man's ordinary state to see more than duality in things.
—*Kathleen Riordan Speeth*

The Neutralizing Force ensures the maintenance of the equilibrium in all of the universe as a regulator between the active and the passive Forces on every plane and at every step. To develop Neutral Force in someone predominately active or passive try observation exercises. Learn to be a spectator, a bystander, indifferent, the one who contemplates and considers and lives within the pause. Watch a skit or small activity, then report the details with accuracy. Taking a mediator position in a debate or discussion where the topic is one that we have a strong opinion or position, then remain uninvolved, restating the various points equally, ultimately doing a good moderator's job. Neutral Force is a noninterventional unaffiliated way of learning. It's ultimate power is through osmosis, a gradual absorption through continual exposure. To gain understanding of Neutral Force is to know emptiness as part of the natural ebb and flow of life. This is the emptiness of the Buddhist paradox that states: *form is emptiness* and *emptiness is form*; the celebrated one who awakens to do away with views, ideas, and perceptions, who looks upon reality without obstructions of the mind.

The neutralizing force or third force in a triad brings the active force and the passive force into relationship. It connects them together, somewhat in the same way as the fulcrum brings the two sides of a balance into relation. Without the neutralizing force, the active and passive forces would cancel each other out, because they are opposed to each other. They are opposites. A connecting or relating force is necessary. Neutralizing force is intermediary between active and passive forces. When the right neutralizing force is present, an active and a passive force no longer oppose one another uselessly, but are brought into a working relationship that creates a manifestation.
—*Maurice Nicoll*

Only when you can be extremely pliable and soft can you be extremely hard and strong. —*Zen Master Dogen*

SYSTEM ELEVEN

VIEWPOINT

PROCESS, EVENT, SOLUTION

The real voyage of discovery consists not in seeking new lands, but in seeing with new eyes. —Marcel Proust

POINT OF VEIW

$\mathcal{E}$xperiences are as rich as the one who is experiencing. Michelangelo painting and you painting differ not in the act but in the awareness. He painted with full presence. To be the experience requires awareness, totality. Life is an experience, not a concept. To know our natural inclination as well as to recognize its manifestations is a way to attain self-knowledge and self-mastery. Knowing how we work opens the door to doing a task with competency and responsibility, from beginning to middle to end. Understanding what our natural Viewpoint is frees our attention for inner work, as well as magnifying our presence.

When your mind is the clear mirror of awareness, you will know that you are the outward expression of the essence of reality. The value of our lives depends on the quality of our thinking, our speech, and our action. —Thich Nhat Hahn

Our frame of mind is a perspective. To understand the range and angle assists the discovery. This is learning what it is to know. Throughout the day there are incidents and occurrences, some consist of various elements, like eating dinner, some are circumstantial, like a letter arriving from an old friend. Things look to be the same. You eating dinner and the Dalai Lama eating dinner. Outwardly the same experience, the difference is not the act, it is the awareness, the presence. The fragrance of the rose is the essence, the rose disappears, we still experience its presence.

The most invisible creators I know are those artists whose medium is life itself. The ones who express the inexpressible—without brush, hammer, clay or guitar. They neither paint nor sculpt—their medium is being. Whatsoever their presence touches has increased life. They are the artists of being alive.
—*Donna J. Stone*

We can look at our own growth as a process. Having a baby is a process, giving birth is the event. Getting married so you can have a baby, or to solve loneliness is a solution. Some people become stuck in one mode, having little access to a different Viewpoint. We might take action in our world in an event way all the while our mind and nature could be firing as a process person. To mature and know your world and to train yourself to ask for assistance in the other world creates and maintains the balance.

You never really understand a person until you consider things from his point of view. —*Harper Lee*

Understanding happens when an experience is total, when we enter fully into it. The experience of unity with existence happens when we are available to connecting with our experiences. The tool, Viewpoint, is a device of knowing. Process, Event, Solution Viewpoint have their own advantages and disadvantages.

The meaning of things lies not in the things themselves, but in our attitude towards them. —*Antoine de Saint-Exupery*

PROCESS

Life should serve up its experiences in a series of courses. —William Golding

A Process person views their experiences as a sequence of activities. This person is comfortable with the steps that are required to start and continue a project, and enjoys the stages along the way. Process people follow the structure of a task, are involved in its arrangement and order. Seeing things as a whole, eating dinner is the entire meal and is approached systematically; starting with the appetizer the meal unfolds.

He who every morning plans the transactions of the day and follows out that plan carries a thread that will guide him through the labyrinth of the most busy life. If the disposal of time is surrendered merely to the chance of incident, chaos will soon reign. —Victor Hugo

Looking at a number of things arranged in a particular order inspires the Process person; finding their creativity and interest engaged throughout a series of events that go from A to Z. Various aspects of the initial project remain and linger. A letter from an old friend continues as a dialogue, each response connected to the earlier letter. Closure is often problematic, since the energy remains connected, difficult to cut off internally, easier to create external boundaries when a reprieve is wanted. In fact, if the boundaries are not set the Process person becomes irritated or angry. A boundary could be not answering a telephone, setting a rule, as long as there are clear distinctions to create an interruption in the routine, situations regain ease. The Process person is often pulled by outside conditions, creating inner questions as how to release themselves and move on. Seeing things as a whole picture, the connections to what has previously happened makes for a rich tapestry.

What makes a person a good artist, a good sculptor, a good musician? Practice. What makes a person a good linguist, a good stenographer? Practice. What makes a person a good person? Practice. Nothing else. —Henry Drummond

A Process person is not necessarily looking towards a solution, an answer or a resolution. The focus is not in finishing the project or the conversation, the energy lies in the pleasure of the open-endedness and the discovery, the surprise of the unraveling and the study of what appears within each framework of the event. This inquiry way of living, oftentimes has an outcome of our rising to a higher level of understanding and maturity through shifting awareness and attention to the circumstances both inner and outer. Ongoing, looking at the bigger picture, not looking towards a result or even having a practical formula, the orientation regards most things as a practice, a discipline that produces substance.

If tomorrow morning the sky falls have clouds for breakfast. If night falls use stars for streetlights. If the moon gets stuck in a tree cover the hole in the sky with a strawberry. If you have butterflies in your stomach invite them into your heart. —Cooper Edens

There is no end to education. It is not that you read a book, pass an examination, and finish with education. The whole of life, from the moment you are born to the moment you die, is a process of learning. —Jiddu Krishnamurti

EVENT

The first fall of snow is not only an event, it is a magical event. You go to bed in one kind of a world and wake up in another quite different, and if this is not enchantment then where is it to be found? —J.B. Priestley

An Event person sees and prefers activities and projects to be an Event and has friction with those things that take many steps along the way. Event people want to be moved by the excitement of the activity, and to rely on their intuition. Certain undertakings do take steps, like writing a book, and others are contained and completed in one time frame, like getting a haircut. Event people enjoy taking each step along the way as the Event, rather than seeing the continuity of sequences that are part of the longer term project. When involved in a situation that has many parts the Event person is most successfully engaged by looking at each part as the total, avoiding engaging with topics like *when will the whole project be completed?* Those solution type questions are debilitating for the person who sees each section as the whole. Photographer Henri Cartier-Bresson speaking about his craft captured the connection between the Event and the moment: *To me, photography is the simultaneous recognition, in a fraction of a second, of the significance of an event.* The systematic steps that are performed to bring a project to an end are not foremost in the mind of an Event person. Producing something emphasizes its uniqueness, creating meaning within each aspect of the larger project. The fun is in the detail of the day's labor, and each part of the larger series is isolated.

The butterfly counts not months but moments, and has time enough.
—*Rabindranath Tagore*

Going to the movies is an Event. Going to college is a process, taking each course is an Event, taking courses that ensure a good grade might be a solution that resolves how one will function at school. An Event person moves into the flow, the steps and time required planning for the long haul take energy from the moment. Eating dinner, spotting what is preferred, all items might land on the plate at once. OK to put the cookie on the plate with the entree, this is the meal and it will be eaten as is, not necessarily step by step. Process people want to lay out and savor the steps, the Event person will squirm, and feel as if the fun is robbed, the moment now drudgery. Blocking out time, scheduling, dividing a task into steps and time-frames with goals, is not the make-up of an Event person. The vitality, drive and delight lies, instead, in the unfolding, seeing the part as the whole. The whole, seen as greater than the sum of its parts, retains its integrity, as each section appears to be complete within itself.

If you want to know the taste of a pear, you must change the pear by eating it yourself. All genuine knowledge originates in direct experience. —*Mao Zedong*

To develop your Event Viewpoint allows for flexibility, intuition; being in the moment. To have access to process is important, not to become discouraged with what you are trying to achieve. The reality; sometimes it is a long process before the Event can happen. A miracle is an Event. There are steps that lead to the miracle. An Event person might find themselves diverted. A process person may kill spontaneity and joy. We don't have to change our orientation, we learn to make bridges. Writer Annie Dillard started her year by saying: *This year I want to stick a net into time and say 'now,' as men plant flags on the ice and snow and say 'here.'* When a process person remains focused, in their identification they lose the humanness that is the nectar of the creative process. The value and beauty of this system is to see something about ourselves as well as others, to have choices, keeping our work and projects juicy, our force vital.

If the clock stops use your own hands to tell time. If the light goes out wear it around your neck and go dancing. If the bus doesn't come catch a fast cloud. If it's the last dance dance backwards. If you find your socks don't match stand in a flowerbed. —*Cooper Edens*

Maybe it's because I'm getting older, I'm finding enjoyment in things that stop time. Just the simple act of tasting a glass of wine is its own event. You're not downing a glass of wine in the midst of doing something else.
—David Hyde Pierce

SOLUTION

Every problem contains within itself the seeds of its own solution.
—Stanley Arnold

Solution oriented people are often linear, not abstract, and feel quite comfortable with information, resolution, and asking for facts and data. Conversations seek out information, details. What did you have for dinner, where was the restaurant; this is not a theory or idea person— the particulars matter. Processing is mostly oriented towards coming up with a solution—to buy a car, figure out a health remedy, take a trip, and so forth. The personal realm is more comforting, and meaning is usually derived from a personal connection. This is not the overview, big roaming mind person.

Suicide is a permanent solution to a temporary problem. —Phil Donahue

Hearing that someone is writing a book, the question becomes what are you writing about, who is the publisher, what is the title and when will it be published? The Solution person understands in a concrete manner. Why would you write a book if you don't want to publish it? Actions have a visible outcome; this is a satisfying way to approach life and produces many successful people. The business world is driven by this mind-set, performance, outcome, details and particulars matter and are valued. There are conditions where this way of regarding the world is productive and effective. In a politically challenged environment, poverty, times of war; it is useful to think about, for example, how education or money will take away much of the abuse and hardship for the people. There is an important use and value to learn each mode, to know our nature and then to have access to the mode that is most beneficial, useful to the moment.

Good management is the art of making problems so interesting and their solutions so constructive that everyone wants to get to work and deal with them. —Paul Hawken

SYSTEM TWELVE

THREE LINES OF WORK

FIRST, SECOND, THIRD

Before you can know your Self, you have to create your Self. —Robert Burton

The order of the Three Lines of Work is important. First line work is on ourself, a practical approach towards our process of self-transformation. Until we understand our own life, and verify how much energy and effort is needed to change our attitudes and patterned ways of thinking, until we see how difficult it is not to be controlled by our emotional life, second and third line work is toxic. First line is work for ourself in the effort to *know ourself* and we proceed by observing, gathering information without judgment, without trying to change or alter what we see. This is practical and straightforward; it's witnessing our life. As the illusions, the lies drop away, as our practice deepens, a certain quality of attention is developed towards self-awareness. It's self-knowledge, understanding and awareness that produce this change.

During moments of self-remembering, attention is divided between the surrounding environment and one's inner self. Perceptions are clear and undistorted, both interiorly and exteriorly. Moments of self-remembering do occur gratuitously in life: most of what is remembered vividly is recorded during these flashes. The deliberate attempt to produce such moments, to sustain them and deepen them, is the backbone of the first line of work. —Kathleen Riordan Speeth

BALANCE ANCHORS UNDERSTANDING

Who am I underneath the chatter and distractions and busyness of doing? Being present frees us to experience our life. When we are not present energy is extracted from us; presence and mindfulness refresh energy. Until we learn to develop ourselves, our relations to others and to the world is theoretical and imaginary. We are robbed of the experience and authentic expression of our self through the pushes and pulls that create reactions and distractions. It is fundamental to come into a relationship with our self for there to be something higher than living a day to day mechanical life. Life provides the lessons, and first line work is for the individual, in second line we look to others, and third line work relates to a greater manifestation beyond ourself. Unless we work on all three we are imbalanced and lack the understanding that anchors transformation.

All search is vain, until we begin to perceive that wisdom is within ourselves.
—*Swami Vivekananda*

Once first line work, self-study, is firmly undertaken, second and third line work become possible. Being conscious of our inner life and what it means to awaken or to have conditioned responses brings us to a place where we effect ourselves and life in a real way. When we notice how we are and make efforts to create an inner struggle between yes and no our self-reflection starts to develop our ability for true inner work.

When you own your breath nobody can steal your peace. —*author unknown*

The images that we form of ourselves obstructs our ability to see, interfering with an authentic experience of life. First line work aims to break the spell, to separate us from the hypnotic power of our self-invented delusional mechanical lives, and through self-recognition to eventually carry us into truth and reality. Only through experiencing life will we know it. The second and third line, once we have created self-awareness, dissolves that fictitious self-image by putting out the practical application of what we have learned. Holding steady to our real experience of ourselves, our practical knowledge teaches us what is usable for our growth. We progress in our inner work in relationship to our willingness to observe our resistance to reality, our attachment to our self-image and our fear. Second line is ourself reflected and in relation to another. Interdependent. Once honoring our own dignity we can dignify another. Breaking the illusion and developing an objective space inside that observes without judgment brings about direction and leads to self-knowledge. True self-knowledge is different from the images we have about how we are.

To *be in the world and not of it*, allows for the separation; to enter life and pass through it we awaken to an inner liberation that brings us to the second and third line. Third line work is to expand, to bring what we have realized out into the world. The value of our efforts are reflected as we cultivate the ability to serve ourself and others, allowing the possibility of action versus reaction. The Three Lines of Work are about being responsible to myself, to others, the planet; to living truthfully, intentionally, mindfully.

To renounce the world means to give up your attachment to the world. It does not mean that you have to separate yourself from it. The very purpose of our doctrine is to serve others. In order to serve others you must remain in the society. You should not isolate yourself from the rest. —the *Dalai Lama*

The Three Lines of Work firmly exemplify: do not work for results, to be thankful for the opportunity to have sincere efforts, to know what to die to and ultimately to be born to understanding and wisdom. This is not about ambition and success, the Three Lines are aimed at non-identification with life itself. To use life as a means of working on ourself, to ask how to use what we have been given, to be willing to experiment, to observe what happens and to learn from that experience is miraculous and worth far more than we could ever pay for it.

To work simply for other people and not on yourself is inexact. To work on yourself and regard other people as a nuisance is mistaken. And again to work on yourself in connection with other people without thinking of the work itself and what it needs is unsound. —Maurice Nicoll

To understand and incorporate the Three Lines of Work makes a dramatic shift in how we live. It directly effects the quality of our relationship to self, to partner, family, community, work, humanity, and whatever else is in our world waiting to be created. To live balanced in this manner we become someone inspiring and uplifting to be with, have a rich inner life, now able to serve the world.

The danger of working only on the First Line is that one imagines one has gained something. The Second and Third Lines help to take us out of that imagination by promoting practical application of what one has gained. —Girard Haven

FIRST LINE WORK

The purpose of practice and the activity you have in everyday life is to study yourself. To study yourself is to forget about yourself. —Shunru Suzuki

First Line Work is work on myself, the efforts made to promote self-understanding. Until I understand myself, it is impossible to understand much about anything around me. What do I want? The first step, self-study, assists in becoming accustomed to watching myself. Learning to observe without identification, impartially, self-understanding develops. Burning from the inside, releasing the stories of my life, discharging everything that has power over me, I am no longer blackmailable. Personal aim representing the level of my understanding begins to form. This assists my inner work. Actively searching for what is needed, what is true, having a clear intention, taking in, incorporating from my own activity and specific intent, this exploration includes reading, self-observation and practical day-to-day living. Following the call to *know thyself* involves collecting data about myself without any effort made towards change or energy placed on judgment. Focused and undistracted, studying and investigating who I am and what I want is First Line Work.

To understand yourself is the beginning of wisdom. You are the content of your consciousness, in knowing yourself you will know the Universe. —*Krishnamurti*

This line is personal, self-centered and egocentric. *The true self,* reports Gangaji, *is a limitless expanse of conscious intelligence.* The risk of working exclusively on First Line is in imagining that I have gained something; that I am already in possession of knowing myself. Acknowledging my limited range of conditioned responses sets the stage for all self-study. To truly help another I must first learn to help myself; helping others is often based on the lazy avoidance to do the harder work of inner evolution.

When you try to understand everything, you will not understand anything. The best way is to understand yourself, and then you will understand everything. —*Shunryu Suzuki*

Buying clothes, brushing teeth, getting a driver's license, therapy sessions, exercising at a spa, spiritual autolysis, meditating, making my lunch, doing my laundry, taking a class, having a yoga practice, anything done for myself; collecting information in this direction of wanting to know who I am, is First Line. Working to change the mechanicalness of my behavior, studying myself and the systems towards this effort is considered to be the crucial and most important work. Self-study requires that I have gathered data about the subject matter, which in this case is myself. How I act in the supermarket, how I feel standing in line, what my body is like as I sit to meditate, do I follow rules as I wait at the office of motor vehicles? If vegetarian, what is it like to eat meat for one week, or to fast for three days, to turn television and cell phone off for the week-end. If left-handed, using my right hand for answering e-mail, maintaining silence until noon, watching and gathering information, I am the experiment, all part of this journey. What distracts me from my intention to keep a daily journal? How are my buttons pushed when driving on the interstate? How do I respond internally when someone doesn't like me or blames me. What is triggered when I am praised and flattered, included or excluded? The journey starts with myself. As the facts come in, I become less engaged with my personality and more involved in the study.

There is a huge amount of freedom that comes to you when you take nothing personally. —Don Miguel Ruiz

Our ordinary ideas, our ordinary knowledge; will not change our being and probably only increase our fixity in our present state of being. If you think that you know already, then you will not take the knowledge of this work seriously. If you are quite sure that you know what is right and wrong, you will not be able to change. To work only for yourself would only increase your self-love, your self-vanity. The more you see in yourself the more you see in other people. If you are blind to yourself you will never understand other people, and, as you know, one of the things we are seeking in this work is understanding which is said to be the most powerful force that we can

create in ourselves. The word 'create' is used in regard to understanding.
—*Maurice Nicoll*

Initially, the friction creates an internal space, jars something loose, and my habits become more apparent. To not be so comfortably unconscious of myself until ultimately the beginnings of a real presence, an observer emerges and self-awareness is born. With awareness, something real can be learned. It is always possible to make efforts, even though there are no guarantees about the result of those efforts. I can still see something more being possible with additional effort or in a different scenario. Looking at, experiencing and accepting myself the way that I am, impartially witnessing, to pay attention, to stop lying about how I manifest, a new level of self-understanding becomes available.

If the First Line is work for yourself, what does that mean when the only 'self' you know is the one you are trying to escape from? —*Girard Haven*

Self-study brings into focus my personality and ambitions, until they become less believable, lose some of their force. The practice of writing down what you think is true, until you come up with something you know is true, is self-digestion, the distillation of self. Jed McKenna describes the practice and calls it spiritual autolysis: *This is not journaling or record keeping, personal awareness or self-exploration, it's not about personal awareness or self-exploration. It's not about feelings or insight. It's not about personal or spiritual evolution. This is about what you know for sure, about what you are sure you know is true, about what you are that is true.* Using your writing to reveal and demystify your beliefs and self-deceptions, to smoke out what is the fiction you have assumed is you, to discover what is true is powerful First Line Work. Write and write more, follow your writing, eliminate the excess, keep slicing out ego, what's called *monkey mind.* Speaking truth, reading truth, writing truth and hearing truth, until one day Truth is acknowledged as reality. Relinquishing the illusion of control, uprooting our idea of ourself carries us across that barrier named *ego*. Now, relationships that require responsibility and self-control become possible, that of being with others, all of this paves the way for second line work.

I observe myself and I come to know others. —Lao-Tzu

Until we understand ourselves, it is not really possible to understand much about anything around us. —Girard Haven

SECOND LINE WORK

The hardest thing for people, is to endure the manifestations of others. —*G.I. Gurdjieff.*

Second Line Work is myself in relation to another. It is about self-awareness, as I interact with others. The friction, irritation, inconvenience, negotiations, compromise, discomfort and reflection, as well as the companionship, friendship, love, partnership and communion, all create the opening and energy needed for the work of transformation. Second Line Work happens inside me, called inner work, and involves the effort to create kindness, consideration, thoughtfulness, truth-telling, sensitivity, compassion towards others. The required self-denial, patience, compromise and sacrifice makes for a larger more beautiful life. This Line involves communicating and sharing what I have recognized in first line work. To know in detail, with clarity, how and who I am, and to be willing to honestly convey that, makes Second Line Work work.

The Second Line of work provides special conditions and support in the effort to become aware of one's way of relating to other people, and opportunities to practice new ways of being with others. —*Kathleen Riordan Speeth*

To be willing to experience other peoples personalities without blaming, criticizing or judging them and to not be reactive is the deepening of my inner work. Seeing the strategies, the attempts at solutions, the self-deception and play of appearances people take on to avoid emptiness, and thereby miss realizing the truth of their being, is a difficult reflection. To learn about myself is the first step, to be able to relate that to the outside world is the fruit or produce. To be with a friend or partner or child as they complain and are negative is a perfect moment for Second Line Work. Having watched myself complain and be negative, remembering the discomfort that caused me, now, finding compassion and forgiveness towards another, this is the practical expression of real love. Love is no longer seen as the goal, it's the cause. Everything in our life is dropped to focus on the moment, with eyes open we are alive.

To endure the manifestations of others is a big thing. Start by making your aim the ability to bear one manifestation of one person that you cannot now endure without nervousness. If you 'wish' you 'can.' Without 'wishing' you never 'can.' Wish is the most powerful thing in the world. With conscious wish everything comes. —G.I. Gurdjieff

Practical application of everything that I learned in the first line happens here. The scale shifts, expands to include the rest of humanity. Bonding, communion, sharing; my openness comes from knowing what a human being is, loosening self-interest, self-importance, and self-involvement: everything is risked to learn to love another. To now move beyond the self-serving self-absorbed reactive relating that is part of first line living, to go beyond resistance and withholding of myself, to sacrifice self-importance, to refrain from only serving myself, I am now moved out of myself into a larger scale. The ego resists the naturalness of good manners and consideration, feeling constrained, sees it as unnatural.

It is you who must help the universe. —Swami Vivekananda

Through first line work I see the challenge to shift and alter myself, yet I arrive at Second Line expecting others to behave differently for my convenience. Here, in this Second Line, I see all people as the manifestation of life, expanding the circle of love to many. Through the reflection of others, releasing my separateness, I become whole. Allowing my hidden places to be exposed, my humaneness extended to others, living with kindness, I am no longer self-absorbed. Finding a way to overcome ego, ignite what I imagined as *my life*, valuing true communication with another, projecting myself as a genuine human being addresses mutual humanness.

External considering, a fundamental exercise in the practice of love, is responding to the others wants or needs without inward identification. Only one who is relatively conscious can play a tune on those he or she meets, rather than reacting helplessly to the world. —Kathleen Riordan Speeth

Knowing how to be truthful and playful as I interact and work with others, not complaining and critical, regardless to the emotional life of my companions, is the focus of Second Line Work. To give and receive, to be honest and direct, to love another; this is the domain of Second Line Work.

One log will not burn by itself, but with a little kindling a number of logs leaning against each other will make a good fire. —Sufi saying

THIRD LINE WORK

Selfless service is the heart of the Third Line of Work, and since any selfless action is beyond the capacity of human beings in the ordinary levels of consciousness, this line of work cannot involve any sustained effort until personality is, at least to some degree, disarmed and the level of consciousness improved. —Kathleen Riordan Speeth

Third Line is work for the community; whether it be family, friends, acquaintances, my sangha, the complex I live in, a school, place of business, city, world or the planet. At this point the harvest of first and second line work is brought forth to manifest all the efforts and fulfillment of what has gone before. In the Third Line the work is from the inside to the outside. The Third Line, built on the efforts of first and second line, is concerned with being in service to the truth of our being, however that service looks; it's where we give from that place where we live. It can be smiling, speaking from the heart, going to a nursing home or orphanage and bringing gift baskets, driving people to voting booths, straightening the exercise studio for my yoga community, preparing dinner for family, tutoring children after school, writing a book, opening my home to a meditation group, giving when the recipients don't know my identity, enabling others to become self-reliant, traveling to disaster areas and assisting in hurricane or tsunami or earthquake relief efforts; any task for community done with care and attention is Third Line Work. It's always about paying attention, attention is energy, connecting ourselves to all others; cultivating interbeing. The principle of service is to give more than I take and to use myself to contribute to the spiritual progress of the world.

Intelligence is impartial; no man is your enemy, no man is your friend. All alike are your teachers. Your enemy becomes a mystery that must be solved even though it takes ages; for man must be understood. Your friend becomes a part of yourself, an extension of yourself, a riddle hard to read. Only one thing is more difficult to know—your own heart. Not until the bonds of personality be loosed can that profound mystery of self begun to be seen. Not till you stand aside from it, will it in any way reveal itself to your understanding. Then, and not until then, can you use all its powers, and devote them to a worthy service. —Mabel Collins

Third Line Work is no longer self-serving and eliminates the self-importance that permeates most people. This Line is about working on the scale of the whole of humanity and higher forces, a bigger sense of myself and my position as a person on this planet. Now I engage spiritual laws, connecting myself to something that exists on a much larger scale. Similar to the movement on the Enneagram circle, once going around the whole circle, 9 returns again to 1 in a new way, (System One) here, too, once mastering Third Line Work I return to a higher level of first line work, now with a expanded new vision. Freed of distractions and the idea of self-importance or success or reward, having burned away the ego of personal agenda, to quote Thoreau: *only that day dawns to which we are awake.* Knowing that a line of time is a curve, to return with a deepened heightened consciousness, to see myself anew and refine what's not in alignment, follows the natural flow of life.

Relating to others depends on the science of external impressions. We do not notice how we behave and so often give a wrong impression to other people. It means acting towards another person in such a way that the other person can understand you. It requires conscious attitude towards the other person. As a rule we are extremely clumsy with one another. We make a wrong impression on someone without knowing it. That is because we do not know ourselves enough through self-observation and therefore do not know about the other person internally. —Maurice Nicoll

Eventually we are working on all Three Lines simultaneously. This is true service, seeing what is needed and being available. Spiritual practices applied in life in loving kindness, friendship, in the recognition and service of truth—our human connections—this is living from the heart. A beautiful, balanced and harmonious way to live. To regard all humankind with tenderhearted empathy, service with devotional commitment, creates this connection. Boundaries vanish, immigration laws and passports seem foolish; this is about one earth, one planet, one people. Third Line Work encourages community, a circle of lovers sometimes located throughout the world. Third Line Work feeds love and compassion, relieves suffering, deepens generosity.

You must not lose faith in humanity. Humanity is an ocean; if a few drops of the ocean are dirty, the ocean does not become dirty. —Mahatma Gandhi

To see that our happiness is not separate from the happiness of others, aware of the suffering in this world we practice looking deeply into ourselves and others to recognize all the causes and conditions that have brought about the difficulties and actively build brotherhood and sisterhood to realize collective awakening. —Thich Nhat Hahn

SYSTEM THIRTEEN

PRIMARY ENERGY LEAKS

IMAGINATION

FORMATORY THINKING

IDENTIFICATION

EXPRESSION OF NEGATIVE EMOTION

UNNECESSARY TALK

Every normal person has quite enough energy to begin work on himself. It is only necessary to learn how to save the greater part of the energy we possess for useful work instead of wasting it unproductively—on the constant waste of attention. —G.I. Gurdjieff

All of life, existence itself, is Energy. Body, mind, soul, and all matter is Energy, each vibrating at different frequencies. The more Energy we misuse, the less we have available, the vitality we conserve and hold becomes available for our work of transformation. Our Leaks of Energy are what exhaust us at the end of a day. We have the option to live weakened, spent, or to experience how to create and preserve Energy, as if plugged into a battery charger, continuously recharging. The psychic energies we waste on useless expenditure is a sign of not understanding ourself, squandering and misspending the substance of ourselves on useless distractions. Throwing away what is needed for the development of our psychic Energy wastes the very substance that is essential, that leads to our real self.

The purpose of life is to transform energies from a lower level to a higher level—and this is the real thrust behind evolution—because as life becomes more advanced and complex, it becomes capable of transmuting higher and higher levels of energy. You are uniquely capable of raising the level of energy you can personally transmute. As you learn to work on yourself, and you awaken and grow more conscious you begin to transmute higher and higher levels of energy. —Allan Clews

Eventually, once understanding how our time and aliveness is mishandled, we work with the habits and routines that developed throughout our life to create our Energy Leaks. Set and conditioned over years, only self-understanding and intentional day labor chips away the sediment to renew ourselves to reclaim vitality, enabling us to live invigorated, with clean, clear, fresh vibrancy, regardless to our age or circumstance.

We are energy itself, with all of its inherent possibilities. Everything is energy and cannot be destroyed. —T. Andrews

ENERGY: UPLIFT, TRANSFORM OR WASTE

Balancing and blending the natural energies of body, emotions and mental processes offers an entry into the spirit world where transformation of Energy takes place, there, unable to be destroyed, only changing form. One Biblical Old Testament reference states that beneath the Almighty's feet was a pavement of sapphire stone, like the very heaven for clearness. Essentially telling us, yes, we can uplift/transform our *bricks*, our obstacles and misfortunes into precious radiant gemstone, making treasure from our suffering, able to transform barbs, swords that are aimed at us, words that come as poison, into gemstones and flowers.

This tool teaches us to become sensitive to our Energy using it economically, understanding when to flow it outward, when to direct it inward; an available tool, a yardstick, a guideline. Conscious use of

Energy is an investment, on the other hand vitality used involuntarily and unnecessarily is a wasteful expenditure. Transforming Energy creates a fresh supply. Energy Leaks detract from the quality of our life, rather we have the option to create as well as to store aliveness. Once we seal these sources of wastage, plug Energy Leaks at their source, our natural power is increased. It's like driving a vehicle with tires that are leaking air, slowing our movement, not the most comfortable ride, often leading to the drama of a flat tire or an accident.

To work on yourself you have to learn how to plug up all of your leaks and conserve your energy, so that you can then use this energy to transform yourself. You waste your energy on things such as identification, internal considering, wrong work of the centers, imagination, daydreaming, negative emotions, unnecessary muscular tension and movements, unnecessary talking and internal dialogue, lying, and the misuse of sexual energy. —Allan Clews

How we live our life does matter. Our preferences—who we spend time with, what movies we see, whether we feel dulled or vital, the books we read, what we think and talk about, the environment we live and work in, nutritional decisions, exercise, habits; all of our choices either enhance or debilitate our Energy. Our moment-by-moment choices either nourish, heal and uplift, or toxify, slowly poisoning our bodies and spirit. Transforming Energy is an essential tool for awakening. The primary obstacle to awakening is that the life force needed to awaken is continuously leaking away. Isn't it an amazement that we have to be taught to live in the present, and to then learn to enjoy the abundance of free available Energy!

G.I. Gurdjieff likened human beings to great balloons that have a constant source of air being pumped into them. But these balloons remain only partially full due to a number of leaks. Our leaks are holes through which available energy flows out and gets wasted. This needless drainage keeps us from feeling fully alive and operating at maximum potential. It keeps us from having the energy and focus to be aware. Plugging the leaks increases available energy. Every time a leak is plugged, our balloon inflates and we feel more alive. Any significant transformation must take into account one's own individual pattern of leaks. —Don, Martha Rosenthal

The following are the five principal sources of energy loss. Find your primary Energy depletion:

I - IMAGINATION

Your thoughts are like a camel driver, and you are the camel. —Rumi

Imagination is a veil that covers reality, and is claimed to be the most persistent obstacle to awakening. It is also the natural state of men and women. In Imagination is where most people live. It's an automatic function ready to interfere with each moment, a result of uncontrolled attention. Our consciousness disappears in the stream of Imagination. The world of drama, illusion, daydreams, self-absorption, distractions, keeping busy, stories; they are all backdrops for daily life. The opposite of Imagination is *to be here now.* To be in control of attention, focused in the present moment, fostering presence, turns off the Imaginary life that is playing in our head. To be in the present moment creates energy. To be in Imagination, to be engaged in the past or busy with the future, not living in the present, worrying and wandering, planning, random associations, reminiscing, sentimentalizing, obsessing, projecting, ruminating, thinking of what could go wrong, feeling that you are not ok, holding grudges, resentment, trying to figure out what might happen, spacing out, holding on to old memories, fantasizing; these are some of the various colorations of Imagination.

Imagination and day-dreaming serve no real useful purpose—because they have no real aim except to gratify the impulse of idle self-indulgence. And so they are not directed towards obtaining anything of real value. The sheer folly and wastefulness of this activity becomes apparent when people use their imaginations negatively and begin to obsess over the terrible things that could happen to them and their loved ones and fret about imagined illnesses and calamities. —Alan Clews

Being in Imagination at different moments throughout the day saps energy, tires us out. We indulge our Imagination to gratify the impulse of idle self-indulgence. All mental gyrations are distractions that rob us from being available, keep us tied up, unable to still ourselves and live peacefully. Our preoccupation, indulgence with anything that is at the expense of our presence is difficult to catch since thoughts that continuously arrive appear more as entertainment than our own state of simple presence. Internal daydreams, fantasizing and intrusive arbitrary thoughts about everything and nothing in particular, called unnecessary thinking, fill a day. An elderly woman once confided to me that everything she had worried about throughout her 84 years had never actually happened. That thought gave her permission to live more spontaneously, releasing the mental concerns that impeded her availability to do what she loved; once renewed, freed of negative Imagination her vitality resurfaced, unworried she was able to take a train from NY to Connecticut to go to her daughter's art show opening, willing to *see what wants to happen*. A powerful and simple practice set forth by Ram Dass is to Ask yourself: *Where am I?* Answer: *Here.* Ask yourself: *What time is it?* Answer: *Now.* Say this until you can hear it.

Remember that there are two kinds of imagination: to imagine what is false to be true, but also, to imagine what is true to be false. One may be shown the way out from the first; but how can one be shown the way out from the second? The problem is how to distinguish between the help we receive and what our own imagination conjures up around it. It does not mean to say that we must have no imagination, nor that we must not elaborate things

for ourselves. But we must know what is original and what we have added. Otherwise all becomes confused. In moments of self-remembering we know the answer, we know our place, we have no pretensions, only certainty.
—Rodney Collin

The directed use of Imagination can bring about creative artistic ventures connecting us to others, while breaking down interfering roadblocks. Culture thrives from a creative use of Imagination. What's not seen or experienced directly, assumed or supposed, drains our inner resources. Seeing what's not here and not seeing what is, we lose our own life. The quality of our consciousness in the present moment is determined by our presence.

Imagination refers to the nearly ceaseless, automatic flow of thoughts through our minds. Because actual thinking is an intentional and disciplined activity. Like Odysseus we need to tie ourselves to the mast to resist these intrusive thoughts. We do not see these intrusive thoughts as a distraction from being present. —the Fellowship of Friends

OUR IMAGINED REALITY

Seeking the inner reality behind Imagination, what seems restrictive becomes liberating. A teacher of mine said, *the real world is hidden by the wall of imagination.* Enjoying what could or might happen; so many live in the game of wishful thinking, happy with the Imaginary, the idea more than the real. The real is always way ahead of what we can Imagine. We Imagine we control—the relationship, the job, the date as we design it, without interference; the mind controls our input and often the outcome. From a distance people live their lives. Not always apparent yet deadly, it often has a tranquil appearance, yet many illnesses are created through Imagination, through receptivity and fear; stress eats away at the physical body and is an underlying factor to all illness constantly robbing us from being present to what is. Imagination will grab our attention leaving us absent minded. In our efforts to transform Imagined or unnecessary suffering we receive Imagined presumed results. Often we trace issues or problems to an event that happened in the past; not understanding that it's our interpretation of the circumstance as well as our personal reaction to it that sets the stage for trauma, not the event. And then we live in that Imagined reality, continuing to retell the story.

In order to awaken, the main difficulty is to continuously see what is in the present and not be in imagination. We must keep trying to break through the clouds of imagination. Omar Khayyam said, 'There was a door to which I found no key: there was the veil through which I could not see.' The veil is imagination, and the key is self-remembering. Imagination consumes energy and intrudes all circumstances so that reality can seem to be a foreign experience. The struggle is always the same—to be present, taste the wine and listen to the music. We forget that the events of imagination never took place. Imagination will be a curse for the rest of our lives. Every second of self-remembering penetrates imagination and pierces eternity. —Robert Earl Burton

The work is to rewrite the past into the present and to drop the story. Being subjective and personal maintains the conditions of Imagination. Imaging something, believing it, and then forgetting it was Imagined, even sometimes imaging what is true to be false creates a barrier and confusion, finally reality becomes unbelievable. When we are present, we are objective, that is, we have no other object but ourself. Penetrating Imagination, seeing through the veil, yielding to the flow of life we drop into the present moment. Many people live their lives under constant conditions of Imagining themselves to be, it is their daily state. Dropping Imagination requires vigilance, as Milarepa reminds us, *Do not wander; remain mindful.*

We are fond of our involuntary thoughts, and that is why they come.

Imagination is a force, an energy, and the mind moves through it. And when the mind moves through it, the body follows. —*Osho*

2 - FORMATORY THINKING

Duality is the real root of our suffering and all our conflicts. —*Chogyal Namkai Norbu*

The mind is energy, and functions through subtle electric waves. Formatory Thinking—seeing duality, either/or, black or white is a divisive pattern. Good or bad, right and wrong, for or against, easy or hard, yes or no; each focuses on a preferred approach, categorized as correct, leaving the other choices unfit, eliminating many possibilities. Whenever we separate ourselves there is suffering; when there is oneness, suffering dissolves. To come out of little mind and move into big universal mind increases energy, eliminating the systematizing of good/bad, right/wrong, yes/no. To see things value-free, breaking routines, habits and conclusions, opens us to discover and step out of a space of division into an open freedom of observation. Division is an illusion. The true self is beyond all divisions of time and space, name and form, of all experiences, because who we are is the experiencer. To find harmony within ourselves and similarly with what is, the pain of separation disappears. To stop seeing opposites and look at how things are complementary, to know light is to pass through darkness, and this is true maturity.

Formatory thinking is not thinking. It can serve many useful purposes, but it is not for thinking. The great majority of people use nothing else. The mechanical part of the intellectual center is called formatory apparatus. A mechanical part works almost automatically, it does not require any attention. It cannot adapt itself to a change of circumstance. Formatory apparatus can only count up to two—it divides everything into two. Catchwords, all popular theories. —*P.D. Ouspensky*

Formatory Thinking happens when a pre-existing thought form interrupts the living process of thinking and forces form to take over, resulting in ideas that are slogans. As a barrier to awakening, thinking becomes automatic. Formatory Thinking stands in the way of inquiry. This obstacle is a barrier to understanding. Dualistic Thinking, fast and easy, blocks depthful thinking, feeds information with its limited perspective, is computer-like, played back like a computer that was data programmed. The Formatory apparatus uses a rote part of the mind that puts things in boxes with associations, limiting everything to two possibilities in absolute terms. Unlike creative thinking it's based on pre-existing programming. The lazy mental habits that obscure real inquiry can be heard in the catchwords and phrases like *they're doing the best they can, whatever, what's up*, as well as verbal associations and unrelated imagery that busily classifies ideas and objects, putting them into pigeon holes, applying words as labels, as slogans, taking everything quite literally. This mental mind-set, thinking without attention, dulls emotions and, in fact, continues to rob energy from our feelings.

Almost all communication with each other in life is by verbal association—no inner content. Lazy, often given to fits of day-dreaming; so it is with the formatory apparatus in us. —C.S. Nott

L I V I N G   E X P A N D E D :   U N I T Y

Without attentiveness, words become labels, deadening our perceptions, most communication has excessive verbal associations, lacking inner content. This lazy mental habit devitalizes creativity, limits understanding and is widespread, dominating the scientific and academic arena, as well as common thought; we have been educated to develop mechanical thinking. Hot and cold, night and day, heaven and hell, conscious and unconscious, right and left brain hemispheres, mind and body, past and future, cause and effect, waking and sleeping; we learn to uncritically live in dualistic thought. Formatory psychological and scientific inquiry have conceptualized mental organization, created conclusions that foster dualities of thought, making things look absolute. Life appears full of opposites, or at least, this is how people conceptualize it. So many possibilities are left undiscovered.

Formatory Thinking will paralyze and create conflict. It is characterized by insensitivity to context, strictly agreeing or disagreeing, and a defensive reply, arguments and denial, which are hallmarks of Formatory Thinking. Seeing two sides, as in good and bad, them or us, right and wrong, necessary or unnecessary, useful or harmful, the decision will be to pick a side or there will be no resolution. To see third force as well as unlimited options breaks our automatic response patterns, brings us into the present moment (explained in System 10, further explored in System 27, Law of Three). Visionary Oscar Ichazo stated: *It has been from the beginning of human culture that every movement is composed of three independent factors.* Considering three or more possibilities opens creative thinking. Stretching out of this limitation, this narrowness, opens up relationships that have been locked into a verdict. Generally it is our own repressed urges, our held back stuck unwillingness to risk take; all our fears bring us to see life in two-tone rulings. Mechanical thinking has its appropriate time and it is useful for recall, for learning driving directions, to spell a word. Formatory responses limit our ability to communicate, and obstructs self-awareness.

The formatory mind is automatic unthinking responses according to fixed patterns or forms; more specifically it's the automatic activity of the mechanical part of the intellectual center. —Robert Burton

Keeping things separated, we are blinded to the ultimate reality of life. The pendulum swinging covers the same ground backwards or forwards. There is no separation, opposites are the same, differing only in degree, opposites are two extremes of the same event. Look at a thermometer to see where hot ends and cold begins. They are degrees, two opposing points called temperature. This can be seen in the form of sharp and dull, light and dark, black and white, high and low, fat and thin, night and day; everything has its season. Attention needs to be given to our emotional life, real emotions do not turn into their opposites, genuine love does not turn into hate, which is why the emotional center does not have a negative part.

Our human experience does not lend itself to absolute statements, for it is too fluid and inclusive to be limited to catch-phrases which satisfy the mind but fall short of describing the paradoxical nature of reality. —Adyashanti

Great teachings speak of unity and oneness, powerful forces that lift us above the limits of Formatory Thinking. Now we are free to see things anew without labeling them. The fullness of experience happens: standing in front of the ocean and allowing it to come into our being, rather than limiting it with cliches, *what a pretty ocean, what a blue ocean.* This is the difference between rowing across the lake with your arms and hands or using two well-made oars. The wave and the ocean are the same. When we try to understand opposites, when we make comparisons and judgments, as in Formatory Thinking, our mind rigidifies, our energy depletes. All things flow out and in, a pendulum like movement, a tide like ebb and flow. As we open ourselves to the expansiveness of seeing connected possibilities, of fluidity, our energy is invigorated. Formatory Thinking is depleting, forcing us to live in the relative world of duality, far away from seeing the reality behind all beliefs and the unity of humankind.

To understand fully, one must transcend from the duality of for and against into one organic unity which is without distinctions. —Bruce Lee

3 - IDENTIFICATION

Identification is a very difficult thing to describe, because no definitions are possible. Such as we are we are never free from identifying. If we believe that we do not identify with something, we are identified with the idea that we are not identified. You cannot describe identification in logical terms. You have to find a moment of identification, catch it, and then compare things with that moment. Identification is everywhere, at every moment of ordinary life. In order to learn not to identify man must first of all not be identified with himself. In the state of identification one does not see and one does not hear. One is shut off from the world around. —P. D. Ouspensky

The third major energy leak is Identification. Who I am is not the car, dinner, a TV show, my opinions and viewpoints, the job I do, my sexual needs, my cravings, my husband/wife/partner and children, or a number on the Enneagram. Our habitual Identification with learned personality traps us into a false self. We Identify with our thoughts, feelings, our sexual energy, with what occurs in the outer life. Being Identified with our personality, profession, self-image, with whatever feelings or sensations capture our attention in-the-moment we continuously lose ourself, pulled away from an inner wholeness through Identifying with our reactions and the contents of our awareness. Watching television, only the show exists, washing the car and becoming critical of how it looks, flirting and being clueless to anything except winning over the object of our affection, absorbed, mesmerized, not mindful, we forget the play, we forget ourselves, oblivious to everything, except the glass of wine, slice of chocolate cake or the injustice we feel. Dressing for a party we discover that the shirt doesn't match the shoes, and suddenly that becomes a predicament, a calamity, because somehow I see the party and the clothing as being part of myself. It's not just a party or just clothing; it becomes as if something had just happened to *me*. The more we work on creating a witness, someone home inside ourselves, the closer we get to catching these moments.

Identification is when all of one's attention is going into one thing. It is exactly like a dog and a bone. When we are identified, we take something that is not truly ourselves to be our identity. If I am identified with making dinner and something happens—I discover halfway that I don't have enough oil—it becomes a crisis because somehow I take the dinner as being part of myself. One does not think about if as being 'just dinner'; instead, it is as if something had happened to 'me'. In any moment we can be more or less identified. —*Girard Haven*

Clarity happens when I know that I am more than my fixation or object of focus. Identifying with our children intrudes on our Identity, fills the space that would be self. Thinking that I am my children blocks me to the true experience of children. The world closes down when we Identify with a small aspect of life as if we owned it and are it. To be free from the constraints of our roles: mother, daughter, teacher, waiter, artist, doctor, lawyer, politician, businessman, athlete, father, godson, grandparent, to explore the limitless possibilities inherent in an authentic relationship—opens doors. Identification, regardless to how important and big one thinks the object is, remains a negative emotion and energy leak, and often goes hand in hand with imagination—Identifying with what one imagines to be real and important. At times, some of the things we take seriously, Identify with, later appear foolish and meaningless and they fill our life, our time. Preoccupied, we lose consciousness.

Identification occurs when our energy and attention is fixed on one aspect of a thing, it is a form of hypnosis, and must be distinguished from concentration and attention which are useful and necessary. —*C.S. Nott*

Often people fail to keep sight of the bigger picture as they make an object, say their job, or happiness, or sex, become so big that it obscures their greater intention. Initially something appears interesting, quite soon we are taken over and become it and no longer do we exist. Feelings heightened, interest piqued; when we allow our self-awareness to collapse we are at the mercy of our experience and thoughts. I am not my job or automobile or thoughts or even my feelings. This narrow focus has been known to suffocate growth. When we Identify we actually lose our Identity. Entering a spiritual and psychological realm we must remember that we are not our mind, not to become fascinated or Identified with our type, or possessive of our children. This energy blockage called tunnel vision suffocates what we love, and stops the possibility of transformation. Most of the world lives in a continuous habit of Identification, with only the object changing. The day begins, the phone rings and a request pulls us away from our aim and into someone else's issues, we lose sight of where we are, shut off the bigger picture, not able to stand aside and witness what is happening. Identifying with events is a major preoccupation and energy drain. Not holding consciousness of ourselves as the witness, we become Identified with other people, sex, money, a party, the super bowl; our attention is so drawn by the subject that our consciousness disappears into it. Slave to most everything that presents itself to sight or mind, especially to those events that *happen* to us.

A major obstacle to working on yourself is the process of identification. When you do not exercise any kind of control or restraint over your attention, you generally become identified with whatever it is that manages to grab your attention. When you are in a state of identification you are an automaton.
—*Alan Clews*

BEING PRESENT

Attached to moods, things and persons, forgetting our core self, it is difficult to distinguish a state of awareness from a state of distraction. Glued to the thought or the television program so that nothing else exists, for most people Identification is a natural unnoticeable ordinary way of living. Thinking that we *are* our headache, or our sexual partner, our childhood traumas, our food or alcohol addiction, our special eating needs of the month, the pain in our stomach, struggles at work, a football game or tennis match, our energy becomes absorbed by that Identity, as if there were nothing more to us than the cold or back pain or dinner date we have that week. Ultimately developing a fondness to our slavery, we are proud of those things that pull us; chocolate, sugar, alcohol, a financial dilemma, our car; ironic to think that we become what we think and do. Buddhist and Indian tradition refer to this as attachment. This hypnotic quality, far removed from concentration or being attentive, becomes fixated on one small aspect of the largeness, the greatness of life.

Man is possessed by all that surrounds him because he can never look sufficiently objectively on his relationship with his surroundings. He can never stand aside and look at himself together with whatever attracts or repels him at the moment. —*G.I. Gurdjieff*

Applying a sense of scale to whatever we are Identified with, placing attention elsewhere, is a start. Allowing consciousness to collapse and disappear, the content of our life to vanish so that we are in a central place in ourself, being present then becomes the focal point of life. Placing, dividing our awareness simultaneously between the object and ourselves as the observer, our consciousness is liberated. Positioning attention on something that we find beautiful: a piece of music or art, the sound of the ocean, can be an effective device to enter a clear space, landing in the pause that follows an activity or thought; relinquishing inner resistance to what appears, primary reality is within. Drawing back the energy to pinpoint a place inside locates us to a quiet central innermost core. By breaking the illusion of Identification again and again, and not being reactive, we release more energy, transcending our state of Identification, opening to presence, the present moment.

One's work is swept away when one becomes identified. If you aren't careful you will spend a large part of your life in identification. Very small things catch us, and we identify with small and large matters with equal intensity. How can we become emotional without becoming identified, because when we identify, we lose our identity, it's by strengthening our immature emotions while controlling artificial emotions that appear through unconscious acting. We need to understand that our problems are illusion. Some of the things we take seriously you couldn't sell for a penny. —Robert Burton

4 - EXPRESSION OF NEGATIVE EMOTIONS

If you let negative emotions and thoughts arise inside you without any sense of restraint, without any mindfulness of their negativity, then in a sense you are giving them free reign. However, if you develop mindfulness of their negativity, then when they occur, you will be able to stamp them out as soon as they arise. You will not give them the opportunity or the space to develop into full-blown negative emotional thoughts. —the Dalai Lama

*L*earning to live without Negative energy—not by repressing it, since Expression not repression is the health—but through transforming it, a tremendous amount of energy is released or stored and saved, rather than discharged. To experience the energy of unnatural emotions like resentment, despondency, irritation, hatred, self-indulgent sentimentality, despair, judgment, self-pity, suspicion, disgust, violence, boredom, depression, anxiety, disappointment; observing, limiting, uplifting our Expression—inwardly and outwardly—we can convert that energy to nourishment for our being. The inner experience is to drop deeper into the understanding, going beyond reaction, by catching and resisting our automatic, mechanical, habitual reactions. The transformation is not from negative to positive, in fact there are people who are mechanically positive, deceiving themselves; it is to drop into a deeper knowing, transforming coarse energy and refining it, an alchemical process of changing lead into gold, offering us fuel for our journey. Eliminating the violence inside ourselves which distracts us from being present, we train ourselves through non-expression to transform our Negative thoughts and feelings.

'The spiritual warrior has no outside enemies' said Abu Bakr. The responsibility for controlling our negative emotions lies with us. We no longer have the luxury of blaming others for our lack of control. Thus, every negative emotion that we express returns home to ourselves, as this is where the enemy truly exists. —Robert Burton

The Expression of Negative Emotions consumes energy, a steep payment for those who are around us. A single burst Expressed recklessly wastes energy that has accumulated throughout a day. Difficult to interrupt; initially noticing and taking care of the tone of our voice and the Expression on our face deactivates further outward Expression. Negativity is at the root of much of what we experience as stress, anxiety and depression, as well as the vast amount of bodily ills, from headaches to heart disease. Learning to disarm, not believe in or justify reactions, weakens and lessens the force of what drains our vital life energy.

In order to transform negative emotions, one must avoid identifying with the subject of one's negativity. It is the source of negativity that one must eventually control, more than the subject. Ouspensky said: 'We have a worm in us that wishes to express itself. Behind all negative emotions lies one's

permission. The term negative emotion means all emotions of violence and depression: self-pity, anger, suspicion, fear, annoyance, boredom, mistrust, jealousy, etc. If a chain of negativity isn't interrupted, it may go on expressing itself. One's evolution hinges upon the transformation of negative emotions.
—*Robert Burton*

NEGATIVITY INCREASES SUFFERING

The experience of our disappointments and loss of hope, our stories that justify the Negative reactions, prevent us from connecting to the uplifted source that is always available. Many times our attitude appears as cynicism, skepticism, discouragement, accusations, blaming, defiance, doubt or gossip; regardless, it is toxic. Ultimately there are no gradations in this energy leak, rooted in the belief that things could be other than they are, unwilling to live into what shows up, there is no *slightly* Negative just the subtle permeations of trying to not appear Negative. Pessimism, fault-finding, being mopey, mean, justifying, punishing, judgmental, feeling victimized, complaining, caustic, brutish, passive-aggressive, defensive, unfriendly, resentful, annoyed, neglectful, crude, argumentative; all cause suffering through resistance. The struggle that arises, that constrains, constricts our stretching from Negative energy into the beautiful flowering of realization is depleting.

Negativity leads nowhere and can only spoil everything. When one has this understanding about negative emotions one is in one way very safe, and in another way very vulnerable. The place left that opens by the departure of negativeness fills with positive understanding, positive certainty, positive love. What immense vistas begin to open up. The transformation of negative emotions direct into affection and understanding. —*Rodney Collin*

To give a voice to a situation that causes stress produces a temporary relief, to complain about someone who has been an irritation feels good in that moment. We appear better, feeling justified, imagining ourself to be vitalized, happier, vindicated, comforted, as if we eliminated the stress inside. And yet Negative Emotions aren't productive or useful. They waste our energy, and result in the suffering and violence of humanity. Many of the Expressed Negative Emotions are seated in conditioned reactions and accusations to external situations, circumstances, as well as to other people whom we presume to have created those reactions, instead, they are due to our own immaturity. Rationalized as a healthy response to situations, it becomes a challenge to teach people to resist, distrust and oppose their Negative Emotions and to work against Expressing them. To see the world as it is, rather than how it could be or how it was; to see the truth is a huge step towards not allowing Negativity to gain a toehold in our life. We are the only one responsible for our reactions, and the great hesitation in our moment of non-reaction shifts us to observant awareness.

The third level of suffering is the most significant—the pervasive suffering of conditioning. This refers to the very fact of our unenlightened existence, the fact that we are ruled by negative emotions and their underlying root cause, namely our own fundamental ignorance of the nature of reality. Buddhism asserts that as long as we are under the control of this fundamental ignorance, we are suffering; this unenlightened existence is suffering by it very nature.
—*the Dalai Lama*

The source for all Negative Emotions are produced inside us, not in the circumstances; realizing this gives us power over its Expression. The discomfort of not Expressing Negativity brings us to live a different kind of life. How we feel and respond is not at the mercy of outside events. Our Expression of Negative Emotions varies from going on a drinking binge, eating a box of cookies when feeling anxious or depressed, showing up late for an appointment, silence as a way of punishing someone, lying, gossiping, shopping and buying unnecessary stuff, driving while drunk, crying in self-pity, littering, playing the victim or martyr, being reductive or demeaning of another; we all have our select favorite styles.

People who are mechanically positive are just as mechanical as people who are mechanically negative. Ouspensky said: 'Some people's false personality functions cheerfully, and thereby they deceive themselves.' One cannot control negative emotions if one cannot control positive emotions, and neither is one's self. Self-remembering is metaphysical and is above the transient dualistic plane. Externally considering another can stop negativity, as can engaging one's moving center, or reading. —Robert Burton

Often in childhood we learn to control and manipulate the world, staging Negative Emotions, ultimately covering our tenderness and sensitivity. Movie, theatre and television abound with examples, ironically, we pay to look at other peoples Negative Expression, as if our lives weren't filled with enough of our own. To intentionally not Express Negative Emotions we tolerate the discomfort of separating from them, not becoming identified through being aware of a self that is separate from the circumstance to experience an acceptance of *that which is*. Asking ourself, *will this really matter in the larger scheme of things*, learning to buffer those around who exploit, to back away from the convincing and salesmanship that is put forth, to protect and value our commitment and dedication to truth; this is the *Way of the Lover*. To see reality is to see the necessity for things to happen as they are.

One realizes that no sane person would choose to be negative. No one wakes up in the morning, looks out the window and says, 'it is a beautiful day. I feel great. I think I will feel self-pity.' Probably we can think of times when our machines have done just that. To see that, as we are we are crazy, not how the machine became that way, but to see it and then to separate from it. —Gerard Haven

TRANSFORMING ENERGY

All Negative thoughts, emotions and actions, resisted, can be transformed into something positive and useful. The shift from Negative energy begins with a refinement of our conversational tone, the way we open and close a door, the manner of placing things on a table, our attitude when we enter a room, our deliberateness and willingness to listen and to not be tricky. Children and animals are sensitive to the timbre of a voice. The tone of our voice carries the intention of our heart, listening to ourself carefully awakens true sensitivity. The intention is not to like or to accept everything, it's to stop the disliking, criticalness and dissatisfaction. Carrying an oppositional demeanor, secretive holding back, illicit relations with a friend's partner, complaining and being uncooperative, eating a candy bar because we feel upset, shopping to relieve anxiety, all ways to allow Negativity to Express itself, drains our energy, creates a heaviness within our projects. Highly detrimental to our journey of awakening, it twists and distorts reality blocking us from seeing what is. Instead we are resisting and rejecting the truth, stopping ourself from accepting the present moment, and is ego building, believing that things could be other than they are. The shift from Negative to neutral or positive carries tremendous impact and requires real mastery over ourselves.

The transformation of negative emotions refers to something more than the mere absence or non-expression of negative emotions. Transformation must be a certain kind of effort which interrupts a negative emotion before it has a chance to get started and changes it into something else. Transformation, therefore, must be a method of redirecting this energy, a method of using it in a different way. With observation and with practice one can learn to place attention, to focus emotional attitudes and direct our manifestations.
—Girard Haven

The Expression of Negativity sabotages group effort and is usually the demise of communal living. This energy leak carries tremendous power and leads to physical, emotional and spiritual exhaustion. Our emotional outbursts; Expressing Negativity not only dissipates the day's energy it has the possibility to use up more than is stored like a power surge effect on our TV or computer, it short circuits cutting us off from the supply we need for our own self-development. The irony in this modern age where we easily fly around the world, go to other planets, is that we still remain not able to resist flying off the handle when a car cuts us off on a highway or someone changes a plan or the weather pattern disrupts our routine. It also is true that we are most apt to Express our Negativity to our closest relationships since they are the immediate representation of ourself—we are mostly angry and judging of ourself— once again, the work begins, therefore, with self.

Negative emotions are a way for us not to see that the world is the way it is. Negative emotions are always based on the imagination of the idea that things could be other than they are, that the world could be different. Like all buffers, it keeps us from seeing the truth. —Girard Haven

One way to work with this leak is to see that we have energy around something rather than reacting with a picture or thought about what makes us angry and to see this as energy. *Energy is an eternal delight,* said William Blake. Breathe; paying attention to the breath shifts our anger. Clearly our reactions are subjective, our friend may have many ways to irritate, but only one that particularly bothers us. Studying ourselves to know what evokes our reactions, shifting attitudes, resisting Expression, always remembering that the source for all Negativity is inside us and that our Negativity is not real. This leads to the deeper and the spiritual work of intentional transformation. True non-expression, inner and outer, opens the door to genuine change. The effort that is made to interrupt a Negative Emotion *before* it starts redirects energy, conserving or using it in an altogether new way. Self-study is still the key, offering us the ability to recognize what and when we are triggered along with the understanding, enabling us to respond differently, thereby transforming Negative Emotions. This is not to reprogram ourselves, it is to transform and uplift. A major difference.

One's evolution hinges upon the transformation of negative emotions.
—R. Burton

5 - UNNECESSARY TALK

The first step toward spiritual freedom is to control the mind, to stop idle chatter, to know silence. —the Buddha

Our inner talk masks presence. Learning to be present internally starts with externally quieting ourself. True silence has a presence, just as true conversation is only of the essential. Chatter, which is both inner and outer clutter, changes the quality of the moment. The inner talk, the one that goes on in the head, as well as mechanical talking, drains us. The gossiping, small talk, questions, quarreling and mindless conversation that people engage in is infectious. We begin to like the noise of our own voice, luring us further away from a space of presence. In fact those words begin to fill the space that presence would occupy. Talking for its own sake, a tension breaker, garnishing attention, displaces mindfulness. The words we choose determines how we experience our lives. Words act upon the world, effecting the sanctity of relationships; uplifting and encouraging someone's day, taking the ordinary and making it sacred, or, words carelessly spoken toxify the tone of a room as well as our own experience. Speech can be poetry, prayer, song, even a weapon. Our words express the contents of our heart.

The words you speak become the house you live in. —*Hafiz*

This energy leak addresses the other four energy leaks. Talking about the past and the future, speaking in duality, opinions and concepts, gossiping and complaining; all are manifestations of four energy leaks through Unnecessary Talk. Conversation can be uplifting and create energy, Unnecessary Talk robs us of energy leaving us tired after speaking. Talking is joyful when we take responsibility for our words. It is isolating and lonely when we are not present, attentive or connected. We understand fasting the body of certain kinds of food, and even briefly, of all food. We also have the possibility of controlling our language. Studies have shown that Unnecessary Talk is at the root of what we experience as anxiety and depression. To cultivate interior silence, stilling the mind and nourishing the body will protect and bring an inner peace and calmness not found in noise and restlessness.

Conversation of a totally different nature is a conversation between friends of spirit and heart. It is a deep listening and transmission of heart as well. Everything in the created cosmos is also in ceaseless conversation, in endless symbiosis and those with attuned ears of the inner heart are able to listen to them. —*Hilary Hart*

Telling and retelling stories, events that we already know, filling space to avert nervousness, gossip and distracting comments, all occupy time while avoiding real contact. Conceptual knowing expressed through *telling about what happened* or *about what you did*, is often limiting, mind-based, creating separation between people. Deeper knowing is non-conceptual, formless, it's knowing through a stillness which calls for an open way of being, a space that joins us in a unifying field of awareness. Lao Tzu called this *the stillness that restores the world.* The fear of silence and emptiness, the inability to tolerate clear empty space and true intimacy leads us to tire ourselves and others with our avoidance of stillness. Most Talk is Unnecessary, is idle conversation, has little meaning, trivial, is of no sense, talk for talk's sake, coming from and supporting self-importance, ego.

The Buddha was unequivocal about the importance of how we employ our human capacity for speech and verbal interaction. Right speech, also called wise speech or virtuous speech, is speech that gives rise to peace and happiness in oneself and others. The Buddha was precise in his description of right speech. He defined it as 'abstinence from false, malicious harsh speech, and abstinence from idle chatter'. —Beth Roth

What we speak about is what we believe to be important. Good conversation is energizing. There is great value in speaking for necessary reasons, such as to communicate ideas. To listen to the gaps in between the words, the silence, listening to our own heartbeat quiets the Unnecessary Talk. Now, words come from within, no longer speaking from the circumference. Words have enormous consequences, harmful as well as beneficial. Unnecessary Talk is noise, an energy leak that sabotages truth.

Whenever I wish to move or to speak, first I examine my state of mind, and firmly act in a suitable way. Whenever my mind becomes attached or angry, I shall not react, nor shall I speak, I shall remain mum and unmoved like a tree. —Shantideva

MINDFUL SPEECH

The restless mind, drawn to amusement and unnecessary information needs to be caretaken. Mindful and discriminating, speech as a rich practice serves. To diminish the Unnecessary inner Talk is to be in an interlude, a parenthesis, an intermission. Then real conversation will not interrupt the silence. Once finding that space, through diminishing

Unnecessary Talk, speaking will not disturb the peace. It directs the energy inwards, containing, rather than diffusing energy, it focuses it. To talk for talk's sake, without a filter attached to the brain, so every thought comes blurting out, not caring if the other person is interested in listening; conversing about empty pursuits wastes energy. The principle of mindful speech is: not lying, slandering, manipulating, convincing, gossiping, chattering, being tricky, speaking unkindly, constantly talking about others; instead, there is the uplifting possibility of directing ourselves to saying what is wholesome, helpful, intelligent, appropriate and necessary. The more we empty ourselves of our chatter the more present we become, the more real conversations show up. Developing skillful conversation involves more than sending and receiving information. It starts with a willingness to emerge a slightly different person and it involves risk. It makes sense and elevates our life to have mindful conversations rather than absent-minded distracted words.

Think before you speak. Read before you think. Great people talk about ideas, average people talk about things, and small people talk about wine. Polite conversation is rarely either. —Fran Lebowitz

Detrimental to consciousness, to harness our thoughts, to struggle with the habit of talking, economizes our energy as well as deepening our spirit. Non-expression, holding energy, creates rich experiences through the effort of resisting the expression of idle talk. Right speech is an important part of the noble eightfold path, a living art put forth by Buddha; a commitment to speak truthfully, to not gossip or speak falsely, not slander, to abstain from harsh speech and idle chatter. Right speech means to use communication as a way to further understanding of ourselves and others, informing, speaking to promote friendship and peacefulness, as a way to develop insight, enabling our words to reflect our inner wisdom. Lying in all forms, whether it be trickiness, misrepresentation or deceit, destroys the ground for trust. The commitment to truth drops us into the present moment; to see things as they are, is the integrity of having our inner and the outer correspond, rather than wishful fantasies that create illusion.

In Sufi circles they say: There's prayer, and a step up from that is meditation, and a step up from that is sohbet or conversation. Who is talking to HU (the pronoun for divine presence). Lover to beloved, teacher to disciple, presence talking to absence, existence to non-existence, periphery to center.
—*Coleman Barks*

UNMINDFUL SPEECH

Slander is considered among the Jewish people as one of the worst sins imaginable, worse than murder. When we become the target of character assassination, we are powerless since we don't even know that we have been murdered; no moment to cry for help or to run away. To be aware of the suffering caused by unmindful speech is to know how words effect happiness or suffering. The ageless wisdom of the ancient rabbinic sages explain: *Three sins are punished in this world and, further, the sinner loses his portion in the world to come—idol worship, forbidden sexual relations, and murder, but Loshon Hora (the evil tongue) is equivalent to all of them. It kills threefold; the speaker, the listener, and the victim.* The Talmud teaches that gossip is like a three-pronged tongue which kills three people: the person who says it, the person who listens to it, and the person about whom it is said. The universe was created through speech. Of the 43 sins recited on Yom Kippur, 11 are known to be committed through speech. The Talmud tells us that the tongue is an instrument so dangerous that it must be kept hidden from view, behind two protective walls, the mouth and the teeth, to prevent its misuse. The harm done by speech is considered worse than the harm done by stealing or cheating someone financially: money lost can be repaid, but the harm done by speech can never be repaired. The *Ways of the Righteous* comments: *Before you speak, you are the master of your words. After you speak, your words master you.*

SPEECH AS A MIRROR OF THE SOUL

One of the Bodhisattva's four methods of guidance, kind speech, is contrary to slander or cruel speech. A good name, livelihood, reputation, can be destroyed by a single word, yet speech originating from a mind of loving kindness seeks peaceful reconciliation and mutual understanding. Unnecessary Talk takes place almost every time we open our mouths to speak. Conversing as entertainment, to stir up a relationship, to convince others—rather than finding a real question from a desire to know and share—is distracting ourselves, wishing we were elsewhere, being in chains of thought, abdicating mature responsibility. Spiritual conversation, presence of mind, being in the moment, reflecting whatever appears, we develop conversations that catch fire. Our conversations, in the spirit of inquiry, informs our life with meaning. *We must be lights unto ourselves*, Buddha said. Being a light in the world, illumining the way for ourselves and others we determine our experiences, our conversations.

Speech is the mirror of the soul, as a man speaks, so is he. —*Pubillus Syrus*

SYSTEM FOURTEEN

GOAL

DISCRIMINATION, ACCEPTANCE RE-EVALUATION, GROWTH, SUBMISSION, DOMINANCE, RELAXATION

My goal is simple. It is a complete understanding of the universe, why it is as it is and why it exists at all. —*Stephen Hawking*

DISCRIMINATION: Positive: sophistication **Negative:** rejection, prejudice

ACCEPTANCE: Positive: unconditional love **Negative:** ingratiation

RE-EVALUATION: Positive: simplicity, efficiency **Negative:** withdrawal

GROWTH: Positive: evolution **Negative:** confusion

SUBMISSION: Positive: dedication, devotion **Negative:** exploited

DOMINANCE: Positive: leadership **Negative:** dictatorship

RELAXATION: Positive: flow, equilibrium **Negative:** stagnation, inertia

We each choose the basic personality characteristics that will overlay our essence and facilitate the lessons that essence wants us to learn in this lifetime, as well as meeting our karmic agreements. Understanding our choices and staying in the positive direction creates the opportunities we need to develop and mature. Of all the traits we select to cover our essence our Goal is the most significant. It is essentially what we want; the thrust, reason and intention, it's a clear indication of where essence wants us to focus as well as what it wants us to attain. Each Goal offers a specific orientation and motivation to our personality.

Reach high, for the stars lies hidden in your soul. Dream deep, for every dream precedes the goal. —Rabindranath Tagore

The Goal we choose gives us direction and is the bottom line issue in all of our experiences. Every life situation pushes us to encounter our Goal, presenting us with circumstances that provide ways to contact and move us in the position of living within that Goal. This is what gives theme and rhythm, impulse and focus, as well as the background for our lessons; essentially it is about our relationship to our life situations. Goal impacts how we experience existence. Our primary motivator, over and above our interests or career aspirations; it is the underlying design determining challenges and issues towards the realization of a destination we would like to reach. Our Goal affects how we interpret our thoughts, what gives meaning to our life. The incentive, encouragement, stimulus, as well as the intention in our life orders itself around our Goal. This objective stirs us to search for something sensed missing in our self, absent or insufficient in life, deficient or lacking in the world.

A man without a goal is like a ship without a rudder. —Thomas Carlyle

WORKING WITH OUR GOAL

Each of the seven Goals determines what our personality pursues. Entering the positive mode of our Goal creates a magnetism that attracts and uplifts. Moving towards the negative direction produces darkness, contraction, fatigue, and blocks us from evolving. To be focused in the positive part of our life is harmonious, in the negative we are uncomfortable, restricted, constrained. Living in the negative part of the personality draws negativity, and holds back growth, whereas living in the positive activates beneficial energy. When we live from the evolved part of the Goal we chose for this lifetime we engage our greatest opportunity for spiritual evolution.

Obstacles are those frightful things you see when you take your eyes off the goal. —Henry Ford

Each Goal, except Relaxation, which is neutral and joins with any other Goal, has a specific partner that it slides to for distinct reasons. An action, expressive, or inspirational Goal will slide to, or use its active, expressive or inspirational partner to fulfill a karma or to find an environment or circumstance that is needed for a period of time. This move offers an opportunity to shift from a negative position to a positive part of the partner Goal, or for a moment to rest and gain access to something needed. Each Goal avoids what the other Goal seeks. Originally the Goal creates a sense of lack, fostering the direction needed to satisfy meaning and purpose in our life. Seeing ourselves as having too much of the opposing Goal we work to neutralize the complementary opposite. Therefore, we see ourselves as being the opposite of who we are in relation to our Goal. Each Goal sees their situation as having an overabundance of the opposing Goal, and we think it's our job to counteract this. In this way, we see ourselves as being the opposite of what we are in relationship to our Goal. A person with the Goal of growth sees their life as too contracted so they look for more experiences, which is neither particularly a deficit or what is needed. Shifting from growth to its partner, re-evaluation sets up a moment to, in the positive, simplify, or in it's negative direction, to withdraw.

If you want to live a happy life, tie it to a goal, not to people or things. —Albert Einstein

The four flavors, distinctive quality and character of each Goal are: expression, inspiration, action and assimilation. Expressive Goals of discrimination and acceptance communicate bringing beauty and feeling into our life, through expression, to motivate harmony, purity, and distinctness. The inspirational goals of re-evaluation and growth stimulate and bring us to new places through inspiring. The action roles of submission and dominance are characterized by doing. Action is not activity, it is an in the moment relevant response. Activity, on the other hand, coming from restlessness and distraction, is not a response to the present moment; it's placing restlessness which comes from the past, into the present. Action is creative, activity is destructive—taking away from presence. Submission and domination are postures of action, postures without action, pulling in energy where deep down there is stillness. The goal of assimilation, relaxation, oriented towards absorption, a neutral goal, therefore unaffiliated, nothing to overcome, becomes a time to incorporate, digest, providing a resource for the other Goals.

Each of the sets of Goals, except neutral relaxation, has two parts, ordinal and exalted. The ordinal Goals deal with the tangible details and are constrictive and contracted; they are the close end of the binoculars. The exalted Goals increase in scope, are wide-range and expansive.

A goal is not always meant to be reached, it often serves simply as something to aim at. —*Bruce Lee*

Ultimately all the Goals work together to create the purpose of why we are here and assist us to realize our interconnectedness with all of life. Each Goal is a facet of a distinct process, within each Goal lies the possibility of learning unconditional love. Each Goal has implicit beauty; for the supreme Goal of life is unconditional acceptance of self and others, no separation. To understand our Goal is to be able to live it mindfully. First, is to know which of the seven is our heart's direction.

Expression		Inspiration	
Ordinal	Exalted	Ordinal	Exalted
DISCRIMINATION	ACCEPTANCE	RE-EVALUATION	GROWTH
+sophistication	+unconditional love	+simplicity, efficiency	+evolution
-rejection, prejudice	-ingratation	-withdrawal	-confusion

Action		Assimilation
Ordinal	Exalted	Neutral
SUBMISSION	DOMINANCE	RELAXATION
+dedication, devotion	+leadership	+flow, equilibrium
-exploited	-dictatorship	-inertia, stagnation

Chart 6: Goals

When you discover your mission, you will feel its demand. It will fill you with enthusiasm and a burning desire to get to work on it. —*W. Clement Stone*

DISCRIMINATION

POSITIVE: SOPHISTICATION

NEGATIVE: REJECTION OR PREJUDICE

Simplicity is the greatest discrimination. —*Leonardo da Vinci*

This is an ordinal expressive goal that is chosen to separate the wheat from the chaff. It hastens to clear unnecessary baggage. With a goal of Discrimination, since it's expressive, I easily share my opinions and preferences. Selecting what is wanted and eliminating what is not wanted in my life, sharpening critical faculties, the goal of Discrimination develops refinement of things that are dense, creating good critical insight.

Voluntary simplicity means going fewer places in one day rather than more, seeing less so I can see more, doing less so I can do more, acquiring less so I can have more. —John Kabat-Zinn

The goal of Discrimination operates to keep my personality free of contamination. Like the kidneys filtering out impurities, this goal is set up to exclude, rather than include. Critically examining, selective, taking things apart, looking for differences, weeding out impurities, breaking down and excluding; the motivation is to make one thing distinct from another. I am the person hand-picking, weeding out the soft and poorly colored grapes in the supermarket, only taking the ripe and juicy ones, screening for impurities, sorting through the potatoes, looking for the unmarked ones of good color, easily saying no to the social invitations that would not work for my lifestyle. Finding contrast in things; the subtle differences most people overlook become underlined and highlighted. Analyzing things, we tend to be connoisseurs and experts in most any chosen field of work. Seeking purity, integrity and distinctive contrast; I take things apart, scrutinizing and examining, until finding the most unique ingredient of what a thing is, its essence, its purity.

Criticism may not be agreeable, but it is necessary. It fulfills the same function as pain in the human body. It calls attention to an unhealthy state of things. —Winston Churchill

Making a *mountain out of a molehill* and the term *hairsplitter* must have referred to those of us with a goal of Discrimination, noting how we belabor, often singling out vague comments that just don't sit right for us. Arguing often appears as an opportunity to examine what is believed and known, picking apart a word of our adversary, to be certain the meaning is accurate. There is no room for ambiguity. Critical faculties are always being refined. Discrimination motivates us to be discerning, choosy, selective, or to categorically outright reject, sometimes unwilling to understand issues on an individual basis. Throughout this process being in the Discrimination mode moves us towards more contraction, feeling that my life is too compliant, I look for more integrity, ironically this is not necessarily what is actually needed since my lifestyle is already stable and constricted. Not a lot of room to add things on in my life, especially as we age; there becomes a fine-tuning until only the things that work, and not much else, fits into my life or schedule.

I won't insult your intelligence by suggesting that you really believe what you just said. —William F. Buckley, Jr.

BALANCING: NEGATIVE AND POSITIVE

There can be a prickly thorny appearance, reflecting our sharp-tongued bristly hypercriticism, on the other hand, a poised, polished look also reflects those of us with a goal of Discrimination. A negative direction leads to bigotry and prejudice, arbitrarily rejecting due to outright bias. In the negative there is automatic displeasure, quickly criticizing and judging in a destructive manner anything not meeting our standards. The range from positive to negative is the distance between finesse, polish, culture, fastidiousness, worldly refinement, and racist, chauvinistic, snobbish, judgmental, sexist, prejudice. In the negative inclination of prejudice our habitual criticism becomes directed, definite and specific, all the while expressing something else as being more desirable. Rejection, another negative aspect of Discrimination, easily overtakes our life. We rebuff and exclude what we don't like, seeking fine distinctions, the best of things. Continuously pushing people away, looking for help and still dismissing even those who are supportive, rejection sets up situations where others will say *no*. The automatic displeasure reaction experienced by those of us in Discrimination mode is because our standards and ideals may be too extreme. Hard to please, the effort made to shift out of the negative part, to look larger, at the whole picture, to value and recognize the worth of things being as they are, uplifts the negative position into positive.

I don't know if people have gotten ruder or if my tolerance level has declined.
—*Tim Gunn*

Discrimination goal rarely cares who likes them or about being loved, unless we value the person doing the loving. The negative part, rejection, liking to be different, aspiring for honesty, often becomes quite unpopular, called cantankerous, a curmudgeon, a grouch. The older soul person with this goal, honest with ourself, acknowledges our limitations in areas we are not proficient, knowing that we are not well studied in a new realm, therefore unable to discriminate with understanding to have appropriate openness and humility. Modest, in this instance, we are willing to see ourselves as a student learning to Discriminate a new subject of interest.

I know as a critic I'm required to have a well-armored heart. I must be a cynical wise guy to show my great sophistication. No push-over me.
—*Roger Ebert*

A popular goal with movie and literary reviewers, art and theatre critics, 4-star chefs, professional tasters of coffee and chocolate, wine, restaurant, and sniffers in the perfume industry. The caution, forethought and care required easily tips into finickiness or irrational opinion and is a fine line to walk. Liking to be appreciated for our individuality, accepted for our uniqueness, as well as having space for our integrity we prefer a partner who is distinctive and unique. Experiencing ourselves as unlike others, in a class by ourselves, this actually is an uncommon goal, only 2% of the population have chosen it. Yet, society and the arts are imprinted by those of us who have chosen this *separate the sheep from the goats* Discrimination goal. Sliding to acceptance, adaptability overcomes the analytical acuteness that predominates, so that our high expectations of others is softened to accept people as they are.

It's a great mistake, I think, to put children off with falsehoods and nonsense, when their growing powers of observation and discrimination excite in them a desire to know about things. —Anne Sullivan

Examples are: *Bob Dylan, William F. Buckley, Julia Child, Fred Astaire, Richard Gere, Denzel Washington, Simone de Beauvoir, Tim Gunn, Gene Siskel, Jack Kerouac, Martha Stewart, Lennie Bruce, Rasputin, Steven Jobs, Johnny Depp, Dick Cavett, Dame Judi Dench, Dr. Edith Wallace, Vincent Van Gogh, Roger Ebert, Mr. Blackwell, Fran Lebowitz.*

ACCEPTANCE

POSITIVE: UNCONDITIONAL LOVE

NEGATIVE: INGRATIATION

Accept—then act. Whatever the present moment contains, accept it as if you had chosen it. Always work with it, not against it. Make it your friend and ally, not your enemy. This will miraculously transform your life. —Eckhart Tolle

Acceptance of others, as well as self-acceptance, is the major theme for those of us with this goal. Rejection is such a painful experience that we go out of our way to be thought well of, to be complimented and included, even at the price of sincerity. We dodge being truthful and forthright so you will like us. It's as if we are handed the task *to be loved.* Lacking the skills to work the assignment we become annoying. A willingness to acknowledge the difficulties that life brings, which is an aspect of this goal, can be a true challenge. In fact, recognizing difficult situations can be quite hard for those of us with this goal. Easy-going, outgoing, friendly, agreeable, adaptive, likeable, easy to be around, once we deal with the fear of not being liked or included, the beauty of total Acceptance shines.

The greatest devotion, greater than learning and praying, consists in accepting the world exactly as it happens to be. —Hasidic saying

The effortlessness of social homogeneity and compatibility, without friction, support my desire to be friendly and harmonious. I am diplomatic, welcoming, inviting, enjoying to make people feel good. A nice time is when people are agreeable. Acceptance is passive, essentially responsive, compliant, often acquiescent to others. Having this goal I am popular, approachable, considered *friendly*, accommodating, a good sport, generally demonstrating goodwill with a cheerful demeanor. Focusing attention on similarities, affinity, and like-mindedness; being in harmony with others and the world is quintessential to my goal.

Every morning a new arrival. A joy, a depression, a meanness. Welcome and entertain them all! —Rumi

Avoiding arguments, rejection, rejecting; I am not an opposing, quarrelsome person, I'm more likely to walk away from an argument, not confront, we do not want to be unpleasant. The ideal is a beautiful dream, yet having difficulty being in challenging circumstances, Accepting situations that are not really Acceptable, compromising integrity; we must do a tremendous amount of work on ourself before being available to agape, to unconditional Acceptance, and learning to live until that time, we just might become stretched out of shape.

Adapt yourself to the life you have been given; and truly love the people with whom destiny has surrounded you. —*Marcus Aurelius*

THE MOVEMENT OF ACCEPTANCE

There is an appearance of stillness, since this is a goal that does not embrace movement. Acceptance is a state of stillness and balance, being peaceful about what happens. The emphasis is Accepting what cannot be changed or overcome, welcoming life and people the way they are. We look open, and have an agreeable nature, not standoffish or aloof. An ultimate place for each of us to touch, Acceptance for who we are.

The nature of love is as the nature of water in the depth of the earth. If we do not dig deep enough, we find mud, not water; but when we dig deep, we find pure water. —*Hazrat Khan*

In the negative mode the fear of being at odds with people, indiscriminately going along with ideas that are against personal integrity, creates dishonesty, discomfort for everyone, a dilemma. Cliches and platitudes abound, we have worked for years to maintain peace and comfort, to shift conversations into trouble-free zones. Avoiding criticism plays a large part in the compromised integrity. Dodging arguments includes missing the ones that contribute and ultimately strengthen intimacy. Speaking truth does not gain popularity, win favor or please everyone.

When we see ourselves in a situation which must be endured and gone through, it is best to meet it with firmness and accommodate everything to it in the best way practicable. This lessens the evil, while fretting and fuming only increase your own torments. —*Thomas Jefferson*

In the positive manifestation, service through offering a loving presence attracts many to us. In the negative mode, I can be an annoying person to be around and one who often avoids the risk-taking of going to the edge to seek truth. There is a sensitivity to rejection, to not being included. This makes it difficult to state our position or to assert ourselves. Agreeing to take on responsibilities rather than saying *no* creates resentment and often manifests in a passive aggressive quality. Quick to manipulate through flattery and praise, a feeling of superficiality and insincerity surfaces. Our graciousness to greet and meet you is expected to be reciprocated or a wounded puppy dog may appear in place of our cheerful greeting. This is our demise, when the *acceptor* wants to be Accepted. The glory is when the *acceptor* separates from our personality and lives in unconditional love.

Things cannot always go your way. Learn to accept in silence the minor aggravations, cultivate the gift of taciturnity and consume your own smoke with an extra draught of hard work, so that those about you may not be annoyed with the dust and soot of your complaints. —*William Osler*

Acceptance slides to the other expressive goal, discrimination, then what appears is a picking and choosing what to Accept and what to reject. When feeling threatened, and to avoid the painful experience of being discarded, we drop into the negative part, giving someone the brush-off before being rejected. People with a goal of Acceptance experience ourself and our life as being too unloving and disharmonious, looking for more conformity and agreeableness, a misperception connected to our slide to discrimination; we need to counteract a complementary yet opposing goal.

Everything in life that we really accept undergoes a change. So suffering must become love. That is the mystery. —*Katherine Mansfield*

We are the lovers of humanity, Accepting others as they are, easily approachable. Admitting what is true brings us to the threshold; to cross and enter the realm of happiness requires Acceptance. Agape or unconditional love which is the pinnacle of Acceptance unveils the secret connection between all things. 30% of the population have this goal.

Flow with whatever may happen and let your mind to be free. Stay centered by accepting whatever you are doing. This is the ultimate. —Chuang-Tzu

Examples are: *Pat Boone, Paula Abdul, Brooke Shields, Bernie Siegel, John Travolta, Robin Williams, Meryl Streep, Bill Cosby, Ronald Reagan, Stevie Wonder, Regis Philbrin, Kelly Ripa, Mathew Broderick, Dolly Parton, Jay Leno, Gene Kelly, Cary Grant, Mata Amritananda Mayi Ma* (known as *Ammachi*).

RE-EVALUATION

POSITIVE: SIMPLICITY, EFFICIENCY

NEGATIVE: WITHDRAWAL

I had three pieces of limestone on my desk, but I was terrified to find that they required to be dusted daily, when the furniture of my mind was all undusted still, and threw them out the window in disgust. Simplicity, simplicity, simplicity! —Thoreau

Choosing a goal of Re-evaluation we focus on looking in depth at singular issues. The boundaries of our life may remain small in order that a concise number of issues receive full coverage. Sometimes referred to as a goal of reduction since my interest is to reduce distractions so as to focus on primary issues. An ordinal inspirational goal, it is inner and past directed, limiting choices, narrowing involvements. To achieve this level of concentration sometimes a physical disability, blindness, autism, brain-damage, retardation, solitary confinement, might be selected, although not always. Disabilities create a simplified lifetime, life becomes pared down, options are limited. Eliminating a wide array of potential life experiences simplifies the task of concentrating more intently on a narrow range of issues. This allows our energy to focus on a task at hand with minimum diversion. When movement and distractions are restricted, the energy stays confined and concentrated. Rather than seeing superficial details there is available time to be thorough and penetrating. The issue may be as large as Stephen Hawkins' quest for a complete understanding of the universe or as encapsulated as Erik Menendez' inner struggle to find meaning to his life in prison.

The ability to simplify means to eliminate the unnecessary so that the necessary may speak. —Hans Hoffman

Often it is a time to slow down, to be introspective or withdrawn, to take a rest, looking at the circumstances in our life that might not be working. Assessing things, determining if they are necessary, this thrifty management and prevention of waste economizes, does not squander. Seeking to discover what is truly essential, discarding nonessentials as uncalled for and excessive, I assign a value system to what really matters, because that's what is kept. These are the garden weeders, managing to keep overgrowth out. To evaluate is to appraise and set a price. To Re-evaluate is to appraise the worth, see how the value has held up, what merits holding on to, what needs to be discarded.

I went to the woods because I wished to live deliberately, to front only the essential facts of life, and see if I could not learn what it had to teach, and not, when I came to die, discover that I have not lived. Our life is frittered away by detail. Simplify! Simplify! Simplicity of life and elevation of purpose. Simplicity! I say let your affairs be as two or three, and not a hundred or a thousand; instead of a million count half a dozen, and keep your accounts on your thumbnail. —Henry David Thoreau

The negative aspect, withdrawal, is experienced as feeling stuck, ruminating, brooding, unclear focus, reducing life to barely anything, handled in isolation and seclusion. Simplicity, clarity, then surrender, maintains the positive direction. Once arriving at the task at hand, being single-minded, close attention in the positive brings us to a beautiful unaffected state of simplicity and wonder. Contemplative, unassuming, a life-long study reveals the manner that Henry David Thoreau and Stephen Hawking have concentrated into their writings.

A man is rich in proportion to the number of things which he can afford to let alone. —*Thoreau*

REVIEW AND REVISE

To look again, from a different point of view about the nature, purpose, or meaning, after changes have taken place; this consideration and examination takes time and focus. To once more assess the condition, extent and importance of anything requires a slowing down, a simplification or withdrawal from the thing or from life. A subtle difference, yet distinctly different. One has to remove the distractions and accouterments that overwhelm and blur focus, to live without complexity, complication or difficulty. Simplicity implies clearness, lucidity, clarity, modesty, naturalness. The other, withdrawal, literally takes something away. Withdrawal implies isolating oneself, separation, pulling back, retraction, recoiling, backing out, cancelling.

If one's life is simple, contentment is to come. —*the Dalai Lama*

I'm at peace with my life because I've accepted that it's ok not to understand. —*Lyle Menendez*

Many children who are committing murder have a goal of Re-evaluation. They are infant and young souls processing and Re-evaluating memories of massacres and abrupt military deaths.

Re-evaluation to this soul-age can come in the guise of revenge and re-enactment of the memory, as in the Columbine School massacre. This is identifying with the aggressor, something that also happens to children who have been incested and raped. They then create a contained imprisoned life, with little external stimulation. People who are institutionalized, incarcerated, often have this goal and are processing their lifetime subliminally or unconsciously. Many are both destructive towards others and self-destructive, violent and revengeful, as in the Connecticut massacre, killing 20 children and 6 adults, and the Parkland Florida High School shooting, with 17 deaths. Living under the custodial care of a family member or agency, little involvement in the intricacies of life is required. People who retreat to the wilderness, having a hermit like existence, seeking quiet and an uncomplicated straightforward life are also among those with this goal.

Simple living will help you to control thoughts. If you lead a simple life, you will have only very few wants and you will have to think a little only.
—*Sivananda*

Avoiding what the complimentary goal of growth seeks, experiences and distractions are kept minimal. The outer travels are replaced with inner traveling. To have a goal of Re-evaluation, the impulse that more contraction is needed happens through the slide to growth, its opposite goal. To recognize the slide supports stretching and opening to new challenges, bringing opportunities for expansion and maturity.

Think simple, as my old master used to say—meaning reduce the whole of its parts into the simplest terms, getting back to its first principles.
—*Frank Lloyd Wright*

Only 1-2% of the population have a goal of Re-Evaluation.

Examples are: *Helen Keller, Christopher Reeve, Erik and Lyle Menendez, Stephen Hawking, Stephen King, Joseph Campbell, Gabrielle Giffords, Henry David Thoreau, George Wallace, Theodore Kaczynski the Unibomber, Nikolas Jacob Cruz the Parkland shooter*

GROWTH

POSITIVE: EVOLUTION

NEGATIVE: CONFUSION

The process of growth is, it seems, the art of falling down. Growth is measured by the gentleness and awareness with which we once again pick ourselves up, the lightness with which we dust ourselves off, the openness with which we continue and take the next unknown step, beyond our edge, beyond our holding, into the remarkable mystery of being. —Stephen Levine

The person with the exalted inspiration goal of Growth finds challenges inspiring. We willingly agree to experiences that push the edge and promote learning. There is a drive to see in a new and different way. Pressed to develop ourselves and stretch beyond the confines of our limits, we present an appearance in the world of being skilled, motivated, busy, knowledgeable and in motion. Eager to have experiences, not always careful to make sure the activities are usable, we sometimes engage in mindless challenges.

It is not the strongest of the species that survives, nor the most intelligent, but the one most responsive to change. —Charles Darwin

Wide in scope, all things seem to have value, options appear unlimited, challenging situations look like opportunities. Interested in most everything, finding that place inside that leads to deeper focus and concentration, discovering what is truly meaningful and important brings understanding. Growth seeks and responds to new stimuli. Distractions cause continual discontent and dissatisfaction, I pursue an endless variety of experiences, following suggestions, responding to invitations, partaking in new activities; I like stretching and learning. Open when talking about our life, liking connections, the sky is the limit. Restrictions feel like missed opportunities, we are a hang-loose, casual, informal social being, not overly guarded about our daily recognitions. Growth implies movement, advancement, progress and evolution; which creates discontent, agitation, a continuous demanding to seek and develop. Wanting a lot, easily revealing personal information, intimacy includes everything. The spark ignites through all-inclusive openness, personal development is in the forefront. Demanding of ourselves, taking on more and more, feeling pushed to the max, every invitation is an opportunity for growth, nothing should slip by, not any experience or circumstance.

Growth is usually considered positive, but nothing can grow forever. If growth of whatever kind, were to go on and on, it would eventually become monstrous and destructive. Dissolution is needed for new growth to happen. One cannot exist without the other. —Eckhart Tolle

In the positive direction, progress is the unfoldment, the continued birthing of becoming. Aspiring to learn and thrive, this goal assists us to become more skillful integrating and improving the quality of life to benefit the lives of others around. In the positive mode we take on a challenge and use it to develop clarity, self-understanding and self-actualization. These moments of lucidity and evolution are often earned through persistent willingness. Growth is an optimistic goal. In the negative posture, overstimulated, we become confused, overwhelmed and insensitive to others. Overextending, life becomes chaotic, unintentional, disorganized, as we flit from one thing to another, energy scattered. The disarray and disorder sabotage Growth, there are only so many roads we travel before the journey sets our head spinning. Priorities become mixed up, distractions eat up progress. The horizontal takes away from the vertical, depth becomes avoided for lack of time and energy. Relationships get tossed away like old sweaters, jobs left unfinished, leases broken, houses bought and sold, one big whirlwind of complications. Little time to integrate, absorb, process, or rest. In the negative position of confusion, we are overwhelmed, not knowing how to use our life for understanding, to develop, to evolve, to go deeper into what's behind the circumstances. Every opportunity cannot be pursued, too much disallows the full appreciation of any particular moment, wanting more, variety here degenerates into disorganization and disorder. Bewildered, complications get mixed up with progress. Focus, limiting options, refining attention; creating boundaries to keep intrusive demands out sets the stage for true understanding and evolution.

A BUSY LIFETIME

Most people don't really grow up. What they do is grow old, they grow tiresome even and self-righteous maybe, for it is very hard to grow. Because it means they must give up something. Usually their ignorance. —Maya Angelou

Growth in itself contains no suffering: distress comes from resistance towards Growth, creating division and conflict. Growth could be growing fat, gathering relationships, collecting experiences, finding situations that inspire progress and development, or growing tumors and any other kind of (*growth*) lump. Inner Growth, continuously becoming, recreating ourselves is a change of being. This is a busy lifetime, and a popular goal; 40% of the population choose it. Fun is less important than developing, until we learn how to have fun innerly. Sitting quietly, stopping and looking deeply, seeing what it is that is always present; inner Growth often happens from not doing anything at all. Growth is not something we achieve, it's through cultivating an attitude, openness, joy.

Change and growth take place when a person has risked himself and dares to become involved with experimenting with his own life. —*Herbert Otto*

Growth is the complement of the ordinal inspirational goal of re-evaluation. Each avoids what the other seeks. In Growth we feel a discomfort in the experience of our life feeling to be too restricted, the opposite of which is true, since available opportunities are quickly noticed. Prone to overstimulation, Growth slides to re-evaluation to catch up, to limit ourself from valuing everything, and instead to engage in only the necessary and essential, to ignore the rest. Open and revealing, people in Growth are willing to share personal stories of their life, while for those in re-evaluation there is a tendency to withdraw, to be selective about what's shared.

For me, the word further was the single most important word in my own journey. It was like my mantra, but it had very specific and poignant meaning. There were many times when the word further came to my aid. Like when I'd think I arrived someplace solid, someplace worth staying, and then I'd remember the word further, and what I understood further to really mean, and I'd realize that as much as I might like it where I was, I really wasn't where I was going yet. Even though I may have attained knowledge and understanding beyond my wildest hopes, even though I may have surpassed my highest expectations of what I might accomplish, even though I may have moved beyond many of my own mentors, the word further was always there, echoing in my mind, reminding me that there's only one objective of the journey and that I wasn't there yet. —*Jed McKenna*

Examples are: *Carlos Casteneda, Maya Angelou, Eckhart Tolle, Steven Spielberg, Allen Ginsberg, Whoopi Goldberg, Dan Rather, Angelina Jolie, Barbara Walters, Helen Keller, Timothy Leary, Yoko Ono, Eddie Murphy.*

SUBMISSION

POSITIVE: DEDICATION, DEVOTION

NEGATIVE: EXPLOITED

I stand here before you not as a prophet but as a humble servant of you, the people. Your tireless and heroic sacrifices have made it possible for me to be here today. I therefore place the remaining years of my life on your hands. I always remember the axiom: a leader is like a shepherd. He stays behind the flock, letting the most nimble go out ahead, whereupon the others follow, not realizing that all along they are being directed from behind. —Nelson Mandela

The person with the ordinal action goal of Submission finds fulfillment in support and dedication, devotion to a cause, job, person, task, family, idea, issue, group. Once actively engaged it might look like a student in an ashram or spiritual school, service to our partner and family, serving our country, enlisting in a monastic order, volunteer charity worker, political campaigning, environmental causes, devotion to the truths of a teaching, or a loyal team member. Putting others needs before our own might be empowering or disempowering. The drive behind this goal is to dissolve a sense of willfulness and self-assertion, called ego and self-importance. Sensitive to the needs of others, the ongoing journey of surrender is to live faithfully, compliantly assenting to whomever or whatever we are dedicated. The loyalty and devotion are offered to a person, issue, country, team, corporation; whatever cause is found to serve and to matter. When an appropriate object is not found, life feels unfulfilled and dissatisfying.

True strength lies in submission which permits one to dedicate his life, through devotion, to something beyond himself. —Henry Miller

Before placing ourself in the service of a cause or person, the feeling of worthlessness and low self-esteem becomes foreground. Submission is a goal on the action axis that involves doing, therefore finding issues and people of merit and value to be dedicated to offers appreciable satisfaction. Finding a raison d'être that inspires allegiance, is the healing. Holocaust survivor Elie Wiesel said: *I decided to devote my life to telling the story because I felt that having survived I owe something to the dead, and anyone who does not remember betrays them again.* An action goal, we dedicate and strive to support what we are behind for it to flourish. It's a wisdom teaching that yielding conquers the resistant, as well as the soft subduing the hard. We learn this in swimming: to resist the current, the large wave, the rip tide, and not be to be swept into it is to bend before it, to swim and follow it offers us the greatest possibility to survive.

As the soft yield of water cleaves obstinate stone, so to yield with life solves the insolvable: To yield, I have learned is to come back again. —*Laozi*

Good followers, although following orders is not always necessary. There are subtle ways to comply. The faithfulness and devotion might display itself in carefully raising a family, living quietly in a religious order, or tirelessly getting behind environmental issues. Attuned to other's needs, my focus of supportiveness inspires. Often looking tired, my eyes are sweet and sad. A readiness to yield, characterizes our tone. My fantasy would be to live in a world where everything is created, nothing new is expected, laws are followed as they are, unfamiliarity becomes a thing of the past. In this world, comradeship and loyalty are meaningful, while deceit or unfaithfulness create a broken-hearted surprise.

Women are the only exploited group in history to have been idealized into powerlessness. —*Erica Jong*

In the negative we are victim to circumstances, exploited, imposed upon and then I become mindlessly compliant. In the positive our sense of helpful caring and devotion are appreciated and bring to us a sense of fulfillment. What goes awry and brings this to a negative direction is being in a space that is out of tune with our values. Then we become subservient, victimized, helpless, in bondage, resigned, exploited. This gainless idea of being ruled and supporting another at the price and risk of our own happiness and development sets a tone for disintegration. In this negative direction we are subservient to circumstances, asking permission to do even small things, to the point of feeling helpless and stuck. Tipped into a subordinate secondary mind-set, personal responsibility is relinquished, handed over to a principle, an official directive, teacher or doctrine, something to adhere to outside of ourself. Having guidelines, a rule book, knowing what is expected offers relief, once a docile, deferential posture takes root. *Tell me what to do,* becomes theme, wanting to move to the back of the group, rather than impact or push a situation.

VALUING SERVICE

I am not the person who insists on having my way. Attached to an organization, whether it be a hospital, educational facility, retreat center, health spa, Fourth Way School, corporation, or even one individual; autonomy is squashed for dependency. A fear of disloyalty, not being dedicated enough, observing others in the organization or my teacher, partner or boss not following the rules; this reinforces a lack of dependability from others, straining expectations, reinforcing the trapped feeling, supporting a negative inclination. Faithful to a fault, this is the person who stands behind their boss, marriage, guru or cause long after the ship sinks. Lacking high-powered, bold, high-octane; I will not be your innovative revolutionary.

True heroism is remarkably sober, very undramatic. It is not the urge to surpass all others at whatever cost, but the urge to serve others at whatever cost. —Arthur Ashe

The shift to the positive track comes from dedication to our principles, chosen relationships and tasks, aligning quality and worth to daily life. Accountability to myself and self-management are key to shifting into the positive mode. Carefully choosing who and what our devotion is attached to, dedication needs to be towards what is truly of value as well as not becoming enslaved to what is loved. Having appropriate causes or people to commit to, the rewards repay the efforts as well as having an inspired life of standing behind our ideals. Replacing blind faith with a seeing intentional conviction brings about trust and confidence in our own being. A person with this quality of faith is not a believer, instead has certainty in truth allowing trust to arise, and with that comes understanding. Treading carefully, heedful, actually perceiving ourselves as too dominant, we avoid forcing a situation. Sliding to domination, I want to counteract and neutralize the opposite goal of domination, feeling a need to become even more yielding, the opposite of what is needed. 10% of the population choose a goal of Submission.

The beauty and charm of selfless love and service should not die away from the face of the earth. The world should know that a life of dedication is possible, that a life inspired by love and service to humanity is possible. —Amma

Examples are: *Dian Fossey, Ralph Nader, Florence Nightingale, Coretta Scott King, Martin Luther King, Jane Fonda, Ralph Nader, Mother Teresa, Mr. Rogers, Albert Schweitzer, Gloria Steinem, Joan D'Arc, Princess Diana, Amma, Nancy Reagan, Michael Jackson, Elie Wiesel, Mahatma Gandhi, Jimmy Carter, Ma Jaya Sati Bhagavati, Nelson Mandela, Joan Baez.*

DOMINANCE

POSITIVE: LEADERSHIP

NEGATIVE: DICTATORSHIP

If you even dream of beating me you'd better wake up and apologize.
—*Muhammad Ali*

When the person with this goal is a winner it's because they want to be. And winning is on my mind. Right from childhood we take over, want to be in charge, control the house, forcefully influence events and to lead the way. The urge to be in command, the one in position of authority has many postures. In one situation it can look like a suicide threat or victim role, in another it might be class president, the disruptive force at a wedding, lead in a school play, the child who won't give up the swing, director of a corporation or a prize fighter. Dominance is always on. We are endlessly attentive to winning and success, leading and directing, from the moment I enter a room or conversation, I am in control, I am in your space, and that's it. The individual with a goal of Dominance remains in the forefront no matter whose needs are prominent. Regardless to who is filming, whose money is paying for the movie, who is directing, we always rise to the top, we cannot help but want to, demand to, gain the upper hand. We are a law unto ourselves, determined, rarely yielding to outside influences, making our own rules and making rules for others to follow. Listen to the words: insist, refuse, willful, control, leadership, ruler, pushy, demanding; within this framework this Dominant person lives.

No matter what you do, be your best at it. If you're going to be a bum, be the best bum there is. —*Robert Mitchum*

Through responsible leadership, which is true service to the other, the purpose of this goal is sometimes experienced and expressed. A good leader does not compromise compassion for authority. I use my high energy to create a winning proposition from every experience and generally, like a good horseman the reins stay in my hands. Right from childhood we are creating situations that show others what to do and where we want to be in charge. To raise a child who has chosen a goal of Dominance it is important to give them areas of control. For example, having the job of setting the table or handing out dessert. Establish clear limits or this will be an unhappy battleground home. You can not coax children out of this goal, and they are always eager to step in where there is weakness, so beware.

It's better to be a pirate than to join the navy. —*Steve Jobs*

In the positive mode, as a determined capable leader, we are willing to step forward and take on responsibilities. This exalted action role in a positive posture is engaging, since there is a win-win quality; a successful leader creates an environment where others can also flourish. Learning to submit to the rules of each situation, to yield and comply, to respect others needs, to be responsible to my own part and to back away from telling others their obligations, to make the effort to be a good sport, a team player, maintains the positive direction of this goal. In the negative arena you will find a bully, a controlling, insensitive person who dictates and takes advantage. In the negative posture there is only the thrust to win, regardless of the other person's loss. Often insensitive to the needs of those around, we become demanding and Dominating, a poor sport. Offering little respect for the rights of others, we claim and demand our rights be respected.

W I N N I N G

If this were a dictatorship it would be a heck of a lot easier as long as I'm the dictator. —*George W. Bush*

This is the only goal that is insistent around not being *gotten*. While we casually jab and chip away, we do not want to be poked back. This has been likened to the hierarchy of the dominant chicken who pecks all the other chickens but none can peck him. Chickens peck or threaten to peck as a means of establishing social rank. In a chicken yard the most Dominant chickens assert their supremacy by pecking at the weaker ones without the fear that the weaker ones will peck back. Considered a *dominance hierarchy*, determining who is the *top chicken*, the *bottom chicken*, and where all the rest fit in between. The term pecking order originated here. This is the entrepreneur who runs his own company, or at least is either at the top of the corporation or in a private mode. Giving orders with ease; taking orders creates discomfort. As a sports coach, prison guard, army captain, board director, serial killer, rapist, president of a corporation, we rise to the occasion. Leading or getting our way, can be by example, by persuasion, by subtly convincing others that they want to do something, although it is actually my agenda. The key is that, subtly or blatantly, we lead.

Winning takes care of everything. —*Tiger Woods*

Wanting to initiate events, with our goal of Dominance we want nothing to happen that we do not cause. Those who behave independent from us are seen as disrespectful, disloyal, undermining, deceitful, disobedient, even treasonous. Experiences that happen apart from our instigation is a betrayal, bringing up a feeling that the people are revolting and need to be subdued, crushed or defeated. This is the one-man/

woman, one-party rule and it is formidable; it's a dilemma to freely show independent behavior in the presence of any of us with the goal of Domination. Unable to let things be, instead, we have to make things materialize as we want them to; once we arrive each event is our orchestration. A moment where we are not in control gets quickly noted and remembered as something to avoid in the near future; it isn't repeated often. Rarely can anyone tell me what to do, instead, we tell most others what to do. Insisting that things happen according to our command, we issue orders with little, if any room for questions. Looking for a life partner, husband or wife that is loyal and faithful, not ever wanting to be betrayed or let down, who will be a good team member; this is the meaning of marriage to the person with the goal of Domination.

I have the same goal I've had ever since I was a girl: I want to rule the world.
—*Madonna Ciccone*

Our noticeable inconsistent behavior is not a looseness or by chance, it is based on our need to change things around so to remain Dominant, to keep shifting course and to remain leader. This does not make us as unreliable or erratic as one may think, the plan changes for the purpose of exercising Dominance, to remain on top of the game plan; to win. A good organizer and take charge person, often we are looking out for a person we have little connection to, making great effort not to let circumstances constrict or oppress us.

I've seen people that are extremely brilliant and they don't have the staying power. They don't have that never give up quality. I've always said that other than bad ideas, which is a reason for failure, the ability to never ever quit, or give up is something that is very very important for success as an entrepreneur. When someone challenges you, fight back, be brutal, be tough.
—*Donald Trump*

People with a goal of Dominance may be remembered as a Nazi, serial killer, mugger, bully, or real estate mogul. We also make a strong military chief, prison warden, corporate leader, heads of State, rock stars, big fish in the pond. With a strong need to be in control, life for us is a challenge and we are determined to overcome or win with victory. With the goal of Dominance in our slide to submission we view ourself as too passive. Wanting to be in a position as a leader, wanting to be respected, with followers in the position behind, we are looking to change the behavior of others, not our own. Seeing ourselves as having too much of our opposite slide, submission, we try to counteract it. Wanting more Dominance, more assertiveness, more ambition, until able to see in perspective we see a distorted self-image. Kings in Dominance—Donald Trump, Madonna, Howard Hughes, Mary Kay Ash, Ted Turner, Frank Sinatra, Katherine Hepburn, P. Diddy, Joan Rivers—are very powerful people. 10% of the population have this exalted action goal.

Winning isn't everything, it's the only thing. It's not a sometime thing, it's an all-time thing. You don't win once in a while, winning is a habit. If winning isn't everything, why do they keep score? There is no room for second place. There is only one place in my game and that is first place. I have never finished second twice in my life, and I never want to finish second again. We didn't lose the game; we just ran out of time. —Vince Lombardi

Examples are: *Ayatollah Khomeini, Madonna, Mohammed Ali, Mr. T, Mohammar Khadafy, George W. Bush Jr., Mike Tyson, Eminem, Napoleon, Mary Kay Ash, Grace Jones, Frank Sinatra, Katherine Hepburn, J. Paul Getty, P. Diddy, Charles Bronson, Ferdinand and Imelda Marcos, Marlon Brando, Fidel Castro, Ho Chi Minh, Tiger Woods, Ray Charles, Annie Duke, Bernie Madoff, Tom Cruise, Joan Rivers, George Gurdjieff, Mae West, Ted Turner, Deepak Chopra, Condoleeza Rice, Sting, John Wayne, Jack the Ripper, Joseph Stalin, Donald Trump, Steve Jobs, Howard Hughes.*

RELAXATION

POSITIVE: FLOW, EQUILIBRIUM

NEGATIVE: STAGNATION, INERTIA

Who has a Goal and yet has not a goal. —A koan and riddle

*L*ife happens smoothly without challenge or drama. In each experience we look like we just won the lottery without buying the ticket. Things drop into my lap and few demands are made. Only by truly understanding how to be in flow and relax can this goal be achieved. Rest, leisure, effortlessness and what the world sees as vacation time is taking life as it arrives. The assimilation goal, neutral and impartial, its point is to let go, rather than make things happen. This is a beautiful opportunity, to portray what others rarely experience. Without interfering or pushing; wealth, satisfaction and pleasure appear. The great teaching in this goal is that life is beautiful when you trust and don't stand in the way.

Just relax, everyone around you is working too hard. —Bauvard

In the positive mode Relaxation appears easy, because it is. In the positive we are in a place of being rather than doing, allowing life to unfold without drama; happy, easygoing, fun-loving, adaptable, free-flowing, and stressless. Floating, lying on top of the water and letting it carry us; Relaxation is a state and can't be forced. Time stops, and both the body and mind surrender. To live in the positive part of the goal of Relaxation, like the proverb, *go with the flow,* is to remain non-judgmental, receiving life as it comes, accepting what appears or disappears. Equilibrium, balance, presence of mind, stability and poise, is a graphic representation of the positive in this goal. Things running smoothly, neither ending nor beginning, with consistence, there are no disruptions. Within this dynamic process of balancing, being available and choiceless, in motion from left to right, passing through dead center, here, balance happens, it comes through the whole experience, not in the frozen, static middle.

Don't underestimate the value of Doing Nothing, of just going along, listening to all the things you can't hear, and not bothering.
—*Pooh's Little Instruction Book*

In the negative mode there is a quality of being stuck, apathetic, sluggish, lazy, uncommitted or too busy, and sometimes there appears an urge to struggle, taking on hard assignments. The negative aspect, stagnation and inertia, lethargic, uncommitted or too busy blocks the flow, so that enjoyment and pleasure get stuck until eventually exhaustion overtakes us. What happens easily in the positive, does not work in the negative. Swimming like a rock, we are no longer suspended in a float, but pulled down like a stone. The stability and comfort in living with things as they are, often holds back development, breakthroughs, innovation and discovery. Little motion forestalls downward movement, at the expense of upward movement. At times taking the path of least resistance, lack of drive and force makes this goal evade, lack ambition, coast through life. Motivated to avoid, eliminate or relieve stress, not much changes in our life. Contradictions and differences are dodged. It's more comfortable to sail along with the status quo, becoming a reliable person, things rarely fall apart, but neither do they improve.

Frankly, I got into the movies because I like movies a lot. With my sunglasses on, I'm Jack Nicholson. Without them, I'm fat and 60. —*Jack Nicholson*

STATUS QUO

Choices are made on the basis of least effort, with the slightest challenge, trouble free. Very little to overcome, we are the surfers and beach people, permanent baby sitters, lay around watching TV soaps, living on inheritance, social security or trust funds, lifetime students, wino street or beach bums, yogis off in the mountains, gigolos and kept women, contented with life. No real ambition, not even to work for favorite material items. Smiling, we look satisfied with life, the eyes wide open and relaxed in the positive, vacant and morose in the negative, not really caring about much. Being concerned with equality, not wanting to owe or be owed, exchanges are preferred to be equitable and completed. Driven to the negative, in a restaurant the bill gets picked apart, even the soda or coffee is computed to the party who ordered it.

What, me worry? Most people are so lazy, we don't even exercise good judgement. —*Alfred E. Neuman*

To shift into action, this neutral goal may have to borrow an appropriate positive aspect from another goal. The neutral assimilation goal of Relaxation has no complementary opposite, it slides to whatever goal it chooses, with the aim to cause no disruption of *what is*. Nothing much to overcome or struggle with, no real ambition, feeling content with life, sort of like a satisfied bovine. Sliding means temporarily shifting to another goal, whatever may appear best at that moment. To flow with the winds of change and not resist the natural flow of the universe allowing it to move smoothly through, brings about this place of Relaxation. As in all goals, choosing Relaxation we still might not learn how to rest or how to go with the flow. In Relaxation our energy does not move, it becomes still, peaceful; we disappear. Wanting leaves, the past and future withdraw, nothing to achieve or acquire, less doing and activity. Look at a balloon as it offers no resistance, this is true present moment harmony. It's tapping into life as it comes along. 7% of the population have this goal.

Relaxation means releasing all concern and tension and letting the natural order of life flow through one's being. —*Donald Curtis*

Examples are: *George Hamilton, Jack Nicholson, Alfred E. Neuman (what, me worry), Georgia O'Keefe, Ringo Starr, Bugs Bunny, Grace Kelly, Buddha.*

SYSTEM FIFTEEN

STYLE

CAUTION, POWER, RESERVED, PASSION, PERSEVERANCE, AGGRESSION, OBSERVATION

We all view the world through individual filters. Those filters—our personalities, attitudes, points of view, our 'styles'—powerfully influence the interpretations that we give to the events in our lives; those interpretations, in turn, determine how we will respond, and therefore how we will ultimately be responded to. The presence of these filters is neither good nor bad; it just is. Some filters may be healthy and constructive, while others may be distorted and destructive. But to live effectively, you've got to recognize the presence of your filters, and take care that they don't distort your perceptions so as to mislead you in your decision making. —Philip McGraw

CAUTION: Positive: deliberation **Negative:** phobia, paranoia

POWER: Positive: authority **Negative:** oppression

RESERVED: Positive: restraint **Negative:** inhibition, repression

PASSION: Positive: self-actualization, enthusiasm **Negative:** identification

PERSEVERANCE: Positive: persistence **Negative:** monotony, unchangeable

AGRESSION: Positive: dynamism **Negative:** belligerence

OBSERVATION: Positive: clarity **Negative:** surveillance

The Style is the approach and manner we choose to arrive at our desired objective or destination. It is our tone, character, appearance, *modus operandi* coloring most of our experiences since it has high visibility as we go about our life. Arriving at the movie theatre in a limousine creates a very different appearance and experience than showing up on a bicycle or on roller blades. Since it is the approach and method in which we most often express ourself, it will also be the way in which we are seen by others. This is the personality trait that we pick that assists us towards our goal. It fills us with a specific energy, then drives us to behave in one of seven ways. As our personality's way of acting on our goal, our approach to life, we are directly effected and impacted since this is the manner in which people respond to us.

Style is not something applied. It is something that permeates. It is of the nature of that in which it is found, whether the poem, the manner of a god, the bearing of a man. It is not a dress. —*Wallace Stevens*

Our Style, or way in which we live our life, whether it is in caution, passion, or through observation, creates a particular kind of experience for us and makes a statement to the world. It's the road we take, the starting place we originate, and the vehicle we operate from: driving in a Hummer we feel different than driving in a Jaguar. Showing up in a Limo makes a distinct impression on people compared to seeing us arrive on a motorcycle. We may not feel or appear the same, regardless, we reach our goal. Essentially our Style is how the world perceives us and our customary way of getting to where we want. We choose a specific Style in order to accomplish and get what we want done, it is the means by which we reach our goal. And is highly visible, so it has tremendous influence on our behavior and energy and on how the world greets and treats us.

Create your own visual style, let it be unique for yourself and yet identifiable for others—*Orson Welles*

Expression		Inspiration	
Ordinal	Exalted	Ordinal	Exalted
CAUTION	POWER	RESERVED	PASSION
+deliberation	+authority	+restraint	+self-actualization
-phobia, paranoia	-oppression	-inhibition, repression	-identification

Action		Assimilation
Ordinal	Exalted	Neutral
PERSEVERANCE	AGGRESSION	OBSERVATION
+persistence	+dynamism	+clarity
-monotony, unchangeable	-belligerance	-surveillance

Chart 7: Style: Our Modus Operandi

Style is a strong coloration for personality and reflects the way in which we prefer to live our life. It is the beginning place or location, defining what path, method, practice or course we follow to reach our goal. It is the underlying behavior pattern of the personality.

Style is knowing who you are, what you want to say, and not giving a damn.
—*Gore Vidal*

Demonstrating Style using the imagery of a vehicle as a description of our Style: the bullet-proof limousine is caution, a Hummer and cement truck is power, a Cadillac, Bentley, Tesla and Mercedes Benz are reserved, a sea foam green Jaguar and a cardinal metallic red Porsche are passion, a snowplow and bulldozer is perseverance, a Harley-Davidson and Sports Utility Vehicles are aggression, a slow train and Greyhound bus is observation. How we approach and achieve our aim is our Style. It is the manner in which a goal is pursued, the primary way issues are approached, the means to the end. Essentially it's the how of living our life; passionately, aggressively, cautiously, in observation, persevering, reserved, or with power. Watching how people act, Style is always visible and apparent, *standard operating procedure*, it exists as a presence.

Style is the mind skating circles around itself as it moves forward.
—*Robert Frost*

CAUTION

POSITIVE: DELIBERATION

NEGATIVE: PHOBIA, PARANOIA

Look-before-you-leap

—the bullet-proof limousine—

*I*n a Caution Style there is an inner directed energy that is watchful, and careful before taking action. It expresses itself as a kinesthetic presence, the body detects and senses, signalling to figure out what might happen before making a decision. Deliberately controlling expression, carefully checking out the highway route before taking the trip, or in the negative direction, just not going, even if they'd like to, feeling it's better to not go. The concern lies in the consequences and the avoidance of making an error, for this person clearly blocks risk-taking. Carefully thinking things through before making a decision, wanting to stay out of harm's way, their game plan is to get to their destination while avoiding any problems. To know what a Caution person feels, imagine being in a foreign country paying for a meal, looking carefully over the receipt and change; the unfamiliarity of different currency justifies this hesitant behavior. Restrained rather than feeling regret, this is not the party goer who will be dancing on the tabletops in a spontaneous leap. This will not be the guy chasing after the bank robber to get the license plate number. Risk-adverse, joining the Auto club of America making certain that home and car insurance are paid for, bases well covered. The location of this path of life is the outer road, riding in a bullet-proof limousine, directed towards reaching their goal.

I need a caution: 'Slippery When Wet' sign, because I just spilled my ego, all over the floor. —Jarod Kintz

When the deliberation becomes endless it creates a stuck frozen quality that turns into a phobia. People who fear flying, escalators, heights, walking under ladders, swimming in the ocean, aversion to spiders, each becomes a reflection of the negative part of Caution. They will be wiping down their silverware in a restaurant, careful to wash their hands. They have an inner, introverted experience of contraction. Taking time so as not to make an error, they appear restrained in personality. The range is from prudent and discreet, showing good judgment, to careful and guarded, sliding to vigilant and exacting, until, finally, unreasonable exaggerated fear. The negative part, phobia and paranoia, may originate as anxiety and can blow up into irrational fears like claustrophobia (enclosed places), monophobia (alone), aerophobia (flying), mysophobia(germs), acrophobia (heights). Apprehensive about unfamiliar situations, shifting away from the anxiety is managed by moving to the positive part of the power style, which is authority. That's giving up the bullet proof limo for a Hummer.

'You still think I've gone cracked in the head,' Ben said, amused. 'Listen, if tomorrow we pulled into Biren and someone told you there were shamble-men in the woods, would you believe them?' My father shook his head. 'What if two people told you?' Another shake. Ben leaned forward on his stump. 'What if a dozen people told you?'. With perfect earnestness, that shamble-men were out in the fields eating.' Of course I wouldn't believe them,' my father said irritated, 'It's ridiculous.' 'Of course it is,' Ben agreed,

raising a finger. But the real question is this, 'Would you go into the woods?'
—*Patrick Rothfuss*

In the positive, they are deliberate and check ocean conditions before going into the water, in the negative, concerned about sharks, sea lice and jellyfish, they just won't go in, saying *I'd like to, but I'd better not.* Careful, tactful and prudent in what they do, a bit unsure of themselves, detailed and exacting in their work and lives, they like to feel certain about the situation and assured before making a decision. Quick to recognize danger, yet, when balanced, they are diplomatic pulling back until feeling safe. This is the bullet-proof limousine, paying close attention; driving is a dangerous venture. Maintaining a specific distance from other cars, this is not a smooth ride, accelerating and decelerating, making corrections, life, also, is a precarious instability.

Don't ever take a fence down until you know why it was put up.
—*Robert Frost*

Accidents or mistakes are unusual, although opportunities are missed while hanging back, holding off, hesitating; the missed opportunities come from anxiety and unreasonable planning, over thinking and doubt. Caution slides to power and is an effective path once deciding upon a course of action and willing to be an authority. Since Caution holds a person back, subduing intensity, taking time, it's sometimes difficult to achieve prominence in the world while having this style. To focus on each step, to be wary of a misstep; allowing a large margin of safety requires a lot of extra stages along the way. An inward private style, often held back, 20% of the population choose this ordinal, expressive style.

Caution is a most valuable asset in fishing, especially if you are the fish.
—*Anonymous*

Examples include: *Stephen King, Dan Rather, Winnie Mandela, Paul Simon, Vanna White, Deepak Chopra.*

POWER

POSITIVE: AUTHORITY

NEGATIVE: OPPRESSION

I'm in charge here.

— *the Hummer, a cement truck, a caterpillar tractor, a bulldozer*—

The buck stops with the guy who signs the checks. The world is changing very fast. Big will not beat small anymore. It will be the fast beating the slow. —Rupert Murdoch

A person with a Power Style approaches life confidently carrying authority and leadership. Their method is to step forth as if they know, speaking with confidence; they are convincing and commanding. One man, bedridden and in a semi-coma, still managed to make his bullying presence felt by clapping and whistling so those around would drop everything and show up. This is the inner road driven in a Hummer, bulldozer or cement truck to reach their goal. If you happen to be in the way they could move over or go around you, but why should they make that effort, when it's easier to drive right over you. Risk-taking, challenges, living on the edge of upheaval, keeps life juicy. Otherwise bored, they take pleasure in daredevil dangerous thrills, not backing off, eagerly taking chances. Powerful and commanding, they enjoy throwing their load around. Circumstances rarely unnerve them, their measure of safety is inside; feeling strong, self-reliant, domineering and certain, the world to them looks to be safe and sound.

Ultimately, the only power to which man should aspire is that which he exercises over himself. —Elie Wiesel

This is the style that drives by in a Hummer, shifting lanes; others move aside so as not to get bashed. They get a kick out of throwing their weight around, you will feel their presence, thrusting outward, bold and uncontained. In a positive mode this influential style, always exudes capability, is effective; they instill assurance. Opportunities are grabbed, adventures are followed with confidence, spunk and spirit, they are always willing to take the bull by the horns and ride out a challenge. Persuasive, directly impacted, people believe they know what they are talking about and feel comfortable when the Power point takes the helm. Actually, when they aren't quite certain, they bluff their way, acting convincingly as if they are self-assured.

The greater the power the more dangerous the abuse. —Edmund Burke

Decisive in behavior, unlike people with a caution style, things are not broken down step by step, they are decided upon fearlessly, regardless to knowing or even understanding the situation. This adventurous Power style feels that victory can be wrestled from the jaws of defeat right at the eleventh hour. Exacting, methodical, meticulousness is not tightly held on to as they pick up the gauntlet to face a challenge. Generally rising in position, rarely hesitant, opportunities hardly ever slide by, becoming natural leaders, they are visible and influential in the realm of politics, spiritual leadership, the medical profession, corporations, entertainment and the business of war.

Power never takes a back step—only in the face of more power. —Malcolm X

When they are negative, behaving as an oppressor, the flagrant heaviness creates a queasy feeling of discomfort for those around. Compliance to the person in this style happens regardless. The oppressive energy continues its spiral, as they become pushy, overly manipulative, obsessed, competitive, browbeating and difficult to deal with. Power is a showy style, a strong presence, intimidating, imposing and heavy-handed. Power neither likes to be criticized nor have their authority questioned. High-handed and dogmatic, they are often unconscious about being unbearably iron-fisted even when told. In matters of detail they are wide-of-the-mark, careless, heavy-footed, not graceful; this will not be the ballet dancer or jeweler setting delicate stones in your wedding ring. Seen in the light of their own relationship to Power, not knowing the difference between real Power and egoic Power, their life has a disharmonious quality.

Power consists not in being able to strike another but in being able to control oneself when anger arises. —*Muhammad*

Real Power can not be taken away without our permission. To shift out of the negative is to move to the positive of caution, which is deliberation. Caution is a helpful place to lay low from excessive strong-arming, this becomes a place to retreat to, taking a big break, out of harm's way. Rather then throw their weight around, the ability to impact others, to be listened to with convincing authority without oppressing others is received positively when coming from an honest, wholesome place of certainty. In the positive Power is flexible, embracing, generous, focused, productive, has good boundaries and is community oriented. Noting whether you feel comfortable or uncomfortable around their presence belies if they are coming from their positive or negative expression of Power. The location of this path of life is the inner road driven in a Hummer to ultimately reach their goal.

Power over others is weakness disguised as strength. True power is within, and it is available to you now. —Eckhart Tolle

10% of the population has this expressive exalted style.

Examples include: *Bill Cosby, Malcolm X, Count Dracula, Rasputin, Rupert Murdoch, Ferdinand and Imelda Marcos, Yoko Ono, Orson Wells, Marlon Brando, Barbara Bush, Al Pacino, Michael Jordin, Werner Erhard, Norman Mailer, Madonna, Frank Sinatra, Socrates, Machiavelli.*

RESERVED

POSITIVE: RESTRAINT

NEGATIVE: INHIBITION, REPRESSION

I express precisely what I want to express.
—a Cadillac, Bentley, Tesla and Mercedes Benz—

This style carries withheld inner developed emotional restraint and self-control. Contained emotions allow time and energy for the pursuit of internal refinement. To hold something back for future use with a specific purpose in mind in our culture is considered polished and courteous, while at the same time, cool reticence or a composed manner is also considered to be inhibited and repressed.

Not to have control over the senses is like sailing a rudderless ship, bound to break into pieces on coming in contact with the very first rock. —Gandhi

The ability to restrain spontaneous outbursts in the service of conserving energy is second nature for the Reserved Style. This is useful for figure skating, martial arts, ballet, dressage, Tai Chi, Gurdjieff movements, painting icons, art restoration and other skills that require poise, presence of mind, level-headedness and moderation. Disciplines that engage contained motion of the body or intricate movements requiring focus and direction are filled with people who have Reserved Style. Vocations and professionals that engage this refinement and sophistication include gourmet cooking, maitre d's, neurosurgery, fashion design, yoga teachers, butlers, diplomats and classical musicians.

If it's not right, don't do it; if it's not true, don't say it. Keep your impulses in reserve. —Marcus Aurelius

One of the reasons I'm excited by what visionary Elon Musk has done with the Tesla is to show that you can reduce global warming and drive a powerful, fun car. A cool car helps make a cooler planet. —Dr. Dean Ornish

Often considered withholding, inhibited, restrained, subdued, essentially they are unaware of their own feelings, moving through life at a deliberate and measured pace. Liking to feel in control of their life, reserved in temperament, they are often seen as *cool as a cucumber.* Civilized behavior, tasteful, the tactful discretion can be seen as either unresponsive and repressed or good breeding. They rarely let their hair down, unless it follows a few stiff drinks, drug use, or hanging out with wild, expressive, acting out people. Energy is drawn up and in, making for held back yet graceful containment.

The big difference between a warrior and a victim is that the victim represses, and the warrior refrains. Victims repress because they are afraid to show the emotions, afraid to say what they want to say. To refrain is not the same thing as repression. To refrain is to hold emotions and to express them in the right moment, not before, not later. —Miguel Ruiz

Driving a Cadillac or Bentley along the low road, composed and unruffled, self-controlled; this is internal refinement. Often a style chosen by ballet dancers, Alexander teachers, Taoist Tai Chi instructors, yoga instructors, gymnasts and brain surgeons. There is a strong positive ability to focus and contain energy. The refinement, good taste and elegance that develops over time allows them to feel in control of their life and serves to add beauty to the world, teaching sophistication, poise and focus. In the negative, this leads to a quality of repression that is blocked and appears as unresponsive and cut off. The quality of constraint, toned down and inhibited, shifts dramatically when they are drunk, doing drugs or hanging around wild party-goers. Sliding to the complementary opposite exalted style, passion, releases the fear of excess, cutting off civilized inhibition; here comes animation, spontaneity, enthusiasm and excitement.

Repression is not the way to virtue. When people restrain themselves out of fear, their lives are by necessity diminished. They become rigid and defensive, and their self stops growing. Only through freely chosen discipline can life be enjoyed, and still kept within the bounds of reason. If a person learns to control his instinctual desires, not because he 'has' to, because he 'wants' to, he can enjoy himself without becoming addicted. —Mihaly Csikszentmihalyi

Nonchalant temperament, rarely displaying being fired up, this internal sophistication permits an expression of emotions that allows them to appear like products of good breeding, i.e. a Mercedes Benz or a classy Tesla. Restrained tastefulness looks at home in formal dress attire, whether in a tuxedo or a long gown. Low key, often avoiding excess, rarely does big trouble show up in their daily personal world. Unlikely to go overboard, subdued, curbed, immediate reactions are well hidden. Relationships may lack clarity, since this is the one style that is difficult to read. Emotions withheld, they are aloof and unimpressionable; others easily misunderstand the signals leaving the person with a style of Reserved misread. Shifting, practicing animation and enthusiasm maintains the positive direction, restrained refined grace, avoiding the negative of inhibition and repression. The location of this path of life is the low road driven in a Bentley, Cadillac, Mercedes Benz or Tesla to reach their goal.

Living apart and at peace with myself, I came to realize more vividly the meaning of the doctrine of acceptance. To refrain from giving advice, to refrain from meddling in the affairs of others, to refrain, even though the motives be the highest, from tampering with another's way of life—so simple, yet so difficult for an active spirit. —Henry Miller

This ordinal inspirational style is in 3% of the population.

Through hard work, restraint and perseverance you can live your dreams. A good leader will learn to harness his gifts toward his goal. —Dr. Ben Carson

Examples include: *Fred Astaire, Bernard Goetz, Marcus Aurelius, Diane Keaton, Jacqueline Kennedy, Nancy Reagan, David Niven, Alec Guiness, Prince Charles, Judy Collins, Ludwig Wittgenstein, Clint Eastwood, Art Garfunkel, Gloria Steinem, Mia Farrow, Martha Stewart, Lisa Marie Presley, George Hamilton, Marlene Dietrich, Pierce Brosnan, Marianne Williamson, Cher, Meryl Streep, Dr. Ben Carson, Denzel Washington, Anna Wintour, Victoria Beckham, Peter Jennings, Cary Grant, Dr. Dean Ornish.*

PASSION

POSITIVE: SELF-ACTUALIZATION, ENTHUSIASM

NEGATIVE: IDENTIFICATION, EXTREMISM

I'm doing this now, who cares about the consequences!
—a seafoam green Jaguar and cardinal red metallic Porsche—

In this style there is intensity in a variety of experiences; beautiful moments, engaging music, and life itself is experienced in the full range of a song. In fact, when the cell phone rings it's Louis Armstrong singing *What a Wonderful World*. The black keys are as important as the white keys, the piano as well as the rest of the orchestra fill in to create a stirring full performance. There is energy, excitement, animation, spontaneity, enthusiasm and ultimately exhaustion for a partner who hangs around without having a Passion Style nature.

Every year I live I am more convinced that the waste of life lies in the love we have not given, the powers we have not used, the selfish prudence that will risk nothing, and which shirking pain, misses happiness as well. No one ever yet was the poorer in the long run for having once in a lifetime 'let out all the length of all the reins.'—Mary Cholomondeley

Intensity is the aim here, life in the Passion zone. People are drawn to this colorful type who casually shares intimate personal facts about their life. Lacking restraint, uninhibited, not your keep the lid on type, they let you know about the nude beach they go to, the masseuse who offered a happy ending massage, their strong opinion about how unkind you are to your mother, or they pick you up and twirl you around to music or to no music. Living in the present moment, following their dream, spontaneous and involved; the possibility for self-actualization through Passion is not just a myth. They get what they want by being enlivened, spirited, high-powered, animated and involved. Enthusiasm and strong emotions, this is the go for it person. Driving along the high road in a fire red Porsche or beautiful sea foam green Jaguar with a fuschia leather interior, or a bright red bicycle with a strikingly vibrant suede seat, life is approached with zest and sparkle. Passion gives the personality the coloration of expressive emotional reactions. *Yes,* with an exclamation point, is a favorite word. Enthusiasm, aliveness, is part of each project. Intense, filled with *Wow! Terrific! Fabulous! Life is beautiful! Heartfelt, Miraculous! Full speed ahead! Life is great and terrible, tragic with yearning as well as celebration!* Sorrow and joy slide easily.

You know, passion is necessary to understand truth—I am using the word 'passion' in its full significance —because to feel strongly, to feel deeply, with all your being, is essential; otherwise that strange thing called reality will never come to you. But your religions, your saints say you must not have desire, you must control, suppress, overcome, destroy, which means that you come to truth burnt out, worn out, empty, dead. You must have passion to meet this strange thing called life, and you cannot have passion, intense feeling, if you are mesmerized by society, by custom, if you are entangled in beliefs, dogmas, rituals. —Jiddu Krishnamurti

Consequences are not forefront. High-spirited and generally success-ful, the play La Cage Aux Folles must have been written about Passion Style, dramatized in the songs: *The Best of Times* and *I Am What I Am.* The movie *La La Land,* where the cast sings and dances on car tops and along the highway stirring hearts and smiles is a great Passion point. Zumba classes to Spanish music on the beach, singing *New York New York* publicly when they arrive in Manhattan, this person is enlivened.

Self-revelation, shouting from the rooftops who they are; privacy or avoiding problems is not a major need. Outrageous behavior, saying things for shock value, usually a colorful person to be around, if you can handle it. Bubbly, they look like they're having a good time, gesticulating as they talk; welcome to the fun in the moment, let's go for it, immediate response person. This is a style that makes choices based on what turns them on.

Passion burns down every branch of exhaustion; Passion's the Supreme Elixir and renews all things; No one can grow exhausted when passion is born! —*Rumi*

In the positive there is heightened awareness, the willingness to live fully, be spontaneous; to live now, minus the worry—regardless to consequences. In the moment, fresh and vital, extreme and outlandish, fervent and eager, inspired and creative, easily achieving what's wanted. Able to realize their dreams, inspiring others, amplifying life, this style exudes the energy to go after whatever is desired, whatever holds excitement.

It's a bonfire at midnight on the top edge of a hill, this meeting again with you. —*Rumi*

In the negative mode, getting caught up in the charge and enthusiasm, losing perspective, overestimating the importance of the thing at hand, drowning in the drama, loose, blatant, outrageous and outlandish; eventually they wear down. This leads to unnecessary suffering. Reactive, even overreacting and exaggerated, things shift out of focus. Mountains out of molehills, little becomes big, until proportion is only a subjective term. Thinking that the slice of pie is the whole pie, an irrational investment or identification occurs. Compromise is not in their vocabulary, restrictions are like poison. The fear of being restrained, which feels like a nail in the foot, heart or intellect, like putting a governor on a racing car, is handled according to the level of their maturity. Flagrant, heedless, head-strong, gesticulating, sometimes obstreperous, feelings become accentuated, suffering is waiting around the corner. Easily irritated, distracted, overwrought, overreacting, irrational, exaggerating, out of proportion; taking on other's difficult stories emotionally as if it was personally happening to them. Identifying with the misfortune, taking the part to be the whole, the feeling of being the problem arises. Losing perspective in the emotions of the moment creates the identification and results in imagining that the immediate circumstances are all that is real. Seeing an accident, looking at disaster on the front page of the paper; these become personal moments for upset, not assisting the issue, instead, identifying and taking on the pain. Dramas, emotional upheavals, involved with other peoples lives and issues, invested in the outcome; Passion Style can slide from: *Life is fabulous* to *Life is exhausting and rough.* Straying from the positive, self-actualization, where we become more of who we really are, we become less ourselves losing our center getting carried away, absorbed into external thoughts and ideas.

Be still when you have nothing to say; when genuine passion moves you, say what you've got to say, and say it hot. —D.H. *Lawrence*

In a Passion Style it is essential to find ways to have freedom from constant emotional involvement so as not to be carried into a whirlwind. Developing self-control, maturity to be thoughtful to self and to others shifts this style into positive enthusiasm, an expressive and eager glow that will naturally permeate their well being. Sliding to reserved style offers time to curb and restrain, to hold back and control their emotions. Reserved assists in compromising which helps the Passion Style resurrect, since their strength of conviction swings like a pendulum sometimes from one extreme position to another. To repair and balance from excess, sitting in reserved internal refinement becomes a possibility. 10% of the population have this exalted inspirational style. Rarely subtle or hidden, they like to do what inspires and moves them the most. This is a grand life, fully consuming, poignant, emotions fly around, sometimes getting lost in a three-ring circus.

Great balls of fire. Drop kick me through the goal post of life. I'm a rompin', stompin', piano playing son of a bitch. Y'know, there's nothin' like tearing up a good club now and then. —Jerry Lee Lewis

Examples include: *Liza Minnelli, William Shakespeare, Stevie Wonder, Lady Godiva, Joan of Arc, Zsa Zsa Gabor, Zorba the Greek, Britney Spears, Vincent Van Gogh, Miley Cyrus, Sofia Vergara, Goethe, Baba Muktananda, Walt Whitman, Rumplestilskin, Lindsey Lohan, Lady GaGa, Dolly Parton, Roberto Benigni, Tammy Faye Bakker, Janis Joplin, Magic Johnson, Dr. Ruth Westheimer, Little Richard, Jerry Lee Lewis, Liberace, Lewis Black, Chris Rock, Bruce Springsteen, John Kennedy, Ray Charles, Lucille Ball, Bette Midler, Peter Allen, Luciano Pavarotti, Roseanne, Cyndi Lauper, Chelsea Handler, Adam Lambert, James Brown, Martin Luther King.*

PERSEVERANCE

POSITIVE: PERSISTENCE

NEGATIVE: MONOTONY,

UNCHANGEABLE

When you come to the end of your rope, tie a knot and hang on.
—Franklin D. Roosevelt

Step-by-step, I never give up.

—a snowplow and bulldozer—

*S*ome words to create the image of this style are diligent, attentive, solid, dependable, unswerving, boring, consistent, hanging in, steadfast, unwavering, uninspiring, monotonous, determined, firm, decisive, relentless. Once an aim and goal is created the project is seen through to its final completion. The original task accomplished, they are successful, although not necessarily rich or famous. Persistent, unfading and disciplined, they offer no excuse to bail or back out, regardless to hardship, agreed upon—it's a done deal.

The difference between perseverance and obstinacy is that one comes from a strong will, and the other from a strong won't. —Henry Ward Beecher

Many who choose this style are accomplished athletes and Olympic stars. This is the driven person in the Guinness Book of World Records. Grounded, establishing routines; years of practice and determination create the hardiness of spirit that makes an athletic champion. Resolutely focused, goal-oriented and driving, once set into motion rules establish the momentum and endurance to bring home the reward. Doctoral dissertation, medical degree, Zen Buddhist meditator, caring for an aged parent or disabled child; this stick-to-itiveness serves well. Not the glittery glamorous person to hang out with, instead a dogged *I'll see this through to the end* ordinal kind of personality. Driving along in a snow-plow, steady, solid, unvarying, a determined relentless routine accomplishes the task. This is the tortoise, patiently, step-by-step, continuing to come along, one speed, certainly not a quitter.

Bear in mind, if you are going to amount to anything, that your success does not depend upon the brilliancy and the impetuosity with which you take hold, but upon the everlasting and sanctified bull-doggedness with which you hang on after you have taken hold. —A.B. Meldrum, Jr.

Consider the postage stamp. It secures success through its ability to stick to one thing until it gets there. —Josh Billings

Repetition, Buddha practiced in the spirit of repetition. Careful, watchful, a practice of routine regularity, over and over, constant consistent training, rooted in reality, no right or wrong; this is the breathing of Buddha. Practiced again and again until becoming the breath of Buddha. Concentration, quiet and stable, ordinary, dependable, plain, simple, calm, not changing from left to right, from fast to slow, self-disciplined; in today's athletic world, it's the endurance of the long-distance runner.

In the battle between the river and the rock, the river will always win. Not through strength but by persistence. —Kongfuzi

In the positive mode this style is based on a persistent way of being, as opposed to dogged stubbornness. Disciplined, long-term tasks are completed, goals achieved. Patient, resolute, relentlessly directed towards completion, well-paced, a hardiness of spirit and resolve that *will not give up the ship*. Their patience, determination, diligence and endurance, like constant drops of water that eventually turn a patch of dry land into a garden, are wonderful ways to mindfully practice inner peace; step-by-step living into the present moment.

Great work requires great and persistent effort for a long time. Character has to be established through a thousand stumbles. —Vivekananda

In the negative there is grim monotonous rigidity, unchangeable, inflexible, humdrum mulish plodding, while the big picture gets lost. Tenacious, they can hold on too long, even when the signs say *bail out* they find the energy to try again. Known to persist once a momentum builds even after it might be better to let go or it is discovered to be unsuitable to the original purpose. This is the person who gets into a rut, who plods on patiently long after it's time to abandon ship. Hanging onto what's known, a fear of change blocks the roads to innovation and controversy. Inflexible, immutable, un-spontaneous and fixed, regardless to appropriateness, they could die trying, not knowing when to exit. Dependable, although colorless and sometimes dullsville, irritating, as they repeat their stories again and again, forgetting they told it as they continue and keep going, unflagging and undistracted. Lacking a spirited outlook, rarely assertive or forceful, don't expect a candid direct answer. Falling into a rut, unable to *get off the hook* or disengage, preferring to stay with the known and familiar, to introduce a new way, to make changes becomes offensive and annoying to their style. Habits are entrenched, regularity is based on their fear of change.

Perseverance alone does not assure success. No amount of stalking will lead to a game in the field that has none. —Yi Jing

Think of the Myth of Sisyphus, eternally compelled to rolling a rock up a steep hill, and just before reaching the top of the hill the rock escapes, then watching it roll back down again returning to the bottom of the mountain to start pushing the rock upward all over again. It is important to know completion, how to contemplate and apply something new, when to move on.

This is the pit bull with locked jaws of steel, they hold on to their prey until the neck snaps. Committed, concentrating on narrow range action until sliding to aggression which brings in dynamic lively energy, expanding the focus, creating a spontaneous impromptu vitality. The slide to aggression brings in a quality of spunk and feistiness, a peppy and spirited demeanor, a bit of a break from the focused discipline and groundedness of Perseverance. 5% of the population have this ordinal action style which slides to the exalted action style of aggression.

Look at a stone cutter hammering away at his rock, perhaps a hundred times without as much as a crack showing in it. Yet at the hundred-and-first blow it will split in two, and I know it was not the last blow that did it, but all that had gone before. —Jacob A. Riis

Examples include: *Thomas Edison, Alan Greenspan, George Bush Jr., Robert Redford, Thich Nhat Hahn, Joan Baez, Shirley MacLaine, Shawn Johnson, Nelson Mandela, Carolyn Myss, Adyshanti, Charlotte Jocko Beck, John Kerry, Dame Judi Dench, Mary Lou Retton, Albert Schweitzer, Terry Waite, Elie Wiesel, Gautama Siddhartha, Franklin D. Roosevelt, Thomas Edison, Mother Teresa, Jesse Jackson.*

AGGRESSION

POSITIVE: DYNAMISM

NEGATIVE: BELLIGERENCE

Keep up or get left behind, it's my way or else! You miss 100% of the shots you never take. —Wayne Gretzky

—a Harley-Davidson and sports utility vehicles—

This approach is expressed through behavior directly aimed outside of self, at you. Dynamic explosive energy, invigorating, spunky, even thrilling to be around, Aggression Style expresses itself through action. Living on the edge and taking chances, they walk up and slap you on the back and you will definitely take notice. This is the risk-taker, not backing off when dark clouds warn trouble. They go after what they want and like the gamble. Often successful at what they do, Muhammad Ali used this mode of driving forcefulness to his advantage. The high energy impact is specifically directed at others, in pursuit of whatever they decide to take a stand on, rarely will you jar them off course.

Sean Penn came across a photographer snooping in his Argentinean hotel room and dangled the man from a ninth floor balcony by his ankles and was arrested for attempted murder. He escaped from Argentinean jail and fled the country. He was also arrested for assaulting a journalist, and again arrested for tying up Madonna to a chair and beating her. —Independent Paper

Outspoken, extroverted and assertive, feeling intimidated people back away. Misunderstood, just being *regular*, those in Aggression Style can be surprised to hear that they are difficult to be around. In their personal world, those unlike them appear sluggish and indecisive. This is Vesuvius and Saint Helens, a compelling style, high-octane, ready to blow; reasonable people prefer not to move in or get too comfortably close. These are the initiators, enthusiastic to actively direct their energy towards others. Routines and rules feel like a daily grind rat race, are irritating, makes them feel tied down. This is the Harley-Davidson, always noticed, taking the active road with gusto, undisciplined, loud, driving and vigorous.

Aggression is how a player stamps their authority on the opposition. It's about intent. It's about power and dominance. The way a scrum locks horns in rugby. The grunt in a tennis forehand. The way Tiger's driver recoils off his back when he hits flat out. It is decisiveness, pace, strength, and commitment. —Neil Harris

In the positive, solution oriented, they choose and go after a goal with enthusiasm and a strong position. Sometimes belligerent, they lead and direct best when not in strong-arm browbeating posture. They will step up to the plate each time, and take a stand when others back away. Self-assertive, a hard-working hustling go-getter, eager beaver fire-ball, energized, rarely displaying weakness. When directed at a goal the capability to lead others and achieve an aim is powerful, taking action when something needs to be done, rising to the occasion, sometimes outperforming all other styles. This zippy Harley conspicuously charges and energetically darts around the track, fascinating to watch. In the boxing ring the high energy bounce, the explosive attack serves them well.

Boys natural play is rough and tumble play, it's the universal play of little boys and it's very different from aggression. And we are a society that's failing to understand the distinction. —Christina Hoff Sommers

In the negative, watch out. Walking around with a *chip on their shoulder,* inviting, competitive, agitating, looking for an opportunity to be jostled or disagreed with; an accident waiting to happen especially since the consequences to rash physical actions are very low on their list of what stands in the way of going after their goal. In battle, they stop short of nothing, always ready to fight, even when unprovoked, rarely knocked off course, peppy, risk-takers, mettlesome, antagonistic, and robust. They are apt to be insensitive to others, lack subtlety, as they energetically insist on their way. Menacing, Aggression becomes volatile and destructive, like a volcano erupting, there is no logic or reason. Harassing, terrorizing, tormenting, Beware!

A society that presumes a norm of violence and celebrates aggression, whether in the subway, on the football field, or in the conduct of its business, cannot help making celebrities of the people who would destroy it. —Lewis H. Lapham

This is the sports utility vehicle taking the terrain off-road with large bumper heights to reach its goal. An exalted action style, focused on concrete actions, high energy is maintained even when doing more than one event at a time. Aggression Style manifests through behavior rather than feelings or thought, which is evident in their noticeable moving in, taking a stand, initiating, insistent. In Chinese terminology this is the most yang of all the styles, which is the masculine principle symbolized by fire and earth. Sliding to its complementary opposite, the ordinal active style of perseverance, the consistency, regularity and patience that has been avoided brings in a smooth more polished and dependable energy. No longer undisciplined eruptive and bouncing off the walls, slowing down, focused, still magnetic and spirited, this is a dynamo style. 5% of the population have an Aggression Style.

Only force rules. Force is the first law. Strength lies not in defense but in attack. The first essential for success is a perfectly constant and regular employment of violence. Any alliance whose purpose is not the intention to wage war is senseless and useless. —Adolf Hitler

Examples include: *Adolf Hitler, Mary Kay Ash, Hulk Hogan, Eddie Murphy, Robin Williams, Steven Jobs, Tony Robbins. John McEnroe, Joan Rivers, Robert De Niro, Arnold Schwarzenegger, Joseph Stalin, Werner Erhard, King Kong, Wayne Gretzky, Richard Simmons, Mike Tyson, Lenny Bruce, Bruce Willis, Mohammed Ali, John Wayne, Mr. T., Sean Penn, Mel Brooks, Fidel Castro, Idi Amin, Grace Jones, Norman Mailer, Cardi B, Donald Duck.*

OBSERVATION

POSITIVE: CLARITY

NEGATIVE: SURVEILLANCE

I look before I leap.

—a slow train and a Greyhound bus—

We have to look at our own inertia, insecurities, self-hate, fear. It is good to know about our terrible selves, not laud or criticize them, just acknowledge them. Then, out of this knowledge, we are better equipped to make a choice for beauty, kind consideration, and clear truth. —Natalie Goldberg

*T*ime is spent paying attention to what is around, noticing what others are doing. So many cultural habits are based on Observation Style. Theatre, spectator sports, movies, celebrity watching, sitting at a cafe or on a beach blanket, window-shopping, parades and television; all engage the neutral Observer onlooker. Watching life happen, to others, spectators and browsers, keeping an eye on life, this style notices and may or may not respond. Good comedy, intelligent journalism, Reality TV shows, Us, People magazine, the C.I.A and other intelligence organizations, the National Enquirer and TV reporting are best from this posture. Throughout the world there is a fascination with watchfulness, whether it's towards the President of a country, a big wheel magnate, superstar, a Nobel prize winner, politician or criminal. It's as interesting to watch a Royal wedding as it is to follow the story line of the muggers who kidnapped, raped and cut up 5 children, the hurricane that hits the Yucatan, the tsunami that wipes out a coastal area, the plane crash that killed local residents and artists, the bombing at the Boston marathon, the Macy's Day Parade, a school shooting, hanging out at the food court at the mall, or sitting on the Beach looking at people. Attention is focused on the current circumstances, what is in the surrounding environment, local TV or newspaper copy.

There are three kinds of men. The one that learns by reading. The few who learn by observation. The rest of them have to pee on the electric fence for themselves. —*Will Roger*

This is the most common and familiar style in the country, filling audiences regardless to venue, which is why a celebrity can't get married without half the world trying to find out where, to whom, who's invited, and what they are wearing. Helicopters overhead, camera crews poised, waiting for hours, watching, absorbing what's around before moving in when the opportunity presents itself. Even a casual dinner for a world-known dignity or popular star becomes a public event, as well as listening to every detail of the illicit affairs of a senator in Congress. We all know an office snitch, a boyfriend in monitoring surveillance mode, someone researching and investigating. Our culture is enthusiastic for private personal information that gets reported about well-known people. Movie, TV, athletic stars, politicians are all hounded by the media, as well as by the public. Their photos as well as the smallest aspect of a celebrities life is made public; we love to read about the most mundane detail. Driving by an accident we slow down, *rubberneck*, to look at and record the event. Popular Television shows with their astute politically incorrect comments, Jon Stewart, Stephen Colbert, Conan O'Brien, Bill Maher, Trevor Noah, David Letterman, D.L. Hugley, Seth Myers, all in Observation Style monitoring and satirizing the tone of the times. Much that we miss is detailed, becoming funny and interesting. We get to peek at, catch a glimpse of things we might not have noticed.

The ultimate court of appeal is observation and experiment, not authority.
—*Thomas Huxley*

So many occupations use and value this style. Police investigators as well as police patrols, television commentators, scientists, detectives, journalists and interviewers, CIA operatives, writers of memoir, comedians, movie, restaurant and theater reviews. An acquaintance casually reporting events, nothing interpretive, reasonably accurate in detail, holds the attention of those around. This is a slow train, a Greyhound bus, taking the combination road, nothing extreme, good windows to look out and to see the details.

Watchfulness is the vital need, for he who does not watch is soon overwhelmed. The sternman need only sleep a moment and the vessel is lost.
—*Epictetus*

In the positive mode this neutral style, while not exciting or colorful, lends to less distortion and more adaptability to suit circumstances than any other style. Observing prior to jumping in, walking into a party or restaurant, looking around, noticing how things are going, waiting before participating, familiar behavior we have all seen. Observation creates clarity through study, reading, watchfulness, examination and insight; being clear and attentive while gathering information. Good Observations are uplifting, open our mind, bring a freshness to our thoughts, stimulate, and offer a new perspective. Sometimes, careful visual detail enhance a novel, a theater setting, appear rich in a movie; all from a well trained Observation Style.

A traveller without observation is like a bird without wings. —Moslih Sa'adi

In the negative, peeping toms and spying are a strategy that keeps this person separate from the world rather than as a participant. Aloof, on the look-out, removed, detached, scrutinizing, disconnected, living as if they are watching what everyone else is doing and are not part of it; looking, yet remaining uninvolved. Continuing in the negative mode, surveillance, they examine and observe things that are actually none of their business, often to catch and control others. Jealous partners, stalking, overly watchful, trying to be invisible, spying with the hope of not being seen, account for a majority of homicides. Observing things that are actually not their concern, makes them murky, keeping them from being sharp and crisp; apparent when you look and see the dumbfounded vacant stare on their face. Television viewers, watching life go by, spaced out, they lose sharp clarity and degenerate into negative aspects.

You can observe a lot just by watching. —Yogi Berra

This is a very common style, half of the population has it, many abuse it, rubbernecking, ogling women, gawking at the scene of an accident, sitting in a mall spaced out; it's the distance between casing out a prospective house break-in or kidnap victim, and the peaceful fly-on-the-wall gatherer of information for the purpose of learning. Virgil wrote about *the snake who lurks in the grass,* and William Butler Yeats poetically described *the long-legged fly upon the stream, his mind moving upon silence, Mary Oliver asked: how many years did I wander slowly through the forest. What wonder and glory I would have missed had I ever been in a hurry!* That's quite a range the neutral Observation style plays within.

All of us are watchers—of television, of time clocks, of traffic on the freeway—but few are observers. Everyone is looking, not many are seeing.
—Peter Leschak

As a neutral style, the constructive value is that the information gathered assimilates knowledge and insight helping to arrive at a place of clarity. As a neutral assimilation style, Observation is the combination of all the other styles. Generally a non-participant, a watcher, the polarity of the other styles allows them to engage in situations, although the preference is to remain a spectator. Generally not stirring the waters, it is sometimes at the expense of having good learning experiences, hesitant to becoming intimate and connected. Avoiding involvement limits learning experiences. Having no complementary opposite to slide towards, Observation Style has the advantage of being able to slide to one of the other six styles. To apply the positive of any of the other styles and choose to express themselves with a tone and appearance of deliberation, or authority, restraint, enthusiasm, persistence or dynamism develops clarity removing the negative manner of surveillance. Using Observation to see where one stands, one can choose to slide to any other style to act. Generally absorbing energy, this is a style that may appear passive and neutral upon meeting, and then decide to borrow a different style to interact. This bus takes many different roads to ultimately reach its goal. The proverb *look before you leap* speaks to the 49% of the population who have Observation style.

I believe in evidence. I believe in observation, measurement, and reasoning, confirmed by independent observers. I'll believe anything, no matter how wild and ridiculous, if there is evidence for it. The wilder and more ridiculous, something is, however, the firmer and more solid the evidence will have to be. —*Isaac Asimov*

Examples include: *Barbara Walters, Georgia O'Keefe, Allen Ginsberg, Gertrude Stein, Joseph McCarthy, Rachel Maddow, Warren Beatty, George Carlin, Tom Cruise, Jon Stewart, Sigmund Freud, John Travolta, James Taylor, Billy Crystal, Carlos Castaneda, Mr. Spock, Dr. Robert Atkins, Tony Blair, Walter Cronkite, Carl Rogers, Susan Sarandon, Steven Spielberg, Julia Child, William Buckley, Trevor Noah, David Letterman, Stephen Colbert, Jerry Seinfeld, Mary Oliver, Bill Maher, Jay Leno, William Shakespeare, Neil Simon, Bryant Gumbel, Ringo Starr, Larry King, Osho Bhagwan Rajneesh, Whoopi Goldberg,* many of the stalkers and loners who isolate themselves.

SYSTEM SIXTEEN

ATTITUDE

SKEPTIC, IDEALIST, STOIC, SPIRITUALIST, CYNIC, REALIST, PRAGMATIST

Life is the movie you see through your own unique eyes. It makes little difference what's happening out there. It's how you take it that counts.
—*Dennis Waitle*

SKEPTIC: Positive: investigation **Negative:** suspicion

IDEALIST: Positive: unification **Negative:** naiveté

STOIC: Positive: tranquility **Negative:** resignation

SPIRITUALIST: Positive: verification **Negative:** blind faith, belief

CYNIC: Positive: contradiction **Negative:** denigrate, belittle

REALIST: Positive: objective **Negative:** subjective, speculation

PRAGMATIST: Positive: practical **Negative:** dogmatic

This is our primary view and mind-set, the way we regard the world. It is the posture or stance in which we are positioned. An artist might describe this as perspective. This, our frame of mind and demeanor, is how we see everything. Our Attitude or disposition is a temperament, orientation, inclination, essentially it is how we view life, our usual and natural slant on life.

Expression		Inspiration	
Ordinal	Exalted	Ordinal	Exalted
SKEPTIC	IDEALIST	STOIC	SPIRITUALIST
+investigation	+unification	+tranquility	+verification
-suspicion	-naiveté	-resignation	-blind faith, belief

Action		Assimilation
Ordinal	Exalted	Neutral
CYNIC	REALIST	PRAGMATIST
+contradiction	+objective	+practical
-denigrate, belittle	-subjective, speculation	-dogmatic

Chart 8: Attitude: Our Mindset

Attitude is more important than the past, than education, than money, than circumstances, than what people do or say. It is more important than appearance, giftedness, or skill. —W.C. Fields

Deep-rooted in our personality are distinguishing qualities that we either use in a positive way or that otherwise show up through negative aspects of our personality. When we come from a place of fear or lack of self-understanding or feeling stressed we drop into the negative characteristics of our personality. This stance, our life-view interpretation, affects and influences our feelings, thoughts, health, relationships as well as our actions. Seeing the world bleak and dangerous, so it becomes; seeing the world as a beautiful dance, so it becomes. Throughout our lifetime the values of our one Attitude change, like light blue darkens to royal blue. How we see our life shifts from naiveté at age twelve to maturity at age fifty, continuously adjusting. Our conscious awareness is reflected in how we live into our Attitude.

A great attitude does much more than turn on the lights in our world; it seems to magically connect us to all sorts of serendipitous opportunities that were somehow absent before the change. —*Earl Nightingale*

To remain in the positive of our Attitude, or outlook, is pivotal, critical, and is fundamental to sustaining a productive daily life. Fortunately, it is the easiest to modify. When we engage in the negative aspect of our Attitude life becomes difficult and our psychological blindspot gets triggered (refer to System 18 Psychological Blindspots) and blocks access to our goal. The movement of our life is directly affected by Attitude. How we see the world impacts every part of our moment-by-moment existence. Emotions are colored by our stance, how we look at life, how we decide, this intellectual position flavored by everything else about us continues to alter as we age and mature. Attitude does not express itself in generalities, our differences impact the colorations of how our Attitude is expressed.

The greatest discovery of my generation is that a human being can alter his life by altering his attitude. —*William James*

There is little difference in people, but that little difference makes a big difference. That little difference is attitude. The big difference is whether it is positive or negative. —*W. Clement Stone*

Attitudes bring out into the open the particular impressions that people project onto the world. Understanding this system deepens self-acceptance, can be used towards realizing our goal, neutralizes our primary obstacle, promotes clarity in communication. Learning about yourself in the light of Attitude offers information that presents the opportunity to make informed choices. Remaining in the positive is a key to eliminating psychological blindspots.

Life is a train of moods like a string of beads; and as we pass through them they prove to be many colored lenses, which paint the world their own hue, and each shows us only what lies in its own focus. —*Ralph Waldo Emerson*

SKEPTIC

POSITIVE: INVESTIGATION

NEGATIVE: SUSPICION

This might not work out as expected, I will check it out, I won't believe it until it's proven.

Me a skeptic? I hope you have proof.

 T he phrase *doubting Thomas* is apt here, he must have been the Skeptic who, when he saw the handwriting on the wall claimed it to be a forgery. The Skeptic will doubt, mistrust, investigate, inquire, have misgivings, disbelieve, be dissatisfied; basically scrutinize even when they appreciate and enjoy something. Looking for the flaw, pointing out imperfections, careful not to get duped, everything is questionable until they actually look at/see the proof with their own eyes. You see this type sitting in the lecture halls, arms folded across their chest, with an expression of *prove it* on their face. They look for possible difficulties, ulterior motives, suspecting there are discrepancies, setting out to find them. Questioning, everything is under consideration. Looking for the underlying reason for what's suspected, probing for clues, asking for evidence, the inquisition begins lightly for insignificant matters and intensifies for subjects of greater importance.

What appears to be the end of the road, may simply be a bend in the road.
—*Robert H. Schuller*

A noticeable scowl, furrowed brow and frown, eyes may slightly squint; sometimes a gloomy sullen look are indicators of a Skeptic temperament. This is a frame of mind that only after checking things out will feel satisfied. Once they have examined the gathered data and a belief system is formed it is equally difficult to shake them out of their new thinking. Firm believers once convinced, life appears to have an ongoing question mark. Not a family member you want to have oppose you around parental deaths and financial questions. Their suspicions will cause relentless probing, might even reach legal subpoenas and interrogations, searching of documentation, questioning of personal income tax records; in the negative they invent ugliness and evil wherever they don't find satisfactory information, whatever they don't understand, once their curiosity is peaked. Only their own subjective insight is valid, others personal opinions are thrown out. Anything not understood is seen as wrong, people are initially deemed guilty until all the evidence is in. Frustrating to deal with, especially when they refuse to go along with something easily taken for granted.

A skeptic is a person who would ask God for his ID card. —E. *Shoaff*

On one hand this attitude misses the inherent beauty and wisdom in the world. What's lacking in imagination, *that's not the real world*, is made up in projections, they see what they want to see, and oftentimes their mental inventions are not so pretty. Neglecting to account for, blind to what can't be known, what is invisible, the abstracted mystery eludes their sensibility; only objective facts are real for this literalist. Subjective insights, unless it's their own, are worthless; imagination and dreams appear foolish, although their projections, often subjective and distorted, seeing what they want to see, projecting their perceptions, is what they consider to be the *real world*. What is factual under appearances is what the Skeptic is digging for and not until it is investigated to satisfaction will the doubt ease. This attitude could be advantageous as a lawyer, detective or investigative reporter.

Do not believe in anything simply because you have heard it. Do not believe in anything simply because it is spoken and rumored by many. Do not believe in anything simply because it is found in your religious books. Do not believe in anything merely on the authority of your teachers and elders. Do not believe in traditions because they have been handed down for many generations. But after observation and analyses, when you find that anything agrees with reason and is conducive to the good and benefit of one and all, then accept it and live up to it. —the Buddha

THE WORLD OF THE SKEPTIC

In the realm of philosophy, Materialism, which holds that everything that actually exists is physical, and Empiricism, stating that knowledge can only be derived through careful observation, are both postures that speak to the Skeptic attitude. Scientific curiosity supports the positive direction of the Skeptic, shifting from the personal to a scientific frame of mind. The world, to the Skeptic, is determined by chance and accident, there is no blueprint, meaning or analogy, one thing is not universally connected to another. Checking out contradictions, the intention is to come to know what is the truth and questioning, examining and considering the facts may lead to what is under appearances. This attitude encourages and supports others to check-up before jumping in, to be prepared for difficulties along the way. It supports becoming well-informed. Many of the philosophical principles of doubt and uncertainty have been supported by well known Skeptic statements such as Nietzsche's: *Do not allow yourselves to be deceived: Great minds are skeptical. There is nothing more necessary than truth, and in comparison with it everything else has only secondary value.* David Hume, another philosophic Skeptic stated: *There is a degree of doubt and caution and modesty which, in all kinds of scrutiny and decision ought for ever to accompany a just reasoner.*

He who has a why to live can bear almost any how. —*Friedrich Nietzsche*

What lies at the base of appearances is a stimulating pursuit for the intellectual person with a Skeptical attitude. The quality of investigation in the positive can ultimately lead to truth, in this manner they are well-informed and a good source for accuracy. In this posture there is no blind faith, things are not accepted at face value. In the negative it leads to creating difficulties that did not already exist. In the negative, being around someone whose attitude conveys to you that you are dishonest, who is studying the details of your life, cross-examining and acting suspicious towards your motives is less than flattering. Never satisfied in their information research quest, bothersome and hard to manage, the investigation is laborious for both sides. Fearful to be deceived, to have the *wool pulled over their eyes*, the Skeptic remains disbelieving. They make a mountain out of a molehill, causing problems that may never have appeared. Locating hidden motives, having a place to hang the blame: it could be other governments, a wild crowd that causes their child to go astray, the economy, the health care system, the son-in-law, their finances, the way their mother treated them; somewhere the blame gets placed. Inherent beauty and wisdom are often overlooked, instead, trickery and mistrust stands in the way.

If you would be a real seeker after truth, it is necessary that at least once in your life you doubt, as far as possible, all things. —*René Descartes*

The Latin Proverb: *Believe nothing and be on your guard against everything* is rooted in the Skeptic mind-set. To shift out of the negative of suspicion is a move towards the positive of the complementary attitude, idealist, which mentally pictures a more ideal world, visualizes the best and then works towards that image. A graphic description states that a Skeptic looks like an idealist who got burned once too often. 5% of the population have an ordinal expression Skeptic attitude.

The unexamined life is not worth living. —Socrates

Examples include: *Woody Allen, Sigmund Freud, Edward R. Murrow, Salman Rushdie, Edgar Casey, Roseanne Barr, William Buckley, Lisa Marie Presley, George Bush Jr., Bob Dylan, Jon Stewart, Jack Benny, David Hume, Katie Couric, Billy Crystal, Sean Connery, Friedrich Nietzsche, Peter Jennings, Courtney Love, Lenny Bruce, Jack Nicholson, Walter Cronkite, Jerry Seinfeld, Mark Twain, Nikos Kazantzakis, Alec Baldwin, Barbara Walters, Thomas Edison, Socrates, George Burns.*

IDEALIST

POSITIVE: UNIFICATION

NEGATIVE: NAIVETÉ

It should be, it ought to be.

Imagine there's no countries It isn't hard to do Nothing to kill or die for And no religion too Imagine all the people Living life in peace. You may say that I'm a dreamer But I'm not the only one I hope someday you'll join us And the world will be as one. —John Lennon

Often a visionary perfectionist, the thought of what could be carries the enthusiasm and energy to create change and bring new opportunity. When the potential, the should and the ought combine, the Idealist meets the purpose of contributing, of making a better world. In this way the vision of an improved society appears through finding healthier products, modernizing buildings for education, better quality apparel, advancing the economy, more functional organizations and smoother running meetings. Value is everywhere, life is filled with meaningful connections. Drugstore fortune cookie philosophy of aphorisms, proverbs and platitudes become matter-of-fact and commonplace. Pithy sayings that contain general truth, *things happen, people are doing the best they know, smile because you can, a stitch in time saves nine, hitch your wagon to a star, it's all for the best, ask not what your country can do for you;* Idealist quotes that reflect a head in the clouds viewpoint. Life is not analyzed, reason and logic is limited, wishful images are projected out into the outer world, until reality pokes through the bubble.

Having two bathrooms ruined the capacity to co-operate. —Margaret Mead

The advertising industry aims towards those with this posture. The commercial media base their hype on the Idealist attitude. TV ads display photos of young attractive men and women, suggesting that buying and using their hair tonic or face cream will ultimately bring you a full head of healthy hair and young supple skin. The Idealist buys the product, earnestly believing in time that they will have movie star quality, eventually it becomes apparent that this is just shampoo or face cream, the mirror portrays the unchanged reality.

An idealist is one who, on noticing that roses smell better than a cabbage, concludes that it will also make better soup. —Bertrand Russell

Large open eyes, optimistic, enthusiastic, seeing the world through rose colored glasses, when the spell is broken and limitations appear disappointment surfaces, although each circumstance might be short-lived. A popular energetic attitude producing many who have successfully pioneered progress. Seeing the world idealistically, having standards that are sometimes castle-building, asking the same criterion of themselves, often brings frustration. Many Idealists through seeing a better way have impacted the world: Mozart, Michelangelo, Van Gogh, Martin Luther King, Steven Speilberg, Frank Lloyd Wright, Margaret Mead and Oprah Winfrey; on the other hand, Idealists having false expectations, trying to reach their ideal naively have found themselves in trouble: Timothy Leary, Jane Fonda, Elvis Presley, John Kennedy, Janis Joplin, Paula Abdul and Evita Peron. The possibility of creating change prevails. Idealist and poet Carl Sandburg stated: *I am an idealist, I don't know where I am going but I'm on my way. I am an idealist. I believe in everything.* Anthropologist Margaret Mead stated: *Never doubt that a small group of thoughtful, committed people can change the world. Indeed it is the only thing that ever has.*

VISIONARY

I don't believe in failure. It is not failure if you enjoyed the process.
—*Oprah Winfrey*

In the positive: ethical strong moral fiber, principled, with sound ideas and enthusiastic drive, they create better educational systems, fair housing, health benefits for the poor, inspired good-will political ambassadors; pulling together the vision as well as the circumstances that manifests improvement. They make their ideals converge with what will happen. Enthusiastic, persuasive, wanting things to improve, hard on themselves, able to easily shift reality to match their mental picture, what doesn't fit into their image gets Xed out.

We must accept finite disappointment, but never not have infinite hope.
—*Martin Luther King, Jr.*

In the negative there is dissatisfaction accompanied with the thought that something still is not good enough, that change always needs to happen. Simple-minded, over trustful and inexperienced, often accompanied by unrealistic gullibility and self-deception sometimes leads to disappointment. Looking for meaningful synchronistic connections, dissatisfaction easily surfaces. This is an attitude that believes that if circumstances were different life would improve.

You can use your idealism to further your aims, if you realize that nothing is Nirvana, nothing is perfect. —Jon Stewart

This is the pioneer who has ideas ahead of time, the visionary who tries to unionize the hospital and protect patients rights who may eventually get fired, the researcher who experiments with drugs to find a better way to treat alcoholism and gets raided by the FBI, the shopper who buys a new beauty cream then doesn't become gorgeous in 10 days; all are visualizing improvement and progress. Unrealistic, they need to move out of naiveté and the abstract to be landed in the world, for then they can become effective and of service and their dreams manifest.

All you can do is the best you can do. —Paula Abdul

Shifting to the ordinal expression mode of skeptic, both are positions that see the world differently than it is and both make the most change. Too much of seeing everyone as a friend till proven untrue, overly trusting, the slide to skepticism, assuming all are enemy 'til proven friend, brings some range and balance. 30% of the population have this exalted expression posture.

Ask not what your country can do for you, but what you can do for your country. —John F. Kennedy

Examples include: *Barack Obama, Tammy Bakker, Richard Simmons, Steve Jobs, Barbra Streisand, Ruth Westheimer, Jane Fonda, Oprah Winfrey, Bill Cosby, Robin Williams, Clint Eastwood, Jay Leno, Steven Spielberg, Carlos Casteneda, Elvis Presley, Goldie Hawn, Ronald Reagan, John F. and*

Robert Kennedy, Evita Peron, Martin Luther King, Coretta Scott King, Paul Simon, Norman Cousins, Janis Joplin, Walt Disney, Steven Hawking, Deepak Chopra, Maya Angelou, Carl Sandburg, Abbie Hoffman, Timothy Leary, Gloria Steinem, Paula Abdul, Mother Teresa, Fidel Castro, Grace Kelly, Yoko Ono, Paul McCartney, Bill Clinton, Joan d'Arc, Sir Galahad, Margaret Mead, Bruce Springsteen, Robert Redford, Osho Bhagwan Rajneesh.

STOIC

POSITIVE: TRANQUILITY

NEGATIVE: RESIGNATION

whatever
I can deal with whatever happens—I can handle it

Slogan of the stoic: 'I don't feel a thing'. —Mason Cooley

The self-disciplined, *patient as Job*, passionless acceptance of life as it is offers a quality of stability to those around. The Stoic attitude displays a calm unmoved face, regardless to the external circumstance. *And the bombs bursting in air*, still no affect on old poker face. They remain contained, no matter what is going on in their world. In certain lifetimes that are politically difficult, or families that are exceptionally dysfunctional, the Stoic attitude affords safety. Nothing has to change and their life is still manageable. Accepting what is, showing patience and endurance in the face of adversity, appearing impassive, self-possessed; to have a peaceful undisturbed environment means more to them then to influence their surroundings.

I will be steel! I will build a steel bridge over my need! I will build a

bomb shelter over my heart! But my future is secret. It is as shy as a mouse.
—*Anne Sexton*

The Stoic attitude has facial benefits that work well at a card table in Las Vegas, as well as being advantageous for surgeons, hostages, athletes, police officers and stressful public occasions. They don't reveal what they are thinking on their facial expression—not hiding their emotions, it's the way they are built. Rarely expressing their feelings, it may appear that there aren't any. Alfred Hitchcock's deadpan expression as he introduced his shows, and Marlon Brando's cool unflappable stoicism contributed to their success as well as to their mystique. Not openly expressing feelings, it is difficult to tell what they are thinking. The news media described O.J. Simpson: *As the verdict was read, Simpson remained stoic, staring straight ahead.* The Stoic likes stability. They actually feel deeply, but speaking up to influence an outcome, stating a position that is opposing, acting frivolous and scatterbrained, making their feelings known, all are unimaginable. Few are privy to or aware of their inner life, a position expressed by Job in his wondering silence: *I will lay mine hand upon my mouth.*

People hide their truest nature. I understood that; I even applauded it. What sort of world would it be if people bled all over the sidewalks, if they wept under trees, smacked whomever they despised, kissed strangers, revealed themselves? —*Alice Hoffman*

A carefully hidden clenched jaw may be a giveaway. Many people in concentration camps survived with this attitude, since it does not provoke the aggressor and offers the inner wherewithal to accept what comes and then continue to go on. Long-suffering, resigned, fatalistic, the outlook of inevitability drags along, *bear it,* feeling overwhelmed they often miss opportunities to learn from difficult moments. Making the best of a hard situation, rather than confront and fight the circumstance, rather than deal with a situation; only when the conditions become extreme and traumatic do they acknowledge something critical is happening. Much of the rest of the time they minimize and overlook, are resolute and unflinching, sober. British writer and philosopher Colin Wilson in a graphic illustration of the austerity of the stoic observed that *the average person accepts miseries and disasters with the stoicism of a cow standing in the rain.*

Imagine smiling after a slap in the face. Then think of doing it 24 hours a day. —Marcus Zusak

Stoic Stability

Chosen when there will be a lifetime that includes a great amount of negativity, since they can insulate from it, as well as minimize it; the Asian populace, for example Tibetans, know this attitude and it has helped them to live in the harshness of China's political and social structure. A headline in a major journal stated: *Tibet's Dalai Lama tours U.S. in stoic quest for self-rule.* The spiritual and political leader of 6 million Tibetans demonstrates the grace and stoicism that has made him one of the world's most admired leaders. The resilience and stoicism of the Tibetan people in the face of Chinese occupation, persecution and displacement is mirrored by the Dalai Lama's emphasis that the path to inner calm and tranquility is to find that peace within ourselves. This attitude portrays his humanitarian compassion.

Education is the ability to listen to almost anything without losing your temper or your self-confidence. —Robert Frost

In a positive posture of tranquility, preferring calm and stability, life is fairly easily handled to support an unexcitable temperament; making the best out of a situation. Not asking for a lot, in harmony with themselves, accepting life as it shows up, they handle what comes along. A high tolerance for irritation, very little shakes their self-control. In the negative attitude of resignation they will not confront conditions regardless to the suffering it brings to the world. They will not speak up, won't influence things and are resigned. The stance is, *things aren't great, but what can you do about it? whatever is, I can handle.* Serenity gives way to compliance and toleration, the urge to make an impact on the world is overtaken by the thought, *what's the use, who cares?* This ability to endure and be long-suffering creates apathy, exhaustion, and submissiveness to whatever arises. This includes an unhappy marriage, unrewarding job, a political climate of tyranny and a toleration of dysfunctional family members.

Grin and bear it at a family event becomes the posture rather than to address the madness, even when it opposes personal values. Hanging in; when most would see the situation as hopeless, the Stoic remains resigned. *Why bother?* is a standard inner response, which keeps them from self-development, rarely motivated to do something, not learning from events, often feeling it will only happen again. This is the *things are tough all over* outlook, which often keeps them immune and insulated, sometimes insensitive and minimizing, overlooking, remaining calm. Since they are unable and unwilling to confront and deal with what should be unacceptable, they are quite stable in a crisis. Whatever the misfortune, remaining composed with self-control, the Stoic gives up rather than disrupt. They are not here to change the world or even make a large impact on their surroundings. Continuing in the negative mode, rather than accept the situation they are resigned, exhausted, non-confrontational, resigned to their life, compliant to its outcome, won't make waves and rarely verbalize their distress. Resignation and composure protects the possibility of experiencing disappointment. Within this tranquil acceptance we can hear that catchy phrase: *whatever.*

At the stumbling of a horse, the fall of a tile, the slightest pin prick, let us promptly chew on this: Well, what if it were death itself? And thereupon let us stiffen and fortify ourselves. —Michel de Montaigne

They make good prisoners of war, Federal Bureau Investigators, great poker players, Zen practitioners, cigar store Indians, carved faces on Mt. Rushmore. Sliding to the complementary attitude, spiritualist, the contracted Stoic expands bringing a hopeful outlook, seeing the possibilities of how life can be, seeing new directions. To shift out of the negative is to look for what is true, thereby coloring in what once was perceived as a *drab* world. Being sensitive to what is happening, practicing meditation, maintaining a spirit of eagerness and promise enables the Stoic to emanate harmony. Stoicism, a school of Hellenistic philosophy taught the avoidance of emotional issues through developing clear judgment and inner calm. Stoic ethics focuses on how being sensible and rational, leading us to be free of passion, especially of suffering, we might reach a placid undisturbed inner state. Stoicism teaches that when living according to reason and virtue it is possible to overcome the discord of the outside world and find peace within oneself. The Stoic slides to spiritualist, seeing the bigger picture. This allows the Stoic to look at the possibilities of how life could be and to dream up hopeful visions. 5% of the population have this ordinal inspirational mind-set.

How ridiculous and how strange to be surprised at anything which happens in life! —Marcus Aurelius

Examples include: *Joan Baez, Johnny Depp, Georgia O'Keefe, Denzel Washington, Willie Nelson, Nelson Mandela, Marcus Aurelius, John Wayne,*

Marlon Brando, Gary Cooper, George Washington, Christopher Reeve, Cher, John Lennon, Bing Crosby, Edward Norton, Michael Caine, Orson Wells, Ringo Starr, Elie Wiesel, Alfred Hitchcock, Andy Warhol, Dalai Lama, Winston Churchill, Jim Morrison, O.J. Simpson, Martina Navratilova, Kate Bush, Brutus, Abraham Lincoln, Gautama Siddhartha, Ed Sullivan.

SPIRITUALIST

POSITIVE: VERIFICATION

NEGATIVE: BLIND FAITH, BELIEF

*It could be, everything is possible
and there are so many ways to get there.*

Here's to the ones who dream, foolish as they may seem, here's to the hearts that ache here's to the mess we make, so bring on the rebels the ripples from pebbles the painters and poets and plays! Here's to the fools who dream, crazy as they may seem. She captured a feeling, sky with no ceiling, sunset inside a frame, smiling through it, she said 'she'd do it again.' —La La Land

The image is *Man of La Mancha* riding into the sky singing *To Dream The Impossible Dream*; this is the optimistic visionary that sees possibilities and dreams visions. When they take care to verify those dreams, visions and experiences, they live in beauty. In this manner taking the most from what appears, and letting go of what is toxic becomes a simple matter. The interest rarely is in the mundane, ordinary, daily routine of life, the energy is toward the bliss and the endless invisible possibilities. Wearing beads blessed by the guru, bank checks with a smiling angelic cherub, that say *remember what's important,* a crystal hanging from the car mirror, stones with beautiful words, a red string on the hand with a shiny star, a salt candle on the desk, a Buddha statue in the bedroom, incensing the home to bring grace; all high priority. *Hitch your wagon to a star*, everything is possible.

Spirituality is completely ordinary. Though we may speak of it as extraordinary, it is the most ordinary thing of all. Spirituality is simply a means of arousing one's spirit, of developing a kind of spiritedness. Through that we begin to have a greater contact with reality. —Chogyam Trungpa

In the business and political arena, they can be powerful leaders, seeing opportunities and creating good prospects from favorable circumstances. Making the most of what is presented and allowing what doesn't work to go, they smudge the hotel room for good energy, hold a white light in their heart, play Tibetan bowls and ring a bell of mindfulness, see auras, remind us that we are all connected, visualize the best of a situation. They look at the high side, what is already working. Not always the best business decision-makers when they are being impractical and unrealistic, taking things on faith, neglecting the demands of the everyday mundane world, they may miss the boat. Disappointment is not easy to bear, turning upsets into opportunities and lessons to learn, the Spiritualist hangs onto the angels and wears a red string around their wrist for good luck. Hoping for the best, envisioning a higher world, one with few problems, asking for healing, heartbreak and a busy mind accompanies the emotionality of stark reality. The drive to live their high ideals, to have moral goodness, shifts sometimes to surprise when others don't share their promising mind-set.

Imagine you come upon a house painted brown. What color would you say the house was? Why brown of course. But what if I came upon it from the other side, and found it to be white? That would be absurd. Who would paint a house two colors? He ignored my question. You say it's brown and I say it's white. Who's right? We're both right. No, he said. We are both wrong. The house isn't brown or white. It's both. You and I only see one side. But that doesn't mean the other side doesn't exist. To not see the whole is to not see the truth. —*Megan Chance*

JOY MOVES TO SORROW

Looking at the world as an endless array of potential possibilities, inspired by what could be accomplished, yet easily influenced; connecting to the details of a situation grounds their airy quality. Disappointment leads to upset, even to inner turmoil, once the vision of a sweet world gets pierced with the reality of teen-agers beating the homeless with baseball bats, neighbors turning away, shark attacks in the ocean, shady real estate deals going south, children being sexually abused, tsunami's wiping out impoverished communities, medical reports showing trouble, family members being abusive, a bomb set off at the Boston marathon, young black men being murdered by the police, women being date-raped; imperfections break the hopeful bubble. Joy moves to sorrow, looking at a world that is infused with suffering.

Spiritual growth comes from absorbing and digesting truth and putting it to practice in daily life. —*White Eagle*

This is the world of Tarot, past life readings, palmists, vibrational healing, botanical elixirs and potions, aromatherapy, Rumi and Hafiz, clairvoyants, numerology, singing bowls, massage, channeling, yoga, hand crafted runes, crystal charms, pagan and magick, pendulums, fairy art, psychic phenomena, shamanism, divination, oneness deeksha, gypsy fortune tellers, meditation, tea leaves, astrology, I-Ching. Faith is felt, and consulting different sources to discover one's fate, even to influence the powers that be, may lead to superstition, beliefs, luck and blind faith. To shift out of the negative is to allow the world to be the way it is, to stop the distractions, neither expecting better or worse, to honor their intuition, to substantiate giving credence to evidence, and to be with what is.

Faith must be enforced by reason. When faith becomes blind it dies.
—*Mahatma Gandhi*

In the positive, inspiring others, holding a vision dedicated to higher purpose, they establish what is true according to what has been experienced. This appears as a connection to higher planes of existence. This is the expansive visionary. Verifying, they establish what is based on evidence as well as their own personal experience. A heart symbolizes the Spiritualist, searching for the Beloved. In the negative, easily influenced and ignoring the practical realities of daily life, there is a naiveté and gullibility that leads to disappointment in what was *believed* to be true. This might be trust in a Guru, business partner, parent, friend or lover. High expectations are dashed as they look towards the world as steadily, unfailingly becoming a better place. Attached to their own beliefs and opinions, tragedies get called opportunities, arrangements are taken on faith, a *white light* is put around things as protection; leading to deluding themselves, avoiding the ordinary practicals of everyday living. Disregarding that the path of the moment appears hopeless, they trot along, impractical and oblivious to the details. Often in pursuit of the eternal good life, they lack groundedness and disregard many important details of living here on the physical plane.

Everyone is sacred. Every time you blink your eye, or I blink my eye, God blinks His eye. God sees through your eyes and my eyes. We are sacred.
—*Mathew King*

To make blind faith conscious is to not live in a belief system, but to live aligned in a truth system. To bear witness and to embrace a world that has many shades and dimensions allows us to more fully inhabit our lives. Sliding to the ordinal attitude of stoic, they become less resistant to live in a world that includes suffering and unscrupulous activities as an ordinary part of life. Serenity and resignation assist acceptance of an imperfect world. Peace of mind is a challenge, disappointments, dashed hopes, what's perceived as bad luck, flaky investments, poor choices, setbacks; often moving to a stoic posture of tranquility eases the inner turmoil. 7% of the population have this exalted inspiration orientation.

This is my quest. To follow that star. No matter how hopeless. No matter how far. And the world will be better for this. That one man, scorned and covered with scars. Still strove with his last ounce of courage. To reach the unreachable star. —The Impossible Dream, Man of La Mancha

Examples include: *Oprah Winfrey, Shirley MacLaine, Thomas Merton, Joan of Arc, Leonard Orr, Ram Dass, Swami Sachidananda, Tammy Fae Bakker, Elvis Presley, Michael Jackson, Kristen Chenoweth, Carl Jung, Marilyn Monroe, Judy Garland, Bernie Siegel, Alice Walker, Mr. Rogers, Jean Robertson, Meryl Streep, Don Juan Matus, Dennis Kucinich, George Harrison, Lena Horne, Andrew Harvey, Jimmy Carter, Patrick Dempsey, Ram Dass, Whitney Houston, Mother Teresa, Billy Graham, Nat King Cole, Liberace, Stevie Wonder, Mahatma Gandhi, Maya Angelou, William Blake, Gwyneth Paltrow, George Gurdjieff, Baba Muktananda.*

CYNIC

POSITIVE: CONTRADICTION

NEGATIVE: DENIGRATE, BELITTLE

Life's a bitch, then you die.

If things can go wrong they will. —Murphy's Law

A cynic is a man who, when he smell flowers, looks around for a coffin.
—H.L. Mencken

*E*xpecting the worst outcome to all situations, there is little surprise or disappointment when things go wrong. This is the mind-set that remembers what has failed in the past, expecting more of the same in the future. Often black humor and sarcastic mocking are based on this attitude. From their perspective they see the ridiculousness and absurdity of most anything and then they expose and satirize it. A gallows humor, warning people not to expect much, doubting is taken over the edge with bitter irony and biting sarcasm in the conviction that things won't work out. The Cynic will then look for probabilities to back their thesis, with an ultimate pleasure when their bleak outlook is confirmed. With this in mind there is little energy geared towards changing the world. The Cynic attitude expresses the viewpoint that I've looked and looked and things don't work, most effort fails and the world sucks. Remembering what has gone wrong, seeing what is amiss with the world, they then expect more of the same.

All I have to be thankful for in this world is that I was sitting down when my garter busted. —Dorothy Parker

Murphy's Law, a popular adage of Western culture, says that *any-*

thing that can go wrong will go wrong. Edward Murphy, a Cynic, was an engineer for U.S. Air Force projects. One experiment, testing human physical tolerance, involved a set of 16 accelerometers mounted to different parts of the body. His assistant wired all 16 accelerometers backwards, the experiment providing a zero reading. At a later news conference Murphy pronounced his infamous quote. *Anything that can go wrong, will go wrong.* Murphy's law, the Cynic attitude, is a light-hearted statement of a need for defensive design, the practice of planning for contingencies in the design stage of an undertaking, anticipating mistakes the end-user is likely to make. Injuries and inaccuracy become rare, the Skeptic taking into account the possibilities for error and then accommodates for that. Defensive design, called *Murphy proofing*, is a procedure that has been instituted in hospital surgical procedures. Using a colorful magic marker on a body part proceeding surgery, naming the part before the operation, the spirit of Murphy's law captures a need to account for human error, to pay attention, to protect ourselves.

A cynic is just a man who found out when he was ten that there wasn't any Santa Claus, and he's still upset. —J.G. Cozzens

The Peter Principle, a theory and book written by Dr. Lawrence Peter is yet another manifestation of the Cynic attitude. The principle states that in a hierarchy every employee tends to rise to his level of incompetence; a competent employee will eventually be promoted to and remain at a position in which he or she is incompetent. Although written in a lighthearted manner, Peter's observations on incompetence have now entered the American Heritage Dictionary as a noun: *Peter Principle: the theory that employees within an organization will advance to their highest level of competence and then be promoted to and remain at a level at which they are incompetent. Etymology: after Lawrence Peter.*

I want my time to be taken up by chores, appointments, errands, arguments. In other words, I want to get married. —*Jarod Kintz*

A further popular expression of the Cynic attitude in this culture is the Dilbert Principle written by Scott Adams, creator of the Dilbert comic strip, giving a voice to millions of Americans in the workplace. Advertised as *the funniest view of a depressing world you'll ever see*, the Dilbert principle claims that companies tend to systematically promote their least competent employees to management in order to limit the amount of damage they are capable of doing. The most ineffective workers will systematically be moved to a place where they can do the least damage—management. Essentially, responding to the Peter Principle, Adams says: *who says these people were ever competent? People are idiots, including me, the only difference among us is that we're idiots about different things at different times. No matter how smart you are, you spend much of your day being an idiot.* Since 1989 Adams has been illustrating this principle each day, lampooning the corporate world in his popular comic strip, Dilbert. Although only a small population carry this attitude, it has managed to permeate the fabric of our culture.

Things probably won't work out. Life sucks, then you die. —*bumper sticker*

The Cynic attitude, sometimes piercing irony, penetrating sarcasm and mirthful ridicule presented as a life philosophy is expressed with the following so-called wisdom quotes: *It will start raining as soon as I start washing my car. When caught in a traffic jam, the lane that you are in will always be the slowest to move. Every solution breeds new problems. Change is inevitable, except from a vending machine. Some people are alive only because it's illegal to kill them. The toothache goes away when the dentist arrives. The light at the end of a tunnel is that of an oncoming train. You will always find something in the last place you look. In order to get a loan, you must first prove you don't need it. When a broken appliance is demonstrated for the repairman, it will work perfectly. The other line always moves faster.* The Cynic sees that if there's more than one way to do a job and one of those ways will result in failure, then somebody will do it that way.

A true friend is a gift from God. Since God doesn't exist, guess what? Neither do true friends. —Scott Dikkers

PREPARATION FOR SURVIVAL

In the depths of my heart I can't help being convinced that my dear fellow-men, with few exceptions, are worthless. —Sigmund Freud

Cynicism began as an informal group of philosophers in Greece and Rome who hung out in the streets like a pack of dogs, the word coming from the Greek term meaning *dog*. The most famous was Diogenes, a street-philosopher who would greet people saying *I am Diogenes the dog. I nuzzle the kind, bark at the greedy, and bite scoundrels.* French philosopher Voltaire centuries later using Cynic wit portrayed the shortcomings and blemishes of humankind. *Animals have these advantages over man: they never hear the clock strike, they die without any idea of death, they have no theologians to instruct them, their last moments are not disturbed by unwelcome and unpleasant ceremonies, their funerals cost them nothing, and no one starts lawsuits over their wills.* —Voltaire

In business it is sometimes hard to complete tasks and projects with this self-defending, self-fulfilling prophecy of disaster. This attitude helps to avoid the worst in abusive family or work environments and is a protective survival position. Little disappointment, not much naiveté encourages the knack to keep oneself off the chopping block. Wary of people's motives, pessimistic about things working out, finally when something does go wrong the Cynic is prepared for it emotionally.

Think of how stupid the average person is and realize half of them are stupider than that. —George Carlin

The Cynic attitude is like an acid. When thought provoking and careful it influences the environment by cutting through the tarnish, still protecting the metal and then leaving it bare. This is not the mindset to shine up the metal or world, there is no drive to provide polish once reaching the metal core, that's in the hands of other attitudes, like spiritualist. This is not the temperament to perfect the world. The Cynic viewpoint when lacking responsibility and thought eats through the metal, and, like acid, ultimately destroys it. Often appearing in humor, comic Lenny Bruce known for his sardonic observations: *If Jesus had been killed twenty years ago, Catholic school children would be wearing little electric chairs around their necks instead of crosses.* Cynical comedian W.C. Fields was fond of telling people *to smile first thing in the morning. Get it over with.* Short with others, prophets of doom, often abrupt and blunt, what falls out of their mouth is often stinging and insulting.

No matter how cynical you become, it's never enough to keep up. —Lily Tomlin

In the positive mode, continuously looking at all angles, seeing how things go wrong, finding the inevitable weak link and failure to projects, opens the door to each side: the absurd, inevitable contradiction inherent in life. This can be empowering since one is prepared; to laugh at the foibles keeps one's spirit moving forward. By looking for mistakes, the Cynic is fortified against scammers, dumb products and empty advertising. Well-protected, watchful for the negative, they aren't likely to fall for political trickery or face-value solicitations. In this way, scanning for contradictions, letdowns are generally avoided. Willing to accept the worst without disappointment, they help us sidestep misfortune. Finding alternative ways, having an offbeat sense of humor, they see things in a piercing satirical way. Continuing in the positive mode, they help us to see the other side, arguing as the devil's advocate, while in the negative direction, they denigrate everything.

I am thankful for laughter, except when milk comes out of my nose. I never think I feel cynical in general. Cynical is reality with an alternate spelling. I feel there's a gigantic amount of injustice and overt crime every day in the world, from emotional crimes to international crimes, and it often carries rewards. —Woody Allen

In a negative mode, looking at bleak probabilities this caustic position turns people away. Extra energy is needed to pursue and accomplish goals; bitter, teasing, biting and harsh, it is easier to be quick-tongued and to ridicule and complain then to get behind a project and hear the possibilities for improving and making life meaningful. Maligning and sarcasm accentuate their negative position of disbelief. Insulting, sometimes sadistic, as children they might torment little animals. So many humorists have cashed in with this provocative attitude, seeing the absurd with well-aimed mockery and an acerbic sense of humor. Sliding to the exalted action realist attitude, no longer taking a negative stance to thwart activity, looking more carefully, less contrary and contentious, the characteristic of contradicting everything softens. 5% of the population have this ordinal action attitude.

A cynic is an idealist whose rose-colored glasses have been removed, snapped in two, and stomped into the ground, immediately improving his vision. —Rick Bayan

One of the more verbal, daring out-spoken Cynics of our time*: Great people talk about ideas, average people talk about things, and small people talk about wine. Life is something to do when you can't get to sleep. Polite conversation is rarely either. As a teen-ager you are at the last stage in your life when you will be happy to hear that the phone is for you. To put it rather bluntly, I am not the type who wants to go back to the land; I am the type who wants to go back to the hotel.* —Fran Lebowitz

Examples include: *Whoopi Goldberg, Lennie Bruce, Lily Tomlin, Woody Allen, George Carlin, Charles Manson, John Belushi, Humphrey Bogart, Billy Crystal, James Dean, Rene Magritte, Richard Pryor, Bob Dylan, Dennis Miller, George Orwell, Joan Rivers, Sigmund Freud, River Phoenix, Bette Davis, Mark Twain, Sandra Bernhard, Frank Sinatra, Mick Jagger, Jonathan Swift, Juvenal, Steve Martin, Larry King, Jean-Paul Sartre, Oscar Levant, J.D. Salinger, Rabelais, Bill Maher, Jon Stewart, Tennessee Williams, Elie Wiesel, Dorothy Parker, Fran Lebowitz, George Bernard Shaw, Mort Sahl, Jules Feiffer, H.H. Munro, Voltaire, Bette Davis, W.C. Fields, Stephen King, Mae West, Fred Allen, Jack Nicolson, James Thurber, Chicken Little, Eeyore,* the donkey who said: *it always rains on my birthday.*

REALIST

POSITIVE: OBJECTIVE, PERCEPTION

NEGATIVE: SUBJECTIVE, SPECULATION

it is what it is

I'm OK—You're OK

what does it look like when it's raining? Like it's raining.

I ain't Martin Luther King. I don't need a dream. I have a plan. —Spike Lee

The attitude of the Realist is depicted in the ancient parable of the farmer whose horse runs away. He maintains the posture of *maybe it's too bad and maybe it's not, only God knows.* The story continues as his horse reappears with five wild horses and the farmer corrals his horse along with the five wild horses. The country folk hearing about this, imagining it as miraculous, arrive to congratulate him for his remarkable addition, and he repeats his view-point, *this is not good or bad, it is what it is.* The next morning his son rides one of the horses and breaks his leg and hearing this the community folk reappear at the farmhouse this time to express their regrets. The farmer repeats his position: *well, maybe it is good, maybe it isn't, only God knows.* Within a week or so an army delegation knocks on the farmer's door to conscript the son to war. They see that the farmer's son has a shattered leg and is in no condition to travel, and so they leave without taking the son with them. The nearby community people again gather, reappear to express their congratulations that the son can stay home to help the farmer with his land. *Could be a good thing, maybe not, it is what is is.* The story continues with the Realist approach of seeing things as they are and living within what appears.

There is no secret. The secret is what is, is; and what isn't, isn't.
—*Werner Erhard*

The Realist is well-grounded, practical, impartial, making decisions with clarity, good in most emergency situations. This popular attitude is not one that makes big changes. It looks objectively at life, accepting situations free of assumption or clarification. Seeing what is happening, noting and talking about it without passing judgment, describing and accepting it, as it is. They enjoy offering accounts of incidents and experiences, stories about things that happen to them or to others, with no particular point or reason except to expound. Their story telling may be aimless and rambling, no real conclusion or statement, simply an accounting of activities. In the positive direction, objective, not reading into situations, they are unsentimental, freed up of judgment. Easily seeing many sides, assets and liabilities, facts and fiction, when in the positive they have no need to rearrange things, they recognize and go along with the *what is*.

There is no need to go to India or anywhere else to find peace. You will find that deep place of silence right in your room, your garden or even your bathtub. —Elisabeth Kübler-Ross

Realist philosopher Immanuel Kant clearly expressed this posture when saying: *There is nothing higher than reason.* Practical-minded, plain commonsense, little need to interpret, enjoying life as it is, everything is assumed to be Ok. The Realist calls a *spade a spade* and in the positive mode is essentially matter-of-fact. Presuming things to be fine, without taking the time or the effort to understand, guesswork becomes a slick pattern and interference towards developing deeper meaning.

The real distinction is between those who adapt their purposes to reality and those who seek to mould reality in the light of their purposes. —Henry Kissinger

LET'S SEE WHAT WANTS TO HAPPEN

Realist Dr. Eric Berne, author of *Games People Play: The Psychology of Human Relationships,* introduced Transactional Analysis, which has influenced millions. The trendy psychology book, self-help genre, simplistic and optimistic, set a tone, spawning the I'm Ok—You're Ok pop culture in the late 1960's and 70's. The *I'm fine* posture offered a user friendly theory of communication and interpersonal interaction. Easily becoming jargon it was sometimes used simplistically to define the selfhood of the individual. One criticism of looking at people through the

Games lens is that in this society there are many sensitive and beautiful people who struggle with their sense of not Okness, and on the other hand there are tyrants and mass murderers who speak about having an elevated sense of being Ok. Focused on externals, on objective realities, understanding is overlooked, instead a tone of superficiality overwhelms depthful investigation.

You don't need to pray to God anymore when there are storms in the sky, but you do have to be insured. —Bertolt Brecht

Moving in the negative direction, what was objective becomes subjective, surmising. Closed to other viewpoints, life is judged personally—from a subjective biased point of view and reality becomes theoretical speculation. Too many choices and influenced by private feelings, they become indecisive and bogged down. Slow coming to a decision, a low tolerance for ambiguity, a resistance to change, evaluating all sides, they become confused with the array of choices. Having lost a neutrally interested perspective, they overextend, gathering too much data. Getting ensnared in a maze of choices, losing sight of the bigger picture they become muddled and unable to come to a conclusion. No longer objective, the reality base that offered clarity falls away. Losing sight of impartial information, influenced by personal opinions things become out of focus, speculative, and are seen as more negative or even more positive than they really are. This leads to big trouble when investing in real estate or the stock market, especially as indecisiveness kicks in creating even more discomfort. Once the negative posture happens, the Realist enters a realm of judgment with strong convictions about how things are not working well, or that people are wrong and aren't informed. Rambling when they speak, taking forever, if ever, to get to their point, they are easy to persuade. This disjointed long-winded wordy quality makes the Realist an easy attitude to identify.

The pessimist complains about the wind; the optimist expects it to change; the realist adjusts the sails. —William Arthur Ward

Our culture enjoys the Realist genre of communication; people telling stories about things that have happened to them, subjective, without a teaching, moral or point; it speaks to the many who live in the Realist attitude. Good as negotiators, judges, scientists, politicians and newscasters. Sliding to the ordinal action attitude of cynic adds the benefit of looking at events and seeing what's not happening or what's wrong, along with the energy to put a stop to it. The fear of looking for what is not right, the contradiction that lies in the heart of the cynic attitude, needs to shift before it gives permission to the Realist to deepen and develop themselves. When a Realist slides to cynic the world, still seen *as it is*, becomes seen *unpleasant as it is*. Both positions approach the world as black or white. The Realist believes their cynical viewpoint is the reality. Stuck in guesswork and hunches, afraid to show disrespect for anything, sliding to cynic, seeing what is wrong helps them to make decisions and find closure. 30% of the population have this exalted action disposition.

The what should be never did exist, but people keep trying to live up to it. There is no 'what should be,' there is only what is. —Lenny Bruce

Examples include: *Spike Lee, Michael Moore, Jennifer Aniston, Tom Brokaw, Werner Erhard, Elisabeth Kübler-Ross, George W. Bush, John Kerry, Alan Greenspan, Colin Powell, Clint Eastwood, Norman Mailer, Sting, Immanuel Kant, Bertolt Brecht, Barbara Boxer, Ernest Hemingway, Sharon Stone, Russell Crowe, Yoko Ono, Lenny Bruce, Alfred Whitehead, Katherine Hepburn, Arnold Schwarznegger, Christie Brinkley, Michael J. Fox, Winnie the Pooh,* who said: *Maybe it will and maybe it won't, let's see.*

PRAGMATIST

POSITIVE: PRACTICAL

NEGATIVE: DOGMATIC

it must be.
Let's all do it my way, it's simple, practical and efficient.

This efficient, practical, matter-of-fact, unsentimental, unromantic, concrete, utilitarian, dogmatic posture is bland and monotonous. This may be hard on the Pragmatist, since choosing the sensible, unremarkable, practical path is rarely the lively, wild, enthusiastic, spontaneous way. So often they miss the fun boat when it happens to sail by since that might take too long. They jump aboard the motor boat, trading pleasure and the scenic tour for down-to-earth speed and efficiency. The beautiful ambling meandering route is impractical, takes too long, might blow a tire because there are ruts in the road, too much extra effort; this direction is just what makes the most sense. Everyone's out in the playground while they're in the library doing homework.

Thought's a luxury. Do you think the peasant sits and thinks of God and Democracy when he gets inside his mud hut at night? —*Graham Greene*

The Pragmatist attitude is a neutral polarity representing the assimilation of all 6 attitudes and offers the capacity to see many aspects of life more clearly, less distorted, while being less colorful. A down to earth, matter of fact, utilitarian, concrete mind-set. While other attitudes pick a color to see the world, as well as taking time to jump in the lake, have a drink or dessert, be romantic and smell the flowers along the way, the Pragmatist does not stop, seeing everything in a monochromatic gray scale.

It doesn't matter whether a cat is black or white; as long as it can catch mice, it's a good cat. —*a Pragmatic unknown author*

Believing value lies in usefulness, this is the pick-up truck, designed for practical circumstances, for performing tasks, for function, not for show or appearance. Seeing what is sensible, effective, economical, good at improving productivity by eliminating waste, they get the job done. Knowing when something becomes a burden, they become irritated by others pie-in-the sky outlook. This is a posture focused on results. Pragmatists are often politicians, deal makers that want you on their side and into their issues. This is an attitude that is popular with accountants, efficiency experts, time management leaders, coaching counselors and consultants. Great at organizing, ask the Pragmatist where to get the best deal on a product, where to find a government auction, home foreclosure or no-fee bank account. Put them in charge of the pot-luck dinner—there won't be all dessert and no main dish–if it's your house mate give them the bill-paying job or checkbook—nothing will bounce, everything will get paid in a timely manner.

I have no dress except the one I wear every day. If you are going to be kind enough to give me one, please let it be practical and dark so that I can put it on afterwards to go to the laboratory. —*Marie Curie*

Along the positive track they create order, have sound judgment, make things work, are mindful of results and find it important to use time well. In fact things not working or not being purposeful becomes an irritant. Disliking impracticality; their best experiences provide interest and function. Never underplay the value of the maintenance person, they arrive to keep the home or business organized, running smoothly; how it *should be*. Concerned with the actual doing or the usability of something rather than with theory and ideas; this is the method person skilled at manual tasks.

DOWN TO EARTH

The Pragmatist attitude likes to create rules so things will be kept in order and also holds others to those rules. They like brainstorming and practical, level-headed, sensible ideas that will be applied. The world is looked at as a place to have experiences, this down-to-earth viewpoint keeps the door open to everything, whether it is beauty or ugliness, sadness or happiness, there is no bias or theory, no ideology or morality. It works, or it doesn't work. Things are good so long as they are suitable and logical. Fun for funs sake is not so functional. Fun because it is during the hours that one is taking care of three children and the structured activity engages the children, becoming utilitarian; and thereby that works.

I'm generally a very pragmatic person: that which works, works. —Linus Torvalds

Lao Tzu, father of Taoism is attributed to the pragmatic proverb: *Give a man a fish and you feed him for a day. Teach him how to fish and you feed him for a lifetime.* Things are perceived in terms of their usefulness. William James, the founder of Pragmatism, an American philosophical movement that was embedded in the reality of life proposed that nothing is true or false—it either works or it doesn't, *practical application is everything.* Sensible, things are assessed by default; what gets the best results. However, what works for one person might not work for another. Often the criterion of function and efficiency ignores lighthearted play and feelings, the project may save money and time, but relationships and emotional life pay on the other side. To be mindful of the plus and minuses before making decisions, to be willing to slide to other positions when useful keeps the air circulating.

With the price of life these days, you got to get everything for free that you can. —*Charles Rogers*

In the negative track the rules take over, hinder growth and evolution, especially through lack of flexibility. Seeing what they think is efficient, ignoring what others think effective, they jump to a solution without looking at other aspects of the issue. Moving into the negative takes on a flavor of long winded preachiness as well as blocking change to retain order. Creating routines and principles, they then become those who enforce those directives. Not liking to be slowed down and pulled into other peoples interruptive and unproductive feelings and needs, that's only ok if it's a good trade-off to get a job done. Dogmatic, biased, insistent, one-sided, opinionated; sticking to a rule book, the rules take over. Boring, pedantic and uninspired becomes the tone, now the code of standards, habits and rituals block unprompted moments, adaptation and transformation. Their mind is made up long before the information is in, changing set opinions is difficult and confusing. Rigidly sticking to the rule book, based on what was established as most appropriate in the past. Reluctant to be wrong or uninformed, without adequate knowledge they profess that they know the situation. Obstructing their own growth, narrow-minded, schedules become worshipped. Not the favorite to invite to the midnight party. No time to *smell the roses*, unless it doesn't interfere with the routine.

Do the difficult things while they are easy and do the great things while they are small. A journey of a thousand miles must begin with a single step. —*Lao Tzu*

One way to shift from the negative is to explore looking at situations through the eyes of other people, to see different angles; this cracks some of the opinions that have been formed, set in concrete that had become overly structured comfortable ideas. Afraid to be wrong or uninformed, their mind is made up sometimes only with favorite familiar opinions. As a neutral assimilation attitude there is no opposite slide, not having a point of view weighted in one direction they see things almost by default in terms of what will succeed, what will get the job done. Representing the combination of the other six attitudes the Pragmatist has the flexibility to slide to any of the other points of view. Combining with a different attitude life has new possibilities. 20% of the population have this attitude.

How many geniuses does it take to change a light bulb? Only one, a pragmatist; to ignore the bureaucratic piles of paperwork and replace the bad bulb with a good one. —anonymous saying

Examples include: *Jesse Jackson, Neil Simon, Cybil Shepherd, George Bush Sr., Charles Bronson, Diana Ross, Werner Erhard, Maria Shriver, Carl Rogers, Lao Tzu, Paul Newman, Susan Sarandon, Lily Tomlin, Nancy Reagan, Dustin Hoffman, Dick Clark, George Washington Carver, Marie Curie, Graham Greene, Marshall McLuhan, Donald Trump, Julia Roberts, Michael Dell, William James, Martha Stewart, Billy Graham, Carly Simon, Mary Kay Ash.*

SYSTEM SEVENTEEN

FIVE NATURAL EMOTIONS

FEAR, ANGER, JEALOUSY, GRIEF, LOVE

Emotions are a key element in self-care because they allow us to enter into the body mind's conversation. By getting in touch with our emotions, both by listening to them and by directing them through the psychosomatic network, we gain access to the healing wisdom that is everyone's natural biological right, acknowledging and claiming all our feelings, not just the so-called positive ones. Anger, grief, fear—these emotional experiences are not negative in themselves, in fact, they are vital for our survival. We need anger to define boundaries, grief to deal with our losses, and fear to protect ourselves from danger. It's only when these feelings are denied, so that they cannot be easily and rapidly processed through the system and released, that the situation becomes toxic. The more we deny them, the greater the ultimate toxicity, which often takes the form of an explosive release of pent-up emotion. That's when emotion can be damaging to both oneself and to others, because its expression becomes overwhelming, sometimes violent. —Candace Pert

*O*ur Natural Emotions effortlessly produce genuine spontaneous responses. Restricted they lead to unnatural reactions and distortions creating conditions that exist in this world—child abuse, murder, criminal behavior, alcohol and drug addiction; personal reactions to the world around us. Healthy people don't react, they act, are responsive. Emotions are energy-in-motion. We are the unchanging ocean, the Emotions are the waves flowing through and past us; the ocean remains ocean even as the waves arrive and disappear.

We think sometimes we are only drawn to the good, but we're actually drawn to the authentic. We like people who are real more than those who hide their true selves under layers of artificial niceties. —Elisabeth Kübler-Ross

	Natural Emotions	Distortions
Fear	natural survival response, caution, startle impulse	anxiety, panic, phobias
Anger	bring about change, self-protection, assertive, firm	rage, hatred, bitterness, resentment, self-hate, holding a grudge, wrath
Jealousy	stimulus that motivates us to grow, improve, emulate another's behavior	envy, put-down of self and others, low self-worth, lack of self-esteem, compare, criticize
Grief	how we deal with the experience of loss	regret, blame, guilt, self-pity, depression, martyrdom
Love	care, concern, giving and receiving nurturing, self-love, maturity, yummy	demanding, possessiveness, expectations, instability, yucky

Chart 9: Natural emotions and their distortions

There are Five Natural Emotions and each has negative unnatural counterparts. What happens in the first six years of life is critically significant. Punishment, bullying, using superior strength and size to force compliance is counter to a child's intuitive understanding of what feels good and loving, bringing up instead a desire for revenge. Children learn through imitation and observation. Generally by the time a child is six years old their unself-conscious pure Emotions have turned into unnatural ones creating survival strategies that continue throughout the life. For most people our Natural Emotions have been repressed and replaced with rather unhealthy, destructive or self-destructive Emotions. Natural Emotions maintain energy—unnatural Emotions strain and create negativity, are fatiguing and toxic, detrimental and self-destructive, leading to turmoil for our life and the life of this planet. Power struggles and wars between nations arise from madness, from unnatural Emotions and desires, creating unnecessary suffering for people and for this earth.

Emotions are the language of the soul: subtle, elusive and cryptic. Often they defy the rationality of the mind and the logic of our society. We need to learn to embrace our emotions because they are the key to our happiness and understanding ourselves. —Jiveny

When we react strongly to people, when someone pushes our buttons, it suggests that we have unfinished business, old issues accumulated from our distortions of unnatural Emotions. These feelings are draining and create physical illness. As children unselfconsciously give voice to their thoughts and feelings their openness is often curtailed by adult rules and regulations under the banner of socialization. Told that it is wrong to feel angry or sad or jealous or afraid, later in life as adults our ability to experience naturalness gets corrupted. When allowed our spontaneous open responses we maintain a healthy attitude and move through our responses quickly before they become backed up and twisted into aberrations.

Emotion is the chief source of all becoming conscious. There can be no transformation of darkness into light without emotion. —Carl Jung

WORLD HISTORY OF EMOTIONS

Chinese medicine connects Emotions to energy meridians that move throughout our body. Emotions that hold on reflect a channel that is out of balance. In this respect Emotions are neither good nor bad, they are our aliveness, indicators of our relationship to ourself and to the world. Traditional Chinese medicine lists five Emotions, and each connects to an organ: fear-kidney, grief-lung, anger-liver, love-heart, distress-spleen. Worry is said to weaken the stomach and stress weakens the heart and brain. Disharmony and illness arises when we overindulge, ignore, repress, overload or become stuck in our Emotions.

Excessive emotions lead to disease, so we practice attaining a state of equanimity. —Chinese medical health care manual

In Chinese medicine the emotions are neither 'good' nor 'bad', they simply are part of being human and alive. There are good reasons to feel fear at times, to be angry, to feel joy, to feel grief. These feelings are indicators of our personal and collective relationship with the world and ourselves. In optimal health, our emotions flow freely, are acknowledged, responded to appropriately, and then we move on to the next 'feeling'. —Dr. Calvin Dale Smith

Homeopathy, a whole medical system developed in Europe 200 plus years ago views the body mind and Emotions as always working together to maintain a relative degree of balance. The homeopathic approach is to understand disease as holistic—evaluated in the context of the whole person—physical, mentally and emotionally.

Homeopathy is the safest and most reliable approach to ailments and has withstood the assaults of established medical practice for over 100 years. —Yehudi Menuhin

Ayurveda, a system of traditional medicine native to the Indian subcontinent first appeared during the Vedic period in India in the second and first millennia BCE, and correlates organs and illness with specific mental/emotional states, creating a mind, body, spirit balance for healing in a natural organic way. The Vedic texts very specifically address those behaviors that enhance the subtle energy of the physical body like yoga, exercise, meditation, and truth telling. The quality of our inner Emotions directly determine the quality of our health. Our physical organs are seats of consciousness that need nourishment to coordinate all our parts into a life-breathing vital whole.

Because we cannot scrub our inner body we need to learn skills to help cleanse our tissues, organs, and mind. This is the art of Ayurveda. —Sebastian Pole

Emotions are real and exist in time and space, located throughout our minds and bodies, and are cross-cultural, the same throughout the world. Distortions are a learned response stemming from the culture that we grow up within. Charles Darwin considered Emotions a pivotal force in evolution, a key to survival. Our Emotions are vital to self-care, to coordinating all the parts of us into a harmonious and healthy whole, they allow us to enter into the body-mind's conversation. When our Emotions are moving and our chemicals flowing we experience a lighter openness that is uplifting. Pay attention to our Emotions for they are the bridge that link and affect our health and well-being. Indigenous cultures worldwide have understood the mind-body connection. When Emotions are expressed all systems are united and made whole, when Emotions are repressed, denied, not allowed to be whatever they may be, our network pathways get blocked, stopping the flow of the all-important feel-good unifying chemicals that run both our biology and our behavior. Our immune system is influenced by this free flow of energy, to interrupt it creates stuck energy, sets up a dis-integrity in the system, causing it to act at cross-purposes rather than as a unified whole.

There are five cardinal emotions with which an Ego is endowed as part of their basic mind. These are the feelings of awe, joy, grief, fear, and anger each of which can be expressed in widely varying intensities. All other emotions are modifications and combinations of these five brought about by societal conditioning during incarnations. The advanced Ego has enhanced their expression of awe and joy and has eliminated further experience of grief, fear, and anger. Emotions are the source of humane sensibility, out of which arises compassion empathy, and sentiment on the Egoic level. —Richard Kieninger

FEAR

Fear protects us from danger. If people do not feel fear, they are a danger to themselves. —*R. Laaksonen*

The first natural emotion is Fear. All children are born with two natural fears; a fear of falling and a fear of loud noises. Fear helps preserve our lives, builds in a quality of caution, providing children with the natural expression of a startle response. As the development of concern for ourselves to feel safe, trusting, secure, centered and relaxed, a natural carefulness brings us into a state of voluntary attention, independent of reactions. All other Fears are learned, taught by parents, family members, society, passed on to children by the projection of outside worries and anxieties to then become twisted into phobias and anxiety.

Childhood is a time for fun and play and not a time to be involved and concerned with adult issues, not a time to be involved with adult decisions regarding where to live, whether parents should get divorced, not to be focused on a parent who erupts, is volatile or drunk and unreliable, not to protect a parent from being hit or yelled at; these type of adult issues create tension and rob children of the natural process of their easy playful time of life. Children who have learned to have Fears, whether they attach that worry to ghosts, dentist, snakes, change, new situations, airplanes, throwing up, dying, dogs or strangers will become emotionally restrained. These are Fears that are trained into children, not Fears that serve to preserve life; trained into the body and stored and lodged in our instinctive center. A child's concern is that once going to bed he might not wake up, while an adult imagines that when we die awareness also dies and there will be nothing—no memory, no consciousness, nothing that ever knew from being alive; identifying with the body, misguided into believing that what we do will continue to preserve our life, when in truth the body will die. Life is impermanent. Only essence is never touched or limited by time or Fear.

It is not that you must be free from fear. The moment you try to free yourself from fear, you create a resistance against fear. Resistance, in any form, does not end fear. What is needed, rather than running away or controlling or suppressing or any other resistance, is understanding fear; that means, watch it, learn about it, come directly into contact with it. We are here to learn about fear, not how to escape from it, not how to resist it through courage and so on. —Jiddu Krishnamurti

The purpose of natural Fear is to build in a practice of caution, to protect and sustain our lives, a tool to help keep our body alive through the understanding that in whatever we do there are ramifications and consequences. Fear is a defensive advantage serving as a motivation to escape to safety, an outgrowth of the love of self, helping us develop self-love and self-worth. It makes our adrenaline flow; although too much paralyzes us, like a rabbit or deer caught in a car's headlights. The ease and flowing movement, as with all natural emotions, maintains our health. All other Fears are learned responses from the environment, educated through the political system, newspapers, schools and universities, television, taught by parents, family members and acquaintances, and they drain our energy while leading to stress, challenges and ill health.

The next time you encounter fear, consider yourself lucky. Usually we think that brave people have no fear. The truth is that they are intimate with fear. —Pema Chodron

Fear that is bottled up becomes panic, an unnatural emotion, creating phobias. The distortions, some of the negative unnatural counterparts of Fear are: anxiety, panic, phobias, dread, fright, alarm, intimidation, apprehension, mistrust, scared, suspicion, terror, worry, awkwardness, foreboding, nightmare, horror, nervousness, distress, agitation. The inhibition of our natural impulses feeds anxiety. The Fear *to be* takes many forms. To recognize and know them is the first step.

There are times when fear is good. It must keep its watchful place at the heart's controls. —Aeschylus

Unnatural Fears create dependent people who have tremendous difficulty meeting their own as well as others needs. Without irrational Fear our suffering would be greatly diminished. The innate response of Fear is as a reminder to be cautious in our actions and to become aware of their effect both on ourself and the world around. As a natural survival response, a startle response and a flight or fight impulse our sensible Fears don't distort reality, are not blinders, do not breed more Fear, do not create paralysis. Self-recognition along with self-understanding—the truth about ourselves can free us. True insight transforms the tyranny of our enslavement.

True fear is the father of courage and the mother of safety. —Henry Tweedy

ANGER

Holding on to anger is like grasping a hot coal with the intent of throwing it at someone else; you are the one who gets burned. —the Buddha

Anger, the second natural emotion, when expressed in a direct constructive way is brief, 15 to 30 seconds. As a tool to learn to say no and create healthy boundaries, it helps to develop our inner authority. Healthy Anger brings about change, is self-protective, teaches assertiveness and firmness. It does not have to be abusive or damaging to another, in fact healthy anger is not directed at others or used to harm. To have not been offered the space to express natural Anger, to have been stopped from saying no as a child, to have been punished, hit or sent away when we responded with a firm, determined no creates a repressed back load of hate and resentment that easily explodes. This is the spark that detonates when we fly off the handle, hit the roof, blow our cool, see red, hit someone or lash out when we are triggered. Not being allowed to say certain swear words; Anger has to be embraced with tenderness, to not be afraid of it for it to be transformed into a nourishing compost that makes love reappear.

Anybody can become angry, that is easy; but to be angry with the right person, and to the right degree, and at the right time, and for the right purpose, and in the right way, that is not within everybody's power, that is not easy.
—Aristotle

Anger denied impinges on our health; hate is corrosive. Stored Anger creates blocked energy eventually leading to illness. Wrath is another distortion of Anger and is about power and control often accompanied with vengeful indignation. Anger as a healthy expression of our emotion is a vital life skill. Anger is constructive when it is instructive. Mahatma Gandhi used that energy to bring India to self-rule. Nelson Mandela having served a 27 year prison sentence said: *Yes, I was angry. And I was a little afraid. After all, I've not been free in so long. But,* he said, *when I felt that anger well up inside of me I realized that if I hated them after I got outside that gate then they would still have me.* And he smiled and said, *I wanted to be free so I let it go.*

Anger is a great force. If you can control it, it can be transmuted into a power which can move the whole world. —Sivananda

The world needs Anger as a monitor to move beyond the acceptance of things that are unacceptable, like genocide and holocaust, child abuse and the mutilation of women and children; some things are really not tolerable. The natural emotion of Anger is a teaching instrument to signal to ourselves that we have a right to say no, before our Anger becomes an unnatural emotion. Anger held or expressed at length is a distortion. Eventually that unexpressed Anger becomes rage, hate, lust for revenge, exasperation, aggravation, animosity, frustration, self-hate, bitterness, agitation, irritability, a grudge, contempt, seething, and we become pissed off, vengeful, offended, sadistic, cold-hearted, belligerent, mean, spiteful, crushed, cross, impatient, hostile, resentful, incensed, indignant, irate. People kill from rage, wars are fanned, bombs are hidden and exploded, terrorists feel justified, guns picked up to kill bystanders; the media feeds us toxic frustration and the public ingests the toxins.

One who controls occurring anger as one would a chariot gone off the track, that one I call a charioteer; other people just hold the reins. —the Buddha

ANGER AND LIBERATION

If you are patient in one moment of anger, you will escape a hundred days of sorrow. —Chinese saying

To grow a beautiful lotus flower we need mud, learning to manage, to embrace our Anger, that alchemical Kali power, the goddess mother known for destroying ignorance, destroying to recreate; Kali destroys the finite to reveal the infinite. The black goddess is death, but to the wise she is also the death of death, for in a profound way life and birth are always bound up with death and destruction. This is the highest form of Anger: the kind that eats our death as well as absorbing the traumas of the world. At the center of this darkness, where our Anger lives lies all the suffering—the unspeakable afflictions that bring us to disappear into a dark silence. The passion and fierceness that is associated with Anger, that burns through self-deception, Kali throws us into the fire burning away illusions, providing liberation.

The world needs anger. The world often continues to allow evil because it isn't angry enough. —*Bes Jarrett*

There is a story about a student asking Buddha why we aren't liberated. Buddha said *go ask people what they want and report back.* The student found that people wanted money, a partner, no stress, a new car, to eat what they desired without getting fat, to travel, a bigger house, better health. No one had asked for or wanted liberation; to awaken. Those places of comfort that people seek: food, money, entertainment don't do much when we are faced with tragedy.

It is important to feel the anger without judging it, without attempting to find meaning in it. It may take many forms: anger at the health-care system, at life, at your loved one for leaving. Life is unfair. Death is unfair. Anger is a natural reaction to the unfairness of loss. —*Elisabeth Kübler-Ross*

Staying with our Anger rather than acting it out or repressing it, gradually it becomes understandable. Steady, being present, all other solutions other than liberation are like throwing a cup of water on a burning house. The courage to face our healthy Anger, to place ourselves into the bright fire of truth; to be a fierce warrior is an initiation into the harsh suffering wisdom of life. No aspect of true Anger can be glossed over, it has secrets to yield as we harness its energy, bringing the light into its darkness, then, within it we grow a fearless examination, the one that ultimately brings about our freedom.

I was angry with my friend I told my wrath, my wrath did end. I was angry with my foe: I told it not, my wrath did grow. —*William Blake*

Anger is a normal emotion if it is expressed when felt. Then it is over with. If one keeps a lid on it, it develops into resentment or hate. Sooner or later, resentment and hate explode, destroying others, or they are held in, destroying oneself. —*Dr. Bernie Siegel*

JEALOUSY

Do not worship any other god, for the Lord, whose name is Jealous, is a jealous God. —*Exodus*

The third natural emotion is Jealousy, the encouragement to improve. Jealousy is the natural emotion that stirs a small child to learn to walk and run the way the big kids do, to be able to read the street sign or menu the way big sister does, to be able to ride the bike like big brother does; the natural emotion that stimulates the urge to emulate and grow. The motivation and inspiration for children to imitate, to mirror their friends, to learn to play the piano, to spell, read, to surprise parents by making a cake for their birthday; all seen and copied, watching what others can do. When children are belittled and discredited, this natural feeling turns into tough competitiveness, into begrudging envy, and forced, driven achievement. Quite visible when we learn the history of athletes and others in the public eye whose demise through drugs, alcohol, endless affairs, sometimes suicide, reflects the pressure and rigors of their childhood conditioning.

Jealousy is both reasonable and belongs to reasonable men, while envy is base and belongs to the base, for the one makes himself get good things by jealousy, while the other does not allow his neighbor to have them through envy. —*Aristotle*

Understanding the difference between Jealousy and envy can be traced through the root meaning of the two words. Jealous comes from the French and Greek root for ardor and zeal, to be watchful and vigilant and is etymologically derived from the Greek *zelos*. Envy, on the other hand, from the Latin *invidia* is characterized by an insatiable desire, resenting that another person has something that we perceive ourselves as lacking, and the wish that the other person be deprived of it. Derived from the French and Latin, envy is to regard maliciously, to bear some-one a grudge. Demanding what is missed from the outside, the reaching out always unobtainable; the French use of *envie* as desire underscores the implicit observation that envy is a passion leading to frustrations. Envy and Jealousy are often used interchangeably, but in correct usage, both words stand for two different distinct emotions. Jealousy is the response and energy that prompts and inspires us to match or surpass by imitation, while envy is the pain or frustration caused by another person having something that we think we do not have.

Children have never been very good at listening to their elders, but they have never failed to imitate them. —*James Baldwin*

Thomas Aquinas described envy as *sorrow for another's good.* Aristotle defined envy as *the pain caused by the good fortune of others,* while Kant defined it as *a reluctance to see our own well-being overshadowed by another's,* explaining that, *the standard we use to see how well off we are is not the intrinsic worth of our own well-being but how it compares with that of others.* Dante defined envy as *love of one's own good perverted to a desire to deprive others of theirs. In Dante's Purgatory the punishment for the envious is to have their eyes sewn shut with wires because they have gained sinful pleasure seeing others brought low.*

JEALOUSY: ANTIDOTE TO ENVY

In Buddhism one of the divine abidings asks us to take joy in the good fortune of another. This virtue is considered the antidote to envy and the opposite of unhappiness at our good fortune. The delicate dance—to not move from Jealousy into envy—holds an attitude of responsibility and practice, we meet the self through some form of a practice which asks for a push from within. The distortion of insulting others, of comparing and criticizing, displays the movement from Jealousy to envy. Envy renders the person unhappy and negative from the envy of wishing to inflict misfortune on others, suffering over another's prosperity.

Envy is a littleness of soul, which cannot see beyond a certain point, and if it does not occupy the whole space feels itself excluded. —Willim Hazlitt

In the Bible being Jealous and being zealous are similar—referring to the changing color of the rising emotions which is associated with zeal or fervor over something dear to us. Jealousy in Scripture involves the desire to have what somebody else has. At times the desire is wholesome, as when we want to develop in our own lives the spiritual qualities we see in others. Envy, feeling displeasure over the blessings others are enjoying, wanting to deprive them of that enjoyment, becomes misguided. Jealousy wants what others have, while envy wants to keep them from having it.

Envy comes from people's ignorance of, or lack of belief in, their own gifts. —Jean Vanier

Jealousy has been observed in infants from 5 months and older. Repressed it moves into the unnaturalness of envy and harmful competitiveness, carrying ranges of guilt and shame. The shame arises with the recognition of the contradiction between the need and the taboo against it, the painful sense of lack and a craving towards that which is felt to be missing. Envy has a self-frustrating aspect stimulating further frustration. To recognize the difference and trace those feelings to their origins allows for our understanding and its clearing.

Example is not the main thing in influencing others. It's the only thing. —Albert Schweitzer

The healthy urge to improve, to learn and to grow like older people, that children see, is a stimulus to impel and motivate us to exceed, to emulate other's behavior. Making effort, paying attention, trying becomes the bedrock of all teachings, for the possibilities are always present and overcoming difficulties is a process that often begins with a Jealous encounter. To return to our own self, to look at our gifts and uniqueness are some of the inner work to dissolve the distortions of unnatural feelings. Jealous is the natural emotion that makes us want to do it again, to try harder, to continue until we succeed. Until we face ourselves, allow the hidden parts to surface, to quote Jung: *we don't become enlightened by imagining figures of light, but by making the darkness conscious.*

Jealousy is like a hot pepper. Use it mildly, and you add spice to the relationship. Use too much of it and it can burn. —*Ayala Pines*

GRIEF

Grief is the rope burns left behind when what we held to most dearly is pulled out of reach, beyond our grasp. —*Stephen Levine*

*G*rief, the fourth natural emotion serves to help us deal with the numerous little deaths that we experience in life. Tears are a gift that enable us to release Grief. Grief is simple natural sorrow and to let ourselves cry, to give ourself the time we need to remember, to mourn; allowing the process that death facilitates within ourselves is our own life cycle transition, eventually we heal. Grief as a natural emotion is the part of ourselves that is allowed to say goodbye when we don't want to say goodbye, that expresses and pushes out the sadness within ourself at our experience of loss. This can range from the daily loss of our dignity incurred by prejudice and cultural humiliations towards women, the disabled, the aged, and to children, or from the unexpected loss of a cell phone, a pet, a job or marriage, to the death of a parent. To live within the pain of truth prepares the ground for all the natural emotions, we all have the capacity to feel Grief, to experience heartbreak, a vehicle for awakening. When we touch the center of Grief and sit with it and let it soften us it has a transformative effect. Our descent also allows for our ascendence, they inspire each other.

The grief which has no vent in tears may make other organs weep.
—Henry Maudsley

The human condition from our separation at birth sets the stage for Grief, not only in major losses but the inevitable Grief that lies in the unknown, in the darkness, in the shadows. The Grief for the loss of a special stuffed animal for a child or their pet dog can be profound, told not to cry or feel loss or to quickly have it replaced; to repress or ignore Grief creates a stuck quality that inhibits movement into new life challenges. Chronic Grief that accumulates over time is the forgetting or loss of self that lies as an underpinning of an ordinary day. So many deaths as we mature, the loss of a favorite tree or a body part not addressed carries over into feelings of being misunderstood, regret, a search for someone or thing to fulfill needs, rather than knowing it is ourself that is responsible for the delight and pleasure that sustains us internally; sharing and communicating these profound experiences encourages healing.

Nothing that grieves us can be called little: by the eternal laws of proportion a child's loss of a doll and a king's loss of a crown are events of the same size.
—Mark Twain

To inhibit the natural expression of Grief will over time create unnatural emotions of despondency, disappointment, discouragement, a heavy heart, a bottomless sorrow, gloom, alienation, hopelessness, melancholy, unhappiness, misery, distress, pain, anguish, heartache, agony, heartbreak, woe, desolation, dejection and chronic depression. The physical exhaustion from unattended Grief is a dead weight, with a long list of symptoms that include sleep disorders, intestinal problems, a dull ache that stiffens our shoulders and cramps our neck. Aggression towards ourselves and others rise as we avoid examining the helplessness we feel. E. L. Doctorow offered a graphic image, saying; *Grief is like driving at night, though you can only see a few feet ahead, you can make the whole journey that way.*

THE TENDERNESS OF GRIEVING

The eye has a dark part and a light part. One can only see through the dark part. —*Tanhuma, Tetzave*

We live in a culture that addresses solutions, that medicates anxiety sorrow and sadness, that disconnects us from our Grief, widening the gulf between the ache that drives us towards our addictions and the strength necessary for the ascent towards open-mindedness and understanding. To find the tenderness in sorrow and offer ourselves compassion enables us to have compassion for others. There is a practice called Tonglen that prepares us to connect to our suffering and to the Grief that is around us. Learning to transform the dark clouds of suffering, extending ourselves, parting with our preciousness, releasing our identification with a limited self we move into the spaciousness of our true nature. Facing our Grief is the prerequisite for this spiritual journey, both the recognition of illusion and our separation from joy and love. The persistence, dedication and devotion to this relentless self-examination is fueled from the recognition that life on the ground level is limited; looking at the human condition, of what we have done to humanity and this earth involves a lionhearted capacity for Grief. Most people are more eager to move into the pleasure, gratification and adventures of living, yet their premature withdrawal from grieving limits their depth, their possibilities, their wisdom. Intentional suffering creates transformation and what follows is a sweetness, our beauty as we birth ourselves into the open heart of compassion.

I saw grief drinking a cup of sorrow. It's sweet, isn't it? Grief said, You put me out of business. How can I sell grief when you know it's sweet? —Rumi

Our expression of loss is often a reflection of the great joys and pleasures we have felt and is a balm or salve, a purification, emptying ourselves from years of wounding and heartbreak, a true medicine for the heart, with time as the great physician. To be in a dialogue that addresses questions about life and death, to learn to live in a world where loss matters, for Grief is a way that bereaved people heal. We are all living in a community of impermanence, we never know when loss will appear, just as we never know when our last breath may be our final, and so how do we enter each day with full aliveness? To soften around our discomfort, to not resist and to meet our Grief with compassion; to embrace loss with soft-hearted kindness we make room for our life.

The five stages—denial, anger, bargaining, depression, and acceptance—are a part of the framework that makes up our learning to live with the one we lost. They are tools to help us frame and identify what we may be feeling. But they are not stops on some linear timeline in grief. —Elisabeth Kübler-Ross

The Grief work that returns us to our naturalness releases the guilt and shame, the despondency and disappointment we feel when we believe that there are things we should have done. Communicating those thoughts, forgiving ourselves, shedding tears, moves us in a healing direction. With our ability to meet our Grief with loving kindness, to enter into it we are freed to rest in the open spaciousness of our being. To not make peace with Grief reduces our life force, to recognize and greet the innumerable losses that pass through our life maintains our vitality. To numb the natural emotion of Grief in a world where everything is impermanent creates a deadness of spirit, limits and constricts, closing off valuable parts of self.

I will build an altar from the broken fragments of my heart.
—*Yehuda HeChasid*

L O V E

Jump to your feet, wave your fists, threaten and warn the whole universe that your heart can no longer live without real love! —Hafiz

The fifth natural emotion is Love. This essential and most important of all the five natural emotions is the basis, the root for all that is human: the presence or absence of Love. From Love's absence, a closed heart, the world often seems the most meaningless. And yet Love is never absent, only we are. Discovering that we are Love, its appearance as both giving and receiving, opening to self-Love, rising as we discover this Love that lives within us, we come to know the meaning of Love. As we learn to know ourselves we learn to know the Love which comes into the world through us, as well as is in the world around us. Repressed Love turns into possessiveness and demanding, creating tension, anxiety, a heavy heart, loneliness, expectations, instability; creates our wounded relationship to Love itself; shifts our essential experience of life from the deliciousness of yummy to the foul taste of yucky.

Reason is powerless in the expression of Love. Love alone is capable of reveal-

ing the truth of Love and being a Lover. This is the Way of Truth. If you want to live, die in Love. Die in Love if you want to remain alive. —*Rumi*

Love is the recognition of beauty, seeing and being seen as the beautiful being that we are, receiving and giving attention, listening inside to the needs of the present moment Love flows into our heart. Our life is sustained through interconnectedness, by the force of Love that sustains human life, what is named *leela,* the play, the Love dance of the universe. To become Love, to become what we Love is who we are, and then we are in the way or presence of Love. Conscious Love, a work of art, has wisdom and knowledge. The great Teachers have brought teachings of Love. As a force in the universe it also exists outside of us. As the cause of existence, goals and illusions disappear and understanding and possibilities arise. It has been said that *when we harness the energies of love we will have again discovered fire.* Finding the knowledge of conscious Love, knowing the world of Love, creates real change. *The Way of the Lover*—this book, which has been my practice, to learn to Love, and this expression of my Love, offers tools to learn to Love consciously, to look at the world through the eyes of Love, to experience life through our heart of Love.

For one human being to love another: that is perhaps the most difficult of our tasks; the ultimate, the last test and proof, the work for which all other work is but preparation. —*Rainer Maria Rilke*

Trunga Rinpoche said: *Everybody loves something, even if it's tortillas.* With practice we can learn to expand our ability to feel, to be vulnerable, to create a crack in the hardness that covers Love, to awaken the tenderness and to pierce through indifference. There is no limit to Love and its expression brings us to living within the spirit of joy. Training to open our heart and mind awakens the Love that is always there. The moat that we construct around our heart is to protect ourselves from life, from the consequences of Love. Love is attention and the slightest lack of attention alters, falsifies, robs Love of its presence. To learn to live in the heart is to remember our natural state as a child. A child with the space to express and receive Love without limitation, embarrassment, shaming, or conditions, who is not tricked and manipulated, develops a natural response to loving, lives in yummy delight. Objective Love is the love of everything.

You can look the whole world over and never find anyone more deserving of love than yourself. —Buddha

NATURAL LOVE

Natural Love has no expectations, respecting others as they are. To experience genuine unconditional Love, minus the if's, we would no longer be looking for external verification, approval or to buy Love with achievements and material objects. Love encompasses being held and holding, to feel physically embraced. Love as a door to higher consciousness, not the sentimental romantic illusion that carries stories of suffering and drama, is what Rilke meant when he said *love is rarely for the young.* Rather, Love entails years of understanding and practice. To Love consciously takes the natural emotion of Love and matures it, bringing our attention, guarding and cherishing what is sacred. Natural Love is holy, as is everything natural. Love as an illumination of the heart, that begins in our childhood, is that look beaming from a babies face, from an open joyful heart to the whole world.

Love is the crowning grace of humanity, the holiest right of the soul, the golden link which binds us to duty and truth, the redeeming principle that chiefly reconciles the heart to life and is prophetic of eternal good. —Petrarch

The universal wound or separation from Love happens early as a protection and distancing from what feels bad; a boulder at the entrance way to our heart, armoring over our heart, a shield over our solar plexus. Swami Prajnanpad, recognizing the chasm between what his students said and how they lived told his students to *bring a certificate from your (husband, wife, child, lover) if you want to study with me.* The day labor becomes the true practice of our inner work. Our inner development and maturity is measured by how we be in the world. How we embody Love is the true measure of our awakening.

Reminded to know the centrality of Love we use our experiences, regardless. This world is here for us. Rumi states that *the fruit is the cause of the tree,* and so we live to reveal the Love, to express it in this world. Reshad Feild stated that *for real change to come about in the world we must know the meaning of conscious love, we have to have the knowledge of love.* Like the earth, we received and were nourished by the light of Love, and we give the light of Love back—look into an infants face for the reflection of that truth. The distortions that are created, the shift from Love to unlove, to grievance to feeling not seen, not understood, not appreciated, distrustful, shut down and constricted, prevents Love from flowing into and through us. And the aberrations that are created when the heart is closed, or confused, bring about sentimentalism, rape, assault, instability, insanity, abuse, abandonment, isolation. How to open again to Love and return to the original state of its natural emotion: says the Indian teacher Sri Poonja: *You must fall in love with the one inside your heart.*

Love is the cause of all creation. Our responsibility in being human is to come to understand that we are placed into this universe, on this planet, in order to know how to love. This planet so desperately needs to be loved, as it gives its life continuously to us, to our life here. —Reshad Feild

SYSTEM EIGHTEEN

PSYCHOLOGICAL BLINDSPOTS

SELF-DESTRUCTION, GREED,

SELF-DEPRECATION, ARROGANCE,

MARTYRDOM, IMPATIENCE,

STUBBORNNESS, ANGER, FEAR,

DOMINANCE AND POWER, TRAMP, VANITY

Each person has one central attribute, a pillar on which the personality structure rests or around which it could be said to revolve. Invisible to one oneself, other people can often give accurate enough information about it.
—*Kathleen Speeth*

SELF-DESTRUCTION: Positive: sacrifice, surrender **Negative:** suicide, violence **Fear:** losing self-control **Shadow:** greed

GREED: Positive: appetite **Negative:** gluttony, excessive **Fear:** losing out **Shadow:** self-destruction

SELF-DEPRECATION: Positive: humility **Negative:** devaluation **Fear:** being inadequate, flawed **Shadow:** arrogance

ARROGANCE: Positive: pride **Negative:** self-importance **Fear:** vulnerability, being found out, being judged negatively **Shadow:** self-deprecation

MARTYRDOM: Positive: selflessness **Negative:** victimization, self-pity

Fear: being restricted, trapped by circumstances **Shadow:** impatience

IMPATIENCE: Positive: presence, audacity **Negative:** intolerance, missing

out **Fear:** not having enough time, missing something important

Shadow: martyrdom

STUBBORNNESS: Positive: determination **Negative:** obstinance

Fear: sudden change, loss of control, authority **Shadow:** neutrally

shifts to any blindspot

ANGER: Positive: assertion **Negative:** aggression, resentment, hostility

Fear: being helpless, out of control **Shadow:** fear

FEAR: Positive: focus, caution, acceptance **Negative:** anxiety, stress,

paranoia, caginess, tricky **Fear:** danger, life and death **Shadow:** anger

DOMINANCE AND POWER: Positive: accomplishment, leadership

Negative: intimidation, dictatorship **Fear:** uncertainty **Shadow:** power

and dominance

TRAMP: Positive: something for nothing **Negative:** something for

nothing, parasitic, laziness, lack of discrimination **Fear:** losing out

Shadow: satisfaction, recognizing enjoying what you have

VANITY: Positive: self, aesthetic sensibility **Negative:** deception,

self-indulgent, self-important **Fear:** non-existence

Shadow: involved with each blind spot

*P*sychological Blindspots, our primary weakness, are acquired characteristics throughout our lifetime, found in our personality. They offer a defensive posture of armoring us particularly in demanding moments at the expense of our growth and transformation. As a limitation to our freedoms, as well as derailing our progress, they ultimately make our life more difficult. Essentially having a life of their own they are archetypical forms of energy. The Blindspot protects and rules the personality, is governed by ego, is a defense, a reaction based on fear, pain and self-involvement, driving us away from the energy of love, sabotaging our happiness and inner peace. To understand and dissolve the obstacle is an immense challenge. Psychological Blindspots represent essential ways we become distorted, walled in behind a prison of isolation, defensiveness, loneliness and illusion. These challenges and obstacles stand as the foremost obstruction to having an intimate deep connection with ourselves and with others. Once they are engaged, we stumble and interrupt clear contact with others. Finding our Blindspots expands consciousness, they hold important information, clues to our freedom. Our attention is pulled in and directed by our primary weakness as we continue to go off on a tangent. Mystic and spiritual teacher G. I. Gurdjieff referred to the Blindspot as a chief feature, saying *it is the most noticeable feature visible upon first meeting a person.*

Every person has a chief feature. It is an outgrowth of their emotional attitude towards themself. Our life is controlled by these chief features.
—*Margaret Anderson*

Psychological Blindspots are giant granite blocks on the path. We chip and chip away at them until they are broken. At certain points in our life we actually like our obstacle, as if it is interesting and great to be arrogant, self-destructive, stubborn, vain or greedy. For most of our life it runs us. It's like a parasite. Destroy it or you will be eaten away, taken over, for our dark patterns are merciless and relentless. This is most apparent in the elderly, if, as we age we avoided or neglected to address our inner life and mechanical impulses. Those earlier free-floating stones rigidify, hardening, setting in shape over time to become permanent landmarks as well as lodging into our physical body. Since the Blindspot activates under stress and is a defense against fear, it strengthens and crystallizes as we age, unless we recognize, identify and neutralize it. Controlling it requires doing what we least like to do: to face our fears, break our habitual behavior, place ourselves in the fire, burn away our ego. Otherwise, our personality pivots around the Blindspot and expresses itself through us as an actual energy that feeds off something in us that is attracted to greed, vanity, anger, arrogance, or any other stumbling block. To not understand and direct our Blindspot, it will run us. The effort is to gain control, to create intention, not just to crush it, instead, to fight against it, to use stubbornness or any impediment intentionally. Identifying a Blindspot takes time and patience, it is not determined solely by actions; the reason for its behavior as well as the qualitative feel of it, its motivation, is the deciding key. Working on any of the identified blindspots also works on our own primary obstruction; and so the study of ourself emerges.

This blind, weak spot appears in several myths of various cultures, most famously embedded in the ancient myth of Achilles. The mighty warrior was invincible to human assault save for a single weakness, through which he was defeated. The Greeks coined that chief and lethal weakness the "Achilles Heel." The prospect of being blind to the hub of our falsehood is most unsettling. —Asaf Braverman

The Blindspots, similar to the *seven deadly sins*, or *passions*, plus these additional five, originate as a reaction to the dysfunction in family and early childhood experiences settling into habit by our teen-age years. Sin, in this sense, means missing the mark and is a flaw disrupting our journey towards wholeness, derails us in life so we get off track missing our aim; as passions they distort our world view. Originally our Blindspot helps us to manage our way through our early family life, eventually, though, it weakens our ability to self-observe, ultimately standing in our way. Studying them allows us to see what runs our life, what limits our freedom. Ordinal Blindspots are self-destruction, self-deprecation, martyrdom, vanity and fear. The five ordinal obstacles have a narrow focus, generally move away from the world, turn inward and against the self. Their consequences are most strongly self-inflicted. Exalted Blindspots are greed, arrogance, impatience, anger, tramp, dominance and power. The six exalted stumbling blocks have a wide focus and move outward to visibly influence their surroundings. Prompted to take action, at times impulsive, they impact those around them. The neutral Blindspot is stubbornness, which affects both the self and the world.

Perhaps all the dragons in our lives are princesses who are only waiting to see us act, just once, with beauty and courage. Perhaps everything that frightens us, in its deepest essence, is something helpless that wants our love.
—*Ranier Maria Rilke*

Each person's obstacle is the core of false personality, the imaginary picture we have of ourself determining the way we view ourself and the world, affecting our actions. Most people have a primary Blindspot supported by a secondary one, both correspond to our internalized self-image. Ready with a rationalization for everyday behavior, it is difficult to recognize our own obstruction since we view it as *who we are*. It exists for us to allow the personality to feel that it is real.

Growth means becoming more of what we already are, not what others want us to be. Growth mean to evolve and wake up, not remaining asleep in the illusion of the learned self. —Brenda Schaffer

OUR CHALLENGE

Our Blindspot essentially determines how we see ourself and the world, our emotional attitude towards ourself. The investigation of finding our primary obstacle, since it is often invisible to us, is to know that it is not us expressing the characteristic it is the quality itself expressing itself through us. Mostly they are not real, our obstructions are imagined, therefore to fight them or to change the obstruction is a waste of time and energy. Rather than switching from one Blindspot to another, from arrogance to stubbornness, from greed to anger, with the illusion that any identification with any obstacle will increase our consciousness or do more than distract us from our purpose; instead, the practice is to separate from them and observe, this is the challenge: to defeat or to intentionally use our obstacle. For each of us the work is to not get triggered, to not be reactive, to not take personally others' subjective reactions. For example, a person with arrogance sees himself as more exalted than he is, viewing himself as the image or illusion, minus the substance. It's as if the person is the experience and is run by it, yet actually there is nothing inside solidly supporting the experience. It is the picture we have of ourself, appearing natural and normal yet difficult to see, understand and grasp, because it is so ingrained in how we think we are, how we imagine ourselves to be. Locked into the mirror reflection, we feel good about our self-image, which perpetuates our reluctance to recognize and shift. Loosening and eventually breaking it allows us to be genuine, not distorted, to develop integrity and character.

A mere machine is evidently incapable of thinking, whereas in man there

exists something perpetually prone to expand, and to burst the chains by which it is confined. —Jean-Jacques Rousseau

Writings on the seven deadly passions date back before 14th century Chaucer: *these visible acts of sin are indications of what is within a man's heart, just as the sign outside the tavern is a sign of the wine that is within the cellar.* In the early 1300's the poets Chaucer and Dante spoke of each capital sin or passion as having a specific healing virtue as its antidote. Seeing them this way they become a source of energy to be used intentionally for our freedom. All of them are neutral energy sources, until the establishment of our intention; just as a car can be used to drive to the supermarket or to run someone over. If the intention is kind then its characteristics are kind.

In their negative mode they are referred to as defense mechanisms, addictions, psychopathology, distractions, attributed to genetics, chemical imbalance, family dysfunction. Sometimes they disempower and incapacitate us into a dysfunctional mess, and yet many times we are rewarded as they push us to achieve or narcotize, posing as something that makes money and drives ambition and success. More often we use our Blindspot for our advantage, to be tricky, to manipulate others, to find weakness and go after it, or, to settle into our lowest common denominator. A Blindspot cares only for itself, having a life of its own. It is an actual energy or entity that feeds off an attraction. Paying attention, being deliberate to uplift our purpose; our stumbling block won't act independently from our self-knowing.

It is with our passions as it is with fire and water, they are good servants, but bad masters. —Aesop

FINDING OUR ACHILLES HEEL

The Blindspot cares only about itself, not about how our overall being or welfare is affected through its gratification. It's opinionated, clever and selfish. Studying and understanding them we decrease their hold enabling us to transform our weakness into our strength. Our primary obstruction, our Achilles heel, is reliably available and, when paid attention to has a positive side. Being intentional, studying, becoming conscious of all of the obstacles assists self-development. The belief that accompanies our Blindspot distorts perception creating self-defeating circumstances. Knowing that our personality is a limitation to our freedom, understanding and making use of this tool, Psychological Blindspots enable us to find what stands in our way, our primary weakness, the handicap which has arisen out of fear and self-indulgence.

An easy childhood allows our obstacles to be like pebbles, but having had an intense and dysfunctional early life we resurrect boulders to wall us in. Recognizing and naming the boulder we move on to see how it controls our life, creates bottlenecks and hurdles, while in its discovery we increase our self-awareness. Often called defense mechanisms they jump out when buttons are pushed as a survival reaction, a protection, standing in the way of our being open and vulnerable. They may work as a quick fix, an easy comfort, yet they thwart and slow down growth. Each of us reacts differently to a similar impediment. Self-deprecation may show up in one person as self-hatred although in another person it appears as criticism towards others. Watching we see where we falter and fumble. The more we slow down and pay attention, the less our challenges rear their head to thwart us, the deeper our connections to self and to others.

It is only after we have seen and accepted the undesirable sides of ourselves that it becomes possible, not necessarily to change them, but to free ourselves from them. In other words, we must first realize that it is not possible to change the machine, that it cannot be anything other than a machine, and only then can we begin to understand in what way it is possible to direct the machine. At this point change does occur, but it is not a change of mechanicality itself; it is a change of attitudes, and change of action follows as a consequence. —Girard Haven

True intimacy requires vulnerability regardless to consequences. Beyond protecting ourselves, we remain an expression of the love that we are. The aim is to separate from these obstacles and bring relativity to the moment, using our day constructively and intentionally. This allows us to direct an energy that feeds off of us, and not mechanically manipulate the weaknesses in other people. The work is to use our efforts as a vehicle for waking up. Erasing our obstacle allows the beauty of our true personality to shine. Psychological Blindspots are a reminder that there are miles to go.

The thing about your blind spot is that you can't see it. —Christa Wolff

Obstacles to spiritual progress, naming our Blindspots, shining a light on our self-delusion, has been said by some to be like finding out a spouse has been unfaithful, that *I have been blindly unfaithful to the spouse of my soul.* In this perspective the obstacle is the seat of illusion, the smoke and mirrors holding the artifice of our personality in place. Boxed in we look out and see the world through the size, shape, and color of our boulder. Obstructions are as unkind to us as they are towards others. The obstacle takes and cares only to support its own existence, ultimately having a life of its own, subjugating our personality. Entire personalities pivot around a Blindspot. One may notice that it's not an individual who is expressing the obstruction, it's the Blindspot expressing itself through the individual. Our obstacle tends to get inflamed in situations that are experienced as threatening to our self-image. Otherwise they quietly control the ego. All obstructions appear positive to us when they are in charge, therefore we have to be vigilantly attentive to see if our good moments are at another's expense or at the loss of our integrity. Acknowledging their presence weakens their hold on our life.

Risk! Risk anything! Care no more for the opinion of others, for those voices. Do the hardest things on earth for you. Act for yourself. Face the truth.
—*Katherine Mansfield*

In our essence we feel loving oneness with everything, as the ego develops so does personality. The trance of personality becomes fixated with one particular pattern, distorting and creating imbalance. The loss of contact to our essential nature is handled by arriving at a strategy to cope with the loss. When we are not present to ourself the solution that replaces presence becomes an underlying feeling that remains with us. The core habitual pattern we choose that characterizes the impediment of acquired personality, the life script, obscures our essence which is otherwise pure, without conflict of thought, emotion or instinct. Recognizing how we stumble, being knowledgeable, truthful, using intuition, not resisting, each passion becomes uplifted and transformed. Knowing that we cannot completely remove all restrictions, through observing and separating we develop the positive qualities of the impediments weakening their control over us. Compassionate tolerance for our stumbling blocks opens a door to understanding and forgiveness for self and for others' obstacles.

Our blind-spot is the way in which we conceal our true Self from ourselves, and conceal this act of concealment. This blind-spot is highly charged, and even as we catch a glimpse of it, it recedes, provoking all sorts of avoidant behaviors. Sometimes, I like to talk about this as the soul's flaw. For every soul—though truly a part of God's holy perfection—is possessed of a 'flaw.' This flaw is not unlike the flaw in an opal, which creates its special 'fire', its charm and attraction. The only difference between the 'fire' and the 'flaw' in the opal is the refraction of light. Likewise, the soul's flaw can be a vice, or in a different light, a virtue. The soul's main task is to work on and with that flaw. One of the most crucial issues in the examination of one's conscience is the search for the awareness of one's basic flaw and fire. The flaw insinuates itself into every facet of our lives; and unfortunately, it is our failures—which are often so close to our successes—that tell us most about it. It is a life-long relationship of struggle and revelation. —Zalman Schachter-Shalomi

Diminishing our obstruction allows the truth of who we are—our pristine nature—to become visible. This happens through self-observation, study, and knowing who we are and how we want to be. When we practice and develop moment to moment attention and awareness, when that is present we create a deeper relationship to our inner world. Diminishing, erasing Psychological Blindspots from our personality while maturing essence is a primary aim of the *Fifth Way*, this *Way of the Lover*. The moments we have of bliss we are featureless.

PRIMARY AND SECONDARY BLINDSPOT

In our early years, especially adolescence, we try out all the obstacles. Like an accessible buffet, we taste and sample each trait until we select a predominant one and a secondary one that suits us and that works well with our karma and goal. We spend our early childhood picking and trying on all the Blindspots, pushing and standing in the way of everyone in our world, and then as an adult we single out our favorite and now stand in our own way. The chosen block is the scar tissue, the scab that covers our woundedness. The secondary one is the obstacle that jumps forward when the first one is quieted. The greater the wound the larger the boulder, the bigger the dramatic scenes that are attracted, and the stronger is the investment to keep all hands off the events before the door of the boulder. Only a strong desire for truth or brutal devastation, along with a gifted teacher/therapist/facilitator/guide assists the decision to look at ourself. The main body of the obstruction is buried beneath the surface, having numerous disguises. Melting these characteristics involves shining a light into darkened recesses. Sincere self-examination allows us to look at what is, take responsibility to not make it a big or little deal. All of the obstacles are imagination, so, rather than wasting energy struggling with the obstacle—which is the impediment fighting against itself—separate and observe. See that the boulder is not *me*.

I want to unfold. I don't want to stay folded anywhere, because where I am folded, there I am untrue. —Ranier Maria Rilke

Having an element of all the obstructions with one particular flaw that is primary; this study is not to notice the presence or absence of each Blindspot, but to observe, pay attention to the degree to which it exists and then to distract and uplift it through developing something positive, to gain control of our predominant obstacle. As long as it possesses us we are run by something that we are not in charge of and therefore we lack an evolving spiritual dimension. Psychological Blindspots are admirable adversaries; successfully challenging and opposing them strengthens, dignifies, offers us fuel for transformation. Salute these roadblocks, as we proceed up and then down the mountain—for they guard and protect the entrance way to bliss! They seduce, entice, distract and are at the heart of every dysfunction, addiction and human-created suffering. Knowing and understanding them arms you; now to recognize and choose freedom!

Each person has one central attribute, a certain feature in his character which is central, a pillar, an axle on which the personality structure rests and revolves. The study of our chief fault and the struggle against it, that is, to destroy its involuntary manifestation is our primary work. —P.D. Ouspensky

People who have used and directed the positive, the transformation of their Blindspots: *Anami Sufi Baba, Meher Baba, Mata Amritananda Mayi Ma* (known as Ammachi).

SELF-DESTRUCTION

POSITIVE: SACRIFICE, SURRENDER

NEGATIVE: SUICIDE, VIOLENCE

FEAR: LOSING SELF-CONTROL

SHADOW: GREED

If one looks with a cold eye at the mess man has made of history, it is difficult to avoid the conclusion that he has been afflicted by some built-in mental disorder which drives him towards self-destruction. —Arthur Koestler

This psychological blindspot is chosen out of a belief that life is not worth living, *I am unworthy to be alive, and will never get whatever it is in life that I want.* Self-Destruction, the fear of losing self-control, the urge to challenge and destroy everything, often shows up as authoritarian, insistent behavior. The conviction and underlying thought is that *you will not destroy me: I will take the controls and undermine myself.* The risk-taker often ups the ante, moving to more dangerous reckless acts as they defy and slowly outmaneuver themselves. Self-hatred has many faces. Drugs, alcohol, gambling, unprotected sex, cigarettes, gangs, self-mutilation, kleptomania, terrorism, anorexia, morbid obesity, wild dare-devil behavior, bulimia; all Self-Destructive acts that continue the cycle of dangerous living. Each road becomes a one-way street, as the tolerance is raised more risk is required, challenging anything, until, eventually only death serves to terminate a life sentence. Living filtered through Self-Destruction one's life has minimal meaning or value.

Suffering is not necessary for man's development; it is the result of violation of spiritual law, but few people seem to rouse themselves from their 'soul sleep' without it. When people are happy, they usually become selfish, and automatically the law of Karma is set in action. Man often suffers loss through lack of appreciation. —*Florence Scovel Shinn*

Modeled on parental imprinting, those choosing this blindspot were often raised in a family where Self-Destruction was the order of the day. Wars, poverty, prison, hospitals, gangs, ritualistic mutilation, professional sports, mental illness, high risk investing, emotional and physical abuse, drugs and alcohol, all fuel this obstacle. This blindspot generally shortens a life through unpredictable living, suicide, drunk driving, dare devil actions, or addictions. The end might come quickly, or as a prolonged side effect of behavior; like hepatitis from needles, HIV from unprotected sex, liver disease from years of drinking, jail sentences that bring exposure to dangerous living, or a challenged immune system from endless partying, accidents, smoking cigarettes or poor fast processed food diets. Gambling with life, the underlying theory reads: if I risk a bit more I might win back what was lost, maybe to borrow and keep at it, I won't stop until I cut my losses. Today, this is the day trader, the Real Estate flipper, the man or woman having successive one-night stands, the Las Vegas high roller, the drink and drive person, the daily pot smoker and cocaine user, street car drag racer; unable to control their appetite and excess, pulled into distractions, hazardous choices and self-sabotage. Destroying the subject of conflict which ultimately is oneself, Self-Destructiveness is deadly.

There are seeds of self-destruction in all of us that will bear only unhappiness if allowed to grow. —Dorothea Brande

Focused on their shortcomings, they experience themselves as too heavy or too thin, too tall or too short, not smart or too slow, not attractive or funny enough, too sloppy, needing more money or stuff, desperate for fame at any price; what they see are their weaknesses not their strengths or appeal. A challenge to inner calmness, inevitably tearing away at something, satisfied to pull themselves apart, reason rarely succeeds. Under stress this obstacle suggests have a drink, medicate myself, go to a casino, take a drug to unwind, light up, get high at this unstable moment. Something is known to be off, seeing flaws and limitation moves them to a behavior that is harmful. The thinking pattern is: *since I am flawed, damaged goods, I will continue the program and not take care to be still and repair the weakness.* Damaging themselves further, whether being accident prone or self-inflicted, they chastise themselves for perceived failings. Most of their transactions feel imbalanced, giving rather than receiving, buying gifts and spending money on others to earn love and praise, losing more than is gained, spending additional time and energy avoiding what is needed. When circumstances are difficult they add hardship, very quick to self-blame, feeling unsupported by the world. Owning extra or luxury items is either a necessity or may be awkward, easier to give things and money away and say *I can't afford that*, having excess creates discomfort or promotes entitlement. The challenge is to develop an appetite for nourishing experiences and personal contacts, not for addictions. Based on the fears of worthlessness and loss of self-control, learning to operate outside of this pattern, to set it aside, to protect one's assets, is the work.

If you are going through hell, keep going. —Winston Churchill

On the other side of the thinking there are megalomaniacal delusions, a pathological egotist who is oblivious and continues until stopped, caught or limited. Much of the Bernie Madoff character whose fantasies of power brought him to life imprisonment fits the Self-Destruction blindspot. He was unable to contain himself until caught, tried, convicted and imprisoned for life. Rarely do we know of a bank robber or rapist who stops himself, there is an ongoing cycle of continuing until caught. We often imagine suicide as immediate self-murder, yet much of what passes as Self-Destruction is a slow painstaking process of taking away one's own life.

Avoid destructive thinking. Improper negative thoughts sink people. A ship can sail around the world many, many times, but just let enough water get into the ship and it will sink. Just so with the human mind. Let enough negative thoughts or improper thoughts get into the human mind and the person sinks just like a ship. —Alfred A. Montapert

SACRIFICE VERSUS SUICIDE

There is a difference between the positive mode of Self-Destruction which is sacrifice and surrender and the negative direction which is suicide and violence. This is visibly apparent in the sacrifice of a Buddhist monk setting himself on fire, a Palestinian Arab attaching a bomb to himself and going into an Israeli marketplace or hi-jacking an airplane and crashing it into the World Trade Center for a protest or idealized cause. Kamikaze pilots led suicide attacks in the closing stages of the Pacific campaign of World War Two. Military aviators, they would intentionally crash their aircraft, often carrying explosives, bombs, torpedoes and full fuel tanks into Allied ships and planes, causing greater damage than a conventional attack such as dropping bombs or using machine guns. People stand behind this blindspot, killing themselves in the name of faith or to serve an ideology. Choosing death as a statement of principles, for political intent, is propelled through believing that the alternative would be more Destructive, would impinge on personal integrity and values. It's considered an act of bravery for soldiers to lay down their life for others, whether it's their companions on the battle-field or the civilian population at home. Mohandas Gandhi engaged in several well-documented hunger strikes to protest British rule of India. Authorities did not allow him to die in custody, knowing that the public believed in a Gandhi that would martyr himself to uphold his truth, and those in charge thwarted his martyrdom.

A man who was completely innocent, offered himself as a sacrifice for the good of others, including his enemies, and became the ransom of the world, it was a perfect act. —Mahatma Gandhi

Self-immolation, suicide by fire, an occurrence in Buddhism and Hinduism, is practised by religious or philosophical monks throughout the ages for political protest, devotion, renouncement and other reasons. Following the self-immolation of several Vietnamese Buddhist monks, Nobel Peace nominee and spiritual teacher Thich Nhat Hanh stated: *the press spoke of suicide, but in the essence it is not. It is not even a protest. What the monks said in the letters they left before burning themselves aimed only at alarming, at moving the hearts of the oppressors, and at calling attention of the world to the suffering endured then by the Vietnamese. To burn oneself by fire is to prove that what one is saying is of the utmost importance, that he can endure the greatest of sufferings to protect his people. To express will by burning oneself, therefore, is not to commit an act of destruction but to perform an act of construction, that is, to suffer and to die for the sake of one's people. This is not suicide. Suicide is an act of self-destruction, having as causes, lack of courage to live and to cope with difficulties, defeat by life and loss of all hope, desire for nonexistence. The monk who burns himself has lost neither courage nor hope; nor does he desire nonexistence. On the contrary, he is very courageous and hopeful and aspires for something good in the future. He does not think that he is destroying himself; he believes in the good fruition of his act of self-sacrifice for the sake of others. The monks who burned themselves did not aim at the death of their oppressors but only at a change in their policy. Their enemies are not man. They are intolerance, fanaticism, dictatorship, cupidity, hatred, and the discrimination which lie within the heart of man.*

SURRENDER

The positive of Self-Destruction lies in the heart of surrender, dropping the false idea that we are separate, are unaffected by all things. It's an unconditional *yes*, dropping expectations, releasing conditions. Surrender is unconditional. Surrender means trust. Even when nothing happens; this is the workings of the universe, leaving the results to an eternal now. Life is sacred, to find meaning in life is a spiritual question.

I know what the greatest cure is: it is to give up, to relinquish, to surrender, so that our little hearts may beat in unison with the great heart of the world.
—*Henry Miller*

To master this obstruction is understanding surrender as both giving and losing control, which is why Twelve-Step programs can work. They say, *admit you are out of control and ask for help.* It takes courage to ask for help. It is strength and confidence that ask for support. Looking at our life, making amends, trusting in a higher power are a few of the strategies in a program that has enabled people to look at and to manage their Self-Destruction. To let go and surrender to our losses is a positive solution to maneuver ourselves out of a downward spiral. The critical shift is in acknowledging that external restraint is not the solution. Over-control, obsessive-compulsive behavior, the belief that external regulation will solve the issue is the illusion. The fear of losing the upper hand, and then trying to be in charge becomes a strategy that is self-defeating. Gaining discipline over our reactions, reigning in the one or two behaviors that are out of control, finding our inner regulator allows room for the external environment to be what and how it is, sometimes out of control. The world continues when we are not in charge of our external world, gaining real power is through letting go of the pretense that we are in command. A life-threatening obstruction to transform, deadly when out of control, carefully moving to the positive part of its shadow side, greed, which is appetite, creates the desire and the vitality to live. A delicate balance to remain in the positive which is a growthful productive satisfying appetite and not to slide to being consumed by out-of-control greedy cravings. The complementary opposite shift to greed eases the idea of being the loser, of giving things away, of imploding.

Your pain is the breaking of the shell that encloses your understanding. Much of your pain is self-chosen. It is the bitter potion by which the physician within you heals your sick self. —Khalil Gibran

The positive mode appears as a parent risking their life to save their child, or diving into the ocean when someone is going under and then drowning, choosing death for principles and political reasons, or as a dangerous mission during wartime to protect our troops. Destroying lies, razing architecture to build again, creating new art forms to overturn old ideas of what is beautiful, killing off the false parts so that the new self can be reborn; for the right reason destructiveness can serve a higher purpose. The negative aspect looks like riding on the back of a motorcycle with no helmet, or getting into a car and driving on a freeway knowing that the driver had been drinking throughout the evening, unprotected sex with a stranger, using needles that might be unclean, bulimia and self-mutilation, prostitution in an unsafe neighborhood, daredevil stunts, addictions like gambling, sex, drugs, and alcoholism, teen-age car dragging, living in the fast-lane, maxing out credit cards, buying drugs and being reckless by mailing them to one's own home, going to the casino with a paycheck that was earmarked for food, medical and family expenses; ultimately not caring or feeling any meaning to life: not valuing one's health and freedom.

When I hear somebody sigh, 'Life is hard,' I am always tempted to ask, 'compared to what?' —*Sydney J. Harris*

The urge is to challenge everything, to tear things apart, continuously taking action, destroying whatever is in conflict, including oneself; to damage and undermine life. The belief that all conflicts can be resolved by destroying the object is the thought form. Change for this attitude comes about through elimination. Rather than having a fast resolution with the idea of no longer having anything to deal with; a solution becomes: ending a marriage, quitting a job, blowing up a church, reactively firing an employee, driving your car and children into a river, suicide; all faster and easier than working on, processing, or seeing what wants to happen as life unfolds. Destructiveness, the tendency to challenge people, theories, ideas, society, prefers not to reason but instead to tear something apart. Sometimes it's a prolonged slow Self-Destruction, other times it's taking foolhardy risks. Popular with critics, getting paid to pull something apart, to trash someone or thing; Destructiveness receives satisfaction breaking things down. It's more natural for them to destroy than to maintain, be patient or to fix. Terrorists, miners, boxers, musicians, artists and movie stars, bull riders, Las Vegas gamers;

particular vocations that magnetize people who live with this primary obstruction.

You suffer from yourself alone; no one compels you. —*the Buddha*

This blindspot turns people against themselves. What is needed to replace panic and despair, to eliminate derailing and putting oneself in jeopardy are internal personality structures that offer self-guidance and support creative living, that imbue meaning to our life. Developing an appetite for healthy living, for fulfilling relationships, clear business transactions; a life free of drama shifts the hold Self-Destruction has on destroying our life. 10% of the population choose this ordinal expression Self-Destruction as their primary or secondary obstacle.

A man will renounce any pleasures you like but he will not give up his suffering. Man is made in such a way that he is never so much attached to anything as he is to his suffering. No one who is not free from suffering, who has not sacrificed his suffering, can work (on himself). Nothing can be attained without suffering but at the same time one must begin by sacrificing suffering. —*G.I. Gurdjieff*

Examples are: *Janis Joplin, Marilyn Monroe, Judy Garland, James Dean, Evel Knievel, Ernest Hemingway, Edgar Allen Poe, Vincent Van Gogh, John Belushi, Jimi Hendrix, Richard Pryor, Lennie Bruce, Mama Cass, Kurt Cobain, Courtney Love, O.J. Simpson, Elvis Presley, Whitney Houston, Bobbbi Brown, Britney Spears, Lindsey Lohan, Mike Tyson, Kristie Allie, Eddie Van Halen, Mel Gibson, Robin Williams, Liza Minelli, Charles Manson, David Carradine, Philp Seymour Hoffman, Amy Winehouse, Nina Simone, Freddie Prinze, Ray Charles, Michael Jackson, Jim Morrison, Anthony Bourdain.*

GREED

Greed is a bottomless pit which exhausts the person in an endless effort to satisfy the need without ever reaching satisfaction. —Erich Fromm

This psychological blindspot, Greed, is grasping, insatiable, craving, gluttonous and hoarding. Its thought pattern of deprivation and dissatisfaction has an underlying belief system that says there is not enough to go around, is concerned with losing out, has great difficulty regulating cravings. Rarely indifferent, it has a large appetite for everything, toxifying our relationship to ourself and to others. This bottomless pit of emptiness lusts after experiences, always wanting more. A fear of not having enough stands in the way of recognizing what we already have. The emotional attitude, Greed, attaches to most anything; ambition, fame, money, material things, information, sex, approval, food, spirituality, longevity, addictions, attention, exercise. Possessions become confused with success. Success becomes blurred with self. Wealth becomes a measure of worth. Spiritual Greed, wanting more and more highs, is a recognizable quality in spiritual seekers who resist returning to the world and, instead, sit by a teacher, Guru, or partner, stealing energy. Looking to what is missing, not seeing what we already have keeps the obstruction of Greed alive.

If you pour the whole sea into a jug, will it hold more than one day's store? The greedy eye, like the jug, is never filled. —Rumi

The self-oriented expression towards the world is: *I have a right to have more, and you owe it to give to me.* The excessive desire to acquire more than is needed has been named one of the seven deadly or cardinal sins, one of the objectionable vices that obscures our essence. On the other hand, virtues, which are non-dual qualities of essence, the natural expression of the awakened heart become an antidote for vices. Sobriety, a sense of gratitude and appreciation for what we already have is the antidote, the virtue that transforms the vice of Greed. Not clinging to anything, either inner or outer, we become touched by everything.

Earth provides enough to satisfy every man's needs, but not every man's greed. —Mahatma Gandhi

Feeling justified in the expectation that life is under the obligation to reward personal moods with pleasurable goodies, this self-indulgent posture works well in the moment, not in the long haul. Addictions based on Greed impact mental well-being. The acquisitiveness that feeds this attitude opposes self-restraint and simplicity; walking a transformational journey turns into spiritual materialism when not addressed. Greed creates the deprivation that stands behind the original impulse. Not enjoying what is, nor understanding the truth behind *less is more*, taking more than their share begins to drive other people away. Dissatisfied with present day reality—-becoming insatiable travelers and collectors of experience—things become a reminder of what's missing. Having routinely received substitutes for intimacy; sweets for love, gifts and promises instead of attention, toys as distraction, bribery, financial rewards for trickery, praise for looking good, admiration for having children, compliments and congratulations for amassing money and stuff, glory for their titles, prizes, their opulence; eventually the substitutes become reminders of the deprivation, fostering suffering until pretense takes over, imagining that these are the real genuine thing.

He who is not contented with what he has, would not be contented with what he would like to have. —*Socrates*

Greed lives in a thought pattern that asks *how will I profit or how will a situation be advantageous to me*. Characteristic to impediments of tramp, sloth or laziness, borrowing without returning, the world owes this person—their interest in others is self-serving—to have their own needs met. How to get something for nothing, poverty-consciousness, Greed is an opportunistic freeloader. Poverty is not comfortable, neither is freely giving. Not valuing things, not pushing to ask: *what really matters*, not caring because often it doesn't know what to value, people with Greed are frequently unreliable to their word. Not quick to sacrifice for others, they pay attention to what is best for themselves. Lacking generosity with their time, energy or their own possessions; learning to give to others, to loosen up blaming, will allow their own energy to step forward while taking responsibility for their own existence. This shift to the positive of self-destruction, sacrifice, releasing something for true meaning; charitable giving of time and money begins to mature the appetite for more. Beginning to recognize a true source of satisfaction, identifying the substitutes that have served as major players in our life, the ones that needed to be continuously renewed, quiets the Greed obstruction.

ENOUGH

Usually Greed attaches to one particular area of a person's life, such as attention, food, sex, drugs, experiences, business, travel, shopping, money; and in that fixated place the person continues to try to get more of what they think they lack, rarely actually feeling satisfied. Under stress, feeling deprived, buying something or eating, drinking, smoking, growing their business, buying lottery tickets, booking an airline ticket to a new place, makes them temporarily feel better. Relationships rarely survive Greed, demanding too much from others, resentment and punishment eats away closeness. Intimacy is compromised since demands are not mutually reciprocated. Greed for knowledge, to travel to new places, unable to go in depth always looking for what will *do it,* there is no real comprehension of experiences, little self-acceptance, an underlying dissatisfaction, along with their attention usually being elsewhere. Thoughts are drawn to the next moment, or competing to be closest to the Guru or whomever is in the seat of power. Love becomes a distortion. Greed will say *it's best to love yourself first*; self-destruction says, *it's good to love yourself last.* Both are misrepresentations; love is equality.

Greed is a bottomless pit which exhausts the person in an endless effort to satisfy the need without ever reaching satisfaction. —Erich Fromm

Bernie Madoff, having both self-destruction and Greed blindspots was fueled foremost by Greed to destroy himself, his demise became a mirror of economic and global proportion. Unrestrained, the pursuit of the unattainable was from a belief system that we have a superior right to an unequal share, carried along with a sense and desire for power over those people who have less. And many, many people with similar blindspots joined Bernie along the ride, eventually blaming Madoff rather than taking responsibility for their own Greed and self-destruction.

The whole government is a Ponzi scheme. —Bernie Madoff

Connecting material wealth and pointless adventures with happiness, Greed and personal relationships are incompatible. Attention wanders to what more can be acquired, inattentiveness is difficult to tolerate.

Whereas the natural emotion of jealousy is a stimulus that impels and motivates growth, moves us to improve, to emulate another's behavior, Greed, on the other hand is closer to the distortion of envy which compares, criticizes, is seated in lack of self-esteem and drives to comparative thinking and putting down the other. Continuing in the negative, this quality is an all-consuming energy that seemingly can never be filled. Uneasy to give up what is owned, Greed expresses itself in a hoarding stinginess. Big egos, self-centered, there are no limits to what brings satisfaction. Feeling to be owed, simply for being alive, the world should provide. This is the opportunist, *how can I profit from this inter-action,* they ask.

That same night, I wrote my first short story. It took me thirty minutes. It was a dark little tale about a man who found a magic cup and learned that if he wept into the cup, his tears turned into pearls. But even though he had always been poor, he was a happy man and rarely shed a tear. So he found ways to make himself sad so that his tears could make him rich. As the tears piled up, so did his greed grow. The story ended with the man sitting on a mountain of pearls, knife in hand, weeping helplessly into the cup with his beloved wife's slain body in his arms. —Khaled Hosseini

FULFILLMENT

Generosity neutralizes Greed by letting others get the credit or praise, giving without having expectations; Greed wants to get its *fair share,* or even a bit more. Need and want are confused and commingled, resentment surfaces as they feel solicited; if, what's in it for me does not fit they feel exploited. Often identifiable by their levels of discontent, children having a lot of stuff, rarely having been asked to wait for gratification, becoming adult will have a difficult time feeling fulfilled, having developed the malcontent that breeds Greed. Focusing on having, creative self-expression—a true means to fulfillment—is ignored.

To be creative means to be in love with life. You can be creative only if you love life enough that you want to enhance its beauty, you want to bring a little more music to it, a little more poetry to it, a little more dance to it. —Osho

The fear of not having brings substitutes into one's life. The pursuit of back-ups, replacements that never truly satisfy creates a person who has difficulty being present; distraction and dissatisfaction feed a fear of life ending before *enough* is found. Looking to get more, fearing to lose out, comparing with others; lack of enjoyment of what is becomes visible. One clue to Greed as a primary stumbling block is a lack of satisfaction in what's accumulated, as well as having to renew the object of desire again and again. The indulgence in substitutes, brief interruptions that take the edge off do not become the connection that thoroughly gratifies. What creates the freedom is an inward experience of a relationship with your deepest self, with others and with the natural world. To neither deprive yourself nor to splurge takes the edge off of this obstacle.

An emotional, a spiritual death, when we are brought to our knees, the passing away of all illusion, dying in life, dying every single moment of our lives; every single moment that we give up the idea that we need anything in life brings us the possibility of having some knowledge of the truth of all life. —Reshad Feild

Rarely looking at shortcomings, little tolerance for giving things up, short-sighted, Greed lacks overview. This is visible in the environmental mind-set to strip the rainforests, the glut for oil, the destruction of indigenous cultures, overgrazing the land, pollution that is destroying oceans that were once teeming with life, all based in the desire for immediate satisfaction regardless to long term consequence. Having no real concern for others, people are valued by what they can give or what can be taken from them. Consuming more than their share, a country, a culture, bankrupts the next generation as well as impacting smaller economies throughout the globe. A huge proportion of illness is rooted in the overconsumption of food, alcohol, sex, electronic goodies, cigarettes, and drugs.

As long as greed is stronger than compassion there will always be suffering.
—R. Eric

The exalted expression blindspot Greed quite often works in partnership with the ordinal expression self-destruction. The two team together creating lawsuits, sometimes prison time, as has occurred with: Martha Stewart, Leona Helmsley, Imelda Marcos, Osho Rajneesh, Timothy Leary, O.J. Simpson, Bernie Madoff, Paris Hilton, Lindsey Lohan, Bill Cosby, Michael Milkin, Enron and other numerous bureaucratic abuses. Corporate misconduct and crime point to the levels of Greed in the business world. In the field of music and the arts the two blindspots lead to disaster as has been displayed in the lives of Ray Charles, Britany Spears, Paris Hilton, James Brown, Bill Cosby, Anna Nicole Smith, Divine, Kirstie Alley, Karen Carpenter, Lindsey Lohan, Mary Kate Olsen, Sandra Dee, Tiger Woods, Mary Tyler Moore, Little Richard, Amy Winehouse, and Nina Simone, all with primary or secondary obstructions of Greed and self-destruction.

In the positive, appetite, there is a zest for living, a longing for something, an ability to create a space for abundance and beautiful things into their life as well as encouraging others, all stemming from a natural desire to satisfy this obstructive need. In its desire to be one step ahead Greed sanctions and promotes technological advancement and innovation. Efforts to free themselves from Greed, to create an outlook of generosity brings more kindness into their personal space. Making Greed passive instead of active, separating from it we see the emotional attitude behind the desire for more. Greed pushes our energy away from feeling satisfied and being in the moment, towards future benefits.

Spiritual materialism rears its head in the richness of the churches and poverty of its people, the wealth of countries and living conditions of its people, even in the competition to be closer to the Guru and the search for spiritual enlightenment. Seeing the blessings already present in our life, feeling the small everyday pleasures, regulating our appetite, temperance and self-restraint, feeling happiness in life as it is, recognizing and enjoying daily moments shifts this obstacle. To begin to use our obstruction consciously, to learn to place our attention inward and make choices from a deeper more central space is the way through, the freedom. Pulled and run by the psychological blindspot of Greed, inner satisfaction and cultivating the integrity of contentment supports a healthy moderate appetite and diminishes unmanageable cravings. 15% of the population have Greed as their predominant or secondary blindspot.

Just as fire dries up a vessel of water, greed dries up the contentment of mind.
—*Sanskrit saying*

Examples are: *P. Diddy, Howard Hughes, Paris Hilton, Scrooge, Jim and Tammy Bakker, Mary Kate Olsen, Lindsey Lohan, Anna Nicole Smith, Ivan Boesky, Donald Trump, Eddie Murphy, Eva Longoria, Kirstie Alley, Bernie Madoff, Richard Simmons, Michael Milken, Martha Stewart, Al Capone, James Brown, Kim Kardashian, Pablo Picasso, Adolf Hitler, Little Richard, Tiger Woods, Bill Cosby, Leona Helmsley, Ferdinand and Imelda Marcos, Paula Abdul, Kanye West, Auto Industry, AIG, Enron and Worldcom bankruptcy scandals.*

SELF-DEPRECATION

POSITIVE: HUMILITY

NEGATIVE: DEVALUATION

FEAR: BEING INADEQUATE, FLAWED

SHADOW: ARROGANCE

When I was born, I was so ugly that the doctor slapped my mother.
—*Rodney Dangerfield*

The feeling of not being worthy accompanies the Self-Deprecation obstruction, eventually gaining a firm foothold in the personality. Deflecting expectations by criticizing themselves, avoiding competition, warning others not to assume too much become strategies to avoid high expectations. Maintaining a low profile, this is the student bringing home C average grades so that school and family will be relieved to see passing marks. Self-evaluation is distorted, blaming themselves for what is not working, then losing faith in their own capability. Self-Deprecators get in their own way when it comes to ambition and success. Difficult interactions give rise to self-hatred falling into self-pity, *woe is me*, eventually attracts humiliating circumstances. Personal put-downs intersperse conversations, apologetically self-critical they become defensive protecting their poor sense of boundaries. Self-conscious, making excuses it becomes easy to join the community of *those who don't value my worth*. This self-blocking obstacle slows personal progress.

Men seldom make passes at girls who wear glasses. I fell into writing, I suppose, being one of those awful children who wrote verse. When asked whether she was Dorothy Parker, she replied, 'Yes, Do you mind?' —*Dorothy Parker*

Underestimating self-value, driven by a fear of inadequacy criticism becomes a comfortable certainty. Holding back talents and potential from visibility, under performing, this self-blocking obstruction limits manifesting in most areas of life. As an outgrowth of our attitude toward ourself, feeling unworthy to have a good relationship, a satisfying job, of looking well-dressed, of the benefits of wealth and success, of being healthy, of stepping into life lessons that promote growth, life is controlled by a roadblock in our character. This self-fulfilling prophesy of defeat and self-doubt at first appears disarming and charmingly humble. Eventually it becomes draining. Non-existence, existing through others, is often a manifestation of Self-Deprecation. Concealing, dissolving one's identity into another person happens from having faulty boundaries, an undefined sense of one's own space, a family who took center stage with their self-involved demands for attention. Not feeling good enough to have quality relationships and possessions, self-pity and victimhood often accompanies this obstacle setting up situations that support hardships.

At the end of a miserable day, instead of grieving my virtual nothing, I can always look at my loaded wastepaper basket and tell myself that if I failed at least I took a few trees down with me. —David Sedaris

To be self-critical is quite self-absorbing, too much concern for one's self; counting one's flaws may appear self-effacing yet the personal involvement is actually upside down vanity. Self-Deprecation although inspirational, the inner feelings of hopelessness sets up situations that foster not feeling inspired, not believing to have what it takes to make the grade. The fear of being inadequate, disappointing or flawed, motivates this self-defeating blindspot, indulging oneself with whining self-pity. *Woe is me,* attracts humiliating circumstances and since *misery loves company* they feel and express sorrow for others. Effecting and limiting financial success, jeopardizing owning a beautiful home, driving a luxurious car, buying appealing good quality clothing, not charging enough money for their work, eventually sets the tone for repeated discouragement. An avoidance of breathing fully, refraining from bringing air deeply into the lungs; when this is prolonged it eventually weakens lung energy interfering with the function of circulating vital energy in and around the body. Self-Deprecation is hard on the body, *why take care of this thing,* leads to poor eating habits, neglect of eyes and teeth, assists in eroding self-confidence. A caved-in chest, often defensive attitude, qualifying statements become irritating for people to be around. Relationships pay their toll.

You're only as good as your last haircut. —Fran Lebowitz

Low self-esteem, undervaluing ourself is the most popular psychological blindspot of old souls who are not overly ambitious and often choose to not be in the public eye. Realizing their insignificance in relationship to the greater universe; simplifying their life becomes a priority. Giving away money to spiritual communities, handing over their power, Self-Deprecatory remarks, allowing less competent people to make decisions, feeling inadequate to step up to the plate and lead; often older souls with well-developed integrity hold back while less scrupulous younger soul people step up to sit in positions of authority and power. Young and mature souls don't take the time or have the experience to understand the processes that goes into the behavior of older souls, this overlooking and lack of valuation feeds Self-Deprecation.

I am the literary equivalent of a Big Mac and Fries. —Stephen King

P E R S O N A

In the positive direction, offering service without the fanfare of acknowledgement, they become unpretentious and truly humble. Mother Teresa was particularly modest and unassuming about her achievements and importance. Awarded the Nobel Peace Prize she backed off from the glamour, insisting that the banquet be cancelled and the money given to the poor. Younger souls, confident and determined taking on executive and political positions are derisive and judging of who they see as the *ne'er-do-wells*. Self-Deprecation in its positive mode offers a sense of empathy, a bridge to nurture compassion towards oneself and others. True humility honors humanity. In the negative, apologizing before and after speaking, not feeling deserving of many of the benefits that life brings, belittling oneself, jokes at a personal expense places a hindrance on manifesting joy or abundance. Self-Deprecation tends to foster passivity, weakening the ability to make decisions, to take action, to avoid risk taking, to have problems allowing acknowledgment and complements. One way to shift out of the negative aspect is to become watchful of apologizing, of inner criticism, to move towards self-validation, accepting complements, taking risks, finding a balanced sense of value and self-confidence that will bring in positive energy.

God will find another person, more humble, more devoted, more obedient to him, and the society will go on. —Mother Teresa

Self-Deprecation has been marketed to the public for products to feel and look top-notch, bringing profit to an advertising industry, keeping the obstruction cleverly disguised. Exploiting themselves with self-derogatory wisecracks, putting their body under the knife for social advances and vanity, the self-contempt is masked to ward off fears of aging in a culture that demands a youthful appearance, that applauds image as success. Many comedians have capitalized on this obstruction as their persona, particularly women: Paula Poundstone, Kathy Griffin, Phyllis Diller, Joan Rivers, Sandra Bernhard, Margaret Cho, there are also male comedians like Don Rickles, Woody Allen, and David Letterman who intersperse self-derogatory comments to create their persona: *How is it possible to find meaning in a finite world, given my waist and shirt size.—Woody Allen. My body is falling so fast my gynecologist is wearing a hard hat.—Joan Rivers*. We have all criticized something personal about ourselves and now we see people publicly giving voice to those secret private thoughts.

Smartness runs in my family. When I went to school I was so smart my teacher was in my class for five years. —Gracie Allen

Arrogance is the shadow to Self-Deprecation and a good antidote, counteracting and neutralizing, a step towards manifesting pride, valuing our worth. The self-important over-inflation of arrogance and the undermining deflation of Self-Deprecation express themselves through the personality, both are self-conscious, two faces of vanity and upside-down vanity; swinging from feeling better than others to feeling less than most others, obstacles that hinder clear perceptions. The willingness to take risks, have new experiences, see ourself as equal to others—not less or more—are some of the paths to release this debilitating blindspot. To observe the presence of this cunning obstruction weakens its hold on our life. Taking action, creating clarity, a more accurate measure of our self-worth, honoring the beauty inside ourself, creating the confidence to take responsibility in life, shifts this obstruction. 10% of the population choose ordinal inspirational Self-Deprecation as their predominant or secondary blindspot.

My one regret in life is that I am not someone else. When I was kidnapped, my parents snapped into action. They rented out my room. —Woody Allen

Examples are: *Woody Allen, Willie Nelson, Ringo Starr, Steven Spielberg, George Carlin, Jerry Garcia, Joan Rivers, Sandra Bernhard, Margaret Cho, Paula Poundstone, Kathy Griffin, Gracie Allen, Rob Kardashian, Larry the cable guy, Don Rickles, Mother Teresa, Fran Lebowitz, Phyllis Diller, Sarah Silverman, Jimmy Carter, Johnny Carson, David Letterman, Fran Drescher, George Harrison, Marianne Williamson, Joni Mitchell.*

ARROGANCE

POSITIVE: PRIDE

NEGATIVE: SELF-IMPORTANCE

FEAR: VULNERABILITY, BEING FOUND OUT, BEING JUDGED NEGATIVELY

SHADOW: SELF-DEPRECATION

The insufferable arrogance of human beings to think that Nature was made solely for their benefit, as if it was conceivable that the sun had been set afire merely to ripen men's apples and head their cabbages. —Shakespeare

The audacious, self-assured, self-important, overconfident presence, high visibility in a room, a cover for low self-esteem and shyness; their fear of vulnerability parades as *just being honest*. While appearing confident, they evade being closely scrutinized, building walls around themselves, carefully avoiding the glare that might reflect their flaws and imperfection. Just as self-deprecation feels that they are worse than others, Arrogance feels better than most. I call the two, vanity and upside down vanity. Taking an offensive posture, *the best defense is a good offense,* this blindspot almost never finds out what others really think of them.

You're so damn arrogant. If you ever met God, the first thing you'd say is 'what are you doing in my chair?' —Lisa Gardner

Arrogance masks the fear of vulnerability through creating a cover, a barrier, so that others won't see the real person. The artifice created is their protection, a shield from being seen, all the while projecting an image of smoke and mirror illusion. Their underlying concern is to avoid being judged, even so, often they are the first to judge themselves privately and others openly as being inferior. Not being the person criticized, keeping censure from penetrating, hiding limitations, learning how to impress, feeling under scrutiny, embarrassed to be with anyone who might be judged, self importance takes over. The hidden inner feeling is: *I can't take it; if I have to hear or see another thing that I did wrong I'll be devastated.* Becoming attractive, dressing in an unmistakable style, covering shyness with a certain appearance, even believing to be that look, Arrogance goes to great lengths to keep up the act. Hiding weak areas, this air of superiority under stress blames others and circumstances for each difficult incident. This is a blamer, sometimes holding others in contempt. The problems are outside—in the environment or in other people. *I told you so,* then retreating behind an unavailable demeanor is a familiar posture. When decisive they let you know where they stand, without moving. They will make it clear they are not going to budge, they will not change their mind.

Arrogance is a creature. It does not have senses. It has only a sharp tongue and the pointed finger. —Toba Beta

This blindspot is good at avoiding being misunderstood and under-valued. Moving away from problems that others create, setting up tight boundaries around themselves fends off criticism. Looking affluent and special, appearing self-confident, boastfulness masks the inner discomfort of feeling undervalued. You might spot them by their swaggering walk or high shoulders. You will hear who they know, how they have connections, that other's success came from the association to them, what importance their life is, and what you might gain from being around or with them. Trying to look better than others, to be different than the way they are, the mask becomes the face. Years of feeling scrutinized creates a sham of self-importance, eroding their own relationship to self. Loneliness and isolation lowers physical resistance and is hard on the immune system. Criticalness pushes people away. Confused about self-worth, an inflated sense of self, an exaggerated sense of their importance limits their range of self-exploration.

Seeing themselves as better than they are, avoiding criticisms becomes paramount; nothing should show them their faults. Unwilling to look or perform poorly or face embarrassment closes down creativity and the flow of sexuality. Negotiating to keep discomfort away makes for a self-imposed smaller world. The self-deluding story, *if only they knew the real me they would really like me, but I keep that for special moments, a busy schedule keeps the real me hidden.* Learning equality means releasing the notion of specialness, means releasing the isolation and invisibility, is about taking risks and leveling the playing field to seeing others as our own true reflection.

Arrogance is a way for a person to cover up shame. After years of arrogance, the arrogant person is so out of touch, he truly doesn't know who he is. This is one of the greatest tragedies of shame cover-ups; not only does the person hide from others, he also hides from himself. —*John Bradshaw*

Self-Image

Self-importance takes up a lot of and space and time and requires expensive possessions. Top of the line car, a status position on the business card, a noteworthy address, an attractive date, picking up restaurant checks that may not be affordable; all this continues until public humiliation appears. This can look like getting fired from the job, the car being repossessed, IRS audit, filing for bankruptcy, house arrest for driving while drinking, sexual dysfunction, or friends your family deem as low life. Shame tortures the Arrogance blindspot. Maintaining a cover with new people, care is taken to appear as if everything is under control, hiding any weakness, deferring to their talented companion by talking about his or her success in public, befriending the person of the day (whether it's a physician, spiritual teacher, entertainer or politician), watching others for clues on how to be; this protects the possibility of being judged, with care not to be embarrassed in public.

In order to help others one must first learn to help oneself. People's consuming interest in changing others is a sign of laziness in working on their own evolution. —G.I. Gurdjieff

Based on a fear of vulnerability, of being examined and discovered to be lacking, deficient, courting people to convince them as well as themselves of superiority, polishing the self-image; being valued is high on the importance chart. The illusion of being better than, guarded and protecting themselves, the offensive position is considered to be the best defense. Quick to set up rules about criticism, they identify with the aggressor, becoming like the one who initially victimized them. The Arrogance blindspot is endlessly self-critical, leaving little room to constructively use and integrate insights or feedback. The inner experience is quite far from the outer, inside is self-consciousness, insecurity, and awkwardness. There is excessive charge in conversations if the inner critic becomes exacerbated. Doors slam, walls go up, making it highly unlikely to get through the fortress. Leaving little room for a cross-conversation, and space to feel judged or be shamed, convincing themselves they are right, they silence opposition. Most often their relationships are with those who would not dare criticize, who are marginalized by age disparity or through being relegated powerless through indebtness to the one carrying the Arrogant over-importance. Lonely at the top, Arrogance cannot have an energetic lively conversation without spirts of contempt and intensity. Looking for clues, watchful as to what will impress others, what people value, then offering that; not showing blemishes or limitations protects the vulnerability.

For one to expect or ask things of others that he himself, if asked, would not be willing to do or give, is the worst kind of arrogance. —Anthony Beal

In the negative mode ostentatious display, like a peacock preening makes others feel less and them more. Exaggeration, narcissism, boastfulness, superiority, conceit, all are characteristics that create a barrier between oneself and others in personal relationships. Showing letters people write extolling and thanking them telling about the generous acts they perform for people, anonymous giving disintegrates the boundaries that define the self as separate from others. This is a character that always lets others know who he assists financially, who he has helped and in what ways; little invisibility about their deeds of kindness and generosity. Arrogance over-inflates the self, sometimes there is a hidden agenda to secretly dislodge others from all imagined pedestal's. People with a primary obstruction of Arrogance won't offer quick apologies, or have a willingness to participate in places where they don't excel. A high opinion of themself, in their movie they brag about their accomplishments, certain that their imperfections are justifiable.

Anointing themselves as those who impart special information, they love to be admired. Overestimating their abilities in the effort to impress, feeds arrogance. Irritated having to deal with mundane ordinary aspects of life, they prefer focusing on their more elaborate projects. Genuine intimacy is difficult from this position; manipulating to their advantage the weaknesses in others, creating a huge pressure, decisions are usually made to support and maintain the viewpoint of the limitation. Most of their close relationships don't have the equality that define a healthy relationship. Personal relationships suffer from an internal dialogue of positioning people. There are no equals; others are higher or lower, better or worse, much younger or older, have more wealth or poverty, smarter or dumber and anyone can be bullied, blackmailed, proven wrong or kicked off the pedestal.

If your self-worth is invested in what you own, as can be the case in our market-driven society, then these things may not hold their value for very long. —Sean Saunders

In the positive, achieving a healthy sense of pride is based on actual efforts and appropriate achievements. A true sense of self-worth gauged on genuine experience begins to dissolve this stumbling block. Cooking a beautiful meal, learning a foreign language, taking risks in undeveloped areas, writing a screenplay, allowing a personal deep partnership that has equality into their life, learning how to play an instrument or to dance, receiving a degree or professional licensing, doing something on their own for themself, learning a skill from a-z; all real accomplishments enables them to feel competent and take pride in their own efforts. In the positive direction they are good people often contributing to the welfare of someone they do care about.

Ah, how the seeds of cockiness blossom when soiled in ignorance. —Steve Alten

Sliding to self-deprecation, the opposite and complementary obstacle, softens the judgments towards self and others. Dropping the facade of greatness, not hanging too long in the worthless mode, seeing themselves as they truly are, daring to be a fool, unchained from respectability, disrupting the pattern, learning equality without diminishing self or elevating another, releasing specialness; this honesty and discipline exercising humility loosens the hold of Arrogance. Seeing, listening, and praising others, dropping into experiencing limitation and showing vulnerability, allowing experiences that expose their weakest areas, intentionally making a fool of themselves, confronting the fear of being judged, they walk towards pride from a place of humility. This shift brings space for criticism, allows assessment and commentary in an effort to see themselves neutrally. When insights or opinions penetrate their barriers, that begins the journey of diminishing this imprisoning boulder. 15% of the population choose exalted inspiration Arrogance as their primary or secondary obstacle.

Try not to become a person of success, but rather try to become a person of value. The true value of a human being can be found in the degree to which he has attained liberation from the self. —Albert Einstein

Examples are: *Kanye West, Adolf Hitler, Mohammed Ali, Liberace, Eddie Murphy, Jack Nicholson, Sylvester Stallone, Donald Trump, Cher, Denzel Washington, Mick Jagger, Mike Tyson, Teresa Giudice, Gertrude Stein, Nicki Minaj, Robin Thicke, Mel Gibson, Salvador Dali.*

MARTYRDOM

POSITIVE: SELFLESSNESS

NEGATIVE: VICTIMIZATION, SELF-PITY

FEAR: BEING RESTRICTED,

TRAPPED BY CIRCUMSTANCES

SHADOW: IMPATIENCE

Martyrdom has always been a proof of the intensity, never of the correctness of a belief. —Arthur Schnitzler

The unnecessary suffering this blindspot creates appears as circumstantial and beyond control. You see the pained look on the face, now notice the spiteful glare in the eyes. The suffering can be silent or like a whining complaining drone. Parents and children in their effort to gain love, attention and affection adopt this stance. People with this blindspot belittle, feel victimized, spark guilt in those around them, enjoy sympathy and assigning blame elsewhere, making the other look bad and themselves look good. Frivolous lawsuits and unnecessary medical expenses; someone accountable for their perceived injustices. Payback might impact the family income while running up medical bills or someone they sue for some imagined infraction. Unnecessary surgery, reveling in extra hospital time, having their body cut, confining themselves to bed, maintaining the lineage of misery, is common place. In the negative mode the lawsuit may be dropped or lost, the lawyer overcharge, this adds to and continues the cycle of suffering they experience. The medical establishment makes a pile of money drugging these clients sorrows into a suppressed place as well as touting their slightly relieved less pinched face in ads for pain-relievers, anti-depressants and sleeping pills.

My grandmother always acted in other people's interests whether they wanted her to or not. If they'd had an Olympics in martyrdom my grandmother would have lost on purpose. —Emily Levine

Based on the belief of being unlovable and the fear of being out of control, feeling trapped by circumstances and helpless to lift out of this viewpoint, the fantasy of being right feeds the hypocrisy. Martyrdom sucks up space and energy. Their face might display a look of prolonged agony, wearing a crown of thorns while being thrown to the lions. The experience is that someone or a situation is causing their misery. If there isn't an issue to despair about they will find it, even feeling sorry for other people as a means of justifying how sorry they feel towards themselves. The energy to control others by provoking guilt for presumed troubles pushes people away making it difficult to successfully support a person manifesting Martyrdom.

The complaining and attitude of being taken advantage of, the resentments, the not accepting responsibility for their own behavior barrage their immune system creating illnesses that fortify Martyr traits. Blaming others perpetuates the story. Listen to the whine in the voice and you will find a Martyr at the other end. The self-fulfilling prophecy continues to draw in the adversity they talk about. *You owe me,* is often a root theme, and can be a parent who expects reward for birthing and raising a child, the boss who blames his employees for the business not succeeding, religious people who glorify suffering, a patient who pays their therapist and is angry they didn't *get better*; the pathways and routes of blame and expectation and disappointment are littered with Martyrdom.

A thing is not necessarily true because a man dies for it. —Oscar Wilde

TAKING RESPONSIBILITY

Misfortune seems to find its way to their door. Self-pity and sympathy are fed through not asking for help. Hoping someone will see their needs, yet in denial to admit their neediness, makes it difficult for others to step forward. Once feeling trapped by circumstances their dreams and possibilities appear impossible to fulfill. Placing the belief of one's unworthiness into the body and seeing negative influences as a confirmation of being victimized by outside forces conspiring against them perpetuates the cycle. Martyrs feel deserving of the treatment they receive. The self-image of a doormat so often portrayed by the mother who sighs a lot, doing subservient things that are annoying supports their other self-image of being a pushover. They will go out of their way to gain approval and sympathy, even doing odd things that others might find undignified to make up for their own lack of self-respect. This is the silent arm-twister cleverly manipulating others, sometimes suggesting someone or something stands in their path of happiness; an unmarried child, loser husband who doesn't make enough money, burdensome parent, the children who don't call, lack of finances, demands at work, their arthritis, bad back, or even the whole medical system. The pleasure of sympathy is a blind alley since it doesn't create change.

Change for this blindspot comes from limiting complaining and blaming while recognizing and identifying manipulation as their personal strategy. Acknowledging and exploring, awareness, paying attention to the sound, tone and mind processes that keep this obstruction alive increases self knowledge and brings space to move within the confinement of the attachment and its limitation. Martyrdom, the fear of being out of control, a victim, worthless, often creates its own agenda, a self-fulfilled prophecy, as one takes on the weight of others karma. Reluctant to release self-pity and continual suffering prevent them from being present in the here and now; painful experiences can be transformed into something valuable and meaningful.

The tyrant dies, and his rule is over. A martyr dies and his rule begins.
—*Soren Kierkegaard*

In the positive direction this person serves and assists others, volunteers for causes, moves beyond their own needs to selflessly focus attention to causes the world has ignored. They bring awareness to the difficulties of the less fortunate, give energy to friends, offer assistance when tragedy strikes, and are cognizant to the misfortune that effects people. Hope, fun, happiness, taking responsibility works to shift this obstruction. The negative direction, living in the illusion of not being in control of one's life attempts to create guilt in anyone who will listen to the sighing, gloom and long-suffering. Will they kill themself? This, too, is offered as a threat to relieve the afflictions caused by the world. Becoming more of a team player, releasing old habits, remembering that life is not *fair*, knowing how to play and have fun, saying no and meaning it, resisting to blame, are tools to move in the positive direction. The lack of inner peace is a high price to pay for this psychological blindspot. The fear of being trapped by circumstances or external elements creates the reality while the complaining and blaming ensures and prolongs it.

The mark of the immature man is that he wants to die nobly for a cause, while the mark of the mature man is that he wants to live humbly for one.
—*Wilhelm Stekel*

Working with Martyrdom means liberating the past, where the perceived injustice was formed and stepping back from the future, where amends are thought to be found. To shift the victim stance into a power-based one requires a recognition of personal neediness and a willingness to stop complaining. Too much concern for oneself, fearful for anyone to know the depth of their neediness crushes and traps. Preferring to keep their victimization secretive, confronting and exposing, quiets them for the time being. The so-called comforts of fault finding, always being right, receiving sympathy, self-righteousness, feeling despair in situations and gaining attention for complaining are difficult habits to give up or to change.

The challenge to break this obstruction lies in a willingness to have needs, to be seen having fun, to deal with loss, being open to share, have tears and release objections and disapproval. Sliding from the ordinal action Martyrdom to the complementary exalted blindspot of impatience, time becomes the ruler. Becoming daring the self-image gets shifted to a strengthening of determined self-respect. Since Martyrs can suffer interminably, using impatience quickens the long-suffering, speeding up, activating affirmation and self-respect. Moving towards the positive mode of impatience, becoming more daring, living outside the box, releases the pressures of the long-suffering trap that has victimized this obstruction. 15% of the population choose ordinal active Martyrdom as their primary or secondary obstacle.

The only difference between martyrdom and suicide is press coverage.
—Chuck Palahniuk

Examples are: *Mother Teresa, Nelson Mandela, Joan of Arc, Elie Wiesel, Abraham Lincoln, Martin Luther King, Terry Waite, Yoko Ono, Winston Churchill, John F. Kennedy, Jesus Christ, Donald Trump, Charles Manson, the Dalai Lama.*

IMPATIENCE

POSITIVE: PRESENCE, AUDACITY

NEGATIVE: INTOLERANCE,

MISSING OUT

FEAR: NOT HAVING ENOUGH TIME,

MISSING SOMETHING IMPORTANT

SHADOW: MARTYRDOM

One moment of patience may ward off great disaster. One moment of impatience may ruin a whole life. —Chinese proverb

To be enslaved to something that is non-existent is the irony of this roadblock. Time is the prison, and Impatience is trapped in the illusion that time is an object to be defeated by or to conquer. Racing the clock to arrive, watching the clock to leave, manifests as agitation, nervousness, intolerance, anxiety, futurizing, impulsive and sometimes restless behavior. Drive casually on any freeway at five p.m. in a big city and experience this obstacle: as people rush, vent, switch lanes, honk and hurry, short-fused and dangerous on public roads, scurrying, moving threateningly close to cars that travel at a slower pace. These are the reactive drivers trying to beat time, pressured by their fear of the finiteness of time, outward sources of power, scrambling to get ahead, to get somewhere else.

How poor are they that have not patience. What wound did ever heal but by degrees? —William Shakespeare

This is yet another psychological blindspot that blames something outside for feeling rushed and anxious. The clock is the culprit of this victimization, and the fear is of *missing out,* that time will *run away.* Ironically, feeling controlled by time eliminates the possibility of being present, in time, or on top of time. This happens as we are speeding ahead thinking about what needs to happen next, feeling pressured by the clock and frustrated that there is not enough time. The Impatience or irrational fear of missing out, of feeling delayed often manifests as abruptness, short-temper and irritability. A fear that things won't get done, life will end without our succeeding, days are being wasted, cranks up the drive to work twice as hard at double the speed.

Time isn't precious at all, because it is an illusion. What you perceive as precious is not time but the one point that is out of time: the Now. That is precious indeed. The more you are focused on time—past and future— the more you miss the Now, the most precious thing there is. —Eckhart Tolle

In the positive mode, daring and spontaneous we are inventive and original. The positive appears as we become mindful, inviting creative options to confusing situations. I remember when a popular well known lecturer was speaking to a large audience and the electricity failed. He stepped forward and continued in the dark suggesting everyone close their eyes and use this moment to go inside and locate a peaceful place. An opportunity to be creative and present, rather than sound off about how long it will take to fix the lights. Open, we receive, light enters. Closed over by this blindspot, clarity is obscured. What loss! An obstacle can be moved away, but in those moments that we block light the loss is irretrievable.

To feel rushed, in a hurry, creates a feeling of limitation so that we miss out on the richness of living in the present moment. Being harassed by the outer world, not paying attention to our inner world; being here for our daily life holds so many possibilities; to be reactive to distractions, going through the motions in a somnambulistic state we lose a finer quality of attention. And attention is love, it penetrates to a deeper level. *Attention, attention, attention,* wrote Zen Master Ikkyu many centuries ago when asked to write down the greatest wisdom. *But what does attention mean? Is that all?* asked his student. Master Ikkyu replied, *Attention means attention.* We could include the word awareness. Attention or awareness is the heart of practice. In awareness there is no space for self-centered thoughts to arise. The life we are living is not in time, it's in experiencing; when we make objects out of our experiences, rather than having an experience we lose the deepening of the experience, that aspect that creates substance and builds soul. To see the barriers, enabling us to be what we essentially are, is to recognize distractions through looking, seeing, through direct experience. Bringing attention to each moment is true presence and awakening.

A tree doesn't force its sap, it stands confidently in the storms of spring, not afraid that summer may not come. It does come. But it comes only to those who are patient, who are there as if eternity lay before them, so unconcernedly silent and vast. I learn it every day of my life, learn it with pain I am grateful for: patience is everything! Be patient toward all that is unsolved in your heart and try to love the questions themselves like locked rooms and like books that are now written in a very foreign tongue. —Rainer Maria Rilke

MANAGING 'TIME'

The Western world is programmed to support this obstruction; high-speed internet access, deadlines to meet, faster cars, small item check-out lanes, drive-through fast food restaurants, pay-first gas stations, caffeine, soda, ginseng, chocolate and amphetamines to keep energy up, corporate philosophy that sees time as a commodity. High energy, super-caffeinated drinks with names like Red Bull, Jolt, Full Throttle and Amp have surged in popularity. We live in a society where businesses use a punch-clock for employees, that has timed parking meters that require 25 cents at 15 minute increments, of rushed errands, horns honking if one hesitates, short-term investments, credit cards used to buy an item before having the money to pay for it, deadlines and appointments, one-day sales. We have bells ringing in school to mark classes, with only brief intervals to get to the next class without receiving a late slip for loitering, we grow up hearing destination oriented questions of *what school are you preparing for,* and *what will you be when you are older?*

Children are trained to feel imprisoned by time as they are rushed and pushed around to fit adult schedules, time gets blamed for jobs poorly executed and used as an excuse for many failed ventures, eventually meals are eaten quickly as are drinks gulped down, we stand at the elevator pressing the button repeatedly thinking that will speed it up, all contributing to the thought form that time is limited. The fear of missing something important, of not having enough time to accomplish things creates the psychological blindspot Impatience. Goal-oriented schooling and parenting promotes the idea of rushing through things to get *there.* Looking forward, difficulty staying focused on the here and now sets up a program of missing what is right here, right now, of digesting and integrating our experiences. Impatience stands in the way of long-term gain. Aborting negotiations before a breakthrough sets the stage and amplifies the underlying fear of missing out.

Impatience breeds anxiety, fear, discouragement and failure. Patience creates confidence, decisiveness, and a rational outlook. Learn the art of patience. Apply discipline to your thoughts when they become anxious over the outcome of a goal. —Brian Adams

During the past 2500 years plus, Aesop's fables have instructed and maintained lasting appeal. How to master the impediment of Impatience, how to make good choices? Fables effectively hold up a mirror, teaching through the engaging form of moral tales. The race between the Tortoise and the Hare, Aesop's story about a boastful hare who challenged anyone to be faster, to race and to win, is completely relevant today. The tortoise, accepting the challenge, paced himself and won the race. The moral, *slow and steady wins the race,* counteracts the Impatience belief that faster accomplishes more. *Rome was not built in a day.* Impatience manifests as carelessness, accidents, sloppiness, imprecision, intolerance, indigestion, bad temper as well as various physical ailments that appear from the commotion and stress of rushing. Haste, vanity and boastfulness disempower disrupting the possibility of feeling peace and contentment.

When someone is impatient and says, 'I haven't got all day' I always wonder, 'How can that be? How can you not have all day?'—George Carlin

Time is an endless moldable limitless movement, a dynamic process influenced by the mind. (further explained under the universal law of Eternal Recurrence, System 27). Quality gets compromised for high numbers in the corporate world encouraging workers to move ahead, to maintain their job, so as not to get fired. Adults acting like babies having tantrums create unsafe situations in public places. Bounced checks and fast financial dealings that sometimes lead to bankruptcy, investor foreclosures, marriages and relationships that could have been saved if the time were taken to slowly, mindfully deepen the partnership; so much unnecessary suffering due to our confusing relationship to time. To be mindful and present places us in a creative relationship to time, able to stretch and bend comings and goings, have synchronistic moments and be available to what is.

Consider the hour-glass; there is nothing to be accomplished by rattling or shaking; you have to wait patiently until the sand, grain by grain, has run from one funnel into the other. —*John Morgenstern*

In the negative direction Impatience manifests as frustration, intolerance, and lack of consideration. The experience is that the supermarket line is too long, the traffic is frustrating and annoying, my companion walks too slowly, there are no available parking places, the movie will start before I get there, the waitress is ignoring me; we feel disappointed, thwarted, and ultimately unsympathetic to the whole situation. Try asking someone in Impatience to wait for you while you go into a store to buy something. Often they leave or are pacing around fully involved in their cell phone picking up calls, texting mindlessly, using the time so their important moments aren't wasted. Their intolerant frustration is the give-away. Drawing attention to themselves, impulsive, often turning out inferior work rather than allowing a process to gradually unfold. Our culture supports this obstruction with overpopulated areas which eventually create long lines in movie theatres, in supermarkets, at post offices, subways, airports, and restaurants; as well as pushing us to deal with schedules, appointments, deadlines, medical and legal professionals who way over book, as well as business phone calls that put us on hold for what seems like an eternity. We are taught that time is limited, we have none to lose or waste, so we had better plan, cram and rush. In truth, time can never be used up, it is a manifestation of our mind.

Being in the moment, attention to the present moment masters this obstacle. It is useful to remember that we can't buy or sell time, although most lives are lived calculating financial payment for allotted time as well as saving money as if that will buy extended time. Choosing to play with the meaning of time, having a clock-free, watch-free day, eliminating plans and leaving large chunks of the day and evening unplanned, strengthens our intuitive sense. To incorporate quiet unstructured days, free of distractions, to practice meditation, watchfulness, paying attention to our breath, to listen to beautiful music, keep a journal, take a slow peaceful walk; useful practices to silence a distracted mind and Impatient life-style.

We smile at the ignorance of the savage who cuts down the tree in order to reach its fruit; but the same blunder is made by every person who is over eager and impatient in the pursuit of pleasure. —William Ellery Channing

The active exalted blindspot Impatience is the complementary opposite of martyrdom. Both are seated in a fear of being victimized by something, moving from intolerance and complaining/blaming to impersonally taking action to change the circumstance. Using this shift to the positive part of martyrdom, selflessness, and to surrender to ongoing situations strengthens the aptitude to listen, to take in, to be tolerant, to quiet anxiety. This creates an opportunity to anchor into a deliberate place from which to give and to serve, attentively, while relinquishing feeling pressured to make up for lost time. 15% of the population choose exalted active Impatience as their primary or secondary blindspot.

One has to wait without impatience for what should come, and yet at the same time do everything within one's power as though one were impatient and as though one were solely responsible. —Rodney Collin

Examples are: *Robin Williams, Billy Crystal, Danny De Vito, Bruce Willis, Sandra Bernhard, Dolly Parton, Andy Cohen, Madonna, Drew Barrymore, Kelly Ripa, John Travolta, Fran Drescher, Harvey Fierstein, Bette Midler, Bruce Vilanch, Jim Carey, Richard Branson, Sean Penn, Frank Sinatra, Steve Martin, Lily Tomlin, Anthony Bourdain.*

STUBBORNNESS

POSITIVE: DETERMINATION

NEGATIVE: OBSTINANCE

FEAR: SUDDEN CHANGE, LOSS

OF CONTROL, AUTHORITY

SHADOW: NEUTRALLY SHIFTS

TO ANY BLINDSPOT

Stubborn and ardent clinging to one's opinion is the best proof of stupidity.
—*Michel de Montaigne*

So many animals walk around with this nick-name: Stubborn as a mule, pigheaded, bullish, dogged. Descriptions abound and are graphic, like wrongheaded, stiff-necked, hard-nosed, ironclad, rocklike, single-minded, lock-jaw, headstrong, hard-shell, immovable, tight-ass, jaw-clencher and brick wall.

Never try to out stubborn a cat. —*Lazarus Long*

The fear of change and loss of control can rigidify and incapacitate, slowing down, refusing to budge, turning a deaf ear; like a mule feeling pushed, digging in there is a bottom line resistance to change. Reduced flexibility lodges in the pelvis, lower back, jaw, knees, joints, neck, feet and ankles. Chronic muscle tension, jaw pain, pinched nerves, muscle spasms and contraction, lack of mobility in the pelvis; unbending in one's nature creates a musculature to match. Teeth grinding at night, tension in the jaw muscles causing temporomandibular joint syndrome, tight back muscles that wear down discs, pulled up shoulders that hunch the back, stomach tightness that creates digestive disorders; ultimately the muscle groups develop a pattern from the resistance and print a fixed tone and a lack of flexibility in the body. Obstructions and blockages cause irritation to the nervous system effecting organs and creating various medical conditions.

This obstacle is commonly used by children and old people, who feel powerless. Nursing homes, nursery schools and early childhood programs are filled with individuals who choose Stubborn as their predominant roadblock. Tantrums, resistance, rebellion, resisting authority, passive aggression, the silent treatment, defiance, are some of the faces of the Stubborn psychological blindspot. Unwilling to change a mind set, inflexible, unyielding, contrary, they hope to block all activity that is connected to what appears as the problem. Often used as a way to brake situations that seem threatening, they plant their heels until the storm passes. The body says *No, I won't;* a false sense of power implies that by refusing to comply, by stopping the action, they become/are the most powerful.

Many are stubborn in pursuit of the path they have chosen, few in pursuit of the goal. —*Fredrich Nieztsche*

Change and impermanence is ultimately the nature of the universe. *Only one thing is constant in this world, and that is change,* observed Greek philosopher Heraclitus. Determined to tough it out, the fear of new situations encourages the rationalization that keeps them from taking in feedback, from even knowing they are not being accommodating. Decision making is based on willfully forging ahead so as to avoid new situations. Uncooperative, Stubbornness sets in at an early age; children are unprepared for the changes and shifts that adults enforce. *Just do it,* pushed to eat what they are told, toilet trained by schedule, argued with, bedtime hours regulated, clean their room or lose privileges, deprived of choices, not taught negotiation, adults controlling children's pleasure by demanding high grades, hours of homework, lengthy practices for discovered talent ranging from piano to basketball sets the arena for obstinacy and headstrong behavior. Having been forced to comply, sitting through situations where autonomy and independence are violated and robbed, the stage is set for the Stubbornness obstruction to set in position, setting the tone for this rock hard obstruction.

Never give in. Never give in. Never, never, never—in nothing, great or small, large or petty—never give in—except to convictions of honour and good sense. Never yield to force. Never yield to the apparently overwhelming might of the enemy. —Winston Churchill

The illusion of winning is based on a loss of the freedom to choose, coming from fear this illusion continues to block decisions that then undermines change and growth. Resistant, often uncooperative, arbitrariness, refusal for the sake of inflexibility, lack of negotiability called poor sport, continues the cycle of frustration, adding to a closed mind; not fun type people to hang out with or take to the party. Quietly defiant in childhood to oppose a bullying environment, lack of flexibility becomes ingrained. Internally sticking with old decisions, they feel martyred: *I've made my decision and now I'll stick it out.*

DETERMINATION

The difference between the impossible and the possible lies in a person's determination. —Tommy Lasorda

In the positive, there is true strength in determination which lays the foundation to develop back-bone along with a willingness to persevere through to achievement. This becomes a solid *yes*, accompanied by strong intentions to forge ahead. Determination; when walking, walk, when driving, drive, no wobble. Steadfast and independent in decisions, achieving aims becomes a reality. In the negative, there is an equally strong *no*, based on a fear of authority, sudden change brings up obstinacy, antagonism and a disregard to look towards options or even be flexible. Missing the bigger picture they hold long after the fact when opposition is imaginary and serves nothing.

Great work requires great and persistent effort for a long time. Character has to be established through a thousand stumbles. —Vivekananda

Going back on old decisions, admitting mistakes is a fundamental tool to melting this obstacle. This shifts the erroneous belief that Stubbornness is based on strength rather than on fear. The posture of Stubbornness being power, they become unyielding, unbendable, immovable, unable to listen, there is the appearance and self-deception of winning based on the ability to stop another's actions. Sometimes disguised as persistence, instead, avoiding change, this is an unnatural position in the order of a universe whose essential nature is change. Not wanting to deal with adjusting they close the way to new situations. To shift this obstruction implies a larger range of possibilities. An Aikido, Tai Chi type stance, focusing on relaxed movement requires far less energy than resisting or aggression. The point of least resistance is attitude. Bracing ourselves for the injuries life brings we are more apt to get hurt unless we are supple and resiliently able to move effortlessly. When we have appropriate response, since life responds, we see that suffering is most often caused by resistance; if we arrive in the moment prepared, little else matters. The outward is simply a reflection of what arises inwardly.

Endurance is one of the most difficult disciplines, but it is to the one who endures that the final victory comes. —*Buddha*

Moving out of the comfort zone, learning to listen, looking for the growth in change along with our acknowledgement of error: a general letting go serves to melt this impediment. Many people settle on this feature to persevere and endure in the face of obstacles, maintaining their life as they stay on course, determined, unpersuadable, struggling internally against impositions, resisting even themselves.

Older souls, opening to new possibilities shift this obstruction living into *don't know mind,* finding an inner authority to deepen their integrity, becoming less resistant through listening to their own inner voice. A willingness to acknowledge poor choice making moves Stubbornness onward; letting go is the ultimate demise for this block—regardless to whether it is to a partner, thought, business or a concept. When something is no longer viable, releasing it is the opening to the possibilities inherent in life. 20% of the population choose this assimilation obstacle Stubbornness, which is a neutral obstruction, the one that shifts to all other obstacles, as a predominant or secondary blindspot. Being assimilative it is sometimes invisible, showing itself less in what it does and more in what it does not do. We feel this blindspot when we run into it; bouncing off a brick wall creates quite an impact. Our bodies shift shape as we try to squeeze by Stubborn people, they are like football blockers holding the line, jamming up the front of the bus or the checkout lane in the supermarket, saying *try to get by me, because I'm not moving.*

I am not more gifted than anybody else. I am just more curious than the average person and will not give up on a problem until I have found the proper solution. —*Albert Einstein*

Examples are: *Fidel Castro, Alan Greenspan, Kevin Costner, Barbra Streisand, Jesse Jackson, Jane Fonda, Billy Graham, Kanye West, Madonna, Steve Jobs, Grace Jones, George W. Bush, Mark Twain, Tina Turner, Winston Churchill, Bruce Springsteen, General George Custer, Stephen King, Helen Keller.*

ANGER

POSITIVE: ASSERTION

NEGATIVE: AGGRESSION, RESENTMENT, HOSTILITY

FEAR: BEING HELPLESS, OUT OF CONTROL

SHADOW: FEAR

Holding on to anger is like grasping a hot coal with the intent of throwing it at someone else; you are the one who gets burned. —the Buddha

Anger walks a thin line, hovering between assertion and persuasion, coercion and aggression. As a classic reaction to injustice and abuse, a protection against pain, Anger supports our defensive system and is a response to our body's fight or flight mechanism. A real or imagined threat when it is internalized and repressed accumulates and is stored in the physical body; from a holistic body perspective that weakens our organ systems, particularly the white blood cells and the liver. In optimal health our emotions flow freely, are acknowledged and responded to appropriately; disharmony arises when we ignore, suppress or are stuck in our emotional body. Annoyance, frustration and displeasure provoked build a slow burn intensifying to become reactive rage and fury. Verbal expressions like boil over, steam up, smoldering fire, blind rage, have a cat fit, seeing red, fly off the handle, hit the roof, roar like a bear, enraged bull, guns booming, fiery temper, blow one's cool, and hot blood, graphically portray the uncontrollable nature of an Anger that loses its containment. Thich Nhat Hahn explains that to retaliate when you are angry is like chasing the arsonist after he sets fire to your home rather than tending to, putting out the fire. Letting your house burn while you run after the arsonist is allowing your home to go up in flames.

Releasing the grip on anger and resentment is an act of self-compassion.
—Sharon Salzberg

Since obstacles or stumbling blocks are connected to the emotional body, separating to observe and to be in our experience in a new way, seeing different possibilities in a manner that evokes understanding rather than reaction we transmute our reactive Anger into a practice, into seeds of love. With the energy of mindfulness, looking into our Anger we transform reactive Anger. Behind appearances there is another reality and stepping away gives us access. Most obstacles are rooted in imagination and express themselves in a particular style. Anger, one of the five natural emotions, the others being fear, grief, jealousy and love, all need to be felt, acknowledged and understood, otherwise they move into aberrations. Anger mishandled develops into distortions like rage, blame, guilt, self-pity, depression, indigestion, physical aggression, rumination, frustration, hatred, bitterness, grudge-holding, displeasure, indignation, annoyance, resentment, self-hate and powerlessness.

Anger is only one letter short of danger. *—popular saying*

We all have the possibility to connect with our Anger, to sit with it, to be non-reactive, to feel the heat that is transmuted into energy. Heat conserved is transmitted into energy; the misinterpretation of emotions collect into a reservoir of unresolved feelings and issues creating what is called *unfinished business*. Anger emerges as a protection against pain. Underneath Anger is sadness, and beneath that is pain. When sadness is activated and our helplessness is overcome there is a relief; on the other hand inactive Anger creates sadness. There are circumstances when Anger would not be permissible, situations where our inactivity sets off a hopelessness noticeable in people who walk around with a downtrodden saddened face. Anger then becomes active sadness and then sadness reflects back inactive Anger. Both are faces of the same repressed energy. The blindspot Anger moves outward interacting with the world. Anger used as a reaction, a force to steam roll people, is not a sign of strength but rather a sign of weakness. What could be strength and assertiveness, now imbalanced and distorted becomes a weapon. Winning an argument does not make us right.

ANGER AND OUR BODY

Anger needs to be controlled, but not hidden from yourself. —the Dalai Lama

Eventually, repressed Anger becomes temporary insanity. Studies have implied that waiting and impatience most typically triggers Anger—there have been more violent attacks in airline terminals, hospital emergency rooms, heavy traffic and other places that have significant wait time, than there are in places that don't have demanding long delays. The legal term, temporary insanity, is often about a crime committed in a moment of expressed Anger, triggered by agitation, a short fuse and fear. When Anger dominates the mind, reality is distorted, like a blind person who visually can't see direction or perspective. Anger generally results from feeling helpless, frustrated or unable to control a situation, feeling trapped by circumstances and seeing no way out. Most people, not knowing how to deal constructively with their Anger will repress or express it in a violating way; learning to express it in a clean way at the appropriate moment keeps it from reaching volcanic levels, staving off long standing depression.

Anger is a normal emotion if it is expressed when felt. Then it is over with. If one keeps a lid on it, it develops into resentment or hate. Sooner or later, resentment and hate explode, destroying others, or they are held in, destroying oneself. —Dr. Bernie Siegel

The perception or sensation of threat or stress, experienced through hormonal change often produced by fatigue, hunger or pain, produces Angry energy that assists the autonomic nervous system to release and then shift back to a relaxed state. Anger as a sensation in the physical body is a biological response that can be converted or redirected. Exercise, sports, dancing, bike riding, martial arts, swimming, walking, running, drumming, writing, singing, talking to a friend, learning to relax, mindful breathing, looking deeply into the nature of our perceptions, compassion towards the other person to realize that he/she suffers and might need help, all are choices to redirect the physical energy, the adrenaline that the body pumps when Anger lights the fire. When the bloodstream is pumped with adrenaline, uplifted to make us more than animal, we begin knowing that we can place ourself in a position to transform, to liberate the power that this energy holds.

It is not the feeling of anger itself that will make changes. It is how you respond to it. You can take the anger that you feel and make it productive rather than raging. You can use it as a catalyst for addressing wrong with great energy and power. —Angel Kyodo Williams

There are many mechanisms available to manage danger; the

natural survival reactions of perceived threats to our livelihood, possessions, loved ones, sense of self and safety, work deadlines and financial
obligations; ultimately to what we call our life. The effect of increased
available energy as part of our physiological make-up is activated once
we feel Angry or stressed. Specific physiological reactions like an increase
in heart rate and breathing as well as constricting blood vessels in many
parts of the body will register as Anger rises to give a signal to become
alert and attentive to our environment. Our brain releases neurochem-
icals into the blood stream which travel through the circulatory system
effecting organs and systems in the body in preparation for a full body
response of fight or flight. Fight or flight is a sympathetic response pattern, also called an acute stress response and is an emergency reaction
whereby the body, feeling alarmed, prepares for combat, faces threat, or
quickly moves to leave. When not expressed or released Anger is held
and stored in our physical form.

Nonverbal signs visible to an onlooker include squaring the torso
for fight, or angling away to prepare for flight, eyebrow-raising, facial
flushing, positioning the body to seem bigger to the eye, swaggering,
larger, upper body strutting; all filling up space to demonstrate power.
Dominance cues are often used to express Anger.

*The ultimate source of my mental happiness is my peace of mind. Nothing
can destroy this except my own anger.* —*the Dalai Lama*

Buddhist practice aims to develop inner calmness, insight, patience
and assertiveness while offering room for Anger and aggression to shift,
to move towards wisdom. Directing outward behavior so as not to react,
rather to maintain a sense of reason, allows us to see the nature of our
blindspot Anger, to become conscious of it. The power of Anger, often

an immediate reaction of fear and loss of self-control is also a jolt of juice and energy which is why Anger becomes a popular choice for so many. Shifting to the positive part of its shadow, fear, and using that to exercise authority confidently, assertively, eases the strong feelings before they build and trigger out of control. Directing fear to caution, attentiveness and focus we gain control over our dispersed energy to be in charge, to not erupt and explode. These are some of the positive aspects of fear that anchor the Anger obstacle. Using humor and creativity rather than division is another possible choice. Gymnast, Mary Lou Retton, writers Ernest Hemingway and Gertrude Stein, boxer Muhammed Ali, actor Marlon Brando, singers Tina Turner and Grace Jones, hard-driven leaders in their fields, forging ahead unafraid to battle when not at the undisciplined edge of their Anger have at times actively disciplined and directed this energy assertively to use it with purpose. 20% of the population choose Anger as their primary or secondary blindspot.

I have learned through bitter experience the one supreme lesson: to conserve my anger, and as heat conserved is transmitted into energy, even so our anger controlled can be transmitted into a power that can move the world.
—*Mahatma Gandhi*

Examples are: *Mike Tyson, Charlton Heston, Golda Meier, Rambo, Mr. T, Grace Jones, Muhammed Ali, Ernest Hemingway, Charles Manson, Kelly Osbourne, Elton John, Chyna, Lena Dunham, Kris Jenner, Serena Williams, Lauren Bacall, Marlon Brando, Sylvester Stallone, Mary Lou Retton, O.J. Simpson, Rebel Wilson, Chris Brown, Kanye West, Judge Judy Sheindlin, Russell Crowe, Sean Penn, Pink, Tina Turner, Charles Bronson, Rosie O'Donnell, Fidel Castro, G.I. Gurdjieff, Gertrude Stein.*

FEAR

POSITIVE: FOCUS, CAUTION, ACCEPTANCE

NEGATIVE: ANXIETY, STRESS,

PARANOIA, CAGINESS, TRICKY

FEAR: DANGER, LIFE AND DEATH

SHADOW: ANGER

It is not that you must be free from fear. The moment you try to free yourself from fear, you create a resistance against fear. Resistance, in any form, does not end fear. What is needed, rather than running away or controlling or suppressing or any other resistance, is understanding fear; that means, watch it, learn about it, come directly into contact with it. We are here to learn about fear, not how to escape from it, not how to resist it through courage and so on. A man who is not afraid is not aggressive, a man who has no sense of fear of any kind is really a free, a peaceful man. —*Krishnamurti*

Fear often arises in a childhood towards a specific thought, then later becomes generalized, spreading until it permeates our life, eventually the personality revolves around Fear. The original Fear of something becomes a complete view of life, of our relationship to the world. Attitudes are filtered through the obstacle. What began as a Fear of my father might expand to a Fear of men, of saying the wrong thing, of change, and continues on to expand and attach, be connected to many things: to traveling, sleep, the ocean, sex, dogs, being alone, relationships, driving, money; decisions are made according to the level of Fears we produce. In Fear we come from lower parts, in love we manifest from higher places. The negative aspects of all the obstacles come from a place of Fear and the positive aspects come from a place of love. The dramas, stories and adventures that are intertwined with Fear create a distorted type of pleasure, excitement, stories that make us feel as if we are alive.

Perhaps everything that frightens us is, in its deepest essence, something help-less that wants our love. —*Rainer Maria Rilke*

Fear is another of the five natural emotions, its distortions being anxiety, panic and numerous phobias. Fear sees itself as being safe or living in danger. Left unattended it develops into paranoia; someone might be angry with me, a partner could have an affair and leave me, swimming in the ocean a shark could attack, a terrorist might be on the airline flight I am scheduled to fly, I may get sick, make a poor decision and lose money, what if the elevator gets stuck, get fired from my job, have a heart attack or get cancer, many things to Fear. Living in concern of something going wrong, both life and death are Feared. When Fear is a false threat it prevents us from dealing with situations effectively. The natural emotion of Fear brings an innate survival response that fosters caution, manifests a startle response and flight or fight impulse. The natural fear of a shark or alligator sets up situations that help avoid danger, whereas unfounded Fears create suffering, separation, paralysis, over caution, defenses, limits life and love and breeds more Fear.

We fear things in proportion to our ignorance of them. —*Livy*

Fear manifests as a mechanism to create a sense of aliveness by feeling there is something real to be lost. Fear, a habit of the mind, loses its power with our willingness to sit with discomfort, knowing that the objects of our Fears are most often an illusion. Dropping into the present moment experiencing its clarity, opening to whatever arises is the freedom. As a protection, founded Fears aid to help avoid senseless accidents when we are in situations of unreasonable danger. Leaving the ocean in a lightening storm, not skiing in an area where there had been a reported avalanche, not walking alone through Central Park at night, knowing your own medical signs, eating and exercising mindfully, trusting your intuition and paying attention to the environment; these are reasonable precautions that when used carefully Fear protects. The tricky part is that many Fears masquerade as sensible and reasonable, with people justifying and rationalizing their Fears to convince themselves and others to their legitimacy.

Fear as a psychological blindspot is a double whammy because irrational Fears fuel and bond to all of the impediments. Fear is fought with Fear. Embracing the Fear, the dark, ourself, others, both the beauty as well as the ugliness, the dark and the light, neutralizes its power over us. Some people are more prone to constitutionally live as Fear types, (see the Enneagram, System One), and although often unaware of this central issue will sometimes recognize it after the Fear lifts.

The enemy is fear, We think it is hate; but, it is fear. —*Gandhi*

FACING FEAR

All of the blindspots are founded on and driven by Fear. They are automatically activated defensively and easily rationalized as plausible. Self-observation leads to disidentification and deprograms the instinctive habitual reaction. This shift in awareness balances, centers, brings an authentic response. Fear, as a source of negativity limits freedom of choice and the expression of love. To have Fear as an obstruction we see in most situations the possibility of something not going right and leading to danger. A child running could fall and get hurt, forgetting to lock the door may be an invitation to a robbery, missing something on a tax report could lead to an IRS audit, swimming in the ocean we might drown or be attacked by a shark, talking to a stranger could lead to an assault; the mind drifts to create negative Fearful scenarios out of casual ordinary experiences. In this negative arena Fear creates stress and anxiety building to an uncomfortable level with its by product of trickiness, anxiety, mental illness, angst, suspicion, panic, depression, a loss of the fun of daily pleasures. Not checked, this is the base line for most illness, accidents and economic financial loss. Circumstances and tension lead to Fear patterns for those who choose this blindspot.

Fear is only as deep as the mind allows. —*Japanese proverb*

In the positive direction, acknowledging impermanence, that there are risks in life, acceptance to what we can do, minimizing arbitrariness with self-awareness, we move onward. Shifting to its opposite and complementary obstacle, anger, helps release us from Fear energy. The positive aspect of anger, assertion, when we are in the grip of Fear, can become a catalyst, bringing attention, a concentration of energy forward. Being in the positive increases clarity, allowing us to operate from a place of truth. Facing our Fears, going into the dark to find the light is essential for spiritual development. Accepting Fear, becoming responsible and having active attention develops self-awareness. Acceptance is non-judgmental neutrality, sometimes taking constructive action, eventually learning to live from a place of love. Blaming blocks awareness, fighting the inner Fear to fight the Fear outside maintains the Fear. Our energy and vitality gets locked or opens; as Fear is extinguished separation vanishes, disunity shifts and harmony arrives. Fear is an absence of love and is created from the imagination that we are separate and as we release our unreasonable Fears our presence automatically liberates others. Unfounded fears feed unnecessary suffering and limits our clarity and ability to experience truth. The other side of every irrational Fear is freedom. People who diminish their Fears, those lurking shadows that grow in darkness and dissipate in the light of love, open their lives to greater treasures and celebration.

35% of the population choose Fear as either their predominant or secondary blindspot.

We now know that the human animal is characterized by two great fears that other animals are protected from: the fear of life and the fear of death.
—*Ernest Becker*

Examples are: *Chicken Little*, small babies, people who manifest phobias, *Tom Arnold, George W. Bush, Adolf Hitler, Sherlock Holmes, Woody Allen, David Letterman, Lamar Odom, Howie Mandel, Helen Palmer, Sigmund Freud, Spike Lee, Simon Cowell, Rosie O'Donnell, Aretha Franklin, Richard Nixon, Charlie Sheen, Adele.*

DOMINANCE AND POWER

POSITIVE: ACCOMPLISHMENT, LEADERSHIP

NEGATIVE: INTIMIDATION, DICTATORSHIP

FEAR: UNCERTAINTY

SHADOW: POWER AND DOMINANCE

Dominance. Control. These things the unjust seek most of all. And so it is the duty of the just to defy dominance and to challenge control. —*Robert Fanny*

Power without wisdom falls of its own weight. —*Horace*

Dominance, less overt and visible than Power, gradually exercising control without explanation, without negotiating, dismissive of public opinion, predominates through creating an environment of dependence. Taking charge, not liking to look weak, those with this obstacle attempt to look as if nothing fazes them. They might be physically unable to go to work, yet will run business from a sickbed. Preferring to be in a position of responsibility, managing and organizing, taking the reigns they gravitate to situations that they can govern. Dominance tries to bring some kind of order, control into situations. Power feels that without visibility others will take advantage, will influence authority over them. Good at getting things done, using whatever is in their nature to make an impact; at times it's bossiness, sometimes through silence, regardless, they step forward. Dominance will retract, become unavailable when the project does not interest them. Refusal to engage, removing availability is a strong control, it's Dominance from the position of inaction.

Power is not neccessarily bad. Its direction is what makes it good or bad.
—*Irene Claremont de Castillejo*

Those under the influence of people with this obstruction often are not aware of it, since it is a gradual take over. Holding out for the win, focused and aimed to come out on top; for Dominance life is a win or lose game, by their rules and at any expense. Power, on the other hand is quick, intimidating and apparent, bullying whenever possible. Camouflaging themselves as spunky, daring and powerful; both psychological blindspots make a forceful impact on the world. Satisfaction, sought after in the outside world, regardless to an official position, careful to maintain an appearance of strength, weakness represents an absence of Power when you live with conditioned thinking. The need to be right is a very common object of the ego and its identification with our obstruction, until we've become just that, one with all of our reactive patterns.

We often speak of love when we really should be speaking of the drive to dominate or to master, so as to confirm ourselves as active agents, in control of our own destinies and worthy of respect from others. —Thomas Szasz

The masculine in our culture, from childhood onward, enjoys stories, movies and games about men who seize power; military commanders, rival warlords, mafia, assassins, Samurai, Ninja; it lives vicariously through enjoying, pleasuring in the energy of Power and Domination. Weakness represents passivity, making things happen is priority. Dominance is often careful, not wanting to look foolish, to win, while Power regards directly impacting, forcing others and being noticed as a primary importance. Both are obstructions that excuse and justify their own shortcomings, that sees life dualistically. Power views life as being controlled or controlling, is more outward-going and conspicuous than Dominance. Dominance sees and lives life as win or lose. Dominance, less forceful, is persuasive, while Power is pervasive and showy. Ironic to be under the power and domination of that which we believe ourselves to be in control of; two obstructions that know how to prevail, having a such a strong hold over our personality.

People dominate because they are afraid, they are not certain about themselves. —Osho, Rajneesh

The blindspots Power and Dominance are highly visible and tempting in a corporate bureaucratic world, in government, in a hierarchical church structure, in the medical world. Ceo's, financial advisers, stock analysts, bankers, mortgage brokers, accountants, physicians, police officers will engage either impediment to influence and gain financial and mental authority over others. Within the church exploitative priests supported by indifferent archbishops have taken sexual Power and Dominance over certain members of their congregation, particularly children. Within government, oppressive military and political action is aimed to Dominate and take command over countries and individuals. The interviews and studies of Nazi war criminals concludes that the lack of empathy, which should have been developed during childhood and adolescence, created indifference enabling atrocities that expressed both Power and Domination. Psychologist Alfred Adler, stated: *The striving for personal power is a disastrous delusion and poisons man's living together. Whoever desires the human community must renounce the striving for personal power.* Adler's co-worker, concentration camp and prisoner of war survivor, Dr. Alexander Mueller, reflected: *Whatever the most basic reasons for dominance and aggression might be, their most significant consequence is to make the other person into an object and not the subject. Our modern life can easily become a struggle for some kind of real or imagined dominance.*

INAUTHENTICITY

True power is the falling away of individual identity. —Sri Saradamani Devi

Dominance and Power are visible blindspots, worn with either an air of authority or duress. Often a leader or model for others, cleverly manipulative, demanding, outward going, sometimes overwhelming, their presence suggests they know what they are talking about, drawing people to look to them for information. Donald Trump as President is a perfect reflection of the bluffing overly confident blindspot pushing and bullying his way and loving to shine in the spotlight regardless to being right, feeling justified by being *the winner.* Appearing self-assured, bluffing when they are not certain, they don't need to appear confident of the circumstance, only of themselves. Both blindspots work well with people who are prison guards or wardens, bullies, bureaucratic heads, military generals, heads of state, serial killers or corporate directors and politicians.

Oh, I just wish someone would try to hurt you so I could kill them for you.
—*Frank Sinatra*

Power and Dominance, when operating as intoxicated energy creates insanity. Whether in a bankruptcy, a hospital bed or prison cell, the individual with this blindspot will be running their business, organizing and controlling, getting others involved. Hitler might have become an institutionalized madman without Power. The newspapers broadcast examples of this psychosis in people who perpetuate crimes of violence during war. Power and Dominance without self-awareness are like a loaded gun in the hands of a child, aimed to harm oneself or others.

The United States has Dominance and Power as its primary obstacles blindly believing that what is right for this country is also right for the rest of the world; to reason or act other than how this country thinks, is not thinking or doing. Dominance and Power lectures, preaches, reassures, instructs, tries to convince both friend and foe; it doesn't aim to completely destroy, since that would ruin the utilitarian value of its subject. The United States Dominates the world both culturally and with military strength. There is no room for a neutral mid-place. There is total control or a moving away, which is still control in its refusal to participate. Dominance looks for a way to set up an environment that fosters dependency. It might set up a bureaucracy using its rules, subtly positioning leadership to sustain Dominance. The energy is directed towards appearing in control, to not be perceived as weak.

AUTHENTIC LEADERSHIP

Power over others is a weakness disguised as strength. True power is within, and it is available to you now. —*Eckhart Tolle*

Moving to the positive characteristics of accomplishment and leadership, being a role model and guide for others while remaining inclusive, shifts the mechanicality. Aligning with the Power that already exists, to be in sync is to resonate with a balance that allows for true surrender. This is no longer the appearance of Power, nor the effort needed for Dominance. Skillful direction for true service to a group and to the individuals within the group, rather than tyranny and coercion to justifying their self-importance and promote self, sets a kindly tone. Turned around and used well this is an obstruction that offers many possibilities.

No legacy is so rich as honesty. —*William Shakespeare*

Accepting the responsibility of Power and Domination and remaining an ordinary person with humility makes for good leadership. The principles of negotiation, reciprocity and cooperation bring about the positive aspects of this hurdle for it to be transformed. The aim is not to defeat the obstructions, Domination or Power, instead, how to use them consciously as tools to awaken. Wasting energy fighting something that is not *us* anyway, observing we learn the nature of our roadblocks which gives us the opportunity to be larger than the hurdle and how best to use it.

15% of the population choose the active Dominance or Power as a primary or secondary blindspot. They often are capable leaders, heads of state, successful entertainers, owners of large successful corporations, or, mafia bosses, gang leaders, heads of sexual rings; determined, enjoying to run the show.

We have confused power with greatness. —*Stewart L. Udall*

Examples are: *Donald Trump, Bill Cosby, Frank Sinatra, Madonna,*

George W. Bush, Dick Cheney, Martha Stewart, Simon Cowell, Mike Tyson, Idi Amin, Fidel Castro, Marlon Brando, Leona Helmsley, P. Diddy, O.J. Simpson, Charles Manson, Adolf Hitler, Marc Anthony, Taylor Swift, Chris Rock, Barbra Walters, Barbra Streisand, Kris Jenner, Kanye West, David Letterman, Justin Beiber, Beyonce, Jay Z, Joan Rivers, Ryan Seacrest, Maks Chmerkovski, Chris Brown, Rihanna, Jillian Michaels, Oprah Winfrey, Angelina Jolie, Robin Thicke, Jennifer Lopez, Martin Scorsese, Malcolm X.

TRAMP

POSITIVE: SOMETHING FOR NOTHING

NEGATIVE: SOMETHING FOR NOTHING,

PARASITIC, LAZINESS,

LACK OF DISCRIMINATION

FEAR: LOSING OUT

SHADOW: SATISFACTION, RECOGNIZING

AND ENJOYING WHAT YOU HAVE

When you seek what is not your own, you lose what actually is your own.
—*Epictetus*

This blindspot creates a person who lacks value towards other peoples things. Something for nothing in the negative implies that a *free* place to stay, a *free* meal, a *free* car ride are what's coming to the person with this impediment. Many times it's publicly acknowledged, like *I just stayed at my friends house in New York, or my cousin's condo in Miami Beach and it was so great.* It's assumed that people will offer, and much of the enjoyment is in the lack of financial payment for these *free* gifts.

Not that most people with this blindspot could not afford to pay out of pocket for these visits and meals, yet the idea that it's *free* is the hook. On the other hand, the positive aspect of this blindspot is the pleasure that is received from manifesting something for nothing.

Makeup artists are always giving me their stuff. My favorite thing is free stuff. I'll take anything. —Cindy Margolis

People having this obstruction are not necessarily poor or without a job; it's a Tramp in their attitude to life. The reluctance to work or to make an effort is one of the clues to spot this blindspot. This is the person who loves to have a *free* place to stay, borrows your clothing when they arrive because they *forgot* to bring something and you have it, who most always lets you pay at the restaurant, at times avoids work, who goes to the lectures when there's a *free* meal, who loves to travel but only if they can stay in someone's house for *free*, and the samples in grocery stores are a highlight for going to a store; the key word is *free*. Receiving something for what they consider is nothing is the draw.

I don't care how much money you have, free stuff is always a good thing. —Queen Latifah

FREE AND EASY

People with a Tramp impediment usually have friends or family who will support this. People will pay for their meals, let them borrow their car, easily loan them some clothes, as well as making their home available and accessible to the person with the Tramp impediment. The strategy and fantasy of the person with this blindspot is often that if visiting a home where their friend has money and things are offered, they are really not taking anything since it has been offered. The belief that someone should satisfy your needs and pay for you, let you stay in their home becomes a way of life. This attitude towards life that a Tramp impediment carries is based on false values. One of their values regards the motive and theory of life. How to make everything easier is often the drive and impetus to proceed.

A man who lies to himself, and believes his own lies, becomes unable to recognize truth, either in himself or in anyone else, and he ends up losing respect for himself and for others. —Fyodor Dostoevsky

The Tramp stumbling block is quite difficult for the person who carries it to recognize. This is primarily because having enough money to pay there is the delusion that *why should I, if it's offered.* When pointed out, most often there will be defensiveness due to what has been their normal everyday behavior for years. The desire for ease at the expense of their growth and development is a hindrance. If it doesn't challenge you, it doesn't change you. To notice when it is influencing our style of living is a primary way to work at transforming it.

What is seductive about Tramp is unique to all the other impediments. Both the positive and the negative *something for nothing,* are the same. The delight in receiving a free buffet or using other peoples homes and belongings, or having someone pay for your airline ticket, are as enticing and pleasurable as well as that they are limiting and confining; as well as having Tramp be in control of your personality. Each of the blindspots are at the heart of every suffering, our addictions and dysfunctions. Tramp is a big obstacle to a person's development.

A person that values its privileges above its principles soon loses both. —Dwight D. Eisenhower

Examples are: many of the people lining up for free things, some coupon carriers, perennial guests who love staying for free, hotel guests who put towels, robes and hair dryers from the hotel in their suitcase before checking out.

Anyone who lives within their means suffers from a lack of imagination.
—*Oscar Wilde*

VANITY

POSITIVE: SELF, AESTHETIC SENSIBILITY

NEGATIVE: DECEPTION, SELF-INDULGENT, SELF-IMPORTANT

FEAR: NON-EXISTENCE

SHADOW: INVOLVED WITH EACH BLINDSPOT

Mr. Self-love and Madame Vanity are the two chief agents of the devil. Vanity is an unnatural, outward manifestation of yourself and leads to untrue inner and outer connections. —*G.I Gurdjieff*

Vanity seeks attention. Boredom is an expression of Vanity, thinking that the world should provide experiences, adventures, things to do. Once discovering that *I* am not the center of the universe, that life does not revolve around *me,* eventually boredom sets in and we look for dramas, stories, entertainment and other distractions. Vanity connects to all of the other obstructions, supporting whatever impediment we have chosen. For example, anger as a primary blindspot and Vanity secondary; identified with building a strong body we look like a prizefighter, strutting as we walk, a determined look, a firm stance. Power or dominance as primary along with Vanity creates a self-important egoist who swells with each *win* regardless to the demise or feelings of the so called *loser/other.* Stubbornness combined with Vanity is proud of digging in their heels: picture the juror that blocks the proceedings by withholding a decision, forcing extra hours of negotiations to make a point, regardless to the expense and time of all others involved, just proud to display firm staying power. A connector to all blindspots, most everyone has Vanity regarding the areas in which we are mechanically inclined, the ones we feel are important, the ones that appear as significant to us. The experience is: if our blindspot is dominance we feel vain about our ability to win and take charge, when it's arrogance we take on speaking up when slighted, insensitive to how we might impact people.

Ego has always been a paradox—it is the point from which you see, but it also makes you blind. —Bill Russell

Society and culture promote activities of Vanity such as fashion shows, the academy awards red carpet, competitive sports, Miss America pageants, exorbitant salaries for athletes, big parades for the winning sports team, television popularity/talent shows, performances, parties and celebrations. Pumped up and ostentatious, inflated, the obstruction of Vanity feeds off attention and comes alive, saying: *Other people notice and pay attention to me, therefore I must be real and important.* Vanity loves receiving attention, cares about others opinions, regardless to caring about that person. The doing of something is secondary to the special consideration that is received from the activity, even negative attention is something. And so the world is filled with particulars about entertainers as well as self-destructive acts and other personal details that people in the news create. Divorce, childhod sexual abuse, alcoholic all night partying; we want to pay attention to all the gory details, feeding the self-indulgence of the one parading their personal life on the headlines.

Vanity wants to be seen, likes having people notice and know what it does. Difficulties and issues become overgrown and significant, the bigger the problem, the more overplayed and important this obstruction inflates. Drama feeds off Vanity to engage others, to have circumstances to draw tension from and towards; to be center stage as hero, heroine, villain, troubled, overlooked person, alcoholic partygoer, school shooter, divorce, marital affair, dramatic suicide threats, the one who saves and helps people, clown, sex tapes, mass murderer, or any other starring role.

The culture devotes itself to the creation and maintenance of a strange and unprecedented 'self' almost entirely cut off from being and thus condemned to ceaseless doing and getting. For such a self, the quality of being alive is simply irrelevant. —George B. Leonard

SELF-INVOLVED NARCISSISM

Vanity, in psychological terms, is identified with narcissism, from Narcissus, who was among the most handsome of young men, his beauty compared to that of Adonis. One of the many nymphs who sought his love and was ignored made a prayer: *So may he love himself, and not gain the thing he loves.* And so Narcissus having come to a pool to quench his thirst saw his reflection mirrored in its smooth surface and fell in love with his own self-image, not able to obtain the object of his love he ultimately died of sorrow at the very same pool. For Narcissus, all things were centered around his own image. Unable to consummate his self-love, Narcissus pined away changing into the flower that bears his name.

There is no limit to the vanity of this world, each spoke thinks the whole strength of the wheel depends upon it. —H.W. Shaw

We all have a degree of Vanity. Self indulgent, self-important, attracting attention, wanting to be noticed and admired, inviting people to know the specifics of what we do, in fact, going on at length about the details of our life to anyone who will listen; that requires vain self-importance, as if our daily doings are so very important that we fill the ears and airwaves with the blow-by-blow details of what's on our mind.

The knowledge of yourself will preserve you from vanity. —*Miguel de Cervantes*

Vanity offers little appreciation to itself, regardless to the praise and attention it receives. Performance, there's never enough, looking for energy that is outside ourself we feel an edge of dissatisfaction. In narcissism our sense of self-worth and self-esteem fluctuates between over-valuation/idealization, called Vanity, and devaluation/self-deprecation of self and others, named upside-down Vanity. This manifests as not being sure we exist or are worth anything. It takes great Vanity and self-involvement to imagine to be so important as to be less valuable than others. In its dualistic nature, Vanity sees itself as being either complimented or criticized. Upside-down Vanity, sensitive to the judgments and opinions of others, professes to be worse off and is apologetic for not being better. Recognition and approval need to be immediate. The chosen job, partner, spiritual path are comparatively imagined to be better or worse than other people's. Life is a movement between polarities looking to be opposite, yet they are complementaries also, the highs don't exist without the lows, the valley needs the mountain, no reason to choose, being choiceless the play of polarities appears. The valley and the peak, allowing for both, the synthesis is natural and releases Vanity from its hindrance, its difficulties, to be free to be in the moment, through the imaginary wall, and then to proceed onward.

The fundamental cause of almost all the misunderstandings arising in the inner world of man, as well as in the process of the communal life of people, is chiefly that psychic factor which is found in man's being during the period of preparatory age exclusively on account of a wrong education, and in the period of responsible age—each stimulation of which gives birth in him to the impulses of Vanity and Self-Conceit. —C.S. Nott

Ben Franklin, conversing about his Vanity obstruction said that *humility was the most difficult thing for him*, when successful he would feel puffed up, rarely humbled by his achievements. Vanity is proud of its humility. To finally be tired of ourselves and the intrigue, self-deception and illusion, this begins the journey of noticing and separating from Vanity. Letting go of our self-identity, which includes ideas about who we are, our expectations and aspirations, eventually diminishes our sense of self-importance. Being more, saying less, having a teacher, a friend offering reflections on our journey, assists us to become familiar with our resistance, releasing our habits, learning to live deliberately.

Go on a journey from self to Self, my friend. Such a journey transforms the earth into a mine of gold. —Rumi

MOST POPULAR BLINDSPOT

Vanity fills us with self-importance, pride, swagger, envy, conceit, unnecessary pieces of baggage that demand our energy and keep us busily engaged. Self-importance, short-sighted, focuses attention on our own identity, not on the bigger picture. Projecting from self keeps the world distanced. This ego-involvement blocks growth and depth, is a barrier to intimacy, stands in the way of coming to face the truth of our self, and impedes awakening. Self-involvement, irritating to some, especially when most conversations return to self-referential associations about ourself, attention continuing to revolve around the little self, about personal adventures, achievements, failures, stories, often tales concerning anecdote and narrative about friends or children. It's still our voice being listened to, telling our story about another, endlessly assuming the listener must be interested. No real question about who is at the other end listening; this Vanity manifests as self-absorption and fascination, the most popular blindspot in America.

We have many independent enemies, but the chief and most active are vanity and self-love. One teaching even calls them representatives and messengers of the devil himself. For some reason they are also called Mrs. Vanity and Mr. Self-Love. We have to deal with our enemies indirectly in order to free ourselves from several at once. These representatives of the devil stand unceasingly at the threshold that separates us from the outside, and prevent not only good but also bad influences from entering. Thus they have a good side as well as a bad side. If a man wishes all influences to enter—for it is impossible to select only the good ones—he must liberate himself from these watchmen. I would advise you to try freeing yourselves and to do so without unnecessary theorizing, by simple reasoning, active reasoning, with yourselves. —G.I Gurdjieff

Ecclesiastes, an accounting for life as illusion, states: *Vanity of vanities, all is vanity.* Here, the meaning of Vanity is everything in this physical world described as transitory and impermanent. We have a choice to chase after the ephemeral in this fleeting world or we can choose the eternal life of awakening unbounded love. Both require energy. To pursue all things under the sun, *that which soon vanishes away* is ultimately meaningless, all worldly possession amount to nothing; power, prestige, pleasure, popularity do not fill the void in our life. Trying to find amusement in idle pointless adventures, in entertaining others with our chatter, mindless self-deception that fuels each obstruction distracts us to live in an imaginary world.

Vanity melts away when life is viewed as a daily gift; all earthly goals and ambitions when pursued as ends in themselves lead to dissatisfaction and frustration. Fulfillment and satisfaction in life is found looking into our interior life, not out; then our separate self continues to dissolve. Choosing and embracing our purpose on this earth brings a peace that eludes us when we focus on earthly things. Ecclesiastes speaks directly to Vanity. *Vanity of vanities,* saith Koheleth; *Vanity of vanities, all is vanity.* An essential theme in this great work, because we identify with Vanity, when it begins to disappear we think we are disappearing. It is a rock that stands in the way of the flow of life. Vanity creates a separation from existence, that separation cultivates suffering separating us from our own nourishing sources. Vanity stands in the way of loving, communicating, relating; it obstructs. Concealed, yet through higher awareness, the choices we make, the way we relate to the world, these all release us into the light of our being.

How can I salute the Self, which is indestructible, which is all Bliss, which in Itself and by Itself pervades everything, and which is inseparable from Itself? I alone am, ever free from all taint. The world exists like a mirage within me. To whom shall I bow? Verily the one Self is all, free from differentiation and non-differentiation. Neither can it be said, 'It is' nor 'It is not.' What a great mystery. —*Mahatma Dattatreya*

The obstruction, Vanity, may be primary, often it is secondary. Regardless, it is a characteristic that remains throughout the journey right up to the door of awakening, serving as a reminder that we are part of this world of imperfect ordinary beings. The positive becomes a paradox. To realize who you are is to realize that you are not. To *be yourself is to be,* know the truth of things as they are, live without endless self-concepts or *I-thoughts*; instead, with fresh immediate direct knowing of self. This authentic knowing comes from our true nature, breaks habits, and elevates Vanity. Once free of who we imagine ourselves to be, the more we open to recognize our bond with everyone. This sensibility used intentionally increases self-awareness, uplifts a difficult space, is peaceful, makes beauty a priority in this world. The rock bottom Vanity is an attribute of the human condition. 37% of the population choose Vanity as their primary or secondary blindspot.

How much ego do you need? Just enough so that you don't step in front of a bus. —*Shunryu Suzuki*

Everything you have done genuinely remains for you and will help you at difficult moments, and everything you have done from vanity is lost to you. —*M. Nicoll*

Examples are: *Lindsay Lohan, Jessica Simpson, Mariah Carey, Kate Hudson, Adam Levine, Kim Kardashian, Katy Perry, Justin Bieber, Janet Jackson, Blake Shelton, Ryan Seacrest, Paris Hilton, Carmen Electra, P. Diddy, Mike Tyson, Britney Spears, Robin Thicke, Maksim Chmerkovskiy, Muhammad Ali, Mick Jagger, Rihanna, Jennifer Lopez, Victoria Beckham, Little Richard, Liza Minelli, Cameron Diaz, Simon Cowell, Paula Abdul,* the peacock.

SYSTEM NINETEEN

MAGNETIC CENTER

Everything is laid out for you. Your path is straight ahead of you. Sometimes it's invisible, but it's there. You may not know where it's going but you have to follow that path. —*Chief Leon Shenandoah*

Our attraction to conscious teachings comes from our Magnetic Center or inner organ of perception as it registers influences that carry traces of awakened energy that are mixed in with life influences which we detect and gather. It is the seat of recognition and perception of influences that lead to and guide esoteric development. It leads us, absorbing influences that direct us towards conscious work and towards an objective understanding of reality. Forming a stable Magnetic Center is an essential stage in our preparation towards awakening. Throughout our lifetime we accumulate internal energy from experiences, sometimes having momentary glimpses of a higher world, and if not resisted we magnetize a life that guides us towards a path that ultimately leads to a Way.

Our Magnetic Center is a rather crude instrument capable of registering the presence of a huge collection of influences ranging from Gregorian church music to the writings of the Bhagavad Gita, from Meister Eckhart to the Pentecostal church, from psychedelics to sacred prose, political cartoons to Rembrandt masterpieces, from the Course in Miracles to a 12-step program, from Sufi practices of Remembrance to Gurdjieff movements and the Enneagram. The spiritual dimension has been named a tower of Babel and it's our work to decipher what originated from energies that originally had consciousness and then became watered down to mix in with life influences.

It is not difficult for us to distinguish influences created in life from influences whose source lies outside life. The beginning of the way depends precisely on this understanding or upon the capacity for discriminating between the two kinds of influences. If a person in receiving these influences begins to discriminate between them and put on one side those which are not created by life itself, then gradually discrimination becomes easier and after a certain time a man can no longer confuse them with the ordinary influences of life. After a certain time they form within him a magnetic center. When the magnetic center attains a certain force and development, a person already understands the idea of the way and he begins to look for the way. They may meet another person who knows the way and who is connected directly or through other people with a center existing outside the law of accident. Influences of the third kind can proceed only from one person to another, directly, by means of oral transmission. —*P.D. Ouspensky*

Our Magnetic Center pulls us towards growth easing us away from temptations that keep us in a mechanical deadened consciousness. Connecting us beyond the realm of ordinary life our magnetism persuades us to seek answers to ageless questions. A rather coarse instrument, in the early stages registering traces of conscious influences we could be uplifted, yet sometimes take missteps and are misled towards diluted, minimized versions of teachings. Magnetic Center is a group of interests which, when they become sufficiently strong serve as a guiding element assisting our understanding and evaluation drawing us to our teachers and teachings; without it ideas of awakening and conscious teachers/teachings hold little appeal. It is that part of the human psychological makeup which is attracted to higher possibilities.

The influences whose source lie outside life collect together within us. After a certain time they form within us a kind of magnetic center, which begins to attract to itself kindred influences and in this manner it grows. If the magnetic center receives sufficient nourishment, and if there is no strong resistance on the part of the other sides of our personality which are the result

of influences created in life, the magnetic center begins to influence our orientation, obliging us to turn round and even to move in a certain direction.
— *P.D. Ouspensky*

Waking up in this lifetime is directly effected by our Magnetic Center, which works like a huge magnet, a sensing instrument, a Geiger counter detecting as we become aware of the levels in the things around us, developing sensitivity, while attracting us to forces that stimulate awakening. Pointing us to move in a direction that knows that there is something else, another kind of life that is not explained in terms of life itself. Our Magnetic Center draws us away from mundane life to resonate with generations of conscious teachings. The strength of its magnetism is built over time with an accumulation of memories collected through our youth. These extraordinary moments grow until one day they spark discontent; a need and desire to develop ourself. This brings us to turn away from conventional society and towards teachings that hook us up with others having a similar vision, as well as someone who serves in some form as a teacher or guide.

Magnetic center is in personality, it is simply a group of interests which, when they become sufficiently strong, serve to a certain degree, as a guiding and controlling factor. —*P.D. Ouspensky*

The Magnetic Center recognizes the traces of an intelligence higher than that of ordinary humans, a level of consciousness beyond that which most people experience. As we search for a deeper meaning to life we are also given invitations, glimpses, signals and reminders that pull us along. Museums, concert halls, libraries, cathedrals and bookstores hold hints of creative works fashioned from moments of great consciousness. The responsibility is to our own judgment, discrimination and common sense to know the false from the true.

It seems to me more and more as though our ordinary consciousness inhabited the apex of a pyramid whose base in us (and, as it were, beneath us) broadens out to such an extent that the farther we are able to let ourselves down into it, the more completely do we appear to be included in the realities of earthly and, in the wildest sense, 'worldly' existence, which are not dependent on time and space. From my earliest youth I have felt the intuition that at some deeper cross-section of this pyramid of consciousness, mere 'being' could become an event, the inviolable presence and simultaneity of everything that we, on the upper, 'normal,' apex of self-consciousness, are permitted to experience only as entropy. —Ranier Maria Rilke

We are magnetically attracted to a path that contains teachings to encourage our true self to emerge. This is created through our frame of mind, by how highly we regard our inner work, along with our willingness to dive deeply, to disengage from frivolous diversions and entertaining distractions. Magnetic Center, developed in our personality, serves as a bridge between false personality and true personality. It grows and improves as we learn to discriminate between the quality of what's out there, eventually separating what is coarse and tasteless to what is refined. Too much running after *new age* fads, workshopping, dappling in cults and life distractions, dramas, unnecessary suffering, traveling adventures, ambition, greed, slowly dulls and erodes the force and power of our Magnetic Center.

If we stand tall it is because we stand on the backs of those who came before us. —Yoruba Saying

Learning to recognize, to distinguish between the imaginary and the real, we use verification, a way to demonstrate to ourself that something is true or not true. Verification opens us to a direct relationship with awakening. The work of the Magnetic Center as it develops and is fine tuned is like owning a thoroughbred horse, and rather than using it for pony rides and letting it wander with any other horse, we choose to train and enhance its skills.

The living self has one purpose only: to come into its own fullness of being, as a tree comes into full blossom, or a bird into spring beauty, or a tiger into luster. —D.H. Lawrence

Attractions radiate and register, and we encounter traces of consciousness, sometimes not knowing what we have touched, nor how to use it, and so become reduced to the common denominator of what's around us, or what it is we think we want in our life. Much of what stimulates our Magnetic Center comes from conscious sources that have been permeated and diminished over time by life influences in this external world, and so, while we need a Center to attract and inspire, it may not get us to any end point.

The spiritual world, a tower of Babel, is filled with writings and teachers that misdirect and mislead. Confusing, with a potpourri of classes and work-shops and books and manuals, sending us messages claiming to be the right or only way, the path is strewn with entertainment, adventures and distractions. Originating from energies that carry traces of truth, the corruption within these sources brings us through a maze until we sift to find the gold nuggets. Often trivialized, ritualistic, lacking the original substance, what originated as *something* becomes relegated to a past time; to be a yogi is much more than to have a preference for taking yoga classes or reading books about yoga. Learning to ask a real question, making blind faith sighted, relinquishing beliefs and personal opinions for universal truth, setting the world aside to produce the birth of consciousness in ourself: what a destination this treasure chest locked away in our heart.

Life did not begin at my birth. Others have been here before me, and I walk in their footsteps. The books I have read were composed by generations of fathers and sons, mothers and daughters, teachers and disciples. I am the sum total of their experiences, and so are you. —Elie Wiesel

Our Magnetic Center directs us to a path, yet is not what brings us up and down the mountain. It draws and points us in a direction, yet is not enough to get us to where we might like to arrive. It points to a mystery, something inexplicable, magical; we need to develop discrimination, self-discipline, desire, understanding, a teacher and a teaching, integrity, attention, study, vulnerability, real listening, patience, dedication and perseverance; the responsibility lies within ourselves along with a grace note. The strength of purpose of the longing in the heart needs the power to push beyond momentary situations; enticements that appear to satisfy. They appear in many forms: recreational drugs, sex, alcohol, glamour, ambition, self-importance, traveling, money; the numerous temptations and pauses along the road. Anything can be a practice, available to be used. Life offers everything. It comes down to what do we *want?*

Esoteric information often hidden, restricted, held secret with difficult methods to understand; for those who are drawn have to both recognize and want *something* through all the mystification. Distractions in life are a great hazard to gathering information. Trusting that there is something beyond the life that we know, and wanting to be part of that something brings us to seek reality, not the illusion of reality. The obstacle that blocks transformation is understanding. Deep understanding is of total being: the intellect, the heart, the guts. Truth, once understood brings freedom.

If I live in forgetfulness, I am, as Albert Camus says in his novel, The Stranger, living 'like a dead person.' Zen masters used to say, 'If we live in forgetfulness, we die in a dream.' How many among us live like a dead person!' The first thing we have to do is to return to life, to wake up and be mindful of each thing we do. Are we aware when we are eating, drinking, in conversation, walking? Or are we wasting our time, living in forgetfulness?
—*Philip Kapleau*

Magnetic Center and the glimpses it offers is essential to directing the experiences that inspire us to embark on a journey of spiritual deepening. The momentary initiations, those indications of another world, accompany us, remain as a reserve to be called upon, often tastes that show up in ordinary conditions. Our recognition is critical, *the secret protects itself,* this unseen sphere lies beyond reason. In this way the Magnetic Center serves to permeate, infuse, saturate us with energy and a longing to participate in the journey to awakening. The dissatisfaction with ordinary life is not enough, what is needed is an unwavering singleness of purpose that sets the Magnetic Center into a permanent spinning, radiating and registering truth in our heart until we know our way to esoteric conscious sources.

The seed of magnetic center is a small part of one, perhaps even from birth, that somehow 'instinctively' knows that there must be something behind life—beyond the pursuits of health, making a living, having a family, acquiring friends, etc. This 'seed' causes one to digest one's experiences accordingly. —*G.I. Gurdjiff, P.D. Ouspensky*

It is necessary to free the mind from acquired attitudes, for they prevent a person from thinking for himself. And unless you begin to think for yourself about your inner work you will never understand it, and receive no help; only through your understanding will you receive the force of enegry. for that reason understanding is the strongest force you can create. —*Maurice Nicoll*

SYSTEM TWENTY

CENTERS OF GRAVITY

LOWER: INSTINCTIVE,

MOVING, INTELLECTUAL,

EMOTIONAL, SEX, SELF-STUDY

HIGHER: INSTINCTIVE, MOVING,

EMOTIONAL, INTELLECTUAL, SEX,

SELF-STUDY

Human beings have a cosmic origin and that origin descends into our functioning. Our centers receive the energy that needs to be transmitted through them. Through the centers, we can receive this energy. If we could look at the stars and forgo our usual self-centered perspective of seeing them as separate from us, and instead see ourselves as an integral part of the whole structure, we would be more able to understand the purpose of our centers and of ourselves. —Dr. Michel Conge

We receive stimulus through one of twelve centers. While the magnetic center is in our personality, these twelve centers are located in our essence. The Centers of Gravity are: intellectual, moving, instinctive, emotional, sex, self-study, higher instinctive, higher moving, higher emotional, higher sex, higher intellectual, and higher self-study center. The independently formed centers are located in the brain, spinal column, solar plexus and genitals. The first five centers are of equal value, none better than the other, only different, the sixth, self-study center has unique characteristics; the six higher centers, fully developed and functioning are as inaccessible as we are, because of the disharmony of the lower centers which are always competing for space. Each of us has one predominant center. Balancing and developing our centers creates harmony in our life. Only through verification and self awareness do we control our centers to come to balance. Essentially, most of civilization is involved with the instinctive, moving and sex centers, which are considered the body of the planet, about five percent engage the emotional center, which is considered culture or worldliness, and two percent with *why*, or the intellectual, which is the mind and understanding.

We are dissatisfied because we do not know how to integrate our conflicting desires. To do so, we have to 'learn' to operate the complicated machine our human body-mind is. When the mind, heart and body are in complete harmony, we can flower to our fullest potential, manifest 'objective consciousness' and our functions of the intellect and emotion will be harmonised into wisdom. —*Evangelos Grammenos*

Conscious work, working on ourself, begins with the creation of one particular permanent Center Of Gravity called, self-study, or, being number four. From this place we first enter a Way and become responsible to our magnetic center (System 19) which births our desire to awaken. A rung on a cosmic ladder, this is transitional man, now conscious that he wants to change, a critical point in our evolution. Most people are unaware and untroubled by their unproductive state, they are seduced by life. Only through becoming aware of the illusory nature of self can we hope to move up on the ladder. We have within us the ability to not follow our habituated conditioning and to develop a self-study center that becomes a doorway to a continuously deepening discovery of who we are. For the majority of people, the six lower centers operate inefficiently and disharmoniously, blocking access to the six higher centers.

OUR PREDOMINANT CENTER

The predominant development of any one center at the expense of the others produces an extremely one-sided type of man, incapable of further development. The principal centers are connected together and, in a normal man, they are always working together. —P.D. Ouspensky

One center right from birth is more central, more primary than the others and is named our Center of Gravity. This becomes fairly apparent as we continue to observe ourself. In times of stress we turn to whatever activity our predominant center prefers. Whether it is taking a walk, reading a book, looking at pornography on the internet, snacking on ice cream and cookies, gardening, studying a map, going to the gym, traveling, calling a friend, or chopping vegetables; these are the moments when our chief center becomes noticeably apparent. Our attractions, inclinations and interests, how we perceive reality, are visible reflections of our Center of Gravity. The first step is to verify the existence of centers, since few of us ever imagined to be other than a one-brained person, of having more than one center or multiple brains. First notice that most people have a predominant response or impulse, a primary way they mechanically enjoy being in life. Next step is to notice our levels of attention; this happens as we create exercises to do things in a new and different way, to break habits, mindfully, since what we notice could eventually become another habit.

As a rule, at every moment of our life, only one centre works in us—either mind or feeling. Our feeling is of one kind when another centre is not looking on, when the ability to criticise is absent. By itself a centre has no consciousness, no memory: it is a chunk of a particular kind of meat without salt, an organ, a certain combination of substances which merely possesses a special capacity of recording—a recording tape. It is completely mechanical. Our mind has no critical faculty in itself, no consciousness, nothing, and all the other centres are the same. What then is our consciousness, our memory, our critical faculty? Its very simple. It's when one centre specially watches another, when it sees and feels what is going on there and, seeing it, records it all within itself. We very seldom watch one centre from another, only sometimes, perhaps one minute a day. —G.I. Gurdjieff

The Centers of Gravity are a control station, like an instrument panel board. Our primary center is the traffic controller that directs our responses to the appropriate place. A person's particular center is an aspect of self that leads, has the initial response to stimuli. The more balanced we become the more all the centers become available, since through our main center we access other centers. The intention is to achieve balance and to maintain our connection to the spiritual being we truly are which manifests through our higher centers. Balancing the centers does not mean the primary center is no longer dominant. Greater flexibility is available along with the ability to choose the appropriate part of centering for any given situation, rather than proceeding from the impulse of one part which usually overloads the circuit board; then later in life we blow a fuse in our overloaded center.

The wrong functioning and interferences of the centers, which are habitual, represent such a waste of energy and loss of quality that for most people a whole preliminary work of putting in order is generally necessary before real work on oneself can begin. —Jean Vaysse

MISWIRING

Each center, or mind, has its own function, knows in its own way. We may know something through a movement—the moving center—that we won't know through a thought—the intellectual center. All of the centers have a separate brain and need to learn to perform their functions with the exception of the instinctive center which has inborn skills. The speed of each center varies; of the first five, the intellectual is the slowest, then the instinctive and moving are faster, and the emotional and sex center have the fastest energy source and are the most volatile. Each center is 30,000 faster than the one preceding. Since we could not exist for one second not taking in impressions it is incredible to imagine the quality of impressions that are received in the fastest centers, our lower centers barely find words to describe them. The sex center moves the most quickly, in fact, 150,000 times faster than the intellectual center. This is helpful in understanding how difficult it is to stop the sex center with the mind, or to *catch* or control the ego of someone who is coming from the sex center. If we were to balance the sex center the other four centers could be controlled. Due to the speed of the centers, it is practical to begin self-study with the slowest center, our intellectual center, ultimately working towards the faster centers. Psychic energy, which is unlimited, is the energy our centers draw upon.

One of the greatest values in understanding this system appears when we come to know that most people are wired incorrectly, like an electric panel that is miswired, causing circuit breaks, blowouts, misfiring and inefficient wasted energy. Studying the Centers of Gravity, learning to rewire, to create circuit breakers and experience the charge and efficiency of good energy flow, accelerates growth. We are looking to free each center from doing things that they are not equipped to do naturally, and then to bring each center back to its own work, the work it is equipped/built to do. The chaos of our individual daily life comes from the fact that these parts or *brains* are not working in sync.

We are like different people living in one organism. In our ordinary state the components of thinking, feeling, and moving are not in communication and only act on each other mechanically, being 'outside' each other. This is inevitably what the study of our centres leads us to see, but it does not come easily. For the greater part of our lives, 'we' are living in only one centre. Our center of gravity moves from thinking to feeling to moving from moment to moment, and we are nearly always identified with the function 'we' happen to be in. But we can make use, when it happens, of the observation by one 'brain' of another, to learn that there are such things as 'brains' associated with the feeling and moving functions as well as with the thinking (where we tend to take it for granted). —J.G. Bennett

THREE LEVELS OF ATTENTION

The lower centers, except for the sex center, are vertically divided into positive and negative halves. From the lower centers we experience ourselves as duality, as pairs of opposites. Our feelings, sensations, thoughts and impressions live in a paradox of polarities: good and bad, beneficial and harmful, important and unimportant, pleasant and unpleasant, pleasure and pain, yes and no, like and dislike; it's from this place that our centers begin. Each center has three horizontal levels of attention, is divided into three parts, which are the levels of attention. The three parts are: mechanical, emotional, and intellectual. First is the mechanical which is steady and stable and requires no attention, no awareness. The mechanical part, working with distracted attention requires little effort, it is on autopilot, and the memory of the center operates there. Most of the global population, over 60%, is centered in the mechanical part: when people are imitative, predictable, repetitive, they are in their mechanical first level. Original or creative thoughts and actions don't originate in the mechanical part, instead, it's the storehouse of the average in people.

The disadvantage of studying these ideas by oneself is that one becomes

accustomed to taking the point of view of one's type, as the only expression of esotericism. In a well-selected group it is exactly the variety of types and the necessity of including and reconciling all their particular points of view that opens the way to new horizons. Little by little one learns that in esotericism apparent contradictions are not of necessity mutually exclusive.
—*Rodney Collin*

The second level, the emotional part, has less stability, more enthusiasm, attention is pulled by an external or internal stimulus and held to a particular kind of object. Attracted by the subject itself, requiring little effort, attention, called identification, generates eagerness and enthusiasm. Not particularly interested in disciplined practice there is a tendency to become involved and to then lose interest in most things that started out as a strong attraction. Projects left unfinished, many books only partially read, and still, people respond to the energy generated by this type, since the gusto and spirited energy for whatever does interest them is contagious. The emotional part represents our greatest need for other people, for spontaneity, excitement and drama. Whatever is in focus becomes more juicy when people are located at the second level of their center. Home life, clubs, birthday parties, theater, sporting events, emotional adventures, social gatherings; it's feelings that count. Holidays and relationships predominate through this center; our sentimental attachments to romance, dating, gifts, greeting cards, family history and connections, flowers and chocolates, advertisements and shocking photos that pull on our heart; the emotional center is a powerful energy. When we are located in this second part of our center we are more easily pulled, less able to root and ground, there is a tendency to get absorbed in the object, as if it were all there is in life.

Feelings, emotions and passions are good servants but poor masters.
—*Khemetic saying*

The third level, which is intellectual, works with consciously directed attention, attention held by effort, or concentration, with the exception of the instinctive brain where the third level controls the energy for the whole person releasing energy as needed. The challenge of discovering new ideas, or trying to complete a mathematical problem, realizing an ultimate formula that nobody else has figured out; these are stimulating experiences for the intellectual level. In Western society we lean towards regarding logic and the intellect as our test of reality. Only recently are we gradually shifting towards valuing other centers, acknowledging the validity of ritual, myth and beauty as sources of truth beyond the dogmas of the scientific realm.

The third level, the least flashy, controls and directs attention, engages the two lower parts. More subtle to spot, least likely to be understood, real learning, thinking and loving happen here. The third level of all the centers work in unison, the lower two levels work separately and are not connected in any way. More inward, this is the threshold and doorway to higher centers, capable of discrimination, appreciation, and understanding. As a gateway to the higher centers, finding a way to access and strengthen this part of ourselves through balancing all the centers, brings a new mode of awareness.

We must look at the lens through which we see the world, as well as the world we see, and understand that the lens itself shapes how we interpret the world. —Stephen Covey

ATTENTION

It is through the twelve centers that we use the energy of attention, and this is the fuel and requirement for transformation and awakening. The effort in the direction of consciousness brings attention to the physical as well as the mental and emotional states. Each center has its own energy source, and processes with a different nutrient, stimulus or speed. The study of parts of centers helps us understand the way the parts move in us—or rather move us like parts of a well oiled machine, without our even being aware of the movement. For example, most of the time when we believe we are thinking meaningful thoughts, the thoughts are really thinking themselves, almost without our participation. They are riding through our minds on rhythms of association, passing through our awareness like ducks crossing a street, pedestrians walking through an intersection.

To pay attention, this is our endless and proper work. —Mary Oliver

Our inner work begins with the control of our attention. Through mindful attention we determine which center is active at any given moment. The possibility of harmonizing the centers then becomes greater. The aim is to have voluntary attention, to take the initiative, independent of mechanical reactions and outside stimulus. On a daily basis we struggle to maintain attention throughout the day. The inability to love is directly related to the inability to pay attention. Consideration, empathy and compassion follow the development and cultivation of our mindful ability to *give* our attention. Love is attentive.

There is no attention in people. You must aim to acquire this. Self observation is only possible after acquiring attention. Start on small things. Make the breaking of a small habit your aim. Ordinarily we have only one attention, directed on what we are doing. Our mind does not see our feelings, and vice versa. Without attention, manifestations vanish. Things should be noted in the memory, otherwise we forget. And what we want is not to forget. —G.I. Gurdjieff

States Of Consciousness

We have the possibility to know four states of consciousness. The first is sleep with dreams. The second is so-called waking state, where we get up and do the day, considered to be a state of hypnosis, mechanical in all that we contact, automatic and reactive, we are open to endless suggestions from family, education and media. The third is a mindful state of self-remembering, self-awareness, where we are awake to ourself and see ourself as we are. The fourth is objective consciousness, where we see the reality behind the way the world appears. Only third and fourth states can communicate with the higher centers, and from these come positive emotions. At times we may have momentary flashes of third and fourth states, not fully understandable as they appear and leave, as they rise and fall.

Each time we make an effort to bring our attention back to ourselves, to what we are doing, to remember ourselves, the centres become connected.
—*C.S. Nott*

The knowledge of centers and the workings of attention offer us the keys to create a life that we want, our work towards presence. This description, Centers Of Gravity, is information to be verified as we observe ourself and others. Our whole beings are controlled by our centers and since the intellectual center is the only one somewhat under our control, it is the one used for verification. Once we train the emotional center (for example, to not be negative) we can also use that center for self study. Our results will go hand-in-hand with our expectations. To watch and study the centers, to know their speed and function; to recognize each is crucial on our journey to know ourself. To study these functions in ourself and in others allows us to see mechanicality as well as our process of development. This is a powerful tool for studying the self!

To awake to myself, to what I am, would mean to find the center of gravity and source of my energies, the root of my being. To be able to bring higher energy in contact with the earth, we must have a harmonious relationship—a right exchange—among our centers. Everything is in movement. The energies of our centers are in movement too, but not in harmony with each other. —Madame de Salzmann

INSTINCTIVE CENTER

POSITIVE: PLEASURE, HEALTH, COMFORT

NEGATIVE: PAIN, DISEASE, MECHANICAL

Fully developed at birth, the instinctive center attends to the inner work of the organism and is itself the representation of our nature. The cleverness of this center is beyond all computation, it is 10,000 better a chemist than any actual chemist or physiologist. The instinctive center is extraordinarily clever. It attends to the inner working of the organism in all its million and one details. —Maurice Nicoll

The spinal cord is the *brain* of this center. The Instinctive or gut Center includes the senses, simple and complex reflexes and the regenerative processes of the body that work without awareness at the cellular/biochemical level. Comprised of the entire body it houses all the other centers. The Instinctive Center is divided into vertical positive and negative halves, experienced as pleasure and pain. In the positive mode we receive gratification, in the negative we get a warning that there is danger. This vertical division represents our capacity for discrimination. The levels of attention are the three horizontal divisions. The function of the Instinctive Center is control of the inner life of the organism. The body is involved with the immediate present, having the ability to internally regulate itself, coordinating innumerable functions, influenced by the will of the Instinctive Center in its impulse to live. Maintaining life is the primary business of this center, and it is relentless in its performance, ignoring the fact that it will ultimately fail.

Impulsive behavior from the instinctive center is motivated from within by a 'program' that is inborn, inherent. Compulsive behavior is motivated from without by a 'program' acquired since birth, called false personality.
—*P. Wittmeyer*

This neutral center of gravity includes: breathing, beating of the heart, digestion, respiration, healing wounds, looking after our bodies temperature, circulation of the blood and the external automatic functions of the reflexes. Unique, it is already highly developed before and at birth, having control over most of our life, in fact, it keeps us alive. Key words for its functioning are *sense* and *sensing*.

The instinctive processes of the body are ready to function at birth. Some of them, such as growth and the circulation of the blood, are at work even long before we are born. First, we have to become aware of the senseless habits that we have. Second, we have to explore the potentials of our bodies and become familiar with how they work. No work of transformation is possible without knowledge of our own body. Third, we have to accustom the body to entirely new usages, and for this purpose the ability to concentrate the sensitive energy on the form of sensation is indispensable. —J.G. Bennett

The Instinctive Center knows the work for each organ and keeps them going properly, shaping our behavior in ways we are barely aware of, regardless to even being overseen. Our breathing demonstrates this urge to survive. We can continue breathing without mind or feelings. Medical reports speak of individuals in a coma, in a prolonged state of deep unconsciousness, all organs still working. Instinctive functions are inborn, forming an entire inner world. Although medical science has gathered information about this center very little is known in comparison to what is unknown. Our fear at being helpless in the event the

Instinctive Center breaks down has invested doctors with great status and higher salaries than most other workers. This wall of protection hides our fears and perpetuates the mythology and mystique around the authority of medical science.

In general, all sicknesses are the outcome of the wrong use of the brains (the centers). —*Samuel Aun Weor*

OUR SENSES

The Instinctive Center is organized around activities of the senses, intuition, the growth of the body, the distribution of energy within the body and telepathy. This can be likened to animal behavior; often Instinctive Centered people will sense, smell and be aware of an experience before it happens. A representation of our animal-like parts, it grasps impressions without translating them. To see, hear, smell, taste are all Instinctive responses that are impulsive and/or developed. The Instinctive Center does not like to be observed, like an animal it feels safer when concealed and uncomfortable when it knows it's being watched. As a population we are trained not to stare, yet feel drawn to look at aberrations of nature often referred to as *the disabled*. Usually it is a reflection of our deep concerns and fears regarding what could happen to our own body.

The culture devotes itself to the creation and maintenance of a strange and unprecedented 'self' almost entirely cut off from being and thus condemned to ceaseless doing and getting. For such a self, the quality of being alive is simply irrelevant. —*George B. Leonard*

When we travel this is the center most often effected; bug bites, sunburn, humidity, sudden storms in warm climates, cold and discomfort in cold weather, sore muscles from long airplane rides, stomach cramps from unfamiliar food and water, tired as the time zones shift and our sleep habits are disturbed, changes in our bowel habits from disruption of routine, sore feet from walking. The moving center eager to get on the road often overlooks the friction that the Instinctive Center will sustain. Caretakers and prisoners of war will betray their personal values and principles, worn down under the pressure of deprivation.

A lifestyle that chooses healthy food, clean air, emotional ease, meditation and daily exercise assists better functioning of this center. The Instinctive Center becomes corrupt when other centers are functioning improperly. For example, held back emotions, stress and obsessive thinking, physical pain that tips us into negativity, are documented to create disease and corrupt the body on a cellular level. Illness is known to direct energy away from other centers and then to drain the immune system. Chronically ill people often become ornery, impatient, short-tempered and unpleasant, losing interest in most aspects of life focusing on their bodily needs, reduced to an animal's struggle to survive. To remain undistracted when the body is challenged requires a quality of presence that provides vigilant attention.

Ask the body to cooperate. Don't eat, or eat less. The body won't listen to ideas, but it will listen to direct commands like this. The body is very important, but it must obey. —Madame de Salzmann

The Instinctive Center takes great pleasure in the sensory experience of food, sex, massage, music, exercise, incense, water, candles, drugs; things that gratify the senses through touch, sight, smell, sound and taste. Words are poor substitutes for real experience. The capacity for sense-pleasure is high. The Instinctive Center governs our pheromones—smells perceived on a subconscious level that determine our Instinctive reaction to others. Entering a room this becomes apparent on the Instinctive level, such as being attracted to someone beyond explanation, or being repelled, feeling danger or vaguely uncomfortable, often for no specific reason, liking or disliking certain odors; the five senses come through the Instinctive Center, data is received automatically. Looking out at the world as an Instinctive Centered person, focused on sensation and how sensation defines reality, our hearing and awareness of potential danger is oftentimes sensitively sharp.

Work that comes naturally to an Instinctive Centered person revolves around gardening, animal training, cooking, a hiking guide, baby sitting, the healing arts, massage, sports and other athleticism, acupuncture, yoga, homeopathy, dog trainer, surfing, dance, playing with small children, being a wilderness guide or forest ranger. Instinctively Centered people are carefully guarded about strong emotional experiences. Influenced by tastes and smell, memories are easily brought forward that have strongly effected the palate or have carried memorable scents. Food and sleep restrictions, challenging weather conditions; unless one has developed their Instinctive Center these are a real problem. This center wants to touch or smell either people or things. Uplifting the center engages experiences of body control, fasting, celibacy, spiritually oriented physical exercises, hands on healing, efforts to save our living planet. Responses are sensed on a gut level.

The various instinctive processes of the body, such as the circulation of the blood, respiration, digestion, and so on, enter into our activity and shape our behavior in a way we are not ordinarily even aware of. The instinctive processes go by themselves and are organized by themselves apart from the rest of us. —J.G. Bennett

The Western world and our educational system has misunderstood and been of great disservice to Instinctive Centered people generating tremendous self-judgment and defensiveness around this center of gravity. Generally less able to express their thoughts or communicate with the ease and facility of people with other centers, often to compensate for their differences they become *as if* personalities. Strongly imagining that they know, backing up their positions with platitudes and random information, they may appear well adjusted but in many circumstances they betray their lack of emotional and intellectual depth. When the thinking center is undeveloped a lack of awareness keeps them caught in this realm, genuine inner experiences are impoverished and life becomes a performance. The idea of who they think they are, repeated often enough, eventually becomes their *truth*. On the other hand, Instinctive Centered people who are comfortable in their own skin, without the urge to intellectually compete and compare, choosing a vocation that is more body-oriented, i.e. a yoga teacher, chef, dancer, golfer, dog walker, baby sitter, swimmer, is closer to being more accurate about who they are and becomes truthful about their inability to verbally express concepts and ideas.

Instinctive applies only to the inner functions of the organism: beating of the heart, breathing, circulation of the blood, digestion—these are instinctive functions. The difference between instinctive and moving functions is: the moving functions of a person, as well as of animals, of a bird, of a dog, must be learned; but instinctive functions are inborn. —P.D. Ouspensky

THE POWER OF OUR INSTINCTIVE CENTER

Divided into three main sections, depending on the attention required and how the attention is directed, the Instinctive Center has control over the energy for other centers, particularly apparent when we are ill or injured; we draw energy away from our other centers until the crisis passes. Interest in most activities diminishes when someone is under physical duress; as in chemotherapy, or in bed with the flu, extremely tired, taking strong medicine, chronic back pain, Atopic Dermatitus, Lyme disease, and other attacks on the immune system. This is a center that has to be reckoned with since ignoring it will disrupt all other centers. The Instinctive Center requires the most attention and energy of all the centers. Left unattended it will wreak havoc on our ability to develop. Deprivation and constant barrage creates a weakening of our efforts. Sleep, food, physical pain, discomfort and exhaustion sets up a cycle of brokenness, diminishes energy and permeates every aspect of our life.

Never underestimate the instinctive center—it is always poised to undermine self-remembering. The instinctive center attempts to destroy hope. One must know it before one can control it, which is a long study, There are few people who can begin to control the instinctive center, because it is evasive and difficult to photograph. Mr. Ouspensky stated that it can only be photographed when one is conscious or approaching consciousness. Controlling its manifestations requires the ability to 'do' by controlling the law of accident.
—Robert Earl Burton

The first level, the mechanical part of the Instinctive Center is unique in that it has already been programmed to its functions at the moment of our birth and yet operates like the first level of all centers, without needing attention or awareness. We pay little mind to our breathing, heartbeat, blood flow, growth of hair and nails; it all just happens. The individual centered in the mechanical part places a lot of attention to their own daily life Instinctive needs. They know their best foods and diets and exercise and vitamins. Traveling they are careful to pack their special shampoos and soaps and brand of tea or coffee, when eating out they notice ingredients as well as smells of food, and to some they appear finicky, liking their food to be separated on their plate, although quite willing to share their information and Instinctive learning.

The second, emotional part, is not as well-intended towards the body. Discrimination may not support bodily needs, a cup of coffee from Starbucks might smell and taste better than a green drink from a local vegetable stand, a Ghiradelli hot fudge sundae might score over salad, cigarettes and alcohol might stimulate and pleasure the emotional part of the Instinctive Center in a manner that engages addictions. This is a powerful center, the mind fixates on pleasure and comfort, gratification and satisfaction, as well as on unpleasant, objectionable sensations. A hot tub, massage, comfortable bed when the center is under pressure; quite a lot of energy is required to pull the mind away from the grips of the second part of this center once it takes hold. Wanting more, a better flavor ice cream, special toppings on the frozen yoghurt, a stronger aroma coffee, a pizza with just the right crust and sauce, a more elegant home, a particular fabric of clothing, a certain body lotion with just the favorable scent; sensuality, desire and impulsiveness fuels this part of the center. Successfully situated in the emotional part of this center are interior decorators who work with beautiful fabrics and colors, gourmet chocolate truffle candy makers, fine perfumers, wine tasters, anyone who specializes in first-class quality products. The ability to jump from strong attraction to disinterest exists in this second part, as it does for all second level people.

The third and intellectual level of the Instinctive Center, attentive, careful, watchful and cautious, does not have its attention directed by the individual, instead, it is said *to be conscious for itself.* What that means is that the third center takes over when needed. The newspapers write about a person running into a burning house to save a child, disregarding the personal pain of his own burns until after the child is brought to safety, or jumping into a lake to pull someone out of a car, not feeling the freezing water throughout the rescue, blocking out all Instinctive needs when walking with a friend who is attacked on a street corner. This aspect, the intellectual part of the center bends time, things happen in a way that allows us to consider and place attention on to what is needed. People speak about extrasensory perception, clairvoyance, unusual healing phenomenon, seeing auras, having a sixth sense; most of this is a result of the intuitive third part of the Instinctive Center. It holds energy for itself from other centers and limits activity through this impulse, borrowing energy from other centers.

The very essence of instinct is that it's followed independently of reason.
—*Charles Darwin*

To go beyond satisfying Instinctive needs births new possibilities. The Instinctive Center strives for well being through things like diet, yoga, and an organic lifestyle. We impair the well being of the Instinctive body with mindless hedonistic habits, lifestyles and unnecessary medical procedures that create malfunction and disease and disrupt the process of wholeness. Meanwhile the potential and higher meaning is inside. It is within the mystery of our own true self—the energy and divine presence of our higher centers. It is realizing the stillness of one's intelligent nature in all aspects of our life.

We control the instinctive center by restricting it. No part of the instinctive center is interested in awakening. The instinctive center is intended to protect the organism during its life on earth. —*Robert Burton*

Examples include: *Jacques-Yves Cousteau, Steve Irwin, Mike Tyson, Stephen King, Pablo Picasso, Marcel Marceau, Katy Perry, Kelly Osbourne, Marilyn Monroe, Jennifer Aniston, Wendy Williams, Keith Urban, Nicole Kidman, Drew Barrymore, Jessica Simpson, Tiger Woods, Ozzy Osborne,*

Bill Shoemaker, Michael Jackson, Cameron Diaz, Charlie Chaplin, Charles Bronson, Britney Spears, Paris Hilton, Miley Cyrus, Mario Lopez, Justin Bieber, Derek Hough, Karina Smirnoff, Kim Kardashian, Caitlyn Jenner, Jessica Simpson, Nicki Minaj, Donald Trump, Randy Jackson, Brad Pitt.

MOVING CENTER

POSITIVE: CREATIVE POTENTIAL, MOVEMENT, PRODUCTIVE NEGATIVE: HABITUAL, RESTLESS, FRENETIC

The moving center is constantly making judgments of the most complicated kind. It can judge exactly and in what way and with what strength you must throw a stone to hit a distant object. The intelligence of the moving center, using no words or numbers, can calculate with the most exquisite precision some complicated series of movements that will give a definite result. —Maurice Nicoll

Based in the spinal cord, this center, like the instinctive, operates almost automatically, habitually, regulating and monitoring itself, otherwise we would injure ourselves. The Moving Center is involved with spatial relationships and our orientation to the physical world and is responsible for the body's perception of motion and for control of all impulses of movement. Working without our giving it attention this center proceeds regardless to how the circumstances shift or develop. The functions of the Moving Center are learned through imitation and early experimentation plus adaptation. We generally move according to the way that we tell ourselves to; right-left-forward-back-up-down-around. Most of our day, including night dreams, is managed by a productive or unsettled Moving Center. The function of the Moving Center is action or inaction, movement or rest; our sense of our body tells us when to move and when not to move; we are learning and recording through both imitation and memory. If there is a question as to whether a function is controlled by the instinctive or Moving brain, consider that if a newborn baby can do the activity, then it is instinctive, if the infant has to learn the activity than the Moving brain is responsible.

The wrong, independent or automatic work of the moving centre deprives the other centers of support and they involuntarily follow the moving centre. Often therefore the sole possibility of making the other centres work in a new way is to begin with the moving centre, the body. A body which is lazy, automatic and full of stupid habits stops any kind of work. —*P.D. Ouspensky*

We use the Moving Center to serve the other centers needs in the physical world. When the emotional center wants to touch someone, if the intellectual center wants to locate a book in the house, as the instinctive center wants food: they all call on their Moving Center. Dealing with the world is the responsibility of this center. This is the world of function, task and creative action. Too often, when tired, aimless unintentional distracted movements, mostly propelled from emotional baggage, are reflected in the Moving Center. Tight muscle tension in the jaw, neck and shoulders, restless hands and feet, twitching of the mouth, shaking the legs, gesturing and fidgeting, telltale defensive body postures; all are a misuse of this center. Any movement requiring sustained attention comes under the province of this center. Under stress there is a relief to automatically focus on one's primary center as a way of dealing with upheaval. Moving Centered people walk around or go for a drive when they are troubled, and under strain go out to a restaurant for dinner, take the dogs for a walk, do laundry and clean the house or some other mechanical Moving activity.

Because the moving center does not daydream most people regard it as uncon-scious. It is the moving center which gives us the power of dealing with the world. Learning by imitation is a power of the moving center. But this imitation is not the copying that turns adults into slaves because it is stimulated by a creative power. It is a very unfortunate thing that the development of the moving intelligence so often comes to a stop even during childhood. The human body has an enormous potential and contemporary education develops very little of it. —J.G. Bennett

Our center is the camera that determines reality. Moving Centered people tend to a lot of distractions, doing things that involve movement. Going out, coming in, changing activities, traveling, walking around, clapping hands, snapping fingers, gesturing, shopping, eating in restaurants, tinkering with a project, like fixing the car or files endlessly, they are agitated and more restless than people with other predominant centers. Visual types, spatially alert, this is the intelligence that orients in space and directs its external movements. Mechanically functioning automatically, without attention; life is experienced through physical movement and action and the preference is the feel of being in motion.

Often people with this center are athletes, dancers, UPS and taxi/ uber drivers, mail carriers, inventors, surgeons, engineers, ski instructors, lecturers that travel the circuit, long distance truck drivers, exercise and fitness professionals, realtors driving clients around to look at properties, waiters and waitresses; skills that involve action and hands-on application. Trapped in purposeless movement, Moving Centered people spend hours playing video games, picking up e-mail, riding their bicycle or motorbike, driving around, walking the mall, looking at Facebook, skiing, going on subways or buses, traveling; anything that entails doing things and sustained movement. Moving Centered people will climb a mountain *just because it's there*. Tennis, swimming, golfing, dancing, acrobatics, I-phone activity, football, soccer, baseball, Tai Chi; all Moving Centered activities. Restricted movement from an accident or injury becomes an insult for this center.

ATTENTIVE OR AUTOMATIC

Ninety-six per cent of our civilization is concerned with the instinctive-moving center, the planetary body; three percent with real culture, the emotions; one percent with 'Why?', the real mind. —*Maurice Nicoll*

We have great potential for creativity with the body, although most of our life is spent in unimaginative, uninspired, habitual postures, body language and gestures. Most movements, once learned, are stored in memory and we function with little attention paid to our abilities. Riding a bike, swimming, using a cell phone or computer to type, walking up and down the stairs, and numerous complex movements are actions that can be performed without any awareness, although initially they all required focus, concentration, repetition and practice. In the beginning learning to ride a bike or tie your shoes required good concentration, control, directed attention. Through repetition the memory is stored and the action is performed without awareness of how the movements are done. Only learned movements remain, the enthusiasm and attention leave, subsequently people in the world move around asleep, inattentive. Most people are able to *sleepwalk*, live without awareness, function without knowing that they are functioning.

There is conscious attention and there is automatic functioning, where the mind is occupied, filled with distractions and thoughts. Walking without placing our mind in our feet, driving a car without knowing we are driving, eating without attention to either the hand that carries the food or to the mouth or teeth that chew the food, are all mechanical automatic functioning. Storing in memory so that we perform actions mindlessly, without awareness, assists in dulled, numbing lack of presence. To make a thing conscious begins to change it. Breaking habits requires directing one's attention, demands voluntary internal attention. To learn something new so as to increase consciousness is to place awareness and intelligence into areas that have been operating habitually, blindly in the dark. This sense which I call *knowing* is actually our sixth sense, and like our other senses—seeing, hearing, smell, taste, touch, can be developed and refined.

Mr. Gurdjieff's movement exercises showed me very clearly that my capacity to direct my attention wherever I liked was less than I had believed it to be. They could not be performed mechanically but only by maintaining the strictest awareness of what one was doing. The slightest wandering of attention threw the whole affair out of gear, and the fact that something had gone radically wrong became as obvious to the pupil as it did to the teacher. The exercises acted therefore as a very sensitive indicator of the performer's inner state and recorded the flickering of his attention. These movements need a very complete attention. —Kenneth Walker

LEVELS OF ATTENTION

There are three horizontal levels of attention in the Moving Center. First is the mechanical, which functions without attention, storing learned movements. Most people repeat learned actions with no awareness; walking, driving, talking, eating, bike riding, swimming, tying shoes, typing, once learned and programmed in the memory bank they no longer require attention and can be performed without awareness. Repetitive tasks such as secretarial work, long distance truck drivers, supermarket cashiers, exercising at the gym, waiting on tables, fall in this category of mechanical Moving Centered routines and can be performed rote and mindlessly.

The second, the emotional level; the attention is held and identified with an object, less steady, it has more energy, motivation and eagerness, enjoying participating or watching movement. The excitement of the Olympic games or looking at a tennis match or world cup, dancing, traveling as an adventure to new unexplored places, placing attention in an exciting sport like hand gliding, mountain climbing, water skiing, parachute jumping; the particular object holds the attention until the activity is over, or our interest is lost.

The third and intellectual part of the Moving Center, careful and intentional with its movements, is used to create, to follow diagrams, for inventions, sustained attention, record-setting athletes who devise new ways to move their body, reconfiguring spacial positioning, as well as engineers and surgeons who perform at their best when working with this intelligence.

It is in the nature of the moving brain to do things, that is, produce changes in the external environment. We have a marvelous capacity for doing things with our bodies, but most of the time is spent in stereotyped postures, gestures and motions. We have the possibilities denied the other animals of acting in this world in a creative manner and yet an honest appraisal of what we do with the earth shows that most of our 'creations' are not only lacking in creativity but deny it entry into our lives. —J.G. Bennett

The Moving Center can execute elaborate and sophisticated tasks. There is high financial reward and great regard for those who excel in this center, particularly professional athletes. Learning skills through imitation; relying on the Moving Center is quicker than learning foreign languages when using the intellectual center. Action directed, spatially guiding us; used to garden, invent things, for all athletic sports, to walk, drive a car, get to places; basically all activities stimulate and feed the Moving Center. Faster than the intellect, a falling book can be grabbed, a hand moves the steering wheel as it hits ice, all before the mind thinks about what to do.

People are born fairly helpless, engaging the creative potential of this center they learn to crawl, climb, walk, run, learn to use their hands for various activities. Many animals are born able to run and keep themselves from falling, not quite as helpless as a human at birth. Humans practically stop their Moving development at a very early age, rarely achieving the skills and potential that are in its capacity. Possibly because its nature is to be inert, passive, only to follow where it is called, it has no initiative on its own. Learning, mostly through imitation, located in the present moment—not daydreaming, ruminating or planning—we tend to regard the Moving Center as unconscious. The world of school, family and society asks for minimal development of this center, and so we live in the mechanical part ignoring its creative potential.

The Moving Center pursues physical achievements. The creative possibilities in the Moving Center are rarely addressed, the education system has a limited viewpoint regarding the promise and undeveloped abilities of what could be done. The physical body has vast untrained, untapped reserves, and it is within the domain of the Moving Center to act upon the world. Intentional movement which happens when we conceptualize, as in architectural drawing, yoga, choreography, martial arts—like Aikido or Tai Chi—and sacred dances that use the Moving Center as an art form, are cognizant of placing attention with conscious awareness towards spacial relations. This is based on the fact that designed movements evoke an inner condition and create a refined energy. Now there becomes beautiful movement, as in Nijinskii creating his ballet leaps; pure grace. Gurdjieff created movements that challenge us to move in a non-habitual way, to release our body from its automatic unconscious locks. The Gurdjieff movements require full attention; practicing directed attention is an indicator of our inner state, to experience what Gurdjieff referred to as the *I am. If with the mind alone you were to repeat I am for a thousand years, it would give you nothing real. What must be aimed for is the totality of the attention, attention in all one's part,* stated P. Travers.

The smallest wandering of attention disrupts our connection to our still point, the ground of our being. Developing a watcher, a witness, someone home within, our center of gravity becomes watchful awareness. The intelligence of movement has been limited to repetitive movement and postures; the world of function has abundant unexplored possibilities. The higher meaning is inside us—our own true self—the divine presence of our own higher centers, to come to learn the truth of who we really are and what can be created from that place.

When all the centers work together then it is conscious living, but one has to learn how to live like this. The least difficult is the moving center, the next the thinking center; the most difficult is the feeling center. —C.S. Nott

Examples include: *John McEnroe, John Travolta, Ted Williams, David Beckham, Paul Newman, Magic Johnson, Maks Chmerkovskiy, Chris Rock, Stevie Wonder, Pippa Middleton, Ben Affleck, George Clooney, Danica Patrick, Serena and Venus Williams, Michael Jordan, Billy Blanks, Wayne Gretsky, Nancy Kerrigan, Justin Timberlake, Ellen De Generes, Pink, Nick Lachey, Jennifer Lopez, Melissa Rycroft, Madonna, Channing Tatum, Rihanna, Justin Theroux, Robert DeNiro, Erin Andrews, Angelina Jolie, Vaslav Nijinsky, Mikhail Baryshnikov.*

INTELLECTUAL CENTER

POSITIVE: YES, AFFIRMATION, REASON

NEGATIVE: NO, NEGATION, SELF-DELUSION

Even at the ordinary level, the head brain of man distinguishes him from other animals. —J.G. Bennett

The Intellectual Center, considered by most people to be the *intelligence*, is actually the least reliable of all the centers. Working with concepts and ideas, reasoning, constructing theories, the formation of words and imagination, comparison and more, this center is complicated and sometimes puzzling to observe. In fact, the functions of the Intellectual Center often prevents us from observing it. Experiences are explained, processes are the processes themselves. Scientific assessment and popular opinion has been that the Intellectual Center is superior, has a corner on the market of intelligence, and is the distinguishing mark between human and animal. Research has now shown a minor qualitative difference between the brains of humans and those of some mammals. Apes have formed rational faculties. Their ability to develop an argument, follow a line of logic, draw conclusions, frame hypotheses, have language with complex grammar and conversations is remarkable. We have named our subspecies Homo sapiens which means *wise man*, although it so happens that as a species we are not so wise, although we are often intelligent. Intelligence predicts the success of individuals without regard to the consequences of their success to others. Wisdom has discernment and judgment and understands the consequences of actions and words.

Who am I standing in the midst of this thought traffic? —Rumi

1149

The mind is the center that is the most under control for us to direct and impact. Located in the brain, this is the slowest of the centers, yet our work on ourself begins here. A starting point to look at self, it's in the brain that the work of understanding begins. The Intellectual Center, unlike the emotional, moving, instinctive and sexual centers, even when not focused, when fragmented, inefficient and haphazard, can still be informed with respect to the possibility of transformation. Training the mind, engaging it for someone to actually live inside, to notice and then bring that awareness into life, creates change. When we are trapped in a thought form, stepping out of it blocks the mechanical momentum of the mind and then true intelligence begins. Intellectually Centered people react slowly, analyzing and considering, looking at all the parts, logically trying to connect, seeing how things relate to each other. Thought is the function of the Intellectual Center. Whether it's watching a television show, painting, or doing income taxes, this center thinks and processes perceptions. Words and ideas are the world of the Intellectual Center, manifesting as thought and reason, analysis and association, concepts, theories, abstractions, sometimes rational, sometimes illogical. Reading, numbers, writing, speaking skills, essentially using the mind, mental activity, linking past and future, is the domain of this center. Symbolic abstractions have their connection to the physical world, sometimes difficult to prove until the Intellect is correctly utilized.

Genuine thinking requires an effort and is something people rarely do. Everyone is advised to 'move his brains' once every day and this means to make a real effort to think. People as a rule do not know what to think about. —Maurice Nicoll

TRAINING OUR MIND

As spiritual beings we are aware of the presence of abstractions, yet how to show the physicality of the divine, of love, grace, of healing, remains part mystery. Research has found the Intellect to be incomprehensible. Most often this center is used mechanically, without understanding or contact with meaning. Experiencing life through thought and analyses is considered to be intelligence as well as the seed of communication. The activity and use of the Intellect places attention on affirmation and negation, yes and no. The ease for quick associative responses to be settled upon, solutions, as opposed to the time it takes for thinking and processing, creates the impression that people who don't understand are smart, while people who access the higher part of the mind, who are slower, who express ideas, appear less informed.

The mechanical part of the Intellect obstructs understanding, the key most important ingredient for awakening. What passes as thought are slogans, platitudes and beliefs, which stop and obstruct thinking processes. Untrained the Intellect is critical and judgmental, on a higher level it is logical with the ability to see at a great range, along with a neutral viewpoint. Most all ideas are mechanical, they are associative, comparative, reactive responses, formatory and robotic. Until a person lives with a level of presence, independent thinking is impossible. Self-observation and mindfulness allow us to see that ideas arise automatically with each impression impinging on the mind.

The mechanical part of the intellectual center registers memories and impressions and associations. It is the fixed part of a person, and they see life in a certain way and say the same things, like a gramophone. They will not change, and nothing can be new in them. —Maurice Nicoll

Change originates in the Intellectual Center, we shift through reshaping our mind-set, our attitude, to see in a new way. The Intellectual Center, even when fragmented will receive a push to develop until we establish a practice, such as bringing awareness into our body. This is how Christopher Reeve, paralyzed, was able to continue to work and make his bodily connections. Ram Dass, following his stroke said: *Before the stroke, I was on a very spiritual plane. I ignored my body, took it for granted. When I look at my life I see that I wanted to be free of the physical plane, the psychological plane, and when I got free of those I didn't want to go anywhere near them. But the stroke reminded me that I had a body and a brain, that I had to honor them.*

From thought and sensation we move to become aware of our feeling state. Expect strong resistance because false personality knows it is being destroyed. Inner work begins by observing what is, when the body is tired self-observation can recognize that fact and deal with it without becoming the *tiredness*. Information is useful. Even to react inappropriately to a situation, the ability and knowledge to recognize what is happening increases self-development. Witnessing inner reactions offers information. Using attention with more consciousness is a beginning step to create a point of awareness beyond mechanical behavior and push us to look at how many of the pictures of ourself are imaginary.

Ponder this universal truth: One way to work on yourself is by being present in the body. Another way is by expanding the heart. A third way is by quieting the mind. Anyone who wants real change, finds a way to work on all three at the same time. —*Riso and Hudson*

We train the Intellect by forcing our mind to pay attention, by understanding what we want to achieve and watching how other centers work. Thoughts come and go constantly; words, images, visions, and dreams. We use this function initially to learn movements, and then its proper use is to let go. Wrong work of the center happens when fear sets in, the Intellect taking over for the faster moving center, most often the results are disastrous. In a moving emergency the mind works too slowly; swiftly moving on a tennis court, skiing, driving and hitting black ice on a foggy road, rock climbing, running down the stairs, riding on a speeding motorcycle or a bucking bronco; for the mind to try to figure out movement while engaged in motion, the slower timing sets up the certainty of injuries and accidents.

You can't change by the mind alone; you must begin with the body, bring body and emotions into line. —Margaret Anderson

MECHANICAL MIND

When we hear a *why* question, the mind looks for a reason and reasoning involves choice and comparison, an affirmation or negation, selecting and rejecting. Intellectual thinking, divided into positive and negative, comes up with a result that our mind sides with—if we think staying up late makes us tired, the Intellect will tell the body to get tired. The Intellect can prove or disprove all theories. Generally referred to as left-brained thinking, the Intellectual Center is primarily linear in function. It makes language possible and uses symbols to make one thing represent another thing. A big diamond ring or expensive car signifies wealth, a pretty body conveys health. Ironically, often we sacrifice the thing that originated the symbol. The wealth may be sacrificed for the ring, the health may be sacrificed for poor nutritional diets or eating disorders. The Intellectual Center often functions without intelligence, discrimination or wisdom.

The head brain is the one with which we think ourselves most familiar.

When the thinking center comes into its own it becomes a direct instrument of our own will. Then we can think what we choose to think and have the power 'to do'. But it is not until we become balanced in the workings of all the brains that it is possible to 'have will.' As we are we spend most of out time is a dream state where mental images automatically form themselves.
—*J.G. Bennett*

Intelligent brilliant minds have arrived at a state of not-knowing. Dionysius called it *agnosia*, no longer any belief or doubt, the paradox of mysticism, through not knowing one comes to know, by knowing one misses. Socrates, of great wisdom stated: *the only true wisdom is in knowing you know nothing. I know that I am intelligent, because I know one thing, and that is that I know nothing.* Today with the millions of published books, and computers loaded with information, Socrates might easily continue to reaffirm that statement. The mind, designed to store information, does not think, it operates as a computer data-base, a file cabinet that stores and retrieves and speaks associatively with slogans. *She's doing her best, look before you leap, money saved is money earned, what's new, I'm fine, nice to meet you, that's interesting, that's the way things are, the book is good,* all pass for thinking. You say you are *cooking a fish,* he says he *went fishing,* you say you *had fish last night in a restaurant,* he says *fish is a good source of omega oil.* Mechanical triggers, no thought here, no real attention; associative thinking prompts a comparative response, similar to playing tennis and batting the ball back and forth.

The storing of information is a cue triggering people to assess a person as smart, as if they understand what has been accumulated. The world of education from first grade through the university as well as our publishing domain is formed and based, rests, in this illusion. Tests and applications are constructed on rote learning, ie. yes or no, fill in the blank, what's wrong with this picture, name 10 things; ways in which our education system imagines to develop intelligence. Originality, innovation, vision, creativity and inspiration are rarely part of the equation in teaching or testing.

The function of the positive side of the intellectual centre is to think Yes, to affirm. The function of the negative part of the intellectual centre is to think No, to negate. Without a negative part in the intellectual centre, it would be impossible to think. The first definition that this system gives is that thinking is comparing. But if a man only has affirmation or yes as an instrument to think with, comparison would not be possible. Comparison requires a quality or a choice between two things, to one of which one says yes and to the other no. All the questions we ask beginning with why (as distinct from those beginning with how) mean that we seek a reason for something: and all reasoning involves comparison and choice—that is selecting this and rejecting that. And it would be impossible to select or reject unless there were in the Intellectual Centre a twin-power—namely, the power of affirmation and the power of negation. —Maurice Nicoll

There are three horizontal levels of attention in the Intellectual Center: first is the mechanical formatory thinking, which leaves no room for creative thinking. It's function is to automatically record, memorize, file, make information available to other centers; to speak in routine reporting statements. It operates by association. No attention is necessary. The second level, emotional, more enthusiastic, the identification consists of fascination and generates energy. Essentially it is held by an object and identified with the object. Going up and down, one's interest may be engaged for a while, eventually one completely loses interest. Books are left unfinished. Ideas are stimulating, even compelling, and people are drawn to listen to the interesting appealing approach to topics this type describes. The third and Intellectual level is where real thinking happens. Absorbed in ideas and concentration, looking to understand and see connections, this is true scholarship at work. Least likely to be understood, the least flashy, the general population will overlook the intelligence of this third part, and, in fact, value the information-gathering of the mechanical first part and the flashy emotional second part more. The third part of all lower centers must be engaged for growth, since they have the ability to direct attention and, therefore, are necessary in creating a witness or observer.

Thought binds a man. Whoever controls his thoughts, is a veritable God on this earth. —*Swami Sivananda*

AWAKENING THE MIND

When we understand how our mind works the practice becomes easy. When delusion is overcome, understanding is there. When sunlight shines, it helps all vegetation grow. When mindfulness shines, it transforms all mental formations. Right view is a flower blooming in the field of mind consciousness. —*Thich Nhat Hahn*

Philosophers, theorists, scholars, tax accountants, lawyers, computer programmers, journalists, academics, debaters, research specialists, internal revenue service specialists, mathematicians and bookworms, live from the Intellectual Center, and games like scrabble, chess, sudoku, backgammon, Go, crossword puzzles, are considered Intellectual pursuits. Enjoying a good documentary at the movie theater, collecting books to read for a rainy day, buying products through name recognition; mental activity is primary. Intellectually Centered persons respond to other people's pain with rational analysis rather than empathy. Emotion is more active as an instrument of perception, personal connections may be strained due to a lack of warmth, feelings thought of as irrational hold back bonding. In this Center feelings follow thought, thinking about bills, then getting upset; in the emotional center someone is happy first, then thinks about something special and fun. Instead of thinking in reaction to a stimulus we could begin to work with the exercise of using our own initiative in the effort to understand/know reality.

Any new invention, regardless of the harm it may do to humanity, is regarded as sacred by the masses—the modern superstition that knowledge is an end in itself. Knowledge without understanding is the root of all kinds of evil.
—*Orage*

The Intellect is effected by our physical being. We think one way when we feel well and another when we feel ill. Poor health, a weak instinctive center is a challenge to maintain clear strong thinking. Without connecting with our emotions and our instincts real understanding can't be formed. Just imagine, if we learned to think for ourselves without habits, old ideas and opinions; about what we want, like, are, why we exist, about our purpose, we would have a new life. Only by really thinking differently, metanoia, can we change our life. It is claimed that only by beginning to think for ourself can change, inner self-evolution, happen; to change is to change our attitudes. *Think beyond your mind!* Our minds are used by our attitudes, and therefore there is no room or energy available for anything new, for growth, for awakening. Our attitudes are subjective and mechanical and can be changed to suit our intention. Our attitudes are not who we are. Learning to use our attitudes, to let them flow into each new moment, and, especially, to study them, as well as choosing ones that uplift in the direction of consciousness, we become mindful. Ultimately this is living suspended in a place of knowing not-knowing, free to experiment, to witness, to record and to act; how we think and thinking in a new way, changing our mind and its habits creates change. To change, we must change.

The Intellectual Center is considered to be the representative of the *will-to-see*, where purpose exists, a world of depth; no longer functioning mechanically. Once we learn to gather lighter energy to fuel the Intellect and are able to think from ourselves we come to know awareness beyond the mind. The Intellectual Center looks for truth in books, yet the higher meaning is inside—it's our own true self—the divine presence of our own higher centers.

The world is not simply there. Everything and everyone we see, we view through the lenses of our thoughts. Your mind is where your thoughts arise and form. It is not simply with your eyes but with your mind that you see the world. So much depends on your mind: How you see yourself, who you think you are, how you see others, what you think the meaning of life is, how you see death, belief, God, darkness and beauty is all determined by the style of mind you have. Your mind is your greatest treasure. We become so taken up with the world, with having and doing more, that we come to ignore who we are and forget what we see the world with. The most powerful way to change your life is to change your mind. When you beautify your mind, you beautify your world. When your mind awakens, your life comes alive and the creative adventure of your soul takes off. —John O'Donohue

Examples include: *Al Gore, Noam Chomsky, Vaclav Havel, Umberto Eco, Salman Rushdie, Stephen Hawking, Gore Vidal, Larry King, Margaret Thatcher, P.D. Ouspensky, Tom Brokaw, Eckhart Tolle, Madeleine Albright, Jean-Paul Sarte, Jiddu Krishnamurti, Dame Iris Murdoch, Maurice Nicoll, Eckhart Tolle, Bertrand Russell, Ludwig Wittgenstein, Gloria Steinem, Houston Smith, Barbara Walters, Soren Kierkegaard, Albert Einstein, Gustave Flaubert, Nikola Tesla*

EMOTIONAL CENTER

POSITIVE: NATURAL EMOTIONS, LIKE

NEGATIVE: NEGATIVE EMOTIONS, DISLIKE

Emotion is the chief source of all becoming conscious. There can be no trans-formation of darkness into light without emotion. —*Carl Jung*

Located in the solar plexus, the umbilical region, the Emotional Center is an energetic force experienced in the region of what is called the pit of the stomach. In many Eastern teachings the solar plexus is considered the seat of power. Feelings are the function of the Emotional Center. The positive includes authentic pure Emotions energized by appreciation and approval, the negative has unnatural distorted Emotions fueled by likes and dislikes, disapproval and condemnation. Negative Emotions have no authentic place in our psychology and are improper work of our functions. We learn them through imitation, culture, education; they live in the false personality. The Emotional quadrant begins to develop from 6 months of age. Most suffering is unnatural and unnecessary. Emotions are essential and important to feel, express, honor and understand. When healthy spontaneous Emotions are not allowed their pure expression and/or development then disturbances in other centers are created. Denial or repression distorts the Emotions which then impacts the psychology and body creating illness and disturbances. Since the solar plexus is the location of the Emotional Center, the inner eye of the soul, referred to as the heart in esoteric teachings, the center of our being, is equated with the source of Emotions.

Emotions are natural, they need to be felt, expressed, acknowledged and understood. Emotions are beautiful, they contribute to our psychological growth, health, learning and communication with others. If the healthy natural emotional processes are not allowed their natural expression and/or development, or if they are repressed or denied for any reason, the result is distortions of these emotions and feelings—which are unhealthy for us both psychologically and physically. There are 5 natural emotions; everything else is a distortion. The distorted emotions make up a big pool of unresolved feelings and issues, this is our unfinished business. —Elisabeth Kübler-Ross

The purpose of the Emotional Center is as an instrument of cognition, a sensitive form of intuitive sight and wisdom. It is the intelligence that establishes value for things and experiences, relates to people and forms a sense of aesthetics, ethics and morality through participation, by entering into things. This is why the Emotional Center needs to be cleansed of negative emotions which are confusing causing misfiring and distortion; once the inner life is shifted from negative to positive its energies are used for experiences of higher consciousness, rather than drained and misdirected by negativity. Ingrained habits of feeling and stereotypical conventional feelings prevent us from deepening intelligent understanding. Developing unused parts of ourself through new thinking, cleaning out old attitudes and creating new connections directs and uplifts our journey. When open and balanced we have a fulfilling Emotional life, feeling the sweetness of life. An overactive center brings large Emotional swings, a malfunctioning center may cause delusions and psychosis, while a blocked center closes us to spiritual energies. The most immature of all the centers, mistrained in the public educational system, dysfunctional in most family units, once trained and matured will bring the desire to become whole with ourself and the world and is considered the *will-to-be*.

We think that negative emotions are produced by circumstances, whereas all negative emotions are in us, inside us. —P.D. Ouspensky

NATURAL EMOTIONS

Each time an impression reaches the Emotional Center it *experiences* an Emotion that is automatically accepted or rejected, so that a positive or negative Emotion is mechanically felt and usually expressed. True feelings are not negative, instead, they carry more or less intensity and the Emotional Center agrees or refuses the feelings. Natural Emotions are fear, anger, jealousy, grief and love. Natural fear is a survival and startle response, a caution impulse. Its distortions include anxiety, panic and phobias. Natural anger, self-protective, brings about change, is assertive, stable, firm and steadfast. The distortions include resentment, self-hate, rage, powerlessness, lack of inner authority, holding a grudge, giving up, bitterness and spite. The natural Emotion of jealousy is a stimulus that impels and motivates to better ourself, grow, develop, progress and refine, imitate, match and emulate another's behavior. Its distortions include envy, comparison, criticism and lack of self-esteem. The natural Emotion of grief, dealing with loss, sometimes through sharing and tears, ultimately transforms heartbreak into a source of strength to make loss meaningful. Some of its distortions are self-pity, depression, martyrdom, guilt, regret and blame. The natural Emotion, love, is self-love, to be loving, nurturing, compassionate. Love is when you have seen who you are and want to share your being with others, it is inclusive. Some of the distortions of love are possessiveness, clinging, neediness, expectations, sentimentality, instability and demandingness. Sentimentality induces nostalgia which leads to moodiness, melancholy, loneliness and fear of loss. Lifting those feelings, seeing the humor, living through feelings and Emotional connections with others allows for more wholesomeness and less suffering in relationships. Distorted Emotions make up a pool of unresolved feelings and issues often called *unfinished business.* These feelings linked together into an endless loop are difficult to work with without guidance and understanding.

We are animals 'in our lower nature.' Our 'emotions' of fear and excitement, anger, curiosity, timidity and courage, irritation and contentment are the same as those we see in the animals. The truly 'human' feelings of love, faith, hope and conscience are possible only in creative beings. Unfortunately we have lost the ability to experience normally the 'positive' emotions and have substituted for them the lower animal passions. —J.G. Bennett

Inner work comes from knowing how to make use of the Emotional Center. Clearing distortions is critical because without defined positive Emotional energy we have interference that stands in the way of deepening our understanding. Our automatic processes lack presence; given certain cues we tune in as if we were paying attention, we tune in as if we were present, lacking awareness, limiting the connection, continuing to disrupt our ability to experience true love and compassion. Disliking a thing or person blocks understanding. Increased consciousness weakens the power of old habituated connections and inaccurate associations. The first step is to not express negative Emotions, next is to study them, see their indulgence as distractions, exhausting us, robbing our presence. They are a misuse of energy. Mostly learned, as with children through imitation: we have trained ourselves to have negative Emotions.

If it's hysterical, it's historical. —Rabbi David Ingber

In the case of a minor irritation, the recognition of the presence of the irritation, along with a smile and a few breaths will usually be enough to transform the irritation into something more positive, like forgiveness, understanding, and love. Irritation is a destructive energy. We cannot destroy the energy; we can only convert it into a more constructive energy. —Thich Nhat Hahn

CREATING SUBSTANCE

The intellectual center is much slower than the Emotional Center so we can't catch Emotions with thought, same with the moving center; mind which is slower can't follow quick movements. This is why the systems in Chapter 12 have great value; to break things down, simplify, to take things apart, then we can work to shift, transform and know ourself. Witnessing, paying attention, impartial self-observation of our Emotional Center, avoiding judgment and justification, we are more able to catch and recognize an event as it happens. To observe ourself as if we are another, that other who is an interesting person to regard, to study, to look at; a research project that opens a door to freedom.

Our only freedom is in knowing, from years of observation and experiencing, that all personally centered thoughts and emotions (and the actions born of them) are empty, but if they are not seen as empty they can be harmful. When we realize this we can abandon them. —Charlotte Joko Beck

The first step towards resolution is to identify *what's wrong? how do I feel? what happened to me?* Next, discharge the feelings. Then move towards the acceptance of your life and yourself. Convert the unhealthy feelings to positive ones. Many Emotions have no cause, they are for their own sake, just as some movements and thoughts have no cause, phenomena that are there to exercise a particular center. The Emotional Center will contract and expand, people will be happy or sad for no reason, trying to make up reasons for their feelings.

Hatred, envy, malice, jealousy and fear all have children, any bad thought breeds others and each of these go on and on, ever repeating until our world is peopled with their offspring. —Ralph Waldo Trine

The most difficult center to control is the Emotional Center. The

Emotionally Centered person processes incoming data from life more quickly than others, not necessarily to do anything, the impulse is to feel. We can work on controlling thoughts or the muscles that are involved with movements, but, liking or disliking is an involuntary response. Indulging, not giving in to unpleasant negative Emotions, is a personal responsibility. Not necessarily to like everything, but to stop the personal disliking. Individual negative Emotions, petty, self-serving and ill-humored, pre-occupies, keeping the focus narrow, blocks our contact with higher centers. Negativity is toxic and contagious. Neutralizing the negative energy of an experience, keeping negative reactions to a circumstance from taking over our Emotions is the beginning of transformation. To choose against expressing negativity in a difficult moment, not to be overcome by vanity and habit, uplifts our Emotions; that ability creates substance, a moment of presence.

We have neither objective nor subjective feeling. The whole realm of our feeling is filled with something alien and completely mechanical. There are three kinds of feeling—subjective, objective and automatic. —G.I. Gurdjieff

Negative Emotions govern life, children absorb them and brood, sulk, whine, nag, argue, eat unconsciously, complain, and are essentially oblivious to being Emotionally negative. Sometimes, especially in children, since Emotional energy is faster than thought, this center can be a firecracker waiting to be lit. Strong likes and dislikes, attached to one item of clothing or a kind of food or color, blowing things out of proportion, low tolerance for boredom, and complaining and bickering, stimulates the Emotional exchange. Mass Emotions, such as everyone at a tennis match standing up and shouting and clapping, a hate crime where a group beats up someone, loyalty to an idea or sports team turns into a mob attacking the other team or fighting with those who think differently, temper tantrums, political violence, crimes of passion; these are feelings overwhelming thought.

Peace. It does not mean to be in a place where there us no noise, trouble, or hard work. It means to be in the midst of those things and still be calm in your heart. —*Anonymous*

With awareness that the poison we feel is toxic we work internally to discriminate and to not accept negative unnatural Emotions. Not to justify or to look for the cause; **all** negative Emotions are unnecessary, no matter what produces them. They prevent development and block access to communicate with the higher Emotional center. There is so much in life that threatens the heart's truth. To remain open, regardless, to maintain the power of love within the heart is the teaching. Our Emotions are not meant to toss us from one feeling to another. This is a center that we rarely educate and train, instead it is left to luck and up to families to program, and that pretty much happens mindlessly and by accident. Schools place little attention towards directing and developing the Emotional Center, and so this culture is filled with people who are reactive, rude, snooping into public figures lives, having erratic mood swings, domestic abuse, gossiping, criminal behavior, indifferent and violent; feeding the Emotions on the lowest of levels.

The proper use of the Emotional Center brings empowerment as well as relaxation and peacefulness, a place where feelings no longer push to carry us into the madness that is called society. Balanced Emotions bring meaning to life and a momentary glimpse of awakening. Life understood through the heart is an Emotional perception of truth. Bringing the mind into the heart opens a quality of conscious awareness that integrates intelligence and Emotion in a way that uplifts, unifies and intensifies perception. Longing and the feeling of inner emptiness, a desire to be more, to feel connected to others, to love, along with the willingness to relinquish using the world to satisfy these cravings, opens us to the journey of awakening.

Within your own house dwells the treasury of joy; so why do you go begging from door to door! —Sufi saying

THE SIXTH SENSE: KNOWING

There is a state of knowing connected with Emotions, knowing is not thinking. To know It's a beautiful day, to feel that my friend is happy, those things are known without mental activity. Knowing what is true is connected to a positive Emotional state, once we tip into the negative space we no longer know. When I am irritated or judging my friend, I no longer see what I originally saw. We glimpse the truth of something and then the Emotional state changes and we no longer see that as truth. The Emotional Center responds to people, to visual impressions and the intrigue of human events, both positive and negative. One may appreciate or be suspicious; the Emotional Center is the root of a personal sense of justice as well as the place of approval or disapproval of people's behavior.

People who are mechanically positive are just as mechanical as people who are mechanically negative. Ouspensky said: 'Some people's false personality functions cheerfully, and thereby they deceive themselves.' One cannot control negative emotions if one cannot control positive emotions, and neither is one's self. Remember that transforming negative emotions is the main method used to awaken, though happily, it is not the only method. —Robert Earl Burton

Our eyes and heart are channels for energy. The way we look at something determines its energy. Negative Emotions like hate, anxiety, bitterness, indignation, self-pity, blame, boredom and all reactive impulses manifesting in our lives are the underlying cause behind disintegration, representing one of the major obstacles blocking our awakening. Each time there is a negative interaction with someone we affect the wholeness and well-being of our life and the world. When our behavior is governed by reactive impulses and self-interest it creates obstructions that when left unchecked lead to breakdowns, health problems, financial troubles. It is our feelings and behavior that determines our day, not the stock market, circumstances or other people. Negative Emotions prevent us from seeing and accepting a situation objectively. They are a sign that something is consuming the present. Yes, they are possible to eliminate!

With ordinary love goes hate. I love this, I hate that, Today I love you, next week or next hour, or next minute, I hate you. He who can really love can be; he who can be, can do; he who can do, is. To know about real love one must forget all about love and must look for direction. As we are we cannot love. We love because something in ourselves combines with another's emanations; this starts pleasant associations, perhaps because of chemico-physical emanations from instinctive center, emotional center, or intellectual center; or it may be from influences of external form. —C.S. Nott

All forms of irritation, frustration, impatience, anxiety, worry, suspicion, resentment, boredom, anxiety, stress, numbness and aggravation are phases of negative Emotions as well as causes of unnecessary suffering. They may feel legitimate and valuable, so long as we imagine that people and circumstances conspire to make us negative. What appears to be a harmless release of energy, accusing and blaming, expressing what we think is our character, is, instead, a pointless sign of Emotional immaturity and shortsighted thinking which corrupts our awareness. Resistance to expressing unpleasant Emotions and instead to transform them, a conscious and intentional choice; directed voluntary attention carries the possibly of our development. The payment for one's *unconscious manifestation is one's conscious life.*

My joy is like spring, so warm it makes flowers bloom in all walks of life. My pain is like a river of tears, so full it fills up the four oceans. Please call me by my true names, so I can hear all my cries and my laughs at once, so I can see that my joy and pain are one. Please call me by my true names, so I can wake up, and so the door of my heart can be left open, the door of compassion. —*Thich Nhat Hahn*

ATTENTION

The three horizontal levels of attention are: first, requiring no attention, expressed mechanically as customary superficial Emotions. Examples are: meeting someone and saying: *nice to see you, how are you, I'm fine, that's interesting, have fun, everything will be Ok,* Emotions at a sporting event, watching TV, sending store bought holiday and birthday cards, the automatic response of shaking hands or nodding when meeting someone, sentimental movies and hit tunes, the social conventions of friendship and family, like sending balloons or candy for Valentine's Day, seeing a couple and feeling envious and dissatisfied because you don't have a partner. These conventional expressions of Emotion, functioning without attention, automatic, lends to people being superficial and insensitive, since the Emotional Center is functioning without attention, without any awareness.

The second level of attention is the most intense and charged of all in our lower centers. The attention in this part of the center is held by and identified with an object. Fixated, like when not eating all day and someone brings a plate of your favorite food, ice cream, pizza, chicken wings, chocolate cake, a cup of coffee, pretzels, blueberries, chocolate chip cookies, something you hold as special, and the attention becomes held by the object. This, the Emotional part of the Emotional Center has passionate swings; love and hate and war live in this place. Self-absorbed as well as self-serving, this center is also a place where one has the capacity to access Emotional sensitivity, to perceive other's feelings.

Few realize that they can control the way they feel and positively affect the things that come into their life experience by deliberately directing their thoughts. —Abraham Hicks

The third level, the intellectual part of the Emotional Center directs attention. More subtle to spot, the neutrality, lack of reacting and *cool* regarding feelings, looks different from other Emotionally Centered types. It is important for all Emotional types to strengthen this part by not expressing negative Emotions, through feeding one's Emotional life with beautiful art, a clear and refined environment, studying great minds, higher vibration music, being amongst sensitive people, good literature, finer impressions. This is the place where we create a bridge to the higher centers. Unconditional love, compassion, gratitude, forgiveness, empathy, an appreciation for the love and beauty in the world all develop here. Faith, hope and love originate here.

Unlike the visible Emotions of the first two parts of the Emotional Center the third, intellectual part of the Emotional Center is silent and inward. This part of us is capable of external consideration—reflecting on what is best for another—rather than the inner consideration of being concerned with what others think of us. The first and second parts want to be understood and to be loved, the third, intellectual part wants to understand and to love. Giving energy to this aspect of our Emotional life protects the energy that is robbed from our sentimental up and down Emotions. This is the threshold and doorway for our spiritual life. The Emotional Center often used as a search for meaning in life, might find faith in something, yet the deepest meaning is inside our true self—the divine presence of our own higher centers.

The whole thing, the most difficult thing, is to wake the heart. Somehow one has to learn to live in the heart, to judge from the heart, as ordinarily we live in a mechanical mind and judge from that. It is shifting the center of attention in oneself. For the movements of the heart are so quick that only if one can learn to live there for some time, is it possible to catch them as they pass and obey them. This also means that we have to learn to feed the heart, taking emotional impressions directly there; just as we now take knowledge directly into the mind. To find truth, head and heart must work together in the right way. —*Rodney Collin*

Examples include: *Nina Simone, Aretha Franklin, Whitney Houston, Oscar Wilde, Edith Piaf, Sarah Bernhardt, Sidney Poitier, Princess Diana, Meryl Streep, Matthew Broderick, Andrea Dworkin, Taylor Swift, Mariah Carey, Virginia Woolf, Kate Winslet, Anne Frank, Dolly Parton, Barbra Streisand, Eisabeth Taylor, Anne Sexton, Robert Frost, Sylvia Plath, Maya Angelou. Oprah Winfrey.*

SEX CENTER

POSITIVE: PLEASURABLE

NEGATIVE: NEUTRAL

All of our manifestations are dependent upon the energy of the sex center.
—*R. Burton*

*T*he Sex Center, located in the genitals, the Sexual glands, works with Sex energy and has the fastest and most refined vibrational energy of all the centers. This center has no negative half, because discrimination and refinement comes from other centers; there is a pleasurable sensation or nothing. Since the energy of the Sex Center manifests, is filtered through the other centers, it can only be directly studied in higher states of consciousness. This is the most misused of all the centers. 75% of our thoughts come from the Sex Center and color all other thoughts. The instinctive center often overrides its functioning. All of the centers deplete the Sex Center, it is of a finer vibrational level and is typically forced to function on a less refined fuel—like running a new car on leaded gas, or a ballet dancer living on a diet of sugar, soda and hotdogs.

It is a very big thing when the sex center works with its own energy, but it happens very seldom. Sex plays a tremendous role in maintaining the mechanicalness of life. It is the center of gravity of all gatherings. What do you think brings people to restaurants, to various celebrations? One thing only. Sex. It is the principal motive force of all mechanicalness. All sleep, all hypnosis, depends upon it. On the contrary sex which exists by itself and is not dependent on anything else is a great achievement. The lie is in the constant self-deception. —P.D. Ouspensky

The Sexual Center is a source of higher energy. Intensity of experiences and wrong work of the center generally leads to feeling distracted and pulled in many directions. This happens when we are captivated by something or someone resulting in a lack of focus to our aim and priority. This is the center where acting out supplies the most energetic intensity. Negative emotions are often based on Sex energy wrongly used. Overindulgence and avoidance continue the perpetuation of misuse. The Sexual Center is the depository for energy in each person. Sex energy, a refined and powerful energy, is extremely explosive when mishandled. Its energy is recognizable when misused in other centers from the quality of enthusiasm, excitement or fierceness which does not appropriately fit the situation. Moving Sex energy upwards, step by step, we are no longer confined by the limitations of the lower center, allowing life itself to become Sexual. Not to repress, in transforming the lower disappears, dissolves into the higher; now we are using this center to move energy into higher planes.

In this law about the power of sex over people are included many different possibilities. It includes the chief form of slavery and it is also the chief possibility of liberation. 'New birth' depends as much on sex energy as do physical birth and the propagation of species. There are no positive and negative sides in the sex centre. There is either a pleasant sensation or nothing. The sex centre plays a very great part in our life. —P.D. Ouspensky

A small proportion of the energy in this center is used for the continuation of life. The nature of Sex energy moves it to flow towards love, but the stumbling block of the *I* has obstructed it like a barrier, a separation, and so love cannot flow. Our life-force can rise upwards, rather than leak out gradually, then it doesn't recede, it rises upwards from within. Energy in the Sex Center is evolution; the preservation of the species and the development of higher consciousness. Sex energy can be used randomly or it can be employed with creative pursuits, creativity itself is a form of Sexual activity. When an artist's concentration and creativity is total, all is dissolved in the work; whether it's a dance, painting, writing or poetry. The world of aesthetics originating from the seed or root of Sex reaching its highest pleasurable peak will transform the world.

Sex lies at the root of life, and we can never learn to reverence life until we know how to understand sex. —*Havelock Ellis*

The transmutation or conversion of Sex energy into energy of a higher order allows the possibility of inner growth and development of an individual. Sexual energy, when unproductive is spent and wasted, on the other hand when intentional and transformed it creates the force which leads to awakening. There is no other force in a human being which could replace Sex energy. Studies show that all other energies, like the intellect and emotions, feed and grow and live on a surplus of Sex energy. In the Sufi world of Rumi and Hafiz Sexuality is a metaphor for opening to the divine dance where we are penetrated to the ultimate state, awakened to life and love with every breath. Sexuality is symbolically expressed by Kabbalists in openly Sexual images of a bride, referring to Sexual ecstasy and higher states of being. Erotic mysticism and direct adoration of the Shekinah as the bride of God were central to many rites as we study the Chassidic mystical masters and their writings.

To Remain Asleep, or to Awaken

We don't understand that sexual energy connects us to the root of life, to the root of our creativity, that sexual energy is what creates life and is what is creating everything around us. Sex lies at the root of life, and we can never learn reverence for life until we learn reverence for sex. —*Margo Anand*

Energy in its lowest basic raw form is called Sex energy. Sex is the natural biological flow of life energy, the source of all life, creativity itself. Sexual activity is an opportunity for a higher transformation of life energy. The work with Sex energy may have little to do with physical Sexual activity. It's about learning to use the Sex Center in a new way, which has been described as *being in love with the world*. Experiencing life with the pleasurable sensations and aliveness that we feel when we are Sexually turned on is using the energy of the center for beautiful living. Energy in itself just *is*, the applied manifestations are how it translates. Expressed through the mind it becomes mental, through a Sexual outlet it becomes Sexual. So we either indulge or direct our Sexual energy into whatever center we choose, lower or higher. Given the excessive amount of energy in the Sex Center, much of our life is concerned with directing Sex energy; essence, personality, higher centers, negative emotions, identification, and imagination, are all using it; therefore we can use Sex energy though this center to remain asleep or to wake up.

The Sexual Center, misused in our lower centers, becomes uselessly aggressive, and over the years, constantly robbed of its energy, it haunts us and becomes coarse, or lifeless, flattened, neutralized, or belligerent and hostile. This energy that is the root of our life, that we oppose and suppress without knowing its sacredness; how to know and direct our energy is how we create a diamond from coal, a pearl in an oyster shell. The Sex Center is a power in the body, not in the mind or feelings. Therefore, it is not concerned with feelings, thoughts, wishes or desires; those are a reflection of the confusion and imbalance in a person. The work of transformation happens only after understanding what the body is and how to use it.

There are three kinds of wine, produced from syrup, grain and honey. But there is a fourth, the darkest of all, the wine of sex, which has intoxicated the whole world. When the mind is uncontrolled, then the body, which is the object of affection to the ignorant, also suffers, and when the mind is controlled, then the body also remains in a good state. —Mahatma Dattatreya

THREE LEVELS OF ATTENTION

The division into three horizontal parts begins with the first level, the automatic mechanical part that works with no attention. Sexual attraction is not by choice. At birth the body carries pleasure; nursing, thumb sucking are parts of the autosexual stage which is biological, a natural phenomenon, the source of all life. At the first level pleasure is a natural expression. Without repression this center brings satisfaction, self-gratification, an interest in life. The second and emotional level takes attention, but this attention does not require effort. Attracted and held by the subject itself usually through identification, we name this: fascination, involvement, infatuation, entertainment, obsession, things we like or enjoy, our preoccupation.

The emotional quality of the second level activates and brings pleasurable feelings that eventually turn into their polar opposite producing unpleasant feelings that feel like unhappiness, roller coasting, until finally dropping, flattening into a neutral place of withdrawal. Between hate and love, between the positive energy and the negative electricity, quite illogical, this paradox is found. Sex addicts and numerous other addictions flourish at the second level which carries tremendous energy, filling many hours of personal life. Aggression and hostility, violence, cruelty and power permeate and become confused as Sexuality often times creating great suffering.

The third and intellectual level has the capacity for recognition, originality, inspiration, resourcefulness, meaning and innovation. Working with an attention that is controlled through effort, Sex energy is transformed into higher planes. This is the beginning awareness that the heart of the Sex Center contains love in an unmanifest form.

Love is a symbol of eternity. It wipes out all sense of time, destroying all memories of a beginning and all fear of an end. —*Madame de Stael*

SHIFTING TO AWARENESS

When the Sex Center is engaged without self-deception, is conscious of itself, it is remarkable. Since this is the one center that has no negative part, there are only pleasant sensations and feelings or no sensations or feelings. Negative or bad Sexual feelings are coming from other centers. Abuse of this center is visible throughout the world. The distortion of dressing and acting in ways to arouse another's Sex Center diverts attention from creating presence, encourages unconsciousness and builds a hypnotic effect. Most sports, war, violence, gambling, excessive digital use, television soap operas, journalistic reporting, gawking at entertainers personal lives, internet pornography, purposeless competition and record setting is done through the Sex Center. The clue lies in noticing the uselessness of the venture. To value our energy, time, body, self, is to make choices that engage meaning and purpose.

Let your lovemaking be like a prayer between you, your god, and your beloved. Talk to and make love to your lover as you would to god. —*Elizabeth Kelley*

To direct our energy toward our higher centers we progress. When the lower centers are out of balance they steal energy from the Sex Center. When the Sex Center perceives it has been robbed, it needs to steal energy from other centers in order to be able to function. So it gets loaded with heavier hydrogens. Thus Sexual imbalance occurs, which in turn unbalances the whole person. This energy can be transformed; controlling negativity and imagination creates an astral body, ignites the pineal gland. Quite difficult to observe, notice as our intensity and speed accelerates, feeling enthusiastic, excited, animated, glowing, zealous in activities, that Sex energy has entered other centers. Once this energy is refined, transformed, it moves upward; it becomes love, prayer, compassion, adoration, intimacy, devotion, it enters every creative dimension.

The key to the understanding of sex is the knowledge that sexual energy is the finest and subtlest naturally produced in the human organism. Thus sexual energy can be turned to any purpose, can express itself on any level. It contains the potentiality of the highest forms of creation, and it also contains the possibility of destroying a man, and wrecking him physically, morally and emotionally. It can combine with his most bestial side, with criminal impulses of cruelty, hatred and fear; or it can combine with his most refined aspirations and keenest sensibilities. And in either case it will immensely heighten the tendency to which it becomes attached. In a very mysterious way, sexual energy contains within itself on a molecular level the universal signature or cosmic pattern. —Rodney Collin

To have a right relationship to Sex is to integrate its higher possibilities into ordinary everyday life. Spiritual evolution is connected to work on oneself, to Sexual health. The unhealthy manifestations of the Sex Center show up as: fear, disgust, distrust, indifference, irritation, disinterest, repressed abstinence, hormonal imbalance, cruelty, impotence, Sexual addiction, phobias, violence, suspicion, distortions of jealousy, repugnance, pseudo-morality, ownership, danger, war, negative attitudes, revenge, condemnation, distraction, wasted energy, crimes like rape, pedophilia, murder, child abuse, pornography and all other crimes of passion.

We will make love an art, and we will love like artists. —Marianne Williamson

The healthy use of the Sex Center contains no danger. This includes relationships based on equality. The healthy use of the Sex Center repels everything that is negative, the beauty of the images, impressions and sensations received in all centers renews energy, is harmonious, has room for Tantric and erotic art. There is no contradiction in the other centers, they are all positive and in agreement. To develop spiritual bodies made up of finer energy-matter than the physical body; healthy Sexuality is vital to direct the flow of energy towards the interests of inner evolution. A conscious use of Sexual energy is rare in relation to a mass culture which promotes promiscuity, pornography, violence, woman hating and religions that chastise masturbation, abortion and promote across the board Sexual abstinence.

LIFE-ENERGY

Everything that people do is connected with sex: politics, religion, art, the theater, music, is all sex. —*G.I. Gurdjieff*

The intentional use of the Sex Center and Sexual energy for the purposes of inner evolution have several dimensions. There are those who choose renunciation, complete abstinence for the possibility of transmutation of Sexual energy. Sex for them is not coordinated with their other functions and does not evolve by itself. Their path includes a struggle against Sex. There are those that regard using the Sex Center for Sexuality to express the sacred as an object of worship. Their Sex is gradually transformed in accordance with the transformation of their other functions. This is the direction of Tantra, an ancient tradition that includes practices used to expand one's understanding. At its purest form, used today, Tantric couples worship each other as equal manifestations of the divine, offering their practice to the service of a higher energy, committed to fidelity and trust, passion and love. In the viewpoint of *The Way of The Lover* Sex is a natural phenomenon, Sex energy moved upwards, life is beautiful, healthy, harmonious and whole.

We all have one energy: Sex. The source of existence, *elan-vital*—life energy, vital force, once refined is transformed and moves upward becoming love, prayer, worship, creative impulse, glimpses of the divine, spirituality. Repressed or acted out it becomes perverse and obsessive, we become uncreative, deadened, imbalanced, compulsive. The Sex Center offers the possibility of mystical states. As the source of life, with clear Sexual energy we give birth: to ourself. We reproduce ourself repeatedly. The Sex Center is closely aligned with the mystery of death. As we suppress Sex, we suppress death. Not to renounce Sex or death, to transcend, disappear, needs vanish and we drop into being here now. To die before we die; our mystical birth rests on our ability to convert Sexual energy.

When you are involved in any deep participation with your total body, it is sexual. When I use the word sexual I mean this experience of totality. The sex center is raw energy, and all energy is sexual. Like a diamond found in the mines it has to be cut, polished; much work is needed. Then it will be possible to recognize that it is a diamond. It has to be transformed for there to be transcendence. —Osho

Examples include: *Marilyn Monroe, Anna Nicole Smith, Jessica Simpson, Paris Hilton, Rihanna, Pamela Anderson, Charlie Sheen, Mario Lopez, Hugh Hefner, Gary Ridgeway the Green River killer, Jeffrey Daumer, Ted Bundy, Miley Cyrus, Avril Lavigne, Carmen Electra, Sofia Vergara, Chris Brown, LaLa, Krishna, Yeshe Tsogyal, Saraha.*

SELF-STUDY CENTER

POSITIVE: DESIRE TO AWAKEN, BALANCE, CERTAINTY

NEGATIVE: UNNECESARY SUFFERING

Study is the first rung on the ladder—the base from which everything ascends. —David Cooper

The Self-Study Center activates an intention towards self-development, separates from a mechanical center of gravity replacing it with an aim to awaken. A permanent center of gravity is established in the ideas, valuation and relationship to inner work. The Self-Study Center is created from being 1, being 2 or being 3 (refer to System 21, Being) with the intention of balancing all five centers: the instinctive, moving, intellectual, emotional and the sex center. The center of gravity, no longer mechanical, is now directed to harmonize all the centers. The memory of the original center we have at birth remains, except now one center no longer is responsible to carry all the weight. Through self-observation a recognition of the difference between thoughts and feelings begins to register. Characterized as *being in the world but not of it*, impressions connect to the Self-Study Center. The impulse to learn and teach replaces movement, sensation, feelings and thinking as the motivational impetus to life. How to be awake in the moment becomes our life curriculum.

Search really begins with seeing the obstructions, the obstacles, the barriers in the way of enabling us to be what we essentially are. And what is not realized sufficiently is that search is no different than a becoming, as one becomes a

lawyer, a doctor, a painter, a truck driver, a cook. One has to know how to search. Here we come to the necessity of being able to concentrate in the same way that if I wish to be a good baker I have to concentrate on baking. In search, one is faced with the necessity of concentrating one's entire attention on this small weak-voiced element in oneself that's crying to be heard. Crying in the wilderness. Search entails recognition of the distractions in the way of looking, of seeing. So perhaps one could come to a definition of search in the sense that it is a seeing with an eye that's not clouded by thought, by intellectualism of a mechanical nature, not distracted by feelings. It requires a watching, a witnessing, of what is. Then the question of 'what is search?' will probably be answered. It will be answered by itself. —William Segal

Being mechanically centered in one of the first five centers becomes a barrier to our natural unfolding, creating a lopsided, distorted, imbalanced person who is dominated by their body, feelings, or their intellect. Self-Study Center is a first step out, a door to the higher centers towards individuality and unity. The desire to be present to our life, to accept anything less than awakening, is the rung on the ladder that creates a witness and loosens us from our unnecessary suffering. To become aware of this external world, while observing how our inner world is stimulated by the outer world, we begin a direct relationship to our awakening. To ask of ourself, *who is in pain and suffering*, we find a perspective, eventually seeing that most suffering is imaginary. What are we if we are not that suffering? Helen Keller demonstrated this when she wrote: *The world is full of suffering, it is also full of overcoming it.* The Self-Study Center is a step towards finding the dimension in ourselves that is beyond form. To be aware of the suffering and to be aware of something that is not suffering is a huge step out.

What appears will also disappear and is therefore impermanent. The Self never appears and disappears and is therefore permanent. It is the only reality. —Ramana Maharshi

In the positive direction, our desire to awaken that force within, our drive to break out from our bondage delivers us from the disquiet of worldly distractions, to see what is behind the veil of ordinary life concerns. Recognizing our thoughts as illusions about self and projections towards others loosens the chains of our sleep. Self-Study brings about self-consciousness, seeing ourselves *as we are.* Experiencing impermanence, the natural disasters of life: deaths of loved ones, hurricanes, fires, tornados, illness, volcanic eruptions, a tsunami, what life brings; so many temptations and circumstances that stand before our being present to our life. A Sufi teacher wrote: *Do not occupy your precious time except with the most precious of human experiences, the state of being occupied with the present.* Many lessons are received at this level, as well as directing energy to simplify, to pull back our involvement with the inessential, the keeping busy.

It is possible to get out of a trap. However, in order to break out of a prison, one must first confess to being in a prison. The trap is man's emotional structure, his character structure. There is little use in devising systems of thought about the nature of the trap if the only thing to do in order to get out of the trap is to know the trap and to find the exit. —Wilhelm Reich

Directed intention is necessary to increase the discrimination that sets the tone for the Self-Study Center. Distractions now have less charge. Our purpose and work begin to have clarity and life falls into place around that discovery. What appears as conflict, the unresolved parts, continue to exist, yet they are less likely to lead to a road of agitation. Self-Study Center is learning how to use life; circumstances are *grist for the mill. Hard* and *difficult* become love words, beginning to know that we are not given an obstacle that we cannot use, learn from, overcome. Understanding and valuing awakening above everything, we are no longer tossed about by the wind; everything revolves around the aim of self-development and awakening. Every detail of our life becomes an opportunity, a work for us to become present to our lives.

You have come here having understood the necessity of struggling with yourself and only with yourself. Therefore thank everyone who gives you the opportunity to do so. —G. I. Gurdjieff

THREE LEVELS OF ATTENTION

The division into three horizontal levels starts with a mechanical part which functions automatically and without awareness, requiring little, if any, attention. The impulse to use everything as a teaching is set, although whether it is received as certainty or as unnecessary suffering is not predetermined. A vacation in New York, no longer a time for aimless wandering distraction, idle partying, time is used with intention: meaningful lectures, being present to the architecture and neighborhoods, yoga classes, meditation, a book fair, walking in nature, places that connect to the values of our lifestyle; meaningful conversations now satisfy, where noise and commotion, shopping and chatting on the phone were once interesting entertainment.

Conversation is the laboratory and workshop of the student. —*Ralph Waldo Emerson*

The second emotional level consists of effortless attention. Attracted and held by the subject itself, most often through identification, the suffering becomes full in bloom. Identified with waking up means that one is asleep, not in the moment, trying to make things other than they are, a further avoidance to being present. Here is the home of personal unsteady feelings, inner considering, excessive exercising, obsessions, security issues, self-deprecation, unworthiness and comparative thinking. Stepping away from the world, often the identification is with a partner, teacher or Guru, a form of spiritual exploration; swept up in its energy, teachings get used to turn against self or others. Alcohol and marijuana sedate the mature and older soul feelings of self-deprecation and societal separation. The second level is a place of excess and overindulgence, and this applies to most anything the person with a Self-Study second level engages in, regardless to its value. Meditation, chanting, politics and causes, relationships, workshopping, pot-luck dinners, week-end retreats; used randomly and in excess become a higher level distraction, yet, still a distraction.

When we are identified, we take something that is not truly ourselves to be our identity. It is exactly like a dog and a bone. We get identified with trivial things. Aware of one thing in all the universe, then for us that is the entire universe, and, if what we are doing represents the whole universe, it is obviously very, very important. To lift our heads out of the water, we need to practice and develop a skill needed for separation, for being aware of things separately, that will keep our sleep from becoming too comfortable, so that we are continuously reminded that there is something we need to do—to separate and try to wake up. —Girard Haven

The third and intellectual level includes the capacity for recognition and meaning; this is attention controlled through effort. From this place we look at suffering differently than those living in the first five centers. The words *hard, difficult, struggle, demanding, work* and *challenge* deepen, continue to take on a new dimension. No longer something to avoid or medicate, instead, seen as opportunities to hold or create energy, for discovery, patience, determination, to create a new level of awareness, to fan the spark of consciousness. Attention and intention are directed to transform the *tough* moments. Here is where understanding plays a large part in our freedom. Understanding is the note that third level sounds.

By understanding everything becomes simple. We see what is, objectively.

Where we stand, objectively. What we can do, objectively. Understanding avoids useless friction, pointless struggle; makes us steady, tolerant, kind, 'understanding.' Gives us weight. To reach real understanding we must study more, much more, verify in worldly terms all that has been said or felt. —Rodney Collin

AWARENESS

A person with a Self-Study Center of gravity is not yet balanced. The difference is that there is an awareness to the imbalance. Studying ourself, to make something of ourself that will resist the influences of life: *to be in the world, but not of it*, is separating from the effects of life, not from life. Through self-inquiry we begin to be in a state where there is a blending and balance between the energies of our bodily sensations and instincts, our feelings and emotions and our mental processes. This process of investigation brings us to familiarity with ourself, to know who we are and how we function The world outside is a true reflection of the world inside, to create stability inside helps us determine the way we respond to circumstances, helps us to repair this planet.

If our center of gravity is in the transformation of negative emotions into positive ones, if we sacrifice the irrelevant, it is because we love nothing more than our aim to awaken. A true relationship can only be successful if both people are living to be present. —Robert Earl Burton

Community, like-minded people generate energy. At this level of inner work a reflection that smiles back is valuable. Gravitating to areas of older soul orientation, places like Sedona, Santa Fe, Berkeley, Boulder, the Florida Keys, Maui, Hawaii and many other coastal areas, Thailand, India and Vietnam become magnets. Meeting at places like organic markets, book fairs, yoga and Buddhist retreats, pot luck dinner meditations, days of mindfulness, classes where clear intentions are set for inner work, as well as living in a sacred space called home, all of these maintain our connections as reminders. Marching to a different tune, conventional society with its bureaucratic organizations and 9-5 working schedule rarely engages those with this center. A search for something more humane and beautiful than the alienating experiences of life in Western Society impels the drive to evolve. Cognizant to the toxicity in the mainstream diet, attention is paid to eating naturally. The medical establishment is no longer a panacea or authority. Sensing the truth to universal laws, the laws of the physical universe and earth energy enter this domain. Eventually one claims responsibility for one's own physical, mental and spiritual development. Living under the law of grace, keeping an eye on the many temptations that pull us away from the essential purpose of our life, attention is placed on harmony and balance.

The magnetic center which leads us to a way of understanding is different than that which leads towards a monastery, a school of yoga or an ashram. It demands another kind of initiative. It demands a broad mind and discernment, that is, the ability to distinguish the mechanical from the conscious in oneself. It requires the awakening of another intelligence. What can be attained does not depend on obedience. The knowledge that results is proportional to the state of awakening, of understanding. —Jeanne de Salzmann

Sacred Psychology is a path that brings people to a Self-Study Center, eventually leading to the Fifth Way, *The Way of the Lover.* Service, working to change the conditions that create discord may show up differently for each individual. The similarity lies in the directed intention and energized presence that each person brings. Higher energy empowers us to live in harmony with existence.

The meaning of your life depends on which ideas you permit to use you. Who you think you are determines where you put your attention. Where you direct your attention creates your life experiences, and brings a new course of events into being. Where you habitually put your attention is what you worship. What do you worship in this mindstream called your life? —Gangaji

It is within ourselves and through ourselves that we ultimately have to find the answers. The self-knowledge we need is an inner experience, consciously lived, of what we are, including the whole range of impressions of oneself which one receives. It gradually becomes clear that self-study has no meaning unless it is placed in the context of life as a whole and the whole world in which we live. Self-study is inseparable from a living study of the cosmos. —Jean Vaysse

Examples include: *Carlos Castaneda, Elisabeth Kübler-Ross, Andrew Weil, David Deida, Deva Premal, Natalie Goldberg, Helen Palmer, David Darling, Kabir Helminski, Reshad Feild, Daniel Ladinsky, David Zeller, Eli-Jaxon-Bear, Lama Surya Das, Pema Chodrin, Joan Halifax, Alan Lew, Chris Griscom, David Cooper, Jack Kornfield, Stephen Levine, Jose Stevens, Andrew Harvey, Jon Kabat-Zinn, Tara Brach, Ken Wilbur, Sharon Salzberg, Coleman Barks.*

HIGHER CENTERS:

INSTINCTIVE, MOVING, EMOTIONAL, INTELLECTUAL, SEX, SELF-STUDY

POSITIVE: STATES OF BEING, PRESENCE

NEGATIVE: NEUTRAL

The beginning of freedom is the moment you realize there is a vast realm of intelligence beyond thought, that all things that truly matter—beauty, love, creativity, joy, inner peace—arise from beyond the mind. You begin to awaken. —Eckhart Tolle

The Higher Centers are associated with symbolic meaning, truth, conscience, love, energy, objective reason and alternate states of reality. The lower centers contain functions and differ in their speed and quality of content. The Higher Centers involve the possibility of higher states of consciousness. To enter the Higher Centers we have to be willing to accept and receive higher moments. The biggest obstacle is thinking that we already are that, therefore not hearing what is required. The greatest ideas and experiences come from the Higher Centers. Our lower centers don't have the language to describe the impressions that are received from Higher Centers, they work inefficiently and at cross purposes. For most people the energy from Higher Centers does not flow to lower centers, blocking access to living in higher states like joy and ecstasy. Higher forces can't get through owing to our self-admiration, our self-importance—our personality.

In higher states gratitude changes into something else. It changes into knowledge of what one has to do, and even —if it is intense enough—into power to carry that out. —Rodney Collin

The Higher Centers are always available at a level greater than we live, a level beyond our personality, always ready to change us, to transmit their force to us, yet we don't hear them or receive their energy owing to our state of sleep. When the lower centers are balanced, when we bring the lower into order and when the lower centers are energized by intentional efforts, then we gradually establish a link with our Higher Centers. This happens through balancing the lower centers to work efficiently and quickly so that energy is left to feed and make sense of the Higher Centers. Otherwise when daily consciousness connects, for example, to the Higher Intellectual Center, and there are moments when it does, the mind refuses to take in the numerous images, ideas, emotions and thoughts, and instead registers a blank, a state of unconsciousness. This displays resistance and resistance is almost always unconscious.

Every moment we spend in higher consciousness helps uplift the consciousness of the whole world. —the lightworkers

DIMINISHING PERSONALITY

Through shifting, non-identifying with ourselves, which begins with self-observation, we begin to see ourself as the invention that we are, looking grown up, mature yet far removed from our essential nature. Taking personal thoughts as real we can't separate ourself to see that we are mostly built on the sands of personality. Higher Centers connect to us when there is truth in us, not when we identify with the kind of person we think and take for granted that we are, since we are not what or who we think we are. Set attitudes obstruct self-change, it is you, *you, yourself,* who must change. Personality has to become passive to escape its prison for there to be a new valuation of self and a realization of freedom and meaning in life. This is not about life and what it has made you. It is about reaching the more silent areas of consciousness, going beyond the noisy region of our mind where we spend the majority of our life.

The highest ideas cannot be understood by the five lower centers, but are reserved for higher centers. Higher centers have their own intelligence, and their own way of receiving information. The only way to discover one's true identity is by experiencing higher centers. The are designed to serve humanity. Higher centers are out of time, it's like being able to see among blind people. They observe the world as it is, without thought patterns. Moments in which one experiences higher centers are imperishable. —Robert Earl Burton

Higher Centers are realized when we are no longer immersed in the personal self. To be self-involved contradicts the possibility of accessing the Higher Centers. It's giving up excessive thinking and talking about ourself as well as the issues that preoccupy our thoughts with self-importance; this opens the door to Higher Centers. Getting rid of ourself, gaining a viewpoint that is outside the personal; feeding the higher part of the self-study center opens the contact, connects the lower centers with the Higher Centers. Self-observation leads to inner separation which is the beginning of awakening. Taking an inner glance at ourself in a neutral way, we begin to detach from our emotional baggage. The Higher Centers are always available, it is we who are not. Through them we penetrate time and space, also called a third or fourth state of consciousness. This state of clarity is the perception of time stopping, being present. Once we connect to the Higher Centers our consciousness expands and we have glimpses into a previously unknown world, symbolic and with mythic meaning.

The presence of higher centers is a reward sufficient unto itself, as they exist in the eternal Now. —*Robert Earl Burton*

STATES OF CONSCIOUSNESS

The Higher Centers are accessed from an altered state of consciousness. The first state of consciousness is ordinary sleep at night time, the second state is daily sleep, the condition that most of the world walks around in, the third state is self-consciousness, self-awareness, or mindfulness, the state in which we are actually conscious of our own existence. Thich Nhat Hanh describes this third state as *keeping our consciousness alive to present reality.* The fourth state, objective consciousness, is consciousness of the nature of things in themselves, where we come into contact with the real world that we have been cut off from by the senses. States of being describe the centers which bring a discovery of true identity. Called, *the eyes of the soul,* Higher Centers offer a finer subtle energy available for us to awaken. Negativity undermines these states, often in the disguise of fear, confusion, anxiety, unhappiness or anger.

You cannot exist one second without impressions. This idea is fantastic. Perhaps it demands a lifetime to understand what it means. It is closely related to another idea which very largely escapes us, and which is that only higher centers can really receive, properly, the food of impressions. When they are functioning what is needed is their proper link with lower centers. —*H. Tracol*

The educational training in the school system does not lead to higher levels of consciousness, nor to balancing ourselves. An excess of information, the social intellectual climate and the information via media encases us within a circle of reason. Freedom from this is only possible via the heart, which is why traditions like the *Way of the Lover* speak to breaking open the heart. Access to emotions is needed to produce the higher hydrogen, energy or substance that activates the Higher Centers. Learning how to bring the mind into the heart, conscious awareness that integrates intelligence and intensifies knowing, the center of our being, is *the peace that passes understanding*, carrying intelligence to the emotions and emotional quality to the intelligence. Verifying that being present to our life is more important than the circumstances in our life we create the efforts to taste presence, the awareness of ourselves in the moment; without presence there is only an imaginary life.

THE WORLD OF HIGHER CENTERS

It is wisdom to know others; it is enlightenment to know one's self. —*Lao-Tzu*

Separating from personality and looking at ourself objectively we enter the realm of Higher Centers. The emotional center, an instrument of perception and compassion, becomes a window into meaning and significance, the cosmic purpose of the world. Brief unexpected random moments, like going to a new city and running into a best friend from childhood, or being in a near-fatal accident, stepping into the ocean after a long day and feeling exhilaration, access these dimensions. The suddenness of that instance jolts us into a state of higher consciousness. The Higher Emotional Center reached through a third state sees images or symbols before translating them into pictures or language. Exceptional moments, an earthquake, a fire, an auto accident: intense emotions that produce a state of clarity open the passageway. Time is experienced as stopping. ESP comes from the functions of the Higher Centers, sometimes through effort, other times triggered by these intensities, when things are experienced vividly. A further characteristic of all the Higher Centers is a sharp and penetrating awareness.

Two levels of conscious functioning above the ordinary are self-consciousness and objective consciousness. Self-consciousness occurs spontaneously for brief moments that often leave particularly vivid memories behind them. These are the high moments that may occur in situations of great danger, intense emotion, or extraordinary stress. Then attention is clear, impartial and relatively complete and is divided between self and environment so that action unfolds spontaneously, appropriately and sometimes even heroically. Self-consciously can also become a way of being. There are many levels of development. It starts with a division into two, as some of the attention is given to one-self and some is available to perceive the environment. In its fullest form, the basic contraction of ego is absent, producing a particular quality of experience. Above self-consciousness there is a higher state, objective consciousness, which also occurs in spontaneous flashes. Such moments are life's 'peak experiences'—or they are totally forgotten as lower centers fall into unconsciousness to protect the body's delicate machinery from unbearably high energy. During states of objective consciousness higher centers are connected to the ordinary ones. One is fully attuned to, and aware of, cosmic laws. One understands, one knows, Along with the 'knowing' comes an ecstatic or blissful quality of joyful acceptance. This condition, too, may become an ever-present state. —Kathleen Riordan Speeth

The Higher Intellectual Center is entered through a fourth state of consciousness, which is objective and develops from self-consciousness. The experience of truth, how life fits together, conscience, contentment, happiness, true self-knowledge and philosophy are Higher Intellectual experiences. Everything is as it really is, no illusions or pretense, no smoke and mirrors. Inner thoughts and feelings, now transparent, create an ease and naturalness. The rate of impressions are increased and deepened. Empathy, mind into heart, a conscious awareness integrates intelligence so that it amplifies perception. In the Higher Centers thinking is often symbolic. Contact with the Higher Intellectual Center is of a transcendent nature, is what lies beyond the reach of the intellect. There is no direct link between the lower and Higher Intellectual Center because the lower intellect stands in the way, analyzing, substituting ideas and representations for the thing itself, replacing immediate perception with imagination, disrupting the immediacy of the contact; the lower centers have no interest in being present. Understanding others, freed of thinking in terms of objects and subjects we begin to see relationships as vehicles of transformation.

OUR AUTHENTIC TRUE IDENTITY

The key to growth is the introduction of higher dimensions of consciousness into our awareness. —Lao Tzu

In esoteric writings the Higher Centers are referred to as a *second birth*, entering *the Kingdom*, the *mystical inner marriage*. A momentary glimpse of Higher Centers may happen, but essentially preparation is needed. The inability to sustain these states rests on the fact that most people look for meaning in their lower centers. Among other places, the intellectual center looks for value in books and lectures; the emotional center looks for meaning in religion, ritual, spiritual groups, and relationships; the instinctive and moving centers look for significance in food, yoga, martial arts, travel, physical achievement; the sex center looks for value in sensations, attractions and humor; the self-study center looks for meaning in the form of workshops, mindful conversation, intentional aims and growth. Instead, the higher meaning is inner, is a wordless presence. Every center has its own different thrust, and we tend to live in a limited pattern of expression not realizing that with directed attention we would have a wider range of experiences and meaning.

If one is awake, one can love. If one is asleep one cannot love. The only way to discover one's true identity is by experiencing higher centers. It is such a vivid experience that a sound person won't forget it. —Robert Earl Burton

Thinking in a new way about everything, including ourself, about our past and present life, shifts us to a higher level of understanding. These undeveloped parts of ourselves are not reached through becoming more ambitious in the world, instead, the higher meaning is inside, experienced through a relationship to our own Higher Centers. The inner work of promoting and prolonging presence, finding presence that resonates in the now, is the connection. Madame de Salzmann expressed this when she remarked: *The energy of the body is too low to make contact with the very high energy which comes from above. The higher part of the mind needs to be connected with the body. The process requires active attention. To respect and serve the finer energy in you—which is not you—life makes sense. The body must obey something higher, otherwise it has no purpose. It cannot serve only itself.*

Mindfulness, sacred dances, chanting, nigguns, meditation, tantra, great art, beautiful poetry, nature and conscious breathing uplift the instinctive, moving, emotional, intellectual, sex and self-study centers. Breath is life. The sex center is uplifted once the breathing system is changed. The breath is the bridge between the body and the soul. Essentially mystic experiences, ecstatic states, are where we have received information about people who connect their lower centers to their Higher Centers. In a Higher Moving Center there is a sense of being connected to the energy of everything. The experience of awe, taking in the energy of an object like the ocean, or a mountain, or a rose; we are absorbing the chemistry through our body and senses.

In higher states gratitude changes into something else. It changes into knowledge of what one has to do, and even—if it is intense enough—into power to carry that out. —*Rodney Collin*

The senses are needed for Higher Centers to be accessed. Listening to music, looking at the ocean, reading or hearing poetry, moments savored alone; time no longer exists. This fourth state of consciousness manifests as presence, as being present. This perception of the connectedness of the universe, beauty, an ecstatic experience, contacts the Higher Moving and Instinctive Centers. Using a different fuel and a finer vibration, we become conscious of our own consciousness. The Higher Self-Study Center knows that there is a story bigger than the personal, even larger than the collective human story. This is the center that connects with the story of life itself and lives as a representative of that life. Higher states do not replace lower states, they add to them, and we become aware of both. Everything is the same, except us; our relationship and attitude to all things expands.

Wonder and I took a vow; we exchanged rings. I fell in love, and she accepted all my desires. I am lying now in a meadow, holding the sky in my arms. If I turn my gaze away from you, this earth, please do not feel ignored. I'll come back and kiss you again. —Rumi

Higher Centers have been called divine intelligence in human form. We might have brief momentary access to them; what has been hidden to us is proportional to our understanding and state of awakening. Opening a door to live in this realm is a possibility. The Higher Centers are out of time. These transforming states of awareness are wordless. We read and learn through the mystics about ecstatic states, visions and revelations, deep penetrating silence; about becoming a universal instrument. Illumination through these centers cause a disappearance of the individual, a unification. As the self remembers to awaken, states appear. We see, we are, present. The Higher Centers are functions of the soul and perceive the connectedness of all things. To penetrate beyond time and space into the eternal reality, we live in a state of peace and detachment. Here in the Higher Centers universal laws become the seat of conscious wisdom; awakened love and compassion.

One of the secrets of awakening is that higher centers cannot be evoked if one is thinking about oneself too much. Higher centers emerge only if one forgets oneself. One's life becomes more interesting to the extent that one doesn't speak about oneself or think about oneself. The presence of higher centers is the hidden meaning of life on earth. Ultimately, they unselfishly serve. —R. Burton

Examples include: *Walt Whitman, Kahlil Gibran, Abraham Joshua Heschel, Jeanne de Salzmann, George Gurdjieff, Gangaji, Zalman Schacter-Shalomi, Thich Nhat Hahn, Ramana, the Dalai Lama, J. Krishnamurti, Osho.*

B E I N G

I   T H R O U G H   7

If one appreciates something with the mind, one **knows** *it; if one appreci-*
ates it with the emotions, one **feels** *it; if one appreciates it with the external*
physical organs, one **senses** *it. But if one simultaneously appreciates it with*
the mind, emotions and physical senses, then one really **understands** *it.*
—Rodney Collin

There are stages in human development; This system Being 1 to 7
divides people into seven categories according to either their state or
by which *brain* predominates. People have similarities, yet it is important to be able to distinguish the differences. Nature in its variation and
contrasts makes it fairly simple to see its differences. Systems such as this
are a resource to recognize diversity in people; their differing kinds of
perceptions, wants, needs, and functioning. Centers of Gravity, System
20, is a useful reference point to study along with this system, Being 1
through 7.

Using the framework of the categories, the first six centers or six
independent minds, which contain what most know as functions and
tasks, includes most of the population born with a center of gravity in
one of the five lower centers. All six can function with or without our
being conscious of them. Unbalanced, mechanical, all on the same level,
differing in their reliance on one function or another, with a misaligned,
unsymmetrical kind of experience and life, people with any of the first
six centers predominant have a style of seeing the world that attracts
and calls to them. Each has the possibility of awakening out of their

limitation. Without unity, all six centers are a mechanical reaction to the moment. Lacking wholeness, an inner life, self-awareness, everything real lies in their outer world, there is rarely any thinking or feeling beyond the personal self. There is little maturity beyond what is personally wanted, nothing much emotionally developed beyond self-love and self-interest, no genuine external consideration or ability to truly feel or think as another might, unless for self-interest or in the realm of personal advantage and credit.

In the world we live in there is this process of conditioning that goes on from an early age which rapidly makes a young person into yet another believer in this whole set of illusions; human behavior that consists of habits and reflexes. Everything that is not a reflexive result of the hard-wired neurological machinery is a matter of habits learned from childhood to the present, and if people were to see that they would experience horror at their condition, but, for the most part, people don't see it. —Kevin Langdon

Relying on one center, not developing other centers, leaves us ill-equipped to move fluidly in the world. This is one of the reasons stress, addictions, and prescription drugs flourish in the Western world. Regardless to success or fame, not having explored other centers we are ill-prepared, poorly equipped to meet new challenges. A person efficient in one area appears steady, yet when conditions and the particulars change and new unfamiliar circumstances appear that sureness wavers. Most people maintain routines and schedules, live in self-deception and illusion, are not flexible to what emerges, are busy keeping up appearances. To function from self, not from impulse and reaction, we need to develop and balance the body, mind, feelings, sexuality and movements.

Becoming aware of what shapes our reactions, our behavior, our influences, our nature and how our reactions have a life of their own is the study. To go beyond the automatic level of attention takes learning and intention. Notice how depression and negativity easily creep in when we are physically challenged with an illness or accident. The study of the different centers in System 20, Centers of Gravity demonstrates the programming, disassociations and disorganization of our activity throughout most of our life. To be informed from the intellect or emotions alone is to characterize human beings, but not to know Being itself, which is where meaning resides, leaves us lacking substance. Therefore, we learn to bring together all the parts of ourself in order to become aware and know the true nature of self and life.

Learning is the best of all wealth; it is easy to carry, thieves cannot steal it, the tyrants cannot seize it; neither water nor fire can destroy it; and far from decreasing, it increases by giving. —Naladiyar

BALANCING

Being 4—Being 7 represent possibilities to actualize states of consciousness. Through developing undeveloped functions we arrive at a place of certainty. Ultimately no longer existing in the image of, we become directly connected to the highest level of understanding, considered the *in-breathing of the spirit*. Without wholeness we live in a world lacking depth of being, diminishing our creative power. To re-educate ourselves and have impulses that serve our well-being, to have resourcefulness in our functions so that we think, move, and feel from a central balanced place, is the strategy for this system. The world lives reactively without direction from an integrated self. To experience ourself as a whole Being, to go beyond the outside of things, we come to a place of understanding, which is *knowing in all centers simultaneously*, and which is necessary for inner evolution.

With conscious effort a new chemical substance is made in one's organism that makes for understanding. You must make personal effort with a newly received idea—you create substances that way, a deposit of new chemical substances. Ideas are like food—must be eaten, digested, even cause nausea. To be sympathetic to ideas is nothing; sympathy is merely chemistry, not understanding. Sympathy=law of fusion of similarities; nothing new is deposited. —*Margaret Anderson*

To use this system we need to learn the difference between states and a permanently established level of Being. States are available and happen on a horizontal plane. They are tastes that come and go, allowing us to briefly enter third and fourth states, the world of Being 5 and 6. The first and second state of consciousness are almost totally a subjective state, in it things are not as they seem. This is the world of illusion and distraction, social lying. The contradiction, the gaps between our knowledge and our understanding results in our one-sided development. The third state creates a witness, an observer, mindfulness. The fourth state of consciousness is objective. Everything is seen as it really is. Experiencing ourself and Universal Laws (refer to System 27) moves us from a horizontal shift to permanently establishing a level of Being which can reshape from one world to another. For a state to become permanent, for knowledge to not be greater or outgrow Being, to know a lot and be able to put it into practice, understanding has to develop. Evolution exists as a possibility for humanity as a whole and for human beings on an individual level. For us it is an alchemical process of accumulating and refining finer energies within Being until awakening to higher consciousness.

You have to climb the stairs and rest your feet firmly on each step to reach the summit. —*Aurobindo*

Being 1, 2 and 3

We are all prisoners. But we sit on the keys. Finitude is our cell. The universe is our prison. Our jailkeeper is the act of being. The keys to liberation are clenched tightly in the fists of our own egos. —Tzi Freeman

Being 1, 2 and 3, are equally mechanical and live in their one predominant center (refer to Centers of Gravity, System 20). They are unable to understand either themselves or one another and are incomplete and undeveloped. When we look at our life we see things we wouldn't have done if we had been balanced in mindful awareness; this is a way to look at our mechanicalness. Based in personal feelings, misunderstandings, confusion, identification, violence, anger, conflict and unnecessary suffering; wars happen from this place. **Being 1** lives from the instinctive-moving-sex center, **Being 2** from the emotional center, **Being 3** lives from the intellectual center. **Being 1, 2 and 3** are created by nature, all equally automatic and mechanical, producing aimless activities and distractions, using up physical energy, creating little substance. **Being 1, 2, 3** move on a horizontal plane, where everything repeats itself. It is unusual for any of the three to be still and observe what is, the bombardment of associations keep up a constant whir of activity. All, **1, 2, 3,** have little interest or ability for self-reflection, see life through their primary center, live in uncertainty, strife, suffering, driven and pulled externally and internally, using energy indiscriminately. All become their own worst enemy, cross wiring centers, undermining productive efficient living. The other centers, jumbled and confused, interfere and actually prevent development of the person. When two centers work together, and co-operate, as opposed to doing the wrong work of the center, or working against each other, there is a greater possibility of being watchful, of beginning to pay attention, of being less asleep. Using the wrong center is disharmonious and tiring. Mechanicalness requires a disconnection of centers. This is apparent when someone becomes unnecessarily emotional when they can't open a package, or overly analytic when listening to music.

Whatever that happens to us is always a response to some stimulus. Do we even have any control over what thought comes into our heads when we see someone on the street? No. It happens because we are machines. Something occurs externally and we might have tried to be happy, but then stop being happy. It just happens to us. From that point of view we are machines. It's no different from any other machine: push a certain button and something happens; put a person in a particular situation, something happens. So one of our first steps towards awakening is to realize that we are not 'doing' anything. Everything is happening. The verification that we are really machines opens the way to self-acceptance rather than judgment or self-pity.
—*Girard Haven*

Using this system, first evaluate if you are predominately moving, instinctive, self-study, sexual, emotional, or intellectually centered. Where does energy first affect you, then what is your initial impulse— to move, have sensations, create physical attractions, to think, teach or feel? What hunger drives you? Is it the hunger to know, coming from the intellectual center, or the hunger to be appreciated, coming from the emotional center, or the impulse to travel and eat out in restaurants? These are the centers of gravity for mechanical habituated humanity and the differences promote misunderstanding and disagreement between people. Stimulus initially impacts your predominant center of gravity, for example: to receive a phone call that loved ones are in a plane accident; **Being 1** engages in moving type action-oriented physical activity, sometimes motivated by an intuitive reaction, the center of gravity is in movement, intuition and instincts; stimulus first effects the instinctive-moving-sex center. **Being 2** responds through the emotional center, emotions rise: feelings happen like fear, upset, jealousy, hurt, worry or anger; they react with moods, feelings and desires. **Being 3** receives the impulse first through the intellect and figures out, thinks about, theorizes, before feeling or taking action, they act from information. The person of reason enters everything from mental considerations. Knowing what dominates us; our thoughts, feelings or instincts, gives us the clue as to which brain is the most active, is predominant.

The lower centers, called lower because they operate with relative coarse energies, work according to habits acquired over a lifetime and are generally not in balance with one another. They are lazy and do not want to do their proper work, borrowing energy from one another, which they are poorly adapted to use; they try to do one another's work, which they are not designed to do and do not do efficiently or without undesirable side effects. —Kevin Langdon

The sex center, because of its high speed and force and having a pleasant sensation or nothing—no positive or negative sides—could stand on a level with the higher emotional center. The sex center energy can be used for the four lower centers or for the higher centers, or both. It ignites the pineal gland, which lies deep in the brain, considered to be the seat of the soul. Through the sex center you reproduce yourself, carrying an energy that can be transformed into higher planes, it's content ultimately being non-sexual. A multitude of our manifestations rely on the energy of the sex center, and from sex to love there is a direct route. The most difficult center to observe because of the finer energy which animates it, when exchanging energy with the other lower centers those centers become charged with a useless enthusiastic zeal while the sex center is essentially robbed of its energy and becomes sluggish; we mostly see the sex center activated in the moving and instinctive centers creating frenetic hyperactivity. Sex energy fills life, often functioning disharmoniously; abstinence is not the solution, when working with its own energy, consciously, we receive the internal alchemy needed for awakening. That might look like abstinence or activity depending on the individual.

The sex center is the depository for energy in the machine. It is a different order of creation than the other lower four centers. Wrong work of centers misuses sex energy. If one cannot control one's machine, one is the machine.
—Robert Earl Burton

MECHANICAL LIVING

Being 1, **2**, and **3**, three types of mechanical, one-sided, one-centered people, considered *ordinary human beings*, are unable to act freely, to understand, are not particularly interested in awakening and rely on their one predominant center. All three share the first and second state of consciousness called resting sleep and waking state, it's like sleep in that we function automatically, without consciousness. Unable to perceive the finer vibrations coming from higher consciousness due to a density and coarseness of their nature, **Beings 1, 2,** and **3** become trapped in distractions, reactivity, wanderings, entertainment, dramas, adventures, compulsions, preoccupations that pull and grab attention. Existence is looked at from a programmed point of view; life and work are separated, jobs are for making a living, not necessarily as an opportunity to evolve. Driven by outside forces, distracted from being present, thinking that external achievements are more important than presence, the possibility of wholeness lacks meaning.

The man married to the world is like someone chained hand and foot.
—*John of the Ladder*

Through this process of self-observation, dividing attention, creating an awareness of our own existence while also placing attention on the situation at hand, we are creating a witness, we become aware of ourselves, and that in itself creates something that is separate from the machine. It is said that : *It is not the changes we experience that matter, it's the observation that matters.* One of the greatest privileges of this human life is this possibility to know who and how we are, why we are here; to awaken to our true nature.

All inner work begins with the control of attention. —*Mme. Ouspensky*

The shift to higher centers, to not be effected by things outside of ourself, to uninterrupted mindfulness, to not be an automaton of reactions changes our view of the universe. The study of self reveals whether we are thinking or feeling; to think or feel when it is necessary to move, to take action, blocks growth; to act without feeling or thought has resulted in a world without compassion. This is the beginning of inner development, of no longer identifying with one point of view. This was clearly stated when William Blake said, *I look through my eyes, not with them.* And the poet John O'Donohue in this century wrote: *It is not simply with your eye but with your mind that you see the world.* Watching the universe within, a wakeful experience of life, we cultivate awareness.

There are four ways toward self realization. The way of the Fakir stresses physical mastery and develops will; the way of the monk uses prayer and devotion to heal the heart and transubstantiate emotion; the way of the yogi deepens understanding for a lucid and clear mind. Then hidden from view and involving physical body, heart and mind, there is the way of the sly man, the fourth of these ways, which works upon all three parts of the human being simultaneously. —*Kathleen Riordan Speeth, Ira Friedlander*

There are three traditional approaches/Ways and two further developed Ways to awakening that correspond to the three types, each aim to develop mastery over their dominant center. The first, **Being 1**, masters the physical body, creating will over the moving/instinctive and sexual brain and leads to the Way of the fakir, **Being 2**, the emotional functions predominates, evolving through a traditional system it becomes the Way of the monk who masters the emotional body through devotion, religious sacrifice and faith, to heal the heart have will over the emotions, elevating the emotional center. **Being 3,** who receiving stimulus initially through the intellectual center masters this center, the Way of the yogi follows the path of knowledge towards a clear mind.

The monk, fakir and the yogi all renounce the world, devoting themselves, their energy, to the Way that speaks to them. The Fourth Way, speaks to working on balancing the centers, all three parts of a person simultaneously. The Fifth Way, *The Way of the Lover,* invites us to awaken through understanding our relationship to ourself and to everything, in loving awareness and kindness, in our spiritual heart, looking deeply at understanding, dismantling the personality and arriving at a quiet inner place that reduces suffering. When a tradition is in line with one of the Ways it is apparent. In all the traditions at the levels of the sacred, *no conscious effort is ever lost.* We are surrounded by great traditions, ours is to recognize the treasure, for the sacred is not a destination, it's an unfolding.

The modern person has no conception of how self-deceptive a life can be that is lived in only one part of oneself. The head, the emotions, and the body each have their own perceptions and actions, and each, in itself, can live a simulacrum of human life. —Jacob Needleman

Examples include: most people throughout the world.

Being 1: *Britney Spears, Mike Tyson, Jessica Simpson, Nikki Minaj, Miley Cyrus, Tyga, Sylvester Stallone.*

Being 2: *Bette Midler, Princes Diana, Edith Piaf, Mariah Carey.*

Being 3: *Madeleine Albright, Ralph Nader, Al Gore, Larry King.*

BEING 4

Understanding with one brain is hallucination; understanding with two brains is semi-hallucination; only understanding with all brains is really understanding. —*G.I Gurdjieff*

Efforts made to discover meaning, to experience the impulse to evolve to become more creates **Being 4**. Born as Being 1, 2, or 3, subsequently through inner work a permanent center of gravity called self-study is established. **Being 4**, motivated by a primary desire to wake up has separated from a mechanical center of gravity and replaces it with the determination to awaken. Life now centers around that desire, is about strengthening attention, becoming watchful, mindful; nothing takes priority to the intention to wake up, entertainment and distractions take a back seat to deepening inner work. The degree of self-understanding has become enough to allow separation from a mechanical center and replace it with a self-study center. The first 3 centers become more balanced, subject to a single authority named a magnetic center. This means that responses and reactions to circumstances and events are based on the relationship to the desire to awaken rather than on the basis of one of the earlier centers. This is a demanding journey and it involves one temptation after another. States come and go, higher centers are impermanent, life as a **Being 4** is insistent, has hardships; it is essential to create a quality life with consistent discriminating standards. Transforming suffering, not expressing negative emotions, not indulging in disappointment and complaints are methods to gather presence. The Tibetan teacher Chogyam Trungpa Rinpoche noted, *If you haven't started on a spiritual path which involves one insult after another, it's best not to begin, but if you have begun, it is best to finish.*

Being 4 looks quite different from the first three types. Beginning to awaken, this is the third state of consciousness, self-consciousness. First and second states are sleep at night and waking hypnotic sleep, vulnerable to suggestions—from the past, from the media, from the voices in our head, which is a typical state in ordinary life. Now appears the realization that we are asleep, absorbed in events, thoughts and emotions and that we have the possibility to be more. Real knowing is direct without any intervention of thought. Questioning, turned toward direct experience, confronting the contradictions of our nature, less rigid, more flexible, yet we show up imbalanced. Pay attention to a tightrope walker constantly altering movements. Great expertise is needed to create and maintain balance. Remember in childhood playing on a see-saw, balancing oneself with a friend, the energy has to match or mirror for the rocking shifting change to happen.

Being 4, with a self-study center of gravity has a choice to respond to the earlier example of a phone call that loved ones had been in an accident appropriate to the circumstance, regardless to their original center of gravity, aiming to be present to see what needs to be done, what wants to happen. Bringing a deepened understanding of life and death the intention to become appropriate in the midst of life situations promotes the response. No longer aimless and tossed about, everything points toward the effort to develop self. Life has direction and purpose, there are authentic moments as well as trying to connect with others, negativity now has a possibility to be controlled. The ability to stand upright in the center of the swinging pendulum of life events exists. The shift follows real psychological work producing inner change and lies in consciousness and the capacity for observation and self-remembering. The ability to see and accept one's own contradictions replace tensions that created separation and frees us from our judgments and limited thought patterns. This is the beginning of real change, both in awareness, understanding and in the ability to observe.

Transformational was the key word. I will tell you one thing that will make you rich for life. There are two struggles—an Inner world struggle and an Outer-world struggle. But these two worlds can never make contact with each other, to make data for Third world. Only one thing can give it: you must make an intentional contact between the two worlds; then you can make data which crystallize for the Third World of man, called by the ancients the World of the Soul. Say: 'I wish the result of this suffering to become my own, for Being.' Yes you can call that kind of wishing suffering, because it is suffering. This saying can maybe take force from your animal and give it to Being. Man is man—he can never be another thing. But he can make his body work for another part of him—his mind. The more the body is forced to struggle, the more labour it does, the more it can give to the mind, and to Being. —Margaret Anderson

UNNECESARY SUFFERING

Not all storms come to disrupt your life, some come to clear your path. —Amen

Don't throw away your suffering. Touch your suffering. Face it directly and your joy will become deeper. —Thicn Nhat Hahn

Being 4 has the ability to understand self and others as well as to overcome the violence and misunderstandings that create strife. Understanding and penetrating awareness are the inner meaning for a **Being 4** having a self-study center of gravity. All experiences used well are possible food for transformation. **Being 4** begins to shift off the horizontal plane and move in a vertical direction. They are able to balance the outer life with an inner life. Sincere hard psychological work produces real inner change. Working on ourself is a guiding principle of life, yet what we develop is still fragile and can disappear. Beginning to know ourself in this delicate place can be lost to a flurry of other interests. The positive moments of self-development are overtaken when the negative part of unnecessary suffering enters the life. A broken relationship, physical hardship, self-criticism, financial upset, addictions, too much stimulation or distraction; all experiences that could create toxic overload and pull us off course. Blaming, feeling victimized, still have the possibility of entering and defeating consciousness, although the seed of change engages wisdom to knock, to penetrate the veil of unnecessary suffering. Drugs, alcohol and a toxic diet dilute the accessibility of higher states. **Being 4** has the possibility to backslide and lose everything, since no state is permanent and inconsistency is a predominant characteristic of **Being 4**. States of suffering may pass, yet so do states of joy. Authentic emotions pay a regular visit, sometimes bringing storms. These penetrating moments can be used as a richness for our practice. Unnecessary suffering prevents **Being 4** from developing. Entering the next level is through the emotional center and the primary way to control the emotional center is through not expressing negativity.

Number 4 vacillates between the heaven of self-remembering and the hell of sleep, and failures outnumber successes, but not indefinitely. If you have a right attitude toward failures, and if you don't identify with them by becoming disappointed, something marvelous can occur: each time you fail, you remember yourself. Number 4 is subject to forgetfulness because higher centers are not permanently functioning within us. We need to be wary of thinking we have something because, when we compare ourself with a man number one, two or three, we do have something, We have relative awakening. But relative awakening is not sufficient; full awakening is the aim and it is a realizable aim. —Robert Earl Burton

There are no concrete organizations or institutions for **Being 4**. They appear and disappear according to needs, teachers, teachings and the times. Intentional communities, ashrams and certain towns offer support and comradeship; yet the majority of individuals in those places have not crystallized a self-study center. They have moments, tastes, memories and thoughts of presence, yet are often unwilling to let go of the distractions and toxicity that jeopardize and pull them out of the present moment. This turns into periods of emotionally reactive times, still identified with something outside us, yet knowing that the opportunity to birth consciousness is within grasp. Having qualities that correspond to **Being 4** is not the same as having the substance or being prepared and in agreement to live what we have seen, what we know. There is no city or community of consciousness retirement, there is only constant day labor.

BALANCE

We see everything through the lens of thought. The way that you think determines what you will actually discover. If your thoughts are impaired or if they are negative or diminished, then you will never discover anything rich or beautiful within your soul. This process of self-discovery is not easy; it may involve suffering, doubt, dismay. We must not shrink from the fullness of our being in attempting to reduce pain. —John O'Donohue

Our life and the world are the environment. Balance is a dynamic process, not a predominating mechanical center, it comes out of the experience of all dimensions of life and takes moment to moment presence. This is the *Fifth Way, the Way of the Lover,* the beginning of a balanced person who is able to have real purpose in life, who can understand what they want and work towards transformation. Life happens through initiative, ordinary efforts are not enough, real change to a higher state requires persisting beyond one's capacity. Life now becomes the teacher, one sees from all the centers. This is the way of living in the world with balanced centers. Centers, like a fuse box when overloaded will short-circuit. Moving centered people who have lived years imbalanced, in overload, often deteriorate in their center of gravity, having to walk with a cane, or confined to a wheelchair, sometimes having to get hip, knee, or joint replacement, at times creating vertigo and other imbalance disorders. Intellectually centered people and scholars blowing out their mind, creating short term memory loss, dementia, Alzheimer's; visit a nursing home and recognize those who have lived in the mind—doctors, lawyers, professors, accountants, historians, business executives—unable to remember the days order or what they did yesterday. Emotionally centered people on anxiety medication, filling mental hospitals after having breakdowns, after having burned out their emotions, flattened out on prescriptions and anti-anxiety medication. **Being 4,** one center no longer having the majority of the responsibility, the centers working together create less overload, an electrical panel proportionally arranged. There is less inappropriate reactions of the different brains, not becoming emotional about changing a tire on a car, each brain becomes more directed to its own functions. Loving nothing more than the aim to awaken, **Being 4** evaluates subjective knowing to enter a path towards an understanding that holds life sacred.

The true way goes over a rope which is not stretched at any great height but just above the ground. It seems more designed to make people stumble than to be walked upon. —*Franz Kafka*

Examples include: *Oprah Winfrey, Helen Palmer, Elisabeth Kübler-Ross, Angelina Jolie, Julia Cameron, Clarissa Pinkola Estes, Simone De Beauvoir, Susan Sontag, Marc Gafni, Meir Schneider, Julia Cameron.*

BEING 5

A man may be born, but in order to be born, he must first die, and in order to die he must first awake. —*G.I. Gurdjieff*

Being 5 moves onto a vertical plane possessing a unified sense of self. What has been fragmented and scattered becomes visible to themselves. They are available to see when they are being mechanically reactive and when they are present to themselves. Someone is home inside to resist outside influences, enabling them to live in the manner that they create. Their imagined sense of self-importance, that great obstacle combined with self-deception, diminishes. The shift is perpendicular from a lower world to a higher world, creating a reliable level of being. Instead of changes of states, highs and lows coming and going, there is a permanent level of being firmly established. Mindful, self-aware, no longer hypnotized by external events, like an oyster making a pearl they try *to be*, having watchful independence. Everything that's known and seen is integrated and complete. Things do not have to be drawn from the outside in order for them to be. To dis-identify with the stories they have heard and learned about themselves, to penetrate false identification and illusion brings about true self-consciousness.

You represent an unknown world that begs you to bring it to voice. Often the joy you feel does not belong to your individual biography but to the clay out of which you are formed. It is wise to let the weather of feeling pass; it is on its way elsewhere. One of the reasons we were sent onto the earth was to make a deep connection with ourselves, this inner friendship. It means that we cannot continue to seek outside ourselves for the things we need from within. —*John O'Donohue*

Being 5 has the ability to pay attention. Lost to ourself is a most typical condition for the majority of the world. **Being 5** understands self and others. Self-aware, self-conscious, objective about themselves, they have balanced centers and see things accurately. **Being 5** can understand themselves without distortion or subjectivity, they are not based in force or violence and have a true sense and understanding of others. A sensitive awareness to background sounds and activities, this begins to be a strong characteristic of beings 5, 6, and 7. Transforming negative emotions into positive; non-expression of negative emotions creates the energy, is the method that enables **Being 5** to live in this realm.

When you are attentive to the moment, there is a natural selection or rejection of impressions which makes you more open. There's an in-built censorship in relation to impressions. This is where one's intention could be important. If I decide to concentrate now, I become more open to better quality vibrations. With intention, one leads a more harmonious existence. With intention one remembers that there's more to life than the mechanical associative actions and thought to which we're subject most of the time. One pauses and in this stop, there's a great in-gathering which can help to change life. Life is joyous. —William Segal

UNITY OF CENTER

Remembering our real individual identity, our own truth, named essence, becomes a permanent center of gravity. Personality slowly diminished, essence is tempered to mature and embody what is true and real. This happens through a continual struggle between essence and personality since both are necessary to develop ourself. Essence would not have the urge to develop without personality. Personality brings the daily issues, the illusions, the temptations, the impediments to overcome. The challenge to resist the temptations that personality brings will strengthen essence. This effort and challenge continues regardless to the circumstances, whether we are living in an ashram, an apartment in New York city, a village in Vermont or a house in New Mexico, with another or alone, working in a restaurant or at a law firm, the internal battle, challenging illusions, confronting habits and patterns, quieting personality ensues. The bigger the self-importance the more resistance and temptation, yet the more food for our increased development.

If you develop yourself you become an individual instead of one of the thousand leaves on a tree. You become a seed. —Margaret Anderson

Being 5 lives from the higher emotional center and is able to act under their own initiative, they are unified. Allowing intense emotional states to penetrate develops higher centers. Friendship becomes the Anam Cara, soul friend, through an act of recognition and belonging. Through effort and attention we develop self-consciousness and have access to higher centers. Living with a magnified sense of background sounds and activity is a challenge as well as a reflection that engages higher centers. Reaching this level without having stood firmly on self-study center, Being 4; we cannot develop further. Experiences of a higher world can be a sign of things to come, not necessarily evidence of attainment. **Being 5** does not go back to previous levels of development and imbalances, unless intentional, through the discovery that our lack of particular inner work is causing others great suffering. This may be an arduous struggle to dissolve and move steps back, to slow the momentum, to repair and fill in the gaps.

What is characteristic of self-remembering? In this state man is not center. He is not separate. Sitting in a room, he is aware of the whole room, of himself as only one of the objects in it. He is likewise aware of others and does not put himself above them or criticize or judge. This is not love, but it is the beginning of love. In this state a man has no self as he is usually aware of it. It is quite impossible for him to consider or become negative, for the moment he does so the state will vanish. —Mme. Ouspensky

The capacity to know deeply and to respond from true understanding is different than that of Being 1-4. The center of gravity now is in the higher emotional center. Bringing information from earlier levels, taking great care, knowing that each moment permeates our whole being; distractions from the outside no longer need to be pulled on to live a beautiful life. **Being 5**, having attained unity of their centers, unity in self, has crystallized an astral body which consists of fine energies, which will survive for a period of time the death of the physical body. The astral body, not subject to time, created through being present, is the formation of an immortal soul, like a caterpillar producing a butterfly. The astral body is the first metaphysical body we can create. An astral body is considered a prerequisite to maintaining a state of self-consciousness. All functions belong to the self, now nothing operates independently or without coordination. What is known is experienced equally in all of our centers. Many powers open, since movement in an inner world is available. What is known is now known with the whole being. This is the *Way of the Lover*, developed self-consciousness with unified objective consciousness.

As we are, we serve the purposes of nature and nothing else in regards to our life. But we can put ourself under different influences if we choose. We can change our level of consciousness and consequently attract different circumstances according to our level. —*Maurice Nicoll*

Examples include: *Llewellyn Vaughan-Lee, Reshad Feild, David Cooper, Matthew Sanford, Chris Griscom, Jed McKenna, Sylvia Boorstein. Kabir Helminski, Pema Chodron, Gangaji, Eckhart Tolle, Stephen Levine, Daniel Ladinsky, Coleman Barks, Ram Dass, Zalman Schachter-Shalomi, Yogi Bhajan, Irina Tweedie, Deepak Chopra, Abraham Joshua Heschel, Joan Halifax, John O'Donohue, Natalie Goldberg, Dr. Paula Bromberg, J.Krishnamurti, Charlotte Joko Beck, Michael Singer.*

BEING 6

The life force and the mind are operating, but the mind will tempt you to believe it is 'you.' Therefore understand always that you are the timeless, spacious witness. And even if the mind tells you that you are the one who is acting, don't believe the mind. Always keep your identity separate from that which is doing the working, thinking and talking. That which has happened—that is, the apparatus which is functioning—has come upon your original essence, but you are not that apparatus. —Sri Nisargadatta

Being 6 has all the qualities of Being 5, a mental body, plus objective consciousness; understanding ourselves and the universe without distortion or subjectivity. Having a center of gravity in the higher intellectual center, which deals with insight and truth, we see both ourself and the world objectively. Not based in violence, which means overcoming all forms of negative emotion, we have a true understanding of others. There appears a recognizable humility, quite noticeably different from Beings 1 through 5. States no longer come and go, there is now a permanent level of awareness. Voluntary attention creates a connection with a higher energy. Personal preoccupation steps aside for universal kinship.

A level of mental maturity is reached when nothing external is of any value and the heart is ready to relinquish all. Before you can say I am, you must be there to say it. —Sri Nisargadatta

Seeing things as they really are, through conscious efforts destroys illusions, life becomes the teacher. Inner development means overcoming violence in ourself through the expansion of consciousness. This happens when we are sealed from ordinary events, the appearances and effects of life. Selecting impressions, **Being 6** is an individual distinct from life and its circumstances. Developed in the ordinary centers as well as being somewhat conscious in the higher emotional and intellectual centers, the ability to know what to do as well as the power to follow through marks this level.

Preparation for the immense task of remaining conscious through death must be to become intensely conscious of oneself in life. —Rodney Collin

Being 6, beyond individual will, living in the world of universal will, has strength of being and is involved in the creation of destiny. They are similar to **Being 7**, except the capacity is not permanently set. There is now complete knowledge, although the possibility of it being lost still remains.

Where can I leave my being? It is my very nature. Now where can I leave my nature? I am it! —Rajneesh

Examples include: *Osho Rajneesh, Thich Nhat Hahn, Dalai Lama, Sri Nisargadatta, Paramanasa Yogananda*

BEING 7

What appears will also disappear and is therefore impermanent, The Self never appears and disappears and is therefore permanent. It is the only reality. Your duty is to be; and not to be this or that. —Ramana Maharshi

Being 7 has unity, free will, a *causal body*, full consciousness, a permanent and unchanging *I*, is free of mechanical impulses, individuality and conscious immortality. The me dropped off, no longer any separate identity, *No-self is true-self; and the greatest being is nobody,* said the mystics. Having achieved all that is possible for a human being, they control all states of consciousness in themselves, nothing can be lost. Fixed in their own field of consciousness, they are freed from the distracting force of life. Understanding others, not based in violence, having full consciousness, objective awareness and higher intellectual function, they are infused with the energy of love, having reached the full development of what is possible for a human being. All unhappy quarrelsome parts of life fall away; there are no illusions, no pretense, no appearances.

Your own self-realization is the greatest form of service you can render. To seek one's Self and merge in it—this is wisdom. —Ramana Maharshi

Developed in an inward direction, **Being 7** is tuned into the fine vibrations and very fine energy-matter of all the higher centers. The language of higher centers are not of time and space, therefore the logical formatory personality cannot hear or understand their messages. Knowledge and being, at their highest level are equal, whatever they *know*, they can *do*. Objective reason is taken to its fullest heights, here we have a truly divine being. (Examples and further explanation are in System Three, Soul age, transcendental and infinite soul.) **Being 7**'s personal identity shifts from ego structures to essence. A complete human being in their intended fullness, unimaginably evolved in relation to others, objective consciousness is the level of enlightened transcendent being. Having unity, will and consciousness independent of any of their functions they are directly connected to the highest level of understanding possible. **Being 7** has the possibility of escape from the cycle of human life through carrying full consciousness and memory over death into the moment of release into the electronic world.

When the goal of life is attained, one achieves the reparation of all wrongs, the healing of all wounds, the righting of all failures, the sweetening of all strivings, the harmonizing of all strife, the unraveling of all enigmas, and the real and full meaning of all life—past, present and future. —Meher Baba

Examples include: *Meher Baba, Mata Amritananda Mayi, Ramana Maharshi, Buddha.*

SYSTEM TWENTY-TWO

SOUND, MOVEMENT, LIGHT, COLOR, CHAKRA, AURA, BREATH, SEVEN BODIES

THE 7 BODIES:

PHYSICAL, ETHERIC, ASTRAL-EMOTIONAL, MENTAL, SPIRITUAL, COSMIC-CAUSAL, NIRVANIC

Despite the appearance of being separate individuals, we are all connected to patterns of intelligence governing the cosmos. —Deepak Chopra

The journey to realize our own true nature entails inner analyses and self-creation, the production of a higher form of being. This system is about becoming aware of the mysterious forces that organize our being, that determine the course of life on earth and that regulate the process of organic evolution. Conscious evolution begins when we choose it. The study of the energies of Sound, Movement, Light, Color and Breath happen through experiencing their energies. Awakening to the reality of other worlds is beyond the visible world; the quality of energy that enters us is more than material. This system of worlds within worlds, of invisible lands, becomes available to us as we develop the senses which reveal the existence of invisible worlds. Throughout our life we are borrowing and taking in energies from the external world. The conscious transformation of energy means that we are no longer at the mercy of what comes our way, or as one spiritual teaching says: *without understanding energy we are just waiting for roast pigeon to fly into our mouths.*

In this life, for those wanting to access the higher world and its planes, our physical world and the universe within, we arrive by descending through the earth vibration or by ascending through the heaven vibration, or both. There is energy that comes up from the earth as well as energy that comes down through higher planes. Having both earth and heaven energies in our bodies balanced creates health. Experienced through resonance, each of us resonates with particular planes and dimensions.

Some part of the psyche—a subliminal form of consciousness, possesses awareness of the background energy landscape and the underlying connectedness of individual bodies below the level of normal consciousness. This results in a subtle condition of tension between different elements of perception—one, sensory, and the other, episensory. —Ali Ansari

Sound, Color, Movement, Light and Breath are all powerful forces in the universe. Every physical manifestation vibrates within a range of frequency. We are energy-emitting beings. Learning to control the rate of vibration opens a door to different levels of consciousness. *The Fifth Way* works with frequency energy to heighten awareness. Breath is life. Conscious breathing, transporting energy from one world to another, being awake to the Breath, brings us into the present moment; the experience of being one with all things and beings. Breathing, a continuous flow from birth to death, connecting us to our body, to the universe, is the bridge. We Breathe air and vitality. Being present with our Breath, watching our mind, opening to whatever presents itself, life appears as it is. To assimilate the consciousness of the energy of each day we use our daily life for the particular purpose we are here for, to live fresh every moment, open, with energy penetrating and burning our toxicity. *The Way of the Lover* is about becoming a knowing instrument of transformation, to realize our oneness with the indivisible Self.

For too long, we have believed that the divine is outside us. Attunement to the senses can limber up the stiffened belief and gentle the hardened outlook. It can warm and heal the atrophied feelings that are the barriers exiling us from ourselves and separating us from each other. Then we are no longer in exile from the wonderful harvest of divinity that is always secretly gathering within us. With a great sense of that interim world between the invisible and the visible; these two worlds are no longer separate. They flow naturally, gracefully, and lyrically in and out of each other. —John O'Donohue

THE VIBRATION OF SOUND

To be present at the last Breath, to Breathe the name *Ram*, as Gandhi uttered when he was shot, brings Breath into harmony with the pulse of the universe. Gandhi suggested that the manner and the moment of his death would reveal whether he was a real Mahatma or not. *If someone shot at me and I received his bullet in my bare chest without a sigh and with Ramana's name on my lips, only then should you say that I was a true Mahatma.* Gandhi often expressed the desire to die with the word *Ram* on his lips. *It is my constant prayer that even if I fall victim to an assassin's bullet I may deliver up my soul with the remembrance of God, with the name of Ram on my lips.* Gandhi was assassinated a few months later. His final word was *Ram*, God's name. A person's entire life is presumed to be captured by the last words or moments, the final gestures. Gandhi had written, *In the end it will be as Rama commands me. Thus I dance as He pulls the strings, I am in His hands and so I am experiencing ineffable peace.*

The rhythm of the body, the melody of the mind, and the harmony of the soul create the symphony of life. —B.K.S. Iyengar

Gandhi, aware how reciting the name Ram could be reduced to a mechanical exercise, cautioned against saying the name Ram except as part of a process of self-realization, or as an effort to call forth the divinity within oneself. Gandhi having observed the unreliable condition of most people, conceded that *in the beginning just lip repetition of his name is a start, since ultimately what is on the lips will possess the heart.* Sound is the original creational tone, language the method of creating expression in the realm of words, frequencies, tones, intentions and resonant intelligent energy organization. When we produce Sound we are relating to the breath and the vibration of the Sound itself. Sound can't be produced unless we breathe. Life, all of existence is made of Sound, of subtle vibrations of Sound.

To transform a grimace into a sound sounds impossible, yet it is possible to transform a vision into music, to go outside an enslaved personality, to become impersonal by transforming into sand, into water, into light.
—*Dejan Stojanovic*

Wordless tunes and melodies in the Jewish mystical tradition, called nigunim, are considered a way we communicate on a soulular transcendent level. Repetitive Sounds, often considered mystical musical prayer, or a spiritual language beyond words, have the power as a musical path to God to elevate us as soul of the universe, opening gates, transcending the limitations of language. *Any breakdown in the verbal communication mode can be repaired by creating a conduit that transcends words,* said Rabbi DovBer Pinson, *a wordless tune which exists on a realm that defies distinctions, separations, and disharmony, is the most fitting remedy against feeling alienated, for it creates a unity of souls; the wordless melody, tears the soul beyond all bounds.*

The ancients of most every culture have said that life begins with the word. Through the Breath and the word we breathe our thoughts into life. Through the vibratory power of word and song we enter the matrix of vibration from which all of life emerges. In the Western world we call it electricity; that the world is made up of electrical vibrations, and Sound is a vibration in the electric energy. To become silent we hear a subtle humming Sound within our own inner self. All Sounds come towards us in circles with us at the center as silence. Listen, not with the ears, but through the navel. To discover within our own being the point of intersection, the still point of the timeless moment, the *soundless sound*. In Zen this silent tone is called the *sound of one hand clapping*. This soundlessness becomes yet another way of entering ourself.

Silence, 'fiaga', is the principal condition of the inner life. Fiaga is the mother of the word, or 'diomon'. To keep silent is to cultivate one's inner dimension. —*Yaya Diallo*

Stars emanate both Sound and Color, their star light entering the body through the eyes. To pay attention to the Breathe to awaken intelligence, for our being to be attuned and resonant to the interconnectedness we partake of the energy that makes up the very substance of the world; it is in this way we make best use of the relative elemental world. The five essential elements; earth, air, water, fire and ether are the pervasive all-inclusive energy that permeate everything. Esoteric traditions have made it clear that the function and purpose of a human being is to become a link, a conduit for higher energy to come down to the earth—to bring heaven down to earth. To discover the spiritual within the material, to find the sparks which carry the blueprint of the entire world, this connection, through the chakras above the head, the crown, is related to the higher vibrations of light and Sound. Our connection with higher energy creates meaning for our life. Our openness allows this flow to enter, to be experienced through our body. In this we are serving something higher.

It is necessary to maintain a contact between the mind and the body, that is to say a sensation. That permits an opening for the energy which comes from above the head. While one is in relationship with that energy there is a sort of freedom which one can sense. We are seeking to approach the unknown, to open the door to what is hidden in us and pass beyond. —Jeanne de Salzmann

The human body, not solid, is held together by Sound, Color, and Light. The body is a map of a person's consciousness, our experience of being. Different Sounds and Colors effect the human psyche. Reality is created by Sound, Light and Color frequencies creating grids that allow human consciousness to experience through spiraling consciousness levels of awareness based on patterns of creation. The entire universe is a musical dance of vibration, with its own resonant frequency. Every atom, electron, as well as our thoughts and consciousness are vibrations, and our thoughts are a signature of our consciousness.

ENERGY FIELD, AURAS

The physical body has subtle bodies layered over it, all with vibrating energy fields. The invisible world of the subtle bodies, called the Aura, carry electro-magnetic waves. The further away from the physical body the more refined and subtle are the vibrations. Our Aura is an electro-photonic vibration response, an energy field that surrounds living and non-living objects. This band of etheric substance surrounding our physical body is an intermediate between the physical and the psychic world. Colors have frequencies and the electromagnetic energy fields or Auras create the myth and metaphor we call reality which carry us into higher awareness. Auras vibrate to different Color, Sound and Light frequencies. The Aura contains our essence. The Color spectrum changes according to our physical, emotional, mental and spiritual state. Shared physical contact creates a common Auric field for a time, as people merge their electromagnetic energies.

The Color of an Aura is determined by our emotions, physical surroundings, health, balance or imbalance in our physical body. Understanding the Colors and intensity of the Aura offers insight into the thoughts, feelings and health of a person. The first layer, one to two inches away from our physical body has the strongest energy, and serves as a force field protection for our body, similar to how the atmosphere protects the earth. The second layer glows with a wide spectrum of Colors and gives health information. The last and largest layer is the essence of our mental, physical and emotional state. Thin and translucent it remains less changeable. An Aura is a unique personal fingerprint, a clue that displays a person's nature and true intentions. If our natural ability to see Auras were cultivated—infants often look above a persons head—once developed this would be a powerful tool for health and communication, providing valuable information.

Watch your own face in the mirror. Try to see the aura. That will be greatly indicative and helpful for your growth, because it will show the color where you are. If it is black, then much has to be done. If it is gray, then you are just in the middle of your growth; half the journey is over. A white aura is the best aura. —*Bhagwan Shree Rajneesh, Osho*

Living harmoniously, in mindful awareness, open, slows the vibration and frequency within the body so as to become attuned to the unmanifest, emptying, preparing the ground. Energy moves upwards to the higher centers. Our energy-field bodies need to receive beautiful impressions to be nourished, to evolve. All things in the universe are in a state of vibration. Vibrational medicine heals illness by manipulating subtle energy fields via directing energy into the body. This recognition, that all matter is energy, forms the foundation of how we are dynamic energetic systems. Einstein's insights proved to the scientific world that energy and matter are dual expressions of the same universal substance; now to incorporate that into the training and approach that the medical world uses to view people and illness.

Holographic vibrational healing working at the level of the higher subtle bodies and Chakras transcends the limitations of time and space. The electromagnetic current that pulls in the cosmic energy that resonates with our light bodies charged with our higher frequencies creates a current as well as an arc of the halo above our head. To access that halo, a communion with the cosmos, we carry the current bringing us a connection to the law of grace which is a final universal law in this chapter, System 27.

The human body is a highly complicated transformer of subtle energies, taking in energies from higher sources and making them available to us. Many of these higher energies would be too strong for us in our ordinary state of existence and so the chakras act as natural filters for our own protection, at the same time affording us the energies that we need to play our part in the reciprocal maintenance of the planet. The chakras also take in the etheric counterparts of the mineral and the vegetable kingdoms. It is through them that color irradiates our whole being. A total alchemical process is taking place. —Reshad Feild

A spiritual light behind the physical spectrum of radiant Colors, similar to a ray of sunlight passing through a prism refracts into seven Colors. Each Color or ray has its quality and its own frequency. Every cell in the body receives energy from the stars, planets and nature. To experience the substance of the universe is to feel its energy running through our physical and subtle bodies. Standing by the ocean, on a mountain, near a flower, stream or tree; the laws of Sound, Light, Movement, scent, Color, Breath, resonate initially on a cellular level, then within the psyche, moving to our central axis from earth to sky. Memories in the energy fields accessed through Movement, Sound, Color, Light, scent and Breath flow; everything vibrates from body to universe.

Gurdjieff wrote: *if our aim is a harmonious development of man, then for us, dances and movements are a means of combining the mind and the feeling with movements of the body and manifesting them together.* The Gurdjieff Movements are an indicator of our inner state as well as our capacity to direct and maintain attention. The smallest blink of attention and all would fall apart. If your attention wanders, is not completely focused it is highly improbable that you could complete the Movements. The aim of totality is a bridge to our awakening.

Dancing symbolizes the rhythmic, patterned movements of life itself. Music and dance amplify and make manifest to our senses the unheard tones and unseen waves that weave together the matter of existence. Even when we are sitting most still or resting in deepest sleep, the atoms, molecules cells, tissues, organs, and systems of our bodies dance in astounding harmony and exchange the ambient energies from air, water, food, and invisible electro-magnetic radiation. —Yaya Diallo

CHAKRAS

The body has seven main energy centers, that look like spinning circles, called Chakras, which means cyclone or wheels in Sanskrit. They are the psychic organs where the essential energies for our emotional, physical and spiritual health are received, transmitted, metabolized and utilized. Nonphysical centers of spinning energy, they are linked to Sound, Light and Color, as are all things in our reality. Each Chakra has all the Colors in it, carrying a frequency specific to certain energetics. To see the Chakras spinning is to see multitudinous fibers of all the Colors, and along those fibers each Color has little conglomerates that look like small globs of seaweed along ropes. We could, with intention, palpate and strengthen our Chakras and Auric fields and extend our light energy out through our solar plexus.

Each of our Chakras is energy vibrating at a certain frequency in an orderly sequence of 7 vibrations, moving up through the elements of earth, water, fire, air, ether, to the spiritual elements of inner Sound and inner Light. The inner Light or white Light is considered the most subtle element from which the entire physical universe is created. They all interact with our physical body through the endocrine and nervous systems. These energy centers function as pumps or valves regulating the flow of energy through our energy system. Similar to the Auras they are not physical but are aspects of consciousness.

Chakras, translated from the Sanskrit language means wheels and are the invisible subtle centres that interpenetrate the physical body. In the East they are often illustrated as being like lotus flowers, each one seen as having a different number of petals. The evolutionary process continues, cannot happen without us, and so we look to correct ways of breathing to keep all these subtle centers and channels open and functioning correctly. Everything is perfectly blended in the heart. Each of the subtle centres, the chakras, work in perfect harmony so that refined energy is made available on earth. Just as the breath is not limited by walls, to no longer need the protection of filters to veil the beauty of the pure light of existence, all becomes One again. —Reshad Feild

The seven main Chakras are aligned in an ascending column from the base of the spine to the top of the head, the crown Chakra represented by a lotus blossom with 1,000 petals. All wisdom passes through the crown Chakra before it is expressed through the lower Chakras. There are thousands of Chakras, both inside and outside the body, the most noteworthy ones are along the spine and at the feet and hands. The following are a description of 11 significant Chakras. The first three relate to our mental perceptions in the physical world, the fourth serves as a bridge and equalizer between our body, mind, emotions and spirit. The fifth, sixth, seventh are Chakras of spirit and connect to our experiences in this world.

The chakras are specialized energy centers which connect us to the multidimensional universe. The chakras are dimensional portals within the subtle bodies which take in and process energy of higher vibrational nature so that it may be properly assimilated and used to transform the physical body.
—*Richard Gerber*

Each Chakra, a dynamic center in our being, has its own unique focus: **The first Chakra**, in Sanskrit, *muladhara,* the sex center, is the root or base, its sound is *lam,* associated with the sound of thunder/ earthquake and is about grounding and survival, located at the base of the spine for men and between the ovaries for women, or the perineum for both, and is represented by the color red. This Chakra is your physical and spiritual foundation. **The second Chakra**, the sacral or navel Chakra, called the *hara,* Sanskrit name *swadhistana* meaning sea of energy, at the lower abdomen, three fingers below the navel, is about emotions and boundaries, connected to the color orange, its sound is *vam,* the sound of the ocean. Often considered to be the gateway into the etheric envelope surrounding the planet, considered by Eastern Asian Cultures to be the seat of internal awareness and energy, the center of our personal connectedness, physically, emotionally, and spiritually. **Third Chakra**, the solar plexus, the *prana,* the bioplasm or bioenergy, the electric energy, located above the navel, *nabhi,* is connected to understanding and energy distribution, represented by the color yellow. Its sound is Ram, a roaring fire.

Fourth, the heart Chakra, Sanskrit name is *anahata*, is located at the center of the chest, the heart, and connects to community, love, the air element and the color green, its sound is *yam*, the sound of wind. Here the lower and the higher meet, the sexual and the spiritual, the worldly and the otherworldly, rooted in the earth and reaching into the heavens. When love awakens in our life through the heart Chakra we marry heaven to earth, we root and spread into the eternal.

The fifth Chakra, called the *vishuddi*, located at the notch of the throat, connects to communication, inner identity, and the color blue. This is the Chakra of communication that listens to the connection between your heart and mind, giving and receiving. As the seat of self expression, it's seen as the crossroads between the head and the heart, the mediator between thought and emotion. This is the Chakra that governs our speech and creative expression in the world, its sound is *ham*, the sound of crickets.

The sixth Chakra, *ajna*, the inner eye, placed at the center of the head, the third eye at the forehead, connects to the intellect and the color indigo, its sound is *sham*, the sound of bells/space. The two hemispheres of the brain meet at the third eye; which is between the two eyes. Responsible for the sixth *sense* connecting us to our internal intuitions the sixth Chakra is responsible for our sharp senses, our ability to read the future and receive non-verbal messages, granting us our sense of observation. This Chakra is the gate leading us and opening to inner realms and spaces of higher consciousness.

The seventh crown chakra, Sanskrit word is *sahasrara*, located at the top of the head is about wisdom, connecting to the color violet, sometimes white. A tool to communicate with our spiritual nature, it's through this vortice that the life force is dispersed from the lower six Chakras. The crown Chakra controls understanding of the inner and outer person, connection is to our higher self, universal understanding and oneness. It's our spiritual connector or communicator, and the sound is *ng, om,* which is the sound of om.

The seven chakras are vital to our health. Negative feelings hamper the spin of the chakras resulting in sickness and disease. Forgiveness releases the charge of old imprints from the mind and the chakras. Then and only then can the energy rise uninhibited through the seven chakras to increase awareness and bring awakening. —Sandra Weaver

COLOR FREQUENCIES

When we are obstructed and constricted our Color frequencies shift, are altered; when our heart is closed off the green in the heart chakra will pull in, the fibers shorten. When we accelerate our energy and extend our perception of subtle body-fields we move out of our third-dimensional self able to see multi-colored energies radiating out from everything: people, animals, plants, all objects.

It's important to clear the decks and to be free of everyday worldly concerns in order to explore fully the world of the spirit. The world can easily distract from this higher endeavor. As well, the soul has an equal task and commitment, to find the treasures and explore the ins and outs of life by being attached. As there is spiritual practice in search of the highest and most refined reaches of human potential, so there is soul practice in pursuit of the juices and nutriments of life's entanglements. —Thomas Moore

The foot Chakras are located at the arches and receive earth energy shades of brown in color they are related to our ability to connect with the earth to stay grounded and receive the earth's energy. Their Sound vibrates to a deep base tone with a low energetic vibration. It helps us channel energies down into the earth to receive earth energy traveling through our body. **The hand Chakras,** located at the center of each palm, usually red, a Chakra for healing, vibrate at a higher frequency working in tandem with the heart Chakra allowing the transmission of loving energy from the heart through the hands.

The soul star or transpersonal Chakra, gold Color, is located 6 inches above the crown Chakra and is the seat of the soul. It's the catalyst to heightening our relationship to the universe. **The earth star** or subpersonal Chakra is located 12-18 inches below the bottom of the feet and is black in Color. Known as the super root, it aligns and connects the body and soul to the powerful energies within the magnetic core of planet earth. Earth star is the grounding point for our Chakra system and its relationship to the planet and the universe. It's similar to the roots of a tree spreading itself out under the earth, anchored with its trunk shooting upwards into the heavens.

Trees are incredible presences. There is incredible symmetry in a tree, between its inner life and its outer life, between its rooted memory and its external active presence. A tree grows up and grows down at once and produces enough branches to incarnate its wild divinity. It doesn't limit itself—it reaches for the sky and it reaches for the source, all in one seamless kind of movement. Landscape is an incredible, mystical teacher, and when you begin to lure its sacred presence, something shifts inside you. —John O'Donohue

To hold our energy at any particular Chakra we are given a momentary glimpse and then can move to the higher integration that awaits us as we travel to experience the unity, the refinement and meeting of other centers. Chakras are our vital energy centers not quite detectable by modern medical means, they are portals between the physical and spiritual planes offering possibilities to explore and balance, uplift and transform. These wheels of energy are vital life forces which keep us vibrant, healthy, and alive. Everything is moving, therefore it's essential that our main Chakras stay open, aligned and fluid.

Everything is animate, Everything moves. It's just that some things move slower than other things, like the mountains or the ground itself. But everything has its movement, has its life. —David Abram

OUR ENERGY SYSTEM

The physical body, emotional body, and brain wave patterns respond to tones and frequencies before becoming harmonically balanced. The modern world impacts us with Sound and Light from cell phones, lamps, i-pads, television, computers, cars, street lights, airplanes; vibrational frequencies all stimulating and affecting our equilibrium. Sea turtles having roamed the earth's ocean and seas for millions of years are threatened towards extinction from the artificial lights, disorienting the sea turtles as they head toward the ocean. The instincts of the ancient sea creature tell them to proceed to the brighter horizon over the sea. Artificial lights on the landward side lead them away from the ocean. Just one bewildering light altering their customary course kills thousands of turtles who would have nested or headed out to sea. So, too, our lives are impacted, our equilibrium jarred, when we allow artificial stimulus, processed toxic food, too much electronic interference, overload our energy system.

As resonant beings we are the instruments. Ours is to attune ourselves to a perfect pitch, full, vibrant and clear. We are here to discover who speaks, who listens. Asking: who am I, how am I, this opening, this investigation, this inquiry leads us by removing the obstacles to reveal what is unchanging. Our bodies are charged with energy that is both measurable and subtle. We are the actual bridge from the physical to the spiritual. Our spiritual body finds expression in the physical world for us to birth ourselves as we enter the cosmic door that frees us from our illusions.

Every sound has its particular color. In Indian music the melody is called raga, which means the color. Each sound has its own color: it is one of the very ancient doctrines of eastern music. And now scientists are coming closer to it: there must be some correspondence between sound and color—because sound is nothing but vibrations of electricity, and electricity is color, light. When a ray of light is broken through a prism, it becomes seven colors. When those seven colors meet again it becomes white. There are seven sounds just as there are seven colors. There is definitely a possibility that seven colors and seven sounds have something in common. Just as seven colors disappear into one color, white, seven sounds disappear into one sound, the sound of silence.
— *Bhagwan Shree Rajneesh*

SEVEN BODIES

Here, within this body, is the Ganges and Jumna—here are Prayaga and Benares—here the sun and the moon. Here are the sacred places, here the Pithas and Upapithas—I have not seen a place of pilgrimage and an abode of bliss like my body. —Saraha

First: PHYSICAL or flesh body, the one we are most familiar with as well as the lowest, most dense of the planes of existence. Represented by red, a dense color, creating the most friction, related to circulation, the heart and the physical body. It's on a horizontal plane.

Second: ETHERIC or energy body, our aura; extends out from the skin an inch and a half, processes energy in the chakras, color is blue, sound is buzzing bees, pulsates at 15-20 cycles per minute. On a horizontal plane.

Third: ASTRAL or emotional body, halo around the head, energy flows through and into the chakras and is stored as holograms, composed of ether and we call this our levitational body, its energy field is 3 to 9 feet from the physical body, attaches at the naval by a silver like cord, color is yellow, psychic phenomena originate here, sound is the ocean. On the astral plane we have awareness within the vapors, not from the body. On a horizontal plane.

Fourth: MENTAL body, its medium is abstract intellectual energy. The aura extends 4 to 10 feet from the physical body. The sound is *om* and carries us into inner silence, into the now where past and future drop away. The color is blue and running waterfall is the tone. On a horizontal plane. Here is the place we call heaven and hell.

Fifth: SPIRITUAL body or atman is on a vertical plane. Here we transcend the limitations of the first 4 bodies, released from desires and off the wheel. Ah—liberation. Method, doors and gate are gone. Effort and labor are no longer useful. When the kundalini awakens in the fourth body we enter the fifth body. This is the plane of bliss: self-realization.

Sixth: COSMIC or causal body, four feet from the physical body. The Akashic records are here, this is universal mind and collective consciousness, the sound of tinkling bells are on this plane, the color is rose.

Seventh body: NIRVANIC or no-body extends, elongates, expands. I and thou are nonexistent. The seventh body loses even existence, to become nothing. Nothing: this is nirvana, the flame goes out. The sound of a flute is heard on this plane of kinetic energy and the color is soft golden.

Death and conception are one. This is the mystery of love and death. At every milestone a more intense energy enters. The energy which unites all things, merges all things into one, just as all wooden objects put into a fire are united in the same heat and the same ash. Ordinary man has not enough consciousness to withstand this energy, so he cannot 'know' what such unification means. With every breath our molecular body dies and is reborn. Beyond the circle of life in the cellular world, another and incommensurable circle of life in the molecular world, and yet another and again incommensurable circle of life in the electronic world, each complete in itself, each leading into the others, and all touching at one point—the simultaneous moment of death and conception, where all is possible. —Rodney Collin

S U B T L E   B O D I E S

Western medicine's lack of recognition of the existence of subtle Bodies allows physicians to enter medicine as if they are going into engineering. We are not simply mechanisms being repaired, or symptoms to be treated. Western medicine often injures our Bodies through invasive procedures. The striking reality is that preventable medical errors persist as the number three killer in the United States, third only to heart disease and cancer, claiming innumerable lives each year, since many errors and mishaps go unreported (2016 statistic from John Hopkins research). Used for diagnostic and emergency procedures, as well as many modern approaches, Western medicine has great value. To heal the Bodies without invading the naturalness of our nature brings a reverence that includes the whole patient. Acupuncture, Homeopathy, Reiki, Ayurveda, Massage, Tibetan medicine all work on the etheric or subtle Body. The mind, emotions and soul have their own distinct Bodies, connected to the physical Body.

What we need is a kind of 'holism' which implies above all a vivid sense of participation in the structured activities of a greater whole—and this greater whole today can not be any less inclusive a field of awareness and activity than humanity and the earth with all its 'spheres' (biosphere, atmosphere, noosphere, etc.) and its many kingdoms of existence. —Dane Rudhyar

The physical Body is the most dense of the 7 Bodies, filling out to the skin. The physical Body offers an experience of separation, not available to any other Body, as well as a solid foundation for all the other Bodies. The physical Body is composed of the energy states of solids, liquids and gases and is dependent upon the etheric Body for its vitality, life organization and other processes that create health. It's significant to know that we have Seven Bodies: the physical or flesh Body, the etheric or energy Body, the astral or emotional Body, the mental Body, the spiritual Body, the cosmic or causal Body, and the nirvanic. Each one is more subtle than the previous.

In this universe of many planes and dimensions we experience the most ordinal plane as physical and concrete energy, the place where we presently reside. This is the world of a dense chemical region of solids, liquids and gases which compose the material world about us. We experience this world through our senses: seeing, hearing, feeling, tasting smelling and knowing. The higher planes are about pure energy, love and truth, while the lower planes manifest them. *As above, so below.* The etheric Body, is the subtle level of the physical Body, the first level beyond the physical Body and extends out from the skin an inch and a half. The etheric regions consist of the higher physical ethers, which are electric, pranic, light and mental. As the energy template around which the physical Body is formed, the etheric is the same size and shape of the physical Body, having an aura that projects slightly beyond the skin. This subtle life-force Body holds the vital energy, the life force.

The etheric Body, also called our Aura, is the real source of all physical vitality, attuning our consciousness to the principle of energy. This energy field is made up of the emanations of our life force. It sustains the life of the physical Body, is the absorber of the vital fluid of life and is identified with the Breath, called spirit, *ruah, spiritus.* The etheric Body accesses energies from the higher Bodies down into our physical consciousness. Vital energy flows through the meridians and is processed in the energy centers or Chakras. The etheric forces are susceptible to control by higher mind and develops will; mind controls life and life controls matter. This life force is found in every living thing; plants, the earth, water and air.

Species—plant, animal and man—cease to be seen as separate entities once the common essence of their being is felt and understood. They are merely different forms of expression—different patterns and frequencies harmonized in the total field of organic interaction of life. —Michael W. Fox

The interactive energy fields, the energetic connection to minerals, plants and animals, make up the living tissue of the biosphere. The vibrations of ether, its wave-motion, give Light, Color and Sound as well as electricity. All plants, animals, rocks and bodies of water are transmitters, receivers and vessels of etheric awareness. The Color attributed to the etheric body is a swirl of blue-violet and the Sound that resonates with this plane is buzzing bees. Particular words sounding repeatedly in the etheric center can create etheric visions. Consciousness cannot function directly through the physical Body, which is our garment that enables us to function in our physical environment. The physical Body must be controlled via the etheric Body; without it the physical Body is immobile. The physical and etheric Bodies are two halves of a whole, which are only completely separated at physical death. As we evolve, our consciousness rises higher through our subtle Bodies.

Surrounding the human body are electromagnetic energy fields. The 'corona' of the human body is the etheric body, and most people can see it with only a little practice. It is a forerunner of the aura, but of a coarser consistency.
— anonymous writer

The emotional and third Body lives at a higher vibratory rate, is more refined than the physical etheric Body and is outside the visual range of the physical eye. This is the astral Body, with more subtle vibrations than the emotions. The vibrations emanating from the third Body are gathered around a person's head where particular colors can be seen, as in the halo in photos around Krishna and Buddha and Rama's heads.

Our experiences store somatic and autonomic sensory experiences of trauma in the emotional Body. Anything that raises the frequency moves the Aura up to a higher color of light, unless there is a serious medical problem. Most physical illness is created in the emotional Body. When the energy flow is blocked, when there are negative emotions, toxicity builds in the emotional Body to create emotional congestion, systemic disease and localized physical illness. When the energy circulates without blockage it flows into the physical world through our energy centers, the Chakras. When the emotional Body is aligned it accelerates the recovery of all forms of emotional trauma that accompanied original events, enabling them to be integrated and the experience resolved, not stored in the physical Body. This harmonizes the emotional forces. Emotional issues stored in the emotional Body become holograms which are energetic thought forms accompanied by a strong emotional charge, creating reactions in the present. The emotional Body, a subtle layer, is associated with the Color yellow.

So here we are—all part of this great hologram called Creation, which is everybody else's Self. It's all a cosmic play, and there is nothing but you.
—Itzhak Bentov

The astral and third Body, a complete Body of conscious energy, composed of astral material, ether, which is lighter than air, is capable of levitation. The astral Body is an exact energy duplication of the physical form and attached to the physical Body, usually at the naval, by a silver-like cord. Its energy field is found three feet from the physical Body and continues for another foot, although it may extend 4 to 9 feet from the physical Body. The astral Body, accompanied by the mind, travels aimlessly or, if directed, intentionally, happening all while the physical Body sleeps. The astral as a vehicle of consciousness has the location of awareness, not the Body. Therefore most people have little memory of their directionless astral travel, called astral projection. The astral Body is a vapor like the second Body, but it is transparent, so the moment you are outside, you will be inside. The astral Body is the same size as the first two Bodies. Up to the fifth Body, the size is the same. With the sixth Body the size will be cosmic, and with the seventh there will be no size at all, not even the cosmic. Psychic phenomena, such as telepathy, dreams and clairvoyance, originate here. The Sound quality of this dimension is the ocean.

Just as there are subtle 'wheels' turning and transforming different aspects of energy, so, in this beautifully complex structure of ours, there are gateways which can open us to further realms of possibility. By opening these gates we can start to develop the higher sense that are indeed available to us once we have made the 5 lower senses our friends and allies. We can, little by little, develop clairvoyance which is the art of seeing or sensing things as they actually are and not only as they appear to be. It is the same with clairaudience, i.e. the ability to hear with the inner ear. With just these two developed senses, nobody can lie to us. —Reshad Feild

The mental and fourth Body facilitates learning, our faculty of knowing, and houses thoughts and belief systems, constructs of the mind. Its medium is abstract intellectual energy emphasizing truth. The mental Body has its own range of feeling assisting the physical Body through mental clarity developing peace of mind by providing increased vibrancy and coherency to our mental faculties. Tension in the mental Body leads to memory lapses in the physical Body and contributes to our aging process. The aura is egg shaped with pointed ends and is a foot from the Body, extending 4 to 10 feet from the physical Body. The *om* Sound originates on this plane. Trust and faith are born here. To enter this place in silence we hear a continuous Sound inside our being which goes on by itself. Falling silent we hear the Sound coming from nowhere, arising from our innermost core. This is the Sound of inner silence, coming from entering the fourth Body through the third Body, the emotional Body. To avoid the third Body, the heart, taking a short-cut, perpetuates a quality of doubt. To enter the mental plane through love, our vision develops psychic eyes. Vision means seeing and hearing things without the use of the sense organs. The limitations of time and space disappear. The color is blue and the Sound of the waterfall, running water, is the tone quality on this plane.

The fourth Body travels into the past and into the future: past, future and present become one. Everything becomes a *now*; no past, no future, and still there is time! The fourth Body is wall-less, from inside the third Body there is not even a transparent wall. To go beyond the fourth there is as much difficulty as there was in going beyond the first. The wall now is between different dimensions, it's of a different plane.

Of what is the body made? It is made of emptiness and rhythm. At the ultimate heart of the body, at the heart of the world, there is no solidity, there is only the dance. —George B. Leonard

The four Bodies are connected to one plane, on a horizontal division. From the next planes the movement becomes vertical. The structure between the fourth and fifth is greater than any of the two lower Bodies because the ordinary way of looking is horizontal not vertical. From the first Body to the fourth Body the movement is from outside to inside, from the fourth to the fifth it is from downward to upward. From the fifth Body: nothing; moving into another realm, another dimension.

The fifth Body and spiritual Body cross the realm of the individual and the realm of time. Only when the kundalini awakens in our fourth Body can we enter the fifth Body; looking upward is the only way to access the fifth Body. In the fourth Body our consciousness becomes like fire—directing the eyes upward, from a center that is above the eyes, upward toward the third eye. All myths of creation have been developed here. Radiating a clear blue light, like the sky on a clear summer day, there is no longer a door or gate or method to move beyond the fifth Body. Zen monks talk about the gateless gate, now there is no gate and still we have to go beyond it. Labor and effort are needed through to the fifth Body, but they are useless from the fifth to the sixth. There is unshakable peace and strength that comes from resting in ourself. Up to the fifth Body a center had to be created; duality ends with the fifth Body. From the fifth Body, the spiritual Body, the answer to *Who am I*, arrives, called self-realization; this is the plane of bliss.

We are made up of many different, inter-penetrating subtle bodies, often called 'etheric bodies' because our composition includes fire, earth, air, water and ether. Ether is considered in physics to be an all-pervading weightless mass which is the carrying force of electro-magnetic waves. These etheric bodies are capable of carrying the electromagnetic force to where it is needed, often through the power of directed thought. Each of these subtle bodies has its counterpart in the world that we can know with the senses, which, for the sake of definition, I have labelled a physical body, a sexual body, an emotional body, a mental-motivated body and an aspirational body, each more refined than the one before. —Reshad Feild

The sixth and cosmic or causal Body, contacted four feet from the physical Body, extending another foot, holds memories and past lives. Located here are the Akashic records, detailed accounts and collections of mystical knowledge that are stored in the causal plane and read in the causal Body. This Body of energy is constructed from the conscious wisdom gained through the efforts of the many lives lived in time and space. A base of knowledge contacted through intuition; this is collective consciousness. The recorded distilled knowledge of the universe is held here. All matter and energy have a recording system and encode and store its information as it occurs. Intentional work with energy builds the causal Body which becomes an active part of soul consciousness called universal mind. Not spatial or time oriented, these are planes of light having the capacity to know and do things the physical mind and Body can not do.

The causal Body holds together a Body of awareness, the casing that determines our level of evolution. It's a molecular DNA determining our awareness of the universe. Meditation is a form of contact. Developing the spiritual energies of love, wisdom and light develops the causal Body. The soul flows energy through the causal Body to each of us, creating a marriage of soul to self which manifests on the planet in compassion and peace. The tinkling of bells are the Sound related to this dimension. This is the plane of truth; here is losing ourself, but not losing existence. The drop becomes the ocean.

In spiritual dimensions our energies flow without abatement, but here we are suddenly subject to constrictive laws of a physical reality. We are cloaked in low, slow vibrations. Remember, the universal hologram is always present. What more profound gift could we give than to restructure our DNA so that all humans inherit health, peace, and the relationship of the highest resonance. We are in a fluid medium, the body, the universe; the hologram. Everything is part of ourselves. We are not just bones and blood and flesh, we are magnificent conduits of energy that make us laugh and dance and live!

As we spin up the spiral vortex of life, all dimensional realities can move to that quickening evolutionary process along with us. We are dancing across the membrane of these dimensions, across the expanse of the universe within divine grace. —Chris Griscom

The seventh Body, the nirvanic or no-Body, extends, elongates, expands, creating wave forms of consciousness. Nirvanic means total cessation, the absolute void, ultimate emptiness. Not spatial or time oriented, no symbols, no images represent it, made up of intelligent light, all a series of interconnecting awareness. Its medium is pure kinetic energy. The spiritual Body guides and balances through the limitations of the physical Body, providing a sense of lightness towards our life experiences. We are sparks from the vast field, particles of its Light. Light makes Color visible. The Sound of a flute is heard on this plane. The spiritual Body expresses itself as tiny threads of shimmering light pulsating.

Listen, friend, this body is his dulcimer. He draws the strings tight, and out of it comes the music of the inner universe, If the strings breaks and the bridge falls, then the dulcimer of dust goes back to dust. Kabir says: The Holy One is the one who can draw music from it. —Kabir

Rumi describes the human Body as a robe for the soul. Seen this way as an outer husk, the seed can't be planted without it. *The soul lives, the body wears out like a cloak.* The spiritual Body contains the archetype, an expansion of identity beyond individuality, elastic, when directed towards an object it expands and elongates. This expansion of consciousness accessed through a state of pure consciousness or presence is a gateway to worlds unlimited by time and space. This is a radiation with a central point that is unified with the one-life that envelops and surrounds the earth. The seventh Body loses even existence, to become nothing.

Man stands as the bridge between heaven and earth. Organic evolution pass-

es through man in an upward and forward moving spiral, whereas conscious evolution comes from completion at the end of time, with the direct purpose of bringing the higher worlds right down here on earth. —Reshad Feild

The world of Light and Sound, unlimited, infinite, what Plato called the *music of the spheres*, is a universal call to enter the *now*. Light, Sound, Color, words and thought used with intention and understanding develop soul consciousness. No longer active in the body, consciousness moves into a world where physical laws are different. Consciousness moves into the astral plane until it withdraws and moves onto the mental plane. We are a gateway to the beyond. A word or phrase, basic Sounds used as mantra, Sound vibration, opens doors to higher centers. Humming, or saying ancient Sounds, *om* or *hu*, phrases like *om namah shivaya*, or, *shema yisroel, ani Adonai*, bring cosmic energy effecting awareness. Movements like yoga, dance, tai chi, Gurdjieff's sacred dances, whirling, the turn, are a preparation, a lifting out of the illusion of time and space. Through these and similar practices we have glimpses into other worlds.

We palpate each other's Auras responding or withdrawing from what we feel in their Auric fields; understanding the nature of the astral and other dimensions we learn to utilize them and access intercommunication between interdimensions. Intelligent releasing of our astral energy to consciousness, we heal, recreate and alter the astral dimension itself. Sound, Color and energetic Movement directed and used intentionally create a harmonious vibration in the physical, mental, astral, etheric, psychic, spiritual and causal levels and Bodies.

What you cannot discover in your own body, you will not discover in any place in the world. —Amiyo Devienne

1247

SYSTEM TWENTY-THREE

PATH OF LOVE

SURVIVAL, DUTY, APPEARANCE,

APPRECIATION, UNDERSTANDING,

ALTRUISM, AGAPE

To love at all is to be vulnerable. Love anything and your heart will be wrung and possibly broken. If you want to make sure of keeping it intact you must give it to no one, not even an animal. Wrap it carefully round with hobbies and little luxuries; avoid all entanglements. Lock it up safe in the casket, safe, dark, motionless, airless, it will change. It will not be broken; it will become unbreakable, impenetrable, irredeemable. To love is to be vulnerable. —C.S. Lewis

We are in the world to learn how to Love. The Path of Love informs us: the impulse to Love is the origin, the root and foundation of all human interaction. To learn to Love consciously is to understand the nature of Love. We work to uproot ourselves from our conditioned responses and pay attention to our reactive ways. Love is the reflection of beauty and oneness in a world of duality. Each of our encounters are a responsibility. To serve Love begins with loving ourself. To look into our own heart is to see the sacred heart of humanity.

Happiness is only possible with true love. True love has the power to heal and transform the situation around us and bring deep meaning to our lives. All of us need love and all of us need to love. All of us have the capacity to love and to understand. But we seem not to believe it and we continue to cause suffering to ourselves and others. Maybe we haven't had the time to look deeply into the nature of our love, to sum up what our love is about, and understand why it is that when we love, suffering arises from it. —Thich Nhat Hahn

The stages along the path are the fruits harvested on the way to Love. As we travel through the gates to higher worlds, Love, the jewel in creation is revealed. To understand the meaning and purpose of Love is to learn to Love consciously, since Love without wisdom is colored with suffering. The earlier stages limit, tether the heart, block the flow and stream of Love. To discipline the heart reveals the illusions and obstacles that create the terrible unnecessary suffering that contort and disfigure our relationships. As we learn, as we practice, as we protect the truth and trust of the other, whether it is animal, plant or person, the flowering, the opening develops our capacity for Love.

Who can tell what miracles Love has in store for us if only we have the courage to become one with it? Everything we think we know now is only the beginning of another knowing that itself has no end. And everything we now can accomplish will seem derisory to us when the powers of our divine nature flower in glory and act through us. —Iqbal

For Love to deepen and surround our world, to reveal the beauty that is Love, is the teaching. This Path, System 23, has seven expressive stages. The teaching, to be in the Way of Love, is to eliminate obstacles that keep us out of the present moment and away from experiencing the true nature of our being, which is Love. *The Way of the Lover* teaches the joy of this vision, how to arrive into a world of unity, how to live in Love. There is no division, only one seamless harmony.

A man who practices the mysteries of love will be in contact not with a reflection, but with truth itself. To know this blessing of human nature, one can find no better helper than love. —Socrates

A LOVE PRACTICE

To learn to Love in a real way, day-to day, as a practice to awaken our heart; to manifest Love in our daily world originates with valuing and loving ourself. *The moment you see how important it is to love yourself, you will stop making others suffer.* Buddha's statement, *You can search the world over and never find anyone more deserving of your love than yourself,* is the first rung on the ladder. Until we learn to Love and serve ourselves, our ability to Love another is severely limited. Only then are we able to practice on another. Healing our own inner division may be the greatest gift we can give to the world. A loving-kindness base prepares the ground; from feeling unlovable and not loved to offering well-being towards ourself. Speaking to ourself as a loved one is a Love practice for all to benefit. Now, rather than being another source of suffering and unhappiness in the world we can become a container and a supply of Love.

Knowing thyself is the first practice of love. —*Thich Nhat Hahn*

Contacting the truth of our own suffering is what cracks the heart open to self-compassion and forgiveness. —*True Refuge*

Through our words and actions we bring Love into the world. Love without knowledge, without consciousness, without knowing what Love is and how to Love, is only the appearance. To respond to Love, for Love to flow through us and take hold of the world there must be understanding. Self-Love is our beginning. Surely it cannot end there, for without further investigation and further growth our traditional customary sentimental, self-important *Love* impedes human society. It Loves nothing higher than itself. Consciousness and awakening is higher than self-Love. For Love to become more than a veiled extension of self-Love it will have to become conscious Love.

The most precious gift we can offer anyone is our attention. When mindfulness embraces those we love, they will bloom like flowers. —*Thich Nhat Hahn*

Love grounded in knowledge is a study for those students in the school of Love. The seven stages along the Path are set forth as a way to study our relationship to Love itself. Love is not the goal, it's the cause, and we are here to open to that; to remember. Numerous awakened beings, Bodhisattvas, mystics; Buddha, Jesus, the Baal Shem Tov, Hafiz, Rumi, Mirabai, Hildegard of Bingen, Meher Baba, Muhammad, Lala, Krishna, Lao Tzu, Saradai Devi, having walked this way before us have left wisdom pearls of light to guide us along, each testifying to Love as the force and power that directed and guided them. To undeniably know that we are not separate from existence, that we are Love, nothing to discover, everything is found. To let Love fully enter us, this energy, continues and continues and continues.

Jump to your feet, wave your fists, threaten and warn the whole universe that your heart can no longer live without real love! —Hafiz

FIRST STAGE

SURVIVAL

When we were engaged in the problems of survival we had no time to have anything to do with culture. —Nursultan Nazarbayev

Providing for and sustained by living in the reality of *I will take care of my own* is the natural root impulse of all living beings to form the foundation of love along this path, the journey of love. This is clearly love on the Survival level, unsophisticated, instinctive, biological, unconscious, self-protective and the most primitive form. Until we can take care of ourselves we are of little use to others. Caretaking our own body, animals safeguarding nurturing their young, this First Stage is practical and instinctive with an imbalance of power. Physical Survival is primary. Food and sex are based on pure impulse; eating is to live, sex is an animalistic urge. At this Stage life is programmed to manage our comings and goings, our concerns regarding the body, physical Survival, all else is foreign. What is known as love is raw primal instinctive energy. Self-centered, looking at the world from our own limited view, what is out there in the world is not important, until, eventually there comes an urge to try it out.

The spirit finds a way to be born, instinct seeks for ways to survive.
—*Toba Beta*

Relationships are based on necessity, our personal need for something that the other can provide. Emotionally undeveloped, Survival is directed towards the preservation of our own body and physical necessities. Children begin from this place, from instinct, circumstance and need. Biological relationships often continue for many years. Resentment, possessiveness, murder, racism, homophobia, kidnapping, sexual abuse, incest, pedophilia, bestiality, emerge from this imbalanced, immature, culturally charged way of viewing relationships. No capacity for remorse or regret, fear and self-involvement shadow all possibility of developing emotional maturity. The beginning impulse of love is conditioned by the rudimentary consciousness from which it appears. Generally instinctive, in the animal world hunting prey is an expression of love with desires to satisfy a bodily impulse, usually hunger. There is no real awareness of morality, conscience, or responsibility towards animals, nature, or humanity.

To put it simply, the lizard brain is purely concerned with survival.
—*Stephen Richards*

The lower form of love obstruct the release of pure love until it is untangled from the limits and obstructions of lower love. Relationships are guarded and sequestered, only when they hit the front pages do we hear about them. Men harboring women or children in a cellar or closet, not free to attend school, sometimes in squalid conditions, couples locking up immigrants and forcing them to work, religious edicts cursing homosexuality, priests molesting children, pimps closely maintaining a stable of women; these are the dark corners of society.

Stars are the scars of the universe. —*Ricky Maye*

This is a home life of relationships that function to satisfy personal needs and cravings; incest, abuse, assault, young people working in factories, voting rights denied for gender and racial reasons, stalking, unsophisticated, self-concern. This early Stage of development is looking for a basic level of subsistence with no feeling for societal consequences.

Without love, nothing in the world would have life. How is an inorganic thing transformed into a plant? How are plants sacrificed to become rich with spirit? How is spirit sacrificed to become breath? —*Rumi*

SECOND STAGE

Duty

Nothing truly valuable arises from a mere sense of duty; it stems from love and devotion towards people and towards objects. —*Albert Einstein*

The expression of the Second Stage of Love encompasses obligation and routine, structure and organization. A relationship rooted in Duty offers security, discipline, allegiance comingled with a quality of loyalty. Love is now about acceptance, looking to authority, group survival and the ability to recognize that another exists. This perspective leads to obligation, rigidity and mechanicalness. Relationships, allegiance to a gang or to family kinship justifies what's named as love. Alliances are connected by beliefs and are rationalized with rhetoric and rules. I love them because they are my family and my value and Duty to protect them regardless to how they behave takes precedence. Jumping into the life of a lie, getting wrapped around protecting the illusion; self-knowledge is impossible when we are immersed in drama.

Little growth or development happens with this alliance and allegiance. This could be an arrangement formed in jail between a guard and a particular prisoner, a gang in or out of the prison system, a community in a repressive country, a wife to her husband, a son or daughter to their family. The sense of obligation and ownership transfers from belongings to people. Supporting and fighting for the gang or clan is imperative; these are *my* people and others are not part of *our* group. This narrow viewpoint limits the world while creating an us and them construct. The NRA, Ku Klux Klan, Mafia, even prison gangs; each have a civilized structure and a moral ring.

We are born into a complex emotional world—our family and society—in a state of total vulnerability. When the adult world—either through misunderstanding, neglect, or outright abuse—fails to see or value us as children, we feel deeply hurt. Our soul experiences a kind of shock, which closes down our natural openness of our being. In shutting down like this, we also close off our access to inner resources that we need for handling life's challenges. Turning away from our pain diminishes our capacity for compassion, the most effective antidote to human suffering. As we lose access to these inner resources, we develop holes or dead spots in our psyche—places where we have gone numb, where the energy of awareness no longer circulates freely. —John Welwood

OBLIGATION AND OWNERSHIP

This stage of love continues the imbalance of power, arrangements rooted in inequality. Maintaining norms takes precedence over protecting the rights of individuals to choose their own values. Police states, countries where the army patrols curfews, enforcing power and fear over the populous, the structure that is felt from the impositions, terrorizing as they are satisfies the need for security and loyalty to *something*. Decisions are made that include whole groups, laws are instituted that infringe on individual rights under the guise of protection and being civilized. Instincts and urges are controlled to fit into the larger group. Beliefs are written in stone; *this is the right way and you better follow it, or you will have measures taken against you,* knowing what's expected and following routines are a relief. This could be a jail regimen, an arranged marriage, evangelical teachings, radical militant groups, condominium rules, political party lines, or unquestioningly/blindly obeying what the doctor orders. Today many of the Muslim communities are proceeding from this place and creating ISIS and terrorist groups to eliminate, to kill those people who aren't in line with their beliefs and religion. No space for creative thought or for questioning authority, this is the one way to do things, and like it or not, understand it or not, I will follow, you will obey.

Duty without love is unfortunate, duty with love is desirable, love without duty is divine. —Sri Satthya Sai Baba

Necessity relationships, called *tagged*, where invisible *tags* of ownership and property value are placed, have a wide range. *My* children, *my* mother, *my* wife, *my* teacher, *my* lover, *my* country, *my* rules, *my* dog, *my* way; the loaded charge coming from early years when dependency and ownership were seen as obligation limits the growth of the individuals. The conservative two parent family value culture supports limiting the possibilities of exploring and deepening relationships under the guise of a lifetime of obligation, named *ownership* and *parenting*. *I am your mother, I am your husband, this is our country leave if you don't like it, I am your husband now have sex with me, I am your father do what I say, it's my dog and I'll tie it up and leave it outside if I want, this is the right religion, anything other is heresy.*

Permission to rape defies any criminality attached to the act. It points to a different standard of civilization being applied as our normal taboos are squelched whenever war is accepted and killing and destruction become commonplace. In this sort of world, the line between duty and cruelty is obscured, for in a wartime environment, full of danger, fear and the thrill of adrenaline, the possession of women becomes the act of a conqueror. —Kevin Gerard Neill

Filled with rules, assumptions, duties leading into expectations, disappointments, constriction, hope, comparison; lives are held back, filled with appointments and right and wrong. Using family, religious, gender, sexual and power roles as a rigid model for public life produces unrealistic, even destructive definitions of community. Viewing the family as the fundamental unit of society limits the creativity and growth of choice making.

Families aren't easy to join. They're like an exclusive country club where membership makes impossible demands and the dues for an outsider are exorbitant. —Erma Bombeck

ALLEGIANCES

Society has few provisions to respectfully caretake the elderly, the bureaucracy of public schools overwhelm, expectations and identification limit the possibility of mutual and *built* relationships for adults to support and respect each others development and fulfillment. Duty is a Stage of Love that does not empower people to maximize or inspire developing personal unique potential. Rarely any insights, life is about *me* and all else is what is *not me* and needs to be controlled or obeyed. Family or gang/group obligations become the slogan, allegiances rank as first order, and others are seen as *other*, not to be considered in the same light as family clan or pod. Individual survival is no longer a focus, expanding to what is considered other in society, the recognition of the world and its rules plays a large part in Duty relationships. Love becomes something outside of self and larger than oneself; it translates as authority, tradition, family loyalty and the Duties required to maintain those connections.

In the effort to perpetuate so-called fundamental moral family values under the theme of the breakdown of the traditional family it's concluded that the logical solution to societal problems are the reunification of the traditional nuclear family structure. This increases government proposals aimed at bolstering traditional family structure. Racism, bigotry, bias, sexual inequality, abortion laws, and religious codes are perpetuated at this stage from a fear of differences threatening the status quo.

The family is the basic group most of us have established in us and it is a barrier to being on a level with each other. The family is technically the small cramped group which most of us never got beyond. It is based on emotion and power. —Anonymous

Goal-oriented and competitive, relationships offer the opportunity to make connections, to reassure getting ahead, pursuing advancement for personal advantage. There is little insight, except to being right and others therefore being wrong. Reinforced behavior and conditioning from family and the culture are difficult to change. The entrenched political structure upholds the rigidity of this Stage. Not questioning motives, lives are devoted to action, not thoughts or feelings. Friendships and relating engage seeing things one way and actually avoiding people of other beliefs.

Blind belief, unthinking respect, and a foolish faith in authority are the greatest enemy of truth. —*Albert Einstein*

THIRD STAGE

Appearance

Love is that sacred feeling which gradually degenerates in people, this sacred impulse of genuine love. Love of consciousness evokes the same in response, love of feeling evokes the opposite, love of body depends only on type and polarity. —*G.I. Gurdjieff*

While there is a sense of you and me in this Third Stage, it is essentially involved with one as the winner and the other as the loser. Relationships have a strong flavor of comparison. Emotionally withheld, mutual dependence forms a love that may not include liking each other. Not great parents, the ability to make strong feeling connections to children is lacking, as well as the reluctance to support the pursuit of what is liked, which is viewed as indulgence, particularly if it is different or *impractical.* The focus is on financial security and daily stability. This is a black and white expression of connections, based on aspiration and common mutual interests. People who don't accept their values, who live out of the mainstream are seen as unconventional and peculiar. The phase of self-promotion called networking begins here.

If we get our self-esteem from superficial places, from our popularity, appearance, business success, financial situation, health, any of these, we will be disappointed, because no one can guarantee we'll have them tomorrow. — *Kathy Ireland*

The expression of love remains conditional. There is a selection of one person, most usually in a conventional form. The concern is with Appearance: how the relationship looks in the eyes of society.

Experimentation with sex will be for adventure and the possessing of people as objects. With sex as power, and relationships as dependence, there is an imbalance of financial and physical power. This Stage of Love is competitive, ambitious, judgmental and goal oriented with shallow emotional connections. Appearance is love as exploitation, the other is used as a means, possessiveness creating bondage, lots of expectations, bringing disappointment.

Parents and grandparents in the Third Stage use their children as objects to show off, talk about, as well as to enhance their own privilege and social status. People are identified as successful doctors, politicians, lawyers, established business owners, those who will make useful children, in-laws, and partners. Relationships are looked to as a means of securing identity. Children are loved as objects to talk about, to show off, a supply to eventually care-take their parents in old age. Trapped by anecdotal memories, sentimentality colors conversations and ways of seeing life.

No man can put a chain about the ankle of his fellow man, without at least finding the other end of it about his own neck. —Frederick Douglass

OBLIGATION AND EXPECTATION

Money is the primary expression at this Stage of Love and gifts at all prices are the display. Love towards oneself comes in the form of keeping the body looking young. Gifting oneself with plastic surgery, beauty products, new electronic toys are the level of self-love that is understood. A youthful attractive demeanor matters, watching how others appear, comparing the styles of the day to how I look, talking about those in my immediate world, a general competitive thought process monitors financial dealings. Gifts for all occasions become a means of exchange, time filled with shopping and distractions, influencing the economy, contributions to shape the political outcome; a visible facade to manifest an inner comfort of success. Facebook is filled with personal photos followed by comments like *you're lookin good, wow-you look young, I like your clothes.*

Conversations about good places to live continues with what's the best place to live as well as sound and clever investment decisions, good financial planning and retirement strategies. The Third Stage monitors what works in the world of achievement, what will create a stable secure future, how being in a relationship and making a family will create a safe pod—a well-contained family unit; all this in the design of winning in the game of life.

To explain why we become attached to our birthplaces we pretend that we are trees and speak of roots. Look under your feet. You will not find gnarled growths sprouting through the soles. Roots, I sometimes think, are a conservative myth, designed to keep us in our places. —Salman Rushdie

Tagged relationships continue. The projected sense of obligation define possibilities and limit truth-telling; early expectations continue to bleed through. Safety in psychological security weighs heavily, children learn well that to tag adults cleverly, financial assistance will be forthcoming. Staying involved with a parent might insure being part of their inheritance or trust fund when he/she dies; wills become a strategy of power and blackmail. Airline tickets and restaurant checks get paid for by the elder family members out of duty and for Appearance rather than choice. Visits remain lopsided, the younger—and this carries through, regardless to the aging process—continue to visit family expecting to receive interested attention, thinking little of true exchange. Maturity is greatly challenged at this stage.

Appearance is something absolute, but reality is not that way—everything is interdependent, not absolute. —the Dalai Lama

Death is pushed aside and substitute words like *lost* and *gone* replace the concept of death, as if the deceased were misplaced, adrift at sea, vanished to be one day found again. This is a one-time occasion, live now, stay looking well, look cheerful, we are our body—dress it well, stay connected to the medical establishment, be productive, and to win, be part of a majority, connected to the people with common mutual interests.

Ordinarily what we call love is not real love, but demands. The ordinary love is a kind of begging—give me, give me more. When love gives, it is true, it radiates, it pulsates. The law of love is: if you go on keeping love it dies. The creative energy that was involved in it becomes destructive. The very energy that was meant to become nectar becomes poison. Give it, let it flow, and it remains nectar. And the more you give, the more you have. —Osho

FOURTH STAGE

Appreciation

The faculty of appreciation makes one light. Life is just like the ocean. When there is no appreciation, no receptivity, man sinks like a piece of iron to the bottom of the sea. He cannot float like the boat which is hollow, which is receptive. —Hazrat Khan

Walking along the path, the Fourth Stage of Love recognizes and values differences. Discrimination, having the ability to look at our life loosens identification, deepens our capacity for relationships and begins a possibility for real change. The stuck places that interfere with our deepening include lust, greed, infatuation, resentment, self-importance, vanity and upside-down vanity, possessiveness, sentimentality and anger. This is still love on the horizontal plane, at the mercy of external forces, obstructions that drain our energy. Comparative thinking and dramas run high, carrying some of the greatest deprivation, pain and suffering we will know. Born out of the mind and constrained by thought, there is often bickering, nagging, working things out, painful separation and divorce; moments of misunderstanding and frustration.

Strong attraction often leads to love/hate relationships, since love and hate are two poles of the same energy. Relationships become complicated, confusing and prolonged. Holding on to familiar but lost love affairs based on the quantity of time invested and dismissing the choice to be single we see long sustained marriages with visible tension. Since love is not a means to anything, not a commodity, love as a way of being eludes Stage Four. Love at this level involves opposite attractions and includes hate as its object.

Couples around the world are living as if love is there. They are living in a world of 'as if.' They are drained of energy, trying to get something out of a false love; it cannot deliver the goods. Hence the frustration, hence the continuous boredom, hence the continuous nagging, fighting between the lovers. They are trying to make their love affairs something of the eternal, impossibility. Love is more of a quality that surrounds you. It has nothing to do with the other. You are loving—you are love—then it is eternal. People carry dead love affairs, carrying it out of fear, clinging—just clinging with the known, with the familiar. —Osho

BOUNDRY CONFLICTS

Kindness, a sense of concern for people in the community, strengthens our capacity to love. Love as the heart of an alliance establishes a reliable base on which bonding can build. Mutual affection opens the door for a force that unites. Affection on one side without reciprocal affection on the other interferes with love entering and rooting itself into the soil of our being. A recognition exists that other people have feelings and so there is a shift to a more evenly based balance of power in Fourth Stage Appreciation. In love there is an active gratefulness, a recognition of the intrinsic worth of the object of love. The deepening of Appreciation brings understanding, valuation, sensitivity and a quality of enjoyment to this stage. Life is expanded, not contracted, more joyful, less suffering; no longer the discomfort and lack of satisfaction, this love now brings about the experience of fulfillment. No longer driven by excitement the days have moments of peacefulness.

The future of the world is dependent upon love. —*Reshad Feild*

Relationships make the effort to have elements of communication. The emotional life opens and boundaries break down. Less focused on success; connections to others, particularly community, matters as much as our career. Love has a tinge of soap opera drama and instability since drugs, alcohol and emotionality create an intensity that is driven from a need to relate. Possessiveness brings us under the tutelage or authority of another which constrains energy, and when thwarted anger and envy appear to obstruct the flow of love. Limiting conditions, personal feelings restrict the movement of the heart, entangles the personality, leading to various complications. Times of privacy create an awkward shift making us appear shut down, swinging from full immersion to withdrawal. Boundary conflicts are a clue to this stage.

CONNECTEDNESS

To take love seriously and to bear and to learn it like a task, the place of love in life is misunderstood, made into play and pleasure as if that is more blissful than work; but there is nothing more happier than work and love, because it is extreme happiness, can be nothing else but work—So whoever loves must try to act as if he had a great work. —Rilke

With reflection, wherever we are the human spirit has a possibility to triumph, never stuck, not trapped. This stage begins the exploration for meaning originating with gratefulness and Appreciation. The Fourth Stage moves from self-concern outward to a recognition of others in our immediate circle being of value. The emotional intensity starts opening up the heart center, the personal aspect of wanting to be liked, cared for, held in regard, creating a sensitivity and a rawness to the life of feelings.

You must fall in love with the one inside your heart, then you will see that it has always been there, but you have wanted something else. To taste bliss, forget all other tastes and taste the wine served within. —Poonja

Love reflects a desire to be Appreciated and an urge to relate. The drama created is from not knowing that the love is within, as well as a need for an intensity of connectedness. Love at the Fourth Stage includes emotional contact, a desire for acceptance and the need to receive as well as to give. The earth is rich and nourished because it takes in and absorbs sun and rain. Only when we allow kindness to penetrate, are receptive, loosening our control, balance our generosity of giving, will we be able to enter the next level. Receptivity requires openness, softening, vulnerability; an entrance way to the understanding that protecting ourselves from the longing to be loved is a barrier from experiencing the presence that is always there.

True love is something far greater than anything that could be called personal. It is the nature of reality itself. Love cares not for the me, it cares only for that which is true, undivided, and whole. When the me dissolves, when it surrenders itself to a unity far greater than anything the mind can comprehend, that is love. —Adyashanti

FIFTH STAGE
Understanding

Love is impossible without understanding. You cannot love someone if you do not understand him or her. If you don't understand and you love, that is not love; it is something else. Without understanding, love can't be true love. We must look deeply in order to see and understand the needs, aspirations, and suffering of the ones we love. —*Thich Nhat Hahn*

*L*ove deepens with a sensing and Understanding of the interrelatedness of all people. To see another; this beautiful encounter of Understanding develops friendship. Now we are able to offer intentionally, accompanied by the Understanding of what the other prefers, what is needed. When giving is from the root of our being we practice loving regardless to our hurts, resistance and intellectual activities. No holding back, what we resist persists, and so to remain the openness we are leaves us free to enjoy and know intimate partnership. Seeking Understanding; a spiritual pull creates distance from the emotional upheavals that toxify relationships. As false personality diminishes and we place attention on mindfulness the ordinary is experienced as remarkable. This nature is who we are. The individuality and unorthodox lifestyle, rarely doing what is not heartfelt, creates inner dialogue and substance called self-worth. Love pursued, this is the step of realizing that the source of love is internal and the desire for union becomes the spirit of truth.

Can we understand at all, ever, where we do not love? —*Sherwood Anderson*

Relationships in the Fifth Stage are built upon truth-telling, openness, a commitment to our inner work. The interest and desire is to know another, what they long for, not to restrict or judge, not to have assumptions or unstated agendas; to love is to see. Here communication steps out of fear, honesty replaces control, deep contact is possible. At this level two people intentionally enter a process where they regard their relationship itself as a vehicle for mutual awakening. Krishnamurti during one of his many talks and teachings stated: *In the understanding of relationship, love comes into being. And in the understanding of love we alter the structure of society.* To Understand our relationship with others we will create a new world.

Love is the true means by which the world is enjoyed: our love to others and others' love to us. We ought therefore above all things to get acquainted with the nature of love. For love is the root and foundation of nature: love is the soul of life and crown of rewards. —*Traherne*

The disparity between our spiritual practice and our human relationships brought the French spiritual teacher Prajnanpad to tell students who wanted to study with him *to bring a certificate from their husband, wife or life partner.* At this level there are no secrets, the heart becomes transparent. The Fifth Stage on the Path of Love dedicates our relationship to consciousness. Everything that happens is food for growth. Personal life comes into alignment with deeper values and purpose, circumstances come and go and now identifications no longer stick. A sense of humor, a desire to teach, Understanding at Stage Five is penetrating this being inside love; the way to know love is through being a lover. The energy that goes into a relationship has to be continuously renewed to rise above our self-contained limitations with an invisible bond that is greater than the sum of all our parts. Here is a glimpse into timelessness, into eternity, into real love.

UNCOVERING THE HEART

The earth and the sand are burning. Put your face on the burning sand and

on the earth of the road, since all those who are wounded by love must have the imprint on their face, and the scar must be seen. Let the scar of the heart be seen, for by their scars are known the persons who are in the way of love.
—*attributed to Prophet Muhammad*

Love is not for the frail, it requires a willing steady heart, a discipline and dedication of the heart that releases us from the prison of the isolated self. It appears *easier* to complain and worry than to live in a state of receptivity with the high stakes of death hovering over the life of your beloved. For the heart to break out of the shell that has held it hostage, unfreezing our emotional responses we feel love and pain as one, a deepening that evolves into compassion. Love is a passageway and once we pass through that door our separateness disappears. The dark night vanishes into a beautiful morning.

For one human being to love another: that is perhaps the most difficult of all our tasks, the ultimate, the last test and proof, the work for which all other work is but preparation. For this reason young people who are beginners in everything, cannot yet know love: they have to learn it. —Rilke

The friction in the Fifth Stage is: until our needs drop away we can not be certain that love is real. Practice to remove the obstacles that hinder love, they are the stagnant water underneath the piles of debris. Quietly holding our imperfections the beauty that we are softens the hardness that covers our heart.

When we walk to the edge of all the light we have and take the step into the darkness of the unknown, we must believe that one of two things will happen. There will be something solid for us to stand on or we will be taught to fly. —Patrick Overton

When we imagine Understanding while disagreeing with another we deceive ourselves; when we Understand someone we are in agreement, and when we disagree we are not Understanding. Understanding is the most powerful force that we create in ourselves—it brings about internal spaciousness. Deep within ourselves is a voice, self-awareness blossoms listening and following that sound to its original longing. Benevolence is always moving towards us. Learn to open the dam, to release the waters, to allow love to flow; stagnant water is not inviting, flowing water stays fresh. To acknowledge and recognize ourself in another births a love that Understands the oneness, eliminating separation. Love is not other than yourself, no one is left out. It arises as our natural being when the obstacles that impede its flowering are surmounted. The duality of lover and beloved maintains the illusory separation. Maintaining this illusion restricts us from love's reflection, from love's oneness.

When you love, may you feel the joy of your heart coming alive as your lover's gaze lands on your eyes, holding them, like the weight of a kiss, deepening. In the gaze of your lover, may you see clearer in the mirror of your own being. —*John O'Donohue*

Tantric sexuality is often an expression of Stage Five relationships, sexuality becomes about gifting ourselves to our partner. *Approach the sex act as if you are approaching the temple of the divine;* accepting the sacredness of sex elevates our partnership. Sharing, giving to another leads to a spiritual incorporation of the beloved in the very being of the lover. The longing and intention to love consciously, to awaken to the truth of who we are is a Path of the heart.

True love is possible only with understanding. When there is understanding, compassion is born. —*Thich Nhat Hahn*

SIXTH STAGE

ALTRUISM

The whole world could be choked with thorns: A lover's heart will stay a rose garden. The wheel of heaven could wind to a halt: The world of lovers will go on turning. Even if every being grew sad, a lover's soul will stay fresh, vibrant, light. Mount the stallion of love and so not fear the path—Love's stallion knows the way exactly. —Rumi

The Sixth expression of love, benevolent, immeasurable, transcendental, originates in the energy of mindfulness. Open presence, *to find the beloved*, Rumi points the direction: *you must become the beloved.* This love affair with the world is for the benefit of all human beings. *If you want others to be happy, practice compassion. If you want to be happy, practice compassion.* This timeless wisdom embodied and stated by the Dalai Lama informs us to direct our energies towards conscious evolution. Listening to the calling of the world, understanding what it means to be human, this Stage of being appears through self-inquiry, self awareness, seeing all people as facets of a diamond light reflection. Every encounter becomes an encounter with a dear friend.

Altruism understands that through giving without conditions, without expectations, we receive. The more we give the more we receive. Distributing our gifts, we join the world of true wealth. This bountiful, kind-hearted state uplifts humanity. It is responsible, incorporating clarity and truth, understanding the sacredness of the world and its connection between all things. Mahatma Gandhi, Yogananda Paramahansa and St. Francis of Assisi, Sixth Stage Altruists, offered their love for the well-being of others, influencing generations. All-embracing human beings, their essential message—to live peacefully a life of service—to bring peace to the world.

When love is the spirit of your life, it will have the freedom and universality of a spirit; it will always live and work in love, not because of this or that, here or there, but because the spirit of love can only love, wherever it is or goes, or whatever is done to it. As the spark knows no motion but that of flying upwards, whether it be in the darkness of night, or in the light of day, so the spirit of love is always in the same course; it knows no difference of time, place or persons; but whether it gives or forgives, bears or forebears, it is equally doing its own delightful work, equally blessed from itself. —W. Law

OPENING

This state of loving where love-energy for all is non-possessive, no longer a relationship, love is a state of being, not about another or falling in love; we become love. Now in love, the other is not the source, love is the source. The neediness of the personality recedes. To become a conduit for love to flow through we arrive at knowing we are loved.

Tonglen, a training in Altruism, is one of the practices of opening our heart to feel the suffering of others, to soften and liberate ourselves from our prison of self-involvement, increasing compassion, offering our presence. Love is a fragrance, a miraculous awakening, a stillness that touches all who appear. In the willingness to surrender, to hold nothing back, for the heart to break open, nothing to protect, love is revealed. In one instant, a look, a sunrise, a child's smile, whether hardship or celebration; the love that's always there arises.

You might quiet the whole world for a second if you pray. And if you love, if you really love, our guns will wilt. —St. John of the Cross

When love enters the Sixth Stage it becomes our inner quality, a field of love, and it determines our relationship to the universe. *Having died to self-interest,* said Rumi, *love risks everything and asks for nothing, love gambles away every gift bestowed.* This vibration transforms, it is the cause of everything, recognizable, service with presence, without demand, free of conditioning and sentimentality. Leaving the horizontal dimension of love which is time based we enter a vertical dimension of love, which is impermanent and eternal. The Sixth Stage of love is not a relationship, it arises from no-mind and no-time. Always there; as the ego, the suffering, the needs, wants, the possessiveness, the exploitation, self-importance, domination, insecurities manipulations, the obstacles are softened, diminished, removed, *you* are removed from the equation and love will be there.

My religion is to live through love. To find the beloved you must become the beloved. —*Rumi*

SEVENTH STAGE

Agape

Love has been identified as being connected with another person. Love is not a person. Love is the individual, collective and universal soul. Love is truth. Love is beauty. Love is self. To know yourself, to surrender to the truth of yourself, is to surrender to love. —*Gangaji*

*U*nconditional openness. There is no cycling off from the physical plane experience without having experienced Agape. The Seventh Stage of love, non-personal, a state of being, is not directed to any one in particular, it is a quality, whoever comes near drinks the wine, smells the fragrance, feels nurtured by the embodiment of unconditional love in the world. *Love is.* No one needs to be the object, no person has to be around, yet the lover still loves. When love will be there the ego will not be there. To know ourselves as this, our very nature being love itself, gifts this presence towards all. You and love cannot exist together. In deep love the other disappears.

The earth has disappeared beneath my feet, it fled from all my ecstasy, now like a singing air creature I feel like the Rose, keep opening. —Hafiz

To access this love, no longer to live with frustration and separation from a struggle with conditional love, this is true nourishment for who appears in the mirror. Relationships serve as the mirror pointing out our imperfections. Drinking from pure love supports us to fully embody human love. Unconditional love is the transcendence of soul over the body, of spirit over matter. The language for two to become one. Love is not a relationship, it is a quality to surround us as a fragrance. Inclusive, infinite, to contain Seventh Stage love, Agape, is like trying to put the sky and sea in a box.

This is love: to fly toward a secret sky, to cause a hundred veils to fall each moment. First to let go of life. Finally to take a step without feet. My place is the Placeless, my trace is the Traceless; 'Tis neither body nor soul, for I belong to the soul of the Beloved. —Rumi

Through the eyes of the lover beauty is revealed. To love one child is to love all children. To embrace the world, all of life opens and expands. This is Agape. The living presence of the love that is eternally available. No conditions in this wide-opened infinite stage. This is the path to reunification. A glance reaches depths, spacious, unbounded, even speaking does not disturb the silence. The power of love is directed in silence and emptiness as the grass reflects the sunlight, as the ocean reflects the sky.

THE EYE OF THE HEART

This bliss-fire of divine love underpins the whole of the universe and is boundless like the heart it streams from forever. Every bird, every stone, every fern, every dancing flea is burning in its flame—it is the flame stuff from

which all the universe is woven in ecstasy. A Hasid knows this and dares to try to empty him or herself so as to be filled with the divine passion of compassion and blaze with its rapture and hunger to serve all beings in the Real. —Andrew Harvey

The world impact of Agape reverberates for thousands of years. Light mixing with light, veiled only as a consequence of our inability to sustain the flood of light. Pure white light. When the eye of the heart opens, we have the physical vision to comprehend directly. In Tibetan Buddhism this is the treasured Bodhisattva, Avolokiteshvatara, who hears the cries of the world, manifesting active compassion, saturating all time and space. Essentially this love is beyond all form, beyond words, not attached to anything, is in everything around us; the lover can never die. Rumi proclaimed: *When we are dead, seek not our tomb in the earth. But find it in the hearts of man.*

This way of love unlocks the heart to the whole world. Known through the form of the awakened Buddha, of Christ, of Kwan Yin, more than a scent, this love surpasses time, enduring in the present moment from thousands of years and forward. Universal human beings have embodied this Seventh Stage, absorbed into its mysteries. Truth speaks through their words as they remind us and provide signposts *to open our hidden eyes and come, return,* says Rumi, *to the root of the root of our own self.* For love is the fire that burns and transforms us, it's in the air we breathe, this love is available to taste, as close as our breath, as near as our heartbeat.

When love will be there you will not be there. There is no coexistence possible: Either you or love, if you are ready to disappear, melt and merge, leave only a pure consciousness behind, love will blossom. —Osho

SYSTEM TWENTY-FOUR

CIRCLE OF LOVERS

A LIVING TEACHING

SELF-EMPOWERMENT:QUEST,

LOVE, KNOWLEDGE-WISDOM-

UNDERSTANDING, COMPASSION,

TEACHER, BEAUTY, CHILD,

HUMOR, DISCIPLINE, ANCHOR,

HEALER, ENLIGHTENMENT, MUSE,

HAPPINESS

'Where am I?' This is the existential question Judaism places at the heart of human experience. Not 'Who am I?' but 'Where am I?' The difference between these two questions is critical. 'Who am I?' sets the self in isolation. To answer this question, you must turn inward. Turning inward, you separate yourself from the world around you. 'Where am I?' sets the self in relationship. To answer this question you must turn inward and outward; you must situate yourself in the world—both the world of self and the world of others. Indeed, to answer the question 'Where' you must drop the notion of inward and outward altogether and see reality as a seamless whole of doing, feeling, thinking, and being. —Rabbi Rami Shapiro

*T*he possibility of creating a Circle of Lovers, of allowing the sacred to enter into our relationships offers us a powerful tool to awaken from the sleep in our life. As we become aware and reach out to connections beyond our immediate family and friends we harness energies to inform ourselves, to stretch, diversify and to deepen. Opening, becoming visible and vulnerable we energetically create expansiveness. Our agreement to sit in a support position in another's Circle extends our presence in the world. Opening ourself is a sign of maturity, our range and willingness to be available to others is an indicator of our good will and magnetism. This is true wealth and prosperity, a bank account carrying resources to sustain and to nurture us, a real investment in our future.

All things and beings in the universe are connected with each other—visibly or invisibly—and through vibrations a communication is established between them on all the planes of existence. —Hazrat Khan

Finding and identifying our Circle of Lovers develops our capacity for intimacy. Here embracing our Circle we create intentional connections, places that resonate and call to us, our refuge and reserve. These energies are available to us as reflections anchored throughout our life. The identities may change, still the images remain retrievable. Imprinting and family role playing, where once we were contained into belief systems that fostered limitation fade away, these mindful choices stretch us as we identify and fill our Circle positions.

One hand can't tie a bundle. —Basa (Liberia/Nigeria) Saying

The Circle of Lovers is a reliable underpinning that upholds structural integrity. It is not necessarily the *helping* that is loosely referred to in popular 12-step programs, self-help groups that focus on support, making life manageable, relieving stress and bringing comfort. We cannot help anyone, we can serve. People and situations are available that authenticate in unequivocal precise ways. This is not dependency, not using someone, not manipulation, not mechanical niceness, not robbing energy. Naming the tricky stealing of someone's energy as *support* is like calling date rape good sex. Exploitation, swindling, deviousness, conquest, misrepresentation, sucking energy and chicanery are not uplifting forms of support. For our connections to reflect our values and intentions, to mirror our meaning and purpose or lack of it, this tool creates a life within a framework of alignment that demonstrates authentic relationship in our Circle of embrace. It is to cultivate what Buddhists call Bodhicitta, the altruistic intention to be of benefit to others, freeing them from bondage and suffering.

It is a fact that in the right formation, the lifting power of many wings can achieve twice the distance of any bird flying alone. —*unknown*

SELF-EMPOWERMENT

Sharing our treasures we connect on deep levels, that of the inexhaustible abundance in a world of being. The vibrations of energy that are carried to us through knowing our Circle, whether we walk though a busy town or in nature, appear miraculously where once there was invisibility. That bond, the connectedness experience and sharing is a reliable source, for we are never disconnected from the whole.

The problem with the world is that we draw our family circle too small. —*Mother Teresa*

Our Circle of Lovers is a harbor, a sanctuary and moorage, a refreshing drink with real nourishment and sustenance. Here we come as a beginner open to each point and viewpoint on our Circle. Bringing beginner's mind to see things as fresh and new makes use of our Circle. Beginners mind, available, connecting to the root; the functional value of a glass is in its emptiness and availability.

We all start out the same way—rich in dreams and nothing more. If we are lucky, we find friends to believe in our dreams with us. When we do, that creative cluster becomes a magnet to attract our good. —Julia Cameron

Each position holds qualities that connect to aspects of our own nature. To awaken to our own true essence, the quality of an awakened Buddha, we need reminders, images, the embodiment of how our nature manifests in this world. Each point on our Circle is a reflection of a quality we have hidden away, to be developed, or an attribute we already have manifested.

Synergy means that the whole is greater than the sum of its parts. It means that the relationship the parts have to each other is a part in and of itself. It is not only a part, but the most catalytic, the most empowering, the most unifying, and the most exciting part. —Stephen Covey

There are 13 positions, plus ourself, in the Circle of Lovers. Having a vital support community is to know that the objects and beings in the configuration are in agreement and in contract with us and are empowered through a mutual acceptance and willingness. The openness to say *yes*, to receiving and giving, stretches our capacity for consciousness as it moves through us, softening to the vulnerability and generosity that allows others to fully enter, further developing our capability, stretching our capacity to embody spiritual maturity.

This system of cooperation must have agreement, permission, accuracy, otherwise the imposition toxifies, robs the power through resistance. Knowing the positions we play on another's Circle provides the

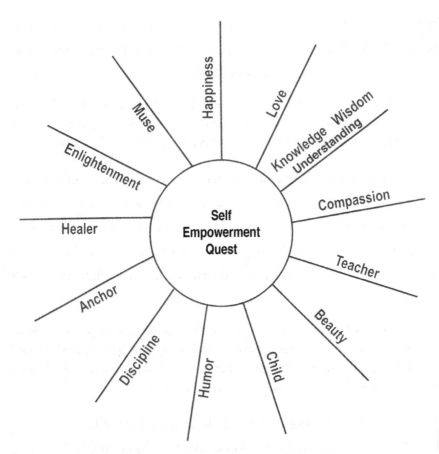

Chart 10: Circle of Lovers: A Living Teaching

ground for a compelling self-aware lifetime. Recognizing the members and objects of our Circle we find a level of sophistication that observes, reaches out, receives, trusts our reliance on our resources, even as gaps are to be filled. The acknowledgment and recognition of a full Circle, who stands in our Circle, and our agreement to serve in another's Circle creates the empowerment.

It is for us to remember that our true relatives are not necessarily those who are connected to us by ties of blood. Our true relatives are those who are nearest akin to us in mind, in soul, in spirit. —*Ralph Waldo Trine*

THIRTEEN POSITIONS

This is a guild and we apprentice ourselves; this is our initiation into conscious living. Recognition of who is in our Circle, who has made agreements with us, is observable by the intensity of the connection, by the persistence of the relationship, by the force that links, like current flowing through an electric circuit.

Human beings long for connection. When we are connected to the community around us and to our spiritual wisdom we are able to live and act with authentic effectiveness. What would it be like if the intensity of human connection and attention could be found here, in addition to all the material wealth that is available? If the human wealth could match the material wealth, what would happen? Heaven could be created, right here.
—*Malidoma Somé*

It is possible for one presence to fill more than one position, although that might also signal us that we have limited our resources. Deceased beings, people we have never met, places, animals and objects, people who move and inspire us, all are vibrationally available to access and fill our Circle positions. The first four positions: Self-Empowerment: quest, love, knowledge-wisdom-understanding, and compassion, affect our most immediate reality, are of primary importance, are basic fundamental needs in a lifetime. In a continuum each position moves further from the personal, the first three are most personal and the last ones are least personal. Teacher, beauty and child are inspirational positions to remind us of the larger perspective in our chosen lessons. Humor, discipline and anchor are energy and beings that help us through lessons on the physical plane. Healer, enlightenment and muse impact abstract lessons and hold clues to themes that continue throughout lifetimes. The happiness position indicates the movement and purpose of our life—towards happiness.

Working with this system is to gather and intentionally create thirteen positions that feed and support awakening the divine essence in ourself: our birthright: self-realization. Learning to categorize and identify, learning how to recognize and call on the appropriate energy teaches us how to nourish ourself, to make conscious the resources that are always available. Once we identify our positions, listening to how energy speaks to us, who to press into service, where to look as situations rise and fall, creating a path to experience reciprocity and mutuality: for, when we follow a path alone we often only arrive at our own ego.

No man is an island entire of itself; every man is a piece of the continent, a part of the main. Any man's death diminishes me, because I am involved in mankind; and therefore never send to know for whom the bell tolls; it tolls for thee. —*John Donne*

SELF-EMPOWERMENT: QUEST

As the sun illuminates, the moon and the stars, so let us illuminate one another. —*Anonymous*

This is you, the person to be loved and supported. Recognition and intention inform our circle as we complete our chart. The acknowledgement and willingness to attract forces that invigorate and reflect back; establishing connections is a practice to discover our place in the community of all beings and things. An initiation to call upon that brings vision, that holds us in relationship to and with our world. Anchored, bridges to a larger reality; to attend to the affairs of our inner life we reach out for a context to provide us with an awareness of the human condition. We, as the center of the circle, are receptive, asked to bow in all directions. Returning to the center, which is ourself, we can then choose to engage with whatever energy we have created on our circle.

Two boats lashed together will never sink. A three-ply rope is not easily broken. —*Epic of Giglamesh*

Our place of strength and protection, within this process self-reliance and surrender are signs of our active connection to skillfully using our circle. Identifying each position expands our life circles, opens a pathway to receive the support that is inherent in each position. The root of spiritual wisdom knows that all things are inseparably connected. This tool is a living testament in that we make use of visible and invisible interconnections. Everything on the circle outside reminds us, reflects who we are inside. To live the experience, to practice this consciousness of inter-being, we pay attention, are focused and determined.

Unions based on sincerity will prosper. The union itself is like an earth-

enware vessel, containing the proceeds of the works of the members. The movement towards union arises from one's innermost convictions; not from persuasion by others. Once one has committed himself to the union, whole-hearted participation will bring rewards. —Yi Jing

As the catalyst, the conduit through which challenges, obstacles, wonders and miracles come into fruition, we take our position and authorize available resources. Acknowledging, endorsing who appears in our life generates vitality to create what we want; working with others shapes our personal force. Power in itself is neutral, it's a potential, a momentum; electrical power can be used to turn on a computer, or to electrocute someone, the intention frames the result. We are the link for the channel, our openness allows the needed amount of energy to come through at an appropriate moment. When there is a *you* separate from *them* then congestion blocks the lines of flow. Duality creates comparison, the idea/illusion of who we are limits our possibilities. Inner disconnection is our primary power loss, the greater the separation the more substantial the isolation, conversely the more connection the more energy and power are available. Support in this light is dying to the illusion of separation, and allowing the current of life to continue its movement. The first step is to know where we are, what we want.

The mountain of aloneness rises only in the valleys of relationship. —Osho

Bridged Chains Of Spinning Circles

A fourteen person Circle of Lovers exists to assist the furtherance of awakening. This is a sophisticated system, not available to support what we *think* we want, instead, geared to protect the development of consciousness. This means that what we want may not always arrive in the form or convenience we imagine. Jesus had 12 apostles, carefully chosen, and each of us have 13 and ourselves, positions that can be identified, sanctioned, encouraged, acknowledged, enlivened to ultimately empower us in return, or to have these positions remain unknown and invisible.

Man is a knot, a web, a mesh, into which relationships are tied. These relationships matter. —Antoine de Saint-Exupery

Through intentional placement and responsibility for our circle community we learn to connect on other planes and prepare ourselves to awaken and live in a celestial world, to talk on the inner planes and dimensions, to call on the upstairs phone line. Co-operation with integrity maintains the reflection. This is what has been meant by the Sanskrit word *sangha*, the community of beings aware of the relationship between all life. When people no longer function as islands, rather to become one with one another, this collaboration, this collective endeavor, community of kindred spirits, is cultivated for ourself. To awaken alone is rare at this time. We no longer live in an era where we journey to a cave or are exiled to a mountaintop, or a time where the endangered snow leopard lives a solitary life. Interdependent, one on the mountaintop, one down in the valley, to cooperate, to join forces, engaged with others the Circle we sit in provides a mirror; what Osho Rajneesh called a *Buddhafield*, surrendered to our own ultimate awakening. And when the circles all intersect, yours and mine, a chain of circles of lovers, interlinked, bridged into global villages originating from Self-Empowerment, the whole world pooling consciousness turns into bridged chains of spinning circles.

It has not been given to one man to have everything in perfection. You have a part to play; I, in my humble way another; here is one who plays a little part; there, another. The perfection is the combination of all these parts. —Vivekananda

THE JOURNEY OF DAILY LIFE

Self-Empowerment: Quest, is the accountability to tell the truth and be aligned with a desire to know ourself. This is support for self-realization, true guidance, regardless to life changes or friction and a willingness to surrender to a circle, for ourself and to others that encourages understanding and wisdom. William Segal, painter and writer named his last exhibition, sixty years of self-portraits, *'In Search of Self, the preoccupation of a lifetime,'* asking with each glimpse of himself: *Who am I?* Segal understood that presence brings an element to art that goes beyond technical skills. The Self-Empowerment position is the hub of the inner circle with the spokes emanating outwards to all other positions. Being wholeheartedly present and attentive, locating ourself—where am I?—feeling the presence of all that we designate to be here with us, to call upon, to listen and know when and how to ask and to receive, we move to transform upward along the vertical.

In the world of experience, the quest is to restore the lost world of innocence-and when the quest has entered our daily life, it can have no end.
—Dr. Edith Wallace

The Quest or journey, in pursuit of Self, begins as we gather and place our representatives, our ambassadors, embodiments to maintain and sustain us for our voyage, the pilgrimage through this lifetime.

Whatever it is you wish to marry, go absorb yourself in that beloved, assume its shape and qualities, bow in worship and draw near. —Rumi

LOVE

Our responsibility in being human is to come to understand that we are placed into this universe, on this planet, in order to know how to love. Love is the greatest force in the universe and the cause of all creation. We are here to know what love is and how to love. —Reshad Feild

A powerful point on everyone's circle, Love is an aliveness and authenticity that lies at the very core of our nature. It's primary placement on our chart is in recognition of Love being the means by which life is enjoyed and the greatest force, the cause of creation, our service to ourself and to others. To use this point well even in the most trying circumstances, this essential ground of our being, the ordinary becomes extraordinary. The Love position is held by the person or energy that opens us to hold Love in our heart. Sometimes limited and mistaken for a sexual or romantic relationship because of its intensity, this might be a sexual partner, family member, therapist, friend, Guru or animal. Regardless to the form of the relationship we learn the secrets of the heart. This being loves us as we are, supporting self-acceptance.

Love is conscious relationship in presence. —Kabir Helminski

The Love position holds us responsible for the Love we offer and receive. Beyond sentimentality, loving is created from study, understanding and the devotion to take Love seriously. Love always creates, brings light to our senses, is the essential energy that makes all things possible; is the energy that brings us to gaze into the eyes of the world. The Love position is one of three on our Circle that are the most directly experienced positions; knowledge-wisdom-understanding, and compassion are the other two. These three positions represent our three fundamental needs in any lifetime. Someone is always at hand to hold this position, a

source to refer to that reminds us to live in a state of Love. It is a particular language that feeds our spirit, the foundation on which the world
is built, the root of peace and compassion. Love reflects its object, is the
force behind everything.

*Love is an ocean whose depth is invisible. Love makes the seas boil like a pot,
and rubbles the mountains to sand, and splits the heavens into fragments,
and makes tremble the entire earth.* —*Rumi*

Mature Love, not based on need, want, possessiveness or emotions,
is rooted in our willingness to go out of ourselves and be present to,
aware of, another. In this person's presence we feel more loving, inspired,
safe; the ego may not recognize the form and block the inspiration but
nevertheless we are still being loved. It is a person or circumstance that
allows us to be who we are and is willing to receive our Love in return.
We feel loved even through our moods, stress, defenses and resistance.
Love accepts imperfection and offers Love even when feeling misunderstood, disliked, unaccepted. This Love which sees and is attentive is
tremendously healing. The Love position remains steady, constant and
openly accepts our Love. Love the reason for creation, the core of our
being; knowing we are loved, guides us to bring Love into the ordinary
daily details of life. *There is no force in the world but love,* said Rilke.

*Love is misunderstood to be an emotion. Actually, it is a state of aware-
ness, a way of being in the world, a way of seeing oneself in others.*
—*David R. Hawkins*

The Love point on our circle ultimately extends further than personal Love. It is said: *what we love we will become.* Drawn into this experience of Love, discovering the Love within ourselves this creative act
unites us with everything that is while transforming our consciousness.
When there is no difference between you and what you Love the circle

is complete. Rumi, poet of Love, said: *Your task is not to seek for love, but merely to seek and find all the barriers within yourself that you have built against it. If you are not giving your life to Love than you are wasting your time here.* Rumi, named by the Sufis as the *Pole of Love*, describes a *love that is stripped bare of ego, broken free from the shell of protection.* This becomes the starting point on the circle, as well as meeting itself as end point.

Jump to your feet, wave your fists, threaten and warn the whole universe, that your heart can no longer live, without real love! —Hafiz

KNOWLEDGE-WISDOM-UNDERSTANDING

Our capacity for knowledge depends upon our degree of emptiness. Remember that knowledge is given and not acquired. Love and knowledge are the two arms of the heart. —Reshad Feild

Knowledge, Wisdom and Understanding saturate existence, are preserved in myths, traditions, sacred symbols, texts, in the numerous paths leading to the Way. As the second of the three primary points on our circle, the sweetness that clarity brings lingers to become a fragrance for all who appear. Knowledge cultivates the mind, Wisdom includes Knowledge, and is limitless. Knowledge offers us the tools to create the energy towards Wisdom, Understanding becomes the bridge. The more we honestly want to learn, preparing the ground, seeding Knowledge to find fertile ground, the closer we come to the bridge of Understanding which connects the two. Knowledge is the doorway to Wisdom, the path that carries us to the Way and in the process of seeking Knowledge we awaken Wisdom. Knowledge can be put into the service of Wisdom. Choose wisely who sits in this point on your circle, with heart, used wisely it brings transformation.

The knowledge of self is wisdom itself. —Madame Blavatsky

This point on our circle offers reliable accurate information, facts, principles, ideas and ways of being. It has a pulse on the times and is available for questions ranging from nutrition and exercise, purchasing a home or car, choosing a school for our child, beautiful places to visit, how to proceed when a relationship hits a rocky place, what to look for in an authentic teacher, how to live mindfully; a support position available for clear feedback. This is our best advisor, a resource position bringing our life into perspective. Oftentimes this place is directing us to discover our own answer, guiding us towards our best interest. It carries an experience of Knowing and Understanding with the willingness to be available while we grow into Wisdom. Digging deep, tasting and digesting our own experience, Wisdom arrives.

And why is perfect wisdom beyond thinking? It is because all its points of reference cannot be thought about but can be apprehended. One is the disappearance of the self-conscious person into pure presence. Another is the simple awakening to reality. Another is the knowing of the essenceless essence of all things of the world. And another is luminous knowledge that knows without a knower. None of these points can sustain ordinary thought because they are not objects or subjects. They can't be imagined or touched or approached in any way by any ordinary mode of consciousness, therefore they are beyond thinking. —the Buddha

The Knowledge-Wisdom-Understanding position exists for us to access as a practical grounded resource, as well as beckoning us to go deeper. Knowledge offers us the tools and Wisdom guides us not to mistake the tools for the treasure. We can't learn Wisdom, we have to awaken it; it's buried and hidden inside us, Knowledge moves so rapidly that we have to renew ourselves to stay afloat, leaving what we knew behind. The Knowledge-Wisdom-Understanding place assists us to speed up, to move along, to raise our level of being.

The more a man understands what he is doing, the greater will be the results of his efforts. Understanding appears only when a man feels and senses what he is connected with. He must feel the idea of mechanicalness with his whole mass, with his whole being. Then he will understand it. Understanding is the resultant of knowledge and being. Results of effort are always proportional to understanding. In order to understand a thing you must see its connections with a bigger whole. —P.D. Ouspensky

The empty glass becomes a metaphor for the Knowledge-Wisdom-Understanding point on our circle. When our glass is full of our ideas, expectations, judgments, opinions and plans, and it fills up quickly, there is no space for anything new, no room for Knowledge. Maintaining the glass to have room to receive, not full and overflowing, otherwise how can we expect to be given anything? Beginner's mind receives, the training is to empty our glass again and again, not to fill it with distractions, concepts, opinions, solutions and suggestions; it takes mindfulness and discrimination to allow the gap, to be actively receptive, to hold out our glass to receive something new and oftentimes surprising.

A single conversation with a wise man is better than ten years of study. —Proverb

CONFERENCE OF THE BIRDS

Knowledge, digging deep, beneath opinions, learnings and formatory ideas, brings us to recognize the Wisdom that is the essence of life. Knowledge moves quickly becoming less relevant as we adapt our level of Understanding to a new dimension of knowing. To know what we are already in possession of becomes our root Knowledge. In this manner the circle exists for us to retrieve the Knowledge hidden within. As we awaken to our own presence in the world, our Knowledge of the universe is from the inside, now, to know ourself is to know the universe and its laws. Through self-knowing comes the creativity that is found through Wisdom. This self-Knowledge is the heart's Knowledge, measureless Wisdom. The link connecting the two is Understanding.

Understanding may be compared to an arithmetical mean between knowledge and being. It shows the necessity for a simultaneous growth of knowledge and being. The growth of only one and diminishing of another will not change the mean. This also explains why 'to understand' means to agree. People who understand one another must not only have an equal knowledge, they must also have an equal being. Only then is mutual understanding possible. There can only be one 'understanding', the rest is non-understanding or incomplete understanding. —P.D. Ouspensky

The classic 12th century allegory, *Conference of the Birds*, has the birds pass through seven valleys on their journey to awaken the heart. The first three are the valley of the quest, the valley of love and the valley of Understanding and Knowledge. It is said that to read this mystical pilgrimage every three years reflects how far we have progressed in our inner evolution. The valley of Knowledge, one of the trials along the path, has no beginning or end, is a long tedious journey to cross. *Underneath the ocean of knowledge there are thousands of pearls of wisdom and mystery, but an expert diver is required who will plunge into the water and bring up those pearls. When those pearls are secure, and the mystery of the essence of existence clearly revealed, the furnace of this earth will be transformed into a flower garden.* This passage from *Conference* reveals the patience and perseverance that is required. Knowledge comes not only from learning about the world but also through immersion, through having a knowing relationship from universe to self, from going through a training rooted in self-discipline. Making the heart a pure mirror Wisdom arrives. This is not ordinary Knowledge, not the learnings from the mental processes of the mind, this is gnosis; at the heart of the Hermetic tradition is the Knowledge that comes from the experience of spiritual mysteries, Knowledge of the divine. In one version of the book it is said that: *to understand it you must have the powers of penetration of the soul, not the ordinary faculties of comprehension.*

Understanding has neither beginning nor end. No way is equal to this way, and the distance to be traveled to cross it is beyond reckoning. Understanding, for each traveler, is enduring; but knowledge is temporary. Understanding can be arrived at variously—some have found the Mihrab, others the idol. When the sun of understanding brightens this road each receives light according to his merit and he finds the degree assigned to him in the understanding of truth. When the mystery of the essence of beings reveals itself clearly to him the furnace of this world becomes a garden of flowers. He who is striving will be able to see the almond in its hard shell. He will no longer be pre-occupied with himself, but will look up at the face of his friend. In each atom he will see the whole; he will ponder over thousands of bright secrets. It is necessary to have a deep and lasting wish to become as we ought to be in order to cross this difficult valley of Understanding. Once you have tasted the secrets you will have a real wish to understand them. —Attar

Knowledge With Understanding

Seeing the spiritual nature of the cosmos is the Sanskrit meaning for Knowledge, *Jnana*, the Wisdom of divine intelligence, the Knowledge that one's self is identical with ultimate reality. This is Knowledge that destroys ignorance, as light removes darkness. This is the Knowledge and Wisdom that is perceived through the senses. Some of this Knowledge comes through reading and assimilating sacred scriptures, listening to self-realized beings, studying self and living harmoniously in relationship to our fellow beings. This is the Knowledge that is the core of our existence, invisible truth always in motion always creating the world; alert and attentive we discover newness within each breath. Jnana, the Yoga of Knowledge uses the intellect as a tool towards Understanding that our true self is behind and beyond our mind. For the purpose of self-discovery, Jnana Yoga probes the nature of the self through the question, *who am I?* Having the actual experience, not the intellectual exercise, placing attention on the source of our being; removing our attention from that which we are not we remember who we are.

Love, work and knowledge are the wellsprings of our lives, they should also govern it. —*Wilhelm Reich*

It is critical to understand that when Knowledge and being are developed unevenly, without the linking walkway of Understanding, the imbalance produces detrimental results. *Knowledge is proportionate to the state of awakening, what you know is your knowledge—all that you are, that is your being or state,* said Ouspensky, a Russian philosopher and spiritual teacher. Beliefs are not Knowledge. If our inner development, our being, does not parallel our Knowledge what we know becomes distorted in us. Knowledge with Understanding uplifts our level of being. Continuously renewed as a living presence we turn to our own experience.

Self-Knowledge not rooted in beliefs, information, or linear thinking, is a living thing, the Wisdom of knowing of digesting our thoughts and feelings. As we refine the process of knowing, through awareness, this river-like evolving dynamic, we enter a land of Wisdom. To make use of this position we learn to sacrifice belief systems, dogma, comparison, projections and opinions. The Knowledge-Wisdom-Understanding position is available to offer perceptive information and direction. To use this support well is to ask real questions, questions from the desire to know, for the greatest Wisdom is awakening to self-Knowledge through Understanding.

Wisdom is the experience of your own nature; it is the expression of your self-being. It is the flowering of your own consciousness. It is not information, it is transformation. —*Osho*

COMPASSION

Compassion is a willingness to offer others, in their suffering the gift of our presence, to share in the suffering of others: to be present to them in their pain and bear it with them, even if only in peace and thought. —*Irma Zaleski*

Compassion vows to remain in this world in order to serve, to help liberate others from their suffering, to embrace the whole cosmos, wanting the world to be freed of suffering. To develop Compassion is to fully develop our Self. To make ourselves vulnerable to other people's pain, to open, and then open more; rather than avoiding our own life we become a conduit lifting and shaping reality in a positive way. Compassion is presence in the face of suffering, vulnerability, our willingness to be present to the suffering, both ours and another's. Reaching out to others as well as into ourselves, to be truly present for another means to be present to ourselves, no easy task as we live into the serious demands that life brings. Expressed poetically in the prayer of St. Francis: *Make me an instrument of thy peace, where there is hatred, sow love, where there is injury, pardon, where there is despair, hope.* Not only empathy to feel another's pain, it is also to work with others, to act, to dwell deeply into the present moment. Compassion is the willingness to share in the sufferings, to be present, Compassion is what we are; our presence. Being vulnerable to our own and to others pain; our gift of presence makes suffering for others less heavy to bear.

When we finally know we are dying, and all other sentient beings are dying with us, we start to have a burning, almost heartbreaking sense of the fragility and preciousness of each moment and each being, and from this can grow a deep, clear limitless compassion for all beings. —Sogyal Rinpoche

For as long as space endures, and for as long as living beings remain, until then may I too abide, to dispel the misery of the world. This Bodhisattva vow of Compassion seeks freedom for all beings both seen and unseen. The Bodhisattva agrees to help other sentient beings, from a tiny insect to a huge mammal. At the heart of the Buddhist teaching we look into samsara, this realm of continual cycles of suffering and how to move towards the world of nirvana, to become liberated from suffering. No longer rooted in the world, possessiveness vanishes. When we are no longer identified, rooted, then we are free to be here, unencumbered. Without suffering there could be no Compassion or love. Compassion literally means *to suffer together.* Released from the rounds of rebirth, choosing to remain in this world in order to help others, to take on the suffering of all other beings and to transfer karmic merit to others, Bodhisattvas undertake voluntary rebirth through Compassion for those still suffering in the processes of the material world.

To not feel compassion for a stranger in trouble is like not feeling that your foot is on fire. —Confucius

THE COMPASSION OF A BODHISATTVA

Buddha once asked his monks, *which do you think is greater: the water in the oceans or the tears we've shed while wandering on?* His answer: *the tears.* Stopping the process of creating worlds of suffering is like giving up an abusive habit, it takes away from suffering through not exploiting and feeding the unhappiness of others. Avalokitsvara, *the one who hears the crying out of the world*, Kuan Yin, goddess of Compassion, *she who hears the cries of the world*, Chenrezig, the embodiment of boundless Compassion, Maitreya, *friend of loving-kindness*, appear in various forms to help all others on our path to liberation. They have put off their perfect enlightenment for the benefit of beings everywhere and will wait as long as there is one being who is not yet awakened. Such is the Compassion of a Bodhisattva. The ultimate goal of spiritual practice, to awaken to our true nature, connecting to the qualities of the above four Bodhisattvas are an example and inspiration. These qualities are reflected aspects of our own nature.

If you feel called upon to alleviate the suffering in the world, that is a very noble thing to do, but remember not to focus exclusively on the outer; otherwise you will encounter frustration and despair. Without a profound change in human consciousness, the world's suffering is a bottomless pit. So don't let your compassion become one-sided. Empathy with someone else's pain or lack and a desire to help need to be balanced with a deeper realization of the eternal nature of all life and the ultimate illusion of all pain. Then let your peace flow into whatever you do and you will be working on the levels of effect and cause simultaneously. —Eckhart Tolle

THE BALANCE POINT: RACHAMIM

The circle of lovers is a living teaching, naming and investigating the root words; the tradition history and meaning of each support reveals the dimension of each position. *Rahamim*, the Hebrew word for Compassion, asks for Compassion at any cost. The root of the Hebrew word is *rechem*, womb; nurturing life we become womb-like, having the wisdom of the womb, able to birth.

During the week, we 'husband' the earth, we 'husband' our strength. Then comes the Sabbath and we become feminine. We receive, we conceive, we are impregnated with a supernal soul, and we give birth to a tenderness. For on the Sabbath, we regenerate a warmth expressed by the term 'rahamim,' a rich emphatic quality. Not quite translatable into English, and yet, how do we generate such tenderness? Once humanity became able to see the earth from space, we ushered in an era where we could be newly-aware of our interconnections. Regardless of nationality or creed, we're all on the same planet. Ultimately the divisions between 'us' and 'them' are illusory. And that's true not only spiritually, but practically. If we pollute a river 'there,' its impact will eventually be felt 'here.' —Reb Zalman Schachter-Shalomi

Jewish mysticism teaches that the world was created through the quality of judgment, *din*, then seeing that the world could not endure on that level alone, the quality of Compassion, *rachamim* was added. The process of creation involved a blending and a balancing of these two qualities. The Kabbalists say that we have the ability to *sweeten the judgments*, a mindfulness practice of opening the heart to see the divine oneness in all things. Knowing the position of anything on the Kabbalistic tree of life, the map of the *sefirot* and how it interacts, reveals an understanding of its nature. Compassion is the divine attribute *tiferet*, the perfect balance point between the expansive right side of the tree where *chesed*, loving kindness and giving are located and the left contraction side of the tree where *gevurah* the strength of restraint is located. At the heart-center, the balance point is *tiferet*, and the harmony that mediates between the two is Compassion which is mindful giving.

By compassion we make others' misery our own, and so, by relieving them, we relieve ourselves, also. —*Thomas Browne*

The Yiddish word, *rachmones*, means that we do not take joy in acts of destruction. We extend a hand, compassionate tears for the little girl whose father died as a terrorist suicide bomber. At Pesach, Jews are reminded that the Israelites were admonished for showing joy at the drowning of the Pharaoh's army in the Red Sea. *Rejoice not, for these are my children, too.* As one of the beautiful names or attributes of God, the Arabic *ya Rahman, ya Raheem*, is the Compassionate, the One who has endless Compassion. All aspects of life can be seen in the names, there is no end to the manifestations for so long as the process of creation exists. To become conscious of the essence of all things means that we become part of everything, alleviating the pain and distress which is hidden in everything.

Compassion for me is just what the word says; it is 'suffering with.' It is an immediate participation in the suffering of another to such a degree that you forget yourself and your own safety and spontaneously do what is necessary.
—*Joseph Campbell*

THE PRACTICE OF COMPASSION

The Tibetan word *tse-wa* is Compassion towards all beings, knowing that we all have an innate desire to be happy and to overcome suffering. This generates genuine universal Compassion, free of attachment and personal feelings. Reliable and consistent, regardless to whether it is a pelican with a fish hook in its mouth, a child falling from a bicycle, a convicted rapist being executed, a friend getting divorced, or immigrant children separated from their parent, Haitians displaced from an earthquake, oil washing into the maze of marshes along the gulf coating the stalks and leaves leaving a toxic stew lethal to fish and wildlife, environmental mishaps; all will affect our mind and heart. A concern for others, the recognition that most of our comforts and daily circumstances arrive through the work, the efforts of others, our appreciation flowers.

Suffering has many masks. Some people have wealth and fame, which is a temporary situation, many have negative thoughts and emotions, others illness and loss; all are aspects of suffering. The distractions of money, fame, entertainment and power all carry us further away from home. The Buddhist understands Compassion through emptiness, the ultimate nature of reality. The cultivation of loving-kindness in Compassion becomes the practice.

Deeds of kindness are equal in weight to all the commandments. —*Talmud*

THE TRUTH OF LOVING-KINDNESS

The Compassion position sees that all beings ultimately want to be happy and free of suffering. This is an expansion of Compassionate situations; circumstances need not be changed, causes may not necessarily be removed; it's the suffering that is wanted to be removed. It's about how we see, the construct of our mind; to live in the world and see its impermanent nature is to grasp the interdependent knowing of the oneness of humanity. To nurture your Compassion for yourself, for the human condition, for all of life, is the only sensible and wise response to understanding and experiencing life. Once passion has transformed its energy, it becomes Compassion and carries a transmuting power of inspiration.

When we come into contact with the other person, our thoughts and actions should express our mind of compassion, even if that person says and does things that are not easy to accept. We practice in this way until we see clearly that our love is not contingent upon the other person being lovable.
—*Thich Nhat Hahn*

Whether you are arrested for selling drugs, relocating, getting married, fired from a job for embezzling money, your son killed in a car accident, you have been diagnosed with cancer; this position holds the truth of loving-kindness. Compassion can be relentless and stern, for truth is ultimately the greatest Compassion we offer. Caring about you and pointing out what you need to see might be penetrating, frank, unembellished; it is painful to face one's own personality. Telling the truth about you in all situations, this position is available to push limits, to see past your fears, to be present. There are moments when Compassion requires saying *no*, certainly it requires a reaching into ourselves. The ingredient for a healthy *no* is to remember the *yes* that *no* is creating room for, this stretches us to embrace all movement of life.

Compassion is not just feeling with someone, but seeking to change the situation. Frequently people think compassion and love are merely sentimental. No! They are very demanding. If you are going to be compassionate, be prepared for action! —*Desmond Tutu*

Make me an instrument of thy peace, this is the Compassion point speaking and holding a space for our desire to bring peace to ourself and the world. The Compassion point focuses on our goodness, sees the divine in us, even when we don't see it; for without Compassion we are unable to truly know anyone or anything. This is the inner secret of understanding otherwise blocked and isolated by concepts, judgment, attitude. Once we connect, are receptive to our own life and then to others, to trees and earth, day and night, then Compassion opens us to experience the continual flow of everything.

Compassion is a priceless jewel. If you want others to be happy, practice compassion. If you want to be happy, practice compassion. It is by means of compassion that we aspire to attain enlightenment. —*the Dalai Lama*

TEACHER

The perfect teacher is one who does not ask for anything for himself, because inwardly he is rich, not he who has built up an organization, nor he who is the instrument of the politician, nor he who is bound to a belief or to a country. —*J. Krishnamurti*

*T*he Teacher position is often someone older and more experienced, who provides guidance and direction, initiation, presence, offers a rite of passage towards a maturing of the heart, uplifting when needed; it's someone with wisdom who has lived what we are now living. This could be a person who has imprinted us, a mentor, guide, therapist, a friend with a high level of being, a place we go to for guidance, teaching and clarity. A Teacher offers instruction in both the theory and the practice of a path. Not only imparting a technique the Teacher develops our understanding and ability towards inner work.

True teaching is always an epiphany: sometimes a clap of thunder but often only a whisper, easily missed. —*Parabola*

Finding a Teacher who points the way to wisdom, a mountain guide who brings us up as well as down the mountain, where conditions for learning opens doors for our possibilities; because in studying the world we are also studying ourselves. It is as easy to find a false Teacher as it is to find a false student, discrimination is the value needed in choosing and refining our entire circle of love. Having an accurate mirror to provide what we resist seeing is essential and validates our efforts to maintain positions on our circle.

The world of the charismatic Teacher is enticing. Deluded Teachers justify what they are doing with explanation, justification, rationalization, encouraging students to donate money, are sexually and emotionally exploitative, misusing power, living outside the laws of morality they often believe they are above the ethical laws that apply to everyone else. To learn from our interactions even when it's to refrain from a certain behavior of a Teacher, continuing to respect their good qualities is to hold to what's true and not diminish ourselves from the negativity of the circumstances. To navigate in the world of spiritual fraud is to have discriminating wisdom.

The transforming teacher senses readiness to change, helps the 'follower' or student respond to more complex needs, transcending the old levels again and yet again. The true teacher is also learning and is transformed by the relationship. The open teacher, like a good therapist, establishes rapport and resonance, sensing unspoken needs, conflicts, hopes, and fears. Respecting the learner's autonomy, the teacher spends more time helping to articulate urgent 'questions' than demanding right answers. —Marilyn Ferguson

It is said that a Teacher is the servant of the student's yearning, their surrendered self-importance and level of being maintains the power of the protection. The Teacher is respected and elevated in order to serve and provide a framework for the intentional work we choose. Reflecting back our inner state, a Teacher shows us the true nature of our mind, reminding us to be ourself.

This very moment is the perfect teacher, and lucky for us it's with us wherever we are. —Pema Chodrin

TEACHERS AND TRADITIONS: DIFFERENT VIEWPOINTS

Many say that an authentic wisdom Teacher is essential for self-development on a spiritual path. The Teacher we find is connected to our motivations and karma. Each Teacher, each tradition, has a very different style. Gurdjieff said it was his job to find the sorest corn on a person's foot and step on it firmly. He supplied conditions for the *super efforts* he required of students, putting them through an odyssey that led them to make extraordinary demands upon themselves. Perseverance cannot be given. We can only teach that which we are.

I cannot teach anybody anything, I can only make them think. —Socrates

Dunstan Morrissey, a Benedictine hermit monk stated that *contemplative solitude is my teacher*; he passed that teaching along to others who found their way to him. Thomas Merton, monk and mystic, taught that driving a disciple into a *dark night* of the soul *makes their breakthrough into true humility and detachment.* A Zen master creates an atmosphere where there is room for both doubt and possibility, to see things as fresh and new, training the ability to see things in a new way, through a beginner's mind. Adyashanti, in his teachings says, *The correct attitude is one where you have no more time to waste.*

The thread of similarity for a spiritual journey is that a most important priority to a Teacher lies in the effort to wake up—and the willingness to place the aim of awakening as a primary value. Thich Nhat Hanh teaches that *our love is not contingent upon the other person being lovable.* The Baal Shem Tov taught that *from everything a person hears or sees in this world he must find a teaching in how we should serve in truth;* the wise person no longer sees a world, he only sees and hears the universe teaching him.

We can only teach that which we are. —Jean Jaures

When the mind of the student and Teacher are experienced directly as one we have found the inner Teacher, that in us which possesses consciousness. Offering guidance, such a relationship exists to create equality, promote genuine experience, lift us to a higher level of understanding. Devotion to the Teacher is not for the Teacher's sake, but for our own. Devotion, rising from a sense of oneness, opens us to what the Teacher has to offer. Through service, *seva*, blockages are cleared and a path is opened towards understanding and freedom. While it may appear on the surface that the service we perform helps the Teacher it is really mutual reciprocity. The Teacher is the servant of the pupil.

Teaching is not a matter of technique it has to do with inner transformation. What is imparted are qualities, sometimes subtle, eventually the creation of a witness, one who is no longer attached. Wanting to help is the downfall, wanting others to change is a misunderstanding. The thread that holds things together throughout many traditions is: no wisdom, no attainment, no thought, no feeling, no non-feeling, no love, no non-love—until we arrive at the pure emptiness which we are.

Teaching is the highest form of understanding. —*Aristotle*

A Teacher has digested the experience of truth in their daily life. We are continuously learning, life is always changing, impermanent, inevitable, fleeting; there is suffering and there is freedom from suffering, everything has meaning and once we learn to observe we are here to teach. Life itself, the circumstances and adventures would be meaningless until taken as an *exercise,* as a *practice*; then it becomes a Teacher. Life itself is not the Teacher, our relationship to it makes it become a Teacher. Wherever our thoughts go we go, either we sink or rise to the level of the teaching and Teacher. Now we allow everything to appear, not avoiding or dodging the difficult. Easy things arrive, difficult things appear, all are here to be met with graciousness.

Without self-knowledge our learning is destructive. Things can be used to destroy or with understanding are used to uplift. To find a Teacher and a teaching, not one that has been arbitrarily invented but one that penetrates to a deeper level, we discover our own means to awakening. Many come forward as Teachers, guides, sheikhs, gurus and many are attractions that serve as obstacles on the way to truth. Grace, baraka, shaktipat, transmission, all arrive through our many traditions.

A TEACHER LINKS HEAVEN AND EARTH

A true teacher is one who opens a space within your mind. If you turn your attention away from everything else and merge with that space, you awaken as that consciousness. This space is the true teacher's gift. It is an open door, but you must walk through it. —Adyashanti

A Sufi expression is: *whoever has no guide has Satan for a guide.* Our mutual responsibility does not make light of a relationship that provides a mature mirror of two hearts. Communication requires equality, both Teacher and student must participate, each wanting truth. Learning to use a Teacher well, not misuse, develops as we come to know ourself and limit our subjective personal thoughts.

Ancient traditions reveal stories of the devoted Teacher-student relationships of Milarepa and Marpa, Shams of Tabriz and Rumi, of the quality of love and transformation imparted. Although their bodies are not here we are surrounded by their teachings. The two, student and Teacher, are essentially interdependent. An old Buddhist scroll reads: *If a spiritual mentor lacks realization, it does not help even if his disciples act with reverence and devotion. If the disciples have no reverence or devotion, it does not help even if the spiritual mentor has realization. This is like a cow having milk, but its calf having no palate.* The Teacher imparts his or her being to the student, not only knowledge.

The Teacher points the way to wisdom, assisting us to discover our own means to freedom. The *inner* Teacher who has been always here, manifests in the form of the *outer* Teacher. The task; to receive the inner knowledge while still making use of outer knowledge. Leading us to our own inner wisdom, helping us to remain on the path; engaging in conversations, there is visible reliability.

The aim of the Teacher is to link heaven and earth, and a direct relationship gives rise to an openness and a reception of energies that is vital. —William Segal

BEAUTY

Let the beauty we love come and fill us. Let the beauty all around get us through. Let the beauty inside be our compass. Let the beauty now be what we do, what we do. —Rumi

*B*eauty provides the mirror to reflect the light of our heart through our eyes and mind. It's what moves us to our aliveness. *Beauty*, explains Kabir Helminski, *is anything that becomes our point of contact with love.* Awakened beings are always beautiful because of their luminous radiance. Their expression of inner vitality reflects their state. This position serves as a reminder that Beauty is a creation of love, opening ourselves we come to know the endlessness, the infiniteness of the Beauty that is love. Nothing destroys the endless expression of Beauty grown from within.

When we appreciate and honor the beauty of life, we will do everything in our power to protect all life. —Thich Nhat Hahn

Through recognition we bring life to the Beauty that is already here, and is *in the eye of the beholder*. Beauty, an inspirational point is a reminder to pay attention, to see, listen and be inspired by the energetic field that creates our physical plane. In attention and awareness, through our loving eye we experience Beauty. To look at this world and see Beauty manifest is a soothing balm, beyond thought and reason. Can we move beyond the limits of conventional conditioned aesthetics to see Beauty in an aging face, a worn out carpet, a declining pet, in shriveled flowers, our wrinkles and aging hands. Our turn towards impermanence is where eternal Beauty lives. Through recognition we become the agents who bring out the inherent Beauty, experiencing even with closed eyes and ears, image and song playing within. Beauty includes compassion for the broken, weary and fallen, as Leonard Cohen sings: *Ring the bells that can still ring. Forget your perfect offering. There is a crack in everything. That's how the light gets in.*

People rarely see the beauty and the greatness around them. They live their life in half sleep. Attention, well developed equips us with the capacity to be open to what would ordinarily escape us. With inside-seeing we awaken to the beauty and the potentiality of ordinary objects. —William Segal

Beauty is the creative expression of life and who holds this position serves, pays attention, opens to never ending unfolding existence. This person, place, or thing holds a space of aesthetic satisfaction. If it's a person they inspire us by their Beauty loosening our conditioned response so that we see the treasures, the wonder. As a reflection they enable us to see our own magnificence. What we have imagined as plain, ugly, old, worn out; our ideas of fixing, judging and criticizing are our resistance to the transient nature of life. Our Beauty point brings us the space to look at what is true original Beauty; the frog kissed turning into a handsome prince freed of his imprisonment through being loved.

The sole purpose of love is beauty. —*Reshad Feild*

In their presence we feel more beautiful and want to enhance ourself through their eyes. If this is an object, like a violin, the experience of playing fills us; feeling our radiance as we play we become that to others who listen to the music. As a place, for example the island of Hawaii, we are moved by the eloquence of the birds of paradise, the sunsets and the native people, to feel beautiful as we relax, smile, tan, wear shorts and tank tops. And so Hawaii holds the Beauty position in our life. In a relationship, this person inspires us to bring energy into our home and life. Their taste imprints us. When our partner is our Beauty point our heart soars each time we really look. This is the deer who walks into the yard and our heart stops, the gazelle or peacock spreading his wings, the koi shimmering in the pond, a horizon bursting into light. It is in the loving eye and heart that Beauty is found, food for the spirit. Living from this consciousness imparts a sensitivity, life becomes a beautiful landscape for our attention bringing greater awareness to what is.

Anyone who keeps the ability to see beauty in every age of life really never grows old. —*Franz Kafka*

A BEAUTI-FULL LIFE

In the ancient wisdom teachings of Kabbalah there are ten divine attributes or principles that emanate out of nothingness to generate a paradigm for all existence. The repairing and restoration of this world, individual and collective evolution is based upon understanding these ten principles which are the tree of life. Beauty, one of the ten principles, is *Tiferet*, symbolizing the pivotal point at the center of the divine realm mediating between kindness and strength the place where spirit and form meet, its goal is the development of a human being to their greatest potential. Portraying the essential foundation of creation the Tree of Life is a representation of the blueprint of the world. As a map to repair this shattered vessel, this esoteric knowledge, the Tree of Life, lives inside us providing information for us to become whole.

There are ten Sephiroth, which means numbers, jewels, the ways the divine is revealed, all linked in a complex figure. Archetypes, each attribute represents one aspect manifesting in the physical and metaphysical universe illuminating our knowledge like precious and radiant gems. These are the personal traits of what is hidden yet mediated through ten knowable qualities. Tiferet, Beauty, one of the ten Sephirah, is the characteristic of divine energy in creation. Beauty has a central relationship to all of the other attributes bringing harmony, seen as the bridge between man and the infinite. The world was created in stages with the Sephiroth as the means and pattern for existence. Tiferet/Beauty, in the middle of the tree represents all the qualities as they descend to the world, as the spiritual aspirations of the world ascend, a ladder of ascent and descent. Learning to emulate them we come to embody the divine attributes of wholeness.

Beauty is the first glimpse of the divine. Wherever you see beauty, remember you are on holy ground. Beauty is an expression of God, in whatsoever form it appears. —*Osho*

The Beauty point on our support wheel is the reminder that everything has Beauty and how to see life from that framework. To live immersed, inspired through Beauty, opens our heart for us to live harmoniously balanced in surprise and wonder, seeing all others as beautiful divine beings, a reflection of who we are.

In Beauty now before me, I walk. In Beauty now behind me, I walk. In Beauty now below me, I walk. In Beauty now above me, I walk. In Beauty all around me, I walk. In Beauty now within me, I walk. It is finished in Beauty. —*Navajo prayer*

CHILD

Help your child's boat across, and your own will reach the shore. —*Proverb*

We choose to put that being in the Child support circle who brings us our experience of parenting. Our attitude, our willingness to take responsibility, to protect and nurture, fosters learning. This is an inspiring position, used well it rekindles purpose and meaning. How to grow in freedom regardless of age is the orientation of this point. How to live in this world sanely, balanced, not half asleep, we offer real intelligence to whomever sits in this position. Intelligence here means knowing what we are doing, the way we walk, the way we talk, the way we eat; it's a mind-set and we live in this manner as we care-take an elder or a pet, or child, as we educate that being to use us well for the deeper questions of living that arise.

This is what you should do; love the earth and sun and the animals, stand up for the stupid and crazy, devote your income and labor to others, have patience and indulgence towards the people, dismiss whatever insults your own soul, and your very flesh shall be a great poem and have the richest fluency not only in its words but in the silent lines of its lips and face and between the lashes of your eyes and in every motion and joint of your body. —*Walt Whitman*

This position is not necessarily held by our own birth Child. This is the being we feel parental towards, inspiring us to be reliable, responsible, nurturing, protective and caring. It might be an aging parent, a dog, cat, bird, elderly neighbor, godchild or friend's daughter. The experience of parenting generates qualities like tenderness, devotion, patience, loving-kindness and responsibility as well as provoking our imperfections and shortcomings. All children are ours, how we live is absorbed into their well-being, creating a foundation and tone.

A human being is like a tree. If you make a scratch on the branch of a full-grown tree, you affect only that branch. But if you make even a miniscule scratch on a seed, it affects the growth of the entire tree. —Menachem Schneerson

Offering a heart-opening environment to support, strengthen and nourish the freedom, trust and independence of the Child is conscious parenting, a true responsibility of this position. Loving that embraces liking; it's not what we say but who we are that creates the learning. The atmosphere, our stability, the environment, the power of our heart, mindful attention, create the persuasion and are the influence.

A POWERFUL REMINDER

Offering protection and caring for the needs of an aging parent or domestic pet are close relationships that speak to the Child position. This offers us a moment to experience our strengths. To be begrudging or resentful robs us of the gifts, the teaching. The responsibility to this position is to be authentic, since trust is born here. Trust, once learned is the foundation to knowing our truth. A Child has his own destiny. Existence is the ultimate parent and our loving-kindness, our giving of who we are, our truthful presence creates this mindful relationship.

To bring up a child in the way he/she should go—travel that way yourself. —Josh Billings

A Child is immediate, imitative, absorbing the examples around. This position asks us to be the most we can be. A Child, being here and now, feels that the visible world is not always what is most important. This impressionable being we choose to put in our care deserves unsentimental truth to maintain the beauty of the wonder that lies in a Child's heart. Learning to encourage rather than punish, to be patient and not bully, to not intimidate, criticize or judge reflects back on how we treat ourself. To nurture, protect and teach; receptivity and vulnerability come from a deep place continuously challenging us to be real.

Children are new editions of consciousness. Children are fresh entities of divinity into life. Be respectful. Be understanding. —Osho

Through the Child connection we learn simplicity and vitality. Every quality exists for a reason and the fresh unfiltered curiosity, vulnerability, and imagination are a teaching for us to study and learn. Most important is not to be arbitrary and casual about the relationship to the beings we are responsible for, they are a powerful reminder to create a purposeful life. To express ourself as a parent is a great art, more extraordinary than giving birth is offering freedom. Caring for these precious souls with sensitivity is an opportunity to clear away the debris that has collected through the years and to remember that existence is the ultimate parent.

Your children are not your children. They are the sons and daughters of Life's longing for itself. They come through you but not from you, and though they are with you yet they belong not to you. —Kahlil Gibran

HUMOR

Blessed are the people who can laugh at themselves—they will never cease to be amused. —Unknown

The Humor position offers a light heart, brings an untroubled sunniness, playfulness, levity, a new perspective, a smile and joviality to our life. Sometimes it is an amusing witty personal acquaintance. It can be an evening television show to relax and laugh with, celebrity comedians like Amy Schumer, Stephen Colbert, Jerry Seinfeld, Robin Williams, Jimmy Kimmel, or Woody Allen movies, a friend who e-mails/texts jokes, looking at cartoons, a person whose temperament is playful or silly. Laughter is the quickest route to ease, nothing to learn, no discipline, skill, talent or study required; a natural activity.

True humor springs not more from the head than from the heart. It is not contempt; its essence is love. It issues not in laughter, but in still smiles, which lie far deeper. —Thomas Carlyle

Laughter releases endorphins which provide natural pain relief, it helps move nutrients and oxygen to body tissues, reduces blood pressure and heart-rate and is a physical and psychological response that often results in an experience of fun. People promote their health by being happy; when people with a good sense of humor experience stress they have lower levels of plasma fibrinogen, a chemical in our bloodstream that indicates the presence of inflammation, an indicator of heart health—the number 1 killer in the world.

This powerful position in our life offers us the benefits of the reduction of muscle tension, lowered production of stress hormones, improved immune system functions as well as increasing our body's ability to utilize oxygen. Our facility to access Humor is one of our most compelling tools. It almost guarantees that our daily mood and emotional state support good health to uplift our life, promoting physical, mental and spiritual health. Developing the ability to find a lighter side to a situation strengthens our sense of Humor and metabolically turns on the immune system to encourage wellness in the face of internal or external threats. Choose well who sits in this position and turn to it often!

Life is not a tragedy, it is a comedy. To be alive means to have a sense of humor, to have a deep loving quality, to have playfulness. —Osho

The simple truth is that people with good humor generally don't remain sick, states Bernie Siegel, M.D.. Humor's ability to protect us against immunosuppression during stress was evident in a study which compared people with a well-developed sense of Humor to people with a poor sense of Humor. Among those with a well-developed sense of Humor, everyday hassles and problems did not weaken their immune system. Their sense of Humor helped keep them from becoming more vulnerable to illness when under stress. Dr. Norman Cousins found Humor to carry analgesic properties that reduce the level of physical pain. There is something about Humor and laughter that causes the immune system to turn on metabolically.

Patch Adams, a medical doctor and clown, has devoted his life to what makes people smile; and, yes, it is quite revealing of a person's character to observe what makes them laugh. Each year he organizes a group to dress as clowns going into hospitals, orphanages, bringing Humor to people in difficult environmental situations. His life inspired the film, *Patch Adams*, starring Robin Williams. His vision is to build a silly hospital where all the activities are infused with fun. Good health is moment-by-moment vitality, not just clear x-rays and normal lab values. The Humor point has a long history: descendents of harlequins, clowns, court jesters, irreverent, inventive merry-makers; even a serious message delivered in clown style can bring a smile deepening into a fuller understanding.

A Sense Of Humor

Life does not cease to be funny when someone dies any more than it ceases to be serious when someone laughs. —*George Bernard Shaw*

In deep laughter the mind disappears. It is impossible to laugh and think. Life is filled with absurdity, paradox, ridiculousness and jokes. Inner laughter is the spirit of laughter; to be happy and make others smile adds quality to our daily living. Humor provides a perspective on life's hard experiences. *It wasn't funny at the time*, expresses the space that shifts our perspective loosening the heaviness that accompanies many circumstances. Humor helps place difficulties in perspective as well as making a predicament manageable. Studies have shown that the use of kind, gentle humor in tragic events is a step towards healthy recovery and healing. Humor allows us to detach from the tragedy, briefly, neutralizing its intensity, and true laughter allows us to go beyond the pain, to rebalance ourselves.

A person without a sense of humor is like a wagon without springs. It's jolted by every pebble on the road. —*Henry Ward Beecher*

The Humor point chosen well, matches what brings comic welcome to us; our sense of Humor gives us the flexibility to release old mental habits and find new ways of seeing. The ability to see funny adds vision to life when life becomes difficult; in a deep laugh the mind quiets and our energy rises. The sage and harlequin have uplifted the spirit of kings and courts through all time; and Humor, playfulness, fun and laughter are the music in the dance of life. Hafiz explains that the Beloved's nature is joy, asking us *to hear God's laughter. I am happy even before I have a reason. What can we now do but Forever Dance!* Humor as a connection to others reduces stress through perspective, replaces distressing emotions with pleasurable feelings, is great for mental health.

If I had no sense of humor, I would long ago have committed suicide.
—*Mahatma Gandhi*

Bringing lightness to our life at challenging times; through death, illness, accidents, politics, divorce, lawsuits, job relocation, moving, is essential when walking a spiritual path. A light heart begins with a smile. In ancient Egypt the heart rather than the brain, was the source of human wisdom and considered the most important of the body's organs. In the final judgment the heart of the deceased was weighed against a feather. A heavy heart would be eaten by a beast and the person would return to earth for a new heart. A heart lighter than the feather, light enough to rise, indicated that the person would pass through to a pleasurable eternity.

HUMOR AS A HEALTHY PERSPECTIVE

Holiness is the life of spontaneity and self-abandonment with humor, which includes the wisdom of serpents as well as the gentleness of doves, because humor is nothing other than perfect self-awareness. It is the delighted self-recognition of one's own absurdity, and a loving cynicism with respect to one's own pretensions. Humor is the transformation of anxiety into laughter: the same trembling but with a different meaning. —*Alan Watts*

This support position is important to contact frequently. Without Humor our thought processes become stuck and narrowly focused leading to increased distress. *Humor is tragedy plus time,* observed humorist

Mark Twain. Humor is the experience of incongruity, a shift in context to see a situation in a useful way, reframing challenges, failings and misunderstandings, a shock absorber for a sometimes bumpy ride, as well as the experience of the forbidden. Often, it is the discrepancy and contradiction between ideas and expectations. Opening to the Humor support brings air and breathing room to venture through the discomfort of disrupted plans and dreams, to meeting failure, obstacles and disappointment with a smile and sometimes a laugh.

Humor has an adhesive quality that connects and bonds people together, sometimes for the length of a funny story or joke, dissolving ego, melting barriers. Making fun of ourselves, playfulness, being silly with wit, a childlike essence, cracking jokes, being foolish, putting a humorous spin on events, exaggerating to the point of the ridiculous, of absurdity; all accessible through the Humor position. Available to cheer us up, a reminder not to take the details too seriously, not to be heavy; a great perspective as well as a cleansing. Laughter, spontaneous and natural, comes when we are relaxed, it is simple, available, bringing in new fresh energy.

Your whole body must be united in laughter—you should shake with merriment from head to foot—I want you to laugh with your whole heart and soul, with all the breath of life—you will then see how the laughter that comes from such a heart defeats the world. —Ammachi

DISCIPLINE

Self-respect is the fruit of discipline; the sense of dignity grows with the ability to say no to oneself. — Abraham J. Heschel

Discipline is a training, a process, and coming from the same Latin root as *disciple,* to learn; it means the immeasurable ceaseless process of learning and knowing. Self-Discipline teaches us how to live as an empowered agent of change, how to remain learning. The commitment, the follow through, the ability to stay focused and inspired is the root foundation for our ascent along a path, for our climb up and down the mountain. The delicate balance of effort and effortlessness, of self-control and surrender, of restraint and wildness, of focus and spontaneity, is the practice and the art.

Those who wish to keep a rule of life must guard their minds in perfect self-possession. Without this guard upon the mind, no discipline can ever be maintained. —Shantideva

True freedom arrives through developing a Disciplined mind. Order is the very root of freedom; refreshed in the remarkable act of living. Discipline is for our freedom and on behalf of all sentient beings. A tool of surrender, Discipline places us where change happens. Disciplining the heart and mind, a fundamental prerequisite of inner work, is the preparation, the action for true growth. Those who have awakened without any apparent effort might have prepared over many lifetimes. We grow in awareness and capacity as we apply our values and ideals into daily practices, as we live in accord with our values and heart rather than through impulse and momentary appetite. This attention to something higher moves us past our little self, beyond moods and thoughts, past the ego, developing strength of character and reliability; to not *desert our post of duty*. Spiritual practice is heart-mind-training a step-by-step exercise of mindful presence.

Maybe you should wake a little earlier, not eat quite so much, and so bring an attempt at discipline as a gift for this friend, to make the meeting more sweet. —Anonymous

Life happens mysteriously. We are in a boat and Discipline with awareness are the rudder and oars that we pick up to help us stay on course. Self-Discipline, not being swallowed up by the trivial or overwhelmed in the drama, assists us to penetrate the present. Difficulties with the world often are a reflection of difficulties with ourself. Having sincerity and paying attention, mysteries hinted at can be understood, the secret recognized, road maps point the direction. The world trains us to divert ourselves from seriousness, is built on distraction to keep us entertained, away from depth and breadth. And so we avoid the commitment to our relationships, our work, our life, that is needed to establish meaningful purposeful intimacy. How to love the world more yet desire it less, apparently stilling our mind and quieting our senses brings about a maturity, a wisdom, and arrives through a dedicated practice.

Whether our action is wholesome or unwholesome depends on whether that action or deed arises from a disciplined or undisciplined state of mind. It is felt that a disciplined mind leads to happiness and an undisciplined mind leads to suffering, and in fact it is said that 'bringing about discipline within one's mind is the essence of the Buddha's teaching'. —the Dalai Lama XIV

THE PRACTICE OF DISCIPLINE

The Discipline point teaches responsibility, understanding, order, calm, regardless to what is happening. It is particularly effective in training and directing our behavior. Benjamin Franklin had a plaque on the wall that reminded him: *He that cannot obey, cannot command.* To be inspired summons an energy, a momentum for the long haul; and so we might choose our Discipline point with that in mind: yoga, our writing practice, Tai Chi, cooking classes, Gurdjieff movements, singing lessons, meditation, something that sparks and encourages, rouses and moves us to dedicate ourself to the fire of our dream.

Discipline offers us the opportunity to be intentional, to have choices that reflect who we are in our lifestyle with a greater range of possibilities. As a preparation and practice we lay the groundwork for creating our life. Self-Discipline is about remaining self-motivated and focused, concentrating on our everyday routine, aiming to live calm and joyful, our mind stable and constant. Disciplined, we are then ever learning. Not known, life is a flux, Discipline is for understanding, not control, it's an ongoing process. True Discipline comes from being involved, from the heart, about what we are doing.

The 'successful' person has the habit of doing the things 'failures' don't like to do. They don't like doing them either necessarily. But their disliking is subordinated to the strength of their purpose, their mission, a clear sense of direction and value, a burning 'yes!' inside that makes it possible to say 'no' to the other things. It also requires independent will, the power to do something when you don't want to do it, to be a function of your values rather than a function of the impulse or desire of any given moment. —Stephen Covey

The Discipline support in our life might be someone who holds us to an obligation. It could be a situation, person, student loan that takes years to pay, an athletic coach, probation officer, teacher, the book we commit to write, our training to play the piano, a Tai Chi practice, a vegan gluten-free lifestyle, an exercise routine. The persistence, perseverance, attitude of celebration needed to realize our dreams grow out of the practice, management, coaching and preparation that this position holds. It creates scenarios that bring our awareness to the impact of our decisions, holding us to our intention to keep focused through our distractions. Choose Discipline coming from the heart not from control, creating substance, finding conditions that bring about true change.

A person without self control is like a city stormed and its walls shattered.
—*Proverbs*

ANCHOR

Every part of this earth is sacred to my people, every hillside, every valley, every clearing and wood, is holy in the memory and experience of my people.
—*Chief Seattle*

This position is held by someone or something that offers us a sense of stability. The Anchor point is dependable. The presence of an Anchor support holds us in place, brings connection and groundedness. Knowing that we have a haven or refuge, a place to turn to refresh; music, the Torah, a mantra, the Bhagavad-Gita, our meditative heart, the ocean, a best friend, grandparent, a sport, home, inward, a special book, dance, our dog, a yoga practice, a certain vacation spot, someone or something to count on—is the reflection of this position. This is our sanctuary and safeguard and since life is impermanent the Anchor position teaches us to hold without clinging. It is a bridge back to ourself, and stands as a reminder of our center and groundedness. A place to go anytime for rejuvenation; its consistency on this physical plane is a reminder that regardless, this thing, place or person is available.

All you need is one safe anchor to keep you grounded when the rest of your life spins out of control. —*Katie Kacvinsky*

This mainstay, can be port and harbor as well as mooring, a provision of stability. Certain practices: lighting candles for the Sabbath, listening to music, an altar, incense, a meditation group, riding our horse, playing the piano, prayers and hymns, our mindfulness practice, a walk in the woods, going to the beach, Tibetan bowls; enjoying our experiences, our rituals, quiets and connects us to remember who is listening as well as looking. Having a sacred space to return to heightens each day. To create an Anchor in the home consecrates the house; an image of Kwan Yin, an icon, our dog's greeting, photos of our children, flowers, a selenite crystal lamp, faces of holy beings, a Buddha, brings a quality of protection for us to draw our strength and inner serenity.

As we move through life: *Thirty spokes are joined together in a wheel, but it is the center hole that allows the wheel to function—Lao Tzu.* Those moments, when we experience magnificence create the well-being of our life, they center and pull us to a place of peacefulness. What we know as the center, the lynch pin, can look like most anything. A writing or meditation practice, working out at the gym, sitting at the piano daily—so long as the experience is a port, an oasis, it serves as an Anchor providing emotional, physical, even spiritual confidence.

MEANINGFUL REMINDERS

Affirmation of life is the spiritual act by which man ceases to live unreflectively and begins to devote himself to his life with reverence in order to raise it to its true value. To affirm life is to deepen, to make more inward, and to exalt the will to live. —Albert Schweitzer

Symbols frame and order the visible world as well as serving as a representative, expressing a higher reality they serve as a continuity of experience for us to shape and to make our experience meaningful. The Mishkan or dwelling place was the portable sanctuary of the Jewish people in the wilderness. The commandment to erect a Mishkan reads, *Let them make me a holy place and I will dwell in their midst.* This has come to mean an inward sanctuary, the true dwelling place we make within our heart, a place that Anchors us to our higher most precious truths; a spiritual center in the midst of the desert.

It is a tree of life to those who hold fast to it, and all who cling to it find happiness. —Mishkan T'Filah

An Anchor exists wherever we allow it. Symbols, and in fact everything we contact can be grounding creating an atmosphere that reminds us of our inner work, that resonates with spirit, requires care. Statues, photographs, malas and prayer beads, a beautiful cup of tea, mindfulness bells, sacred opportunities root us, carrying richness and meaning. Used well these are our reminders of what we yearn for, mirroring our own true nature, reflections that Anchor us into the present moment.

There is no need to go to India or anywhere else to find peace. You will find that deep place of silence right in your room, your garden, or even your bathtub. —Elisabeth Kübler-Ross

HEALER

Healing is possible only when your energy enters the other person and becomes his energy. If it comes up to the door and returns, no healing happens. —Rajneesh

This position might be held by a massage therapist, an acupuncturist, homeopath, a yoga teacher, physician or counselor, cook, Tai Chi teacher, musician, or our dog. It may be a friend whose presence brings Healing to the physical, spiritual and emotional bodies. Sometimes it is a physical experience like a treatment, other times a conversation. Restorative, this presence generates comfort and Healing. The importance of this point is to reconnect us to our own Healing source. This is the gardener of love and it can be our home, a temple, the ocean, mountain, Shabbat, whatever opens us to our wholeness. The Healer reconnects us to the source not through doing, through being. The more empty the Healer, the deeper connection to the whole; once connected our energy flows.

The time will come when the work of the physician will not be to treat and attempt to heal the body, but to heal the mind, which in turn will heal the body. In other words, the true physician will be a teacher; his work will be to keep people well, instead of attempting to make them well after sickness and disease comes on; and still beyond this there will come a time when each will be his own physician. —Ralph Waldo Trine.

This position teaches us to not consider illness the enemy. It might be an experience of cleansing, a purging, and our intervention assists the wisdom that allows the body to Heal itself. The breath of life, regardless to what medical or Healing system we use is a link between life and death. The Healer's considerations are the mental, physical and spiritual realms of existence. The Healer is not the *cure*, it's a guide on a path to self-Healing. To deeply experience our sickness and health we create a possibility to create health, not only combat sickness. The Healer uses illness as an ally offering a new perspective, opening doors to healthier new ways of living.

We are the pain and what cures pain, both. You suppose you are the trouble but you are the cure. Don't look for the remedy outside yourself. We are the medicine, We are the cure. —*Rumi*

Healing is to become joined with the whole and the Healer serves to reconnect what is cut off, to rejoin the heart, spirit and mind; the barrier before the door is crafted from our illusions. Opening the passageway to experience no division we enter this world heart open, everything reflecting everything else. This is Healing, uniting all parts.

Complete health and awakening are really the same. —*Tarthang Tulku*

Stress, a primary disease of this century, creates a disruption in our body's energy system. Healing, to bring our life into a harmonious balance necessitates a mindful change. We forget to breathe and instead separate from the body, from the naturalness of a life well lived. The Healer position on our circle is to remind us to refresh our connection to the innermost core of our being, to become whole. This Temple we call body, how to inhabit, nourish and align it to live a balanced life? It is in the body that we ground and root, the human self is called upon to give expression to the greatness of this body—from that the soul arises.

RECEPTIVITY

All life in the relative world has to do with healing. Each moment can be a healing experience for we are never given more pain than we can bear. Reshad Feild accesses a dimension of healing that brings insight into that which lives as a link between Healer and Healee. Reshad states: *the first step towards true healing is to know that you are loved.* To die to the illusion that we are separate, to be present, is to be Healed. The mind connects the heart and the breath to a place of unity.

We are here to heal. —Reshad Feild

Often the Healer does not show up until we step forward and take responsibility for our own Healing process. Who is the doctor? The mind and heart of the patient. Repairing, mending, processing the deeper effects of experience, this being or non-physical guide, an instrument of Healing, helps us assimilate life. This might happen in a dream state, through meditation, oftentimes listening to music. We missed the one person we were born to Heal when we don't Heal ourself.

The only way to heal this world is to heal ourself. —Elisabeth Kübler-Ross

Our Healer position on our circle of lovers must be someone we trust, first the energy approaches us—then we open for it to enter. It is our participation, our state of ease which allows the energy to penetrate. They may provide treatment and advice, as well as a *kiss of protection* on our journey. What cures a patient may not be what the practitioner *knows,* but who the practitioner *is*; real and prolonged contact can be crucial. To use our time here well, to make the Healing path spiritually fertile, this figure, protector, guides us to the heart of Healing, insistent that the resources to proceed can be found within. So choose well!

For every illness is every cure, except old age. This very body that we have, that's sitting right here now, with its aches and its pleasures, is exactly what we need to be fully human, fully awake, fully alive. —Pema Chodron

ENLIGHTENMENT

When your real, effortless, joyful nature is realized, it will not be inconsistent with the ordinary activities of life. —Ramana Maharshi

This position is held by an awakened presence; it may be a teacher, a Guru, a being who is no longer in body, a Mahatma, a saint. You feel uplifted and lightened, connected to your higher centers, inspired; this is a battery charge for your life. Reading their books, owning photos, listening to their talks; there are many ways to integrate the personal with the universal. This is a significant resource, a reminder of what is true. To be Enlightened is to be intimate with all things. This position inspires the soul, enriching our life, fostering the process of transformation. It is a love affair and the boundaries disappear, like a raindrop falling into a river, until the appearance vanishes, then there is no longer any form. If you meet the Buddha on the road, kill him. Nothing stands in the way, and now this point will serve, and serve and serve.

The 'authentic person' not only transcends himself in various ways; he also transcends his culture. He resists enculturation. He becomes more detached from his culture and from his society. He becomes more a member of his species; this is clearly a basis for universalism. —Abraham Maslow

Guru literally means one who dispels darkness, in form they are human; perfection lies in conscious transcendence not in concrete manifestation. This position is awakened, guided by wisdom, love and compassion. When a Buddha is present recognition is often dismissed because we don't image our own possibility. Providing a framework for us to be in the big picture of our life the Enlightenment position brings us an invitation to directly experience our aliveness within the great mystery. The inspiration is a compass that serves as a reminder of consciousness in this lifetime. A finger pointing to our awakening from a dream, of being aware and knowing reality, the Enlightenment point is a steady light, the polestar of a spiritual path. This truth is always here for us to awaken and celebrate our simple everyday moments.

This world is only one drop in an infinite ocean, one link in an infinite chain. —Swami Vivekananda

AWAKENING

Proper effort is not the effort to make something particular happen. It is the effort to be aware and awake each moment. —Ajahn Chah

Our ability to live in the reality of awakening, the attention to day-to-day tasks, moment-to-moment living, letting the actions of our life speak, reflect our spirit like the jewels of royalty. When there is no resistance or grasping to life, nothing to seek, then Enlightenment becomes a presence, a being here and now. Enlightenment is a discovery, a disappearance; effort stops, the search is over. Walking this labyrinth, this great spiral; the points on our circle of lovers are a formula for remembrance. The Enlightenment point insists that this place on our chart reflects pristine awareness: an awakened heart, like a finger pointing to the moon—this is the map. The popular Zen proverb: *before enlightenment; chop wood, carry water. After enlightenment; chop wood, carry water* is emphasized by the Vietnamese monk Thich Nhat Hahn when he said *there is no enlightenment outside of daily life.* The risk is that we search far away for what is as close as our heartbeat. A conscious life lived in the world, ongoing, seeing the sacred in all things; spiritual life is the ordinary practice. The circumstances of our daily life act as a reminder, are an invitation to enter the stream of life, and this point serves to hold, to uplift our attention through the difficult.

Enlightenment is your natural state of felt oneness with Being, It is a state of connectedness with something immeasurable and indestructible, something that, almost paradoxically, is essentially you and yet is much greater than you. It is finding your true nature beyond name and form. —Eckhart Tolle

Within our circle of love this point is a window and through that window we see out. Ours is not to worship the window but to use it to see presence and absence, emptiness, reflection and light. Sometimes we look out to see sun and sky, other times our own reflection. The Buddhist word for Enlightenment is Nirvana, cessation of the ego, elimination of suffering and all desires, that state where nothing happens anymore, the darkness disappears and a being appears filled with light. Nothing is gained, awareness is present at all times and is a blissful silence. The Enlightenment point is a messenger, a letter arrives, read it. Simplicity, awakening to the sacred in the ordinary, right here, is what this point expresses.

Just as solid rock remains unmoved by the wind, even so, neither sense impressions or contacts of any kind, pleasant or unpleasant, desired or undesired, can cause the heart of one who has truly awakened to waver. —the Buddha

MUSE

The muse is like the angel one sometimes meets on a path while seeking wisdom, peace, and compassion. The muse with her sweet breath or fiery torch stands in the dark place and lights our way. —Deena Metzger

This source of inspiration impacts creative powers. The Muse is a person or an ideal we are in alignment with such as painting, poetry, music or truth. Holding to this concept or ideal inspires and intensifies desire, vision, artistic heart and creative imagination. The Muse is a deep experience, a great joy, a source that lights our fire and recharges our battery. A Muse position brings out our creativity. Not to imitate, but to actualize our own potential. Soul age plays a part in this position. Younger souls might make fame, ambition, money, or success their Muse. Wanting to be a big-name writer, wealthy businessman, well-known painter becomes the goal. Older souls yearn towards a spiritual awakening; devoted to Buddha, or the Beloved, Rumi, Hafiz, freedom, understanding, awakening, creativity, divine love, Torah, a Guru. Whatever one chooses becomes the highest value—our Muse.

Our life is the instrument with which we experiment with Truth. —*Thich Nhat Hahn*

The nine Muses in Greek mythology were the daughters of Zeus and Mnemosyne (Memory). Each Muse was in charge of one of the arts; poetry, history, music, theater, hymns and religious songs, literature, dance, comedy and astronomy. Artists invoke their Muse for help. In the modern world the Muse is the guardian angel or the daimon of creativity. This position is the pure aspiration with which we measure our life and personally strive to attain. Acknowledging who personifies our Muse and being able to identify its quality constructs the road map.

The Muse gives the greatest clue to why we arrived, incarnated in the first place. Sometimes we confuse the source of the Muse, its spirit, with the Muse itself. This source of inspiration, guiding spirit, capturing our heart, invites us to create.

This is the other secret that real artists know and wannabe writers don't. When we sit down each day and do our work, power concentrates around us. The Muse takes note of our dedication. She approves. We have earned favor in her sight. When we sit down and work, we become like a magnetized rod that attracts iron fillings. Ideas come. Insights accrete. —Steven Pressfield

INVOKING OUR MUSE

The Muse engages our attention to what we devote ourself to in this lifetime and offers the necessary strength needed to birth our creative moment. Once the spark is established, maintaining the momentum, finding the endurance, the focus; carving the way includes discovering and inventing to keep the freshness alive. To honor our Muse is looking at the world new, loving the process, the journey, the adventure. Not the goal, but how we approach life, relinquishing illusions to play in the world of artistic inspiration. The creative powers which will assist, exist, wait to be summoned.

One reason I don't suffer writer's block is that I don't wait on the muse, I summon it at need. —Piers Anthony

This is where the dancer becomes the dance, the writer disappears into words, our identity is shattered. When Rumi turned his whirling became the turn of the universe, bringing spirit into form. The real Muse is the thing itself: the writing, the painting, the music; creation is a response and as long as we are alive we are able to answer from that place where we stand. For older souls it is not to sacrifice the burning of the heart for celebrity status, ambition, approval; not to make a business out of our art. Wherever we are in the entry point, wherever we stand is holy. To make our art soar is to place ourselves in the fire. This outpouring has its greatness in the union between the artist and the work. To be an instrument, to be reminded who is the real creator; co-partnering with the Divine is a humbling moment. To enter that door where the Muse resides art is created and takes on its own life.

I am my own muse, the subject I know best. The subject I want to better.
—*Frida Kahlo*

You, the artist, you're not the puppet of the piano, you're not the puppet of the muse, but you're not the monster, either. It's a relationship, it's a conversation, and all it wants is to be treated with respect and dignity—and it will return ten thousand times over.—*Elizabeth Gilbert*

The spirit of exploration lies in invoking the Muse, both divine being and messenger, bringing gifts as well as making demands. The Muse takes us out of our own small personal world and opens the sky, cracks the earth and actuates us forward, to enter the world. Who then, is our Muse; the one we light candles and incense to before we write. The one who broke our heart as we learned to love yet felt abandoned and broken by in our dark night of the soul. The one we carefully choose music for, before we go to the alter of inspiration. Entering the world of Hafiz, Rumi, Gurdjieff's hymns and dances, Leonard Cohen's soulful singing, Deva Premal's chanting, we invent heritage out of the context of inspiration, we take refuge in our dialogue, carried daily, to realize our own creation. The Muse is not about changing ourself, it is about meeting ourself.

He suggested I pray to the Muse, get down on my knees and pray right there in the corner and he said he meant it literally. —*W.S. Merwin*

HAPPINESS

The most revolutionary act we can commit today in our world is to be happy. If you want to change the world than be your own focus for a celebration of life. —Patch Adams

*T*his is a decisive point on the Circle of Love, a reminder to take responsibility for our Happiness. Everything outside is a stimulus and it's our state of mind, our inner posture that receives it. When experiences are relative and personal, what once brought pleasure at one time might bring displeasure or unhappiness at another. To go beyond dualities brings us to discover, to experience an amazing array; real happiness is located within. Life is a fabulous showroom and we sample and taste many things that stimulate our sensations; our work is to find the real inside. That's where the Happiness is secured.

If you want happiness for an hour, take a nap. If you want happiness for a day, go fishing. If you want happiness for a month, get married. If you want happiness for a year, inherit a fortune. If you want happiness for a lifetime, help someone else. If you want eternal happiness, know yourself. —Saying

It takes the same effort to be Happy as to be miserable. It is said that everything can be done with joy, even remorse can be done with joy. Seeing our responsibility to be Happy strengthens the determination that creates the fuel for this commitment. Once the investment to unhappiness is released know that Happiness is not incidental to the journey, it is vital. Once you start living in Happiness, joy and ease follow.

The thing is to be happy. No matter what. Just try that. You can. It gets to be easier and easier. It's nothing to do with circumstances. You wouldn't believe how good it is. Accept everything and the tragedy disappears. Or tragedy lightens, anyway, and you're just there, going along easy in the world. —Alice Munro

So easily found in early childhood, Happiness is often relinquished through the process of aging. Ask many elderly people in their 80's if they are Happy and rarely from their heart will they say, yes; even though they have wined and dined, tasted and sampled, romanced, traveled; it's change, impermanence, that effects their attitude. Everything changes: the body ages, people come and go, our minds change, and all the while there is something to discover that is unchanging: the Self. This is the bedrock, the foundation for real Happiness.

Nothing can make you happier than you are. All search for happiness is misery and leads to more misery. The only happiness worth the name is the natural happiness of conscious being. —*Nasargadatta*

HAPPINESS AS A PRACTICE

Don't Worry—Be Happy. —*Meher Baba*

I remember reading that life, from beginning to end, could be described in either one of two words: Yucky or Yummy. Children see with simplicity—fun or not fun, playing or not playing; toddlers remain present to the moment, engaged in their inner playfulness. Our culture having extensively researched sadness, anxiety, stress, despair, misery, mourning and depression has yet to look at the neurochemistry of Happiness. What a study! as well as an aim and intention. To practice Happiness as a study not unlike practicing cooking, meditation, playing piano, painting lessons, for the outcome—to be an accomplished cook, pianist, golfer, or accomplished at creating a life rooted in Happiness.

When people seek excessive entertainment and amusement what are they doing but confessing their lack of happiness and their need to forget this fact? —*Paul Brunton*

The search for Happiness leads to uncertainty because looking to find it *somewhere* is based on an immature belief that it is someplace else. Outside sources are by their very nature undependable; you are overlooking your true nature, which is Happiness. You are overlooking yourself. Within, inward, found in the self, *there is no way to happiness; happiness is the way*, said Buddha. This is the journey. To know yourself, to recognize who you already are, the Happiness that is alive within, for no reason. After many lifetimes on earth we need to refine the focus, Happiness—spiritual alchemy transforms painful experiences.

Nearly all of mankind is more or less unhappy because nearly all do not know the true Self. Real happiness abides in Self-knowledge alone. All else is fleeting. To know one's Self is to be blissful always. On the day of liberation, you will laugh, but what is on the day of laughter is also now.
—*Sri Ramana Mararshi*

In the Jewish tradition, the Talmud explains that if a wedding and funeral procession were to meet the wedding procession takes precedence and the mourners move to a side street so their tears do not sadden the wedding party. Mourning is suspended during the Happy occasion of Shabbat. The biblical image is that we all are walking towards Happiness. Even in the darkest of times, goodness and hope can be seen in the world. What's named as Paradise here on earth is our place of celebration and dance.

He who is unattached to the external world and its objects and attached to the inner Self, will attain Happiness, an everlasting state. —*Bhagavad Gita*

Happiness on the circle of love serves to keep us pointed in the direction of awakening good will and delight and is a primary focus of *The Fifth Way, The Way of the Lover.* Exploring the true source of Happiness disengages unnecessary suffering. Having and doing lose their glamour, take a lesser position to enjoying who we are and what we know; being, aliveness and presence. The satisfaction creates the state, the enjoyment of what we have, opening our heart becomes greater than the desire to have more or other. The mindfulness practice of understanding what leads to Happiness and what creates suffering, the very turning towards Happiness deepens big-heartedness, life now becomes the art. The beloved poet Hafiz described this place: *I am happy even before I have a reason. I am full of light even before the sky can greet the sun or the moon. Dear companions, what can Hafiz now do but forever dance!*

Happiness as an optimal state of being, as an appreciation of the present moment is measured by our inner freedom, the stable inner well-being that we develop. To cultivate Happiness, to overcome unnecessary suffering requires mindfulness. This includes looking at our limitations with dignity and grace as well as facing what appears as obstacles to our enjoyment of life. How we live, what we make of our days creates paradise. Greeting life as it is, as it unfolds may we awaken to the *ten thousand joys and the ten thousand sorrows* of the Tao. How to live during the difficult times is an important usage of this point. Compassion towards ourself is a meaningful spiritual framework to enhance a Happier life leading towards peace and kindness to all. Yes, Happiness is who and what we are, a conscious way of traveling.

I believe that the very purpose of our life is to seek happiness. The very motion of our life is toward happiness. —*the Dalai Lama*

SYSTEM TWENTY-FIVE

MINDFULNESS
MINDFUL CONVERSATION

Mindfulness is knowing what you're experiencing while you are experiencing it. —Guy Armstrong

Mindfulness has been a core theme at the center of all major teaching traditions. It speaks universal truth expressed through numerous diversified distinct voices. The inner teachings, the essence of most all traditions, express this one essential truth. The wisdom of each perspective is its common ground, is in the long history embodied in the attributes that speak to our inner state. Referred to in Judaism as kavanah—connecting and directing the heart and mind, this is the mind-set for prayer. In the Sufi tradition it's named dhikr—the devotional act of remembrance, remembering that we exist and that our lives become the dhikr in action. The fourth Way, a Gurdjieff tradition, names it self-remembering—placing intentional attention, consciousness of our being, a practice to contact ourself into this present moment. In Buddhism and Hinduism it's dhyana—deep concentration, the yoga of meditation. The practice of living Mindfully, of bringing our distracted scattered mind home, focuses on the inwardness of our actions, the inner meaning; thoughtful, understanding attention

The mind, the mind, the mind—This is the beginning and the end of it all. The quality of one's life depends on Nothing but the mind. —the Buddha

Studies report that the average person has more than 200 thoughts a minute. Our minds are overcrowded, without the space for watchfulness we miss a glimpse of the mystery as it appears. A state of open readiness brings us to experience our aliveness in a new way, each moment fresh and vibrant. When Mindfulness is strengthened, when we learn how to better manage our jumping monkey mind this is the great gift we offer to ourself. To engage in Mindfulness we cultivate contemplative self-awareness, enjoying the freedom of no anticipation, embarking on a solid practice; space in the mind generates clarity and alertness.

By letting go of the banana, the monkey becomes a monk.
—*Swami Sarvapriyananda*

NON-REACTIVE ATTENTIVENESS

By silencing the mind, we can experience real peace. —*Henepola Gunaratana*

The following story speaks to cultivating uninterrupted Mindfulness: Once upon a time a person who had been inattentive and distracted throughout his lifetime died and found himself seated facing a high wall which revolved gradually before his eyes. It was made known to him that once every 1,000 years a gate would come level to where he sat, the gate leading into Paradise, momentarily open to him. He must wait in patience for that moment, he understood that to be Mindful would bring him to enter Paradise; this was his opportunity to step into eternal joy. For 999 years 11 months and some days the person sat Mindfully bringing his attention to the wall which revolved slowly before him. But there came a moment when his mind wandered and was distracted, a past memory, a thought, a concern, a worry: in that moment the gate came level and opened and then continued its round. Another possibly 1,000 years of practice before him.

An attentive mind is an empty mind. —*Jiddu Krishnamurti*

This forgetfulness, these numerous distractions are our condition. When we forget we are forgotten. The landscape does not vanish because a blind man cannot see it. Our mindlessness, our inattention does not affect reality, which is what it is. To be Mindful is what makes us human. The constant unwavering attention does not easily turn away, being Mindful we live a non-reactive life attentive to present time reality.

Let things come and abide in our heart. Let our heart return and abide in things. All through the day and night. —Dogen

Looking at the sky before our mind says sky, before there are words to name it, this original moment that embraces the essence of what we see is a practice to prolong, brings us into the present moment: to see what is as it is. When we remember the movie we saw last night that is memory, when we become aware that we are remembering the movie, that is Mindfulness. When we conceptualize the process telling ourself: I am remembering, now we are thinking.

Mindfulness, which goes back thousands of years, is the development of practices to cultivate wakefulness, kindness, and compassion. And by cultivating it, I mean living and embodying it. It's an experience, a way of being, a doorway into oneself. Mindfulness is the awareness that arises from paying attention on purpose in the present moment nonjudgmentally.
—Jon Kabat-Zinn

Forgetfulness puts attention to sleep. To bring our mind to the here and now, to drop into what is, this is Mindfulness. Wisdom traditions have for thousands of years put forth bodies of teachings that continue to remain with us. The living teachings are Mindfulness manifesting in our daily lives. Intentionally created states become an enduring trait for long-term changes in our brain structure, and have demonstrated measurable improvements in our immune functions.

PRACTICING MINDFULNESS

What is a Mindfulness practice? *We practice so that each moment of our life becomes real life.* —*Thich Nhat Hanh*

We practice and look deeply to gain understanding. This is Mindfulness: looking deeply to cultivate awareness. From this place comes a vision of kindness, compassion, understanding and love; of living Mindfully. Mindfulness practice is being present, trusting our direct experience, one moment at a time, observing and describing without judgment; it's letting the thoughts come without engaging them.

We nourish Mindfulness through our practices: inviting, hearing the sound of the bell call to us, walking and remaining calm and aware in the midst of motion, staying connected to ourself through the changes and shifts of the day. We practice regardless to our resistance and intellectual ideas. No holding back. Practice to remove the obstacles that obstruct our conversations and understanding. The heart of the process is taught from personal experience as well as attuning to our own internal life for us to become attuned to the internal lives of others. Practicing Mindfulness we become intimate with the workings of our own mind.

If your mind becomes firm like a rock and no longer shakes In a world where everything is shaking, Your mind will be your greatest friend And suffering will not come your way. —*Theragatha*

Seeing the sacred in all things is the ordinary practice. The circumstances of our daily life serve as a reminder, are the invitation. Living now becomes an art for every moment of our daily life. Answering our phone we practice Mindful talking. Washing the dishes, getting dressed, sitting at the computer, eating breakfast; life is the laboratory. Practice is available to us in each moment. Everything that is in our daily life can be accessed as our practice. Cooking, shopping, walking, conversing; all is food for Mindful living. Being present to the things we do throughout the day: we are practicing. While we are walking, if we know we are walking and not distracted; attentive, we are walking Mindfully. The key is in the knowing. This is a journey of the present moment. Knowing comes through awareness and is a state of knowing. We've been taught about our five senses: hearing, seeing, touching, tasting, smelling. Our sixth sense is knowing. When we walk we know we are walking, as we eat we know we are eating. The key is in the knowing.

Mindfulness is: Every time we breath in we will know we are breathing in, every time we breath out we will know we are breathing out. In this way, we are fully ourselves. —Thich Nhat Hahn

One form available to us that engages wisdom teaching as a practice are bells and singing bowls. According to oral tradition the existence of singing bowls dates back to the time of the historical Buddha. Traveling smiths would gather material of seven metals, each symbolically representing a different planet in the solar system: sun-gold, moon-silver, mercury-mercury, mars-iron, copper-venus, jupiter-tin, saturn-lead. The smitty monks, as they hammered and turned the bowls, would sing and chant prayers and mantras which then became woven into the fabric of the bowls. So every time we use the striker to awaken our bowl the monk's prayers are released into the universe and we are embraced by the prayers that were sung into the bowls. The ancient sounds and prayers that still carry sacred energy carry us deep into silence. It has been said that the singing bowls emit the music of the void, the sound of the universe manifesting. When striking the bowl listen to the reverberation and to the silence between the ringing, for that becomes the attention that leads to Mindfulness.

This is Mindfulness, a space that holds silence. When our mind is spacious it is not distracted. This is paying attention without resistance, without avoiding or negating. When the mind is not crowded or busy we listen. Then the mind is a living thing, it is not dead. Hearing a Tibetan bowl, stop and let the sound carry us back to our own true self. This is sounding Mindfulness, and when it sings listen to its tone echoing inside us connecting us to our breath, to our heart, to the center of the universe.

This mind, perfectly and fully realized, moves with a clear, tranquil spiritual awareness. It encompasses heaven, covers the earth, penetrates form, and rides with forbidden abruptness. It is a radiant light shining from the crown of your head, illuminating wherever you are; it is an awesome wind, rising up at each step you take, enveloping all things. If you are able to make this mind your own, then even though you do not seek excellence yourself, excellence comes to you of its own accord. Without seeking emancipation, you are not hindered by a single thing. —Daito

To truly enter and penetrate the world of experience with awareness creates the shift and change that opens a door to shine a light on understanding. Applying the practice into our daily life, being Mindful of something, of whatever we encounter; *once we open ourselves, then we land on what is,* commented Chogyam Trungpa.

Man's mind is his essence; he is where his thoughts are. —Nachman of Breslov

Mindfulness is the capacity to shine the light of awareness onto what's going on here and now. Mindfulness is the heart of meditation practice. —Thich Nhat Hanh

MINDFUL CONVERSATION: WORLD PEACE

It has been said that when we speak we teach, when we dialogue we clarify, when we listen we learn. A good Conversation strengthens who we are. We become familiar with what is important. True Conversation empowers and changes lives. To engage in a Conversation, not talk or idle chatter, deepens us. It is always a process, an experiment, involving risk, an adventure where we agree to belong to the Conversation. Practice and study, like every art, makes our words sing, have real meaning, can bring us to a new part of ourselves. This is Conversation as a practice, the ingredients are presence, being active as well as receptive, asking a real question, Mindful inquiry, moving away from colloquialisms, pat expressions, generalizations, allowing for space, and, ultimately, our being sincerely authentic.

A single conversation with a wise man is better than ten years of study.
—*Chinese proverb*

Mindful Conversation as a practice aims to train us to listen and speak from our heart. It restores communication within ourselves. True listening asks us to open and receive before we respond. To begin to dialogue in a manner that reveals fresh newness is an invitation to minimize suffering and places our attention towards authentically living in a way that honors our integrity and our true values. To enter deeply into Conversation as a path brings us into the present moment.

We need to pay attention to the ways in which we speak, and to the beauty of our word and our ways of putting words together—so that we speak to each other not as disembodied minds but as embodied feeling-ful, animal-beings.
—*David Abram*

RULES FOR A MINDFUL CONVERSATION

In Asian languages, the word for 'mind' and the word for 'heart' tend to be the same word. So if you are not hearing the word 'heartfulness' when you are hearing the word 'mindfulness,' you're really not understanding what it is all about. You're going into thought, and you're going into your concept of mindfulness, but mindfulness is pointing at something beyond words, underneath words, underneath thinking. —Jon Kabat-Zinn

FINDING OUR VOICE

1. Slow down. Know that you are breathing.

2. Be present. Mindfulness is present moment awareness, taking place in the here and now.

3. Be specific, not rambling or associative.

4. Is this a story that others need to hear, is there a teaching in what wants to be expressed?

5. Know the difference between speaking as entertainment, attention seeking, idle chatter and what is true expression.

6. Idle chatter is when there is no filter attached to the brain. Speak Mindfully, be changed from the experience.

7. In a dialogue we leave space for the development of a conversation, of asking a real question, of living in the *I don't know.*

8. Speak to communicate, to reflect your inner state.

9. Bring your mind to your words. Observe how you speak to others.

10. True conversation is distinguished by a purposeful content. Literal-mindedness is hollow heavy deadness. Not *how are you?* or *what's new?* — instead, the challenge is to make a real bridge to the person with whom we speak.

11. Small talk, surface or horizontal socializing, undermines and diverts us from intimate conversation; it becomes the norm, sabotaging real talking. Examples of small talk: *What kind of work do you do? Where are you from? What's up or what's new?*

12. Belong to the conversation. Know your Intention. We dedicate our conversation and hold that in front of us. Intention is present in every moment of Mindfulness. The words we say create the life we experience.

13. Listen deeply with agreement. Disagreement blocks understanding. You cannot understand and disagree. Understanding is the most powerful force that we create in ourselves—it creates internal spaciousness.

14. Being willing to be truthful is what allows truth to emerge.

15. Listen deeply to the words of the heart, ours and the other.

16. Smile.

Those who do not have power over the story that dominates their lives, power to retell it, deconstruct it, joke about it, and change it as times change, truly are powerless, because they cannot think new thoughts. —*Salman Rushdie*

SYMPTOMS OF MINDFULNESS

Be on the lookout for symptoms of Mindfulness. As we are exposed to Mindfulness there is a possibility as well as a hope that people might catch it in epidemic proportions. This would pose a serious threat to what has been a lifelong condition of stress and unhappiness in the world.

Some signs and symptoms of Mindfulness are:

• A tendency to pay attention

• Wishing yourself and others to be happy

• A loss of interest in judging, criticizing, negativity, opinions, comparing and gossiping

• Eating slowly while savoring your food

• A loss of ability to worry (this is a serious symptom since it cancels out most fears)

• Frequent episodes of gratefulness and appreciation

- An increasing tendency to walk with awareness
- A habit of listening and speaking purposefully
- Smiling for no reason
- Paying attention, open-hearted; having surges of loving-kindness
- Warning: If you have some or all of the above symptoms, be advised that your condition of living Mindfully may be quite advanced and not curable. If you are exposed to anyone exhibiting any of the above symptoms remain calm because you are at risk. The threat to bring about a peaceful world is a real possibility.

Mindful communication happens when you are truly present in this moment with curiosity, kindness, and compassion. You listen with open, non-judgmental heart to the other person. You speak skillfully, generally avoiding lying, harsh language, gossip, divisive speech. Before you speak, you ask yourself is it useful, true, beneficial, and timely. —*T.E. Atkins*

A L C H E M Y

You will transmute nothing if you have not transmuted yourself before.
—*Paracelsus*

*A*lchemy seeks to transform base metals into gold, and we are the Alchemists—the ones who practice Alchemy. This is a mystical chemistry, miracle-working, an essential theme on our path of awakening. We each have access to levels of Alchemy. As the Alchemists had specific processes to transform lead into gold, we, too, have tools to raise the energetic vibration of our consciousness. The seven metals of Alchemy are: lead, tin, iron, copper, mercury, silver and gold. For the Alchemist the symbol of gold has represented the perfection of matter on all levels, including that of the mind, spirit, and soul. The quality of our life is reflected in our connection to higher energy. Alchemy as a way to transmute the frequency of thought, altering the harmonics of matter, is a way of living with awareness and intention through contacting and connecting with higher energy. Thoughts are electrical, emotions are magnetic; the dimension that we operate in is subject to universal laws. The universe reflects and mirrors our vibration. Shifting our perspective and understanding reshapes and raises or lowers our vibration.

Mind, as well as metals and elements, may be transmuted from state to state; degree to degree; condition to condition; pole to pole; vibration to vibration.
—*Hermes Trismegistus*

Discovering the secret of transmutation was the Alchemist's dream. The transmutation of base metals into gold was pursued for over 2,000 years, eventually the Alchemists learned that to accumulate a penny's worth of gold from mercury would take 1,000,000,000,000,000,000, 000,000 years. That level of patience matches the old proverb: *in the struggle between the stone and the water, in time, the water wins.*

Children play a hand game of rock, paper, scissors, fire and water; rock blunts or breaks scissors, scissors cuts paper, paper covers or captures rock, fire meets scissors and burns paper while water erodes rock, puts out fire and rusts scissors. Water being the strongest. The ancient Greeks understood the unique properties and power of water, a most precious resource on our planet. From liquid to solid to vapor—water is the epitomal symbol for metamorphosis and transformation.

Nothing is softer or more flexible than water, yet nothing can resist it.
—*Lao Tzu*

Water is not only oxygen and hydrogen, it also has memory and can be positively stimulated by energetic sources. Energy scholar and researcher Dr. Mararu Emoto claimed that human consciousness effects the molecular structure of water. *Water is a blueprint for our reality* and that emotional energies and *vibrations* change the physical structure of water. We know that the average human body is made up of 50-70 % water, and the earth is made up of approximately 60% water. Our bodies and the world around us are directly effected by our mind.

CHANGING LEAD TO GOLD

You are an alchemist; make gold of that. —*William Shakespeare*

Through persistent interior work we come to directly experience energy in its primal and fundamental form. The Alchemists tirelessly repeated experiments which offered us glimpses of the historical goal of Alchemical transmutation. The corresponding internal process taking place within the human psyche is our evolving consciousness and transformation. The search for an elusive substance, the philosopher's stone that might turn inexpensive base metals into valuable gold was an Alchemist's dream. The legendary substance was viewed as an elixir that held the secrets of life, the knowledge of creation.

Alchemy considered the levels of transformation a metaphor for uplifting and refining the spiritual and mental life, of transmuting thoughts and energy; this is about the evolution of consciousness in the Alchemy of spiritual processes. Gold has symbolized a quality of perfection and refinement and Alchemy has used images and metaphor to express chemical teachings to spiritual processes. The *philosopher's stone* became a symbol for the inner urge of the spirit to transform, like base metals being transformed and refined. Today we see our heart as the philosopher's stone, our elixir of love.

'This is why alchemy exists', the boy said, 'So that everyone will search for his treasure, find it, and then want to be better than he was in his former life. Lead will play its role until the world has no further need for lead; and then lead will have to turn itself into gold. That's what alchemists do. They show that, when we strive to become better than we are, everything around us becomes better, too.' —Paulo Coelho

The Alchemical process brings about a mysterious shift in consciousness, what is referred to as awakening. The Alchemist's dream was to transmute lead into gold. We become an Alchemist of our beingness as we transform our life creating substance and meaning through being present. We are born with a refinement or baseness and from that place we decide to uplift our Alchemy, lower it, or live as it is. To transmute the lead of our personality and everyday life into the gold of our higher nature is a practice of spiritual Alchemy. The corresponding internal process of changing lead to gold has not been codified or bound by any doctrines. This psychology of the gods here on earth is directed towards wholeness and vitality.

No mirror ever became iron again; no bread ever became wheat; no ripened grape ever became sour fruit. Mature yourself and be secure from a change for the worse. Become the light. —Rumi

Observing our daily routine we notice if our clothing is lead Alchemy—old, torn, in disarray or unclean. We uplift through choosing a fabric and color with a higher vibration. The same is true of our home environment. Small acts create a shift, like taking books off the floor and designing beautiful shelving, or changing dark heavy brown burlap bed-spreads to a light yellow pima cotton or rayon fabric. Replacing a dingy stained scarf with a delicate lavender or pale rose silk scarf, a ballpoint pen we picked up from the bank is put aside for a Montblanc pen with a closed top balanced weight and smooth feel; all these possibilities shift our Alchemy to a higher tone and vibration.

UPLIFTED OR DEPLETED

Destruction perfects that which is good; for the good cannot appear on account of that which conceals it. The good is least good whilst it is thus concealed. The concealment must be removed so that the good may be able freely to appear in its own brightness. For example, the mountain, the sand, the earth, or the stone in which a metal has grown is such a concealment. Each one of the visible metals is a concealment of the other six metals. —Paracelsus von Hohenheim

Moving outward to the planetary environment, some cities have historical committees that make decisions to preserve, maintain as well as uplift architecture and land. Painting the interior of our home colors that emanate light will alter our state as we enter; everything in our outer surroundings affect us. To be connected to and uplift our outer and inner world creates a gentle energy circulation in our life. The world composed of vital energy or life force that vibrates at different frequencies permeates our body, the building where we live, as well as each item we wear and use. We absorb, project and deflect energy and what we live with affects us with its energy field. Breathing in toxins is like taking a fish out of a clean lake and putting it into contaminated water. Eating toxic food, encountering course negative people, driving on highways breathing in carbon, hanging out in smoky bars, or eating beautiful organic food, sitting at the ocean breathing in pure ozone, being gentle with ourself; we are either uplifted or depleted through every interaction.

Correcting oneself is correcting the whole world. The sun is simply bright. It does not correct anyone. Because it shines, the whole world is full of light. Transforming yourself is a means of giving light to the whole world.
—*Ramana Maharshi*

Interacting with our belongings, the intention for our life surrounds us; changing and shifting the outer template of home, car, clothing, affects our consciousness. At some deeper level of reality all things in the universe are infinitely interconnected. In a holographic universe everything in reality would have to be seen as a metaphor, even the most haphazard events express some underlying symmetry. Our thoughts, our home, acquaintances, our belongings can be healers or dark forces. Cleansing our energy field increases circulation, heightens awareness, as we make choices to nurture and invigorate rather than poison and deplete. Clear loving intention uplifts the quality of our life. We create environments, everything else follows.

The secrets of alchemy exist to transform mortals from a state of suffering and ignorance to a state of enlightenment and bliss. —*Deepak Chopra*

OUR ALCHEMICAL JOURNEY

The primary goal of the Alchemists evolved and transformed into something of a different nature. When looked at through a symbolic lens the Alchemical experiments of transforming base worthless metals into precious gold unconsciously reflected an internal developmental process of health in the human psyche. Symbols are patterns of energy and on a deeper level a symbol is a pattern of etheric energy underlying its different forms. The progressively deepening encounter with the inner spiritual dimension of our being is a treasure hunt lived daily. Extracting the essence of a particular quality, purifying and gathering it to become an inner resource offers us something we can touch upon at will. Finding a symbol that captures the essence of that quality we sense some indication of this process begin to rise out of and separate from the specific symbols and feelings connected with that quality. To encourage this process we remember what we value as we gather, collect, digest and distill our experiences until we have an available tincture. To nurture and sustain this infusion as a trace, an elixir in our inner world, creates our Alchemical journey. When this tincture becomes fixed within our being we can draw upon it at will. A part of our inner forces retains an echo of the work we have done so that we reconnect with this reservoir whenever we wish. Evoking the inner tincture of an experience enables us to call upon this resource in our life as needed. This is invaluable on our transformative path for our ability to maintain contact with our essence.

Transmute yourselves from dead stones into living philosophical stones.
—G.Dorn

Alchemy as a tool accelerates lightening the load of worldly burdens. A generous heart accompanied by a knowing mind sees through to the very nature of things. The original Alchemical law: *in order to make gold, it is first of all necessary to have a certain quality of gold. If no gold whatever is possessed, there is no means whatever of making it*, speaks to the preparation, the practices we create to upgrade our energies, transforming in order to awaken. We are all composed of cycling energies and Alchemy draws out, purifies and magnifies us so that we shift and uplift how we interact with the world. To evolve we have to transform, and friction is our opportunity; an Alchemical process taking place in the Alchemical laboratory of life itself. The transformation of the self is about creating something new, a change in the substance of our being. Freed from our conditioned self, liberated from our personal reactions, we sacrifice ourselves into the *fire of love*. Francis Bacon said of this process: *Alchemy may be compared to the man who told his sons he had left the gold buried somewhere in his vineyard; where they by digging found no gold, but by turning up the mould, about the roots of their vines, procured a plentiful vintage.*

Our journey, when filled with hard work, challenges, and difficult life experiences can be redeemed through carrying meaning into understanding. Now the search for gold shines a new light, brings about a new world. As we approach the end of our seeking, we may no longer need to dig up buried treasure in hopes of a big find, we may no longer be drawn to travel to India to sit at the feet of a Guru; closer is the treasure which is sitting in our own heart, as close as our breath, our efforts are counted, our efforts not so easily tossed away, ourselves not so easily tossed away; we may discover within the absolute truth of who we are; conscious awareness.

The real alchemy is transforming the base self into gold or into spiritual awareness. That's really what new alchemy is all about. —*Fred Alan Wolf*

SHIFTING THE WORLD

The true alchemists do not change lead into gold; they change the world into words. —*William H. Glass*

This ancient path of purification and transformation is used by Alchemists to purify themselves through dissolving the base material of the self until reaching the gold of enlightenment. The symbols used creates energy to amplify higher states of consciousness. Symbols are patterns of energy. For a human being to awaken, to deepen in the realization of truth is a spiritually transformative process. To evolve is to recognize that Alchemical work takes place on many different levels. We can train ourselves to see Alchemically. Objects carry levels that transmit impressions for us to absorb. Along the *Fifth Way, The Way of the Lover*, our work is to transform and uplift all energy. We can transform scientific psychology into Sacred Psychology, uplift ordinary sexuality into tantric sexuality, our daily walks into mindful steps, conversation into sohbet, and routine religious observance into prayer. What is in our daily life need not pull us down, all can be transformed—uplifted—through this Alchemical process we learn to go from gravity to grace.

The alchemist knows that there is a very solid link between matter, life and consciousness. Alchemy is the art of manipulating life and consciousness in matter to help it evolve or to solve problems of inner disharmony. —*Jean Dubuis*

UNIVERSAL LAWS

We are an image of the world, created by the same laws which created the whole of the world. Knowing and understanding ourself we will know and understand the whole world, all the laws that create and govern the world. And at the same time by studying the world and the laws that govern the world we will learn and understand the laws that govern us. Some laws are understood and assimilated more easily by studying the objective world, and we can only understand other laws by studying ourself. The study of the world and the study of ourself must therefore run parallel, one helping the other. —G.I.Gurdjieff

*U*niversal Laws govern this universe. Beyond the world of appear-ance there is a world of Universal Laws, often invisible, at times predictable and repeatable; some of the Laws belong to this earth, the same everywhere, they maintain balance and harmony. Universal Laws just are, and we have the possibility to discover them. The earth is under the Laws of the solar system, the solar system is under the Laws of the galaxy, the galaxy is under the Laws of all the galaxies; to understand this opens us to deeper appreciation of the miraculous harmony of this universe. Training our mind to look deeply and to penetrate into the reality of this universe with a true mind, rather than an obstructed mind of imaginary beliefs, we are able to touch the nature of things and to enlist the ongoing process of transformation. The Laws of gravity, grace, cause and effect, fate and destiny were here before we acknowledged them. Gravity existed prior to Newton's discovery. Things fell before we understood to create a science of falling.

When we look into any phenomenon—material, physiological, or psycholog-ical—we can see how much individuality and how much collectivity is in it. Let us go together to climb the nameless mountain, let us sit on the ageless blue-green stone, quietly watching time weave the silken thread that creates the dimension called space. —Thich Nhat Hahn

True knowledge is knowing that there are invisible worlds and that the Laws we live under in our individual life are personal and subjective. We have access to a large dimension of consciousness although most of the world restricts consciousness to a single plane of reality to maintain feeling protected while living in an impermanent ever-changing world. This creates isolation and separation. Laws operate in the outer universe as well as on spiritual planes and inner realms of consciousness. To gain access and know other realms, to find and cross that bridge is to recognize *what is.*

Universal Laws are objective and show us that the real work is hap-pening not only in this world but also on other planes and dimensions. Ultimately, knowledge, information and understanding are the tools that bring us freedom. We live under Universal Laws, the Laws that transcend all religions, philosophies and individual beliefs. To learn and understand Universal Laws is to see what and how life provides us with a tangible way to create a harmonious life.

All the doors remain bolted, except for those who enter through the door of the laws. —ancient Sufi saying

To live focused on this miniature cosmos called *our world* consisting of self-interests, self-involvement and the small group called *family and friends* confines our energy. To think about the little world of this planet earth and see that it is a part of the planetary world which is in turn part of the solar system demands an interest that is beyond ourself.

Most people are riveted to a microscopic focal point and see only the wall of the cave as in Plato's Republic, seeing only the shadows of the images. To develop the desire to want more, see more, know and understand more, to have interests outside ourself, to live in a world of wonder—a place we once knew as children—is what's required in the investigation of Universal Laws. To be connected to higher meaning, open to receive information and understanding beyond our armspan, to be in the process called awakening, all happens from taking in new thoughts, new ideas, from looking out through fresh eyes, from an imaginative place.

The larger the island of knowledge, the longer the shoreline of wonder.
—*Ralph W. Sockman*

Universal Laws Direct Us

Universal Laws are the basic principles of life and transcend the diversity of individual beliefs and philosophies that govern every aspect of the universe. They transcend all time as well as form. As we evolve we live under fewer Laws. The more Laws, the greater the limitations. Universal Laws direct us. Using the systems described in this chapter, we have options to free ourselves from some Universal Laws. The more we study to know ourselves, the more Laws we are liberated from the fewer are our constraints. We are created to be self-evolving and we have the ability to know which Laws we are influenced by and how to position our lives for that to happen. Essentially our lives depend on Universal Laws and principles. Sometimes we have an intuitive effortless understanding of a Universal Law from a young age, like sensing that this is not our first or last lifetime. Universal Laws cannot be broken in the same manner we can break life laws, such as running a red light, hacking into a computer line, or not paying child custody. Suffering happens when we try to resist or oppose them. Being in flow with the Laws diminishes suffering, collapses time. They are, in fact, a bond that connect all experience allowing each person the possibility of total knowing.

Science fulfills its purpose, not when it explains the reasons for the dark spots in the sun, but when it understands and explains the laws of our own life, and the consequences of violating these laws. —*John Ruskin*

When Buddha was about to die, Ananda and the other disciples wept. *Have I not already told you that it is the nature of things that they must pass away. All things dissolve, but the Truth will always remain. I am resolved. Why should I preserve this body when the body of the excellent Law will endure.* The teachings continue. Although never appointing a successor his teachings continue to manifest within Universal Laws that forever remain. Buddha taught that the greatest of conquests was not the subjugation of others but of the self. In the Dhammapada it is taught: *Even though a man conquers ten thousand men in battle, he who conquers but himself is the greatest of conquerors.* Understanding the Laws, living the Laws in any form is the freedom.

For anything to function effectively there needs to be some kind of structure. There are laws that govern our universe that apply to everything, everywhere at all times in our universe. These laws enable our universe to function in an orderly fashion. Without these laws there would be chaos in the universe. Study, understand, cooperate, apply these Universal Laws into our daily life. —*Kathleen Rainbow*

MAN-MADE LAWS AND UNIVERSAL LAWS

We live in a world subject to forty-eight mechanical orders of Laws. Whatever efforts we make to externally change our world, for example through science, we still remain under forty-eight Laws. Some Laws reflect the principles of how the mystery of physical life unfolds, others reflect Laws that rule spiritual planes and inner realms of consciousness. For everything invented of a beneficial nature there is also something created with an opposite nature that is destructive. We discover penicillin, then through research invent the atomic bomb. In the world of medicine, as one disease lessens—tuberculosis and small pox—another disease increases—aids, cancer, severe acute respiratory syndrome, ebola, zika virus, or will reappear on another part of the planet. We try to create financial stability and then something else enters as our world is rocked by natural disasters; hurricanes, earthquakes, floods, tornados, tsunamis.

The discrepancy eludes us so long as the focus remains to improve the outer world without working on the inner world. The way to create a better world is through accessing our deeper parts and living mindfully, otherwise we are building a home on shifting sands. *Know! This world is a very narrow bridge*, said Reb Nachman of Breslov. Proceed mindfully; on the bridge we are suspended, connected to the earth on either side of us by something we have constructed for ourselves. These are the Laws we create, the meanings which have no reality apart from what we give to them. Remember that we have constructed it ourselves, an illusion created and sustained by human beings. On the other side of the bridge where nature is not interrupted are Universal Laws available for us to live into and to know.

Self-realization is almost maximally difficult owing to the extreme density of mechanical laws that operate on our planet so that, although human beings are designed with the potential for increasing their level of being, the chance that any particular individual will succeed in doing so is very slim. This effort begins when one realizes the truth about the human condition. Plato likened the human being to someone fascinated by the shadows dancing on the rear wall of a cave, who is so engrossed that he is heedless of the world behind him. —*Kathleen Riordan Speeth*

There are a hierarchy of Laws; Laws that apply to the sun, Laws that apply to the solar system as a whole and Laws applying to the individual planets. It is difficult to liberate ourselves from the larger number of Laws, that group of Laws connected to the moon which is governed by ninety-six orders of Laws. The forty-eight categories of Laws that apply to the earth effect us directly as Law and indirectly from the intermediate levels. A Law coming from the level of the sun states that the earth rotates around the sun, and this accounts for the seasons and the length of the day and night. The Laws that we are influenced by that are determined by the earth are, for example, the gravity of the earth and the electromagnetic field of the earth. A Law of nature is: As part of the ecosystem, if there is global warming we will be directly affected. Once we free ourselves from many of the forty-eight Laws then we are no longer constrained by mechanical Laws that restrict us, this is the path of self-realization, the *Fifth Way, The Way of the Lover.*

Science fulfills its purpose, not when it explains the reasons for the dark spots on the sun, but when it understands and explains the laws of our own life, and the consequences of violating these laws. —*John Ruskin*

There are classes of man-made laws that maintain society, some as formality, some arbitrary, and many self-imposed. In our communities knowing the rules and working within their context we are offered greater mobility and freedom. An accountant understanding the income tax structure can use that information to enhance his work or, conversely, to take advantage of the system.

Society has set rules and regulations. They can be broken. Breaking laws we find ourselves under more laws. Stealing or drinking and driving opens the door to adding the principles and laws of the court, the criminal system, jail, into our life. For some there is comfort to know the boundaries of rules and regulations. Not complying to man-made laws brings us under additional laws. There are periods in our life when we are placed under legal restrictions: prison, military, schools, hospitals and corporations. When we break laws, like in school or in the military, we come under even more rules of conduct. When we go to prison not only are there new extra regulations, but also strict schedules to follow.

The laws people construct and live by have been created to protect social growth and change. When society recognizes new needs and demands, laws change. In some countries women are not allowed to breast feed in public. The guidelines we self-impose have levels of importance, arbitrariness and even religious values. Freed from these impositions as older souls we feel a surge of energy. The transition between worlds opens energy as well as providing a deepening experience.

Learning To Liberate Ourselves

To the scientist, the universality of physical laws makes the cosmos a marvelously simple place. By comparison, human nature—the psychologist's domain—is infinitely more daunting The remarkable feature of physical laws is that they apply everywhere, whether or not you choose to believe in them. After the laws of physics, everything else is opinion. —Neil deGrasse Tyson

We don't need law enforcement agencies to maintain Universal Laws: the speed of light, gravity, thermodynamics, momentum, causality are not just good ideas, they are the Law.

There are many laws of the universe that govern the way things are. How is it that human beings forget the dimension of consciousness and remain 'unachieved?' That is, 'Is there a law of forgetfulness?' Does one live under it? How to carry the question and not forget it?—Fran Shaw

Learning and working with Universal Laws offers powerful tools that contribute to clarity and awareness, used well we spend less energy and direct our life more efficiently and wisely. Universal Laws studied for understanding, not out of fear but out of a desire for knowledge and freedom, will liberate.

It is said that Laws govern us, while habits direct us. With study we discover that not all Universal Laws are obligatory. Universal Laws can be found in mythology, fables, fairy tales, esoteric metaphysical writings, allegories and always in the workings of our life. *As luck would have it*, and *coincidence*, are names for Laws not recognized; for everything happens according to Law. Fear itself can be diminished through knowledge and understanding of Universal Laws.

The universe is perfectly balanced by natural and moral laws with regulatory vibrations to maintain order. —*Dick Sutphen*

The father of the space program, Dr. Werner Von Brand commenting on physical Laws stated that: *The natural laws of the universe are so precise that we do not have any difficulty building a space ship, sending a person to the moon and we can time the landing within a fraction of a second.* The physical Laws, like gravity, visibly show themselves. An apple falls and we see the Law of gravity. Life may not appear fair, yet natural Laws exist, not always apparent to the eye, and they influence our everyday lives. We sow what we reap, surrendered to the meaning of the Law.

World 1, the highest world, totally beyond anything, unfathomable, has only one Law, which is the unity of the will of creation. The Law of three is indistinguishable, nothing can be distinguished from anything else. In the next world, world 3, we are under three orders of Laws, in the next, world 6, we are under six orders of Laws, in the next twelve, then twenty-four; on our earth there are forty-eight orders of Laws under which we must live. The only place in creation that would be more difficult to liberate ourselves, would be the moon, which is governed by ninety-six orders of Laws. The Will of the absolute manifests only in the worlds it directly creates, then goes on mechanically until it reaches the end of creation which is in our case the moon. Since we live under forty-eight orders of Laws we are far from the Will of the Absolute, if we free ourselves from many of those Laws we would be closer; therefore liberating ourselves from the mechanical Laws that constrain us to move toward the Absolute; this, then, is the path of self-realization.

WORLDS

There are different orders of laws that Man can be under, lowest is the Law of Accident. This includes all mechanical people. A mechanical man has no psychology. He is a machine. He reacts always in the same way to any external stimulus; a machine has no psychology. Only a man who begins to know himself and work on himself can be said to begin to have a psychology. The Law of Fate, the Law of Will; those are Laws that conscious men are under. —Maurice Nicoll

World 1 and 3 are uncreated, creation begins with World 6. World 3 is a link between the unfathomable source and creation and is a seat of Buddha, of the Holy Trinity and the Divine, since it exists through love. The relationship between the three forces brings about the six orders of the Laws of creation, World 6, which is the world of unity in diversity, yet lacks the distinction of one and many. Out of World 6 comes the unity of life, all suns; we enter that world by dropping the *I*. The Bodhisattva, pure spirit, known as Compassion, has chosen to remain unliberated until all beings are free. This is World 6 of the highest mystical realm where nothing is separate. These are the 7 worlds, each with a different number of Laws. World 1 is unfathomable, World 3 is divine will, World 6 is compassion, World 12 is individuality, World 24 is essence, World 48 is personality and World 96 is delusion.

Self-remembering outlives galaxies and stars. Hydrogen 6 and 12 are clinical labels for one's embryonic soul. Each time we suffer a shock we produce a trace of this imperishable, divine substance. Apollo ruling the four horses that pull his chariot esoterically refers to World 6 controlling the four lower centers. It is a law that higher centers can emerge only if one forgets oneself. One's life becomes more interesting to the extent that one doesn't speak about oneself or think about oneself. Higher centers cannot come into being when one is immersed in imaginary problems. —Robert Earl Burton

World 12, our sun, the world of individuality is connected to that place where we have our own *I* and individual wills. Here, there is one and many, time and space taking on a different meaning. Will is similar to the air, we all breathe it, yet it is one. The materiality makes this world fixed and predictable. World 24, the next lower world of all planets, is where we live in time and space. This is the world of essence, where our inner life becomes real.

False personality is under 96 orders of laws. Personality is under 48 orders of laws. Essence is under 24 orders of laws. —Rodney Collin

Being One, Two, and Three are under forty-eight to ninety-six orders of Laws. Being Four lives in World 24. Being Five is established in World 24 and comes under the Laws of World 12. Being Six lives in World 6, and Being Seven is under the three Laws of World 3. (Refer to System 21, Being). Numbers are fundamental, certain numbers like three and seven determine the existence and maintenance of a living whole, a cosmos. In psychological language, World 6 is the higher intellectual center, which is wisdom. World 12 is the higher emotional center, the world of lover and beloved. World 24 is essence, our authentic self, World 48 the level of true personality and world 96 the level of false personality.

Laws are the same everywhere, but they manifest themselves in a different, or at least, in not quite the same way on different planes of the Universe, that is, on different levels. —P.D. Ouspensky

TO SEE BEYOND OURSELVES

This is oral tradition esoteric information. There has never been a completed published study of Universal Laws. Know that as we develop our relationship to ourself, to earth and to each other, amazing possibilities lie ahead. *The Way of the Lover* offers tools, explanations and understanding of this remarkable journey into freedom.

Go out one clear starlit night to some open space and look up at the sky, at those millions of worlds over your head. Remember that perhaps on each of them swarm billions of beings, similar to you or perhaps superior to you in their organization. Look at the Milky Way. The earth cannot even be called a grain of sand in this infinity. It dissolves and vanishes, and with it, you. Where are you? And is what you want simply madness? Before all these worlds ask yourself what are your aims and hopes, your intentions and means of fulfilling them, the demands that may be made upon you and your preparedness to meet them. A long and difficult journey is before you. Remember where you are and why you are here. Do not protect yourselves and remember that no effort is made in vain. And now you can set out on the way. —G.I. Gurdjieff

Universal Laws are a bond that link all experiences attracting an energetic force that connects us to higher qualities eventually preparing a way for us to absorb knowing and meaning. To begin to know ourself, loosening contact with the world that builds personality creates growth in states of consciousness through the richness of experiencing understanding along with our ability to live consciously. Meaning brings about an inner richness that increases the light. Now, instead of seeing only ourself we see the earth, galaxies, the expanding universe. This heavenly reflection is a reflection of our state of consciousness. Wider, expansive, multi-dimensional, until we are in harmony with everything.

To think beyond ourself, to have our interest focused beyond our immediate life interests takes a developed consciousness and strong force. Seeing in a new way deepens the process of awakening. To look at life and its events through understanding Universal Laws brings new meaning, sheds light on, creates substance, changes our being, heightens the force in our life. Conscious evolution begins with individual evolution.

To think and see beyond ourselves, is to join in the evolution of the entire cosmos. The following are twenty-one Universal Laws accompanied by brief descriptions and explanations. The creativity and exploration lie in continuing this study—adding our own list and commentary—once understanding how to recognize and identify a Universal Law. In studying the world and its Universal Laws, we study and elevate ourself.

The way of achieving consciousness by overcoming thought is the way of transmuting thought into understanding. To subject the meaningless wanderings of the mind to the pattern of cosmic laws, by trying to think of everything that happens to us, of everyone we meet, not in relation to our personal likes and dislikes, but in relation to great principles. In this way we gradually become liberated from a subjective point of view and acquire objective understanding, provided that we actually try to live all sides of our life by the great laws which we study or discover. —Rodney Collin

Universal Laws

Be sincere—that is, find yourself.

Be honest—that is, pay your debts.

Be truthful—that is, leave your egoism and live through understanding of universal laws.—Rodney Collin

1. AS ABOVE, SO BELOW
AS BELOW, SO ABOVE

What is above is like what is below. What is below is like what is above. The miracle of unity is to be attained. —Emerald Tablet

*T*his law holds the key to all mysteries. Carved on the Emerald Tablet, wording by Hermes Trismegistus, with bas-relief lettering in an alphabet similar to ancient Phoenician with magnificent workmanship, this early artifact was molded out of a single piece of emerald green crystal over 10,000 years ago. The tablet translated into Greek was put on display in Egypt in BC; claimed to have been taken aboard the Arc by Noah and hidden in caves after the flood, it is a revered document, synonymous with ancient wisdom. The tablet inspired 3500 years of alchemy guiding alchemists in their meditation and practical work. A source for most religious, mystical and spiritual traditions, it is the foundation of astrology and alchemy and shares similarities with Taoism, Buddhism, Hinduism, Judaism, Christianity, Islam, Gnosticism, Kabbalists and the Masons. The Emerald Tablet, held in high regard; legend claims it holds the key to all mysteries and reveals the secrets of the universe.

The Emerald Tablet is an ancient artifact that reveals a profound spiritual technology, which has survived to this day despite centuries of effort to suppress it. Encoded within the tablet's mysterious wording is a powerful formula that works in very specific and comprehensible steps on all levels of reality at once—the physical, the mental, and the spiritual. —Dennis Hauck

Encoded within the tablet is a prophetic message. To transform energy is to be aligned with a greater force, tapping into the energy of the cosmos. Encoded within the tablet's wording is a teaching for personal transformation as well as a teaching to accelerate the evolution of our species. The tablet's universal message made it forbidden knowledge, censured by patriarchal authority for thousands of years, censured by the medieval church, the Egyptian priesthood and numerous religious and political leaders. About the year 400AD it was buried on the Giza plateau and is imagined to still be there. Having been publicly exhibited in Egypt in 330BC there are many alchemical drawings which are considered to be schematic diagrams of the Emerald Formula.

As Above, So Below, is the Hermetic doctrine of correspondences between micro-and macrocosm. The text of the Emerald Tablet, with numerous significant translators including Indries Shah, Helena Blavatsky, Isaac Newton, Roger Bacon is thirteen lines, and reads:

As below, so above; and as above, so below. With this knowledge alone you may work miracles. All things have their birth from this one thing by adaptation. Its father is the sun, its mother the moon, the wind carried it in its belly; its nurse is the earth. Every wonder is from it. Converted into earth its power will remain one and undivided. Separate earth from fire, the subtle from the dense, with gentle heat and artistic devotion. Through wisdom it rises slowly from the world to heaven. Then it descends to the world combining the power of the upper and the lower. Thus you will have the light of all the world, and darkness will disappear. With this elixir you can master subtle things and penetrate all mysteries. In this manner, the world was created, but the map of this road is hidden. This is the way. I am Hermes Trismegistus, one in essence, but three in aspect. In this trinity is the wisdom of the whole world, having three parts of the philosophy of the whole world.

The origin of this text is shrouded in antiquity, transforms reality and reinstates our rightful relationship to the universe. The foundation of astrology and alchemy, the tablet reveals that the microcosm of mankind and the earth is a reflection of the heavens. This is a Kabbalistic world view of emanation. In Kabbalistic cosmology all of creation emanates in ever expanding layers of complexity, yet all are at the same time part of an unknowable limitless power. It says that there is an interaction between celestial and terrestrial affairs and that all the manifold forms in which matter occurs have one origin. A universal soul or spirit permeates both microcosm and macrocosm and that unity in diversity implies the possibility of transmutation. To unite the microcosm with the macrocosm, to join with human consciousness; when such a supreme union is achieved the subject and object becomes one. To feel this unison with the universe we reach our higher or true self and ascend from earth to heaven and descend to earth again and miracles are now possible; the goal is the direct union; all this is encoded on the tablet.

OUR MIRROR REFLECTION

If you do not make yourself equal to God, you cannot apprehend God; for like is known by like. —Hermes Trismegistus

This is yoga, satori, Buddhism, the experience of divine union spoken of in mystic tractates the world over. Some say it's true meaning must be found in every human soul. The Lord's Prayer echoes, stating, *on earth as it is in heaven.* Homeopathy, allopathy and science greatly influenced by the Hermetic formula all teach that when the earth's immune system, called the ozone layer, erodes, the human immune system erodes. *As Above, So Below.*

Understanding our relationship to all of existence challenges the definitions we grew up with, visions, dreams and energy from the spirit plane expand to attain the *miracle of unity*. This universal law works in specific steps on all levels of reality at once—the physical, mental and the spiritual.

What happens *Above* has a corresponding and parallel occurrence in the world *Below*. This law states that the world is harmonious, objective and unified. Everything is related and connected to everything else. *As Above, So Below*, enables us to reason from the known to the unknown. It teaches that if it's anywhere, it is everywhere. Understanding how my life is connected to the sun, moon, stars and planets, brings me to understand my position in the universe. As a miniature universe what exists *Above* can be known through a study of human composition, and similarly, to understand the matter of the cosmos is to understand the laws that guide my life.

Understanding this universal law, it follows that there is nothing outside that is not within, that what is above is mirrored below, therefore, to know myself, that I am a microcosm of the macrocosm, I grasp that I have the key capable of unlocking all the doors of knowing.

They know themselves; they know the Cosmos as well. —Khemetic saying

2 . BENEFICENCE

The childish work for their own benefit, The Buddha's work for the benefit of others, Just look at the difference between them. —Tibetan mystic

To embrace human love with spiritual love, emotional connections with spiritual wisdom, to live in a way that serves the benefit of others is the universal law of Beneficence. To benefit people in their immediate circumstance helping them toward liberation is the deeper meaning of Beneficence. In Mahayana Buddhism the Bodhisattva postpones attainment of nirvana to alleviate the suffering of others. The Bodhisattva takes a vow to attain supreme enlightenment for the sake of all beings.

Beings are numberless—I vow to free them. Delusions are inexhaustible, I vow to end them. —the Bodhisattva vow of compassion

Love is an unqualified absolute wish for the happiness of another, in the words of Rumi, *love is known only by those who become lovers.* We are all interconnected. A deep love for all life on the planet is a place from which we can truly serve. This law considered to be the first principle of morality, the love of mankind, is unbiased kindness, to regard the welfare of others, charitableness, love of humanity accompanied with a desire to promote well-being and happiness. Everything in creation is considered good in so far as it exists and in so far as it fulfills the potential for which it was created. Accordingly, human beings are good because of their inherent created worth, their human dignity.

Practice kindness all day to everybody and you will realize you're already in heaven now. —Jack Kerouac

Beneficence is not a moral rule, it's connected to awareness. Finding qualities that benefit humanity rather than judging and condemning, bringing light into the dark, uplifting rather than discarding, Beneficence completes the cycle of knowing and embraces appreciation, charity, goodwill and gratitude. To release a circumstance we first appreciate the gifts it brings; this law ensures that you complete your knowing and take to heart all that is before moving on. The understanding that completes the lesson accelerates growth and change; being grateful, seeing beauty and goodness regardless to how insurmountable the situation appears is behind the thought: *as long as I have breath there is something to be grateful for.*

SHIFTING OUR PERSPECTIVE

Deeds of kindness are equal in weight to all the commandments. —*Talmud*

Pain is a wake up call—imagine your hand on a hot stove, your pain reflux helps preserve you from greater harm. Difficulties and challenges seen through the beauty of everything from the micro to the macro promotes a path of meaning. All beings have a seed of perfection, tremendous potential, an angelic Buddha nature, therefore we practice looking for divine sparks to be redeemed. This shifts our responsibility from removing negativity to looking for the spark of love, to erase hate while watering the seeds of kindheartedness, promoting the good, Beneficence. This law finds its expression in compassion, charitableness and kindness, in helping others further their purpose and legitimate interests, to benefit others; to lift people up we elevate our own heart.

You are good when you are one with yourself. Yet when you are not one with yourself you are not bad. You are good in countless ways, and you are not bad when you are not good, you are only loitering and sluggard. —*Kahlil Gibran*

On the earth plane good and bad manifest, while on a universal plane Beneficence embraces everything, including the totality of good and bad. How connected we are to goodness lies in our soul age and the desire to awaken. Good is whatever brings us closer to an awakened presence and the opposite is what draws us away. Consciousness is a force or magnet and life has an opposing magnet. The constant tension of opposing forces is a universal law of polarity which says that all paradoxes may be reconciled. On the mental plane, this principle manifests itself in the heart center of each person as a light or as a dark mind. The principle of polarity makes possible the choices made between good and bad, right and wrong, generosity and greed, truth and lies. Mold can be seen as useless or converted into penicillin, a person may be negative or we could look further to find some quality that is redeemable.

If one broke the law of gravity one broke one's neck, if one broke this law of forgiveness one inflicted a mortal wound on one's spirit and became once again a member of the chain gang of mere cause and effect from which life has labored so long and so painfully to escape. —*Laurens van der Post*

PROMOTING THE GOOD: FORGIVENESS AND GENEROSITY

The Buddhist path speaks to fourfold Beneficence: heaven and earth, parents, brethren, and law. We receive life from the universal Beneficence of nature and parents, and to live with charitableness and goodwill in our heart, with the aim of doing no harm, is a deep teaching and true study. This law offers good for good and good for what is not good. Its natural consequence lies in the heart of all medical practice; *primum non nocere—first, do no harm.* The ethical principle of respect for individual self-determination, the nature and dignity of human beings; to help others further their true interests, Beneficence asks that we promote the good, and hold gratefulness and forgiveness in our heart.

Forgiveness is the fragrance the violet sheds on the heel that has crushed it. —*Mark Twain*

In the Jewish tradition a characteristic of a holy person is one with extraordinary generosity. Through *tzeddakah/generosity/righteousness* we become holy and improve the world's balance by giving to those in need. Money and wisdom have been loaned and offer us a possibility of becoming more giving when we take on Divine qualities. This means that the money and intelligence we are born with or earn offers us a great opportunity to create a richer wiser world through sharing what we have and what we understand.

It is said that:

Ten strong things have been created in the world. Rock is hard, but iron smashes it. Iron is hard, but fire softens it. Fire is hard, but water extinguishes it. Water is strong, but clouds carry it. Clouds are strong, but wind scatters them. Wind is strong, but the body breathes it. The body is strong, but fear defeats it. Fear is strong, but wine expels it. Wine is strong, but sleep dissipates it. Death is stronger than all, and tzeddakah (generosity) saves us from death, as it is written, tzeddakah delivers from death. —Talmud, Proverbs

To understand the inner meaning of this law changes the way we see ourselves and our property. The inner law is: if you hold back you lose, if you give you will keep. What we offer to existence is returned a thousand times. Knowing the dimension to creation and living with gracious generosity of spirit is a key to the secret of death and the harmonious beauty of this universe. *Do unto others as you would have them do unto you.*

For the law of beneficence teaches this: that goodness is worth while which can withstand even badness: that kindness is valuable which can withstand tyranny. —Hazrat Inyat Khan

3 . CREATION

What is necessary to grasp is that creation necessarily implies laws, there can be no creation without laws and this means that every created thing is inevitably under laws—that is, nothing is created free. —Maurice Nicoll

$\mathscr{E}$verything in Creation, in the universe, is alive and connects to everything and flows into all things. *Man is expressed,* says the Upanishad, *when he realizes all creation in himself and himself in all creation.* The primary purpose of Creation is for life to experience itself, for you to experience yourself. All Creation is governed by laws otherwise there would be only chaos and disorder. There are laws that operate in the outer universe and more subtle laws that rule the spiritual planes and the inner realm of consciousness. Universal laws are a bond that connect all experience so as to achieve total knowing. This mutuality, reciprocal exchange, takes place in everything and we come to know ourselves by materializing knowingness, eventually experiencing and converting that knowing through understanding which creates substance as we evolve into higher levels of being. Rumi states this poetically: *I was a hidden treasure and I longed to be known, so I created both worlds, the visible and the invisible, in order that my hidden treasure of generosity and loving kindness would be known.* Universal laws are displayed throughout Creation; the teaching is that through our understanding we use the magnetic force that develops from the awareness of being interconnected with all of creation.

Man is the microcosm, creation the macrocosm—the unity. All comes from One. By joining of the power of contemplation all can be attained. This essence must be separated from the body first, then combined with the body. This is the work. Start with yourself, end with all. Before man, beyond man, transformation. —Indries Shah

The law of Creation, as stated in the Emerald Tablet, says that there are corresponding planes in every level of Creation. We exist at a certain level on earth and as part of nature, *a part of the thin film of organic life that covers the globe.* It is in the nature of things that everything is under laws—*nothing created is free.* Creation takes place in this material world, home for us for three million years, as a later stage in the process of evolution, compared to the sea, rock and vegetation, we are capable of consciousness, awakening, of further transformation. To see the whole phenomenal world as a product of laws, which are laws in action, is our creative ability to be alive and ever-evolving.

There is a hierarchy of laws, laws that apply to the sun, laws which apply to the solar system and laws that are for individual planets. A law from the sun says that the earth rotates around the sun and this determines the seasons and the length of day and night. We are created to evolve to live under less laws, gaining more freedom, although we also can decline to then live under more laws. This is reflected in our institutions and bureaucracies. The school superintendant is under less rules than the school principal, who is still under less regulations than the teacher, who is still under less rules than the students. This is a reflection of the law of Creation; from the top downward increasing laws exist.

CREATION AND LAWS

If we are able to connect with the immediacy of ongoing creation, we have the potential to enter the advanced contemplative state called Nothingness, a level of interconnectedness of all things where there is no separation of space and no limitation of time. The continuous radiation of creative force never ceases from the world. —Levi Yitzhak

The seven different worlds originate with World 1 which is unfathomable and uncreated, its law is the unity of the will of Creation. World 3, all possible systems of worlds, is divine will and is uncreated. World 6, the milky way, is unity in diversity, and Creation begins as all suns. World 12, our sun, is the world of individuality. World 24, the planets as one mass, is where we live in time and space, the world of essence, where our inner life becomes real. Essence is under twenty-four laws. World 48, the Earth, the world of personality, demonstrates a distinction between objective and subjective states where we are not connected to things as they are. This is the world of our material and reactional selves. Personality is under forty-eight laws, which is actually forty-eight categories of laws. World 96, the moon, is the delusional world which is the root of our psychological problems. False personality is under ninety-six categories of laws where life is lived for pleasure; when that is interrupted we become negative and lose ourselves. There are ninety-six laws, and all the laws of World 48 have a negative counterpart. Most people tend to live between World 48 and 96, under the influence of between forty-eight and ninety-six categories of laws.

Life is a series of beginnings, not endings. Just as graduations are not terminations, but commencements. Creation is an ongoing process, and when we create a perfect world where love and compassion are shared by all, suffering will cease. —Dr. Bernie Siegel

Each person has, as above, so below, their own *moon, earth, planets* and *sun*. These correspond to false personality, true personality, essence and the authentic self, and they are subject to the laws of their corresponding worlds. False personality as the most mechanical is under ninety-six orders of laws and under the influence of the moon. All things are governed by laws of one kind or another. All the laws of this universe are found in any completed phenomenon, and understanding the meaning of the laws bring opportunities to use this information in the service of our freedom as well as to serve others.

Sometimes, when a bird cries out, or the wind sweeps through a tree, or a dog howls in a far-off farm, I hold still and listen a long time. My world turns and goes back to the place where, a thousand forgotten years ago, the bird and the blowing wind were like me, and were my brothers. My soul turns into a tree, and an animal and a cloud bank. Then changed and odd it comes home and asks me questions. What should I reply? —Hermann Hesse

4 . RENUNCIATION

Renunciation of some kind, voluntary or involuntary, is the condition of all growth and all existence; this is the universal law of sacrifice. That which before renunciation was pleasure, enjoyed with desire which was uncertain and dependent on circumstances and objects, has become after renunciation bliss pure, now seated in ourselves, self-existent and universal, we enjoy without desire, not struggling to gain possession of what does not belong to us, but as is, already in possession of all that the world contains. —Sri Aurobindo

Sacrifice is at the threshold of the law of Renunciation. What we are asked to give up are our illusions. We sacrifice the belief that we have anything, ultimately giving up unnecessary suffering, this is actually Renouncing nothing to begin the adventure of knowing the self. When we Renounce the world we are really only Renouncing that which is harmful to our peace and the peace of the world, now peace can become the prevalent experience in life. Since it is impossible to empty our hands before they hold something, the journey happens over time and through our investments and acquisitions.

The sacrifice through which one thing reaches its fulfillment is not a sacrifice that leads to death; it is the casting off of chains and the attainment of freedom. —Rabindranath Tagore

Under this law we learn to transcend those things that make life overwhelming, for the world to no longer have authority over our essential nature. Since the mind carries all objects, is the source of thought, this is the obstacle to overcome. We sacrifice what holds us prisoner, our anxieties, worries, tension, all the things that enslave us. Freedom comes from Renouncing the old ways and what we receive is in direct proportion to what we give up. Life then loses its power of fascination and distraction. This Renunciation is an inner sacrifice, to arrive at a surrender of desire and attachment. To realize we own nothing, to not possess what we have is a road to happiness. We have been reminded that *the world was created for my sake*, and on the other hand we are reminded that *we are dust and ashes*. A young poet wrote: *I create nothing, I can't create nothing.* What is this I, this ego that we slowly dissolve to live in our vast universe?

Pray to God that your attachment to such transitory things as wealth, name, and creature comforts may become less and less every day. —Ramakrishna

This law instructs us not to remove one habit for another habit, *to slip quietly out of the noose of our habitual self, releasing all grasping and relax into our true nature*, writes Sogyal Rinpoche, this, then, is the blessing, not substitution; it's living mindfully within the ordinary. All gain is loss and all loss is gain. To become more than our gain is to rise above it otherwise what we have overwhelms and crushes us. This is to know the happiness that is true and unchanging. Essentially we are sacrificing what we imagine we have, particularly our mechanical suffering, which is everything that represents our personality. This consists of things like resentments, sentimentality, self-pity, irritation, impatience, aggravation; only then will we move forward, out of reactivity and onto a different and higher level.

SACRIFICE

There is no need to surrender your job, only surrender yourself.
—*Ramana Maharshi*

The gift is discovered within the journey of sacrifice. What we give is what we get to keep. We receive in proportion to the payment we make, becoming smaller than what we want and greater than what we give away. It is in the giving where we achieve greatness. Our life force once in contact with higher values requires active attention. Movement of energy as a constant makes impermanence a truthful reality, to live in this experience, having confidence in a peaceful inner quiet place we touch stillness. Liberated from reactions, nothing left to Renounce.

Even if you stay in quiet and serene places deep in the mountains and sit silently in quiet contemplation, as long as the road of the mind-monkey's horse of conceptualization is not cut off, you will only be wasting time.
—*Man-An*

The law of Renunciation operates irrespective of personal attitudes; it simply is. Its consequence responds to behavior, to resist or ignore this law one is unconsciously or mindlessly carried away by personal whims, reactions and impulses, engaged in unnecessary suffering, inflicting suffering onto others. Much of what we imagine and are troubled about are irritations that represent our personality. Ideas like inequity, victimization, right and wrong, have a stronghold in imagination. The subduing of the personality ultimately sets the stage for the birthing of a real *I*. We sacrifice our negative impulse to destroy and we create and birth a desire for self-awareness.

To 'leave the world' means that you do not let the feelings of worldly people hang on your mind. —*Eithi Dogen*

To embody mindfulness and self-sacrifice, to refine the beauty of who we are is embodied spirituality. Renunciation as a law leaves this life without possessing anything permanently; when we die we leave all attachments and possessions. To live this law we deepen into an inner and outer world of peace. To resist it creates distress. Once we recognize illusion as illusion unnecessary suffering begins to dissolve. Attachment, greed, ambition; this law speaks instead to living in emptiness. To live without the thought of *mine,* without *me* or *my story.* The real riches, living in peaceful awareness, no price can be placed upon it. This is one of the laws of our solar system, the controlling factor on the physical plane; the destruction of form so that evolving life becomes one of the fundamental methods of evolution.

Giving does not exhaust your resources. At the deepest level, there is no giver, no gift, no receiver. Only the Universe rearranging itself. —*Jon Kabat-Zinn*

Through the law of Renunciation we arrive at a value system that is greater than life. The significance and meaning of life appears once we find something higher than life itself. Our willingness to offer up attachments in the name of our values becomes a dedication, for the spirit of Renunciation is our willingness once we rise above the things we surrender. Truth, love, freedom, bliss can not be renounced, instead we sacrifice to keep what matters alive. Letting go of those things that give us pleasure is easier than giving up what we imagine we have, our beliefs and struggles all leading towards the big and essential Renunciation, automatic suffering. This includes fears, self-pity, self-righteousness, self-importance, negativity and freedom from our mechanical life. Often we prefer to hold on and keep our habits and still want to get the *jewels,* the peace and harmony that might be exchanged for relinquishing habits. Understanding the law of Renunciation teaches us to establish values and priorities. This law is a powerful tool to carry us along a road of impermanence, maturity, and awakening.

Without sacrifice nothing can be attained. We sacrifice only what we imagine we have and which in reality we do not have. We sacrifice our fantasies. This is very difficult. It is much easier to sacrifice real things. We must sacrifice our suffering. Nothing is attained without suffering but at the same time we must begin by sacrificing automatic suffering. We expect, in a superstitious way, to gain something by sacrificing our pleasure, but we can't expect something from sacrificing our suffering. —P.D. Ouspensky

5. EQUILIBRIUM

The bird is teaching the balance between form and formless. Stillness and sound, always fresh and new. That's the art of living. To live in both dimensions, form and formless. The entire civilization is lost in form, in objects, in thoughts, in that dimension of things. Balance needs to reestablish itself. Because no civilization can survive without the balance between form and formless. —Eckhart Tolle

The natural universal law of Equilibrium, that things balance out over time, is often invisible. Balance is in play regardless to whether we see it or not. Equilibrium is a dynamic process, not a static condition. This law balances our payment. Life is movement, not to live in the static middle, rather, to be available to the range: the up and down, high and low, the joy and grief, left and right. Life is dynamic movement. The middle/balance, a brief interval, like the old grandfather clock swinging from left to right and passing through the middle—if we held the momentum, time would stop. Holding the swinging pendulum still, the clock stops. When the middle is passed through, that nonresistant moment maintains the flow. We cannot force Equilibrium, it's brought about through agreement and acceptance of all and everything.

Sacrifice the first portions of the harvest that your strength and faith to bring about what you desire may be increased. Give the first portion to avoid danger of worldly indulgence. Give that you may receive. Fulfill the requirement of the universal law of equilibrium. —Khemetic saying

Life is tension between the opposites. Balance, remaining available to both polarities, is living under the law of Equilibrium. Contraction and expansion, day and night, life and death, young and old, long and short, happy and sad, safe and dangerous, light and dark; Equilibrium comes about through experiencing all dimensions. What is constant throughout movement is our witnessing; that is the balance.

The point in life is to find equilibrium in what is inherently unstable. —Pierre Reverdy

Equilibrium is finding who you are beyond form, in the space, in the stillness, it's bringing a balance into life, between form and formless, between the human made world and the inner state of consciousness, between technical knowledge and spiritual energy. Time and form go together, to come to balance is to not lose ourselves by overly focusing on form. The transition, the state that is balanced, is the unmanifested and the manifested; you become that which is transparent to the formless, to the divine. The human made world will be changed. This is dropping into the law of Equilibrium, remaining connected to the sacred, while living in form, living in time, remembering spirit. Conditioned consciousness is form, self-remembering is to know the knower, the self who stands beyond the mind, aware, not unconcerned. The timeless dimension, where everything dissolves, energetic fields; things come into form, appear and disappear, unfold, disintegrate, renews to reappear.

When you simply are, you are in alignment with the isness of all things; and through that alignment, you may have anything you desire—and you have to do nothing except be! —Ramtha

Balance is to live between both worlds, the world of form and the world of being. The universe as a continuous and endless process of creation adjusts all that concerns the material and spiritual evolution of the cosmos with the least expenditure of force, with the least possible effort, with the proper adjustment of Equilibrium and with the necessary rate of rhythm. Evenness of rhythm is really an illusion of time and does not exist in the cosmic center. Equilibrium happens, it arrives of its own accord out of fullness and totality. Once finding what is permanent, eternal, then all else—good/bad, high/low—disappear. For there is no balanced middle static way to live; living in totality, balance appears. All that is left is witnessing, presence, Equilibrium.

The great universal law of equilibrium governs all the processes of which we have any knowledge, from the movements of the planets to the vagaries of the human mind; all things which exist are currently tending toward positions of balance or equilibrium. —Tansley

6. PHYSICAL LAWS

Recognize that the very molecules that make up your body, the atoms that construct the molecules, are traceable to the crucibles that were once the centers of high mass stars that exploded their chemically rich guts into the galaxy, enriching pristine gas clouds with the chemistry of life. So that we are all connected to each other biologically, to the Earth chemically and to the rest of the universe atomically. It's not that we are better than the universe, we are part of the universe. We are in the universe and the universe is in us. This universality of physical laws tells us that if we land on another planet with a thriving alien civilization, they will be running on the same laws that we have discovered and tested here on Earth—even if the aliens harbor different social and political beliefs. —Neil deGrasse Tyson

The Physical universe has Laws that describe and define how the Physical world operates. The explanation and understanding of these Laws may alter or deepen over time, yet the Laws themselves do not change. They are immutable as well as universal. These Laws reflect the principles of how the mysteries of Physical life unfolds. Examples of universal Laws on the Physical plane follow: We only digest certain foods. We have to eat, or we will die. We live within a certain temperature range to maintain our body. Requiring a specific amount of humidity in the air is essential. The air must have a specific chemical composition to enable us to breathe. A certain amount of sleep, and specific portions of liquid are necessary to stay alive. To survive on this earth we have and have had basic human needs: oxygen, water, food, shelter and sleep. After fifteen minutes without oxygen the brain damage becomes irreversible. It's estimated the without water for more than 4 days the possibilities for survival are slim to none. The destruction of form so that life progresses is one of the fundamental methods of evolution. These are factors on the Physical plane.

We live in a universe that functions by laws; predictable, repeatable, under-standable laws. Natural laws is the uniform and orderly method of energy. You can act in accordance with these laws, or you can disregard them, but you can in no way alter them. The laws forever operate and hold you to strict accountability, and there is not the slightest allowance for ignorance. Once a person learns and obeys these laws, he will get rich with mathematical cer-tainty. The foundation for clarity is that: All laws fall under one great law namely 'Energy is.'—Wallace Wattles

ENERGY

The power and beauty of physical laws is that they apply everywhere, whether or not you choose to believe in them. —Neil deGrasse Tyson

Our love and attention must be placed in the body as well as in the heart and spirit. The inner body which lies buried within the impermanent limited aging body connects us to the eternal present. The energy field within the body anchors us once we learn to hold our attention. To be rooted inside the body while remaining aware of our surroundings and present to our thoughts so that nothing can toss us away is a powerful practice. There is a Japanese phrase *ne aka, ne kura*. Bright root, dark root. To find yourself at the root of everything, to know that brightness and darkness at their root are the same, we become like a mountain, strong and stable regardless to seasonal change, regardless to a battering by the wind and rain, the rock-hard interior remains stable and calm.

All things and forces are in a powerful and dynamic relationship. When we each take responsibility to sustain the health of our own piece of the universe, then we are cooperating to sustain the health of the whole. —*Roger Jahnke*

Within the Physical plane energy moves through time and space. Energy contacts energy and creates reactions, responses and consequences. Modern quantum physics demonstrates that matter is actually vibrating energy. The spiritual world vibrates at a frequency not easily accessible to our Physical senses. The body not fixed or stable, in flux, is a flowing field of vibration and energy. The body is a place where above and below meet, where something shines through us that no longer has anything to do with us or any of our personal history once we choose to live in a state of presence. Forms are here with us and something beyond form is also present; the Physical Laws point to the limitations that are part of every form. To attune to earth's core energy, to inhabit the body, to know we are not separate from the world, to say yes to what is; now the presence we radiate causes everything to radiate presence.

Everything in existence is crying out for a particular quality of consciousness that only humans can give, reflected Peter Kingsley. Paying attention to Physical Laws, knowing how to use them, how to open to our senses, to use the Laws, the body, the senses consciously, rather than be used by them, is a study and an art. Consciousness as an act of service is to embody love and understanding for the world. To learn and know the Physical Laws provides beauty and harmony in our lives when we use them in the highest manner.

If all mankind were to disappear, the world would regenerate back to the rich state of equilibrium that existed 10,000 years ago. If insects were to vanish, the environment would collapse into chaos. —E.O. Wilson

MIND AND BODY

The Physical world is the world of personality. Since there is a definite relationship between mind and body, negative dark states of the mind change the chemistry of the cells in the body. A good state makes good food for all the cells of the body and helps us work with the Law that speaks to impermanence: that our Physical body wears out.

Humanity represents the stage of the Earth's unfoldment at which the planetary soul becomes not only self-aware but functionally and creatively conscious of the processes through which growth, awareness, and the exteriorization of spirit through form takes place. —The Findhorn Community

Mindfulness, paying attention, bringing our consciousness into each activity, whether eating, breathing or drinking, maintains our rootedness. Once we connect our inner body to presence we have access to a formless place. Walking along this bridge carries us across and into the realm of Physical Laws. There is one truth for the world of spirit, there is one science based on the unity of Physical Laws for all of humanity. The Laws can be studied by observing them in ourself, to gain freedom from the Laws, knowledge and study is necessary so as not to create another Law in its place.

The universe is immense and gorgeous and magnificent. I salute it. Every speck, every little fly on the window salutes the universe. Every leaf has meaning. In the physical body in which we are, in the life which we are involved, we can all add our share of love without leaving the room. —Helen Nearing

7 . G R A V I T Y

In the school I went to, they asked a kid to prove the law of gravity and he threw the teacher out of the window. —Rodney Dangerfield

*I*f people were oblivious to the law of Gravity and always surprised by its effect they would have little understanding of life on earth as we know it. We are subject to the law of Gravity and respect it whether we believe in it, like it, or understand how it works. Otherwise we would be driving off a cliff, jumping from high buildings, and surprised with each object as it falls. The law of Gravity could be superseded, we could use the law of aerodynamic lift to overcome Gravity and still the gravitational attraction between the Earth and objects will continue to pull them towards the ground. The law of Gravity works for everyone. We do not need a vast knowledge of the laws of physics to understand how Gravity works. We know that if we step off a high balcony we will fall. We also experience that if we align ourselves with this law correctly, there is greater ease.

Scientists speaking about the law of gravity tell us that the fastest animal on earth with a top speed of 120ft/sec, is a cow that has been dropped out of a helicopter. —Dave Barry

The universal law of Gravity is one of the physical laws that govern earth. Gravity is a mathematical formulation applied throughout the universe. Newton understood that the same Gravity that caused an apple to fall held the moon in its orbit. Comparing the acceleration of an apple falling from a tree to that of the moon's orbit led to a simple conclusion regarding the nature of Gravity and the forces of the entire universe. Everything attracts with the same gravitational force. Discovering the law of Gravity, a fundamental constant in nature, Newton extended the understanding of Gravity beyond earth. Newton did not create the law but simply discovered that which had already existed universally, by itself. Newton's explanation of the law of Gravity serves to create a formula of calculation for all movement.

When asked about which scientist he'd like to meet, Neil deGrasse Tyson said, 'Isaac Newton. No question about it. The smartest person ever to walk the face of this earth. The man was connected to the universe in spooky ways. He discovered the laws of motion, the laws of gravity, the laws of optics. Then he turned 26'. —Neil deGrasse Tyson

The universe is always in motion, it is a vibrating, pulsating, resonating, magnetizing force; at the molecular level everything is in motion. It is pure energy. We are an electromagnetic force field, sending out a frequency of vibrations which magnetize and connect with energy waves. The impartial flow of substance, how we tap into a stream of consciousness with thoughts, determination; the pure formless substance of the universe is the source of everything. It awaits our recognition and will create, attract, magnetize and mold itself to whatever form we desire, once we align with it through universal laws. Gravity as a force exists when length, breadth and height are structured, it can only exist if time does, therefore it works on our body more than it works on atoms. Particles don't know time, whereas our atomic structure is conditioned by our thinking, for example, we can decide to change our shape from thin to fat. We are not a constant.

If I have seen further it is only by standing on the shoulder of giants. I can calculate the motions of the heavenly bodies, but not the madness of people. —Isaac Newton

Gravity works best out of third dimensional consciousness. Consciousness arrives at truth first, then science follows and makes sense of consciousness. Gravitation is powerless to exhibit the property of weight in a perfected yogi as he/she materialize and dematerialize their bodies and other objects moving with the velocity of light while utilizing creative light rays bringing instant visibility into physical manifestation. The yogi demonstrates consciousness freed from three dimensions of space as well as the fourth dimension of time. Certain awakened beings can transfer their body of light with ease through the light rays of earth, water, and air. As we raise our consciousness we free ourselves from certain laws.

GRAVITATIONAL FORCE

In swimming at my level it's about control of the small movements. A good ballet dancer floats across the stage, the best sprinters virtually abolish gravity. All motion occurs in the right direction. —Alexander Dale Oen

The laws of the universe serve as a useful tool for self-study. We understand the structure of our own psychology by understanding how the law of Gravity effects us. Just as the compelling force of attraction holds our solar system, holds our planets to revolve around the sun, it holds the lesser systems of atomic and molecular matter circulating around a center in the planet and that of the subtle bodies coordinated around their microscopic center. This is a primary law. To use the law of Gravity for self-study we look at how Gravity expresses itself in our own orbit. Gravity is in us as well as outside us, and as well as a cosmological significance it has a psychological and spiritual significance. To understand that freedom is not through struggle or resistance, to circumnavigate the ego is to surrender—and laws like Gravity are a reminder that we are not in control. To understand the laws, to pay attention, *to chop wood and carry water*; this is the way.

If you look more deeply you will see that in just five or six days, the rose will become part of the garbage. You do not need to wait five days to see it. If you look at the rose, and you look deeply, you can see it now. And if you looked into the garbage can, you see that in a few months its contents can be transformed into lovely vegetables, and even a rose. If you are a good organic gardener and you have the eyes of a Bodhisattva, looking at a rose you can see the garbage, and looking at the garbage you can see a rose. Roses and garbage inter-are. Without a rose, we cannot have garbage; and without garbage, we cannot have a rose. They need each other very much. The rose and garbage are equal. The garbage is just as precious as the rose. If we look deeply at the concepts of defilement and immaculateness, we return to the notion of interbeing. —*Thich Nhat Hahn*

A magnetic center, its function being to attract teachings, since Gravity always attracts, speaks to a person's center of Gravity which draws either mechanical impulses or esoteric information. We are a corresponding reflection of what's above therefore Gravity acts on us psychologically. Creating something in ourself that resists Gravity we isolate from the effects of life on us—not from life itself. The Gravitational force of the moon influences the ocean tides as well as the earth and people's psychology. The moon, as a permanent center of Gravity, balances our physical life. As we develop and make something in ourselves that resists influences, we create a conscious center of Gravity, which brings us to a new level. The law of Gravity, a formula used for calculation, affects humanity through planetary influences. We are capable of incorporating the principles of Gravity when we are in possession of a permanent center of Gravity, and then we are able to determine the direction we are traveling.

I do not know what I may appear to the world, but to myself I seem to have been only like a boy playing on the sea-shore, and diverting myself in now and then finding a smoother pebble or a prettier shell than ordinary, whilst the great ocean of truth lay all undiscovered before me. —Sir Isaac Newton

8. RECIPROCAL MAINTENANCE LADDER THEORY

In the system of reciprocal maintenance the universe fulfills its destiny. —J.G. Bennett

Reciprocal exchange maintains all organic and inorganic matter for the universe to proceed and fulfill its destiny. The universe operates through dynamic exchange, nothing stands still. The Reciprocal feeding of everything that exists happens in both organic and inorganic matter. Similarly, we create relationships that maintain Reciprocal agreements in order to sustain the motion and momentum of our journey. As a miniature universe our spiritual path mirrors that of the cosmos. A Ladder exists as we see earth and sky, day and night, a beautiful exchange that maintains our balance.

They know themselves; they know the Cosmos as well. —Khemetic saying

Life as an organic unity remains connected. We have an affinity with a flower and a dog, just as the flower and dog have an affinity to us. The illusion of separateness that allows division is unmasked in this law. With all things absorbing or serving, Reciprocal Maintenance allows the world to proceed. The imperfection of all things means that a borrowing happens, since incompleteness allows for evolution and involution. An ancient Buddhist and Navajo formula states that *the imperfection of all things is a prerequisite for their existence.* And so, for our own life, we look for moments to exchange with others, for this encourages our aliveness. Our liberation follows our union with all and everything. We collaborate and exchange in our common effort to strengthen and nourish ourselves. In our effort to awaken we refine our being.

The golden rule or the ethics of reciprocity is to love for humanity what you love for yourself; spread peace of goodness between yourselves. —Amina Elias

Through our life or death we contribute to the transformation of energy upon which the Reciprocal Maintenance of all existence depends. The law of Reciprocal Maintenance, as within so without, determines that our lives serve to maintain something considerable or negligible in the world. Universal laws are clear in all traditions, stated and restated in each generation, through each tradition, throughout the centuries, note the following:

Tsze-Kung asked, 'Is there one word which may serve as a rule of practice for all of one's life?' The Master said, 'Is not reciprocity such a word? What you do not want done to yourself, do not do to others.' —Kongfuzi

What is hateful to you, do not to your fellow man. That is the entire law; all the rest is commentary. —Hillel, Talmud

All things whatsoever ye would that men should do to you, do ye even so to them: for this is the Law and the Prophets. —Jesus of Nazareth

A LADDER OF RESPONSIBILITY

Compassion towards the suffering of humanity is the payment, from the cosmic drama there emerges the miraculous destiny of awakening, once we are willing to pay the price. The ocean of suffering is immense, yet when we turn around we also see land. The Dalai Lama translated the Bodhisattva's vow to say: *So long as space remains, so long as sentient beings remain, I will remain in order to help, in order to serve, in order to make my own contribution.* Universal teachings, liberation from bondage, compassion, seeing world suffering, we are here until all beings reach a place that is free of suffering. Dissolving the conditioning of the mind, Reciprocity is offered back to the world in service and responsibility, treating others with the understanding that we have been offered; for love and respect and manners flow both ways. What is given is returned.

From everyone who has been given much, much will be demanded; and from the one who has been entrusted with much, much will be asked.
—*Jesus Christ*

As a student has a teacher to ascend, a teacher has a student to ascend. Each is necessary for the other's evolution. And the law says that through the relation of teacher to pupil when the teacher rises the pupil also is lifted. This happens as influences energetically flow from above down and through one person and another, eventually out into life. The true teacher is an opening, one who has broken the barrier of separation and lives in friendship, not superiority. Good students make good teachers, good teachers make good students. Mutual responsibility. The teacher is an opening, student and teacher mutually interdependent; the teacher's sincerity reflects the students receptivity. The teacher imparts his or her consciousness as a Ladder of responsibility that creates an atmosphere and reflects back the determination of the student. Everything absorbs, we are all food and Reciprocal exchange is taking place in our organic and inorganic world, both transforming substances as well as receiving and transmitting vibrations. What passes through us results in a Ladder appearance. Everything absorbs as well as serves; Reciprocal exchange takes place in everything.

The teacher is the servant of the student's yearning and can only give as much as the student's yearning allows. —*Kabir Helminski*

To sit with somebody who is transparent enough so that the stillness comes through unhindered, there's a reciprocal movement in you because the presence of stillness suddenly recognizes itself. —Eckhart Tolle

9 . REDUCTION, LEVELS

Laws are the same everywhere. But they manifest themselves in a different, or at least, in not quite the same way on different planes of the Universe, that is, on different levels. —P.D. Ouspensky

When we awaken out of our identification with form, reality shifts. Awakening from the dream we call life, having sat in the cave we have known as the body, we experience the world as it really is. Recognition of another Level from a mindful recognition and place of understanding our experience, births consciousness, shifts our point of view. Although we can't alter the fact that circumstances create things to happen, seeing new, the meanings shift. Until we drop our illusions we project a world through our own imagination. The real world will function only as a screen and we project our dreams onto it, not seeing the real world. This is living in the world of maya, a mist or veil of ignorance of the self that comes between us and the Truth. Mind is illusion, not the world. The true world is not illusory, only the world created by the mind is illusion, and the distance between the two reveals the quality of an enlightened perspective.

Reality is simply the loss of ego. Destroy the ego by seeking its identity. It will automatically vanish and reality will shine forth by itself. This is the direct method. There is no greater mystery than this, that we keep seeking reality though in fact we are reality. We think there is something hiding our reality and that it must be destroyed before reality is gained. How ridiculous! A day will dawn when you will laugh at all your past efforts. That which will be on the last day you laugh is also here and now. —Ramana Maharshi

We transform energies from a lower to a higher Level, which serves the universe. Raising the Level of energy, transmuting it into something higher, we become more than a mechanical generator of energy. This becomes the charge, the meaning behind evolution: through consciousness we see the world as it is. Our Level of being is dependent upon our Level of consciousness, and that is dependent upon the highest Level of energy we transmute. All the Levels co-exist, interdependently. To sacrifice who and what we think we are, our illusions, makes it possible to enter a new Level. Being adaptive to a higher frequency; tuning in to it transforms us while the acceleration curve goes vertical.

Nothing in the world can bother you as much as your own mind. I tell you a fact, others seem to be bothering you but it is not others, it is your own mind. —Sri Sri Ravi Shankar

Whatever blinds us is less important than that there is a barrier between awareness and sleep. Asleep, yet turning in our sleep is a beginning. Preparing the ground to move to a new Level, to increase the quantity and quality of seeing continues until becoming eyes with our whole being. People struggle to tear each other from one set of illusions and focus them instead on another set of illusions. What influences the material world is the perception, the seeing of the world differently, from a conscious Level. These visions, have brought something unnameable into life that has effected humanity throughout the ages.

When a person musters the strength and overcomes his obstacles, continuously progressing higher and higher according to his level, he is actually benefiting another person who was on the higher level that he is now entering, because the other person must now rise to a higher level, since two people cannot be on the same level. —Rebbe Nachman

The world is like a dream, but how will we know that we are in a dream if we do not wake up the next morning! Until we wake up we won't know we are asleep. Our consciousness creates the world we inhabit. In *The Republic*, the myth of the cave, the shadows of the wall create a compelling image of everyday life. The cave speaks to different Levels of awareness and understanding. Imagine prisoners who have been chained deep inside a cave for all of their lives. They face a wall in the cave and can never look at the entrance of the cave. Whatever passes the entrance casts a shadow on the wall inside the cave and the prisoners see the shadows on the wall mistakenly viewing the shadows as reality. However, one man breaks free from his chains and leaves the cave seeing the real world. Returning he tells the prisoners, what is outside the cave, about the light, yet they don't believe him. To them the shadows are reality and the escaped prisoner is a madman. When the prisoners are released from the *chains of illusion,* they turn their heads to see the real objects instead of the world of delusion where they had lived. To unchain ourselves from shadowy illusions and surmount the barrier separating ourself from the sunlight of reality, to purge ourself of self-interest and wrong thinking we first must unchain ourself. This steep and rugged ascent from ignorance to true knowledge is an exhausting journey of searching and working on ourself.

We can never understand the being of a man who is on a higher level than our own—A.R. Orage.

Plato's myth is a reminder of where we came from, who we are, and where we are going. Myths preserve memories for those times when we forget our inner vision. The laws are here and as we learn to understand them we give birth to what we carry hidden inside us, the spiritual foundation of our world. Plato teaches in his cave allegory: *the minds of the masses are filled with the shadows of the images.* Mistaking appearance for reality, people are directed by the image rather than the direct experience of reality. It is difficult to penetrate the light, reality can be blinding. And many believe their reality is the light, rather than the veil. It is said that *the threshold of reality is veiled by golden light.* We see according to our Level of consciousness.

Mind is indeed the source of bondage and also the source of liberation. To be bound to the things of this world: this is bondage. To be free from them: this is liberation. —Upanishads

If you correct your mind, the rest of your life will fall into place. —Lao Tzu

WITNESSING

Everything changes once we indentify with being the witness to the story, instead of the actor in it. —Ram Dass

The universal character of the trickster, the wise fool, the shape-shifter who lives between the Levels, where there are no boundaries to reality, carries teaching stories, which are a link to truth. The everyday perceptions used as a reflective surface contain hidden meanings, communicate higher learning and echo Plato's cave. Nothing is as it seems, as one awakens to a new Level of reality. Behind the words of the stories lies our true self. Nasrudin, wise in his foolishness and foolish in his wisdom, has inherited and carried the tradition as a legendary figure able to instruct from his ordinary realm. One such story has Nasrudin enjoying walking into town as his son rides a donkey. People passing by comment, *look at the poor man walking while the strong child rides, the youth of today have poor values.* To make the correction Nasrudin exchanges places, now riding, until people passing by comment, *look at that selfish man riding a donkey while his son walks in the hot sun.* So the two get on the donkey and ride together until people passing by comment, *that poor donkey has to carry the weight of two.* They both get off and decide to walk beside the donkey. Soon people pass, commenting, *look at those fools, both of them walking under the hot sun, with no one riding the donkey.* Nasrudin says to his son, *this shows us how difficult it is to adjust to other people's opinions.* One ending has Nasrudin riding his donkey while facing backwards still arriving at his intended destination ridiculing our assumptions; life is a predicament, sometimes backwards, at times upside down. Absurd and ridiculous as life is shown to be, once understood it becomes miraculous; certainly we are here to awaken from our illusion of our separateness.

We do not see things as they are. We see them as we are. —*Talmud*

Cassandra, in Greek mythology, daughter of the King of Troy, given the gift of prophecy, the knowledge of future events, was additionally cursed with a warning that no one would believe her warnings, her predictions. In our time Elie Wiesel, in a like manner, writes about Moishe the Beadle, caretaker of the Hasidic shteibel, the house of prayer, who in June 1941 expelled as a Jew from his small town in Sighet, Romania, crammed into a cattle car, was taken to Poland. He describes how the train was overtaken by the Gestapo, the German secret police as it arrived into Poland. Brought to the forest, forced to dig pits, he saw Jews shot and dropped into graves, children thrown alive into fires, women, children murdered; miraculously he was taken for dead, and escaped his fate. Eluding death, he saw as a sign to return to his hometown and warn the Jews of the impending disaster; to save the Jews of Sighet. Telling the tales of what he had seen in Poland, the Jews of Sighet did not pay attention, could not comprehend, calling him a madman, making Moishe a significant disregarded witness. In March, 1944 the Germans invaded Sighet and the rest is history.

Do not stand idly by if you witness injustice. You must intervene. You must interfere. Never will I forget that night, the first night in camp, which has turned my life into one long night, seven times cursed and seven times sealed. Never shall I forget that smoke. Never shall I forget the faces of the little children, whose bodies I saw turned into wreaths of smoke beneath a silent blue sky. Never shall I forget those flames which consumed my faith forever. Never shall I forget that nocturnal silence, which deprived me, for all eternity, of the desire to live. Never shall I forget these things even if I am condemned to live as long as God himself. Never. —Elie Wiesel

LEVELS OF REALITY

Existence is everything that can be known, but it is not all that is real. —J. G. Bennett

The possibility of becoming conscious of our own existence, of uplifting ourselves is a higher Level for us to reach. As we leave the confines of the cave we come to experience the world as increasingly beyond ourselves and that experience nurtures selflessness and changes the way we look at the world. Awakening shows us how to look at the world of shadows in a different light, not to escape from this world, instead, to have a sense of transcendent possibility. To know the law of Levels is to empty ourself. The lower cannot see the higher. Just as a child does not grasp the life of an aged person, a young soul cannot see an old soul. The depth of our humility lies in understanding how many more dimensions exist other than what we are seeing. This opens the door to glimpse invisible worlds that exist.

People travel to wonder at the height of the mountain, at the huge waves of the seas, at the long course of the rivers, at the vast compass of the ocean, at the circular motion of the stars, and yet they pass by themselves without wondering. —Augustine of Hippo

On a practical level, in the physical world: the world of action, emanation, doing, named *assiyah*—on an emotional level, named *yetzirah*, in the world of feelings, world of formation—in the world of creation, understanding, the creative world named *briyah*, the intellectual plane in the world of infinite light, wisdom, *atzilut*, the closest to divinity, a brush with the mystery, these four worlds are always available to us to live into, to deepen our lives. The physical world, the emotional world, the intellectual world, the spiritual world—these four worlds or Levels of reality, reflect the understanding that existence is multilayered and in a state of dynamic flux. People tend to reduce everything to the Level they are on, interpreting from their own position. Laws are the same on every plane, although they manifest themselves in different ways on each Level. This is why true understanding is so difficult; associations, meanings, states of consciousness; within all of these differences lies room for misunderstanding.

Try for a moment to accept the idea that you are not what you believe yourself to be, that you overestimate yourself, in fact that you lie to yourself. That this lying rules you to such an extent that you cannot control it anymore. But you never stop yourself in what you are doing or in what you are saying because you believe in yourself. You must stop inwardly and observe. Observe without preconception, accepting for a time this idea of lying. And if you observe in this way, without self-pity, giving up all your supposed riches for a moment of reality, perhaps you will suddenly see something you have never before seen in yourself until this day. —G.I.Gurdjieff

The material world is influenced through our perceptions. The characteristics and status of a person might be noteworthy, achievements attained could be laudable, yet the being might be at a Level that is petty, vain and less than remarkable. Different Levels provide the polarity to give life its force, the more invisible we remain, the more that force penetrates our life. Harmonizing what seems irreconcilable heals the division and allows the expression of truth.

People living on the earth can belong to very different levels, although in appearance they look exactly the same. A man may be an able scientist, and at the same time he may be, and has the right to be, an envious, egoistic, mean, vain, and absent minded man. —*P. D. Ouspensky*

10. ACCIDENT

As long as the outer side or personality is active and takes the lead, you are under the law of accident, that is, anything, however meaningless, can happen to you. —*Maurice Nicoll*

*E*verything happens, living under the law of Accident. Things come about through association, sometimes through earlier efforts, other times, guesswork. Most of humanity, not present to their lives, reacting from personality, remain under the law of Accident. When the inner life takes place for no reason, random thoughts popping into the mind creating worries or smiles, things in the external life unexpectedly turn up. Accident means that something appears without a direct relation to actions. Most people find their meaning through a world that is externally presented, not through getting meaning from themselves. An incident happens with no apparent connection to the visible circumstance. Withdrawing from the scattered mind to live attentively deepens our awareness and intention, directing and guiding the mind we are less under the influence of this law. By strengthening our will we are liberated from the effects of Accident. Studying, learning about ourselves, becoming intentional, breaking habits, being in charge of ourselves, having some control over our thoughts, frees us from being directly impacted and living directly under the law of Accident.

The universe needs the Law of Accident because accident—change—unpredictability—is what creates possibility. And it appears to be a brilliant stroke of not only risk-taking, but intelligence: to create a universe where radical new possibilities are realized through a remarkably strict structural order which nonetheless incorporates an inherent unpredictability. Humans find themselves in a universe with an essential randomness at the very heart of the machine—the quantum state—from which all observable levels of order inevitably emerge. —Lee van Laer

The events that take place under the law of Accident are caused in the present moment. I am in a super market, a man bumps into me, rushes ahead and out the door. I fall and break my hip. He leaves the store and I never see him again, although my year is filled with mementos of the occasion. Surgery, wheelchair, cane, physical therapy; one moment elongated into many sequences. This type of incident, with no past, and whose cause is in the present moment, is called *Accident*.

A man has not sufficient will to do, that is to control himself and all his actions, but he has sufficient will to obey another person. And only in this way can he escape from the law of accident. There is no other way. He may meet another man who knows the way and who is connected directly or through other people with a centre existing outside the law of accident. —P.D. Ouspensky

Our being, which is under certain laws and is a mix of personality and essence attracts the life that we live. As personality and false personality is quieted and essence grows we are no longer directly effected and living under the law of Accident. Driven by outer circumstances called life, we don't realize that we could actually live in a different way. The continual reactions of false personality that have power over us confine us to live under the law of Accident. The more reactive we are the more we are influenced by the law of Accident, which means that anything can happen; our intuition and sensing before hand is compromised.

You will continue to suffer if you have an emotional reaction to everything that is said to you. True power is sitting and observing everything with logic. True power is restraint. If words control you that means that everyone else can control you. Breathe and allow things to pass. —Pinterest

Imitating others, living out of ego we put ourselves in situations that don't belong to us, are Accidental. We might get arrested hanging out with friends who are doing drugs, ride in a car with a driver who's been drinking and be in a collision, or running after a moving bus and slipping we are injured, take a gambling risk on stocks or at a casino and lose a significant amount of money, or take a dare to dive off a board and break our neck; meaningless situations that alter our daily and future life. Our thoughts roam around in our head and at times become obsessive or negative, our emotions get jostled by other peoples opinions and comments, our feelings are played with by sentimental movies and flattering or unflattering comments, regardless, we are barely in charge. We are at the mercy of Accidental remarks and incidents. On the other hand, under the law of Accident we might survive a horrendous experience randomly getting into the wrong subway, avoiding a holdup, or miss getting on a flight of an airplane that is hijacked or goes down in a storm. There are stories of people who had a flat tire and missed getting to work at the World Trade Center on the day that it was bombed. New Age communities have sayings and slogans that misrepresent the law of Accident by presuming that when a lucky random *accident* appears there are *angels* or *consciousness* involved, although when a misfortunate *accident* happens that's treated differently. Both are equal, both Accidental from a lack of self-awareness and part of a scheme of a life lived primarily directed and influenced from the outside.

Watchfulness is the vital need, for he who does not watch is soon over-whelmed. The sternman need only sleep a moment and the vessel is lost.
—*Epictetus*

The important events that happen to those living under this law are Accidental; meeting a partner or friend by chance, winning a lottery or inheriting a fortune, great looks, contracting hepatitis, being hit by a car, buying property and the value inflating or deflating to make or lose money, meeting a spiritual teacher or visiting an ashram, and so on. Rarely, if ever, will this person stay with spiritual or inner work—since an Accident brought them to a teacher, so will Accidental circumstances take them away from remaining at a community or holding steadfast in their dedication to their own inner work.

EASING FREE FROM LAW OF ACCIDENT

As you open your awareness, life will improve of itself, you won't even have to try. It's a beautiful paradox; the more you open your consciousness, the fewer unpleasant events intrude themselves into your awareness. —*Thaddeus Golas*

The law of Accident is a law of world 48. Personality is under the law of the earth, the law of Accident, forty-eight orders of laws. False personality is also under the law of Accident, and the moon, ninety-six orders of laws. To be under this law one lives with a narrow conscious-ness, which applies to mechanical person number one, two, three (refer to system 21, Being). Most of humanity lives under the law of Accident as well as under two types of influences also ruled by Accident. The first influence is life itself which creates circumstances: country, climate, family, society, profession, finances, politics of the time. The second are conscious influences imprinted to us through evolved beings, sources and artifacts: like Buddha, the Dalai Lama, Ammachi, Jesus, the Torah,

Rembrandt, Vivaldi, Tibetan bowls.

Old soul awakened beings imprint the culture and generations are affected for no reason other than being born at times that are impacted by a particular energy. Intermingled in the daily fabric of living life, expressed in teachings through art, music, poetry, religion, eventually watered down, falling under the law of Accident, this, then mechanically imprints cultures and future populations. Sometimes we respond, sometimes we don't. The ability to use these influences is relative to our understanding and capacity to discriminate.

Inner growth, a change of being, depends entirely upon the work which a person must do on himself. —G.I. Gurdjieff

To be under the law of Accident is to allow the meaning of our life to be external. We feel happy because we have a good job, angry when we are fired, depressed when a date turns us down, proud when we are invited to join a prestigious group, important when someone publicly dedicates a song to us, bad when our speech receives a poor review, neglected when our parents forget our birthday, delighted when people clap because they like our appearance, yet shamed if they stare and disapprove. Our sense of ourself and the meaning of who we are rests on externals, being driven by life and placed under the law of Accident. Until we receive meaning from ourselves life is precarious and anything can happen.

If part of our body is wounded and we must walk through a jostling crowd, we shall be especially careful to guard and cover that wound. In a similar manner, when we are dwelling amongst harmful people or objects that cause our delusions to arise, we should guard the wound of our mind carefully. If we are anxious to protect an ordinary wound that can at most give us but a little temporary pain, then surely we should be highly motivated to guard the wound of our mind. If our mind remains unprotected and uncontrolled, it can lead us into hellish experiences of deep suffering and torment until we feel we are being crushed between two mighty mountains. —Shantideva

Self-study, inner work, recognition with a desire to change moves us away from the influence and the effects of the law of Accident. Our thoughts and external circumstances, randomly occurring, distractions predominate our ordinary life; and then we become strongly impacted by the law of Accident. Sometimes the events are beneficial, sometimes detrimental. Under the law of Accident we have little to do with the cause of the thought or circumstance. Much of what happens under this law has little to do with us, who we are or our nature, bringing a quality of meaninglessness to our life. Accidents are not foreseen. As inner Accidents are reigned in, reactions diminished, external Accidents become less frequent.

The outward work will never be puny if the inward work is great. —Meister Eckhart

Living life under the law of Accident produces victimhood and feelings of emptiness, we become reactive rather than proactive, and have a diminished sense of personal responsibility. A society that lives under the law of Accident has high crime rates, full prisons, road rage, liability litigation, and poor workplace performance. What appears as an unjust circumstance for one person may be, in fact, a beneficial gain for another. Living in unconsciousness everything is Accidental. When we are mindful life takes on a new meaning. Incidents in ordinary life happen mechanically. Thoughts, the inner life is as much randomly affected by circumstances as are the circumstances; there is no reason in them, and while we think Accidents are rare the opposite is true. Accidents are commonplace. To change this we need to take control of ourselves—our reactions, our emotions, our thoughts, our habits, our eating, our body;

then we avoid certain influences. As we study ourselves the relation to the law of Accident changes, *we* fill the space.

There is only one meditation—the rigorous refusal to harbor thoughts. To be free from thoughts is itself meditation. —Nisargadatta

To make a commitment to self-study, to break free from this law, things begin to happen, both great and sometimes unpleasant which now really do belong to us. This points the way to recognize what is arbitrary, what is intentional, to see when we are slacking off or becoming lazy, careless or mechanical. When difficulties ease we feel a deep satisfaction. Finding someone who lives outside the law of Accident, gradually accidents practically disappear.

It is the very nature of things that they must pass away, but the Truth will always remain. —Buddha

Although our life is shaped around existing bureacratic structures, forming a stable magnetic center serves to guide us towards higher possiblities (System 19, Magnetic Center). When the magnetic center builds enough force one looks for a Way, even drawing in like minded people and a teacher. At this time one may be freed from the law of Accident and effected by a third influence—oral transmission. Finding and choosing a Way, possibly the Fifth Way, *The Way of the Lover,* loosens the hold this law has on us. Eventually we shift to living under the law of cause and effect; subsequently, as we awaken we move to live under the law of fate and destiny. To act out of our consciousness, not living unconsciously, is the step out from under the power of the law of Accident.

Accidents need space and time. The more our time is occupied with conscious work the less room will be left for accidental happenings. We can mould the law of accident only by moulding ourselves. Work on ourself, occupying a big place in your life creates balance and eventually dispenses with accident.

When inner accidents stop in us, it will make us more free from external accidents. Things happen in human life according to the following laws: The law of accident, the law of cause and effect, the laws of fate and destiny, the law of karma and the law of will. —*P.D. Ouspensky*

11. CAUSE AND EFFECT
EFFECT AND CAUSE

Every cause has its effect; every effect has its cause; everything happens according to law; chance is but a name for law not recognized; there are many planes of causation, but nothing escapes the law. —*Hermes Trismegistus*

*L*ife is a causal link. Wherever we start, Cause or Effect, all will follow. We create an Effect a Cause evolves, we initiate a Cause and the Effect follows. To create intentional Causes in our life allows the law of accident to loosen its hold, now results have less possibility for accident. When there are seeds there will be trees. Where there are trees there have been seeds. What happens is connected to a previous action. Every thought we think, each action taken, the choices made allow for new Effects that continuously shape and alter our life. This, too, is a reflection of the entire universe—as the world is always dynamically changing and Effected, so are we.

The reasons are not necessarily the answer. Since the cause is the effect of its own effect. —*Reshad Feild*

What Effects us also Causes change. Something happens because of the action taken. This is the chain—create the Cause or create the Effect. Once we create the Cause, the Effect will eventually happen. Five days a week we drive over the speed limit through a small town. On the fifteenth week we are stopped and fined for speeding. Getting caught has little to do with the activity of the fifteenth week. Eventually we are bound to get caught, and so it is the result of the 75 times and fifteen weeks that went before. Cause is followed by Effect, and we invite it towards ourself; the Effect is within. Once we choose to be intentional we create the Effect, and the Cause will follow. Choose to learn and see what happens, choose to be happy and a new world opens. To change the way we frame our life, seeing obstacles as clues to what business we are here to finish, to meet challenges and difficulties with appreciation and kindness; by choosing the Effect, the Cause follows. Inner peace and happiness, the result: everything follows. Begin anywhere—create the Cause or create the Effect. Effect is within us—Cause surrounds us, they follow each other.

The source is within you. And this whole world is springing up to it. —*Rumi*

No longer dependent on the law of accident for the essential and important events of our personal life, the meaningful events of our life are the result of a previous action. The law of Cause and Effect is an intermediary step, one of the stages, a different level as we develop from the law of accident towards the law of will. At this new level we are learning to control our thoughts, actions, states of consciousness; to guide ourself in a direction that will not be accidental. This may be a long slow process, an escape route, impossible for the ordinary person who is incapable of reliability and constancy, who gets waylaid and diverted by *things not working*, by coincidences, mental formulations and challenges. Once the center of gravity of our life becomes the desire to awaken there is little room left for accidents to fill the occupied space; a freedom from most accidents arrives. Direction becomes foremost, and we are released from having puppet strings pulled by each of our distractions, entertainments and fascinations.

CREATING OUR WORLD

In this world, which we call the 'world of appearances,' we can see that there is something called 'cause and effect' because it is necessary that there is a mirror in which we see ourselves. We see cause and effect as happening here in this world, and yet: 'There is no creation in the relative world, there is only the becoming of being'. Thus Ibn' Arabi tells us that 'the cause is the effect of its own effect.' As long as we find ourselves limited by linear and rational thinking we do not come to the true nature of our being.
—Reshad Feild

Inherent in this law is the realization that once we set our intention, with time the garden will grow. We begin by having choice over inner accidents. Effect is within us, and in fact is us. Thoughts are as we image ourself to be. Thoughts are real and they have an Effect on the energy that permeates and makes up all life in our universe. The thoughts that we think are vibrations, that are attracted to and joined with like vibrations which create what we have come to know and see in our physical world as our current reality, is called *our life*. Thought is Cause and Effect in its manifest likeness. If we plant seeds of corn, we will harvest corn, not watermelon. Watering seeds of love, compassion and happiness, creates a beautiful world.

Everything we do is sowing, and all of our experiences are harvests.
—Khemetic saying

Choose to be joyful, to love, and then watch what happens. What we plant might be harvested by someone else in a far off moment. The illusion of separateness once dissolved allows us to not expect results. There are seven dimensions of reality in which Causation occurs. When we cultivate service something gets built and eventually manifests in the spiritual dimension. Through choosing an Effect, like, to choose to be happy, we create the Effect to surround us. We see happiness by making the Cause follow. The Effect is within. The connection between Cause and Effect, often a mystery, appears because Cause and Effect are on different levels.

If you plant turnips you will not harvest grapes. —Akan (West African) saying

We cannot change the law, yet we can free ourself through changing the present, through the present the future and through the future the past. Since today is the result of the past, this day can change the past. One obvious way is by coming back, yet another is through paying off obligations and debts. To see everything as literal Cause and Effect, makes transforming life impossible. Transformation happens through being under different sets of influences. Life is not literally as we see it. Once we make the significant events in our life happen through our own efforts, we are freed up from the law of accident and are moved, influenced, living under the law of Cause and Effect.

Our life is shaped by our mind; we become what we think. Suffering follows an evil thought as the wheels of a cart follow the oxen that draws it. Joy follows a pure thought like a shadow that never leaves. —The Dhammapada

1 2 .   K A R M A

As the blazing fire reduces wood to ashes, similarly the fire of Self-knowledge reduces all karma to ashes. —The Bhagavad Gita

This is the residue of the acts and the fruits of our actions and every aspect of life is effected. Karma is the tangle of cause and effect that we establish in ourself by our actions. It is what we are identified with when we die, it's thought to influence the conditions of the next life. The word Karma, from the Sanskrit root *Kri*, literally means to do, an action, a deed. What *we sow is what we reap* expresses this law, indicating that our actions generate energetic force. We think sowing and reaping are essentially different and fail to understand, they are the same. Karma is the currency of our life, with it we buy as well as create all life experience, which includes fun, suffering, happy, interesting and sorrowful moments. Every action, the careless carefree ones, spontaneous sexual encounters, random impulses, angry words, thoughtless decisions, poor financial dealings, pleasant or unpleasant they all have consequences and bring about a chain of results. The immediacy of our actions resonates in our heart.

When we respond to life consciously, thoughtfully, intentionally, without identifying, we change our Karma, which is the line of personal cause and effect in our life created by our actions. Life itself is not the teacher, it's our relationship to it that brings meaning; when we are in a Karmic circumstance how we behave towards it may not change the situation, instead, we have the possibility to change how we look at, understand and respond to the circumstance.

This Law of Karma—whether conscious or unconscious—predestines nothing and no one. It exists from and in eternity, truly, for it is eternity itself; and as such, since no act can be co-equal with eternity, it cannot be said to act, for it is action itself: karma creates nothing, nor does it design. It is man who plans and creates causes, and karmic law adjusts the effects; which adjustment is not an act, but universal harmony tending ever to resume its original position. —Helena Blavatsky

The law of Karma is the moral equivalent of cosmic evolution, which is the tendency of the interconnected universe towards balance. Learning to take action with intention and awareness we change our Karma. To meet pleasant experiences with the same breath as we greet unpleasant ones allows life to be the teacher; this transforms the meaning of life and makes our purpose here become visible to ourself.

Because the self that is identified with any form is an illusion, this looking beyond form brings us under the law of our fate which is a deeper cause and effect. As we mature our essence we change our fate and start to move under the law of will. The aphorism: *substitute intentional doing for accidental happening* loosens us from the law of Karma as well as easing us away from the law of accident. We begin under the law of accident, move to the law of cause and effect, then Karma, then fate and destiny, ultimately to live under the law of will.

The law of karma is an impersonal energy dynamic. When its effects are personalized, that is, experienced from the point of view of the personality, they are experienced as a reversal in the direction, a coming back to the intender, of the energy of his or her intention. The person who intends hatred for others experiences the intention of hatred from others. The person who intends love for others experiences the intention of love from others, and so forth. The Golden Rule is a behavioral guide that is based upon the dynamic of karma. A personalized statement of karma would be: you receive from the world what you give to the world. —Gary Zukav

LIVING IN AWARENESS

There are three aspects to Karma. The first is the accumulation of our past lives. Every event, reaction, desire, missed opportunity, achievement, thought and feeling make up the first aspect of Karma. It is the everything; all thoughts as well as activities that did or did not happen, yet were felt, desired or feared. The second part of Karma is what actually gets worked out in this lifetime, specific parts of our Karma that will get cleared. A portion of our Karma is passed through, lived out, realized in this lifespan of possibly eighty to ninety years or more. The third aspect is a continuation of the second just a smaller portion chosen to be cleared in this lifetime, small enough to be handled in our day-to-day living. Someone pushes in front of you in the movie line, or cuts you off on the highway and you yell or react in some way, our reactions continue this large reservoir, the one with full accumulation. Creating a witness, choosing a new creative posture, eventually eliminating reactions we discover what is important, what is the reason for our life, our purpose. Reactions blur the truth, allow us to think that the circumstances, that life itself is the object. Not reacting, some minute piece of Karma is fulfilled.

The third aspect, in the moment day-to-day Karma, is present moment transformation that ultimately completes and depletes the reservoir of Karma. In this third part we open to life as a teaching with a willingness to be where we are, with love and understanding. Allowing the meaning and purpose of existence to unfold, our awareness diminishes our Karma. Living mindfully drains the reservoir of Karma, living unconsciously the reservoir fills as new accounts are added. Our enslavement to the past continues in the present moment based on our senseless oblivious behavior. All mindless action add to our Karma account; they are reactions—only mindful acts done with awareness are responses that will diminish our Karmic bank account.

Any work, any action, any thought that produces an effect is called a karma. Thus the law of karma means the law of causation, of inevitable cause and sequence. Wheresoever there is a cause, there an effect must be produced; this necessity cannot be resisted, and this law of karma, according to our philosophy, is true throughout the universe. Whatever we see, or feel, or do, whatever action there is anywhere in the universe, while being the effect of past work on the one hand, becomes, on the other, a cause in its turn, and produces its own effect. Every thought we think, every deed we do, after a certain time becomes fine, goes into seed form, so to speak, and lives in the fine body in a potential form, and after a time it emerges again and bears its results. These results condition the life of man. Thus he molds his own life. Our thoughts, our words and deeds are the threads of the net which we

throw around ourselves for good or evil. Once we set in motion a certain power, we have to take the full consequences of it. This is the law of karma.
—*Vivekananda*

In Buddhist teaching the law of Karma places the responsibility for unskillful actions, which are events that are intended to have a negative effect on the person who commits them. An unskillful event is accompanied by craving, resistance or delusions, while a skillful event is a pure and present moment. Situations are not skillful in themselves rather they resonate the mental events that occur along with them. Your Karma is intimately connected to your motivation. Living without reacting and completing right intentions eventually frees us from our Karma. Bondage, on the other hand lies in living unaware, what we do when we are unaware is not an action, it is a reaction and creates Karma. When we live in mindful self-awareness our actions have completion, wholeness, and leave no trace, the second part of our Karma, daily, moment by moment, goes away as the reservoir begins to empty.

THE WHEEL OF KARMA

Every time we communicate we either produce more compassion, love, and harmony or we produce more suffering and violence. Our communication is what we put out into the world and what remains after we have left it. In this way, our communication is our karma. The Sanskrit word 'karma' means 'action,' and it refers not just to bodily action but to what we express with our bodies, our words, and our thoughts and intentions. Throughout our day, we produce energies of thought, speech, and action. You are your action. Karma is the triple action of our thoughts, our speech, and our bodily action. —*Thich Nhat Hahn*

Karma relies heavily on action; past actions influence consequences affecting our position and progression in life. To be one with knowledge we pass through the wheel of Karma. The work we do as well as the attitude with which we go about it are currency; making a personal decision to love and to learn within our employed work strengthens the meaningful value of monetary payment. Karma-yoga as a science of action with non-identification is about meeting pleasant and unpleasant situations similarly. In this way life becomes the teacher and its meaning and quality allows life to become a screen, an exercise used for glimpses of what is real. Acting without emotional attachments to the fruits of our deeds, detached from the consequences we lose the idea of control over an outcome. Peaceful living brings us to live harmoniously as a way of life. To not have expectations or motives or anticipation of an outcome gradually purifies our mind. When we create energy imbalance through violating someone's being, someone's space, Karma is established.

Situations seem to happen to people, but in reality they unfold from deeper karmic causes. The universe unfolds to itself, bringing to bear any cause that needs to be included. Don't take this process personally. The working out of cause and effect is eternal. You are part of this rising and falling that never ends, and only by riding the wave can you ensure that the waves don't drown you. The ego takes everything personally, leaving no room for higher guidance or purpose. If you can, realize that a cosmic plan is unfolding and appreciate the incredibly woven tapestry for what it is, a design of unparalleled marvel. —Deepak Chopra

REDESIGNING OUR INHERITANCE

Observing self uncritically allows us to shift from the customary habitual attitudes that deaden aliveness and perpetuate unnecessary suffering. Rather, to look at situations we are in Karmically, not to change the situation, instead to redesign the way we are, in the experience. Choosing a different attitude towards a circumstance may not change the situation itself yet it does alter the way we are so we can move out of our ordinary mechanical reactions, our conditioned self. Understanding and the willingness to work with universal laws brings us to live under the law of grace (a final law in this chapter) rather than accumulating Karma, which is restrictive.

I am the owner of my karma. I inherit my karma. I am born of my karma. I am related to my karma. I am supported by my karma. Whatever karma I create, whether good or evil, that I shall inherit. —the Buddha

There are times when personal challenges interrupt, become forefront in our daily life, and we become overwhelmed and unable to clear them. This is often self-Karma, and it manifests and is met differently from person to person. It could appear as personal issues regarding smoking, insomnia, gambling, alcohol, destructive relationships, weight issues, debt, bankruptcy, divorce; situations and experiences that create internal discord and disharmony. To resist, to try and obstruct or fight the challenge intensifies and stokes it. Rather to sit with it, study, dissect, find an objectivity or neutrality, to surrender to it gracefully, examine what surrounds and creates it allows for us to diffuse and use it as a learning as well as diminishing the negativity of the Karma and its impact on our life. There is the opportunity to realign and balance ourselves rather than act out or be swept into the vortex of our Karma; for us to evolve is to embrace and use our experiences towards learning and maturing, neutralizing their impact, softening and rebalancing the debt and our life.

Self-karma is caused by false self-limiting beliefs acquired in past experiences, either in past lives or earlier in the lifetime. This can result in a disease, for instance, that requires a righting of the internal imbalance in order to heal. —Shepherd Hoodwin

A contract between individuals can be karmic. It might be a doctor and patient, married couple, two friends, business partners, an aunt and a neice, a boy and his god-mother; each pair remaining together until the Karma is completed. The possibility of releasing the contract without having to manifest it physically happens through compassion, forgiveness and the law of grace. Desire is a strong chain that binds, for Karma is attracted where the magnet of the personal ego still exists. In action, without reaction, there is completion; Karma disappears. Master of your thoughts, freedom from reactive living loosens us from this law.

Karma neither punishes not rewards, it is simply the one Universal Law which guides accurately, and so to say, blindly, all other laws productive of certain effects along the grooves of their respective causations. It is not Karma that rewards or punishes, but it is we, who reward or punish ourselves according to whether we work with, through and along with nature, abiding by the laws on which that harmony spends, or—break them.
—*Helena Blavatsky*

13. FATE AND DESTINY

From birth to death, every person is weaving thread by thread around himself, as a spider does his cobweb, his destiny. When the last strand is woven, and we are seemingly enwrapped in the net-work of our own doing, then we find ourself completely under the empire of this self-made destiny. It then either fixes us like the inert shell against the immovable rock, or carries us away like a feather in a whirlwind raised by our own actions, and this is karma. —*Helena Blavatsky*

Fate and Destiny include birth, death and planetary influences, all circumstances that occur before we create causes. The planetary influences which control Fate, like our type and essence, effect us only after we weaken our personality. The cause of my Fate exists in eternity, not in the present, and exists as my Fate. To live under the law of Fate we must be connected to our essence, our more internal side. This means that what we do comes from a choice of understanding, not from a mechanical external place. When we have experiences from a mechanical place we are living under the law of accident because personality and the outer self are directly under the law of accident.

A man can have the fate which corresponds to his type but he practically never does have it. This arises because fate has relation to only one part of man, namely to his essence. —P. D. Ouspensky

The configuration of the planets create a birth horoscope and that directs our Fate. We have many ways to reveal our nature, and how we express ourselves influences the reality that we experience. The elements arrive and the play is subject to interpretation, improvisation and creativity; for example, having a good imagination we could become an artist or we might become a tricky con. Personality, changeable acquired habits, opinions and defenses, created or influenced by the world outside ourself is under the law of accident.

Our essence, the authentic part that we develop, is under the law of Fate. Essence, inherent at birth, develops during our early years to be covered by false personality and imprinting; some teachings refer to essence as the higher self and soul. Real growth happens in our essence which is what belongs to us, not in our personality. It's a growth of our understanding; essence is under the law of Fate. Personality is what gets developed and learned through our contact with external life. If we have to memorize something in order to pass a test that does not grow our essence, it magnifies our personality. Developing our essence increases our consciousness, which is light, and therefore gradually illuminates our being as well as bringing more light into the world.

The moment I penetrated into my innermost core I found it was as if suddenly millions of suns had arisen. When love has flowered totally there is a bright light, as if, suddenly, millions of suns have arisen all around you. —Kabir

The law of Fate that belongs to our essence has less laws (twenty-four) than those that govern personality (forty-eight). As we relinquish habitual suffering and negative emotions, moving to live under the twenty-four orders of laws of Fate, we become less invented and more true to who we are intended. Fate is what we should be, becoming this essential individual we pass under fewer laws. Fate means our own real Destiny. When the falseness of personality weakens which happens through our perception of its unrealness, we disconnect from the law of accident and connect to our Fate, until then, we are separated from our Fate.

To Derive Meaning From Ourselves

We have already had to re-think so many of our conceptions of motion, we will also gradually learn to realize that which we call destiny goes forth from within people, not from without into them. —Ranier Maria Rilke

Intentional choices that refer to our own self move us from the law of accident to live under the law of Fate. For example, recognizing that when cooking a meal your negative energy will permeate the food and strain your digestion—you choose to make the effort to clear yourself as you cook and eat. This effort to derive meaning from ourself creates a responsibility towards self-development, moving us under the law of Fate. Acting from understanding creates an authentic self bringing us under world 24 and the law of Fate, now we prepare for what is coming; under the law of accident there was no preparation.

When an inner situation is not made conscious, it appears outside as fate. —Carl Jung

Fate is ordained, Destiny is our own, once we create will into our life, we move towards growth and into our Destiny. So much falls away, situations are not attracted to us as we create a resistance to life through being non-reactive, internal, intentional—responding from a thoughtful place of understanding. As the saying goes: *who controls the past controls the future. Who controls the present controls the past.* Our innate essence, essential nature, our individuality is what belongs to us. Personality is a useful tool, providing information for growth. We acquire our personality from the outside world, our essence, inherent at birth must be retrieved and developed.

We have a two-fold destiny, either to live only as the unconscious slave of the all-universal purpose, or to pay the debt of our own existence and thus attain independent individuality, with all that this brings of further possibilities of self-perfecting. —J.G. Bennett

Organic life is under the influence of all planets, the sun and the moon. Major events like war, earthquakes, tsunamis, all have planetary influences. Once we notice how we are, as we work on developing an inner life, as unnecessary emotions disappear, we move towards what is vital in us, the real part, bringing us under the law of our essential Fate. Weakening our personality creates room for planetary influences to contact us. Strengthening our personality builds a shell around our essence, now few outside influences can come through, then we are barely effected by Fate except for birth and death. Outside influences, except for birth and death, can loosen their power over us.

If it be true that we are working out our own destiny here within this short space of time, if it be true that everything must have a cause as we see it now, it must also be true that that which we are now is the effect of the whole of our past; therefore, no other person is necessary to shape the destiny of mankind but man himself. —Vivekananda

IMPERMANENCE: OUR VERY LIFE
IS THE BLESSING

Destiny, meaning from the stars, exists to direct us towards our purpose. In Greek mythology the Fates, the three goddesses of Destiny and Fate, daughters of the night, decided the Fate of all humanity, they represented time—past, present and future. The goddesses of Fate personified the inescapable Destiny, assigning every person their Fate or share in the scheme of things and their decisions were unchangeable. Weavers and singers, Lachesis, the lot-giver, spins, singing of things that were, measuring the thread of life, Clotho, the spinner, the youngest, puts the wool round the spindle, singing of things that are, spinning the thread of life, and Antropos, the unavoidable, the never-turn-back eldest, sings about the things that will be, and cuts the thread when death arrives. They make the thread of each person's life. When the thread is cut, we die. While the goddesses are three, Fate is one.

From womb to tomb-impermanence, we rehearse our death. —David Ingber

Fate is spun at birth, according to the legend, and life has its limit, called death. As goddesses of birth they prophesied, as goddesses of Fate they revealed the future, as goddesses of death, they represent the greatest mystery. Clotho, spins the thread of life, Lachesis, allots the length of the yarn, and Atropos does the snip, the final cut. At the birth of each person, the goddesses spin out the thread of our future life, follow our steps, directing the consequences of our actions according to the counsel of gods. As our Fate, terminated at death, the goddesses of Fate become the goddesses of death.

The flux and the shape of the present are not the whole story. There remains to answer the most important question: Through what do we have a hold or influence on existence? This is from our will. We are committed to a pattern of living that will recur throughout our lives. This is in part due to what is generally called character and includes choices made perhaps long ago in early childhood. This pattern tell us who we are and gives us the sense that 'this is my life.' There is also a freedom of decision. It is decision that creates a new future beyond recurrence. It is decision that embraces the unknown and the unforeseeable. Here decision is not making up our mind, but intentional creativity. If the recurrent pattern signifies fate, then the realm of free decision must signify destiny. —A.G.E. Blake

In the Jewish tradition the holidays of Rosh Hashonah and Yom Kippur express that our Fate is set up year by year, as an outline, yet we are able to become an instrument to raise ourself and thereby elevate the world to higher consciousness. The liturgy says: *on Rosh Hashonah it is inscribed and on Yom Kippur sealed (in the book of fate) how many will die at the preordained time, and who before this time—who will rest, who will wander, who will be tranquil, who will suffer, who will be poor, who will be rich.* Following this, the congregation all say: *but teshuvah (a return from estrangement/renewal), tefillah (prayer/praise), and tzeddakah (generosity/justice), cancel the harshness of this stern decree.* To open ourselves, to reframe priorities, have an active interest in humanity, in service, we change our world. Through mending our soul we are mending the world, we are healing, mending, repairing, transforming the brokenness; for whatever we do in our life affects everything in the universe.

Watch your thoughts, for they become words. Watch your words, for they become actions. Watch your actions, for they become habits. Watch your habits, for they become character. Watch your character, for it becomes your destiny. —Unknown

14. WILL

In order to have will we need to be conscious and responsible to the world around us. First we need to have something to offer and then perhaps we can be used by the higher will. Develop your will and your strengths, so that one day you may be allowed to be of service and manifest will here on earth. —Reshad Feild

The age old saying: *Patience is the Mother of Will,* speaks to the inner meaning of the law of Will. Impatience implies a need to impose yourself, to be willful. Patience, living in deep trust, is surrender. To take action is important, the results unfold in their own time. To wait, open, certain that something is possible, yet with no expectation, is active patience, that space between idea and manifestation. Real Will comes from above, not from life and its interests. To have above in you, in your attitude or thoughts, is an open connection and develops Will. Inner observation, sincerity and perseverance are the necessary ingredients for realizing that there is something higher than ourself, universal laws, something that directs us. Will is from higher and subtle influences, ideas that act upon us and are responded to by us as we sense them. What the majority of people call Will are the result of their wants and desires, their whims, self-importance, duty, willfulness; a thin line between willingness and unwillingness. Will develops in us as we become aware of internally being in contact, connected to its ideas. Then we become self-initiated, not obligatory.

We seek the gift of a new quality of will, this new quality of will cannot be the same as the self-will. Self-will is based on self-love. The latter constantly feels resentment if not flattered. A Conscious man, totally different from an ordinary man, would not be impressed by any of the manifestations of the self-love so unpleasantly rampant in us. That would be one sign to know him by. A further sign would be an absence of resentment, pointing to the possession of a new will. A conscious man could not have a will founded on self-love. As long as self-love remains you will continue to obey yourself. You will not inwardly acknowledge anything above yourself. 'A conscious man is under the Law of Will.' —Maurice Nicoll

To develop Will we eventually diminish self-will and willfulness. Self-will is self-opinions. What we name as our will is generally ourselves. Will is connected with our emotional life and so developing our emotional center is the beginning of creating Will. We may think to drive more carefully, or to lose weight, but that does not mean that we will. We may want our way, which is indiscriminate self-involved willing, or unwillingness. These are the wills that eventually are left behind for absolute Will. First is to see ourself, then to know ourself. To act and interact without any self-seeking is to take part not trying to enhance our sense of self, then we are no longer seeking for anything to identify with out there as we go beyond the material world.

Will is created by effort and needs to be educated. Self-will and willfulness, are the result of constantly shifting desires; Will arrives from intention and struggle. Working on our actions allows us to see our desire to do or not to do something; extending beyond possibilities actually doing more than we can, creates the shift. This is to do all we can about what concerns us, and then to do more. St. Francis of Assisi wrote: *Start by doing what is necessary, then what is possible, and suddenly you are doing the impossible.* To dream the impossible dream is *to reach the unreachable star.* This type of stretching develops being, from where Will is built.

Take some small thing you wish to do, which you cannot now do, and compel yourself to do it, whim is the beginning of will. Take a whim you have, a

harmless whim, and make an effort to gratify it. This is a beginning, a step, towards the state of real will. —C.S. Nott

DEVELOPING WILL

In the first part of life we struggle: to know the ways of the world, we strengthen sharpness, intelligence, ego and will power. To know the inner world we need the stamina for the continuous process of surrender. This type of letting go, from a place of power, is an act of Will. Essentially we live under the law of accident, fate or upon another's and our own will, and in this manner we have to weaken our personality to form Will. This process happens after we release self-love, self-will, self-admiration, selfishness, self-prejudices and self-interest. Putting forth extra effort, more than we imagine we have, builds Will. Standing behind decisions, directing and maintaining clear intentions with effort, creating completion; all help form Will. This act of resolve accumulates energy by exhausting our usual supply of energy, doing more than what is necessary, what has been referred to as *intentionally walking an extra 2 miles after hiking for 25 miles.* Will develops from intention, extra effort and perseverance; a commitment to accomplish what we intend. What we have known as will comes from our desires, which shift, change, are influenced by popular opinion and schooling, often rooted in strong opposition. *I will carry that table and ask no one for help*, moves to willfulness, the habitual pushing ourself. Once surrendered to a higher Will we have the capacity for conscious decisions; this surrender takes courage and strength and is the inner meaning of the law of Will.

Mr. Gurdjieff completely denies the possibility of will being in the common presence of the average man. Will is a certain combination obtained from the results of certain properties specially elaborated in themselves by people

who can do. In the presence of average people what they call will is exclusively only the resultant of desires. Real will is a sign of a very high degree of Being, in comparison with the Being of an ordinary man. But only those people who possess such Being can do. —G.I. Gurdjieff

What the majority of people refer to as will is the result of desires often experienced by an adjustment between willingness and unwillingness. Will develops from an unbiased attitude and an integration of self. After the personality is weakened, essence matured and inner sincerity created, Will develops. This, from a genuine, sincere place, fed from a level that values and is kept alive for and by ourself—because all that is beautiful in us wants it and feels the loss when it is not present. Outer is for ambition, praise, self-image, attention, self-interest. Surrendered to enter the silence, the uncharted desert or field of temptation activates our energy to press forward onward towards developing something, a substance called Will.

Taking what happens in our daily life as grist for the mill, connecting the circumstances of each moment to waking up and then moving inwards, beneath and behind ourself, attracts Will. Sharpness of intelligence, created in our younger years through struggle builds a Will involved with life. A strong ego, confident, coming from a place of power is needed for surrender. Renunciation is meaningful after we have something to renounce; lose ourself in life we gain ourself in surrender. Will and surrender are mirror images, reflections of the same energies. To loosen the ego takes tremendous courage; before we renounce we need to have something to renounce. This is the surrender that follows maturity; surrender is the leap from ego to lightening ego, from the idea that we are separate to the understanding of seeing that I am not separate. Will comes from connecting to, feeling influences, presence reaching us; getting rid of our *self* for change to happen, surrendering to universal laws breaks us from our own self-will.

TO FEEL THE PRESENCE OF WILL

Today something is open that calls me toward a relation with the higher, but this does not come about by itself. I feel I have to obey a higher energy, an authority, which I recognize as the sole authority because I am a particle of it. And I need to serve it in order not to lose my relation with it. In the act of being present, I voluntarily obey and submit, renouncing my own will and at the same time asserting a different will over the functions.
—*Jeanne de Salzmann*

Real Will comes down from a higher level, there has to be something aware and present in us to make that contact. What is higher is innermost. *Above* is the same as *inner*. To become internal, to weaken personality, requires heartfelt sincerity. Knowing when we are genuine, taking responsibility for our intentions through agreement are steps on a path of living under the law of Will. It begins with an impulse, an inspiration and continues growing with our effort. Once we have Will we can use it to surrender and be a vehicle; we can be driven (like a car) from the inside, rather than being pulled and pushed by outward illusions. This preparation, to be available to higher influences, requires not doing things the customary way. This Will is not concerned with the external world, it is not about giving up smoking, losing weight, exercise, sleep, or negations. It is about making conscious connections, being present, not mechanical; consciousness and Will as forces awaken through our efforts. Will is freedom from conditioned consciousness, it's a liberation from living a mechanized life.

There is no alternative to making efforts to be present, daily for the rest of one's life. Consciousness cannot be given, it must be earned through one's own efforts, aided by higher forces. When I listen to a concert, for example, I feel there is as much responsibility in me to hear every note as there is on the artist to play those notes. —Robert Burton

The Lord's Prayer states: *May Thy will be done on earth.* This is to allow higher influence to reach us. Filled with self-will and willfulness we are unable to feel the presence of higher influence Will. When we hear: *Let Thy Will be done, not my Will,* this is the step towards our responsibility of fulfilling Will on this planet, by saying *I Will,* then our actions are an expression of a greater Will. Changing, growing our essence, which is a genuine part of us, is essential, since that's where real Will lives. The familiar Lord's Prayer, *May Thy will be done on earth,* asks to connect us to this greater Will, breaking us from our own self-will; *Thy Will,* not my will. When we feel that force, which is not a power that we have, instead as one in which *we are,* an energy enters us, a current, and life expands in us; this happens when we are still, not blind submission, instead we are touched by a Will to be what we are, to awaken to our true nature.

*The object of will is to bring order into manifestation. We need to be able to say **I** consciously, then **I will**. —Reshad Feild*

15. MIRACLES

A miracle is the manifestation in this world of the laws of another world, unknown to us or rarely met with. There can be no other kind of miracle. A miracle is not a breaking of laws, nor is it a phenomenon outside laws. These laws are incomprehensible and unknown to us, and are therefore miraculous. —P.D. Ouspensky

In this universal law, the cause of events are neither in the past, present, or in recurrence. Miracles are commonplace, existence in each moment is a Miracle. Life, the great Miracle, carries experiences that provide no reasonable explanation; visible manifestations offer proof, so the law of Miracles continuously demonstrates. An event that runs counter to, or at least stretches the laws of nature, sometimes referred to as supernatural, a divine intervention or a psychic happening, often becomes the description of a Miracle. As we expand our understanding of life it becomes apparent that we are already wired for Miracles, they happen with ease through normal everyday circumstances. The events of our life are the natural interplay of the powers of the above and the below, manifestations of universal laws (refer to the law of, *as above, so below*). The *above* of the Emerald Tablet is the realm where the creative action of spirit originates, and the *below* is the material world where creative action appears.

The miraculous is the entry into an action of a conscious force that knows why and how the action is performed. This will bring me a new way of living. —*Jeanne de Salzmann*

What are considered Miracles are the manifestation of universal laws in the physical world. As we awaken to interface our intelligence with the natural intelligence of the universe, what we see in the sub-atomic world of quantum physics parallels seeing Miracles. Limited thinking has denied access to the information regarding our power over our thoughts. Industrialist Henry Ford said, *If you think you can or if you think you can't, either way, you're right.* Yes, we make the world with our mind! Change your thoughts to change your world.

Miracles are more important for what they teach than for what they accomplish. The purpose of a miracle is not just deliverance, but to transform the consciousness of the one who experiences it. —*Eliezer Shore*

The literature of religion is filled with Miraculous events, most holidays are based on Miracles that happened centuries ago. Here in this ordinary world lies the Miraculous nature of creation which is an ongoing process. Once we look at the depth in this creation and understand causality, seeing the law of Miracles we know that in one instant all life could be crushed, yet, instead, creation continues to support life.

Mystical cosmologies contain at least seven levels. So many of the classic stories that we have learned concern substances that change their material structure in a manner that does not fit our understanding. If a rock were to fly like a bird, or a man walk on water like a duck, these events would appear Miraculous on this plane and the level in this cosmos that we have come to know. It appears fitting that the stories we hear to be Miracles belong to another dimension, level or cosmos. Universal laws, as in the law of gravity, make for the intricacies of the universe. Ultimately, when we feel the connectedness, the wonder of all of life, we are living the Miraculous.

In Search Of The Miraculous

One disciple said: My master stands on one side of the river. I stand on the other holding a piece of paper. He draws a picture in the air and the picture appears on the paper. He works miracles. The other disciple said: My master works greater miracles than that. When he sleeps, he sleeps. When he eats, he eats. When he works, he works. When he meditates, he meditates.
—Zen Buddhist story

The power of Miracle energy, often a glimpse of higher reality, exists as a potential form for us to tap into, to know and to assist our lives. To understand that opportunities are within this universe regardless of adversity, we might create and see the Miracles we desire. The force and strength of Miracles replace life struggles and offer positive change for all humanity. When we see what is inexplicable we stretch beyond physics in defining reality as well as opening to know that physical laws also are Miraculous. To recognize the magic throughout everyday requires maturity. The human body and our brain with its enormous capacities are examples of mechanisms that appear to be Miraculous, their every working a Miracle. Reality has already been broken down under analysis. With a few equational strokes of his pen Einstein challenged many fixed realities.

Miracles are nature unimpeded, which is a good way of saying that if you take your hand off the tiller, the boat will steer itself and do a vastly better job of it than you ever could. —*Jed McKenna*

A single flap of a seagull's wing's would be enough to change the course of all future weather systems on this earth. In a scientific context the *butterfly effect* states that the flap of a butterfly's wings in Central Park could cause an earthquake in China. The notion of unpredictability in a scientific view of the universe challenged and changed understanding. This lack of order in a system that nevertheless obeys particular rules serves as a reminder to the notion of the Miraculous. In personal terms, looking for our keys and leaving the house five minutes late we might miss a life-threatening incident and be safely protected; several New Yorkers who worked for years in the twin towers building did not show up the morning of 9/11 due to a child's sore throat or a flat tire. A hurricane with tornado winds that destroyed houses on either side leaves our home intact. Thinking about a long ago friend from high school as the phone rings and voilá, it's her voice on the other end. Wondering what kind of radio to buy, an e-mail arrives with the descriptions of the 5 best radios.

MIRACLES ARE COMMONPLACE

According to Vedanta, there are only two symptoms of enlightenment, two indications that a transformation is taking place within you toward a higher consciousness. The first symptom is that you stop worrying. Things don't bother you anymore. You become light-hearted and full of joy. The second symptom is that you encounter more and more meaningful coincidences in your life, more and more synchronicities and this accelerates to the point where you actually experience the miraculous. —Deepak Chopra

Synchronicity is a word coined by Carl Jung to describe temporally coincident occurrences of causal events. The experience of having meaningful coincidences Jung saw as a dynamic that underlay human history, not due to chance but as the manifestation of parallel events or circumstances reflecting a governing dynamic. *Effects* without *cause* are looked upon by many as Miracles. There is wisdom that we can know and learn from the endless possibilities that emerge from ordinary daily moments. Unrealized Miracles are constantly happening in other dimensions. Miracles are guidance from the universe. Understanding that all energy and matter are interconnected, two seemingly disconnected events are actually interconnected. We are part of the universe and the universe is communicating with itself.

Around the awakened Self, miracles dance naturally. Healing takes place and revelations occur quite simply, like the heat in a pot cooks vegetables. —Andrew Harvey

Coming from the Latin verb *mirari*, to wonder, the suffix—*cle* makes a noun: a Miracle is that which elicits wonder. In Tibet a Miracle is seen as power, a quality of awakened mind, a spontaneous manifestation of compassion, a cosmic energy; it is as it is, a happening. The Miraculous arrives as a surprise and like children we look in wonder. Rabbi Shlomo Carlebach explained a story about a small Miracle during the Jewish new year service of Rosh Hashonah: *on the first day of Rosh Hashonah we ask God for what is possible, on the second day, we are to ask for what is impossible.* The holiday of Passover recounts miracles that allowed the Jewish people to leave Egypt. The Hebrew word for Miracle is *nes*, a sign that is abbreviated on the dreidel, children's spinning tops. The words for the letters on the dreidel are *nes, gadol, hayahm sham,* meaning, *a great miracle happened here.* Signs in the Hebrew tradition lead towards seeing the wisdom and wonders of this great creation. *Nes* is a clear sign of a greater reality, a vision that expands consciousness taking us beyond the limits of the form we knew, stretching our imagination. In the Kabbalistic tradition it's the efforts that go into repairing this world, the day labor that creates the bridge for realizing a Miracle. Rabbinic commentary literature, the Midrash, says that *the world cannot exist without miracles.* They inspire and remind us of the greatest Miracle: that of an expanded consciousness.

In Jewish mysticism, the instant we open our eyes to the true dimensions of creation and causality, we find ourselves immersed in a sea of miracles. This realization is astonishing. At any instant, creation might unfold in a way that would be disastrous for us; therefore, each moment is bursting with the gift of life. Indeed, as a result of this awareness, the mystic loves life intensely and feels loved by it. A miracle is not a singular event in contrast to the flow of nature, but rather that miracles are an ongoing process. The only reason we think that a miracle is opposed to the ordinary flow of nature is because we do not have a broad enough scope of these other dimensions of reality. If we did we would see that everything is dependent upon miracles.
—*David A. Cooper*

The law of Miracles, the teaching of universal laws, in their implications is in the transformation that takes place afterwards. There is a story that Buddha reprimanded a monk for his fascination with the Miracle of walking through walls. As long as our attention moves only from one fascination to another, we then miss the deeper essence of the inner meaning of the work. The glamour and allure of experiences draw many a seeker and the search becomes the adventure, as we get further and further away from the esoteric meaning.

The actual Miracle is a change of heart, is to alter a negative habit, to drink a cup of tea so reverently that you experience the whole universe slowly revolving; a Miracle is the freshness and astonishment of each passing moment. Miracles, random coincidences seemingly beyond comprehension pointing to the mystery of life urge us to open and participate offering reminders; they are always here, receive them in this world filled with surprise, prizes and wonder.

Who makes much of a miracle? As to me, I know of nothing else but miracles. To me, every hour of the light and dark is a miracle, every cubic inch of space is a miracle, every square yard of the surface of the earth is spread with the same; Every spear of grass—the frames, limbs, organs of men and women and all that concerns them, all these to me are unspeakably perfect miracles. —Walt Whitman

16. THREE

Threeness is one of the master ideas of human culture. It is integrally linked with a vision of creativity, of making the new from the old. It draws upon our intuitions of a spiritual order intervening in the workings of the world— without violating any of the restrictions under which we exist, such as cause and effect. It is an open-ended principle, capable of endless interpretations. —A.G.E. Blake

The law of Three, one of the fundamental laws of the universe, is the basis of everything in the universe, all structures and processes, and applies to all events; it is the root of all ancient systems. This is the law of *how things happen.* Every manifestation is the result of Three forces. This is the law of the Three principles of action, resistance and equipoise. Nothing ever happens without a combination of Three independently different and opposing forces that have the nature of active, passive and reconciling or positive, negative and neutralizing. The first and highest level of creation is produced by Three forces. Most of us live not really seeing how the law of Three works, how things come about and change.

Creation depends on the conjunction of three forces; nothing can take place unless all three are present. —Kathleen Riordan Speeth

When we perceive through our head, heart and body, then the law of Three becomes a reality. For there to be true understanding is to think, feel and sense together, and this is the law of Three working within us. *We understand this law by making it happen in ourselves. It is this that enables us to link with the phenomena of the physical world and begin to see how real change is possible,* wrote A.G.E. Blake. Without neutralizing force, active and passive forces stand in useless opposition; nothing new happens. The Enneagram, one of the symbols on the cover of this book, is a triangle within a circle, an expression of the law of Three forces.

All knowledge can be included in the Enneagram and with the help of the Enneagram it can be interpreted. And in this connection only what a man is able to put into the Enneagram does he actually know, that is understand. Everything can be included and read in the Enneagram, with instruction from a man who knows. —G.I. Gurdjieff

An active force initiates an action, is the active principle that drives an impulse and is met by a passive force moving in an equal and opposite direction, it resists or opposes this drive. In this situation nothing takes place, unless a Third, or neutralizing force enters to carry the energy of the active and passive forces in a particular direction. The Third force reconciles them. When this occurs, a triad takes place. A simple example of this is when the active force of water is brought together with the passive force of wheat and they meet the reconciling force of heat, the result is bread.

Every experience we have and all phenomenon we see, from constructing a building to creating a painting is the result of one of six different triads corresponding to the six combinations of the active, passive and neutralizing forces in the position of first, second and Third force. Third force is invisible to us, and is the force in any triad that is not under our direct control. We either make something happen or wait for circumstances to change; our own interest or enthusiasm, although essential, will not themselves produce a result. Recognition of Three forces as well as opening or connecting ourself to a Third force accelerates self-development.

THIRD FORCE

There are two great laws in the cosmos: the law of three and the law of seven. The law of three describes the necessity for three forces: active, passive and neutralizing, which must be present in order for any event to take place. These two laws are shown on one ninefold symbol, the Enneagram, in which the inner triangle reflects the Law of Three. —G.I. Gurdjieff

The law of Three is essential to transforming the energy of every person; introducing Third force as a representative of consciousness broadens our mental process. Every phenomenon in all worlds are the result of a simultaneous action of Three forces—the positive, active, creative, initiating, affirming first force; the negative, passive, reaction, resisting, material, denying second force; and the neutralizing, balancing, relating, mediating, formative, connecting Third force. The mind does not have a natural ability to discern the Three forces at work, is not geared towards seeing beyond duality, it registers formatory thinking of yes and no and right or wrong. There are many Three-part structures in our world. In the realm of physics there are (phenomenon) atoms, made up of (first force) neutrons, (second force) electrons, and (Third force) electromagnetic field. In law, there is (first force) the plaintiff, (second force) the defendant, (Third force) the judge; the phenomenon might be the settlement of the dispute.

The three forces reflect the three basic conditions of the Universe. The passive force is a derivative of the static condition, space; the active force is derivative of the dynamic condition, time; the neutralizing force ensures the maintenance of equilibrium in all the Universe, on every plane, and at every step. —Boris Mouravieff

We are not trained to recognize Third force, nor is it easily accessible. Essentially, we can't see phenomena as manifestations of Three forces because we don't witness the objective world when we see through our subjective states of consciousness. When we see the world in its Three forces in each action, we see the world as it actually is. To do this is to study ourselves seeing the actions of Three forces; we are a miniature universe, laws are the same on every plane. For example, I want to lose weight to create a healthier body. My desire and first step is the active force. The pulling of old habits that oppose the first step will be the passive or negative force. The two forces will either counterbalance each other or one will overwhelm the other in the same time, weakening one, absorbing another, until eventually there will be no result, or it will go around and around for a complete lifetime. So we feel desire, we feel initiative, but until Third force arrives we have nothing left to use towards our own initiative.

Third force may come as a new eating plan with studies and group meetings that show the benefits to taking off weight. This supports the initial drive plus adds fuel to conquer old habits as well as the inertia that was passive or negative force. Now, we become active in the direction of our desire. We are the result of the convergence of Three independent forces. The active force expresses itself as our mind and intellect, the passive force manifests as our body, while the reconciling force comes alive as our emotions.

THIRD FORCE: INSTRUMENTALLY CREATIVE

Attempting to take this law out of context and understand it, we see that it's part of a whole system. Understanding the integrated nature of the whole system is essential. The law of three is not constrained to a single level. The energy from the law of three emanates directly from the highest level of the universe, and it percolates downward through octaves, providing motive forces (shocks) to help the octaves evolve properly and complete themselves.
—Lee Van Laer

To want something—a car, a relationship, to write a book; that is first force. Eventually we meet the opposing force to what we want, the resisting second force. This might be finding that a car is more expensive than we can afford, the partner is unavailable or not attracted to us, a time to work on the book is filled with appointments and distractions. All negative second force interferes with our desire to manifest first force proposal. If we don't calculate second force, the opposition to what we want, little is accomplished. Through opening to second force and expecting and understanding it we have the opportunity to remain positive, not depressed, angry, frustrated, or to give up. Then Third force meets and connects active first force and passive second force to create the manifestation. The stronger the active force, the stronger is the passive opposing force. To understand this is to stop feeling/being defeated in life. Third force brings first and second force together. The judge (Third force) brings the plaintiff (first force) and the defendant (second force) together. The relationship between first and second force is established by the nature and quality of Third force. Second force actually helps us to develop our individuality. Through working with the second force in ourself, we learn to evolve and live a richer more satisfying life.

Our life is generally lived under the impact of the neutralizing force of life—outer circumstances, inward attitudes and illusions continually shape our behavior. To make our personality passive, consciousness will influence our actions and understanding. —Theodore Nottingham

Results and creation itself rests on the combination and the balance of the Three forces. The universe is a being with Three centers corresponding to our own. The forces of nature and fundamental attributes have been used Triadically for centuries and are reflected in Christianity as Father, Son and Holy Spirit; in the Taoist tradition as Yin, Yang and Tao; in Hinduism as Brahma, Vishnu and Shiva. The Triadic scientific formulas that describe forces and relationships in nature include Einstein's equation E=mc2, and the Pythagorean formula a2=b2+c2.

There is the Three-fold nature of man, which is body, soul and spirit, in art there are Three primary colors, red, yellow and blue, because the triangle is the principle of figures it is considered to be the mistress of geometry, in music there are Three primary tones of the musical scale, in aeronautics Three spacial coordinates, longitude, latitude and altitude. In language there is past, present and future tenses. Looking at life this way, rather than the dualistic posture of, them and us or right and wrong; seeing without black and white duality opens the immense world of possibilities which are available once recognized and acknowledged.

Everything is created and knit together from the heights to the depths of the Universe by the double action of the law of 3 and the law of 7.
—*Maurice Nicoll*

17. SEVEN: THE OCTAVE
THE ORDER OF CREATION

I had sweated for years to understand something of the Law of Seven, the Octave. Unless and until a person has experienced the working of the law in himself, he cannot understand it—it remains just information for the curious. —*C.S. Nott*

*T*here are two fundamental cosmic laws behind all things and they govern the universe, the law of three forces of creation and the law of Seven, the Order of Creation. Creative forces have order, otherwise everything would be in chaos. The law of Seven restricts creation, the law of three, checks everything at two points. Both are fundamental laws and cannot be reduced further, they are the quintessence and kernel; meaning they just *are*.

When the three forces do meet and an act of creation takes place, a chain of manifestations may develop in which third force in one event becomes active force in the next event—for the three forces change sign with respect to one another as they go about spinning or braiding the thread of occurrences. Now the second fundamental law, the Law of Seven, begins to operate, governing successions of events. It states that whenever any manifestation evolves, it does so nonlinearly. There is an orderly discontinuity in every progression of things, in every series. —*Kathleen Riordan Speeth*

The law of Seven, which controls the development of all processes in the universe, is that nothing remains at rest, all things move in the direction of evolution or involution—and there is a limit to both these movements. This law governs the steps of events. There are two points where all processes in the world have an interruption. The law of Seven explains why everything does not continue forever. Things do not keep up ad infinitum; snow and rain, anger and pain, do not go on uninterrupted, there are no straight lines in nature—everything takes a curve, has a break.

Understanding how to use this law assists the maintenance and momentum of our personal work and daily life. The beginnings of Octaves are visible in our daily life, and by their very nature they make our projects and plans a challenge. Everything needs to be pushed at two definite places and is unable to proceed without outside external help. This is because certain shocks are needed in the unfolding of all things; the law of Seven causes narrow places to appear as we progress on our journey.

The law of seven can become a tool that can help you understand how to keep your efforts moving. The law of seven, also called the law of octaves, that nothing continues forever, can be observed everywhere in the natural world and in everything we do internally and externally. If we understood the law of octaves, we could see more clearly how the universe unfolds, or how a tree grows, or how learning requires special efforts at special, very specific points. —William Page

The law of Seven describes the way a sequence of events eventually loses force or direction and states that what we create has order until difficulties or constriction appear at two visible points. These gaps, checks or intervals happen in every process—from writing a book to cooking a meal, from decay to growth; it is the Octave relationship to the law of Seven. When applied to music it is divided into 7 notes, with a repetition of the first note. *Do, re, mi, fa, sol, la, ti, do.* Each note signifies qualities of energy as well as aspects of time. The initial note, *do*, is the intention. The decision to do something is the *do,* and the more strength and conviction sounding this note the greater the chance of completing the task.

It's apparent in the musical scale that the Octave is made up of unequal steps. *Do re mi* are equally distant from each other, yet between *mi* and *fa* is a half-step, *Sol, la* and *ti* have full steps, yet *ti do,* again, has a half step. When we get to *re* and *mi,* it takes a shock to assist us to get to *fa.* Without that shock peoples lives are filled with broken Octaves—incomplete, restricted and redirected plans. Otherwise, everything begun would proceed to its final destination. Everything shifts at definite intervals, meaning that vibrations are either increasing or decreasing at a consistent rate, and then either slow down, speed up, or change direction.

The Law of Seven/Octave states that there is a slowing down of vibrations at two points. According to the Law of Octaves the notes of the descending octave involve more and more laws, and vice versa. A part is under more laws than the whole. Now all evolution is an ascent of an octave. Psychological evolution is an increase of Consciousness, a bringing together of more things into a unity—because Consciousness means a knowing together. The more one studies the Law of Seven the more one sees that it is a uniting framework, a skeleton, as it were, for all forms of life, psychological or physical. Everything is united, everything is connected together, nothing can exist independently, yet each thing has its own individual existence although it is connected with what is below it and what is above it. —Maurice Nicoll

HOLDING TO THE DIFFICULT

Only by fulfilling the law of Seven can anything develop to its intended conclusion, which is why an alternative name has been to call this the law of shocks, the Order of Manifestation, the law that provides the relationship of the part to the whole. To understand anything we have to know something about the whole before understanding the part. To really know the earth we need to understand the solar system and the galaxy. Everything is connected; knowing our significance on this planet is connected to knowing ourself. Eckhart Tolle, spiritual teacher and author, expressed this, stating: *The world can only change from within. You are here to enable the divine purpose of the universe to unfold. That is how important you are.*

Every note of an Octave is itself a whole Octave. We begin our task with enthusiasm, yet irritation, doubt and resentment start to take away the high energy that originated with our project. Effort, intention and presence are needed to continue on this journey of fulfilling our purpose. We work on many Octaves simultaneously during the day, hour, week, month, year. What helps to hold us to the Octave and completion is remembering the energy and strength of our original intention. To maintain a creative flow we release the energetic connection to the Octave to allow something new to enter.

Octave relationships are in all processes, in everything we undertake. Whenever we choose a project, or are working on something, the tendency is to slow down—decrease interest—get tired—loose momentum before the task is completed. The timing to give ourself the shock, which is considered to be needed at the first and second interval, assists in continuing a project's intended direction. It is in the nature of all things that they are held up, constricted in two places, needing a shock to continue—this is the law of Seven.

All the finer 'hydrogens' needed for the working, the growth, and the evolution of the organism were prepared from three kinds of food, eatables and drink, air, and impressions. Neither air nor food can be changed. But we can improve our impressions to a very high degree and in this way introduce fine 'hydrogens' into the organism. It is precisely on this that the possibility of evolution is based. —*P.D. Ouspensky*

The combination of the laws of three and Seven meet in the diagram hydrogens of the Enneagram and also in the Kabbalistic Tree of Life. Contained within this law lies the origin of free will, for without intervals there would only be predeterminism. Things do not develop uniformly, they have spaces that are filled with acceleration and slow downs. Once we understand and experience the law of Seven within ourself, we can recognize this law in relationship to the universe.

This too shall pass. —*popular saying, refers to universal law of Seven*

The law of Seven, which governs the order of creation assists us in understanding when to add conditions or shocks, as we continue our possibility for self-development. Everything we set out to have happen is the beginning of an Octave. We want an exercise program and so we join a local gym. If the intention, *do,* is sounded with a force and effort to keep up the direction the program is maintained and we reach the *mi* note. When there are misunderstandings or confusion the direction gets rerouted, and *mi* is not reached. If the gym locker room smells, or the well-liked instructor leaves, or the distance seems too far or expensive, our disappointment with the gym sabotages the original commitment to exercise. The direction of the project becomes switched to now be something else. Next door to the gym is a clothing store, the direction moves to buying clothes that fit better. Once the place of shock arrives, to go on to the *fa,* owing to the nature of the law of Seven a shock is needed. To stop here is a failure. The shock may come from life; friends reminding us how out of shape we look, even in new clothes, or from ourself—now we remember why we began the original Octave and we are revitalized to continue—making a renewed effort to maintain the original intention of the exercise program. The slowing down of vibrations at two points, between *mi* and *fa*, and *ti* and *do* requires an exceptional effort to sustain, continue and complete our aims, projects and intentions.

DIRECTING OUR LIFE

This law of Seven explains why there are no straight lines in nature and also why we can neither think nor do, why everything with us is thought, why everything happens with us and happens usually in a way opposed to what we want or expect. All this is the clear and direct effect of the 'intervals', or retardations in the development of vibrations. —P.D. Ouspensky

All matter is energy condensing as it moves further away from its source. The world consists of vibrations, from coarse to finer vibrations. The law of Seven breaks a process into 7 steps, or 8, with the last step equivalent to the first, with the points of slowing down the rate of increase of vibrations, called intervals. The law of Octaves can be found in heat, light, chemical, magnetic and other vibrations. The law of Seven in cosmology is a teaching about the ordering of creation on different levels, in the macrocosm of the universe and in the microcosm of man.

Structures, as in living organisms, and processes, as in becoming in time, can be understood as sevenfold: the 7 day system we use is based on ancient astrological knowledge regarding the 7 known celestial bodies, 7 days in creation, as well as 7 steps in the musical octave, 7 deadly sins, 7 wonders of the world, 7 continents of the world, 7 sacraments of the Catholic church, sail the 7 seas, there are 7 dwarfs, 7 colors in the rainbow. To understand the law of Seven is to realize that beyond the law of accident we want to have something happen short of relying on luck to create shocks, at a perfect moment we need to make special efforts or the direction of our aim will change.

The law of octaves explains many phenomena in our lives which are incomprehensible. —*G.I. Gurdjieff*

Historically, the Hebrew word for Egypt, *Mitzrayim*, has meant narrow places. Mitzrayim confined the Israelites physically, emotionally and spiritually. We personally enslave ourselves and also we can free ourselves. The comfort and security of the familiar and often oppressive, the journey of growth and revelation often through the wilderness out of the narrow places into the open brings us through the Octave. Each Octave has a narrow place and a point of liberation. Understanding the difficult or narrow places, of being held back, is in somehow knowing that it is impossible to be free from one influence without becoming subject to another.

All work on ourself involves choosing the influence we want to subject ourself to and actually positioning ourself under that influence. Observing ourselves, knowing when these difficult moments appear we learn how to place our energy, what efforts we want to make and which ones are necessary to make so as to continue. As we learn to harness our thoughts and live mindfully, expanding consciousness, we are less at the mercy of the narrow places. This is how to live a harmonious life, sounding each note to live peacefully, melodiously.

All things face constriction or a narrow place. Visible in nature; animals are born, not all survive, birds migrate, not all make it. There are instances; a voice inside stops us from losing our temper, we give ourself a shock to hesitate before acting impulsively. These difficult moments teach us what is needed, how to get energy, what efforts to make to achieve aims. Understanding the law of Octaves, recognizing an interval;

when we understand what stages an activity will go through we can predict the intervals and prepare to successfully cross them. Learning about the law of Seven, the law of Octaves, is understanding that all notes have to be sounded in harmony.

Understanding the law of Seven, the processes that are happening in and outside ourselves, we learn to create the necessary shocks to direct our life. Knowing how and at what moment to give an additional shock to an Octave we keep the line straight, otherwise we won't discover much. This new way of living, when it takes root brings a connection with something deep and something that is beyond that which ordinary life usually provides, a way of living that's on a different level.

Everything goes by octaves, no vibration, no movement, no activity can go any other way. With knowledge of the Law of the Octave the place of everything is known and vice versa, if the place is known, one knows what exists there and its quality. Everything can be calculated, only one must know how to calculate the passage from one octave to another. —P.D. Ouspensky

18. WORLD SIX

A world of the fourth order subject to a greater number of laws is world six: the accumulation of stars we call the Milky Way. —P.D. Ouspensky

The Milky Way Galaxy, home of our solar system, offers Six fundamental laws of World creation and World maintenance. The Milky Way is but one of billions of stars in the universe visible from earth as a band of light in the evening sky. The Milky Way, large and spiral, contains about 200 billion stars. One of billions of other galaxies in the universe, it's home to earth and to our solar system. Galaxies are large systems of stars and interstellar matter; our sun is a star in the Milky

Way galaxy. The fact that the Milky Way divides the night sky into two roughly equal hemispheres indicates that our solar system lies close to the galactic plane.

Planets are enormous beings, and have relations between themselves as people do. They are reactions, tensions. They communicate by emanations—a pure force which does not operate through and by means of matter; and by radiations which operate through and by means of matter. —A. R. Orage

World Six, a second order of creation is under three laws and three of its own; Six orders of laws. This process proceeds downwards to every level of creation. Understanding these laws directly relates to understanding our own true nature. World Six drops separateness and distinction, is a World of inclusiveness in differences, the World of the highest mystical experience, the *Bodhisattva*. This is the compassion that remains in a body, available to all humanity. World Six, the Milky Way, has three conscious and three mechanical laws. Space, which is limitation, begins only in World Six. World Six is the source of laws for the World.

There can be no creation without laws and this means that everything is inevitably under laws, nothing created is free. The vertical line of creation means if we could ascend it, we would pass under fewer laws, and gain more freedom. —Maurice Nicoll

The following three laws have to do with World creation:

1. The law of *expansion*, or *Involution* which allows for variety, contrast and differences.

2. The complementary law of *Evolution* or *concentration*; through this law variety returns to unity, things are able to return to their source.

3. The law of *Freedom*; through this law it's possible to freely initiate and act in the creation.

The following three laws have to do with the order, continuity and preservation of the World:

4. The law of *Order*, says that everything has an innate pattern.

5. The law of *Interaction*, a law of universal connectedness through which everything can interact with everything else, concerns the particular way in which matter, fields, atomic and subatomic particles affect each other—like through gravitation or electromagnetism.

6. The law of *Identity*, says that everything can sustain and claim its own nature.

THE CONSCIOUSNESS OF OUR ACTIONS

The atoms of our bodies are traceable to stars that manufactured them in their cores and exploded these enriched ingredients across our galaxy, billions of years ago. For this reason, we are biologically connected to every other living thing in the world. We are chemically connected to all molecules on Earth. And we are atomically connected to all atoms in the universe. We are not figuratively, but literally stardust. —Neil deGrasse Tyson

Processes are developments over time and since there is no time in World 3 there are no processes or sequences. Quantum physics addresses World 3, which is within World Six. World Six, derived from and lower than World 3, has Six processes. Time and space in World Six are distinct. These Six processes are the Six points of the Enneagram, the points on the circle that aren't points of the triangle. Three factors in time can combine in Six ways. The Six sequences and the World above them are the law of seven. The seventh process is Do. To look at our own life and study these Six processes develops self-understanding.

A fourth state of consciousness, objective consciousness, awakens out-of-time memory. Living from this place called cosmic consciousness, light is present, help is available; at this level we see things as they really are. Different levels of consciousness exist, and from World Six we receive understanding and perspective, intentionally developed consciousness and being, active real conscience and the will to do. From a World Six consciousness comes authenticity and living out meaning and purpose. Guided and inspired there is a total lack of violence. When knowledge and being are at their highest level and are equal all understanding is practical. This means that there is nothing we know that we can not do.

'To do' means to act consciously and according to one's will, and by one's own initiative. Man differs from the animal by his capacity for conscious action, his capacity for doing. This definition makes it possible to single out man from a series of other beings not possessing the power of conscious action, and at the same time according to the degree of his consciousness in his actions. Without any exaggeration we can say that all the differences which strike us among men can be reduced to the consciousness of their actions, but among ordinary men, as well as among those who are considered extraordinary, there is no one who can 'do.' In their case, everything from beginning to end is 'done,' there is nothing they can 'do.'—G.I. Gurdjieff

The process of creation repeats itself relying on the laws of the Worlds, manifesting forces of their own they are represented by the number Six. Each successive World has twice the number of laws as the preceding World. Conscious access to the molecular World brings about access to the consciousness of the planetary World. World 3 is within World Six is within World 12 and so on. Systems on different scales have their own autonomy, although they are always in submission to the law of three and seven, this assures the diversity of the universe. We are primarily influenced by the World of which we have a part, and while we are created through nature it only develops us to a certain point. After that point we develop ourselves.

World Six, directly accesses objective consciousness. Earth is one of the planets of the solar system and the sun is one of the stars of the Milky Way. Planetary influences penetrate to the earth. When we deeply know that the order within ourselves corresponds to the harmony of the universe we understand that our inner work helps maintain order in the Universe.

Go out and stare at the sun in the sky. Why are you blinded? Why are you unable to define or describe what you see? Why is the impression incomparable with anything you know? It is because you are looking through a hole in our three-dimensional scenery, out into the six-dimensional world.
—*P.D. Ouspensky*

19. ETERNAL RECURRENCE

We shall not cease from exploration. And the end of all our exploring will be to arrive where we started for the first time. And know the place for the first time. —*T.S. Eliot*

The law of Eternal Recurrence maintains that the universe has been Recurring, and will continue to Reoccur in a self-similar form an infinite number of times; the universe has no starting or ending limitation. The matter comprising the universe is constantly changing its state, cycling through the same events infinitely, until eventually the same state Recurs. This law has been notably significant through the ages in all cultures. Prominent in Indian philosophy, where life is not considered to begin with birth and end in death, moving as a continuous flow that extends beyond. Visible in ancient Egypt, the scarab, the valuable amulet was seen as a sign of eternal renewal and re-emergence of life. Behind this was the perception of existence as eternal and circular; what had happened at the first moment of creation would be repeated over and over again. From predynastic times the Egyptians were a farming people, they were familiar with the fact that seeds planted in the ground returned as harvest the following year, just like the sun rose every morning.

A splendid centre of infinity's whirl pushed to its zenith's height, its last expanse, felt the divinity of its own self-bliss repeated in its numberless other selves. —Sri Aurobindo

The symbol of a serpent or dragon swallowing its own tail and forming a circle, constantly re-creating itself, traces back to Ancient Egypt. The alchemists adopted the symbol named Ouroboros, representing self-reflexivity or cyclicality, cycles that begin anew as soon as they end, and put forth the image of the snake or dragon eating its tail as a sign of Eternal Return. Karl Jung regarded the archetype as the basic mandala of alchemy, writing: *The Ouroboros has been said to have a meaning of infinity or wholeness. In the age-old image of the Ouroboros lies the thought of devouring oneself into a circulatory process, for it was clear to the more astute alchemists that the prima materia of the art was man himself. A dramatic symbol for the integration and assimilation of the opposite, the shadow. This feed-back process is at the same time a symbol of immortality, since it is said of the Ouroboros that he slays himself and brings himself to life, fertilizes himself and gives birth to himself.*

The world was before the creation, and at an end before it had a beginning; and thus was I dead before I was alive, though my grave be England, my dying place was Paradise, and Eve miscarried me before she conceived Cain. —Thomas Browne

Pythagorean teachings brought to Greece theories about the origin of the universe expanding ad infinitum distinguishing between two kinds of repetition. Pythagoras put forth that the same things are repeated again and again and exist a number of times; one is the natural order of things, like seasons, the other is that there is no difference in time. In our three-dimensional world we don't seeing space-time-eternity, that requires five dimensions, the fourth dimension being time. Each moment of the universe refers to billions and billions of years. This process is the macrocosm of everything that happens in nature. According to Pythagoras, the universe is a constant cycle of separation and reunion. All the notes together compose celestial music to encompass the harmony of the spheres.

Above the cloud with its shadow is the star with its light. Above all things reverence thyself. There is geometry in the humming of the strings, there is music in the spacing of the spheres. —*Pythagoras*

THE WHEEL OF TIME

Gautama the Buddha taught the law of Eternal Recurrence as the wheel of lives. The wheel, one of the most important Buddhist symbols, represents endless cycles, that all formations are impermanent, as an indication of the way things are, as a mirror to study and to understand the eternal laws. In Tantric Buddhism, Kalachakra is a teaching portraying our endless cycle. Kalachakra, wheel of time, is the flow of all events, past, present, and future. The Kalachakra deity represents omniscience, one with all time, therefore knowing all. The wheel, with no beginning and no ending, is also the universal symbol of Buddhism. The Dalai Lama has portrayed Kalachakra as the teaching for our time.

The natural seasonal changes are a visible appearance of this law; summer disappears as fall appears, winter arrives year after year, the moon is new, later in the month full, and then new again. We live within the framework of this repetition knowing it as movements of the heavenly bodies which produce phenomena such as solstice and equinox; in our three-dimensional world this is our reality. Evolution, through inner growth moves us into the fourth and fifth dimension. Loosened from the wheel of the fifth dimension we pass into the spiral of the sixth dimension.

A mountain is composed of tiny grains of earth. The ocean is made of of tiny drops of water. Life is an endless series of little details, actions, speeeches and thoughts. And the consequences are far-reaching. —*Swami Sivananda*

Within the world of nature the caterpillar forms a chrysalis and one day splits open emerging as a beautiful butterfly. Passing to a new level, no longer appearing in its previous form, disappearing from the caterpillar realm; many mark this transformation as a mysterious magical happening yet it is also a manifestation of the universal law of Eternal Recurrence.

'How does one become a butterfly? 'Pooh asked pensively. 'You must want to fly so much that you're willing to give up being a caterpillar.' Piglet replied 'You mean you die?' asked Pooh. 'Yes and no,' he answered. 'What looks like you will die, but what's really you will live on.' —*A. A. Milne*

To Change Ourselves Internally

To understand eternity is to know the present moment. In this timeless spaceless realm all creation is interconnected and interdependent. A simple continuous unfolding of the present; understanding the law of Eternal Recurrence is to realize the consciousness within us in this moment. In the world of Eternal return the responsibility lies firmly on every move we make. Director Harold Ramis' popular film Groundhog

Day, based on the theme of Eternal Recurrence, states: *the antidote to the existential dilemma at the core of my movie, is expressed by Ouspensky; trapped as we are on the karmic wheel of cause and effect, our only means of escape is to assume responsibility for our own destiny and find the personal meaning that imparts a purposeful vitality to life.*

Ouspensky's masterful classic novel, *Strange Life of Ivan Osokin*, inspired the film Ground Hog Day imaginatively exploring Eternal Recurrence. This theme has engaged great minds like Schopenhauer and Nietzsche. We live our lives over and over again in a kind of endlessly repeating film; nothing will change in this ceaseless merry-go-round unless we ourselves change—deeply and fundamentally.

Ivan Osokin, protagonist in Oupensky's book *Strange Life of Ivan Osokin*, demonstrates that even to be given, to be gifted with free-will to alter events in our life, the same events will happen, regardless. Ivan goes to a magician, tells him bitterly of all the chances he has thrown away in his life. If he had only known beforehand the outcome of his actions he imagined that he would not have had such disappointment. The magician laughs and tells him that nothing would be changed. Then, with Ivan's surprise and agreement, he offers to prove it by sending him back twelve years. He may relive his life, and may even remember at every stage—if he wants to—what the consequences will be. Ivan wakes up in the same dormitory at school, where he proceeds to misbehave and get expelled, just as he did before. He brings emotional distress, hurting his mother just as he did before. What had been his past is now his future; he knows it but cannot avoid it. He gets into the same scrapes, has the same adventures with women. By the time he again meets the woman he once loved, Zinaida, he has forgotten that he had ever met her. The story repeats itself down to the last detail—until, once again, he finds himself visiting the magician. But when he reaches the point of asking the magician to send him back, he suddenly remembers everything. *But this is simply turning round on a wheel,* says Osokin. The old man smiles. *My dear friend,* he says, *you must realize that you yourself can change nothing and that you must seek help. And to live with this realization means to sacrifice something big for it. This is the law of human nature.*

Osokin is told by the magician to *remember.* The knowledge of having lived before is a great but unsafe secret, given to us only once, to be made use of or to use us. The Magician tells Ivan: *A man can be given only what he can use; and he can use only that for which he has sacrificed something. So if a man wants to acquire important knowledge or new powers, he must sacrifice other things important to him at the moment. Moreover, he can only get as much as he has given up for it. You cannot have results without causes. By your sacrifice you create causes. Now the question of what to sacrifice and how to sacrifice. You say you have nothing. Not quite, You have your life, So you can sacrifice your life. It is a very small price to pay since you meant to throw it away in any case. Instead of that, give me your life and I will see what can be made of you. I shall not require the whole of your life. Twenty, even fifteen years will be sufficient. When this time is over you will be able to use your knowledge for yourself.*

If a man could understand all the horror of the lives of ordinary people who are turning round in a circle of insignificant interests and insignificant aims, if he could understand what they are losing, he would understand that there can only be one thing that is serious for him—to escape from the general law, to be free. What can be serious for a man in prison who is condemned to death? Only one thing: How to save himself, how to escape: nothing else is serious. —G.I. Gurdjieff

Recurrence is a fact—to escape requires sacrifice. Nothing will change in this endless life of distractions unless we ourselves change internally. To not change anything in ourselves, everything will be the same again. The sacrifice is to withdraw energy from life which feeds personality; to withdraw energy from our personality allows essence to grow. Essence changes as we see and understand that we must change something in ourselves. The growth of essence, outside of time and therefore not limited to any particular time, creates an Eternal, not worldly change. It is our essence which recurs, in Eternity, not in life time. Our body is in time, our essence on the vertical, is above time. Essence will attract new circumstances and retain memory, and memory is our relationship to time (refer to System 9, Essence Nature, for further explanation of essence).

TIME AS INFINITE CIRCLES

We seldom realize, for example that our most frequent thoughts are not actually our own. For we think in terms of languages and images which we did not invent, but which were given to us by our society. —*Alan Wilson Watts*

To enter again the same circle and change our being; to stand in presence assists all who have ever and will now enter our circle. We reshape everything in the past, present and future, since time is a circle. Time is infinite circles all turning on themselves, some inter-connecting; the past becomes as living as the present and future. Nothing in nature follows a straight line, time follows a curve, eternity another dimension of time, just as life itself, for us, is time. As a line that bends round on itself and then returns to the same place, which is a circle, our lives are curved and return to the same place; the moment of birth. Developing ourselves, we change the now, as well as the past and future. Knowing that the line of time is a curve, not a straight line, is the explanation for other dimensions and for Eternity.

That which has been is that which will be, and that which has been done is that which will be done. So there is nothing new under the sun. —*Ecclesiastes*

The earth was once perceived as flat, as a plane or disc; that the world stopped at the end of the horizon. Following the invention of the compass and improved map-making and with the return of Christopher Columbus from his trans-Atlantic voyage, the concept of the earth as flat was shattered. Here we see time, too, is round. In the present moment, time disappears. Different planes and dimensions exist, parallel universes spin off and merge, essentially there is an endless contraction and expansion. On each parallel there may be a different outcome for us. Some of us acknowledge experiencing more than one reality.

If we do not change anything in ourselves everything will be the same again. Developing our essence changes our life and our memory; now, at a difficult moment one remembers what to do and we make new choices. Looking at this life, at the cross-roads where we might have taken a different turn, remembering those moments consciously might alter the course of our whole life. Things no longer need to be avoided, since completion will happen, or we will be brought back to the same point again and again. Goethe explaining this idea claimed that: *All wise thoughts have been thought already thousands of times; but to make them truly ours, we must think them over again honestly, till they take root in our personal experience.*

Albert Camus, in the Myth of Sysyphus, has the hero condemned to repeating a process, accomplishing nothing, yet states that *the struggle itself towards the heights is enough to fill a man's heart.* The gratification we discover through hard work becomes the accomplishment, work not always rewarded with a monetary paycheck. Only if Sysyphus becomes conscious of his task, if during the descent he develops awareness he becomes superior to his fate. Camus states that *he is stronger than his rock, superior to his fate. Our fate is the only thing that we can shape, and in doing so, that fate belongs to us. Sisyphus' rock belongs to him. There is no end, the rock is still rolling, I leave Sysyphus at the foot of the mountain. The struggle itself towards the heights is enough to fill a man's heart. One must imagine Sysyphus happy.*

A Taste Of The Eternal Now

Nietzsche in his poetic writings of *Zarathustra* created an identity that became *the teacher of eternal recurrence*. Eternity means another dimension, not extension of time, no longer before or after. The fourth dimension is time and the fifth dimension, Eternity. Recurrence, everything being connected, says our circles connect with other circles and that developing ourselves impacts now, the past, and the future. There being no time as we imagine it, everything is living and present. No permanence, the world does not aim at a final state, it is always changing, and, like a body of water, is energy. Nietzsche writes about *seeking an eternity for everything, for everything seems far too valuable to be fleeting.* To treasure life, the joy found here and now, is the affirmation that makes our life and its possibilities come alive. This allows us to be freed *from* the world to be freed *for* the world, to be in it authentically, with full heart. Forms dissolve and the world of light is still. The law of Eternal Recurrence brings a taste of the Eternal now.

At death we have the possibility, claims author and teacher of consciousness Maurice Nicoll, *of acquiring part of this life for our own use; with work, effort of the right kind, this life becomes for us imperishable being.* Charles Nott, writer and student of Gurdjieff, offered the view-point that: *If a man works on himself, then circumstances will change with him. His characteristics will be similar, but his essence may be different. He may be freer and so avoid many stupid mistakes.*

What is the use of a man knowing about recurrence if he is not conscious of it and if he himself does not change? One can even say that if a man does not change, repetition does not exist for him. —G.I. Gurdjieff

To remember is meaningless without the memory combined with a moment in the present which brings a view of the same image; our memory must see double. This combination of dissimilar objects in memory offers the clarity, our awareness, perception.

*Ouspensky's picture of eternal recurrence, in which we do the same thing over and over again is expressed in his novel Strange Life of Ivan Osokin. The hero is powerless to change his endless repetition even when he has access to the knowledge that this is happening. It is not enough to be aware of recurrence, we have to be 'able to do' something about it. We can meditate forever but we 'are not there.' To receive and be aware of impressions in a conscious way is linked to 'self-remembering'. Building inner substance allows us to become aware of recurrence and can begin to do something about it. Now we are growing from essence—the state in which we were born and not the state which has accumulated through external impacts. The main characteristic of essence is that it does not rely on memory or calculation but deals with things as they are without images or explanations. Our spiritual practice is what we do with our inner lives apart from our involvement in the world, our work on ourself. From within, our key to integrity in life, is about our communication with ourselves. What we have called the unconscious is true consciousness. To know what we are doing is intentional creativity. Now 'we know the place for the first time.' Feeding the body of the soul, we become entirely spontaneous. Salvation is associated with the transformation of negative emotions. Recurrence is ended. With this, we leave the Enneagram.
—A.G.E. Blake*

Objective consciousness frees us from the confinement of Eternal Recurrence. Awakened, life becomes the teacher, and we do not have to return to the same place. Rodney Collins in *The Theory of Eternal Life* writes: *We may compare the circle of man's life to an electric circuit which is broken at death, and has memory to the current. This 'break' is quite sufficient to prevent the flow of current at its ordinary intensity from one side to the other. But were the electric tension to be very greatly increased, the current might be expected to arc across the gap, thus creating an intense light and at the same time completing the circuit and permitting a 'flow' from one side to the other. The escape of the self from a cellular into an electronic state is like an atomic explosion.* Lives develop sequentially one out of another in Recurrence; the moment of death in one life is the moment of conception in the next. Let us continue to develop consciousness so that we can use this lifetime well, bringing memory, not collapsing into unconsciousness, remaining awake as we cross the threshold into the realm of spirit.

The path up and the path down is one and the same. Identical the beginning and the end. Living and dead are the same, and so awake and asleep, young and old: the former shifted become the latter, and the latter shifted the former. —Heraclitus

20. IMPERMANENCE AND CONTINUATION

If we are not empty, we become a block of matter. We cannot breathe, we cannot think. To be empty means to be alive, to breathe in and to breathe out. We cannot be alive if we are not empty. Emptiness is impermanence, it is change. We should not complain about impermanence, because without impermanence, nothing is possible. —Thich Nhat Hahn

The universal law of Impermanence and Continuation teaches us to drop into true joy and the preciousness of every moment. Buddha understood after he left the palace that all things desired and cherished pass away and rather than being caught up in worldly considerations he sought to look deeply, to understand the true nature of life and death.

Our attachment to a particular form is what brings us pain and suffering. The courage and awareness to understand Impermanence, to be present and practice Impermanence and Continuation, is to touch the body of suffering and experience both joy and sorrow, seeing into the heart of existence. Relaxing into our true nature, life unfolds. To not investigate and look deeply into the nature of life and death many people live in fear and suffering. Our efforts to live in the present moment is a training for understanding Impermanence. Experiencing comings and goings and process and continuation we become vulnerable to the wondrous honest simplicity of life. To look deeply at the concepts of birth and death, that the wave disappears and becomes ocean, we learn to value what is here now and teach ourselves to shift suffering into joy.

Ii is not impermanence that makes us suffer. What makes us suffer is wanting things to be permanent when they are not. —Thich Nhat Hahn

Past, present and future are concepts that most often keep us from living in the present. And life is happening in the present moment. *The cause of all pain and suffering is ignorance* has been a guiding statement ascribed to Buddha. *We are imprisoned by the world of ignorance, birth, and death because we take this imaginary, constructed world created by our mind as reality,* states Thich Nhat Hahn. Seeing things as they are, life, death, money, finances, political institutions, mountains, health, aging, the interdependence of all things; freed of judgments opens the door to love, understanding and inner peace.

Is not impermanence the very fragrance of our days? —*Rainer Maria Rilke*

All things change, nothing remains the same and so there are no permanent identities. I read today that an Antarctic iceberg glacier was breaking apart. Does that mean that the glacier dies, or does it absorb into the moving waters to become less solid as it joins the sea? Continuing, continuing, the glacier moves along into its changed form. When we look deeply into ourselves we too can step into the realm of moving waters that become the sea. Looking into the nature of Impermanence and Continuation we loosen our confinement to time and space, we look deeply to live deeply.

THE NATURE OF LIFE

Impermanence is the law of the universe. —*Carlene Hatcher Polite*

There is a tendency for people to get lost in the distractions and activities of life, to pull away from the immediacy of life's Impermanence. Pain killers, alcohol, gambling and other substances indulged as addictions are used to cover the truth of the law of Impermanence. To experience this law and also the beauty, meaning, sadness, joy, and the flux and flow of life brings us to the depth of this law. To practice living under this law brings us to value and cherish what we have: to treat with kindness and love our beloved, home, friends, health, all the beautiful things that surround us, for they are Impermanent and will change.

When you swim, be a part of the sea; when you walk, be a part of the road! Integrate with the universe! See it not as a distinct entity, but as your own continuation, as your own self! –Mehmet Murat Ildan

Our culture emphasizes identifying with the externals, the ego, with those things that we imagine to be real and permanent. Depression, medication, bitterness and dissatisfaction mask the avoidance of learning how to live within a law that is designed to liberate us from fear and to see our true nature.

Impermanence is a principle of harmony. When we don't struggle against it, we are in harmony with reality. —Pema Chodron

All is fleeting. Impermanence is the core and essential quality of all phenomenal existence. The fragrance of the flowers, the beauty of the butterflies, the sun as it rises, the sound of the bell, the moment-by-moment arising and passing reveal the pure nature of things. Our ideas of the way things should be, our viewpoint and senses mislead us to live in illusion. Understanding process and movement, that people and thoughts come into being and pass away, change form and energetically continue, are a reminder of the nature of life.

Some people, sweet and attractive, and strong and healthy, happen to die young. They are masters in disguise teaching us about impermanence. —Dalai Lama

THE FIVE REMEMBRANCES

We arrive into this world as a Continuation; the illusion of permanence, the concept of a fixed identity cultivates a suffering that fills this world. Do we remember that we were already here before birth? Thay says if we ask a sheet of paper if it was here before it was this book it would answer, *Yes, in the form of a tree, in the form of sunshine, in the form of a cloud and the rain, in the form of minerals and the earth. The moment of becoming a sheet of paper was a moment of continuation.* In our world the avoidance of looking deeply at life and death brings aging to become a dodged experience. So many eagerly make tremendous efforts to create changes that sidestep telltale signs of youthfulness. Erasing wrinkles, coloring the grey, transplanting thinning hair, all part of the illusion that protects and relieves us from the thought of dying.

If you look deeply into the palm of your hand, you will see all generations of your ancestors. All of them are alive in this moment. Each is present in your body. You are the continuation of each of these people. Before your so-called birthday, you were already there, in your mother. So that moment of child-birth is only a moment of continuation. —Thich Nhat Hahn

Our lives with their shifts and changes from childhood to adolescence to this present moment, our physical changes, brown hair to grey, are a reflection of this law. Understanding arrives through living fully, not as concept and theory, instead, fully living, being present to know and to touch what is our life. Being open, to be with our life, as Ram Dass reminds us, to *be here now.*

A ground and central teaching of the Eastern tradition are the Five Remembrances:

1. *I am of the nature to grow old. There is no way to escape growing old.*

2. *I am of the nature to have ill health. There is no way to escape having ill health.*

3. *I am of the nature to die. There is no way to escape death.*

4. *All that is dear to me and everyone I love are of the nature to change. There is no way to escape being separated from them.*

5. *My actions are my only true belongings. I cannot escape the consequences of my actions. My actions are the ground on which I stand.*

The Law of Impermanence and Continuation is expressed in the Five Remembrances and what we learn to cultivate is a consciousness that diminishes our suffering, does not add to the suffering of others and opens a heart of compassion towards ourselves and humanity.

There is nothing permanent except change. Everything flows and nothing abides; everything gives way and nothing stays fixed. Cool things become warm, the warm grows cool; the moist dries, the parched becomes moist. It is in changing that things find repose. You cannot step twice into the same river, for fresh waters are ever flowing in upon you. —Heraclitus

21. GRACE

All the natural movements of the soul are controlled by laws analogous to those of physical gravity. Grace is the only exception. —*Simone Weil*

The law of Grace is an invisible power that lifts and is all and everything. Grace carries kindness, mercy, compassion, favor, goodwill, benevolence, beneficence, forgiveness, harmony, blessing and wisdom. It is unending and amazing, this state of Grace. To be open to receive is to live in the question that arises from the heart. As we allow life to unfold through us, Grace is always present. Living in a state of Grace, that silent light of presence, is a culminating crowning law.

Grace is a mirror of eternal energies teaching us to transform seeing into contemplation and enabling us to view the world in eternal beauty. —*I Ching or Book of Changes*

Think of this law pulling upwards, the opposite of the law of gravity which is usually a downward force. Beauty and harmony the cycle of the earthly and divine are expressed through this law. Opening to a state of Grace often communicated through the power of silence, we arrive into the present moment, sitting in presence. It's where we really are, landing in an instant. A moment of recognition carrying a breath of fresh air, inexhaustible. Yet what place does Grace have in our ordinary life? Subtle, concealed, an often unnoticed gift.

Grace is the beauty of form under the influence of freedom. —*Friedrich Schiller*

In French, Grace, as acknowledgement means *thank you*. The *I Ching* or Book of Changes, names Grace, or Pi, a hexagram, the tranquility of pure contemplation, composed of creative heaven and receptive earth. The saying of Grace at meal time is an expression of appreciation and gratitude towards the food that appears on our table and to all who made it possible for our benefit, our nurturance; all things can become our bread of life. *There is no death,* said poet Gary Snyder, *that is not somebody's food, no life that is not somebody's death.* Sacrifice feeds us, and we learn to live within the law of Grace instead of accumulating karma. As we loosen ourselves from universal laws, Grace is living in harmony within the invisible, increasing the flow of thanksgiving in our hearts.

THE LAW OF FALLING UPWARDS

Grace is God as heart surgeon, cracking open your chest, removing your heart—poisoned as it is with pride and pain—and replacing it with his own. Grace is the voice that calls us to change and then gives us the power to pull it off. —Max Lucado

Grace, always becoming, never static; the law of falling upwards. This is the mystery of love, individuality disappears. To risk and enter the unknowable, for all happening to disappear is to have a love affair with everything and nothing. Grace is the blessing, the benediction. Surrender, and then life is conquered. St. Augustine portrayed Grace as a love that is our preparation, a beginning and end, stating that: *God provides the wind, man must raise the sail. Will is to grace as the horse is to the rider.*

The winds of grace are always blowing, but you have to raise the sail. —Sri Ramakrishna

In ancient Greece, the three Graces were goddesses of joy, charm and beauty, endowing creativity and love. Defined as the powers of giving, receiving and returning, a circle of divine love given, received, returned; creation and evolution. *Charis,* the Greek word for Grace is a name that means shining veil. In the myth of Charis, the *Iliad* of Homer, Grace is concealed in daily events where its presence goes unnoticed, entering the simple moments, practical graciousness lifts the mundane to meaningfulness. So often repeated in the prayer: *Hail Mary, full of grace*, earthly and divine love completing a circle, offering that we, too, be filled with Grace. The Hail Mary, traditionally known as the Ave Maria, greeted as a simple woman, a mother living on earth, one *full of grace*, is a bridge between the human and the divine worlds.

The Old Testament refers to her as Sophia, the incarnation of the wisdom beneath all spiritual knowledge. Charis and Maria both carry Grace as the feminine representation of the queen and goddess of heaven and earth, also called Shekinah, the dwelling of the Divine Presence, radiant beautiful being of light, a manifestation of a loving maternal entity.

Love is the crowning Grace of humanity, the holiest right of the soul, the golden link which binds us to duty and truth, the redeeming principle that chiefly reconciles the heart to life, and is prophetic of eternal good. —*Petrarch*

RESTING IN AWARENESS

Ram Dass, who influenced a generation of spiritual beings, in the later part of his life, created a documentary feature film, *Fierce Grace*. The film explores the evolution of the New Age and Ram Dass' life including the massive stroke which left him paralyzed on the right side, confined to a wheelchair and with speech aphasia. The brain damage that affected his language center made it difficult for him to find words, bringing him to value the long silence between words which deepened his spirit. In an interview, describing the stroke as *fierce grace*, he speaks to the question: *what is grace?*

Grace is when one lives in the spirit. When we are able to get away from the ego plane, to our souls, where we can see things as God sees them, we experience our lives as grace. Those who take the spiritual trip too lightly will receive 'fierce grace.' If you have faith, then grace will stay. Stroke, grace, stroke, grace, stroke, grace. This has been my major spiritual exercise during the stroke, bringing these two together. The suffering comes when you try to hold on to continuity. —Ram Dass

Ram Dass, king on a throne, not victim in a wheelchair, experienced Grace as a presence that *just is. When I focus on who I used to be or on who I thought I was going to be, it brings up suffering. But if I just rest in awareness, I'm fine.* This invitation from the universe, called stroke, echoes teachers who offer the message to stop and call off the search, and to then see what is revealed. Being stroked, Ram Dass has continued to inspire and serve, humbled by his physical limitations, living his teaching in a new way. The Grace that effects transformation, that invites change, is possible only to a receptive heart.

When you die you will not be called to account for the illegitimate things you did do, but for all the legitimate pleasures you might have tasted and did not: You will give account for what you saw, yet did not take the time to appreciate. —Jewish Proverb

The smallest offering made with sincerity and a reverent attitude knows that Grace lives in the midst of our daily work. The mystic sees the miraculous as constant reminders of divine harmony. To open our eyes to the ongoing process of everyday miracles is to know the law of Grace. The invisible sustains us and has the ability to overlap the inner and outer worlds.

The things that we pray for, give us the grace to labour. —Thomas Moore

There is a moment in life when everything comes into focus and makes perfect sense. The incongruities, the pain, hidden messages, all fall into place; in the larger picture a weight is lifted off our shoulders as we drop into the understanding that things are exactly as they are. The recognition, the invisible becoming visible, this opening to the creative source lies in our awareness as the power of Grace. Outside and independent of time, the Grace of transformation enters. Always here, like gravity, for us to be vessels of that presence. In this generation Mick Jagger expresses this state in the lyrics of *Jump for Joy*: *My soul is like a ruby And I threw it on the earth But now my hands are bleeding From scrabbling in the dirt And I look up to the heavens And a light is on my face I never never thought I'd find a state of grace.*

To live in this oneness, unity; this is the uplifting universal law. Surrender. And those who have lived this law: Buddha, Moses, Krishna, Rumi; they lived spiritually levitated. This, then, is the law of falling upwards—rising in love until we disappear.

Grace is not a magic substance which is filtered into our souls to act as a spiritual penicillin. Grace is unity, oneness within ourselves, oneness with the universe. —*Thomas Merton*

CHAPTER THIRTEEN

Epilogue: Final Thoughts
The Way of Understanding

Life At Its Best

If understood, life is simply a jest;

If misunderstood, life becomes a pest.

Once overcome, life is ever at rest.

For pilgrims of the Path, life is a test,

When relinquished through love,

Life is at its best.

—Meher Baba

FINAL THOUGHTS
The Way Of Understanding

When we want to understand something, we cannot just stand outside and observe it. We have to enter deeply into it and be one with it in order to really understand. If we want to understand a person, we have to feel their feelings, suffer their sufferings, and enjoy their joy. Love is impossible without understanding. Understanding is the fruit of meditation. Understanding is the basis of everything. No understanding, no attainment. Understanding is the essence of a Buddha. Perfect Understanding is the destroyer of all suffering, the highest, the unequalled mantra. —Thich Nhat Hahn

*T*he Way of the Lover, The Fifth Way, considers each person from a heart of Understanding and what in the present moment we want; not from what we have, had or will be, not by our status or wealth or looks, or how much we know. What we want arises from our capacity for Understanding. Knowledge, solid, if not reinvented and renewed, blocks our open penetrating flow of Understanding. We are our Understanding and out of that emerges what we want. A demand for Understanding is the principal claim made upon us, the most powerful, strongest force we can create.

If we have reached some creative insight or some deeper perception, we find it difficult to remember how it came about. It is for that reason that we consider the creative step to be spontaneous, unconscious, and generally out of our control. We do not know how to make it happen again. As T.S. Eliot says: 'We had the experience but missed the meaning.' What we have to do is build a bridge of remembrance, a way of recapitulation that can reengineer the same event again. This then is true mastery. The completion of understanding is to be able to recreate an insight at will. Progress takes place within the present moment as we integrate our experience in and out of time. —A.G.E.Blake

Throughout this book are ways of Understanding. Offerings to enhance presence. To recognize and Understand deepens our being. Understanding comes about through inward change, illuminates the mind, to be freed from the world, to be freed for the world, to enter worlds that previously were unavailable. We are responsible only for what we Understand. To do something because we Understand, rather than because we are told, makes a tremendous difference. To react is easy, to Understand comes through mindful awareness. The greater we Understand what we are doing the greater are the results of our efforts. Results are proportionate to the consciousness we bring to our task. You cannot disagree and Understand. To Understand reveals interior connections. There are not many Understandings, there is only one.

If a person does not become what he understands, he does not really understand it. —*Soren Kierrkegaad*

Often we meet people dissatisfied with their lack of knowledge, rarely are people discontent with their level of being; that place of stillness, inner being, which is our true source of strength and stability. To react mechanically is easy, to Understand is sophisticated and deepens maturity. Living fearfully reactive to external influences impedes our psychological development. To live for the sake of our reputation causes us to live inauthentically in a well-dressed world outside and often an unpeaceful interior psychological world.

A lifetime is so precious and brief, and can be used so beautifully. —*Pema Chodron*

Growth arrives through patience and self-valuation, as we respond from our Understanding, connecting to a place deep inside ourselves. Until the word *practice* becomes our friend learning remains a remote abstract idea; we are learned when we pay attention to what appears in our life using it as our practice. Practice loving, practice with relationships, practice paying attention to ourself; everything we want arrives through preparation and self-reflection. Polished to a beautiful patina, everything becomes our practice, and eventually, one day, our life is lived with our beautiful presence as a meditation.

Understanding is hidden, inward, a result less of changing what we know than of changing ourselves and the way in which we exist. To understand more, we have to be more, have to become transformed. The true test of our understanding is not that it gives our ordinary selves more to talk about but that it enables us to create these higher worlds within ourselves, to enter into the higher worlds which, until then, must remain for us only words. And to make this entry, we may find that we have to learn how to empty ourselves, then everything can enter into us. If we learn to get out of the way, then everything can come. When we truly 'understand,' it is to 'stand under,' that is, to be subject to the laws of the higher worlds. —J.G. Bennett

EVERYTHING BECOMES OUR PRACTICE

We are our Understanding, therefore how we live our knowledge is with wisdom and creativity, or obstructive and harmful. A person taking gun lessons may have knowledge of how to shoot a gun, yet lacking Understanding use it mindlessly to kill someone. The shift is internal. This journey of self-empowerment brings us to our own true face. To have self-awareness we have everything ever needed. To think in a new way learning to navigate the depths of human nature, discovering ourselves, these works in progress, we awaken to another level of life. Awakening is the most precious possibility we have, how we use our consciousness, what we place it on, there we are. We cast a light on positive or negative things; where our consciousness is, there we will be. Inner work is step number one on the ladder, to own the projections we put out onto the world. Without standing on this first rung of the ladder we see out into the world through a glass darkly, through a frosted window painted grey, with no light coming in; self-awareness increases the light, penetrates the dark.

Understanding is the strongest force that we can create in ourselves. We must remember the moments of understanding that we have had. —*Nicoll*

Through Understanding we develop being; knowledge and being equally matured bring us to greater internal freedom replacing the imbalance that originally created our dissatisfaction. Fear, anxiety and lack of presence is a reflection of lack of Understanding, a deficiency of inner development. Understanding, increased consciousness and love are all identical. Understanding is the internal quality that holds us to the difficult, it is the rope, the ladder, the raft.

Understanding arises naturally from the dismantling of the patterns that prevent us from knowing what we are. To dismantle reactive patterns we need to cultivate attention, and to cultivate attention we need to bring order into our lives. Understanding comes from the direct experience of being. It changes how we think, feel, and behave. If understanding doesn't change how we think, feel, perceive, and act, it isn't really understanding. —*Ken Mcleod*

This world is a very narrow bridge, don't build your house on it. When everything is taken away, know that it was not you. There is always something that can not be taken away; Nelson Mandela knew this during his years in prison, Jesus lived this truth, Eckhart Tolle and Thich Nhat Hahn give voice to this. When we truly absorb something it enters, becomes part of who we are, a certainty that erases all doubt, a discovery and a way of being not to be taken away.

We are all falling above the infinite groundlessness of life, and we learn

to become stable in flight, and to support others to become free of the fear that arises from feeling unmoored. The final resting place is not the ground at all but rather the freedom that arises from knowing there will never be a ground, and yet we are here, together, navigating the boundless space of life, not attached, yet intimate. 'Wherever you may be, your life is sustained and supported by the whole universe. The main purpose of human life is to maintian this sanctuary. It is not to climb a ladder to develop your own personal life.' The unity of heart, mind, body, the world, and this moment is the sanctuary, a place of no resistance, a place of refuge. This very moment is that place. Not seeking, not fleeing, but resting in the midst...this is why we practice, so we can actualize awakening inside the life that we have.
—*Joan Halifax*

In his teachings Gurdjieff speaks to a universal law that *the quality of what is perceived by anyone* when another person tells us something, *either for our knowledge or our understanding, depends on the quality of the data formed in the person speaking.* So often we go to lectures and classes and nothing happens or passes through us. Gurdjieff insisted that *Understanding is the first requirement of his teaching.* In that we can only Understand others as much as we Understand ourself, and then seeing the connection with a larger whole, with a greater perspective, is how and why to use the teachings of universal laws and the systems in this second part of this book. To see ourselves under the influence of greater laws, to truly know that to see more we have to be more, engages practice. As we create these higher worlds within ourselves, how to step out of the way and pay attention, opens us towards our awakening.

If one appreciates something with the mind, one 'knows' it, if one appreciates it with the emotions one 'feels' it, if one appreciates it with the external physical organs one 'senses' it, but, if one simultaneously appreciates it with the mind, emotions and physical senses then one really 'understands' it. This is very rare as we are. It can be developed. —*Rodney Collin*

UNDERSTANDING IS LOVES NAME

To learn to respond from our Understanding rather than our impulses, to disengage from our reactivity, to awaken and be present is the aim and purpose of using the tools in Part Two. Mechanized humanity thinks concretely with justification, explanation, rationalization; clinging to form. To become self-aware is to think psychologically, spiritually, mindfully, consciously as individuals with an inner life looking to make connections and meaning. The development of knowledge and being form our Understanding, which does not remain static, it increases or diminishes. How we speak, how we think, the words we choose determine how we experience our lives. And this is the essential ground for *The Way of the Lover.*

Right understanding. Our understanding is not to be only an intellectual understanding. True understanding is actual practice itself. Our understanding at the same time is its own expression, is the practice itself. Not by reading or contemplation of philosophy, but only through practice, actual practice, can we understand. —Shunryu Suzuki

Understand for yourself why you want to deepen awareness. Our personality is something that develops outside of us and does not really belong to us, like clothing from a store it is bought and worn; on the other hand, essence which is born to us, matures; through Understanding it matures and marks a growth in our consciousness. Essence grows from our internal side. As we respond from a deeper place this move inward feeds essence, locates us to where we are, who we are, to our purpose. The light increases, connections turn on, light bulbs now illuminate broadly sweeping expanses.

True love is possible only with understanding. When there is understanding, compassion is born. To love without knowing how to love wounds the person we love. Understanding is love's other name. If you don't understand, you can't love. If our parents didn't love and understand each other, how are we to know what love looks like? The most precious inheritance that parents can give their children is their own happiness. If we have happy parents, we have received the richest inheritance of all. —Thich Nhat Hahn

The tools in Part Two offer strategies to catch glimpses of what we are really like; to experience another is first to recognize ourself. To see our personal psychology and make changes in our inner world happens through psychological effort. If the physical body were as sloppy as our inner world most people would clean up the mess. Creating a witness leads to self-awareness; now we notice where we are inside and create an intention to where we want to be. The offerings in this book are open systems presented as challenge and investigation, ongoing processes continuously reinvented. Using this book well, studying ourselves, finding the contradictions, seeing what prevents us from shaking up the false images brings light into our inner darkness.

There is no coming to consciousness without pain. People will do anything, no matter how absurd, to avoid facing their own soul. One does not become enlightened by imagining figures of light, but by making the darkness conscious. —Carl Gustav Jung

There are many ways to read this book; alone and/or with others, studied as themes, discussions, note-taking to discover and learn the systems and laws, slowly carefully digesting, as well as continuing to read it again. To walk in the foot-steps of those who have gone before, to experience all worlds penetrating everything, seeing and participating in the laws as we are affected, we become more. The moments of sudden Understanding, of open clear states, of loving and living into our smile offer the possibility of setting the direction; to live authentically aware and awake, is the spirit and determination for our life.

When we talk about understanding, surely it takes place only when the mind listens completely—the mind being your heart, your nerves, your ears—when you give your whole attention to it. —Jiddu Krishnamurti

AWAKENING

To know and understand real change requires a long preparation and to want it very much for a very long time. A passing desire or a vague desire based on dissatisfaction with external conditions will not create a sufficient impulse. One's evolution depends on individual understanding of what one might get and what must give for it. —P.D. Ouspensky

That pure seed of awakening when attended, watered and well-fed is priceless and reveals everything as it is. Here are maps and direction, methods, practices and tools, keys to unlock the great mysteries, the *how* of awakening. Each teaching changes us, they are doors into ourself to stabilize our Understanding, glimpses into the universe. We are capable of further transformation, of awakening; in this manner we keep our self-renewing process in motion.

GIVING THE GIFTS: RECEIVING THE PRIZES

To give to humanity what we find within ourselves opens the heart of the world. In this journey of self-discovery, *The Way of the Lover,* we come to know ourself through our interaction with life. We are mid-wives to a new awakening, the process itself is the gift. To remember the simplicity of the journey, illusions drop and we see the wonder of our own true nature. The first step is to know ourself. To contact the hidden treasure so we can be of service, to distribute the wealth, the jewels: our gifts. The invisible becomes visible as it joins eternity, and in love our beauty is revealed. A sudden glimpse into what's hidden, the invisible worlds, is our pure moment. Our evolution is inner. To evolve the ability to concentrate attention on inner states: to become aware of ourself, to drop our consciousness back into a space where there is no story, where there is no longer attachment to our thoughts, when thoughts arise to let them pass through; in those moments of silence everything becomes sacred.

Stop measuring days by degree of productivity and start experiencing them by degree of presence. —Alan Watts

This book speaks to awakening, a sustained inner capacity, an earned state freed from reactivity, delusion of separateness, habituated conditioning and unnecessary suffering: these become our wealth—our prizes. Individual effort, combined with grace, moments that bring a taste of bliss—gifts, surprises, prizes received appear; both are necessary for self-evolution. States which manifest in the heart are passing moments, higher states become miraculous, transporting us, this is the polish, the reminder of paradise, a beautiful heaven on earth.

To be yourself in a world that is constantly trying to make you something else is the greatest accomplishment. —Ralph Waldo Emerson

WHY I LISTEN

Holy listening—to 'listen' another's soul into life, into a condition of disclosure and discovery—may be almost the greatest service that any human being ever performs for another. —Douglas V. Steere

Flowers open because they hear something. Fruits grow in exchange for the warm tenderness of the sun's rays. This exchange cultivated, this energy that moves us, opens our heart. We speak and listen, subject to object, you and I, exchanging. Paying attention, standing as witness to another, what a privilege to bring a new possibility of being intimate, connected, present, in presence with another. Through years of practice, developing the quality of attention, precision and intention, we train ourselves to open to a higher energy. Deep listening demands honesty, authenticity, requires that we guard ourselves from closing our heart and our intuition. To awaken to self-awareness, to what is, to be in this moment, listening to beyond, brings awareness of an unconditioned place beyond the fiction of biography, beyond the masks of cinematic movies. Listening to a sacred voice, hearing it speak in our ordinary encounters creates a bridge to flow reciprocally.

Stay close to any sounds that make you glad you are alive. —*Hafiz*

Often when we investigate this thing we do in life called *our work* we find that its thread runs continuously throughout our lifetime. Mine certainly has. From *forever* I have focused on listening, studying, engaging, processing, digesting my life and the life of others. Throughout my university years the study of phenomenology and intersubjectivity, particularly the 51 year personal relationship of Jean-Paul Sartre and Simone de Beauvoir captured my attention.

When you are listening to somebody, completely, attentively, then you are listening not only to the words, but also to the feeling of what is being conveyed, to the whole of it, not part of it. —*Jiddu Krishnamurti*

Sitting with countless people hearing their narrative, training myself to open to the force of attention, anchored into the service of this instrument, I love those precious moments and bless that I am engaged in a tender work in a community with those who show up, and in our fearless inquiry we uplift our lives. To learn to love, to hear the genuine, the real within myself, the vulnerability that dissolves walls, has created precious relationships that have carried me throughout the years. What a lucky lifetime!

Peace. It does not mean to be in a place where there is no noise, trouble or hard work, it means to be in the midst of those things and still be calm in your heart. —*Unknown*

SPIRITUAL ECONOMICS

We see nothing truly till we understand it. —*John Constable*

The essential teaching of the Jewish tradition, the Sh'ma, begins with the words: Listen, Hear. Pay attention. Telling us to become attentive and inward, silent, and from that a voice can be heard: *Ve'ahavta, and you shall love, and you will love.* An invitation to soften, to know and to hear, a great responsibility, to be present and to love. What a directive!

What was said to the rose that made it open was said to me here in my chest. What was told the cypress that made it strong and straight, what was whispered to the jasmine so it is what it is, whatever made sugarcane sweet; whatsoever was said to the inhabitants of the town of Chigil in Turkestan that makes them so handsome, whatever lets the pomegranate flower blush like a human face, that is being said to me now, I blush. Whatever put eloquence in language, that's happening here. The great warehouse doors open, I fill with gratitude, chewing a piece of sugarcane, in love with the one to whom every 'that' belongs. —*Rumi*

All of the systems and practices when used intentionally, with open awareness, create substance. They hold us steady to remain mindful. As we awaken and polish the heart, we know that each one of us is a universe. Our smile and joy, the sun; our grief and longing, the dark night; our silence and romance, the moon; our thoughts like the burning stars, the star-stuff of which we are made; our body and form, the earth, our tears and perspiration the ocean, lakes and rivers; wherever there is hair, the trees, grasses and forests. Each season is a portion of our life: from the childhood of spring, adolescence of summer, maturing into autumn, to our late in winter. *Late in winter my heart is still a rose in bloom.* And so the study of ourselves is as the study of the universe, this alchemical work, its potential as boundless as love itself.

Tell me the story of how the sun loved the moon so much, he died every night to let her breathe. —*Hanako Ishii*

Giving away our gifts is our practice. Our payment is what we receive back. This is spiritual economics. We are called upon to co-create the mystery, to birth and build a new future. As partners in the creation, as voyagers and agents of the light, we know when asked, *who is rich?* it's whoever is happy with their lot. To love, to risk is everything, to go forward is to welcome and live in the heightened sensitivity that awakening brings. To live a spiritual life means to live a human life, where our greatest passion is compassion.

Bring joy to others, and you shall attain joy. Because the others and us are not different. We are one and the same. To bring joy to others, we must serve them. This is one of the best ways of being in bliss. —*Swami Vivekananda*

MYTHIC IMAGINATION

My heart holds every form. It is a pasture for gazelles, a monastery for monks, an abode for idols, the holy site of the pilgrim, the tablets of the Torah. My religion is love—wherever one turns, love is my belief, my faith. —*Ibn al-Arabi*

We live in mythic times. Shattering old concepts of reality, humanity is challenged with an atmosphere and climate that seeks to control and dominate nature and people. *The Way of the Lover* speaks to a sacred cosmos, a marriage of masculine and feminine principles. We are asked to create a conscious relationship to ourselves that restores and reflects our relationship to our sacred earth and conscious cosmos. The mythic imagination, song of the universe, speaks to the heroic, a life lived in self-discovery that develops wisdom and the power to serve others. The experience of being alive, a music of the spirit, serves as a mirror that reflects back to that place where we are standing. The challenge is not to dismantle society and its institutions, the illusion to be destroyed is the self: false personality, ego, imprinting with all its accompanying blindness. To then inquire into our own deep inward mystery is to live a harmonious relationship to reality. To cultivate the mythic imagination is to treasure the journey of the human spirit in its longing for truth. We no longer have troubadours and wandering scholars to teach us, to link us together; humanity is cut off from its source of tradition. It's not the meaning for life that is lacking, it's the enthusiasm, the exaltation, surprise and delight of being alive, the fire that cultivates our creative imagination.

Put everything at stake. Be a gambler! Risk everything, because the next moment is not certain, so why bother? Why be concerned? Live dangerously, live joyously. Live without fear, live without guilt. Live without any fear of hell, or any greed for heaven. Just live! —Osho

As we are, the ego is an earthly veil of separation that stands in between our ability to experience states that move our inner being and an absence/lack ofconsciousness. For the seeker and the sought to dissolve, for only the present moment to remain, is the source of all wisdom. Stories, myths, the words of the mystics, saints and sages enrich our inner world. This freedom from the mind is consciousness as a reflecting mirror. The device called mythic imagination engages us as it brings about a new level of consciousness. Nothing to solve, only to dissolve. Timeless, beyond birth and death, permeating everything, that link of understanding, a universal convergence as we fully enter into ageless experiences.

We must become ignorant of all we've been taught, and, be, instead, bewildered. Run from what's profitable and comfortable. If you drink those liquors, you'll spill the spring water of your real life. Forget safety! Live where you fear to live. Destroy your reputation. Be notorious. I have tried prudent planning long enough, from now on, I'll live mad. —Rumi

THE KINGDOM OF THE SEA

A boat may stay in the water, but water should not stay in the boat. An aspirant may live in the world, but the world should not live in him. —Sri Ramakrishna

According to legend a reclusive middle-aged mud frog lived at the bottom of a well. This particular frog with huge eyes, a full rounded body and an eerie voice imagined that the whole world was his dark damp well. As time slowly passed the green of his frog color faded like a forest after winter, the croaking deep voice shifted its resonant tone.

One morning, a morning like every other morning, something new happened, an elder frog jumped down into the well to pay a visit. They sat on a small rock talking, and the mud frog questioned and wondered where the elder frog lived. Explaining that he was from the large and beautiful sea, the mud frog said he imagined that the sea was just half the size of his well. The elder frog found that to be the funniest most absurd thing he'd ever heard and laughed and laughed causing his echoing laughter to spill over and fill the tall narrow well with resounding tones. Seeing that the mud frog didn't really understand what is the sea, dismayed at his laughter, elder frog explained the joke.

Imagining the sea to fit in a well was humorous since the sea stretches across the entire world and so he asked: *would the mud frog like to visit the sea?* Yes, followed by a *no,* once realizing the difficult nature of the proposed journey. Numerous excuses of resistance, the *yes* eventually resurfaced and they soon both prepared to leave on a journey, to find the sea.

Traveling far and long, persevering despite tiring challenges, moving towards something radiating intensely, one day they reached the sea. Looking out at this vast stretch of water, the infinity of the ocean, standing at the seashore, yet only able to touch the small waves at the edge of that greatness, there was a recognition of the spaciousness of the infinite, having never seen anything like this, having never imagined this reality, finally being total, the mud frog jumped, slipping into the great ocean. In a flash, a split second of surrender, mud frog's head exploded into a thousand pieces.

The personal self of the frog who had lived quietly at the bottom of a well, contained, isolated yet constrained by his small mind, was broken, blown up, exploded as frog into thousands and thousands of pieces. Now, frog was everywhere, in each drop of the sea, in every frog face, admidst the waves, in stones and stars. All-breaking, bursting into pieces, nothingness exploded into creation. Frog arrived! A sudden realization, his heart awakened to truth. Transformed, never to return to the small dark dank well of illusion, frog exploded into awakening. Rather to be awake than live on the vapor of a dungeon!

Light the incense! You have to burn to be fragrant. —*Rumi*

Frog understood that a prison made of mud or a prison made of gold makes no difference, to come out of the prison of the mind, to disappear, to be one with the whole, so simple, and yet we fail to see it at all. Elder frog understood the cosmic joke. When silence is too much it becomes laughter. *Take your place in the presence of the wordless,* said elder frog, awakening transcends all imagination. Finally, aware of presence and distance, now there becomes fulfillment. The years of quiet preparation, living simply, alone, free of distraction, grounded at the bottom of a well, prepared the mud frog. He became ready. Aloneness is when we are finding ourself listening to that inner place of stillness, uncontainable; as the flower cannot contain its fragrance, it has to be released.

It is in the infinite ocean of myself that the mind-creation called the world takes place. —*Ashtavakra Gita*

This story reflects life simple, awakening immediate, prepared, practicing, grace arrives, certainty, no hesitation, and then in the blink of an eye there is no before or after and no in-between. Behind the split second, within the story the invisible speaks to years of silent preparation; waiting without a goal.

I let go of me. In Hebrew, letting go is called bitul, which really means suspension of self. Most of us fear the moment of suspension, to jump, to let go, when our feet leave the ground. —*Simon Jacobson*

Buried within the twinkling of an eye lies diligence, patience and beyond. Following the instantaneous final release from the mind, where the prison and prisoner are one and the same, there is only silence and joy. For what is asleep awakens after the responsibility for falling asleep is recognized. Devices direct and push, yet it is us that has to wake up. A game plan, strategy, maneuvers, all preparation; in the world of birds only when the birds wings are strong enough will they fly. Somehow the elder frog sensed that moment of truth; here is the leap into the unknown; to jump upward or to crash to earth.

You can't cross the sea merely by standing and staring at the water. —*Rabindranath Tagore*

Many are those who live sequestered. Not separate, regardless, we are part of everything that exists. The sea, energy vortex, the fabric of the universe, extremely delicate, subtle fibers of energies present in our entire creation. In fairy tales the frog, an amphibious animal, associated with a fountain or deep well lives both in the water and on land. Frog connects the ethereal unconscious energies symbolized by water with the tangible physical conscious energies symbolized by land. The inner secret is disclosed at the door of the sea which carry the waters of life. Breaking form, the source shows us what we are seeking, whoever seeks it finds their own, not the sea's. The trust that entered the ocean washed all thoughts away. One such act exceeds all other moments. Drowning with no expectation, this tale unfolded, surrendered into union with the water, frog gained deliverance from the body of earth.

Open to life, freed from the illusion of his small personal world, frog, as most of us, had liked the familiar, what was known—even without liking it so very much. Not to give that familiar security up for a journey without guarantees. The challenge of the spiritual journey is that the comfort in the familiar and predictable get relinquished. To dip into the deeper places is to uproot and move ahead, as things change, the journey continues. Jump totally into life, as high as we can, dive deeply, unchartered, into the unknown; it's up to us. Free, now to live in the wonder of the great sea, that covers the whole of earth. Is this the end or the beginning? Is this life or death? A Sufi teaching says: *Spiritual maturity is to live as a mystic in the world, being fully responsible in everyday life while knowing the world is a fragile illusion. Now, trained to stay centered, holding onto the thin thread that is suspended between the worlds.* The whole point of being here, is to arrive here. Radiantly nothing, emptiness that is full, emptiness that is everything.

In 1970 I was on my way to India, though I didn't know it at the time. Crossing Turkey, I caught a ride with a Swiss truck driver who was the spitting image of John Lennon. I rode with him for three days as we navigated the frighteningly narrow roads in the Turkish highlands. Not infrequently, he closed his eyes as he turned the steering wheel to round a curve, with a sheer, thousand-foot drop on one side and a mountain wall on the other. 'It's best if I close my eyes' he said. 'Then I don't freeze up' He had made more than thirty trips across these highlands and the deserts of Iran and Afganistan and had had more than a few adventures. All those hours alone, however, had also given him time to reflect on life and the nature of things. 'I have a friend,' he said, one day, 'who lives in a small village in Switzerland. We are about the same age. She has never traveled outside her village. and I've been all over Asia and Europe. I'm not sure which of us has had the better life.' His comment has always stayed with me, pointing me away from concern about the content of life back to the importance of being present in the experience of life itself. —Ken Mcleod

THE HEART UNVEILED

Tradition is the core of truth, the one single current at the heart of all the real teachings. It is a message from a higher consciousness. It is knowledge of the laws that govern the sacred hierarchy of being, and such knowledge cannot contradict nor disagree with itself. —D.M.Dooling

Within the realm of the sacred are our myths, archetypes, legends, fables, koans, allegories, symbols, old tales and parables. The keepers of the wisdom stories, usually handed down word of mouth to live with the immortals, beyond, beyond, beyond. These carriers, shamans, magicians, guides, making the invisible accessible, who move between worlds and dimensions, parting veils and holding tradition, bring the sacred into this mundane world. Stories, words, define and instruct us, create us, they determine the meaning of our experiences. So many of the transmissions have been communicated orally, are esoteric and directly inspired from a level of true experience and universal understanding.

And it is said that all traditions must die unless they are renewed through direct experience. We have had Shakespeare, Homer, Dante, Torah, Talmud, Rumi, Jesus, Hafiz, Buddha, the IChing, all bringing us into the sacred as we experience the possibility of transformation through a larger story, through the wisdom that penetrates the realms of the visible and invisible.

The challenge, then, is to be the creative myth-maker that we are, to consciously choose our myth, lest it be chosen for us, by the collective mind.
—*Mary Elizabeth Marlow*

The celebrated classic 12th century Persian allegorical poem, *Conference of the Birds*, as well as a modern version, *The Birds Who Flew Beyond Time*, like the legend of the frog, is a journey to awaken the heart, a pilgrimage of the soul as it seeks union with the divine. The birds, representing the various types of human beings journey to fly beyond time to find the dwelling place of the great being who is the life of all life. The earth sends a message to the birds that she is dying, requesting their help. They must fly through seven immense valleys, until they find the great being who is the life of all life. Then they must bring back to earth the message that they receive through this great being. Undergoing many trials they attempt to free themselves of their self-importance, to loosen their attachments, and to shift their beliefs, attitudes, perspective and habituated conditioning. The birds are on a pilgrimage that is ours as well as theirs—the journey toward self-realization, the ultimate contribution we can offer to the earth.

As a great fish swims between the banks of a river as it likes, so does the shining Self move between the states of dreaming and waking. As an eagle, weary after soaring in the sky, folds its wings and flies down to rest in its nest, so does the shining Self enter the state of dreamless sleep, where one is freed from all desires. —The Upanishads

Initially there is great excitement and eagerness to embark on this adventure, until, one by one, seeing how arduous, long, as well as the sacrifices necessary, each bird finds excuses, justification to curtail the journey. The nightingale, that aspect of self caught in the exterior form of things cannot leave the rose, is satisfied by the love of the rose, all the while being warned against living as a slave of a passing love that interferes with seeking self-perfection. Duck is too content with water to look into his own heart. Hawk is well pleased with his position at court waiting on earthly kings. The sparrow is too afraid even to set out, Sparrow is reprimanded for taking pride in humility, directed to get rid of his fear.

Here are our human foibles, attachments, defenses, the stories we have constructed to support our illusions are mirrored in each birds' pretext. So many reasons we give to evade the hardship, the payment required to wake up. We are instructed to sacrifice the only real thing we have: our life. This is a pilgrimage for those willing to take a leap, for those prepared to lose, not for the fearful, prideful, indolent, vain or lazy. Ultimately, those who embark on the journey, and so many fall by the wayside; for those few who reach the destination, and lose themselves to find themself, this is the heart unveiled.

From the terrestrial to the celestial domain all veils are torn for he who serves the goblet which shows the universe. —Hafiz

The pilgrimage, a long and perilous one, takes them through seven valleys. First is the valley of the quest where desires are renounced, next, the valley of love, a limitless place where the seeker is consumed by a yearning for the beloved, then the valleys of understanding, independence and detachment, unity, bewilderment, and finally poverty and fulfillment in nothingness, or extinction. These are the valleys of doubt, false dreams, envy, hate, power, cruelty and despair. No matter how discouraging the voices there is always a deeper truth that takes them further. Ultimately the birds arrived to Understand that the great being is not going to save the earth for them, but through them. The divine message they carry back to earth is their own transformed selves.

On finding and contemplating universal truth the birds discover their essential life and identity by annihilating their individual selves to become one. Nothing gained; liberation is a loss—the loss of the sense that there ever was a separate self, being is already all that is; this is the awakening.

I want a man to reach a stage of understanding so that he can be bent, twisted and turned and yet he will always point in the same direction.
—*saying attributed to Gurdjieff*

Spiritual Maturity

When I say maturity, I mean an inner integrity. This is the first step towards maturity: I am responsible. Whatsoever is happening, it is my doing. Maturity is innocence reclaimed, it is innocence recaptured. Maturity is a rebirth, a spiritual rebirth. With silence and innocence you penetrate your own innermost core. Lose the ego and gain the self or no-self, and you are mature. Die to the past and be born to the present and you are mature. Maturity is living in the present, fully alert and aware of all the beauty and splendor of existence. —*Rajneesh, Osho*

The shocks and the stripping away carry us to the ocean of our soul, to become what we know. Attachments to the world, to distractions, recede as we overcome illusions about ourself, bringing inner change and awakening our Understanding. This Understanding is attained from within. The training and preparation, supporting self-discipline, ultimately realizes clarity, certainty; the heart becomes a reflecting mirror.

The birds realized freedom. Mud frog found his way to a sanctuary, recovering and restoring the connection between the body of the earth and the soul of the ocean, from his isolated place in the well to surrender, jumping into the depths. Mud frog was a leap into the ocean—*he* didn't disappear, he became oceanic—mud frog became the ocean itself, part of the vastness. No longer to find mud frog, no longer to find each bird; and that is our hesitation, how we keep ourselves, our need to be someone, a special identity, keeps us from disappearing into the ocean, the sky, whatever it is that stands before our becoming.

The voyage of the mud frog and the birds is ours as well as theirs—a journey that transforms the destructive elements of the soul, freeing us to act on behalf of life. The journey led to the sea of the soul, through effort and surrender to the elder frog, dying to the old. The mud frog woke up. He lived in darkness, at the bottom of a well and found the sea, standing in front of it in a flash of lightning, awareness brought a new context. That is awakening. He arrived and entered.

Self is everywhere, shining forth from all beings, vaster than the vast, subtler than the most subtle, unreachable, yet nearer than breath, than heartbeat. Eye cannot see it, ear cannot hear it nor tongue utter it; only in deep absorption can the mind, grown pure and silent, merge with the formless truth. As soon as you find it, you are free; you have found yourself; you have solved the great riddle; your heart is forever at peace. Whole, you enter the Whole. Your personal self returns to its radiant, intimate, deathless source.
—Mundaka Upanishad

AWAKENING TO THE SACRED

Come into the heart. Where the great mystery lives. Look, here is the Way!
—*Rumi*

Daily life presents moments that imprison as well as bring freedom. The journey begins with a glimpse, a taste, step by step we proceed on the alchemical path of turning copper into gold. Here, inside is everything, the gift, raw, available, not yet arranged. The task is to create a container, reliable and present for the everyday details of life to resonate, vibrate, permeate. Once ignited, the fire lit; the danger lies in illusion and fascination. *Remember to change your consciousness from the imaginary to the real.*

Projecting onto the screen keeps us from seeing the real, holding us to live in maya, illusion. The marketplace, entertainment that binds us blindly to samsara, this world, the wheel; separated from the nourishment that feeds our heart—our identification with ourselves brings us to feel that we are dying when we relinquish those temptations that hold us in self-satisfaction. *The rung of a ladder was never meant to rest upon but only to hold a foot long enough to enable us to put the other somewhat higher,* wrote Thomas Huxley. The journey brings us into ourselves and into life, until the personal drops away. The ordinary, mundane life becomes the path, becomes the profound.

Stand on a beach and watch the gigantic play of lightening in the sky and on the sea, and all art pales. Watch the sun explode into a thousand soft reds at sunset over the Himalayas, and the most glorious poem becomes a faint memory. Enter into the bliss of presence, and even the deepest pleasure of the mind, even the most extreme, most refined aesthetic delight are as nothing, straws in a vast bonfire. Rumi cries, 'One hour of love is worth a hundred worlds. Language is a handful of dust/a breath of His blows away.'
—*Andrew Harvey*

Chop wood and carry water, drink a cup of tea slowly, mindfully. Life is simple, we are ordinary. The spiritual path is about loving ourself and loving others. Being sincere, considerate, ethical, respectful, having manners, mindful, of service, a good sport, a team player, with patience, constancy, present and positive to self and others. Absence of these qualities raises a red flag as to what path a person is traveling. Self-deception inflates the self, an authentic path demands vulnerability and simple tasks of service.

Towards the final part of the journey, when patience and perseverance are necessary, reflecting an ordinary life that lacks glamour and adventure, this is the shedding of the dinosaur scales of the earlier illusions of an exciting life; for now little is left that stands in the way of realizing our true nature, our inner stillness. To be present, to carry the clear high energy right here in daily life, to be attentive to true needs, physical, material and spiritual, and to live a balanced life in the world; with this we enter a new spiral of evolution.

Even if you have pushed yourself and feel you've broken through, push yourself further. If you are on, ride that wave as long as you can. Don't stop in the middle. That moment won't come back exactly in that way again. Go further than you think you can. —Natalie Goldberg

LIFE IS AT ITS BEST

The mud frog journeyed and found freedom, the birds returned to earth transformed. Our pilgrimage brings us to the ends of the earth, and we, too, don't know what the treasure is until we become the treasure itself. We carry the gifts hidden within ourselves to live harmoniously, participating joyfully in the sorrows of the world. Discernment with wisdom is our tool and weapon, our dynamic process of Understanding and taking appropriate action, our gift of presence, our openness to others. This is a very great gift, the prize, to find that place within ourself, the center of quietness and core of peace. Right here, in the midst of life. This, is *The Way of the Lover*, the Way of Understanding.

When the goal of life is attained, one achieves the reparation of all wrongs, the healing of all wounds, the righting of all failures, the sweetening of all sufferings, the relaxation of all strivings, the harmonizing of all strife, the unraveling of all enigmas, and the real and full meaning of all life—past, present and future. When relinquished through love, life is at its best.
—Meher Baba

If you have time to chatter

Read books.

If you have time to read

Walk into mountain, desert and ocean

If you have time to walk

sing songs and dance

If you have time to dance

Sit quietly, you Happy Lucky Idiot

—Nanao

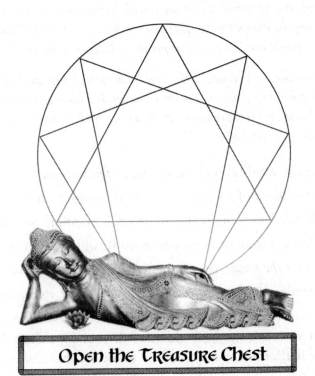

Open the Treasure Chest

OPEN THE TREASURE CHEST

Books are the carriers of civilization. Without books, history is silent, literature dumb, science crippled, thought and speculation at a standstill. Without books the development of a civilization would have been impossible. They are the engines of change, windows on the world, lighthouses erected in the sea of time. They are the companions, teachers, magicians, bankers of the treasures of the mind. Books are humanity in print. — Barbara Tuchman

It seems to me that one should only read books which bite and sting one. If the book we are reading does not wake us up with a blow to the head, what's the point of reading? A book ought to be an ice pick to break up the frozen sea within us. —Franz Kafka

To bring the wordless into words, as, *in the beginning was the word,* carries the flavor of a writer's inner world, written on the measure of their breath, filled with the energy of original intention. So choose well, to breathe in the breath of those whose words will penetrate your heart. *Words are forces the breath lets go,* wrote Robert Duncan. The words we choose determine how we experience our lives. Our voice, our writing voice, tells readers the content of our life. In the Native American tradition, Spider Woman sang the world into existence a word at a time. Love of language itself, accompanied by love for others, has crafted beautiful books. The following are books from writers of substance. I have found them to be companions along the way, books that I cherish:

—*The Subject Tonight Is Love: The Purity of Desire poems of Rumi, 60 wild and sweet poems of Hafiz, I Heard God Laughing, The Gift,* and *Love Poems from God,* five books by Daniel Ladinsky

—*Strange Life of Ivan Osokin,* by P.D. Ouspensky

—*The Illuminated Prayer,* and *The Illuminated Rumi,* both by Coleman Barks and Michael Green

—*One God Clapping, This Is Real and You Are Completely Unprepared,* and *Be Still and Get Going,* three books by Alan Lew

—*The Last Barrier, The Invisible Way, The Alchemy of the Heart,* all three by Reshad Field

—*One Song,* by Michael Green

—*Hidden Journey, a Spiritual Awakening,* and *The Way of Passion,* two by Andrew Harvey

—*Happiness,* by Matthieu Ricard

—*And You Shall Love, Hasidic Tales,* both by Rami M. Shapiro

—*The Chasm of Fire,* by Irina Tweedie

—*The Hidden Lamp,* edited by Florence Caplow, Susan Moon

—*The Essential Rumi,* and *The Soul of Rumi,* and *Rumi the Book of Love,* three books translations by Coleman Barks

—*A Voice at the Borders of Silence,* by William Segal

—*At Home in the World, The Heart of Understanding, True Love, The Art of Communicating, Cultivating the Mind of Love, Fragrant Palm Leaves, Being Peace,* seven books by Thich Nhat Hanh

—*The Happy Prince* and *The Selfish Giant,* both by Oscar Wilde

—*The Theory of Conscious Harmony,* by Rodney Collin

—*Self-Healing My Life and Vision,* by Meir Schneider

—*From the Kingdom of Memory, Open Heart,* and *Legends Of Our Time,* three by Elie Wiesel

—*Hasidic Tales of the Holocaust,* by Yaffa Eliach

—*Long Quiet Highway, Writing Down the Bones, Wild Mind, Thunder and Lightening, The Great Failure, Living Color, True Secret of Writing, The Great Spring,* eight books by Natalie Goldberg

—*Love you Forever,* by Robert Munsch

—*Anam Cara, To Bless The Space Between Us,* both by John O'Donohue

—*The Wheel Of Life, a Memoir of Living and Dying,* by Dr. Elisabeth Kübler-Ross

—*Ocean Born: Birth as Initiation,* by Chris Griscom

—*The Little Prince,* by Antoine De Saint-Exupery

—*Life at Its Best,* by Meher Baba

—*God Is a Verb,* by David A. Cooper

—*Self Remembering,* by Robert Earl Burton

—*Quest For God, I Asked for Wonder, The Sabbath,* three books by Abraham Joshua Heschel

—*The Birds Who Flew Beyond Time,* Anne Baring and Thetis Blacker

—*Conference of the Birds,* by Attar, introduction by Andrew Harvey

—*Bringing Heaven Down to Earth,* compiled and interpreted by Tzvi Freeman

—*The Power of Myth,* by Joseph Campbell

—*Death, the Greatest Fiction,* and *The Book of The Secrets,* both by Bhagwan Shree Rajneesh, Osho

—*Making Loss Matter: Creating Meaning in Difficult Times,* by Rabbi David Wolpe

—*The Truth of This Life,* by Katherine Thanas

—*The Fruitful Darkness, Standing at the Edge,* both by Joan Halifax

—*Long Life, Felicity,* both by Mary Oliver

—*Wounds into Wisdom,* by Tirzah Firestone

—*After the Ecstasy, the Laundry,* by Jack Kornfield

—*The Two Step, the Dance Toward Intimacy,* by Eileen McCann

—*The Man Who Thought He Was Messiah,* by Curt Leviant

—*Spiritual Enlightenment,* and *Spiritually Incorrect Enlightenment,* and *Spiritual Warfare, The Notebook, A theory of Everything,* all by Jed McKenna

—*The Geologist of the Soul,* and *Davening,* and *From Age-ing to Sage-ing,* three by Rabbi Zalman Schacter-Sholomi

—*The Reality of Being,* by Jeanne de Salzmann

—*Eyes Wide Open,* by Mariana Caplan

—*Everyday Zen,* by Charlotte Joko Beck

—*The Talmud and the Internet, a Journey between Worlds,* by Jonathan Rosen

—*Break the Mirror,* by Nanao Sakaki

—*Fierce Attachments,* by Vivian Gornick

—*Pay Attention, For Goodness' Sake, That's Funny, You Don't Look Buddhist,* and *Don't Just Do Something, Sit There,* all three by Sylvia Boorstein

—*The Jew in the Lotus,* by Roger Kamenetz

—*Letter to my Daughter, Celebrations, A Song Flung Up To Heaven, Hallelujah: The Welcome Table, All God's Children Need Traveling Shoes,* all by Maya Angelou (listening on CD has the sound of her magnificent voice.)

—*Coming To Our Senses,* by Jon Kabat-Zinn

—*Zen Seeds,* by Shundo Adyama

—*The World Could be Otherwise,* by Norman Fischer

—*Zen Confidential, Single White Monk,* both by Shozan Jack Haubner

—*Reflections on Silver Pond,* by Ken McLeod

—*The Choice,* by Dr. Edith Eva Eger

—Talks and writings, by Sadhguru Jaggi Vasudev

—*The December Project,* by Sara Davidson

—*On Love and Other Difficulties,* and *Letters To A Young Poet,* both by Ranier Maria Rilke, translation by John Mood

Read the best books first, or you might not have a chance to read them at all. —Henry David Thoreau

Don't read anything except what destroys the insulation between yourself and your experience or what pulls down or what strikes at or what shatters this ruse you call necessity. —Louise Erdich

Some people think of reading only as a kind of escape. Books are much more. They are a way of being fully human. —Susan Sontag

AND ESPECIALLY FOR THE WRITER

Write what will stop your breath if you don't write. —Grace Paley

Better to write for yourself and have no public, than to write for the public and have no self. —Cyril Connolly

Whenever I have endured or accomplished some difficult task—such as watching television, going out socially or sleeping—I always look forward to rewarding myself with the small pleasure of getting back to my computer and writing something. This enables me to store up enough strength to endure the next interruption. —Isaac Asimov

—*The Writing Life,* by Annie Dillard

—*Negotiating with the Dead, A Writer On Writing,* by Margaret Atwood

—*The Writing Life,* edited by Marie Arana

—*The Lie that tells A Truth*, by John Dufresne

—*On Writing, a memoir of the craft*, by Stephen King

—*Belief and Technique for Modern Prose*, by Jack Kerouac

To write, a person has to take off her coat, shirt, and skin. I have to be unarmored. —Jane Hirshfield

They can be a great help—words. They can become the spirit's hands and lift and caress you. —Meister Eckhart

Books, not which afford us a cowering enjoyment, but in which each thought is of unusual daring; such as an idle man cannot read, and a timid one would not be entertained by, which even make us dangerous to existing institutions—such call I good books. —Henry David Thoreau

Writing is the act of discovery. Know that you will eventually have to leave everything behind. The writing will demand it of you. Writers are great lovers. They fall in love with other writers. That's how they learn to write. They take on a writer, read everything by him or her, read it over again until they understand how the writer moves, pauses and sees. That's what being a lover is: stepping out of yourself, stepping into someone else's skin. As writers we live life twice, like a cow that eats its food once, and then regurgitates it to chew and digest it again. We have a second chance at biting into our experience and examining it. —Natalie Goldberg

LIST OF ESSENTIALS FOR THE WRITER

BY JACK KEROUAC

1. Scribbled secret notebooks, and wild typewritten pages, for yr own joy.

2. Submissive to everything, open, listening.

3. Be in love with yr life.

4. Something that you feel will find its own form.

5. Be crazy dumbsaint of the mind.

6. Blow as deep as you want to blow.

7. Write what you want bottomless from bottom of the mind.

8. Accept loss forever.

9. Believe in the holy contour of life.

10. Write for the world to read and see yr exact picture of it.

One of the few things I know about writing is this: spend it all, shoot it, play it, lose it, all, right away, every time. Do not hoard what seems good for a later place in the book, or for another book; give it, give it all, give it now. The impulse to save something good for a better place later is the signal to spend it now. Something more will arise for later, something better. These things fill from behind, from beneath, like well water. Similarly, the impulse to keep to yourself what you have learned is not only shameful, it is destructive. Anything you do not give freely and abundantly becomes lost to you. You open your safe and find ashes. —Annie Dillard

Writing is a sacred vocation, there is no preciousness or pretense about its sanctity—only earnest and inexorable purposefulness. If your commitment isn't to truth, then you are in the wrong line of work. Try to release yourself from attachment to results, to awards, publications, praise, to indifference, rejection, and misunderstanding. Immerse yourself in the common ground of the universe so that your true voice —not the egoistic voice that clamors vainly for power (for it will ruin you if you listen to it)—your authentic voice, supported by sacred reality, may be heard. May your words illuminate your vision, find you compassionate, attuned to human suffering and committed to its alleviation. —Melissa Pitchard

What more could one ask of a companion? To be forever new and yet forever steady. To be strange and familiar all at once, with enough change to quicken my mind, enough steadiness to give sanctuary to my heart. The books on my shelf never asked to come together, and they would not trust or want to listen to one another; but each is a piece of a stained-glass whole without which I couldn't make sense to myself, or to the world outside. —Pico Iyer

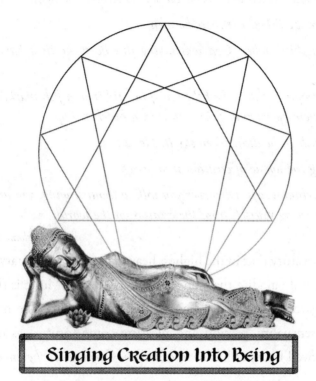

Singing Creation Into Being

SINGING CREATION
INTO BEING

When God created the world, He said: Let there be light.

Let there be fishes. Let there be men.

Do you think when God was saying this he spoke in a harsh voice?

For example: let there be fishes! as if he said it in a fish market? or let there be cows! as if he said it in a butcher shop?

The truth is, he didn't even say it. He sang it.

He sang the whole of creation into being.

Reb Nachman says, whenever you talk without singing, you are disconnecting yourself from the creation of the world.

—Shlomo Carlebach

There is a story that in the highest heaven there is a sanctuary, a sacred and joyful paradise that song alone can unlock. Music is the key to open the gates. Music stirs whatever lies in the heart. The mixture of devotion, sensuality, passion and pleasure come forward as our inner being is moved by what has been called *the language of the angels.*

Music gives a soul to the universe, wings to the mind, flight to the imagination, and life to everything. —Plato

In the great Emperors court lived a musician, a master of inner sound. Without words he could make bells sing in the heart, bringing whomever listened to enter a fragrant garden, the scent and colors filling great space. His music brought flowers to plants that had never bloomed. His secret was knowing that all of existence is made up of sound, the vibration of energy. He would sit by his instruments, surrounded by unlit lamps and eventually they would come aflame. Music creates heat; he knew that from having heard the soundless sound, the humming in his heart, his inner melody. Breathing brings oxygen, which flames the fire, heats the water our body stores, igniting the heart. Such is the nature of music. Water flows downwards and fire rises upwards. For the court musician understood that life itself is music, food for the soul, an infinite heavenly concert.

He who has realized that sun and stars and souls do not ramble in a vacuum will keep his heart in readiness for the hour when the world is entranced. For things are not mute: Out of the world comes he behest to instill into the air a rapturous song for God. —Abraham Joshua Heschel

Sound and music are a source of peace, healing and nurturance to draw upon, a universal language. Music holds history, heritage, and cosmos, making the world radiate. Breathing in melody, rhythm and sound quiets the mind as well as builds stamina and life force. I have a wonderful music system on my desk that has a play list and as I write it alternates from tune to tune. The music captures my thoughts, quiets my mind, accesses an empty portal so that *I* am not in the way as I write. Calm, peaceful, happy, inner harmony, mind not straying, this solitude is truly a refuge that I return and return to; sitting on my desk chair, music turned on, deepening the present moment, sweet time of writing. Music reveals the voice of our soul.

Many say that life entered the human body by the help of music, but the truth is that life itself is music. —Hafiz

Music lives in the present moment. Heightening our sensitivity, entering a world of harmony—this is the place where the music never stops. Tucked within our own true selves, bringing us home into this universe—we become the music. The sound between the notes fill us, reverberate to return to the silence which is the root of our being.

If you cannot teach me to fly, teach me to sing. —*J.M. Barrie*

THE FOLLOWING ARE A FEW OF THE MUSICIANS AND MUSIC THAT UPLIFT MY SPIRIT

—*The Essence, Love Is Space, Embrace, Moola Mantra,* and *Dakshina, Password, Satsang, Deva and Miten In Concert with Manose, Ocean of Love/So Much Magnificence,* all by Deva Premal

—*I Will Not Be Sad In This World,* by Djivan Gasparyan

—*Journey Within,* by Dominique Starck

—*Ruach, Aliveness, Good Night My Sweetest Children,* all by David Zeller

—*Synchronicity,* by Master Charles

—*Buddha Bar*

—*Eight String Religion, Prayer for Compassion,* both by David Darling

—*Eclipse* and *A Wish,* both by Hamza El Din

—*Flying,* by Garth Stevenson

—*Shamanic Dream,* by Anugama

—*In the Garden of Souls,* by Vas

—*Silk Road,* by Kitaro

—*Praise,* by Ahmed Tijani

—*On Sacred Ground,* by Chinmaya Dunster

—Yo Yo Ma

—Itzhak Perlman

—*Olam Chesed Yibaneh,* by Menachem Creditor

—Cantor Azi Schwartz

—Fairouz

—*Hallelujah,* by Daniel Kahn

—*Stardust,* by Willie Nelson

—*Trance Dance,* by Shiva Rea

—*Gurdjieff, Chants, Hymns and Dances,* by Tsabropoulos

—*Resonance,* by Rochester Folk Art Guild

—*Chopin Collection Nocturns, Beethoven Piano #4,5* by Arthur Rubenstein

—*Sura,* by Chloe Goodchild

—*Water Down the Ganges,* by Prem Joshua & Manish Vyas

—*The Beloved,* by Bhakti

—*Garden of the Gods* and *Tibet* and *Nada Himalaya,* by Deuter

—*Sacred Chants of Shiva,* singers of the Art of Living

—*Moola Mantra*—Deeksha transmission

—*In The Arms of Love,* by Ottmar Liebert

—*Prayer For Healing,* by Netanel Goldberg

—*Gurdjieff/De Hartmann,* by Amaral, Andres, Rodrigues

—*Zen,* by Chris Hinze

—*Fly Away,* by Omar Faruk Tekbilik

—*Crossing the Bridge,* by Baba Zula

—*I Am Sam,* music inspired by the motion picture

—*Best of Sound of Goreme,* by Firuza and Divan

—*Meetings With Remarkable Men,* De Hartmann, Rosenthal

—*Bridge to The Unseen,* Melanie Monsur

—*Call of the Mystic,* Bharanji and Manesh De Moor

—*The Prayer Cycle*

—*Lachin,* by Anna RF

—*Sound of Goreme*

—*Rain of Blessings,* by Lama Gyurme, Jean-Phillippe Rykiel

—*Old Ideas, Ten New Songs, Live in London,* all by Leonard Cohen

—*Beyond Children,* by Tina Turner

—The Beatles

—Yuval Ron Ensemble

—Nina Simone

—Snatam Kaur

—Maria Callas

—Anthony Mordechai Tzvi Russell

—Luciano Pavarotti

—Gregorian Chants

To play a wrong note is insignificant, to play without passion is inexcusable.
—Ludwig van Beethoven

There's a music for everything. Didn't you ever hear the earth spinning? It makes a sound like a humming top. Dear me, yes! Everything in the world—trees, rocks and stars and human beings—they all have their own true music. —P.L. Travers

Music is about as physical as it gets: your essential rhythm is your heartbeat; your essential sound, the breath. We're walking temples of noise, and when you add tender hearts to this mix, it somehow lets us meet in places we couldn't get to any other way. —Annie Lamont

THANK YOU

*G*rateful acknowledgment is made to Daniel Ladinsky for permission to reprint his beautiful translations, the love songs of Hafiz, and the timeless voice and light of Rumi. Thank you Daniel for reflecting that sweet playfulness and laughter, and for our telephone poetry reading. I loved that.

Gratitude to Coleman Barks for permission to reprint his inspired renderings of Rumi. Thank you Coleman for keeping the breath of Mevlana fragrant.

Tom, sitting together we formatted this book—you are a blessing. Your computer skills, creative attention, integrity and care; a book designer from heaven.

Manjari for the photographic creation, the compelling presentation of the cover of this book. I knew when I first saw your photos in Sedona that your camera would bring this Buddha to life.

Ingrid Sorensen, your creative spirit allowed the photo of me on the back flap to express a natural essence.

To my parents Adele and Manuel Bromberg who live in my heart, *I will build an alter from the broken fragments of my heart.* Your memory endures, thank you for this precious life.

Udbodha, our beautiful conversations, smiling and bowing to each other, a lotus for us both, friendship, reflection: *One loyal friend is worth 10,000 relatives.*

To the Mindfulness Community and dear sweet Thay, Thich Nhat

Hahn, envisioning me as *Joyful Awakening of the Source*. May I unfold to live as that beautiful Dharma name.

Amma who embraces me as *Ambika Ma, Compassionate Mother*, a beautiful reflection of her heart.

Mitchell, my godson, *when you untie your wings everyone around you will fly up like doves*, our connection began in this lifetime the moment I saw you. Tender child; *the rose opens, and opens, and when it falls, falls outward*. Petals released, your blossoming to diminish the world's pain.

To Linda, your years of consistent loving friendship is a priceless treasure. Your lighthearted lightness of being beams smiles.

To the great hearts who have penetrated me, whose breath ignited my fire: Beloved Mother Guru Ammachi, Rebbe Zalman Schachter-Sholomi, Jean Robertson, Bonnie Whittingham. As well as the beautiful companion family, the sisters and brothers, the teachers I have traveled with along side: Reshad Feild, Kabir Helminski, Adnan Sarhan, Gangaji, Ammachi, Jean Robertson, Elisabeth Kübler-Ross, Sufi Baba, Yogi Bhajan, Ma Jaya Sati Bhagavati, Natalie Goldberg; companion guides in this great circle of lovers.

As well as the inspired teachings of Thich Nhat Hahn, Osho, Krishnamurti, Alan Lew, Mevlana Rumi, Mary Oliver, Eve Esler, David Ingber, Hafiz, G.I. Gurdjieff.

A deep bow to my colleagues: Jose Stevens, Chris Griscom, David Deida, Alvaro Lopez-Waterman, Deborah Kane, Ram Dass, Andrea Dworkin, Helen Palmer, as well as the Rosh Hodesh community; our deep conversations and moments together have brought treasures of love to this life.

Stay close to anything that makes you glad that you are alive. Bring your cup near me, for a drink from Love's Hands. So I will always lean my heart as close to your soul as I can. —*Hafiz*

To the countless people, those who have allowed their lives to be witnessed, who have been patient, resilient, who with vulnerability have brought their life stories; breathing together we have witnessed the narratives dissolve, dropping the suffering, creating a wider, wilder, deeper life. The remarkable privilege—my life filled with the emergence of beautiful beings; relationships with purpose: the consciously examined life is worth living. The day labor, the spiritual conversations, the transcendence of wounding, illusions revealed on the voyage towards understanding: what a miraculous work. Deep gratitude to all those who have shared their self-inquiry. I feel like the true Ambika Ma, the Mother, who is blessed with countless magnificent, loving, kind children.

TO THE VOICES THROUGH THE
TELEPHONE LINES: TENDER CHILDREN

I seem to have loved you in numberless forms, numberless times..
In life afterlife, in age after age, forever.
My spellbound heart has made and remade the necklace of songs,
That you take as a gift, wear round your neck in your many forms,
In life after life, in age after age, forever.
Whenever I hear old chronicles of love, it's age old pain,
It's ancient tale of being apart or together.
As I stare on and on into the past, in the end you emerge,
Clad in the light of a pole-star, piercing the darkness of time.
You become an image of what is remembered forever.
You and I have floated here on the stream that brings from the fount.
At the heart of time, love of one for another.
We have played along side millions of lovers,
Shared in the same shy sweetness of meeting
the distressful tears of farewell,
Old love but in shapes that renew and renew forever.

—*Rabindranath Tagore*

Thank you for everything.
I have no complaint whatsoever.

——*Zen Master Sono*

May this book offer that vision of a universe created by love, and may Rumi and Hafiz and all sacred teachings embrace and carry you kindly, intimately, along *The Way of the Lover*.

TO ALEXANDRA

Beloved of my Soul, Sashie, thank you for everything, for every day. Listening, reading, feeding, loving. *I am blessed, choosing again what I chose before. I seemed to have loved you in numberless forms, numberless times—in life after life, in age after age, forever. Surely there is a window from heart to heart.*

Alexandra Isadora
The Wild Rose

Sometimes hidden from me
in daily custom and in trust,
so that I live by you unaware
as if by the beating of my heart.

Suddenly you flare in my sight,
a wild rose blooming at the edge
of thicket, grace and light
where yesterday was only shade,

and once again I am blessed, choosing
again what I chose before. —w.b

Balibt und galibteh vi eyne—Beloved and lover as one

Libav-tini b'ahat may-ae-naiykh —You have stolen my heart with a single glance

CONSOLATIO

(FOR ALEXANDRA)

When I die I want your hands on my eyes: I want the light and the wheat of your beloved hands to pass their freshness over me one more time to feel the smoothness that changed my destiny.

I want you to live while I wait for you, asleep. I want for your ears to go on hearing the wind, for you to smell the sea that we loved together and for you to go on walking the sand where we walked,

I want for what I loved to go on living and as for you I loved you and sang you above everything, for that, go on flowering, flowery one,

so that you reach all that my love orders for you, so that my shadow passes through your hair, so that they know by this the reason for my song.
—*Pablo Neruda*

FURTHER DEEP WORK

Telephone sessions, e-mail and text are available to learn to use the systems and tools for self-study and inner investigation and personal growth. Mindful conversation, finding our voice, brings a deeper understanding enabling us to develop a practice of presence to live freed from habituated conditioned patterns, awake to the mystery of being.

Contact Dr. Paula Bromberg at email: Goldoceandrive@gmail.com or through Facebook: Paula Ambika Bromberg.

ABOUT THE AUTHOR

*D*r. Paula Bromberg: psychologist, teacher, para-rabbi, writer, has been dedicated and inspired by a personal journey that brought her to experience many paths, teachers, spiritual communities and methods. *The Way of the Lover* draws on direct experience—her professional encounters of over 50 years. It is written with the authority that comes from decades of study and teaching. Traveling and receiving initiation into Eastern and Western lineages: Sufi, Buddhist, Jewish Renewal, Gurdjieffian, East Indian; learning within living traditions, transcending formal boundaries to teach from those places; to kindle that fire in the heart of others.

The author has a Doctorate in Philosophy in Clinical Psychology, maintains a telephone practice as a counselor and spiritual teacher, recorded a live television series *Conversations with Doctor Paula*. Her creation, *The Fifth Way: The Way of the Lover* is the foundation of her work. The living interconnectedness makes up the *real* world and all traditions are part of this; and the creative force is Love.

During her years at the New School for Social Research, Paula worked as an educator: director and teacher at the Little Village Rudolph Steiner School, teacher for Head Start, Blueberry School for Autistic and Schizophrenic children, taught at Bellevue Psychiatric Hospital, and represented the State of New York Office of Developmental Disabilities as a psychologist. Living in New Mexico she continued her private practice as well as a special education public school teacher and served on the Governor's Mental Health Council.

She trained and was supervised by Dr. Laura and Dr. Fritz Perls, and studied and worked with J.L. Moreno M.D. and Zerka Moreno at the Moreno Psychodrama Institute in NewYork. She presented position papers at Queens College, Columbia University and New York University as well as facilitating *Spontaneity Groups* and workshops in New York City and Massachusetts, while maintaining her private counseling practice. Her training brought her to study extensively and oftentimes travel with many innovators: Dr. Rollo May, Elisabeth Kübler-Ross M.D., Rabbi Zalman Schachter-Shalomi, Rabbi Gershon Winkler, Helen Palmer, Dr. Moshe Feldenkrais, Dr. Ida Rolf, Rabbi Nahum Ward-Lev, Edith Wallace M.D., Otto Kernberg M.D., Ram Dass, Allen Ginsberg, Natalie Goldberg. Living and studying at a Fourth Way School in the Gurdjieffian tradition, traveling worldwide with Sufi teachers has been a prominent part of her life.

Paula was on the faculty of the Elisabeth Kübler-Ross Institute at Northern New Mexico College teaching and training hospice workers. She has been a guest on the radio show: Health Through Knowledge with Zoe Lewis, M.D. A consultant and frequent guest speaker for a Regenerative Medicine television series with A. Farschian, M.D.

An in depth full-time training at the Institute for Traditional Medicine, Ayurvedic Medicine, under the direction of Dr. Vasant Lad to understand the intricacies and connection between Eastern and Western medicine, specializing in speech pathology at Emerson College for three years she continued her integrative development as a clinician and practitioner. Receiving a BA from the New School for Social Research and advanced studies at the Graduate Faculty of the New School, Ph.D from Sierra University, learning to promote well-being has been at the forefront of her multidisciplinary studies. Dr. Paula created three counseling centers in New York City, conducted seminars throughout the United States, lectured at universities and was a frequent guest on radio and television shows.

Her many years of direct practice and travels with inspired spiritual teachers: Gangaji, Yogi Bhajan, Adnan Sarhan, Mata Amritananda Mayi Ma Amma, Kabir Helminski, Reshad Feild, Jean Robertson, Adyshanti, Chris Griscom, Ma Jaya Sati Bhagavati deepened her wisdom of understanding. A lucky lifetime.

She has developed and created a psychological/spiritual system called *The Fifth Way, The Way of the Lover* throughout her fifty years of working with people. To discover and study our essential nature, to experience the meaning and purpose of our life awakens us through concrete teachings that transform us to live our life mindfully, with presence. It is our birthright to be initiated into the truths that will evoke the powers that are our natural gifts, enabling us to find the hidden meaning and higher guidance that is inherent in our life.

From an early age Dr. Paula demonstrated an irrepressible striving to understand and to awaken. A voice of clarity and presence of heart, Paula has written a remarkable book of timeless wisdom that will change your life. Her work and writings have been praised by many of the foremost spiritual leaders from numerous traditions.

Her e-mail address is: Goldoceandrive@gmail.com

Facebook: Paula Ambika Bromberg

L IST OF C HARTS

BOOK ORDER INFORMATION

Your Name:_____

Address:_____

City:_____State/Country:_____

Zip/Postal:_____Phone:_____

Email Address:_____

Instructions: You may <u>Email</u> your orders to: Goldoceandrive@gmail.com
Facebook contact: Paula Ambika Bromberg
Please indicate the quantity of books you wish to order:
The Way of the Lover, per book= $ <u>Suggested $49.95</u>_____

<u>Shipping & Handling</u>
U.S.A. $10.00 for first book, add $3.00 for each additional book.
International: $15.00 for first book, add $4.00 for each additional.

Shipping & Handling= $_____

TOTAL PAYMENT= $_____

<u>Please indicate type of Payment</u>
Credit Card: __Visa __MasterCard __American Express __Discover_PayPal

Name as it appears on Credit Card:_____

Credit Card number:_____

Expiration Date:_____

*Enter the digits from the signature strip on the back of card:_____

Your Signature:_____

Print name:_____

<u>Shipping Address (if different from billing address above)</u>

Name:_____

Address:_____

City/State/Country:_____

Zip/Postal:_____